Marketing

Principles & Perspectives
Third Edition

Series in Marketing

Marketing

Principles & Perspectives
Third Edition

William O. Bearden
University of South Carolina

Thomas N. Ingram
Colorado State University

Raymond W. LaForge
University of Louisville

McGraw-Hill
Irwin

Boston Burr Ridge, IL Dubuque, IA Madison, WI
New York San Francisco St. Louis
Bangkok Bogotá Caracas Lisbon London Madrid Mexico City
Milan New Delhi Seoul Singapore Sydney Taipei Toronto

McGraw-Hill Higher Education

*A Division of The **McGraw-Hill** Companies*

MARKETING: PRINCIPLES & PERSPECTIVES
Published by McGraw-Hill/Irwin, an imprint of The McGraw-Hill Companies, Inc. 1221 Avenue of the Americas, New York, NY, 10020. Copyright © 2001, 1998, 1995, by The McGraw-Hill Companies, Inc. All rights reserved. No part of this publication may be reproduced or distributed in any form or by any means, or stored in a database or retrieval system, without the prior written consent of The McGraw-Hill Companies, Inc., including, but not limited to, in any network or other electronic storage or transmission, or broadcast for distance learning. Some ancillaries, including electronic and print components, may not be available to customers outside the United States.

This book is printed on acid-free paper.

domestic   1 2 3 4 5 6 7 8 9 0 VNH/VNH 0 9 8 7 6 5 4 3 2 1 0
international 1 2 3 4 5 6 7 8 9 0 VNH/VNH 0 9 8 7 6 5 4 3 2 1 0

ISBN 0-07-232297-7

Publisher: *David Kendric Brake*
Executive editor: *Gary L. Bauer*
Developmental editor: *Barrett Koger*
Marketing manager: *Kimberley Kanakes/Colleen Suljic*
Project manager: *Karen Nelson*
Production supervisor: *Melonie Salvati*
Senior designer: *Jennifer McQueen Hollingsworth*
Supplement coordinator: *Elizabeth Hadala*
Media technology producer: *Ann Rogula*
Cover design: *Rebecca Lloyd Lemma*
Compositor: *Carlisle Communications, Ltd.*
Typeface: *10.5/12 Sabon*
Printer: *Von Hoffmann Press, Inc.*

Library of Congress Cataloging-in-Publication Data

Bearden, William O. (date)
    Marketing, principles & perspectives / William O. Bearden, Thomas N. Ingram, Raymond W. LaForge.—3rd ed.
       p. cm.
    ISBN 0-07-232297-7 (alk. paper) (McGraw-Hill/Irwin series in marketing)
    Includes index.
    1. Marketing—United States.   I. Ingram, Thomas N.   II. LaForge, Raymond W.   III. Title.
IV. Series.
HF5415.1.B4155   2001
658.8—dc21   00-056238

INTERNATIONAL EDITION ISBN 0071180257
Copyright © 2001. Exclusive rights by The McGraw-Hill Companies, Inc. for manufacture and export.
This book cannot be re-exported from the country to which it is sold by McGraw-Hill.
The International Edition is not available in North America.

www.mhhe.com

To Patti, Anna, Wallace, and my mother, and in memory of my father.

Bill Bearden

To Jacque and Rocky.

Tom Ingram

To Susan, Alexandra, Kelly, my dad and in memory of my mom.

Buddy LaForge

Meet the Authors

William O. Bearden

(Ph.D., University of South Carolina) University of South Carolina

Bill Bearden is the Bank of America Professor of Business Administration at the University of South Carolina. He has focused his teaching and research interests in consumer behavior and marketing research. In addition, Bill teaches principles of marketing and marketing management. His teaching awards include Outstanding MBA Teacher, the College of Business Administration Alfred G. Smith Excellence in Teaching Award, and the University of South Carolina AMOCO Award for Excellence in Undergraduate Teaching.

He is currently a member of the Editorial Review Boards for the *Journal of Consumer Research,* the *Journal of Marketing Research,* the *Journal of Marketing,* the *Journal of Retailing,* the *Journal of Business Research,* and the *Marketing Education Review.* His professional experience includes past president of the Southern Marketing Association and the Education Division of the American Marketing Association, and member of the American Marketing Association Board of Directors. Previously, he served as Co-Director of the USC Lilly Endowment Teaching Fellows Program and currently coordinates the Ph.D. Program in Marketing at USC.

Bill lives in Columbia, South Carolina, with his wife Patti, while his two daughters, Anna and Wallace, work for the Environmental Protection Agency in Washington and teach high school math in Greenville, SC, respectively. Bill and his entire family are active in tennis and enjoy frequent trips to the South Carolina coast.

Thomas N. Ingram

(Ph.D., Georgia State) Colorado State University

Tom Ingram is Professor of Marketing at Colorado State University, where he teaches principles of marketing, marketing management, and sales management courses. Before commencing his academic career, Tom worked in sales, product management, and sales management with Exxon and Mobil.

Tom has received numerous teaching and research awards, including being named the Marketing Educator of the Year by Sales and Marketing Executives International (SMEI). He is a recipient of the Mu Kappa Tau National Marketing Honor Society Recognition Award for Outstanding Scholarly Contributions to the Sales Discipline. Tom has served as the Editor of *Journal of Personal Selling and Sales Management,* Chairman of the SMEI Accreditation Institute, and as a member of the SMEI Board of Directors. Currently, he is editor of the *Journal of Marketing Theory and Practice.*

Tom has published extensively in professional journals, including the *Journal of Marketing,* the *Journal of Marketing Research,* the *Journal of the Academy of Marketing Science,* and the *Journal of Personal Selling and Sales Management.* He is co-author of *Sales Management: Analysis and Decision Making,* 4th ed.; and *Professional Selling: A Trust-Based Approach.* He and his wife Jacque enjoy skiing, golf, and exploring the mountains of Colorado.

Raymond W. (Buddy) LaForge

(DBA, University of Tennessee) University of Louisville

Raymond W. (Buddy) LaForge is the Brown-Forman Professor of marketing at the University of Louisville (*http://cbpa.louisville.edu/buddyl*). He founded the *Marketing Education Review* (*http://cbpa.louisville.edu/mer*), served as Editor for 8 years, and is currently Executive Editor. Buddy has co-authored *Marketing: Principles & Perspectives, Sales Management: Analysis and Decision Making, Professional Selling: A Trust-Based Approach, The Professional Selling Skills Workbook,* and co-edited *Emerging Trends in Sales Thought and Practice.* His research is published in many journals to include the *Journal of Marketing, Journal of Marketing Research, Journal of the Academy of Marketing Science,* and *Journal of Personal Selling and Sales Management.* Buddy currently serves on the Direct Selling Education Foundation Board of Directors and Executive Committee, DuPont Corporate Marketing Faculty Advisory Team for the Sales Enhancement Process, Family Business Center Advisory Board

(*http://cbpa.louisville.edu/fbc*), as Vice President of Conferences and Research for the American Marketing Association Academic Council, and as Vice President/Marketing for the Academy of Business Education. He is developing The Sales Program at the University of Louisville and establishing The Sales Professional Network (*http://cbpa.louisville.edu/salesnetwork*) linking sales faculty, students, and executives to improve sales careers, education, research, and practice. Buddy and his wife, Susan, and daughters, Alexandra and Kelly, enjoy tennis, golf, and thoroughbred racing in Louisville, Kentucky.

Preface

The marketing world is changing rapidly. Global economic conditions, political situations, and competitive landscapes are in constant flux. Marketing approaches that worked yesterday may not work tomorrow. Increasingly, marketing success requires doing things differently. Students will face a marketing environment different from the one discussed in our classes today. Learning what was done in the past will not prepare them entirely for what they need to do tomorrow. Consequently, in the third edition of *Marketing: Principles & Perspectives,* we have presented the topics that remain relevant and important, while simultaneously emphasizing new thinking and approaches to marketing practice. Because students need to be prepared to operate in the complex and dynamic marketing world of the future, they need to develop the capacity to think and act like marketers in a difficult and uncertain environment. This requires the ability to assess complex and changing marketing situations, to determine the best marketing strategies for these situations, and to execute the strategies effectively.

Every idea presented in the text and expanded upon in the accompanying teaching resources is intended to help students develop the understanding and skills to become successful marketers. The text is designed to facilitate student learning from individual reading and study. The teaching resources provide useful tools for instructors to go beyond what is covered in the text. Together, the text and teaching resources represent an integrated package for preparing students for marketing in the future.

This package differs from currently available products in many important ways. The critical advantages include the integration of key marketing perspectives, the presentation of comments from practicing marketers, the implementation of an integrated marketing communications (IMC) approach, and an emphasis on decision making.

Key Features and Changes

In this version of our text, we have made a number of substantial changes, while at the same time revising some of the features from the second edition of *Marketing: Principles and Perspectives.* Each chapter has been revised to include the most current marketing thought and practice. New and updated examples, cases, and chapter openings have been incorporated into what we believe is a very up-to-date presentation.

The major features and changes include the following.

Prologue

The text begins with an exciting prologue that tells the marketing story of America Online, one of the most innovative marketers heading into the twenty-first century. The brief introduction provides a description of marketing practice at a well-known company of interest to students, which will get them enthused about the study of marketing. Two new America Online video segments, created specifically for this text, accompany the Prologue and Chapter 1; taken together, this in-depth examination of a leading-edge company creates an exciting introduction to the principles of marketing course.

Electronic Commerce

In our previous editions, the authors have emphasized the role of technology as a source of new products and as a means of enhancing marketing practices. In the last edition, at a time when marketing on the Internet was in its infancy, we included Web pages as part of each chapter opener and Web exercises for each chapter. In addition, we discussed the role of technology in marketing throughout the text. In the current edition, we continue to offer these features and have added a complete chapter on electronic commerce (Chapter 21). In this new chapter, we discuss the primary e-commerce business models, address key marketing issues in e-commerce, and provide in-depth coverage of ethical and legal issues in the electronic arena. Still in its formative years, e-commerce—as well as the more comprehensive practice of e-business—is often treated as if it is distinct from other business activities. However, e-commerce is fast becoming a crucial part of the very fabric of business, not a separate activity conducted only by Internet-based companies. The growing importance of e-commerce is recognized throughout this edition, and its importance is underscored with an additional chapter on the topic.

Marketing Perspectives

In this edition, we continue to integrate seven perspectives that are critical to effective marketing practice; these are discussed within the text where appropriate. These key perspectives are as follows: global, relationship, ethics, customer value, productivity, technology, and entrepreneurship. They are integrated throughout the text by direct discussion, examples, photos, and ads. Student exercises, boxed inserts, and cases address these timely themes as well. Briefly, the perspectives can be summarized as follows:

 Global—A global perspective includes searching for marketing opportunities around the world, competing effectively against international competitors, and working with multicultural suppliers, employees, channel partners, and customers.

 Relationship—A relationship perspective consists of building partnerships with firms outside the organization, encouraging teamwork among different functions within the organization, and developing long-term customer relationships.

 Ethics—The ethics perspective stresses the importance of incorporating moral and social responsibility issues, including ecological concerns, within marketing decision making.

 Customer Value—A customer value perspective means constantly looking for ways to give customers "more for less," often by continually striving to improve product and service quality.

 Productivity—The productivity perspective focuses attention on improving the management of marketing resources for optimum results.

 Technology—The technology perspective encourages marketers to incorporate the latest technological advances to improve both marketing practice and the development of new products.

 Entrepreneurship—The entrepreneurship perspective encourages marketers to emphasize creativity, innovation, and risk taking in their marketing efforts.

An Emphasis on Student Learning

We see important trends emerging in marketing education. For one thing, teaching is receiving more emphasis at most colleges and universities—but not teaching as traditionally viewed and practiced. It really does not matter *what* we teach, if students do not learn. And student learning is viewed differently, too. Learning is not just the recall of facts by passive students, but the understanding of concepts and the ability to apply them appropriately. Such learning requires the active participation of students.

The complete package for *Marketing: Principles & Perspectives, third edition,* is oriented toward student learning, and the text and the teaching resource materials are designed to complement each other toward that end. In keeping with our philosophy that students should be able to understand the text largely from their own reading and study, we write in a lively, interesting, informal manner to capture their attention and interest. Major concepts are presented clearly and simply in a way that students can understand. Encouraged by our reviewing panels, we did not include everything we know about every topic, but only what we believe students at this level need to know. We streamlined the discussion of concepts and then reinforced them with interesting examples and exciting visuals, and incorporated a number of learning tools to facilitate the learning process. The pedagogical features emphasize our student-focused learning approach:

HOME-PAGE CHAPTER OPENERS   Every chapter opens with an actual home page and discussion of how that site is being used to market the company or organization that created it. Companies represented include eBay, Pfizer, Information Resources Incorporated, British Airways, and Dell Computer Corporation to name a few. The book's home page will include a hot link to all of the Web sites mentioned in the text, including these chapter openers.

THINKING CRITICALLY   Two critical thinking questions are included within each chapter to help emphasize the importance of effective decision making. Each question relates to one of the concepts within the chapter and is constructed to encourage the student to think critically about a complex issue. The decision-making scenarios presented here are drawn from both real and theoretical companies.

SPEAKING FROM EXPERIENCE   This edition also includes comments about marketing from business professionals. We highlight one such person in each chapter and include three of his or her comments on key issues discussed in that chapter. By inclusion of these "Speaking from Experience" remarks, practitioners help bring to life the text material and add additional depth of explanation. The marketers included represent a range of large and small companies from a variety of industries. Example companies include Bank of America, Ralston-Purina, The Pampered Chef, Brown-Forman, Doe-Anderson, Inc., Lucent Technologies, and DuPont. Interestingly, the positions represented by these marketers include both senior individuals and young professionals in the early years of their careers. Consequently, students should be better able to identify and understand the varied opportunities available in marketing and how important marketing can be to professionals in other functional areas of business.

USING THE WWW IN MARKETING   Internet exercises are found at the end of each chapter. These questions require the student to consider how the Internet can be used to address marketing concepts or decisions. In addition, you can visit our home page where additional marketing examples and up-to-the-minute information will be posted.

Other Student Features   All chapters in the third edition have been formatted so that each pedagogical feature contributes to student learning by supporting the text material, including the principles and concepts covered in the chapter.

STUDENT LEARNING OBJECTIVES   Every chapter begins with several learning guides to help students focus attention on major concepts in reading and studying the chapter. At the end of each chapter, the summary is organized around these introductory learning objectives.

BOXED INSERTS   Each chapter contains two boxed inserts designed to provide current examples of three important topics: **Earning Customer Loyalty, Being Entrepreneurial,** and **Using Technology.**

EXHIBITS AND PHOTOS   The visual aspects of each chapter were designed to increase student learning. The exhibits, photos, and ads visually enhance and expand upon the chapter discussion.

UNDERSTANDING MARKETING TERMS AND CONCEPTS   The most important terms and concepts are in boldface and defined when first introduced. Each boldface term is listed at the end of each chapter with the page number where it is defined. A glossary of terms and definitions is also included at the back of the text.

THINKING ABOUT MARKETING   Ten review and discussion questions also are included at the end of each chapter. These questions reinforce the decision-making aspects of the text by including both critical thinking questions and recall of the most important material covered in the chapter.

APPLYING MARKETING SKILLS   Every chapter includes three application exercises. These exercises can be used as either homework assignments or as in-class discussion topics. The exercises provide varied and interesting ways for students to apply what they have read or are covering in class.

MAKING MARKETING DECISIONS   All chapters conclude with two cases representing well-known companies and current situations. At least one of each pair is global in orientation. Questions are included to encourage students to make decisions regarding the current activities of each company. A mix of both consumer and business-to-business cases, cases involving both multinational firms and small businesses, and cases reflecting both service and retail situations reflects the current diversity of the business world.

Organization

Marketing Principles and Perspectives, 3rd Edition, is divided into eight parts. *Part One, Marketing in a Dynamic Environment,* defines and examines the scope of marketing. The first chapter, *An Overview of Contemporary Marketing,* presents an overview of marketing including a historical perspective and the different philosophies that have guided marketing. An explanation of the marketing concept and the importance of satisfying customer needs and developing long-term profitable relationships with customers are also discussed. Chapter 1, also describes the seven key marketing perspectives—global, relationship, ethics, productivity, customer value, technology, and entrepreneurship—that are integrated within the text and the many reasons why their consideration is needed for effective marketing practice. *Chapter 2, The Global Marketing Environment,* emphasizes the global marketplace and the external environments (e.g., social, economic, political, and competitive) that influence marketer decision making. *Chapter 3, Marketing's Strategic Role in the Organization,* describes the role of marketing at different levels within the organization and the importance of effective marketing strategy.

    Part Two, Buying Behavior, contains two chapters that describe, first, the concepts and influences on consumer buying behavior and decision making, and second, business-to-business markets and organizational buying behavior. *Part Three, Marketing Research and Market Segmentation,* contains two chapters as well. In *Chapter 6, Marketing Research and Decision Support Systems,* an overview of the marketing research *process* and information systems is presented. *Chapter 7, Market Segmentation and Targeting,* includes the concepts of segmentation, targeting, positioning, and product differentiation.

    The remaining four parts cover the marketing mix elements—product, price, distribution, and promotion or integrated marketing communications. In *Part Four, Product and Service Concepts and Strategies,* three chapters present basic product and service concepts (Chapter 8), new-product development (Chapter 9), and product and service strategies (Chapter 10). Marketing services are emphasized throughout this section of the book.

    The next part of the text, *Part Five, Pricing Concepts and Strategies,* covers fundamental pricing concepts and customer evaluations of prices (Chapter 11) and price determination and the managerial strategies used to guide pricing decisions (Chapter 12).

The distribution aspects of the marketing mix are covered in *Part Six, Marketing Channels and Logistics.* In *Chapter 13, Marketing Channels,* the different types of direct and indirect channels are discussed. Retailing is covered in a separate chapter (Chapter 14), which includes the many new advances in retailing technology and methods. The place or distribution component of the text concludes with a chapter on wholesaling and logistics management (Chapter 15).

Part Seven, Integrated Marketing Communications, contains six chapters. First, an overview of promotion and integrated communications is presented in Chapter 16. This chapter describes the communications process and marketing communications planning. The major components of the promotions *mix* are then discussed in the remaining four chapters. First, up-to-date coverage of advertising and public relations is offered in Chapter 17. The objectives and methods of both consumer and trade sales promotions are described in Chapter 18. Personal selling and sales management, with particular emphasis given to relationship selling, are the focus of Chapter 19. A separate chapter on direct marketing is included in Part Seven; specifically, the newest direct marketing techniques are covered in Chapter 20, as well as the interactive aspects of marketing communications.

Chapter 21, *Electronic Commerce,* provides additional discussion of marketing's role in electronic commerce. While many aspects of e-commerce have been discussed in earlier chapters, Chapter 21 examines prevalent business models and crucial issues facing electronic marketers.

Appendix A describes many of the frequently used mathematical and financial tools used to make marketing decisions. *Appendix B* presents an expanded marketing plan and a discussion of how to develop one. A detailed glossary of terms and three indexes conclude the text. These indexes enumerate authors cited, companies and brands used as examples, and the subjects covered within the text.

Teaching Resources

INSTRUCTOR'S MANUAL   The instructor's manual comprises chapter outlines, lecture notes with supplemental lecture materials, answers to end-of-chapter questions, and ideas for individual and group student learning activities.

TEST BANK AND COMPUTEST   The test bank comprises more than 3,000 questions, including multiple choice, short answer, fill-in-the-blank, and critical-thinking essay questions.

VIDEO LIBRARY   This current, dynamic video library includes 22 video segments, one for each chapter plus the prologue. The video segments, which run between 6 and 15 minutes, demonstrate the marketing concepts from the text and are tied to specific chapter concepts. Some of the companies featured include America Online, BMW, Reebok, Rollerblade, and Specialized Bike to name just a few.

INSTRUCTOR CD-ROM   This exciting presentation CD-ROM allows the professor to customize a multimedia lecture with original material and material from our supplements package. It includes video clips, all of the electronic slides and acetates, art from the text, the computerized test bank, and the print supplements.

COLOR ACETATES   The acetate package contains 100 original, full-color acetates of compelling ads and striking line art that illustrate key marketing concepts. We have changed the ratio of images to 50 percent text sources and 50 percent outside sources. Our research indicated that some adopters missed not having text graphics in the package. Detailed teaching notes accompany each acetate and include provocative questions to stimulate class discussion and promote active learning.

ELECTRONIC SLIDES   PowerPoint slides are rapidly becoming a staple in the presentation tools that instructors use. Three hundred slides, approximately 15 per chapter, are available to adopters of the text.

MEDIA RESOURCE GUIDE   This manual includes a summary of every segment within the video library, along with specific student learning objectives. Creative and thought-provoking application exercises are also included to further enhance the video experience.

HOME PAGE   The book's home page can be found at www.mhhe.com. business/marketing/bearden. It contains Web Exploration Links (hotlinks to other Web sites) and Keeping Current (abstracts of issues in the news, referenced to a chapter in the book and accompanied by a list of discussion questions). For instructors, it will also offer updates of the examples and cases in the text, additional sources of marketing information, and downloads of key supplements.

Student Resources
The book's home page can be found at www.mhhe.com. business/marketing/bearden. It contains Think Links, provocative Web links with accompanying questions, and StudentSpeak, a forum designed to encourage students to interact with one another.

Acknowledgments
Writing a text requires a team effort, and we have enjoyed a collaboration with the best teammates imaginable. Cooperative, knowledgeable, creative, candid, and always encouraging—these are but a few of the positive things we found in our teammates. We are especially appreciative of the countless number of people involved in this project who time after time put forth the extra effort necessary to accomplish our mutual goals.

- The professionals at McGraw-Hill/Irwin led the way on what we feel is a terrific revision. Thanks to many, many people at McGraw-Hill/Irwin, including Jill Braaten (sponsoring editor), Colleen Suljic (marketing), Karen Nelson (production), Jennifer Hollingsworth (designer), Keri Johnson and Mike Hruby (photo research), Harriet Stockanes (permissions), and Barrett Koger (developmental editor).

- We would also like to thank several people who have been with us since the early days of this project. Eleanore Snow was our developmental editor on the first edition, and her early direction still serves as an inspiration to us. Rob Zwettler signed us to our first book contract years ago, and we truly appreciate his continuing support. Nina McGuffin and Lynn Mooney worked with us on previous editions—and sweated the deadlines as much as we did. Steve Patterson and Greg Patterson were instrumental in our decision to work with McGraw-Hill/Irwin on this book.

- We would also like to thank several individuals who have contributed significantly to the supplementary materials accompanying the text. Craig Hollinghead and Barbara R. Oates, both of Texas A&M, Kingsville, put together the comprehensive *Instructor's Manual.* An extensive set of objective test questions was developed by Ronald L. Weir of East Tennessee State University. The PowerPoint slides developed by Mary Mobley of Augusta College, and Kevin Bittle of Johnson and Wales University will provide monthly updates to the book's Web site.

- Our book has been improved by a long list of reviewers—both national and international—of three drafts of the manuscript. We were stimulated and encouraged by their comments and suggestions, and we incorporated many of their ideas into the text. Our thanks to our marketing colleagues listed below and to additional reviewers who prefer to remain anonymous. Because of length considerations we were not able to incorporate every good suggestion, but we considered all of them carefully and appreciate the reasoning behind them. We believe *Marketing: Principles & Perspectives* comes much closer to meeting your teaching needs and the learning needs of your students because of your efforts.

First, we would like to thank the following focus group participants and reviewers of the third edition:

Steven Engel
University of Colorado

Ronald E. Goldsmith
Florida State University

David C. Jones
Otterbein College

Robert Key
University of Phoenix

Dale A. Lunsford
University of Tulsa

Glen Reiken
East Tennessee State University

Nick Sarantakes
Austin Community College

Lois Smith
University of Wisconsin–Whitewater

Michael Welker
Franciscan University

We would also like to thank the many survey respondents who helped to shape this new edition and thank again the reviewers of our first and second editions:

Ronald J. Adams
University of North Florida

Nancy J. G. Adelson
North Seattle Community College

Arni Arnthorsson
College of St. Francis

Ramon Avila
Ball State University

Joe Ballenger
Stephen F. Austin University

Terri Feldman Barr
Thomas Moore College

Kenneth Bartkus
Utah State University

Stephanie Bibb
Chicago State University

Connie T. Boyd
University of Tennessee–Martin

John R. (Rusty) Brooks
Houston Baptist University

Phyllis Campbell
Bethel College

Paul Chao
University of Northern Iowa

Robert Collins
University of Nevada at Las Vegas

Kent Cox
University of Houston-Central

Lyndon Dawson
Louisiana Tech University

Oscar DeShields
California State University–Northridge

Ann M. Devine
Alverno College

Kathryn Dobie
University of Wisconsin at Eau Claire

John Doering
Minot State University

Casey Donoho
Northern Arizona University

Michael Dore
University of Oregon

Robert Doukas
Westchester Community College

Michael Drafke
College of DuPage

Cemel Ekin
Providence College

Leisa Reinecke Flynn
Florida State University

Bob Franz
Southwestern Louisiana State University

Barry Freeman
Bergen Community College

Ralph Gallay
Rider College

William G. Glynn
University College Dublin, Ireland

Pradeep Golpalakrishna
Pace University

Sandra K. Smith Gooding
Loyola College in Maryland

Bill Green
Sul Ross State University

Steve Grove
Clemson University

Robert F. Gwinner
Arizona State University

Fleming Hansen
Copenhagen Business School, Denmark

James B. Hunt
University of North Carolina at Wilmington

Eva M. Hyatt
Appalachian State University

David B. Jones
LaSalle University

Robert King
University of Hawaii at Hilo

Fredric Kropp
University of Oregon

Priscilla A. La Barbera
New York University

Irene Lange
California State University–Fullerton

J. Ford Laumer, Jr.
Auburn University

Paul Londrigan
Mott Community College

Mike Luckett
University of Central Florida

Dale Lunsford
University of Tulsa

Mary Ann Machanic
University of Massachusetts

Ed McQuarrie
Santa Clara University

H. Lee Meadow
Northern Illinois University

Carla Meeske
University of Oregon

Carla Millar
City University Business School, London

Michael S. Minor
University of Texas–Pan American

Robert Morgan
University of Alabama

Linda Morris
University of Idaho

William F. Motz Jr.
Lansing Community College

Erik B. Ness
Norwegian School of Management, Oslo, Norway

William Perttula
San Francisco State University

Linda Pettijohn
Southwest Missouri State

Marie A. Pietak
Bucks County Community College

David Prensky
College of New Jersey

Milt Pressley
University of New Orleans

Andrea Prothero
Cardiff Business School, University of Wales

Daniel Rajaratnam
Baylor University

Rich Rexeisen
St. Thomas University

Glen Riecken
East Tennessee State University

Bob Robicheaux
University of Alabama

Carlos M. Rodriguez
Governors State University

Joel Saegert
University of Texas at San Antonio

Nick Sarantakes
Austin Community College

Charlie Schwepker
Central Missouri State University

Don Self
Auburn University at Montgomery

C. David Shepherd
University of Tennessee–Chattanooga

Richard Sjolander
University of West Florida

Jane Sojka
Ohio University

Carol Soroos
North Carolina State University

Michael J. Swenson
Brigham Young University

David Szymanski
Texas A&M University

Janice Taylor
Miami University

Ronald D. Taylor
Mississippi State University

Lou Turley
Western Kentucky University

Michael Tuttle
Northwood University

Sushila Umashanker
University of Arizona

David J. Urban
Virginia Commonwealth University

Rockney G. Walters
Indiana University

Jim Wilkins
Southwestern Louisiana University

Susan D. Williams
Jersey City State College

Ken Williamson
James Madison University

Kenneth Willig
LaSalle University

Robert Winsor
Loyola Marymount University

Terrence H. Witkowski
California State University–Long Beach

Helen R. Woodruffe
University of Salford, England

Alyce Zahorsky
Golden Gate University

Sherilyn Zeigler
University of Hawaii–Manoa

Bill Bearden
Tom Ingram
Buddy LaForge

Contents in Brief

Contents

Part Four
Product and Service Concepts and Strategies

Chapter Eight

Chapter Nine

Part Six
Marketing Channels and Logistics

Chapter Thirteen
Marketing Channels

Chapter Fourteen
Retailing

Chapter Eighteen

Chapter Nineteen

Where to Find . . .

Chapter-Openers

Speaking from Experience

End-of-Chapter Cases

Prologue: America Online

**So effective,
no wonder it's #1**

You whip out your cell phone on the way to work and send an AOL instant message to your boss to discuss the day's schedule. While lunching at McDonald's, you check your AOL stock portfolio on your pocket organizer. After dinner, you flip on AOL TV to watch the news or use your PC to buy some gifts at Shop@AOL. As you climb into bed, you remember another gift you need to buy. So, you use the mini-Web terminal at your bedside to place this order.[1]

Does this sound farfetched? Not if America Online (AOL) has its way. Beginning in early 2000, AOL will begin to implement its strategy called AOL Anywhere. This strategy is intended to make AOL accessible through the new information appliances that are becoming available. These include smart phones, TV setup boxes, and a host of other gizmos.

America Online was launched in 1985 and went public in 1992 with 155,000 members. Today, AOL has more than 21 million members and generates annual revenues in excess of $5 billion from subscribers' fees, advertising, and e-commerce sales. Its stock is up over 6,000 percent since it went public. So, if you had invested $1,000 in AOL stock in 1992, it would be worth over $150,000 today![2]

Why has AOL been so successful? There are many reasons. One is certainly the leadership provided by founder, chairman, and CEO Steve Case. He has established a vision that drives everything at AOL. The vision is simply "to build a global medium as central to people's lives as the telephone or television . . . and even more

valuable."[3] The AOL Anywhere strategy is intended to achieve this vision.

Effective marketing is another reason for AOL's success. We have studied leading marketing companies, such as AOL, and identified seven key perspectives that help these companies better identify and respond to market opportunities, and that improve marketing decision making. Our objective is to present each key marketing perspective and illustrate the importance of each perspective to the success of AOL. Although the perspectives are highly interrelated, we address them separately in this discussion. Many interrelationships among the perspectives are discussed at the end of the Prologue and throughout the remainder of the book.

A Global Perspective

A global perspective means that marketers should view the world as their potential marketplace. Customers, suppliers, competitors, partners, and employees can come from anywhere on the globe, no matter where a firm is located or where its product is marketed. The rapid growth of the Internet as a truly global medium increases the importance of a global perspective. For example, anyone anywhere in the world with Internet access can interact with AOL by typing

[1]Adapted from Catherine Yang, Steve Brull, Peter Burrows, Linda Himelstein, and Steve Hamm, "There's No Escaping AOL," *Business Week*, December 6, 1999, p. 92.

[2]Malcolm Campbell, "What Makes AOL Click?" *Selling Power*, September 1999, pp. 56–62.

[3]Ibid., p. 56.

www.aol.com. This site is open to those who are not AOL members. Astute marketers take a global perspective in identifying growth opportunities, and when developing and executing marketing strategies.

Identifying Growth Opportunities

Many firms operate in mature domestic markets that provide only limited opportunities for future growth. These firms can often find attractive growth opportunities in international markets. This is especially true for most companies operating on the Internet, and certainly for AOL.

The United States currently dominates the Internet with more than half of the individuals who are on-line and three-quarters of Internet commerce. However, Iceland, Finland, and Sweden have more Internet usage per capita than does the United States. And, Internet usage is increasing rapidly in Europe, Asia, and Latin America.[4] AOL recognizes that the fastest Internet growth in the future will be outside of the United States. It is taking steps to establish itself in various international markets, but competition is fierce and marketing strategies must be adapted to the specific requirements of each international market.

Successful Marketing Strategies

A global perspective is needed not only to identify potential growth opportunities, but also to guide firms in the development and execution of marketing strategies in order to take advantage of these opportunities. Understanding the culture, language, customs, and other unique aspects of an international market or cultural target market is critical for marketing success.

The need to adjust marketing strategies to meet the needs of different international markets is evident in Europe. Many Europeans think that American sites have too many bells and whistles, so European sites need to be more customer-oriented. The colors used on sites are also a consideration. For example, in America red is the color of love, but in Spain it is associated with socialism.[5] In addition to these types of preference differences, AOL faces a difficult problem in pricing. Its basic strategy in the United States is to offer unlimited access through a local or toll-free telephone number for a flat monthly fee. However, in many European countries local telephone calls are still charged by the minute. This adds considerably to the cost of using AOL in these countries based on its monthly fee pricing strategy. Thus, AOL has had to change its pricing in some countries. For example, the company reduced its monthly fee from $21.95 to $16 in Britain. It is even considering offering the service for free to compete against Freeserve, the no-fee Internet service in Britain with the largest number of users.[6]

A Relationship Perspective

The increasingly complex business environment drives companies and marketers to work together for mutual benefit. No longer can one individual or one company have all of the knowledge, skills, or resources necessary for marketing success. Instead, networks of various relationships are required. A **relationship perspective** consists of building partnerships with firms outside the organization and encouraging teamwork among different functions within the organization to develop long-term customer relationships.

[4]Irene Kunii, "The Internet Economy: The World's Next Growth Engine," *Business Week,* October 4, 1999, p. 77.

[5]Ibid., p. 77.

[6]Catherine Yang, Kerry Capell, Jack Ewing, and Marsha Johnston, "I Claim This Land . . . Whoops!" *Business Week,* June 14, 1999, pp. 115–19.

Customer Relationships

Marketing has traditionally been viewed as the sales-generating business function. Its importance is reflected in the adage "nothing happens until a sale is made." This sales orientation sometimes leads firms to focus entirely on generating sales in the short run, with little consideration for profitability or the activities used to produce sales. Fortunately, the emphasis on generating sales in the short run at any cost is being replaced by an emphasis on developing, maintaining, and expanding long-term, profitable relationships with selected customers.

AOL is concerned with two types of customer relationships. The first is relationships with the 21 million subscribers who typically pay $21.95 per month for unlimited access to AOL. Maintaining and expanding relationships with subscriber customers is one key to AOL's success. The second is relationships with business customers using AOL for advertising and electronic commerce. The Interactive Marketing Group was established in 1996 to serve these customers. The group's sales were $102 million in 1996 but exceeded $1 billion in 1999. A sales organization consisting of 38 outside salespeople and 20 inside sales representatives is responsible for developing relationships with these business customers.[7]

Organizational Partnerships

Few firms can themselves perform all of the necessary marketing activities productively and profitably; therefore, it is necessary to work with different organizations to carry out many marketing activities. Examples include relationships with marketing research firms to perform marketing studies, advertising agencies to develop integrated marketing communications programs, and wholesalers and retailers to distribute a firm's products. A firm's success in developing long-term customer relationships typically requires close working partnerships with many different organizations.

AOL represents a network of partnerships with many different organizations. For example, the success of its AOL Anywhere strategy depends largely on several recent partnership agreements:[8]

- A partnership with Gateway to develop and co-market Internet appliances and home networking devices, such as Web terminals.

- A partnership to put AOL e-mail on Palm Pilot handheld devices.

- A partnership with Motorola to put AOL's Instant Messenger service on Motorola's new smart wireless devices.

- A partnership with DirecTV to bring AOL to the satellite TV screen.

[7]Campbell, "What Makes AOL Click?" pp. 56–62.
[8]Yang et al., "I Claim This Land . . ." p. 92.

These partnerships are intended to ensure that AOL is available on all of the new information appliances available now or expected to be introduced in the future.

Teamwork Relationships

The days when marketing managers operated in isolation from other business functions are over. Success in the current business environment requires that all company members work as a team toward achieving common objectives. No single individual or function performs effectively as an independent entity. Cooperation and teamwork are necessary to succeed in an increasingly complex and rapidly changing business environment.

Teamwork within and across business functions is extremely important at AOL. This is especially evident within the Interactive Marketing Group. AOL salespeople identify the specific needs of each business customer and then prepare customized proposals to meet these needs. Once accepted, the customer works closely with the marketing, advertising, and media professionals in AOL's account services department. The objective of the account services department is to get results for the customer so that the customer is satisfied and will do more business with AOL in the future.[9] Effective teamwork between the sales and service function and within the service function is critical to the success of the Interactive Marketing Group.

An Ethics Perspective

Because marketers work at the interface between the company and its customers, partners, and other groups, ethical and social responsibility considerations are important and complex. An **ethics perspective** involves proactively addressing the morality of marketing decisions and practicing social responsibility to include ecological considerations.

Marketing Ethics

A company must project a high level of morality to establish trust between itself and its customers and other stakeholders. Trust provides the foundation for long-term relationships with customers and organizational partnerships.

AOL builds trust with customers by guaranteeing satisfaction, security, and privacy. Specific policies in all of these areas are available to AOL members on-line. For example, customers are protected against any liability from credit card fraud when making purchases from any of AOL's Certified Merchants. AOL also protects member privacy by indicating that AOL or its affiliates will never ask for a credit card number or password, except when a customer is making a specific purchase. The company appears to deliver on these promises, as evident in the following statement:

Since the creation of AOL's shopping area and the inception of our Guarantee in October 1996, the Shopping Channel has never received a report of a credit card that was compromised during a shopping transaction with Certified Merchants on AOL.[10]

Social Responsibility

Social responsibility refers to ensuring that marketing actions have a positive impact on society. This includes minimizing social costs, such as environmental damage, and taking specific actions that benefit society. Businesses are social institutions with a responsibility to contribute to social welfare.

AOL takes this social responsibility seriously. One example is in the area of Internet access by children. Although the openness of the Internet is one of its strengths, the flip side is that children can be exposed to pornographic and other objectionable materials. AOL has taken a proactive stance in this area by providing parents with the ability to control what their children can view. This Parental

---

[9]Campbell, "What Makes AOL Click?" pp. 56–62.
[10]Reported in AOL Certified Merchant Guarantee, viewed on December 9, 1999.

Control function allows parents to decide exactly what to make available to their children. Parents can control access to e-mail, chat rooms, instant messaging, Web sites, downloading, newsgroups, and premium services. Four basic levels of access are available: Kids Only (12 and under), Young Teens (13–15), Mature Teens (16–17), and General Access (18+). Parents set a level of access for each child and can make changes whenever desired.

Ecological Orientation

Marketers practicing an ecological orientation consider the environmental impacts of all marketing decisions. This can result in making changes, such as using recyclable materials, in order to reduce the negative environmental impact of marketing activities. At the same time, however, astute marketers are finding many profitable opportunities in satisfying the needs of the increasing number of environmentally concerned consumers.

One of the advantages of the Internet is the reduction of the need for paper and other packaging materials due to products and services being provided on-line. AOL communicates most of its information to subscribers electronically and offers subscribers the opportunity to download a variety of materials. For example, subscribers using AOL 4.0 and new subscribers were able to download and install AOL 5.0 directly. This reduced the need for the production of CDs and related packaging considerably. And, updates to AOL 5.0 are typically handled electronically as well. In addition, as more consumers shop and perform other activities on AOL, the need to travel to stores and other places diminishes greatly; this should help reduce traffic congestion and pollution in many areas.

A Customer Value Perspective

Business buyers and consumers are continually trying to get more for less. Both groups assess what they get for what they give. "What they get" includes the basic features of the product, but also other important factors related to the purchase, use, and disposal of the product. These might include the convenience of the purchase, training in product use, dependability of delivery, after-the-sale service, ease of disposing of the product, and other factors. "What they give" includes the monetary price of the product, but also time and effort to purchase the product, costs associated with using the product, and other factors. Buyers determine value by comparing the "get" and "give" components. A **customer value perspective** means constantly looking for ways to give customers more for less.

Increasing customer value drives AOL. The company introduced a flat-rate pricing plan in 1996. This provides value to customers because they get more AOL access for the same price. AOL also improves its content and services on a regular basis. AOL 5.0 was introduced in 1999 and offers customers both improvements in the previous version as well as new offerings. For example, e-mail capabilities have been greatly expanded and a new calendar function has been added; there are also many more opportunities for subscribers to customize various areas to meet their specific preferences. Customers receive more value because they get these improvements and new features at the same price as AOL 4.0.

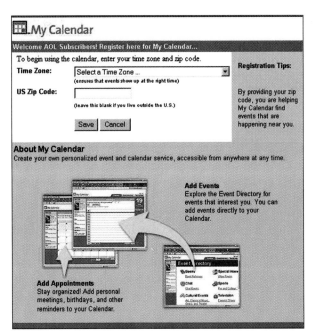

A Productivity Perspective

A **productivity perspective** is trying to get the most output for each marketing dollar spent. Productivity is typically defined in terms of output per input ratios. For marketers, outputs might be sales or market share. Inputs include dollars spent on advertising, number of salespeople, number of sales calls, or any other marketing activity. Therefore, sales per advertising dollar or sales per salesperson are important productivity ratios for marketers.

Marketing expenditures represent a significant expenditure for many firms, especially those building brand identity worldwide. For example, Coca-Cola spends about 20 percent of its revenue on marketing. Many of the large Internet firms are trying to establish their brands globally and spending a great deal on marketing efforts. AOL's 1999 marketing budget was $807 million. This compares to marketing budgets of $206 million for Yahoo! and $402 million for Amazon.com.[11]

A key issue is how productive are these marketing expenditures. Evidence indicates that AOL has been very productive in spending its marketing dollars. Although AOL spends more on marketing than does Yahoo! and Amazon.com, its marketing expenditures are a much lower percentage of its sales (16.9% versus 35.9% versus 25.9%, respectively). These expenditures are also having results, as AOL was recently ranked in the top 60 of global brands, and considerably higher than both Yahoo! and Amazon.com.[12] Another productivity measure is revenue per marketing dollar spent. AOL generated almost $7 in revenue for each marketing dollar spent in 1998. This is a 74 percent increase from 1997 and much higher than that of Yahoo!, Amazon.com, and most other Internet firms.[13]

A Technology Perspective

Technology is advancing at a tremendous pace. New developments in artificial intelligence, biotechnology, optoelectronics, and many other areas are reported daily. The dizzying pace of technological change challenges marketers to embrace a **technology perspective** so they can translate new and emerging technologies into successful products and services and use technology to improve marketing practice.

Developing New Products

Failure to keep up with new products based on the latest technology can affect a company's market position very quickly. This is especially true on the Internet, where companies are constantly introducing new products and services to customers around the world.

AOL is a leader in translating technology developments into new products and services for its customers. One example is the "You've Got Pictures" service offered on AOL 5.0. Customers can drop off film at participating retailers and get the prints and negatives back as usual. However, the pictures will also be delivered directly to the customer's AOL account. These electronic images can then be shared with anyone on the Internet and sent to specific individuals with e-mail. And, the AOL Anywhere strategy discussed earlier is based on providing AOL products and services to users of new technology information devices.

[11]Paul C. Judge, Heather Green, Amy Barrett, and Catherine Yang, "The Name's the Thing," *Business Week*, November 15, 1999, pp. 36–39.

[12]Ibid., p. 37.

[13]Debra Sparks, "Who's Getting More Bang for the Marketing Buck?" *Business Week*, May 31, 1999, pp. 148–50.

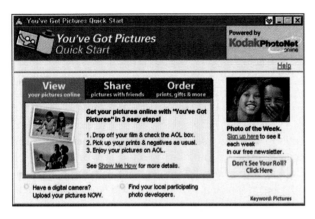

Improve Marketing Practice

Today, marketers are accustomed to using information and communications technologies in many marketing activities. Cellular telephones, fax machines, notebook PCs, multimedia technology, and other technologies offer marketers the potential to achieve competitive advantages.

AOL uses new technologies to improve marketing efforts to its customers, but its Interactive Marketing Group's purpose is to help business customers use these technologies to improve their marketing practices. One example in the nonprofit sector illustrates the potential for Internet technologies to improve marketing. AOL established helping.org to assist nonprofit organizations to increase the number of volunteers and charitable giving to their organizations. One of the site features is VolunteerMatch where individuals can punch in their zip code, areas of interest, and times available for volunteer work. The individual will then be provided with a listing of volunteer opportunities that meet these criteria. Easy, Secure Online Giving provides information about all of the charities recognized by the IRS and makes it possible to make a donation on-line with the same security protections as for on-line shopping. Helping.org has the potential both to dramatically improve the marketing practices of nonprofit organizations that are trying to get more volunteers and to increase charitable contributions.

An Entrepreneurship Perspective

A dynamic business environment creates a need for firms to be flexible and responsive to marketplace demands. Slow and rigid business bureaucracies need to be replaced by streamlined organizational structures and processes. Success often depends on being able to do some things differently from, sooner than, or better than competitors. This requires that marketers bring an entrepreneurial perspective to their work. An **entrepreneurial perspective** has three basic dimensions: innovation, risk taking, and proactiveness. Marketers adopting an entrepreneurial perspective attempt to do things in new and unique ways, to make important decisions in the face of uncertainty, and attempt to be the first to try something different.

The founding of AOL by Steve Case in 1985 is certainly an entrepreneurial event. However, the company has gone to great lengths to maintain its entrepreneurial spirit, even though it has grown to be very large. The AOL Anywhere strategy is a good example. AOL is being proactive, innovative, and risk-taking in capitalizing on the many different types of information appliances that are becoming available. And while it has a strong position in Internet access through PCs, it is not resting on its laurels. AOL sees many opportunities in the future and is developing strategies to seize these opportunities.

Integrating the Perspectives

Although we have discussed each perspective separately, the perspectives are very interrelated. For example, continuing developments in information and communications technologies make it easier for firms to productively engage in business globally and to develop relationships with customers, partnerships with other organizations, and teamwork within firms, even when employees are located in different areas. These new technologies also introduce

Ich kann eMails sogar aufs Handy schicken.

new ethical issues that must be addressed if companies are going to be able to earn the trust necessary for successful relationships of all types. The rapid and continuous changes in the business environment require firms to be entrepreneurial, especially in trying to provide customers with more value. The interrelationships among the perspectives will be emphasized in more detail throughout the remainder of the book.

A New Development

AOL shocked the business world on January 10, 2000, by announcing an agreement to purchase Time Warner for stock valued in excess of $160 billion. If the deal is completed as expected, it will combine the #1 Internet provider with the #1 media company. Time Warner consists of movie and TV studios, cable operations, music companies, and books and magazines. Its well-known brand names include *Time, Sports Illustrated, Fortune,* Warner Brothers Studios, Warner Music, CNN, TBS, and HBO. AOL is expected to use content from these various sources in its on-line service. Steve Case will be chairman of AOL Time Warner which he sees as the first attempt to converge entertainment, information, communications, and on-line services into one company. If all goes well, the two companies will be merged by late 2000.[14]

[14]David Lieberman, "Merger fulfills needs of each," *USA Today,* January 11, 2000, pp. B1–B2 and Richard Siklos, Catherine Yang, Andy Reinhardt, Peter Burrows, and Rob Hof, "Welcome to the 21st Century," *Business Week,* January 24, 2000, pp. 37–44.

Chapter One

An Overview of Contemporary Marketing

After studying this chapter you should be able to:

1 Discuss what marketing is and why it is important to organizations and individuals.

2 Distinguish between marketing as an organizational philosophy and a societal process.

3 Understand the components of a marketing strategy and the different activities involved in marketing products and services.

4 Be aware of the various types of marketing institutions and the different marketing positions available in these institutions.

5 Appreciate how marketing has evolved from earlier times to the present.

6 Understand the basic elements and relationships in the contemporary marketing framework.

The Amazon.com Web site represents an interesting entrepreneurial story. Jeff Bezos was employed in a computer systems job in 1994 when he came across the statistic that worldwide Web usage was growing at 2,300 percent a year. Because of this high growth rate, he began investigating potential business opportunities for the Internet. His approach was to evaluate different business ideas against the Internet's strong points to determine the business best suited for the Internet. The result of this analysis was the book business.

So, in July 1995, Amazon.com was introduced as a book retailer. The company's mission was to use the Internet to transform book buying into the fastest, easiest, and most enjoyable shopping experience available. Since Amazon.com did not have an inventory of books in a retail location, it could offer customers an enormous selection of books over its Web site. Customers could also shop and place orders 24 hours a day and seven days a week. The shopping experience was easy and fun, and various services were added to create value. For example, customers could post reviews of books read on the Amazon.com Web site, and those thinking about purchasing a specific book could read these reviews. This was the beginning, and growth has been phenomenal.

Amazon.com now offers many different products and services, including music CDs, videos, electronic products and software, toys and games, and home-improvement products. It also offers an auction service, a Special Occasions Reminder service, an e-mail subscription service where customers automatically receive information about new products in categories of interest, a scheduler/address book, and a comparison shopping tool; further, it provides customers instant personalized product recommendations the moment they log on. International sites are being developed with local content, such as Amazon.co.uk for the United Kingdom and Amazon.de for Germany. The company stands behind all of its services with the Amazon.com Safe Shopping Guarantee and the Amazon.com Auctions Guarantee.

Amazon.com has also developed partnerships with and made investments in other companies. For example, the Amazon.com Associate program makes it possible for other Internet sites to earn money by selling Amazon's products on their sites. It has also invested in leading Internet retailers like drugstore.com, Gear.com, Home-Grocer.com, and Pets.com.

One of the major reasons for the success of Amazon.com is its rapidly growing number of satisfied and loyal customers. The customer base grew from around 3.3 million in June 1998 to about 10.7 million in June 1999 and is over 13 million today. Although the company has yet to earn a profit, its stock price has skyrocketed, making Jeff Bezos a multibillionaire. Amazon.com is expected to be very profitable in the long term, but is incurring losses now due to heavy investments in distribution systems, other Web businesses, and customer development.

Sources: www.amazon.com and www.hoovers.com, December 16, 1999.

The Amazon.com story illustrates a basic principle of successful marketing: Identify market opportunities, and respond by developing and executing marketing strategies to take advantage of the opportunities better than competitors do. Jeff Bezos realized that the Internet had the potential to offer customers new and exciting shopping experiences. He started in book retailing, because Amazon.com could provide a better book selection, customized services, and lower prices than could typical book retailers. Finally, and most important, Amazon.com focuses on the customer; the company's key advantage is its large and growing base of loyal customers.

In a dynamic and turbulent business environment, marketers must continually revise their strategies to meet growth objectives. Amazon.com has done this by adding new product categories and new services. The firm now faces Internet competitors as well as traditional retail rivals. So it must continually look for ways to improve its existing operations and expand its offerings to increase the value provided to customers. Its rapidly growing customer base suggests that it is doing a good job in this area.

Amazon.com is actively involved in marketing. The most accepted definition of **marketing** is that adopted by the American Marketing Association:

Marketing is the process of planning and executing the conception, pricing, promotion, and distribution of ideas, goods, and services to create exchanges that satisfy individual and organizational goals.[1]

This definition views marketing as a process involving marketing exchanges, strategies, activities, positions, and institutions. Before discussing each of these areas in detail, we examine the importance of marketing and different views of marketing.

The Importance of Marketing

Marketing is usually associated with business organizations. Most people are probably familiar with the marketing activities of consumer product firms such as Procter & Gamble, Sony, Nike, McDonald's, General Motors, and Kmart. They also may be aware of marketing efforts by firms—such as Xerox, Monsanto, Caterpillar, Boeing, and DuPont—that market to other organizations.

Marketing also plays an important role in a wide variety of situations. Consider the following examples of nonprofit, place, idea, and person marketing:

Marketing is increasingly important to many nonprofit organizations. The Boy Scouts uses advertising to increase membership

- *Edgewood Symphony Orchestra*—This community symphony orchestra performs four regular concerts in Edgewood, Pennsylvania, and special performances at local and regional events. The board of directors wanted to increase concert attendance. They surveyed residents and used the collected information to develop a detailed marketing plan. The marketing plan included complimentary tickets to residents who had never attended a concert, a publicity campaign to enhance the orchestra's good image, and cooperative marketing alliances with local corporations. By the second concert of the season, attendance had quadrupled.[2]

- *Portland, Indiana*—First National Bank of Portland dominates the market in this town of 6,000. Bank growth depends on the growth of the community. The bank and its advertising agency studied the town's strengths and weaknesses, talked with residents, and devised a 38-point plan to stimulate the town's growth. The plan focused on building relationships with youth so they would remain in the community when they got older and bring new business and residents into the community. After the plan was implemented, new businesses were started and existing businesses expanded. The bank expects the town's population to double in size within 10 years.[3]

- *Certified public accountants (CPAs)*—The American Institute of Certified Public Accountants is marketing the idea that CPAs are the premier providers of business and financial services. The marketing theme is: "The CPA. Never Underestimate the Value." Advertisements communicating this theme were run in major national daily newspapers and business publications and during prime-time news and business programs on network and cable TV. A CPA logo was also developed for promotional items such as mugs and pens.[4]

- *Presidential campaigns*—The 2000 U.S. presidential campaign is being driven by integrated marketing communications programs. Mass advertising is still important, but all of the candidates are integrating other marketing communication's tools to support advertising efforts. These programs typically include a mixture of advertising, telemarketing, direct mail, town meetings, "grassroots" visits to voters' homes, debates, appearances on news shows, and then there is the Internet. All of the candidates have Web sites that allow them to communicate and interact with voters. George W. Bush has done an especially good job of raising money from his web site. This is the first presidential election where the Internet is playing a major role in campaign marketing efforts.[5]

These examples illustrate marketing's importance to a nonprofit organization, a community, a professional association, and political candidates. Today, more organizations and individuals realize that effective marketing is a critical determinant of success.

Views of Marketing

Most of the emphasis in this book is on marketing as the process defined at the beginning of the chapter. Nevertheless, marketing can also be viewed as an organizational philosophy and as a societal process.

Marketing as an Organizational Philosophy

An organization typically has some type of philosophy that directs the efforts of everyone in it. The philosophy might be stated formally, as in a mission statement, or it might become established informally through the communications and actions of top management. An organizational philosophy indicates the types of activities the organization values. Three different philosophies deserve mention.

A **production philosophy** exists when an organization emphasizes the production function. An organization following such a philosophy values activities related to improving production efficiency or producing sophisticated products and services. Production drives the organization. Marketing plays a secondary role because the organization thinks the best-produced products can be easily marketed. High-technology companies often follow a production philosophy.

A **selling philosophy** predominates where the selling function is most valued. The assumption is that any product can be sold if enough selling effort is given to it. Marketing's job is to sell whatever the organization decides to produce. Although selling is one component of marketing, organizations driven by a selling philosophy emphasize selling efforts to the exclusion of other marketing activities.

A **marketing philosophy** suggests that the organization focuses on satisfying the needs of customers. This focus applies to people in the marketing function as well as to those in production, personnel, accounting, finance, and other functions. Production and selling are still important, but the organization is driven by satisfying customer needs. Applied Materials reinforces the importance of a marketing philosophy every payday. "Your payroll dollars are provided by Applied Materials customers" appears on the front of every employee's paycheck.[6]

MARKETING CONCEPT Marketing as an organizational philosophy has been based on the **marketing concept**. This concept consists of three interrelated principles:

1. An organization's basic purpose is to satisfy customer needs.

2. Satisfying customer needs requires integrated and coordinated efforts throughout the organization.

3. Organizations should focus on long-term success.

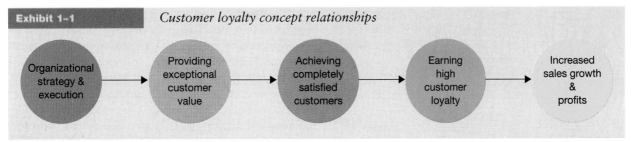

| Exhibit 1–1 | *Customer loyalty concept relationships* |

Organizational strategy & execution → Providing exceptional customer value → Achieving completely satisfied customers → Earning high customer loyalty → Increased sales growth & profits

Sources: Adapted from James L. Heskett, Thomas O. Jones, Gary W. Loveman, W. Earl Sasser, Jr., and Leonard A. Schlesinger, "Putting the Service-Profit Chain to Work," *Harvard Business Review,* March–April 1994, pp. 164–74; and Frederick F. Reichheld, *The Loyalty Effect: The Hidden Force behind Growth, Profits, and Lasting Value* (Boston: Harvard Business School Press, 1996).

The marketing concept has been embraced by many firms since the 1950s.[7] However, the competitive business climate of the 2000s suggests that merely satisfying customers is not enough.

Satisfied customers often leave and purchase from competitors. For example, Xerox polls 480,000 customers per year regarding their level of satisfaction using a five-point scale from 5 (high) to 1 (low). Analysis of these data indicated that customers giving 5s were six times more likely to repurchase Xerox equipment than those giving 4s. Now, Xerox's objective is to have 100 percent of its customers being totally satisfied with Xerox products and services.[8] Xerox and other successful marketers are extending the focus beyond just customer satisfaction to customer loyalty.

CUSTOMER LOYALTY CONCEPT   The **customer loyalty concept,** illustrated in Exhibit 1–1, consists of three basic relationships:

1. Earning high levels of customer loyalty leads to increased sales growth and higher profitability.

2. Completely satisfying and delighting customers is the best route for earning customer loyalty.

3. Providing exceptional value is needed to delight and completely satisfy customers.

The basic reasons for the close relationship between customer loyalty and sales and profits are presented in Exhibit 1–2. Loyal customers contribute to increased sales growth because they tend to buy more over time and are an excellent source of new business referrals. Some companies calculate the **lifetime value of a loyal customer** as the revenue stream from repeat purchases and referrals. For example, the lifetime value of a loyal pizza eater can be $8,000, of a Cadillac owner, $332,000.[9]

Typically, loyal customers involve limited acquisition costs, low operating costs, and higher profit margins. The conventional wisdom is that it costs at least five times as much to serve a new customer as an existing one. Sometimes the efforts to get new customers may not even be profitable. For example, MBNA was spending 98 percent of its marketing dollars on getting new customers. It found that it cost about $50 to get a new credit card customer, these customers were not profitable

| Exhibit 1–2 | *Customer loyalty, sales, and profits* |

1. Keeping loyal customers requires no acquisition costs. Getting new customers often requires high acquisition costs.
2. The longer a firm keeps a customer, the more base profit earned from continuing purchases over time.
3. Loyal customers tend to buy more from a firm over time.
4. It usually costs less to deal with loyal customers than with new customers.
5. Loyal customers are typically an excellent source of referrals for new business.
6. Loyal customers are often willing to pay a price premium to receive desired value.

Source: Frederick F. Reichheld, *The Loyalty Effect: The Hidden Force behind Growth, Profits, and Lasting Value* (Boston: Harvard Business School Press, 1996), pp. 39–50.

One way to promote customer loyalty is to reward customers for their loyalty. Friday's awards points to customers based on the amount spent. These points can be redeemed for free food at subsequent visits.

until the second year, and many left before the second year. The company changed its strategy and focused on keeping existing customers. It increased the customer retention rate to 50 percent and became one of the most profitable banks in the country.[10]

The link between customer satisfaction and customer loyalty is especially interesting. One study of this link in the automobile, business personal computer, hospital, airlines, and local telephone service markets concluded that completely satisfied customers are much more loyal than merely satisfied customers. Another study in the banking industry found that completely satisfied customers were 42 percent more likely to be loyal than merely satisfied customers.[11] These results are consistent with the Xerox example presented earlier. There is increasing evidence of the close relationship between complete customer satisfaction and customer loyalty.

How can organizations completely satisfy their customers? The simple answer is by continuously providing customers with exceptional value. **Customer value** is defined as what a customer *gets* (benefits from product use, related services) for what a customer *gives* (price paid, costs to acquire and use the product). Value is determined by the customer. For example, Southwest Airlines is the only major airline to be profitable for the past 20 years. One of the reasons for this success is that Southwest's customers value frequent departures, on-time service, friendly employees, and low fares. Southwest consistently provides customers exceptional value that translates into complete satisfaction, loyal customers, and increased sales and profits. Southwest does not assign seats, offer meals, or provide tickets as most other airlines do. Its customers do not value these services, so they are not offered.[12]

Organizations are faced with a difficult challenge in continually providing exceptional customer value, completely satisfying needs, and earning customer loyalty. Those successful in these endeavors are likely to achieve higher levels of sales growth and profitability than those that do not. Organizations increasingly have to be market-driven and customer-focused to compete effectively in the future. Some guidelines for executing a marketing philosophy that incorporates the marketing and customer loyalty concepts are presented in Exhibit 1–3. These guidelines are relevant for those in marketing and nonmarketing functions within an organization.

Exhibit 1–3	*Executing a marketing philosophy*

1. Create customer focus throughout the business.
2. Listen to the customer.
3. Define and nurture your distinctive competence.
4. Define marketing as market intelligence.
5. Target customers precisely.
6. Manage for profitability, not sales volume.
7. Make customer value the guiding star.
8. Let the customer define quality.
9. Measure and manage customer expectations.
10. Build customer relationships and loyalty.
11. Define the business as a service business.
12. Commit to continuous improvement and innovation.
13. Manage culture along with strategy and structure.
14. Grow with partners and alliances.
15. Destroy marketing bureaucracy.

Source: Frederick E. Webster, Jr., "Executing the New Marketing Concept," *Marketing Management* 3, no. 1, p. 10.

David Power
President
Power Creative Inc.

Power Creative provides integrated marketing communications services for the domestic and international operations of large blue-chip corporations. David received a BS in marketing from the University of Louisville in 1993 and joined Power Creative as an account executive, handling the RCA brand for Thomson Electronics. He has since been promoted to senior account executive, Vice President, and was recently named President of the company.

"Power Creative was regarded as just a supplier of advertising and marketing materials for many years. But in today's business world, with tight budgets and pressure to deliver higher margins, our customers view us as true business partners. Our objective is to improve the client's bottom line. Consistently delivering on this commitment has two major benefits. First, completely satisfied customers remain loyal. For example, we have worked with General Electric Appliances for many years. Second, loyal customers help us get new business. A recent example illustrates this. An individual we worked with at General Electric Appliances took a job as vice president and general manager of sales, marketing, and distribution for Lennox. He contacted us to develop programs to promote Lennox furnaces and air conditioners to housing contractors. We would never have been considered for this business without our previous successful relationship."

Marketing as a Societal Process

Marketing as a societal process can be defined as a process that facilitates the flow of goods and services from producers to consumers in a society. At this level, the emphasis is on issues such as:

- What institutions are involved in the societal marketing system?
- What activities do these institutions perform?
- How effective is the marketing system in satisfying consumer needs?
- How efficient is the marketing system in providing consumers with desired goods and services?

Thinking Critically

- Compare the political, economic, and marketing systems of a developed country with those of a developing country.
- Compare the political, economic, and marketing systems of the following countries: China, Poland, and the United States.
- On the basis of these comparisons, what can you conclude about the interrelationships among a country's political, economic, and marketing systems?

A society's marketing system is closely related to its political and economic systems. These close relationships are vividly illustrated by the tremendous changes that continue in Eastern Europe. Countries that operated under a communist political system with centrally planned economies did have some sort of marketing system, because products and services were provided to consumers. The marketing systems, however, were woefully ineffective and inefficient, largely because most "marketing" decisions were made centrally by government bureaucrats. With little consideration of customer needs, these officials decided what to produce, in what quantities, how products were to be made available to consumers, and at what prices.

Ineffective marketing systems contributed to the overthrow of the communist regimes in Eastern Europe, and these countries continue to struggle with developing democratic political systems and market-based economies. A market-based economy requires an effective and efficient marketing system that can identify and satisfy consumer needs for products and services. Although transforming political, economic, and marketing systems is painful and difficult in the short run, the changes promise to improve the standards of living in these countries in the long run.

However, the transformation process is often slow and the benefits from a market economy are not distributed equally. Consider the following family situations in China, which is trying to move to a market economy but keep its existing political system:

- Liu Fengtong used to be a welder at a coal plant a few miles away from Beijing. But he was laid off and now gives dance lessons to customers paying a 25¢ admission fee. Liu earns about $90 a month, about half of what he earned as a welder. This is the only work he can find to support his family.

The move to free-market economies and more open marketing systems offers tremendous opportunities for many firms. Dell is expanding its business in the China market.

- Frank Liu lives 700 miles away, in Shanghai. He heads a government agency that recruits foreign investors for the Waigaoqiao Free Trade Zone. He works in a wood-paneled office and wears expensive suits. His son attends an exclusive private school, and his family just bought a new apartment. Liu regularly meets with executives from Intel, Hewlett-Packard, and Dell and travels to the United States and other countries to develop business for the trade zone.[13]

These situations illustrate very different results from the move to a market economy and new marketing system. Over time, more people are likely to benefit from these changes, but market economies and marketing systems are not perfect. For example, a recent study of the contributions of the aggregate marketing system to U.S. society found both benefits and criticisms. Benefits included economic well-being, quality of life, and social/psychological benefits to individual workers and consumers. Criticisms included negative effects on societal values, unethical marketing practices, and ecological problems. This analysis did, however, conclude that the contributions from the U.S. aggregate marketing system outweighed the negative impacts.[14]

Important relationships exist between marketing at the organizational and societal levels. People moving from a planned to a market-based economic system must learn and implement basic marketing practices. The success of a society's marketing system depends on the ability of individuals in organizations to identify and respond to consumer needs effectively and efficiently. These individuals face the following problems, as expressed in a study of managers in several Eastern European countries:[15]

- Becoming more market-oriented and consumer-responsive.
- Improving product quality.
- Changing product design, assortment, finishing, and packaging.
- Increasing communications efforts such as personal selling and point-of-purchase sales.
- Increasing merchandising efforts.
- Using competitive pricing.
- Instituting promotional pricing and price discounts.

Poland and Malaysia are two developing countries with improving marketing systems. Colgate-Palmolive is taking advantage of opportunities in these countries by marketing a variety of consumer products.

Marketing as a Process

Marketing as an organizational philosophy and a societal process are related to the way marketing is performed by organizations and individuals. We are now ready to discuss the major aspects of marketing as a process.

Marketing Exchanges

Exchange is generally viewed as the core element of marketing.[16] **Exchange** has been defined as the "transfer of something tangible or intangible, actual or symbolic, between two or more social actors."[17] Thus, the basic purpose of marketing is to get individuals or organizations to transfer something of value (tangible or intangible, actual or symbolic) to each other. The most familiar type of exchange occurs when a customer exchanges money with a retail store for a product. Every time a customer pays a Papa John's pizza delivery person and receives a pizza, a marketing exchange takes place.

Marketing exchanges are not confined to transactions of money for products, as shown in Exhibit 1–4. Businesses engage in barter where they exchange their goods and services for the goods and services of another firm. Nonprofit organizations, colleges and universities, politicians, and many other "social actors" are also involved in exchanges. Volunteers and contributors to nonprofit organizations, for example, exchange their time and money for the satisfaction derived from helping a good cause. Or consider the tuition that students pay a university or college in ex-

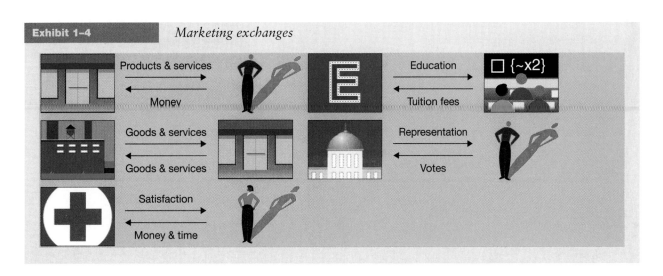

Exhibit 1–4   *Marketing exchanges*

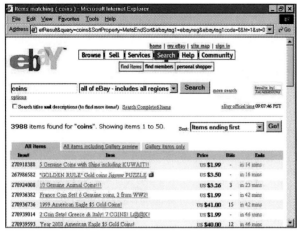

The basic purpose of marketing is to facilitate exchanges. eBay facilitates exchanges through auctions on the Internet.

change for the education they receive. Even politics involves exchanges, with people trading their votes for the promise of representation from a political candidate.

The major objective of marketing exchanges is to satisfy the needs of the individuals and organizations involved. For an exchange to take place, each party must be willing to give up something to get something. What each party gets must be as satisfying as what it gives up. If someone decides to buy a delivered pizza from Papa John's, the pizza must be as important as the money exchanged to get it. Similarly, Papa John's must think the money it receives from the customer is as important as the delivered pizza it exchanges.

Creating exchanges that satisfy customer needs requires that marketing strategies be developed and marketing activities performed. The process involves people in various marketing positions who determine what is to be done (they plan) and then do it (they execute). Some people in marketing positions are employed by the firm that produces the product and some by other organizations that specialize in specific marketing activities.

Marketing Strategies

Marketing strategies consist of selecting a target market and developing a marketing mix to satisfy that market's needs. A **target market** is a defined group of consumers or organizations with whom a firm wants to create marketing exchanges. A **marketing mix** is the overall marketing offer to appeal to the target market. It consists of decisions in four basic areas: product (development of a product, service, or idea to

Exhibit 1–5   *Marketing mix decisions*

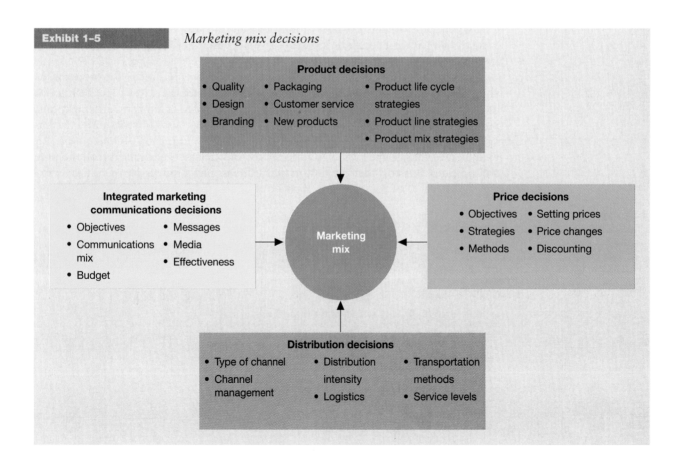

exchange), pricing (what to charge for the exchange), integrated marketing communications (how to communicate with the target market about the possible exchange), and distribution (how to get the product, service, or idea to the target market to consummate the exchange). As is evident from Exhibit 1–5, many marketing decisions must be made within the product, pricing, communications, and distribution areas.

The cosmetics industry is a good place to look for examples of different marketing strategies. Note in Exhibit 1–6 that Maybelline, Mary Kay, and Clinique all market a variety of cosmetic products to defined target markets. Brands differ, as do the prices charged, the methods of distribution, and the types of marketing communications. Each company effectively blends product, price, distribution, and integrated marketing communications decisions into a different marketing mix designed to serve its target market.

Marketing Activities

Regardless of an organization's specific marketing strategy, a number of different marketing activities must be performed to move products from producers to end users. Exhibit 1–7 illustrates these important activities schematically.

Buying and selling activities are required to finalize an exchange. The product assortments desired by buyers must be transported to appropriate locations and stored in inventory. The inventories must be financed and the risk associated with holding the inventory assortment assumed. Quality and quantity of product assortments must be standardized and graded. Finally, marketing information about buyers and competitors is needed to make marketing decisions.

Say you want to buy a DVD player. A number of producers of DVD players—Toshiba, Sharp, Panasonic, Sony—would like to sell you their brand. But it would be inefficient if you had to visit each producer to examine its product and then purchase directly from the factory. To facilitate the exchange process, the producers market their DVD players through various types of retailers, such as Circuit City.

Exhibit 1–6	*Marketing strategies*		
	Maybeline	**Mary Kay**	**Clinique**
Target market	Low end	Middle	High end
Product	Cosmetics	Cosmetics	Cosmetics
Price	Low	Moderate	High
Distribution	Mass merchandisers	Direct to consumers	Upscale department stores
Marketing communications	Advertising through mass media	Personal selling to consumers in home	Targeted advertising and personal selling to consumers in stores

Exhibit 1–7   *Marketing activities*

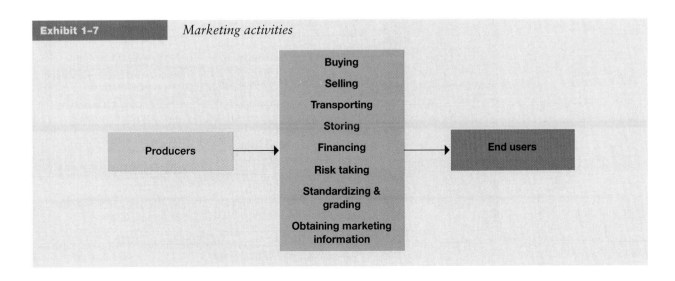

Thinking Critically

All of the key marketing activities must be performed for marketing exchanges to take place. Many of these marketing activities are increasingly being performed over the Internet. Assume you were interested in buying a new car.

- How would each of the key marketing activities be performed if you purchased the car from a local car dealer and did not use the Internet in any way?

- How could you and car producers and marketers use the Internet to perform these marketing activities?

So now you can go to Circuit City, try out different DVD-player brands, and easily purchase the one best suited to your needs. Circuit City has performed many of the marketing activities shown in Exhibit 1–7 that are required to complete an exchange between you and the producer of DVD players. Circuit City buys an assortment of DVD-player brands, transports them to its retail outlets, and stores them there in inventory. It assumes the expense and risk of holding this inventory. It standardizes and grades the product quality and quantity. Because it wants to move the DVD players from inventory to end users, it advertises and promotes the brands it carries and the price at which it is willing to exchange each brand. Buyers come to the stores, talk with salespeople, and purchase desired brands.

This would be the typical approach for getting DVD players from producers to consumers. However, with the tremendous growth of the Internet, other options are available. You might go to the Web site of one of the DVD producers and obtain information about DVD players, locate dealers for its brand, and possibly make a purchase. Or, you could go to a shopping site, such as Amazon.com, and compare various DVD brands and purchase the one that best meets your needs.

One way or another, certain marketing activities must be performed for exchanges to occur between producers and end users. In some cases, marketing institutions, such as retailers like Circuit City, perform many of the marketing activities for producers. In others, most activities are performed by individuals within the producing firm. Sometimes consumers perform some of the required marketing activities.

Marketing Positions

There are a variety of marketing positions within most organizations. Examples are shown in Exhibit 1–8. Some of these positions, such as advertising manager, distribution manager, or sales manager, indicate specialization in one area of marketing. Others suggest working across marketing areas (marketing manager, product manager, marketing research manager). The reality is that most marketing positions require close working relationships among different marketing and business

Marketing research firms specialize in performing marketing research activities to help firms make better decisions. ACNielsen is a global marketing research firm.

Exhibit 1.8	*Marketing positions*
Position/Alternative titles	**Duties**
Marketing manager Vice president of marketing, director of marketing	Directs all company's marketing activities, including planning, organizing, staffing, directing, controlling, evaluating performance
Product manager Brand manager	Develops goals, objectives, plans, strategies, marketing mixes for product line or brand
Advertising manager Advertising director, director of communications	Devises advertising policy and strategy, selects advertising agencies, develops promotional campaigns, selects media, allocates advertising expenditures
Distribution manager Logistics manager, traffic manager, transportation manager	Manages distribution system, including storage and transportation for all products, services
Purchasing manager Director of purchasing, director of procurement	Manages all purchasing activities, including buying product ingredients or components, supplies, equipment, needed materials
Marketing research manager Director of commercial research, director of market research	Develops research designs for specific problems; collects, analyzes, interprets data; presents results to top management
Public relations manager Director of public relations, director of communications, public affairs officer	Manages all communications with media and company stakeholders, to present favorable public image
Customer service manager Director of customer relations	Provides customer service, handles customer complaints
Sales manager Vice president of sales, director of sales, national sales manager, regional, district, or branch sales manager	Organizes, develops, directs, controls, evaluates salesforce

Source: Rolph Anderson, *Professional Personal Selling.* © 1991, p. 105. Reprinted by permission of Prentice-Hall. Englewood Cliffs, New Jersey.

functions. For example, advertising, sales, product, marketing, production, and accounting managers typically work together to develop and execute marketing plans for specific products.

Marketing positions are most prevalent in business firms, although similar positions exist in nonprofit organizations, hospitals, government agencies, museums, accounting firms, and other organizations. For organizations that follow a marketing philosophy, many employees are involved in marketing activities even though they may not hold formal marketing positions.

David Power, President, Power Creative, talks about being involved in marketing throughout his career: "Successful organizations are becoming increasingly customer-focused and are investing in ways to develop one-to-one relationships. These companies rely on everyone in the enterprise, from CEO to product development engineer to receptionist, to contribute to customer relationships. This means that everyone in the organization is involved in some marketing activities. And, different positions perform different marketing activities. For example, as an account manager most of my job was to maintain and expand our relationship with one large account. Now, as President, I am involved in more strategic issues that span all of our customers. I still, however, call on prospects to get new business and on existing customers to keep their business."

Marketing Institutions

Some organizations specialize in specific marketing activities and become experts in performing them. Thus, a firm may work with several of these organizations to handle the required marketing activities.

We have already discussed the important role that retailers, such as Circuit City, play in making a variety of different products and brands available to consumers. Sometimes wholesalers also undertake specific marketing activities for producers and retailers. Wholesalers engage in exchanges with producers and subsequently exchange these products from their inventory to meet the needs of retailers. They might also perform specialized services for producers and retailers. Some of the leading wholesalers are McKesson Corporation (health care products), Fleming Co.

(food), Produce Specialties (exotic fruits and vegetables), and United Stationers (office supplies).

Marketing research firms and advertising agencies also provide specialized services for client firms. Some firms emphasize specific types of marketing research, but the largest firms offer a full array of research services, including focus groups, concept tests, customer interviews, mail surveys, experiments, or other types of marketing research. The largest marketing research firms include ACNielsen, IMS International, Information Resources, Inc., and the Arbitron Co.

Advertising agencies also provide various services to help firms develop and implement marketing communications campaigns. Again, some of these firms specialize in specific areas; others provide full services, often including marketing research. The leading advertising agencies include Young & Rubicam, Saatchi and Saatchi, BBDO Worldwide, DDB Needham Worldwide, and Ogilvy & Mather Worldwide.

How Has Marketing Evolved?
Traditionally, the roots of modern marketing have been traced to the 1950s, when the marketing concept was first articulated. Before then, according to this view, most firms were driven by either production or sales philosophies, even though they engaged in marketing activities. So in the 1950s, leading firms presumably embraced the customer-oriented marketing concept. However, recent historical analysis provides strong evidence that marketing activities and customer orientations were commonplace in firms much earlier than the 1950s in the United States, Germany, and England.[18]

The Early Years
In the early 1500s in Germany and England and in the 1600s in North America, most of the population was rural and largely self-sufficient. Production and transportation were primitive, and capitalism was not well developed. Some astute marketers emerged nevertheless. Typically they marketed luxury goods to the nobility and the growing urban middle class, armaments to governments, or textiles and basic staples to selected elements of the population. Important marketing institutions and activities originating during this period include fixed-location retail shops, advertising, wholesale trade, warehouses, and traveling salespeople.

Modern Marketing Begins
The Industrial Revolution, from about 1750 in England and 1830 in the United States and Germany, produced tremendous changes in marketing. Production methods and transportation systems greatly improved. A substantial migration from rural areas to urban centers created potentially large markets. Marketing became a pervasive and central activity as firms tried to serve these developing markets. Because of intense competition, firms targeted particular population groups, developed products specifically for them, and promoted the products vigorously. The important marketing activities that we know as market segmentation, target marketing, and promotion were carried out by many firms during this period.

Modern Marketing Develops
Beginning with the Industrial Revolution, institutions and activities associated with modern marketing became more widespread. Here are some ways firms implemented a customer orientation in the nineteenth century:

- During the 1880s, Waltham Watch Co. moved from marketing whatever the factory decided to produce to producing exactly what customers wanted.

- Hampshire Paper Co. gave its salesforce extensive training in the philosophy that salespeople were expected to help customers solve their problems.

These ads were popular around 1900. Although marketing at Coca-Cola, Kellogg, and Ford has changed drastically since then, these companies were practicing basic marketing concepts many years ago.

- Parker Pen Co. realized that all customers did not want the same type of pen; its 1899 catalog included 40 pens priced from $1.50 to $20.

Even though the marketing concept was not formally articulated until the 1950s, some firms were clearly practicing it much earlier, as shown by a business text published in 1916:

Today the progressive business man makes careful, intensive studies not merely of the consumer's recognized wants but of his tastes, his habits, his tendencies in all the common activities and relations of life. This he does in order to track down unconscious needs, to manufacture goods to satisfy them, to bring these products to the attention of the consumer in the most appealing ways, and finally to complete the cycle by transporting the goods to him in response to an expressed demand.[19]

Modern Marketing Evolves

Marketing has built on past accomplishments as it has evolved. Many firms for many years have taken a customer orientation and performed basic marketing activities. What has changed most in recent years is the way marketing activities are performed. For example, the practice of dividing the market for a product into segments with different needs (market segmentation) has been used by at least some firms for over two centuries. However, segmentation procedures have changed drastically from simple, judgmental approaches to the use of sophisticated statistical techniques and large databases today. Even the tremendous changes brought about by Internet and e-commerce do not change the basics of marketing. How marketers do things has and will change dramatically, but the basics of a marketing philosophy and organizational process remain the same. This book focuses on both the marketing basics and the changes that have taken place in recent years and are expected to occur in the future.

A Contemporary Marketing Framework
The contemporary marketing framework that underlies the focus for this book is presented in Exhibit 1–9. The framework has three major elements: marketing, the marketing environment, and marketing perspectives.

Exhibit 1–9   *A contemporary marketing framework*

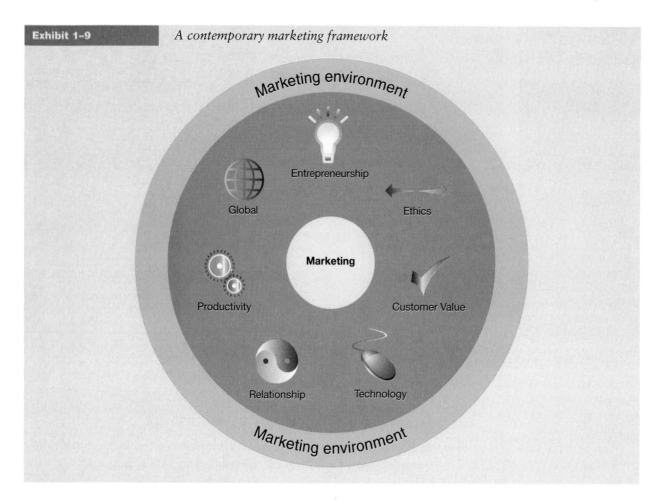

Marketing

The inner circle represents marketing as an organizational philosophy and organizational process. Most of this book expands on topics that fit within this circle: the marketing concept and marketing exchanges, strategies, activities, positions, and institutions. The marketing circle contains the largely controllable decision areas for marketers in all types of organizations.

Marketing Environment

The larger circle represents the uncontrollable environment within which marketers must operate. The marketing environment is categorized further into social, economic, competitive, technological, legal/political, and institutional environments. Each of these categories is examined in detail in Chapter 2.

Marketing is largely concerned with identifying market opportunities and responding to these opportunities by developing and executing effective marketing strategies. Market opportunities are typically the result of conditions or changes in the marketing environment.

Thus, successful marketing requires constant assessment of the marketing environment to identify opportunities and to determine the best way to capitalize on them. The difficulty is that the marketing environment is complex, turbulent, and uncertain.

Key Marketing Perspectives

We have identified seven key marketing perspectives to guide marketers in responding effectively to opportunities offered by the marketing environment (see

Exhibit 1–10	*Key marketing perspectives*	
Marketing Perspective	**Icon**	**Definition**
GLOBAL		Viewing the world as the potential marketplace to include identifying and responding both to market opportunities around the world and to different cultural groups within each market.
RELATIONSHIP		Building partnerships with firms outside the organization and encouraging teamwork among different functions within the organization in order to develop long-term customer relationships.
ETHICS		Addressing the morality of marketing decisions and practicing social responsibility to include ecological considerations.
CUSTOMER VALUE		Constantly looking for ways to give customers more for less.
PRODUCTIVITY		Trying to get the best return for each marketing dollar spent.
TECHNOLOGY		Translating new and emerging technologies into successful products and services, and using technology to improve marketing practice.
ENTREPRENEURSHIP		Focusing on innovation, on risk taking, and on being proactive in marketing efforts.

Exhibit 1–9). These perspectives provide links between marketing and the marketing environment. The seven key marketing perspectives are presented in Exhibit 1–10 and were discussed in the Prologue about America Online.

David Power, President, Power Creative, comments on the importance of these key marketing perspectives: "These key marketing perspectives are extremely important in my business. Our clients operate globally, so we must have a global perspective to meet their needs. Relationships with customers and teamwork within our company are critical to our success. We must continuously look for ways to create value for our customers and to ensure we do business ethically. Increasing our productivity and the productivity of our clients is a constant concern. Often, this requires being entrepreneurial, especially in using new technologies. We must be at the "cutting edge" in applying new technologies in innovative ways. This will continue to be a challenge as the use of the Internet in marketing and e-commerce grows."

Because these perspectives are important considerations in all aspects of marketing, we integrate them throughout the remaining chapters in several ways.

First, the appropriate perspectives are discussed in relevant places in each chapter. Icons in the margin or in-text and italicized references indicate when a specific perspective is being discussed.

Second, many chapters also include sidebars entitled "Using Technology" and "Being Entrepreneurial." These present examples of a technology and entrepreneurship perspective toward the material covered in the chapter. In addition, some chapters feature sidebars entitled "Earning Customer Loyalty," which highlight the relationship perspective.

Third, many chapters conclude with a section addressing important ethical issues relevant to the chapter topics.

Finally, in each chapter's "Speaking from Experience" features, professionals address the perspectives in various ways through their comments.

Summary

1. **Discuss what marketing is and why it is important to organizations and individuals.** Marketing "is the process of planning and executing the conception, pricing, promotion, and distribution of ideas, goods, and services to create exchanges that satisfy individual and organizational goals." Marketing is important to all types of organizations because it focuses on satisfying the needs of customers. Individuals, such as politicians, also engage in marketing during campaigns for election and when developing and implementing policies. Marketing activities are performed by people in various positions at different organizations. Interacting with people is a major component of most marketing positions.

2. **Distinguish between marketing as an organizational philosophy and a societal process.** Marketing can be defined in different ways. As an organizational philosophy, marketing is an orientation where everyone in the organization is driven by the marketing concept to satisfy customer needs. At the societal level, marketing is the process that determines the flow of goods and services from producers to consumers in a society.

3. **Understand the components of a marketing strategy and the different activities involved in marketing products and services.** A marketing strategy consists of the selection of a target market and the development of a marketing mix to appeal to that target market. The marketing mix is an integration of product, price, communications, and distribution decisions to serve a target market better than competitors.

   Implementing marketing strategies to facilitate exchanges requires many activities, including buying, selling, transporting, storing, financing, risk taking, standardizing and grading, and obtaining marketing information.

4. **Be aware of the various types of marketing institutions and the different marketing positions available in these institutions.** The necessary marketing activities are performed by different institutions and various positions within these institutions. Although some producers can perform all required marketing activities, organizations specializing in specific marketing activities are often used. Typical marketing institutions are wholesalers, retailers, distributors, marketing research firms, and advertising agencies.

   Important marketing positions include marketing managers, product managers, advertising managers, purchasing managers, sales managers, marketing research managers, and individuals who report to these managers. Marketing activities are also performed by people in nonmarketing positions.

5. **Appreciate how marketing has evolved from earlier times to the present.** Marketing has evolved substantially. This evolution moved from the origins of retailing to improved production and transportation methods (brought about by the Industrial Revolution) to the consumer orientation of modern marketing. The biggest change in marketing today is the way in which marketing activities are performed—for instance, segmenting markets by using statistical technology and databases.

6. **Understand the basic elements and relationships in the contemporary marketing framework.** The contemporary marketing framework depicts the important relationship between marketing and the marketing environment. Seven key marketing perspectives are presented as orientations that drive marketing's interactions with the external environment.

Understanding Marketing Terms and Concepts

Thinking about Marketing

1. How can top management in an organization ensure that all employees are driven by a marketing philosophy?

2. What is an example of barter as a marketing exchange?

3. How would you describe the major target market and marketing mix for your college or university?

4. What are the marketing activities required to get toothpaste from a producer, such as Colgate-Palmolive, to a consumer, such as yourself?

5. What marketing activities do Internet auctions like ebay.com perform?

6. What are the relationships between marketing as a societal process and the economic and political systems in a country?

7. What do you think is the most innovative development in marketing practice during the past few years? Why?

8. What types of marketing positions interest you? Why?

9. What role do the seven key marketing perspectives play in the contemporary marketing framework?

10. How does the marketing environment affect marketing?

Applying Marketing Skills

1. Pick a retail store at which you frequently shop. Identify and discuss the store's target market and the specific product, price, integrated marketing communications, and distribution decisions the management has made to develop a marketing mix.

2. Interview someone in a marketing position. Ask him or her about the activities involved in the position, about any expected future changes in the position, and about career opportunities.

3. Identify a nonprofit organization in your community. Determine the role of marketing in this organization by reading promotional materials and talking with someone in the organization.

Using the www in Marketing

Activity One   Go to Amazon.com's home page (http://www.amazon.com).

1. What are the latest products and services offered by Amazon.com?

2. What services does Amazon.com offer to help you select a DVD player that will best meet your needs?

3. Evaluate the selection and services offered by Amazon.com to help customers in purchasing books.

Activity Two   Go to the Barnes & Noble home page (http://www.bn.com).

1. Compare and contrast the home pages of Amazon.com and Barnes & Noble.

2. Evaluate the selection and services offered by Barnes & Noble to help customers in purchasing books and compare with what Amazon.com offers.

3. What would you recommend Barnes & Noble do in order to provide more value to its book customers?

Making Marketing Decisions

Case 1-1 Coca-Cola: Reviving a Marketing Philosophy

Coca-Cola has been one of the world's great marketers. Under the tutelage of Roberto C. Goizueta, Coke built a strong market position around the world and achieved strong sales and earnings growth for 16 straight years. Its stock increased a whopping 3,500 percent during this period. Unfortunately, Mr. Goizueta died of cancer in 1997. M. Douglas Ivester, chief financial officer at the time, took over as CEO.

Mr. Ivester has faced a number of challenges during his tenure. Coke's international growth has slowed considerably due largely to poor economic conditions and other problems in several international markets. For example, economic problems in two of Coke's biggest

international markets, Japan and Brazil, translated into no growth in 1998. Coke has invested $700 million in Russia during the past eight years, but the economic collapse in Russia has Coke operating at only 50 percent capacity. Some of Coke's efforts to expand in Europe and Latin America have been rebuffed by regulators concerned that Coke will dominate local markets. And reported contamination of Coke in Belgium hurt the company's image considerably.

The situation in the United States is also difficult. American consumers already drink more soft drinks than in any country in the world, except Mexico; therefore, domestic sales growth will have to come from increases in market share. But Coke's major competitor, Pepsi, is fighting for every piece of the market. Pepsi's "Joy of Cola" communications campaign has been very successful and has overshadowed Coke's long-running "Always" theme. Pepsi is also fighting hard in the lucrative restaurant-chain market and has increased the number of its vending machines considerably. Although Coke still leads Pepsi, this heightened competition is costly, putting further pressure on earnings growth. One response has been to raise the price of syrup to Coke's independent bottlers by 7.7 percent in 2000; this is twice the normal price increase and has infuriated the bottlers.

Although Coke's problems are not all Ivester's fault, the company's lackluster performance has reduced its stock price substantially and put Ivester under enormous pressure. On December 6, 1999, he stunned everyone by announcing his pending retirement in April 2000 and the appointment of Douglas N. Daft as the new CEO.

Daft had been in charge of Coke's Asia operations. Whereas Ivester had a financial background and spent most of his career at Coke's headquarters in Atlanta, Daft is a marketing person with extensive experience around the world including the Middle East and China. Though the economic conditions in Asia and Latin America are improving, Daft faces the same problems Ivester did—difficult challenges both domestically and internationally—and is nonetheless expected to return Coke to its glory days under Goizueta.

Questions

1. What is the first thing you would do if you were the new Coke CEO?

2. Ivester employed a production-oriented philosophy during his tenure as CEO. What does Daft need to do to instill a marketing philosophy throughout Coke?

3. What would you recommend Coke do to compete more effectively against Pepsi in the U.S. market?

4. What would you recommend Coke do to increase its growth internationally?

SOURCES: Dean Foust, Geri Smith, and David Rocks, "Man on the Spot," *Business Week,* May 3, 1999, pp. 142–51; Dean Foust, David Rocks, and Mark L. Clifford, "Is Douglas Daft the Real Thing?" *Business Week,* December 20, 1999, pp. 44–45.

Case 1-2 *Jollibee: Beating McDonald's in Burgers*

McDonald's is clearly the most successful fast-food brand in the world, with annual sales around $30 billion. It dominates most markets by providing customers with consistent product quality and service—but not in the Philippines.

Jollibee Foods Corp. is a family-owned chain with about $250 million annual sales. It has, however, captured about 52 percent of the Philippines market (compared with 16 percent for McDonald's). The company has twice as many stores in the Philippines as McDonald's does. How has Jollibee's been able to beat McDonald's in this market?

The major key to success is understanding and meeting the needs of the local market. Jollibee offers spicy burgers, fried chicken, and spaghetti and serves rice with all entrees. The food is similar to what "a Filipino mother would cook at home" and is designed "to suit the Filipino palate." And Jollibee charges prices from 5 to 10 percent lower than McDonald's. This combination of the right food at a lower price gives customers real value.

Jollibee also uses some marketing approaches that have been borrowed from McDonald's. It works hard to attract kids by targeting ads to children, providing in-store play activities, and offering signature characters and other licensed toys and products. The company locates restaurants in prime spots often surrounding a McDonald's outlet. And Jollibee maintains high standards for fast service and cleanliness.

The company is trying to duplicate its success in the Philippines in other international markets. It currently has 27 restaurants in 10 countries—even one in the United States. Jollibee will open six restaurants in Los Angeles and San Francisco to appeal to the large Filipino communities in these cities. Longer term, the firm thinks Chicago, New York, Houston, and Miami will be good markets because of their large Asian and Hispanic populations.

Jollibee cannot rest on its laurels in the Philippines or elsewhere. Government restrictions on foreign firms, such as McDonald's, are being lifted within the next two years. This should make McDonald's a more formidable competitor. Also, McDonald's is not likely to sit back and make it easy for Jollibee to gain footholds in other Asian and U.S. markets. Competition in the United States could be especially fierce.

Questions

1. Why do you think McDonald's has not been more successful against Jollibee in the Philippines?

2. What would you recommend McDonald's do to increase its market share in the Philippines?

3. What is your evaluation of Jollibee's strategy to expand into Asian, Middle East, and U.S. markets?

4. What marketing strategy would you recommend to Jollibee for successful operations in the U.S. market? How do you think McDonald's will respond as Jollibee enters the U.S. market?

SOURCE: Hugh Filman, "Happy Meals for a McDonald's Rival," *Business Week,* July 29, 1996, p. 77; "King of Fast Food at Home, Jollibee Plans Six More Stores in the U.S.," *Fox Market Wire,* March 12, 1999, pp. 1–3.

Chapter Two

The Global Marketing Environment

After studying this chapter, you should be able to:

1 Understand the nature of the marketing environment and why it is important to marketers.

2 Describe the major components of the social environment and how trends in the social environment affect marketing.

3 Understand how the economic environment affects marketing.

4 See how the political/legal environment offers opportunities and threats to marketers.

5 Appreciate the importance of the technological environment to marketers.

6 Understand differences in the competitive environment.

7 Know how changes in the institutional environment affect marketers.

Michael Dell founded Dell Computer Corporation with $1,000 when he was a college student at the University of Texas at Austin in 1984. Today, Dell is the world's leading direct computer systems company with annual revenues in excess of $24 billion. The company has over 33,000 employees, with sales offices in 34 countries around the world. Dell serves customers in more than 170 countries and territories.

Why has Dell been so successful? The major reason is that Michael Dell revolutionized the computer industry by introducing the direct model. Prior to Dell, most personal computers were sold through various middlemen—wholesalers and retailers—to the final customer. Dell did not think these middlemen added much value, so he developed a model to bypass them. The basic direct model aims "to deliver a superior customer experience through direct, comprehensive customer relationships, cooperative research and development with technology partners, computer systems custom-built to customer specifications, and service and support programs tailored to customer needs." So, if you go to the Dell Web site, you can select from various options to create the exact PC you desire. The computer will then be shipped directly to you. You can also check the Web site to follow your PC throughout the assembly process and keep track of it throughout the shipping process.

Dell now sells PCs to business customers, government agencies, educational institutions, and consumers. The company is enhancing the direct model by applying the Internet to its entire business. Over $35 million worth of PCs are purchased from Dell's Web site each day, accounting for about 43 percent of total sales. Approximately 40 percent of technical-support activities and 50 percent of order-status transactions are conducted over the Internet. Dell maintains 44 country-specific Web sites to meet the needs of customers in different international markets. The company's objective is to deliver faster, better, and more-convenient service to customers over the Internet.

But Dell is not just an Internet company. Many of its customers are large corporations, educational institutions, and government agencies. A field salesforce is used to initiate and develop relationships with these customers. Dedicated account teams, consisting of sales, customer-service, and technical-support representatives, serve the largest customers. Global account teams provide multinational customers with a single point of contact and offer global marketing programs. Still, although these customers receive personal attention from Dell, more and more communication and interaction is being accomplished over the Internet.

Sources: www.dell.com, December 22, 1999; Dell Computer Corporation, Form 10-K, 1999.

The Dell example illustrates how the marketing environment affects a firm's operations. The **marketing environment** consists of all factors external to an organization that can affect the organization's marketing activities. These factors are largely uncontrollable, although marketers can influence some of them. All marketers face the difficult task of identifying the important elements of the marketing environment for their organization, assessing current and likely future relationships between these factors, and developing effective strategies for a changing environment. This task has become increasingly difficult in recent years, as many elements of the marketing environment change rapidly and unpredictably. The objective of this chapter is to help you understand the important elements and relationships in the marketing environment.

The Marketing Environment

In the contemporary marketing framework diagrammed in Chapter One (Exhibit 1–9), the marketing environment appears in the outer circle. We now expand that framework by describing the major elements of the marketing environment. Exhibit 2–1 presents the addition of the social, economic, political/legal, technological, competitive, and institutional environments to the original diagram.

The best way to understand the marketing environment is to place yourself in the middle of the marketing circle. You are now a marketer for some organization and must make decisions about the marketing exchanges, strategies, activities, positions, and institutions employed by your organization. However, the decisions you *can* control depend on factors and trends in the marketing environment that you

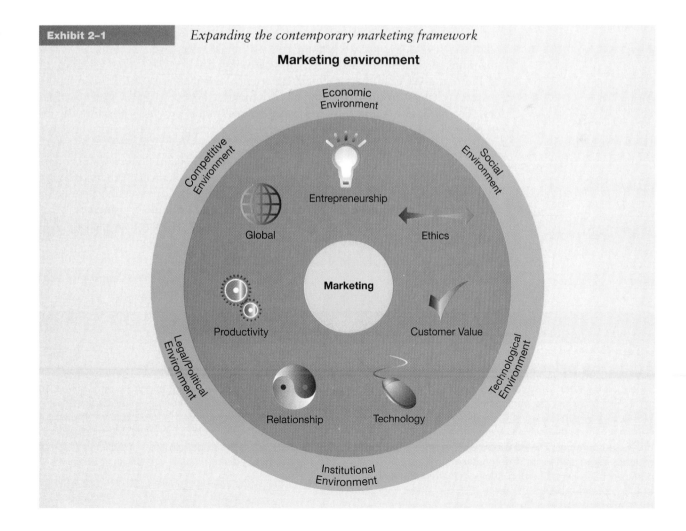

Exhibit 2–1   *Expanding the contemporary marketing framework*

cannot control. Thus, your task as a marketer is largely to identify opportunities or threats in the marketing environment and then make marketing decisions that capitalize on the opportunities and minimize the threats.

Creation of Market Opportunities and Threats

The marketing environment creates opportunities or threats in two basic ways. First, changes in the marketing environment can directly affect specific markets. A **market** is a group of people or organizations with common needs to satisfy or problems to solve, with the money to spend to satisfy needs or solve problems, and with the authority to make expenditure decisions. Changes in the marketing environment can make markets larger or smaller or sometimes create new markets. Market opportunities typically arise when markets increase in size or new markets are created.

Take the Dell Computer situation. Rapid technological developments have steadily reduced the price of personal computers, making them affordable to more individuals and organizations. In the mid-1980s this increased the size of the personal computer market. Michael Dell recognized this and realized he could take advantage of this market opportunity by implementing the direct model. The direct model would differentiate his company from PC competitors and be a way to satisfy customer needs in a profitable manner.

The second way the marketing environment produces opportunities or threats is through direct influences on specific marketing activities. Rapid advancements in Internet technology have provided Dell with opportunities to reach new markets and to serve customers more effectively and efficiently. Customers can now order customized computers, receive customer service, and get technical support 24 hours a day and seven days a week. Interacting with customers over the Internet is not only more convenient to customers, but is also less costly to Dell. So, utilization of the Internet gives customers a better experience and increases Dell's profitability. However, changes in the marketing environment also pose threats. Many companies, such as Gateway and IBM, are using a direct model and incorporating the Internet into marketing operations. This increases the competitive intensity within the industry.

The critical point of this discussion is that marketers need to understand the marketing environment to be able to make good decisions. Changes in the marketing environment may create opportunities or threats either by affecting markets or by directly influencing marketing activities. An interesting example of using new technology to respond to changes in the weather is presented in "Using Technology: Adjusting Prices to Temperature Changes."

Using Technology

Adjusting prices to temperature changes

When the weather gets warmer, the market for soft drinks increases. More people purchase more soft drinks and are willing to pay a higher price. Coca-Cola is testing a new vending machine that will allow them to adjust prices based on the temperature. The vending machine is equipped with a temperature sensor and computer chip that can automatically raise prices for drinks in hot weather; the technology is already being used in Japan, where wireless modems are used to adjust prices based on temperature.

Coke also already uses vending machines with a wireless signal in Australia and North Carolina—in these cases to relay which drinks are selling at what rates and where. About 12 percent of soft-drink sales worldwide come from vending machines, so Coke could generate significant revenue from the ability to adjust prices to temperature changes.

Source: "A Case of Supply and Demand," *Marketing News*, November 22, 1999, p. 3

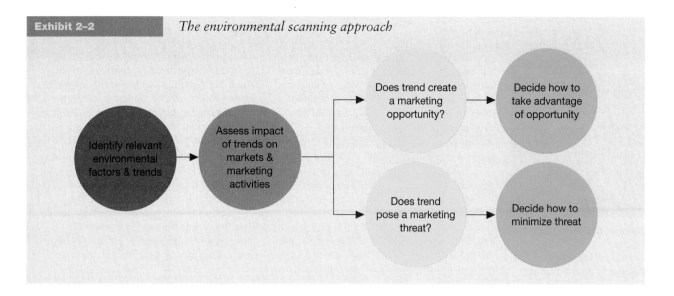

Exhibit 2–2   *The environmental scanning approach*

Identifying Market Opportunities and Threats

Many firms use **environmental scanning** to identify important trends and determine whether they represent present or future market opportunities or threats. As illustrated in Exhibit 2–2, this procedure consists of identifying relevant factors and assessing their potential impact on the organization's markets and marketing activities. This is simpler to say than do, because many of the potentially important environmental factors are interrelated and many of them change constantly.

Skandia, the $7 billion Swedish financial services giant, used an interesting approach to identify future growth opportunities. The company established a new unit, Skandia Future Center, and selected 30 diverse people from around the world to form five Future Teams. Each Future Team consisted of a mix of people from three generations (20-somethings to 60-somethings), who also represented a variety of functional roles, organizational experiences, and cultural backgrounds. The mission of each Future Team was to explore one of five major environmental forces (the European insurance market, demographics, technology, the world economy, and organizations and leadership) and develop a vision of the future for Skandia. The Future Teams presented their ideas to a group of 150 executives. The executives then formed 20 small groups to brainstorm responses to the ideas developed by the Future Teams. The process produced several innovative ways for Skandia to grow in the future.[1]

One way to deal with a volatile marketing environment is to use the seven key marketing perspectives discussed in Chapter One. As shown in Exhibit 2–1, these perspectives are at the interface between the controllable marketing circle and the uncontrollable marketing environment. They thereby provide important orientations for viewing the marketing environment, assessing market opportunities and threats, and determining the best marketing responses to the changing environment. The perspectives work both ways: They guide both a marketer's outward evaluation of the environment and inward response to the environment through marketing decisions.

Social Environment

The **social environment** includes all factors and trends related to groups of people, including their number, characteristics, behavior, and growth projections. Since consumer markets have specific needs and problems, changes in the social environment can affect markets differently. Trends in the social

Speaking from Experience

Samuel Chi-Hung Lee
President
International Marketing
Consultants Company Limited

Based in Hong Kong, Samuel Chi-Hung Lee's company has established extensive business networks in southeast Asian countries, such as Indonesia, Malaysia, Singapore, Burma, Vietnam, and southern China. Samuel has been a senior sales and marketing management executive for several North American corporations with operations in Hong Kong and has an MBA. He describes some of the business opportunities made possible by the rapidly changing marketing environment in Hong Kong.

"Hong Kong and other Asian countries were hurt badly by the economic and financial crisis in 1997. This crisis produced a tremendous decline in the Hong Kong stock market and the property market. Many individuals lost 40 percent-50 percent of their personal assets. This reduced the purchasing power of consumers, which had a negative effect on many businesses. Although the situation is improving, the marketing opportunities are different. There is no longer the opportunity to make high profits in the property market. Therefore, property developers are diversifying their investments into the high technology area. The opportunities are now in cyberspace. The property wars are being replaced with cyberspace wars in Hong Kong."

Twoje biuro może być tam gdzie zechcesz

IBM ThinkPad 755 CD

Różnica jest oczywista

The markets for many products and services are global. This ad for the IBM Thinkpad in Poland uses an appeal that can be used in any part of the world. "Your office can be wherever you want it to be."

environment might increase the size of some markets, decrease the size of others, or even help to create new markets. We discuss two important components of the social environment: the demographic environment and the cultural environment.

Demographic Environment

The **demographic environment** refers to the size, distribution, and growth rate of groups of people with different characteristics. The demographic characteristics of interest to marketers relate in some way to purchasing behavior, because people from different countries, cultures, age groups, or household arrangements often exhibit different purchasing behaviors. A *global perspective* requires that marketers be familiar with important demographic trends around the world as well as within the United States.

GLOBAL POPULATION SIZE AND GROWTH

Population size and growth rates provide one indication of potential market opportunities. The world population is now more than six billion, with almost 100 million people added each year during the 1990s. Thus, the world population grew about one billion during the decade of the 1990s. Approximately 95 percent of that growth took place in developing countries in Asia, Africa, and Latin America.[2] Population in the developed countries grew at a much slower rate. For example, the U.S. population grew by approximately 1 percent per year throughout the 1990s. These trends are expected to continue.

There is a tremendous disparity in population size and growth rates across countries, as shown in Exhibit 2–3. China currently has the largest population, followed by India, with the United States a distant third. The rapid growth of the Indian population is expected to make it the world's most populous nation by the year 2100. Other countries with large and growing populations are the developing nations of Indonesia, Brazil, Pakistan, Bangladesh, and Nigeria.

Exhibit 2–3   *The most populous countries*

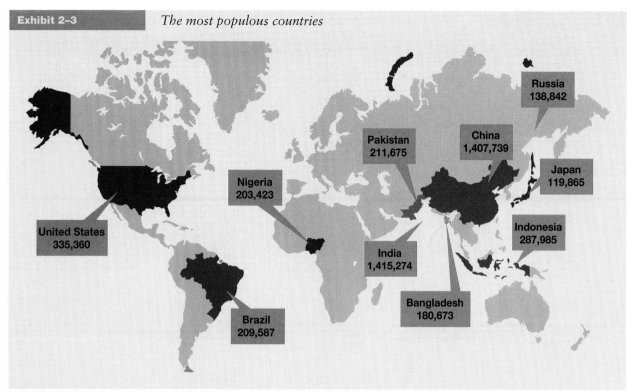

Russia
138,842

Pakistan
211,675

China
1,407,739

Japan
119,865

Nigeria
203,423

Indonesia
287,985

United States
335,360

India
1,415,274

Bangladesh
180,673

Brazil
209,587

Note: Population in thousands—Year 2025 (estimated)

Source: Excerpt from *The World Almanac and Book of Facts 2000* (World Almanac Books, 1999), pp. 878–879. Used with permission of the publisher. All rights reserved.

The world population situation can be summarized as follows. About every two seconds, nine babies are born and three people die, for a net increase of three people each second. This leads to a growth rate of 10,600 people per hour, 254,000 per day, 1.8 million per week, 7.7 million per month, and 93 million per year. Of this annual increase, developing countries will have 87 million new people, and developed countries, 6 million. Annual growth will increase to 94 million by the year 2000; by 2020 it will be 98 million, with 98 percent occurring in developing countries.[3]

These world population statistics make it clear that marketers cannot rely on population growth in developed countries alone for general increases in market size. The largest growth markets, measured by population size, are in the developing countries. Yet, lower income levels in developing countries may limit the actual market size for many products. Thus, marketers will have to look hard to find attractive growth markets in developed and developing countries.

GLOBAL DEMOGRAPHIC CHARACTERISTICS AND TRENDS Overall world and country population statistics are important, but most marketers target subgroups within these large populations. Trends in population subgroups are therefore typically the most useful to marketers.

An important trend in many countries is growth of the urban population. Current and projected populations for the world's largest cities are presented in Exhibit 2–4. In general, the largest cities and the highest city growth rates are in developing countries such as Mexico, Brazil, and India; however, growth in urban population is evident in many developed countries. For example, in 1900, the U.S. population was 39.6 percent urban and 60.4 percent rural; in 1990, the figures were 75.2 percent urban and 24.8 percent rural.[4] This means the largest and fastest-growing markets for many products are located in the urban areas of most countries.

Another interesting trend is the aging of the population in many countries. Current and projected median ages for selected countries are presented in Exhibit 2–5.

Exhibit 2–4	*The world's largest cities*		
City		**1995 (in thousands)**	**2015 (est.) (in thousands)**
1. Tokyo, Japan		26,959	28,887
2. Mexico City, Mexico		16,562	19,190
3. Sao Paulo, Brazil		16,533	20,320
4. New York, USA		16,332	17,602
5. Mumbai (Bombay), India		15,138	26,218
6. Shanghai, China		13,584	17,969
7. Los Angeles, U.S.		12,410	14,217
8. Calcutta, India		11,923	17,305
9. Buenos Aires, Argentina		11,802	13,856
10. Seoul, South Korea		11,609	12,980

Source: *The World Almanac and Book of Facts 2000,* (World Almanac Books, 1999), p. 878.

Exhibit 2–5	*Median age in selected countries*		
		Median Ages Past & Projected	
Country		**1990**	**2010**
Italy		36.2	42.4
Japan		37.2	42.2
Britain		35.7	40.0
U.S.		32.9	37.4
Korea (North & South)		25.7	34.4
China		25.4	33.9
Brazil		22.9	29.2
Mexico		20.0	26.5
Nigeria		16.3	18.1

Source: Data from United Nations Population Division.

The aging of the population is especially evident in Italy, Japan, Britain, and the United States. Notice, however, the relatively young populations in the developing countries, such as Nigeria, Mexico, Brazil, and China.

Age distribution trends in the United States are presented in more detail in Exhibit 2–6. The largest percentage of growth is occurring in the 45–64 and 65+ age brackets, with slight to moderate decreases in all younger age categories. These trends have important implications for marketers; older consumers have different needs and purchasing habits than do younger consumers. Marketers are responding to different age markets in a number of ways. For instance,

- Take Home Instead Senior Care is responding to the needs of those in their 70s and 80s. The company provides "nonmedical companionship" through services such as mail sorting, letter writing, meal preparation, incidental transportation, laundry, and helping clients remember to take medication. Business is booming; 1999 sales were up 91 percent from 1998.[5]

- Financial institutions have increased marketing efforts to attract mature Americans. Mutual fund giants T. Rowe Price and Vanguard offer software programs to help older consumers plan for retirement. Merrill Lynch hired a gerontologist to understand mature consumers better and to develop products to suit their goals.[6]

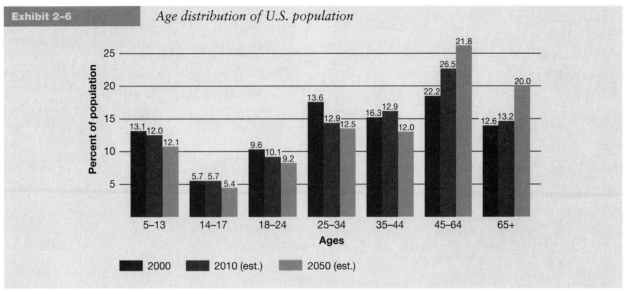

Exhibit 2–6   *Age distribution of U.S. population*

Percent of population

- ■ 2000   ■ 2010 (est.)   ■ 2050 (est.)

Ages	2000	2010 (est.)	2050 (est.)
5–13	13.1	12.0	12.1
14–17	5.7	5.7	5.4
18–24	9.6	10.1	9.2
25–34	13.6	12.9	12.5
35–44	16.3	12.9	12.0
45–64	22.2	26.5	21.8
65+	12.6	13.2	20.0

- ESPN developed the Alternative Sports Olympics to appeal to consumers aged 18 to 29. Also called The Extreme Games, the program features sports that attract the so-called Generation X (bungee jumping, street luging, sky surfing, and barefoot water-ski jumping) and are sponsored by companies trying to target those young consumers (Taco Bell, Mountain Dew, Nike, AT&T, and Pontiac). More than 130,000 spectators see the games live and millions watch on television.[7]

- Sega of America spends a great amount of time trying to understand teens. The company's advertising agency visits the homes of 150 teens and goes shopping with them at the malls. This information helps Sega introduce new video games successfully.[8]

Yet another relevant demographic trend is the declining number of household units consisting of the "typical" family: married couples with children living at home. Only 26 percent of U.S. households fall into this category, down from 45 percent in 1972. People living with nonrelatives is a fast-growing household type, up 62 percent since 1972.[9] In addition, about 23 million Americans live by themselves. This is an increase of 91 percent for women and 156 percent for men since 1980.[10] The needs and purchasing behaviors of different household arrangements represent important trends affecting marketers.

Cultural Environment

The **cultural environment** refers to factors and trends related to how people live and behave. Cultural factors, including the values, ideas, attitudes, beliefs, and activities of specific population subgroups, greatly affect consumers' purchasing behavior. Thus, marketers must understand important cultural characteristics and trends in different markets.

CULTURAL DIVERSITY   Cultural differences are important in both international and domestic markets. A cultural group's characteristics affect the types of products it desires and how it purchases and uses those products. Different cultural groups in international markets often require marketers to develop strategies specifically for them.

Campbell's Soup has had some successes and some failures in doing this. The successes include hearty vegetable and fat-free soups in Australia, duck-gizzard soup in Hong Kong, and the Godiva Chocolatier line in Japan. But the company has had

Populations in developed countries are aging, while those in developing countries are much younger. These different demographic trends represent challenging marketing opportunities for many firms.

some failures due to lack of understanding cultural differences in some markets. German consumers did not like Campbell's canned condensed soup. They prefer dry soups in envelopes. Polish consumers did not like Campbell's prepared soups, since they would rather cook soup at home.[11]

Much of the population growth in the United States is and will be accounted for by different cultural groups. The majority U.S. population is expected to grow by about 3 percent between 1990 and 2000. Compare this with the 14 to 52 percent growth rates of different ethnic groups. A large portion of this population growth is accounted for by African-Americans, Asian-Americans, and Hispanics.[12] However, significant growth is also expected from other cultural groups: Arabs, Russians, Eastern Europeans, and Caribbeans.[13]

These different cultural groups retain many of their habits, attitudes, interests, and behaviors even though they are proud to be Americans. The United States is not a melting pot; it's a mosaic of unique people with a variety of cultures. Successful marketers understand the delicate balance between important cultural differences and similarities that unite different cultures.[14] For example, the Arab-American sector consists of a diverse group of people from 22 different countries, with the largest subgroups being Egyptians, Syrians, Lebanese, Palestinians, and Iraqis. Although these subgroups differ in various ways, there is also a cohesiveness among them due to their common Arab heritage.[15]

Another interesting trend is a blending of races and ethnic groups. It is estimated that by 2050, the percentage of the U.S. population that claims some combination of black, white, Hispanic, or Asian ancestry will triple to 21 percent. Singer Mariah Carey and TV news anchor Soledad O'Brien (black, white, and Hispanic) and golfer Tiger Woods (black, white, American Indian, and Asian) are prominent examples of this trend.[16]

This cultural complexity provides marketers with a continual challenge. Take the Hispanic market as an example. The Hispanic population in the United States is

More women are playing golf. This expanding market offers attractive opportunities for many firms.

currently 31 million, with more than $300 billion in purchasing power. Effectively marketing to Hispanics requires much more than translating marketing communications into Spanish. The California Milk Processor Board (CMPB) found this out. It had used the theme "got milk?" to increase milk consumption by the mass market. When it tried to translate this theme to the Hispanic women's market, two interesting things were discovered. First, running out of milk is not funny to Hispanic women, it is an insult. Second, the translation of "got milk?" into Spanish means "are you lactating?" Based on these findings, the CMPB developed a multigenerational, family-focused campaign about passing down milk-based recipes. Interestingly, Hispanic teens responded enthusiastically to the "got milk?" campaign.[17]

These examples in the Hispanic market illustrate the importance of understanding the diversity among and within different cultural markets for developing successful marketing strategies. There are typically opportunities to market products across some cultural groups and to also target specific cultural groups. Sometimes, products from one culture can appeal to consumers in another culture. Princess Asie Acansey of Ghana capitalized on such an opportunity when she formed Advanced Business Connections (ABC). She was disturbed about the imagery of Africa as typically presented in the United States and decided to do something about it. ABC infuses African culture into the American teddy bear. The teddy bears represent African royalty and follow African royal customs. The first teddy bear was the king's protocol officer, Kwesi-Bear, then King Tutu Bear, followed by Queen Abena. Most of ABC's marketing has been on the QVC home shopping network. The products have been well received beyond the African-American market in the United States, illustrating the potential from mixing different cultures.[18]

CHANGING ROLES   As more women enter the workforce and household compositions change, typical household roles are altered. No longer are financially supporting the household and developing a career solely the responsibility of men. No longer are household chores, child care, or grocery shopping solely the responsibility of women. In many households, roles have shifted and distinctions have become blurred. More men spend time on household and shopping chores, and many women are involved in career development and provide much or most of the financial resources for a household. Tremendous market opportunities exist for firms that can develop effective strategies for appealing to these changing roles.

Take golf as an example. Women now account for 21 percent of the 25 million golfers in the United States. And this percentage is growing. Some of this growth is due to more women playing golf as part of their business or professional life. Others play the sport entirely for pleasure. In any case, women spend about $3 billion annually on golf equipment, clothing, travel, greens fees, and other related products. One study found that women are more likely to take golf lessons, are less price sensitive, and are more concerned about wearing fashionable clothing than are men golfers. This growing, upscale market of female golfers is attractive to marketers of golf products as well as marketers of other products.[19]

EMPHASIS ON HEALTH AND FITNESS   Another cultural trend is an increased emphasis on health and fitness. The pursuit of a healthier lifestyle includes eating more nutritious foods, exercising regularly, participating in various sports activities, and focusing on wellness. This translates into potential market

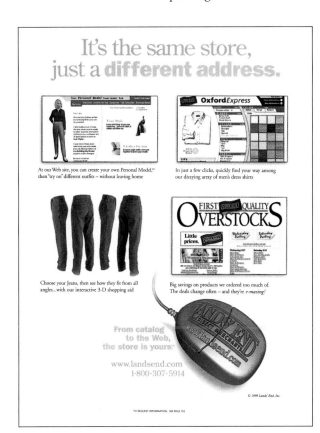

Busy people look for ways to make life easier. Lands' End provides a convenient way for men and women to shop for clothes.

opportunities for firms that provide products and services geared toward improving health and fitness.

Consider how firms are taking advantage of this social trend in the beverage industry:

- Nutriceuticals combine exotic fruits with medicinal plants and herbs to promote various health benefits. For example, Mrs. Wiggle's Rocket juice offers Papaya Ginseng to boost energy; Nantucket Super Nectars markets Ginko Mango to enhance mental acuity; and Fresh Samantha introduced Spirulina Fruit Blend to strengthen the immune system.[20]
- John Bello founded South Beach Beverage Company to market a line of herb-spiked teas and tonics. The drinks are intended "to uplift the mind, body, and spirit" and carry exotic names, such as Jing and Qi. Sales have been brisk, increasing from $2.1 million in 1996 to $67 million in 1998.[21]

DESIRE FOR CONVENIENCE   Changes in household composition, increases in the number of working women, and a general shortage of time underlie an increased desire for convenience. Two-paycheck households often have more money than time. And they are willing to spend this money to avoid spending time doing undesirable chores, such as cooking, cleaning, or auto maintenance. Thus, many consumers buy products and services to minimize time devoted to such chores, opening new market opportunities for companies able to meet these needs.

One of the major reasons the Internet is becoming so popular is the convenience it provides in so many areas of consumers' lives. Assume you wanted to buy a book, a CD, a DVD player, some software, and some toys. You would ordinarily have to visit a variety of different stores during business hours to make these purchases. Or, you might be able to look through several catalogs and place several phone calls to order your products. Or, you might go to a Web site like Amazon.com any time you want and order all of the products at one time and have everything delivered directly to your door in a couple of days. Which shopping approach offers the most convenience to you and other shoppers?

CONSUMERISM   *Consumerism* is the movement to establish and protect the rights of buyers. Some say the consumerism movement will intensify as we move through the twenty-first century. Consumers are more educated, knowledgeable, and organized. They will demand better consumer information, quality, service, and dependability, and fair prices.[22] The consumerism movement is one reason marketers need to adopt an *ethics perspective*. Giving consumers products that work, charging fair prices, being honest, and practicing social responsibility are the best ways to respond to consumerism.

One increasingly important consumer issue is environmentalism. As consumers worldwide become concerned with environmental issues, their purchasing behavior will change. Successful marketers can respond by developing environmentally safe products and communicating their environmental contributions.

Ogallala Down Co. is taking advantage of this trend. The company's philosophy is, "Healthy products for people and the environment." It markets down comforters and pillows that are hypoallergenic, warm, lightweight, breathable, and guaranteed for 10 years. Established in 1989, the company has enjoyed rapid sales growth in an industry long dominated by large firms. The American Marketing Association recognized the

ICH WAR EIN AUTO.

Ford-Automobile sind in hohem Maße aus wiederverwertbaren Teilen gefertigt. Da kann es vorkommen, daß manche dieser Teile in einem völlig anderen Produkt wieder auftauchen.

Wichtiger ist uns jedoch die umfassende und sinnvolle Wiederverwendung aller eingesetzten Werkstoffe im Automobilbau. Deshalb untersucht Ford in einer Pilot-Demontageanlage die optimale Zerlegung von Altfahrzeugen.

Mit den dort gewonnenen Erkenntnissen verbessern wir ständig die Recyclingfähigkeit neuer Ford-Modelle. So können wir bereits seit Oktober 1991 die kostenlose Rücknahme aller ab diesem Zeitpunkt vom Band gelaufenen Fahrzeuge der Escort-/Orion-Baureihe garantieren.

Wenn Sie mehr über Recycling oder andere umweltentlastende Maßnahmen beim Produktionsprozeß bei Ford wissen möchten, rufen Sie uns einfach an: 0130 42 42.

FORD. BEI UNS DREHT SICH ALLES UM SIE.

Consumers worldwide are becoming more concerned about the environment. Fordwerke appeals to these concerns by marketing a toy made from recycled auto parts. The headline reads: "I was a car."

environmental achievements of Ogallala Down by presenting it with an Edison Environmental Award.[23]

POPULAR CULTURE   The final cultural trend we note is the popularization of the U.S. culture throughout much of the world. Movies, television shows, and commercials typically express a culture's values and attitudes, and U.S. food, fashion, and entertainment trends are becoming increasingly popular worldwide. Technological advances and globalization of the media allow the export of this popular culture, resulting in a variety of market opportunities.

China represents a good example of this trend. The Chinese market consists of 1.2 billion people and 305 million TV sets. Foreign shows are limited to 25 percent of all TV programming with ESPN, CNN, and MTV among the cable channels allowed. Much of this programming contains U.S. popular culture. For example, Disney provides the Dragon Club Show on 100 cable systems, and Viacom offers one to five hours daily of MTV on 36 cable systems. The Chinese people seem to enjoy these shows. Peng Jinglong, a Beijing high school student, is a fan of the Cartoon Network's *Tom and Jerry* cartoons:

Chinese cartoons can't compare. American cartoons are more lighthearted and funnier. And the stories are better.[24]

Economic Environment   The **economic environment** includes factors and

trends related to income levels and the production of goods and services. Whereas demographic and cultural trends generally affect the size and needs of various markets, economic trends affect the purchasing power of these markets. Thus, it is not enough for a population to be large or fast growing, as in many developing countries, to offer good market opportunities; the economy must provide sufficient purchasing power for consumers to satisfy their wants and needs.

Economic trends in different parts of the world can affect marketing activities in other parts of the world. For example, changes in interest rates in Europe affect the value of the dollar on world currency markets, which affects the price, and subsequently sales, of American exports and imports.

Market opportunities are a function of both economic size and growth. The **gross domestic product (GDP)** represents the total size of a country's economy measured in the amount of goods and services produced. Changes in GDP indicate trends in economic activity. However, changes in economic growth around the world mean that market opportunities are often shifting. For example, many Asian countries experienced negative GDP growth in 1997 and 1998, but returned to positive growth in 1999 with this trend expected to continue into 2000. Korea represents a good example. Japan, however, continues to experience slow growth. Many other areas of the world expect economic growth in 2000 and beyond. Latin America countries have generally recovered from economic problems in 1998 and 1999, and typically expect economic growth to resume in 2000. European countries and the United States are expected to continue the economic growth of recent years.

Another important economic factor is the level of economic activity per person. Per capita data integrate population and economic data to provide an assessment of the purchasing power of individual consumers in a country. The United States ranks at the top of the pack in per capita GDP, followed by Switzerland, Canada, Luxembourg, Germany, and Japan. Some smaller countries, such as the United Arab Emirates and Kuwait, have large GDPs relative to their small populations, although their overall level of economic activity is small in comparison with the larger countries. Consumers in these countries may have a lot of purchasing power, but there are not that many of them. These countries typically offer attractive market opportunities for luxury products.

Many developing countries have large and growing segments of middle-class consumers. Gillette targets the 250 million middle-class consumers in India.

Conversely, many developing countries have large populations relative to their economic strength; that is, individual consumers do not have much purchasing power. However, subgroups within these countries may have substantial purchasing power, or economic growth may offer substantial opportunities in the future. India, for example, has a large and growing population but a low per capita income. Within this relatively poor country, however, are 250 million middle-class consumers. This is larger than the total U.S. market. Coca-Cola, Walt Disney, Kentucky Fried Chicken, Frito-Lay, and many other companies have recently started Indian operations to take advantage of this opportunity. Motorola estimates 40 to 50 million middle-class families there have the buying power to purchase a telephone or pager. It considers India one of the largest untapped markets in the world.[25]

Samuel Chi-Hung Lee, President, International Marketing Consultants Company Limited, discusses the marketing opportunities available in China: "China is making efforts to open its markets and to integrate its economy more fully into the world market. If this continues, it will increase economic growth, generate many new jobs, and produce attractive business opportunities. Hong Kong will benefit from this trend, since it is a window for China. For example, the government of the Hong Kong Special Administration Region sees many opportunities in this economic environment. It is trying to develop the tourism industry through a joint venture with Disney World. It is also developing a new technology highway through the Cyber Port Project. Many new infrastructure projects, such as new highways and railways, are being undertaken. These projects will all contribute to economic growth in the area and generate many market opportunities."

Political/Legal Environment

The **political/legal environment** encompasses factors and trends related to governmental activities and specific laws and regulations that affect marketing practice. The political/legal environment is closely tied to the social and economic environments. That is, pressures from the social environment, such as ecological or health concerns, or the economic environment, such as slow economic growth or high unemployment, typically motivate legislation intended to improve the particular situation. Regulatory agencies implement legislation by developing and enforcing regulations. Therefore, it is important for marketers to understand specific political processes, laws, and regulations, as well as important trends in each of these areas.

Global Political Trends

In today's world economy, international political events greatly affect marketing activities. One significant trend is a move from government-dominated economies and socialist political systems toward free market economies and, in many countries, democratic governments. Russia and the republics from the former Soviet

Being Entrepreneurial

Marketing opportunities during war

During the 78-day NATO bombing of Serbia, the economy in Belgrade was shattered and anti-American sentiment was high. A visible American icon, McDonald's, was attacked when the bombing began. Everything from windows to chairs was smashed, and the restaurant was forced to close down. However, less than a month later, manager Dragoljub Jakic reopened the store. It was covered with cardboard and plastic sheeting and posters saying "McDonald's is yours." A traditional Serbian cap was placed on the golden arches, prices were lowered, and free hamburgers given to anti-NATO protesters. Slowly, customers returned. Four months after the bombing ceased, McDonald's was restored to its former condition and business had returned to prewar levels.

Source: Katarina Kratovac, "At Least One U.S. Icon Survives in Belgrade," *Marketing News*, October 11, 1999, p. 29.

Union and former communist countries in Eastern Europe, such as Hungary, Romania, and Poland, are moving in this direction at various rates. China is taking a different tack: trying to promote a free market economy within its socialist political system. This objective may be difficult to achieve, as rapid economic growth is generating pressure for a more democratic political system.

These historic developments offer potentially huge market opportunities for many firms, given that these populations need many different types of products and services. Creating effective free market economies is likely to take a long time and considerable effort. Many countries continue to struggle with new political and economic systems. But, marketing opportunities can be found in the most unusual situations as presented in "Being Entrepreneurial: Marketing Opportunities During War."

A second important political trend is movement toward free trade and away from protectionism. One approach is the development of trading blocs throughout the world. One of the most significant is the European Union (EU). It consists of 11 European countries representing 290 million consumers and a combined GDP of $6.5 trillion. Another is the North American Free Trade Agreement (NAFTA). It consists of the United States, Mexico, and Canada and includes 360 million consumers and $6 trillion GDP.[26] The aim is to eliminate trade barriers and to promote easier access to the markets in each participating country. As this development continues, trading blocs have the potential to generate many opportunities for marketers.

The free trade trend goes beyond trading blocs and encompasses a *global perspective*. The best example of this perspective is the General Agreement on Tariffs and Trade, or GATT. This agreement was signed by 124 countries in 1994 to eliminate trade barriers worldwide. The World Trade Organization (WTO) was established as the watchdog organization, and a world court was set up in Geneva to arbitrate trade disputes. Although results have been mixed, the WTO is making slow but steady progress toward free trade around the world.[27]

A final trend is the use of embargoes or sanctions by the UN or individual governments to limit trade to specific countries, a popular political weapon in recent years. For example, the United States participated in embargoes against Iraq, South Africa, Libya, and Vietnam. An embargo, of course, eliminates many potential market opportunities. In contrast, the lifting of trade sanctions, as in the case of South Africa, can release pent-up demand and produce tremendous opportunities.

Unilateral embargoes are especially difficult for affected firms. A case in point involves Vietnam, against which the United States had a near total economic embargo for 18 years. When the embargo was lifted in February 1994, Boeing, Marriott, Johnson & Johnson, Coca-Cola, Kodak, Du Pont, Kellogg, and American Express initiated efforts to enter the Vietnamese market. This is a potentially attractive market because of its size (72 million people) and its sporadic movement toward a market-based economy. However, American firms are at a competitive disadvantage. Firms from Asia, Australia, and Europe have invested over $7.5 billion in Vietnam since 1987. Sanyo, Toshiba, and Honda are among the firms that have already established strong competitive positions. U.S. firms will have to work hard to overcome the problems caused by the embargo.[28] The Vietnamese bureaucracy has also been difficult to deal with, resulting in the pulling out of companies like Raytheon and Sheraton Hotels. Things might improve in the future, as the U.S. and Vietnam governments have completed an agreement to give U.S. companies greater market access and lower tariffs and Vietnam normal trade status with the United States.[29]

One specific issue of enormous interest around the world was the reversion of Hong Kong to Chinese control. Hong Kong became a Special Administrative Region (SAR) of China on July 1, 1997. C. H. Tung was selected the first chief executive of the SAR. Under British control, Hong Kong had grown economically under a democratic government. Although China has largely embraced free market capitalism, it remains largely a tightly controlled communist state.[30]

Samuel Chi-Hung Lee, President, International Marketing Consultants Company Limited, talks about the political environment in Hong Kong since July 1, 1997:
"Hong Kong became a part of China on July 1, 1997. This has had an impact on

the political situation in Hong Kong. The Chinese central government in Beijing now governs Hong Kong, although it largely operates behind the scenes. The government of Hong Kong does, however, have a high degree of autonomy under this one country, two systems approach. But, the Hong Kong government must operate within guidelines established by the Chinese government. This has changed the situation in Hong Kong somewhat. Hong Kong used to be an economically-driven city. Now, there is much more attention paid to political considerations."

Legislation

Organizations must deal with laws at the international, federal, state, and local levels. U.S. laws directly affecting marketing typically fall into two categories: those promoting competition among firms and those protecting consumers and society. Exhibit 2–7 presents examples of each type.

Laws promoting competition focus on outlawing practices that give a few firms unfair competitive advantages over others. The specific impact of these laws depends on court rulings that may change over time or differ at the state and national levels. One of the highest profile cases in recent years is *United States* v. *Microsoft*. The government charged that Microsoft routinely used its monopoly power to crush competitors. The first round went to the government, when U.S. District Judge Thomas P. Jackson released his finding of facts in its favor. The breakup of Microsoft to increase competition is a possibility, but far from a certainty. There are likely to be some changes as the case continues in the courts or a settlement is negotiated between Microsoft and the government.[31]

Consumer protection laws generally indicate what firms must do to give consumers the information they need to make sound purchasing decisions or to ensure that the products they buy are safe. For example, the Fair Packaging and Labeling Act requires packages to be labeled honestly; the Child Protection Act regulates the amount of advertising that can appear on children's television programs.

| Exhibit 2–7 | *Key U.S. laws affecting marketing* |

A. Promoting Competition

Act	Purpose
• Sherman Act (1890)	Prohibits monopolistic practices
• Clayton Act (1914)	Prohibits anticompetitive activities
• Federal Trade Commission Act (1914)	Establishes regulatory agency to enforce laws against unfair competition
• Robinson–Patman Act (1936)	Prohibits price discrimination
• Lanham Trademark Act (1946)	Protects trademarks and brand names
• Magnusson–Moss Act (1975)	Regulates warranties
• United States–Canada Trade Act (1988)	Allows free trade between United States and Canada

B. Protecting Consumers & Society

Act	Purpose
• Food, Drug, and Cosmetics Act (1938)	Regulates food, drug, and cosmetic industries
• Fair Packaging and Labeling Act (1966)	Regulates packaging and labeling
• Consumer Credit Protection Act (1968)	Requires full disclosure of financial charges for loans
• Child Protection and Toy Safety Act (1969)	Prevents marketing of dangerous products to children
• Fair Credit Report Act (1970)	Regulates reporting and use of credit information
• Fair Debt Collections Practice Act (1970)	Regulates methods for collecting debts
• Child Protection Act (1990)	Regulates advertising on children's television programs
• Americans with Disabilities Act (1990)	Prohibits discrimination against consumers with disabilities

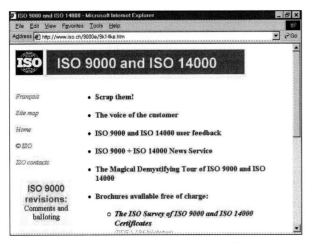

The globalization of markets increases the need for international standards. ISO 9000 and ISO 14000 represent an important approach to facilitate international trade.

Laws typically affect marketing activities by indicating what can or cannot be done. Until recently, Germany had a law that forced most retail stores to close at 6:30 PM on weekdays and 2 PM on Saturdays, and it did not allow commercial baking on Sunday. This restricted the operations of retailers. A new law expanded allowable shopping hours to 8 PM on weekdays and 4 PM on Saturdays; it also allowed bakeries to sell fresh bread on Sunday mornings. Other stores must remain closed on Sunday.[32]

Some laws are directed at providing marketing opportunities. Syria, for example, in trying to open its economy to the private sector and foreign investment, passed a law that exempts investors in approved projects from taxes for five to nine years, waives customs duties on certain imports, and removes regulations that at one time made it difficult to do business in Syria. Known as No. 10, it has contributed to a 7 to 8 percent growth in the Syrian economy.[33]

Regulation and Regulatory Agencies

Most legislation in the United States is enforced through regulations developed by a variety of agencies, and marketers must often work with regulatory authorities at the federal, state, and local levels. Often, regulations are not the same at different governmental levels. For example, the Federal Trade Commission (FTC) enforces guidelines for how firms promote the environmental advantages of their products, but these guidelines do not supersede state laws or regulations. Now, 12 states regulate environmental claims in some way, with more states likely to follow in the future. Sorting through different regulations is a complex task for marketers.[34]

Several of the most important federal agencies are described in Exhibit 2–8. Some of these regulatory agencies cut across industries (FTC, CPSC, EPA); others focus on specific industries (FDA, ICC, FCC). The impact of these regulatory agencies is especially evident in the pharmaceutical industry. The FDA must approve a new drug before it is marketed and can place limitations on its use. For example, the FDA approved Warner-Lambert's anticonvulsant, Neurontin, but only as an add-on therapy for patients taking other epilepsy medications. This stipulation limits Warner-Lambert's marketing efforts for Neurontin.[35] FDA actions can also produce marketing opportunities. The approval of smoking-cessation nicotine drugs as over-the-counter products opened up a large market to marketers of nicotine gum and patches.[36]

As more firms participate in the global marketplace, the need for international regulations is emerging. One example is the International Standards Organization's set of quality standards called *ISO 9000*. For example, the ISO 9000 and ISO

Exhibit 2–8	*Important U.S. regulatory agencies*	
Agency	**Responsibilities**
• Federal Trade Commission (FTC)	Regulates business practices
• Consumer Product Safety Commission (CPSC)	Protects consumers from unsafe products
• Environmental Protection Agency (EPA)	Protects environment
• Food & Drug Administration (FDA)	Regulates food, drug, and cosmetic industries
• Interstate Commerce Commission (ICC)	Regulates interstate transportation industry
• Federal Communications Commission (FCC)	Regulates interstate communications industry

14000 standards apply to 20 different functions within a company, such as product design, process control, purchasing, customer service, inspection and testing, and training, and are being incorporated into laws of the European Union (EU) to regulate trade in Europe. A company must go through a long and expensive process to become ISO 9000–certified, which would indicate it meets world standards in many areas. Companies not ISO 9000–certified may not do business in Europe or many other countries. Even individual companies, like General Motors and Siemens, require their suppliers to be ISO 9000–certified.[37]

Technological Environment

The **technological environment** includes factors and trends related to innovations that affect the development of new products or the marketing process. Rapid technological advances make it imperative that marketers take a *technology perspective*. These technological trends can provide opportunities for new-product development, affect how marketing activities are performed, or both. For example, advances in information and communication technologies provide new products for firms to market, and the buyers of these products often use them to change the way they market their own products. Using these technological products can help marketers be more productive. Fax machines and cellular telephones are illustrative.

New technologies can spawn new industries, new businesses, or new products for existing business. Firms at the leading edge of technological developments are in a favorable position. Thus, marketers need to monitor the technological environment constantly to look for potential opportunities that will improve their positions.

Marketers also need to monitor the technological environment to minimize threats to their companies or industries. New technologies can, after all, *disrupt* entire industries as well as enhance them. For example, optical networks are affecting the telecommunications industry, diagnostic technologies are affecting the health care industry, systems-on-a-chip technologies are pressuring the microprocessor industry, and the Internet is having a significant impact on retailing, financial services, and education.[38]

In general, the level of R&D expenditures and patents provides an indicator of technological development. Although U.S.-based companies rank high in many overall measures, firms in other countries are increasing R&D expenditures and receiving patents at a higher rate than are U.S. firms. One study compared 25 nations on an overall innovation index based on R&D funding and other similar measures. The United States was at the top in the 1980s and 1990s. However, based on current trends, Japan, Finland, Denmark, and Sweden would pass the United States by 2005. The United States suffers from inadequate spending on basic research and education, as well as a shrinking percentage of technical workers. The weakest areas are in advanced material science, solid-state physics, and software.[39]

To compete successfully, firms must monitor developments in specific technologies. Important technological developments will likely include those in computers, robotics, and computer-aided design and manufacturing (CAD/CAM), and their potential impact on how people live and work; in artificial intelligence and expert systems, and how they are used to solve problems; in superconductors and potential applications for new products; in transportation technologies, such as magnetically levitated trains,

New technologies provide many opportunities to improve products and services. Advances in wireless technology are generating many new products and services.

supersonic aircraft, and "smart" cars; and in communications technologies, and their effects on individuals and organizations.[40]

Competitive Environment

The **competitive environment** consists of all the organizations that attempt to serve similar customers. Two types of competitors are of major concern: brand competitors and product competitors. **Brand competitors** provide the most direct competition, offering the same types of products as competing firms. For example, Nike is a brand competitor of Reebok, Adidas, and other firms that market different brands of the same types of sport shoes. These firms target the same markets and typically try to take customers away from one another.

Product competitors offer different types of products to satisfy the same general need. Domino's Pizza, McDonald's, and Kentucky Fried Chicken are product competitors. They attempt to satisfy a consumer need for fast food, but they offer somewhat different menus and services. Domino's, McDonald's, and KFC also have brand competitors, which market the same types of fast food to the same customers. Brand competitors of Domino's, for example, are Pizza Hut, Papa John's Pizza, and Little Caesar's Pizza.

The competitive environment for most firms is fierce and often global. Marketers must identify their relevant brand and product competitors in order to identify market opportunities and develop marketing strategies. One trend affecting many industries is the changing competitive landscape. Some product competitors have become brand competitors by expanding their product offerings.

Consider the financial services industry. Banks used to compete against banks, insurance companies against insurance companies, brokerage firms against brokerage firms. Now, many banks, insurance companies, and brokerage houses offer a range of financial services products that compete directly with one another. And new competitors are entering the market, especially through the Internet. It is now possible to do banking, buy and sell securities, and purchase many other financial service products on-line.

Keeping track of the number, types, and actions of competitors is becoming increasingly important, but much more complex and difficult. However, recent evidence suggests that it might be worth the effort. One study found that companies placing a premium on competitor information grew 200 percent faster than firms that did not. The three most crucial types of competitor information were changes in competitor pricing, new-product development, and changes in corporate strategy.[41]

Thinking Critically

The text discusses how competitive boundaries are being dissolved in the financial services industry. Consider the changes in the telecommunications industry to include local telephone service, long distance, cellular telephone service, and Internet access:

- Who are the major competitors in the local, long distance, cellular, and Internet access markets?
- What marketing strategies are these companies using?
- What competitive changes are taking place in the telecommunications industry?
- What changes do you predict for the future?

Institutional Environment

The **institutional environment** consists of all the organizations involved in marketing products and services. These include marketing research firms, advertising agencies, wholesalers, retailers, suppliers, and customers. Specific trends and characteristics of these institutions are discussed in detail in subsequent chapters.

Many organizations are changing how they are structured and managed. These trends in the institutional environment include reengineering, restructuring, the virtual corporation, horizontal organizations, and empowerment. An organization's adoption of any of these concepts means that it is changing some elements of its structure and processes. These changes are likely to affect the amount and types of products the firm needs as well as the purchasing processes it uses. The potential marketing implications of organizational changes are illustrated by the restructuring efforts of many firms.

Many organizations are restructuring in various ways. Many programs emphasize long-term relationships with selected suppliers instead of short-term transactions with a large number of suppliers. Xerox, for example, has cut its supplier base from several thousand to several hundred. This trend means that the pool of potential customers for many marketers is becoming limited. Success in this type

Consolidation is an important trend in many industries. The combining of Norfolk Southern and Conrail is an example in the railroad industry.

of environment requires that marketers take a *relationship perspective* and focus on doing more business with fewer customers.

The downsizing of organizations is also commonplace. Sometimes entire departments are eliminated; in other cases, the number of employees within departments is reduced. The major purpose of downsizing is to lower costs and make the organization "leaner and meaner."

When an organization eliminates departments, it typically hires outside firms to replace them. This can offer market opportunities for accounting firms, advertising agencies, personnel firms, and other businesses that can perform the needed functions. When department personnel are reduced, fewer people are available to do the work. For example, many firms have downsized their purchasing departments, and purchasing managers at these companies are responsible for purchasing more products and services than in the past. Marketers can take advantage of this situation. Professional salespeople can work closely with these busy purchasing managers to help purchase quality products that add value to their businesses.

Consolidation throughout industries is another important trend. In the future, many industries will consist of a few large firms enjoying most of the market share, plus many small firms, each with limited market share. One source made specific predictions illustrating this trend.[42] It reported that nine domestic U.S. airlines accounted for 80 percent of the market, with smaller carriers getting only 20 percent. By 2001 there will be only four major domestic carriers. Also, there are now 20 major auto firms around the world, with market shares ranging from 1 to 18 percent. By 2001, only five will be left. Whether these specific predictions come true or not, the overriding trend toward consolidation is clear, as witnessed by the pharmaceutical, financial services, and retail industries.

Consolidation has two important implications for marketers. First, organizations must develop marketing strategies to hold their own in a competitive environment consisting of a few large firms and many small firms. Second, they must develop effective marketing strategies to serve both very large and very small customers.

These and other institutional trends affect the way organizations operate. Marketers that serve organizational customers must examine these trends to identify market opportunities and develop effective marketing strategies. Moreover, these trends affect the competitive structure for all marketers and have important implications for the types of marketing strategies likely to be effective.

The Future

The only certainty about the future is that it will be uncertain and change will occur at an increasing rate. Despite this caveat, there are hopeful signs that the world economy will exhibit strong growth. The world growth rate for the past three years was nearly double that of the past two decades. The expansion of economic freedom and property rights, more fiscal restraint by governments, increases in investment, freer trade, and exploding technological innovation are some of the forces supporting world economic growth. Although a large scale war, environmental catastrophe, political upheaval, or other event could change the picture, the current prognosis is expressed by Jeffrey Sachs, economist at Harvard University: "The positive side is spectacular. Economic growth will raise the living standards of more people in more parts of the world than at any time in prior history."[43]

Summary

1. **Understand the nature of the marketing environment and why it is important to marketers.** The marketing environment consists of all factors external to an organization that can affect its marketing activities. Elements of the marketing environment are largely uncontrollable, although marketers have influence over some factors. Environmental factors can affect the size and growth rate of markets and can influence marketing activities. Thus, changes in the marketing environment offer opportunities and threats to marketers. Identifying and responding effectively to these opportunities and threats is a major challenge.

2. **Describe the major components of the social environment and how trends in the social environment affect marketing.** The social environment comprises all factors and trends related to groups of people, including their number, characteristics, behavior, and growth projections. Its major components are the demographic and cultural environments. The demographic environment refers to the size, distribution, and growth rate of people with different characteristics. The cultural environment refers to factors and trends related to how people live and behave. Demographic factors typically relate to the number of people in different markets, whereas cultural factors generally influence the needs of these markets.

3. **Understand how the economic environment affects marketing.** The economic environment includes factors and trends related to the production of goods and services and the relationships between this production and income levels. The economic environment affects the purchasing power of consumers, which is an important determinant of the size of a market.

4. **See how the political/legal environment offers opportunities and threats to marketers.** The political/legal environment, encompassing factors related to governmental activities and laws and regulations, directly affects marketing activities. Laws and regulations normally present constraints within which marketers must operate. These laws and regulations are closely related to current political trends. Some marketers, however, can identify market opportunities arising from these laws and regulations.

5. **Appreciate the importance of the technological environment to marketers.** The technological environment includes factors and trends related to innovations that affect the development of new products or improving marketing practice. Technological advances are happening so rapidly that marketers must constantly monitor the technological environment to keep abreast of latest developments.

6. **Understand differences in the competitive environment.** The competitive environment consists of all the organizations that attempt to serve the same customers. Brand competitors compete directly by offering the same type of product to the same market. Product competitors compete more indirectly by offering different types of products to satisfy the same basic need.

7. **Know how changes in the institutional environment affect marketers.** The institutional environment consists of all the organizations involved in marketing products and services. These include marketing research firms, advertising agencies, wholesalers, and retailers. As the characteristics of these and other institutions change, so will the marketing strategies necessary to serve different customers and to compete effectively in different industries.

Understanding Marketing Terms and Concepts

Thinking About Marketing

1. How do changes in the marketing environment generate opportunities and threats for marketers?

2. What are the major differences between the demographic and cultural environments?

3. Why are trends in the institutional environment important to marketers?

4. How does the Internet affect the competitive environment facing many firms?

5. Look at **"Using Technology: Adjusting Prices to Temperature Changes."** What are other examples of how marketers respond to changes in the weather?

6. How do political changes affect regulations and regulatory agencies?

7. What are the most important social trends facing marketers in the twenty-first century?

8. Refer to **Being Entrepreneurial: Marketing Opportunities During War.** Identify examples of what McDonald's did that represent entrepreneurial behavior (innovative, proactive, and risk-taking).

9. How are the social and economic environments interrelated?

10. How can new technologies be used to help marketers scan and monitor the marketing environment?

Applying Marketing Skills

1. Identify several marketing environment trends that you think might affect enrollment at your college. Discuss whether each trend represents an opportunity or a threat. What strategy might your institution use to take advantage of the opportunity or minimize the threat?

2. Watch the complete evening news show on one of the major networks. Make a note of significant marketing environment trends examined during the newscast. After the news show is over, suggest the potential effect of each trend on marketing practice. Which trends represent opportunities? Which trends represent threats? Could any of the potential threats become opportunities if a marketer viewed it from an entrepreneurship perspective?

3. Contact a marketing executive at a local company and ask how he or she assesses changes in the marketing environment. Identify who in the company is involved in what types of environmental scanning. Ask the executive to identify the key trends affecting his or her company and what the firm is doing to respond appropriately to these trends.

Using the www in Marketing

Activity One
Go to Dell's Web site (http://www.dell.com).

1. How does Dell's Web site add value to customers?

2. Using information on the Web site, describe and evaluate Dell's global marketing efforts.

3. What ideas do you have for improving Dell's Web site?

Activity Two
As discussed in the chapter, laws and regulations typically are designed to promote competition among firms or to protect consumers and society. Some Web sites that present legal information are:
Federal Trade Commission (http://www.ftc.gov)
FedWorld Information Network (http://www.fedworld.gov)
Consumer Information Center (http://www.pueblo.gsa.gov)
United States Information Agency (http://www.usia.gov)

THOMAS: Legislative Information on the Internet (http://thomas.loc.gov)
National Archives and Records Administration (http://www.nara.gov)
Visit several of these sites and:

1. Select an example of legislation intended to promote competition among firms. Provide a brief synopsis of this legislation and indicate how the legislation affects marketing practice.

2. Select an example of legislation intended to protect consumers and society. Provide a brief synopsis of this legislation and discuss how the legislation affects marketing practice.

3. Which of these sites would you recommend that marketers monitor on a regular basis? Why?

Making Marketing Decisions
Case 2-1 Women's NBA: Women's Team Sports Taking Off

Women's individual sports, such as golf and tennis, have been successful for many years. The same cannot be said for team sports. Prior to 1997, at least three attempts had been made to establish women's professional basketball leagues. All had failed. So, why would anyone try again? Because the marketing environment changed.

Women's collegiate sports programs have expanded tremendously in recent years. This has produced a new generation of women athletes and fans. And the stunning success of women athletes at the 1996 Summer Olympic Games in Atlanta added to this interest. The result is the formation of four new women's professional leagues being formed since the Olympics. One is the Women's National Basketball Association (WNBA).

The tip-off of the WNBA was in June 1997. The league initially consisted of eight teams operated by NBA teams in eight cities. The Western Conference included the Los Angeles Lakers, Phoenix Suns, Sacramento Kings, and Utah Jazz. The Eastern Conference teams were the Charlotte Hornets, Cleveland Cavaliers, Houston Rockets, and New York Knicks. The season began after the NBA play-offs in June and concluded with a championship game on August 30.

The WNBA worked hard to make the new league a success. Sponsors were obtained and contracts to televise selected regular season and playoff games were secured. The league advertised during the NBA's regular season and playoff games. The results of these marketing efforts appear to have been successful.

The fourth WNBA season begins with preseason games on May 13, 2000. The league started with 8 teams, expanded to 12 in 1999, and will have 16 teams competing in 2000. More games will be televised on NBC, but games are also being broadcast to 125 countries in 18 different languages. Attendance initially averaged around 4,000 per game, but has increased to about 10,000 fans a game in 1998 and 1999. The league drew 1.96 million fans in 1999. Contrast this with the 20 years it took for the NBA to draw more than 1.9 million fans in a year. Sponsors, such as Nike, Sears, and Anheuser-Busch, have extended their sponsorship deals and new sponsors, such as Gatorade, are being added.

The future looks good as well. The Sydney Olympics in 2000 will provide the league with international exposure. It is expected that teams from the U.S., Brazil, Australia, Russia, and Poland will include WNBA players. The league also has a popular Web site (*www.wnba.com*). The WNBA is considering more expansion in the near future and continues to improve existing operations.

Questions

1. What trends in the marketing environment helped the WNBA be successful?

2. What trends in the marketing environment represent threats to the WNBA?

3. Why would companies like Nike, Sears, Anheuser-Busch, and Gatorade want to be sponsors of the WNBA?

4. What role does the WNBA Web site (*www.wnba.com*) play in the league's marketing strategy?

Sources: Margaret Littman, "Sponsors Take to the Court with New Women's NBA," *Marketing News,* March 3, 1997, pp. 1 and 6; Gigi Barnett and Skip Rozin, "A Lot of Leagues of Their Own," *Business Week,* March 3, 1997, pp. 54–56; www.wnba.com, February 15, 2000.

Case 2-2 Gold's Gym: A Western Health Club in Moscow

The move toward a free market economy has opened new opportunities for entrepreneurs in Russia. One such entrepreneur is 23-year-old Jake Weinstock. After graduating from the University of Pennsylvania, Jake worked as a business consultant for Ernst & Young and moonlighted as marketing manager for Dynamo, the Red Army hockey team that is now a farm team for the Pittsburgh Penguins professional hockey team. Despite being very busy, Jake wanted to start his own business in sports or fitness.

He first developed a partnership with fellow American Paul Kuebler and Russian Vladimir Grumlik. The partners spent the winter of 1995 studying the successes and failures of new businesses in Moscow. This work generated the idea of starting a Western-style health club. The concept was to bring a new level of service and management to health clubs in Moscow.

Because there is a limited middle class in Russia, the target market for the health club was determined to be people who had money to spend now. This included about 100,000 expatriates and 400,000 rich Muscovites, based on the best available information. The partners calculated they would need 1,000 members paying $1,500–$2,500 annually to break even and 3,000 to generate the profits needed to attract Western capital. Limited availability of capital in Russia led them to seek capital from American firms, such as Commonwealth Property Investors.

Once the capital was obtained, getting the needed fitness equipment to Moscow was addressed. The partners ordered 24 shipments of very expensive, high-tech Cybex fitness equipment and a basketball court supplied by Nike. Since the government levies heavy storage fees for each day that imported goods are not released, it was important to get the equipment through customs as soon as possible. Vladimir Grumlik used his personal connections to facilitate the customs process. Relationships and alliances with other important people were also necessary to get the business established.

Gold's Gym opened in Moscow in February 1997. The gym balances Russian and American culture. The staff is entirely Russian, but they have all been trained to deliver high levels of Western service. Other clubs in Russia had the mentality "that they're doing you a favor by letting you use their club." Gold's Gym is much more customer-oriented. The partners hope the mix of the best equipment and the best service will lead to success.

Source: Julia Vitullo-Martin, "Moscow Entrepreneurs Seize Golden Opportunity," *The Wall Street Journal,* January 20, 1997, p. A14.

Questions

1. What aspects of the marketing environment in Russia made it difficult to open Gold's Gym?

2. What is the basic marketing strategy of Gold's Gym?

3. In what ways is a relationship perspective important to the success of Gold's Gym?

4. What future marketing environment trends do you think represent opportunities or threats to the success of Gold's Gym?

Chapter Three

Marketing's Strategic Role in the Organization

After studying this chapter, you should be able to:

1 Discuss the three basic levels in an organization and the types of strategic plans developed at each level.

2 Understand the organizational strategic planning process and the role of marketing in this process.

3 Describe the key decisions in the development of corporate strategy.

4 Understand the different general business strategies and their relationship to business marketing, product marketing, and international marketing strategies.

5 Realize the importance of relationships and teamwork in executing strategic plans.

Honeywell International, Inc., is an advanced technology and manufacturing company serving customers worldwide. The company is organized around nine businesses: aerospace, consumer products, electronic materials, friction materials, home and building control, industrial control, performance polymers, specialty chemicals, and transportation and power systems. The firm employs approximately 120,000 individuals in 95 countries.

The Web site for Honeywell provides a wealth of information. Details about the corporate businesses, as well as about individual products and services, are offered for potential customers. The Web site also provides information for investors, instructions and summaries for members of the media interested in the company's background, and information on careers for students and other potential employees. The in-depth company history describes the evolution of the organization beginning with the first thermostat ads run in 1893, to the recent $14 billion merger of Honeywell and Allied Signal in December 1999.

Honeywell is making extensive use of its Internet site to enhance the performance of its employees and to improve relationships with its customers. Moreover, its Web-based capabilities are also being used to strengthen its supply-chain management. For example, Honeywell is offering Web-based distance learning solutions and employee training through MyPlant.com (http://www.myplant.com). This offering reduces the cost of training systems and the need for company staff to travel, while making continuing education more available. Honeywell has also introduced a Web-based customer resource designed to help homeowners recognize and locate home solutions, as well as suppliers and installers for improving home control systems (e.g., heating and cooling controls). **Sources:** http://www.honeywell.com/about/; http://biz.yahoo.com/bw/991202/nj_allieds_1.html; Robert P. Mader, "Honeywell to Merge with Allied Signal," *Contractor,* July 1999, p. 46; Geoffrey Colvin, "Honeywell Packs Its Bags," *Fortune,* July 5, 1999, p. 31; Jessica Davis, "Mentors Corner: Intranet Gives Honeywell Control Over Documents," *InfoWorld,* March 15, 1999, p. 56.

The complexity of the Honeywell conglomerate illustrates the importance of a well-designed corporate marketing strategy. The firm consists of unique business units, each offering an extensive array of products and services. Strategies and implementation of strategies must be developed and executed at the corporate, business-unit, and product levels. Overall, strategy and long-term planning are guided by the firm's vision as stated in their mission statement. At the business level, planning begins with an examination of the current situation, including technological changes and competitive effects. From this analysis, both threats and new business opportunities are identified. Decisions to pursue new opportunities are followed by the establishment of objectives, often stated in terms of market share, sales volume, or profitability. Subsequently, business and marketing strategies are developed to achieve those objectives. Effective execution of strategy in implementation must then occur for objectives to be realized.

Many of the most familiar firms around the world are complex organizations that market many different products in many different business areas. Take, for example, Asea Brown Boveri (ABB), the worldwide heavy-industry giant. The ABB corporation consists of eight major business segments, 65 business areas, 1,300 independently incorporated companies, and about 5,000 autonomous profit centers.[1] Marketing efforts require planning and implementation across all the various business segments, business areas, incorporated companies, and profit centers.

The Honeywell experience exemplifies a typical success scenario. First, a small company markets a few products to a well-defined market. Although this sort of marketing is not easy, the company directs all its efforts toward the initial products and market. If the firm succeeds and grows, competitors enter with similar products. Over time, the company's opportunities for marketing the same products to the same market decline. To continue growing, the firm must develop new strategies. Typically, it must either market different types of products to its current market, the same products to different markets, or new products to new markets. The relatively simple single-business, few-products firm becomes a complex multibusiness, multiproduct company.

The complexities facing Honeywell, ABB, and other firms produce many of the key challenges for today's marketers. In this chapter, we examine the important role of marketing in the contemporary multibusiness, multiproduct firm. We classify organizations into corporate, business, and functional levels, and discuss strategic planning and strategic decision making at each level. Our focus is on the role of marketing. The chapter concludes with a discussion of teamwork in the execution of strategic plans.

Think of all the ideas you put on paper. In China, that's a lot of paper.

That's why we helped Asia Pulp and Paper build the fastest mill in the world. ABB also created a new generation of integrated automation that can monitor and operate the entire plant from a single screen. At ABB, we believe the most important thing we build today is knowledge. Because the power that will drive the next hundred years is the power of ideas.

www.abb.com

Brain Power.   **ABB**

Many corporations have individual business units. ABB, a global technology company has multibusiness operations in many different markets and for a variety of products.

Organizational Levels

The **corporate level** is the highest level in any organization. Corporate managers address issues concerning the overall organization, and their decisions and actions affect all other organizational levels. The **business level** consists of units within the overall organization that are generally managed as self-contained businesses. The idea is to break a complex organization into smaller units to be operated like independent businesses. This is the level at which competition takes place; that is, business units typically compete against competitor business units, not corporate levels versus corporate levels. For example, Blockbuster consists of six business units: domestic home video, international home video, domestic music retailing, international music retailing, new-technology ventures, and other entertainment venues.

The **functional level** includes all the various functional areas within a business unit. Most of the work of a business unit is performed in its different functions. A typical university provides a good illustration of different organizational levels. The president, vice presidents, and other central administration positions represent the corporate level. The different colleges within the university, such as the college of business or college of arts and sciences, can be considered business units. There are also different functions performed within each college. The typical functions are teaching, research, and administration carried out by faculty, staff, and administrators.

Organizational Strategic Planning

Strategic planning for multibusiness, multiproduct organizations typically occurs at each organizational level. Strategic plans at higher organizational levels provide direction for strategic plans at lower levels. In a sense, lower-level plans are developed to execute higher-level plans. Because of this relationship, strategic planning must be integrated and consistent throughout levels.

A study of U.S. and South African firms provides a general description of strategic planning.[2] These firms reported that the major benefits of strategic planning are improved performance relative to objectives and a better organizational focus and vision. Most of the firms prepare formal strategic plans at the corporate, business, and product levels, with different functional managers participating in the planning process. These include sales managers, product managers, marketing researchers, production managers, and financial managers. Many firms also incorporate customers into the process. Over 75 percent of the firms in this study said their strategic planning was well coordinated.

Types of Strategic Plans

The different types of strategic plans and important strategic decisions are illustrated in Exhibit 3–1. A **corporate strategic plan** provides guidance for strategic planning at all other organizational levels. Important corporate strategy decisions concern development of a corporate vision, formulation of corporate objectives, allocation of resources, determination of how to achieve desired growth, and establishment of business units. These decisions determine what type of company the firm is and wants to become.

A **business strategic plan** indicates how each business unit in the corporate family expects to compete effectively in the marketplace, given the vision, objectives,

Exhibit 3–1	Organizational strategic plans	
Organization Level	**Type of Strategic Plan**	**Key Strategic Decisions**
Corporate	Corporate strategic plan	• Corporate vision • Corporate objectives and resource allocation • Corporate growth strategies • Business-unit composition
Business	Business strategic plan	• Market scope • Competitive advantage
Marketing	Marketing strategic plan	• Target market approach • Marketing mix approach
	Product marketing plan	• Specific target market • Specific marketing mix • Execution action plan

and growth strategies in the corporate strategic plan. Different businesses within the same organization are likely to have different objectives and business strategies. For example, the Hilton Hotels Corp. emphasizes growth of its gambling casino business by expanding throughout the United States and into foreign markets such as Egypt, Turkey, and Uruguay. Hilton is selling some downscale hotels to concentrate on ritzy resort hotels. These changes in corporate strategy influence the company's business strategies and are turning Hilton into more of a gaming than a hotel company.[3] Each business needs to make decisions concerning the scope of the market it serves and the types of competitive advantages to emphasize. Decisions in these areas contribute to a general business strategy.

Each business consists of different functions to be performed, and strategic plans may be developed for each major function. Thus, many organizations will have marketing, financial, R&D, manufacturing, and other functional strategic plans. A **marketing strategic plan** describes how marketing managers will execute the business strategic plan. It addresses the general target market and marketing mix approaches.

Each business unit has its own product marketing plans that focus on specific target markets and marketing mixes for each product. A **product marketing plan** typically includes both strategic decisions (what to do) and execution decisions (how to do it).

Pitney Bowes, originally founded as a producer of mailing equipment and postage meters, is now a multibusiness, multiproduct corporation. The Copier Systems Division, one of the company's new business units, develops and executes marketing and product plans to compete against Xerox, Canon, Minolta, and Konica. The division's basic business strategy is to target large Fortune 1000 companies and to differentiate its products from the competition on the basis of product quality and efficiency of distribution. Unlike many newcomers to an industry, Pitney Bowes does not claim to offer the lowest prices in the industry.[4]

It is extremely important that organizations integrate their strategic plans across all levels. Coordination of business, marketing, and product plans is especially critical. For example, P&G has a general strategic plan for its detergent business and specific product plans for the different brands such as Tide and Cheer. Brand managers for each of P&G's detergent products must clear marketing strategies for their individual brands through the detergent business marketing manager. Without this coordination, P&G would find itself competing more against its own brands (Tide versus Cheer) than against those of other companies (P&G versus Dial and versus Unilever).[5]

The Strategic Planning Process

Although individual organizations will differ in the way they approach strategic planning, a general process is illustrated in Exhibit 3–2. This process applies to strategic planning at every level. We present it as a step-by-step approach to make it easier to understand strategic planning. In the business world, most organizations are involved in different stages of the process simultaneously and do not necessarily follow such a step-by-step approach.

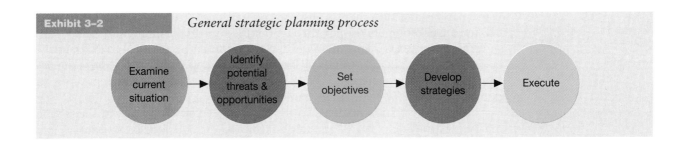

Exhibit 3–2   *General strategic planning process*

Examine current situation → Identify potential threats & opportunities → Set objectives → Develop strategies → Execute

EXAMINE THE CURRENT SITUATION   First, the managers evaluate the existing situation for the corporate, business, marketing, or product level. They typically analyze historical information to describe current strategies, assess recent performance, and evaluate the competitive situation. This background information provides a benchmark for the remainder of the strategic planning process.

IDENTIFY POTENTIAL THREATS AND OPPORTUNITIES   Next, the focus changes from what has happened to what might happen. Managers identify key trends in the marketing environment, assess the possible impact of these trends on the current situation, and classify them as either threats or opportunities. Threats represent potential problems that might adversely affect the current situation; opportunities represent areas where performance might be improved. Thus, Specialized Bicycle Components must recognize trends in retailing and changing preferences among consumers. Similarly, Blockbuster saw new technological developments, like Philips's Imagination Machine, as opportunities. Managers typically rank potential threats and opportunities, addressing the most important ones first in the next strategic planning stage.

SET OBJECTIVES   Managers must now establish specific objectives for the corporate, business, marketing, and product levels. Typical objectives involve sales, market share, and profitability. The specific objectives should be based on the analysis of the current situation and the marketing environment. As we discuss later, objectives at the different organizational levels must be consistent. For example, the sales objectives for all businesses must be set so that meeting them means meeting the corporate level sales objectives.

DEVELOP STRATEGIES   Finally, managers develop strategies for achieving the objectives. These strategies will indicate how the organization will minimize potential threats and capitalize on specific opportunities. The strategies developed at this stage represent what an organization plans to do to meet its objectives, given the current situation and expected changes in the marketing environment. A sample product marketing plan is presented in Appendix B at the end of the text.

EXECUTE   A clear strategy and well-crafted programs may still fail if execution and implementation efforts are misdirected or inadequate. Effective execution is enhanced when employees share common values and are properly trained and when sufficient resources and staff are provided to support implementation. It is important to note that both a sense of organizational-wide commitment to the adopted strategy and a sense of commitment by those managers responsible for implementation have been shown to be primary determinants of effective execution.[6]

The Role of Marketing

Marketing plays an important role in the strategic planning process for many organizations. Although some marketing positions are represented at the corporate level, most are at the functional level within the business units of an organization. As shown in Exhibit 3–3, however, marketing is involved in strategic planning at all organizational levels.

Strategic marketing describes marketing activities that affect corporate, business, and marketing strategic plans. Strategic marketing activities can be classified into three basic functions. First, marketers help orient everyone in the organization toward markets and customers. Thus, they are responsible for helping organizations execute a marketing philosophy throughout the strategic planning process.

Second, marketers help gather and analyze information required to examine the current situation, identify trends in the marketing environment, and assess the potential impact of these trends. This information and analysis provides input for corporate, business, and marketing strategic plans.

Third, marketers are involved in the development of corporate, business, and marketing strategic plans. Marketing's influence varies across organizations. For

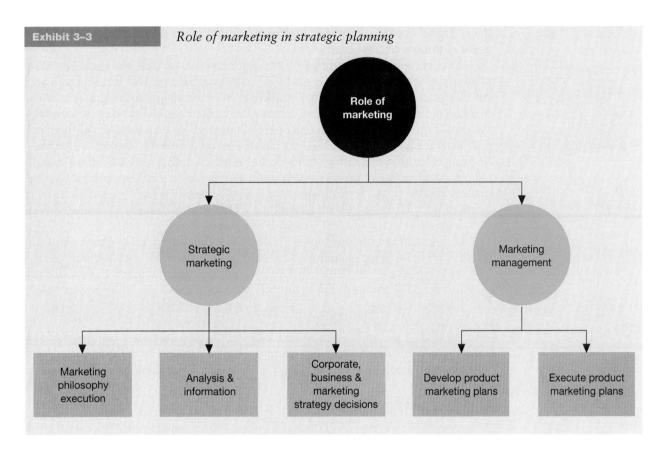

Exhibit 3–3   *Role of marketing in strategic planning*

organizations driven by a marketing philosophy, marketing necessarily plays a key role in strategic decision making. The trend toward pushing strategic planning responsibility further down the organization is increasing marketing's clout in an organization's strategic planning process.[7]

Marketing management relates to specific product marketing strategies. It differs from strategic marketing in its basic orientation. Strategic marketing focuses on broad strategic decisions at the corporate and business levels. Marketing management is concerned, by contrast, with specific strategic decisions for individual products and the day-to-day activities needed to execute these strategies successfully. At the operating level, marketing managers must focus on the four Ps of the marketing mix: price, product, promotion, and place (distribution).[8]

The strategic role of marketing and marketing management are now in a period of considerable change and evolution. These changes are due to a number of important environmental phenomena that are affecting the way many firms do business. To begin, many well-known companies work closely with dedicated partners on the supply side (often using single supply partners) and the distributor side of their business, expecting their distributors to play proactive roles in the development of services and marketing strategy. For example, on the supply side, the modern-day Nike does very little manufacturing of its own and focuses largely on marketing. In this vein, companies such as this are actually embedded in **business networks,** comprising strategic alliances among suppliers, distributors, and the marketing firm.[9]

Other influences on marketing include the connected-knowledge economy; globalized and consolidated industries; fragmented markets; and demanding customers and consumers. With these changes, new kinds of competitors will emerge, markets will continue to become homogenized across country boundaries, and mass markets will erode in the face of mass customization. Business customers and individual consumers expect diversity and have multiple means of obtaining products, as well as learning about company offerings. Some observers foresee a future in which the Web will enable automated purchasing, anonymous transactions, and the by-passing of most intermediaries.[10]

The role of marketing within the firm is in transition as well. For example, some scholarly observers have argued that the marketing function will be reduced as the values embodied in the firm's market orientation permeate the firm. That is, a cross-functional dispersion of marketing activities will occur as the firm becomes market-oriented throughout. In a test of this premise, one study of managers across functions (i.e., marketing, human relations, operations, accounting, and finance) within their firms revealed that marketing as a separate function still contributes to a firm's financial performance, customer-relationship performance, and new-product performance beyond the performance attributable to the firm's general market orientation.[11] Therefore, an understanding of the strategic planning process is even more important in today's ever-changing marketplace.

Our discussion of organizational strategic planning provides an overview of different types of strategic plans, a general strategic planning process, and marketing's basic role in these areas. With this background, we are now ready to examine the major strategic decisions at the corporate, business, marketing, and product levels.

Corporate Strategy Decisions

The key corporate strategy decision areas defined in Exhibit 3–1 are corporate vision, corporate objectives and resource allocation, corporate growth strategies, and business-unit composition.

Corporate Vision

A **corporate vision** represents the basic values of an organization. The vision specifies what the organization stands for, where it plans to go, and how it plans to get there. As indicated in Exhibit 3–4, a comprehensive vision should address the organization's markets, principal products and services, geographic domain, core competencies, objectives, basic philosophy, self-concept, and desired public image.[12] Specialized Bicycle, for example, addressed these issues in its stated vision: "customer satisfaction, quality, innovativeness, teamwork, and profitability."

The ability to develop vision depends on the company's understanding of what should be enduring and what is subject to change. Companies that enjoy enduring success, such as Hewlett-Packard, 3M, Motorola, and Procter & Gamble, have core values and core purposes that remain fixed; but they endlessly adapt their strategies and practices to a changing world. A company's **core values** are the small set of guiding principles that represent the enduring tenets of an organization. The Disney Company's emphasis on imagination and wholesomeness reflect its essential core values. **Core purpose** reflects the company's reason for being or its idealistic motivation for doing work. Disney's core purpose is to entertain people; 3M's is "to solve problems innovatively" (see Exhibit 3–5).[13]

Sometimes organizations develop a formal mission statement to communicate the corporate vision to all interested parties. A mission statement can be an important element in the strategic planning process because it specifies the boundaries within which business units, marketing, and other functions must operate.

The mission statement for Ben & Jerry's is threefold: (1) to make and distribute the finest quality all-natural ice cream and related products; (2) to operate the Company on a sound financial basis of profitable growth, increasing value for our shareholders, and creating career opportunities and financial rewards for our employees; and (3) to operate the company in a way that actively recognizes the central role that business plays in the structure of society by initiating innovative ways to improve the quality of life of a broad community.[14]

Exhibit 3–4

Corporate vision components

- Markets
- Products and services
- Geographic domain
- Core competencies
- Organizational objectives
- Organizational philosophy
- Organizational self-concept
- Desired public image

Exhibit 3–5 · *Core purpose: A company's reason for being*

3M: To solve problems innovatively.

Cargill: To improve the standard of living around the world.

Fannie Mae: To strengthen the social fabric by continually democratizing homeownership.

Hewlett-Packard: To make technical contributions for the advancement and welfare of humanity.

Lost Arrow Corporation: To be a role model and a tool for social change.

Pacific Theatres: To provide a place for people to flourish and to enhance the community.

Mary Kay Cosmetics: To give unlimited opportunity to women.

McKinsey & Company: To help leading corporations and governments to be more successful.

Merck: To preserve and improve human life.

Nike: To experience the emotion of competition, winning, and crushing competitors.

Sony: To experience the joy of advancing and applying technology for the benefit of the public.

Telecare Corporation: To help people with mental impairments realize their full potential.

Wal-Mart: To give ordinary folk the chance to buy the same things as rich people.

Walt Disney: To make people happy.

Source: James C. Collins and Jerry I. Porras, "Building Your Company's Vision," *Harvard Business Review*, September–October, 1996, p. 69.

Mission statements provide direction for corporate leadership and help guide marketing strategy. At Ortho Biotech, a shared vision helps an increasingly diverse workforce make day-to-day decisions about what needs to be done.

The statement emphasizes the importance of quality products, company performance and employee success, and the social responsibility aspects of business.

The vision statement for Whirlpool is similar but does not mention the role of business in society: "We create the world's best home appliances that make life a little easier and more enjoyable for all people. Our goal is a Whirlpool product in every home, everywhere. Created by: pride in our work and each other; passion for creating unmatched customer loyalty for our brands; and, performance results that excite and reward global investors."[15]

One study found that companies with a formal vision outperformed similar companies without a formal vision by more than six to one. Marriott illustrates what some companies are doing. After management developed mission statements for the corporation and hotel division, each of the company's 250 hotels crafted its own mission statement. Staff members at each hotel spent three days participating in "visioning" exercises to develop the mission statements.[16]

Exhibit 3–6 lists questions that a firm's top managers should continually ask themselves in efforts to install a corporate vision for effectively competing in the future.

The last two questions form the basis for recent views of successful competition; that is, the firm's comparative advantages and distinctive core competencies are the

Speaking from Experience

Bobbie Oglesby
Director of Windows Branding and Communications
Microsoft, Redmond, WA

Bobbie Oglesby holds a master's degree in marketing from the University of South Carolina. She was attracted to Microsoft because of the opportunity to shape how technology is developed and used. Advancements in technology, particularly the Internet, are opening up a new world of opportunities and challenges.

"Computer technology has become pervasive in businesses and is fundamental to almost every business process. As a result, the information technology professionals inside businesses have an increasingly complex array of products and services they must elevate and manage. Recognizing this, we are changing the way we market products at Microsoft from focusing on the individual products to combining products into specific solution sets. We are moving from an organization focused on product marketing to teams focused on solution marketing. By doing this, we reduce the complexity of the IT managers' decision process and better meet the customer's needs."

| Exhibit 3–6 | *Questions leading to an effective corporate vision* |

1. Which customers will you be serving in the future?
2. Through which channels will you reach customers in the future?
3. Who will be your competitors in the future?
4. Where will your margins come from in the future?
5. In what end-product markets will you participate in the future?
6. What will be the basis for your competitive advantage in the future?
7. What skills or capabilities will make you unique in the future?

Source: Gary Hamel and C. K. Prahalad, *Competing for the Future* (Boston: Harvard Business School Press, 1994), p. 18.

resources for competitive advantage. **Core competency** reflects a bundle of skills that are possessed by individuals across the organization. The core competency Federal Express possesses in package routing and delivery rests on the integration of bar technology, wireless communications, and network management. Boeing, the international manufacturer of airplanes, lists three core competencies on their web site: (1) detailed customer knowledge and focus; (2) large-scale system integration; and (3) lean, efficient design and production systems.[17] Competitive advantage derived from these core competencies in turn yields superior financial performance. In summary, a successful corporate vision reflects the sequence from core competency to competitive advantage to financial performance.

Corporate Objectives and Resource Allocation

The second major corporate strategy decision area involves setting objectives for the entire organization and assigning objectives and resources to business units and products. Although the corporate vision provides general overall direction for the organization, corporate objectives specify the achievement of desired levels of performance during particular time periods. Corporate objectives are established for many areas, but the most visible tend to be financial objectives. Typical financial objectives concern sales, sales growth, profits, profit growth, earnings per share, return on investment, and stock price.

Sales and sales growth objectives are often of direct concern to marketers. Although sales-related objectives are set at the corporate level, actual sales are achieved by marketing individual products to individual customers. Therefore, corporate sales objectives influence marketing activities throughout the organization, as illustrated in Exhibit 3–7.

Suppose the corporate sales growth objective is to increase this year's sales by 10 percent over the previous year's total. To achieve the desired results, management must break down this objective into goals for each business unit and product. If all products and business units meet the assigned objectives, the organization will achieve the desired growth.

In Exhibit 3–7, 10 percent of the desired sales growth is assigned to Business 1, 8 percent to Business 2, and 12 percent to Business 3. The sales growth objectives for each business unit are then further assigned to the specific products marketed by each business. Again, the sales growth objectives are not equally divided across products, because the various products have different opportunities for increasing sales. But if each product achieves the desired sales increase, the business unit will meet its sales growth objective. And, if each business unit does so, the organization will meet its 10 percent objective.

This hierarchy of objectives represents the organization's sales growth plan. Now, corporate resources are allocated to the business units and business-unit resources are allocated to products. Business 1 receives more corporate resources than

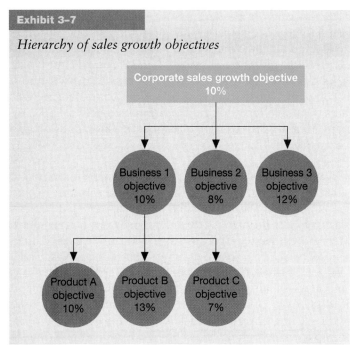

Sources: Shelby D. Hunt and Robert M. Morgan, "The Comparative Advantage Theory of Competition," *Journal of Marketing,* April 1995, pp. 1–15; and Gary Hamel and C. K. Prahalad, *Competing for the Future* (Boston: Harvard Business School Press, 1994), p. 223.

some other business units, and Product B receives more of the resources from Business 1 than the other two products it markets. The more sales growth required from a business unit or product, the more resources it typically needs to achieve the desired increases.

Corporate objectives and resource allocation affect marketers in two basic ways. First, marketers are involved in setting the objectives for different organizational levels. Although the amount of marketing participation varies across firms, setting realistic objectives requires the market information and analysis that marketers can provide. Assessments of trends in the size and growth rates of markets and the potential actions of competitors are inputs for setting objectives and allocating resources.

Second, corporate objectives and resource allocation decisions provide guidance for the development and implementation of business and marketing strategies. For example, the marketing managers for Products B and C in Business 1 have different objectives and receive different levels of resources to achieve them. Therefore, they are likely to develop and implement different marketing strategies for their products.

Although growth and new-customer generation are traditionally important, companies are increasingly framing objectives in terms of customer relationships and customer retention. Frequently cited corporate objectives based on relationships with customers are (1) retain most profitable customers, (2) increase sales volume from existing customers, and (3) protect core customers from competition.

Corporate Growth Strategies

Corporate growth strategies describe the general approach for achieving corporate growth objectives. The basic strategic alternatives involve limiting corporate operations to the same products and markets or expanding into new ones. Exhibit 3–8 presents four general options.

A **market penetration strategy** represents a decision to achieve corporate growth objectives with existing products within existing markets. The organization needs to persuade current customers to purchase more of its product or to capture new customers. This typically necessitates an aggressive marketing strategy, which means increasing marketing communications, implementing sales promotion programs, lowering prices, or taking other actions intended to generate more business.

A **market expansion strategy** entails marketing existing products to new markets. The new markets might be different market segments in the same geographic area or the same target market in different geographic areas. Specialized Bicycle Components for example, has expanded into new markets by obtaining expanded distribution through new retail outlets.[18]

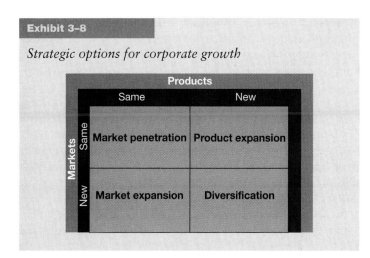

A **product expansion strategy** calls for marketing new products to the same market. The organization wants to generate more business from the existing customer base. Nike is not about to abandon athletic footwear, a business it dominates worldwide with more than $4 billion in revenues. However, footwear is a mature business, and Nike is embarking on an expansion strategy to transform itself into a global sports and fitness company.[19] As part of this expansion, Nike plans to offer 82 new stock keeping units (SKUs) in footwear for the committed golfer. These additions will be headlined by 50 Tiger Woods signature models. The expansion into golf products will be accompanied by "Nike Golf" operating as a separate company division with their own unique logo.[20]

More and more companies are looking to new products for profitability and away from downsizing and cost cutting. However, the focus is on product expansion ideas with the least risk and the greatest potential margins.

A **diversification strategy** requires the firm to expand into new products and new markets. This is the riskiest growth strategy, because the organization cannot build directly on its strengths in its current markets or with its current products. There are, however, varying degrees of diversification. **Unrelated diversification** means that the new products and markets have nothing in common with existing operations. **Related diversification** occurs when the new products and markets have something in common with existing operations. Blockbuster's move into music retailing has some relationship to video rentals since both are retailing operations in the electronic entertainment business.

A sound corporate growth strategy is important to an organization's long-term performance. Many firms employ several growth strategies simultaneously. However, other firms pursue one basic corporate growth strategy. Tootsie Roll Industries, for example, has remained in the candy business for 97 years. The company produces 37 million Tootsie Rolls and 16 million Tootsie Pops annually from factories in the United States and Mexico City. Although the company emphasizes market penetration, it has purchased 17 different candy brands to generate some growth from new products.[21]

Bobbie Oglesby comments on new strategies with which to grow business:
"Microsoft is a strong believer and practitioner of strategic planning. Each year, Microsoft's chairman and president set key objectives for the company that ultimately drive all business and marketing plans for the year. In addition, we also create a three-year plan to ensure we are anticipating the right products and infrastructure for the future."

Business-Unit Composition

In pursuing its corporate growth strategy, an organization may operate in a number of different product and market areas. It does so through business units designed to implement specific business strategies. A **strategic business unit** (SBU) focuses on "a single product or brand, a line of products, or mix of related products that meets a common market need or a group of related needs, and the unit's management is responsible for all (or most) of the basic business functions."[22]

SBUs are sometimes separate businesses from a legal standpoint. For example, Sears at one time consisted of Dean Witter Reynolds (investments), Coldwell Banker (real estate), Allstate Insurance, and the basic retailing business, Sears Merchandise Group. In other cases, corporate management establishes SBUs to facilitate planning and control operations. Additionally, they can change these SBU designations when conditions warrant. For example, Digital Equipment once organized itself into 150 SBUs. With recent cost cutting, however, management consolidated the 150 into 9 SBUs that focus on specific industries. Now, management looks at the company as if operating in only 9 separate businesses, rather than the previous 150.[23]

Thinking Critically

Consider a set of strategic business units for a corporation.

- What factors influence market growth rate and market attractiveness for these SBUs?

- What business strengths and weaknesses might be most important in the evaluation of SBUs for a manufacturer of surgical products for use by hospitals?

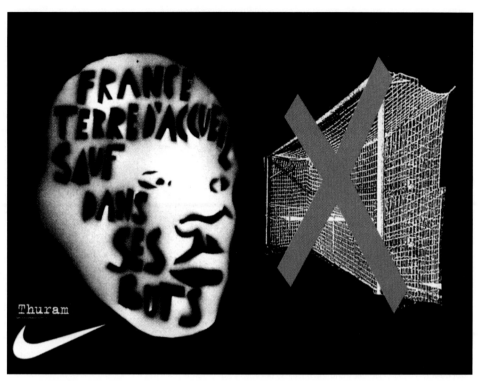

Nike has developed a broad mix of athletic product lines and regularly evaluates their relative growth potential and profitability.

An overriding decision for many companies is the determination of the firm's mix of strategic business units. Household products, specialty nonfood products, and dressings and sauces represent three of Clorox's strategic business units.

Changing a firm's business composition is not unusual these days. Corporate downsizing often causes a firm to exit from some business areas. Sears, for example, sold all or parts of its investment, real estate, and insurance businesses to concentrate on its retail business.[24] Whether the corporate decision is to increase or decrease the number of SBUs, once a given business composition is established, separate strategies are developed for each business unit.

Marketing strategy is the emphasis at the SBU level, where the focus is on market segmentation, targeting, and positioning (topics covered in detail in Chapter 7) in defining how the firm is to compete in its chosen businesses.[25] Historically, the configuration of a firm's business units has been evaluated in terms of market share and market growth using some variation of the Boston Consulting Group growth-share matrix. A simple depiction of this matrix is shown in Exhibit 3–9.

The matrix classifies the company's portfolio of SBUs into four categories: stars, cash cows, dogs, and question marks. Stars have a large share in growth markets. These products are profitable and require investment by the firm to support their continued performance. In contrast, cash cows have large market shares in slower-growth markets. These products generate significant cash relative to the expenses required to maintain share; hence, cash cows provide funds in support of other SBUs. Dogs, candidates for deletion or divestment, have modest market shares in low-growth markets. The remaining category, question marks, includes strategic business units that are problems. Ideally, these units with low market share but residence in high-growth markets should be supported and invested in to spur market share. If possible, the question marks should be shifted toward the star cell.

This view has proven useful over the years as a method for organizing and evaluating the mix of SBUs contained in company product/business portfolios. Consideration of strategy at the business-unit level enables management to stay in closer

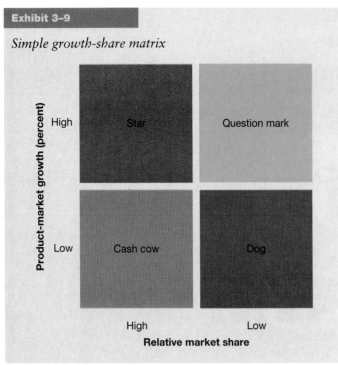

Exhibit 3–9

Simple growth-share matrix

Sources: B. Heldey, "Strategy and the Business Portfolio," *Long Range Planning*, February 1977, p. 12; and George S. Day, "Organizing the Product Portfolio," *Journal of Marketing*, April 1977, p. 34.

touch with customers, competitors, and costs and to maintain strategic focus. Further, this simplistic matrix based on market share and market growth has been expanded to include more complete definitions of market attractiveness (beyond market growth) and business strength (beyond market share).[26] Unfortunately, these business portfolios have been criticized for placing too much emphasis on market-share growth and entry into high-growth businesses to the neglect of managing current businesses well.[27]

More recent views of strategy formulation have evolved beyond discussion of star and question mark SBUs. New marketing strategic thinking emphasizes what can be, rather than what is. The emphasis is upon identifying opportunities for growth that do not naturally match the skills of existing business units. After years of downsizing, companies have begun to redefine strategy generation and to search for creative ways to grow and compete effectively. Instead of figuring out how to position products and businesses within an industry, strategy should focus on challenging industry rules and creating tomorrow's industries, such as Wal-Mart did in retailing or as Charles Schwab did in the brokerage business.[28]

Business Strategy Decisions

The basic objective of a business strategy is to determine how the business unit will compete successfully—that is, how the business unit's skills and resources can be translated into positional advantages in the marketplace. Management wants to craft a strategy difficult for competitors to copy so the business can sustain any advantages it has. For example, some retailers achieve sustainable advantages by selecting the best locations for their retail stores, effectively shutting out competitors from those areas. Other retailers try to gain advantages by offering the lowest prices. Price advantages are often difficult to sustain, however, because competitors can usually match them.

A business strategy consists of a general strategy as well as specific strategies for the different business functions such as marketing. The general strategy is based on two dimensions: market scope and competitive advantage.

Market Scope

Market scope refers to how broadly the business views its target market. At one extreme, a business unit can select a broad market scope and try to appeal to most consumers in the market. The business might consider all consumers part of one mass market; more likely, it will divide the total market into segments and target all or most of those. An example of a broad market scope strategy is the move by Nike beyond shoes into most every sports market. At the other extreme, a business unit can focus on only a small portion of the market. An example of a focused market scope strategy for a large, known international firm is Honda's introduction of a limited number of new car models compared with the broad offerings of U.S. automobile manufacturers.

Wal-Mart competes globally on the basis of providing name brands at lower prices, made possible by low cost structure.

Competitive Advantage

Competitive advantage refers to the way a business tries to get consumers to purchase its products over those offered by competitors. Two basic strategies are again possible. A business can try to compete by offering similar products and services as competitors, but at lower prices. Succeeding in a low-price strategy typically requires the business unit to have a lower cost structure than that of competitors. Wal-Mart is a good example of a business that prospers with a low-price strategy. It offers the same brands as many other retailers, but at lower prices. Wal-Mart can sustain this advantage and be profitable because it has a very low cost structure and constantly looks for ways to reduce costs.

A business may also compete through differentiation, that is, offering consumers something different from and better than competitors' products. If it is successful in achieving the desired differentiation, the business can typically charge higher prices than its competitors do. Neiman Marcus, for example, offers a unique product mix and exceptional service to differentiate itself from competition. Consumers are willing to pay higher prices to receive these benefits.

Bobbie Oglesby comments on competitive advantage: "Increasingly, competitive advantage in business is being powered by instant access to information. In addition, kids today carry pagers and phones so they are constantly connected to friends and family. Microsoft understands access to information will be one of the fundamental necessities in the twenty-first century. As a result, we've updated our corporate mission to state our vision of providing 'access to information anytime, anywhere, and on any device.' As a result, all our products are developed to be Internet-savvy, plus our corporate tag line 'Where Do You Want To Go Today' was developed to reflect this vision."

Earning Customer Loyalty

Lands' End: Retention based on quality

Companies that focus on obtaining and keeping profitable customers, productive employees, and loyal investors generate consistently superior results. Lands' End, the second-largest clothing catalog retailer in the United States, is one such company. Lands' End maintains unusually high inventories to enhance its ability to fill customer orders. Every effort is made to retain customers, as repeat business is required to cover the costs of obtaining buyers. Michael J. Smith, new CEO for Lands' End, asserts that its customers will pay for great quality sold by employees who treat them well. Providing high-quality merchandise and excellent service are the two pillars that form the basis of Lands' End's efforts to retain customers and build customer loyalty. This basic strategy, coupled with deliberate innovation through international expansion and specialized catalogs for certain segments (such as petites for women), has spurred growth to projected sales over $1.1 billion.

Lands' End has also devised a Web site that works as a complement to its well-known catalog. In fact, as of late 1999, LandsEnd.com and Gap.com rank 1 and 2 among apparel retailers in sales lured by Web sites. The on-line site offers the entire line of clothes, as well as other products and several unique services. Color swatches enable color combinations to be evaluated, for example, and the Shopping Aids Division provides two unique resources: With Oxford Express, shoppers can peruse the selection of more than 10,000 button-down dress shirts, and Your Personal Model allows women to enter their measurements and then receive fashion advice.

Sources: Susan Chandler, "Lands' End Looks for Terra Firma," *Business Week*, July 8, 1996, pp. 128 and 131; Robert C. Blattberg and John Deighton, "Manage Marketing by the Customer Equity," *Harvard Business Review*, July–August 1996, pp. 136–44; Frederick F. Reichheld, *The Loyalty Effect: The Hidden Force behind Growth, Profits, and Lasting Value* (Chicago: Bain and Company, 1996); Julie Skur Hill, "Online Selling Puts Dent in Stores, Catalogs," *Advertising Age*, September 27, 1999, p. S18; and "Mail-Order Legend Masters E-Commerce," *Computer Shopper*, May 1999, p. 280.

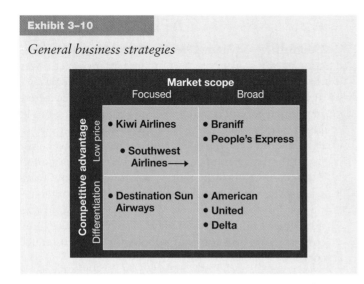

Exhibit 3–10

General business strategies

General Business Strategies

Combining the market scope and competitive advantage decisions produces the four general business strategies presented in Exhibit 3–10. The exhibit provides examples of each strategy for the airline industry.[29]

Kiwi Airlines targets the small-business or leisure traveler on routes between Newark, Chicago, Atlanta, and Orlando. Thus, its market scope is focused on only two segments and a few routes. Kiwi achieves competitive advantage by offering low fares with no purchase or travel restrictions.

Destination Sun Airways focuses on flights from the Eastern seaboard to Florida destinations such as Fort Lauderdale and West Palm Beach. It flies only routes abandoned by the major carriers. Therefore, it maintains an advantage by providing airline service not available from other carriers.

Most of the major airlines, such as American, United, and Delta, employ broad, differentiated strategies. These global carriers compete on many of the same routes, but try to differentiate themselves through service, frequent flier programs, and other benefits. These airlines must be price competitive, but their major strategic focus is to find ways to differentiate themselves on nonprice factors.

Although a strategy of broad scope and low price has been seen in the airline industry, several carriers have been unsuccessful in implementing it. Examples are People's Express, Braniff, and Eastern Airlines. These carriers all failed, largely because none could reduce its cost structure enough to be profitable at the low fares.

One airline that might succeed with this strategy is Southwest Airlines. Southwest began as a narrow-scope, low-price airline in 1971, and the company has posted profits for 20 consecutive years. The airline now serves 36 different cities and is expanding into several others. Thus, its market scope is broadening. Southwest may be able to do what most other airlines have not: make its no-frills approach work even with a broad market scope.[30]

As Southwest expands its market scope, many major carriers have announced plans to go after the short-haul market. Continental has already entered the short-haul business with CALite. USAir, Delta, and United have similar plans. The major carriers are trying to borrow from the strategies that have made Southwest successful.[31] Delta, for example, has partnered with Air France and Swissair in strategic alliances to expand its offerings. In addition, Delta Connection is affiliated with other southeastern airlines to cover short-haul travel, and it recently purchased Comair, enabling even greater accessibility throughout the eastern United States.[32]

Strategic alliances enhance the ability of companies to provide added value. United Airlines has joined forces with SAS and other airlines to provide expanded market coverage.

Marketing Strategy Decisions

Recall from Chapter 1 that a marketing strategy addresses the selection of a target market and the development of a marketing mix. The remaining chapters in this book discuss these areas in great detail. Our purpose here is to provide an overview of the two basic types of marketing strategies and to discuss international marketing strategy.

Marketing strategies are developed as functional strategies at the business-unit level and as operating strategies at the product level. The two strategies differ in specificity of decisions. Business strategy decisions are relatively general, intended to provide direction for all business-level marketing activities. Product strategy decisions are very specific, because they guide the actual execution of marketing activities for individual products. Exhibit 3–11 compares the decisions for the two types of marketing strategies.

Business Marketing Strategies

A business marketing strategy must be consistent with the general business strategy. For example, if the general business strategy includes a focused market scope, the target market strategy must concentrate on only a few market segments, perhaps only one. If the general business strategy is low price, the price strategy must be low price. Aside from these obvious constraints, several strategic options are typically available in each marketing strategy area.

Saturn Corporation provides a good illustration of a business marketing strategy.[33] General Motors established its Saturn business unit to develop new approaches for manufacturing and marketing cars, and the unit reported its first profit in 1993. Saturn's original general business strategy was a broad market scope and

---

Exhibit 3–11	Business and product marketing strategies	
Decision Area	**Business Marketing Strategy**	**Product Marketing Strategy**
Target market	Segmented or mass approach	Specific definition of target market to be served
Product	Number of different products	Specific features of each product
Price	General competitive price level	Specific price
Distribution	General distribution policy	Specific distributors
Marketing communications	General emphasis on marketing communications tools	Specific marketing communications program

---

Being Entrepreneurial

Gap: "Clicks and mortar . . ."

GAP has succeeded in the retail clothing business by offering value and unique style, as well as a sense of belonging to its customers. This approach has now been extended to their very successful Internet operations. By aggressively promoting both the store operations and the Web site, Gap enables both to benefit from the strengths of each. In fact, among apparel chains, Gap is now the leading seller in on-line sales. In spite of the difficulty of selling clothing, as opposed to less-personal types of items, such as books and computers, Gap's record is attributable to the following. Overall, Gap recognizes the importance of minimizing the cannibalization of retail sales due to on-line purchases. This is achieved through its savvy returns policy: Nonfitting on-line purchases may be returned without hassle to local Gap stores. At the same time, computer users visiting the store are encouraged to register on Gap's Web site; this allows Gap to send weekly e-mails announcing sales and new styles.

Sources: Julie Skur Hill, "Online Selling Puts Dent in Stores, Catalogs," *Advertising Age,* September 27, 1999, p. S18; Louise Lee, " 'Clicks and Mortar' at Gap.Com," *Business Week,* October 18, 1999, pp. 150, 152; and Edward O. Wells, "The Diva of Retail," *Inc.,* October 1999, p. 38.

Technological advances are often the central theme for competitive service strategies. In addition, this Peapod brochure promotes convenience and the ability to enhance shopping decisions through such features as comparison shopping and coupon-redemption capabilities.

a differentiated competitive advantage. The strategy includes a segmented target market, a relatively narrow product line, value-based pricing, selective distribution, and balanced marketing communications. Recently, Saturn has revamped its strategy to include an expanded product line with a sport-utility and mid-sized sedan. The sport-utility vehicle is targeted at the comparable Honda and Toyota vehicles. These additions are the result of pleas by Saturn dealers for expanded product lines.[34]

Saturn focuses on the broad market but divides it into specific segments and develops strategies for each. It offers a relatively narrow product line with many options available for each product. Pricing is based on value, and dealers typically do not negotiate. Distribution is selective, with only certain dealers chosen to market the Saturn vehicles. Marketing communications are balanced between advertising to inform consumers and get them into the dealers, and personal selling to sell the cars.

Product Marketing Strategies

Product marketing strategies require very specific decisions (see Exhibit 3–11). The target market is defined in detail, the product features and options specified, exact prices established, actual dealers identified, and a detailed communications program developed.

These decisions must be consistent with both the general business and the business marketing strategies. For example, Saturn's target market for each product fits within the market scope of the general business strategy. The unit decides on each product within the business product line, sets prices within the business product guidelines, uses appropriate dealers, and develops a communications strategy similar to the business communications strategy.

International Marketing Strategies

Marketers must address two key areas when developing international marketing strategies: selecting an entry strategy and deciding on a strategic orientation.

ENTRY STRATEGY   An **entry strategy** is the approach used to market products in an international market. The basic options include exporting, joint ventures, and

BENEATH *the surface of* SOME FINE BRITISH TRADITIONS *you may find* SOME FINE BRITISH TECHNOLOGY

Each morning, on the willow-banked rivers of England, a quiet ritual takes place. For more than a hundred years, teams of college rowers have broken the stillness of the river waters with the synchronized pull of their oars. To the traveler, it's a quintessentially English scene,

dignified and serene, as if torn from the pages of a novel by Waugh or Forster.

Indeed. However, down on the water, the rowers themselves may be taking a very different view of the action. Today's teams use computers to maximize their stroke and space-age materials to improve the performance of their boats. Team pride is everything. And competition is fierce.

Perhaps this unique combination of tradition, teamwork and forward-thinking is one of the reasons behind the success of our Derbyshire manufacturing operations. Where, since 1992, local team members have produced more than one million Toyota vehicles for markets within the UK and Europe.

In 25 countries around the world, local people are the real strength behind the production of quality Toyota cars and trucks. Here in America, Toyota vehicles are produced using many U.S. parts. And the talents of more than 25,000 local men and women have helped Toyota become the fourth-largest automaker in America.

Toyota recognizes that our success as a global automaker depends on our commitment to creating successful local partnerships.

It takes teamwork to move forward. Just ask any rower.

TOYOTA People Drive Us

Successful product strategies emphasize desired end benefits. Toyota promotes their cars' technology in foreign markets.

direct investment. Each option has advantages and disadvantages in level of investment and amount of control.

Exporting is a method of selling products to buyers in international markets. The exporter might sell directly to international buyers or use intermediaries, such as exporting firms from the home country or importing firms in the foreign country. Exporting typically requires the lowest level of investment, but it offers limited control to the marketer. Carrier (commercial air conditioners), Caterpillar (construction equipment), and Chrysler (cars) are firms actively engaged in exporting.[35]

At the other extreme is **direct investment,** where the marketer invests in production, sales, distribution, or other operations in the foreign country. This normally requires the largest investment of resources, but it gives the marketer the most control over marketing operations. Wang Laboratories, for example, emphasizes direct investment by operating 175 sales and distribution offices worldwide.[36] United Kingdom's Cadbury Schweppes PLC purchased Industrias Dulciora SA to give Cadbury the second-largest market share in Spain's confectionery market.[37]

In between these extremes are various joint-venture approaches. **Joint ventures** include any arrangement between two or more organizations to market products in an international market. Options are licensing agreements, contract manufacturing deals, and equity investments in strategic partnerships. Investment requirements and marketing control are usually moderate, although this depends upon the details of each joint venture. Examples of joint-venture strategies include Apple Computer's licensing of its new PowerPC chip to Asian firms such as Taiwan's Acer; the joint venture for pesticides, named Qingdao Ciba Agro Ltd., between Switzerland's Ciba-Geigy AG and China's Qingdao Pesticides Factory; and the marketing partnership between Delta Airlines and Virgin Atlantic Airways to coordinate flights and give access to London's Heathrow Airport.[38]

INTERNATIONAL STRATEGIC ORIENTATION Firms operating in international markets can use two different orientations toward marketing strategy. With a **standardized marketing strategy,** a firm develops and implements the same product, price, distribution, and promotion programs in all international markets. With

Standardized and customized marketing strategies suggest two alternative approaches for the design of international marketing strategy. Coca-Cola uses a standardized approach for certain apsects of its marketing mix.

a **customized marketing strategy,** a firm develops and implements a different marketing mix for each target market country.[39] Most international marketing strategies lie somewhere between these extremes, leaning toward one or the other.

These different marketing mixes may involve changes to the communications mix, the product itself, or both. At the corporate level, a **global strategy** views the whole world as a global market. A **multinational strategy** recognizes national differences and views the collection of other countries as a portfolio of markets.

Coca-Cola, for example, uses a largely standardized marketing strategy, where the brand name, concentrate formula, positioning, and advertising are virtually the same worldwide, but the artificial sweetener and packaging differ across countries.[40] TGI Friday's restaurants are successful in the Far East using the same concepts as in the United States. The mix of American memorabilia and chatty, high-fiving waiters produces high sales per store. In fact, the TGI Friday's in Seoul generates double the sales volume of an average restaurant in the United States.[41]

Nissan, in contrast, uses a more customized marketing strategy by tailoring cars to local needs and tastes. One success has been the Nissan Micra, designed specifically to negotiate the narrow streets in England.[42] Similarly, Campbell's Soup gets higher sales by adapting its products to local tastes. For example, sales accelerated when it introduced a cream of chile poblano soup to the Mexican market.[43]

Some companies are moving from customized to standardized marketing strategies. Appliance marketers traditionally customized products for each country. But Whirlpool, through extensive research, found that homemakers from Portugal to Finland have much in common. It now markets the same appliances with the same basic marketing strategy in 25 countries.[44]

The adaptation versus standardization decision is subject to a number of sometimes conflicting factors. Factors encouraging standardization include economy-of-scale advantages in production, marketing effort, and research and development. In addition, increasing economic integration in Europe and intensifying global competition also favor standardization. In many cases, however, demand and usage conditions differ sufficiently to warrant some modifications in marketing-mix offerings. The factors favoring adaptation in international strategy include differing use conditions, governmental and regulatory influences, differing consumer behavior patterns, and local competition. Adaptation is also consistent with the market orientation principles of the marketing concept. Accordingly, standardization may only hold for brands with universal name recognition and for products that require little knowledge for effective use, such as soft drinks and jeans.[45]

One study of 35 companies in Japan, Europe, and the United States that have successfully strong brands across countries revealed four common ideas about effective global branding:

1. Stimulate the sharing of insights and best practices across countries.

2. Support a common global brand-planning process.

3. Assign managerial responsibility for brands in order to create cross-country synergies and to fight local bias.

4. Execute brilliant brand-building strategies.[46]

Executing Strategic Plans

Developing strategic plans is one thing; executing them effectively is another. One route to effective execution of strategic plans is encouraging individuals within an organization to work together to achieve organizational objectives, reflecting the development of relationships within the organization. Two forms of teamwork are important: across the different functional areas and within the marketing function. In addition, comarketing alliances enable pursuit of strategic objectives under certain conditions.

Cross-Functional Teamwork

Traditionally, the different functions within an organization worked largely in isolation. Manufacturers manufactured, engineers engineered, marketers marketed, and accountants accounted. With little direct communication between these functions, their orientations were often more adversarial than cooperative, especially since each function has somewhat different objectives and operates from a different vantage point.

Exhibit 3–12 presents the different orientations between marketing and the other organizational functions. The potential difficulties in getting different functions to work together as a team are clear. Why should production care about marketing's interests when it is supposed to produce as much as possible as cheaply as possible? There was no reason for one function to care about another in this type of situation, and typically they did not.

The problem is that if an organization does not produce products that consumers will purchase, it does not matter how low production costs are. More and more organizations are realizing this and adopting a marketing philosophy, which means that everyone within the organization focuses on satisfying customer needs. And satisfying customer needs requires teamwork within an organization.

Many organizations have overcome differences in functional objectives and orientations by communicating the importance of teamwork. They reward the meeting of organizational goals such as customer satisfaction instead of merely functional goals such as low-cost production.

An interesting example of cross-functional teamwork is in the use of multifunctional teams to work with organizational customers. Companies such as Hewlett-Packard, Du Pont, Polaroid, and CIGNA send multifunctional teams from marketing, manufacturing, engineering, and R&D to visit specific customers regularly. The objective is to promote teamwork among employees from different functional areas, to develop a customer focus in all functional areas, to collect useful marketing information about customers, and to improve customer relationships. The value of these multifunctional customer visits is expressed by an R&D manager:

> In the past, engineering and marketing would argue about a product. . . . Instead, now we have marketing, manufacturing, and engineering all together deciding on the goal from the beginning. It's more of a trust and team-building kind of thing. We traveled together and went to all of these customers together. And we had conversations following it so that we trust each person's opinion more.[47]

Exhibit 3–12

Business function orientations

Function	Basic Orientation
Marketing	To attract and retain customers
Production	To produce products at lowest cost
Finance	To keep within budgets
Accounting	To standardize financial reports
Purchasing	To purchase products at lowest cost
R&D	To develop newest technologies
Engineering	To design product specifications

Many organizations have emphasized cross-functional teamwork to overcome barriers caused by pursuit of functional objectives, such as low-cost production, rather than long-term customer satisfaction. Hewlett-Packard combines new products with teamwork across functions to enhance market acceptance.

Marketing Teamwork

Even within marketing functions, teamwork is not universal. Different marketing functions often operate somewhat independently—advertising people perform advertising activities, salespeople sell products, brand managers manage their brands, and marketing researchers engage in marketing research. Many firms have little coordination among the different marketing functions. Today, however, the leading organizations are coordinating their marketing efforts and requiring close contact among the different marketing functions.

Many consumer product manufacturers, for example, foster close coordination among brand managers, salespeople and sales managers, and marketing researchers to execute tailored marketing programs for individual retail stores. Working as a team, they uncover information about the customers of each store. The sales and brand managers then work together to execute specific marketing programs for each store to improve sales and profits.

Kodak's reorganization illustrates the importance of marketing teamwork. In changing from a product-driven to a marketing-driven philosophy, the company established a group to integrate marketing functions that had been run separately, such as advertising, sales promotions, public relations, sales, and marketing research. The integrated group will work together in developing and executing all marketing plans.[48]

P&G uses a "business management team" approach to run each of its 11 product categories in efforts to encourage global brand success. The teams consist of four managers, headed by an executive vice-president, who have line authority for research and development, manufacturing, and marketing in each region. For example, the head of health and beauty aids in Europe also chairs the hair global category team. Because the teams are headed by top level executives, there are no organizational barriers to carrying out decisions.[49]

Bobbie Oglesby comments on growth challenges: "The Internet is fundamentally changing how we market products at Microsoft. With our Web sites and e-mail alerts/newsletters, we are able to form direct relationships with customers. We are also able to provide much more personalized and customized information to meet their individual needs, making one-to-one marketing much more cost-effective than it was in the past."

Co-Marketing Alliances

Co-marketing alliances include contractual arrangements between companies offering complementary products in the marketplace. The alliance between Microsoft and IBM was instrumental in the growth of Microsoft. Such alliances are increasing in frequency and enable firms to gain specialized resources from previously competing organizations. The success of co-marketing alliances is dependent on the care exhibited in partner selection and the extent to which relationships are balanced in power and benefit to both partners. Like in relationships between suppliers, customers, and employees, trust and commitment to the relationship in a co-marketing alliance engender cooperation and profitable network performance.[50]

Solution selling, in which products are marketed together as a means to construct a meal, has become quite popular. Interestingly, this approach has brought together previous competitors, such as Tyson and Pillsbury. Their coordinated effort to sell Sliced and Diced vegetables and chicken involved all aspects of partnering, from using national advertising to encouraging retailer support.[51]

Other alliances include Northwest Airlines and Visa, Kellogg's Pop-Tarts and Smuckers Jelly, and Krup's coffeemakers and Godiva chocolate. So, too, has Quaker Oats partnered with Nestlé in the development of granola bars with candy-bar appeal. Mattel and P&G are combining to share information and to promote their diaper brand, Pampers Playtime. And the co-branding of credit cards (e.g., Rich's and Visa) by retailers is also increasing; it enhances the visibility of the participating retailer. Determinants of the success of these alliances include prior attitudes toward the two brands and the perceived appropriateness of both brand fit and product fit. More-familiar and well-known brands are most effective at generating positive reactions to brand alliances. In particular, a branded component (e.g., Intel, NutraSweet) carries a certain equity and signals quality and performance more strongly than conventional attributes.[52]

Summary

1. **Discuss the three basic levels in an organization and the types of strategic plans developed at each level.** Organizations can be defined at three basic levels. The corporate level is the highest and responsible for addressing issues concerning the overall organization. The business level is the basic level of competition in the marketplace. It consists of units within the organization that are operated like independent businesses. The functional level includes all the different functions within a business unit. Strategic plans are developed at each level. Corporate and business strategic plans provide guidelines for the development of marketing strategic plans and product marketing plans.

2. **Understand the organizational strategic planning process and the role of marketing in this process.** The general strategic planning process consists of examining the current situation, evaluating trends in the marketing environment to identify potential threats and opportunities, setting objectives based on this analysis, and developing strategies to achieve these objectives. Strategic marketing describes marketing activities at the corporate and business levels. Marketing management emphasizes the development and implementation of marketing strategies for individual products and services.

3. **Describe the key decisions in the development of corporate strategy.** The key corporate-level decisions include establishing a corporate vision, developing corporate objectives and allocating resources, determining a corporate growth strategy, and defining the business-unit composition. Corporate strategy decisions affect strategic planning at all lower organizational levels. And strategic plans at lower organizational levels are designed to execute the corporate strategy.

4. **Understand the different general business strategies and their relationship to business marketing, product marketing, and international marketing strategies.** General business strategies require decisions concerning market scope and competitive advantage. Market scope can range from focused to broad; competitive advantage might be based on pricing or differentiation. Combining the market scope and competitive advantage options produces four general business strategies. A firm's business marketing strategy must be consistent with its general business strategy. Decisions on market scope and competitive advantage directly affect business marketing strategies. Product marketing strategies must also be consistent with and serve to execute business marketing strategies. International marketing strategies require decisions about entry method and strategic orientation.

5. **Realize the importance of relationships and teamwork in executing strategic plans.** The complexity of today's business environment requires cooperation both across different business functional areas and within the marketing function itself. Cross-functional and marketing teamwork are necessary to execute strategic plans effectively.

Understanding Marketing Terms and Concepts

Thinking About Marketing

1. How does a firm's corporate vision affect its marketing operations?

2. How does marketing differ for a new, single-product venture and a large, multiproduct corporation?

3. What are the basic options for a corporate growth strategy?

4. Look at "Earning Customer Loyalty: Lands' End: Retention based on quality." How might Lands' End grow through market penetration?

5. How do business marketing strategies and product marketing strategies differ?

6. What are the keys to effective execution of strategic plans?

7. Refer to "Being Entrepreneurial: Gap: 'Clicks and Mortar.'" What core competency drives Gap's Internet success?

8. How does an understanding of the marketing environment, as discussed in Chapter 2, help in the development of strategic plans?

9. Why do firms change their business composition?

10. How do corporate objectives affect marketing operations?

Applying Marketing Skills

1. Read an annual report for any company. Using only the information in the report, describe the firm's corporate, business, and marketing strategies.

2. Pick a recent issue of *Business Week, Fortune,* or any other business publication. Review it to identify examples of corporate growth strategies used by different firms.

3. Interview a marketing executive at a local firm. Ask the executive what types of strategic plans the firm develops and what is included in each strategic plan. Also, inquire about the firm's strategic planning process.

Using the www in Marketing

Activity One   Go to the home page of Honeywell (http://www.honeywell.com).

1. What does the site say about core competencies and corporate vision?

2. How are the businesses organized within the larger corporation?

3. How does the site describe Honeywell's emphasis on the production of quality products?

Activity Two   Find the Internet home page of a company that you admire and that offers multiple product lines.

1. What company did you choose? Why?

2. What strategic business units make up the company?

3. What is the overall mission for the firm? What marketing strategies are used to support that mission?

4. Describe the primary product benefits used as the focal point for the marketing strategy of one of the company's products.

Making Marketing Decisions

Case 3-1 Bank of America: Appealing to Multiple Customer Categories

The merger between previous BankAmerica and NationsBank to form Bank of America now leaves Hugh McColl in charge of an organization with $614 billion in assets. This makes Bank of America the largest and most nationwide bank, larger than Citicorp and Chase Manhattan. The bank has some form of relationship with more than two million businesses, 85 percent of the nation's largest businesses, and over 30 million households. Now earnings growth hinges on making the bank's 4,500 branches and 14,000 ATMs run smoothly. The results of frequent acquisitions to build a company this size, as well as managerial turnover associated with buying firms, have caused problems in transition and loss of market share in some areas. In addition, operating

costs are increasing. The general process following the bank's acquisitions is to feature streamlined, lightly staffed branches.

The eventual key to success will be the ability of Bank of America to handle its various customer types and its own employees. For example, the identification of customers by profitability is a concern. Bankers encourage profitable customers by offering CDs at premium rates and discourage nonprofitable customers by charging them higher checking fees; the ability to make these distinctions was limited after the merger with Barnett Banks in Florida. Bank of America also lost a significant share of its private trust customers after it took over Boatman's Bancshares in Missouri. As Bank of

America develops its new product identity, plans include a new initiative to train branch bankers to handle more small-business products. On the positive side, Bank of America Corp. has announced it will no longer give out customer information to telemarketers.

McColl argues that the mergers enhance scale, which enables the company to spread costs over a larger customer base and is more important as the financial services industry becomes more technology driven. Moreover, consolidation in the industry has been fueled by the encroachment of nonbank competitors and changing regulations that have allowed banks to expand into new product categories, as well as into new geographic regions.

Questions

1. What obstacles does Bank of America face in its operations as a national bank operating across such a diverse geographical area?

2. How do banks organize their operations in regard to customer categories?

3. What difficulties arise in providing customer service for such large and complex organizations?

4. What opportunities for competition confront Bank of America?

SOURCES: http://www.bankofamerica.com/annualreport/html/sharemsg.cfm; "Bonding," *The Economist,* April 18, 1998, p. 7; Eryn Brown, "BankAmerica: An Open Dialogue," *Fortune,* August 3, 1999; Bernard Condon, "Who's Minding the Branches of BofA?" *Forbes,* September 6, 1999, p. 58; Timothy L. O'Brien, "Big Bank Says It Won't Share Customer Data," *The New York Times,* June 12, 1999, p. B1; and "A Megabank in the Making," *Business Week,* September 13, 1999, p. 144.

Case 3–2 Virgin Atlantic Airways: Flying toward U.S. Markets

Virgin is best known for its competition with the larger and more staid British Airways. Virgin has benefited greatly in Great Britain from its underdog role in competing for the lucrative transatlantic travel business. In the smaller and confined British environment, Virgin has gained wide recognition. The company aggressively promotes and prices air travel fees and services and has developed very strong brand recognition. Its corporate reputation, regardless of the business endeavor, is clear: innovation, value for the money, and an element of fun.

Virgin is now applying this philosophy in its efforts to break into the U.S. market. Questions remain, however, about its ability to succeed in the U.S. market where it will face both more competitors and an environment in which companies typically spend a lot more on marketing. One action taken by Virgin was the opening of a 75,000-square-foot megastore in New York's Times Square. The store is described as the world's largest record, movie, book, and multimedia store. Virgin's soft-drink brand, ranked in Great Britain above Pepsi, has been introduced in selected U.S. markets. Its airline does indeed possess considerable name recognition among business travelers in the United Kingdom. Recently, Virgin has begun aggressively promoting incentive vouchers that can be purchased and applied for whole or part payments on package holidays, flights, hotel accommodations, and car fares.

Virgin gets much credit for competing with British Airways, and its "cool" image has established a nice niche in the United Kingdom. The cola success has been due to price; the airline success has been due to unique customer

services and creative promotions and advertising. Yet, the hurdles confronted by Virgin in its efforts to successfully compete in the United States are formidable.

Virgin Airways continues to make heavy use of a variety of promotions and media in efforts to strengthen its position in competition for cross-Atlantic travel. For example, Virgin Atlantic has targeted United and American airlines for travelers between Chicago and London using billboards mentioning the Chicago fire. In an effort to boost awareness in the United States, Virgin Atlantic has advertised using billboards and full-page ads promoting their Web site. Other promotions tied the company to the debut of the second Austin Powers movie, *The Spy Who Shagged Me.* A cross-promotion between Virgin and Joe Boxer promotes round-trip travel to London. In addition to the airline, Richard Branson has now attached his name to dozens of unrelated ventures and some marketing experts warn the brand name is in risk of becoming diluted. Many of these ventures involve Branson only putting up his name for controlling interests, while wealthy partners provide the required funds.

Questions

1. What major obstacles will Virgin face in the U.S. expansion that are not part of marketing within the United Kingdom?

2. What is your evaluation of Virgin's fun-oriented marketing strategy?

3. What problems occur when products from the same corporate brand (Virgin) are differentiated on different bases (price versus service)?

SOURCE: "Advantages of the Versatile Voucher," *Marketing: Incentive 95 Preview,* April 27, 1995, pp. 5–6; Edmond Lawler, "How Underdogs Outmarket Leaders," *Advertising Age,* November 13, 1995, p. 24; Cyndee Miller, "The British Invasion," *Marketing News,* June 3, 1996, pp. 1, 10; and "Virgin Atlantic Shortlisted for Advertising Campaign of the Year," *Marketing Week,* February 3, 1995, p. 5; Becky Ebenkamp, "JB, Virgin Unite Again for U.K. Trip," *Brandweek,* March 8, 1999, p. 14; Julia Flynn, Wendy Zeller, Larry Light, and Joseph Weber, "Then Came Branson," *Business Week,* October 26, 1998, pp. 116–20; "Virgin Atlantic Ads Take Aim at United, American," *Brandweek,* October 11, 1999, p. 8; and "Virgin Aims to 'Shag' Greater Awareness in U.S.," *Adweek,* June 7, 1999, p. 5.

Chapter Four

Consumer Buying Behavior and Decision Making

After studying this chapter, you should be able to:

1 Discuss the importance of consumer behavior.

2 Understand consumer decision making and some of the important influences on those decisions.

3 Distinguish between low-involvement and high-involvement consumer behavior.

4 Understand how attitudes influence consumer purchases.

5 Appreciate how the social environment affects consumer behavior.

6 Recognize many of the individual consumer differences that influence purchase decisions and behavior.

7 Recognize the outcomes of consumers' decisions to purchase or not to purchase and how they affect marketing success.

Kodak is consistently listed among America's best brands in surveys of brand attitudes, recognition, and equity. Kodak is cited for "representing feelings of caring and sentimentality, making photographic technology easy and something everyone can enjoy." Recognizing the underlying motives for consumer behavior and the important "ease of use" consumer benefit are excellent examples of how understanding consumer behavior enhances firm success.

Kodak's knowledge of consumer behavior is also evident in the design of the company's attractive and useful Web site (http://www.kodak.com). While providing the usual information about the company and its organization, the Kodak Web location offers consumers information about new products, a means of "chatting" with other photography enthusiasts, and helpful suggestions about product use. In addition, Kodak's site enables consumers to search for, and obtain information for evaluating, alternative photographic film and camera products. As such, consumers are better able to make more informed decisions. An important outcome of this enhanced decision making is a more satisfied and loyal consumer base.

The challenges faced by Kodak as the firm enters the new millennium are formidable. These challenges will only be successful if faced by a thorough understanding of how consumers buy Kodak brands, as well as competing brands. Its market share in film has dropped from 80 percent in 1984 to 65 percent in 1999, due largely to the growth and aggressive pricing of Fuji. To experience continued success, it is important that Kodak be competitive in the digital imaging business; currently, Kodak is second behind Sony in the U.S. market. Kodak's future depends upon its ability to make money on different media, such as CDs and the Internet. **Sources:** Jeff Green, "Kodak Tries to Circumvent Summer Price War with Promotional Lures," *Brandweek,* May 17, 1999, p. 19; "Keeping Kodak Focused," *Money,* January 1999, p. 46; Geoffrey Smith, "Film vs. Digital: Can Kodak Build a Bridge?" *Business Week,* August 2, 1999, pp. 66–68; and Chanoine Webb, "The Picture Just Keeps Getting Darker at Kodak," *Fortune,* June 21, 1999, p. 206.

Kodak's success is due to the company's ability to adapt to rapidly changing environments and evolving customer needs. Kodak's adherence to the principles of the marketing concept has depended on the company's understanding of consumer decision making and the many internal and external factors that affect consumer choices.

In the development and execution of a marketing program, a company must consider consumer preferences, the motivations behind purchase decisions, and subsequent product use. Remember that the marketing concept is based on identification of consumer needs and customer satisfaction. Likewise, building customer loyalty and long-term profitability are not possible without a firm grasp of the company's current and future customers. The success of marketing strategy, including the identification of target segments and the design of marketing mix combinations, depends on knowing what motivates consumers and how they form preferences and make decisions.

Consumer behavior is a complex topic and difficult to cover in a single chapter. In fact, consumer behavior is a separate course in many marketing programs. Additionally, the study of consumer behavior has historically been a multidisciplinary phenomenon. Researchers from psychology, anthropology, economics, and sociology, as well marketing and consumer-behavior specialists, have all contributed greatly to our understanding of consumer preferences and decision making.

In this chapter, we try to describe many of the most important aspects of consumer behavior. Again, the study of consumer behavior is critical in helping to ensure adherence to the principles of the marketing concept and the development of effective marketing strategy. First, we offer a formal definition of consumer behavior and explain why the topic is so important. Then we use a model of consumer decision processes to explore consumer problem solving and decision making. Next, we describe important environmental, individual, and situational influences that affect consumer behavior. The chapter concludes with a discussion of the primary outcomes that can follow the purchase and use of products and services, as well as a number of ethical issues that involve individual consumer behavior.

The Nature of Consumer Behavior and Decision Making

Consumer behavior can be defined as the mental and emotional processes and the physical activities that people engage in when they select, purchase, use, and dispose of products or services to satisfy particular needs and desires. Identifying and understanding consumer needs and preferences and their determinants is critical in the pursuit of profitable business opportunities.

Today a number of factors make it all the more important to understand consumer markets and individual consumer behavior: the mere size of the consumer market, ongoing changes in consumer shopping habits and purchase decisions, the continuing emphasis on consumer-oriented marketing, and the design of effective marketing strategy.

Size of the Consumer Market

The U.S. consumer market consists of all individuals in the United States. In 1999, the consumption expenditures for this market were huge: $6.3 trillion out of a total gross domestic product of $9.3 trillion.[1] Demand of this magnitude is well worth understanding. Moreover, competition for consumer dollars will increase as populations in the United States and other countries age, resulting in declining expenditures for some products. Firms that understand consumer behavior will be best able to compete effectively.

Your favorite Filet-O-Fish sandwich is back...
bigger and better than ever! Crispy on
the outside, tender and flaky on the inside.
Plus, that famous, tangy tartar sauce
with American Cheese!

FILET-O-FISH®
Now 33% more fish than the Original Filet-O-Fish!

Shifts in consumer preferences for some markets have been driven by growing concerns about health and nutrition. Many food marketers have incorporated such preference shifts into the design of their menus.

Mahogany cards celebrate
African-American culture
every day of the year.

From Kwanzaa to birthdays, Mahogany cards from Hallmark
offer a whole new way to say you care. Now at selected Hallmark retailers.

Mahogany

♔
Hallmark
The ways to say you care.

Multicultural differences offer opportunities for marketers to capitalize on unique preferences among segments of consumers. Hallmark recognizes these important multicultural effects in the design of their product mix.

Changes in the Consumer Market

Of equal importance are changes occurring in the consumer market. Some important trends affecting consumer buying behavior are detailed in Exhibit 4–1. They include consumers' concern for quality at reasonable and fair prices, for the effects of their purchases on the environment, and for health and diet.

Several fundamental demographic changes will affect the underpinnings of the consumer market in 2000 and beyond. These include the aging of the baby-boom generation, the increasing importance of children as consumers, differences between the haves and have-nots, and society's increasingly diverse population. Household budget expenditures will increase dramatically for health care and computers relative to declining dollars for furniture, food, and apparel. The growing popularity of khakis and casual shirts relative to business suits is but one example.[2]

Other trends that have increased dramatically in the last five years and will continue past 2000 include the following: the growing importance of convenience such as bottled water; ready-to-eat consumption such as frozen pizza and refrigerated dinners and fresh salads; and the doubling of sales of health and self-care products, such as antismoking products, hair coloring, and nutritional supplements. Consumer markets will be affected by diversity changes as well. While Blacks and Hispanics account for only 18 percent of middle-aged Americans, they account for 33 percent of the country's youth. Include a fast-growing Asian-American population, and collectively these groups will transform markets for items such as clothing, entertainment, and housing.[3]

One of the largest transformations in households has been the changes that have occurred in gender roles and division of responsibilities between husbands and wives. In 1960, 42 percent of women (ages 25–64) were employed in the workforce outside of the home; the figure in 1995 was 72 percent. The implications of this enormous change for the design of product and service offerings, as well as for the intended audience of advertising, are profound.[4]

Nowhere are the complexities more obvious than in the food industry. The paradox here is that consumers may want low-fat, low-cholesterol salads for lunch and fish for dinner, but many also choose a hot fudge sundae for dessert. This means that some old-fashioned, middle-of-the-road products like ordinary ice cream are being squeezed by low-cal frozen yogurts on one side and extra-luscious, superpremium ice creams on the other.[5]

McDonald's and other restaurants have reacted to consumer demands by offering new products with less fat and fewer calories, such as lean chicken sandwiches and salads, and by focusing on wholesomeness in ads. In addition, themes of value and high quality/low price are widely trumpeted to consumers.

Procter & Gamble continues to prosper and is growing worldwide. The primary impetus for the company's growth and profitability is its understanding of consumer demands for value. P&G's emphasis on volume growth, driven by innovation and lower prices, has been the primary contributor to higher earnings. The company's stated objective is to offer superior performance at competitive prices. It pursues this objective through price reductions on recognized brands, cost control throughout the organization, and the introduction of economy-priced products worldwide.[6]

Exhibit 4–1	*A sampling of trends affecting consumer behavior and consumer marketing*

- The increasing diversity of the marketplace and the increasing importance of understanding multicultural differences and their influence on consumer preferences and choices.
- Shoppers increasingly economizing or downscaling to less expensive brands, searching for deals, waiting longer to rebuy, balancing quality and price consciousness.
- Consumers increasingly factoring environmental considerations of brand and company reputation into buying decisions.
- People finding shopping more distasteful, frustrating, time-consuming.
- Nontraditional methods of selling and buying—direct mail, catalog, home shopping—growing at remarkable rate; changes supported by improving communications technology.
- In-store selling evolving rapidly—as seen in electronic ads above aisles and coupon dispensers attached to shelves.
- Consumers moving from conspicuous consumption to rational consumption and cautious use of finances.
- Consumers altering behaviors and diets to reflect greater concern for health and physical fitness.
- The aging of the population; longer life expectancies and lower birth rates making the over-50 segment a dominant force in society.
- Changes in family and workforce composition making men and women increasingly similar in choices of products and services.

Consumer-Oriented Marketing

To become more consumer-oriented and to build long-lasting relationships with their customers, companies need to understand what motivates buyers. This is an important aspect of the marketing concept. Ford Motor Company, for example, focuses on increased customer satisfaction and employee commitment. The company

- Is dedicated to being customer-driven.
- Makes carefully thought-out decisions about the customers to whom each product is to appeal.
- Studies potential customers and what they most want.
- Develops detailed product attributes to fulfill customer wants; doesn't copy what someone else is doing.
- Follows up with customers to confirm that products and marketing programs meet objectives.[7]

To consistently deliver high-quality products and services, marketers must understand and respond to continually changing consumer needs and expectations.[8] And marketers with the best understanding and the least biased perceptions of consumer needs will be the most competitive.[9] This constant striving to understand and better serve consumers reflects the pursuit of total quality management (TQM) principles.

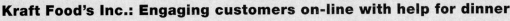

Earning Customer Loyalty

Kraft Food's Inc.: Engaging customers on-line with help for dinner

The recipe for success of Internet sites may be seen at the Kraft Food's Interactive Kitchen (www.kraftfoods.com) site. According to one digital measurement firm, the site is the highest-trafficked consumer packaged-goods site. The site is informational and customer-oriented, as opposed to being focused on product advertising. Repeat returns to the site are encouraged, in part, by their "Make It Now" link, which helps design meals from ingredients currently on hand. Data suggest that 71 percent of the site's visitors have "bookmarked" the site—a considerable amount of evidence pointing to the benefits of the information and assistance to consumers. As the company acknowledges, there is real advantage in solving consumer needs and building brand loyalty if it means customers realize the depth and breadth of Kraft products.

Source: Sheree R. Curry, "Kraft Site Shows CPG Firms How It's Done," *Marketing News,* October 11, 1999, p. 20.

Design of Strategy

Last, an understanding of consumer behavior is required for the effective design and implementation of marketing strategy. Knowledge gained through experience and marketing research provides the basis for the development of brand images and market positioning strategies. The success of these efforts determines subsequent brand strength, or what is commonly called *brand equity,* the marketplace value of a brand. A strong, well-known consumer brand, such as Kodak, Gap, Coke, Nabisco, and others, can induce quick and favorable consumer reactions to the particular company's products and enable the successful introduction of new products using the same brand name.

Exhibit 4–2   *A general model of consumer decision making and influences*

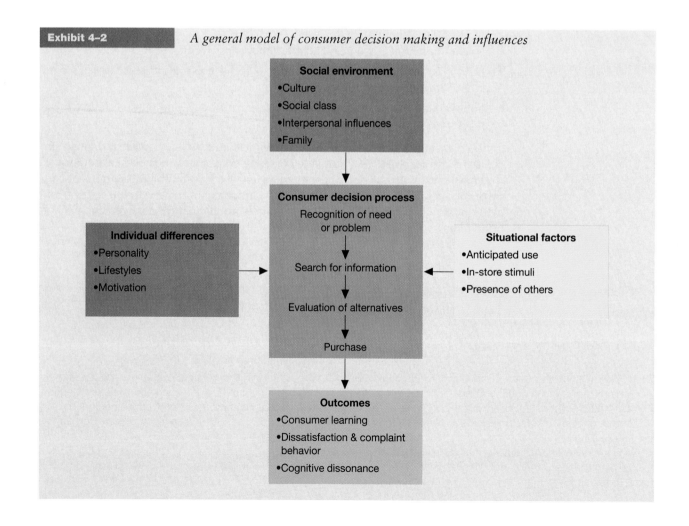

Consumer Decision Making

A general model of consumer decision making and influences on these decisions is presented in Exhibit 4–2. The consumer decision process, shown in the center of the model, assumes a conscious and logical decision-making process: from recognition of a need or problem to information search to evaluation of alternatives to purchase. This sequence can be affected by the social environment, individual differences, and situational factors. All have implications for the design and implementation of successful marketing strategy.

The Consumer Decision Process

A consumer's recognition of a *need* or *problem* may stem from an internal desire, the absence or failure of a product, or some external influence such as advertising. It can be as simple as getting thirsty and wanting a soda, or having to replace a used or outdated product or one that has lost its appeal. Advertising may also trigger the consumer's perception of a need or serve as a reminder.

After recognizing a problem, the consumer engages in a search for information. An *internal search* involves a review of information stored in memory. Although readily available, internal information may be incomplete or inaccurate. An *external search* involves gathering information from marketing sources such as advertising or from nonmarketing sources such as friends or *Consumer Reports*. Nonmarketing sources of information may be particularly useful because they are likely unbiased. The degree of search can vary by the number of brands examined, the number of stores visited, the variety of attributes considered, the number of information sources consulted, and the time spent on searching. An understanding of consumer search behavior is important to defining a product's or brand's competition.

The effects of on-line search and evaluation are already very evident and are profoundly affecting the manner in which consumers shop and the way in which firms compete. The Internet acts as a readily accessible source of external information and a facilitator of alternative evaluation. Psychologists and marketing experts have found that consumers who search on-line are impatient, in control, and quick to shift from Web site to Web site. Consumers in cyberspace are demanding more choices and more information. The most important attributes for encouraging consumers to shop a particular Web site are assurance of privacy, larger price discounts, ability to return products to a bricks-and-mortar store, and ability to speak with a customer representative. The shoppingbot phenomenon also has revised the decision-making process. A typical shoppingbot sequence might begin with a series of questions to narrow choices, then offer manufacturer-provided, detailed product descriptions, then end with links to retailers. In other instances, auction sites, such as *www.eBay.com,* provide input regarding the possibility of bidding for decided-upon items.[10]

After searching for information, the consumer evaluates possibilities (products, brands). This *evaluation of alternatives* is based on the individual's beliefs about the products and their features or characteristics. These beliefs form the basis for the consumer's attitudes, which influence both intentions to buy and purchase behavior. Following purchase, outcomes such as feelings of satisfaction or dissatisfaction and the development of brand loyalty may occur.

Consumer behavior is a complex phenomenon, and many internal and external factors may influence an individual decision. Many decisions are motivated by specific needs and values; some involve a conscious and logical decision process; others are made with little or no thought. One in-store field study of 4,200 grocery and mass-merchandiser shoppers revealed the following findings regarding consumer decision making:

1. Fifty-nine percent of purchases were unplanned, 30 percent were specifically planned, and the rest were generally planned or brand switches.

2. In-store decision making is greater for larger households, for higher-income households, and for women.

3. Consumers are more likely to make an unplanned decision when the product is displayed at the end of an aisle.[11]

Two other concepts relate to consumer decision making. First, **conversion rates** are used to describe the percent of shoppers who are converted into buyers. Conversion rates vary widely depending upon the kind of store or department involved. In some parts of the grocery store, conversion rates are near 100 percent. In art galleries, the conversion rates are near zero. Second, **surrogate shoppers** are involved in a significant portion of consumer decisions. A surrogate shopper is defined as a commercial enterprise, consciously engaged and paid by the consumer or other interested partner on behalf of the consumer to make or facilitate consumer decisions. Familiar examples include financial advisers, travel agents, and wardrobe consultants. Surrogates may perform any or all of the activities involved in consumer decision making—from search to determination of the brand consideration set to choice.[12]

High- and Low-Involvement Decisions

Involvement represents the level of importance or interest generated by a product or a decision. It varies by the situation or the product decision at hand and is influenced by the person's needs or motives. Frequently, involvement is affected by how closely the purchase decision is linked to the consumer's self-concept and how personally relevant the product is to the consumer.

Involvement is an important concept because it affects the nature or complexity of the communications appropriate for promoting products and services. Relatedly, involvement influences the nature of information processing engaged in by consumers. **Consumer information processing** represents the cognitive processes by which consumers interpret and integrate information from the environment.[13]

High-involvement decisions are characterized by high levels of importance, thorough information processing, and substantial differences between alternatives. The choice of a college to attend, the purchase of a home or vehicle, or the purchase of a bike for a sports enthusiast are all examples of high-involvement decisions. As such, high-involvement decisions are consistent with the logical and thoughtful sequence shown in the center of the consumer behavior model in Exhibit 4–2.

High involvement may be caused by a number of personal, product, and situational factors.[14] Again, importance of the purchase to one's self-concept increases involvement. If financial or performance risk is high, the decision is more likely to have high involvement. High involvement is also more likely when a gift is purchased or social pressures occur.

Low-involvement decisions occur when relatively little personal interest, relevance, or importance is associated with a purchase. These decisions involve much simpler decision processes, and little information processing, than the sequence described in Exhibit 4–2. For low-involvement decisions, consumers do not actively seek large amounts of information. Low-involvement purchases may include soft drinks, fast foods, toothpaste, and many snack foods. In these instances, repetitive purchase behavior may develop. Since these decisions involve little risk, trial purchases are often the consumer's major means of information search and product or brand evaluation.[15]

Consumer Problem Solving

Consumer decisions are often described as involving one of three types of problem-solving effort: routinized response behavior and extensive or limited problem solving. The type of decision is important to marketers because it influences the nature of the communications they should use to market their products, and hence, affects the productivity of their expenditures.

In **routinized response behavior,** some need results in a quick, habitual decision with limited search for information: If you are out of your favorite shampoo, you

Thinking Critically

Most snack foods are thought to represent low-involvement purchases. However, snack-food products now often compete on the basis of nutritional value and health-related themes, such as low calories, low sodium, and low fat.

- If snack-food purchases are indeed low-involvement decisions, how can companies use this nutritional and health information to influence consumer purchase behavior?

buy some more. The decision process is quite simple and results in a purchase from the consumer's set of acceptable brands. Generally, the consumer requires information only about price and availability. These decisions are relatively automatic, with minimal mental effort and little related search for alternative brands. Routinized response behavior, then, is often reflected in low-involvement decision making and in brand-loyal purchase patterns.

At the other extreme, **extensive problem solving** involves considerable mental effort and substantial search for information. Many high-involvement decisions result in extensive problem solving. The first purchase occasion for many complex and expensive products, for example, typically involves extensive problem solving. Even the criteria on which the choice will be made (the product attributes) must be learned. In the first purchase of a computer or a stereo system, unless the decision is turned over to someone else, the buyer may obtain much information about features, makes, models, and prices. He or she must then process this information and consider the alternative brands.

Limited problem solving reflects an intermediate situation. Here the consumer encounters an unfamiliar brand in a familiar product class. For instance, a sports enthusiast may see a new brand of running shoes or golf clubs. Although the consumer may understand the relevant product attributes, he or she must obtain sufficient information to evaluate the new brand on these criteria.

Types of Consumer Choices

Actually, the acquisition of goods and services is made up of many choices. At least six generic choices may be involved in consumer behavior: product, brand, shopping area, store type, store, and to an increasing degree, nonstore source (catalogs, PC and TV shopping).[16] The decision-making processes and the influences on those decisions discussed in this chapter apply to all six of these choices.

Consumers also must allocate their limited budgets across product categories. The average U.S. metropolitan household devotes half of its spending to housing, utilities, transportation, and food. Other categories allocated at least 5 percent annually are apparel, insurance, health care, and entertainment. As such, much consumer marketing funds are directed at these categories.[17]

Attitudes

Attitudes and attitude formation are related to the evaluation stage of the consumer decision process. **Consumer attitudes** are learned predispositions to respond favorably or unfavorably to a product or brand. Most of us take for granted our attitudes toward our favorite restaurant or soft drink. However, attitudes are instrumental in determining which alternative products and brands will be purchased and used. Attitudes have certain characteristics that make understanding them important to marketers trying to convince consumers to either buy their products for the first time or to remain loyal. First, attitudes have valence. That is, attitudes can be positive, negative, or neutral. Firms use creative messages and allocate huge amounts of funds to create or encourage positive attitudes. Second, attitudes that are strongly held and/or which are held with confidence are resistant to change. Therefore, the establishment of positive brand attitudes in the marketplace is a strategic objective for marketers. Last, attitudes can erode over time if not reinforced; hence, one role of advertising, as you will learn in Chapter 17, is to maintain awareness and to reinforce existing positive brand impressions and attitudes. It is particularly important to note that attitudes are a primary determinant of purchase behavior and their role in consumer behavior is a frequent area of inquiry for marketing researchers.

Consumer products, such as shampoo, typically stress a single end benefit in efforts to encourage information processing for what is typically a low-involvement purchase. Organics Shampoo employs unique visuals in their efforts to promote consumer message processing.

An understanding of consumer attitudes has very basic implications for marketing, for two reasons. Attitudes are based on beliefs consumers hold about the attributes or features (price, level of service, quality) of the products they are evaluating. In many instances, these attributes form the basis for the development of marketing strategies. And attitudes are primary causes of behavior, which makes them very relevant to marketers who want to understand why consumers buy—or do not buy—their products.

Consistent with one well-known psychological model, attitudes are often depicted as the combination of beliefs about the salient product attributes that consumers consider in evaluating alternative choices. The model and an example are presented in detail in the textbook's appendix. This theoretical view of consumer attitudes is rich in implications for developing effective marketing strategy. Briefly, attitudes are assumed to reflect the consumer's beliefs about product attributes (e.g., price, ability to clean, durability) and the weights or evaluation the individual has assigned to the different attributes. This multi-attribute view of consumer attitudes helps marketers assess which attributes are important to consumers, the strengths and weaknesses of brands based on those attributes, and areas in which the greatest improvement in attitudes might be realized.

Experiential Choices

So far, we have described consumer decision making as a logical process involving the conscious consideration of product information related to the attributes or the characteristics of the alternatives under consideration. The assumption is that consumers' long-term goals guide their preferences and that they make purchase decisions thoughtfully and logically. Routinized or habitual decision making is the only exception we have discussed to this point. However, consumers frequently make choices based on their emotions and feelings, adding an experiential perspective to the decision process. One such choice heuristic is termed **affect referral.** In such instances, consumers simply elicit from memory their overall evaluations of products and choose the alternative for which they have the most positive feelings. Affect referral explains why so many convenience items are purchased habitually. Another category of buying decisions that are made with little or no cognitive effort are **impulse purchases.** Impulse purchases are choices made on the spur of the moment, often without prior problem recognition, but associated with strong positive feelings.[18]

Consumers also often make irrational choices in which they act against their own better judgment and engage in behavior they would normally reject. These decisions are called *time-inconsistent choices* and, like impulse purchases, reflect consumer impatience and the urge to splurge. Psychologists have studied these choices as related to dieting and addiction for years. Yet all of us at one time or another have felt the urge to buy when better judgment suggests otherwise.[19]

Influence of the Social Environment
A number of external influences affect consumer behavior and purchase decision processes. The social environment directly affects sources of information consumers use in decision making and product evaluations. In many instances, personal sources, such as family and friends, may be more credible and influential to consumers than any other source of information.

The most important social influences are culture, subculture, social class, family, and interpersonal or reference group influences. These flows of influence within the social environment are summarized in Exhibit 4–3.

Cultural Influences

Culture refers to the values, ideas, attitudes, and symbols that people adopt to communicate, interpret, and interact as members of society. In fact, culture describes a

Exhibit 4–3   *Flows of influence within the social environment*

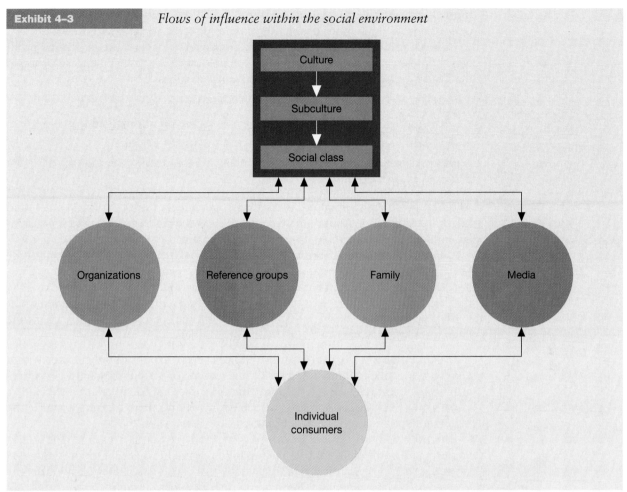

Source: J. Paul Peter and Jerry C. Olson, *Understanding Consumer Behavior,* 5th ed. (Burr Ridge, IL: Irwin/McGraw-Hill, 1999) p. 250.

society's way of life. Culture is learned and transmitted from one generation to the next. It includes abstract elements (values, attitudes, ideas, religion) and material elements (symbols, buildings, products, brands). The process of absorbing a culture is called **socialization.** It continues throughout one's life and produces many specific preferences for products and services, shopping patterns, and interactions with others. Applied to marketing and consumer behavior, it is referred to as *consumer socialization.*

In particular, the culture of a country has been shown to affect the appropriateness of different advertising strategies. Using the well-known categories of culture developed by an IBM executive, Geert Hofstede, one researcher discovered that in countries where people are not highly focused on social roles and group affiliation, such as Germany and Argentina, functional brand images are most effective. In countries where social roles are important, such as France and Belgium, images based on social and sensory messages are appropriate. Relatedly, cultures with low individualism (e.g., Asian countries) are also amenable to social appeals that emphasize group affiliation.[20]

The concept of culture has two primary implications for marketing: It determines the most basic values that influence consumer behavior patterns, and it can be used to distinguish subcultures that represent substantial market segments and opportunities.

VALUES   **Values** are shared beliefs or cultural norms about what is important or right. Values, such as the need to belong or to succeed, represent important goals to which consumers subscribe. A society's values are transmitted to the individual through the family, through organizations (schools, religious institutions, businesses), and through other people (the community, the social environment).

Cultural values directly influence how consumers view and use individual products, brands, and services. One typology of values used by consumer researchers is the List of Values (LOV).[21] It includes nine basic values:

- Self-respect
- Warm relationships with others
- Self-fulfillment
- Respect from others
- Excitement
- Security
- Sense of accomplishment
- Sense of belonging
- Fun and enjoyment in life

Another commercial method researching consumer values is the Values and Lifestyles program (VALS), which identifies eight market segments that share similar end values. This segmentation scheme is explained in more detail in Chapter 7.

Values influence the goals people pursue and the behavior used to pursue those goals. Many marketing communication campaigns recognize the importance of values as the basis for advertising themes and justification for purchase. For example, the desire for recognition and self-fulfillment is frequently used by companies selling self-improvement and exercise products. Or, the sense of belonging forms the basis for marketing many personal and gift products.

SUBCULTURES   The norms and values of specific groups or subcultures within a society are called **ethnic patterns.** Ethnic groups or subcultures may be formed around national, religious, racial, or geographic factors. Members of a subculture share similar values and patterns of behavior, making them attractive marketing targets for specific products and brands.

Unique subcultures often develop in geographic areas of a nation. The southwestern part of the United States is known for casual lifestyles, outdoor living, and active sports.[22] The Southeast is associated with a conservative lifestyle and friendly atmosphere. One system divides North America into "nine nations": the Foundry (industrial Northeast); Dixie; Ectopia (northern Pacific Rim); Mexamericana (southwestern area); the Breadbasket (Kansas, Nebraska, Iowa, etc.); Quebec (French-speaking Canada); the Empty Quarter (northwestern Canada); the Islands (tip of southern Florida, Caribbean Islands, some Latin American influence); and New England.[23] Each region contains many individuals who share similar values and lifestyles.

The black and Hispanic subcultures, while diverse themselves, are the largest ethnic subcultures. The black subculture is growing in size and spending power. Hispanics make up the second-fastest-growing subculture, behind the Asian subculture. Many Hispanics share a common language and a strong family orientation. Conservative Christian areas and Jewish centers also represent subcultures of influence.

Numerous demographic characteristics have been used to identify subcultures. Examples of these include:

Nationality—Hispanics, Italians.

Race—African-American, American Indian, Asian.

Region—New England, the South.

Age—elderly, teenager.

Religion—Catholic, Jewish, fundamentalist.

These subcultures include large numbers of consumers who share common values, behavior patterns, and beliefs that relate to consumer behavior. (Note that an individual can belong to more than

Cultural differences offer opportunities for marketers. Among the largest and fastest growing segment is the Hispanic market. *Latina,* a bilingual magazine for Hispanic women, is designed to appeal to those consumers who maintain ties with their heritage.

one subculture.) The consumer socialization of individuals within those subcultures affects their purchase decisions.[24]

Demographic analysis can be used in other ways for understanding consumer phenomena. For example, the enduring characteristics of the generation from which consumers come remain important as individuals age. Marketers are increasingly using these shared generational experiences to reach and effectively appeal to consumer segments. For the Depression generation, that may mean stressing thrift; for the World War II generation, patriotism; boomers are often seen as independent types stretching society's bounds. The point is, as the young get older, their habits stick with them.[25]

Social Class Influences

Some products are designed to appeal to the busy lifestyles of many working class families. Lunchables provides benefits to working parents in need of support for their families.

Social classes are relatively homogeneous divisions within a society that contain people with similar values, needs, lifestyles, and behavior. One approach for consumer analysis describes four social classes: upper, middle, working, and lower class, each of which can be further subdivided.[26] Identification with a social class is influenced most strongly by level of education and occupation. Social class is also affected by social skill, status aspirations, community participation, cultural level, and family history.[27] Social classes are relatively stable, but educational experiences and career moves enable individuals to shift from one class to another. Today, the middle class is declining in size. Economic conditions have limited upward mobility of the working class and caused many borderline families to fall into poverty.[28]

One recent study asked individuals to classify themselves as lower, working, middle, or upper class. Forty-six and 47 percent categorized themselves as working and middle class, respectively. Occupation and education were again the primary reasons individuals gave for their assignments. Research suggests that the working class is becoming younger, more ethnically diverse, and more female. These changes offer opportunities for marketers in their desire to understand consumer behavior and to identify large segments of potential buyers.[29]

Social class influences the types of purchases consumers make and the activities they pursue. Who goes to wrestling matches and who goes to the opera? Who plays polo and who goes bowling? Exhibit 4–4 summarizes some of the differences among subclasses of the middle class. Although preferences do change within classes over time, as evidenced by the differences between the 1980s and 1990s, more-significant differences in purchases and behaviors occur *between* classes.

Family Influences and the Family Life Cycle

Family influences play two important roles: in the socialization of people and in affecting individual purchase decisions. Families are the most influential factor on an individual's behavior, values, and attitudes. Patterns of behavior and values learned early in life are not easily changed. Lifestyles (athleticism, fondness for the outdoors) are usually learned from parents through **childhood consumer socialization**—the process by which young people acquire skills, knowledge, and attitudes relevant to their functioning as consumers in the marketplace.[30]

Individual family members also influence purchase decisions through their performance of different roles within the family. Members of a family or household may assume different roles—and roles may change, depending on the situation. In

Exhibit 4–4		*Class distinctions: You are what you choose*		
		Lower Middle	**Middle**	**Upper Middle**
Car	1980s	Hyundai	Chevrolet Celebrity	Mercedes
	1990s	Geo	Chrysler minivan	Range Rover
Business shoe (men)	1980s	Sneakers	Wingtips	Cap toes
	1990s	Boots	Rockports	Loafers
Business shoe (women)	1980s	Spike-heel pumps	Mid-heel pumps	High-heel pumps
	1990s	High-heel pumps	Dressy flats	One-inch pumps
Alcoholic beverage	1980s	Domestic beer	White wine spritzer	Dom Perignon
	1990s	Domestic light beer	California Chardonnay	Cristal
Leisure pursuit	1980s	Watching sports	Going to movies	Golf
	1990s	Playing sports	Renting movies	Playing with computers
Hero	1980s	Roseanne Barr	Ronald Reagan	Michael Milken
	1990s	Kathie Lee Gifford	Janet Reno	Rush Limbaugh

Source: Adapted from Kenneth Lubich, "Class in America, *Fortune,* February 7, 1994, p. 116. © 1994 Time Inc. All rights reserved.

the choice of toys, for example, parents often determine the acceptable set of brands from which children may select. The parents make the decision to buy, yet the child makes the brand choice. In other cases, all family members may influence decisions to purchase large-ticket items such as homes and automobiles, and increasingly, men and teenagers are doing the grocery shopping; marketers target these shoppers with ads in the magazines they buy.

Today, the role of children and teenagers within a family, and even as a market themselves, cannot be underestimated. Children's direct spending tripled in the 1990s. A typical 10-year-old goes shopping two or three times per week with parents. Apparel spending is the fastest-growing category of expenditures, and preferences formed by the young influence brand recognition and success among other age groups. One estimate is that 4- to 12-year-olds indirectly or directly influence purchases valued at more than $500 billion annually.[31] These influences affect choices of food items, clothing, restaurants, entertainment, and even automobiles. A grid showing how family influences relate to different product decisions appears in Exhibit 4–5. It crosses the number of decision makers with the number of users, identifying nine categories of family influence, depending on who makes the purchase decision and who uses the item. Cereal, as shown in cell 4, might be consumed by multiple members of the family but selected by the primary grocery shopper.[32]

Television, the Internet, and other media are affecting teenagers globally. One consequence is a common culture of consumption among young people worldwide. For example, MTV networks are directly influencing the spending habits and brand preferences of young people everywhere. As in the United States and the United Kingdom, well-known brands like Levi's, Nike, and Timberland are preferred worldwide among teenagers and other young consumers.[33]

Family life cycle is also relevant to consumer behavior. It describes the sequence of steps a family goes through: from young, single adults, to the married couple whose children have left home, to, possibly, the retired survivor. The family life cycle suggests ways to develop marketing strategies and design products and services. Household consumption patterns vary dramatically across the

Exhibit 4–5

Family buyer and user differences across purchase categories

		Purchase decision maker		
		One member	Some members	All members
User	One member	1 Book	2 Dad & Eric buy tennis racquet for Eric	3 Birthday gift
	Some members	4 Mom buys breakfast cereal for kids	5 Wine for dinner party	6 Private school for children
	All members	7 Refrigerator	8 Personal computer	9 Everyone helps pick toppings on a pizza

Source: Adapted from Robert Boutilier, "Pulling the Family Strings," *American Demographics,* August 1993, p. 46. © American Demographics, Inc., Ithaca, NY.

Exhibit 4–6

Changing shares of household types

	Percentages		
	1978	**1988**	**1998**
Married, no children	31	31	30
Married, children	39	28	26
Not married, no children	19	28	32
Not married, children	11	13	12

Source: Tom W. Smith, "The Emerging 21st Century American Family," *GSS Social Exchange Report No. 42.* National Opinion Research Center, University of Chicago, Chicago, IL, November 24, 1999, p. 28.

family life cycle. Appliances and insurance are bought for the first time during the early stages, for instance. Luxury products, travel, and recreation are typical expenditures for middle-aged adults with no children at home. Companies tailor product variations for specific stages of the family life cycle, such as Campbell's soups or Chef-Boy-R-Dee pasta packaged in smaller sizes for households of single or older consumers.

Changing family life cycles also have implications for product needs and buying behavior. Dramatic increases in age associated with first marriages, women working outside the home, single parents, premarital births, single-person households, childless couples, divorces, remarriages, alternate forms of living arrangements, and lower fertility rates have produced striking changes in families and households.[34] Exhibit 4–6 shows the decline in the number of households comprising married couples with children at home and the increase in single-parent and single-person households. These trends may decrease demand for large dining room tables, but they are good news for businesses that sell smaller tables, refrigerators, televisions, cleaning products, and other one-to-a-household items.[35]

Among the changes to the traditional family life cycle, the prevalence of dual-earner households and adult children living at home are phenomena well recognized by marketers. Today, companies study dual-income households just as intently as they studied homemakers a quarter of a century ago. For example, college-educated households make large-ticket purchase decisions jointly. Less-educated dual-income couples often both work to just buy increasingly expensive necessities. Young adults are now waiting longer to leave the home. In most cases, the prolonged stay enables the young adult to spend wages on luxuries instead of paying rent.[36]

Interpersonal Influences

Marketers also recognize interpersonal influences beyond the family, including friends, co-workers, and others. These sources of influence are often referred to as **reference groups,** or those others look to for help and guidance. They may be groups a person belongs to and ones she or he admires or wants to join.

INTERPERSONAL INFLUENCE PROCESSES   Three types of interpersonal processes—informational, utilitarian, and value-expressive—form the basis for interpersonal influences. **Informational influence** is based on the consumer's desire to make informed choices and reduce uncertainty. When we need to buy a complex product or face a new decision, we often seek information and advice from others we trust.

Utilitarian influence is reflected in compliance with the expectations, real or imagined, of others. These expectations are referred to as *norms.* Compliance to norms occurs in efforts to achieve rewards or avoid punishments. Rewards and punishments in day-to-day consumer behavior involve acceptance and peer approval and disapproval. These normative influences are particularly acute for young people. Sometimes these can be negative influences, such as peer pressure to use drugs, alcohol, or tobacco.

Value-expressive influence stems from a desire to enhance self-concept through identification with others. These influences are seen in the frequent use of popular spokespersons and attractive models in much consumer advertising. Celebrity endorsements

Cindy Crawford's Choice

OMEGA
The sign of excellence

The use of popular figures as product endorsers makes use of value-expressive interpersonal influences.

Peer influences among adolescents are important determinants of consumer behavior worldwide. Products are often purchased consistent with the need to identify with others and/or to express desired images.

from personalities such as actor Bill Cosby and model Cindy Crawford are intended to encourage identification with these figures through brand purchases. In other instances, products or brands are purchased in support of one's real or desired image.

The latter two forms of influence are sometimes combined into a more general category labeled **normative influence.** Marketers attempt to use normative social influences by showing favorable consequences that can occur when their brands are used or unfavorable consequences that occur when not used. What many want, particularly young consumers, is to be acceptable to their peers. So what determines "cool" for teenagers is partly about individuality and partly about belonging. Companies like Levi Strauss spend millions generating associations with their products that reflect positive acceptance among peer groups.[37]

LUXURIES AND NECESSITIES   Interpersonal influences on buying behavior vary across product types and depend on two conditions: whether a product is a luxury or a necessity and whether it will be used largely in public or in private.[38] If the product is consumed visibly, social approval and the effects of others' opinions may be important. Necessity products are owned by virtually everyone; hence the influence of others for necessities is on the brand purchased, not on product ownership.

Exhibit 4–7 gives an overview of the effects of public versus private consumption. Note that interpersonal influence on product *and* brand decisions is weak in the case of private necessities. In the case of public luxuries, interpersonal influence is thought to be strong for both product ownership and brand selection decisions. The strength of interpersonal influence varies for other combinations of luxury/necessity and public/private buying behavior.

Individual Differences   A vast number of individual differences can influence consumer behavior. Many people are swayed by various forms of word-of-mouth communications. Individual differences also stem from personality, lifestyles and psychographics, and motivation.

Exhibit 4–7	*Reference-group influence on product and brand purchase decisions*	
Product / Brand	**Weak reference group influence (−)**	**Strong reference group influence (+)**
Strong reference group influence (+)	**Public necessities** *Influence:* Weak product & strong brand *Examples:* Wristwatch, automobile, business suit	**Public luxuries** *Influence:* Strong product & brand *Examples:* Golf clubs, snow skis, sailboat
Weak reference group influence (−)	**Private necessities** *Influence:* Weak product & brand *Examples:* Mattress, floor lamp, refrigerator	**Private luxuries** *Influence:* Strong product & weak brand *Examples:* Video game, pool table, CD player

Word-of-Mouth Communications

Some people, traditionally labeled **opinion leaders,** influence consumer behavior through word-of-mouth communications. Opinion leaders were originally viewed as intermediaries between sources of information, such as advertising and other media, and the consumer. Their influence often stems from their involvement and interest or expertise in particular products. Marketers now recognize that communication flows both from and toward opinion leaders. In an application of the opinion leader concept, one research company focuses upon the 10 percent of Americans labeled "influentials." This segment of 20 million, by their inclination to use cutting-edge products, their income, their status, and their voice, exerts an inordinate amount of influence on the goods and services adopted by friends, co-workers, and acquaintances. Fifty-two percent of this segment of influentials had in-home access to the Internet as opposed to 23 percent of other Americans at the end of 1998.[39]

Market mavens are another type of information diffuser. These are consumers who know about many kinds of products, places to shop, and other facets of the market, and they like to share this information with other consumers.[40] Unlike opinion leaders, who know a lot about a few products, mavens know something about many products and enjoy discussing them. Market mavenism is a more general concept than opinion leadership in that mavens' influence results from the passing of information and expertise in the course of just making conversation. Mavens do not necessarily adopt new products or even use the products they are knowledgeable about, but they influence other people's choices and diffuse information on new products.

Word-of-mouth communications from friends and family are among the most important influences on consumer behavior. Because of the credibility of word-of-mouth information, others we know can easily affect purchasing decisions, particularly by limiting the choices we consider. More than 40 percent of Americans seek the advice of family and friends when shopping for doctors, lawyers, and auto mechanics. Word-of-mouth information is also crucial to decisions about restaurants, entertainment, banking, and personal services.[41] A recent large-scale study of college students revealed that the influence of word-of-mouth (44 percent) is twice as influential in new-product purchases than either price (22 percent) or advertising (22 percent).[42]

Personality

Personality reflects a person's consistent response to his or her environment. It has been linked to differences in susceptibility to persuasion and social influence and thereby to purchase behavior. General personality traits related to consumer behavior include extroversion, self-esteem, dogmatism (closed-mindedness), and aggressiveness. For example, dogmatism might limit product trial or the adoption of product innovations for some consumers; aggressiveness may be related to the purchase of certain types of sporty cars and to consumer complaint behavior in reaction to unsatisfactory purchases. Self-esteem is thought to be inversely related to persuasibility—the more self-esteem, the less subject to persuasion—and has implications for the effectiveness of marketing communications.

The use of general personality measures to explain purchase behavior has been disappointing. Researchers need to develop marketing or consumer-related measures to determine the role of personality in the consumer decision process and explore whether findings can be generalized across product and service classes. Such consumer-related measures would help in identifying market segments and creating and sustaining effective promotional campaigns.

The notion of *self-concept* is one idea used to explain the products consumers buy and use. Self-concept is the overall perception and feeling that one has about herself or himself. Consumers buy products and brands that are consistent with or enhance their self-concept.[43]

Marketers try to create relationships between their products or services and consumers. Marketers can affect consumers' motivation to learn about, shop for, and buy the sponsored brand by influencing the degree to which people perceive a product to be related to their self-concept. This objective is clear in the many ads that emphasize image enhancement and personal improvement through use of the advertiser's brand of product or service.[44]

Different views of self-concept have been offered. Self-concept has been referred to as actual self-concept, ideal self-concept, and social self-concept, the latter often deemed the "looking glass" view of an individual's self-concept. The notion of ideal, or desired, self-concept reflects the image the individual would like to display to others. The social self-concept reflects the image the individual believes others hold. Consumers purchase, display, and use goods that reflect these views of themselves or that enhance self-concept through the consumption of products as symbols. Possessions play an important role in defining individual identities in today's contemporary Western economies.[45]

Lifestyles and Psychographics

An outgrowth from attempts to use personality measures to explain consumer behavior are the concepts of lifestyle and psychographics. *Lifestyle* describes a person's pattern of living as expressed in activities, interests, and opinions (AIO statements are discussed in more detail in Chapter 7). Lifestyle traits are more concrete than personality traits and more directly linked to the acquisition, use, and disposition of goods and services.[46]

Psychographics divide a market into lifestyle segments on the basis of consumer interests, values, opinions, personality characteristics, attitudes, and demographics.[47] Marketers use lifestyle and psychographic information to develop marketing communications and product strategies. For example, responses to questions about the frequency of outdoor activity, cultural arts viewing, and opinions on social issues can be related to product use and then used as the basis for advertising themes and other marketing communications.

Chet Zalesky notes: "The basis for segmentation will determine its usefulness throughout the organization. An attitudinal-based segmentation (lifestyles/psychographics) will be useful in advertising, communications, and positioning. On the other hand, a customer needs/benefits-based segmentation will identify unique product benefit segments that can be used to redesign current offerings, launch new offerings, or highlight the need for initiatives to change how the organization interacts with its customers."

Motivation

Motivation refers to a state or condition within a person that prompts goal-directed behavior. Motivation generally occurs with recognition of some need or problem and can affect information search, information processing, and purchase behavior.[48] For example, washing machine owners are not routinely motivated to evaluate washing machine ads. But if their Maytag fails, they will be motivated to evaluate washing machine brands. Motivation involves both energy and focus. Motives themselves may be obvious or hidden.

Researchers frequently cite the classification of motives proposed by Abraham Maslow.[49] In this approach, individuals evolve in their personal growth, with higher-level needs (esteem, self-actualization) becoming important only after lower-level needs (physiological, safety) are satisfied. Any unfulfilled needs are assumed to be "prepotent" and provide the most immediate motivation for behavior. Levels of needs in Maslow's hierarchy and examples of associated product purchases include:

Self-actualization needs—Art, books, recreation.

Esteem needs—Clothing, home furnishings.

Love and belonging needs—Mementos, gifts, photographs.

Safety needs—Burglar alarms, seat belts.

Physiological needs—Food, heat, shelter.

Motives that drive consumer behavior are affected by an individual's environment, including marketing communications and reference-group influences. The productivity of marketing communications is enhanced when marketers position products to satisfy consumers' needs and the motivations that generate them.

Situational Factors

In addition to the social environment and individual consumer characteristics, situational influences also affect consumer behavior.[50] Situational influences can involve purchases for anticipated situations, such as special occasions, and unanticipated occurrences, such as time pressures, unexpected expenses, and changed plans. In-store sales promotions and advertising can exert situational influences on consumers as they often make buying decisions while shopping. A common in-store situational factor is music, long considered an effective means for triggering moods. One study reveals that grocery-store sales volume was significantly higher with slow rather than with fast music.[51]

Situational determinants of consumer behavior can be summarized as follows:

- Consumers purchase many goods for use in certain situations, and the anticipated use influences choice. Gift giving and social occasions are often important determinants of purchase behavior.

- Situational factors can be inhibitors as well as motivators. Inhibitors that constrain consumer behavior include time or budget constraints.

- The likely influence of situations varies with the product. Consumers buy clothing items, books, and many food products with anticipated uses in mind.

Situational store factors within the retail environment are also important. These store conditions include physical layout, atmospherics, location, the presence of others, the assistance of salespeople, and in-store stimuli. Merchandisers also try to capitalize on situational factors in developing their marketing plans. Gas stations have evolved into multiline convenience stores, for instance, and fast-food chains cater to situational needs with drive-through services.

Advertising often incorporates situational use into its message themes. For example, consider the well-known message "use Arm & Hammer Baking Soda as a refrigerator deodorant." This ad suggests the target brand (Arm & Hammer) as a reasonable choice for the target situation. In contrast, some ads compare the target brand with another product already associated with that situation ("Eat Orville Redenbacher Popcorn instead of potato chips as an afternoon snack"). Other ads compare the use of the target brand in a new situation with its use in a more familiar situation ("Special K breakfast cereal is as good at snack time as it is at breakfast").[52]

Using Technology

Shopbots and consumer search

Companies now recognize that comparison shopping has become commonplace in cyberterritory. As such, consumer search behavior and alternative evaluation capabilities have become greatly enhanced. As part of that phenomenon, "shopbots" are the latest craze. Shopbots can be divided into three categories: (1) product brokerlike options that recommend products based upon criteria specified by the buyer (one example being www.Deal-Time.com, which asks users to provide the type of product desired, the amount they are willing to pay, and how long they can wait); (2) merchant brokering shopbots that collect price and availability information (for example, www.best-bookbuy.com, which factors shipping costs into a comparison of total prices for books, giving a more realistic estimate of total prices); and (3) negotiating shopbots that buy, sell, and bargain, often in auctionlike services. The potential for these negotiation services is great in business-to-business situations, particularly for large-volume purchases of commoditylike products.

Sources: Mike D'Onofrio, "IntelliQuest: Bots to Replace Researchers," *Advertising Age's Business Marketing,* August 1999, p. 8; Susan Kuchinskas, "It's 'Dealtime' for Users with a New Shopping Bot," *Brandweek,* June 21, 1999, p. 30; Patricia Riedman, "Portals Rethink Retail Strategies, Shopping Agents," *Advertising Age,* February 1, 1999, p. 28; Joe Rudich, "Shopbots," *Link-Up,* July/August 1999, p. 26; and Rob Turner, "The Price Is Right," *Money,* May 1999, p. 199.

Consumer Behavior Outcomes

The study of consumer behavior does not end at purchase. Other phenomena or outcomes may and often do occur. These include consumer learning; consumer satisfaction, dissatisfaction, and complaint behavior; and cognitive dissonance.

Consumer Learning

When marketers set out to influence consumers, they typically try to impart knowledge through advertising, product labels, and personal selling—methods that are efficient and can be controlled by the marketer. Marketers hope consumers will attend to, comprehend, and then remember these messages. Yet, consumers also learn by experience. Experiential learning is highly interactive, and consumers often give it special status—experience is the best teacher.

Consumer learning happens when changes occur in knowledge or behavior patterns. Learning as knowledge gained is consistent with the decision process we have described.[53] Learning as behavior is also a critical outcome. Because successful marketing depends on repeat purchase behavior, providing positive reinforcement for the desired behavior is crucial.[54] Briefly, learning involves or is based on the combination of individual drives (needs), cues or stimuli in the environment, responses (consumer behavior), and reinforcement of those behaviors.

Consumer Satisfaction, Dissatisfaction, and Complaint Behavior

Consumer satisfaction, dissatisfaction, and complaint behavior are also important outcomes of consumer purchase-decision processes. *Satisfaction* and *dissatisfaction* describe the positive, neutral, or negative feelings that may occur after purchase; *consumer complaints* are overt expressions of dissatisfaction. Consumer satisfaction is central to the marketing concept and is a dominant cause of customer loyalty. Increased loyalty enhances revenues, lowers the costs of individual transactions, and decreases price sensitivity. Satisfaction also has benefits within the firm; costs associated with handling returns and warranty claims are reduced, as are those associated with managing complaints.[55]

Judgments of satisfaction and dissatisfaction are generally thought to result from comparisons between a person's expectations about a purchased product and the product's actual performance.[56] Purchases that turn out worse than expected result in **negative disconfirmation** and negative feelings. Purchases that turn out better than expected (resulting in **positive disconfirmation**) are evaluated positively.

A simple model of consumer satisfaction–dissatisfaction relationships is depicted in Exhibit 4–8. First, the consumer's prior experiences with products and brands establish expectations. Marketing communications, including advertising, and word-of-mouth communications also influence expectations. When you take your car to be serviced or repaired, what expectations do you have? Consumers thus develop expectations about what a product or service should be able to provide. Comparison between the buyer's expectations and the product or service performance levels results in the confirmation or disconfirmation of expectations and the outcomes of satisfaction or dissatisfaction. These positive or negative feelings serve then as input into the formation of future attitudes and expectations. Although disconfirmation is generally considered the most important determinant of satisfaction, expectations and performance directly influence satisfaction also. This is consistent with research showing that consumers with higher expectations experience higher levels of satisfaction and that performance, independent of positive or negative disconfirmation, exerts a direct effect on feelings of satisfaction.[57] Similarly, research on cars shows that consumers with high product involvement tend to be more satisfied with their purchases than less-involved car owners.[58] Regardless, however,

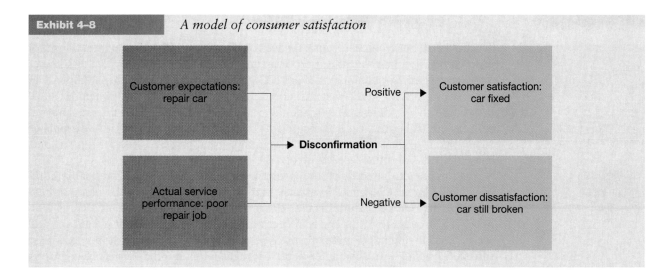

Exhibit 4–8	*A model of consumer satisfaction*

firms adopting a *customer value perspective* must employ marketing communications that convey realistic expectations.

Companies now regularly measure satisfaction and recognize it as an important determinant of customer retention. However, the measurement of satisfaction must consider not only what the customer did receive but what he or she could have received. That is, companies must study their competition as well. Overall quality has been shown to be a better predictor than satisfaction of customers' willingness to keep buying.[59] Practitioners now agree that only stellar performance makes a real difference in customer loyalty. The success of programs that measure satisfaction levels are dependent on benchmarking, either against competitor performance or performance goals established by management. Customer satisfaction measurement is useful for identifying areas in need of improvement to strengthen relationships with customers, as well as subsequent assessment of how efficiently and satisfactorily services and products are being provided.[60]

Besides influencing subsequent expectations, purchase behavior, and loyalty, dissatisfaction can result in several forms of consumer complaints: **voice responses** (seeking satisfaction directly from the seller), **private responses** (bad-mouthing to friends), and **third-party responses** (taking legal action, filing complaints with consumer affairs agencies).[61] Remember that word-of-mouth personal communications are very credible and influential.

Complaints are customer feedback about products, services, and company performance that marketers should never take lightly. Dissatisfied customers talk to more people than satisfied customers; often dissatisfied customers never make a complaint to the company.[62] Because new customers are harder to find, maintaining satisfaction among existing customers should be paramount.

To gain feedback, some companies even encourage their customers to complain. Companies that know what is bothering their customers have a better chance of correcting problems, retaining sales, and preventing further damage.[63] At Dell Computer Corporation, the mail-order PC marketer, staff, and managers meet every Friday morning to review customer complaints. The Dell vision is that every customer must be pleased, not merely satisfied.[64] In the same way, Coca-Cola wants to hear from its customers when they have a problem. According to its consumer affairs department, "Consumers who have a good experience with our company tell an average of five other people; but those who have a bad experience will tell twice as many people."[65]

Buick promotes safety features to appeal to its middle-class, traditional market segment.

Cognitive Dissonance

The final consumer behavior outcome we consider is **cognitive dissonance,** a form of postpurchase doubt about the appropriateness of a decision.[66] Cognitive dissonance may occur over major choices, such as college decisions and purchases of homes and expensive furniture, stereo systems, and appliances. Most students remember some uneasiness about whether they made the best choice of a college to attend. This uneasiness occurs because each alternative has attractive features. Cognitive dissonance is most likely to occur when the purchase is important, perceived risk is high, the purchase is visible, and the decision involves a long-term commitment.

Dissonance can affect postpurchase attitudes, change behavior, and cause additional information seeking. Strategies marketers can use to reduce postpurchase cognitive dissonance include regular programs of follow-up communications with buyers to discourage doubt and reinforce convictions about product strengths; solid service and maintenance plans to provide reassurance and increase postpurchase satisfaction; and warranty agreements arranged after purchase to protect buyers against problems that may occur.

Ethical and Social Issues

Some instances of consumer and business behavior raise ethical and social concerns.

Consumer Behavior

Unethical consumer behaviors include shoplifting and abuse of return policies. Shoplifting losses represent a tremendous cost to retailers and eventually to other consumers as retailers pass on the costs. Abuse of a company's return policies is also unethical; returns should be made only for reasonable problems.[67]

On the positive side, consumers are increasingly incorporating social concerns into their buying decisions. Environmentally concerned consumers show high awareness of label information and product content. Companies often market their products with messages and product information that recognize these environmental concerns.

Other consumer behaviors driven by ethical and social motivations are less personal and more political. For example, 1970s boycotts of infant formula products sold in Third World countries, and suspended in the mid-1980s, have reemerged because consumers believe the manufacturer failed to live up to its promise of ethical practice. Minority and gay rights groups use their buying power to express opinions about political issues.[68] "Buy American" campaigns recognize the effects of individual consumer behavior on jobs and local economies. The motivation for many boycotts is simple. Sellers should abide by certain ethical standards. Products produced by child labor or workers severely taken advantage of is an issue that has drawn attention on occasion. Some argue that buyers have responsibilities to be informed about sellers' ethical behavior and to consider that behavior in deciding to make purchases.[69]

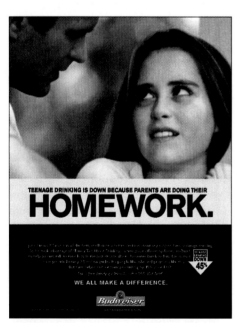

Both consumers and marketers have responsibilities to act ethically. Anheuser-Busch tries to inform parents about the best ways to communicate responsible behavior to young consumers.

Business Behavior

Business behavior is evaluated in terms of two standards: corporate social responsibility and business ethics. For example, firms are expected to provide safe products for reasonable prices. Their actions are not expected to detract from the general well-being of consumers. Efforts to monitor waste and the effects of production on the environment stem from these firm responsibilities. Likewise, marketing practices should not offend individuals or specific groups. Hence, liquor and tobacco advertising has been moderated in recent years, and tobacco advertising has been banned from the networks. Many beer companies, such as Coors and Budweiser, now emphasize responsible use of their products.

Summary

1. **Discuss the importance of consumer behavior.** Marketers must understand consumer behavior to develop successful strategies and identify target market segments. Furthermore, awareness of emerging trends in the consumer marketplace is essential for quick recognition of and response to problems and opportunities with sound marketing strategies.

2. **Understand consumer decision making and some of the important influences on those decisions.** Consumer behavior describes the mental and physical activities that people engage in when they select, purchase, use, and dispose of products and services purchased to satisfy needs and desires. The traditional view of consumer decision making is sequential: recognition of problem, search for information (either internal or external), evaluation of alternatives, purchase, and postpurchase evaluation.

3. **Distinguish between low-involvement and high-involvement consumer behavior.** Involvement represents the level of importance or interest generated by a product or a decision. A person highly involved in a decision (the purchase is personally relevant) will likely go through the entire decision-making sequence, from problem recognition to postpurchase evaluation. High-involvement decisions are characterized by thorough information processing, significant personal relevance of the decision, and substantial differences between alternatives.

   Consumers with low involvement will probably not engage in an extensive information search. Low-involvement decisions have minimal personal relevance and are likely routine or habitual. Consequently, they require less mental or physical effort than extended or limited problem solving.

4. **Understand how attitudes influence consumer purchases.** Consumer attitudes, which are learned predispositions to respond favorably or unfavorably toward a product or service, are important primary causes of behavior. They are important for both explaining consumer behavior and designing marketing communications for changing consumer behavior. One useful view depicts attitudes toward purchase behavior as a combination of beliefs about the product's attributes and the relative evaluation of those attributes.

5. **Appreciate how the social environment affects consumer behavior.** Social influences on behavior must be understood prior to the development of sound marketing strategies. Social class and family influences affect consumer behavior and can be used to identify market segments.

   The culture in which consumers are raised is also critical in determining the values that matter to them; culture may be used to identify segments with unique needs (subcultures). A great deal of learning also comes from observing and interacting with others (informational interpersonal influence). Some behavior occurs with the expectations of others in mind (utilitarian influences) and some with how they will react to our own behavior (value-expressiveness). The latter two are normative social influences. Consumers are also influenced by the situations in which behavior occurs or is expected to occur.

6. **Recognize many of the individual consumer differences that influence purchase decisions and behavior.** Individual consumer differences affect consumer decision making and behavior. These include: personality differences; lifestyle differences, which are often measured as consumer activities, interests, and opinions; and differences in motivation.

7. **Recognize the outcomes of consumers' decisions to purchase or not to purchase and how they affect marketing success.** Some of the more important outcomes that occur after purchase are consumer learning, feelings of satisfaction or dissatisfaction, and cognitive dissonance. Learning may result from experience and knowledge gained through advertisements and marketing communications.

   Feelings of satisfaction and dissatisfaction occur when product performance exceeds or falls short of expectations. Dissatisfaction may lead to consumer complaints and loss of future business. Cognitive dissonance is postpurchase doubt about the appropriateness of a decision. It is most likely to occur when the purchase is important or involved, perceived risk is high, the purchase is visible, and the decision involves a long-term commitment.

Understanding Marketing Terms and Concepts

Thinking About Marketing

1. Describe the importance of understanding consumer behavior. How does this understanding relate to the identification of target markets?

2. Outline and discuss the steps involved in the consumer decision-making process. How might this sequence differ for routinized response behavior and limited problem solving?

3. What is meant by low-involvement consumer behavior?

4. Why are consumer attitudes important? What role do consumer beliefs about product attributes play in consumer decision making?

5. Outline the three types of interpersonal influence, and explain how each may affect purchase behavior.

6. Explain how understanding social class and the family life cycle can enhance marketing effectiveness.

7. How does culture affect consumer behavior, and what are the implications for marketers?

8. Discuss the ethical responsibilities that consumers have in the marketplace.

9. Contrast cognitive dissonance with consumer dissatisfaction. What determines feelings of satisfaction and dissatisfaction?

10. Refer to the "Earning Customer Loyalty" box. How can Web sites be used to generate loyalty, and what characteristics of Internet search and shopping behavior work against customer loyalty?

Applying Marketing Skills

1. Contrast the decision sequence you made for two recent purchases—one expensive or complex decision, and one simple decision.

2. Discuss two examples of the way marketers could use interpersonal influence to their advantage. Under what conditions would you consider using interpersonal influence as a marketing tool to be unethical?

3. Find examples of ads that exemplify the following consumer behavior concepts: safety needs, consumer satisfaction, family influences, and subcultures.

4. Compare a product's print advertisement in a popular magazine targeted toward the general population with the same product's advertisement in a Latino/Hispanic magazine or an African-American magazine. Do the ads emphasize the same product benefits? Are different cultural values used in the message themes for both ads? Do these differences reflect the firm's customer orientation or just opportunistic efforts to capitalize on ethnic identification?

Using the www in Marketing

Activity One   Consider one of the following shopping comparison sites: www.activebuyersguide.com, www.snap.com, or www.productopia.com. These sources can be used in the selection of untold types of products.

1. How is the information organized and how do these sources affect the logical decision-making process around which this chapter was organized?

2. How do these sites make a profit or earn revenues?

3. Comment on the search and alternative information generated as it benefits the consumer, as opposed to information obtained from an in-store search designed to benefit the retailer?

Activity Two
For the Kodak home page, http://www.kodak.com, identify the following influences on consumer purchase behavior that Kodak is trying to capitalize on:

a. Social influence

b. Family

c. Gift-giving situations

d. Impulse purchase

Making Marketing Decisions
Case 4-1 Merrill Lynch: Technology and Consumer Buying

The environmental phenomena impinging upon Merrill Lynch and other financial institutions continue to be dramatic. Technological and global trends are affecting this large financial giant in ways the firm has been slow to address. Like so many financial service firms, Merrill Lynch is under siege from the Internet. The firm is being battered by much lower margins caused by the growth of electronic trading systems, which are forcing fundamental changes in financial markets. Merrill Lynch initially became the frequently cited example of Internet anxiety, a laggard of almost two years.

The company recently launched a series of on-line trading Web sites. These alternatives enable both small investors and corporate clients to track their holdings, as well as buy and sell a wide variety of products. As part of that introduction, commercials promoted the ongoing availability of Merrill Lynch employees for discussions and advice. The firm must ensure that the Merrill Lynch brand, which represents advice and consulting, is merged smoothly with its current offerings.

The switch to the Internet has been hard; the firm was slow to adapt, and competitive inroads by such competitors as Charles Schwab and E*Trade have led many consumers to on-line trading. These changes are felt in-house in the way Merrill Lynch conducts business.

Brokers who are used to making money by charging commissions will now have to rely on fees charged for advice. The "disintermediating" effects of the Net are making previous distribution channels redundant by connecting sellers directly with consumers. As of late 1999, Merrill was rethinking every one of its businesses, from research to asset management to brokerage, and concluded that the firm had to become an Internet-based company.

Questions

1. What are the implications of Internet trading for price sensitivity among consumer stock buyers?

2. What are the implications of demographic shifts in the American economy for the design of advertisements promoting financial services?

3. How might Merrill Lynch use an understanding of consumer decision making to help avoid cannibalizing sales from existing customers?

4. How can Merrill Lynch capitalize on the value of its analysts, traders, and brokers in efforts to maintain positive attitudes toward the company in the marketplace?

SOURCES: Beth Snyder, "Retail Financial Expertise Suits O'Donnell for JWT Post," *Advertising Age,* November 8, 1999, p. 96; "Even Merrill Can't Evade This Net," *Business Week,* June 14, 1999, p. 174; "Merrill Lynch Expects Higher Global Economic Growth in 2000," *Xinhua News Agency,* December 15, 1999 (http://www.comtexnews.com); "Merrill's E-Battle," *Business Week,* November 15, 1999, p. 256; and "Merrill Lynch in Japan," *The Economist,* January 9, 1999, p. 71.

Case 4-2 The Gap, Inc.: Appealing to the Global Teenager

 The list of "coolest" brands among U.S. teenagers includes Gap. Included in Gap Inc.'s set of over 2,400 stores are The Gap outlets, GapKids, Banana Republic, and Old Navy Clothing. Best known for casual and active clothing, Gap began in 1969 in San Francisco as a small store named after the "generation gap." During the 1970s, the company expanded its focus beyond sole emphasis on teenagers in efforts to appeal to a larger spectrum of consumers. Now the retail specialty chain has stores in 48 states, as well as in Canada, France, Puerto Rico, and the

United Kingdom. In addition, the company is in the process of opening stores in Japan and exploring other ventures in Asia. Fourth-quarter 1998 sales rose to $3 billion, up 40 percent from the year before.

Japanese customers are not unlike American consumers in their desire for well-known brands for some products. However, cultural and value differences in Japan make competition more difficult. Retailers that are successful expanding across borders typically appeal to a common lifestyle that the company fully understands. Other recent trends are also influencing the purchase of casual clothing. In particular, demand for designer jeans is on the rise, jeans that often are priced at twice what a pair of Gap or Levi jeans cost. And a new array of colors and bright shades are now chic among consumers of all ages.

Gap traditionally had viewed its store windows as the primary means of advertising. As a result, the company's ad spending was below that of many competing retailers. Industry experts questioned the company's reluctance to use radio and television, media popular with the Gap's young target audience.

Gap has now gone global with its advertising as part of worldwide campaigns to battle Dockers for a portion of the growing khaki market. Their advertising has remained focused upon attractive models displaying their products, often in dance-oriented themes. This approach has been very successful, and it contrasts with the awkwardness of some of Levi's mixed-message advertising. In a very competitive retail environment, Gap, Inc., has been effective at maintaining a distinct identity for the firm's core brands—Gap, Banana Republic, and Old Navy.

Questions

1. What role will the global teenager concept have in Gap's efforts to expand in Japan? Will the modest use of broadcast advertising influence consumer decision making enough to make the Japanese entries successful?

2. Once young consumers in an area learn about a new store's presence, is the decision to patronize the store an extended or limited problem-solving situation?

3. How will culture and subcultural factors affect Gap's performance in non–U.S. areas such as Japan?

4. In the United States, are the purchase of Gap-branded products subject to normative interpersonal influence? If so, are these influences predominantly utilitarian, value-expressive, or informational?

SOURCES: Alice C. Cuneo, "Gap's Ad Guru Departs," *Advertising Age,* May 6, 1996, pp. 1, 56; "Marketing Briefs," *Marketing News,* July 1, 1996, p. 2; Cyndee Miller, "Another Win for Retro: Designer Jeans Are Back," *Marketing News,* June 3, 1996, pp. 18–19; Kelly Barron, "Gaplash," *Forbes,* June 14, 1999, pp. 110–12; Alice Cuneo, "Gap's First Global Ads Confront Dockers on a Khaki Battlefield," *Advertising Age,* April 20, 1998, pp. 3, 49; "Daddy Gap," *Business Week,* January 11, 1999, p. 63; Hal Espen, "Levi's Blues," *New York Times Magazine,* March 21, 1999, p. 54; Bob Garfield, "Gap Secretes Sweet Smell of Ad Success," *Advertising Age,* August 16, 1999, p. 55; and Alan Treadgold, "The Outlook for Asian Retailing," *Discount Merchandiser,* May 1999, pp. 45–46.

Chapter Five

Business-to-Business Markets and Buying Behavior

After studying this chapter, you should be able to:

1 Define the nature of business-to-business buying behavior and markets.

2 Explain the differences between business-to-business buying and consumer purchase behavior.

3 Recognize the different types of buying decisions.

4 Define the different stages of the business buying process.

5 Describe the buying-center concept and the determinants of influence within the buying center.

6 Understand the nature of government, reseller, and other institutional markets.

www.tumyeto.com

Tum Yeto, the world's third-largest seller of skateboards and related items, was a temporary victim of its own success. The San Diego company's manufacturing capacity was significantly less than the demand for its skateboards. It was hard for Tum Yeto to get an adequate supply delivered on a timely basis to retail accounts. To ignore the problem would ultimately open the door wider for its competitors, so Tum Yeto went to work with its suppliers to remedy the situation.

Tum Yeto persuaded its suppliers to deliver the materials needed for producing skateboards just before they were needed in the production process. This allowed Tum Yeto to simplify and reduce its inventory, produce skateboards faster, and improve its cash flow. As a result, suppliers now devote a larger portion of their production to Tum Yeto because the flow of purchase orders and payments is more reliable than in the past.

Retailers also like the changes at Tum Yeto. In the past, lack of reliable supply had been the retailers'

largest complaint. Now, working off a twelve-month forecast, Tum Yeto is able to provide a predictable flow of products to the retailers every month. Shawn Zappo, skateboard buyer for the Boston chain store Blades, says he prefers to deal with Tum Yeto because "It's nice to work with a company that's this organized. They have a huge selection, and it's pretty much always available when you want it. They have everything covered."

By working closely with its suppliers, Tum Yeto can also offer dependable service direct to its customers via the Internet, which now accounts for 10 percent of its sales. Overall sales have grown by 50 percent, and Tum Yeto has increased the number of retailers selling its products to 1,100, also an 50 percent increase. In a market that is only growing at 15 to 20 percent, Tum Yeto owes a lot of its success to its suppliers and a much-improved purchasing process. **Sources:** Libby Estell, "Unchained Profits," *Sales & Marketing Management,* February 1999, pp. 63–67; and information from the Tum Yeto Web site, www.tumyeto.com, November 30, 1999.

Companies like Tum Yeto spend enormous amounts on products and services for business operations, and then market products and services to other consumer or business buyers. As indicated in the Tum Yeto example, these firms are making many changes to improve purchasing performance. Companies marketing to businesses and other organizations need to understand purchasing behavior to develop and execute marketing strategies successfully.

In this chapter, we define business-to-business buying, discuss its importance, identify emerging trends, examine important business purchasing concepts, describe government, reseller, and other institutional buying practices, and address relevant ethical considerations. As marketers, our objective is to understand what these buyers do and want, so we can market to them effectively.

The Nature of Business-to-Business Buying

Business-to-Business Buying Behavior Defined

Business-to-business buying behavior refers to decision making and other activities of organizations as buyers. It involves transactions between buying and selling organizations. A primary element in business-to-business buying is the selection of **suppliers, sources, or vendors.** These are interchangeable terms for companies or individuals who sell products and services directly to buying organizations. In practice, industrial or manufacturing firms distinguish between two kinds of purchases: those involving production and operational products routinely needed in ongoing production or maintenance (raw materials, fasteners, bearings, paint) and those involving capital products (milling machines, power-generating devices, computers and telecommunications systems).

Organizations fall into four general categories: *business firms,* including manufacturers of tangible goods and firms that provide services such as health care, entertainment, and transportation; *government markets,* federal, state, and local; *reseller markets,* such as the many wholesalers and retailers; and other *institutional markets,* such as hospitals (profit and nonprofit), educational and religious institutions, and trade associations. Each of these categories includes organizations that purchase from other organizations. Increasingly, business buyers are involved in **supply-chain management,** or "the integration of business processes from end user through original suppliers that provides products, services, and information that add value for customers."[1] The basic concept is to cut across organizational and company boundaries to better serve the customer, thereby gaining a competitive advantage. Thus, purchasing personnel work with others inside and outside their companies as a key part of supply chain management. In doing so, purchasing personnel may be involved in information gathering and dissemination, negotiating, monitoring the system, evaluating suppliers, and other roles in addition to making purchases.

Supply chain management is distinguished from typical purchasing operations in several ways. In the former, there is a focus on end-to-end processes rather than on individual functional departments such as purchasing, manufacturing, and marketing. Supplier relations require more commitment from the involved parties, and information is more freely shared. In addition to goals for financial performance, targets are set for improved customer satisfaction, and measurement of progress toward these goals becomes more important.

Characteristics of Business-to-Business Buying Behavior

There are some similarities but many differences between consumer and organizational buying behavior and decision making. Principally, consumers buy for their

Exhibit 5-1	*How business-to-business buying behavior differs from consumer buying*

1. Business-to-business buyers are fewer in number, larger, and more concentrated geographically than consumer buyers. This necessitates heavy emphasis on personal selling and trade advertising in business-to-business marketing.

2. Business purchase decisions often involve a more deliberate or thorough product evaluation and are subject to influence from multiple sources (purchasing, engineering) within a firm.

3. The demand for consumer products drives the purchases made by product manufacturers. Business purchase behavior is thus closely tied to economic fluctuations in the consumer market.

4. The demand for some products is related to the purchase of other products (joint demand). For example, if the demand for business personal computers declines, the demand for software applications and business computer printers may decline also.

5. Purchased industrial products are often complex, expensive, and bought in large quantity. Thus, many purchase decisions are based on detailed product specifications or choice criteria. Business markets also make greater use of leasing.

6. There is much more interdependence between business buyers and sellers. This underlies the need to build long-term buyer–seller relationships and leads to greater emphasis on after-sale service.

own use and for household consumption. Business buyers purchase for further production (raw materials, components), for use in their firm's operations (office supplies, insurance), or for resale to other customers. Major distinguishing characteristics of business-to-business buying behavior are presented in Exhibit 5–1.

Demand for business-to-business products is often dependent on demand in consumer markets. This phenomenon is referred to as **derived demand.** For example, the demand for many products is derived from consumer demand for new automobiles. When demand for new autos goes up, the demand for products used to make them, such as steel, plastic, and textiles also goes up. The reverse is also true.

Evaluating Business-to-Business Markets

Marketers can evaluate the size and growth rates of consumer markets using demographic characteristics. Many information sources report population statistics by characteristics like age or income level for different geographical areas. These demographic characteristics are not useful for evaluating business markets.

The federal government has developed a numerical scheme called the **North American Industry Classification System (NAICS)** for categorizing businesses. As shown in Exhibit 5–2, NAICS uses the first two digits to identify an industry sector such as the information industry. The third digit identifies an industry subsector (broadcasting and telecommunications), the fourth an industry group (telecommunications), the fifth an NAICS industry (wireless telecommunications carriers, except satellite), and the sixth a U.S. industry—in this case, the paging industry.

For each classification within NAICS, important economic data are available. This includes number of companies and employees, sales revenues, and percentage of sales occurring in large and small organizations. Such data are useful to marketers for estimating the size and growth rates of business markets. Developed in the late 1990s, NAICS offers several advantages over the

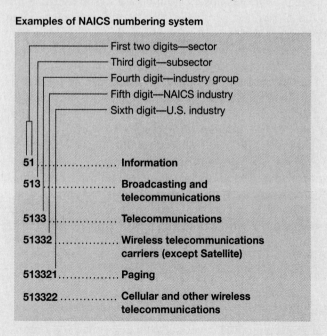

Exhibit 5-2

North American Industry Classification System

Examples of NAICS numbering system

- First two digits—sector
- Third digit—subsector
- Fourth digit—industry group
- Fifth digit—NAICS industry
- Sixth digit—U.S. industry

51 .... **Information**

513 .... **Broadcasting and telecommunications**

5133 .... **Telecommunications**

51332 .... **Wireless telecommunications carriers (except Satellite)**

513321 .... **Paging**

513322 .... **Cellular and other wireless telecommunications**

Source: United States Census Bureau, www.ntis.gov/naics, November 30, 1999.

previous Standard Industrial System. Mexico and Canada are also using the NAICS format, which allows comparisons for the entire North American market. Also, NAICS data include important industries that have recently emerged, another advantage over the Standard Industrial System. For example, NAICS tracks several high-tech industries, casinos, warehouse clubs and superstores, and HMO health care organizations, all ignored under the Standard Industrial Classification system.

The Importance of Business-to-Business Buying

Business-to-business markets and purchasing behavior are important for two basic reasons. First, the size of business markets offers many opportunities for astute marketers. Second, many firms are trying to increase profits by improving purchasing practices.

Business purchasing far exceeds consumer purchasing in total dollars. Businesses are the prime buyers of raw materials, such as minerals and farm products that are further processed and resold in whole or as part of other products. Businesses and other organizations also purchase services from advertising agents, accountants, consultants, attorneys, airlines, railroads, and so on.

The purchasing budgets of General Electric, Du Pont, GMC, Ford, and other companies exceed the gross national product of many countries. It is easy to see that businesses represent potentially lucrative markets for the products and services of many companies.

Lowering the cost of purchased products can be an effective way to increase profits. Consider this simple example. Assume a firm has annual sales of $100 million and a net profit margin of 5 percent. If this firm wanted to increase profits by $1 million, it would have to increase sales by 20 percent ($20 million sales increase × .05 net profit margin = $1 million profit increase). This type of sales increase may be difficult to accomplish in the slow-growth markets facing many firms. But if the company reduced costs by $1 million through improved purchasing, it would achieve the profit growth objective. This may be more doable in many situations.

The reality is that most firms are trying to increase profits by both increasing sales and reducing costs. However, more and more firms realize the powerful impact that purchasing improvements can have on profits. As business buyers change purchasing practices, marketers need to be aware of the changes and adapt marketing efforts appropriately.

Trends in Business-to-Business Buying   The purchasing operations at many firms are undergoing substantial changes. Key results of an extensive study about the future of purchasing are shown in Exhibit 5–3. In this study, 160 purchasing executives were asked to identify important trends for purchasing through the year 2008. An examination of Exhibit 5–3 indicates that several key marketing perspectives are particularly relevant for business marketers who seek to effectively meet the needs of purchasers.

Exhibit 5–3	*Selected purchasing trends 1998–2008*

1. Electronic commerce	7. Global-supplier development
2. Strategic cost management	8. Third-party purchasing
3. Strategic sourcing	9. Competitive bidding
4. Supply-chain partner selection and contribution	10. Strategic supplier alliances
5. Relationship management	11. Win–win negotiation strategy
6. Performance measurement	12. Complexity management

Source: Phillip L. Carter, Joseph R. Carter, Robert M. Monczka, Thomas H. Slaight, and Andrew J. Swan. *The Future of Purchasing and Supply: A Five- and Ten-Year Forecast.* Arizona State University: The Center for Advanced Purchasing Studies, 1998, pp. 27–36.

Productivity Improvement

Productivity improvement is emphasized throughout many companies. This affects purchasing in at least three major ways. First, firms find that it is often more productive to purchase products and services from other companies than to make the products or perform the services internally. This is called **outsourcing.** Second, corporate downsizing has often involved downsizing of the purchasing function. And third, purchasing is paying greater attention to reducing **cycle time,** or the total elapsed time to complete a business process.

Outsourcing first became popular in the manufacturing sector, but has now spread to all sectors of the economy, including services and the government. Arthur Andersen, the worldwide consulting firm, has benefited greatly from outsourcing in recent years as organizations seek help with logistics, human resource management, and other management functions. In New Zealand, for example, Arthur Andersen provides outsourced services for several government agencies, saving the country an estimated $100 million per year.[2] As indicated in Exhibit 5–4, the importance of outsourcing is gaining even more momentum.

A primary motivation to outsource is potential cost savings. According to some industry experts, the opportunity to save money through outsourcing is still important, but companies are also using outsourcing to better focus on strategic priorities. According to Scott Lever, vice president of Michael F. Corbett & Associates, there is "a shift away from short-term cost savings as the primary rationale for outsourcing. Outsourcing is increasingly being used as a long-term strategic tool to help firms focus on their core competencies, to share their presence in the marketplace, and to transform their business models."[3]

Purchasing personnel are often involved in strategic planning, new-product development, and other diverse activities. Downsizing the purchasing function has been facilitated by technology, especially the automation of routine reordering from established suppliers. Beyond the gains made possible by technology, productivity improvements have been made by fewer people doing more work.

Business buyers often focus on improving productivity within their organizations. GE Capital appeals to such buyers, pointing out in this ad that they helped one company reduce order delivery time from 28 days to 4.

Use of Technology

Buyers are increasingly employing a *technology perspective* to improve the productivity of purchasing operations. Reducing cycle time is an important purchasing trend (see Exhibit 5–3). Because time is money, buyers are interested in ways to reduce the purchasing, product-development, product-delivery, manufacturing, and inventory cycles. Reducing cycle times increases productivity by lowering the costs of doing business and can help increase sales. The use of new technologies often leads to shorter cycle times. Toyota, for example, now custom-builds its Solara coupe within five days of receiving the customer's order. Most manufacturers take 30 days to custom-build a car, and even Honda, usually the most efficient automaker, takes

Electronic commerce applications in purchasing

Business buyers frequently use the Internet for these activities:

- Requesting proposals and price quotes.
- Posting bids.
- Transmitting purchase orders.
- Using Electronic Data Interchanges.
- Ordering with electronic catalogs.
- Seeking suppliers.
- Tracking delivery schedules.
- Managing contracts.
- Managing inventory.
- Paying invoices/making payments.

Source: Terri Tracey, "The State of Electronic Commerce," *Purchasing Today,* August 1999, pp. 21–24.

15 days. Toyota's system relies on 360 key suppliers linked by computer in a virtual supply chain. Parts are loaded onto trucks in the order in which they will be installed, and trucks must meet precise delivery schedules. In a highly competitive market, Toyota's productivity improvement in business purchasing has led to an advantage in its consumer marketplace.[4]

Perhaps the most exciting technological development in recent years is the advent of electronic commerce in the purchasing function. In many industries, computer-to-computer systems link customers and suppliers, allowing automatic replenishment of inventory on a timely basis. Such systems include the shared networks of Wal-Mart and Procter & Gamble, Saturn and its automotive parts suppliers, and numerous hospitals and Allegiance (formerly Baxter). These company-to-company systems may link companies' private internal systems, which are called intranets. When two or more companies' Intranets are linked, this forms an extranet. Increasingly, electronic data interchanges run over the Internet are also referred to as Extranets. Conducting company-to-company exchanges over the Internet offers two key advantages over private and value-added networks: significantly lower per-transaction costs and widespread easy access.[5] For an illustration of how a supply network can be set up via the Internet, see "Using Technology: Adaptec Chips Away at Competition."

Business buyers agree that security is the biggest obstacle to using the Internet in purchasing. But with over 90 percent of business buyers reporting access to the Internet, electronic commerce in business markets is well established and growing rapidly. Exhibit 5–5 indicates how business buyers use the Internet.

A Relationship Perspective

The focus on supplier relationships by buyers is driving the emphasis on relationship marketing by sellers. Many of the purchasing trends reflect an emphasis on a *relationship perspective* (see Exhibit 5–3). These include supply-chain partner selection, relationship management, performance measurement, global-supplier development, strategic-supplier alliances, and win–win negotiation strategies. The goals of strong buyer–seller relationships, as shown in Exhibit 5–6, are to foster innovation and improve business efficiencies. By achieving these goals, customer satisfaction and profitability can be positively influenced. Over time, suppliers can

Using Technology

Adaptec chips away at competition

Adaptec, a California-based computer-chip supplier, was facing intense competition from other chipmakers that manufacture their own silicon. Rather than build a silicon-manufacturing plant at an estimated cost of $1.2 billion, Adaptec invested a million dollars in software and consulting to link their purchasing with silicon suppliers via the Internet. In doing so, they reduced chip delivery time from 15 to 8 weeks, and significantly improved customer satisfaction. Adaptec also realized considerable inventory savings

and improved communications with suppliers in Taiwan, Hong Kong, Singapore, and Japan. Its success with chips has Adaptec looking at how it can link all of its suppliers in an integrated supply chain. Saving while simultaneously improving customer service with the Internet is indeed a powerful combination.

Source: Cherish Karoway White, "We're Not There Yet!" *Purchasing Today,* January 1999, pp. 40–49.

Speaking from Experience

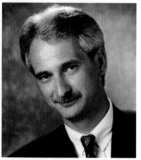

W. Wayne Whitworth
The Strategic Purchasing Group

W. Wayne Whitworth, C.P.M., is President of the Strategic Purchasing Group, a consulting firm specializing in purchasing and supply-chain management strategies. His prior experience includes purchasing management positions with Brown-Forman Corporation and Dover Resources, Incorporated. He is a Certified Purchasing Manager (C.P.M.) and earned his BSBA degree from the University of Louisville and an MBA from Bellarmine College.

"Technology is having and will continue to have a significant impact on both sales and purchasing professionals. Electronic commerce will move the transactional based, non-strategic purchases to the Internet in a market place forum. From the seller's point of view, new skills will be required to service buyers on a more strategic level. Buyers, in turn, will be the visionary link within the supply chain bringing the full resources from strategic partners to manage total cost of ownership and supplier relationships."

Exhibit 5–6   *Important features of strong buyer–seller relationships*

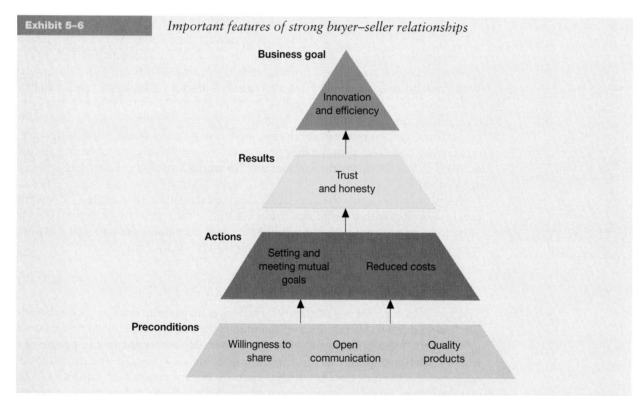

Source: A. T. Kearney, as reported in Phillip P. Carter, Joseph R. Carter, Richard M. Monczka, Thomas H. Slaight, and Andrew J. Swan, "The Future of Purchasing and Supply: A Five- and Ten-Year Forecast,"p. 23. Copyright the Center for Advanced Purchasing Studies, Arizona State University, 1998.

earn loyalty from their buyers, as illustrated in "Earning Customer Loyalty: Genuine Parts Is the Real Deal."

Buyers are in a rather unique situation because they work directly with suppliers to purchase products for their firm (internal customers) that are used to produce products for external customers. Although it is important for buyers to meet the needs of their internal customers, ultimate success depends on contributing to the success of external customers. Buyers are spending more time with external customers to better understand how the products they purchase from suppliers affect the products purchased by external customers. This helps them make purchases that can both reduce costs and increase customer satisfaction.

An important element of supplier relationships is an *ethics perspective*. Successful relationships must be based on trust. As indicated in the Tum Yeto example at the beginning of the chapter, buyers and sellers share a great deal of information and must

Focus all aspects of **your business** on **your customers.**

Lucent
Customer
Relationship
Management
Solutions.

If you could bring together all your business resources with everything you know about your customers (whether they contact you by mail, e-mail, Web site, phone or fax), what would it amount to?

A more consistently satisfying experience for your customers (keep 'em coming back). A more profitable revenue-generating opportunity for your business.

That's the idea behind Lucent Customer Relationship Management Solutions.

Now the company that helps more businesses connect with their customers (in more ways than anyone else) can help you do more business with each of your customers.

How? Lucent CRM Solutions focus every part of your enterprise (from Internet, to call centers, to databases, to fulfillment and beyond) on customers' needs and preferences, building long-term customer loyalty to deliver on your business goals.

Our leading-edge intelligent software links customer interactions across your entire company. We have technology to integrate your voice and data applications (around the block and around the world), eliminating barriers to doing business. It adds up to a more seamless experience for your customers.

The power of our strategic alliances with leading software applications, technology and integration partners assures you a total CRM Solution.

And (rest easy) Lucent NetCare® CRM Professional Services can help you plan, design, integrate and manage your solution (24x7x365).

See how Lucent CRM Solutions bring it all together to make customer relationships more rewarding for everyone. Give us a call.

1-877-FOR-CRM1 (1-877-367-2761)
www.lucent.com/crmnow

And the rewards
add up for everyone.

Lucent Technologies
Bell Labs Innovations
231 alt. Ave Road
Basking Ridge, NJ 07920
www.lucent.com/crmnow
1-877-FOR-CRM1

We make the things that make communications work.

Business marketers can assist their customers in building better relationships with their own customers. Lucent Technologies offers business customers a way to improve service with its smart Contact Solution, a customer-service management program.

Thinking Critically

Assume you are the buyer for liquid floor cleaner in the following situations. For each situation, specify what would be the most important purchase criteria that you would use to select a supplier.

- A buyer for a national chain of retail hardware stores.
- A buyer for a large manufacturing facility in Pittsburgh.
- A buyer for a janitorial-supplies wholesaler.

trust that this information will remain confidential. Both parties must trust each is working for mutual benefit. Honest and open communication is necessary. Once developed, trust is a powerful asset in a supplier relationship. Once lost, it is very difficult—and maybe impossible—to reestablish.

Gerber, a major manufacturer of baby foods, lost trust in some of its suppliers who were using genetic engineering in their corn and soybean products. After an inquiry from the environmental group Greenpeace raised health concerns, Gerber severed relationships with these suppliers, who were genetically altering their products to be resistant to pests and weed-killing chemicals.[6]

MCI provides a contrasting example of how a supplier can build better relationships by earning customer trust. MCI's Proof Positive program for business customers offers the lowest-cost calling program based on actual phone usage. Each month, customers receive a detailed statement and price comparisons with AT&T. If customer usage patterns change, MCI automatically switches them to a lower cost program. The Positive Proof program resulted in significant sales growth and customer retention.[7]

The final aspect of a *relationship perspective* is teamwork within the firm. Buyers are working more as teams with engineers and other functions in the selection

Earning Customer Loyalty

Genuine Parts is the real deal

Genuine Parts earns the loyalty of its 5,200 local auto-parts distributors by concentrating on its business needs along with the needs of the end user, or final buyer. Operating out of 63 distribution centers, Genuine offers a higher rate of filled orders than do other suppliers. By operating its distribution centers efficiently, the company holds shipping costs to a minimum, which ultimately translates into attractive profit margins for the local distributors. Genuine also offers its distributors a time-saving electronic interface with customers, suppliers, and distributors. Further, Genuine uses its buying power to negotiate favorable prices from its suppliers, which ensures that its local distributors can buy at the lower prices usually available only to large companies.

Source: Steven Wheeler and Evan Hirsh, *Channel Champions* (San Francisco: Jossey-Bass Publishers, 1999), pp. 14–15.

of suppliers. In many respects, buyers orchestrate the purchasing process within their firms. They coordinate the flow of information between the seller and buyer and rely on people within and outside their firm for expertise in evaluating different products and suppliers.

Wayne Whitworth emphasizes the importance of relationships in purchasing:
"The traditional role of purchasing will continue to change toward supplier management. This shift will place higher demands on interpersonal skills and the management of relationships with internal and external customers. The very nature of purchasing's new role will require a unique ability to develop collaborative partnerships with internal and external stakeholders to bring new products to market and to reduce total cost of ownership. Bringing multiple disciplines, functions, and cross-functional teams together to promote strategic organizational goals can only be accomplished by building relationships of trust, support and willingness to adapt to change."

Customer Value Considerations

One of the keys to successful supplier relationships is building customer value. Buyers are interested in suppliers that can add value to their business by continually increasing quality and lowering costs. Quality and cost considerations go beyond just the product being purchased to everything related to doing business together.

Over the years, Procter & Gamble has worked diligently to continuously increase the value received by Wal-Mart, one of its most important customers.[8] According to P&G's director of management information systems, the relationship between P&G and Wal-Mart used to be adversarial, and Wal-Mart did not like doing business with P&G. Procter & Gamble pushed for sales irrespective of what the customer wanted and was inflexible in meeting Wal-Mart's needs. By forming a joint Wal-Mart/P&G business team, executives from both companies now value the relationship and look forward to a prosperous future together. P&G has added value by driving down costs and sharing data that enable a better understanding of the ultimate consumer, consequently increasing sales for both companies.

Ethical Considerations

Many buyers emphasize an *ethics perspective* by examining the costs associated with product disposal and looking for ways to recycle or reuse products. These types of programs are likely to be more important in the future, as buyers become more actively involved in the environmental area.

In an effort to make business practices more environmentally friendly and safe, 47 nations are working to implement ISO 14000 standards for environmental management. Many companies, most of which are certified under ISO 9000 standards (refer to Chapter 2), are now seeking certification under ISO 14000. For purchasers, there are several implications. First, purchasers should identify activities, products, and services that have an environmental impact. This includes recycling programs, emissions to air, discharges to water, use of raw materials, and storage and movement of hazardous materials and the impact of both on land and communities. Purchasers can work with suppliers to reduce excessive packaging, conserve natural resources, and minimize the dangers of products and processes that may harm the environment.

Herman Miller, a manufacturer of office equipment, has worked with suppliers to promote environmentally friendly purchasing practices. Wood is a critical raw material for Herman Miller. Nations with tropical wood forests are a main source of supply. These nations are often developing nations in which indiscriminate logging practices destroy entire forests and various species of wildlife and vegetation. Herman Miller has eliminated the use of certain woods in its furniture and buys only from suppliers that can document responsible forestry activities. The company and its suppliers also work with organizations such as the International Tropical Timber Organization to promote the long-term viability of forest lands.[9]

"It's kind of hard to have a **fishing industry without fish**. That's exactly what happened in Sicily due to industrial pollution. Then we came in and helped mix things up—literally. We designed and provided the big, dependable, submersible pumps and mixers that drive their new water purification process. And once it started operating, the water started coming back to life—fish and all. Hallelujah!"

Zbigniew Czarnota, Research Engineer, Stockholm

ITT Industries
Engineered for life

Environmental issues are important to many business buyers. ITT Industries provided a treatment system in Sicily that improved water quality and fish habitat.

Types of Buying Decisions

In Chapter Four, we classified consumer decisions on a continuum ranging from extensive problem solving (requiring development of criteria for a decision) to routinized response behavior (requiring only price and availability information). Business-to-business purchase decisions can be classed similarly: straight rebuy, modified rebuy, and new-task decisions.[10] These categories are described in a grid in Exhibit 5–7. Note that the classes are distinguished according to the newness of the purchase decision, the information required, and the need to consider alternatives in the purchase, such as different suppliers.

New-Task Decisions

In **new-task decisions,** as shown in Exhibit 5–7, the buying problem is new and a great deal of information must be gathered. New-task decisions are relatively infrequent for a company, and the cost of making a wrong decision is high. Suppliers must convince the buyer their product will solve the buyer's problem; they cannot count on merely offering a price advantage to win the sale. New-task decisions are generally consistent with the sequence of activities in the buying process (discussed later).

When NBC purchases new technology products for use in its studios, the purchase is considered from every angle. A nationwide team of television engineers,

Exhibit 5–7	*The buying decision grid*			
	Type of Buying Decision	**Newness of the Problem**	**Information Requirements**	**Consideration of New Alternatives**
	New task	High	Maximum	Important
	Modified rebuy	Medium	Moderate	Limited
	Straight rebuy	Low	Minimal	None

Source: Erin Anderson, Wujin Shu, and Barton Weitz, "Industrial Purchasing: An Empirical Examination of the Buyclass Framework," *Journal of Marketing,* July 1987, p. 72. © 1987 by the American Marketing Association. Reprinted with permission.

Insupplier salespeople provide ideas and programs to help their customers build their businesses. This Colgate-Palmolive salesperson provides advice on in-store displays and merchandising to a retailer in China.

production staffers, and buyers is assembled. Major electronic corporations, generally about seven, from the United States, Europe, and Japan are asked to submit proposals. Engineers evaluate their technical capabilities. Production people evaluate their ability to produce quality pictures easily. Then written evaluations from these examinations are used, along with input from NBC's buyers, to make a selection.[11]

Modified Rebuy Decisions

Modified rebuy decisions call for the evaluation of new alternatives for purchase decisions. A modified rebuy could involve considering either new suppliers for current purchase needs or new products offered by current suppliers. The amount of information required and the need to consider new alternatives are less than for new-task decisions but more than for straight rebuy decisions. More familiarity with the decision means less uncertainty and perceived risk than for new-task decisions.[12] Purchases of complex component parts from a new supplier are typical modified rebuy decisions. In these situations, the firm's buyer, often with some input from management, will make the decision.

Straight Rebuy Decisions

Straight rebuy decisions are the most common type. Products and services bought previously are simply repurchased. Delivery, performance, and price are the critical considerations in a straight rebuy. "Outsuppliers," or suppliers not currently being used, are at a considerable disadvantage in this case because "insuppliers" have achieved their status by fulfilling purchase expectations over time. This being the case, the buyer is often reluctant to spend time evaluating other suppliers or risk changing suppliers. Purchase of office supplies, raw materials, lubricants, castings, and frequently used component parts involve straight rebuy decisions. Business buyers typically make these decisions.

The Buying Process

The buying process is presented in Exhibit 5–8. Like many consumer decisions, the decision sequence begins with problem or opportunity recognition. Problem recognition may be triggered by the depletion of supplies, worn-out equipment, or the need for improved technology. It may arise in various departments: operations, production, purchasing, engineering, or planning. New business opportunities may also generate the need for purchases. Once the firm recognizes need to purchase, it determines the desired product characteristics and the quantity to buy. Then production, R&D, or engineering personnel determine specific details for each item. These "specs" are the needed levels of product characteristics.

Next, the firm searches for qualified sources or suppliers. Information about potential suppliers may be available from salespeople, exhibitions and trade shows,

Exhibit 5–8	*The business buying process*

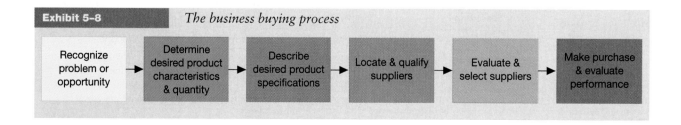

Recognize problem or opportunity → Determine desired product characteristics & quantity → Describe desired product specifications → Locate & qualify suppliers → Evaluate & select suppliers → Make purchase & evaluate performance

Thinking Critically

Assume you are the sales representative for a reputable company in the industrial-packaging business. You have just replaced another sales representative who recently resigned from the company. In making your initial sales calls, one of your customers tells you that he will never buy from your company again because he lost trust in the previous salesperson, who had lied to him.

- What can you do to rebuild trust with this customer?

direct-mail advertising, press releases, trade news and trade advertising, word-of-mouth, and professional conferences. Suppliers are evaluated to ensure they can produce and deliver the product as needed and provide service after the purchase. Surveys indicate that buyers are also looking for more than a quality product and excellent service performance in their suppliers. More buyers are expecting that suppliers will work closely with them to improve performance levels, contain costs, and develop new technologies. Buyers also prefer suppliers that will share data and resources to accomplish mutual goals, help improve the buyer's operations, and respond quickly to emergencies.[13] A formal procedure for evaluating suppliers is presented in Appendix A.

Wayne Whitworth considers several factors when choosing among potential suppliers: "There are a myriad of factors to consider when evaluating a potential or existing supplier. The most visible and quantifiable are those relating to price and quality. These attributes are readily identified and relatively easy to measure. The most difficult portion to quantify, however, is service since it entails a broad range of activities that are subjective in nature. When evaluating this component, I prefer to examine a supplier's cost contribution. Suppliers are rewarded based on cost savings contributions, innovations, new-product development activities and quantifiable measures that impact our total cost of ownership. The objective of this process is to remove subjective criteria from the evaluation process and recognize those suppliers that continually contribute value added, cost effective products and services."

Once a decision has been reached, the firm makes the purchase. Typically, buyers negotiate the final purchase. Buyers try to get the best deal for their company and often negotiate for better payment terms, delivery schedules, or other benefits. After the purchase is finalized, buyers continually monitor the suppliers' performance.

The business buying process varies according to the type of buying decision. New-task decisions are the most complex and typically follow the process we discussed. Modified rebuy situations are less complex, but normally include most of the stages in the buying process. Straight rebuys are usually a reorder from a current supplier.

The Buying Center

Sometimes one individual in a firm makes the buying decisions. Decisions made by a single individual occur most frequently for casual, routine, low priority, and simple modified repurchase decisions. In many instances, however, purchases are joint decisions of a buying center involving more than just a professional buyer. The **buying center,** a primary concept in business purchasing, includes more than the purchasing department or the purchasing function; it is made up of people throughout the organization at all levels. Moreover, the makeup of the buying center may vary as decisions change.

The number of people and departments represented and the levels of management involved are greater for new-task and complex modified rebuy decisions. The roles that people assume in influencing a purchase decision include initiator, decider, influencer, purchaser, gatekeeper, and user. These terms are largely self-explanatory, except for **gatekeepers,** those who control the flow of information and communication among the buying-center participants.

Vendors selling to industrial firms must recognize these multiple roles. The potential supplier may have to reach everyone involved in the decision process. That is, the seller must go beyond engineering and purchasing departments and talk to the gatekeeper, those who influence the decision, and the decision maker, for instance. IBM is a legendary example of how to do this well. IBM salespeople try to identify everyone involved in the purchase decision, the interrelationships among these individuals, the contribution of each, and the criteria each uses in making product or service evaluations.

Firms pursuing a *global perspective* face additional challenges since international purchases can make buying decisions and processes even more complicated. Most firms prefer to use overseas purchasing offices, typically staffed with foreign nationals with both purchasing and technical training. Some companies hire import brokers to handle their international purchases.

Buying-center members, connected by both workflow and communication networks, receive information from several sources. These sources of information may be personal or impersonal, commercial or noncommercial. Commercial sources come from some *sponsor* that advocates purchase of a particular product or service. Noncommercial personal sources, such as professional contacts, are influential because they include actual users of the product. They also have more credibility because of their likely unbiased perspective.

Marketing efforts targeted toward businesses depend heavily on personal selling. However, commercial nonpersonal advertising through trade publications and other sales literature can stimulate customer leads, enhance a vendor's image, and generally support personal selling efforts. Once again, the Internet can be a valuable source of information for business buyers. In Asia, for example, the business-to-business segment is the fastest-growing area of e-commerce. With supply chains in Asia often extending from Taiwan to mainland China to the Philippines and the United States, the Internet is a tremendous resource for business buyers. As a result, marketers are rapidly seizing the opportunity to connect with purchasers by adding the Internet to their mix of communications tools for reaching business markets. In Asia, where face-to-face contact between buyers and sellers has been preferred for centuries, technology again comes to the forefront in business buying.[14]

Government Markets

In the United States, the **government market** includes federal, state, and local government organizations that purchase goods and services for use in many activities. With total expenditures in the trillions of dollars, the government market is the largest in the world, with the United States federal government the largest customer in this market. The Department of Defense, traditionally the federal government's biggest spender, now trails the Department of Health and Human Services and the Treasury Department in expenditures.[15] Waste in government purchasing is a perennial topic of discussion, but government buying practices have been reformed significantly in recent years. Taxpayers are less tolerant of frivolous purchases, and government buyers have responded.

The *Commerce Business Daily (CBD)* publishes notices of government procurement needs, contract awards, sales of government property, and other procurement information for the federal government. A new edition of the *CBD* is issued every business day. Each edition contains approximately 500 to 1,000 notices, and each notice appears only once. All federal procurement offices are required to announce in the *CBD* all contracts or subcontracts involving expenditures over $25,000.[16]

Competing for government business is a complex, time-consuming, and often frustrating endeavor. Government purchase decisions are subject to legislative direction and, in the case of the federal government, monitored by outside agencies such as the Office of Management and Budget (OMB). Most governments, whether national, state, or local, purchase through open bids or negotiated contracts. **Bids** are written proposals from qualified suppliers in response to published governmental requirements or specifications. The lowest bidder is typically selected. In some instances, small business suppliers get preferential treatment in bid evaluations. A negotiated contract is reached when a government unit works with a company to determine contract terms.

At 9:00 am
Rock salt for the Commonwealth of Pennsylvania cost $33.0 million.

At 6:05 pm
It cost $30.5 million.

In one day, the FreeMarkets® process obtained 615 bids from 9 bidders, reducing the cost of rock salt by 7%, and saving $2.5 million for the taxpayers of Pennsylvania.

■ Free**Markets**

On-line auction sites are becoming popular with government units that buy from the lowest bidder.

Food companies advertise to both consumer and reseller markets. Tyson advertises its chicken to resellers, offering restaurant operators easy-to-prepare recipes and menu suggestions.

Reseller Markets

The **reseller market** is made up of firms that purchase goods and in turn sell them to others at a gain. This market includes wholesalers and retailers, totaling approximately 2.5 million companies with more than 25 million employees. Retailers and wholesalers are covered in detail in Chapters 14 and 15.

Retail businesses are everywhere. They make goods and services available to consumers at reasonable prices and in wide assortments. Most goods sold directly to consumers are first purchased by resellers. Wholesale firms tend to be more concentrated in trade centers surrounding larger population areas.

Retail establishments frequently use professional buyers to make their purchase choices. In many instances, say, for grocery chains, salespeople call on the buyers at central wholesale locations. Buyers at other retail firms, such as department stores, frequent trade shows where they place purchase orders directly with manufacturers.

Small retailers not part of large chain or franchise arrangements often band together to make purchases. Through buying-group memberships, these retailers get merchandise discounts or rebates they could not typically get on their own.

Assortment and quantity decisions are the cornerstones of retailing and wholesaling success. Resellers must be able to purchase products with significant consumer demand or appeal. Their success also depends heavily on their ability to purchase products that they can resell at prices above their purchase price. Competitive pressures and growing consumer price sensitivity have greatly increased the need to make correct decisions.

Other Institutional Markets

Nonprofit organizations must also purchase goods and services to support their activities. These organizations include educational institutions, public and private hospitals, religious and charitable organizations, and trade associations. As buyers, they represent viable marketing opportunities, and many specialized firms meet needs in these unique market niches. For example, some architects specialize in church or school design and construction. Other companies specialize in supplies for public and private schools. And of course, institutional buyers have standard business needs too. Many firms produce and sell health care equipment and supplies. Concerns about communicable diseases have given rise to an entire industry of protective health equipment such as disposable gloves.

Business buyers sometimes visit supplier locations to become more knowledgeable about the products they purchase. Siemens Medical Systems, a supplier of medical equipment, has a fully operational demonstration facility in its New Jersey headquarters.

Ethical Issues

Ethics is a constant concern in business-to-business negotiations and transactions. Bribery is a particularly troublesome area. Bribery can take many forms: gifts from vendors to people involved in decision making, "money under the table," and promises for the future. Suppliers offer these financial inducements to increase their chances of being selected by firms. Another related practice that may occur in purchase interactions between organizations is **reciprocity.** Reciprocity is when firm A purchases from supplier B who in turn buys A's own products and services. Such practices are illegal if they restrict competition and must not be used in decisions to select suppliers unless the arrangements can be made legally.

The important values of fairness, honesty, and trust are cornerstones of the *ethics perspective.* They should influence all negotiations between business purchasers and their suppliers, including the selection of suppliers or vendors. Judgments of suppliers should be made impartially and fairly. Unfair trade promises should not be extracted from companies that are in dire need of business or at some other disadvantage. This is the inverse of price discrimination, when firms unethically and illegally charge different prices to different customers for similar products and services. Purchasers should not unfairly require different suppliers to charge different prices for similar goods and services.[17]

For firms pursuing a *global perspective,* the possibility of encountering ethical dilemmas is multiplied many times. Practices in some countries differ dramatically from domestic expectations. In Japan, South Korea, and Taiwan, for example, failure to accept a business gift can imply insensitivity and disrespect. Many international companies have therefore had to develop well-defined policies that address the issue of receiving favors and gifts from overseas suppliers.

Summary

1. **Define the nature of business-to-business buying behavior and markets.** Business-to-business buying behavior refers to the process through which organizations make purchase decisions involving other organizations as suppliers. Increasingly, business buyers are concerned with supply-chain management, which integrates business processes from end users through original suppliers, providing products, services, and information that add value for customers. The four broad business markets are business firms, including manufacturers and service providers; federal, state, and local governments; wholesale and retail firms that buy products and then resell them; and institutional firms, including hospitals, educational institutions, and trade associations.

2. **Explain the differences between business-to-business buying and consumer purchase behavior.** Business buyers differ from consumer buyers in important ways. Overall, industrial and business buyers are more geographically concentrated, purchases are larger, decisions are subject to multiple influences and often approached more analytically, and demand is derived from consumer markets and trends in those markets. Organizational buying decisions typically rely on a number of choice criteria, including quality and reliability of performance, price, inventory service, reputation of supplier, and the ability to provide technical and service support.

3. **Recognize the different types of buying decisions.** Business-to-business purchase decisions can be classified into one of three categories, differentiated by complexity: new-task decisions, where the choice criteria must be determined and substantial information gathered; modified rebuys, where new sources of supply may be evaluated for situations previously encountered or the decisions are only moderately complex; and straight rebuys, where products and services bought previously are repurchased from known vendors.

4. **Define the different stages of the business buying process.** The most complex purchase decisions involve this sequence: (1) Recognize the problem or opportunity; (2) determine desired product characteristics and quantity; (3) describe desired product specifications; (4) locate and qualify suppliers; (5) evaluate and select suppliers; and (6) evaluate performance.

5. **Describe the buying-center concept and the determinants of influence within the buying center.** The buying center for an organization is responsible for selecting suppliers and arranging purchase terms. It is made up of people involved in routine and nonroutine purchase decisions. They may come from different departments (purchasing, engineering, production) and levels within the organization and may play one or more roles: initiator, decider, influencer, purchaser, gatekeeper, or user. Buying-center members vary in their influence on decisions, and a number of factors affect the relative power they hold in business-to-business purchases.

6. **Understand the nature of government, reseller, and other institutional markets.** The primary organizational markets include the government market, resellers, and other institutional firms. The federal government is the largest single purchaser. State and local governments make many purchases as well. Resellers are wholesale and retail firms that purchase goods to resell to other organizations or directly to consumers at higher prices.

Understanding Marketing Terms and Concepts

Thinking About Marketing

1. What are the distinguishing characteristics of business-to-business buying behavior?

2. What is the North American Industry Classification System? How can it be used to assist in marketing to business buyers?

3. Describe some of the current trends in business-to-business buying behavior.

4. Refer to "Using Technology: Adaptec Chips Away at Competition." What are some key benefits of using the Internet to facilitate purchasing and supply-chain management?

5. Refer to "Earning Customer Loyalty: Genuine Parts Is the Real Deal." Comment on this statement: Buyer–seller relationships are not just about economics; trust is just as important. Agree or disagree and give your reasoning.

6. What are the different types of buying decisions, and how do the information requirements vary across the decisions?

7. What is the general sequence of activities in new-task purchase decisions?

8. What is the buying center? Who are some of its typical members?

9. Contrast personal and impersonal sources of information. How might credibility differ across sources of information that are available to organizational buyers?

10. What is reciprocity? Why might it be illegal?

Applying Marketing Skills

1. Assume you must purchase new personal computers for your medium-sized company. What decision criteria would be involved, and how might the decision be reached?

2. Assume your manufacturing company has made the decision to begin importing critical component parts from country X. It is common practice for companies in that country to offer their customers personal gifts and small amounts of cash for their business. These parts, which are critical to your company's success, can be purchased abroad in country X at a much lower price and at a quality that matches that of current U.S. suppliers' products. What policies should be established for guiding the behavior and decision making of your company's purchasing personnel?

3. Describe the way the buying needs of a small retail clothier (the business owner and four employees) might differ from the needs of a manufacturer of industrial forklifts. The manufacturer makes purchases through its buying center. Discuss the likely differences in the decision processes involved for the two businesses.

Using the www in Marketing

Activity One   Compare the on-line purchasing sites for OfficeMax (www.officemax.com) and Staples (www.staples.com). Assume you are a buyer for office supplies for a large national manufacturer in the United States and that you want to purchase the majority of your office supplies from one vendor. In making your assessment, compare these attributes: ease of navigation, product availability, customer support, and ease of ordering. Rate each site on each attribute, and make an overall assessment of the strengths and weaknesses of each site.

Activity Two   On-line auctions have become part of business buying. Go to www.tradeout.com to investigate an on-line auction site. How useful do you think on-line auctions could be for business buyers?

Based on what you see at www.tradeout.com, does it seem that some business buyers might benefit more from on-line auctions than would others? If so, for which product categories would on-line auctions seem most promising for business buyers?

Activity Three   Dell Computers uses its Internet site to appeal to different categories of business and government buyers. Go to www.dell.com and compare the information available to federal government buyers with the information available to medium and large businesses (those with over 400 employees). What specific information does Dell offer potential buyers in these two categories? Is it adequate? Are there significant differences in the available information for buyers in the two categories?

Making Marketing Decisions

Case 5-1 Harley Davidson's Customer-Centered Supply Chain

Harley Davidson is best known for its high-quality motorcycles, but the company is also getting a lot of press about its customer-centered supply chain. By listening to its customers, and getting its suppliers to also listen to customers, Harley has built a strong foundation for its supply chain. In the process, Harley reinforces customer loyalty in a customer base already fiercely loyal to the leading American manufacturer of motorcycles.

In building its supply chain, Harley subscribes to several axioms developed in conjunction with the National Initiative for Supply Chain Integration and the Center for Advanced Manufacturing International. Among the axioms: a shared specific focus on satisfying the end consumer; a fundamental level of cooperation and trust; open and effective communications; and all supply-chain members' being committed to the generation of long-term mutual benefits.

It all starts with the customer, and Harley hits the road to learn from its ultimate buyers. Among the most important venues for listening to the customer are semiannual biker rallies in Florida and South Dakota. Bikers from all over the United States attend these rallies, where Harley sets up booths, display areas, and test rides. Key suppliers join Harley at these rallies to gather customer input through surveys, interviews, and less-formal one-on-one conversations with riders. This connection of customers with Harley personnel and suppliers helps ensure that consistent information is passed back from customers to the critical parties in the supply chain.

In addition to the rallies, Harley hosts dealer shows, also attended by supplier representatives. Harley can learn about dealer concerns at these shows, and key suppliers can provide information about technical concerns. All dealer information, as is the case with ultimate consumers at rallies, is documented and entered into the supply-chain database for appropriate follow-up.

Eventually, Harley compares notes with suppliers, and joint decisions are made that better meet the needs of all parties.

The level of detail in this information-gathering process is impressive. For example, Harley riders are sticklers for detail when it comes to paint and chrome. Harley and its suppliers ask for customer input on bike colors and just how much chrome it needs in order to give the bikes that unmistakable Harley look.

By implementing a customer-centered supply chain, Harley enjoys many benefits. It helps attract world-class suppliers such as Delphi Automotive Delco Electronics Systems, which supplies speedometers, tachometers, cruise control, and other electrical devices. The efficient supply chain also makes it easier for dealers to be competitive against rival retailers. Harley also supports its dealers through its on-line RoadStore. Though introduced as solely an information site, its usefulness will likely expand, as Harley plans to implement on-line sales through its dealers in the year 2000.

Questions

1. How can Harley Davidson marketing and sales personnel interact with its purchasing personnel to further strengthen the supply chain and improve customer loyalty?

2. What is the role of technology in Harley's supply chain? What additional uses of technology can you identify that might be useful to Harley's focus on the dealer and the ultimate customer?

3. Some of Harley's suppliers also supply key Harley competitors. How can Harley be sure these suppliers will not share competitive information with its competitors? How important is trust between suppliers and business buyers?

SOURCES: Julie Murphree, "Building a Customer-Centered Supply Chain," *Purchasing Today,* June 1999, pp. 34–42; "Harley Davidson Goes Live with Blue Martini Software for Its Dealer-Centered E-commerce Program," *Business Wire,* November 29, 1999, at www.businesswire.com; "Harley Davidson Opens Doors on the RoadStore," *PR Newswire,* November 22, 1999, at www.prnewswire.com; and "Delphi Formalizes Supply Relationship with Harley-Davidson Motor Company through Signing of Master Agreement," *PR Newswire,* November 5, 1999, at www.prnewswire.com.

Case 5-2 General Motors Flexes Its Purchasing Muscles

 Working with 30,000 suppliers, General Motors spends about $87 billion dollars a year on parts, equipment, components and sub-assemblies, raw materials, services, operating supplies, and other items. This makes GM the second-largest customer in the United States, trailing only the federal government. For years, the purchasing practices of General Motors have focused on reducing costs. Former purchasing chief J. Ignacio Lopez de Arriortua was credited with combining GM's 27 purchasing organizations into a single, powerful, and sometimes ruthless buying entity. Under Lopez, it was not uncommon for GM to tear up contracts with suppliers and run multiple rounds of bidding to get lower prices. Lopez departed in 1997, and General Motors is moving aggressively to further establish its presence as one of the premier buying organizations in the world.

General Motors continues its efforts to reduce the costs of everything the company purchases. In a time when the company lags arch rivals such as Ford and DaimlerChrysler AG in car design, marketing, and labor-cost management, purchasing has been GM's savior. The company has shown improved earnings and a stronger balance sheet in recent years, much to the credit of the purchasing function. Purchasing is saving GM approximately three to four billion dollars on an annual basis.

Using the power of technology, the company has created GM TradeXchange, which the company claims is the world's largest Internet "virtual marketplace" for buyers and sellers of products, parts, services, and raw materials. This is GM's first major business-to-business e-commerce initiative. Benefits to site users include reduction of purchasing cycle times, automatic purchase authorization, and integration of accounting and contractual procedures.

Harold Kutner, GM's current purchasing chief, says GM can't dictate prices suppliers charge on TradeXchange, but he expects lower prices. He adds that GM will monitor the site and perhaps look for new suppliers if suppliers' prices aren't competitive. Mr. Kutner notes that prior to TradeXchange, "GM had a fat, healthy, uncompetitive Midwest supply base."

GM's strategic purchasing initiatives include strongly encouraging suppliers to link into TradeXchange; speaking with "one voice" to suppliers, or ensuring that regional buyers give suppliers a consistent message; coordinating production-parts with service-parts purchases, a sign that supply-chain management has been strengthened at GM; and further emphasizing a "zero-defects mentality" with respect to product quality.

Suppliers are expected to provide accurate just-in-time deliveries, use electronic data interchanges for transactions and customer support, provide GM support in product development, share technological advances, meet worldwide quality standards, and continuously improve the value they provide to GM. Suppliers that

meet these standards reap huge rewards, and it is becoming increasingly common for other large purchasing organizations to have such expectations of their suppliers.

Not only is GM using the Internet to extend its global reach, but it searches the globe for new suppliers in other ways. For example, the weakened economies of many Asian countries have created excess capacity in the tool-manufacturing industry in Korea, Taiwan, Thailand, and Japan. Realizing that excess capacity anywhere in the world might help GM secure lower prices for stamping dies used to make fenders and hoods, GM deployed the equivalent of a purchasing SWAT team to find new suppliers. Two new companies were selected, saving GM millions of dollars.

Industry observers expect GM to continue its emphasis on cost reduction. The impact of its TradeXchange site could be monumental in terms of stimulating growth in electronic commerce. Interestingly, Ford has announced plans for a similar site, and with many companies supplying both General Motors and Ford, things could get sticky. For one thing, it is expected that GM will demand that all of its suppliers do all of their business on GM's site, and Ford will demand the same. Smaller customers of the suppliers might then be able to see the lower prices paid by the large customers, thus creating an additional problem for suppliers. In addition to operating their own purchasing websites, GM and Ford are joining with Daimler/Chrysler to operate a joint purchasing site on the Web. Through it all, GM will continue to leverage its size in negotiating with suppliers.

Questions

1. Can the General Motors emphasis on lower costs have any detrimental effects on the company's ultimate ability to deliver a competitive product to automobile buyers?

2. Do you see any ethical issues in the way that General Motors conducts its purchasing operations?

3. What can suppliers do to negotiate mutually beneficial contracts with General Motors? How do you think potential suppliers will react to GM's requirement that all of the suppliers' business be conducted through GM's TradeXchange?

SOURCES: Gregory L. White, "How GM, Ford Think the Internet Can Make Splash in Their Factories," *The Wall Street Journal Interactive Edition,* December 3, 1999, at www.interactive.wsj.com; Robert L. Simison, "General Motors Drives Some Hard Bargains with Asian Suppliers," *The Wall Street Journal,* April 2, 1999, pp. A1, A6; "General Motors Joins Forces with Commerce One to Move into Business-to-Business E-Commerce with Innovative Internet Purchasing Enterprise," from GM's home page at www.gm.com, November 4, 1999; and "Selling to GM," from www.gmsupplier.com, November 4, 1999.

Chapter Six

Marketing Research and Decision Support Systems

After studying this chapter, you should be able to:

1 Understand the purpose and functions of marketing research.

2 Be familiar with the stages of the marketing research process.

3 Discuss different types of research designs, data collection methods, and sources of secondary and primary marketing research data.

4 Understand many of the major issues involved with survey design and sampling.

5 Appreciate the role of marketing research within decision support systems.

Information Resources, Inc. (IRI), a Chicago-based research firm, was founded in 1978. The company's mission is straightforward: to be the leading provider of business information services in the consumer packaged goods industry. Their main competitor is A. C. Nielsen. Revenues in 1998 were $511.3 million, making IRI the fifth-largest research organization worldwide.

Much of IRI's revenue comes from their InfoScan product line. InfoScan is a syndicated market-tracking service that provides information on weekly sales, price, and store condition for products sold in a sample of over 4,000 food, drug, and mass-merchandise stores. IRI's services also include a national sample of 60,000 households whose purchases are recorded by store scanners. An additional 55,000 households use hand-held scanners to record purchases regardless of store type. BehaviorScan links household television viewing, print readership, and purchase behavior into a source rich in marketing information and is capable of testing new products and/or new marketing programs. IRI's expanded InfoScan Census now includes data from 30,000 food and drug stores. Other research services offered by IRI include electronic test-marketing services, data analysis application tools, and distribution planning software. These offerings are designed to provide solutions that focus on the functional areas of sales, marketing, supply chain, and retail operations.

The IRI Web site provides an overview of the company's extensive offerings to consumer packaged goods marketers, as well as summaries of the research methods used to collect the data. Other information ranges from employment opportunities to a full presentation of IRI's annual report. The site uses key terms to guide interested customers to descriptions of problem solutions and key applications of the company's data services. For example, the pricing section describes how IRI data can be used to assess the effectiveness of different pricing strategies, to measure the price sensitivity of individual brands, and to predict sales across a range of prices. ReviewNet offers Internet access to syndicated data via IRI's Web site. **Sources:** Jack Honomichl, "Firms Play Name Game As Acquisitions Ruled in 1998," *Marketing News,* June 7, 1999, pp. 47–48; "Information Resources," *Standard & Poors NASDAQ Stock Reports,* March 25, 1996, p. 4247K; "Solutions for the Consumer Packaged Goods Industry," *Information Resources, Inc., 1995 Annual Report;* and "Information Resources," http://www.infores.com/public/marketing/press/new/nzzmocrm.htm, December 3, 1999.

Marketing research is used in planning to identify the needs of product users and in problem solving to evaluate the types of products to offer. Flavors marketed by Ortega were developed based on information from marketing research.

Marketing research companies like Information Resources, Inc., and A. C. Nielsen are among the largest providers of marketing research data and offer a wide variety of services. Smaller research firms often specialize in industry types or individual services, such as measurement of customer retention and customer satisfaction. IRI makes a large portion of its revenues from the sale of product-movement tracking data derived from large surveys of grocery stores and drug stores; whereas, other research firms provide for their clients individually designed studies that address particular situations or problems. IRI's research enables its customers to monitor sales and promotional activities across product categories, to understand the effects of promotions on consumer activity, and to identify problems and opportunities in distribution.

The overall objective of marketing research is to reduce risk in decision making by helping management understand its uncertain and changing marketplace and the consumers and competitors that make up its markets. The marketing research process involves the collection, interpretation, and use of data to make decisions. Such understanding makes a firm better able to provide products and services that meet customer expectations and needs. Marketing research enhances communication between a firm and its markets with the aim of improving managerial decision making. The aim of research is not to confirm that decisions already made are correct, but to identify alternative choices and to support the decision-making process.[1]

What Is Marketing Research?

In its definition of **marketing research,** the American Marketing Association recognizes the complexity of the process and the different activities that may be performed.

Marketing research links the consumer, the customer, and the public through information used to:

- Identify and define marketing opportunities.

- Generate, refine, and evaluate marketing actions.

- Monitor marketing performance.

- Improve understanding of marketing as a process.

Marketing research:

- Specifies the information required to address these issues.

- Designs the methods for collecting information.

- Manages and implements the data collection process.

- Analyzes the results.

- Communicates the findings and implications.[2]

This definition emphasizes the generation of information that assists in managerial decision making. We adapted the second half of the definition as an outline for discussing the stages of the marketing research process in this chapter.

Marketing research is useful in planning, problem solving, and control, as shown in Exhibit 6–1. Marketers use marketing research to provide guidance in decision making. This enables them to spend their resources more effectively. Researchers must understand the research process, the marketing process, and the industries in which the firm operates.[3] Take the research team for Stouffers, a national organization that manages private restaurants and clubs, for example. Stouffers researchers must understand the growth and image objectives of the organization, besides identifying new market opportunities and conducting customer satisfaction surveys. Only by knowing the club business can meaningful research be conducted

Speaking from Experience

Terry Vavra
President
Marketing Metrics, Inc.

Terry Vavra has a B.S. degree in marketing from the University of California, Irvine, and a Ph.D. degree in marketing from the University of Illinois. Marketing Metrics, Inc., founded in 1983, is a marketing research firm that specializes in customer retention and global marketing strategy. Vavra discusses the growing importance of research.

"Make no mistake about it, marketing researchers are sometimes criticized, especially by individuals in positions where personal creativity is viewed as paramount (e.g., brand managers, creative directors). But the tide is turning. Fewer and fewer upper-level managers will commit company resources based on only one person's intuition. They increasingly demand supportive evidence available only from research."

Exhibit 6–1   *Kinds of questions marketing research can help answer*

I. Planning

  A. What kinds of people buy our products? Where do they live? How much do they earn? How many of them are there?

  B. Are the markets for our products increasing or decreasing? Are there promising markets that we have not yet reached?

  C. Are the channels of distribution for our products changing? Are new types of marketing institutions likely to evolve?

II. Problem solving

  A. Product

    1. Which of various product designs is likely to be the most successful?

    2. What kind of packaging should we use?

  B. Price

    1. What price should we charge for our products?

    2. As production costs decline, should we lower our prices or try to develop higher quality products?

  C. Place

    1. Where, and by whom, should our products be sold?

    2. What kinds of incentives should we offer the trade to push our products?

  D. Promotion

    1. How much should we spend on promotion? How should it be allocated to products and to geographic areas?

    2. What combination of media—newspapers, radio, television, magazines—should we use?

III. Control

  A. What is our market share overall? In each geographic area? By each customer type?

  B. Are customers satisfied with our products? How is our record for service? Are there many returns?

  C. How does the public perceive our company? What is our reputation with the trade?

---

to support the Stouffers organization. Pizza Hut now links its unit managers' bonuses to the results of customer satisfaction surveys. Questions address satisfaction with service, food quality, and other issues.

Marketing research is often used to evaluate the characteristics and potential of markets prior to making decisions about product introductions and new-market entry. Research is helpful in evaluating new-product concepts and advertising campaigns under consideration. It is also used to monitor market performance and competitive reaction. Nielsen Inc., one of the oldest and largest marketing research firms, provides data to packaged-goods manufacturers like Coca-Cola and Nabisco about their product sales. Research is also used to identify and solve problems. Municipalities, for example, frequently conduct marketing research to identify citizens' needs and methods for attracting shoppers to the area.

Most important, marketing research should support the firm's overall market orientation. Research links marketers to markets through information and scientific study. It is used to explore opportunities and problems, monitor performance, refine marketing strategy, and improve understanding of marketing efforts and markets themselves. As such, research enhances a firm's closeness with its customers and enables the marketer to anticipate latent unfulfilled needs and wants.[4]

Marketing Research in the New Millennium

Significant environmental phenomena will affect the marketing research industry in the next decade and beyond. First, the traditional time line of four to six weeks for the typical research project will no longer be acceptable in many cases. However, researchers will still need to balance time pressures with quality. Second, gatekeeper technology, such as caller ID and privacy-related services, will limit researcher access to consumers. And, discussed later, pending federal and state legislation may restrict the data collection process as well. Marketing research is also becoming more a part of the marketing strategy development process. This shift to more of an advisory role represents less emphasis on the more traditional marketing research roles of testing and evaluation.[5]

Interactivity, e-commerce, and the Internet are certainly affecting the practice of marketing, and likewise are affecting the conduct of marketing research. New consumer information is pouring in at incredible speed from scanners, loyalty program tapes, syndicated data services, and the Internet. Marketing researchers within firms and researchers within the marketing research industry itself are going to be required to adapt to this technological wave of change. The problem is no longer how to get information; the problem today is how will data be managed. As examples, the research departments at the Campbell's Soup Company and Procter & Gamble have been renamed "Information Management" and "Consumer Market and Knowledge," respectively.

At GM, the company now has a database of 12 million credit card holders, giving access to the buying habits of their customers. Blockbuster has a database of 36 million households. The information is used to determine movie choices and to cross-promote its affiliates such as Discovery Zone for children. Analyses of these databases also reaffirm Pareto's Law. For example, 13 percent of Diet Coke drinkers represent 83 percent of the product's volume; for Taster's Choice, 4 percent of their customers generated 73 percent of their sales. These databases and information at the customer level will be instrumental in enabling companies to build long-term relationships with their core and loyal segments.[6]

The marketing research industry itself is in transition. Consolidation among companies has resulted in market dominance by the top 25 firms. Companies like A. C. Nielsen, IMS, IRI, and Kantar hold significant industry market share. And, these companies are truly global in their customer base and offerings. It is important to note the evolution of firms from market and opinion research firms to suppliers of information, consulting, and data exchange. These changes have made easy entry into the industry much harder. Previously, small firms could easily exist and succeed, even with minimal capital investment.[7]

The Marketing Research Process

Exhibit 6–2 presents the stages of the **marketing research process.** The sequence begins with an understanding of the problem and ends with analysis and interpretation.[8] The overall objective should be to generate useful, timely, and cost-effective information. That is, the resulting reduced risk and improved decision making should justify the research costs involved. Even a small study involving 500 local telephone interviews can cost more than $10,000 when researcher time and other costs are considered. Consequently, the cost–benefit trade-off of doing research is always an issue for a firm.

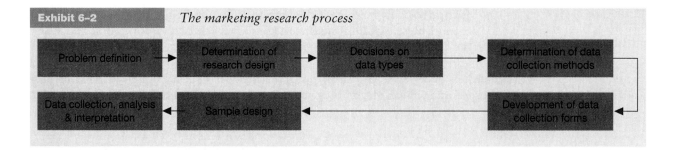

Exhibit 6–2   *The marketing research process*

Problem definition → Determination of research design → Decisions on data types → Determination of data collection methods → Development of data collection forms → Sample design → Data collection, analysis & interpretation

Thinking Critically

The marketing research process is typically thought of as beginning with problem definition (see Exhibit 6–2). However, as the text explains, significant research occurs without problem definition.

- Assume you are marketing research manager for a large regional bank. What kinds of research might your bank engage in without formal problem identification (e.g., declining profits)?

Problem Definition

Problem definition is depicted in Exhibit 6–2 as the first step in any marketing research project and is critical to its success. Problems in a business are often defined as differences between the way things should be and the way they are. Both researchers and management (the users of the research) need to understand the research problem clearly.

It should be noted that a substantial amount of research is ongoing and is used for general control and planning purposes. For example, the many companies that use data on in-store sales and product movement provided by IRI or A. C. Nielsen engage in research continuously in their efforts to monitor competitive activity in the marketplace. Thus, often in the problem definition stage of the research process, a problem is not formally identified. Instead, ongoing research may lead to identification of a problem, such as declining sales, low turnover, declining brand appeal, or the emergence of competitive offerings.

The problem definition stage is often difficult because the expectations and desires of managers and researchers frequently differ. Researchers generally take an exploratory perspective, whereas managers may prefer research that confirms their expectations and provides few surprises. For best results, all parties involved must take a constructive stance in defining the research problem. They must focus on the real problem and not the symptoms; anticipate how the information will be used; and avoid prescribing a specific study until the problem is fully understood and defined.

Research Designs

Marketing research designs are general strategies or plans of action for addressing the research problem and the data collection and analysis process. The problem definition stage is likely to suggest approaches for determining which marketing research design to use. Research generally has three purposes: exploration, description, and explanation.[9] They result in three general types of research designs: exploratory, descriptive, and causal. Common methods and example studies for each of these designs are shown in Exhibit 6–3.

EXPLORATORY DESIGNS Exploratory research is typically carried out to satisfy the researcher's desire for better understanding, or to develop preliminary background and suggest issues for a more detailed follow-up study.

As shown in Exhibit 6–3, exploratory research can be conducted using literature reviews, case analyses, interviews, and focus groups.[10] Better understanding of a problem might begin with a review of prior research. A researcher working for a bank would not begin a study of the bank's image, for example, without some review of the banking literature on what determines a bank's image. In-depth interviews with individuals who already have some knowledge of the problem may shed some light on the issue.

DESCRIPTIVE DESIGNS Descriptive research is normally directed by one or more formal research questions or hypotheses. Typically, a survey or questionnaire is administered to a sample from a population of interest to the firm, such as female

Exhibit 6–3	*Three general research designs*	
Type	**Common Methods**	**Example Studies**
Exploratory designs	Literature reviews Case analyses Interviews with knowledgeable persons In-depth interviews, focus groups	Evaluation of new-product concepts, environmental-trend analysis, identification of product attribute importance
Descriptive designs	Cross-sectional surveys Panel studies Product movement surveys Store audits Telephone, mail, personal interviews	Market potential, image studies, competitive-positioning analysis, market characteristic examinations, customer-satisfaction studies
Causal designs	Experimental designs (lab and field studies) Market tests	Evaluation of alternative marketing mix combinations (varying price levels, changing promotional appeals, reallocation of salesforce efforts)

Focus groups are commonly used to explore new concepts and to obtain consumer reactions to ad campaigns under development. South Seas Plantation used focus groups of guests and resort prospects to help make decisions about themes, logos, TV spots, and brochures.

household heads or purchasing agents in an industry. Examples include consumer surveys to estimate market potential, segmentation research to identify demographic consumer segments, attitude and opinion surveys, and product usage surveys.

Descriptive studies may be cross-sectional or longitudinal, depending on the timing of the observation. For example, a survey of customers administered at a given time to assess perceived satisfaction with service is a *cross-sectional study*. Consumers who participate in panel studies of purchase behavior over a period of time are involved in *longitudinal research*.

CAUSAL DESIGNS Exploratory and descriptive studies can help answer certain questions, but identification of cause-and-effect relationships requires **causal research**. Causal designs call for *experiments*, in which researchers manipulate independent variables and then observe or measure the dependent variable or variables of interest.

Suppose a direct marketing company wants to see the effect on sales of increasing its 50¢ coupon to $1. To test this, the company matches two markets, using key variables such as product sales, consumer demographics, and market size. In one market, consumers receive the $1 coupon; in the other market, they receive the 50¢ coupon. At the end of the experiment, the company compares sales in the two markets and learns that the $1 coupon generates more sales. When it incorporates the cost/profitability of each coupon value into the analysis, however, the company finds the $1 coupon results in a loss, while the 50¢ coupon is profitable. This analysis convinces the company to continue its 50¢ coupon promotion.

Data Types

Marketing research information is categorized as either primary data or secondary data. Interrelationships among the different types of data and the various data collection methods are summarized in Exhibit 6–4.

PRIMARY DATA Primary data are collected specifically for a particular research problem. This is the type of information most frequently associated with marketing research, such as survey data from a sample of customers about satisfaction with services. Polls on the standing of political candidates prior to elections are another example. Primary data have the advantage of currency and relevance for a specific research problem. Their primary disadvantage is cost.

Exhibit 6–4	*Data collection methods and examples*

Sources of Information

Primary Data	Secondary Data
SURVEYS • Mail • Telephone	**INTERNAL DATA** • Company records • Data from marketing design support systems
INTERVIEWS • Mall intercepts • Personal interviews	**EXTERNAL DATA** Proprietary • Custom research • Syndicated services
FOCUS GROUPS **OBSERVATION** • Personal • Mechanical	Nonproprietary • Published reports • Census data • Periodicals

Large research firms provide proprietary, secondary research data for use by other firms in analyzing consumer purchase patterns and brand switching. A. C. Nielsen's Homescan panel of 40,000 households tracks consumer purchases at the household level across all types of store outlets.

SECONDARY DATA　Secondary data are those already collected for some other purpose and are available from a variety of sources. As a rule, researchers should consult secondary data before collecting primary data. Corporate libraries and outside vendors (firms that specialize in providing research data) provide secondary data. Some public and private universities offer secondary research services. Japanese firms have long recognized the value of secondary data within their firms and regularly use it to compare product movement.[11]

Internal secondary data are collected within a firm and include accounting records, salesforce reports, or customer feedback reports. *External secondary data* may be nonproprietary or proprietary. *Nonproprietary* secondary data are available in libraries and other public sources. For example, information from *Sales & Marketing Management*'s "Survey of Buying Power" about population, income, and age groups can help managers estimate market potentials and identify likely market segments.

Obviously, the fastest growing source of secondary data is the Internet. The Internet represents the infrastructure (the machinery, computers, lines, and equipment) that supports what has become known as the World Wide Web or the "the Web." Individuals and firms with personal computers, a modem, and software access or browser can generate information from both Web sites and home pages around the Web. Information sources include product and company data, business and article reviews, as well as data from companies such as Dow Jones and Dun & Bradstreet.[12]

Terry Vavra talks about the use of available secondary sources of information:
"The marketing research community needs to fully mine the value of existing information—the so-called secondary data. All too frequently, good money is spent collecting information that already exists in some government or industry database. Given the existing database tools and the Internet search tools now available, the marketing researcher should first search for existing information rather than initiating immediately a separate primary study."

Primary data are collected for a specific product or situation. In-home surveys, a means of collecting primary data, can provide detailed explanations regarding actual product use.

Purchase data collected on samples of consumers can identify what consumers are buying, who are new adopters, and which firms represent the competition.

On-line computer databases using CD technology are often free or available in libraries for minimal fees. Many companies now purchase demographic and geographic census data on CD-ROM for use in selecting store sites, mapping sales territories, and segmenting markets.[13]

Proprietary secondary data are provided by commercial marketing research firms that sell their services to other firms. Commercial firms can establish *diary panels* of representative households that record product and brand purchases. These data can help companies evaluate market share and purchase patterns. **Scanner data** obtained from Universal Product Code (UPC) information read in grocery stores provide timely information on actual purchase behavior. Scanner information is forecast to eventually enable companies to model their decisions and to allow management to allocate advertising and promotional dollars across actions to achieve optimum marketplace performance.[14]

Advances like these enable retailers to monitor product movement and to assess the effectiveness of advertising and in-store promotions. Several firms, including Nielsen and Information Resources, Inc., developed proprietary systems that combine information on product purchasing behavior with TV viewing behavior to produce **single-source data**.[15]

Computer technology is used in novel ways to combine U.S. census data with internal customer data. For example, *geographic information systems (GIS)* provide digitized maps that can be displayed on color computer terminals.[16] There is a huge difference between a stack of printed customer names and addresses and a color-coded map showing where the customers are located. GIS systems save marketing researchers hours of tedious plotting. GIS maps were used in the Clinton/Gore presidential campaign to improve volunteer and media efforts.[17]

Geographic displays have significant potential for marketing research use in the next decade. The Bureau of Census now sells street maps with economic and population data detailed to city blocks on compact discs. Programmers can mesh customer data with these spatial databases, allowing display of three-dimensional plots of customers. Chemical Bank uses GIS to ensure the bank acts in a socially responsible manner and lends money fairly in poor neighborhoods.[18]

Using Technology

Virtual-reality shopping: Simulating shopping experiences

Virtual reality refers to the practice of using technology to simulate real-world experiences. Research companies are now creating virtual-reality shopping environments using CD-ROMs to see how consumers react to package designs, store layouts, and shelf-space positioning. Packages can be "picked up" and examined on all sides and even placed in a cart. During the shopping process, the computer unobtrusively records the amount of time the consumer spends shopping in each product category, the quantity purchased, and the order of decision making. Virtual shopping procedures enable research firms to use their imagination without the huge expenses associated with

full-fledged market tests. As the price of computers comes down and as 3-D graphics become easier to create and manipulate, the use of simulations will grow dramatically, as virtual market research becomes more relevant for smaller companies.

Sources: Raymond R. Burke, "Virtual Shopping: Breakthrough in Marketing Research," *Harvard Business Review*, March–April 1996, pp. 120–31; William C. Copacino, "Logistics and the World of 'Virtual Retailing,'" *Logistics Management*, March 1996, p. 3; Tom Dellecave, Jr., "Curing Market Research Headaches," *Sales and Marketing Research*, July 1996, pp. 84–85; Joshua Macht, "The New Market Research," *Inc.*, July 1998, pp. 86–94; and Margaret R. Roller, "Virtual Research Exists, but How Real Is It?" *Marketing News*, January 1, 1996, pp. 13, 15.

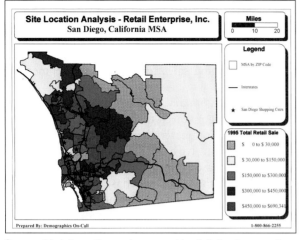

Geographic information systems provide digitalized maps of customer markets that are easily color coded to display differences in area effective buying income or other characteristics. These systems have been used effectively in making retail site selection decisions.

Data Collection Methods

Some of the more popular methods of primary data collection include focus groups, telephone surveys, mail surveys, personal interviews, mall intercepts, and Internet surveys. Their principal advantages and disadvantages are summarized in Exhibit 6–5.

FOCUS GROUPS   The most common exploratory procedure is the **focus group.** Focus groups usually comprise 8 to 12 individuals led by a moderator in a focused, in-depth discussion on a specific topic. Usually lasting no more than two hours, the sessions are designed to obtain participant feedback on a particular subject. Focus groups of consumers are well suited for examining new-product concepts and advertising themes, investigating the criteria underlying purchase decisions, and generating information for developing consumer questionnaires.[19]

The guidelines for using focus groups often vary by the research problem or situation of the firm. For example, groups of executives who may hold strong opinions or teenage consumers who can be shy argue for mini–focus groups of four to six participants. Also, focus groups need not necessarily be homogeneous demographically. The rule of thumb is that subjects should be comfortable with one another and that some diversity is beneficial. In many cases, budgets do not afford the luxury of separate focus groups, which can run as high as $20,000, for each demographic group in each market.[20]

Marriott, in an attempt to strengthen relationships with its customers, conducts ongoing focus groups with its customers and its service personnel. The focus groups used to develop Tylenol's new cough medicine revealed that the brand symbol, an elongated "C," reminded them of cough and care. In focus groups for Crayola, consumers were asked to draw the product's package from memory. The results revealed the green and yellow colors are synonymous with the product and demonstrated the importance of keeping these colors in the package design.[21] Fo-

Being Entrepreneurial

Creative ways of doing research

Marketers are constantly searching for what will be the next market craze—for what motivates and turns on the consumer. Sometimes this search is referred to as the "cool hunt." Examples of "cool" include the Converse One Star, the signature shoe of the retro era. Efforts to find the next craze often involve creative ways of doing market research. In some instances, the research is very unstructured and includes personal involvement in the marketplace through observation and in-depth discussions, frequently with the young and the hip, who now are the trendsetters for much of society. Another approach uses beepers to track the activities people engage in when using a product. During one "beeper study," consumers recorded what they were doing when beeped. This approach was used to learn how consumers mix listening to music with their everyday lives.

Another novel approach is the Zaltman Metaphor Elicitation Technique or ZMET, developed by Jerry Zaltman, a Harvard Business School professor. The method combines neurobiology, psychoanalysis, linguistics, and art theory to try to uncover the mental models that guide consumer behavior—to illuminate the unspoken aspects of the customer brain. The procedure involves consumers' collecting pictures that represent their thoughts and feeling about a product. The pictures can be taken from magazines, catalogs, and other sources. Collages of these pictures are developed by the research participants to express their deepest thoughts. This technique has been used successfully to improve the marketing of panty hose to women. The premise underlying the approach is that metaphor (i.e., viewing one thing in terms of another) is central to thought processes and crucial to understanding the needs and emotions underlying consumer preferences.

Sources: Malcolm Gladwell, "The Cool Hunt," *The New Yorker,* March 17, 1997, pp. 78–88; Daniel H. Pink, "Metaphor Marketing," *Fast Company,* April/May 1998, pp. 214–29; Melanie Wells, "New Ways to Get into Our Heads," *USA Today,* March 2, 1999, pp. 1B–2B.

Exhibit 6–5	*Advantages and disadvantages of frequently used data collection methods*	
Method	**Advantages**	**Disadvantages**
Focus groups	• Depth of information collected • Flexibility in use • Relatively low cost • Data collected quickly	• Requires expert moderator • Questions of group size and acquaintanceships of participants • Potential for bias from moderator • Small sample size
Telephone surveys	• Centralized control of data collection • More cost-effective than personal interviews • Data collected quickly	• Resistance in collecting income, financial data • Limited depth of response • Disproportionate coverage of low-income segments • Abuse of phone by solicitors • Perceived intrusiveness
Mail surveys	• Cost-effective per completed response • Broad geographic dispersion • Ease of administration • Data collected quickly	• Refusal and contact problems with certain segments • Limited depth of response • Difficult to estimate nonresponse biases • Resistance and bias in collecting income, financial data • Lack of control following mailing
Personal (in-depth) interviews	• More depth of response than telephone interviews • Generate substantial number of ideas compared with group methods	• Easy to transmit biasing cues • Not-at-homes • Broad coverage often infeasible • Cost per contact high • Data collection time may be excessive
Mall intercepts	• Flexibility in collecting data, answering questions, probing respondents • Data collected quickly • Excellent for concept tests, copy evaluations, other visuals • Fairly high response rates	• Limited time • Sample composition or representativeness is suspect • Costs depend on incidence rates • Interviewer supervision difficult
Internet surveys	• Inexpensive, quickly executed • Visual stimuli can be evaluated • Real-time data processing possible • Can be answered at convenience of respondent	• Responses must be checked for duplication, bogus responses • Respondent self-selection bias • Limited ability to qualify respondents and confirm responses • Difficulty in generating sample frames for probability sampling
Projective techniques	• Useful in word association tests of new brand names • Less threatening to respondents for sensitive topics • Can identify important motives underlying choices	• Require trained interviewers • Cost per interview high
Observation	• Can collect sensitive data • Accuracy of measuring overt behaviors • Different perspective than survey self-reports • Useful in studies of cross-cultural differences	• Appropriate only for frequently occurring behaviors • Unable to assess opinions of attitudes causing behaviors • May be expensive in data-collection-time costs

cus groups have even been asked to watch test versions of Hollywood movies and then provide endings.

Focus groups, along with some research information obtained from in-depth interviews and the observation research methods described later, provide **qualitative data.** Qualitative data are characterized by the depth of responses obtained and richness of description. The open-ended nature of the responses, coupled with typically smaller samples, makes predictions and generalizations tentative or difficult. However, qualitative information from focus groups, for example, is particularly useful in exploratory studies where problem understanding and initial insights are needed.

In contrast, descriptive surveys using large-sample telephone surveys or sales-tracking data from store panels such as IRI yield **quantitative data.** These data, collected using structured response formats, can be easily analyzed and projected to larger populations. For example, quantitative information from political polls can be used to predict voter opinion. Or, marketing surveys can be used to identify the content and rank order of reasons underlying customer satisfaction.

TELEPHONE SURVEYS Telephone interviews are relatively cost-effective; a large number of them over a wide geographical area can be conducted quickly and efficiently. Many firms use telephone interviews as their primary means of conducting survey research.

Telephone interviews also enable centralized control and supervision of data collection. *Random digit dialing* and *plus-one dialing* methods have become increasingly popular in the telephone interview process. In one popular version of random-digit dialing, four random digits are added to three-digit telephone exchanges. In plus-one dialing, a telephone number is randomly selected from the local directory, and a digit or digits added to it. This enables the inclusion of unlisted numbers in the sample and increases the likelihood of sampling a working number.

Problems with the use of telephone interviews limit their effectiveness. Questionable ethical practices, such as the use of marketing research as a sales ploy, hurt the research industry. Both the European Society for Opinion and Marketing Research (ESOMAR) and Council of American Survey Research Organizations (CASRO) have called for self-regulation among companies doing telephone interviews to stem the growing backlash against researchers.[22] Many states are contemplating legislation to restrict telephone survey research. In addition, the breadth and depth of information that can be obtained from telephone interviews is limited.[23]

MAIL SURVEYS Mail surveys can obtain broad geographical market coverage, are generally less expensive per completed survey than other methods, and can be used to collect data rather quickly. Surveys can address a range of issues in a single questionnaire. Studies based on mail questionnaires, and to lesser degrees those using telephone and personal interviews, suffer from nonresponse. Inaccurate mailing lists, questions about who exactly answers the survey, and the inability to handle respondent questions are additional shortcomings of mail surveys.

Although mail questionnaires are relatively inexpensive, conducting a mail survey can involve investments that may be prohibitive for smaller firms. Costs can be reduced by a number of means. For example, Plymart Company, a large southeastern building supply company, chose a university professor over an independent marketing research contractor to design and administer a survey of customer perceptions. The results persuaded management to add framing supplies, which increased sales by 22 percent. For less than $5,000, the company received $100,000 worth of information.[24]

Personal interviews enable the collection of in-depth information in one-on-one situations. Such interviews can be conducted in-house or in-store. For in-store situations, researchers may actually observe behaviors and choices as evaluations and decisions are made.

PERSONAL INTERVIEWS Personal interviews involve one-on-one interactions between a consumer, customer, or respondent and the researcher or some field interviewer paid to conduct the interviews. Personal interviews have relatively high response rates. In addition, they are conducive to the collection of substantial in-depth information and provide visual stimuli such as products and advertisements. Some researchers believe personal interviews are even more flexible than focus groups in that questioning adjustments can be made between interviews if necessary.[25] In addition, shy respondents can have their say, and sensitive topics can be more easily covered than in focus groups.

Thinking Critically

• For each stage of the research process discussed in this chapter, develop a list of questions that researchers should consider answering.

Disadvantages of personal interviews include the time and travel costs, concerns of personal safety of the interviewer, and inability to cover a wide geographical area. Although personal interview response rates average 70 percent, participation varies widely over types of neighborhoods. People living in metropolitan areas tend to be the least responsive.[26]

MALL INTERCEPTS   The shortcomings of personal interviews have led to increased use of **mall intercept interviews.** In a mall intercept, consumers are approached and interviewed while on shopping trips. One-on-one interaction provides the chance to show visual cues, while overcoming many of the time, travel, and safety concerns associated with door-to-door personal interviewing. Research has shown mall intercept interviewing to provide findings and quality of responses similar to telephone and mail survey collection methods.[27]

Technological advances have enhanced the productivity of mall intercept research. MarketWare Corporation solicits participants for their "virtually real shopping" simulation: "strolling" through store aisles via computer screen. Research can be conducted on any number of variables simultaneously, such as price, package information, and shelf location.[28]

INTERNET SURVEYS   The Internet is fast becoming a popular means of conducting survey research, as are modified focus group discussions. With technology changing rapidly, the future of Internet-based research is both promising and hard to predict. However, and as shown in Exhibit 6–5, Internet-based survey research has its advantages and disadvantages like other methods of conducting surveys. On the positive side, research can be done faster, easier, and more cheaply than surveys conducted by mail, in the mall, or over the phone. The surveys are less intrusive and more convenient for respondents, and the potential exists to present visual cues, unlike traditional telephone interviews.

Concerns have been raised regarding privacy and validity. Regarding the latter, the primary concern for now is that Internet surveys provide largely self-selected, convenience samples. Sample frames are more difficult to define than for telephone and mail surveys. Relatedly, most Internet surveys are volunteer-based, as participants can select which studies interest them. Hence, care must be taken to ensure that Internet surveys are not just 1-800 or 1-900 polls.[29]

PROJECTIVE TECHNIQUES AND OBSERVATION   Marketing researchers sometimes use projective techniques and observation for data collection. **Projective techniques,** such as word association or sentence completion, allow a researcher to elicit feelings that normally go unexpressed. They may be particularly useful in eliciting honest opinions about sensitive subjects. They can be used effectively in focus groups, mall intercepts, and personal interviews. In one application, consumers are asked to react to different forms of an advertisement or pictures without any brand or product information included in the mock-up. Reactions are reassessed when brand names are added.[30]

Observation research monitors customer behavior by a researcher or by video camera. Much can be learned by unobtrusively observing how customers use a firm's or its competitor's products. In some instances, observation may provide more accurate information than might survey data.[31] Observation research is also useful when traditional survey methods may not reveal the process by which goods and services are bought and used.

In another form of observation research, mystery shoppers evaluate the consistency and quality of services offered. Banks frequently use this practice to evaluate the service quality provided by their tellers and service personnel. Field observation requires patience, discipline, and enthusiasm on the part of the observer. However, in-store observations coupled with a few open-ended questions can yield insights into the role of price, the importance of ingredients, the effects of packages, and so on. In all cases, the researcher or field worker is there when the consumer or buyer behavior happens.[32]

Ethnographic research attempts to record how consumers actually use products, brands, and services in day-to-day activity. This form of direct observation, called *ethnography,* is based on techniques borrowed from sociology and anthropology. For example, a researcher may actually enter a consumer's home, observe consumption behavior, and record pantry and even garbage content, which can result in the collection of realistic data and richer descriptions of consumer behavior.[33]

Data Collection Instruments

The collection of marketing research information typically involves construction of a data collection instrument called a *survey* or *questionnaire.* Once a survey has been drafted, the instrument should be pretested on a representative sample and revised accordingly. The final instrument should consist of unambiguous, concise, and unbiased questions that respondents will be able and willing to answer.

Data collection instruments vary in structure. The degree of structure is influenced both by the research design (exploratory versus descriptive) and the method of data collection (focus group versus mail survey). Questions may take an open-ended, multiple choice, or scaled response format. Examples of questions and response formats are shown in Exhibit 6–6.

Errors in question design include at least five types:

- *Double-barreled wording:* "How would you rate the handling ability and gas economy of your new Taurus?" very good, good, fair, poor, very poor.

- *Loaded wording:* "Given the growing rate of product recalls, how likely would you be to complain about problems with a new car purchase?" likely, unlikely.

- *Ambiguous wording:* "Have you purchased a home appliance within the last six months?" yes, no.

- *Inappropriate vocabulary:* "Do you feel the current discount rate is too high?" yes, no.

- *Missing alternatives:* "Which of the following includes your age?" 25 and under, 26 to 49, and over 50.[34]

Exhibit 6–6   *Types of questions used in survey research*

Scaled

  Likert agree-disagree

    I favor the increased use of nuclear power. (Circle one)

    Strongly Agree Neither agree Disagree Strongly
    agree   nor disagree   disagree

  Semantic differential

    For me, tennis is . . .

    Important _____ : _____ : _____ : _____ : _____ : Unimportant

Multichotomous (multiple choice)

  Which of the following is the primary reason you selected our bank for your personal checking account?

  _____ Location   _____ Service

  _____ Interest rates _____ Other _____ (Please specify)

  _____ Reputation _____

Categorical

  Which of the following categories includes your total income for 199x? (Please check)

  _____ $30,000 and under

  _____ $30,001–$35,000

  _____ $35,001–$50,000

  _____ $50,001–$65,000

  _____ Over $65,000

Open-ended

  What suggestions can you make to improve our service? _____

"Margaret, I want to know the real you...subject to a sampling error plus or minus three percentage points, of course.

Sampling and nonsampling errors may affect marketing research results. When even carefully selected probability samples do not exactly mirror the population, sampling error occurs. Nonsampling errors are due to such factors as interviewer bias, nonresponse bias, and improperly worded questions.

Sample Design

The decisions and sequences involved in sampling are presented in Exhibit 6–7. The particular purpose of any research greatly influences the nature of the sampling process; of course, the population or group to be studied is determined by the issue of interest. If a wholesale bakery experiences declining product sales at the store level, it would want to sample individual purchasers and users of bakery products. Researchers might decide to sample household heads who regularly purchase bakery products.

Sampling saves money and time in that a smaller subgroup (or sample) is assumed to represent a larger population. Inferences from sample responses are then made to the population. The quality of these projections depends largely on how representative the sample is.

PROBABILITY SAMPLING In **probability sampling**, each person or unit in the population has a known, nonzero chance of being selected by some objective procedure. Probability samples are desirable, because the use of an objective, unbiased selection technique enhances the representativeness of the sample. There are several probability sampling approaches. In *simple random sampling*, each unit has an equal chance of being selected, such as the use of a random number table to select phone numbers. *Stratified sampling* occurs when the population is divided into mutually exclusive groups, such as consumers with different income levels, and random samples are taken from each group. *Cluster sampling* consists of organizing units into smaller groups or clusters, such as similar neighborhoods or census tracks, then selecting clusters randomly and including each house in the selected clusters in the sample.

NONPROBABILITY SAMPLING In **nonprobability sampling,** the selection of a sample is based on the judgment of the researcher or field worker. When funds or time are limited, or when only preliminary insight into a problem is needed, nonprobability samples may be appropriate. Nonprobability samples include convenience samples: for instance, the use of student samples in academic research; quota samples, in which a sample is selected to conform to some known distribution such as half female or 30 percent minority; and judgment samples, in which sample members are selected because researchers believe they bring some unique perspective to the research problem.

SAMPLING FRAME Once the type of sample and the target population have been determined, the **sampling frame** is specified. The sampling frame is the outline or working description of the population used in sample selection. A frequently

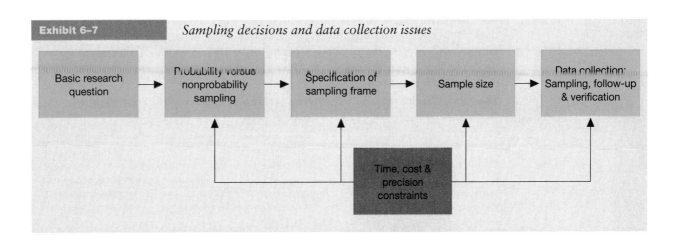

Exhibit 6-7   *Sampling decisions and data collection issues*

Basic research question → Probability versus nonprobability sampling → Specification of sampling frame → Sample size → Data collection: Sampling, follow-up & verification

Time, cost & precision constraints

used sampling frame is the telephone book. For business-to-business marketing research, customer or firm lists might serve as the sampling frame. Today, firms often purchase sample lists from companies that specialize in providing them. Care must be exercised in selecting a sampling frame (say, a telephone listing) to minimize the exclusion of relevant population members. Telephone directories do not include unlisted households and households without telephones.

SAMPLE SIZE   The desired **sample size** is based on a combination of factors: the anticipated response rate, the variability in the data, cost and time considerations, and the desired level of precision.

In practice, a sample size is often some even number (say, 500 or 1,000) large enough to give the user confidence in the results, on which he or she will base decisions. As a rule, researchers may benefit by taking smaller samples selected by more rigorous but possibly more expensive probability sampling procedures. That is, research users will be more confident in the representativeness of samples selected by some unbiased selection process.

RESPONSE RATES   A disturbing trend in the past quarter century has been the slow but steady decline in sample cooperation. The causes of this trend include an increase in percentage of working women, the increase of telemarketing, and the growth of screening devices. High-quality samples will be possible only with greater cost and effort. The changes required to generate higher response rates will include increased compensation to respondents and interviewers, more contact attempts to locate respondents, and greater use of mixed modes of survey administration, including e-mail and Internet research.

The primary concern with nonresponse is the realization that nonrespondents differ from respondents in terms of their opinions about the issues being studied and in terms of their demographic composition. Hence, it is necessary to contact a subset of nonrespondents so that findings can be adjusted. In addition, the computation of response rates is required and should be included in marketing research reports and summaries. For example, the response for a telephone survey can be computed as follows:

$$\text{Response rate} = \frac{\text{Number of complete from those contacted}}{\text{Number of complete} + \text{number of refusals} + \text{number of terminations}^{[35]}}$$

Fieldwork

Fieldwork is the process of contacting respondents, conducting interviews, and completing surveys. In the case of mail surveys, field workers must prepare mailing labels, develop introductory and follow-up letters, and carry out the mailings. Telephone surveys, personal interviews, and mall intercepts require the recruitment and training of interviewers to collect the data from the designated sample.

In many instances, the data collection process, and perhaps data analysis, will be subcontracted out to a supplier or field service firm. That is, the actual interviews may be performed by a company that specializes in collecting marketing research data. Under these circumstances, the subcontractor supervises the data collection process and verifies the quality of the information collected. This should include verifying that the interviews were indeed conducted and that the responses to certain key questions are valid or correct.

Terry Vavra underscores the pitfalls of failing to monitor data collection fieldwork: "Although many research projects are well conceived and designed, all too frequently they fail where 'the rubber meets the road'—the fieldwork component. Much fieldwork is subcontracted to specialty fieldwork companies (e.g., telephone interviewing firms). As researchers look for cost efficiencies in conducting their fieldwork, they often rely on poorly trained and inadequately supervised field staffs. As you become involved in marketing research, monitor very carefully how your data are collected from respondents. Fieldwork is often the weakest link in the research process chain."

Analysis and Interpretation

There are a variety of techniques for analyzing marketing research data, ranging in complexity from straightforward frequency distributions, means, and percentages to complex multivariate statistical tests. Statistical analyses typically look at group differences (males versus females, users versus nonusers) or the strength of association between marketing variables (advertising and sales, prices and sales). The most frequently used statistical tests include those of mean differences (*t*-tests, analysis of variance) and correlation tests (chi-square cross-classification tests, Pearson correlations, regression).

The types of analysis to be performed on the data should be anticipated at the design stage so the appropriate data collection forms are developed. As a rule, managers prefer simple understandable presentations of findings. Reports should focus on the original problem and objectives of the research.

Changing Technology

Technology has both positive and negative effects on the conduct of marketing research. As mentioned previously, scanner data and the ability to collect single-source data from households are dramatically affecting the research industry. On the positive side, the availability of computer-assisted telephone (CAT) interviewing has enhanced sampling, data entry, and data processing. Interviewers can read questions from a computer screen and record answers directly on the computer. This process results in instantaneously updating data. Moreover, WATS services have lowered the cost of telephone surveying. Yet technology has some negative effects on the use of telephone interviews too. Answering machines and voice-mail responses inhibit both consumer and business-to-business telephone research.[36] Call waiting also hampers the conduct of telephone surveys and is another factor contributing to the decline of telephone response rates. Sadly, the large increase in telephone sales calls and the difficulty of distinguishing between sales calls and survey research are the primary determinants of declining response rates.[37]

Technology is affecting other aspects of marketing research as well. For example, videoconferencing capabilities enable clients from a distance to monitor focus groups and provide the opportunity to involve more participants in observation. The savings from videoconferencing result because clients do not have to travel to locations to view focus group sessions. Breakthroughs in technology have also increased the potential for using faxes in survey research. Early research on survey effects suggests that fax surveys could make the administration of short questionnaires less expensive and faster than mail surveys. Likewise, e-mail offers the potential for increasing survey efficiency. Last, freestanding touch-screen computers at retail kiosks are now programmed to administer complicated surveys, show full-color images and video clips, and play stereo clips. With little need for instruction, in-store patrons freely use the interactive kiosks without reservation.[38]

International Considerations

Rote application of U.S. research practices to other countries is not likely to be appropriate. Firms operating globally must understand that cultural and economic differences between countries add a layer of complexity. One researcher identified eight common errors in conducting an international research project:[39]

1. *Selecting a domestic research company to do international research*—It is best to choose a company with experience in conducting global research.

2. *Rigidly standardizing methods across countries*—In certain countries, postal problems present unique difficulties; and in many countries, communications systems are inadequate for telephone interviews.

3. *Interviewing in English around the world*—Depth of responses is greatest when the local language is used.

4. *Implementing inappropriate sampling techniques*—Probability sampling designs are difficult to implement in many foreign countries.

5. *Failing to communicate effectively with local research companies*—Everything should be put in writing and all deadlines should be specified exactly to avoid delays.

6. *Lack of consideration given to language*—For some research studies, measurement instruments should be "back translated" to ensure equivalence in meaning.

7. *Misinterpreting data across countries*—Cultural and ethnic differences can affect response, the meaning of concepts, and even responses to measurement scales. For example, Asians may use the midpoints of scales, whereas the English tend to understate responses.

8. *Failing to understand preferences of foreign researchers regarding the effective conduct of qualitative research*—For example, Europeans expect focus group moderators to have training in psychology; Asian mixed-sex group discussions do not yield useful information.

Conducting research using Japanese participants in particular requires some adjustment of American and European methods. Moderators or interviewers must repeatedly reassure Japanese respondents that negative statements are acceptable. Open-ended questions, lacking some illustration, will not elicit adequate responses from Japanese consumers. Nonverbal responses, such as body movement and facial expressions, often yield more information than will verbal answers.[40] Responses to scale items can vary across cultures as well. Three respondents, all equally likely to buy a product from a market test, may give different responses based upon their interpretation of rating scales. Interpreting these meanings in global research can become even more difficult. For example, in a study of Brazilian and Japanese consumers, a "5" from a seven-point scale corresponded to 75 percent probability of purchase. For the Japanese data, a score of about 3.8 corresponded to a 75 percent probability of purchase.[41]

Conducting research across cultures can be difficult. International marketing researchers encounter such added problems as language differences, product use differences, and technological differences that limit data collection alternatives. Lea & Perrins used marketing research to investigate cultural differences prior to positioning their new flavoring product in Singapore.

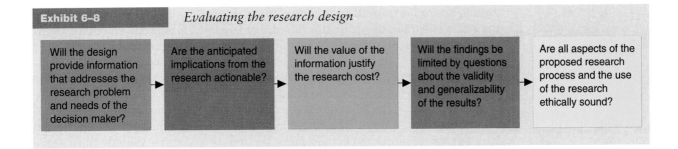

Exhibit 6–8	*Evaluating the research design*

| Will the design provide information that addresses the research problem and needs of the decision maker? | Are the anticipated implications from the research actionable? | Will the value of the information justify the research cost? | Will the findings be limited by questions about the validity and generalizability of the results? | Are all aspects of the proposed research process and the use of the research ethically sound? |

Evaluating Marketing Research

A research proposal is often developed prior to conducting a research study. These proposals outline the purpose of the research, the activities of the project, the costs and time constraints, and the likely implications or outcomes. The most important questions to ask in evaluating a research design prior to conducting research are presented in Exhibit 6–8.

Once a research project has been completed, the validity and reliability of the procedures used should be evaluated. **Validity** of questions on a survey refers to the extent to which the measures truly assess the concepts being studied. Consider the item, "I like BMW sedans." Results showing significant agreement with this statement would not be a valid measure of consumer opinions about purchase attitudes; rather, they would indicate an overall liking for the brand. **Reliability** reflects the consistency of responses or the extent to which measurement results are reproducible. A related validity issue, and important in determining the value of many research projects, is the concept of external validity. *External validity* reflects the extent to which the results from a research study can be generalized to other contexts, situations, and populations.[42]

Ethical Issues in Marketing Research

Research ethics are increasingly debated. The American Marketing Association (AMA), the Advertising Research Foundation (ARF), and the Council of American Survey Research Organizations (CASRO) are collaborating on a code of ethics. Self-regulation among firms conducting research is increasingly being called for in efforts to improve the practice of marketing research. If these efforts are not successful, respondent cooperation will continue to erode.[43]

Questionable tactics in marketing research that are frequently criticized include excessive interviewing, lack of consideration and abuse of respondents, and delivering sales pitches under the guise of marketing research.[44] The latter is particularly important for the research industry, as two-thirds of Americans consider survey research and telemarketing to be the same thing.[45] Legislation that now addresses only unsolicited commercial telephone calls could easily be extended to cover survey research.[46] Legislation already exists in most European Community nations that restricts the research industry by protecting privacy rights of consumers.

Ethical considerations are involved in researchers' relationships with all parties in the process, including respondents, the general public, and clients. First, marketers have the responsibility to treat respondents fairly by being candid about the nature and purposes of the research, by not using research as a sales ploy, and by not violating the confidentiality of respondents' answers. Researchers' obligations to the general public include being unintrusive, being considerate, and protecting the rights of privacy.

At the same time, researchers have a responsibility to gather accurate and reliable data for their clients.[47] Researchers should not manipulate findings to present a more favorable image of themselves or the firm. The significance of results should not be overstated. Questionable research practices, such as incomplete reporting of results, misleading reporting, and nonobjective research, can bring the integrity of the entire research process into question. For example, a cigarette ad once claimed that "an amazing 60 percent" of a sample said Triumph cigarettes tasted "as good as or better than Merit." Although this statement was technically correct, the results also indicated that 64 percent said Merit tasted as good as or better than Triumph, which was not reported to the public.[48]

Another issue is the subsequent use of data and the confidentiality of information collected for a client by a firm specializing in marketing research. Consistent with the *relationship perspective*, data collected for one client should not be made available to other clients.

Advertising on television programs shown in public schools has been criticized as being exploitative of children and as being excessively commercial. Similar issues are arising regarding the conduct of marketing research. Increasingly, schools are partnering with research firms in programs that allow those firms access to students for research purposes in exchange for funds to support school needs. As an example, Noggin cable television in Montclair, New York, recently paid $7,100 to support the purchase of school word processors for the right to use students once per week during school time in 30-minute focus groups. The ethics of these and other programs are certainly an issue.[49]

Marketing Decision Support Systems (MDSS)

Glaxo Inc., a pharmaceutical maker in Research Triangle Park, North Carolina, spends about $2 million a year on its sales and marketing decision support system for hardware, software, user training, and personnel. Donald Rao, manager of market analysis and decision support at Glaxo, claimed a return on investment of 1,000 percent since the system's development in 1987. The system provides detailed data on physician locations within sales territories, which allows managers to fine-tune marketing plans and product-sample allocations. In addition, it allows substantial savings in managerial time.[50]

Like Glaxo, many firms view all marketing data and information as part of a larger entity called a **marketing decision support system** (**MDSS**). All activities and computerized elements used to process information relevant to marketing decisions are components. These systems are now commonplace in many Fortune 500 business-to-business giants in industries such as airlines, banking, insurance, and pharmaceuticals.

A schematic overview of an MDSS is shown in Exhibit 6–9. Such systems represent a comprehensive perspective allowing a combination of different sources of information from different departments. MDSS are useful for both manufacturing and service companies.

Marketing decision support systems are generally designed to:[51]

- Support but not supplant management decision making.
- Apply to semistructured decisions of middle and upper management, such as pricing, promotion, and location decisions.

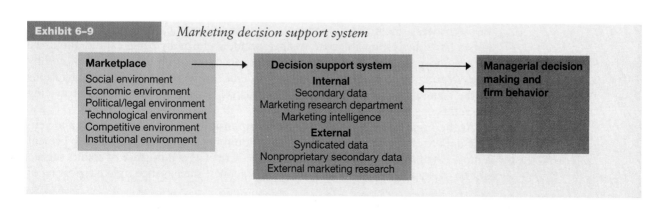

| Exhibit 6–9 | *Marketing decision support system* |

Marketplace
Social environment
Economic environment
Political/legal environment
Technological environment
Competitive environment
Institutional environment

Decision support system
Internal
Secondary data
Marketing research department
Marketing intelligence
External
Syndicated data
Nonproprietary secondary data
External marketing research

Managerial decision making and firm behavior

- Provide interaction between and among people and systems.
- Center on a segment of related decisions (the allocation of marketing effort and resources).
- Be user-friendly.

An MDSS is designed to enhance managerial decision making and firm performance by providing relevant and timely internal and external information. Input comes from many sources: the economic environment, social trends and changing consumer tastes, and the legal environment. Data from consumers, customers, and competitors are relevant. Prior experiences and decisions are also fed back into the system. Even permanent links with customers are now included in some MDSS systems. For example, a system linking Levi Strauss and Milliken, a textile manufacturer, significantly reduced costs for both companies and enabled Levi Strauss to respond to fashion changes and bring new products to market more quickly.[52]

External marketing research data may come from syndicated sources or various nonproprietary sources of secondary data. Syndicated market databases are useful for comparison with internal sales data to gauge market penetration. Internal data normally come from the marketing research department's own input, accounting records, and salesforce reports.

Computer technology now enables a variety of outputs from an MDSS. Output might include forecasts of sales, comparison of sales relative to forecasts, analysis of competitor performance, estimation of market potentials, evaluation of advertising effectiveness, and monitoring of consumer expectations and satisfaction. Some researchers predict that in the coming decades, a growing proportion of marketing decisions will be automated by ever-more-powerful combinations of data, models, and computers. As such, some aspects of marketing decision support systems will involve marketing decision *automation*. These changes will occur as firms increase their marketing activities into smaller units (i.e., individual stores, customers, and transactions). The resulting amount of data and numerous decision-making points can be more effectively handled by automated systems.[53]

Database Marketing

A significant technological innovation is **database marketing,** the collection and use of individual customer-specific information to make marketing more efficient. The term *database* refers to customer/prospect information stored in a computer with software to process the information. Computer technology provides the ability to pull apart and recombine information in ways previously impossible. Knowing which customers are predisposed to which products allows a firm to tailor marketing efforts to individual customers.

Database marketing can be instrumental in the success of companies' direct-marketing efforts. In many cases, customers respond to such efforts by making orders and inquiries via toll-free phone numbers. Companies use marketing research principles in developing customer databases and analyzing the information obtained from customer responses to direct-marketing efforts, such as telemarketing and direct mail. This information can enable a company to tailor individual messages at the customer level. Database marketing extends the traditional customer address list by including purchase records, demographics, psychographics, and information on media use. Note, however, that consumer advocates and government officials are increasingly raising ethical concerns about individual privacy as a result of the use of such data.

Vipont Pharmaceutical, a Fort Collins, Colorado, marketer of oral hygiene products, grew from start-up sales of $13,000 to $37 million in 10 years. The company credits its success to its relationships with its customers, both consumers and dentists, which the compilation of individual information files helped establish.[54] Similarly, relationship marketing has been strengthened for the Bank of A. Levy, of Ventura, California, by its implementation of a system that catalogs and sorts marketing customer information files. Manipulation of individual customer files

Database marketing involves the collection and use of individual customer-specific information. Catalog companies now analyze individual customer purchase patterns to tailor their direct marketing efforts.

through some database marketing program is becoming increasingly important to relationship marketing.[55]

One important aspect of data-based marketing is the ability to evaluate return on investment (ROI) of marketing expenditures. By merging descriptive attitudinal data with behavioral purchase records, direct marketers can both target mailings and craft messages to their most profitable customers. The behavioral data can be used to estimate incremental purchases from a targeted campaign with certain estimated costs. Moreover, such information, as expected return on investment, can be used to argue for additional resources and support for marketing effort within the firm.[56]

With better targeting of prospects for products and promotions, data-based marketing clearly contributes to increased efficiency. When practiced properly, data-based marketing yields double-digit response rates, compared with 2 to 4 percent for "junk mail." For example, Hilton Hotels offers targeted promotions to senior citizens in its Senior Honors program, prompting almost half of the members to take previously unplanned trips that included stays at the Hilton.[57]

Last, the development and use of databases comprising information on individual customers raises ethical concerns regarding privacy. First, marketers must thus continue to work at self-regulation regarding privacy protection. Second, it should be noted that firms that build their databases from within, as opposed to purchasing lists from other sources, are able to maintain the privacy of their customers. Third, customer permission and notification should be regularly sought. And fourth, firms should take into consideration that customers generally want firms to reduce the volume of catalog and advertising mail while simultaneously increasing the relevance of that information.[58]

Summary

1. **Understand the purpose and functions of marketing research.** The function of marketing research is to generate information that assists the firm's managers in making decisions. Marketing research helps managers respond to the ever-changing environment in which businesses operate. It is useful in problem solving, planning for the future, and controlling or monitoring ongoing performance. Marketing research links the marketer, the customer, and the public through information used to identify and define marketing opportunities; generate, refine, and evaluate marketing actions; monitor marketing performance; and improve understanding of marketing as a process.

2. **Be familiar with the stages of the marketing research process.** There are six stages of the marketing research process, through which primary data are generated to address a specific marketing problem or issue. In the first stage, problem definition, both the researcher and the user develop a clear conception of the problem that the research is intended to address.

    The second stage is specification of the appropriate research design, which is then used in the third stage, determination of the types of data to be collected and the methods of collection.

    In the fourth stage, researchers develop a data collection form, often a survey or questionnaire. In the fifth stage researchers design the sample, specifying the fieldwork required to collect the data. Finally, the data collected are analyzed, summarized, and presented to the users or firm management.

3. **Discuss different types of research designs, data collection methods, and sources of secondary and primary marketing research data.** Exploratory research designs are used to obtain general familiarity with a topic or problem. Focus groups, literature reviews, case analyses, interviews with knowledgeable individuals, and convenience sampling are examples of exploratory research.

    Descriptive designs are typically guided by some specific research question or hypothesis. Cross-sectional designs involve surveys administered at a given time. Longitudinal designs examine research questions over time through repeated measures of a common sample. Causal designs involve experiments, in which researchers manipulate independent variables of interest, such as price or advertising.

    Marketing data can be primary or secondary. Secondary data may be either internal, coming from within the firm, or external. External secondary data may be either nonproprietary (noncommercial) or proprietary.

4. **Understand many of the major issues involved with survey design and sampling.** Each survey method has its advantages and disadvantages. The different survey methods include telephone interviews, mail questionnaires, personal interviews, and mall intercepts. Researchers must carefully construct items or questions in a survey to ensure that the data collected are reliable (yield consistent responses) and valid (reflect the concepts being studied).

    Researchers can use probability or nonprobability samples, depending on the objectives, characteristics, and budget of the research. Probability samples are selected by some objective, unbiased process. Simple random samples are the most typical example.

    To assemble a nonprobability sample, the judgment of the researcher enters into the selection. Examples of nonprobability samples are convenience samples and quota samples. The researcher must decide on the population to be sampled, the sample size, and the sampling frame.

5. **Appreciate the role of marketing research within decision support systems.** Within the firm, the marketing decision support system (MDSS) consists of all activities and the hardware and software regularly used to process and provide marketing information relevant to marketing decisions. The firm may also employ outside agencies to provide marketing input.

Understanding Marketing Terms and Concepts

Thinking About Marketing

1. How might a clothes manufacturer employ focus groups in their search for what is "cool"? Would observation be a better approach? (See Being Entrepreneurial: Creative Ways of Doing Research.)

2. What is the purpose of marketing research? What are the primary stages of the marketing research process?

3. Explain differences among exploratory, descriptive, and causal designs, and give examples of each.

4. Differentiate these pairs of concepts:
   a. Cross-sectional versus longitudinal designs.
   b. Secondary versus primary data.
   c. Field market tests versus simulated market tests.

5. Describe the primary advantages and disadvantages of mail surveys, telephone interviews, personal interviews, and mall intercepts. What advantages are offered by virtual shopping technology over simulated test markets?

6. What are the different types of probability and nonprobability samples? Give examples of each.

7. What is the difference between projective techniques and observation research? What is ethnographic observation?

8. What factors determine sample size? What is involved in fieldwork?

9. What is an MDSS? Describe its primary advantages.

10. Identify three ethical issues in marketing research. Cite some concerns faced by firms conducting marketing research.

Applying Marketing Skills

1. Develop a sampling plan to conduct a telephone survey of residents in the county where your university is located. Assume you want to investigate opinions about the construction of a nuclear power plant in a nearby county. Who should be interviewed? How will the sample be drawn?

2. A manufacturer of roller blades is interested in assessing the satisfaction of its retailer customers. What are the advantages and disadvantages of the alternative data collection methods in gathering customer satisfaction data for the firm?

3. Design a research project for examining racial and gender differences in opinions about a sensitive subject such as presidential candidate preferences. Would the same design be appropriate for differences in new-product acceptance?

4. Research Incorporated, a regional marketing research firm that does tailored primary research projects in California, has been contacted by ABC Company for what appears to be a very profitable research project involving the demand for catalog shopping services. Research Incorporated recently completed a similar project for XYZ Company, a competitor of ABC. Both ABC and XYZ are large retail discount chains with over 50 stores in the Southwest. Should Research Incorporated accept the project? Should the information obtained for XYZ be given or sold to ABC?

Using the www in Marketing

Activity One   This chapter is organized around a description of the marketing research process. Consider this explanation as you access the NPD Group's Internet site (http://www.npd.com).

1. The NPD Group is one of the world's largest research firms. What can be learned about information on the Internet as a source of secondary data?

2. If a company were considering advertising on the Internet, what sites offer significant potential for marketing consumer goods?

3. What services does NPD offer regarding the collection of primary data?

4. How can "PC-Meter Q3 Sweeps" help companies understand what consumers are doing on the Internet?

Activity Two   Consider the Web site of IRI, Inc., the company whose home page opened the chapter.

a. What services and products are offered by the company?

b. Do their information services represent primary or secondary data?

c. What kinds of companies could make the best use of the information this company provides?

Making Marketing Decisions

Case 6-1 Sun-drop: Refocusing on New Segments

Sun-drop is a regional Southeastern soda brand, manufactured by Dr Pepper/7 Up. The drink is citrus-based, and competition within the product category is considerable. In particular, Mello-Yellow and Mountain Dew offer very well-known products that appeal to segments of all types. Until recently, Sun-drop had not targeted any particular market segment or segments.

Marketers have many choices, including the balance between focusing on the brand or the target market. Spurred by their increased competition, Sun-drop has now launched ad campaigns designed to reach teen consumers. In particular, teens located in smaller communities are the focus of the company's strategy; its themes stress "regular" teens in real-life situations. The decision to divide their market into smaller and smaller segments was apparently not based upon any market

research. While teens are the largest segment of soda drinkers, this very targeted strategy seems counter to most advertising aimed at youthful consumers that stresses the hip and unique in image and expression-laden advertising. However, developing loyalty among young consumers in any segment may be a long-term advantage.

Questions

1. What type of research should Sun-drop consider prior to expanding into other geographical areas?

2. What aspects of appealing to youthful consumers make the use of marketing research more important?

3. How should Sun-drop monitor changes in competition for its customers?

SOURCES: Don Peppers and Martha Rogers, "Do You Really Know Your Customers?" *Sales & Marketing Management,* January 1999, pp. 26–27; Rachel X. Weissman, "The Little Brand Fights Back," *American Demographics,* July 1999, pp. 35–36.

Case 6-2 Avon Products: Questions Abroad

Avon is currently the largest direct seller of cosmetics, with annual sales of approximately $5.2 billion. Avon sells to women in 135 countries through 2.8 million independent sales representatives. About two-thirds of its business is outside the United States. Sales have been weak in the United States, and they've been volatile in international markets due to currency fluctuations and other problems. The company's stock lost about 40 percent of its value when it recently indicated earnings would not meet Wall Street expectations.

Sales and profit results around the world are mixed, based on second quarter 1999 figures. U.S. operations posted a 4 percent sales and 11 percent profit increase. Sales in Latin America were down 3 percent, but up 16 percent if currency translations are excluded. Profits were up in Brazil, Mexico, Venezuela, and Central America, but down in Chile and Argentina. In the Pacific region, sales and profits were up strongly. There was substantial improvement in China, where Avon was forced to cease operations temporarily last year due to China's ban on direct selling. Sales in Europe were down overall, but up when currency exchanges were excluded. Profits were up everywhere in Europe, except in Russia, which is still plagued by economic turmoil.

When Andrea Jung was recently named CEO, Avon became the second-largest U.S. company to be run by a woman. Jung started as an Avon consultant in 1993 and became president and COO in 1998. Her vision is to "make Avon the most relevant beauty brand for women in the world."

Further expansion into global markets would require careful planning and decision making. While the demand for quality products in previously untapped markets was evident and there was a ready available source of willing salespersons, uncertainties about markets and buyer behavior in countries such as China, Vietnam, Romania, and Ukraine suggested the need for marketing research.

Avon promotes predominantly using female salespersons in their widely known direct personal-selling strategy. In addition, orders can be made from catalogs, e-mail, and faxes. Support for Avon's image is enhanced worldwide through the company's cause-related marketing (CRM) program. Avon focuses on different issues in different countries: breast cancer in the United States, Canada, Mexico, and Spain; care for senior citizens in Japan; AIDS in Thailand; and support for mothers in Germany. These programs demonstrate the firm's social responsibility via charitable contributions by Avon from revenues produced through sale of its products.

Questions

1. What information could be collected to assist Avon in deciding which countries to emphasize?

2. How can marketing research be used to investigate cultural differences affecting the use of cosmetics? What secondary data sources might be helpful in estimating market potentials for East European countries?

3. How might research be employed to evaluate the effectiveness of Avon's cause-related marketing program?

4. Can marketing research determine the likely effects of crude distribution and retail systems in lesser developed markets? If so, how?

SOURCES: Eric N. Berkowitz, Roger A. Kerin, Steven Hartley, and William Rudelius, *Marketing,* 5th ed. (Chicago, IL: Richard D. Irwin, 1997), p. 112; Philip Kotler, *Marketing Management: Analysis, Planning, Implementation, and Control,* 9th ed., (Upper Saddle River, NJ: Prentice-Hall, 1997); Pat Sloan, "Rapid Gains Set Table for Jung Move at Avon," *Advertising Age,* February 3, 1997, p. S12; "Avon Names Asian-American Woman as CEO," *USA Today,* November 5, 1999, p. B1; Andrew Edgecliffe-Johnson, "Avon Lady Promoted to Chief Post," *The Financial Times Limited,* November 5, 1999, p. 32; Rachel Beck, "Avon Calls on Woman to Be Chief Executive," *The Coloradoan,* November 5, 1999, p. B4; Dana Canedy, "Opportunity Re-Knocks at Avon," *The New York Times,* November 5, 1999, p. C1.

Chapter Seven

Market Segmentation and Targeting

After studying this chapter, you should be able to:

1 Define and explain market segmentation, target markets, and product differentiation and positioning.

2 Understand the criteria used for evaluating the likely success of a segmentation strategy.

3 Know the role of market segmentation in the development of marketing strategies and programs.

4 Describe the issues involved in product and brand positioning.

5 Understand the alternative bases for segmenting consumer and business-to-business markets.

6 Evaluate alternative approaches for pursuing segmentation strategies.

www.Future.sri.com

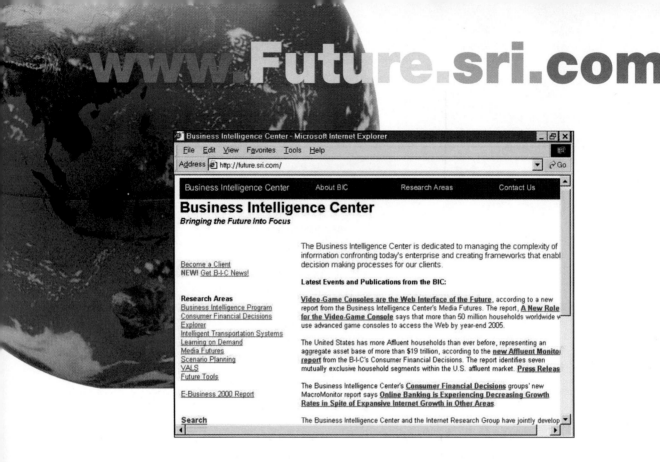

SRI's Values and Lifestyles (VALS) Program, established in 1978, developed the first commercial market segmentation system. In 1989, the original VALS system was revised to more closely identify psychological attitudes that predicted consumer buying behavior and media preferences. The current system, VALS 2, uses demographic characteristics such as age, income, education, and gender, in combination with psychological attitudes about one's self to provide a richer description of U.S. consumers. VALS groups American consumers into one of eight segments based on how they respond to the VALS questionnaire. This questionnaire is integrated in large national surveys of products, services, and media to discover the preferences by VALS type. Clients also use the VALS questionnaire in their custom research.

As described on their Web site, typical applications of VALS include new-product development, identification of target-market advertising design, media planning, and public relations. For example, a beverage company used VALS to identify its target market and to create an image and communications strategy for appealing to that market. One analysis examined geographic differences. The results revealed that Southeasterners score highest in the two most physically active groups: the young, rebellious excitement-seeking "experiencers" and the "makers," who are people with construction skills and who value self-

sufficiency. According to SRI researchers, this suggests that marketers in the Southeast must consider both "How does the product make me feel?" as well as "What does the product do for me?"

VALS can also be used as a tool for understanding new-product acceptance and innovation. For example, "experiencers" are quick to pick up on new products that provide an outlet for social interaction, fun, and excitement. "Believers," on the other hand, tend to stick with products and brands that they know, so it is not usually wise to target this group with a brand-new product. Also, SRI now offers consulting to clients who want to advertise on the Internet by helping them understand the attitudes and preferences of on-line service and Internet users. The VALS Web site allows visitors to take the VALS questionnaire and to see which consumer type they are most like. Through this process, VALS captures the psychographic profile of people who use the site. Interestingly, the results indicate that the largest segment of Web users falls into the upscale, well-educated "actualizer" VALS type. **Sources:** Rebecca

Piirto Heath, "The Frontier of Psychographics," *American Demographics,* July 1996, pp. 38–43; Rebecca Piirto Heath, "Psychographics," *Marketing Tools,* November/December 1995, pp. 75–79; Anne Marie Chaker, "Lifestyles: They Know What They Like," *The Wall Street Journal,* September 15, 1999, p. F4; and Anne Marie Chaker, "Lifestyles: No Life of Leisure," *The Wall Street Journal,* May 19, 1999, p. S3. Written comments by Carrie Hollenberg, the VALS Program.

Market segmentation involves the identification of market segments that will respond differently to varying marketing mix combinations. Ford offers products and communications designed to appeal to car-buyer segments formed on the basis of desired end benefits.

The VALS typology offers firms that employ the approach a unique understanding of differences in consumer segments identified using a combination of survey responses to questions about individual lifestyles, values, and demographics. A firm's researchers can use the variables to group consumers into eight market segments and then examine those segments for differences in product preferences and desires. Market segmentation allows a company to treat distinct consumer groups differently, thus enhancing its competitive advantage. That is, the company can effectively vary product offerings and marketing communications to capitalize on segment differences.

Market segmentation is among the most popular and important topics in the entire field of marketing. Market segmentation is consistent with the marketing concept and enhances a firm's ability to understand its core customers or who its core customers will be in the future. As such, segmentation helps the marketer identify important consumption patterns. Furthermore, market segmentation strategies are necessary both for consumer goods and services marketers and for firms operating in business-to-business markets. In this chapter, we explore the concept of market segmentation and how firms develop their market segmentation strategies. We define target markets and product differentiation and positioning, and we discuss the stages involved in developing a segmentation strategy.

Market Segmentation, Target Markets, and Product Differentiation

Mass markets and widespread brand loyalty, once taken for granted in business, have given way today to market segments of widely varying tastes, needs, and sensitivity to competing products. The emergence of these fragmented markets, new economic demands, changing technology, and intense international competition have altered the ways firms must compete.

In this section, we distinguish between market segmentation, target markets, and product differentiation. Throughout the section and the chapter, issues related to market segments, target segments, and targeting are discussed. Although similar terms, these reflect different concepts. Briefly, market segments are groups of prospective customers who share similar needs and wants. No firm can operate in every market and satisfy every need, nor can firms operate effectively within very broadly defined markets. Thus, target segments represent those groups the firm selects to focus on with separate marketing mixes. Targeting then involves selecting which market segments to emphasize and designing efforts to appeal to the unique differences and motivations that define those selected segments.

Market Segmentation

Firms often pursue a market segmentation approach to meet today's market realities. As discussed in Chapter 1, a market is a group of consumers or organizations with which a firm desires to create marketing exchanges. **Market segmentation** divides a market into subsets of prospective customers who behave in the same way, have similar wants, or have similar characteristics that relate to purchase behavior. The overall market for a product consists of segments of customers who vary in their responses to different marketing mix offerings. Market segmentation attempts to explain differences among groups of consumers who share similar characteristics and to turn these differences into an advantage.[1] As such, marketing effectiveness is enhanced by an understanding of who the firm's best customers are, what's on their minds, where and how they can be reached, and what they are buying.

A segmentation strategy can be pursued through variations in some or all aspects (product, marketing communications, price, distribution) of the marketing mix elements. For example, many widely purchased products such as soft drinks, computers, and clothing involve variation in both product and marketing communications to reach market segments and increase sales. In other instances, a single product may be marketed to different segments using different marketing communication campaigns. For example, a pharmaceutical manufacturer may promote the same new drug product to physicians, pharmacists, and hospitals using a different communication program for each. Sheraton's loyalty programs, costing up to $50 million annually, are based upon the data-based segmentation scheme comprising business travelers and leisure guests.[2]

Compaq Computer Corp. segments its consumer market using differences in price sensitivity and demand for product features. In a recent introduction, Compaq's consumer products varied in price from $1,699 to $3,999. The machines varied in size from small laptops to complex multimedia machines. The higher-end models may seem pricey for an industry increasingly offering less-expensive, scaled-down products. However, the company believed there were enough consumers who would buy the high-priced and, more important, the high-margin products.[3]

A number of factors are making understanding market segmentation more important:

- Slower rates of market growth, coupled with increased foreign competition, have fostered more competition, increasing the need to identify target markets with unique needs.

- Social and economic forces, including expanding media, increased educational levels, and general world awareness, have produced customers with more-varied and sophisticated needs, tastes, and lifestyles.

- Technological advances make it possible for marketers to devise marketing programs that focus efficiently on precisely defined segments of the market.[4]

- Marketers now find that minority buyers do not necessarily adopt the social and economic habits of the mainstream. As one market researcher observed, America is no longer a melting pot, but more of a mosaic or "salad bowl."[5]

Market segmentation is appropriate not just for firms marketing tangible products; nonprofit and service organizations also find it useful. For example, realizing that it had many different types of donors and volunteers, the Arthritis Foundation looked for an effective way to reach the right person, at the right time, with the proper request amount, and with the right message. To address the diversity in possible donors and volunteers, the foundation identified 12 categories of individual households defined by location, housing type, and income. The foundation found the segment labeled "urban gentry" (upper-income city dwellers) four times more likely than any other group to contribute both money and time.[6]

International marketing may be based on the cultivation of **intermarket segments,** which are well-defined, similar clusters of customers across national boundaries. This view of segmentation allows firms to develop marketing programs and offerings for each identified segment on a global basis.[7] Reliance on a single standardized global strategy can cause a firm to miss important target markets or to position products inappropriately. Similarly, customizing marketing strategy only to individual countries may result in a firm's losing either potential economies of scale or opportunities for exploiting product ideas on a wider scale.[8]

Some consumer-product businesses, such as McDonald's, Coca-Cola, and Colgate-Palmolive, use globally standardized products and marketing themes for some of their products. For most consumer products and brands, however, international marketing benefits from segmentation principles. In these instances, customized strategies may be developed for different countries or groups of countries. One recent study of

Speaking from Experience

Meredith Heckman
Senior Director, Marketing
Research
Sodexho-Marriott Services

Meredith Heckman earned her Bachelor of Science degree in Marketing from the University of Tennessee and now works for Sodexho-Marriott Services in Gaithersburg, Maryland. She was previously employed by American Express and Burke Research, Inc.

"Sodexho-Marriott Services provides on-site foodservice to over 4,000 clients across the United States and Canada, so understanding and reacting to customer differences are critical. Our clients view on-site foodservice as an important contributor to overall employee/student/patient satisfaction and, in some cases, even their productivity. Segmentation of on-site foodservice customers is an important tool for achieving that understanding and helping our clients reach their goals."

soap and toothpaste preferences, for example, revealed four segments across consumers in the United States, Mexico, the Netherlands, Turkey, Thailand, and Saudi Arabia. The largest segment comprised substantial numbers of consumers from Saudi Arabia, Mexico, and the Netherlands. These people all shared preferences for selected product benefits.

Many international marketers believe that teenagers represent the first truly global segment. Teens worldwide show remarkably similar attitudes and preferences. For instance, common clothing preferences are baggy jeans, T-shirts, and Doc Martens. An interest in MTV is also prevalent. There are similarities in the way teens look and the consumption patterns they exhibit. The emergence of this common ground will make marketing to this global segment more efficient. However, companies must still acknowledge subtle differences in culture and national preferences, particularly in the advertising messages used to promote nonlocal brands.

India has a very heterogeneous population, but the mere size of the market is attractive to consumer goods marketers. With 950 million people, the potential

Evian multinational campaign recognizes the existence of segments across country lines. The ads are included in women's magazines in Switzerland, Japan, France, Spain, Singapore, Italy, Austria, Hong Kong, Germany, the United Kingdom, and the United States.

demand is obvious. Consumer goods marketers like Pizza Hut, Kentucky Fried Chicken, Honda, and General Motors have simplified their strategies by focusing on the middle-class segment of the 250 million well-educated, Westernized residents of the largest cities.[9]

Target Markets

Market segmentation lets a firm tailor or develop products and strategies to appeal to the preferences and unique needs of specific groups of customers. These groups are typically referred to as target markets: groups of consumers or organizations with whom a firm wants to create marketing exchanges.[10] Examples include the elderly, the Hispanic, or the college-student markets, each of which can be targeted for specific products and reached through specific marketing programs. **Targeting** involves selecting which segments in a market are appropriate to focus on and designing the means of reaching them. Appealing to an entire market is often too costly. Moreover, a focus on certain markets can increase the efficiency and effectiveness of marketing efforts. However, a firm should target only those markets it can effectively reach and serve. Further, finely defined segments with their own marketing-mix strategies should be justified only on a return-on-investment evaluation.

As we shall see later in this chapter, segmentation may be appropriate for businesses of all sizes, not just for large firms with many products. Many small- and medium-sized companies find it better to concentrate on gaining a large share of one segment or a few, rather than small shares of all possible segments in a product market. For example, Liberty Bank of Philadelphia generates a profitable business from a market segment overlooked by many of its competitors: small businesses. Liberty Bank exhibited an *entrepreneurial perspective* through its efforts to establish itself as the bank for small-business customers, thereby increasing its share of an important target market.[11]

Product Differentiation

Related to market segmentation is **product differentiation**. Product differentiation exists when a firm's offerings differ or are perceived to differ from those of competing firms on any attribute, including price. A product differentiation strategy positions a product within the market. Marketers attempt to position a product or service in customers' minds—to convince customers the product has unique and desirable characteristics. By developing these perceptions, marketers seek to establish a competitive advantage relative to competing firms that offer similar products or brands.

In the mid-1980s, for example, brands in the frozen entrée market were differentiated on convenience, and consumers traded taste for that convenience. Stouffer's changed that balance by introducing a line of entrées positioned on taste but offered at a premium price. By focusing on a key benefit previously missing from other frozen dinners, Stouffer's expanded the market and became the category leader. Product differentiation and positioning are explained in more detail later in this chapter.

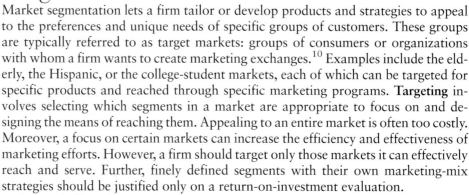

From Mass Marketing to Mass Customization

Among the most notable changes in this century has been the shift from mass marketing to **mass customization**. Companies like Dell Computers have proven that complex manufactured products can be made to order. Now, companies throughout the world have embraced mass customization in an attempt to satisfy the diverse needs of their customers and to provide unique value. The concept is made possible by advances in manufacturing and information technology that enable firms to provide product variety and customization through flexibility and quick responsiveness.

Various approaches have been used, and these approaches can range in the extent to which interactions with customers occur. "Collaborative customizers" conduct direct dialogue with customers to determine their needs and to identify the precise offering that is required to satisfy those needs. Other firms only package the offering individually in what is termed "cosmetic customization." The National Bicycle Company of Japan serves both ends of the mass market to mass customization continuum by operating two separate manufacturing facilities. The mass-production facility caters to their large market segment and is organized around traditional production facility efficiency. The mass-custom bicycle plant is directly linked to retail outlets where customers can choose from among eight million possible variations.[12]

One summary of the possibilities describes the alternatives as follows. At the least-specific level, mass marketing involves the company offering a standard product to markets worldwide, such as Diet Coke. Companies that practice target marketing focus upon niches in the market. Godiva Chocolate is directed at a more focused market comprising consumers with specific tastes. Sometimes companies focus upon market cells, many more in number and varied in description than typical larger target markets. These cells are derived from company databases through the process of **data mining,** which uses sophisticated analytical and statistical procedures to discover interesting patterns within company data sets. Data mining enabled Capital One to market 7,000 different MasterCard and Visa variations.

The most focused form of marketing is customer-level marketing. At the customer level, a distinction is made between "mass customization" in which the seller combines basic modules in different ways for each customer, versus "customized marketing" in which products are developed from scratch for each individual customer. Especially in business-to-business markets, many firms are starting to involve their customers in the product development process. On the consumer side, Chrysler allows potential customers to design their ideal car on the company's Web site in a special design section that calculates the price based upon those specifications.[13]

When Is Market Segmentation Appropriate?

Market segmentation can be useful for both new ventures and mature brands. In the case of new products, marketers target segments likely to respond positively to the introduction. Products that have been on the market for a while face an increasing number of competitive offerings, making it more difficult for any mass marketer to dominate in its product categories. Some frequently used approaches include developing brand-line extensions, repositioning the product for additional uses, or identifying the needs of a particular segment, or segments, and developing marketing strategies for each.[14]

The frozen entrée category again provides an example of a combined approach. Once Stouffer's successfully introduced its line of frozen entrées, the competitors came running. Stouffer's built on its success by extending its product line, tapping another key segment in the marketplace: the weight-conscious consumer. Stouffer's Lean Cuisine frozen entrées offered this segment low-calorie, tasty meals and the convenience of quick preparation. The frozen entrée category continues to be one of the most competitive in the grocery store, but Stouffer's maintains dominance through its target marketing approach.

A market segmentation strategy is not always appropriate, however. Advertising and marketing research practitioners suggest segmentation may not be useful when the overall market is so small that marketing to a portion of it is not profitable, or when the brand is dominant in the market and draws its appeal from all segments.[15]

Criteria for Effective Segmentation

Successful execution of a market segmentation strategy depends on the presence of several characteristics in the overall market and its various segments. In determining strategies to pursue, marketers should judge potential segments against five criteria: measurability, accessibility, substantialness, durability, and differential responsiveness.

Hispanic-Americans represent a substantial and responsive demographic segment.
Qué pasa.com makes effective use of market segmentation by offering products designed for this consumer segment.

MEASURABILITY   **Measurability** reflects the degree to which the size and purchasing power of segments can be assessed. Measurability is enhanced if segments are defined by concrete variables enabling easily obtainable data. Demographic characteristics, such as income and age, are examples. Firms can use such data to reach segments and to estimate the size and potential of target markets. The Buying Power Index method described in the appendix of this book can be used to measure potentials for geographic areas.

ACCESSIBILITY   **Accessibility** describes the degree to which a firm can reach intended target segments efficiently. That is, the selected market segments must be reachable with unique marketing communications and distribution strategies. The Hispanic market is an example of a growing segment that can be reached by specific media (newspapers, radio, television). More than 14 percent of U.S. residents aged five and over speak a language other than English at home. Hence, the total market for non-English programs could reach a figure of more than 40 million residents by the end of 2000. The growth of cable and satellite television programs for targeted audiences give advertisers the opportunity to access in-language television audiences.[16] In another example, previously successful albums now available on CDs, such as Led Zeppelin albums, are marketed to middle-aged consumers by ads on the cable channels ESPN and Arts and Entertainment.[17]

SUBSTANTIALNESS   **Substantialness** refers to the degree to which identified target segments are large enough or have sufficient sales and profit potential to warrant unique or separate marketing programs. The growing Hispanic population is a sizable market that merits specifically designed products, advertising campaigns, and even distribution approaches. African-Americans make up another important demographic segment. With annual earnings over $275 billion, the segment has buying power well worth targeting.[18] In contrast, some sports retailers feel that the left-handed segment is too small to warrant carrying left-handed golf clubs in inventory.

Market segments are often defined in terms of price sensitivity. Hartmarx Corporation offers multiple product lines to various price sensitive segments. These offerings include Hart Schaffner & Marx and Hickey Freeman, the latter of which appeals to the more price-conscious segment.

DURABILITY **Durability** has to do with stability of segments—whether distinctions between segments will diminish or disappear as the product category or the markets themselves mature.[19] The development of differentiated products, communication campaigns, or distribution strategies often involves considerable financial and time commitments. Segments selected for targeting should offer reasonably enduring business opportunities. The Hispanic market meets this criterion, as it is a significant and, perhaps more important, a growing segment of the population. Current population trends indicate the Hispanic population will be a key segment for marketers for many years to come. Another is the aging U.S. population. As of the end of 2000, there are expected to be 59 million people over 55 years of age. This segment is ripe for targeting products and services oriented toward health and conservation of income.[20]

DIFFERENTIAL RESPONSIVENESS **Differential responsiveness** refers to the extent to which market segments exhibit different responses to different marketing mixes.[21] If segments do not respond differently to varying marketing communications or product offerings, there is little need to segment. People interested in price will respond differently to low prices from people who seek high quality and assume price and quality are related.

Hartmarx Corporation provides a good example of the way a manufacturer segments target markets by price sensitivity. Hartmarx, a national producer and marketer of men's and women's fashions, developed brands and strategies to fill unique market voids.[22] Once Hartmarx acknowledges that different groups of consumers are sensitive to different price levels, it designs marketing strategies to differentiate variations in product (quality), communications (types of ads), and distribution (types of retail outlets). For example, the company targets Hart Schaffner & Marx to the upscale segment. Jaymar dress slacks and Sansabelt slacks are sold to the moderate segment. Kuppenheimer Men's Clothiers and Allyn St. George are included in the popular value offerings. Each brand name provides a product designed for different price-sensitive segments. Exhibit 7–1 is an example of how a retailer might segment men's clothing by price range.

Satisfying the Segmentation Criteria

By satisfying these various criteria, a company can choose market segments that can be described in managerially useful terms (measurability); that can utilize its communication and distribution channels (accessibility); that are sufficient in profit potential (substantialness); that will persist for some reasonable period (durability); and that vary in their reactions to different marketing efforts (differential responsiveness).

The Hispanic market provides a good example of combining segmentation criteria to evaluate a market. Although there are subsegments within it, the overall Hispanic market possesses unique cultural characteristics that make it an attractive target segment. The unique language and cultural characteristics of this market clearly make the segment *measurable* and *responsive* to appeals designed directly

Exhibit 7–1	*Hypothetical retail market segments and price points*						
	Business Clothing			**Furnishings**		**Casual Wear**	
Retail market segments	**Suits**	**Jackets**	**Dress slacks**	**Dress shirts**	**Neckties**	**Sport shirts**	**Casual slacks**
Upscale	$600 & over	$475 & over	$150 & over	$55 & over	$45 & over	$47.50 & over	$95 & over
Upscale moderate	$450–$600	$350–$475	$100–$150	$39.50–$55	$37.50–$45	$37.50–$47.50	$65–$95
Moderate	$375–$450	$250–$350	$75–$100	$39–$39.50	$25–$37.50	$32.50–$37.50	$45–$65
Value conscious	Under $375	Under $250	Under $75	Under $30	Under $25	Under $32.50	Under $45

for it. Hispanic-Americans will account for over one-fourth of the population by the end of 2000; the market thus represents both a *substantial* and *durable* opportunity. The market is also *accessible*—both broadcast (radio, television) and print (newspapers, magazines) media reach the Hispanic community efficiently with specialized ads.

Marketing to Hispanic consumers has international implications as well. Wal-Mart, Sears, McDonald's, Ford, General Motors, and PepsiCo target Mexico for expanded export and local operations. McDonald's earmarked $500 million to open 250 new restaurants in Mexico by the year 2000, and relaxed trade restrictions have opened opportunities for Ford and GM to export luxury automobile models.[23]

In fact, ethnic commonalities make marketing in native languages to subcultures within countries worldwide, particularly in the United States, worthwhile. For example, the purchasing power of Arab, Asian, Hispanic, Russian, Eastern European, African, and Caribbean immigrants in the United States is now over $400 billion. Increasingly, mainstream marketers are capitalizing on the tendency of people of ethnic similarity to live long term within close-knit communities that maintain ties with the countries of origin.[24]

Stages in Developing Market Segmentation Strategies

Stages required in the development of a market segmentation strategy are summarized in Exhibit 7–2. The organization's core business determines the product or service market in which it operates, be it the restaurant industry, computer software, lawnmowers, cleaning services for office buildings, or whatever. Given its overall product or service market, a firm identifies the distinguishing characteristics, or **bases of segmentation,** for the segments within that market. After describing these segments, the firm evaluates them for potential and likely success, then selects the key segment or segments to target. Finally, the firm develops marketing mix strategies, including various product and service forms, and price and distribution strategies and communication appeals for each segment.[25]

Bases for Segmentation

Logical bases to define market segments have to do with characteristics of the firm's customers or their behaviors. Exhibit 7–3 describes some of these bases for both consumer and business-to-business marketing situations.[26] The Levi Strauss strategy uses some of the most easily identified consumer segmentation bases, including age, race, and gender. Brand-loyalty segments and the heavy-user segment are among the most important and now are the focus of many customer retention efforts. For business-to-business marketing, computer companies provide an example. They frequently organize their selling efforts around different industries, such as banking, insurance, and educational institutions.

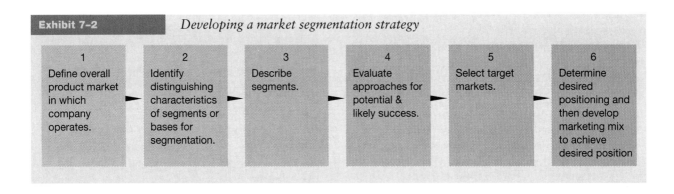

Exhibit 7–2   *Developing a market segmentation strategy*

1	2	3	4	5	6
Define overall product market in which company operates.	Identify distinguishing characteristics of segments or bases for segmentation.	Describe segments.	Evaluate approaches for potential & likely success.	Select target markets.	Determine desired positioning and then develop marketing mix to achieve desired position

| Exhibit 7–3 | *Frequently used consumer and business-to-business segmentation bases* |

Consumer Marketing

USER-RELATED

Demographics: age, gender, race, income, education, family size, family life cycle stage

Social class: lower, middle, upper

Culture: religion, nationality, subculture

Geographic: region, state, metropolitan location and size, urban versus rural

Lifestyles and psychographics: quiet family person, traditionalist attitudes, progressive, conservative

BEHAVIORAL

Benefits: desired product attributes

Usage: users versus nonusers, light versus heavy

Price or promotional sensitivity: high versus low

Brand loyalty: loyal versus nonloyal

Buying situation: kind of store, gift giving (kind of shopping)

Economic: profitability and potential

Business-to-business

USER-RELATED

Customer size: annual sales

Geographic location: Northeast versus West Coast

Organizational structure: centralized versus decentralized

Stage of buying process: decision at hand versus initial stages of decision making

Attitude toward vendor: current purchaser versus new account

Buying decision criterion: price versus quality

Type of product: installations, supplies, services, raw materials, component parts

Type of organization: manufacturing, government, public utility

BEHAVIORAL

End use: resale versus production component

Usage: users versus nonusers, light versus heavy

Product/service application: insurance versus banking

Economic: profitability and potential

Being Entrepreneurial

Fingerhut: Data-based segmentation

Fingerhut, the second-largest consumer catalog marketer in the United States, demonstrates its entrepreneurial orientation by an aggressive marketing program, which includes segmentation, risk taking, and product expansion. First, the company has not ignored the low-income segment of consumers as many companies do. With prices and monthly payments prominently displayed in its catalogs, Fingerhut recognizes the lucrative opportunities in extending credit to less-affluent consumers. Second, using the information obtained from its catalog and credit relationships, Fingerhut has created a cutting-edge database that allows the company to target the best credit risks among low- and moderate-income households. And more recently, its expansion into credit card services has generated unexpected revenue growth.

Fingerhut's abilities as a manager of customer data and Internet presence led to the purchase of Fingerhut by Federated Department Stores. Fingerhut's expertise in handling orders through catalogs and the Internet, plus its strength in database management, will greatly help Federated's retail businesses. Fingerhut now uses 300 predictive models to investigate the likelihood of consumer responses to different offerings. Such data mining has produced important findings, such as the not surprising, but still widely unrealized, notion that customers who have changed their address triple their purchasing in the next three months. As such, Fingerhut's "mover's catalog" was developed for that segment.

Sources: Susan Chandler, "Data Is Power: Just Ask Fingerhut," *Business Week,* June 3, 1996, p. 69; Kathleen Kiley, "Smarter Mailing Ups Some Sales and Earnings," *Catalog Age,* May 1996, p. 8; and Kathryn M. Welling, "Boring Doubles," *Barron's,* June 10, 1996, pp. 22–26. Jennifer Lach, "Data Mining Digs In," *American Demographics,* July 1999, pp. 38–45; and "Retailer Buys Fingerhut Marketing Company," *Marketing News,* March 15, 1999, p. 15.

DEMOGRAPHICS   For consumer marketing, demographic segments are particularly significant. Some products are targeted for teenagers and others for the elderly; others are designed for young couples just beginning a family. Vacation decisions are uniquely related to family life cycle characteristics, with children having significant input even at young ages. Marketing researchers often rely heavily on occupation and education to form social-class segments.

Ethnic and racial characteristics are also important segment descriptors. According to the 1990 census, there are now 29.8 million African-Americans in the United States, up 13.2 percent from 1980; 22.3 million Hispanics, up 53 percent; and 7.3 million Asian-Americans, up 108 percent.[27] The increasing importance of diversity will make understanding ethnic, racial, and cultural differences between segments a determinant of the successful design of segmentation strategies. In fact, Blacks, Asians, Native Americans, and Hispanics will attain the U.S. majority around 2050. These dramatic shifts will transform business over the next 50 years.[28]

The demographic makeup of the typical American household continues to change. Married couples are now barely the majority. Households are growing more slowly and getting older. College-educated people earn a lot more than less-educated consumers, and sadly, the gap between these two groups is growing wider. More and more jobs are being found in service industries, and the population shift to Western and Southern states continues.[29]

These trends and demographic phenomena are important to marketers' understanding of segment characteristics. For example, age differences are often used individually or with other demographic variables, such as gender, income, and education, to describe market segments. Five generations are often used to categorize age differences:

* *The millennial generation*—Born between 1977 and 1994, this large new generation numbers 70 million.

* *Generation X*—Born between 1965 and 1976, this well-educated, media-savvy generation now makes up the young adult population of the United States.

* *Baby-boom generation*—Born between 1946 and 1964, this is the largest single generation of Americans and remains a focus of marketers.

* *Swing generation*—Born between 1933 and 1945, this small generation of Americans now holds top positions in business and government.

* *World War II generation*—Born before 1933, the oldest consumers are the most affluent in history.[30]

Three of these age groups are particularly important in terms of marketing: teens, Xers, and boomers; and similarities among these groups offer unique insights into differences in consumer behavior. Of note, teens spend over $65 billion each year of their own money and influence considerably more in aggregate expenditures by either spending their family's money or determining how their parents make decisions.

Xers are more likely than boomers to seek a balance between leisure and work activities as young adults. They care deeply about buying "cool" brands that match their own image needs and often serve as trendsetters for the population at large. In addition, following their college years, young adults now more often live at home as their careers are formed; hence, they have considerable discretionary income. This group actually consists of three significant and overlapping submarkets: college and graduate students, up-and-coming professionals, and married couples. Firms who have been successful in reaching this group typically use the Internet as part of a larger campaign, particularly TV advertising. However, care must be exercised in the design of these campaigns, since Generation X consumers are often cynical about advertising.[31]

With boomers continuing to age, the marketing opportunities associated with an aging population are profound. Previous generations retired and lived off fixed incomes. Boomers are expected to continue working in the marketplace and to place a positive spin on aging. Consequently, products and services that appeal to older

Perception.   Reality.

For a new generation of Rolling Stone readers, drugs are out of their minds and into the frying pan. They know the truth; that if you tune in and turn on, you burn out. For twenty five years, Rolling Stone magazine has reflected the changing attitudes, ideas and lifestyles of the people who are changing the world. If you want to reach seven million of these people, we invite you to alter a few minds in the pages of Rolling Stone.

Rolling Stone

Music audiences can be segmented as well. Clearly, *Rolling Stone* magazine appeals to a certain lifestyle and/or younger-aged consumer segment.

Thinking Critically

- What media might be effective for reaching the most profitable consumer customers for large banks?

- What bases would be appropriate for use in the development of a segmentation of business-to-business marketers? Evaluate this scheme using the five criteria for effective segmentation.

consumers with younger, positive self-images will be effective. Moreover, major life events like diet changes, divorce, and retirement open fertile ground for marketers.[32]

Children between 2 and 12 years spent over $24 billion in 1997. Aggregate data suggest that the rate of spending by children tripled in the 1990s. Moreover, and as explained earlier in Chapter 4 on consumer behavior, children influence untold billions of purchases as well. In total, one source estimated that children influenced either directly or indirectly $500 billion in consumer expenditures in 1997. And, children are important to marketers as the consumer base of the future, since brand and product preferences and habits are often formed early in life. Regulators are working noticeably hard to erect barriers between children and the marketers who want to sell to them, particularly regarding purchases on the Internet.[33]

GEOGRAPHICS   Geographic differences are sometimes important in the development of marketing strategies. For example, cellular-phone marketers use geographic analyses to evaluate their distribution effectiveness. In addition, gaps in geographic coverage can also signal effective area campaigns by cellular-phone competitors that must be countered.[34]

One method of categorizing geographic differences uses census data to identify metropolitan areas. There are three types: **metropolitan statistical areas** (MSAs), **primary metropolitan statistical areas** (PMSAs), and **consolidated metropolitan statistical areas** (CMSAs). MSAs must have a city with a population of at least 50,000 or be an "urbanized area" with 50,000 people that is part of a county of at least 100,000 residents. The largest designation is CMSA. These are the approximately 20 largest markets in the United States that contain at least two PMSAs. PMSAs are major urban areas, often located within a CMSA, that have at least one million inhabitants. New York, Los Angeles, and Chicago are among the largest CMSAs. Populated areas within these markets, such as Marietta near Atlanta and Ventura near Los Angeles, represent PMSAs.

The combination of geographic information and demographic characteristics is called **geodemographics**. Much published geodemographic data are available that firms can use in evaluating the size of potential market segments. Products are often directed toward geographic markets, particularly when tastes differ between regions. Further, it is important for marketers to know which areas are the fastest growing and represent the greatest future opportunities.

Meridith Heckman notes: "Our approach uses a mix of off-the-shelf geodemographic clustering and proprietary psychographic/benefits segmentation approaches. This mix gives us segments which are identifiable, marketable, effective, and relevant. The end result is a method that can be applied in any of our foodservice categories to identify and serve the interests of tightly defined and lucrative 'target segments.' "

Firms use geodemographic data systems to integrate geographic information with census data. The fundamental premise in such geodemographic systems is that households in neighborhoods share similar lifestyles ("birds of a feather flock together") and that such neighborhoods repeat themselves, allowing similar neighborhoods to be classified into market segments.[35] Using a geographic information system (popularly labeled GIS), the lifestyle cluster system groups households into one of 40 residential types. Marketers can append lifestyle codes to customer records to expand their customer profiles and to enhance the study of the relationship of lifestyles to purchasing patterns.[36] Southwestern Bell Corporation (SBC) uses geodemographic analysis to develop marketing strategies for its European cable operations in the United Kingdom. The company uses the data to identify neighborhoods susceptible to sales through direct marketing campaigns and to screen bad-debt areas.[37]

Geographic clusters reflect segmentation targets that enable marketers to more efficiently employ their resources. Consider your own neighborhood. The cars and homes are probably of similar value. The mailboxes contain many of the same magazines, the cabinets the same products. The households have similar incomes and educations, as well as attitudes and product preferences.[38]

PSYCHOGRAPHICS AND LIFESTYLES Psychographic or **lifestyle research** attempts to segment customers according to their activities, interests, and opinions.[39] Such research uses survey responses to items concerning individual *activities, interests,* and *opinions*—called **AIO statements**—to develop in-depth profiles of consumer groups or segments. Examples of AIO statements are:

- "A person can save a lot of money by shopping around for bargains" (*price conscious*).
- "An important part of my life is dressing smartly" (*fashion conscious*).
- "I would rather spend a quiet evening at home than go to a party" (*homebody*).
- "I am uncomfortable when my house is not completely clean" (*compulsive housekeeper*).[40]

Psychographic research has been used successfully in a variety of segmentation applications. As an example, one study of women over 65 combined psychographic research with an analysis of segments identified by media preferences. This study of the growing over-65 market described the following media consumption patterns:

- *The engaged*—High levels of newspaper readership and high viewing levels of television news programming.
- *The autonomous*—Moderate levels of newspaper readership, and low use of media in general.
- *The receptive*—High viewing levels of television comedy programs and moderate levels of newspaper readership.[41]

A follow-up study using responses to a series of AIO agree–disagree statements provided a richer description of lifestyles within these segments. For example, women in the engaged segment were heavier users of cosmetics, considered cooking and baking extremely important, and were quite negative toward large companies and business practices.

Psychographic segmentation has also been applied successfully to the very lucrative baby-boomer market for pharmaceutical drugs. This segment, which represents $8.40 of every $10 spent on prescription drugs, has been divided into four segments: the proactives, the faithful patients, the optimists, and the disillusioned—

Andersen Consulting emphasizes a primary benefit to businesses—how to compete effectively in e-commerce.

defined in terms of their opinions and attitudes regarding health care and the use of prescription drugs. The first two segments, the proactives and the faithful patients, contain 70 percent of the over-40 market but differ greatly in their motivation and use of media; these differences have implications for market segmentation. For example, a "pull strategy" is effective with proactives, who are heavy consumers of health-oriented media. That is, advertising directly to the consumer will generate demand that "pulls" the product through the distribution chain. In contrast, the faithfuls attend to their physician communications; hence, marketing communications directed toward the prescribers will "push" drug sales through distribution to the consumer.[42]

A popular application of the lifestyle and psychographic approach to segmentation is the **Values and Lifestyles Program** of SRI International. VALS segments consumers into eight groups: actualizers, fulfilleds, believers, achievers, strivers, experiencers, makers, and strugglers. Firms can use this system to effectively develop advertising and promotional campaigns, including the selection of media and the design of message content. As shown in Exhibit 7–4, the groups are arranged along two dimensions: self-orientation and resources. Self-orientation refers to the attitudes and activities people use to maintain their social self-image and self-esteem. Resources include attributes such as education, income, age, energy, self-confidence, and even health.[43] For example, the actualizers, the smallest segment at 8 percent of the U.S. population, have the highest incomes and self-esteem. The remaining seven segments each represent from 11 to 16 percent of the population.[44]

BENEFIT SEGMENTATION   Many firms segment markets according to the particular attributes or benefits that consumers want.[45] **Benefit segmentation** enhances the design and marketing of a product to meet expressed consumer needs for quality, service, or unique features. In fact, benefit segmentation is most consistent with assumption of demand variation between segments. For example, Apple targeted a segment that wanted easy-to-use computers, consumers put off by

Business-to-business situations can benefit from segmentation practices. For example, JCPenney targets minority-owned businesses as potential suppliers.

Exhibit 7–4

VALS2: Eight values and lifestyles segments from SRI International

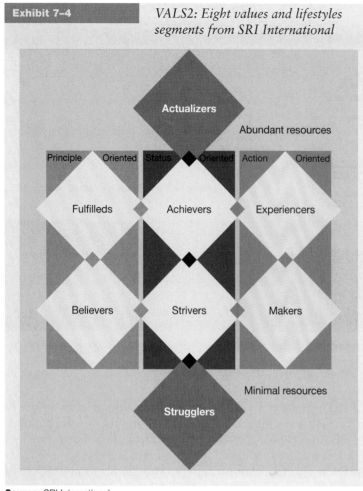

Source: SRI International.

what they saw as complications in operating other PCs. Defining this niche and simplifying the process of learning built Apple into a major factor in this market.

Benefit segmentation is consistent with the provision of *customer value* and the marketing concept—that is, to be customer-oriented and to provide consumer benefits to generate long-term customer satisfaction. The belief underlying benefit segmentation is that true segments are best described in terms of the causal factors or basic reasons for purchase.[46]

Benefit segmentation works in marketing services as well as products. Through its novel promotional messages, Andersen Consulting markets itself as a provider of much-needed benefits to many companies—information systems that do not threaten the firm's employees and that make computer technology a real contributor to the firm's performance. Users of the Internet have been segmented into those seeking adventure and exploration, information, entertainment, and on-line purchase of products and services. These segments of Internet users are labeled (1) adventurers (37 percent); (2) fact collectors (28 percent); (3) entertainment seekers (12 percent); and (4) social shoppers (9 percent).[47]

ECONOMIC SEGMENTATION Firms are increasingly segmenting their customers based upon the profit potential associated with individual accounts. Such economic-based segmentation occurs in both consumer marketing situations and business-to-business competitive markets. As shown in Exhibit 7–3, economic considerations are a behavioral-based segmentation characteristic. For example, banks often segment their customers into A, B, and C categories based upon profitability data generated through information on customer accounts and their previous account activity. The low revenue/low profit customers will receive minimum service, and in the case of banks, may be charged higher fees. In contrast, high revenue/high profit customers are targeted with personal communications, while direct mail is used for moderate revenue/moderate profit accounts. Factors such as cost of retention, potential for expansion, and customer contributions to profits are instrumental in determining these segment identifications.[48]

INTERNATIONAL SEGMENTATION Segmentation is an important part of international marketing as well. Firms can employ one—or some combination—of three approaches. First, companies may use a single standardized strategy in all international marketing. Second, customized strategies may be developed for different countries or groups of countries. In these cases, the countries represent different segments. Third, and as explained earlier, intermarket segments, comprising similar clusters of consumers across national boundaries, may be identified. Variables that are typically used to form country segments include income and GNP per capita, telephones and TV sets per capita, percent of population in agriculture, and political stability. For example, a company considering the sale of durable electronic products (VCRs and CD players) identified two important segments formed by combining countries: (1) Holland, Japan, Sweden, and the United Kingdom; and

(2) Austria, Belgium, Denmark, Finland, France, Norway, and Switzerland. Those segments were found to share similar patterns of new-product adoption and, hence, were addressed with similar marketing efforts.[49]

Combining Bases of Market Segmentation

Exhibit 7–5 diagrams one way a firm might combine consumer characteristics to decide on a market segmentation strategy. Here a two-stage process begins with research designed to identify the heavy users of a product or service. If the heavy-user segment has unique or consistent demographic characteristics, such as income or education, the firm's decisions about how to reach that segment are easier; that is, which magazines or television programs can be used efficiently. Similarly, identifying certain lifestyle characteristics of the heavy-user segment gives the firm additional insight about which product configuration or advertising theme is likely to be successful.

Exhibit 7–6 gives another approach for combining different variables to describe segments of consumers. Here, five demographic and household characteristics

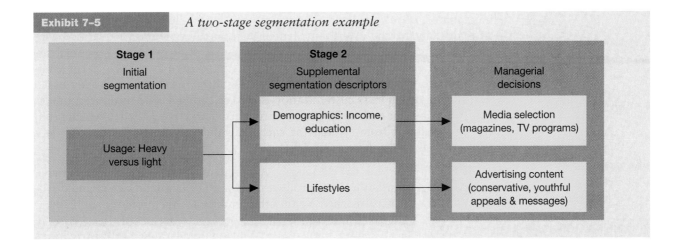

Exhibit 7–5   *A two-stage segmentation example*

Exhibit 7–6   *Segmentation bases and related product purchases: A lifestage analysis*

Lifestage Segment	Predicting Variables	Products of Interest
New, unmarried households	Income $0–$24,999 Head of household age 18–24 Unmarried Renters No children present	Credit Basic household supplies, furnishings Consumer electronics Appliances Career clothes, materials
Upscale, married, new children	Income $75k+ Head of household ages 35–44 Married Homeowner Children present, age 0–5	Insurance Financial planning Toys Educational plans Vehicles with high safety ratings Home entertainment products (cameras, film)
Preretired, upscale, empty nesters	Income $75k+ Head of household age 50–64 Married, widowed, divorced (three distinct subsegments) Homeowners or renters (additional subsegments) No children present, only one or two adults present	Remodeling services Real estate services Travel services, equipment, clothes Retirement planning Health care planning Upscale vehicles Recreational items (golf, tennis, sailing)

describe segment membership: income, age of head of household, marital status, home ownership, and presence of children in the household. Marketers can add these variables to their data files of current and potential customers and tailor products and services according to this analysis. For example, target products relevant to the "pre-retired, upscale, empty nester" segment include remodeling services, real estate services, health care planning, upscale vehicles, and recreational equipment.[50]

Basically then, firms identify and combine distinguishing buyer segment bases to:

- Help them design product or service offerings to market to targeted consumer segments.
- Help them choose media vehicles.
- Help them develop marketing themes for use in communicating to a particular segment or segments.

Segmentation Strategies

Strategies for engaging in segmentation are often categorized as undifferentiated, differentiated, or concentrated. These approaches provide firms alternative methods for enhancing the execution of their marketing programs. These strategies range from appeals based upon "mass marketing" to strategy focused on predetermined target markets. From our earlier discussion, other more-specific segmentation approaches target large numbers of market cells, or involve customer-based marketing, in which mass customization is used to combine basic product modules in different ways for each customer or customized marketing is used in which products are developed from scratch for each individual customer. Exhibit 7–7 is a schematic view of the three approaches.

UNDIFFERENTIATED STRATEGY A company adopts an **undifferentiated strategy** when it markets a single product using a single communication and distribution mix for the mass market. Neither the product nor the promotional theme is varied or differentiated. Undifferentiated approaches are most often used early in the life of a product category. Initial product introductions, such as the early introduction of the automobile, often use a single mass-marketing approach. The undifferentiated strategy offers some advantages because of economies of scale but opens the firm to competition. Today, even water is marketed in brands to different segments. Truly undifferentiated strategies are largely a theoretical impracticability, or at least, a phenomenon that occurs infrequently.

DIFFERENTIATED STRATEGY At the other end of the scale is the **differentiated strategy,** under which a firm uses different strategies for most or a large number of different segments. In some cases, a unique product and communications campaign may be developed for each segment. In other instances, a common product may be marketed to different segments with varying communication strategies. Of note, a differentiated strategy does not simply mean a change in product, although it may. Frequently, variations in multiple aspects of the marketing mix are involved. The Hartmarx and Levi Strauss approaches, with their multiple product versions and advertising campaigns, are examples of complex segmentation schemes. Differentiated strategies are often the choice of companies such as soft-drink manufacturers and life insur-

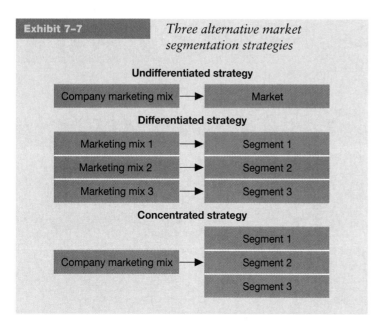

Exhibit 7–7   *Three alternative market segmentation strategies*

Undifferentiated strategy

Company marketing mix → Market

Differentiated strategy

Marketing mix 1 → Segment 1
Marketing mix 2 → Segment 2
Marketing mix 3 → Segment 3

Concentrated strategy

Company marketing mix → Segment 1 / Segment 2 / Segment 3

ance firms, which offer many product versions to meet different preferences. McDonald's, for example, embodies segmentation principles in its offerings. Happy Meals and playgrounds are offered for children, while nutritional information on trays and commercials showing parent/child interactions are targeted toward adults. Likewise, traditional burgers are offered along with healthier salads and sandwiches. Although a differentiated strategy is often useful for increasing sales and profits, continual adjustments to segmentation programs may prove expensive.

CONCENTRATED STRATEGY   A firm pursues a **concentrated strategy** when it seeks a large share of just a few profitable segments, perhaps only one, of the total market. With such a strategy, a company concentrates more on serving segments innovatively and creatively than on pricing.[51] American Express, for example, has traditionally sought upscale instead of middle-income customers. Thus, the company concentrates its advertising resources in pursuit of a large share of the higher-income consumer market.

COUNTERSEGMENTATION STRATEGY   **Countersegmentation** is an alternative strategy to traditional segmentation approaches. It involves combining market segments and assumes an increasing consumer willingness to accept fewer product and service variations for lower prices. Countersegmentation is seen in the move toward generic brands and retail superstores and warehouse stores and reflects segmentation by demand for low price. Sam's outlets and Toys "R" Us appeal to a broad range of consumers and do not emphasize finely focused target segments. Countersegmentation is seen also at IBM and Chrysler, which have streamlined their product lines by combining operations and eliminating some brands.

FACTORS INFLUENCING SEGMENTATION STRATEGY   A number of market, product, and competitive factors may influence a firm's choice of segmentation strategy. They include size and type of the market and a variety of competitive factors.

If consumers are not particularly sensitive to product differences, an undifferentiated strategy may be appropriate. But if the firm sells to an overall product market with many different segments, a differentiated or concentrated approach is the better choice. Two product-related factors are also relevant: stage in the product life cycle, and the degree to which the product may be varied or modified. If the product is new, a concentrated segmentation strategy may be best—that is, offering only one product version or a few at most. If the firm's interest is to develop primary demand, an undifferentiated strategy may be appropriate. In the later stages of a product's life, large firms tend to pursue a differentiated segmentation strategy.

For example, consumer product giant Procter & Gamble pursues a differentiated strategy in the laundry detergent category. P&G markets powdered laundry detergents such as Cheer and Tide to different segments of the product market. The company constantly differentiates its products within and across brands to address the segments vital to its success. Potential growth segments are prime candidates for differentiated products. When the liquid detergent segment was growing, P&G introduced a liquid version of Tide; later, the company addressed another potential growth segment with Concentrated Tide.

Competitive factors are particularly important in a firm's market segmentation strategy. If its major competitors pursue an undifferentiated approach, a firm may decide to engage in a differentiated or concentrated approach. If a firm has many competitors, its best strategy may be to concentrate on developing strong brand loyalty and buyer preferences in one target segment or perhaps a few. Finally, a firm's size and financial position can influence the choice of strategy. Smaller firms with relatively limited resources often find it necessary to pursue a concentrated segmentation strategy.

A firm adopting an undifferentiated approach or pursuing only the largest segments may well invite substantial competition. This is the **majority fallacy:** although large "majority" segments may appear to offer a firm potential gains, pursuing only them may involve confronting overwhelming competition. In this case, it is better for a firm to pursue a concentrated strategy, focusing on one segment, or a few, to obtain larger shares of markets in which it can compete effectively.

Targeting Market Segments and Positioning Products

Once a firm has chosen its overall market segmentation strategy, it then must select specific segments and position products for effective appeal to those segments. Factors that affect the choice of a segmentation strategy also influence which specific segments should be targeted.

Estimating Segment Potentials

To estimate market potential and likely sales, the firm should distinguish between firm and industry potentials and between forecasts of the best possible results and expected results. As Exhibit 7–8 shows, **market potential** is the maximum amount of industry sales possible for a product or service for a specific period. The **market forecast** for that same period is a function of the amount of marketing effort (expenditures) put forth by all companies competing in that market. Total market potential then represents an upper limit on total sales. **Sales potential** is the maximum amount of sales a specific firm can obtain for a specified time period.

To produce a sales forecast, a company should screen out market segments that represent insufficient potential sales and analyze further the remaining segments. Company forecasts must consider competitive activity and the availability of channels of distribution and marketing media. What brands are already in the market? What are the strengths and weaknesses of the competition? What distribution outlets and supporting channels of distribution are available? What is the cost of access to the appropriate media? One set of steps firms can use to estimate potential for a segment is:

1. Set time period of interest.
2. Define product level.
3. Specify segment characteristics or bases.
4. Identify geographic market boundaries.
5. Make assumptions about marketing environment (uncontrollable factors such as competitive activity).
6. Make assumptions about company's own marketing efforts and programs (controllable factors).
7. Make estimates of market potential, industry sales, and company sales.[52]

Exhibit 7–9 sets out data on market potential for pizza across four age groups. Population information of this sort is obtainable from U.S. census or state records. The product purchase percentage data can be obtained from an annual "Survey of Buying Power" in *Sales & Marketing Management*. The use of these data are explained in Appendix A.

Developing Forecasts

Forecasts represent the amount the company expects to sell in a market over a specific time period. The period will vary by company and use of the forecast. Forecasts are used to evaluate opportunities, budget marketing efforts, control

Exhibit 7–8	*Firm and market potentials and forecasts*	
	Best possible results	Expected results for given strategy
Industry level	Market potential	Market forecast
Firm level	Sales potential	Sales forecast

Exhibit 7–9		*Estimating market potential for frozen pizza for Arizona and Colorado (in thousands)*				
Age Group	**Percent Purchasing Frozen Pizza**	**Population**		**Potential Pizza Sales**		
		Arizona	**Colorado**	**Arizona**	**Colorado**	
18–24	10.4	384	341	39.94	35.46	
25–34	25.8	634	607	163.57	156.61	
35–44	24.3	568	622	138.02	151.15	
45–54	14.5	381	384	55.25	55.68	
				396.78	398.90	

Source: Joseph P. Guiltinan, Gordon W. Paul, and Thomas J. Madden, *Marketing Management: Strategies and Programs,* 6th ed. (New York, NY: The McGraw-Hill Companies, 1997), p. 111.

Thinking Critically

Trend analysis involves extrapolating the trend pattern in historical data.

- Using the following eight quarters of sales data for a product for the years 1998 and 1999, forecast sales for the first quarter of 2000 using both a three-period moving average and a four-period moving average: 24, 26, 28, 27, 29, 33, 32, and 33.

- Which of the two forecasting systems would be most sensitive to abrupt changes in the overall trend pattern?

expenditures, and assess subsequent sales performance. High forecasts can lead to excessive investment and expenditures, whereas low forecasts can result in lost opportunities.

There are a number of methods for forecasting sales, some of which are explained below. These methods can be grouped into *qualitative* procedures, which employ judgmental opinion and insight, and *quantitative* methods, which use historical data to make trend extensions or numerical estimates of forecasted sales. The primary qualitative forecasting methods are a survey of buyers' intentions, expert opinion, and a composite of salesforce estimates. The primary quantitative methods are trend analysis, market tests, and statistical demand analysis.

A **survey of buyers' intentions** is useful in certain situations. Under this method, forecasts are based on surveys of what consumers or organizational buyers say they will do. First, the buyers must have well-formed intentions and be willing to follow those intentions. In addition, they must be willing to disclose their intentions accurately. These conditions are most often satisfied for durable consumer goods and for large purchases in business-to-business marketing.

Expert opinion represents another qualitative or judgmental approach to forecasting. Using this approach, analysts ask executives within the company or other experts to provide forecasts based on their own judgments or experiences. This can be a quick and perhaps inexpensive method; however, the forecast accuracy depends on the knowledge of the executives or experts involved and their ability to provide realistic estimates.

A **composite of salesforce estimates** provides another means of forecasting sales. Under this method, sales representatives give forecasts for their individual territories, which can then be combined across territories. Sales reps have unique exposure to the competition and market trends. Plus, these estimates can be obtained cheaply and regularly. However, reps may give low forecasts in efforts to keep their own sales quotas low.

Trend analysis, a quantitative forecasting approach, often referred to as *time-series analysis,* examines historical sales data for predictable patterns. If the environment is reasonably stable, extrapolating past sales data can provide a quick and efficient means of making forecasts. Often the firm will identify trend, cyclical (economic cycles), and seasonal effects in its past sales pattern. Exponential smoothing is a frequently used form of trend analysis in which the most recent sales data are weighted the heaviest in determining each new forecast. The major problem with time-series or trend analysis is that the firm is assuming that what happened in the past will continue in the future, making no attempt to determine what caused the sales.

When the firm is uncertain about its subjective judgment or the ability of past data to forecast the future, a market test may be necessary. Market tests are particularly useful for evaluating the likely success of new-product introductions. **Market tests** involve marketing the product in test locations using the planned communications, pricing, and distribution strategies. Forecasts for other areas can then be obtained from sales in the test markets.

Statistical demand analysis involves developing forecasts from the factors thought to be most important in determining sales. Under this method, sales are forecasted from equations in which price, advertising and sales promotion, distribution, competitive, and economic factors serve as independent variables. Regression analysis is the most frequently used estimation procedure. Statistical demand analysis is advantageous in that it forces the firm to consider the causal factors that determine sales. Also, the relative importance of the independent factors can be evaluated. Although computers have made demand analysis readily available to forecasters, the usefulness of the method depends on appropriate application. Some sophistication in data analysis procedures is clearly a prerequisite to their use.

Forecasting is not a rigorous science, in spite of the availability of some very sophisticated methods. When using any of the methods described above, forecasters should be careful to avoid several common errors. These errors include the failure to carefully examine any assumptions made, such as anticipated social and technological changes; excessive optimism that inhibits consideration of the downside risks involved; failure to specify the time frame involved and the intended purpose of the forecast; and the failure to blend both quantitative and qualitative methods such that mechanical extrapolation is combined with reasoned judgment.[53]

Targeting Market Segments

To select target segments, the firm must consider a combination of factors, including the segment's potential sales volume and profits, competition currently selling to the segments, and the firm's abilities and objectives.

Marketing children's products requires targeting parents. Playskool promotes product durability and child enjoyment as primary benefits to interested parents. Such ads must be placed in magazines and broadcast media that will reach parents with young children.

Although large segments with a substantial number of buyers seem to promise high potential sales volume and profits, smaller segments served by a unique marketing mix may also provide lucrative business opportunities. Specialty stores in large malls serve many of these segments. For example, General Nutrition Center targets health-conscious people, and Lady Foot Locker, women sports enthusiasts.

The large markets may also attract the greatest number of competing firms (the majority fallacy). In general, a firm will have to assess market potential in light of competitive issues. If the firm has a competitive advantage that cannot be easily copied, it may attempt to approach the larger market segments.

The selection of target markets has a lot to do with the firm's objectives and distinctive competence. A firm specializing in innovative technological products, for example, may compete on total value, rather than on price alone, focusing on one segment or a few segments where high-quality, innovative products appeal.

Targeting also requires designing advertising and promotional mixes to reach the intended segments. Resources are wasted if the advertising results in duplication of audience or reaches nontarget market consumers. Accurate identification of the marketing segments appropriate for a particular product is critical if firms are to target those segments efficiently.

Technology brings new precision to both the selection of specific target segments and the ability to reach them. When Buick's analysis of the large station wagon segment revealed that upscale suburbs, particularly in the Midwest and Northeast, were potentially lucrative markets, it targeted consumers with ads in magazines sent to the relevant zip codes. Targeted ads promoting the Roadmaster station wagon ran in issues going to 4,940 of the more than 40,000 U.S. zip codes. That was 20 percent of U.S. households, but those households represented 50 percent of the buyers of large wagons.[54]

The benefits of targeting are prevalent in the marketplace—the grocery, clothing, and shoe industries included. For example, the use of in-store scanners and grocery card loyalty programs are enabling grocery retailers to more precisely target their consumers. In an application of economic segmentation, Sav-O's Piggly Wiggly stores are focusing on the top 50 percent of their customers, who represent 90 percent of their business. These customers are targeted with special promotions and advertisements designed to increase their transaction numbers per store visit. Moreover, data on the preferences of these desirable consumers are useful in determining shelf-space allocations among competing brands. Targeting specifically toward baby boomers has also enabled New Balance to compete successfully with Nike in the very competitive athletic-shoe market.[55]

Meridith Heckman stresses the importance of the knowledge gained from segmentation: "By using customer segmentation to understand the unique requirements among foodservice patrons—whether they are in a school, college/university, office/factory, or health-care facility—we are able to offer the optimal mix of menus, service, food promotions, merchandising, atmosphere, etc. Depending on the needs of customers at an account (needs that may exist within a few key segments or go across all segments), we can tailor our total package to address specific taste preferences, nutritional concerns, price sensitivities, and values/personal interests."

Positioning

Once segments have been selected and targeted, the firm must position its products and services in the minds of its customers. **Positioning** a product or service involves designing a marketing program, including the product mix, that is consistent with how the company wants its products or services to be perceived. The strategy a firm adopts is driven then by the desired positioning. Positioning aims to influence or adjust customer perceptions of a product or brand. An effective position lets a brand occupy a preferred and unique position in the customers' minds while being consistent with the firm's overall marketing strategy.[56] As such, positioning involves the selection of target segments and the formulation of product attributes that make up the brand. Recently, Snackwell's successfully halted dramatically falling sales volume by repositioning itself. This repositioning included product reformulation, an increased marketing budget, and a drastic shift in advertising redirected toward the brand's new core audience—women. Nabisco is also building its relationship with its primary target market by creating a Web site directed at women and an ongoing direct-mail campaign augmented by women-targeted promotions.[57]

Earning Customer Loyalty

Universal music: Moving switchers to on-line

E-commerce will become a nightmare for some marketers but a dream come true for some buyers, who incur little or no search costs for considering competitive offerings. Marketers can no longer rely on switching costs and incomplete consumer information to sustain customer loyalty. Instead, sellers must find genuine ways to differentiate their products to maintain a loyal customer base and to charge profitable prices. These phenomena hold especially for companies like Universal Music (http://www.umusic.com),

as on-line selling becomes commonplace. Their goal is to compete with smaller labels already on-line and ensure that Universal is not cut out as the middleman between artist and audience. Universal will have to provide more than just the search for music, but offer other special events such as interactions with musicians to build site loyalty.

Sources: Faye Brookman, "Companies Invest in Customer Loyalty," *Marketing News,* March 2, 1998, p. 12; Nanette Byrnes, "Internet Anxiety," *Business Week,* June 28, 1999, p. 81; and Bob Donath, "No, Really, the Marketing Concept Never Left," *Marketing News,* July 19, 1999, p. 10.

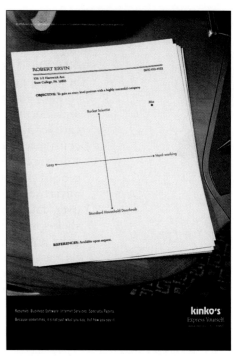

These Kinko's advertisements depict a humorous perceptual map which makes the important point that even students must 'position' themselves in the marketplace.

Positioning a new brand requires distinguishing it from other brands. Customers must perceive it as sharing important attributes with other brands in the product category but as being superior on differentiating attributes.[58] **Repositioning,** called for when a firm wants to shift consumer opinions about an existing brand, requires development of new marketing programs.

Product attributes, price, and image enhancements are major components in positioning. **Perceptual maps,** spatial representations of consumer perceptions of products or brands, are often used to evaluate brand positions in a market. Exhibit 7–10 is a perceptual map for the automobile market. Cars are positioned on the map according to consumer perceptions of price and brand expressiveness. Note that over time, a brand's market position can shift.

Perceptual maps often show positions for competitors' brands. They also convey to a company how much it must change consumer perceptions in order to achieve parity with or differentiation from competitors. By combining segmentation and positioning research, a company can learn which segments are attractive and how consumers in specific segments perceive the company's products relative to competing products and brands.[59]

Micromarketing

The ultimate in target marketing is **micromarketing,** which frequently combines census and demographic data to identify clusters of households that share similar consumption patterns. The PRIZM market segmentation system is one example. Demographic descriptions of county, zip code, and census tract locations combined with information about area values, preferences, and purchasing habits enable companies to pinpoint likely or desired customers. Firms use micromarketing to increase the productivity of their marketing expenditures. Micromarketing enhances the effectiveness of marketing efforts by enabling marketers to:

- Identify potential markets for direct selling through mail and telemarketing campaigns.

- Profile their customers by matching them to demographic and lifestyle clusters.

| Exhibit 7–10 | *General Motors car markets* |

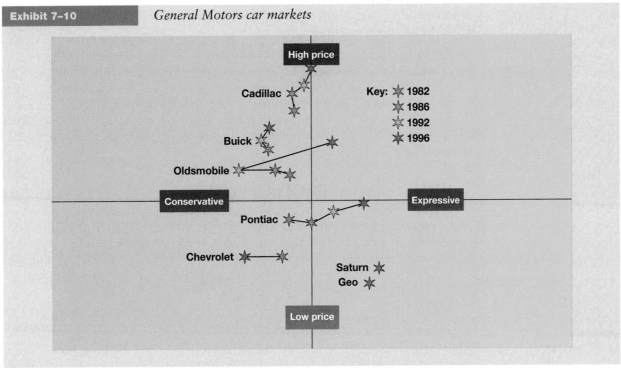

Source: *Automotive News,* May 11, 1992, pp. 1, 42; and William R. Dillon, Thomas J. Madden, and Neil N. Firtle, *Essentials of Marketing Research* (Homewood, IL: Richard D. Irwin, 1993), p. 353.

- Learn which areas offer the greatest potential in site selection for new stores or offices.
- Tailor their advertising themes and plan their media.[60]

As an example of the latter, *Reader's Digest* will soon print 40 different versions of its monthly editions. The advertising in each version will be designed for different areas of the country. This will enable advertisers, who provide much of the publication's income, to reach high-potential market segments.[61]

Market Segmentation and Ethics

Targeting selected market segments can provide substantial benefits to both marketers and consumers: the marketer gains sales and the consumers receive the particular products and services they most want and value. Yet, segmentation practices can be so effective that they are fraught with opportunities for exploitation. Marketers must consider the ethical issues associated with some segmentation and targeting practices.

Advertising to Children

Advertising to children, a large and influential market segment, can stimulate demand for expensive and unnecessary products. Such advertising has been criticized for developing unrealistic expectations and demands for some youthful consumers who can least afford unnecessary expenditures. Demand for expensive athletic shoes or certain kinds of jackets or jewelry is easily fostered. Further, very young children sometimes have difficulty differentiating between program content and commercial messages.

Reaching children, whose influence and discretionary-funds growth exceeds inflation, is big business. However, some of the member countries of the European Union believe that overtly selling to children via television advertising is unethical. As an example, the British Independent Television Commission states that ads targeting children must not:

- Take advantage of their natural credulity.
- Lead them to believe they will be inferior if they do not have the advertised product.

- Harm them.
- Force them to pester their parents.

The same concerns hold in the United States for young consumers. The results from congressional legislation and government restrictions will place tight reins on the ability of firms to collect information from children via the Internet. In particular, the Children's Online Privacy Protection rules are in response to parental concerns and Federal Trade Commission study regarding the susceptibility of children to marketing tactics, predominantly those associated with interactive communications available on the Internet.[62]

Gender-Role Stereotyping

To capture universalities among members of market segments and to simplify messages, marketers often resort to stereotypes. Portrayals of women in advertising are frequently criticized. For instance, some have argued that the "traditional housewife" shown primarily in a kitchen or laundry room and the bikini-clad model in beer ads are inaccurate stereotypes that negatively influence gender-role formation for both men and women.[63]

Harmful Products

Marketing harmful products, such as cigarettes and alcohol, to young people raises important ethical issues. Some brands of cigarettes, such as Virginia Slims, are positioned to attract young women. Models in cigarette and beer ads are youthful, active, and attractive individuals. Messages for these products often emphasize the social acceptability of smoking and drinking, minimizing the impact of package warnings regarding the negative effects of their use.

Privacy Issues

As marketers are increasingly able to target precise consumer segments, concerns about privacy arise. Consumer purchase histories, credit histories, and telephone numbers can be combined for use in developing and targeting direct marketing campaigns. Care must be exercised in the use of this information.

Product Proliferation

Over 30 food products are introduced every day, or 25,000-plus per year in packaged goods, including food, beverages, health and beauty aids, household products, and pet products. Is this ever-increasing proliferation needed? The continuing segmentation of markets and products to serve those products seems endless. Consumers are often bewildered by the number of choice alternatives.[64]

Some researchers and practitioners are now arguing for a plan labeled the "Efficient Consumer Response." One pillar of this grocery-industry recommendation is **efficient assortment**. While product issues are addressed in the three chapters that follow, keep in mind that the practice of developing finer and finer product distinctions designed in part to appeal to more-specific market segments has been questioned from both the perspective of improving consumer decision making and retailer performance. In fact, a number of studies have shown that the number of brands and brand sizes (i.e., stock-keeping units) can be reduced without affecting sales or consumers' perceptions of variety. In addition to simplifying decisions for consumers, cutbacks in category SKUs allow the retailer to reduce the occurrence of out-of-stocks, to cut back on stacking frequency, and to lower warehouse costs. For example, one summary of industry research reported a study in which the number of alternatives of cat-box filler was reduced from 26 to 16. There were no effects on category sales, but savings in logistics costs increased operating profit 87 percent.[65]

Summary

1. **Define and explain market segmentation, target markets, and product differentiation and positioning.** Market segmentation is used when consumer groups (segments) share needs or preferences that differ from other segments. Market segmentation strategies attempt to take advantage of these differences and to meet each segment's demands. The segments served by firms are often called *target markets.*

    Product differentiation exists when customers perceive that a firm's product offerings differ from those of competing firms on any physical or nonphysical attribute. Positioning a product within a market is the process of exercising a differentiation strategy to convince consumers that the product has unique desirable characteristics.

2. **Understand the criteria used for evaluating the likely success of a segmentation strategy.** Five criteria are relevant in the design of a market segmentation strategy. Measurability refers to the extent to which the size and purchasing power of segments can be defined. Accessibility is the degree to which firms can efficiently reach intended target segments. Substantialness addresses the size of the target segment and its potential sales and profits. Durability refers to a persistence—the extent to which segments will persist over time as good business opportunities. Differential responsiveness is the degree to which market segments differ in their response to varying marketing mix combinations.

3. **Know the role of market segmentation in the development of marketing strategies and programs.** Market segmentation can be useful for both new and mature products or services. New products can be targeted to segments promising opportunities for introduction and growth. Mature brands can be repositioned, extended, or marketed to appeal to specific segments. An appropriate market segmentation strategy can help marketers focus on growth and expansion opportunities in an increasingly competitive marketplace.

4. **Describe the issues involved in product and brand positioning.** After determining the segmentation strategy, the marketer must take care in selecting the appropriate segments and positioning the firm's brands for those seg-

ments. Positioning refers to consumers' perceptions of the particular product or brand in relation to its competitors. Overall, the firm must identify the existing competitive products and brands within a market. It then must assess which attributes determine product preferences for the brands in that market. An examination of the fit between existing preferences and beliefs, ideal preferences, and brand capabilities will assist the firm either in positioning a new brand or in repositioning an already available brand.

5. **Understand the alternative bases for segmenting consumer and business-to-business markets.** Variables used to develop segmentation schemes may be either user- or behavior-based, and they may apply in either consumer or business-to-business marketing situations. User-related characteristics include demographic and psychographic variables for consumers, and customer size and geographic location for business-to-business applications. Behavior-related characteristics include benefits desired and extent of usage for consumers, and product application for business-to-business markets.

6. **Evaluate alternative approaches for pursuing segmentation strategies.** Segmentation strategies are of three types: undifferentiated, differentiated, and concentrated. An undifferentiated strategy involves the use of only one combination of marketing mix variables to meet the demands of the entire market. This strategy is appropriate if consumers are insensitive to product variations, if the competition is light, or if the product itself cannot be easily varied.

    A differentiated strategy involves the use of different marketing mix combinations to meet all or many of the segments constituting a market. A concentrated strategy aims to achieve a large share in just one or a few segments.

    In practice, many firms evolve from using an undifferentiated or concentrated strategy to adopting a differentiated approach, either as the firm can produce variations of the product or as the product develops beyond its introductory stage. An alternative approach, countersegmentation, combines market segments to provide consumers lower-priced products with fewer product variations.

Understanding Marketing Terms and Concepts

Thinking About Marketing

1. What is market segmentation, and how does it differ from product differentiation?

2. How might a marketer attempt to differentiate a product from competing products?

3. What are the criteria for segmenting a market, and what is meant by each one? Contrast differential responsiveness with segment accessibility.

4. Describe the different bases for segmentation. In doing so, explain the differences between user-related and behavior-related characteristics. How does PRIZM, described in Case 7-1 make use of these bases?

5. What bases might be used to define segments for these products: cassette recorders, hand calculators, personal computers, and public universities?

6. What is benefit segmentation? How does demographic segmentation differ from psychographic segmentation?

7. Define the different segmentation strategies. Compare and contrast each strategy with the others, and explain the conditions under which each may be appropriate.

8. What implications does the majority fallacy hypothesis have for the pursuit of a concentrated segmentation strategy?

9. How might Fingerhut use its databases to strengthen its marketing efforts?

10. Why is the practice of market segmentation and targeting now more important than ever?

Applying Marketing Skills

1. Compare the audiences of *Time* and *Rolling Stone* magazines. How does advertising in these magazines relate to market segmentation?

2. A large U.S. manufacturer of heavy-duty carpet for use in office buildings is considering expanding its marketing efforts to include European countries. The company has segmented its marketing efforts geographically and by company size. What market segmentation decisions does the company face as it expands its efforts to include both Eastern and Western European countries?

3. Bicycle manufacturers pursue a benefit segmentation strategy to address the U.S. adult market. Using this method, they can market essentially the same product for exercise, for leisure, or for just plain fun. Bicycles are also popular worldwide. How would you go about segmenting the bicycle market in, say, the Netherlands and Egypt?

Using the www in Marketing

Activity One   This chapter's opening discussed the VALS Web site (http://Future.sri.com). Select the Values and Lifestyles Program, and then at the bottom of the page click on "Find your own VALS-type now."

1. What demographic descriptors are used to define the VALS segments?

2. Comment on the number and nature of the agree–disagree attitude statements? Do your

responses reflect stable or temporary opinions about yourself? Were you surprised by your own VALS categorization? How do your own values and lifestyles compare with others?

3. What other information must companies have before this segmentation scheme is useful in a practical sense?

Activity Two　　Many e-commerce companies are now using heavy advertising to market their on-line services. Consider the Barnes and Noble site: http://www.barnesandnoble.com.

a. What aspects of this site are designed to develop a "loyal" segment?

b. How does Barnes and Noble compete with Amazon.com?

c. What behavioral segmentation characteristics of on-line book buyers would be helpful in the design of marketing strategy?

Making Marketing Decisions
Case 7-1 PRIZM by Claritas: You Are Where You Live

For the past two decades, the Alexandria, Virginia–based company Claritas Inc.'s geodemographic segmentation product, PRIZM (potential rating index by zip market), has been one of the most highly used tools to identify consumers. PRIZM is a micromarketing tool that categorizes consumers into lifestyle segments. The basic notion behind PRIZM is that "birds of a feather flock together"; that is, people who live together often purchase the same types of items. The original designer of the PRIZM database, Jonathan Robbin, categorized U.S. Census Bureau data in zip codes and analyzed each for social rank, mobility, ethnicity, family life cycle, and housing. These data are supplemented by market research surveys and other statistics obtained from the A. C. Nielsen Co. and 1,600 municipal and regional agencies. Currently, PRIZM also segments consumers by block tracts and zip-plus-four. The newest version of the PRIZM software consists of 62 consumer segments. This growing number of consumer segments is an indication of the increasing economic and ethnic complexity within consumer markets.

The 62 clusters are organized into 15 standard social groups, indicated by the degree of urbanization, from the rural countryside to urban high-rises. The 15 groups cover the range of affluence, from "rural-landed gentry" to "urban cores." Survey Sampling, Inc., adds PRIZM codes to their random telephone samples to add lifestyle information such as interests, hobbies, education, and spending patterns. By identifying the neighborhood types where existing customers are located, accurate predictions can be made where prospective customers are located. This information can then be used in designing direct-mail campaigns, media planning, site analysis, and product positioning.

Users of PRIZM include restaurant chains, banks, and stores in search of the best locations for new outlets. For example, Premier Bank in Baton Rouge, Louisiana, merges PRIZM with its internal database to find neighborhoods with households that match the traits of its best customers. Additionally, direct marketers develop target mailings based on information provided by PRIZM. Finally, advertising agencies explore the PRIZM database for insights concerning consumers.

Having successfully developed the original PRIZM software, Claritas Inc. has recently introduced a segmentation system that can accurately profile a market's workday population as well as illustrate the difference between the area's daytime and nighttime demographics. This segmentation product, Workplace PRIZM, provides marketers with valuable information concerning the daytime demographics of an area. Therefore, companies can evaluate whether their products and services are needed for the daytime population.

The development of the Workplace PRIZM software was based on the original PRIZM residential tracts. Workplace PRIZM weights the original tracts by the percentage of residents commuting to specific employment tracts. These newly developed workday tracts are often quite different than the original population tracts.

Overall, the PRIZM system is based on the theory that by knowing the location, education level, traits, and habits of each cluster in a community, retailers and shopping-center marketers can market to specific clusters. Therefore, the use of PRIZM software as a consumer segmentation tool should provide marketers with valuable information concerning consumers.

Questions

1. Why is PRIZM software an effective marketing tool?

2. How has PRIZM software been used in the past, and how might this software be used by others in the future?

3. Discuss the privacy issues that may be associated with PRIZM software. Is the use of PRIZM software by companies unethical?

4. What are the advantages of the newly developed Workplace PRIZM software?

SOURCES: Debra Hazel, "Marketing to Your Clusters," *Chain Store Age Executive,* August 1994, p. 76; Christina Del Valle, "They Know Where You Live—and How You Buy," *Business Week,* February 7, 1994, p. 89; "Claritas Eases Marketing to Commuters," *Bank Marketing,* September 1995, p. 97; "A Higher Profile for Audience Measurement," *Broadcasting & Cable,* December 1, 1997, p. S20; "The PRIZM Advantage," *The Frame* (Fairfield, CT: Survey Sampling, Inc.), August 1999, p. 1; and http://yawl.claritas.com/about.asp, December 12, 1999.

Case 7-2 Marriott International: "Suite Deals"

Marriott International is a worldwide operator and franchiser of hotels and senior living communities. Marriott has subsidiaries in 55 countries and regions, and its business volume reached $16 billion last year. The lodging business includes over 1,700 operated or franchised properties. Marriott, which operates eight chains of hotels and suites, focuses its hotel marketing efforts on two groups: middle-class families and business travelers. Unlike other hotel competitors, Marriott uses separate brand names on their different lines. Examples of their product mix, approximate prices, and the intended target market for each are as follows:

Fairfield Inn—$45–$65; the economizing business and leisure markets.

SpringHill Suites—$75–$95; members of business and leisure markets looking for more space, amenities.

Courtyard—$75–$105; the "road warrior."

Residence Inn—$85–$110; travelers seeking residential-style hotel.

Marriott Hotels/Resorts—$90–$235; members of the discerning business and leisure markets.

Ritz-Carlton—$175–$300; senior executives and others looking for luxury.

Recently, Marriott restructured its management to ensure more-effective coordination of their complex operations. Specifically, three business categories were established, each headed by a senior VP: full service (e.g., Marriott Hotels), extended stay (e.g., Residence Inns), and select services (e.g., Courtyard, SpringHill). This organization allows shared resources for such activities as strategic development, market analyses, and the Rewards loyalty program. Category teams structured around these three groupings should enhance decision making and implementation of marketing changes and strategies.

The SpringHill introduction is Marriott's most recent product-line addition. The rooms are large and practical. In late 1999, the new brand had 30 hotels open and another 100 under construction or planned for construction. This addition has been so far one of the fastest-growing launches in Marriott history.

Questions

1. What are benefits and drawbacks from such a diverse offering of hotel chains?

2. What segments remain untapped?

3. To what extent does price sensitivity affect choice of alternatives within the line of hotels and suites?

4. If the lodging market is $60 billion in total, is Marriott slicing the market too thin?

SOURCES: Christina Brinkley, "Marriott Outfits an Old Chain for a Brand-New Market," *The Wall Street Journal,* October 13, 1998, http://interactive.wsj.com/articles/; "Marriott's New View of Downtown," *Business Week,* July 26, 1999, p. 78; Marty Whitford, "Marriott International Restructures Management," *Hotel & Management,* October 18, 1999, p. 23; and Marty Whitford, "Old and New Flags Vanish with Rebranding Strategy," *Hotel & Management,* October 4, 1999, p. 30

Chapter Eight

Product and Service Concepts

After studying this chapter, you should be able to:

1 Understand the differences between goods and services.

2 Differentiate between consumer and business products, and discuss the different types of each.

3 Recognize that marketers need to appreciate the perspective of the consumer.

4 Define and discuss the importance of product quality, product design, branding, packaging, and customer service.

5 Explain how the different product components need to be integrated to meet the needs of customers.

The Frito-Lay Web site presents useful information to consumers, retail customers, investors, and potential employees. In addition to basic information about the company, its history, and its products, the site adds value to consumers by providing dietary information and recipes that incorporate Frito-Lay products.

The history of Frito-Lay is especially interesting. Elmer Doolin started The Frito Company in 1932 based on the new product Frito Corn Chips. Herman W. Lay founded the H. W. Lay & Company in 1938 to market potato chips. In 1945, The Frito Company granted H. W. Lay & Company an exclusive franchise to manufacture and distribute Frito Corn Chips in the Southeast. The two companies developed a close affiliation and merged in 1961 to form Frito-Lay, Inc. In 1965, Frito-Lay, Inc., and the Pepsi-Cola Company merged into PepsiCo. Frito-Lay remains a separate operating division of PepsiCo producing almost 60 percent of the parent company's profits.

Today, Frito-Lay has sales in excess of $9.6 billion a year. The company has more than 100 product lines with many well-known brands such as Lay's, Ruffles, Doritos, Tostitos, Fritos, Rold Gold, and Sun Chips. Nine of Frito-Lay's brands are among the 10 best-selling snack food brands in major U.S. supermarkets. Lay's and Ruffles potato chips and Doritos tortilla chips are the leaders in the potato chip and salty snack food categories. Doritos, Chee-tos, Lay's, 3D's, and Ruffles are global brands. The company operates 44 manufacturing plants with the world's largest snack food plant in Frankfort, Indiana.

Frito-Lay is noted for the quality of products it provides to consumers and the exceptional service it gives to retail customers. The company's basic business philosophy is: "Make the best product possible; sell it at a fair profit; and make service a fundamental part of doing business." This philosophy guided The Frito Company and H. W. Lay & Company from the beginning and continues to drive Frito-Lay today. **Source:** The Frito-Lay Web site, http://www.fritolay.com

The Frito-Lay example illustrates the importance of quality products, strong brands, and exceptional service to a company's success. This chapter explores the key product and service concepts. We define the different types of products and discuss the important components of a product: quality, design, branding, packaging, and customer service.

What Is a Product?

The term **product** is defined as an idea, a physical entity (a good), a service, or any combination of the three that is an element of exchange to satisfy individual or business objectives.[1] From a marketing viewpoint, the key element of this definition is "to satisfy individual or business objectives." Individuals and businesses purchase products to solve problems or satisfy needs. That is, products provide benefits. Successful marketers focus on the benefits products supply to customers.

Let's examine the term *product* from a consumer's viewpoint. Say a consumer bought some product—maybe purchased a notebook for a course, or bought lunch at a local restaurant, or perhaps picked up some dry cleaning. Why did the consumer make each purchase? The major reason is the consumer wanted the benefits offered by the purchased product. The notebook, the lunch, and the dry cleaning provided benefits—in the ability to take notes in class, to satisfy hunger, and/or to have clean clothing. The specific features of each product (the type of notebook, specific restaurant and meal, characteristics of the dry cleaner) are important only insofar as they are translated into the specific benefits the consumer wants.

While reading these three chapters in Part Four, it is critical to think about products from a customer's viewpoint. Customers purchase products for their benefits, and astute marketers emphasize product benefits in their marketing efforts. For example, focusing on customer benefits is the basic marketing philosophy of Hewlett-Packard: "Many companies build a product and look for a market. We listen to our customers, research their needs, and build products that provide solutions for their problems."[2]

Consumers purchase products to receive benefits. Gold's Gym suggests the benefits from using its bodybuilding facilities.

Types of Products

Marketers often classify products into specific categories. We focus on the categories of goods and services, and consumer and business products. We then discuss different types of consumer and business products.

Goods and Services

Goods are usually defined as physical products such as cars, golf clubs, soft drinks, or other concrete entities. **Services,** in contrast, are normally defined as nonphysical products such as a haircut, a football game, or a doctor's diagnosis.

Products, however, do not necessarily fall into one category or the other. Almost all products incorporate some characteristics of both goods and services. "Being Entrepreneurial: Food on the Internet" illustrates the close relationship between goods and services.

A useful way to view goods and services is on a continuum, as presented in Exhibit 8–1. Where a product lies on this continuum affects how it should be marketed, because goods and services possess several unique characteristics. The more a product lies toward the services end of the continuum, the more it is intangible, perishable, inseparable, and variable in quality. The more a product lies toward the goods end, the more it is tangible, storable, separable from the producer, and standardized in quality.

The purchase of a soft drink such as Pepsi-Cola in a restaurant can illustrate these differences. The soft drink is a good. It is tangible; it can be touched when it is served from the can. The restaurant can stockpile cases of Pepsi-Cola to serve when needed. The companies manufacturing and distributing the Pepsi are separated from the customer when the product is consumed. Finally, the quality of the Pepsi is expected to be the same from can to can, because the manufacturing process is standardized.

The service provided by the restaurant, however, is different. The activity of serving the Pepsi is not tangible; it cannot be touched. The restaurant cannot store the service provided by a waiter; if there are no customers, the potential service of a waiter is wasted. The waiter's service cannot be separated from the restaurant, and it is performed in the presence of the customer. Consumers consider the waiter and the restaurant to be the same. And finally, the service provided by the same waiter to different customers, or by different waiters, is likely to vary in quality.

GOODS AND SERVICES STRATEGIES Although the tangibility, perishability, separability, and variability characteristics differentiate many products and services, new technological developments are blurring some of these differences.

Being Entrepreneurial

Food on the Internet

Everybody has to eat and most people have to integrate eating into very busy schedules. Entrepreneurs are capitalizing on this opportunity by using the Internet to provide time-starved consumers with convenient ways to satisfy the need to eat.

Cooking.com and Tavolo.com focus on those who want to cook. Both sites sell gourmet food and cooking products, but they also offer various services to customers. These services include weekly menu planners with menu suggestions, as well as features that convert standard to metric measurements, tailor recipes to the number of people being served, and create a shopping list based on the weekly menu.

For those who want to eat out or order food for takeout, there are new options. Foodline.com and OpenTable.com offer Web-based reservation systems, while Food.com provides on-line ordering and local delivery from more than 13,000 restaurants nationwide. All customers have to do is enter their zip code and then place an order from the menu offerings.

CookExpress.com presents an option between cooking from scratch and eating out or takeout: a gourmet, ready-to-cook meal sent directly to a customer's home by Federal Express. These three-part meals require less than 30 minutes to fix.

Source: Alessandra Bianchi, "What's Cooking On-Line?" *INC.,* January 2000, pp. 23–25.

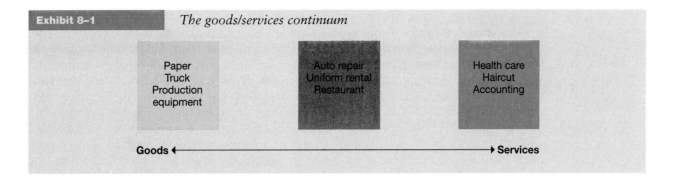

Exhibit 8–1   *The goods/services continuum*

| Paper
Truck
Production
equipment | Auto repair
Uniform rental
Restaurant | Health care
Haircut
Accounting |

Goods ◄─────────────────────────────────────► Services

Some services have characteristics similar to those of goods. For example, on-line databases are services, but the information provided is tangible, it can be stored until a customer needs it, the provider of the service is separated from the user, and there is little service variability.

In addition, the service content of many goods is a key component of the value received by customers. Take computers as an example. The hardware is clearly a good, but much of the value provided to customers is through the services accompanying the good, such as customizing a system to meet the specific needs of a customer. These services might include installation, software modifications, training, and ongoing support.

As suggested earlier, it is important to think about products from a customer's viewpoint. Customers are making purchases to satisfy needs or solve problems. Increasingly, this often requires marketers to offer products that represent a mix of goods and services. It is still important, however, to understand the typical differences between goods and services and how these characteristics lead to different strategies for the goods and service components of a product offering. We discuss these differences below and present specific strategies for services in Exhibit 8–2.

TANGIBILITY   One of the most interesting differences between goods and services relates to tangibility. Because goods are tangible, marketing strategies typically emphasize the intangible benefits derived from consuming the product. For example, many ads for Coke convey an intangible excitement associated with drinking the product. On the other hand, because services are intangible, marketers often try to associate them with something tangible. This approach is evident in the insurance industry: Consider the "good hands" of Allstate, the "rock" of Prudential, the "cavalry" of Kemper, and the "good neighbor" of State Farm.

PERISHABILITY   Perishability also has an important effect on the marketing of services. Services cannot normally be stored, so marketers of services use different

Exhibit 8–2   *Characteristics and strategies for services*

Service Characteristic	Service Strategy	Examples
Intangible	Associate the service with something tangible.	General Motors' Mr. Goodwrench; models of buildings prepared by architects.
Perishable	Manage demand to utilize supply.	Reduced prices for afternoon movies; lower rates for off-season accommodations at tourist attractions.
Inseparable	Capitalize on advantages of person providing the service.	Motivate service providers through compensation and recognition programs; continual training of all customer contact personnel.
Variable	Standardize service delivery as much as possible.	Use of technologies, such as automated teller machines, to provide service; implementation of quality-improvement programs.

strategies to manage demand. For example, higher prices are charged when demand is expected to be high, but prices are lowered when demand is expected to be low.

Airlines offer a good example of this type of strategy. Passengers flying to the same destination often pay very different fares, depending on flight schedule and time of booking. During holiday periods, fewer discounted tickets are available. Various types of discounted tickets are offered at other times to fill planes that would otherwise fly with empty seats not purchased at regular fares. The earlier customers make reservations and pay for tickets, the lower the fare. Low fares also go to those on standby, that is, customers willing to wait for an available seat after all reserved passengers are boarded. Airlines use standby to generate revenue for seats that have not been purchased in advance and would otherwise go to waste.

The production and consumption of services are often inseparable. Singapore Airlines emphasizes the importance of its flight attendants in delivering services to customers.

SEPARABILITY Goods like tennis racquets, tuxedos, or tomatoes can be produced, stored, and then sold to customers. Services, on the other hand, are typically produced and consumed simultaneously. For example, a dentist produces dental service at the same time the patient consumes it. The customer, then, tends to see the person and the business providing the service as one and the same. Thus, bank tellers are the bank, nurses or billing personnel are the hospital, and salespeople are the firm.

The close relationships between the production and consumption of services and between the person and the business providing the service have significant implications. Whether a business provides goods or services, it must be concerned with the management of service employees. Every employee who has contact with customers is part of the firm's service offering. Therefore, effective management and training of employees who see customers is critical for providing quality services. Training of executive-level managers is not enough; service employees at all levels need the appropriate attention if they are to "be" the company.

VARIABILITY The difficulty of standardizing services, especially when they are delivered by people, has important implications for marketers. Even well-trained and professional service providers have bad days. Therefore, there will always be some variability in service quality. Even so, leading firms analyze their service processes and develop standards and procedures to minimize variability to the extent they can.

Consumer and Business Products

Another important distinction is between consumer and business products. This categorization is based on the way a product is used, and not on the specific characteristics of the product. **Consumer products** are those purchased by consumers for their own personal use. **Business products** are those purchased by a firm or organization for its own use. Thus, the same product could be classified differently depending on the purchase and use. For example, if Elena buys a pencil to use at home, it is considered a consumer product. If Elena's employer purchases the same pencil for her to use at work, it is considered a business product.

We have seen that the buying behaviors of consumers and businesses differ in important ways. These differences motivate different strategies, depending on whether a product is marketed to consumers or businesses. There are also different types of consumer products and business products, as Exhibit 8–3 demonstrates.

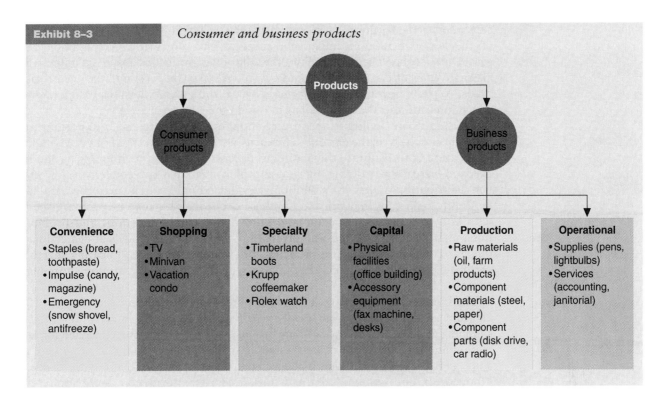

Exhibit 8–3   *Consumer and business products*

Convenience	Shopping	Specialty	Capital	Production	Operational
• Staples (bread, toothpaste) • Impulse (candy, magazine) • Emergency (snow shovel, antifreeze)	• TV • Minivan • Vacation condo	• Timberland boots • Krupp coffeemaker • Rolex watch	• Physical facilities (office building) • Accessory equipment (fax machine, desks)	• Raw materials (oil, farm products) • Component materials (steel, paper) • Component parts (disk drive, car radio)	• Supplies (pens, lightbulbs) • Services (accounting, janitorial)

TYPES OF CONSUMER PRODUCTS   There are millions of consumer products, and they can be classified in a number of ways. One especially useful approach is to classify products according to how consumers shop. Such an approach is valuable because it suggests that specific marketing strategies are relevant for a particular consumer-product category. Relevant shopping behavior by category is described in Exhibit 8–4. Of course, the same product can be classified differently by different buyers.

Convenience products are items consumers do not want to spend much time shopping for. Buyers of convenience products typically want to make a quick purchase at the most convenient location. Although they may prefer a specific brand, they will buy something else if that brand is not available. Convenience products are normally low-priced, often-purchased goods. They might range from staples (toothpaste, bread, or mustard), to products bought on impulse (chewing gum, magazines, or candy bars) or in an emergency (umbrellas, antifreeze, or snow shovels).

A key to marketing convenience products is to obtain extensive distribution. Marketers should make such products available at all convenient locations so consumers will be able to find the brand they want and not have to switch to another. Widespread distribution is especially important for products bought on impulse, because consumers purchase them only when they see them during their shopping trip. Distribution is also important for products bought in emergencies.

Soft drinks are convenience products for most consumers. Although consumers might prefer Coke over Pepsi or vice versa, they tend to switch to the other if the preferred brand is not available. Coke and Pepsi marketing strategies are designed to ensure that their brands are readily available. Thus, the brands are marketed through all types of retail outlets, restaurants, vending machines, and now at the checkout counters in many grocery stores.

Shopping products, in contrast, are items consumers are willing to spend time shopping for. When

Exhibit 8–4

Types of consumer products

	Prefer Specific Brand	Willing to Shop
Convenience	May	No
Shopping	No	Yes
Specialty	Yes	Yes

consumers perceive all the product alternatives as similar, they often shop around for the best price. A family might shop at several electronics stores, for example, to get the best deal on a television. For other shopping products, consumers might see alternatives as differing in important ways and shop for the one that best meets their needs. A family might shop at Chrysler, Toyota, and Ford dealerships to determine which minivan suits them, as well as to obtain the best price.

Consumers are willing to spend time shopping if the purchase is important to them, particularly if the product is expensive. For marketers, the key strategic implication is to facilitate the shopping process. Typically, a shopping product needs to be readily available, but not as widely available as a convenience product. Distribution outlets for a shopping product should provide extensive information to help consumers in the purchase decision. This may be accomplished with knowledgeable salespeople and informative communications and promotional materials. Salespeople and printed brochures for car models at dealerships illustrate typical marketing approaches for shopping products. Locating several car dealers in the same general area also would help to facilitate the shopping process.

The Internet has, however, changed the purchasing process for shopping goods. Consumers do not have to physically visit retail stores to get information about shopping goods. They can now "click" to many different sites to get needed information and then decide to make the purchase on-line or at a retail store. In fact, consumers can go to sites developed by companies such as Active Buyer's Guide, Productopia, and Epinions.com and have access to information about products from product experts or users. Consumers still spend time on shopping good purchases, but the Internet makes it possible for them to get more and better purchasing information in a convenient manner.

Specialty products are different yet, in that consumers both want to purchase a specific brand and are willing to look to find it. They are neither willing to switch brands, as they are for convenience products, nor shop to evaluate product alternatives, as for shopping products. They want one brand, and they will travel to buy it.

Marketers might limit distribution of specialty products to exclusive outlets and can typically charge high prices. Such marketing efforts should focus on maintaining the loyalty of customers and the image of the product. Certainly, most marketers would enjoy selling a brand considered a specialty product. These are rare circumstances, however, for few consumers are committed to only one brand in many product categories.

TYPES OF BUSINESS PRODUCTS Classifying business products is difficult because a vast number of different products are used by for-profit firms, nonprofit organizations, and government agencies. Our categorization groups products according to the way they are used in the operation of a business (see Exhibit 8–3).

Capital products are expensive items used in business operations but do not become part of any type of finished product. Because they are used over long periods of time, their cost is normally depreciated or spread over some useful life rather than expensed completely in the year of purchase. Capital products range from physical facilities such as manufacturing plants, office buildings, and major equipment, to accessory equipment such as desks, copy machines, fax machines, or forklifts.

The purchasing process for capital products may be long and involve many individuals. Marketers of capital products emphasize personal selling as the major communication tool. Prices are often negotiated, and sometimes businesses decide to rent or lease capital products rather than buy them outright.

Capital products are expensive items used in business operations. PACCAR markets heavy-duty trucks to business customers.

Production products become part of some finished product. Raw materials, such as coal, oil, or farm products, are the basic type of production product. Component materials and component parts are also production products. Component materials are products that require further processing to be included in the finished product. Examples are steel, paper, and textiles. Component parts are fabricated for the finished product. They may require some minor processing or be used as is in the finished product. Thermostats and disk drives are examples.

The purchasing process for production products is extensive but typically less involved than for capital products. Businesses want to receive quality production products when they are needed, otherwise the production process may be interrupted. Marketers of production products therefore must emphasize both product quality and reliability in meeting delivery schedules. A buyer does not necessarily select the supplier with the lowest initial price. Increasingly, the long-run cost of doing business with suppliers is more important to firms than the short-run price of the product.

Operational products are used in a firm's activities but do not become part of any type of finished product. Maintenance, repair, and operating supplies are considered operational products. These include lightbulbs, cleaning materials, repair parts, and office supplies. Also included are services such as accounting, engineering, and advertising that are purchased from outside vendors rather than provided from within the business.

The purchasing process for many operational products is the least extensive for any business product. After an initial purchase, and assuming the business is satisfied, subsequent purchases may be straight rebuys; that is, the buyer merely places an additional order with the same supplier. Thus, it is important for a seller to get the initial order and to ensure that the buyer is satisfied with all aspects of the purchase. If this happens, it is almost impossible for a competitor to get its foot in the door.

Product Components

We have said that consumers purchase products to satisfy needs. Another way to say this is that people really want a "bundle" of benefits when they purchase a product, and different consumers are likely to want different benefits from the same type of product. For example, some consumers purchase Rollerblade skates for fun, others as a way to increase health and fitness, and others because of the excitement involved with in-line roller skating.

To provide the benefits consumers want, marketers need to integrate the components that make up a product effectively. These consist of the product and customer service features illustrated in Exhibit 8–5. Product features include quality, design, branding, and packaging. Customer service encompasses various purchase and usage services. Different blends of product features and customer service provide different benefit bundles.

Credit cards offer a good example. Although all credit cards provide a basic benefit (credit), they offer different mixes of benefits to appeal to specific consumers. Credit cards differ in annual fees, rewards for use of the card, payment terms, design of the card, brand name, and services provided. All these components interact to produce the product, or the benefits, consumers purchase. For example, American Express recently launched a new credit card, the Blue card. In addition to offering typical credit card features and benefits, the Blue card offers users access to the American Express Online Wallet. This new feature provides customers with the benefit of faster and more-secure on-line purchases. Consumers concerned about Internet security are likely to value the benefit bundle offered by the Blue card.[3]

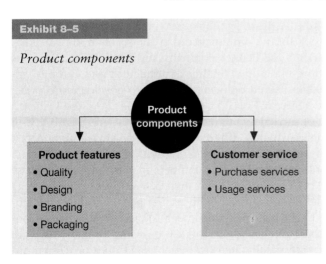

Exhibit 8–5

Product components

Doris K. Christopher
President and Founder
The Pampered Chef

Doris started The Pampered Chef as a direct-seller of high-quality kitchen tools in her suburban-Chicago basement in 1980. Company sales are expected to exceed $700 million in 2000 with over 55,000 Kitchen Consultants working in the United States, Canada, and the United Kingdom. Doris has served as the Chairperson of the Direct Selling Association, was named a regional winner of Ernst & Young's National Entrepreneur of the Year Award, and wrote *Come to the Table: A Celebration of Family Life.* She earned a B.S. in Home Economics from the University of Illinois at Urbana-Champaign. Doris talks about how her company integrates the different product components to provide the benefits desired by customers:

"Satisfying the needs of customers is the key to our success. The philosophy of direct selling is based on one-on-one interacton with customers. Through this direct interaction, customers provide feedback directly to the company regarding product quality, design, and service. At the Pampered Chef we believe that our products should earn the right to be in your kitchen. We say 'This is a good product, now how can we make it better?' We've made our mark by listening to our customers, improving our products, and offering them at competitive prices."

Some firms are practicing **mass customization** by offering each customer a customized bundle of benefits. New information and communications technologies are making this possible. For example, many Internet sites allow each individual user to select specific types of information to be continuously downloaded and displayed on the user's screen. Each customer can select the stock prices to be reported, the cities for weather forecasts, the types of sports information desired, and other specific types of information to be communicated. Another example is the marketing by Levi's of custom-fitted jeans to women. As technology develops, more opportunities to increase customer value through mass customization will become available.

Quality

As a product component, product quality represents how well a product does what it is supposed to do as defined by the customer. Rational, a German manufacturer of computer-controlled ovens that combine convection and steam heat, recognizes the importance of defining product quality from the customer's viewpoint. Everywhere in the plant, signs say, "Gut genug? Der Kunde entscheidet" ("Good enough? The customer will decide").[4]

Improving product quality as consumers define it can be an effective way to increase product sales. For example, most consumers probably consider a quality turtleneck to be one that looks good, fits well, and lasts a long time. JCPenney found that its turtlenecks were of lower quality than those offered by competitors like The Gap, Lands' End, and L.L. Bean. Penney's turtlenecks lost their fit and did not last very long, because they shrank and puckered at the seams upon washing. To improve the product's quality, the Penney company stiffened its specifications for fabric, fit, and construction, and added Spandex to the neck and cuffs. By introducing higher-quality turtlenecks and reducing the price to provide more value, the company saw sales triple in a year.[5]

Consumers define quality of turtlenecks in terms of looks, fit, and durability. In other markets, consumers define quality differently. In the prestige fountain pen market, for example, consumers consider utility along with glamour and distinction. Cross, Waterman, Montblanc, and Parker compete in this market. All these products offer similar utility, but each provides prestige differently. One maker may emphasize glamour, citing the famous people who use its pens; another may emphasize distinction, pointing to the historical documents signed with its pens. Consumers have responded to these pitches about quality by using as many as eight different pens during a year, with specific pens to match wardrobes or to sign different sorts of documents.[6]

Thinking Critically

You have decided to open a pizza restaurant that would provide customers with the highest-quality pizzas.

- What are the characteristics of a quality pizza as defined by most customers?

- How do you evaluate the quality of the pizzas offered by the existing pizza restaurants (Pizza Hut, Godfather's, Papa John's, etc.)?

- What do you plan to do to make your pizzas higher quality than what competitors offer?

Product quality is defined by customers. Ping emphasizes how its drivers will help golfers keep their drives in the fairway which should lower their scores.

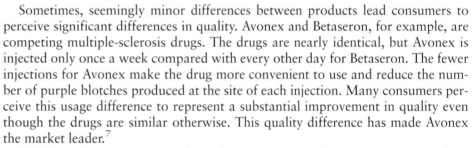

Sometimes, seemingly minor differences between products lead consumers to perceive significant differences in quality. Avonex and Betaseron, for example, are competing multiple-sclerosis drugs. The drugs are nearly identical, but Avonex is injected only once a week compared with every other day for Betaseron. The fewer injections for Avonex make the drug more convenient to use and reduce the number of purple blotches produced at the site of each injection. Many consumers perceive this usage difference to represent a substantial improvement in quality even though the drugs are similar otherwise. This quality difference has made Avonex the market leader.[7]

Marketers, however, cannot always be sure consumers have accurate perceptions of the quality of their products. This was an especially difficult problem for the U.S. automobile industry. Objective assessments of quality by trade observers or groups such as J. D. Power have consistently shown improvements in the quality of American cars. Yet, many consumers were not aware of these quality improvements. They typically based purchase decisions on personal perceptions of quality, not necessarily objective evaluations, and these perceptions lagged reality.

Quality is what consumers consider it to be. Marketers should ensure that their products provide the desired level of quality, work to constantly improve this quality, and convey to consumers an accurate picture of the quality. These are difficult tasks, but they are essential for success in today's competitive marketplace.

Design

Product design includes the styling, aesthetics, and function of a product. How a product is designed affects how it works, how it feels, how easy it is to assemble and fix, and how easy it is to recycle.

Product design decisions can be pivotal in a product's success. Consider one example: the introduction by Reebok and Nike of basketball sneakers with inflatable air cushions for better ankle support. The Nike shoe required the wearer to carry a separate hand pump to inflate the shoe. The Reebok shoe design included a pump tucked neatly into the shoe's tongue. Reebok's Pump was successful; Nike had to drop its shoe from the market.[8]

Much of the current focus on product design is to improve the performance of a product and to reduce the cost of producing it. Boeing did this when it designed the

Product design is an important product component for both goods and services.

fighter jet for the twenty-first century. The design was very innovative with an unusual modular wing, a front-mounted engine, and stealth capabilities. This design improved jet fighter performance, but it also significantly reduced production costs.[9]

Ford took a slightly different approach in designing the 1997 Taurus. It asked workers and engineers at Taurus factories to come up with ideas to make the car more cheaply without reducing performance. Most of the design changes are invisible to consumers and represent cost reductions of a $1 here and 50¢ there. The total savings per car amounted to about $180. Although this does not sound like much, the redesign will save Ford about $73 million a year.[10]

Product design is becoming increasingly important for all types of products, even low-cost ones. For example, Century Cuddle Tub & Huggy Bath is a baby bathtub. The company knew that it is difficult to bathe a newborn, since one hand has to hold the baby's head and the other the washcloth. So it designed a baby bathtub that consists of a simple hammock in the tub with a headrest to hold the baby's head securely. This leaves the parent's hands free to do the washing. The cost of the product is $19.99. As suggested by William Stumpf, a judge for the Industrial Design Excellence Awards, "Good design is now across all product lines, from computers to appliances."[11]

Building strong brands and protecting brand names and brand marks is critical for many firms. General Mills presents many of its successful brands in this trade ad.

Branding

It is critical that a firm identifies its products to distinguish them from similar products offered by competitors. This is the **branding** process. Several key terms need defining for this discussion:

- **Brand**—A name, term, sign, symbol, design, or combination that a firm uses to identify its products and differentiate them from those of competitors.

- **Brand name**—The element of a brand that can be vocalized, such as IBM, Tide, Snickers, or Diet Coke.

- **Brand mark**—The element of a brand that cannot be vocalized, such as the MGM lion, the Buick symbol, or the Texaco star.

- **Trademark**—A brand or part of a brand that is registered with the U.S. Patent and Trademark Office. This registration gives the owner exclusive right to use the brand and may even preclude other firms from using brand names or marks that are similar.

The global marketplace and new technologies are adding to the complexity of protecting brand names and brand marks. For example, Hilton Hotels Corp. owns U.S. rights to the Hilton name, but Ladbroke Group PLC of Britain controlled the name outside the United States. Unable to use the Hilton name for a series of luxury international hotels, Hilton Hotels branded them as Conrad International Hotels. Recently, Hilton and Ladbroke formed a strategic alliance and are using the Hilton name for U.S. and international hotels. In fact, Ladbroke changed its name to Hilton Group PLC.[12]

The increasing use of the Internet is causing similar problems. The publisher of a Web site called candyland.com was sued by the toy manufacturer Hasbro because it infringed on its trademarked Candy Land game. Hasbro won the suit and the Web site changed its name to adultplayground.com. Web site names can be protected by first registering them with the Internet Network Information Center. This will help to keep others from using a name that is already registered. But to get more complete protection, the name should be registered with the U.S. Patent and Trademark Office.[13] Additional protection for brands and trademarks on-line is now available due to the passage of the Anticybersquatting Consumer Protection Act. This law applies basic trademark law to the on-line world and provides on-line firms with a process to prosecute offenders.[14]

IMPORTANCE OF BRANDING   Branding is important to both consumers and marketers. From a consumer's viewpoint, branding facilitates buying. If there were no brands, consumers would have to evaluate the nonbranded products available every time they went shopping. They could never be sure they were purchasing the specific desired products and would have difficulty evaluating the quality of some. When selecting from among branded products, consumers can purchase specific ones and be reasonably certain of their quality. For example, one study found that 67 percent of consumers felt more confident buying familiar brands.[15]

Branding also provides psychological benefits to consumers. Some buyers derive satisfaction from owning brands with images of prestige. These brands convey status. Examples are Rolex watches, Mercedes-Benz automobiles, and Waterford crystal.

From a marketer's viewpoint, branding has considerable value. A brand differentiates a firm's product from those of competitors and helps to focus and facilitate marketing efforts. To build a strong brand, marketers need to first determine the brand identity. A **brand identity** is the brand concept from the brand owner's viewpoint. It should be relatively simple and clearly understood by everyone in the company. All marketing communications should be designed to support and reinforce this brand identity. Examples of effective brand identities are profit-with-a-principle (Body Shop); thicker, creamier, and pricier than any other ice cream on the market (Haagen-Dazs); and low-cost watch of excellent Swiss quality with a stylish, fun, youthful, provocative, and joyful brand personality (Swatch).[16]

BUILDING BRANDS   Because brands are important to consumers and marketers, many firms focus considerable attention to building brands. The basic brand-building process is depicted in Exhibit 8–6.

The first step in brand building typically focuses on generating brand awareness. **Brand awareness** is achieved when target consumers know about a brand and call it to mind when thinking about the product category. For example, Procter & Gamble has achieved brand awareness with Tide, which many consumers automatically recall when thinking about buying laundry detergent.

Brand awareness must then be translated into a **brand image,** or the impression that consumers have about a brand. Marketers should ensure that consumers have accurate ideas of the brand's advantages and positive impressions of it. P&G is successful if consumers perceive that Tide gets clothes cleaner than do competitive brands. Consumers' image of a brand should match the brand identity established by the company.

With a positive brand image established in their minds, some consumers will normally purchase Tide when shopping for laundry detergent. Such buyers exhibit **brand loyalty.** The most brand-loyal customers will select Tide on almost every purchasing opportunity.

The culmination of brand awareness, image, and loyalty is the development of **brand equity,** or the value that the brand has in the marketplace. Brand equity has

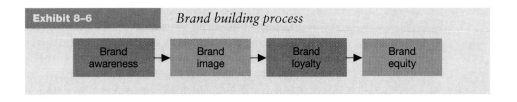

Exhibit 8–6   *Brand building process*

Brand awareness → Brand image → Brand loyalty → Brand equity

Exhibit 8-7   *Brands to watch—twenty-first century*

1. Amazon.com
2. America Online
3. Banana Republic
4. Dell
5. Dryel
6. ESPN (includes ESPN2, ESPN Magazine, ESPN Zone)
7. eBay
8. Excite@Home
9. Fidelity Investments
10. Tommy Hilfiger
11. Krispy Kreme

12. Lucent Technologies
13. Mountain Dew
14. Nickelodeon (includes Nick at Nite)
15. Nintendo
16. Nokia
17. Priceline.com
18. SBC Communications
19. Starbucks
20. Vanguard
21. Yahoo

—Republished with permission of The New York Times

a financial dimension, especially important in any merger or acquisition transaction. The financial value of P&G's Tide would be significant in any discussion of an acquisition price, for instance.

Brand equity also affects marketing efforts. The same marketing strategy and level of expenditures used for different brands are likely to have different results, depending on brand equity. Typically, marketing efforts built on an established positive brand awareness, image, and loyalty—or high brand equity—are more successful. Exhibit 8–7 presents examples of brands that are being built in the twenty-first century.

Many of the brands listed in Exhibit 8–7 are Internet companies. Building strong brands is extremely important to these companies. The typical approach is to focus efforts on media advertising to generate brand awareness, to develop a desired brand image, and to get consumers to visit their sites. This is important, but only part of the brand building process. Research indicates that strong brands are built on the favorable experiences consumers have with a firm's products and services. Effective advertising can only drive consumers to an Internet site or retail store or to try a product or service. Brand loyalty and brand equity depend on the experiences consumers have once at the Internet site, retail store, or when the product or service is purchased. Charles Schwab and eToys are examples of companies that have built strong brands by developing solid relationships through positive interactions with customers.[17]

Doris Christopher, President and Founder, The Pampered Chef, discusses the brand building process: "Building brands is important for many firms. In the direct-selling industry, to build a brand means to build a trusting relationship with customers. Customers will continue to buy products from companies with whom they have good experiences. The Pampered Chef believes in building brands through fulfilling promises. We make a promise to our customers that with every product we sell they will get the best quality product at the best price, with service that exceeds their expectations.

TYPES OF BRANDS Marketers must decide early on whether to brand a product, and if so, which type of brand to use. **Generics** are products that are not branded. They are labeled instead by their generic name and may be of lower quality and cost less than branded competitors. Usually, plain black-and-white labels identify the product by its generic name, such as peas, aluminum foil, or tomato soup.

In the pharmaceutical industry, generic products must meet the quality standards set by the Food and Drug Administration. Many doctors specify generic drugs in an effort to reduce the patient's costs. Indeed, pharmaceutical companies that once marketed only branded products are hopping on the generic bandwagon. Merck, for example, has established its West Point Pharma division to market generic pharmaceuticals for brands no longer protected by patents. It will continue to market its branded products through other divisions.

Private labels provide retailers the opportunity to charge low prices and earn high profit margins.

If a firm decides to brand its products, it can choose one of two types of brands. The first and most familiar type is a **manufacturer brand.** Sometimes referred to as a **national brand** or **regional brand,** it is sponsored by the manufacturer of the product. The manufacturer is responsible for the product's quality and marketing. Many firms, such as P&G, IBM, Gillette, and Xerox, use manufacturer brands for their products.

The other type is a **distributor brand.** Also called **store brand, private brand,** or **private label,** it is sponsored by a distributor such as a wholesaler or retailer. Although the manufacturer's name may be indicated somewhere on the label, the distributor is responsible for the product's quality and marketing. Familiar store brands are Craftsman tools (Sears) and President's Choice grocery products (Loblaw). Many distributors are introducing their own brands. The lower marketing costs for private-label brands make it possible for distributors to maintain high profit margins while charging lower prices than for manufacturer brands.

Intense competition today between manufacturer and distributor brands has been termed the *battle of the brands.* Initially, the mass-marketing power of large manufacturers gave them the edge in this battle. Recently, however, large retailers with tremendous amounts of consumer purchasing information have improved their position substantially.

The competition for market share involves the value provided to consumers. They typically perceive manufacturer brands as of higher quality than distributor brands. Yet, the quality and cost differences vary considerably. When consumers perceive large quality differences, manufacturer brands may provide the most value and are purchased. When consumers perceive small quality differences, then distributor brands may provide the best value and are purchased.

Federated Department Stores is one company that is trying to push private brands throughout its network of department stores. These private brands help to differentiate its stores from competitors and contribute to improved profitability. Instead of the typical 50 percent markup on manufacturer brands, Federated can take as much as an 80 percent markup on private labels and still give customers lower prices. Current private brands for Federated include Charter Club, Alfani, Arnold Palmer, Club Room, I.N.C., M.T., Studio, The Cellar, and Tools of the Trade.[18]

The battle between manufacturer and distributor brands is likely to intensify in the foreseeable future. Private-label sales are increasing more than those of manufacturer brands in many product categories.

CHOOSING A BRAND NAME   Choosing an effective brand name is an important decision for both manufacturer and distributor brands. The brand name communicates a great deal, which can facilitate brand awareness and brand image. In general, an effective brand name suggests something about the product's benefits; is easy to pronounce, recognize, and remember; is distinctive in some way; and can be translated into other languages.

Ideally, a brand name should help to communicate to consumers the major benefits of the firm's product. If this is achieved, the brand name helps to link brand awareness with brand image. As consumers become aware of the brand name, they begin to associate it with specific product benefits. Sometimes this association can make it difficult for companies to change strategies. Take the banking industry as an example. Many banks are trying to expand into different financial service areas, such as investment management and insurance. A problem is that many consumers perceive banks to be very conservative and not innovative, friendly, or aggressive. Thus, many banks either avoid using the word *bank* in their name or play down the *bank* part of their name. Examples include Chase Manhattan and Wells Fargo.[19]

Thinking Critically

The increasing attention given to private brands by many retailers is causing problems for manufacturer brands.

- What strategies would you recommend manufacturers employ in order to strengthen their brands and combat the increasing penetration of private brands?

- What strategies should retailers use to offer the best mix of manufacturer and private brands?

A brand name that is easy to pronounce, recognize, and remember helps in establishing brand awareness. The name should also be distinctive. Brand names that meet these criteria are Mustang, Kodak, and Crest. Sometimes a brand name can be effective and not really mean anything in real words. Manfred Gotta develops brand names using "artificial nomenclature." Names he has created for companies include Vitek (fitness products), Tornac (umbrellas), Dogstix (dog snacks), and Ernty (baby food). For cars, his specialty, he has come up with the Opel Calibra, Mazda Xedos, and Volkswagen Corrado. None of these brand names is a real word, but each communicates an image and is distinctive and easy to pronounce, recognize, and remember.[20]

A brand name should be translatable into different languages for global business. Many a firm has been embarrassed when introducing a brand name into a different language; others have been able to capitalize on effective brand names. For example, brands that translate well into Russian include Sony, Adidas, and Ford. As P&G introduces brands in Russia, it alters its usual names somewhat. Oil of Olay becomes Oil of Ulay, Tide becomes Ariel, and Pert Plus is Vidal Sassoon Wash & Go.[21]

An alternative to developing a brand name is licensing an existing name or logo. **Licensing** typically consists of the right to use a trademark in exchange for paying royalties on the sale of the licensed product. For example, Coors licensed the name of its upscale beer Irish Red from a long-defunct brewery.[22] A familiar use of licensing is putting a university's name or seal on different products. Sales of licensed university products are around $2.5 billion a year. Notre Dame and the University of Michigan are at the top in sales of licensed products.[23]

Another approach is **co-branding,** where two brand names are used on a product. The objective is to capitalize on the brand equity in each brand as a way to appeal to defined target markets more effectively. Co-branding has become commonplace in the credit card industry. For example, the Visa brand name is often combined with another brand name to focus on specific markets. The other brand might be another company trying to generate sales for its products, such as Ford, Traveler's Advantage, or Churchill Downs, or a nonprofit organization trying to generate revenue, such as your university or its alumni association. Another example of co-branding is the inclusion of "Intel Inside" on specific personal computer brands. Although there are similarities in many co-branding relationships, the details of each situation are typically negotiated and formalized into a contractual arrangement.

Co-branding combines two brand names on the same product. BOLData and Intel illustrate co-branding for a computer server.

Packaging

Packaging is an important component for many products. A *package* is the container or wrapper for a product. It typically includes a *label,* a printed description of the product on the package. Packaging is important to both consumers and distributors of a product. A product's package might perform a number of different functions, including protecting the product until consumed, storing the product until consumed, facilitating consumption of the product, promoting the product, and facilitating disposal of the product.

Because many retailers are self-service sellers, a product's package must communicate the brand's image and help to sell the product. Distinctive packages help capture the attention of consumers as they view competitive products. Both package

Packaging is an important component of many products. Black & Decker uses different packages for its different brands.

and label also provide important information that consumers use in evaluating competing brands.

Black & Decker markets Quantum tools to the do-it-yourself market and DeWalt tools to the professional market. The Quantum package is green to appeal to the dominantly masculine market and has a photograph of the product and the Black & Decker name prominently displayed on the package, because the Black & Decker name had credibility in the nonprofessional market. Packaging for the DeWalt products features a neon yellow background and black type and has no references to Black & Decker, since professionals do not associate the Black & Decker name with professional tools. The different packages have helped to increase sales of both brands by appealing to the targeted market segments.[24]

Innovations in packaging offer ways to differentiate brands that consumers might otherwise perceive as very similar. Whereas once all toothpaste brands were packaged in tubes, they now come in pumps, squeeze containers, and stand-up tubes. This new packaging accounts for almost 20 percent of toothpaste sales.[25] It is normally hard to sustain an advantage with new packages, however, because competitors are quick to imitate successful innovations.

An ecological concern is critical to packaging success in the current environment. Many consumers complain about packages that use too much material or material that is difficult to dispose of. Compact discs were introduced with excessive packaging, and many people remember the flap over McDonald's Styrofoam containers. Today, the CD industry uses a new standardized package that is much smaller than the original versions, and McDonald's now packages all its hamburgers in paper wrappers. L'eggs has replaced its plastic egg with a recyclable cardboard box; Kodak has eliminated its cardboard box. And P&G markets superconcentrated liquid detergents. There are many opportunities for marketers to develop innovative packages that help sell a brand, improve its function, and have environmental advantages.

Customer Service

The final product component is **customer service,** which describes the assistance provided to help a customer with the purchase or use of a product. Customer service applies to both goods and services. For example, a consumer purchasing phone lines from Bell South for a new home is buying the basic service of being able to communicate by phone from specified locations within the home. These are the basic features of the phone service. However, customer service concerns all the contacts the customer has with Bell South employees. This includes the person taking the order and the employee installing the phone line. For instance, customers might evaluate the service according to how well the service options were explained, whether the installer arrived on time, and whether the work was completed as promised.[26]

For many products, especially business goods, customer service differentiates competitors. One study found that the best customer service was provided by MCI, Nordstrom, Home Depot, American Express, Saturn, Lands' End, and Starbucks. These companies differentiate themselves from competitors by providing better customer service regardless of whether marketing goods or services.[27]

Providing exceptional customer service can give a firm a marketing advantage. Since competitors can quickly copy changes in basic product components, the key to success in many industries is beating the competition in customer service. An innovative customer service can sometimes provide exceptional and unique value to customers as indicated in "Earning Customer Loyalty: Thanking Customers."

Few things can help a firm more than giving customers exceptional service, even under trying conditions. An example will illustrate. The warehouse manager of Miller Business Systems received an order for 20 desks, 20 executive chairs, 40 side

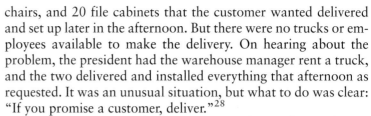

"OUR NEW DESK CLERK LENT HIS CUFF LINKS TO A GUEST FOR A CRUCIAL MEETING. INSTANTLY WE KNEW WE HIRED THE RIGHT GUY."

Bill Marriott

That's a true story. There are many others. They are just one of the many reasons frequent business travelers prefer Marriott. Call your travel agent or 1-800-228-9290.

Marriott
WE MAKE IT HAPPEN FOR YOU.

Providing exceptional customer service is one way to gain competitive advantage. Marriott celebrates how one employee did something exceptional to help a hotel guest.

chairs, and 20 file cabinets that the customer wanted delivered and set up later in the afternoon. But there were no trucks or employees available to make the delivery. On hearing about the problem, the president had the warehouse manager rent a truck, and the two delivered and installed everything that afternoon as requested. It was an unusual situation, but what to do was clear: "If you promise a customer, deliver."[28]

Important elements of customer service during the purchasing process include providing information about product alternatives, training in product use, and credit and financing services. Exceptional customer service prior to a purchase can produce competitive advantages. Consider the case of Curry Hardware in Boston. This small hardware store is located next to a huge Home Depot store that offers much lower prices. Curry thrives in this situation because it has lots of salespeople available to answer customers' "how to fix it" questions. Customers are willing to pay more to receive this valuable service.[29]

Important elements of customer service after the purchase include fast and reliable delivery, quick installation, accessible technical information and advice, repair services, and warranties. Sometimes just showing concern for customers after the sale can do wonders. An interesting example is Yolanda Eijgenstein, head of Wie Mailt Wat? (Who's Mailing What?) in Rotterdam. Her company collects, categorizes, and reports on every piece of direct mail in the Netherlands. Clients are mostly banks and consumer-product companies. After reports are sent to clients, she calls to see how they like the service. Most are astonished that she has called, and many place additional orders.[30]

Doris Christopher, President and Founder, The Pampered Chef, emphasizes the importance of providing customers with excellent service: "Selling a product is only the first step in building a relationship with customers. Many times when a customer takes home a product they are unsure how to use it. At The Pampered Chef we make sure this does not happen. At our Kitchen Shows, the customer has the opportunity to try the product before he or she buys it. We also ensure that once the customer gets the product home, they know how it will meet their needs in the kitchen. With each product we provide easy-to-read instructions detailing how to properly care for and use it, along with recipes that utilize the product. Our Kitchen Consultants also offer ongoing customer service and support after the sale."

The critical task facing marketers is to combine quality, design, branding, packaging, and customer service components into an effective product offering. A product must meet the needs of the target market and also have advantages over competitors on important product components. Moreover, businesses must constantly be ready to alter product components to adapt to a dynamic marketing environment.

Earning Customer Loyalty

Thanking customers

Surprisingly few companies thank their best customers for doing business with them. The Sunset Station, a casino and hotel in Henderson, Nevada, wanted to stick out from the crowd by thanking their most loyal customers in an innovative way. The hotel invited 25,000 of its most loyal customers to "Free Hug Friday." More than 5,000 customers attended. Each customer received a mug full of Hershey's Kisses and hugs from the hotel's executive team.

Since this was the first "Free Hug Friday," customers did not know what to expect. The friendly atmosphere was a

pleasant surprise. Brad Goldberg, Sunset's vice president of marketing, came up with the idea for "Free Hug Friday." It was a big success according to Brad: "I've gotten personal cards and letters saying how much they enjoyed it." The company plans to repeat the event next year and will probably see many of these appreciated customers throughout the year.

Source: Tricia Campbell, "Cozying Up to Customers," *Sales and Marketing Management,* December 1999, p. 15.

Summary

1. **Understand the differences between goods and services.** Products can be viewed as a continuum, with goods at one end and services at the other. Goods are physical products; services are nonphysical products. Goods are more tangible, perishable, separable, and standardized than services. Most products represent a mixture of goods and services.

2. **Differentiate between consumer and business products, and discuss the different types of each.** Consumer products are those purchased by consumers for their personal use. Business products are those purchased by a firm for its own use.

   Different types of consumer products include convenience, shopping, and specialty products, which differ in the amount of shopping consumers are willing to undertake. Consumers are not willing to shop for convenience products, will shop to make the best purchase for shopping products, and will shop to purchase a specific product for specialty products.

   Business products include capital, production, and operational products. Capital products are expensive goods that do not become part of a company's finished product. Production goods become part of a finished product; operational goods are used in a company's operations but do not become part of a finished product.

3. **Recognize that marketers need to appreciate the perspective of the consumer.** People purchase products to satisfy needs or solve problems. They perceive products as bundles of benefits that can help them satisfy needs or solve problems. To view products from the customer's perspective, marketers must focus on the benefits that product components provide to customers.

4. **Define and discuss the importance of product quality, product design, branding, packaging, and customer service.** Marketers need to look at products as consisting of various components that provide benefits to consumers. The major components are product quality, product design, branding, packaging, and customer service. Product quality could be described as an assessment of how well a product does what it is supposed to do from the customer's viewpoint. Product design includes how the product looks and feels, and how easy it is to assemble and use.

   Branding describes the way a firm identifies its products from those offered by competitors. Packaging addresses the container or wrapper for a product and any labeling that might be provided. Customer service refers to any activity intended to facilitate the purchasing or use of a product.

5. **Explain how the different product components need to be integrated to meet the needs of customers.** Marketers must integrate all product components to offer the bundle of benefits desired by customers. Marketers can achieve competitive advantages by skillfully mixing the different product components into an effective, complete product offering.

Understanding Marketing Terms and Concepts

Thinking About Marketing

1. What are the basic differences between goods and services?
2. Why is it important to differentiate between consumer and business products and among different types of each?
3. Refer to "Being Entrepreneurial: Food on the Internet." How do these companies represent a blend of goods and services?
4. Refer to "Earning Customer Loyalty: Thanking Customers." What are other things firms can do to thank their best customers?
5. Why is brand equity important?
6. Explain what product quality is. Why might it be important to your classmates?
7. Explain how firms can develop competitive advantages through customer service.
8. How does a global perspective affect product component decisions?
9. Why is it important to take an ecological perspective toward packaging?
10. Why is a customer value perspective toward customer service important?

Applying Marketing Skills

1. Go to a large chain supermarket. Select any one specific product and identify the manufacturer brands, distributor brands, and generics that this store stocks. List each specific brand under each type and compare the product components for each. Summarize your findings to report the results.
2. Assume you have developed a new type of microwave popcorn that tastes as good as competitive products but takes only half the time to prepare. Develop a manufacturer brand name for this product. Compare the name you have chosen with brand names for other microwave popcorn brands. Discuss why you think your brand name will be effective.
3. Look through the ads in the local newspaper. Identify all the examples of customer service you find. Summarize your findings into a list of the ways marketers are using customer service to differentiate their products.

Using the www in Marketing

Activity One   Go to Frito-Lay's home page (http://www.fritolay.com).

1. For most consumers, are Frito-Lay's products convenience, shopping, or specialty products? Citing evidence from the Web site, is Frito-Lay's marketing strategy consistent with your classification?
2. How would you evaluate the brand names of Frito-Lay products? Which are the best? Why?
3. How does this Web site help Frito-Lay provide added value to customers and retailers?

Activity Two   The most obvious examples of product design are for physical goods such as cars and home appliances. However, product design is also important for services. View the following Web sites:

Yahoo! (http://www.yahoo.com)
SNAP (http://www.snap.com)

1. How does product design apply to these services?
2. Compare the design of each of these sites.
3. What recommendations do you have to improve the design of each site?

Making Marketing Decisions

Case 8-1 Fed Ex and UPS: Competing Electronically and Globally

 Federal Express and UPS are major competitors in the express-delivery business. Each offers similar services to individual and business customers. Marketing strategies for both firms have focused on pricing and advertising in recent years. But the development of new technologies is changing the basis for competition.

Both companies are using technology to facilitate communication with customers and to allow customers to track shipments electronically. The services available from each can be viewed on the Web: Federal Express—http://www.fedex.com; and UPS—http://www.ups.com.

Growth in the overnight shipping business in the United States is slowing down. Fed Ex, UPS, and the

United States Postal Service (USPS) all report slower growth in overnight shipments during the past year. Interestingly, the effect of the Internet on this business is mixed. On the positive side, increases in purchases over the Internet are increasing business because these purchases must be shipped to homes or offices. UPS is getting a large share of this business. One study indicated that UPS shipped 55 percent of items bought on the Internet last Christmas, compared with 32 percent for USPS, and 10 percent for Fed Ex. On the negative side, the Internet is reducing business in several areas. Documents, data, photographs, and other similar parcels that were once sent overnight are now being sent electronically. These can be sent more quickly and easily as e-mail or e-mail attachments, reducing the demand for overnight shipments.

The companies are focusing more attention on growth opportunities in international markets. Several likely developments will make this international business easier. First, trade ministers from 34 countries recently agreed to a Free Trade Area of the Americas (FTAA) to develop and implement procedures that would expedite customs clearance for express shipments. Second, the World Trade Organization (WTO) met to launch the Millennium Round of global trade talks and is expected to consider an agreement similar to the FTAA. Third, Hong Kong is contemplating separate regulations for air cargo and passenger air traffic. All of these measures would facilitate the growth of international express cargo business.

Both UPS and Fed Ex are emphasizing international business. Fed Ex is performing especially well with its premium global service, International Priority. UPS raised around $5 billion from its recent IPO and is investing aggressively in the international business, such as international operations facilities in Louisville.

Questions

1. Describe the general product components for Fed Ex and UPS.

2. Visit each company's Web site and compare the electronic services offered to customers.

3. What changes in product components might Federal Express or UPS have to make to be successful in the new Internet world?

4. What strategy would you recommend UPS use to obtain a stronger competitive position globally than that of Federal Express?

SOURCES: Kevin G. Hall, "FTAA Efforts to Ease Restraints May Surface at WTO Meeting," *Journal of Commerce,* November 8, 1999, p. 19; Joseph Lo, "Fed Ex Chief Seeks Change to Air Cargo Operations," *South China Morning Post,* November 6, 1999, p. 3; and David Rocks, "UPS: Will It Deliver?" *Business Week,* November 15, 1999, p. 41.

Case 8-2 Oink Oink: Building a Brand Name

Miles Handy has built a $10 million pet food company by turning pigs' ears into a dog snack. He came across the idea almost by accident. Five years ago he returned from a pet-food industry trade show in Germany with a roasted pig ear. His beagle, Heide, gobbled it up even though she did not normally like dog treats. Based on this experience, Miles decided to start a business.

Instead of importing the pig ears from Germany, he decided to produce them. The process consisted of buying cast-off pig ears for 15¢ a pound and roasting them in his own smokehouse. Heide served as the official taste-tester. Since the establishment of Oink Oink, Inc., in 1991, sales are about one million pig ears each month, produced in five smokehouses.

A large part of the company's success is due to effective marketing. Realizing that consumers might not want to buy slimy pig ears, the ears were enclosed in colorful packages decorated with playful pigs and pooches. He used the brand name Oinkers for the pig ears. This has helped to generate brand awareness. A nationwide contest is in progress to select a board of advisers for Heide. Pet owners from across the country are writing letters indicating why their pets love Oinkers.

Oink Oink has introduced a few other products, such as Pork Tenderloin. However, the company has had some problems with the Agriculture Department because it must be made clear that these products are not for human consumption. Despite this, Miles expects his company to continue to grow. Competition is heating up due to the success of Oinkers.

Questions

1. What are the important product components of Oinkers?

2. What role does packaging play in the marketing of Oinkers?

3. How would you evaluate Oinkers as a brand name?

4. What strategies would you recommend to increase customer loyalty to Oinkers?

SOURCE: Tom Stein, "Build a Brand Name," *Success,* July/August 1996, p. 28.

Chapter Nine

Developing New Products and Services

After studying this chapter, you should be able to:

1. Recognize the different types of new products.

2. Discuss the different sources of new products.

3. Understand the stages in the new-product development process.

4. Describe the way marketing research is used in the new-product development process.

5. Appreciate the keys to new-product success.

www.3m.com

3M Worldwide - Microsoft Internet Explorer

File Edit View Favorites Tools Help

Address http://www.3m.com/

Explore 3M around the world
Select a country Go >

Creating solutions for
business, industry, and home

3M Worldwide

About 3M
Learn about our culture of
innovation or read the
latest financial reports.
More...

3M Innovation
When you need to make
snow, 3M markers show
where to go. More...

Copyright 3M 1999 | Legal information | Privacy policy

The 3M Web site is consistent with the innovative nature of the firm. 3M is a $15 billion company with more than 70,000 employees who create, manufacture, and sell 50,000 products in 200 countries around the world. The company has operations in 60 countries and the Web site provides a menu for accessing information about 3M in specific countries and offers that information in different languages. Some of 3M's products, such as Scotch Magic Tape, are well-known brands purchased by individual consumers and organizations. Other products are components for automobiles and computers purchased only by business customers.

The real distinguishing characteristic of 3M is its continuous emphasis on innovation. One of the company's major objectives is to generate 30 percent of each year's sales from products that are less than four years old. This means that 3M must continually develop and introduce successful new products.

Thus, one of the driving principles at 3M is "the promotion of entrepreneurship and insistence upon freedom in the workplace to pursue innovative ideas."

The 3M innovation culture is evident throughout its Web site. One section is entitled "Our Pioneers." This section profiles over 20 inventors and the inventions that led to successful 3M products. Another section presents a timeline history of 3M, with a special emphasis on the important innovations that have driven the company's growth since its inception.

In addition to being a leader in innovation, 3M tries to be a good corporate citizen; specific 3M initiatives to protect the environment are thus also presented and discussed on their Web site. The company also practices social responsibility by supporting community efforts to improve education as well as to further economic and social development. **Source:** www.3m.com, January 12, 2000.

3M provides an especially interesting example of the importance of new-product development. If the company generates 30 percent of sales from products less than four years old, then over $4 billion of its $15 billion total sales come from relatively new products. To meet this objective year after year, 3M must continuously churn out new products and effectively market many of them. New products are clearly the key to 3M's growth and success.

In this chapter we examine new-product development. We begin by discussing the types and sources of new products. Then, we discuss the various stages of the new-product development process. Finally, we suggest several keys for successful new-product development.

New-Product Overview

Developing successful new products drives sales and profit growth for many companies. One study found that companies leading their industries in profitability and sales growth gain 49 percent of their revenues from products developed in the most recent five years. Companies at the bottom in sales and profit growth achieve only 11 percent of sales from new products.[1]

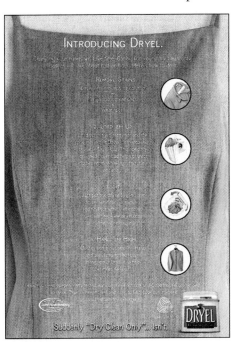

New-product development is a key element of success for many firms. Dryel is a new product to help consumers care for their clothes.

Another study of 2,000 companies predicted that new products would account for 37 percent of total sales by the year 2000, up from the then-current level of 28 percent.[2] This seems reasonable since companies often set specific goals for new products. We have already mentioned 3M's new-product goals. Rubbermaid is an additional example. Rubbermaid wants to enter a new-product category every 12 to 18 months and expects to get 33 percent of sales from products introduced within the past five years.[3]

Companies also use new products to try to gain market share from competitors. Take the fast-food industry. Total industry sales are slowly declining. Major industry players, such as McDonald's, Burger King, and Wendy's, are engaged in fierce competition to grow in this declining industry. The introduction of new products is one strategy they are trying, but with mixed results. Wendy's stuffed pita sandwich was one of the most successful new products in the fast-food industry and helped increase sales at existing Wendy's restaurants. McDonald's, on the other hand, spent around $250 million to capture sales from adults with its Arch Deluxe hamburger. The product was a failure because it did not generate the growth desired by McDonald's.[4]

Despite the importance of developing new products, a large percentage of them fail. One study of 11,000 new products launched by 77 manufacturing, service, and consumer products companies reported that only 56 percent of these products were still on the market five years later.[5] Other studies have suggested the failure rate is even higher, maybe up to 80 percent. Whatever the exact figure, new-product failures are costly. The failures of Ford's Edsel, Du Pont's Corfam, Polaroid's Polarvision, RCA's Videodisc, Cadillac's Allante, and IBM's PCjr cost each company millions.

These and other costly failures motivate companies to take a *productivity perspective* toward new-product development. The aim is to decrease the percentage of new-product failures, reduce the cost of development, and shorten the time required to get new products to market. These objectives drive most of the changes companies are making in the new-product development process. Herman Miller, for example, incorporated customers, cross-functional teams, and computer software to develop new office furniture that satisfies customer needs. This approach shortened the new-product development cycle by 50 percent, lowered costs substantially, and led to an 11 percent sales increase in a sluggish market.[6] A study of consumer product manufacturers found that most are shortening product development time to meet the needs of retailers. Study results indicated that 36 percent had one- to

Speaking from Experience

L.A. Mitchell is Account Executive for Large Business Accounts at Lucent Technologies. She has worked on developing sales forecasts for new and existing products, developed marketing plans for various sales teams, and currently assists local phone companies in marketing communications features to large business accounts. L.A. earned her M.S. in Marketing from Colorado State University. She emphasizes the importance of shortening the time required to get new products to the market.

L. A. Mitchell
Account Executive for Large
Business Accounts
Lucent Technologies

"Getting new products to market quickly is critical to success in today's business environment. If you can't be the first to market, you run the risk of your competitor being several jumps ahead by the time you introduce a new me-too product. Small, innovative companies with first-to-market products often find themselves acquired by larger companies who are willing to pay high premiums for the advantages of early market entry. The challenge Lucent faces in the communication industry is in being able to take advantage of technological advancements while not forcing your customer to continuously replace costly infrastructure. The difficulty lies in anticipating technological advances and being able to integrate them into existing products. Lucent is no longer just in the business of producing telephones. Today, we must compete in unfamiliar industries such as cable, the Internet, and wireless data transmission."

three-month development cycles, 36 percent had three- to six-month cycles, and 28 percent took six months to a year for new-product development.[7]

Types of New Products

At first glance, defining a new product would seem to be easy. Yet, the term *new* can be defined from different vantage points and in a number of ways. The first issue is, new to whom? The first time a customer uses a product, it is a new product to him or her, even if it has been available and used by others for a long time. In this case, though the product newness affects the customer's purchasing behavior and the firm's marketing strategies, it does not have a major impact on an organization's new-product development process.

What does directly affect this process is how new the product is to the organization. And even from an organizational perspective, there are degrees of newness. Exhibit 9–1 presents several categories of new products, organized by how new they are to the company developing and marketing the product.

New-to-the-world products are the only ones that are new to both consumers and organizations. These products have never been offered before to any group of consumers; and if successful, they spawn a completely new industry. Obvious examples are the introduction of the first car leading to today's automobile industry, the first airplane and the aircraft and airline industries, and the first microcomputer and the personal computer industry.

The other types of new products in Exhibit 9–1 describe products new to the marketing firm but not new to some other firms or to consumers. From the firm's point of view, the product could be a new-category entry, an addition to an existing product line, an improvement to an existing product, or a new use of an existing product.

A large percentage of new products introduced each year are in the less innovative categories, particularly in many consumer product areas. One study found that of the 15,866 health, beauty, household, food, and pet products introduced, nearly 70 percent were different varieties, formulations, sizes, or packages of existing brands; only 5.7 percent of new products in these categories represented breakthroughs in technology, formulation, packaging, or even positioning.[8]

New-to-the-world products create new industries. The Kelly-Springfield Tire Company was established when the automobile was introduced to replace travel by horse with travel by car.

Exhibit 9–1	*Types of new products*

- **New-to-the-world products:** Product inventions, such as Polaroid instant camera, the first car, rayon, the laser printer, in-line skates.
- **New-category entries:** Products new to the firm, but not to the world, such as P&G's first shampoo, Hallmark gift items, AT&T's Universal Card.
- **Additions to product lines:** Line extensions or flankers on the firm's current markets, such as Tide Liquid detergent, Chrysler K cars.
- **Product improvements.** Current products made better; virtually every product on the market today has been improved, often many times.
- **Repositionings:** Products retargeted for a new use or application, such as Kellogg's Frosted Flakes cereal (now targeted to adults), and pork repositioned by National Pork Producers in recent years from being similar to beef to being the "other white meat."

Source: Adapted from C. Merle Crawford, *New Products Management,* 4th ed. (Burr Ridge, IL: Richard D. Irwin, 1994), p. 11.

Some companies are involved in all of the new-product categories. Sony, for example, introduces around 1,000 new products each year, about 4 every business day. About 800 of these are improved versions of existing products. Typically, improvements consist of new features, better performance, or a lower price. The other 200 Sony products are aimed at creating new markets. They may not all be completely new to the world, but they are very innovative. Recent examples include Data Discman, PalmTop, and Mini Disc.[9]

Moving down the list of product types from new-to-the-world products to repositionings, the product is less new to the firm. This means that its development and introduction is less risky too, because the firm is building on areas of experience. Lower risk also typically makes the new-product development process shorter and less rigorous.

Remember that in our discussion of the new-product development process we use the general term *product* to refer to both goods and services as well as to consumer and business products. The stages in the new-product development process generally apply to all types of products. Examples throughout the chapter include goods, services, and consumer and business products.

Sources of New Products

Firms can obtain new products in a number of ways, with the two extremes being through external sourcing or through internal development. **External sourcing** is any approach by which a firm receives either ownership of another organization's products or the right to market the products of another organization. In such a case, products are new to the firm but not to consumers.

A number of alternative arrangements describe external sourcing. In an acquisition, the buying firm purchases another firm to obtain ownership of all the latter's products. The buying firm owns these products and may either merge them into its existing operations or allow the acquired firm to continue current operations. Newell Rubbermaid represents a good example of this approach. The Newell Co. started as a drapery hardware manufacturer. Since the 1960s, the company has acquired 75 consumer product companies. During the 1990s, the company made 18 major acquisitions adding $2 billion in sales. The most noteworthy was the acquisition of Rubbermaid completed in March 1999. This acquisition led the company to change its name to Newell Rubbermaid. Newell Rubbermaid generates sales in excess of $6 billion annually by manufacturing and marketing consumer products through mass retailers and home centers. Its acquisitions over the years have added many new products into the corporate family, such as Rubbermaid plastic products, Anchor Hocking glassware, Levelor blinds, and Rolodex files.[10]

Sometimes a firm purchases only specific brands from another firm. This approach is often used to enter international markets. For example, Colgate-Palmolive purchased all of S. C. Johnson's liquid hand-and-body soap brands in Europe and the South Pacific. Sales of these brands were about $75 million. The purchase was

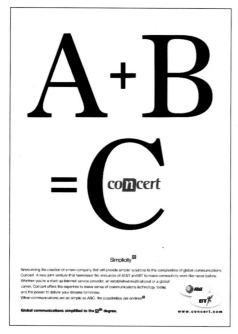

Collaborative ventures are an increasingly important approach for developing new products, AT&T celebrates the formation of a collaborative venture with BT to offer new global communications products.

viewed as a quick means for Colgate-Palmolive to add new products for the European and South Pacific markets.[11]

Other arrangements can be classified as some type of **collaborative venture.** Collaborative ventures allow two or more firms to share in the rights to market specified products. Often-used collaborative arrangements include strategic partnerships, strategic alliances, joint ventures, and licensing agreements. Although the specifics may vary considerably, in every case there is some agreement that allows a firm to market products new to it.

The French pharmaceutical company Sanofi SA has used this approach very successfully. Sanofi has about 30 new drugs under development, with each costing up to $400 million. It cannot afford to spend this amount of money on product development. So its strategy is to find partners that will share in the development costs of a product for a license to sell the product when, and if, it is approved. These collaborative ventures allow Sanofi and partners to share the risks and rewards of new-product development.[12]

Internal development means that a firm develops new products itself. The firm may work with other firms for some parts of the process; it might subcontract product design, engineering, or test marketing to other firms. Or it might work in partnership with another firm throughout the entire process. The key point is that in internal development the firm is directly involved in the development of a new product, even though it may not accomplish every step by itself. An interesting approach to helping firms develop new products is presented in "Being Entrepreneurial: A New-Product Museum."

Internal development is riskier than acquiring new products from external sources. A firm developing new products assumes all or most of the costs and risks involved. When acquiring through external sources, a firm purchases or receives the rights to sell products that have a history in the market. External sourcing requires a firm to identify products of other firms, make the necessary agreements to obtain the desired products, and market them. Many firms use both external sourcing and internal development for new products.

New-Product Development Process

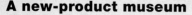

The new-product development process can be conceived as consisting of the seven stages presented in Exhibit 9–2.[13] The process is presented as a logical series of steps for discussion purposes. In reality, the lines between each step are often blurred as companies are in-

Being Entrepreneurial

A new-product museum

Jean and Robert McMath have established the New Products Showcase & Learning Center in Ithaca, New York. This new-product museum contains over 65,000 consumer products organized by categories such as foods, beverages, health, beauty, and household products. The collection includes 57 different kinds of chutney, 87 assorted nectars, 67 mildew removers, and 82 flea-and-tick repellents. The McMaths get test-marketed consumer items and new-product samples from stores and trade shows across the country.

The museum is the foundation for the McMath's new-product consulting business. The couple helps large and

small companies with new-product development. Their focus is on the history of failed products. The idea is that if companies understand the history of failed products in their industry, the firms are more likely to avoid mistakes made by other companies in the past. The McMath's also share their new-product knowledge with clients, and Mr. McMath co-authored a book with Thom Forbes entitled *What Were They Thinking? Marketing Lessons I've Learned from Over 80,000 New-Product Innovations and Idiocies.*

Source: Louis Jacobson, "Dream Keepers," *The Wall Street Journal Interactive Edition,* September 27, 1999, pp. 1–7.

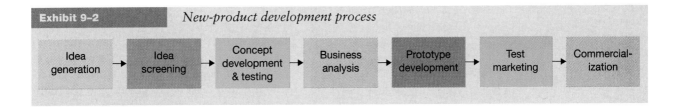

Exhibit 9-2 *New-product development process*

| Idea generation | → | Idea screening | → | Concept development & testing | → | Business analysis | → | Prototype development | → | Test marketing | → | Commercial-ization |

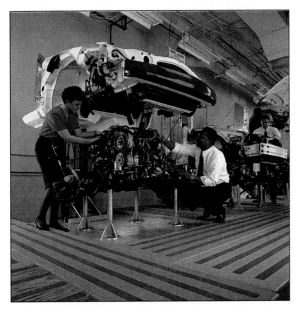

Reducing new-product development time can produce a competitive advantage for many firms. Ford's World Class Timing process has trimmed the time from design studio to showroom by 25 percent.

volved in different stages at the same time; sometimes they even eliminate specific stages. Also, the specific process for any one product will vary by company, industry, and type of new product.

Two issues related to the new-product development process deserve some discussion. First, as a firm moves from one step in the process to the next, costs increase substantially. A major objective is to weed out potential failures as early as possible without eliminating products that might be successful. This is a difficult balancing act, but one that cannot be avoided. Rigorous analysis to evaluate products at each stage and to determine which warrant further attention can help firms be both productive and successful in developing new products. Because of this, each stage requires a "go" or "no-go" decision. And since approximately 46 percent of new-product development costs are wasted on products that ultimately fail, firms must make such decisions as early as possible.[14]

The second issue of note is that the traditional approach to new-product development has been a functional, linear process as shown in Exhibit 9–3. Typically each functional area works on specific stages of a process in isolation. When one step is concluded, the results go to the following functional area for the next step. For example, R&D might conceive a product idea and give it to the design function, which would design the product. Design passes it to engineering, which develops engineering specifications and gives it to manufacturing to produce. Manufacturing produces the product and gives it to marketing to sell. Although this type of approach has resulted in some successes, the process can be very slow and costly.

Many firms have improved the new-product development process by adopting a multifunctional, simultaneous approach as shown in Exhibit 9–3. This approach requires all relevant functions to work together during all stages, with several steps typically performed simultaneously. Some firms benefit from including suppliers, distributors, customers, and other interest groups.

3M has formalized this approach through its Pacing Plus initiative. This initiative is intended to accelerate the development of high-impact new products and bring them to market faster. Criteria for qualifying for the Pacing Plus program are new-product development projects that change the basis for competition in new or existing markets, offer large sales and profit potential, receive priority access to 3M resources, operate in an accelerated time frame, and employ the best available commercialization processes. About 25 Pacing Plus programs are underway for products ranging from microflex circuits for electronic products to films that increase the brightness of notebook computer screens.[15]

Boeing is another company implementing a teamwork approach. After losing billions of dollars in the past, the airline industry wants planes that cost less and operate more efficiently. Boeing is developing new planes with these characteristics by grouping experts from design, manufacturing, maintenance, finance, and marketing into new-product development teams. The 737X, a passenger jet, is one result of this teamwork approach.[16]

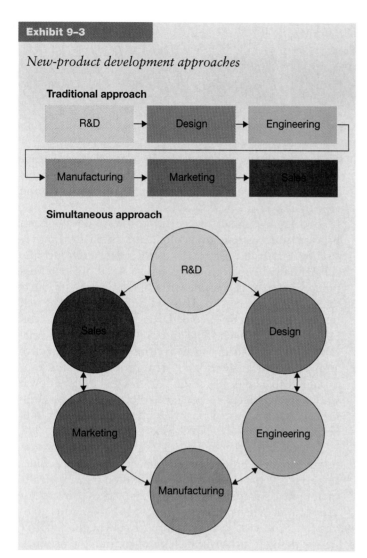

Exhibit 9-3

New-product development approaches

Traditional approach

R&D → Design → Engineering

Manufacturing → Marketing → Sales

Simultaneous approach

R&D
Design
Engineering
Manufacturing
Marketing
Sales

Idea Generation

Idea generation is the initial stage of the new-product-development process. A new product begins as someone's idea. Firms typically generate a large number of ideas relative to the number of successful products introduced. One study reported that 13 new-product ideas were needed for every successful new product.[17]

Ideas for new products can come from different methods and sources. Analyzing the products offered by competitors can generate ideas for new products or improvements in existing products. Typically, these ideas are ways to differentiate a firm's new product from competitive offerings. Ford used this approach in designing its new Mercury Mystique. The company evaluated the characteristics of the Honda Accord, Pontiac Grand Am, Mazda 626, Nissan Altima, and Mitsubishi Galant. As a result of this analysis, the Mystique is larger, roomier, and much easier to maintain than competing cars. Its engine needs a tune-up only every 100,000 miles.[18]

By watching customers use existing products, firms can generate ideas for new products. Employees at John Deere visit dealers and farmers to observe their products in use and to talk about potential problems. These visits often produce ideas for improved products for farmers or better ways to service John Deere dealers.[19] Karen Bertiger wanted to place a cellular call from the Bahamas to her home in Arizona, but she could not get through. She asked Bary Bertiger, her husband and vice president of the satellite systems group for Motorola, why the cellular phone won't work everywhere. Because of his wife's question, he came up with the idea to create a satellite-based wireless-telephone system that would allow anyone to call anybody from anywhere in the world. Over 10 years and $5 billion later, the system is called Iridium.[20]

In addition, technological developments can be a useful source of new-product ideas. Firms think about ways they might transform emerging technologies into successful new products. Even the government is getting into the act. Government agencies of all types are introducing a growing number of electronic services. It is the beginning of the e-government era. The state of Georgia offers citizens the opportunity to purchase hunting, fishing, and boating licenses over the Internet. College students can apply for financial aid from an Education Department student aid Web site. The National Science Foundation is currently conducting a study of the feasibility of "cybervoting." These new electronic services provide convenience to citizens while also reducing the cost of government. For example, Maryland saved $1.6 million when 250,000 professionals renewed their annual licenses on-line.[21]

Employees often suggest ideas for new products, and some firms reward them for doing so. Since salespeople have the most direct contact with customers, some companies motivate them through rewards for reporting new-product ideas to their managers.[22] Creative group methods, such as brainstorming, to stimulate thinking about new-product ideas are also useful. Sharing information and ideas can also be valuable, especially across international markets. For example, Pillsbury invites executives to training sessions to swap ideas. One success from this approach is the dulce de leche flavor for its Häagen-Dazs ice cream. This supersweet, butterscotch-like flavor was developed and introduced at the only Häagen-Dazs store in Buenos Aires. It immediately became the store's best seller. When this idea was presented at a training session, Häagen-Dazs executives from the United States and Europe decided to introduce the new flavor in their markets. It has been a terrific success in both markets. In the United States, dulce de leche sells better than any flavor except vanilla, with monthly sales in excess of $1 million.[23]

L.A. Mitchell, Account Executive for Large Business Accounts, Lucent Technologies, discusses sources for new product ideas: "New-product ideas can come from just about anywhere. Lucent has entire organizations whose sole function is to continually explore and develop new-product ideas. These organizations frequently employ focus groups, surveys, and other marketing research techniques to generate new ideas. Some of the best ideas come from needing to solve a significant customer problem. For example, the increase in automobile accidents due to people talking on cell phones while driving has generated many ideas for new products and features. Some of these include products that allow cell phones to be used "hands free" and new features that make it possible to dial a number by simply speaking the name of the person or business you wish to call."

Idea Screening

Since the idea-generation stage is relatively inexpensive, the major objective is to create a large pool of ideas for potential new products. The purpose of **idea screening** is to evaluate the idea pool and reduce it to a smaller and more attractive set of potential new products. The ideas should be screened for consistency with company vision and strategic objectives, potential market acceptance, fit with firm's capabilities, and possible long-term contribution to profit. A major objective is to eliminate as early as possible ideas that have little chance of resulting in successful new products. Ideas that remain after screening move to the next stage in the new-product development process.

A popular idea-screening approach is to use a checklist. The basic procedure is to identify the factors that are important to a firm and to evaluate each new-product idea against each factor. Adding the individual factor scores for each idea produces an overall idea-screening score. The higher this score, the better the new-product idea. Sometimes firms have a cutoff score; they drop ideas scoring below the cutoff and retain those scoring above for further development. Or companies might rank the idea-screening scores from highest to lowest and focus efforts on the ideas with the highest scores.

Exhibit 9–4 presents an example of a checklist used by 3M. 3M decided that customer need, competition, technology, marketing, manufacturing, price versus competition, and performance versus competition are important factors. The company rates ideas against each factor on a scale ranging from zero to five. The individual factor ratings are then summed to produce a total score. As shown in the exhibit, the idea is evaluated very high on each factor, for a total score of 30. On the basis of this score, a go decision is likely. If the score had been very low, say 15, the new-product idea would not have been developed any further.

Concept Development and Testing

Concept development is the process of shaping and refining the idea into a more complete product concept. In the generation and screening stages, the product idea is typically very general, perhaps a soft drink with added nutrients for health-conscious consumers or a direct-mail service for marketing textbooks to students. The evaluation of product ideas to this point is generally done by people within the firm, with little if any assessment by potential customers.

The major objective of concept development and testing is to formalize product concepts and have them evaluated by potential customers. Formalizing the product concept means describing the basic product idea in detail. This usually entails describing all of the product's components, including its projected price. If possible, a picture of the product should be included with the concept description. Exhibit 9–5 presents a product concept for a new healthful soft drink.

Thinking Critically

Identify a new product you think has the potential to be successful. Develop a concept statement for this new product with at least two variations of the product. If possible, draw pictures of each product variation. Then develop a short concept test and administer it to at least five other students. Evaluate the results of this exercise:

- What information did the concept test provide?
- Given this information, what would you do next if you really wanted to develop and market this new product?

Exhibit 9–4	*3M's idea-screening checklist*

	Scale							Rating
Factor	**0**	**1**	**2**	**3**	**4**	**5**		
CUSTOMER NEED		Nice		Definte utility		Critical		5
COMPETITION		Many		Limited		None		4
TECHNOLOGY		None in 3M		Within 3M		Within ISD*		4
MARKETING		None in 3M		Tape Group		ISD		5
MANUFACTURING		None in 3M		Equipment modification		Existing equipment		4
PRICE VERSUS COMPETITION		Competitive advantage		Neutral		Strong 3M		3
PERFORMANCE VERSUS COMPETITION		Strong competitive		Neutral		Strong 3M		5
*Industrial Specialties Division.						Total		30

Source: James J. McKeown, "New Products from New Techologies," *Journal of Business and Industrial Marketing,* Winter-Spring 1990, p. 70.

Exhibit 9–5	*Product concept test*

NEW HEALTHFUL SOFT DRINK

This new drink is as refreshing and thirst-quenching as a normal soft drink, but much more healthful. It contains only natural ingredients. Three 12-ounce cans contain the normal vitamin and mineral daily requirements for an average adult. The drink will be available in several fruit flavors, will be clear in appearance, and will be packaged in recyclable aluminum cans. The cost of a 12-ounce can will be 69¢.

1. **How likely are you to buy this product?**
   Definitely would buy _____
   Probably would buy _____
   Might or might not buy _____
   Probably would not buy _____
   Definitely would not buy _____

2. **What do you like the most about this product?**

3. **How could this product be improved?**

   Concept tests are then used to get potential customers to evaluate the product concept. Sometimes multiple variations of the basic product concept are provided, so consumers can indicate which they like best. In other cases (see Exhibit 9–5), consumers are asked to respond to various questions about only one product concept. Besides assessing the concept provided to them, consumers are usually given an opportunity to suggest improvements. Concept tests are most often conducted as personal interviews, but they can be performed through mail surveys.

   If the concept tests indicate a low level of consumer acceptance and low likelihood of purchase, the firm makes a no-go decision. If the tests indicate a high level of consumer acceptance and high probability of purchase, the firm makes a go decision. The results of the tests may also provide ideas for revising the concept to better meet the needs of consumers.

Business Analysis

Ideas that survive concept development and testing are subjected to detailed business analysis. The **business analysis** stage of the new-development process calls for preparing initial marketing plans for the product. This requires developing a tentative marketing strategy and estimating expected sales, costs, and profitability for the product. A product idea reaching this point has passed general company screening criteria and been accepted by consumers. The purpose of the business analysis is to determine if it makes business sense to introduce the product.

The firm must assess whether it can market the new product profitably. This requires estimating costs, which is difficult but easier than forecasting sales. Several types of sales estimates may be necessary. For infrequently purchased products, such as appliances, production equipment, or personal computers, the firm must estimate initial sales and long-term replacement sales. For frequently purchased products, like toothpaste, business supplies, or cookies, it must forecast both first-time sales and repeat sales over time.

The firm must attempt to predict sales over several purchasing cycles, because the ultimate success of a new product depends on consumers' trying the product and then repurchasing it. Pillsbury's experience with Oven Lovin' Cookie Dough shows what can happen. Within months of introduction, the product was available in 90 percent of supermarkets and sales were growing. In less than two years, however, sales crumbled. After using the product, consumers did not think it was much different from the dough they were using previously, so they switched back to their old product.[24]

Because it is so difficult to estimate new-product sales and costs, the real value of the business analysis is in identifying products that are not likely to succeed commercially. Consumers might like the product, and it might meet the firm's general criteria, but the market might be too small or the marketing costs too high for the new product to have a reasonable chance of long-term profitability. If this is the case, the firm makes a no-go decision. Although a no-go decision at this point has some costs, it can save the firm the very high costs associated with the remainder of the new-product development process. A go decision means that the new product offers the potential profitability to warrant continued development.

Chrysler provides an example of a no-go decision. The company put together a formidable team to develop a luxury car code-named LX. The LX would be a rear-wheel drive luxury car with a new 32-valve V-8 engine of over 300 horsepower. The car would be fast, but it would handle well and be able to compete with BMW, Mercedes, Jaguar, Lexus, Infiniti, and Cadillac. Everyone was excited about the project as Chrysler moved closer to actually producing the car. However, after analyzing the market, management concluded that increased competition would reduce margins to a level where the product would not generate sufficient profits. Although everyone involved wanted to produce the car, management made a no-go decision because of the limited profit potential.[25]

Prototype Development

Prototype development means converting the concept into an actual product. The objective is to use the information obtained from the concept tests to design an actual product that can be further tested. New-product costs begin to escalate at this stage because developing a prototype normally requires a considerable investment. Product ideas that make it to this stage should have a high probability of succeeding. Firms are doing a better job of weeding out poor product ideas earlier in the development process, as evidenced by a decrease in the number of new products that make it to the prototype stage from about 50 percent to 20 percent.[26]

Firms following a *customer value perspective* focus on two areas during prototype development. The first is to design the product to satisfy the needs expressed by consumers in the concept tests. One approach is through **quality function**

Exhibit 9–6   *Product function deployment matrix*

NEW COPIER PRODUCT						
Product characteristics						
Customer requirements	Multiple-size paper tray	Touch controls	Energy-efficient	Slip-in toner cartridges	Long-term warranty	High speed
Fast copies						X
Versatile	X					
Durable		X	X		X	
Low maintenance		X	X	X		
Easy to operate	X	X		X		X
Low operating cost			X			

X = Specific product characteristics designed to meet specific customer requirements

deployment (QFD), a procedure that links specific consumer requirements with specific product characteristics. A simplified QFD matrix for a new copier product to be marketed to business users is presented in Exhibit 9–6. In this example, each product characteristic is designed to provide at least one benefit desired by customers. This approach directly links product features to customer requirements.

The second area is to build quality into the product. In the past, a product would be designed and then given to manufacturing to produce. Sometimes it would be difficult and costly to produce to the design specifications. Now, many firms include people from product design, engineering, and manufacturing in designing the prototype. Manufacturing considerations are incorporated directly into product design. This approach ensures not only that the prototype will satisfy customer needs on paper, but that it can be produced to the desired quality level. An interesting example of developing prototypes is presented in "Using Technology: Robotic Pets."

Using Technology

Robotic pets

Sony's Digital Creatures Laboratory recently introduced the world's most sophisticated entertainment robot. The new product is a robotic dog that can bark for attention, sit up, lie down, scratch its face, wag its tail, play ball, change eye color, and learn as it grows. It is named AIBO, which is a Japanese word for "companion" and short for Artificial Intelligence Robot. The price for AIBO is $2,000. Sony hopes this is the first in a line of robotic dogs, cats, monkeys, and other creatures.

But, getting AIBO to market was a real challenge. The product development team built six prototypes over five years before coming up with one that had the desired quality. It took five prototypes before they were able to get one that could walk. The seventh prototype required tremendous work to "debug" software glitches and to finalize the desired appearance of the robotic dog. The AIBO launched in 1999 was based on the seventh prototype. Interestingly, Sony is not selling AIBO through its normal retail distribution channels, but only selling it over the Internet from the company's Web site.

Source: Irene Kunii, "This Cute Little Pet Is a Robot," *Business Week,* May 24, 1999, pp. 56–57.

Test Marketing

Once a product prototype is developed, it can be tested. **Test marketing** involves testing the product prototype and marketing strategy in simulated or actual market situations. Test marketing can be both expensive and risky. Full-scale test marketing can cost over $1 million and last up to 18 months. Competitive reactions have taught even savvy marketers like Procter & Gamble to be cautious in their testing. Several years ago, P&G was testing a ready-to-spread frosting brand. Taking note of the test, General Mills rushed to introduce its own Betty Crocker brand, which now dominates the market.[27] The two primary methods for testing are simulated test marketing and standard test marketing.

Simulated test marketing refers to evaluating a new product in situations contrived to be similar to how consumers would purchase and use it. A typical simulated test involves intercepting shoppers at a high-traffic location in a mall. Surveyors ask them about their use of various products and expose them to a concept or commercial for a new product. Respondents then participate in a shopping exercise during which they can purchase the new product. After the exercise, they are asked about their purchases. They are then contacted at a later date about their use of and intentions to repurchase the product.[28]

In **standard test marketing,** a firm tests a new product and its marketing strategy in actual market situations. The size and number of test markets depend on the need for reliable information, the costs associated with test marketing, and the potential reactions from competitors. Selected test markets should be representative of the characteristics of the target market for the new product. A typical approach is to execute the marketing strategy for the new product in the selected test markets and to carefully track results. Sometimes firms vary elements of the marketing mix in different test markets to identify the most effective marketing strategy.

Ameritech uses an interesting approach to test marketing. It goes to small towns in its region and has the citizens test new products and services. For example, the company enlisted more than 100 people in Woodstock, Illinois, to evaluate its Clearpath digital cellular service. The feedback from these test-market towns has provided useful information for improving Ameritech's new products prior to launch. Interestingly, people from these towns who have actually participated in the test-marketing programs are often used in Ameritech's "Human Factors" advertising campaign. These ads show the people using the new products in sometimes humorous ways. The underlying logic behind the test marketing and advertising is that "if technology doesn't work for people, it doesn't work."[29]

Test marketing represents the final exam for a new product. If the new product passes this exam, a go decision will lead to the commercialization stage. If the new product fails this exam, a no-go decision will lead to dropping the new product or going back to the drawing board to make significant changes. Even though test marketing is expensive, it is typically much less costly than commercializing the product. So a firm is much better off stopping an unsuccessful product at this stage than during the commercialization stage.

Test marketing products is one way to gauge consumer response prior to launching a product. Goodyear uses test marketing to evaluate new tire products.

Commercialization

During the **commercialization** stage, the firm introduces the product on a full-scale basis. The level of investment and risk is generally the highest at this stage. Investments in production, distribution, and marketing support can be extremely high. However, the firm can reduce some of this risk by performing the other stages of the new-product development process appropriately. Successful

Exhibit 9–7	*Consumer adoption process*	

Consumer adoption stage	Marketing strategy objective
Awareness	Communicate the availability of the new product.
Interest	Communicate benefits of new product to gain consumer interest.
Evaluation	Emphasize the advantages of new product over alternatives currently on the market.
Trial	Motivate consumers to try the new product.
Adoption	Make sure consumers are satisfied with use of the new product.

commercialization requires understanding consumer adoption, timing decisions, and coordinating efforts.

CONSUMER ADOPTION   The **adoption process** describes the steps consumers follow in deciding whether or not to use a new product. The stages in the adoption process are presented in Exhibit 9–7. Marketing strategies must be designed to move consumers through these stages to achieve the adoption of new products.

Research suggests two important considerations about the adoption process. First, consumers differ in their rates of adoption. There is usually a small group of consumers who are the most willing to adopt new products. Typically called **innovators,** they normally represent the first 2.5 percent of the adopters. Identifying the innovators and targeting marketing efforts to this group are keys to successful commercialization of a new product.

Second, the characteristics of a new product affect its rate of adoption. The more complex the product, the slower the rate. For example, it takes 5 to 15 years before new electronic technologies (e.g., VCRs, cable TVs, PCs, and cell phones) catch on

Innovative approaches are often used to introduce new products. Apple emphasizes the Desktop Movies feature as an advantage of its new iMac computers.

among consumers and penetrate a large portion of the market.[30] The rate of adoption is facilitated, however, when the new product is compatible with existing products, has clear and readily observable advantages over those products, and can be tried on a limited basis. Marketing strategies should capitalize on the characteristics that facilitate adoption and minimize the characteristics that slow adoption.

L.A. Mitchell, Account Executive for Large Business Accounts, Lucent Technologies, talks about facilitating the adoption of new products: "Even good new products can become old products very quickly if the customer has difficulty in accepting the new product. High-tech products traditionally have very high initial costs. For these new products, Lucent targets customers in very competitive industries where product differentiation is critical to a company's success. It is here that we will most likely find early adopters willing to take on new products. In order to capture the early adopter market, we need to present a product that can integrate quickly into the customer's product offering and demonstrates a quick return on investment or a significant competitive advantage."

TIMING   In most cases a firm can introduce a new product on its own timetable. A threat of competitive entry, however, can pressure a firm to launch the product quickly. The first entry in a market can often establish a long-term advantage. One study found that for technology-based companies, the profitability of new products is related more to getting to the market on time than to staying within the product development budget.[31]

Late entry can be advantageous if competitors have entered the market and developed interest and demand for the new product. Later entrants may be able to reduce the costs of market entry, avoid some of the mistakes made by the early entrants, or introduce better products. Compaq did this with its subnotebook computer. After many competitors were in the market, Compaq introduced a subnotebook similar to what was available but priced $1,000 below the competition. This entry appealed effectively to the home market.[32]

COORDINATION   As the new-product development stages have progressed, a marketing strategy for commercialization has evolved. A firm needs to coordinate all functions to implement this strategy effectively. Production, distribution, and all other marketing and company efforts must ensure that sufficient product is produced and available to satisfy the demand generated from the commercialization strategy.

One study found that new-product launches were more likely to be successful when the firm had a structured commercialization process that was understood by everyone involved and when there was frequent communication within and across department and divisional boundaries. It is also important that the product launch be given priority status with objectives set and specific responsibilities for all tasks assigned. Once the product is introduced, tracking results and providing feedback are critical.[33]

Rawlings Radar Ball™
Speed Sensing Baseball

Adoption of new products is facilitated if the new product has clear advantages over existing products. Rawlings emphasizes the advantage of its new Radar Ball over normal baseballs.

One of the worst things that can happen is to get consumers interested in a new product and then not have it available when they are ready to purchase. For example, photography retailers were promoting the Advanced Photo System with the line, "The dawn of a new era in photography is here!" Developed by five of the world's largest photo manufacturers, the system was supposed to solve many picture-taking problems. Small, light cameras would be available in various designs. The cameras would take three different sizes of pictures on the same roll of film, and many picture-taking errors could be corrected during photofinishing. Consumers were ready to purchase, but the cameras were not available. Six months after introduction, few retailers had the products because of production problems and demand miscalculations. The net result was frustrated retailers and consumers and, in the words of one executive, "the worst product launch in the history of the photographic industry."[34]

Exhibit 9–8	*Keys to new-product success*

- Number-one factor: unique, superior, differentiated product that delivers unique benefits and superior value to customer.
- Market-driven and customer-focused new-product process.
- More predevelopment work before development gets under way.
- Sharp and early product definition.
- Right organizational structure.

- New-product success is predictable: Use profile of winner to sharpen project-selection decisions.
- New-product success is controllable: Emphasize completeness, consistency, quality of execution.
- Speed is everything! But not at the expense of quality of execution.
- Companies that follow multistage, disciplined new-product game plans fare much better.

Source: Adapted from Robert G. Cooper and Elko J. Kleinschmidt, "Stage Gate Systems for New-Product Success," *Marketing Management* 1, no. 4, pp. 20–29. Reprinted by permission of the American Marketing Association.

Keys to New-Product Success

Studies of new-product introductions identify a number of reasons for failures and successes. Many executives are not satisfied with the speed of new-product development in their companies and have difficulty in planning and budgeting for new projects. Front-end planning is critical to improving the new-product development process.[35] A synthesis of these studies provides the keys for new-product success, as presented in Exhibit 9–8.[36]

Many of these keys to new-product success are consistent with the perspectives emphasized throughout this book. New-product development should be market-driven and customer-focused, aimed at developing superior products that offer consumers unique benefits and exceptional value. The predevelopment efforts, such as idea screening, concept development and testing, and business analysis, appear to be critical to new-product success. In fact, establishment of a disciplined and rigorous new-product development process, effectively executed at each step of the process, is an important determinant of success.

Organizational Approaches

The use of cross-functional teams working simultaneously on different steps helps shorten the new-product development process and increases chances for success.

Teamwork is often required to make the new-product development process successful. Thermos used a cross-functional team to develop a new electric grill that won four design awards.

Three organizational arrangements have been found to work well. A **balanced matrix organization** calls for a project manager to oversee the project and to share responsibility and authority with functional managers. Decision making and approval are a joint process.

A **project matrix organization** assigns a project manager to take primary responsibility and authority for the process. Functional managers then assign personnel as needed to perform various activities throughout the process.

In a **project team organization,** a project manager heads a core group of people selected from various functional areas. Managers from the different functional areas are not formally involved in the process.

Teamwork across functional areas is essential for new-product success. The emphasis throughout the process should be on producing products that offer the quality and value desired by consumers. In many cases, this means constant awareness of how new technologies may be used to solve customer problems. Although many of the keys to success seem obvious, the majority of new products still fail. The reason for many of these failures may be that firms did some of the obvious things wrong or failed to do them at all.

Source: William R. Dillon, Thomas J. Madden, and Neil H. Firtle, *Essentials of Marketing Research* (Homewood, IL: Richard D. Irwin, 1993), p. 50.

Marketing-Research Support

Marketing research can make important contributions to the new-product development process. Concept tests and test marketing were discussed earlier in this chapter, and other marketing research approaches were covered in Chapter 6. Exhibit 9–9 highlights some of the types of marketing research that might be used throughout the new-product development process.

Prelaunch activities refer to marketing-research studies prior to commercialization. These types of studies typically introduce consumer input into the decisions made at each stage of the new-product development process. *Rollout studies* are performed after the product has been introduced in the commercialization stage. These studies assess consumer response to the new product and its marketing strategy.

The successful introduction of Banana Nut Crunch illustrates the important role that marketing research can play. The cereal maker, C. W. Post, wanted to develop a banana-flavored cereal. Bananas are America's favorite cereal fruit and consumers had responded favorably to the banana-flavored cereal concept. The initial cereal included dried banana pieces, but this flopped in product tests. Then, the idea to make the cereal like banana-nut bread was generated. Consumers responded positively to this new concept. Prototypes were produced and tested in several hundred households. Again, the response was positive. Banana Nut Crunch was then introduced, and tracking studies indicated strong initial and repurchase demand. Today, the cereal is a strong success and one of Post's hottest brands. Information provided by consumers through various marketing-research approaches produced the key information to make the product introduction successful.[37]

Successful New Products

Although many new products are failures, there are always many interesting successes. Let's conclude our discussion of new-product development by looking at several products selected as "The Best Products for 1999":[38]

- The Olympus EyeTrek hooks to a DVD player and gives the impression of viewing a 52-inch screen from 6.5 feet away while you listen to stereo sound.

- Kozmo.com (www.kozmo.com) and Urbanfetch (www.urbanfetch.com) target "couch potatoes" by delivering magazines, junk food, and videos in under an hour.

- Viactiv candy contains 500 milligrams of calcium—and only 20 calories—in a tasty chocolate and caramel flavor.

- Outlast clothing contains new fibers that absorb body heat and then release it when the body chills. It warms skiers on the lifts and cools them when skiing down the slopes.

- The GE Advantium microwave combines microwaves with halogen lights to produce an oven that cooks in record time. It is also preprogrammed to cook more than 100 different meals.

Summary

1. **Recognize the different types of new products.** Products differ in how new they are to customers or to the firm introducing them. From a firm's perspective, new products can be classified as new-to-the-world products, new-category entries, additions to product lines, product improvements, or repositionings.

2. **Discuss the different sources of new products.** New products can come from external sources or be developed internally. External sourcing includes acquisitions or various types of collaborative arrangements allowing a firm the right to market the products of another firm. Internal development is when a firm is directly involved in the development of new products. The firm might work with other firms on some new-product activities, but it is actively involved in the process.

3. **Understand the stages in the new-product development process.** The new-product development process consists of the interrelated stages of idea generation, idea screening, concept development, business analysis, prototype development, test marketing, and commercialization. As a firm moves through this process, costs rise substantially. A prime objective is to eliminate potential product failures as early as possible and to spend time and resources on the ideas with the largest chances for success.

4. **Describe the way marketing research is used in the new-product development process.** Marketing research goes on throughout the new-product development process. Specific types of marketing research are valuable in the prelaunch stages. These studies help to assess market acceptance of the product and the likely success of particular marketing alternatives. Different marketing research approaches are used to monitor and evaluate results during the commercialization stage.

5. **Appreciate the keys to new-product success.** A synthesis of new-product research suggests the nine keys to new-product success presented in Exhibit 9–8. In general, the keys to success are market orientation, customer focus, effective execution of a rigorous new-product development process, adoption of a multifunctional new-product organizational approach, and development of products that deliver the benefits and value desired by consumers.

Understanding Marketing Terms and Concepts

Thinking About Marketing

1. How does the new-product development process differ for different types of products?

2. What are the advantages and disadvantages of using external sources for new products?

3. Look at "Using Technology: Robotic Pets." Suggest five new-product ideas using robots that are not pets.

4. Should all new products be test marketed? Why or why not?

5. What should be included in a business analysis for a new product?

6. Reread "Being Entrepreneurial: A New Product Museum." What are the three mistakes you think companies have made in developing and marketing new products?

7. Describe the use of marketing research throughout the new-product development process.

8. What factors should be considered during the idea-screening stage of the new-product development process?

9. How is the development of new services likely to differ from the development of new goods?

10. How is the development of consumer products likely to differ from the development of business products?

Applying Marketing Skills

1. Assume that students are complaining about how hard it is to get information about scheduled school events. Being entrepreneurially oriented, you would like to develop a product to solve this problem. Go through the idea-generation, idea-screening, and concept-development stages of the new-product development process. Bring one or more new-product concepts to class for testing.

2. Contact a local firm in your area that is active in new-product development. Interview people at the firm, and find out as much as possible about the company's new-product development process.

3. Identify a recent new product that you think has been very successful. Select a product that allows you to obtain information from both published sources and company officials. Evaluate how well the firm introducing this product followed the keys to new-product success presented in Exhibit 9–8.

Using the www in Marketing

Activity One   Go to the 3M web site
(http://www.3m.com).

1. Select one of the inventors in the "Our Pioneers" section. Describe the invention and how it led to new 3M products.

2. Based on information available from the Web site, why do you think 3M has been so successful in developing new products?

3. What are 3M's plans for new product development in the future?

Activity Two   One example of a truly
innovative product can be found at http://www.sleddogs.com.

1. Describe this product.

2. Why is this product so innovative?

3. What are the keys to marketing this innovative product successfully? How does understanding adoption and diffusion help you in developing a successful strategy for introducing a new, innovative product such as this?

Making Marketing Decisions

Case 9-1 The Automobile Industry: New-Product Competition

Pickup trucks and sport utility vehicles (SUVs) have been big sellers in recent years. The automobile companies are racing to develop a hybrid vehicle that will combine the comforts and off-road capabilities of an SUV with the cargo capabilities of a pickup. Nissan and Dodge introduced the first version of this type of vehicle in 1999. These were basically small pickups with four full-sized passenger doors.

Ford and General Motors are rushing to enter this market. Ford decided it was important to beat GM to market, so it will introduce the Explorer Sport Trac and Ford F-150 SuperCrew in early 2000. The SuperCrew is a full-size pickup with four SUV doors. It also plans to introduce the Lincoln Blackwood, a Lincoln Navigator SUV with a box in the back and exotic wood along its sides, in late 2000. These vehicles have clear advantages over the Nissan and Dodge products already available. Ford hopes its early entry will help it achieve market dominance before GM enters the market.

General Motors is following a different strategy. It has spent considerable time and money trying to develop a superior product for this market. The result of this effort is the Chevrolet Avalanche to be available in early 2001. The Avalanche will have four sedanlike doors and an open, but enclosable, cargo bed with enough room for a couple of

mountain bikes. This vehicle is more than a composite of basic features. GM engineers spent considerable time designing a production-ready door for between the cab and the pickup bed, and much effort was devoted to giving the Avalanche an aggressive, macho look. The Avalanche was also tested in an expensive simulated test marketing trial. All of these efforts were intended to help GM develop the best possible product. Although GM will enter the market a year later than Ford, it hopes that consumers will buy its superior product.

The stakes in this new product race are high. Ford and GM have spent over $1 billion in developing vehicles for this market. The company that dominates this market is likely to be rewarded with billions in profits.

Questions

1. What type of new product are these new vehicles?

2. What are the key differences and similarities in the Ford and GM strategies?

3. Which strategy do you think will be most successful? Why?

4. What strategy would you recommend a company like Toyota follow for this market? Why?

SOURCE: Fara Warner and Gregory L. White, "Auto Rivals Cross SUV with Pickup in Hopes That a Star Will Be Born," *The Wall Street Journal Interactive Edition,* January 3, 2000, pp. 1–5. Permission conveyed through the Copyright Clearance Center, Inc.

Case 9-2 Water Joe: A New-Product Idea from a Student

David Marcheschi was a typical student. When it was time for a test, he would stay up all night and cram. David had more difficulty than others staying up, because he hated the taste of both coffee and sodas. He wished someone would caffeinate plain water.

After college, he was still looking for a caffeinated drink without the caffeine flavor. He mentioned this idea to a friend whose father owned a beverage company. The chemist at the beverage company helped David develop a formula for a spring water product that incorporated as much caffeine as an eight-ounce cup of coffee. David took the formula, named it Water Joe, put it in a half-liter bottle, created a label, and prepared to launch the product.

Bottling Water Joe required special equipment that most bottlers did not have and were not willing to purchase. He spent two years talking to bottlers before he found Nicolet Forest Bottling. The company already had a water distribution system in place and wanted to form a partnership to market Water Joe. David jumped at this opportunity and formed Water Concepts LLC.

The market for Water Joe was large and diverse, including athletes, individuals who work late at night, and people tired of their teeth turning brown from coffee. Reaching these consumers required getting distribution in convenience stores, truck stops, and other retail outlets. David also wanted to position Water Joe as an alternative to soft drinks like Coke and Pepsi. His strategy was to situate Water Joe next to soft drinks in stores.

By the end of 1996, Water Joe was shipping 400,000 bottles a week to retailers in every state in the United States. Annual sales have grown to $12 million. David is pleased with his success. Competition has noticed and is introducing similar products. He must now consider how to continue growth in the future.

Questions

1. Why do you think Water Joe has been such a successful new product?

2. What other market segments might Water Joe target?

3. What new products do you think David might develop to ensure future growth?

4. Think of your experiences as a student. Can you generate any ideas for new products from these experiences?

SOURCE: Gianna Jacobson, "A Jolt of Inspiration," *Success,* January/February 1997, p. 21. Reprinted with permission. Copyright 1997 by Success Holdings Company, L.I.C.

Chapter Ten

Product and Service Strategies

After studying this chapter, you should be able to:

1 Understand the different characteristics of a product mix.

2 Recognize the stages and characteristics of the product life cycle.

3 Identify appropriate marketing strategies for products in different life cycle stages.

4 Describe the limitations of the product life cycle concept.

5 Discuss different product-mix and product-line strategies.

www.starbucks.com

The first Starbucks coffee shop was at Pike Place Market in Seattle in 1971. The concept was successful, and 165 Starbucks locations were opened in 1992, when the company went public. The chain now has more than 2,800 retail locations in the United States and Canada and another 300 in Europe and Asia. The Starbucks strategy is to create a unique experience based on mellow ambience, premium coffee beans, and coffee beverages.

Future growth will come from several areas. There are many international opportunities, and Starbucks hopes to have 1,000 international locations within the next five years; Japanese outlets are doing well, and the company recently entered China and the Middle East. There are also growth opportunities in the United States, where gourmet-coffee sales have increased by 46 percent during the past two years. Starbucks has less than 6% of the coffee market allowing plenty of room for growth. Starbucks is also expanding its in-store product line with more coffee choices and has added tea by

purchasing Tazo, a premium tea company. It also plans to start selling lunches in some stores. Further, there is an effort to expand market share in the office-coffee service market and to open licensed stores on university campuses and in grocery stores.

The Starbucks Web site focuses on coffee and tea, as expected, but offers other products as well. Customers can order CDs from hearmusic.com, a Starbucks subsidiary purchased for $10 million. The company has also made an equity investment in cooking.com. Customers can click to this site and purchase dishes, cutlery, and other related products.

On balance, the future looks bright for Starbucks. It has a promising growth strategy for its retail shops and an interesting strategy for electronic commerce. Profits were up 25 percent in 1999 and are expected to increase 20 to 25 percent for the next several years. **Sources:** www.starbucks.com, January 18, 2000; and Jeff Schlegel, "Something Brewin'," *Individual Investor,* February 2000, pp. 60–61.

Most companies market many different products. Colgate-Palmolive shows some of the many products in its product mix.

The experiences Starbucks has had illustrate the challenge of marketing multiple products and services, where success depends upon developing and implementing effective strategies for specific products, individual product lines, as well as the entire product mix. The task becomes even more difficult for companies such as Starbucks because product strategies for their stores must be integrated with those for electronic commerce. But, this is the task faced by more and more firms.

Even small, entrepreneurial firms based on a single product normally add new products to achieve growth objectives. One reason for this is that once a new product passes the commercialization stage and is introduced into the market, it typically goes through some type of life cycle. At the later stages of this life cycle, sales and profits decrease significantly. Thus, firms introduce new versions of existing products to extend this life cycle or new products in other areas to meet company growth objectives and take advantage of market opportunities. Smart companies employ effective product and service strategies to direct this growth.

In this chapter we introduce the product mix concept and discuss strategies for individual products, product lines, and the overall product mix. We emphasize the role of the product life cycle as a basis for strategy development.

Product Mix

A **product mix** is the total assortment of products and services marketed by a firm. Every product mix consists of at least one product line, often more. A **product line** is a group of individual products that are closely related in some way. An **individual product** is any brand or variant of a brand in a product line. Thus, a product mix is a combination of product lines, which are combinations of individual products.

A product mix, relevant product lines, and individual products can be defined at different levels. In Chapter 3, we discussed organizational strategic planning at the corporate, business, and marketing levels. At the corporate level, the product mix

Exhibit 10–1	*Product mix characteristics*

Kodak Camera Product Mix

Consumer Cameras	Digital Cameras	Industrial Cameras	Motion Analysis Products
•KODAK ADVANTIX 2000 AUTO Camera •KODAK ADVANTIX 2100 AUTO Camera •KODAK ADVANTIX 3100AF Camera •KODAK ADVANTIX 3200AF Camera •KODAK ADVANTIX 3600ix Camera •KODAK ADVANTIX 3700ix Camera •KODAK ADVANTIX 4100ix Zoom Camera •KODAK ADVANTIX 5600 MRX Text-Date Camera •KODAK ADVANTIX Cameras •KODAK CAMEO Auto Focus Camera •KODAK CAMEO cameras •KODAK CAMEO Focus Free Camera •KODAK CAMEO Motor 110 Camera •KODAK CAMEO Motor EX Camera •KODAK CAMEO Zoom Plus Camera •KODAK FIESTA 35 Camera •KODAK FUN SAVER 35 Camera •KODAK FUN SAVER 35 Camera with Flash •KODAK FUN SAVER 35 Camera with Flash Wedding Edition •KODAK FUN SAVER ADVANTIX Single-Use Flash Camera ...and 15 others	•KODAK DC25 Digital Camera •KODAK DIGITAL SCIENCE 420 Color Infrared Camera •KODAK DIGITAL SCIENCE 420 GPS Camera •KODAK DIGITAL SCIENCE DC20 Camera •KODAK DIGITAL SCIENCE DC40 Camera •KODAK DIGITAL SCIENCE DC50 Zoom Camera •KODAK DIGITAL SCIENCE Professional DCS 410 Camera •KODAK DIGITAL SCIENCE Professional EOS-DCS 3 Digital Camera •KODAK Megapixel Image Technology Camera System •KODAK Professional DCS 420 Digital Camera •KODAK Professional DCS 460 Digital Camera •KODAK Professional DCS 465 Digital Camera Back •KODAK Professional DCS IR Digital Cameras •KODAK Professional EOS-DCS 1 Digital Camera •KODAK Professional EOS-DCS 5 Digital Camera	•KODAK MEGAPLUS Camera, Model 1.4 •KODAK MEGAPLUS Camera, Model 1.6 •KODAK MEGAPLUS Camera, Model 4.2	•KODAK EKTAPRO EM Motion Analyzer, Model 1012 •KODAK EKTAPRO EMP Motion Analyzer •KODAK EKTAPRO HS Motion Analyzer, Model 4540 •KODAK EKTAPRO Hi-Spec Motion Analyzer •KODAK EKTAPRO Intensified Imager, Model SI •KODAK EKTAPRO Intensified Imager, Model UVX •KODAK EKTAPRO Intensified Imager, Model VSG •KODAK EKTAPRO Motion Analysis Workstation

Product Line Length / **Product Mix Width**

would be defined as all products marketed by the entire corporate entity, with each business unit typically representing one or more product lines. Each business unit, however, also has its own relevant product lines made up of related products. There can also be multiple product mixes within a business unit.

Any product mix can be defined in terms of width, length, and consistency. Exhibit 10–1 illustrates these characteristics for the camera product mix at Kodak. **Product mix width** refers to the number of product lines in the product mix. The more product lines, the wider the product mix. The camera product mix is relatively narrow, because it consists of only four product lines: consumer cameras, digital cameras, industrial cameras, and motion analysis products.

Product line length refers to the number of products in a product line. In the Kodak example, the consumer cameras product line is the longest, with 35 products. The industrial cameras product line is the shortest, with only three products. It is also sometimes useful to talk about the average product-line length across a firm's product mix. For Kodak cameras, the average product-line length is 15.25, since there are 61 products organized into four product lines.

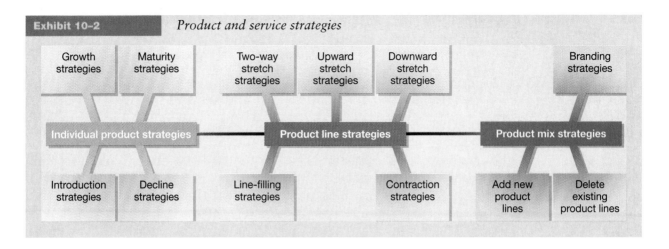

Exhibit 10-2   *Product and service strategies*

Product and service strategies diagram:

Top row: Growth strategies | Maturity strategies | Two-way stretch strategies | Upward stretch strategies | Downward stretch strategies | Branding strategies

Middle row: Individual product strategies — Product line strategies — Product mix strategies

Bottom row: Introduction strategies | Decline strategies | Line-filling strategies | Contraction strategies | Add new product lines | Delete existing product lines

Product mix consistency refers to the relatedness of the different product lines in a product mix. The product mix throughout Kodak is very consistent, because all of the products are related to imaging. So even if we expanded our focus to the corporate or business-unit level, the product mix would still be relatively consistent. The products would not all be cameras, but they would be associated with imaging.

Firms marketing multiple products and services must devise strategies for individual products, specific product lines, and the overall product mix. Key strategies at each level are presented in Exhibit 10–2. Although we discuss each level separately, the strategies are interrelated. Effective firms integrate product and service strategies across these levels. "Using Technology: Building Brands on the Internet" provides an interesting example in the book industry.

Individual Product Strategies

An important factor in the development of marketing strategies for individual products is the product life cycle. The **product life cycle (PLC),** like the biological life cycle, describes the advancement of products through identifiable stages of their existence. The stages are introduction, growth, maturity, and decline, as shown in Exhibit 10–3. The product life cycle

Using Technology

Building brands on the Internet

Unilever is a $50 billion global food, home, and personal care products company with familiar brands like Lipton, Ragu, Dove, Popsicle, Q-tips, and many others. The company realizes that brand differentiation depends as much on service as on product features and on the power of the Internet to provide desired services to consumers. Some of the actions Unilever is taking to build its brands over the Internet include the following:

- It currently has separate Web sites for 50 of its brands and intends to expand this to all brands in the future.

- It has negotiated marketing deals with AOL, Microsoft, and Excite at Home to promote its brands.

- It is building a database of 10 million customers in order to accumulate information that will subsequently help develop customer relationships.

- Many of its sites provide valuable services to consumers. For example, Recipe Secrets on the Lipton site presents daily suggestions for dinner as well as step-by-step narrated and illustrated preparation instructions in full-motion video.

- It is shifting advertising efforts from traditional media to interactive media.

Richard A. Goldstein, President and CEO of Unilever United States, expressed the firm's basic approach for using the Internet to provide value to consumers: "We must engage, inform, entertain, and provide real value in terms of trial offers, usage tips, and time-saving information."

Source: Michael Krauss, "Unilever Evolves, Perhaps Should Revolt," *Marketing News,* September 29, 1999, pp. 20–21.

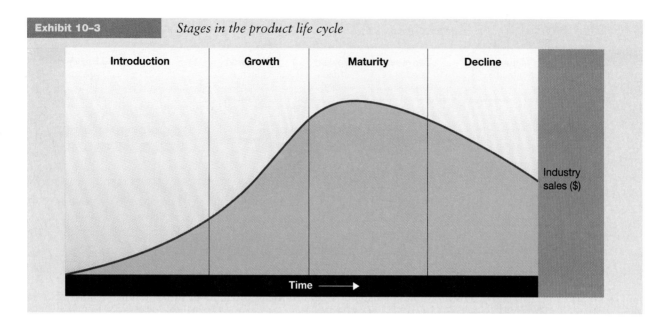

Exhibit 10–3 — *Stages in the product life cycle*

Introduction | Growth | Maturity | Decline

Industry sales ($)

Time →

concept applies best to new product forms; it does not work as well to describe stages for general product classes or for the specific life of individual brands.[1] Thus, marketers at AT&T would find the product life cycle concept of most value for product forms such as portable telephones, cellular telephones, or video telephones. The concept is less useful in analysis of the basic product class of telephones or of specific AT&T brands of telephones.

The product life cycle concept is based on four premises:

- Products have a limited life.
- Product sales pass through distinct stages, each with different marketing implications.
- Profits from a product vary at different stages in the life cycle.
- Products require different strategies at different life cycle stages.[2]

Before discussing relevant stages, characteristics, and marketing strategies, we should examine the diffusion process as a basis for the product life cycle concept.

Diffusion Process

When a new product form, such as the cellular telephone or the compact disc, is first introduced to the market, consumers go through a process in determining whether or not to adopt it. We discussed this process and factors that facilitate adoption in Chapter 9. Research suggests that different groups of consumers adopt innovations at different rates. Some consumers adopt a new product when it is first introduced; others wait until the innovation has been on the market for some time. These different adoption rates mean that it typically takes time for an innovative new product form to diffuse throughout a market. The **diffusion process** describes the adoption of an innovation over time.

The general diffusion process is presented in Exhibit 10–4. The process is depicted as a bell-shaped curve with five different adoption groups. As discussed in Chapter 9, **innovators** are the first to adopt a new product; they represent about 2.5 percent of a market. The diffusion process then moves to the **early adopters** (13.5%), **early majority** (34%), **late majority** (34%), and finally the **laggards** (16%). The types of consumers in each group differ depending on the type of innovation. However, as shown in Exhibit 10–4, consumers within each category have several common characteristics.

The different categories of adopters in the diffusion process are one reason new products go through life cycles. As an innovative product diffuses through these

Exhibit 10-4 *Diffusion process*

| **Innovators:** 2.5% Venturesome, higher educated, use multiple information sources | **Early adoptors:** 13.5% Leaders in social setting, slightly above-average education | **Early majority:** 34% Deliberate, many informal social contacts | **Late majority:** 34% Skeptical, below-average social status | **Laggards:** 16% Fear of debt, neighbors & friends are information sources |

Source: Adapted from Eric N. Berkowitz, Roger A. Kerin, Steven W. Hartley, and William Redslius, *Marketing,* 4th ed. (Burr Ridge IL: Richard D. Irwin, 1994), p. 327.

adopter categories, competitors enter the market and marketing strategies change. The interaction of the diffusion process and firm competition means that marketers face a different situation at each stage of the product life cycle (see Exhibit 10–5).

PLC Stages and Characteristics

The **introduction stage** starts with the launch of a newly developed product into the marketplace. Thus, the introduction stage of the product life cycle extends the commercialization stage of the new-product development process discussed in Chapter 9. Sales growth in the introduction stage is often slow because innovators typically represent a small portion of the market. Profits are low or nonexistent because of heavy expenses incurred in product development and intensive marketing to launch the product. There are no direct competitors for the first market entry, but competitors will likely enter over time.

Ideally, a new product would remain in the introduction stage for only a short time. However, some products never get out of this stage or remain in it for much longer than desired. A case in point is the introduction of handheld computing products. Apple's Newton MessagePad was among the first entries in this market. Adoption was much slower than expected because consumers did not perceive sufficient value from the initial product. Apple responded by introducing new models, the Newton MessagePad 110, and 2100, with many new features. However, consumers did not value these new features either, and sales of handheld computing products languished. The situation changed when 3Com Corporation introduced its Palm Pilot 1000 and Palm Pilot 5000 handheld products in 1996. These products were simple, easy to use, extremely portable, and able to be automatically synchronized with the data on a personal computer. Consumers saw real value in these products, and sales took off.[3]

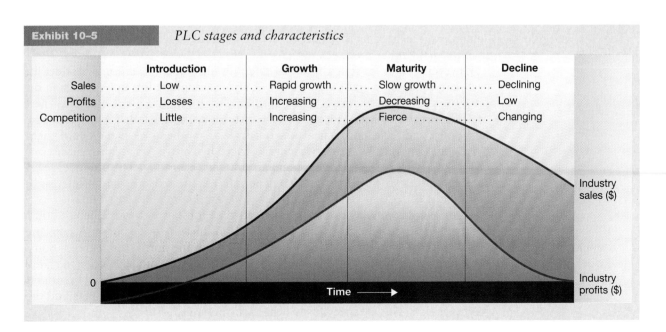

Exhibit 10-5 *PLC stages and characteristics*

	Introduction	**Growth**	**Maturity**	**Decline**
Sales	Low	Rapid growth	Slow growth	Declining
Profits	Losses	Increasing	Decreasing	Low
Competition	Little	Increasing	Fierce	Changing

Industry sales ($)

Industry profits ($)

Time ⟶

0

The second phase in the product life cycle is the **growth stage.** During this time, sales and profits increase rapidly. Innovators, early adopters, and the early majority buy the product. Recognizing the potential for profits, additional competitors enter the market with different product versions. The number of competitors and the rate at which they enter affect how long the growth stage will last. It will be shorter the faster competitors enter the market and the more aggressive their marketing strategies. Handheld computing products are now in the growth stage. Sales are expected to increase from the approximately 3,000,000 units in 1997 to more than 13,000,000 units in 2001. The Palm Computing organizers hold about 72 percent of the market, with distribution in 35 countries. Competitors are entering the market with different versions, but the Palm III, Palm V, and Palm VII have been introduced with new and better features. For example, the Palm VII offers wireless access to the Internet.[4]

When the marketing efforts of all competitors begin to get adoptions from the late majority, the **maturity stage** begins. Profits peak, then begin to decline, reflecting intensified competition, especially on price. Competition becomes even more fierce during the latter part of the maturity stage, when laggards adopt the product. The market gets saturated such that increased sales come more from taking business away from competitors than from getting business from new adopter categories. Most companies market products in the maturity stage of the product life cycle.

When falling sales persist past the short run, a product enters the **decline stage.** Profits decline and competition is changing. A product can reach this stage for a variety of reasons. One, most consumers who could buy the product may have done so. Another reason may be a shift in consumers' tastes, which is common in the clothing industry. Sales can also decline because of technological advances. The rotary telephone, for example, has largely been replaced by touch-tone phones that make it easier and quicker to place a call. Compact discs and digital audiotape formats hastened the decline of long-playing records. Digital imaging could have the same effect on film photography.

PLC Length and Shape

The length of a product life cycle depends on how well the product meets the needs of the marketplace. Products such as the basic household refrigerator have endured for a long time by offering consumers a good value. For less than $1,000, consumers can buy 20 years or more of convenient food storage.

In many industries, technology is advancing rapidly, which tends to shorten product life cycles. The life cycle for laptop computers was only a few years, as technology paved the way for introduction of equally powerful but smaller notebook computers. The product life cycles for styles, fashions, and fads are similarly shorter than for many other products.

Life cycle curves for styles, fashions, and fads differ from traditional product life cycle curves, as shown in Exhibit 10–6. A *style* is a unique form of expression defined by certain characteristics of the product. Decorating is a good example. There are different styles of furniture and home furnishings, such as early American, contemporary, and French provincial, and one style or another goes in and out of vogue over time. The Southwestern style, characterized by Native American and Mexican design and influence, is currently popular in home decorating. The product life cycle curve for a style fluctuates, reflecting periods of renewed and waning interest by consumers.

Fashion is a component of style. It reflects the more currently accepted or popular style. Fashions tend to follow the typical product life cycle curve. A few consumers interested in differentiating themselves from the norm start a trend. Soon, more consumers follow the lead of these innovators in the desire to copy the latest fashion. The mass market adopts the popular fashion as the norm, and eventually the fashion goes into decline as the cycle starts all over with another new and different fashion. This is especially evident in the apparel industry.

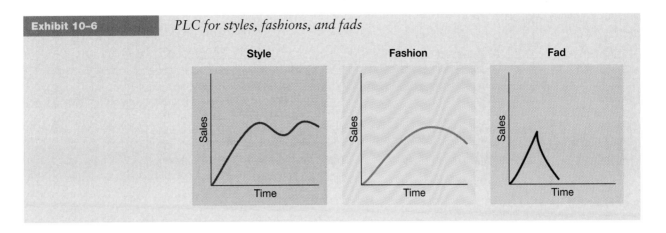

Exhibit 10–6   *PLC for styles, fashions, and fads*

However, sometimes fashions return to popularity. For example, designer jeans were very popular in the late 1970s and early 1980s. The tight, blue, straight-legged, denim jeans with designer labels then went out of fashion. But they are coming back, although with a lot more flair. Designers are adding rhinestone buttons, groovy new hues and prints, and laminate trims, and they are blending other fabrics with the denim. Apparel companies Pepe Jeans, Versace, Tommy Hilfiger, and Ralph Lauren are all introducing products to take advantage of the fashionable return to designer jeans.[5]

Finally, *fads* are a subcategory of fashion. Fads have dramatic product life cycles. They capture attention and grow quickly, but last only a short time and attract a limited number of consumers. Fads do not last long because of their limited benefits. They merely satisfy the need to be different and interesting. Some examples of fads are Cabbage Patch dolls, high-power water pistols, and games such as Trivial Pursuit. The life cycle of a fad is thus a very steep curve over a short period.

Sometimes it is difficult to determine if a sharp gain in sales is a fad or whether sales growth will continue. Harley-Davidson faced this situation when its large motorcylces gained popularity and stretched production capability. Management was contemplating a large expenditure to increase production but was concerned that the sales spike was due to a short-lived fad. Further analysis indicated this was not the case, Harley-Davidson increased production capacity, and sales have continued to grow.

Shortening lengths of product life cycles and their different shapes increase the complexity of marketing decisions. Firms respond to these trends by developing marketing strategies to take advantage of each life cycle stage. Some marketing strategies for each stage in a typical life cycle (Exhibit 10–5) are presented in Exhibit 10–7.

Introduction Strategies

The overall objective in the introduction stage is to increase awareness and stimulate trial of the new product. If there are no competitors, marketing efforts focus on generating **primary demand,** or demand for the new product form. As competitive brands are introduced, the focus shifts to generating **secondary demand,** or demand for the firm's specific brand.

Two different pricing strategies are possible. Firms often set high introductory prices for new products to quickly recover the costs associated with development and introduction. Examples of this type of strategy are seen frequently in high-tech products. Most technologically advanced products start out at a high price that innovators are willing to pay. VCRs, home computers, and cellular phones, for example, were all introduced at a high price. Firms modified their pricing strategies as these products moved through the life cycle, making them much more affordable to the mass market.

Exhibit 10-7	*PLC marketing strategies*	
Stage	**Objective**	**Marketing strategy**
Introduction	Awareness and trial	Communicate general product benefits to consumers and channel members.
Growth	Usage of firm's brand	Specific brand marketing communications, lower prices and expanding distribution
Maturity	Maintain market share and extend life cycle	Sales promotion, lower prices, expanding distribution, new uses, and new versions of product
Decline	Decide what to do with product	Maintain, harvest, or divest

Another strategy is to set a low introductory price. This approach is intended to generate faster market penetration. Because of the low price, it will take longer for a firm to recover new-product development costs. However, the low-price strategy can lead to a larger market share and long-term profits.

Distribution in the introduction stage is typically limited. Marketing efforts must be targeted to channel members as well as final customers. Marketers use different communication tools to persuade resellers to stock the product and to get consumers to try it.

Growth Strategies

When a product enters the growth stage, the firm's basic objective is to build consumer preference for its brand. Because of the favorable characteristics of the growth stage, many competitors are likely to enter the market. These competitors usually challenge existing brands by offering improved versions of the product. Early fax machines, for example, were in the growth stage when they were challenged by plain-paper versions.

Increased competition often results in the lowering of prices, especially toward the end of the growth stage. In addition, marketers usually expand distribution to make it easier for consumers to purchase the product. Communication efforts emphasize the competitive advantages of each firm's brand.

Marketing strategies during the growth stage typically focus on the competitive advantages of a firm's brand. Olympus is emphasizing its brand of digital cameras.

Maturity Strategies

The overall objectives at the maturity stage are to defend market share and extend the product life cycle. With the diffusion process nearing completion, opportunities to get new adopters are limited. Marketing efforts focus more on taking customers away from competitors than bringing new adopters into the market. But this is difficult and costly. Several strategies might be used during the maturity stage.

One popular strategy is to offer incentives to consumers for purchasing the firm's brand. These include lowering the brand's price relative to that of competitors or using sales promotions, such as coupons or rebates, to reduce the brand's price. Although incentives can produce more sales from existing customers and take sales from competitors, their cost reduces a firm's profit margins.

Another approach is to get consumers to use the product in different ways. This strategy can lead to more purchases from existing customers or might extend the product life cycle by bringing new consumers into the market. For example, Arm & Hammer successfully expanded the uses of its baking soda product. Originally used in cooking, baking soda is now used as a deodorizer in refrigerators, in carpet cleaning, in toothpaste, in antiperspirants, and

Introducing new and improved versions of a product is one strategy for extending a product's life cycle. Cheerios began as Cheerioats in 1941 and has been improved many times to extend its life cycle to over 50 years.

most recently in wintergreen-flavored gum. These new uses for Arm & Hammer baking soda led to a 15 percent sales increase in 1999. Eagle Brand Sweetened Condensed Milk has followed a similar strategy. It has been used for more than a century in Mom's Thanksgiving pumpkin pies. The brand is now being marketed to busy moms for use in all types of recipes, such as no-bake bars, shareable crumble treats, and an after-school beverage.[6]

A final approach is to extend the life cycle by continually introducing new and improved versions of the product. Since these new versions are not new product forms, they do not start a new product life cycle. They do, however, help prevent the product from moving into the decline stage. Procter & Gamble uses this strategy often. For example, P&G has improved Tide detergent many times during its long history.

Hasbro uses an interesting approach to extend the life of some of its toys for toddlers. It has developed a process to make the toys 99.9 percent germ-free. The plastic in the toys is embedded with Microban, a germ-killing chemical. The chemical is nontoxic and will not wash off because it is incorporated chemically into the plastic. Hasbro will add the germ-free concept to all of its Playskool toys beginning with the Roll and Rattle Ball and Busy Band Walker.[7]

The sales, profit, and competitive characteristics of the maturity stage produce a difficult situation for marketers. Marketing strategies used in the introductory and growth stages are not normally successful in the maturity stage. Firms often try many different strategies to maintain market share and extend the product life cycle.

Decline Strategies

When a product reaches the decline stage, marketers must make tough decisions on what to do with their brand. Sales and profits are decreasing and competition is strong. However, the picture can change depending on what competitors do. If many competitors decide to leave the market, sales and profit opportunities increase. If most competitors stay in the market, opportunities are limited. Thus, the appropriate strategy depends a great deal on the actions of competitors.

Three basic strategic choices are available: maintaining, harvesting, or deleting the product. Maintaining refers to keeping a product going without reducing marketing support, hoping that competitors will eventually leave the market. Some people, for example, still prefer (or can only afford) black-and-white televisions. Similarly, rotary or dial telephones persist in some areas of the country for reasons of technology.

A harvesting strategy focuses on reducing the costs associated with a product in the decline stage as much as possible. Advertising, salesforce time, and research and development budgets are limited. The objective is to wring out as much profit as possible during the decline stage.

Finally, deleting refers to dropping a product altogether. A firm might withdraw the product from the market, ending its life cycle, or might be able to sell it to another firm. Deleting products is difficult for many firms, but it may be the best strategy. The resources expended on a product in the decline stage may produce only minimal returns. Productivity can normally be increased by allocating these resources to products that will produce higher returns.

Limitations of the PLC

The product life cycle is meant to be a tool to help analyze the characteristics of products and design marketing strategies. The concept, however, has limitations. Marketers should be aware of these before jumping to conclusions based solely on the product life cycle.

First, remember that the life cycle concept applies best to product forms rather than to classes of products or specific brands. If marketers look only at the brand and not the overall product form, they may not see the whole picture. Brand sales can fluctuate for reasons unrelated to the product life cycle.

Second, the life cycle concept may lead marketers to think that a product has a predetermined life, which may produce problems in interpreting sales and profits. A dip in sales, for example, may be taken to mean that a product is entering the decline stage. Managers could prematurely drop the product when the dip represents only a temporary blip in the marketplace. Many products have survived for decades without decline because they were managed correctly. Ivory Soap (introduced in 1879) and Morton's Salt remain stalwart competitors. In other cases, declining products can experience a jump in sales with some new development in the environment, as was the case with cereals. When medical research seemed to show that oat consumption reduces cholesterol, sales of Quaker Oats Bran soared.

The final and most important limitation of the product life cycle is that it is merely a descriptive way of looking at the behavior of a product. There is no way the life cycle can predict the behavior of a product. That is, the product life cycle has limited relevance for forecasting future performance. Rather, marketing strategies help move a product along the life cycle. It is an interesting paradox that the strategies marketers adopt are both a cause and result of the product's life cycle.

Product-Line Strategies

Individual products that are related in some way form product lines. Firms must integrate strategies for individual products within the strategy for a product line. The basic strategic alternatives are to increase or decrease the length of a product line.

Increasing the Product Line

Most firms have growth objectives, so they tend to adopt strategies that add products to a product line. Since few firms have product lines that cover all market segments, they focus on where to add products. Sometimes additions to product lines are needed to keep customers coming back. An example of this strategy is presented in "Earning Customer Loyalty: Keeping Customers at Old Navy."

A **downward-stretch strategy** is an attempt to add products to the lower end of the product line. The microcomputer industry offers an excellent example of this strategy. IBM, Compaq, and Apple traditionally operated at the upper end of the microcomputer market, with the clone marketers at the lower end. With sluggish sales and more value-sensitive consumers, the three companies introduced several low-priced microcomputers. This strategy has effectively revived sales for all three companies.

WE DIDN'T INVENT THE BED & BREAKFAST, WE JUST BROUGHT IT UP TO DATE.

Today's bed and breakfast is always right around the corner, with over 400 Holiday Inn Express® locations from coast to coast. Each one offering a warm welcome, clean, comfortable rooms and a free continental breakfast every morning. Plus, we provide services like fax and photocopying, free local phone calls and the opportunity to collect Priority Club® points. So next time you're looking for great value and a good night's sleep, look no further than Holiday Inn Express hotels. America's new bed and breakfast.

1·800·HOLIDAY

Holiday Inn
EXPRESS

Inn Keeping with the Times.™

©1998, Holiday Inns, Inc. All rights reserved. Most hotels are independently owned and operated.

A downward-stretch strategy adds products to the lower-cost end of the product line. Holiday Inn Express was introduced to appeal to customers who value a lower price and fewer amenities.

An **upward-stretch strategy** is just the opposite: Products are added at the higher end of a product line. This has been a favorite approach for Japanese companies in the U.S. market. All the Japanese car marketers initially entered the U.S. market at the low-priced end. As companies achieved success with these products, they gradually added higher-priced products. Now, most Japanese companies market products at all levels, even at the luxury end of the market with products such as Lexus and Infiniti.

A **two-way-stretch strategy** entails adding products at both the high and low ends of the product line. Firms that have focused on the mass market might use this strategy to appeal to both price-conscious and luxury-seeking consumers. Marriott has used this strategy for its hotel product line, adding Marriott Marquis at the high end and Courtyard and Fairfield Inn at the low end. Marriott's product line now cuts across most segments of the lodging industry.

A **line-filling strategy** involves adding products in different places within a product line. A firm might use this strategy to fill gaps in its product line that are not at the high or low end. Candy marketers have used this approach with varying degrees of success. Hershey Chocolate successfully added Hershey's Hugs to its Hershey's Kisses product line. But it experienced disappointing results when it added Crunchy Peanut Butter Cups to the Reese's product line.[8] Honda has always trailed import rival Toyota in U.S. sales, even though its Accord is very successful. One reason is that Honda does not have pickup trucks to compete with Toyota's Tacoma or Tundra or the pickups offered by General Motors and Ford. The company realizes its growth in the United States is limited unless it adds pickups within its product mix. Although an expensive proposition, analysts predict that Honda *will* offer pickups in the United States within two years.[9]

A key concern in adding products to a product line is evaluating whether a new product will add new sales or take sales away from current products in the line. **Cannibalization** occurs when a new product takes sales away from existing products. A great deal of cannibalization shifts sales from one product to the new product, with little overall gain for the firm.

Strategies for adding products to a product line are typically most successful when cannibalization is low. For example, Yoo-Hoo has been around for 70 years and is the number-one chocolate beverage in the United States. The company wanted to increase sales, so it added new flavors to its product line. Called Yoo-Hoo Mix-ups, they are blends of the basic chocolate drink with other flavors such

Earning Customer Loyalty

Keeping customers at Old Navy

Old Navy is a clothing company that was launched in 1994 and now has 450 stores with plans to open more than 100 new stores during each of the next few years. The unique atmosphere of the company's stores is attributable to things such as 1950s Chevies and merchandise piled high in freezers. Sales at existing stores have been growing at about 20 percent annually.

Much of Old Navy's success is due to getting and keeping customers. And, customers come and stay because of the new products that are continuously being added to the product mix. Jenny Ming, president, is largely responsible for this. She tries to predict which hip-looking clothes of the moment will appeal to the masses and then produces them in large quantities and markets them aggressively. Fleece pullovers, baggy cotton pants, and cargo pants are three recent successes.

Customers have responded by spending more of their clothing dollars at Old Navy. Case in point: Cheryl Ellis discovered the value offered at Old Navy and now is a loyal customer; she spends $100 to $150 a month (that she allots for clothes for herself and her children) at Old Navy.

Sources: Louise Lee, "A Savvy Captain for Old Navy," *Business Week,* November 8, 1999, pp. 133–34; and Louis Lee, "Why Gap Isn't Galloping Anymore," *Business Week,* November 8, 1999, p. 136.

A line-filling strategy adds products throughout a product line. Ford is introducing new products in different product lines.

as coconut, mint, banana, and strawberry. An initial concern was that sales of Mix-ups would merely replace those of the original chocolate beverage. However, early focus groups and initial sales indicate that cannibalization will be minimal and the Mix-ups will increase total sales for the company.[10]

Jack Kennard, Senior Vice President, Executive Director of Global Brand Development, Brown-Forman Beverages Worldwide talks about increasing a product line: "Effective strategies for increasing a product line should enhance product image and satisfy different customer needs. Brown-Forman has used upward-stretch strategies to increase sales and enhance product image. For example, our best selling brand is Jack Daniel's Tennessee Whiskey. We successfully introduced Gentleman Jack Tennessee Whiskey as a premium quality addition to the original line. Then, Jack Daniel's Single Barrel Tennessee Whiskey was released as a new super-premium product. Cannibalization has been zero, as these new product "family members" met different customer needs, boosted volume and profit, and enhanced brand image both within the United States and internationally."

Decreasing the Product Line

Firms must consider deleting products when they are not successful, when they have reached the decline stage of the life cycle, or when the costs of marketing long product lines are high. Such **product line contraction** is normally painful but often necessary to improve performance. For example, because of intense price competition and decreasing consumer demand, ConAgra deleted breaded fish patties and breakfast sandwiches from its Healthy Choice product line.[11]

The more products a company sells in a product line, the higher its marketing expenses tend to be. Deleting products reduces expenses and can lead to improved profitability. For example, Borden reported disappointing financial results for several quarters. In examining strategies to turn performance around, the company realized it had 2,800 products in its snack-food product line, compared with 445 for industry leader Frito-Lay. The revised strategy was to discard marginal products and eliminate product items so that the remaining products could be better supported.[12]

Product-line strategies are extremely important, and they are the result of complex and difficult decisions. The products in a product line represent a firm's offerings to its customers. As customer needs change or competitors introduce new products, a firm must be able to respond. One proper response might be to add products to a product line; another response, to delete some.

Product-Mix Strategies

The product mix consists of all product lines and individual products marketed by a firm. Strategies at all levels must be consistent for maximum effectiveness.

Strategic Alternatives

Thinking Critically

Adding product lines to a product mix is a difficult task. Although there are some reported successes, there appear to be many more failures. Assume that you were asked to advise a company that was considering the addition of a product line.

- What are the key factors this firm should consider?
- How can the company best evaluate these factors to arrive at a decision?
- What strategy would you recommend to introduce this new product line?

The basic product mix strategic alternatives are to add new product lines or to delete existing ones. Many firms achieve growth objectives by expanding the product mix through the addition of new product lines. Successes are most likely to occur when a new product line has some similarity to existing product lines. For example, Fidelity Investments is an established mutual funds marketer. When its business plateaued at 6.2 million accounts, Fidelity decided to expand its focus from mutual fund investment to serving all of a customer's financial needs. It added several new financial service product lines, from credit cards to insurance. The new strategy was successful, resulting in record revenues.[13]

Some similarities between product lines may not seem obvious at first glance. For example, Circuit City has added used cars to its product mix. How are used cars similar to Circuit City's established consumer electronics and major-appliance product lines? President and chief executive officer Richard L. Sharp commented: "We believe that automobile retailing offers opportunities to capitalize on Circuit City's strengths in customer service and big-ticket retailing."[14]

Although expanding into new product lines might seem to be an easy growth strategy, many firms find such success elusive. Adding new product lines can be risky. The more different a new product line is from existing lines, the more risk involved. This is especially true for firms that move into products outside their areas of expertise. The popular business press presents almost daily examples of firms that have downsized by dropping unrelated product lines. For example, Gerber dropped its trucking and furniture product lines to concentrate on its mainstay: baby food.[15] Similarly, Coors shed diverse product lines, such as ceramic multilayer computer boards, dog food, and packages for soaps, to focus on beer.[16] Gillette is considering dropping product lines such as household appliances and pens so that it can concentrate on its core product lines: razor blades, batteries, and toothbrushes.[17]

There are, however, many success stories of firms moving into new product and service areas. Texas Instruments, for example, has performed well with a product mix consisting of semiconductors, defense electronics, printers, notebook computers, productivity software, and consumer electronics products. And the company is capitalizing on recent technological advances to position itself to move into different areas of the emerging information super highway.[18]

Jack Kennard, Senior Vice President, Executive Director of Global Brand Development, Brown-Forman Beverages Worldwide emphasizes the value of adding new product lines: "Adding new product lines can provide an ongoing source of novelty, create excitement, and help capture new customers. Jack Daniel's Country Cocktails is one example. This new product line helped Brown-Forman enter the premium low-alcohol beverage market. Jack Daniel's Country Cocktails expanded the Jack Daniel's brand into new consumer markets, particularly females. By attracting new customers, Brown-Forman increased sales and enhanced the Jack Daniel's brand."

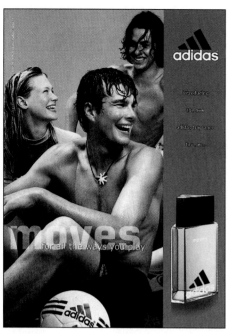

Many companies market a diverse product mix. Adidas emphasizes a product mix to meet different customer needs.

Sometimes firms add product lines in new business areas. When Arthur Andersen introduced new service lines, it had to convince clients that the company was capable of providing the new services.

Branding Strategies

Our discussion of branding in Chapter 8 focuses on branding decisions for a single product. As firms expand product mixes and extend product lines, brand decisions become more complicated. Companies marketing multiple products and services need a strategy to guide branding decisions. The basic options are presented in Exhibit 10–8.

One option is to use an **individual brand name strategy;** that is, the firm establishes specific brand names for each individual product in a product line. This approach allows a firm to choose what seems like an effective brand name for a particular product. The drawback is that because individual brand names are unrelated, products stand alone. Brand equity from one brand cannot benefit another. Procter & Gamble is probably the most famous user of individual brand names. P&G's objective is for all products to compete on their merits, so each product has its own brand name. For instance, P&G's detergent products have well-known individual brand names such as Tide, Cheer, Bold, Dash, and Oxydol.

The other basic option is to adopt a **family brand name strategy;** in this case, all brand names are associated with some type of family brand name. One approach is to brand all product items in the product mix with the company name, as Heinz

Exhibit 10–8	Branding strategies

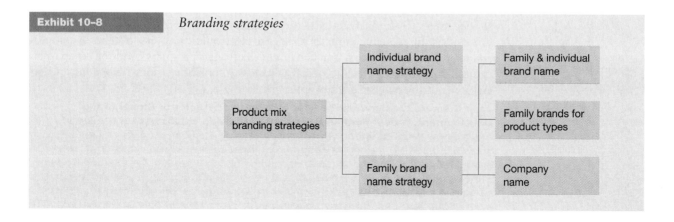

Product mix branding strategies

Individual brand name strategy
— Family & individual brand name

Family brand name strategy
— Family brands for product types
— Company name

and General Electric do. Another choice is to use different family brands for different product lines, with all items in a given product line bearing that same family brand name. Sears does this by using the Craftsman brand for tools, the Kenmore brand for appliances, and the Die Hard brand for batteries. A final alternative is to use both a family and an individual brand name for each product—for example, Kellogg's Rice Krispies and Kellogg's Raisin Bran.

Family brand name strategies can help firms increase product lines or add product lines. New products that build on the brand equity of an established brand are called *brand extensions*. Research indicates that the positive associations consumers have with a brand can be transferred to new products in the same category (increasing product lines) as well as to new products in different product lines (adding product lines). If successful, these extensions build additional brand equity.[19] Milky Way has used a family brand name strategy successfully in adding products to its candy-bar line and establishing an ice-cream product line.[20] There is some risk to using a family brand name strategy, however, because unsuccessful new products could weaken the brand equity of the established brand.

Ethical Issues in Product and Service Strategies

Marketers following an *ethics perspective* ensure that products are safe and not harmful, consumers receive relevant product information, there are meaningful differences among products in a product line, and if something goes wrong, there is a mechanism for redress.[21] It is important to continuously assess performance and safety issues from the new-product development process through production and marketing. Any identified problems should be corrected as soon as possible. Failure to do so can lead to dissatisfied customers, product recalls, and expensive lawsuits.[22]

Product recalls mean the marketer must allow customers to return the product to get the performance or safety defect corrected. This can be very expensive and harmful to a company's image. Companies can limit expenses and harmful effects by establishing a procedure to recall the product voluntarily. Without an established procedure, the process is likely to be inefficient and costly. If marketers do not proactively recall the product, they can be coerced to do so by various government agencies. For example, the National Highway Traffic Safety Commission forced Chrysler's three recalls of its new Neon car, and the Consumer Product Safety Commission recalled several brands of crayons containing hazardous lead levels.[23]

Potential harmful effects from products is a difficult issue. Should firms market products that consumers want but that are harmful to them? Some observers argue consumers should be allowed to decide through their purchasing practices; others think companies should not market products with harmful effects. The current battle over the marketing of cigarettes is an example of this issue. Another example is movie-theater popcorn. Most movie theaters prepare popcorn with coconut oil, which raises blood cholesterol more than any other fat or oil. Movie theaters could change to a more healthful way of preparing their popcorn, but consumers like the smell and taste of coconut

Product counterfeiting is an increasing problem for many products. A U.S. Customs agent drives a steamroller over 17,000 counterfeit designer watches smuggled into the country. These watches were worth $620,000.

oil–popped popcorn better. This issue will continue to receive attention because it is being pushed by the Center for Science in the Public Interest.[24]

The issue of harmful effects goes beyond individual consumers to society at large. Products that are not harmful to consumers may create environmental problems for society as a whole, such as emissions from automobiles, nonbiodegradable packaging, and polluting chemicals. Marketers emphasizing an *ethics perspective* act in a socially responsible manner by addressing the potential environmental problems associated with product use and disposal.

An increasingly important ethical and legal issue from a *global perspective* is product counterfeiting. *Product counterfeiting* occurs when a company copies another firm's trademark, copyright, or patent. Although this sometimes happens with U.S. firms, product counterfeiting by foreign companies is a major problem. The U.S. International Trade Commission estimated that counterfeit products by foreign companies cost U.S. firms between $6 and $8 billion a year in sales.[25]

The problem is especially difficult in China. Chinese stores carry products that look like Colgate toothpaste, Del Monte canned food, or Kellogg's Corn Flakes. But the toothpaste isn't Cologate, the canned food is made by a company called Jia Long, and the cereal is Kongalu Corn Strips. The damage from product counterfeiting in China is estimated to be $800 million a year. Microsoft argued that Chinese software pirates cost it $30 million annually, and this cost is growing. The developing legal system in China makes it difficult to stop these infringements on property rights.[26]

To ensure they are operating in an ethical manner, marketers need to answer the following questions appropriately:[27]

- Is the product safe when used as intended?
- Is the product safe when misused in a way that is foreseeable?
- Have any competitors' patents or copyrights been violated?
- Is the product compatible with the physical environment?
- Is the product environmentally compatible when disposed of?
- Do any organizational stakeholders object to the product?

Conclusions

As this chapter clearly shows, product and service strategies are extremely important. These decisions must be integrated at different levels of the organization, and they provide direction for the other areas of the marketing mix. Pricing, distribution, and marketing-communications decisions are all influenced by the product and service strategies of a firm.

Summary

1. **Understand the different characteristics of a product mix.** A product mix is the assortment of products marketed by a firm. It consists of individual products organized into product lines. The basic characteristics of a product mix are its width, length, and consistency. Product mix width refers to the number of different product lines in the mix; product line length to the number of different products in a product line; product mix consistency to how related the product lines are.

2. **Recognize the stages and characteristics of the product life cycle.** Products go through a life cycle similar to a biological life cycle. The basic stages of the product life cycle are introduction, growth, maturity, and decline. Sales and profits change over the life cycle as competitors enter the industry and markets become saturated.

3. **Identify appropriate marketing strategies for products in different life cycle stages.** Marketing strategies differ for products as they move through different life cycle stages. In the introduction stage, the firm emphasizes generating consumer awareness and stimulating trial of the product. During the growth stage, it focuses on building consumer brand preference to secure a strong market po-

sition. The maturity stage calls for a variety of strategies to maintain market share and extend the life cycle. During the decline stage, the firm must consider options to maintain, harvest, or drop the product.

4. **Describe the limitations of the product life cycle concept.** The product life cycle concept applies mainly to product forms rather than to product classes or specific brands. If, because of the concept, a marketer thinks a product has a predetermined life, it could adopt a marketing strategy that limits the product's life. The product life cycle concept is descriptive, not predictive.

5. **Discuss different product-mix and product-line strategies.** The basic product-mix strategic alternatives are to add to or drop product lines from the mix. The similarity between product lines and the use of a firm's strengths are key considerations in making these strategic decisions. Branding strategies are also important as firms add products to a product mix.

    The basic product-line strategies are to increase or decrease the length of a line. Downward-stretch, upward-stretch, two-way-stretch, and line-filling strategies can be used to increase product line length. Product line contraction will decrease product line length.

Understanding Marketing Terms and Concepts

Thinking About Marketing

1. What are the major differences between the growth and maturity stages of the product life cycle?

2. What are the alternative marketing strategies firms might use for products in the maturity stage?

3. What are the major differences between style, fashion, and fad?

4. How do shortened product life cycles affect marketers?

5. Look at "Using Technology: Building Brands on the Internet." Evaluate Unilever's Internet strategy.

6. How would you define the product mix for any firm?

7. Reread "Earning Customer Loyalty: Keeping Customers at Old Navy." What else might Old Navy do to increase customer loyalty?

8. Why is product line contraction so difficult?

9. What is meant by the term *cannibalization*?

10. What are the risks associated with adding new product lines that differ greatly from a firm's existing product lines?

Applying Marketing Skills

1. Go to a local supermarket, drug store, or discount store. Walk through the packaged-goods aisles, consider promotional and packaging information, and identify at least five examples of marketing strategies for mature products. Evaluate each marketing strategy example.

2. Obtain the annual report for any firm. Draw a chart that illustrates the product mix for this firm. Evaluate the firm's product mix.

3. Assume you have just invented a new-to-the-world product. Describe the product, and develop the marketing strategies you would use in the introduction and growth stages of the product life cycle.

Using the www in Marketing

Activity One   Go to the Starbucks Web site (http://www.starbucks.com)

1. Discuss the product mix offered by Starbucks.

2. How does Starbucks use this Web site to expand relationships with customers?

3. What recommendations can you offer to improve the Schwab Web site?

Activity Two   Fender Musical Instruments is one of the largest and most famous guitar manufacturers in the world. The Guitar Center retail chain is the largest reseller of Fender products. Go to the following Web sites:
Fender (http://www.fender.com)
Guitar Center (http://www.guitarcenter.com)

1. Describe the product mixes offered by each company.

2. Describe the product lines offered by each company.

3. Discuss the reasons for the similarities and differences in the product mixes and product lines offered by the two companies.

Making Marketing Decisions

Case 10-1 American Express: Expanding Electronically

American Express has developed a trusted brand name in its 140-year history. The company is a giant in the financial services and travel industries with over 24 million customers. Several new products and product lines are being introduced to make American Express a giant on the Web. It wants to provide customers with a seamless web of financial planning, banking, travel, and shopping services.

One service is an addition to the American Express credit card product line. The Blue card is being introduced with very low interest rates: zero interest for six months, followed by fixed rates of 9.99 percent to 15.99 percent with no annual fee. It includes a "digital wallet," which stores all of a customer's key shopping information—for example, addresses and credit card numbers—on a secure American Express site. The Blue card has a built-in computer chip; the card can be plugged into a special reader attached to the customer's computer to verify the shopper's identity and unlock the "digital wallet." Once this is done, American Express zaps the information to the electronic merchant and the purchase is completed. This approach is easier than filling out forms with each digital retailer and provides the security desired by many customers.

American Express also has a new product line called Membership B@nking. This is an on-line bank providing many financial services. In order to attract customers, the bank is currently paying top rates for one-year certificates of deposit. It hopes to move many of its existing customers to electronic banking and expand relationships with them by selling them credit cards, insurance, and financial planning services.

The company's final new product line is AmEx Brokerage. American Express tried to enter the on-line brokerage market with Financial Direct but was unsuccessful. This second attempt is more promising: AmEx Brokerage will provide stock trades, with neither commissions nor money-management fees, to customers who keep at least $100,000 on deposit. These customers can also tap into research used by the company's mutual-fund managers and use new on-line financial planning tools. The expectation is that brokerage customers will translate into more business for the firm's financial planners and advisors.

American Express is trying to leverage its brand name into the on-line world. It is, however, using a low-price strategy to attract customers. This is a different pricing strategy for the firm and raises questions as to how profitable these new on-line products will be.

Questions

1. How do the new on-line products and product lines change the American Express product mix?

2. What is your evaluation of the strategy for AmEx Brokerage? Do you think the firm will be successful in its second on-line brokerage attempt? Why or why not?

3. How important is the American Express brand name to the success of the firm's electronic strategy?

4. What is your evaluation of the low-price strategy for these on-line products in the short run and in the long term?

SOURCE: Mike McNamee, "Don't Leave Home without a Freebie," *Business Week,* November 8, 1999, pp. 150, 152.

Case 10-2 Poppy Industries: A Young Entrepreneur

When Poppy King was 16, she searched stores in Melbourne, Australia, for lipsticks in rich colors. She could not find any. During her search, salespeople in department stores told her that other consumers were looking for the same thing. Nothing happened for three years.

At the age of 19, she left school and founded Poppy Industries, Inc. to provide consumers with rich-colored lipsticks. Poppy found a mentor who gave business advice and also invested in the company. It took her a year to develop the company's first lipstick line of seven colors. She designed the packaging herself and devised unusual names, such as "Ambition" and "Inspiration," for each color. An accountant was hired to develop a business plan.

She then set out to get retailers to stock her products. By the end of the first month, 40 retail outlets in Melbourne and Sydney were selling her lipstick. Then, Australia's largest retailer, Myer Grace Brothers, came on board. Wanting to move into international markets, Poppy contacted and won the business of American fashion retailer Barneys. Her products were introduced during the launch of Barneys' Madison Avenue branch opening and featured in *Vogue, Mirabella,* and *Elle* magazines. Sales were brisk.

Today, Poppy Industries sells its cosmetics through hundreds of exclusive retail outlets in Australia, Singapore, India, Pakistan, and the United States. Despite intense competition in the cosmetic industry, sales are in excess of $8 million. Operations are being moved from Melbourne to New York in anticipation of future expansion. The strategy is to strengthen the product in the United States and then move into additional international markets.

The company has expanded its product mix to include more cosmetics and accessory lines. However, Poppy intends to stick close to the formula that brought such success: "We're never going to have hundreds and hundreds and hundreds of products and colors. It's a very tight and focused brand."

Questions

1. Why do you think Poppy Industries has been so successful?

2. How would you describe the product mix for Poppy Industries?

3. What strategy would you recommend for expanding the product mix of Poppy Industries?

4. In what ways does Poppy King illustrate an entrepreneurship perspective toward marketing cosmetic products?

SOURCE: Brent Pollock, "From Teen to Titan: How an Australian Entrepreneur Turns a Pretty Profit," *Success,* December 1996, p. 12.

Chapter Eleven

Pricing Concepts

After studying this chapter, you should be able to:

1 Realize the importance of price and understand its role in the marketing mix.

2 Understand the characteristics of the different pricing objectives that companies can adopt.

3 Identify many of the influences on marketers' pricing decisions.

4 Explain how consumers form perceptions of quality and value.

5 Understand price/quality relationships and internal and external reference prices.

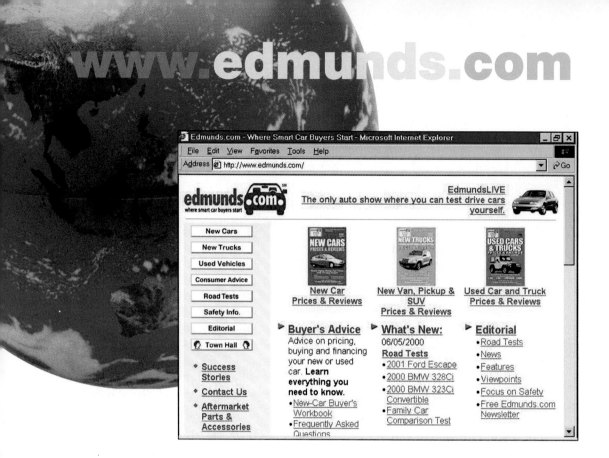

Headquartered in Santa Monica, California, Edmunds.com is the Internet's pioneer and leader in providing free unbiased automotive information. Users are offered automotive pricing data, automobile and other vehicle reviews, and rebate and incentive information. Edmunds.com was ranked #1 in *The Wall Street Journal's* Survey of Car-Shopping Web sites. Edmunds.com, which spends millions of dollars on outdoor, print, and radio ads to promote itself as an unbiased source of vehicle pricing and reviews, makes its money from referrals to marketing partners.

Edmunds.com is now planning for global expansion. The company's first entry will be into the United Kingdom in the Fall of 2000, followed with additional sites scheduled for France, Italy, Germany, and Spain. As part of this expansion, Edmunds.com has partnered with UK-based Autologic, a market leader in automotive logistics and outsourcing. Like the original U.S. site, pricing and financial information will provide consumers the increased opportunity to make informed choices and save money.

Pricing information offered by Internet Web sites like Edmunds.com has forced major manufacturers, such as Ford and General Motors, to reconsider their traditional price advertising, which historically has been based upon "manufacturer suggested retail prices." However, expanded price information on the Internet now allows consumers to negotiate based upon wholesale prices gathered free on the Web. In reaction to pressure to provide more information to their consumers, Ford has already run a pilot program in Arizona in which consumers are able to click from Ford's Web site to dealer information that includes price points closer to the invoice price Ford charges the dealer. The ability of consumers to gather price information from sites like Edmunds.com will increase their ability to judge offered prices and to make purchase decisions with more confidence.

Sources: *http://www.edmunds.com/edweb/about;* Jeff Green, "Auto Info Source Edmunds.com Revs Ad Plans after Getting Holiday Lift," *Brandweek,* February 7, 2000, p. 55; David Welch, "Car Dealers Say: Follow that Mouse," *Business Week,* April 10, 2000, pp. 106, 100; Joseph B. White and Fara Warner, "Car Makers Try to Alter Pricing Practices," *The Wall Street Journal,* January 24, 2000, p. A4.

Many factors influence price, which in turn influences sales and profits. Companies can charge premium prices because they offer high-quality products that consumers value. The premium prices enable distributors of the products to maintain sizable margins (the difference between price and cost of goods sold) and gain healthy profits. Perceptions of value at the consumer level allow higher prices, which can be used to maintain high quality in production and gain enthusiastic support by distributors and retailers.

Determining prices for complex product lines is an important task. Prices set too high will discourage sales; prices set too low may result in unprofitable business and a revenue stream that does not cover costs and expenses. Buyers in business-to-business markets, as well as individual consumers, often evaluate other factors, but price remains a primary choice determinant. And the interaction of prices with promotional activities often affects the firm's image.

In this chapter, we discuss the role of price and the major influences on pricing decisions. We explore the various pricing objectives governing marketers' decisions. Finally we discuss how advertised prices affect consumer perceptions of value and decision making.

The Role of Price

Price is the amount of money a buyer pays to a seller in exchange for products and services. It reflects the economic sacrifice a buyer must make to acquire something. This is the traditional economic concept of price, called the **objective price.** Where barter and exchanges pass for currency, prices may be nonmonetary. Much trade between developed and less-developed countries involves barter. This practice, called *countertrade* by economists, holds particular promise as a means of helping Eastern European economies. For instance, Germany has traded Mercedes-Benz trucks to Ecuador for bananas, and Russia has traded passenger aircraft to China for some consumer goods.

Prices frequently have other labels. The price of a university or college education is called *tuition*. The prices charged by professionals such as doctors and lawyers are referred to as *fees*. Loans are paid for by *interest payments*; charges for meter violations and overdue books are paid as *fines*; apartment charges are called *rents*. Other terms used to describe prices include *premiums, taxes,* and *wages*. In nonprofit situations, *donations* and *time* represent prices to support charities and political candidates. In all cases, however, these terms reflect prices associated with the receipt of something of value.

Speaking from Experience

Mack Turner
Managing Director
Bank of America

Turner joined Bank of America in 1981 after completing his MBA at the University of South Carolina. Previously, he managed marketing research and the bank's service quality and incentive plan management divisions. Turner stresses the importance of relationships and the value of services. If the banker does a good job understanding the customer's business strategy and truly finds creative solutions to his or her clients' business needs, he or she will be rewarded with additional business and less price sensitivity. Research has consistently shown that customers do have relationships with banks and within that small set of relationship banks they have "lead" banks. The lead bank receives the majority of the revenue the customer awards his or her banks.

"Banks have learned that a key to influencing price elasticity is the management of the perceived importance of the bank to the customer. In corporate and investment banking, firms strive to be perceived as their customer's top bank. This is frequently referred to as 'relationship banking.' The customer looks to the relationship bank not only for products (services) but for advice and guidance. The value of the relationship and proactive attention is seen by the customer as justification for a higher price."

Telephones and telephone services have become quite price competitive and frequent dealing is used to attract price sensitive customers.

List prices, set before any discounts or reductions, may differ from the actual market price or price paid. Price discounts, allowances, and rebates may make the market price different from the list price. Also a product's price may differ for particular uses or segments. In pharmaceuticals, for example, a drug might have a prescription price, a hospital price, and a Medicare price.[1]

Basic Price Mix versus Price Promotion Mix

A recent view of the marketing mix (price, product, marketing communications, distribution) makes a distinction between the firm's basic price mix and the price promotion mix,[2] described in Exhibit 11–1. The **basic price mix** includes those components that define the size and means of payment exchanged for goods or services. Examples include the list price, usual terms of payment, and terms of credit. The **price promotion mix** includes supplemental components of price, which aim at encouraging purchase behavior by strengthening the basic price mix during relatively short periods of time. These include sale prices, end-of-season sales, coupons, temporary discounts, and favorable terms of payment and credit. For business-to-business marketers, a number of factors may reduce the invoice price to a final transaction price. The most common include prompt payment discounts, volume buying incentives, and cooperative advertising incentives.[3]

Examples of these mixes are common in the marketplace. Dry cleaners that reduce prices on certain days offer both standard and discounted prices. Automobile dealers vary dramatically in their price mixes. Many dealers offer temporary reductions and favorable credit terms to stimulate demand. Other auto dealers may offer fixed but low prices and terms to appeal to "negotiation haters."

Price promotions are designed to attract nonusers of products and services, as well as product users of competing brands. Price promotions may also be intended to increase the quantity amount and/or frequency of consumption among current brand users. Marketers must be careful, however, that price promotions do not detract from perceptions of quality, which eventually lowers overall perceived value and intentions to buy. Some argue that consumers who buy only because of the promotion will cease to buy once the price reduction is retracted. For these reasons, nonmonetary promotions such as premiums and extra quantity may be as effective in generating loyal behavior in the long term.

Often retail-grocery and discount-store prices are described as being either EDLP ("everyday low price") or HiLo ("high-low"). The latter strategy involves offering

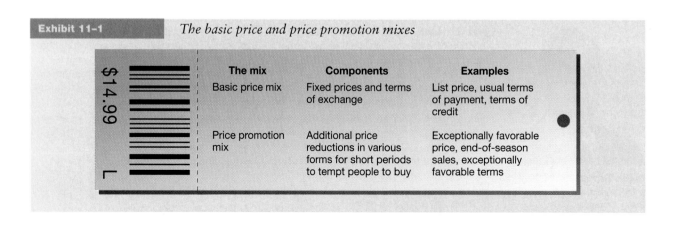

Exhibit 11–1   *The basic price and price promotion mixes*

The mix	Components	Examples
Basic price mix	Fixed prices and terms of exchange	List price, usual terms of payment, terms of credit
Price promotion mix	Additional price reductions in various forms for short periods to tempt people to buy	Exceptionally favorable price, end-of-season sales, exceptionally favorable terms

temporary but deep discounts in a small group of product categories. EDLP assumes constant low prices across a wide assortment of product categories. In practice, retailers do not adopt a single position, but customize their pricing strategies and tactics to market conditions, to categories, and to brands. In fact, price strategies can vary on at least four dimensions. *Price consistency* reflects the EDLP/HiLo continuum. *Price promotion intensity* represents the frequency, depth, and duration of price discounts. *Price/promotion coordination* represents the extent to which price discounts occur with supporting in-store displays and/or newspaper feature advertising. Last, the brand price level relative to the cost of other brands in a category is important. For example, higher-priced national brands are often effectively price discounted.[4]

The Importance of Price and Pricing Decisions

Price is the one aspect of the marketing mix that is most easily changed. Setting a price does not require the investment involved with advertising or developing products or establishing distribution channels. Price changes are certainly more easily implemented than distribution and product changes. Consequently, the fastest and most effective way for a company to realize its maximum profit is to get its pricing right.[5]

Price also affects customer demand. **Price elasticity of demand,** or the responsiveness of demand to changes in price, is more than 10 times higher than advertising elasticity. That is, a certain percentage change in price can lead to 10 to 20 times stronger effects on sales than the same percentage change in advertising expenditures.[6] For these reasons pricing decisions are among the most important decisions that marketers regularly confront.

Price promotions or price reductions have become so common in some consumer product categories that sale prices represent the norm. Price reductions provide many benefits to consumers, manufacturers, wholesalers, and retailers. The primary benefits are listed in Exhibit 11–2.

Both the importance and difficulty of pricing decisions have increased in recent years. These changes have arisen because of several environmental phenomena.[7]

- Introduction of look-alike products increases sensitivity to small price differences.

- Internet access to price and competitive information have made price comparisons easier and have increased pressures on prices.

- Demand for services, which are labor-intensive, hard to price, and sensitive to inflation, has increased.

Thinking Critically

The effects of price on sales are greater than corresponding changes in advertising.

- Does this hold for both price increases and price decreases?

- Does the long-term lagged effects of advertising account for the lower average elasticity for advertising relative to price elasticity?

Exhibit 11–2	*Benefits of price promotions*

- Stimulate retailer sales and store traffic.
- Enable manufacturers to adjust to variations in supply and demand without changing list prices.
- Enable regional businesses to compete against brands with large advertising budgets.
- Reduce retailer's risk in stocking new brands by encouraging consumer trial and clearing retail inventories of obsolete or unsold merchandise.
- Satisfy trade agreements between retailers and manufacturers.
- Stimulate demand for both promoted products and complementary (nonpromoted) products.
- Give consumers the satisfaction of being smart shoppers who are taking advantage of price specials.

Source: Adapted from John A. Farris and John A. Quelch, "In Defense of Price Promotion," *Sloan Management Review,* Fall 1989, p. 64; and Rockney G. Walters, "Assessing the Impact of Retail Price Promotions on Product Substitution, Complementary Purchase, and Interstore Displacement," *Journal of Marketing,* April 1991, p. 17.

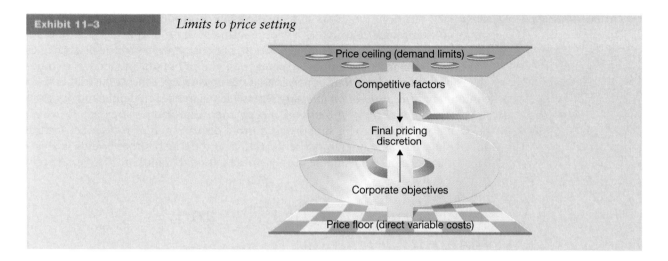

Exhibit 11-3   *Limits to price setting*

- Increased foreign competition has placed added pressure on firms' pricing decisions.
- Changes within the legal environment and economic uncertainty have made pricing decisions more complex.
- Shifts in the relative power within distribution channels from manufacturers to retailers, who are more price-oriented, also has increased the importance of price decisions.
- A bottom-line emphasis places more pressure on performance. Price reductions boost short-term earnings more effectively than does advertising.
- Technology that has reduced the time from new-product idea generation to production also shortens the average life span of products.

The general limits on prices are depicted graphically in Exhibit 11–3. Prices are limited on the high side by what the market will accept and by competitive prices. On the low side, prices must cover costs plus some return on investment. Corporate objectives generally increase pressure toward higher prices to cover overhead and fixed costs and generate an adequate return or profit level. The exhibit depicts the limited latitude that managers may actually have in setting prices.

Price as a Part of the Marketing Mix

A common mistake in marketing is setting a product's price independently of the rest of the marketing mix rather than as an intrinsic part of market positioning strategy.[8] In making pricing decisions, marketers should consider the role of price in consumer perceptions of product quality and image. Interrelationships among items in product lines and between complementary products offered by a firm must be considered in setting prices. Likewise, prices should be set such that all parties in the distribution chain are able to add profitable markups. In addition, prices should not be set without knowledge of market changes and differences between market segments. And last, all marketing messages and communications supporting a product should be integrated and "speak" with a common voice. Hence, pricing objectives must be consistent with the overall communication objectives of the firm as they relate to products and their prices.

Internet Pricing Effects

Interactive shopping on the Internet continues to improve consumer customer access to price and quality information. And, across-store and across-source comparisons are facilitated. These phenomena hold for individual consumers and business-to-business buyers. Questions remain, however, as to whether price sensitivity will increase from this easier access to information or whether easier access to other information that differentiates products will offset these pressures toward price sensitivity.[9]

For goods that are common across stores or business-to-business sellers, price sensitivity will undoubtedly increase. Prices for many products sold on the Internet are being pulled downward by cost-conscious consumers who cross-comparison shop. Auctioneers, such as eBay.com and icollector.com, offer competitive prices for even hard-to-locate items and are particularly well suited to marketing smaller items that can be scanned for viewing and easily shipped.[10]

For sellers, savings come from lower real-estate and rental costs and reduced outlays for advertising, inventory, and transportation. However, price is not the only avenue to success for marketing on the Internet. Customer satisfaction and customer service are paramount. Customers lured on-line with low prices, no search costs, and easy ordering are demanding service like traditional customers. Increasingly, companies are making available service reps, offering the ability to track orders, and responding more quickly to e-mail. Recently, Compaq Computer Corporation had to offer $250 gift certificates to appease customers who were dissatisfied with their Internet shopping service.

Of particular importance, marketers who begin to sell on-line face problems in balancing their on-line efforts with their traditional outlets. This balance has been particularly difficult for computer companies like Dell and Gateway that sell to both individual consumers and businesses. Dell sells direct to consumers and uses the Internet to sell and support corporate buyers. On-line sellers must consider the effects of both their Internet efforts and the prices they are charging on their own dealers and outlets.[11]

Global Pricing Considerations

Pricing in international markets is particularly difficult. Firms pursuing global opportunities find that prices for the same item can be extraordinarily different across countries, even within countries; prices seem to be driven by different dynamics in each situation. For example, one brand of portable TVs was priced at 408 deutsche marks (DM) in the Netherlands, 434 DM in Germany, 560 DM in Italy, and 596 DM in Spain. Understanding price structures and managing prices internationally in these situations can be difficult.[12]

International pricing is also made difficult by exchange-rate differences and the need to present prices in foreign currency values. The **exchange rate** is the price of one country's currency in terms of another country's currency. Changes in exchange rates can affect the prices consumers in different countries have to pay for imported goods. Also, prices of goods are often driven up by taxes, tariffs, and transportation costs. *Protective tariffs* are taxes levied on imported products to raise the prices of those products in efforts to keep local prices competitive.

With the transition in Europe to the euro monetary system, marketers will encounter a market system that rivals that of the United States. The use of a single currency will force marketers to restructure their pricing decisions. This adoption of a single currency will weaken what has been a powerful marketing tool—price differentiation by country. Once the single currency is completely operative, price differences between countries that are now hidden by currency differences will be apparent and will force companies to differentiate their products in other ways.[13]

Pricing Objectives

Pricing decisions are made to achieve certain objectives consistent with a firm's overall mission and marketing strategy. Five objectives commonly guide pricing decisions: ensuring market survival; enhancing sales growth; maximizing company profits; deterring competition from entering a company's niche or market position; and establishing or maintaining a particular product-quality image.[14]

Firms may pursue a combination of these objectives. The objective at Texas Instruments in pricing calculators is to achieve a cost advantage by virtue of growth in sales and dominant market share.[15] For Texas Instruments, large market share translates into competitive advantage through economies of scale from high-volume production and marketing operations. Kmart emphasizes low prices in efforts to generate sales growth and volume. Such objectives provide long-term direction to a company's pricing and promotion decisions.

Market Survival

In some instances, a firm must set prices to ensure its short-term survival. That is, the firm adjusts prices so it can stay in business. Excess production capacity, for example, may require a firm to lower prices so it can keep plants open and maintain operations. In some instances, a firm may adjust prices upward if increased revenues are required.

Recently, the cruise industry's top two carriers, Carnival Cruise Line and Royal Caribbean Cruise Line, for example, broke all reservation records. To fill their rooms, however, they had to resort to deep price discounts. Increasing price consciousness and worries about the economy had led consumers to postpone trips, to trade down to less-expensive accommodations, and to demand lower prices.[16]

Frequent end-of-season deals by retailers represent efforts to move inventory and thereby recoup cash for investment in continuing operations and for purchasing new merchandise. Similarly, manufacturers may reduce prices as new products are introduced in place of existing models. In some cases, even very successful companies like Procter & Gamble have lowered prices to lessen erosion in sales.[17] Pricing for survival is a short-term objective, however. At some point, profitability and return on investment must be satisfactory to ensure long-term success.

Banks in recent years have seen their market share erode significantly and have begun to price aggressively. In efforts to combat this erosion of interest income, banks have resorted to charging extra fees for some services, such as ATM machines and credit cards. These fee increases represent higher prices to consumers. However, many feel these charges are unethical and reflect unnecessary gouging of customers in efforts to earn extraordinary profits.[18]

Sales Growth

Often companies set prices to stimulate sales growth, realizing that price and sales volume are inversely related such that lower prices will normally increase volume. The benefits from higher volume are based on the assumption that increased sales lower unit production costs, increase total revenues, and enhance profits at lower unit prices. **Penetration pricing** is often the strategy used to accomplish this objective. Firms set penetration prices low to encourage initial product trial and generate sales growth, often as part of market entry strategies. The assumption is that the market is sensitive to price differences and that low prices will drive up sales. In this case, short-term profits are sacrificed for future growth. Penetration pricing is also useful for deterring new competitors and reducing short-term costs through high-volume production runs. For international market entry, particularly for unknown companies or companies entering developing countries, a penetration approach is often useful. The initial success of Nissan, Toyota, and other foreign car manufacturers was due, in part, to the use of penetration pricing strategies.

Banks compete on the basis of different charges and fees associated with their line of services.

Often firms set a high list price but then use a low introductory offer to generate initial sales. This approach is advantageous in that the high list price can signal product quality; otherwise, some buyers may question the quality if a low introductory price is used alone.[19]

Market share describes the firm's portion, or percentage, of the total market or total industry sales. Price setting to maximize market share is similar to price setting in pursuit of sales growth. Greater market share increases a firm's market power, which enables it to extract more-favorable channel arrangements (price and distribution advantages with suppliers) and, in turn, to maintain higher margins.[20]

Mack Turner discusses the short-term effects of price reductions and the attraction of new business: "When interest rates are high, many banks offer high promotional rates in hopes of attracting new customers. However, some of these offers only attract short-term investments that quickly leave the bank for even more attractive deals elsewhere. Relatedly, some banks give away free checking hoping the new customers will purchase other loans and credit cards. Yet, banks that follow this strategy but do not have specific sales strategies in place to cross-sell additional services to these new customers frequently find this tactic to be unprofitable."

Market share and firm profitability are often related. As in the case of Texas Instruments, greater market share leads to economies of scale. Economies of scale produce competitive advantages because of increased experience and efficiency; that is, companies learn to produce more efficiently with experience, and per-unit costs decline as volume increases.

Even companies with high market shares can be affected by price competition. Gerber, for example, held 72 percent of the $1.1 billion baby-food market. When it raised prices by 5.5 percent, however, competitors Beech-Nut and Heinz began discounting their prices. Monthly sales for Gerber fell quickly by 16 percent.[21] Similarly, price competition between Kellogg's, the number-one marketer of cereals, and Post has forced Kellogg's to reduce prices on some of its most popular brands, like Rice Krispies and Fruit Loops, to fight declining market share.[22]

An increase in market share is a reasonable pricing objective, but not when competitors have lower unit costs. In such instances, it may be impossible to build market share by lowering prices. Similarly, it is foolish for a company to use pricing strategies to increase market share when customers are not price sensitive.[23] In this case, a firm may be better served by targeting particular market segments in which new products have a competitive advantage other than price.

For many companies, the immediate emphasis will be growth in volume, irrespective of market share. This may occur when there are many firms in a market and all have low share. In addition, growth in sales may be derived from generating new customers or getting current customers to buy more per occasion or to buy more frequently, beyond increased growth from attracting competitors' customers.

Profitability

Maximization of profits is a frequently stated objective for many companies. Yet, this objective is difficult to implement. Profit maximization requires complete understanding of cost and demand relationships; and estimates of cost and demand for different price alternatives are difficult to obtain. As Exhibit 11–4 demonstrates, if prices are set too low, marketers' profits are insufficient; if set too high, no one will buy. Clearly, however, adequate profits are required, and companies are sensitive to changes in profits over time as indications of performance.

Increased prices can affect profitability three to four times more than increases in sales volume at constant prices. One consumer-durable-products company increased operating profits by nearly 30 percent with only a 2.5 percent increase in average prices. An industrial-equipment manufacturer boosted operating profits by 35 percent by raising prices only 3 percent.[24]

Price skimming is a strategy often associated with profit maximization. It includes setting prices high initially to appeal to consumers who are not price

| Exhibit 11–4 | *Optimal pricing decisions* |

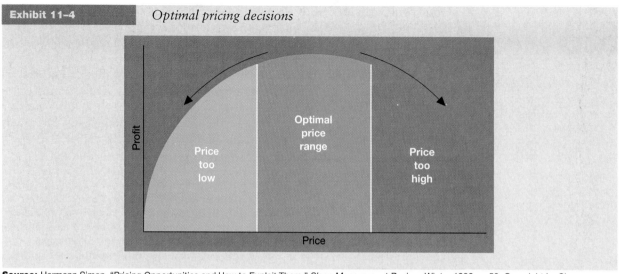

sensitive. In sequential skimming, the firm subsequently lowers prices to appeal to the next most lucrative segments.[25] This strategy allows companies to maximize profits across segments. Besides improving short-term profitability, price skimming lessens demand on production capacity, recoups R&D expenditures, and obtains profits before competitors enter the market. Moreover, consumers may associate product prestige and quality with the high introductory prices prevalent in a skimming approach. Du Pont and IBM are well known for using high introductory prices and skimming practices in marketing new products.[26]

Profitability is often related to **return on investment (ROI)**. ROI is the ratio of income before taxes to total operating assets associated with the product, such as plant and equipment and inventory. As for profitability objectives, the evaluation of the effects of alternative prices on ROI requires realistic estimates of cost and demand for a product or service at different prices. Firms attempting to obtain a desired ROI must take a longer-term, visionary view.

Competitive Pricing

Prices may also be set in reaction to competition. As in penetration pricing, a firm may keep prices low to inhibit competition from entering. Or it may set prices close to those of lower-priced competitors to avoid losing sales. **Price competition** occurs most often when the competing brands are very similar, or when differences between brands are not apparent to prospective buyers.

ITT Sheraton's simplified pricing system, modeled on the airlines' pricing approach, has been criticized by competitors as "rate cutting." The Sheraton pricing structure involves one room rate for business travelers, another for 14-day advance reservations, and a third for weekend rates. Sheraton also lowered its standard price. Not surprisingly, Hilton and Hyatt spokespeople warned that price competition would hurt the industry.[27]

Price competition may result in price wars, with prices spiraling downward in succeeding rounds of price cuts. They may lead to such low prices that all competitors operate at a loss in the short run. Price wars are frequent in the airline and computer software industries. Recent price wars over software in Europe may reduce the sizable margins U.S. companies once obtained for their products, margins once justified by the costs of translation.

In **nonprice competition,** the firm attempts to develop buyer interest in benefits such as quality, specific product features, or service. For this to work, customers must view the distinguishing attributes as desirable. Finally, focusing on unserved target markets in which competition is minimal may allow a firm to charge higher

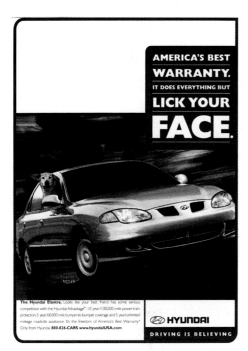

Prices charged for products must cover the entire bundle of product attributes. Warranties are used to enhance the value associated with products; however, their costs should be considered in the prices of products.

prices. For example, Charles Schwab uses its technological communications advantages to offer low competitive prices for financial services.

Competitive strategies have been described as being arrayed on a continuum labeled the **competitive strategy-positioning continuum.** This continuum is anchored by "low-cost leadership" on one end and "differentiation" on the other. For example, one furniture store may emphasize low costs of overhead and operation, a "no frills" warehouse positioning. Alternatively, a competing store may emphasize a more luxurious atmosphere with extensive decorations that appeals to more sophisticated customers. This latter store is more likely to compete on attributes other than price, while the former retail outlet attempts to attract consumers largely by low prices.[28]

Quality and Image Enhancement

Firms often keep prices at a premium to maintain an image of product-quality leadership. **Prestige pricing** is based on the premise that some buyers associate price with quality and avoid products or services for which they perceive prices as too low. The American Express Gold Card and Lexus are examples of products that have images of exclusivity generated through premium prices. Professionals such as lawyers, doctors, and consultants often charge high fees for similar reasons. In these instances, low prices might imply lower-quality service or expertise; the reputations of these service providers allow the higher prices to be charged. The prestige associated with high-price/high-quality products and services is particularly important in gift-giving situations.

When the costs of malfunction are high, business buyers often purchase the highest-quality product available, regardless of price. They believe the risk of nonperformance—say, shutting down an entire production line or process—outweighs the risk of paying too much. Likewise, critical component parts that

Using Technology

Scanner technology: Concerns about price accuracy

Scanner technology has become an integral part of the consumer environment. The benefits to retailers are well documented: decreased labor costs, improved inventory control, and enhanced information about buying patterns. In addition, customers benefit from less waiting due to faster checkout processing. These benefits and improvements in technology will undoubtedly yield further development of scanner technology. For example, Safeway has introduced a self-scanning system where customers charge themselves for their own shopping. Scanner technology also provides benefits to retailers by making available inventory reports to show vendors exactly what is moving and what is not. As such, the retailer is better able to negotiate orders for products that are actually selling. The acquisition of scanner data also facilitates the analysis of historical data by region, which yields insight into the effects of demographics on product category movement.

Concerns remain, however, regarding the effects on consumer welfare stemming from errors in prices charged

to consumers at the cash register. Opinions vary widely, and retailers are often uneasy about discussing the accuracy of scanner systems. However, the cumulative effects of inaccurate pricing is an important issue that directly affects customer satisfaction. In California, Kmart was ordered to institute a program to correct inaccurate shelf prices; the program involved $3 discounts on items scanned higher than the advertised price. One study of 15 grocery stores found that errors in prices systematically favored the retailer for purchases of advertised specials and items on end-of-aisle displays.

Sources: "Getting the Bugs Out," *Progressive Grocer,* March 1996, p. 56; Ronald Goodstein, "UPC Scanner Pricing Systems: Are They Accurate?" *Journal of Marketing,* April 1994, pp. 20–30; Tim Triplett, "Scanning Errors Likely to Take Toll on Customer Satisfaction," *Marketing News,* August 8, 1994, pp. 1, 6; Bill Commun, "Don't Just Scan, Analyze," *Journal of Petroleum Marketing,* May 1999, p. 19; and Amanda Loudin, " 'Been There, Done That' with Scanner Technology," *Warehousing Management,* June 1999, pp. 38–41.

form the core of manufactured goods, such as electronic circuit boards, are likely to carry high prices.

Influences on Pricing Decisions: The Five Cs of Pricing

To ensure that pricing decisions are effective and consistent with the firm's objectives, marketers should consider the **five Cs of pricing** shown in Exhibit 11–5: costs, customers, channels of distribution, competition, and compatibility.[29] These five elements represent the critical influences on pricing decisions.

Costs

Costs associated with producing, distributing, and promoting a product or service are instrumental in establishing the minimum price or floor for pricing decisions. Prices must cover, at least over the long term, the investment and support behind the product, as well as provide enough income and profit to the company. In some instances, costs must be reduced to maintain price competitiveness. This phenomenon is evident in the airline industry. Low-cost providers such as Southwest Airlines have forced full-service airlines, such as American, United, and Delta, to control costs in efforts to maintain competitive prices. These cost reductions have been forced by consumers who are willing to accept fewer extras in service for lower fares.[30]

Exhibit 11–6 details the various costs that must be covered by a $15 price for a CD. The largest of these costs are marketing related: retailer overhead, including operating expenses and profit margin, is 38 percent of the total price; record company overhead, including promotion, advertising, and profit, is 22 percent; and distribution is 13 percent. For this product, nonproduction costs far exceed the other sources of costs that must be covered by price.

Timex also bases its pricing and production decisions on cost considerations. Timex used to make most of its parts itself. Today, the company outsources its components (buys the parts from other manufacturers) so it can make production changes quickly. It is able to use its position as a dominant buyer of watch components to keep costs competitive and get faster payback on watches with shorter life cycles.[31] Old Navy maintains low prices by keeping the design of its products simple and by making use of less-costly fabrics. Through clever packaging and color design, Old Navy successfully offers products, unlikely to go out of style, at cut-rate prices. Procter & Gamble has reduced costs by standardizing product formulas and packaging, reducing reliance on consumer promotion, as well as trade promotions, and limiting costly new-product launches. Intel Corporation has instituted a cost-reduction program aimed at limiting costs of materials through purchasing from their suppliers. Their emphasis is on the entire supply chain and on programs that regularly identify low-cost alternatives that maximize value to Intel.[32]

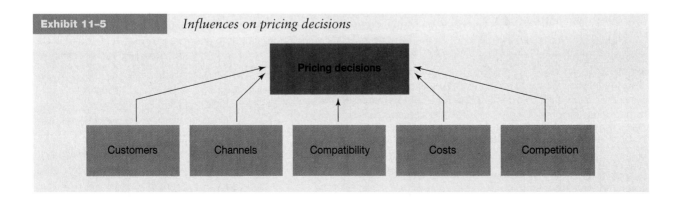

| Exhibit 11–5 | *Influences on pricing decisions* |

Pricing decisions

Customers   Channels   Compatibility   Costs   Competition

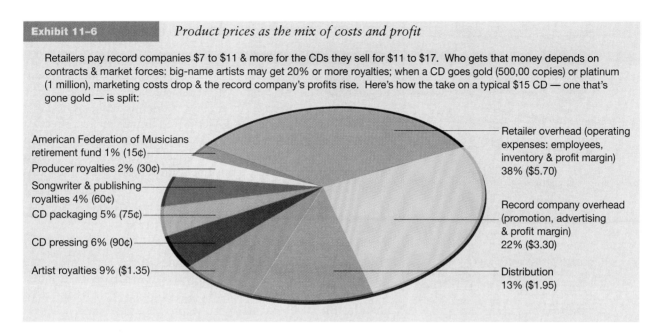

Exhibit 11-6   *Product prices as the mix of costs and profit*

Retailers pay record companies $7 to $11 & more for the CDs they sell for $11 to $17. Who gets that money depends on contracts & market forces: big-name artists may get 20% or more royalties; when a CD goes gold (500,00 copies) or platinum (1 million), marketing costs drop & the record company's profits rise. Here's how the take on a typical $15 CD — one that's gone gold — is split:

American Federation of Musicians retirement fund 1% (15¢)

Producer royalties 2% (30¢)

Songwriter & publishing royalties 4% (60¢)

CD packaging 5% (75¢)

CD pressing 6% (90¢)

Artist royalties 9% ($1.35)

Retailer overhead (operating expenses: employees, inventory & profit margin) 38% ($5.70)

Record company overhead (promotion, advertising & profit margin) 22% ($3.30)

Distribution 13% ($1.95)

Customers

Customer expectations and willingness to pay are important influences on pricing decisions. Buyer reactions are primary determinants of demand. In some instances, customers may be willing to trade off increased prices for more benefits or enhanced product features.

The customer interest in value has not gone unnoticed. Many firms now emphasize value by offering lower prices and higher quality. Penney's returned to its original position as a moderately priced merchant. General Motors has seen substantial customer approval of its value-pricing approach that reduces the prices of its cars, including those models with attractive options.[33]

The health industry has also responded to price-conscious consumers. Today, prescription drug manufacturers like Miles Laboratories compete on price. Normally, new drugs are marketed on their medical advantages, and traditionally drug companies have used studies showing some medical advantages as the basis for maintaining high prices.

Service companies occasionally use **value-in-use pricing** to factor customer input directly into pricing decisions. They base prices on customer estimates of the costs if the service could not be obtained. Such firms are responding to consumer perceptions of value. Computer repair services, for example, might be based on some percentage of the savings to the company from limiting computer downtime. This approach, while requiring some market research, satisfies customer needs and requirements for service at the price the customer defines as reasonable value.[34]

Target costing, a concept developed in Japan, combines both cost and customer input into price decisions. The process results in a market-driven cost estimation procedure to determine for a product what the manufacturing costs must be to achieve (1) the profit margin the company desires, (2) the features sought by customers, and (3) the prices that will be attractive to potential buyers. The result is the development of a product geared toward the needs of buyers at prices they are willing to pay.[35]

Consumers vary in their reactions to price. For example, one study found that more-educated consumers and consumers with

Pricing strategies, product image, and distribution exclusivity must be coordinated. For example, some higher priced and upscale products, like Johnston & Murphy shoes for men, are sold through only a limited number of outlets.

Prices charged by manufacturers to their distribution partners should be set such that members of the channel of distribution can profit as well. Distributors and retailers must be able to establish sufficient margins to profit from their purchase and resale of manufacturer's goods.

less income constraints were less price sensitive. In addition, the effects of price promotions on consumers are often described as being asymmetric. First, reactions to price reductions vary by brand type, with price reductions for premium brands drawing consumers from segments who regularly buy competing brands and consumers who usually buy moderate or private-label brands. Price reductions for lower-priced brands are less effective at generating incremental sales. Second, and as will be explained in Chapter 12, consumers react more strongly to price increases than decreases. Hence, consumer effects on price increases should be carefully considered.[36]

Channels of Distribution

Prices must be set so that other members of the channel of distribution earn adequate returns on sales of the firm's products. Marketers must consider the margins that others in the channel can make. If channel intermediaries cannot realize a sufficient margin, they will not market the products adequately. Moreover, the product's image must be consistent with the channels of distribution. For a product that attracts buyers with a low price, the goal would be low-cost distribution. For a product that attracts buyers with its superior attributes despite a high price, distribution must complement those attributes.[37] For example, certain cosmetics are marketed only through exclusive-image departments. And some exclusive sportswear lines, such as Ellesse and Head, are marketed largely through restricted distribution networks.

Marketers give special sales promotion allowances and support to channel members to encourage purchase. These trade sales promotions now represent the largest of all marketing communications expenditures. Channel arrangements also involve restrictions on resale price, although manufacturers cannot require independent wholesalers and retailers to charge certain prices. Price guarantees stating that prices are the lowest available are also often given to retailers and wholesalers to encourage their patronage.

Competition

Prices charged by competing firms and the reaction of competitors to price changes also influence pricing decisions. Haggar cotton pants and Levi's Dockers are but one example of products that actively compete on price. As a rule, pricing decisions should not be made simply to make the next sale or to meet some short-term pricing objective. Companies that price successfully in competitive markets know that the goal is not just winning sales; they want to maintain those sales in the future.

When competing products and services are very similar, the prevailing prices are a natural limit on the ability of the firm to adjust prices. Prices set significantly higher than the competition will attract only limited demand and cause buyers to switch brands; low prices may result in heavy price competition or futile price wars. Burger King and Wendy's reacted to Checker Drive-In Restaurants by aggressive pricing of their "value" meals and products. Competitive prices also are a factor in the way consumers rate the fairness of a firm's prices.

American products are experiencing increasing competition in Eastern Europe as shoppers become hesitant about higher-priced brands from Western companies. For example, given the still-small average monthly salary in Poland (about $300), consumers are returning to cheaper homegrown merchandise. In response, Western companies are introducing low-cost, low-priced alternatives to compete with the cheaper Polish products. For example, Germany's Benckiser compensated for its expensive laundry detergent, Lanza, by introducing a much cheaper brand, Dosia.

This strategy enabled the German firm to still compete with lower-priced Polish products without damaging the reputation of its higher-priced Lanza brand.[38]

Competitive effects on prices are complex and can vary due to technological influences, the market position of the brands involved, and regulatory changes affecting some industries. For example, competitive pressures from the Internet and the ability of consumers to make price comparisons across outlets are helping pull prices downward. One study noted that, even after accounting for shipping costs, prices for prescription drugs and apparel were over 20 percent less than those in traditional retail outlets.[39]

For many consumer packaged goods, competition among products of different quality is asymmetric. Price promotions by higher-quality brands draw disproportionately more market share from lower-quality brands. Firms in previously regulated industries, such as utilities, are finding much more intense competition and must manage pricing decisions carefully.[40]

Thinking Critically

- Comment on the relevance of the cross-elasticity formula given in Appendix A for the compatibility factor as a determinant of prices for products in a product line. That is, how does cross-elasticity of demand relate to prices of products that make up a firm's product line?

Compatibility

Finally, the price of a product must be compatible with the overall objectives of the firm. Again, a firm's long-term image considerations will influence the prices it establishes. High brand equity enables a firm to launch brand extensions, to extract better arrangements from distributors and retailers, and to charge higher prices.[41] Dial soap, after 40 years, is still the category leader; Chips Ahoy, a 25-year-old brand, is still the leading chocolate chip cookie. These brands have strong brand equity and hence high prices and excellent margins. In both cases, the prices charged are compatible with the overall marketing strategy for the brand.

In pricing a product, a firm must also consider the prices of other products within its product line. The price of one product or brand should not cannibalize sales, that is, shift sales from other brands within the same line of products. If a top-of-the-line model in a line of running shoes is priced at $150, a low-end model targeted to the novice runner should be priced so as not to steal sales from the higher-end model. Likewise, Boeing prices its line of commercial airlines so that low-end models do not detract from the larger, top-of-the-line airplanes.

Ethical and Legal Restraints on Pricing

Marketers must consider more than the influences of the five Cs in price decisions. Pricing practices must also conform to laws and regulations and ethical expectations of customers and society in general. A variety of legislation affects the pricing decisions of firms. The objectives of this legislation are largely twofold: to protect competition among companies within markets and to protect the rights of consumers. The most important of these laws, summarized in chronological order of enactment in Exhibit 11–7, influence the ethical aspects of pricing decisions.

The Sherman Act (1890) inhibited price fixing and restraint of trade among competitors. Pricing practices designed to drive competitors from the market and conspiracy among competitors are limited by the case law established following this legislation. The act represents one of the government's first attempts to establish antitrust policies. A recent case involved allegations that 55 private educational institutions engaged in price-fixing agreements that resulted in overly high student fees. The Sherman Act was also used by the American Football League in its suit against the National Football League.

The Federal Trade Commission Act (1914) established the FTC as the administrative organization for monitoring unfair and anticompetitive business practices. The FTC is charged with limiting deceptive pricing and advertising practices.

The Clayton Act (1914) restricted price discrimination and purchase agreements between buyers and sellers and strengthened the antitrust limits on mergers and competitor arrangements of the Sherman Act. The act also limited requirements that a purchaser of one product must buy other products from the seller.

Exhibit 11-7   *Significant U.S. legislation influencing price decisions*

- **Sherman Act, 1890:** Establishes illegality of restraint of trade and price fixing. First antitrust policy instituted by U.S. government. Predatory pricing to drive competitors from market is also restricted.
- **Federal Trade Commission Act, 1914:** Establishes Federal Trade Commission, which is charged with limiting unfair and anticompetitive practices of business.
- **Clayton Act, 1914:** Restricts price discrimination and purchase agreements between buyers and sellers; strengthens antitrust limits on mergers.
- **Robinson-Patman Act, 1936:** Limits the ability of firms to sell the same product at different prices to different customers. Price differentials can lessen or harm competition, particularly among resellers.
- **Wheeler-Lea Act, 1938:** Allows the Federal Trade Commission to investigate deceptive practices and to regulate advertising. Also ensures that pricing practices do not deceive customers.
- **Consumer Goods Pricing Act, 1975:** Eliminates some control over retail pricing by wholesalers and manufacturers and allows retailers to establish final retail prices in most instances. Places limits on resale-price-maintenance agreements among manufacturers, wholesalers, and retailers.

The Robinson-Patman Act (1936) placed more stringent restrictions on **price discrimination** practices—selling the same product to different customers at different prices. Price discrimination can inhibit competition, particularly among resellers. It is legal to charge final consumers different prices (senior citizen discounts, student rates), because this does not impair competition. A manufacturer, however, may violate the law by charging different prices to different retailers. Quantity discounts are not an issue so long as all buyers can take advantage of uniform discount policies.

All price discrimination is not illegal, however. Under certain conditions, price discrimination may be permissible if the buyers are not competitors; the prices charged do not limit competition; the price differentials reflect differences in costs of serving the different customers; and the price differences occur because of efforts to meet competitor prices.

Acceptable price discrimination may reflect price differences based on time, place, customer, and product distinctions. For example, different prices are charged for telephone use and movies depending on the time of the day. Place differences account for differences in prices at hotels and entertainment events. Even individual customers may be charged different prices based on negotiations or differences in need.

Charges of price discrimination do occur in the marketplace. For example, many pharmacists charge that they pay more for prescription drugs than managed care providers who command discounts for large purchase quantities. In past years, drug manufacturers have pledged to limit price increases to inflation rates or less. However, recent price increases in prescription drugs have risen above those rates as health care reform pressures subsided. Now many pharmacists claim that they are unfairly burdened and at a competitive disadvantage to hospitals and HMOs that pay lower prices for drugs.[42]

Dumping—selling a product in a foreign country at a price lower than its price in the domestic country, and lower than its marginal cost of production—is a form of price discrimination. Most governments have antidumping regulations that protect their own industries against unfair foreign pricing practices. Typically, appeals for government assistance are based on the argument that offending firms are practicing **predatory dumping**—pricing intended to drive rivals out of business. A successful predator firm raises prices once the rival is driven from the market. One famous case involved Sony Corporation of Japan. Sony was selling TV sets for $180 in the United States, while charging $333 in Japan for the same Japanese-made product. Threats of increased tariffs on Japanese TVs eventually forced increases in the prices of those exported to the United States.

The Wheeler-Lea Act (1938) expanded the FTC's role to monitor deceptive and misleading pricing and advertising practices. More recently, the Consumer Goods Pricing Act (1975) supported the right of retailers to determine final prices. The ef-

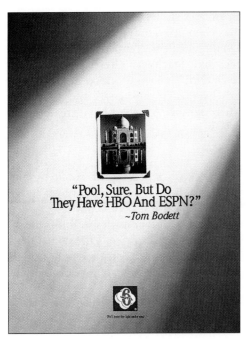

"Pool, Sure. But Do
They Have HBO And ESPN?"
~Tom Bodett

Even ads that do not promote prices should be consistent with the overall pricing strategy of the firm. This nonprice communication subtly reinforces the low price positioning of Motel 6.

fect of the legislation is to limit the ability of manufacturers to control prices in their channels of distribution.

Implications for Pricing Decisions

Primary implications of legislation and case law for pricing include the following:

- Horizontal price fixing among companies at the same level of a distribution channel is illegal.

- In most cases, retailers are free to establish their own final selling prices. Prices charged by manufacturer- or wholesaler-owned retailers may still be restricted by the owner.

- Some states have enacted minimum price laws that prevent retailers from selling merchandise for less than cost.

- Prices must not be presented in a way that deceives customers.

- Discrimination that reflects extremely low prices to eliminate competition, or that does not reflect cost differentials, may be illegal.

- In industries with a few large firms, it is generally acceptable for the pricing behavior of smaller firms to parallel that of larger firms.

International Agreements and Organizations

The prices charged for products and services are also affected by a number of international agreements or organizations. Among the more important agreements are the General Agreement on Tariffs and Trade (GATT); the Organization of Petroleum Exporting Countries (OPEC); the European Union (EU); and the North American Free Trade Agreement (NAFTA). All have wide-ranging effects on the prices charged in global markets.

For example, OPEC is a loose federation of many of the oil-producing countries. This cooperative arrangement is designed to influence market prices and short-term profits for crude oil. The cartel has been affected by acts of cheating on production

Earning Customer Loyalty

Emachines: PC prices eroding brand loyalty

In no other industry have the effects of declining prices on brand loyalty been more evident than in the personal computer industry. Loyalty to brands, such as IBM and Macintosh, has been significantly undermined as PC prices have dropped with improvements in technology and lowering costs. Packard Bell-NEC, which marketed both premium- and low-priced machines, has found sales particularly hard to generate. In contrast, sub-$1,000 PC sales have increased market share for Compaq, Hewlett-Packard, and direct-order companies Dell and Gateway. How low will prices drop as new entrants produce and sell even lower priced models? One noteworthy example, emachines Inc., represents one of the fastest takeoffs in high-tech history.

Their priciest machines were being offered at $599 in early 2000. Their intended target market is the 15 million-plus households who are the next to purchase their first PC. Emachines Inc. and other new entrants into the low-priced market are now increasing pressure on the profits of the large firms in the market, as prices continue to undermine brand loyalty. However, like other situations, those firms who are successful in the sub-$1,000 market will be those that couple low price with attractive features and service.

Sources: Peter Burrows, "Fast, Cheap, and Ahead of the Pack," *Business Week,* April 5, 1999, pp. 36–37; and Jim Carlton, "Cheaper PCs Start to Attract New Customers," *The Wall Street Journal,* January 26, 1998, p. B1.

among its own members as well as nonmembers' independent pricing actions. OPEC's effectiveness at controlling prices has been uneven in recent years.

Coffee cartels in South America actually enhanced the competitive positions of high-priced marketers of coffee—companies like Starbucks. Restrictions placed upon production of coffee, similar to those of OPEC on oil production, have hurt lower- and moderate-priced national brands by raising their costs and squeezing their already low margins. Starbucks and other high-priced sellers have greater margins to absorb the rising costs.

Customer Price Evaluations
We have talked so far about pricing from the perspective of the marketer or the seller. But how does the buyer judge prices? What determines a customer's evaluation of a product or brand?

The key to learning how prices influence purchase decisions lies in understanding how buyers perceive prices.[43] This **perceived monetary price** is the consumer's reaction that the price is high or low, fair or unfair. Further, consumers do not always remember prices, even within the store, and often encode or process them in personally meaningful ways.[44]

Judgments of Perceived Value

Perceived value describes the buyer's overall assessment of a product's utility based on what is received and what is given. It represents a trade-off between the "give" and the "get" components of a purchase transaction and plays a critical role in purchase decisions.[45] Some observers describe perceived value as "quality per dollar."[46]

The give is mainly the product's price. Increasingly, consumers base brand decisions on their notions of a "reasonable price" and compare prices regularly.[47] Exhibit 11–8 summarizes the effects of price on buyer judgments of value. Perceived value ultimately determines willingness to buy. Perceived value in turn is determined by a combination of the perceived benefits, or quality received, and the monetary sacrifice made; higher benefits enhance value; higher monetary sacrifice detracts from it. These offsetting effects reflect the trade-off of the give and get components inherent in consumer perceptions of value.

The power of consumer perceptions of value has not gone unnoticed by marketers. Well-known consumer companies whose stated primary emphasis is on consumer value include McDonald's, Wal-Mart, Sara Lee, Toyota, and Taco Bell. Business-to-business marketers now focusing on value through lower prices and enhanced quality include Emerson Electric, Electronic Data Systems (EDS), and 3M.

| Exhibit 11–8 | *Relationships among price, perceived value, and willingness to buy* |

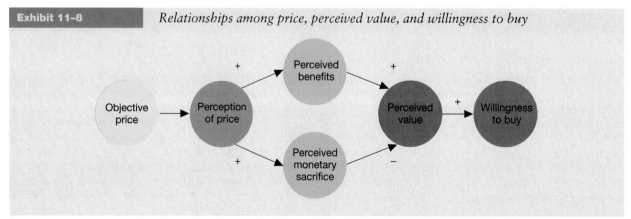

Source: Adapted from Kent B. Monroe, *Pricing: Making Profitable Decisions,* 2nd ed. (New York: McGraw-Hill, 1990), p. 46; and William B. Dodds, Kent B. Monroe, and Druv Grewal, "Effects of Price, Brand, and Store Information on Buyers' Product Evaluations," *Journal of Marketing Research,* August 1991, p. 308.

The determinants of value for services are even more critical to understand. As one noted expert in services marketing emphasizes, the lack of differentiation among many competing services encourages managers to overuse price as a marketing tool; the mistake is thus made that price and value are equivalent. In truth, value represents the benefits received for burdens endured. These burdens not only include price, but also slow service, busy telephone lines, and rude boundary employees who interact directly with the customers of service providers.[48]

Price/Quality Relationships

Consumers trade off prices paid for benefits received, or product or service quality. The **price/quality relationship** describes the extent to which the consumer associates the product's price with higher quality. Higher prices do not always signal higher quality, however. Evidence suggests that, if there is a positive relationship, it is not very strong.[49] Sometimes uninformed consumers mistakenly use price to make quality judgments. When price and quality are not related, buying a higher-priced brand is a poor decision.

One study of *Consumer Reports* ratings revealed some interesting findings regarding the existence of actual price/quality relationships.[50] In tests across brands within nine product classes, prices and objective quality ratings were found to be positively related, negatively related, and not related, depending upon the products investigated. For example, positive relationships between price and quality existed for bicycles, washing machines, and frozen pizza. Negative relationships were observed for stereo speakers, blenders, and spray cleaners. Thus, consistently assuming higher prices mean higher quality does not always result in wise decisions.

Consumer Use of Price Information

The effect of prices on consumers varies across people and situations.[51] Uncertainty about prices and quality can make purchase decisions difficult. The importance of quality and a buyer's previous experience determine the role of price in consumer evaluations. Ideally, consumers should use a **best-value strategy,** picking the lowest-cost brand available with the desired level of quality. In a **price-seeking strategy,** some consumers make a price/quality assumption and choose the highest-priced brand to maximize expected quality. Other consumers follow a **price-aversion strategy,** buying the lowest-priced brand simply to minimize risks of having spent more than necessary.

Mack Turner comments on pricing strategy: "With e-commerce achieving critical mass, the consumer—both the retail and corporate consumer—has the tool to gain broad knowledge of product offerings, deep knowledge of product benefits, and the ability to act on that knowledge immediately. From a pricing point of view, e-commerce creates the potential of a 24-hour-by-7-day auction. The customer can quickly visit multiple on-line stores, shop prices and availability, and select the lowest price. New channels for borrowing have been created in which several e-commerce lenders compete head-on for the borrower's business. E-commerce retailers will have to aggressively manage their product availability, distribution, and after-sale service. Service providers, such as banks, will have to provide more-current and complete on-line research and information, as well as excellent execution and after-sale support."

Recognition that consumers use different purchase approaches can influence the firm's marketing strategies. If product quality is not obvious to the consumer but has high importance (imported wines, for example), firms often use a *price signaling strategy:* They set prices higher to imply higher quality. Where quality information is more readily available and the importance of quality is high (appliances, perhaps), firms often pursue a value-based strategy and use informative advertising. In this case, the firm keeps prices competitive and focuses marketing communications on the benefits and quality of the product. Firms market generic brands and brands that compete largely on low price in recognition that some consumers are price-averse. Interestingly, low prices or heavy advertising expenditures can signal high quality in some instances. When quality is not observable and can only be assessed through consumption (i.e., experience goods), "wasteful" expenditures by the firm via low introductory prices or an expensive ad campaign may signal high quality for products dependent on repeat business.[52]

How Are Price Judgments Made?

Consumer expectations about market prices affect decisions to buy. Prices noticeably above and below expectations can lead to unfavorable reactions to product offerings.

How do people judge whether prices are too low, too high, or fair? Consumers compare product prices with internal and, in some cases, external reference prices. **External reference prices** include those charged by other retailers or comparison prices that a retailer provides to enhance perceptions of the published price.

Internal reference prices are comparison standards that consumers remember and use to make their judgments. There are several internal reference prices. One is the expected price, a primary determinant of whether a buyer perceives a price as fair and reasonable. Another is the **reservation price,** an economic term for the highest price a person is willing to pay. Expectation of future prices is also a key internal reference, as the forward-looking consumer evaluates the costs and benefits of buying now versus buying at some future time.[53] Other internal reference prices include "the price last paid, the average retail price, and the price I would like to pay."[54] Consumers sometimes infer motives for prices, particularly unexpected high prices, and these motives affect perceptions of price fairness. When high prices are assumed to reflect marketer "greed," fair-price perceptions generate negative inferences to the seller. As such, fair price is an important internal reference price in certain circumstances.[55]

A model of consumer evaluations of prices is presented in Exhibit 11–9.[56] It assumes that consumers have price information through past experiences with purchases of the same product or similar products.[57] Most people may be uncertain about specific

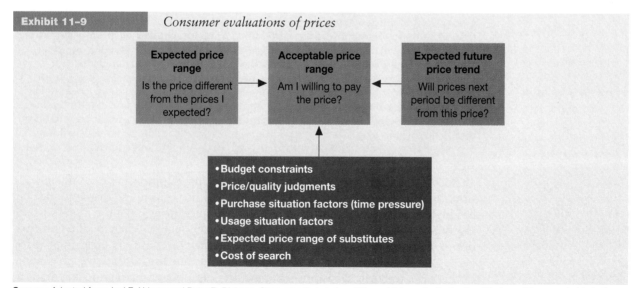

Exhibit 11–9	*Consumer evaluations of prices*

Expected price range
Is the price different from the prices I expected?

→

Acceptable price range
Am I willing to pay the price?

←

Expected future price trend
Will prices next period be different from this price?

↑

- Budget constraints
- Price/quality judgments
- Purchase situation factors (time pressure)
- Usage situation factors
- Expected price range of substitutes
- Cost of search

Source: Adapted from Joel E. Urbany and Peter R. Dickson, *Consumer Knowledge of Normal Prices: An Exploratory Study and Framework,* Marketing Science Institute, report no. 90-112 (Cambridge, MA: 1990), p. 18.

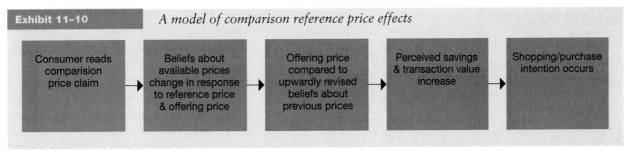

Exhibit 11–10 *A model of comparison reference price effects*

| Consumer reads comparison price claim | → | Beliefs about available prices change in response to reference price & offering price | → | Offering price compared to upwardly revised beliefs about previous prices | → | Perceived savings & transaction value increase | → | Shopping/purchase intention occurs |

Source: Adapted from Abhijit Biswas and Edward A. Blair, "Contextual Effects of Reference Prices in Retail Advertisement," *Journal of Marketing,* July 1991, p. 4. © 1991 by the American Marketing Association. Reprinted with permission.

prices but have some general expectations about market prices and a range of acceptable prices. They evaluate how the price of a product fits these expectations. They may interpret prices judged as too low as indicating suspect product quality; prices judged as too high are dismissed as out of the question or associated with a different product category.

Individual price evaluations may be influenced by external factors such as budget constraints, time pressure, anticipated use situations, or the cost of further search for lower-priced items. Consumers are generally less willing to pay higher prices for brands they perceive to have frequent price promotions.[58]

Advertised Comparison Prices

Advertisers often provide comparison prices (external reference prices) to persuade shoppers to buy. Comparison prices generally take one of three forms: prices previously charged by the retailer, prices charged by other retailers in the area, or manufacturer-suggested prices. Exhibit 11–10 summarizes the effect of comparison prices.[59] Comparison pricing increases the perceived **transaction value** of the purchase (the perceived merits of the deal) by raising the shopper's internal price standard, which makes the advertised price appear more attractive.[60] Increased transaction value then enhances overall acquisition value, which increases the likelihood of purchase. Such price-induced incentives are particularly effective for positioning products that are relatively undifferentiated from those of competitors. These transaction value-enhancing strategies are prevalent for jewelry, luggage, and some electronic products. In fact, retailers such as Best Buy and Circuit City often present sale prices coupled with either "previously offered prices" or manufacturers' suggested prices.[61]

This is one ECHO that doesn't repeat anything.

www.isthistoyota.com
CHANGING, EVERY DAY. TOYOTA

Comparison prices are used to "frame" offerings as a good deal or high value. In this comparative pricing ad, Toyota promotes both sale price and the MSRP price

Summary

1. **Realize the importance of price and understand its role in the marketing mix.** For every good or service sold, the determination of price is critically important to the level of demand and the profits earned. A price set too high will discourage demand; a price set too low will result in less revenue; both lead to lower total profits. Determining an optimal price is becoming more difficult with changing marketplace trends, including faster technological progress, the proliferation of new products, increased demand for services, and growing global competition.

   Relationships between the determined price and the other marketing mix variables affect sales of the product and others the company offers. Price is only one aspect of the firm's marketing mix; other aspects, such as product and distribution, must be considered in pricing decisions. Further, price offers the selling firm a basis for competing whenever other differences among competing brands are not apparent to buyers.

2. **Understand the characteristics of the different pricing objectives that companies can adopt.** Common objectives that guide company pricing decisions include ensuring market survival, enhancing sales growth, increasing market share, maximizing profits, realizing a certain return on investment, deterring competition, and establishing or maintaining a particular quality image. Firms often pursue profitability objectives by a price-skimming strategy and growth and competitive deterrence by a penetration-pricing strategy. Prestige pricing is consistent with quality and image-enhancement objectives.

3. **Identify many of the influences on marketers' pricing decisions.** Pricing decisions are influenced by the five Cs of pricing: costs, customers, channels of distribution, competition, and compatibility. Costs determine the minimum level of prices. Prices must at least cover costs in the long term, or insufficient profits and income result. Customer expectations, as well as perceptions of value and fairness, determine price acceptability.

   Price determination must also take into account of other members of the channel of distribution. Intermediaries in the channel must be able to earn sufficient margins. Competitive factors also influence prices. When products are similar and price differences are important to consumers, prices will tend to move toward the going price.

   Pricing decisions must also be compatible with the overall marketing and communications objectives of the firm. Finally, national and international laws and agreements also influence price decisions.

4. **Explain how consumers form perceptions of quality and value.** Potential buyers, including individuals and business buyers, form perceptions of value that influence their willingness to buy (purchase behavior). Perceived value is the overall assessment of the utility of a product, depending on what is received and what is given or paid. Price influences perceived value in terms of perceived benefits and perceived monetary sacrifice. Consumers vary in their reactions to price, but they typically adopt one of three strategies: a best-value strategy, a price-seeking strategy, or a price-aversion strategy.

5. **Understand price/quality relationships and internal and external reference prices.** Consumers frequently infer quality from prices. This reaction describes the price/quality relationship. These opinions, regardless of their accuracy, influence the buyer's decision; customers are more likely to pay a higher price if they believe a product to be of higher quality.

   Many consumers compare advertised prices with expected prices, a frequently used internal reference price. If prices are above expectations, perceived value of a product declines; lower-than-expected prices may cause perceived value to rise. Companies often provide external reference prices by pairing an offered price with a higher comparison price designed to make the lower price more attractive. These comparison prices may be previously charged prices, manufacturer-suggested prices, or competitive prices.

Understanding Marketing Terms and Concepts

Thinking About Marketing

1. What is the meaning of price? Contrast the basic price mix with the price promotion mix.

2. Why are pricing decisions so important? What are the effects of setting prices too low? Too high?

3. What environmental conditions make pricing decisions so difficult? How might these effects influence estimation of costs and revenues?

4. How do these pricing objectives differ: quality enhancement versus market survival? Sales growth versus profitability?

5. Describe briefly how information on the Internet affects price sensitivity? How might these effects differ for well-known versus less-familiar brands?

6. How does Charles Schwab compete with other brokerage houses such as Merrill Lynch? What influences Schwab's pricing strategy?

7. What are some of the primary legal restrictions on marketers' pricing decisions?

8. Contrast external reference prices with internal reference prices. Give several examples of each. How do reference prices affect consumer reactions to prices?

9. Define consumer perceived value and explain what determines it. How do price and perceived quality affect perceptions of value? Explain the relationship between price and quality.

10. Explain these purchase strategies that consumers use to evaluate prices: best value, price seeking, price aversion.

Applying Marketing Skills

1. Interview a small retailer. Ask how prices are determined and how products put on sale are selected. Does support from the manufacturer influence the initial price of goods? What role does consumer demand play?

2. Find in your local newspaper reference-price advertisements from two different retailers. What are the original prices and the sale prices? What are the percent reductions? With whom or with what is the sale price compared? What wording is used to make the reference-price claim?

3. Interview a close friend or relative. Ask the question: "What comes to mind when you consider the purchase of a personal computer?" At what point does the person mention price? To what extent does the order of the attributes mentioned reflect their importance in determining the purchase?

Using the www in Marketing

Activity One As you know, more and more consumers are using the Internet to shop and gather information. This phenomenon is particularly prevalent in the sports industry. Consider the price information for two brands of tennis rackets. Wilson, Prince, and Dunlop offer a variety of models:

1. How is the price information presented? Can consumers make easy price comparisons within lines?

2. Why are the dealer companies unable to present discounted-price information for the most recent models?

3. Why have price discounters for sports equipment been so successful? Is it ethical for consumers to shop at local retail stores—and even borrow equipment from the store for trial use—but then purchase from a price discounter using a magazine advertisement or the Internet?

Activity Two Assume that you are shopping for a Tommy Hilfiger casual shirt for a younger brother in high school.

1. How might price comparisons differ between shopping on the Internet versus a trip to the mall?

2. Describe the differences in price between those presented on the Tommy Hilfiger site versus in-store prices. How do the total prices charged compare (i.e., including shipping costs)?

3. What role does price play in the overall strategy of Tommy Hilfiger?

Making Marketing Decisions
Case 11-1 Silver Fox: Wily Competitive Pricing

For specialty stores such as Silver Fox, pricing decisions take on some unique characteristics. Silver Fox is a small retail store offering tennis clothing and accessories. Near the store are a number of country clubs and a large high school, and there are many adult tennis teams in the area. Open six days a week, the store operates with four part-time employees and the owner, John Atkinson.

Silver Fox has annual sales of around $375,000. Tennis clothing, such as warm-up outfits, shorts and skirts, and T-shirts, constitutes 40 percent of the store's total sales, 50 percent including shoes. An additional 40 percent of sales is made up of tennis rackets and balls; the final 10 percent comes from the store's racket-stringing service. Tennis clothing is a very important component of the store's business, as it sells these items at a 100 percent markup over cost during peak seasons. The store offers national brand names of clothing and, at least during the spring and summer, enjoys an acceptable sales level of tennis clothing.

During the spring and summer, demand for tennis supplies is much higher than during other months. This increased demand allows Silver Fox to mark up its clothing items a full 100 percent, a pricing strategy Atkinson believes is necessary to achieve the desired profitability. During these peak seasons, Silver Fox and its competitors charge comparable prices. With its convenient location, the store is able to maintain a steady stream of sales.

During the fall and winter, however, demand for tennis clothes and accessories declines sharply, and the store's larger competitors really hold an advantage. By offering clothing and equipment for other sporting activities, these competitors can maintain overall high sales levels. Silver Fox does not offer any merchandise to offset slow tennis-related sales during these months, so it cannot compete on price with its competitors. Instead, the store is forced to come down considerably on its 100 percent markup just to maintain sales. Because the store purchases its merchandise directly from local sales representatives, costs for tennis clothing do not fluctuate during the year.

Reducing markup on clothing items during the fall and winter months provides some advantages. The store can increase its sales of tennis apparel during this otherwise slow period. Moreover, the lower clothing prices serve to increase the store's customer traffic flow during these

months, although not to the height of its traffic flow during the spring or summer. This increase in customer traffic serves to increase sales for nonclothing merchandise.

Several environmental influences have caused Silver Fox to consider a drastic change in strategy. The shop is considering offering for sale only a limited line of tennis products (e.g., rackets, balls, and grips). Other products (largely tennis shoes) could be ordered individually on demand by the Fox for its members and walk-in customers. The reasons for these contemplated changes are threefold: (1) the emergence of several large sporting-goods stores in a large regional mall located only two miles from the Silver Fox location; (2) the establishment of a competing tennis facility within one mile; and (3) the growing practice of shoppers using Silver Fox as a means of determining personal shoe and clothing sizes just prior to making purchases via direct interaction with other suppliers—such as those who advertise regularly in tennis magazines or those who sell direct via the Internet. In addition, tennis magazines serve as monthly delivered catalogs, as all major tennis periodicals offer tennis equipment and clothing for direct sale at very competitive prices.

To offset these phenomena and the lost income from the sale of tennis clothes, several changes in strategy by Silver Fox are being considered. However, the changes in strategy are not without risk. The effects on club membership and the existing positioning of the Fox are unknown. First, the interior of the club could be remodeled and used as a source of rental income for parties, receptions, and business meetings. Second, greater emphasis on private tennis lessons could be more heavily emphasized, with part of this income going to support the club's activities.

Questions

1. Explain why Silver Fox's clothing pricing strategy seems to be cost-oriented during the spring and summer months but more demand-oriented during other months.

2. Would you classify the demand for tennis clothing as elastic or inelastic? Explain your reasoning.

3. Should Silver Fox adopt the proposed new strategy? Why or why not?

Case 11-2 Priceline.com: Price Search and Competition

Priceline.com has pioneered a unique type of e-commerce known as a "demand collection system" that enables consumers to use the Internet to save money on a wide range of products and services, while enabling sellers to generate incremental revenue. Priceline.com has generated substantial success in the sales of airline tickets and hotel rooms. The firm now offers the ability to buy cars, long-distance telephone services, and grocery products for home delivery, while other purchase opportunities are available or under development. Home loans can even be arranged using priceline.com.

Priceline.com makes money on the spread between what a customer is willing to pay and the price offered by the vendor. Priceline.com collects information regarding the numbers of customers, their product and service preferences, and the amount willing to pay. Partnerships between priceline.com and other companies provide the opportunity to generate incremental demand for the partnering firms, without disturbing partner-firm normal pricing structures. Consumers must guarantee their offer by credit card, must agree to keep their offer open for a certain period of time, and must be flexible regarding brand selection.

Competition for priceline.com on the Internet in terms of price services and auctions is evolving at a very fast rate, and on-line haggling is now among the hottest phenomena in e-commerce. As examples, Amazon.com has begun an auction service and America On-Line now offers eBay as one of its features. Potentially, cyberauctions could push aside normal sticker prices and begin an era of dynamic pricing. The no-cost aspects of using the Internet make price bargaining an easy means of shopping.

Questions

1. What effects will priceline.com have on brand integrity for the companies with which it is involved?

2. What other industries represent potential opportunities for priceline.com?

3. What effects, if any, will Internet offerings like priceline.com have on both consumer search behavior and sensitivity to prices?

4. As auction alternatives expand on the Internet, what will priceline.com have to do to maintain its competitive advantage?

SOURCES: Robert D. Hof, Heather Green, and Paul Judge, "Going, Going, Gone," *Business Week,* April 12, 1999, pp. 30–32; Nick Wingfield, "Priceline Adds Three Airlines to System, Resulting in a Charge of $1.1 Billion," *The Wall Street Journal,* November 17, 1999, p. B2; Nick Wingfield, "Priceline.com Names Microsoft in Suit, Alleging Violation of One of Its Patents," *The Wall Street Journal,* October 14, 1999, p. B18; Nick Wingfield, "Priceline.com Plans to Let Customers Bid for Long-Distance Phone Service," *The Wall Street Journal,* November 8, 1999, p. B6; and http://www.priceline.com/PriceLine ASOPourCompany?asp/company.asp.

Price Determination and Pricing Strategies

After studying this chapter, you should be able to:

1 Discuss the interrelationships among price, demand, demand elasticity, and revenue.

2 Understand methods for determining price.

3 Recognize the different pricing strategies and the conditions that best suit the choice of a strategy.

4 Recognize the importance of adapting prices under shifting economic and competitive situations.

5 Understand the ethical considerations involved in setting and communicating prices.

The eBay site offers on-line trading opportunities in which consumers can bid on products and in which sellers can auction items for sale. Of particular importance, and unlike traditional exchange relationships in the marketplace, buyers have significant input into the determination of prices. Through eBay, individuals can buy and sell items in more than 1,000 categories in an auction format. The number of individuals collecting items, ranging from match covers to *Three Stooges* memorabilia, is incredible. At the beginning of 2000, eBay had some 7.7 million registered users bidding on some three million items.

As one of the few dot com companies to have made a profit from the beginning, the site tries to establish a sense of community by drawing together people with similar perspectives and interests. eBay enables consumers to pursue their individuality and offers sellers financial opportunities. eBay enables one-to-one transactions across divisions caused by geography and class. Trust among individuals is critical to the success of relationships, and fraud on the site has been remarkably infrequent. eBay offers free insurance in case transactions go bad, as well as escrow accounts that, for a fee, hold funds until deals are complete. Trust is engendered by the site's feedback forum, in which auction winners are encouraged to describe their experiences and transactions. Sellers on eBay with positive comments are subsequently sought out by others and command better prices.

The site has experienced its troubles, however. Hardware shortcomings prevented the company from keeping up with the site's phenomenal growth in mid-1999, and several disturbing site crashes occurred. Moreover, the cite was severely affected in early 2000 by "hack-attacks." Meg Whitman, eBay's CEO, now has a firm understanding of what technology means to her company and is determined to develop the kind of e-commerce system previously believed impossible. Continued development of eBay should enable the company to continue to prosper, as growth projections suggest significant potential market demand. For example, Prudential Securities estimates that consumer-to-consumer and small business-to-small business gross sales will reach $41.6 billion by 2003. **Sources:** Sally B. Donnelly and Mitch Frank, "Auction Nation: Town Square Community Center, Social Scene—eBay Turned into Much More than Auction," *Time,* December 27, 1999, p. 82; Michael Krantz, "The Attic of e:>>From Yesteryear's Treasures to Yesterday's Garbage, There's a Price and a Place for Everything; What Are You Collecting?" *Time,* December 27, 1999, p. 74; Kathleen Melymuka, "Internet Intuition," *Computer World,* January 10, 2000, p. 48; and Don Tapscott, "Customer Woes: The New Big Internet Industry," *Computerworld,* November 1, 1999, p. 30.

Internet influences on consumer prices and the prices charged for products have been profound. In this example, the eBay situation underscores the importance of price when products can be reasonably evaluated and when consumers have some idea of their needs and the kinds of products and services that can satisfy those needs. The example illustrates only one approach to pricing, however. In this chapter, we examine the processes companies use to select a specific pricing strategy. Additionally, we discuss some theoretical and practical issues affecting the determination of prices. Some of these issues involve ethical considerations. Price determination and evaluation of appropriate pricing strategies are a continual managerial challenge.

As many now believe, electronic commerce is leading to fundamental changes in the way companies relate to their customers and, in the case of auctions, the way consumers relate to one another. The effects are being felt as much as anywhere in the area of pricing. For example, comparing insurance rates from hundreds of companies would take hundreds of calls. Now, price comparisons are possible with the click of a mouse. Allstate has already reduced its labor force and begun selling on the Internet. Sites such as eCoverage and Quotesmith.com make comparisons readily available. In contrast to auction sites, other sites on the Internet are collecting bargain hunters in efforts to build power for negotiations in search of low prices. For www.mercata.com, the process bands together consumers who have common needs in search of "volume discounts."[1]

Price Determination: An Overview

The step-by-step procedure diagrammed in Exhibit 12–1 presents a logical approach for setting prices.[2] Execution of this process requires an understanding of the concepts described in

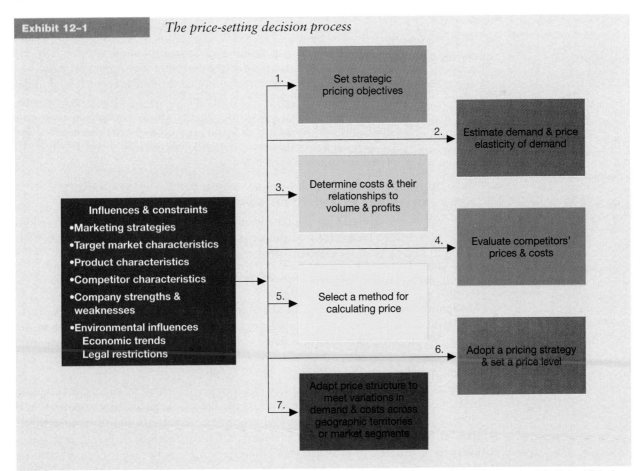

Exhibit 12–1   *The price-setting decision process*

Influences & constraints
- Marketing strategies
- Target market characteristics
- Product characteristics
- Competitor characteristics
- Company strengths & weaknesses
- Environmental influences
  Economic trends
  Legal restrictions

1. Set strategic pricing objectives
2. Estimate demand & price elasticity of demand
3. Determine costs & their relationships to volume & profits
4. Evaluate competitors' prices & costs
5. Select a method for calculating price
6. Adopt a pricing strategy & set a price level
7. Adapt price structure to meet variations in demand & costs across geographic territories or market segments

Source: Adapted from Harper W. Boyd, Jr., and Orville C. Walker, Jr., *Marketing Management: A Strategic Approach* (Homewood, IL: Richard D. Irwin, 1990), p. 461.

Chapter 11. First, the firm must set pricing objectives consistent with its overall marketing and strategic efforts and with the product's image and quality. Common pricing objectives are to maximize profits or sales growth. Second, the firm must consider market demand and the responsiveness of demand to different prices. What will the level of sales be at different prices? How do sales change as prices vary?

Next, the firm determines the costs to manufacture products or provide services and the relationship of costs to volume. The company evaluates competitor prices and costs. If prices are set well above market prices, consumers will not purchase. If prices are too low, revenues and profits may be lost. Then the firm may use one of various methods for determining prices, including markup pricing, break-even analysis, and target-return pricing methods.

Finally, the firm must set specific prices, often using one of the common pricing strategies. After setting prices, the firm monitors and adjusts them to adapt to differences in demand and costs across market segments or to meet competitive reactions.

As Exhibit 12–1 shows, the stages in this pricing process are subject to several influences and constraints. These include product characteristics, company strengths and weaknesses, and legal constraints. Moreover, both costs and demand are difficult to estimate. Sometimes, price determination involves setting a price first, then revising in response to market performance.

Price and Demand

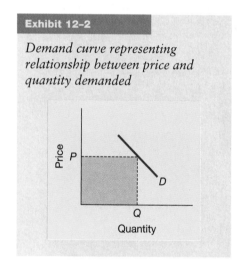

Exhibit 12–2

Demand curve representing relationship between price and quantity demanded

Demand Curves

The relationship between price and demand is expressed in the traditional market **demand curve** labeled D in Exhibit 12–2. Under normal conditions, customers buy more as prices drop; they buy less when prices rise. Price is only one determinant of demand, however. Others include household income, tastes and preferences, population growth, and prices of related products. For many business-to-business situations, demand is driven by general economic conditions and consumer demand, as well as by the preferences and needs of the firm's buyers. This is the concept of derived demand discussed in Chapter 5.

Price Elasticity of Demand

Price elasticity of demand is a basic business concept. The relationship between price and quantity demanded varies; as one increases, the other decreases. Price elasticity of demand is computed as:

$$\text{Price elasticity of demand} = \frac{\text{Percent change in quantity demanded}}{\text{Percent change in price}}$$

Computational procedures and an example are shown in Appendix A.

Elastic demand exists when small price changes result in large changes in demand. When demand is elastic, a small decrease in price increases total revenues. Elastic demand prevails in the motor vehicles, engineering products, furniture, and professional services industries.

Inelastic demand exists when price changes do not result in significant changes in demand. Inelastic demand often occurs for books, magazines, newspapers, and clothing, as well as in the banking and insurance, beverage, and utility industries.[3] Exhibit 12–3 depicts elastic and inelastic demand situations. Overall, demand is likely to be inelastic to price changes when there are few or no product substitutes; when buyers do not readily notice the higher price and are slow to change their buying habits or to search for lower prices, or when they think higher prices are justi-

Speaking from Experience

Colleen Suljic obtained her bachelor of science degree from the University of Illinois, Urbana/Champaign, School of Communications, with a minor in business administration. She is active in the marketing of business and economics texts for four-year institutions. Her duties include the development of complete textbook marketing plans, as well as coordination of marketing efforts with editorial and production staff.

"The college textbook market has not traditionally been price sensitive. However, it has recently become more sensitive to price, allowing greater price elasticity. The price of the product was rarely a deciding factor in the past for the professor, the decision maker. In some cases, it is now a leading factor. We've found that a small difference in price does not change buying behavior, but a difference of $15 to $20 does. For a student using this book, it is very possible that your professor is concerned about the cost, since this book is available in a loose-leaf, low-cost alternative."

Colleen Suljic
Senior Marketing Manager
McGraw-Hill/Irwin Higher
Education Group

Exhibit 12–3

Elastic and inelastic demand

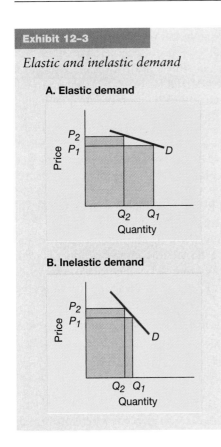

A. Elastic demand

B. Inelastic demand

fied by product improvements or inflation; and when the product or service represents a small portion of their household income.[4]

Where demand is price-elastic, marketers must carefully evaluate any proposed increases in price. Price changes may cause significant change in quantity demanded. Long-term elasticities may differ from short-term ones as customers become aware of changing prices and have time to search for alternative products or services.

Cross elasticity of demand relates the percentage change in quantity demanded for one product to percentage price changes for other products. For example, products are often part of a line of similar products; and changes in the price of one brand may affect the demand for other items in the product line. When products are close *substitutes*, such as cola beverages, a rise in the price of one will increase the demand for the other. For businesses, a sharp increase in prices of steel fasteners used in the construction of trucks would cause increased demand for less-expensive plastic or aluminum fasteners.

Alternatively, when products are *complements*, a price increase of one may decrease the demand for the other. For example, large price increases for personal computers would cause a decrease in the demand for printers. And price reductions of taco shells may increase sales of taco sauce.[5]

Some marketers believe that a primary objective is to create inelasticity for their products. This requires a thorough understanding of demand, allowing the firm to offer brands with attributes that customers find irresistible regardless of price. That is, brands are designed to offer benefits that entice consumers to pay prices high

Being Entrepreneurial

Net serves up quotes

As the insurance industry moves slowly to react to the Internet, Net upstarts, such as Quotesmith.com, are making on-line sales much easier than dealing with local insurance agents. The database for Quotesmith.com provides instant price quotes on auto, life, medical, and other forms of insurance from over 300 insurers. The site provides ready access to useful reference tools and comparative price information. Moreover, Quotesmith.com allows consumers to purchase from the company of their choice without having to deal with commissioned salespersons. The Internet company also offers two unique guarantees: (1) view the lowest rates on term life insurance or receive $500; and, (2) the quote will be accurate or receive $500.

Source: Diane Brady, "Insurers Step Gingerly into Cyberspace," *Business Week*, November 22, 1999, pp. 160–161; http://investor.quotesmith.com, February 18, 2000.

enough to be profitable to the firm. Relatedly, efforts to retain customers through loyalty programs and specialized services are designed to inhibit shifts in demand resulting from changing prices of the firm's products or competing products.

Costs, Volume, and Profits

We have seen the trade-offs between prices and quantity demanded. Yet price determination must also consider the costs incurred in the production and sale of goods. **Fixed costs** (FC) such as plant and large equipment investments, interest paid on loans, and the costs of production facilities, cannot be changed in the short run and do not vary with the quantity produced. These costs would occur even if the quantity produced were zero. Many advertising costs are viewed as fixed costs, at least over a predetermined period.[6]

Variable costs (VC) such as wages and raw materials change with the level of output. Marketing variable costs include packaging and promotional costs tied to each unit produced.

Total costs (TC) are the sum of variable costs (VC) and fixed costs (FC). Variable costs are made up of the variable cost per unit times the number or quantity of units manufactured (Q):

$$TC = (VC \times Q) + FC$$

Marginal costs (MC) are incurred in producing one additional unit of output. They typically decline early over some level of production because of economies of scale, but eventually begin to increase as the firm approaches capacity and returns diminish.

Marginal revenue (MR) is the additional revenue the firm will receive if one more unit of product is sold. This amount typically represents the price of the product. **Total revenue** (TR) is total sales, or price times the quantity sold:

$$\text{Total revenue} = \text{Price} \times \text{Quantity}$$

To determine the price that maximizes profits, the firm combines cost information with demand or revenue information. Simply viewed:

$$\text{Profits} = \text{Total revenue} (TR) - \text{Total costs} (TC)$$

This difference is greatest at the point where profits are maximized, where the firm's marginal revenue (MR) equals marginal cost (MC). When marginal revenue exceeds marginal cost, additional profits can be made by producing and selling more product. An example of these computations is presented in Appendix A.

Colleen J. Suljic, McGraw-Hill/Irwin Marketing Manager, had this to say about pricing strategies:
"When determining the price of our textbooks, we have to consider the costs associated with producing the product and the supplements that support the book. Our fixed costs include the EDP Plant (Editing, Design, Production) and Editorial Plant (marketing research, grants, product development honoraria)— all of the costs associated with developing a book before it's actually printed. These costs are considered "fixed," because they do not vary with the number of copies printed or sold. Our variable

Price plays a critical role in competition among firms for some industries. Here, UPS promotes efficient service and prices that cover only the distance packages travel.

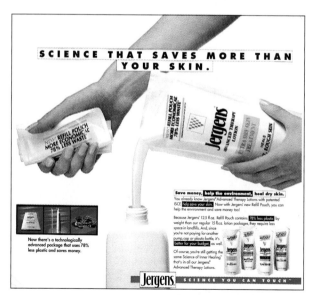

Improved packaging enables lower prices to consumers and helps the environment. In the case of Jergens, refill pouches cut costs and require less landfill space.

costs include typesetting paper, binding, and author royalties. These are variable costs because they vary with the number of copies printed or sold. We calculate our total costs and refer to our initial pricing strategy. We may choose to price our text competitively, or we may use price as a competitive advantage. We experiment with tentative prices by using a break-even analysis—we calculate the number of units we need to sell in the first year to cover our investment."

Price Determination Methods

A firm may choose from several methods of determining price. It may subjectively determine a price based on what management feels is appropriate at the time. Or it may use a combination of methods or procedures. It is important to note that firms should stress both demand and cost considerations in determining prices. Following initial price setting, firms can adjust prices according to trial-and-error experiences and fluctuations in demand. Some basic approaches are markup pricing, break-even analysis, target-return pricing, and price sensitivity measurement.

Markup Pricing

Retailers typically use some form of **markup pricing,** where markup is the difference between the cost of an item and the retail price, expressed as a percentage. A product's price is determined by adding a set percentage to the cost of the product. These percentages are often standardized across product categories. Formally:

$$\text{Price} = \text{Unit cost} + \text{Markup, or}$$
$$\text{Price} = \text{Unit cost}/(1 - k)$$

where k = desired percent markup.

Assume, for example, that a retailer purchases a popular branded tennis racket at $80 and adds $40 to the cost, for a retail price of $120.

$$\text{Markup as a percentage of selling price} = \frac{\text{Markup}}{\text{Selling price}}$$
$$= \frac{\$40}{\$120} = 33\%$$
$$\text{Markup as a percentage of cost} = \frac{\text{Markup}}{\text{Cost}}$$
$$= \frac{\$40}{\$80} = 50\%$$

In some cases, the retailer may wish to know the markup charged for a product given the price and the original cost. This markup percentage can be computed simply as:

$$\text{Markup (\%)} = [(\text{Price} - \text{Unit cost})/\text{Price}] \times 100\%$$

Using Technology

Pricing discrimination

Revenue management systems, also called yield management systems, are already in use by airlines, which use them constantly to adjust prices and the number of seats allocated to different fares. Hotels now employ these systems to discriminate among different classes of patrons. Varying prices across days and length-of-stay restrictions are commonplace. Now, experts predict massive expansion in price discrimination practices as computing technology and data processing capabilities increase. Staples sends out catalogs with different prices to the same customers, knowing that the price-sensitive customers will know which one to buy from. Like some practices already in place, Bill Gates predicts Web sites will soon recognize customers and charge them based upon their history of buying. Perhaps, for example, the "clickstream" navigated by a consumer on Amazon.com can be employed to target that person as being price sensitive and consequently lower prices may be offered.

Sources: Neal Templin, "Hotels Adopt System Used by Airlines That Helps to Maximize Revenue," *The Wall Street Journal,* http://interactive.wsj.com, May 5, 1999; and Scott Woolly, "I Got It Cheaper than You," *Forbes,* November 2, 1998, pp. 82, 84.

Other procedures and examples for determining retail prices and markups are summarized in Appendix A.

Break-Even Analysis

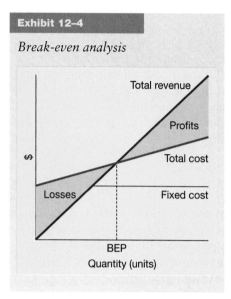

Exhibit 12–4

Break-even analysis

Break-even analysis is a useful guide for pricing decisions. It involves calculating the number of units that must be sold at a certain price for the firm to cover costs and, hence, break even. The approach is shown graphically in Exhibit 12–4. The *break-even point* (BEP) is determined by the intersection of the total revenue line ($TR = P \times Q$) and the total cost line ($TC = FC + VC \times Q$). The area between the two lines and to the right of the intersection represents profits. To make a profit, the quantity sold must exceed the BEP.

The slope of the total revenue line is determined by the price charged. A higher price would make the total revenue line steeper, and the BEP would be lower. Lower costs would also reduce the BEP.

Washburn Guitars provides an excellent example of the relationships between total revenues, total costs, contribution margin, and break-even quantity. The instruments Washburn sells to first-time buyers are mass-produced items; thus they have much lower variable costs in terms of labor and materials per unit than the guitars designed individually for rock stars. In addition, the lower prices appeal to the more price-sensitive entry-level buyer. Consequently, lower variable costs per unit enable Washburn to price its mass-produced items competitively and to sell beyond needed break-even quantity levels at modest market prices.

The BEP in units is

$$Q(BEP) = FC/(P - VC)$$

where P = unit price and $Q(BEP)$ = break-even quantity. The quantity $(P - VC)$ is typically referred to as the product's **contribution margin.**

Consider a case of plastic medical gloves priced at $7.25 and entailing $2.25 in variable costs. At total fixed costs of $200,000, the required break-even quantity would be 40,000 units. That is,

$$40,000 = \$200,000/(\$7.25 - \$2.25)$$

If the price were raised to $12.25, and assuming sufficient demand existed, the BEP would drop to 20,000 units.

BEP can also be expressed in dollars:

$$Q(BEP\$) = FC/(1 - VC/P)$$

Using the previous medical gloves example, the BEP in dollars would be:

$$\$289,855 = \$200,000/(1 - \$2.25/\$7.25)$$

Break-even analysis is useful for evaluating the effects of various price and cost structures on needed demand levels. And by adding a desired profit amount to the fixed-cost portion of the equation, a firm can calculate the number of units that must be sold at a certain price to achieve a certain profit level.

Break-even analysis can be expanded to consider different price and quantity combinations. This modified break-even analysis (described in Appendix A) recognizes that the BEP can vary depending on the price chosen. Profits do not necessarily increase as quantity increases, as lower prices may be needed to generate the increased demand.

Thinking Critically

Break-even analysis is useful for evaluating how alternative cost and price combinations affect the quantity required to break even.

- The break-even point can be lowered by raising the price. However, what if similar products in the marketplace are offered at prices below the higher price under consideration?

- Likewise, the break-even point can be lowered by reducing variable costs. However what if reducing variable costs hurts product quality?

Target-Return Pricing

Target-return pricing is a cost-oriented approach that sets prices to achieve some desired rate of return. Cost and profit estimates are based on some expected volume or sales level. The price is determined using the equation:

$$\text{Price} = \text{Unit cost} + \frac{(\text{Desired return} \times \text{Invested capital})}{\text{Expected unit sales}}$$

Assume a national manufacturer of office supplies sells a computer-paper organizer. Average variable costs for the product are $8; total assets employed in the business are $4,500,000. The firm desires a 15 percent return and expects to sell 200,000 units. Therefore, the target-return price is:

$$\text{Price} = \text{Unit cost} + \frac{\text{Desired return} \times \text{Invested capital}}{\text{Unit sales}}$$
$$= \$8 + (0.15 \times \$4,500,000)/200,000 = \$11.38$$

The firm would price the product at $11.38. Again, the success of the approach assumes the supplier can reach the expected sales volume of 200,000 units.

Target-return pricing forecasts a fair or needed rate of return. However, the effects of other variables in the marketing mix and competitive factors are not considered directly; and target-return pricing, like break-even analysis, is best used in combination with consideration of other determinants of demand.

Some Japanese firms use an approach to pricing that recognizes the effects of price on demand and the role of costs in determining demand. As Exhibit 12–5 shows, the Japanese specify a target cost based on the price they believe the market is most likely to accept. Designers and engineers then meet target costs. This approach emphasizes the product's ability to achieve market acceptance by considering more directly the interface between the prices buyers are likely to accept and the costs necessary to produce products at those prices. As such, the Japanese recognize the effects of both demand and cost considerations in determining their prices. Nissan, Sharp, and Toyota use this approach.

Some U.S. and European companies design a new product first, and then calculate the cost. If the cost is too high, the product must be redesigned or the company must settle for a lower profit level.[7] Generally, the Japanese worry less than American and European manufacturers about cost accounting. They work backward from a price and make sure the product can be produced with the quality demanded at that price.

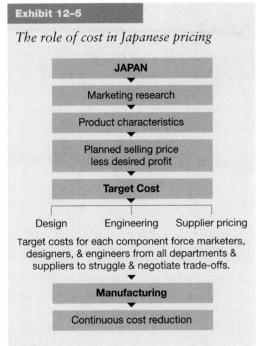

Exhibit 12–5

The role of cost in Japanese pricing

JAPAN
↓
Marketing research
↓
Product characteristics
↓
Planned selling price less desired profit
↓
Target Cost
↓
Design   Engineering   Supplier pricing

Target costs for each component force marketers, designers, & engineers from all departments & suppliers to struggle & negotiate trade-offs.
↓
Manufacturing
↓
Continuous cost reduction

Source: Adapted from Ford S. Worthy, "Japan's Smart Secret Weapon," *Fortune,* August 12, 1991, p. 73. © 1991 Time Inc. All rights reserved.

Income-Based Pricing

One important and often-used pricing approach involves the determination of price based upon the income to be generated by the product under consideration. **Income-based pricing** is frequently used for pricing real estate property, marketable securities, and businesses. For example, consider a business that is for sale that has annual net income (i.e., income after salaries and so forth are paid) of $600,000. The typical return on investment for similar companies in this industry is 18 percent. A beginning purchase price would be $3.33 million ($600,000/.18). This selling price for the business might be adjusted for unique competitive strengths or the likelihood of improved revenue streams in the future.[8]

Prices and Customer Value

Effective value creation is based upon a thorough understanding of target customers, including an exploration of how value is created. Determining price is a critical aspect of this valuation creation. Prices set too high result in limited trial, while prices set too low result in poor positioning and missed opportunities.[9]

A useful approach for incorporating customer input into determination of prices is **price sensitivity measurement (PSM).** Developed in the early 1970s, this procedure

Exhibit 12–6   *Consumers' price sensitivity measurement for electric razors*

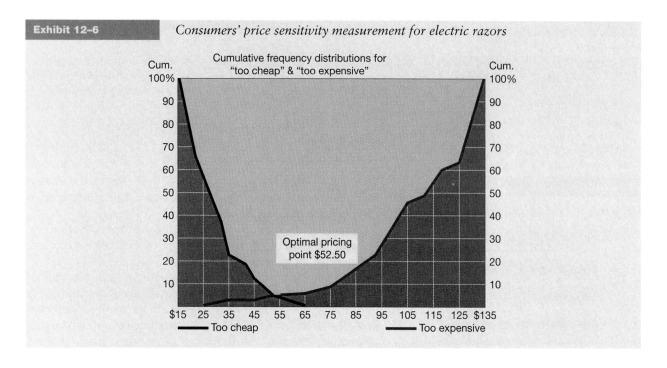

is still used today by some firms to estimate prices for new consumer and industrial products. First, a sample of potential buyers reads a product description and views any available pictures or diagrams. Then the buyers are shown a pricing scale that begins with $0 and includes up to 30 different price points. The scale measures the points at which buyers consider a price too expensive or so cheap they would question the product's quality. The PSM then yields price estimates high enough to reflect the product's perceived value and low enough to avoid sticker shock.[10]

A version of the PSM approach is shown in Exhibit 12–6, which plots the reactions of 249 European respondents to a new electric razor. The intersection between ratings of prices that are "too cheap" and "too expensive" provides an estimate of the price to charge. This approach considers consumer price sensitivity and perceptions of value as primary determinants of price.

Value in use (VIU) analysis is a useful approach for determining the economic value that a product has relative to an existing competitive offering. This approach is useful for assisting in the determination of what price to charge and in the determination of the arguments suppliers can use to justify higher prices. An example is shown in Exhibit 12–7. In this case, the analysis reveals the new product has seven times the value of an existing product and that a price for the new product well above the $5 being charged already would be appropriate. If the product cost $10 and the price were set at $25, the purchasing company would be $10 better off (i.e., $25 versus $35 VIU) if the switch were made to the new product.[11]

Pricing Strategies

Setting prices to achieve the firm's objectives requires the selection of a specific pricing strategy or a combination of strategies.[12] The eleven pricing strategies shown in Exhibit 12–8 fall into four categories: differential pricing, where the same brand is sold to consumers under different prices; competitive pricing, where prices are set to take advantage of competitive market conditions; product-line pricing, where related brands are sold at prices to take advantage of interdependencies among brands; and psychological pricing, where prices are based on consideration of consumer perceptions or expectations.

The appropriateness of a particular pricing strategy depends on several circumstances: the variability of demand (the presence of different market segments), the competitive situation, the characteristics of consumers in the market, and the expectations or perceptions of consumers.

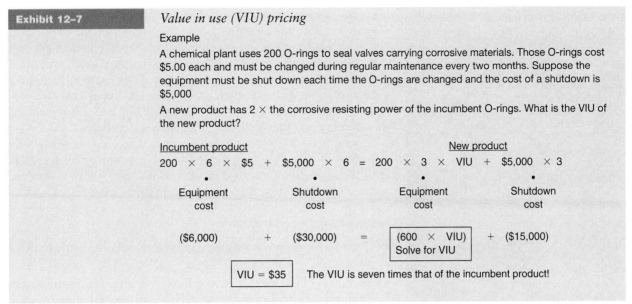

Source: Timothy Matanovich, Gary L. Lilien, and Arvind Rangaswamy, "Engineering the Price-Value Relationship," *Marketing Management,* Spring 1999, p. 49.

Exhibit 12–8	*Example pricing strategies*		
Differential pricing	**Competitive pricing**	**Product-line pricing**	**Psychological pricing**
Second-market discounting	Penetration pricing	Bundling	Odd–even pricing
Periodic discounting	Price signaling	Premium pricing	Customary pricing
	Going-rate pricing	Partitional pricing	One-sided claims

Several commonsense assumptions about buyers underlie all pricing strategies. First, some buyers have search costs in taking time and effort to obtain information about which firms sell what products and at what prices. Second, some buyers have low reservation prices, the highest prices they are willing to pay. That is, some price-sensitive buyers do not need a product enough to pay the high price others pay.

Differential Pricing

Differential pricing involves selling the same product to different buyers under a variety of prices. This is price discrimination, or the practice of charging different buyers different prices for the same quantity and quality of products or services.[13] Differential pricing works because the market is heterogeneous, or more simply, differences in reactions to price exist among consumers or consumer segments in the market.

The ability to engage in differential pricing has been facilitated greatly by the ever-growing number of on-line auction sites, such as priceline.com, and shopbots that search the Web for low prices. If a business sells a product or service that rapidly depreciates in value, such as computers, or that becomes worthless in a moment, such as airline seats, then on-line auctions with their ability to differentiate prices are viable sales channels. Moreover, one additional benefit from consigning products to on-line auction houses is that the auction site sells to end consumers and sellers avoid the perception of undercutting their own prices.[14]

SECOND-MARKET DISCOUNTING   The most common form of differential pricing, **second-market discounting,** occurs when different prices are charged in different market segments. (Recall that this practice may be legal in retail, but illegal in wholesale if it harms competition.) Second-market discounting is useful when the

Prices are often varied across segments. Reduced prices for senior consumers are a frequently and effectively used form of price discrimination.

firm has excess capacity and different market segments exist. Generic brands and some foreign markets often provide opportunities for second-market discounting. For example, if a firm can sell its product cost-effectively in a foreign market, it may be profitable to export even at a price below local prices. The exporting firm must have excess production capacity (so no new fixed costs are required), and the markets must be sufficiently separated so that transaction costs prevent interaction between markets.

Second-market discounting also occurs when the company sells a portion of its output as generic brands at lower prices to price-sensitive segments. Other examples include differences in student and senior citizen discounts for entertainment ticket prices.

For price discrimination to be successful, some rather restrictive conditions must be satisfied:

- The market must have segments that respond differently to price variations.
- Members of the market paying the lower price must not be able to resell the product to the people paying the higher price.
- Competitors should not be able to undercut the prices charged to the higher-price segment.
- The cost of segmenting and policing the market should not exceed the extra revenue derived from charging the higher prices.
- The practice should not cause consumer resentment.
- The form of price discrimination used should be legal.[15]

PERIODIC DISCOUNTING   In some cases, it is advantageous for a firm to offer periodic or occasional discounts. **Periodic discounting** enables a firm to take advantage of the presence of consumer segments that differ in price sensitivity. This approach includes **price skimming,** where an initial high price is determined for new products to skim the market. Price skimming allows product development costs to be recovered when introductory sales are growing. People willing to pay the high price purchase first, and then the firm lowers prices as sales slow to attract the next-highest level of price-sensitive buyer. Du Pont, a well-known innovator of industrial products, frequently uses a price-skimming strategy.

Competitive Pricing

Competitive pricing strategies, based on the firm's position in relation to its competition, include penetration pricing, limit pricing, price signaling, and going-rate pricing.

Penetration pricing calls for a low initial price to generate sales volume and take advantage of economies of scale (larger production runs at lower unit costs). It is often used when the marketer wants to maximize sales growth or market share. Penetration pricing may be particularly beneficial when there are a significant number of price-sensitive consumers in the market (demand is price-elastic) or the firm fears early entry of a competitor if prices are set high and margins appear attractive. **Limit pricing,** another term for low penetration pricing, also entails setting prices low to discourage new competition. In situations in which competitive reaction is unlikely, firms may engage in price skimming, described earlier.

Price signaling puts high prices on low-quality products. This approach, while clearly not beneficial to buyers, may reflect unethical behavior; but firms can pursue it successfully if several conditions are satisfied. First, there must be a segment of buyers whose experience is consistent with a price/quality relationship, who believe firms spend more to provide higher quality, or who trust the market and assume a positive relationship between price and quality exists.[16] Second, information on the level of quality should be hard for buyers to obtain.[17] *Consumer*

Thinking Critically

The elasticity of demand has a big impact on the pricing policy of new products. Depending upon whether a product has elastic or inelastic demand, how will this affect the decisions made to price a new product or change the price for an existing product?

Rebates and trial products are used with introductory low prices to stimulate initial product sales and to build sales volume.

Reports regularly reports examples of successful brands that have high prices and suspect quality.

Going-rate pricing reflects the tendency of firms to price at or near industry averages. This approach is frequently used when products compete on the basis of attributes or benefits other than price. Going-rate pricing has the additional advantage of lessening the threat of aggressive price wars, which may be unprofitable to all competitors.

Competitive pricing strategies also determine the positioning of many retail organizations. Value retailers, like Family Dollar and Dollar General, are becoming the newest high-growth concept. These low-overhead, low-price general merchandisers compete with the "big three"—Wal-Mart, Kmart, and Target—by offering lower prices to the growing segment of households earning $25,000 or less. Both Family Dollar and Dollar General target lower-income and fixed-income families, often in neglected geographical markets.[18]

Product-Line Pricing

Firms often offer a line of multiple versions of the same product, such as Radio Shack stereo speakers priced from $59.99 to $149.99. Low- and high-end prices may influence buyer perceptions of quality and set standards for comparing items within the product line.

Low-end prices frequently influence doubtful or price-conscious buyers to purchase and are often used as traffic builders. The high-end price has considerable influence on the quality image of the entire product line. Marketers must be sensitive to price changes in the product line. A price change in one product can detract from sales of other products in the line, because they are often substitutes for one another.[19]

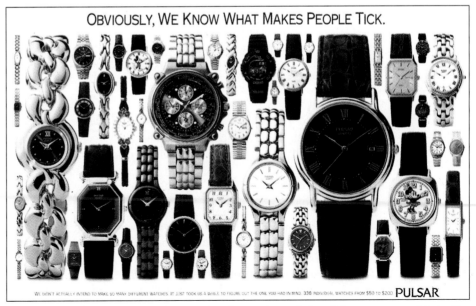

OBVIOUSLY, WE KNOW WHAT MAKES PEOPLE TICK.

PULSAR

Product-line pricing decisions pose a common dilemma for marketers. Price ranges associated with items in a line affect the perceived levels of quality for the line, while individual prices must be set so that sales are increased for the line without negatively affecting the sales of items within the line.

BUNDLING   Increasingly, companies are realizing the value of combining separate products into bundles. **Bundling** is marketing two or more products or services in a single "package" for a single price.[20] The practice is seen frequently in the marketing of ski packages, hotel services, restaurant meals, and stereo and computer systems. Bundling also occurs in the purchase of health care equipment by hospitals. In these cases, the bundle price is typically less than if each item in the package is bought separately.

Pure price bundling occurs when the bundle includes a number of the *same* product, such as multiple candy bars or golf balls sold in a package for a single price. Two-for-one offers in travel packages or restaurant orders are price bundles often used to regulate demand levels. Product tie-ins or multiproduct bundles involve *different* products included in a single offering for a single price. The products may be complementary, for example, a personal computer and a printer.[21] In addition to often selling at lower prices than if unbundled, bundling reduces the costs to consumers from searching and the cost to sellers from individual transactions. New computers come bundled with software, the shopping for which most consumers desire to avoid. Bundling has other benefits to the seller as well: Price bundling can increase frequency of purchase profitability. This conclusion is based upon recent findings that suggest consumers allocate lower cost to each bundled unit following purchase. Therefore, products such as prepaid phone and photocopy cards have the potential to increase both the amount and rate of consumption.[22]

PREMIUM PRICING   When a firm offers several alternative models, it often uses a premium-pricing strategy. **Premium pricing** sets higher (premium) prices on more deluxe product versions. The various models are designed to appeal to different price-sensitive segments or to segments wanting different combinations of features. Typically the firm (the manufacturer or the retailer) makes most of its profits on the expensive models and less on lower-priced models in a product line. Premium pricing occurs often for beer, clothing, appliances, and automobiles. Hewlett-Packard successfully competed with IBM for corporate data-center business by aggressively promoting its top-line models in its HP9000 series.[23]

PARTITIONED PRICING   Many firms divide the prices they charge into parts, in lieu of charging a single price. These "part" prices are often termed the *base price* and the *surcharge*. This practice is called **partitioned pricing.** Examples include catalog or Internet prices for items on sale, plus the shipping and handling charges associated with delivery. A Sony telephone from a mail catalog for $69.95, plus $12.95 for shipping and handling, is one specific combination used in a well-designed study of partitioned prices. Recent research suggests that this practice is common in the marketplace because consumers do not process the base price and surcharges completely and accurately, and as such, the total cost remembered is less and therefore demand is increased.[24]

Psychological Pricing

Psychological pricing recognizes that buyer perceptions and beliefs affect their price evaluations. Prestige or premium pricing and comparing competitors' prices with a firm's lower sale prices deal with the psychological aspects of consumer reactions to prices. Odd–even pricing and customary pricing are other applications of psychological pricing.

ODD–EVEN PRICING   **Odd–even pricing** presents prices at values just below an even amount, a common practice. Instead of pricing contact lenses at $200, for example, the price is set at $199.95. The marketer intends for consumers to associate the price with the $100 to $200 range, assuming that demand for the contacts will be less at $200 than at $199.95. In addition, the precision associated with the $199.95 price implies a bargain.

Odd–even pricing, or just-below pricing as it is sometimes called, may be beneficial for other reasons as well. First, evidence suggests that when low price is important to the consumer, the just-below price is more effective at getting consumers' attention. Second, just-below prices may have memory effects; that is, the left-most digits of a price represent the greater amounts of money and are therefore the most important. Some studies have revealed that people recall the just-below endings as underestimates from memory. Odd prices created from round-number prices have been shown to be the most effective. For example, a price such as $199.95 would likely lead to a substantially lower average recalled price than $249.95.[25]

CUSTOMARY PRICING   In the past, consumers associated a **customary price** with a product, but frequent price promotions and price increases have made this practice less prevalent today. The classic example of customary price is the much-dated 5-cent candy bar; today's customary price might be 50 cents. Customary-price beliefs represent consumers' strongly held expectations. Pricing strategies that set customary prices typically modify the quality, feature, or service of a product without adjusting the price. The many versions of Swatch watches, for example, are often set at the customary price of $40.

ONE-SIDED PRICE CLAIMS   Concerns arise regarding the implications of one-sided price claims in which superiority in price for one attribute or offering is made. However, what happens when the prices of firms' other offerings are actually higher? One study of prices for mail delivery services found that consumers overgeneralize one-sided price claims to the prices for other but omitted services. Specifically, a significant number of subjects in a recent study erroneously concluded that a well-known mail carrier had the lowest overall prices just because the firm promoted its low price for guaranteed morning delivery, when in fact its prices were higher for package pickup and delivery by 5 PM the next day. These issues are important to those concerned with consumer welfare to the extent that such practices lead to deception and inaccurate decision making.[26]

Adapting Prices

Determining a pricing strategy and setting prices are only the beginning. Prices change as competition occurs and as the firm's marketing and production expertise improve. The firm must react to competitive price changes as well, constantly considering how often and how much to change prices. Price discounts and geographical pricing decisions also require marketers to adapt their prices.

Price Decreases and Increases

Firms often must reduce prices to generate sales. Sometimes, lowering price improves profits through higher sales. When market share is declining or excess production capacity exists, the firm may lower prices. This may stimulate demand and allow greater use of production or plant investments. Depressed economic conditions may also necessitate price reductions.

Price reductions, however, are risky. Competitive retaliation to price decreases is particularly important. Firms may encounter three traps in reducing prices:[27]

- **Low-quality trap**—Buyers may question the quality of low-priced products.
- **Fragile market share trap**—Price-sensitive buyers may switch to the next lower-priced product that comes along.
- **Shallow pockets trap**—Higher-priced competitors that reduce prices also may have longer staying power due to higher margins.

Price decreases may be implemented in several ways, with direct reductions from the original price most common. Firms may also reduce prices by offering quantity discounts or rebates. Bundling additional products or services with the basic product, while maintaining the current price, is another tactic.

Price promotions by manufacturers affect the strategies engaged in by resellers of grocery and other packaged goods. In fact, many grocery retailers and wholesalers are dependent upon the purchase of products at reduced manufacturer prices. In these instances, reseller firms become dependent upon forward buying, a practice in which large quantities of products are bought on sale, enabling the wholesalers and retailers to subsequently have larger margins when the products are then sold to consumers. These practices lead then to consumers' spending heavily for products that are on sale. For example, almost 71 percent of total supermarket sales for carbonated beverages in one 52-week period occurred when the products were being price promoted.[28]

Price increases are also common. A primary reason is inflationary pressure; increases in the costs of inputs and production force prices upward. In Central and South America, price increases from inflationary pressures are common, often requiring high increases over very short time periods. Also, when demand is great, firms often raise prices. Moreover, they may do so indirectly by reducing or eliminating quantity discounts, cash discounts for prompt payment, and trade allowances. Services once included with a product may be unbundled so the buyer actually receives less for the same price. In effect, these tactics enable firms to adjust real prices upward without raising list prices.

Both price increases and decreases must be noticeable to affect purchase decisions. For example, a reduction from $5.75 to $5.45 may not influence demand, while a reduction to $5.15 might be meaningful. Buyers have **price thresholds** for products, and they notice when prices go under or above those limits. Thresholds depend on the average price of the product. A 10-cent reduction on a $10 product, for example, differs from the same reduction on a 50-cent product.

Ranges of acceptable prices also exist. The **acceptable price range** includes prices buyers are willing to pay. Airwalks, for example, demonstrates the role of price as part of a product's marketing mix. With its low-cost structure, due largely to outsourced foreign manufacturing and corresponding low price, the Airwalks shoe offers an acceptable and generally low price range to a segment of young consumers. Buyers may react negatively when prices move outside the acceptable range, above or below. Prices raised too high may exceed buyer budgets or be judged as unfair. Marketers that gouge buyers by charging excessively high prices are often publicly criticized. Prices reduced below the acceptable range generate concerns about product or service quality, the low-quality trap.[29]

Buyers, both consumer buyers and organizational buyers, often resist price increases and are particularly hesitant to pay prices perceived as unfair. Price changes that result in undue profits for the firm are perceived as unfair, while price increases that just maintain firm profit levels are judged as fair. This notion is referred to as the "principle of dual entitlement." Relatedly, there is growing irritation among many business travelers with increasing airline fares and rules that guarantee that executive travelers are charged the highest prices.[30]

In situations where large price increases may be justified, the increases, even when driven by unexpected or unknown market conditions, may have to be justified to the firm's buyers or customers. Communication with customers is critical in these price-increase situations. As an example, Roasterie, a wholesaler of gourmet coffee in Kansas City, Missouri, recently faced a doubling of grower prices in a three-month period. In justification for increasing their own prices, Roasterie sent a lengthy letter and copies of news articles to their 300 customers detailing the environmental influences affecting the cost of coffee.[31]

Reacting to Competitive Price Changes

Competitive pressures affect pricing decisions of retailers and companies that sell to other businesses. Price competition among retail marketers is particularly acute with the advent of Wal-Mart, grocery superstores, and club warehouses. Recently, Target ads accused Wal-Mart of using misleading pricing tactics. Price comparisons by large retailers are likely to intensify as Wal-Mart, Kmart, Target, and others run out of territories to conquer.[32]

Brand managers should react to competitive price changes case by case. If price decreases among competitors do not increase total market demand, then price competition can hurt all competitors. The firm must try to determine the purpose of its competitive price change, its likely duration, and the reaction of other competitors in the market.

If buyers make decisions on nonprice characteristics, a reactive price decrease to meet the competition may not be necessary. Competitors instead might try to compete on service, quality, and features. When competition is based largely on price, however, a price decrease to match the competition may be required.

Examples of competitive price reactions are easy to find even among the most well-known companies. Pressures to reduce prices have been particularly strong in the computer software market, where competitors have undercut rivals by as much as six times. IBM reacted to the success of Toshiba and Compaq in the PC notebook market by aggressively promoting the capabilities of its line and offering competitive prices. In a similar move, Apple reduced its base price by more than $1,000 to stimulate sales of notebook computers.[33] Hertz cut its car-rental rates to match competition from Alamo Rent-A-Car and Budget. Hershey Foods was forced to match price reductions by M&M Mars.[34]

Deregulation has forced many utilities to consider competitive effects for the first time in the development of their marketing strategies. As states deregulate in the United States, customers can comparison shop and, in many cases, reduce monthly bills by changing suppliers. The effects of competition on the services provided and the prices offered by gas and electric utility companies to their customers in many markets have yet to be fully understood. Profit margins are very small in customer transactions. Hence, there is little room for error in setting prices. During one recent shortage in the Midwest, utilities in Ohio and Illinois lost millions by paying $5 for power from their wholesalers that they were selling to residential customers for a dime or so.[35]

GENERALIZATIONS ABOUT PRICE CHANGES   Considerable research has been conducted regarding the effects of price changes. These studies have involved experiments in which price levels were systematically varied and analyses of scanner data collected in-store. A review of these studies yielded the following conclusions:

- Temporary retail price reductions substantially increase store traffic and sales.
- Large-market-share brands are hurt less by price changes from smaller competitors.
- Frequent price dealing lowers consumers' reference prices, which may hurt brand equity.
- Price changes for high-quality brands affect weaker brands and private-label brands disproportionately.[36]

Colleen J. Suljic, McGraw-Hill/Irwin Marketing Manager, talks about competitive packaging: "One way we try to strategically compete against other publishers and the used-book companies is with value packages. For example, we often package a study guide at a reduced price, or even for free, to encourage the student to purchase the new book and not a used one. The total package of the new text and the supplement is often lower than the price of purchasing a used textbook and the supplement. It is a win/win situation for the student and the publisher: The student gets an exceptional value and the publisher sells more units."

Marketing policy and practice that continually allocates large percentages of budgets to price-related promotions serves only to reduce baseline revenues from higher-margin and unpromoted sales. As such, many brand managers worry that funds are being taken away from image advertising designed to nurture brands for the long haul and that constant price-promotion activity will only damage brand equity that enables firms to charge more-profitable premium prices.[37]

Price discounts and trade allowances are used by manufacturers to encourage retailers to carry their products. In this General Mills trade ad to retail buyers, the message emphasizes advertising support and price discounts to retailers.

Price Discounts and Allowances

The actual price a customer pays may differ from the market or list price, perhaps because of discounts from the original price. Discounts, which take many forms, occur in consumer and reseller transactions. They include cash discounts, trade promotion allowances, and quantity discounts.

Marketers often offer *cash discounts* for prompt payment by retailers. For example, terms of payment may be "3/10, net 30," indicating that the full amount of purchase is due in 30 days with a 3 percent discount available if the customer pays the bill in 10 days.

Trade sales promotion allowances are concessions a manufacturer pays or allocates to wholesalers or retailers to promote its products. The manufacturer or wholesaler may reduce prices on certain items so retailers can offer sale prices. Or the manufacturer may give additional marketing communications incentives to help the retailer pay for advertising. In fact, much of the newspaper advertising for grocery stores is actually supported by manufacturers' cooperative advertising payments.

Marketers give *quantity discounts* when the customer buys large quantities of a product. For example, full price might be charged for 500 or fewer reams of computer paper. For purchasing 501 to 1,000 reams, the customer receives a 3 percent discount per ream. For purchases over 1,000 reams, a 5 percent reduction off list price would be offered. A cumulative quantity discount entitles the purchaser to a larger discount as the sum of purchases within a specified time period, usually a year, exceeds a certain amount. Noncumulative quantity discounts apply to onetime purchases and are based on the size of the order.

Geographical Pricing

Companies with geographically dispersed customers sometimes adjust prices because of costs resulting from distance. Shipping costs may be substantial and detract from profit if they are not included in the price. Marketers use geographical pricing approaches to address these issues.

One of the more commonly used methods is **FOB origin pricing.** FOB stands for free on board, meaning the goods are placed on a carrier (truck, train, barge) and shipped to the customer. FOB pricing requires customers to pay the unit cost of the goods plus shipping costs, which differ with location or market. An opposite strategy is to charge the same price and transportation cost to all customers. Using a **uniform delivered price,** the company charges each customer an average freight amount. A principal advantage of this method is ease of administration.

Zone pricing is an approach between FOB pricing and uniform delivered pricing. Customers within an area (say, the Northeast) are charged a common price. More-distant zones or areas are charged higher freight amounts.

Freight absorption pricing is another form of geographical pricing. Here the seller absorbs freight costs—offers free or reduced costs of delivery—to attract more business. This practice occurs when competition among sellers is heavy.

Competitive Bidding and Negotiated Pricing

In the United States, retail prices for most consumer goods normally are not negotiable. However, outside the United States, price negotiations for consumer goods occur regularly. Likewise, almost all business-to-business purchases are negotiated to some extent. In fact, many organizational buyers now view every aspect of their purchase transactions as negotiable. Negotiated pricing is the norm in marketing to the federal government, the largest purchaser of goods and services.

Exhibit 12–9	*Alternative bid prices and expected values (in $000)*			
Submitted price (bid)	Costs	Contribution to profit	Probability of selection	Expected value
$250	$170	$ 80	.75	$60.00
275	170	105	.70	73.50
300	170	130	.65	84.50
325	170	155	.50	77.50
350	170	180	.45	81.00

Note: Expected value = (Contribution to profit) × (Probability of selection).

Sealed-bid pricing is unique in that the buyer determines the pricing approach and the eventual price. The buyer encourages sellers to submit sealed bids, or prices, for providing their products or services;[38] the sellers set prices on the basis of cost considerations and expectations about what competitors will bid.

Sealed-bid pricing may be difficult for the seller. First, the seller must determine the costs involved in providing the product or service. The seller must then set a price according to the prices it expects competing firms to submit. The price must cover costs, provide a reasonable return, and be low enough to be selected by the purchaser. Overall, the bidding company must be able to evaluate the chances of winning a particular contract at different prices, determine the profit potential under various bidding outcomes, and identify projects for which the expense of preparing and submitting a bid is economically justified.[39]

An example bidding situation is shown in Exhibit 12–9. This framework allows the seller to evaluate alternative bids in terms of the costs of the project, the contribution of each alternative to profits, and the probability of winning the job at each bid price. As the price or submitted bid increases, the probability of winning decreases.

Negotiated pricing is common for large investments, such as building or other installations, and for consulting arrangements, many professional services, or governmental work. Negotiation between vendor and supplier replaces evaluation of multiple bids. If these are long-term arrangements, or agreements likely to involve future negotiations, concern for developing and maintaining relationships is critical. In some smaller deals, sales reps may negotiate prices and margins for the company in the field on a transaction-by-transaction basis. Field salespeople can help identify situations when price quotes need to be more competitive to avoid losing profitable business.[40]

Pricing Services

The unique characteristics of services—intangible, perishable, inseparable, and nonstandardized—make their pricing difficult. Price determination is influenced by the nature of the service involved. For professional services, such as those provided by attorneys and accountants, prices vary according to the complexity of the service and the amount of work or services provided. However, pricing decisions for services, as for tangible products, should consider expenses or costs involved with service delivery, price expectations of customers, management objectives of a reasonable return, and pricing for similar services by competitors.[41] Generally, the larger the share of the market held by a service provider, the higher the price it can charge relative to competition.

One difficulty in pricing services is the need to manage off-peak periods of demand. Movies, airlines, and car-rental firms, for example, price services to shift demand to periods of excess capacity.

Pricing services and utilities can be difficult. As deregulation spreads, utility companies will face increasing pressures to price competitively.

The perishable nature of these services makes creative pricing and demand management an important aspect of service pricing. That is, once a movie starts, an airline flight takes off, or a rental car remains unused over a weekend, the potential income from these unpurchased intangibles is lost.

In some industries, pricing of services is extremely competitive. The airlines industry has wide differences in prices across markets, time periods, and competitors. The entry of competitive firms can influence prices dramatically. Recently, Morris Air, one of a handful of low-cost, low-fare airlines, forced Delta Airlines to cut its fares up to 80 percent and to offer double miles to frequent fliers in efforts to retain customers. Morris normally flies only short routes under 500 miles and offers no hot meals. Morris's discounted fares are more flexible than Delta's and those of other large airlines. In addition, prices are kept low by flying only Boeing 737s, which saves money on parts inventory and maintenance demands.[42]

Bundling of services into a single package and price is a common strategy. Hotels (lodging, meals), banks (large deposits yield free travelers' checks), physicians (exams, diagnostic tests), and airlines (travel, rental cars), for example, provide services for a single bundle price.[43] Bundling increases demand by providing increased savings and convenience to the consumer.

Ethical Issues and Deceptive Practices

Ethical problems associated with business pricing are not uncommon and are often the focus of much public scrutiny. A recent congressional investigation into the pricing practices of a national hospital company revealed significant bill padding. Patients were charged $44 for saline solutions (salt water) costing 81 cents and $103 for crutches costing $8.[44] Pharmaceutical companies have been cited for overpricing life-saving drugs, as in the case of AIDS vaccines.[45] Claims of price gouging have also been leveled against major airlines for their pricing during peak travel times or in geographic areas where a major carrier dominates. Following Hurricane Andrew, Florida's attorney general subpoenaed top plywood manufacturers for records justifying soaring prices. Evidence of profiteering and consumer gouging was found among sellers of batteries, chain saws, and flashlights. Similar accusations arose after the 1994 Los Angeles earthquake. In contrast, Home Depot, a national retailer of home building supplies, sold its products at cost immediately following Andrew.[46] Undoubtedly, Home Depot's positive response earned the company much goodwill.

FTC Guidelines and Deceptive Pricing

Many advertised prices include comparison prices. These can enhance the attractiveness of the offer by making the price reduction appear lower than merely stating it alone. Comparison price advertising typically pairs the sale price with prices formerly charged by the retailer, competing retailer prices, or manufacturer-suggested prices.

Comparison price advertising is effective, and it provides useful information to buyers. Unfortunately, the ease with which claims can be made and their influence on buyers increase the likelihood of deceptive pricing practices. Federal Trade Commission (FTC) guidelines provide specific procedures for avoiding deceptive price advertising. The most common practices addressed by the guidelines include:[47]

- **Comparisons with former prices**—Prices claimed as former prices charged by the retailer ("Regularly $XX, Now Only $YY") must have been offered to the public on a regular basis for a "reasonable" period of time. Although sales are not required at the higher price, the former price must have been a genuine offer for some period.

- **Comparisons with other retailer prices**—When prices are said to be lower than those being charged by other retailers for the same merchandise in the advertiser's trade area, the advertised higher prices must be based on fact.

- **Comparisons with prices suggested by manufacturers or other nonretail distributors**—If prices are said to be reductions from the manufacturer's list price or suggested retail price, these comparison prices must correspond to the prices at which a substantial proportion of the product's sales are made.

Several years ago May Department Stores in Denver was cited by the attorney general of Colorado for "engaging in continuous and repeated patterns of deceptive price advertising and sales practices." Examples included houseware products "on sale" at the same sale prices for two years and luggage advertised as discounted from "regular" prices that never were May's prevailing prices and that were double the luggage prices for the same items charged by other local retailers.[48]

The context under which consumers make decisions can affect the ethics of marketing practices as well. For example, in cases where individuals are suffering from extreme grief, such as following the death of a loved one, decisions regarding funeral arrangements are difficult. Retailing experts have learned that presenting only corners of caskets in a product line arrangement, instead of using large showrooms displaying numbers of whole caskets, makes decisions easier for the buyer. However, the practice raises the average price paid from $200 to $400, as consumers avoid lower-end models. The ethics and fairness of this product-line pricing strategy certainly warrant evaluation.[49]

Bait and Switch

Grocery stores and department stores advertise some brands at cost or near cost to attract consumers. These marketers hope that low-priced items or *loss leaders* will generate traffic and sales of other items in the store. A **bait and switch** occurs when the retailer advertises but does not actually offer a reasonable amount of the promoted product. If the product is not, or was not, actually available, consumers may trade up and buy a more expensive version of the advertised loss leader. This bait-and-switch practice is illegal and unethical.

Predatory Pricing

In some instances, companies charge very low prices to drive competition from the market. Any losses incurred can be recouped later by charging higher monopoly prices once competition has been discouraged. This practice is called **predatory pricing.** A company that claims predatory pricing by a competitor must demonstrate that the low-priced firm, typically a larger firm, charges prices below its average total costs, with the *intent* to harm competitors.

Predatory pricing is difficult to prove in the courts, for juries are skeptical of these claims.[50] The company that sues must show not only that a rival firm prices below cost but also that it does so intending to raise prices later. Wal-Mart was once accused of predatory pricing by pharmacy chains because of its aggressive drug pricing practices. The Justice Department charged American Airlines of illegally forcing smaller competitors out of its Dallas hub. After the smaller carriers left, prices to consumers were raised. Predatory pricing has also been discussed in the government's case against Microsoft, which often gives away software to build market share.[51]

Unit Pricing

The number of products, brands, and package sizes in the marketplace presents a bewildering array of choices. The potential to be misled or at least confused is likewise great. Many states have passed **unit pricing** legislation to help consumers process in-store price information. Unit pricing presents price information on a per-unit weight or volume basis to facilitate price comparisons across brands and across package sizes within brands. Unit pricing is intended to help low-income consumers and price-vigilant shoppers.[52] Although not an ethical issue per se, unit pricing is designed to improve consumer decision making and to reduce the potential for being misled or misinformed by the vast amount of in-store information.

Summary

1. **Discuss the interrelationships among price, demand, demand elasticity, and revenue.** Marketplace conditions influence prices. The higher the price of most goods or services, the lower the demand. These relationships are depicted in the familiar economic demand curve. The extent to which demand changes as price changes is the price elasticity of demand. Inelastic demand exists when a seller increases price and sees little decrease in sales. Demand is elastic when small changes in price cause large changes in the quantity demanded.

   The profit-maximizing price level is the point where total revenues minus total costs is highest. This point occurs at the price where marginal revenue equals marginal cost. This expression of profit maximization does not consider factors such as the seller's ability to influence demand through promotional activities.

2. **Understand methods for determining price.** Cost-oriented methods for determining price include markup pricing, where the price is set as a certain percentage increase above its cost; break-even analysis, which calculates the number of units required to be sold to cover costs at a certain price; and target-return pricing, where the price is set to provide some specific desired rate of return on investment. A competition orientation to determining price suggests firms charge prices similar to competitors' prices.

3. **Recognize the different pricing strategies and the conditions that best suit the choice of a strategy.** Four broad categories of pricing strategies are differential pricing, competitive pricing, product-line pricing, and psychological pricing.

   When differences exist across consumer segments, differential pricing is effective. Examples include second-market discounting, where different prices are charged to different segments, and periodic discounting.

   Competitive pricing includes penetration pricing, where a firm sets an initial low price to stimulate demand or deter competition, and price signaling, or offering a high price for a low-quality brand in hopes consumers will infer high quality.

   Product-line strategies are important for firms that sell a variety of brands of the same product, as the price set for one of the brands often affects sales of the entire product line. Some firms use bundling strategies, where separate products or services in a line are sold as a single bundle. Premium pricing, when the firm charges higher prices for deluxe brands within a product line, is most successful when market segments want different combinations of features. Psychological pricing includes the practice of odd–even pricing and customary pricing.

4. **Recognize the importance of adapting prices under shifting economic and competitive situations.** Prices are reduced under several circumstances: declining market share, changing customer preferences, or lower competitive prices. If competitors can easily detect price reductions and are willing to retaliate, price reductions are risky. Lowering prices may also affect consumer perceptions of quality, may work only until an even lower-priced product is available, and may be difficult to maintain in the presence of larger and stronger competitors.

   When products compete on attributes other than price (service, features), price changes in face of competitive price shifts may not be required. In homogeneous markets, however, where products are similar and compete largely on price, price reductions by competitors will probably have to be matched. Inflation or excessive demand sometimes leads to price increases.

   For a price change to affect demand, the increase or decrease must exceed some minimal threshold so as to be noticeable. Buyers also have a range of acceptable prices. Prices reduced below the lowest acceptable price may generate perceptions of inferior quality; prices above the highest acceptable price will be rejected.

5. **Understand the ethical considerations involved in setting and communicating prices.** Ethical considerations are an issue in pricing decisions. Prices must not potentially mislead or take advantage of customers. The FTC offers guidelines that govern advertised price specials and comparison pricing. The most common aspects of comparison pricing governed by the FTC include comparisons with former prices, comparisons with other retail prices, and comparisons with prices suggested by manufacturers or distributors.

   Another unethical practice involves predatory pricing: pricing below average cost until competitors are forced out of the market. After driving out competitors, the firm raises its prices. Unit pricing is required in some states to provide information on prices on a per-unit or volume basis to enhance consumer decision making.

Understanding Marketing Terms and Concepts

Thinking About Marketing

1. Define price elasticity, and explain its relationship to demand.

2. Briefly explain the steps that should be considered in determination of a price.

3. Why are pricing decisions so important, and why are these decisions becoming more difficult?

4. Why may pricing decisions involving international marketing be so problematic?

5. Contrast break-even analysis pricing with markup pricing. What are the shortcomings of each approach?

6. How might the pricing strategies for a line of low-calorie Chinese grocery items vary over time?

7. Contrast penetration pricing with price skimming.

8. Identify two examples of both pure price bundling and product bundling.

9. Consider the pricing of services. What will determine the prices charged by firms that provide accounting services to small businesses?

10. How does the Federal Trade Commission view reference claims for advertisements involving *(a)* former price comparisons and *(b)* comparisons with competing retailers?

Applying Marketing Skills

1. Identify a new-brand entry in two different product categories. How do its prices compare to competing brands in each category? What factors might account for differences between prices within the categories?

2. Are the following practices ethical? Explain.

   a. John Doe is a retailer of brand X fountain pens, which cost him $5 each. His usual markup is 50 percent over cost, or $7.50. Doe first offers the pens for $10, realizing he will be able to sell very few if any. This offer lasts for only a few days. He then reduces the price to $7.50 and promotes as follows: "Terrific bargain: X Pens, Were $10, Now Only $7.50!"

   b. Retailer Doe advertises brand X pens as having "Retail Value $15, My Price $7.50," when only a few distant suburban outlets charge $15.

3. Explain why long-distance telephone suppliers charge different prices at different times of the day. Explain how the competition between AT&T and MCI influences their pricing behavior.

Using the www in Marketing

Activity One   The eBay Web site discussed in the introduction of this chapter has been influential in affecting how consumers search for low prices. Consider the following questions as they relate to price search using eBay:

1. What activities are required for an individual consumer to offer products for sale on eBay?

2. What are the characteristics of products that are most consistent with selling on sites such as eBay?

3. What advantages does eBay offer traditional retailers?

4. For what kinds of pricing situations are on-line auctions likely to be most effective?

Activity Two   Identify and describe the
pricing strategies for the following products. Explain why
these pricing objectives are appropriate for the respective
environments in which the organization operates:

1. Florida Power and Light http://www.fpl.com
2. Boeing http://www.boeing.com
3. L'Eggs http://www.pantyhose.com
4. Goodyear http://www.goodyear.com

Making Marketing Decisions
Case 12–1 P&G's Price-Promotion Approach

The world's largest advertiser, Procter &
Gamble, invented EDLP, or everyday low
pricing, in efforts to enhance brand loyalty,
cut costs, and end the wide fluctuations
caused by price promotions. More recently, the strategy
has been introduced into Europe by P&G for the same
reasons. So far, EDLP has been used for certain products
in Italy, the United Kingdom, and Germany. However, the
success of this approach in international markets, such as
Europe, remains to be determined.

Deep price discounts in European retailer markets,
particularly in the United Kingdom and Germany, are
commonplace. According to consumer surveys of
customer preferences and purchases, 44 percent of
German customers said they take home the cheapest
brand they can buy. Fifty-three percent of U.K. consumers
said retailers' private labels are just as good as
manufacturer brands. This suggests that retailers would
prefer high-low pricing strategies, where brands are
offered on temporary discounts. Again, these price cuts
would be largely supported by trade allowances from
manufacturers to the retailers. Yet in spite of these
conditions, P&G has moved ahead with its introduction of
EDLP pricing into European markets.

One interesting aspect of the pricing strategies used in
Europe is that price cuts are being made without
increases in media spending. That is, firms are seeking
more efficiently targeted media, in addition to cutting
prices and reducing sales promotion expenditures. The
switch to EDLP, which is being funded in the United
Kingdom from reductions in advertising and promotional
budgets, is an attempt to halt the aggressive growth of
retailers' own-label brands. In addition, firms are
announcing price cuts first to the news media prior to
discussions with retailers, which places increased
pressure on retailers to support the EDLP pricing strategy.

Procter & Gamble's move from high-low pricing to
everyday low pricing (or value pricing) was first met with
considerable resistance by the grocery industry. By now,
the P&G position is established. The objective is to
establish the value of product to the retailer or wholesaler
and then to charge prices consistent with that value

"every day." Prices are set so that the cost of goods sold
to the retailer would be the same under either plan,
adjusting for the differential costs under the high-low plan
and the additional costs of inventory required when goods
are purchased in quantity under the high-low plan. Beliefs
among managers regarding consumer behavior are also
important. Coupons are expensive, particularly when
values are doubled, and many managers believe coupon
and other price-reduction campaigns only serve to make
consumers perennial bargain hunters.

The initial move to limit price promotions in Europe
caused a slight decrease in sales and some friction with
retailers. EDLP defenders at Procter & Gamble respond
that retail multi-buying practices lowers turnover and
argue that value pricing has become successful in the
United States after some initial year sales declines.

Procter & Gamble has lost 10 percent of market share in
the last five years and has failed to introduce any truly
innovative products. New CEO Durk Jager, a Dutch longtime
P&G employee, has recently introduced a progressive global
plan. The new organization will comprise seven global
business units, organized by product category. Other
changes include plant closings and renewed responsibility
to managers for individual products; the latter change is
designed to increase the rate of innovation within P&G.

Questions

1. What risks does Procter & Gamble face in this global
pricing decision?

2. What factors make pricing decisions for foreign
markets so difficult?

3. Why do retailers prefer that manufacturers offer deep
price discounts in efforts to get them to stock certain
products? How does EDLP in the United States or
elsewhere affect retailer markups as part of the
distribution chain?

4. Why are private-label brands, or own-labels as they
are called in Europe, so price competitive?

5. Some argue that price elasticities are up to 10 times
greater than advertising elasticities. Comment on the
consistency of the low-price strategy.

SOURCES: Amy Barone and Laurel Wentz, "Artzt Steering Barilla into EDLP Strategy," *Advertising Age,* February 26, 1996, p. 10; "Low Prices," *Ad Age
International,* March 11, 1996, p. 18; Claire Murphy, "P&G Escalates Pricing Conflict," *Marketing,* April 4, 1996, p. 3; Jack Neff, "Price Cuts Move into
Media Mix," *Advertising Age,* March 6, 1996, p. 16; Amanda Richards, "P&G Price Cuts to Hit Own-Label," *Marketing,* February 15, 1996, p. 1; Barbara E.
Kahn and Leigh McAlister, *Grocery Revolution: The New Focus on the Consumer* (Reading, MA: Addison-Wesley, 1997); Dagmar Mussey and Amy
Barone, "Heat's on Value Pricing: Sales Drop Only a Blip Say EDLP Backers," *Advertising Age* 68, no. 2 (January 13, 1997), p. 121; Raju Narisetti, "P&G
Bets on Low Prices 'Every Day' to Cut Out Need for Company Coupons," *The Wall Street Journal,* January 8, 1996, p. 15B; and "Procter's Gamble," *The
Economist* 351 (June 12, 1999), p. 10.

Case 12–2 Loctite: Business-to-Business Global Strategies

Loctite Corp., the Hartford, Connecticut, maker and marketer of industrial sealants and adhesives used in manufacturing processes by other firms, has equity in companies in 24 countries, and its 1,000 products are sold in 80 nations. Loctite products are used in making motor vehicles, compact disc players, videocassette recorders, and other products. Because many of its customers produce with nonmetallic products, Loctite has developed adhesives for use on plastics, fiberglass, and ceramics.

Nearly 80 percent of Loctite's profits come from overseas sales. The company's growth strategy is to invest in developing nations and recently opened markets, ensuring a toehold in economies poised for rapid growth.

Loctite is optimistic that the North American Free Trade Agreement (NAFTA), the establishment of European Union (EU), the opening up of the Eastern bloc and China will give Loctite an even wider market to operate in. This global orientation is based on management's often-stated understanding that 95 percent of the world's population does not live in the United States.

Loctite's international strategy is straightforward. The company seeks local partners and gives them good margins that enable prices to be set at profitable levels. The company is patient in letting its subsidiaries develop. For example, its Chinese operations took 10 years to turn a profit. Local managers make their own marketing and pricing decisions. Products are priced according to value in each of the company's markets. However, price decisions are subject to a wide variety of pricing situations, currency factors, and inflation rates in the numerous countries in which the company does business.

Today, Loctite is organized around four geographic regions (i.e., North America, Europe, Latin America, and Asia) and five marketing channels (i.e., industrial automotive, electronics, industrial maintenance, industrial production, and medical equipment). Computers, automobiles, vacuum cleaners, speakers, cosmetics, and compact disc players are just some of the products that are made with Loctite products. The continuing success of Loctite comes from its research, development, and engineering centers located in the United States, Germany, Japan, and Ireland. In fact, 20 percent of its sales are derived from products developed and introduced in the last five years. This continuous stream of new-product introductions enables Loctite to maintain competitive advantage for its products while still charging prices that offer profitable margins to the company.

Several other developments have occurred that will further improve Loctite's ability as a business-to-business marketer. First, Loctite has earned ISO 9002 Quality System Registration. This recognition is a unique signal of quality that industrial buyers can use in their decisions regarding supplier selection. In addition, Loctite recently has partnered with Du Pont in a strategic alliance to market a new line of lubricants. This alliance will further strengthen the perception of Loctite as a major player in Du Pont's targeted markets. Both phenomena will also facilitate Loctite's ability to charge premium prices.

Questions

1. What cultural considerations must be considered in setting prices for Loctite's industrial products?

2. What strategies have accounted for the success of Loctite?

3. What are Loctite's major pricing objectives?

SOURCES: Bill Kelley, "Sticking to His Guns," *Sales & Marketing Management,* July 1993, pp. 54–57; Elizabeth S. Kiesche, "Loctite Secures a Grip in a Broader Market," *Chemical Week,* March 3, 1993, pp. 37, 40; Tim Smart, "Why Ignore 95% of the World's Market?" *Business Week,* October 23, 1992, p. 64; "Small Manufacturing Facility Features Big-Company Support," *Design News,* April 19, 1999, p. 47; and company Web site: www.loctite.com.

Chapter Thirteen

Marketing Channels

After studying this chapter, you should be able to:

1 Explain the functions and key activities of marketing channels.

2 Discuss the role of intermediaries in marketing channels.

3 Distinguish between direct and indirect marketing channels.

4 Illustrate how some firms use multiple channels successfully.

5 See how marketing-channel decisions are related to other key marketing decision variables.

6 Understand how power, conflict, and cooperation affect the operation of a marketing channel.

7 Give examples of ethical and legal issues encountered in the operations of marketing channels.

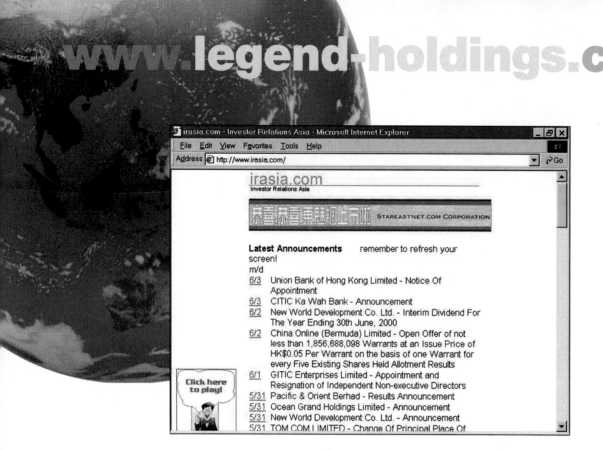

Despite their best efforts, multinational powerhouses such as Compaq, IBM, and Hewlett-Packard are not the leading sellers of personal computers in China. It is state-owned Legend Holdings, a company that badly trailed these three companies heading into the late 1990s, that leads China's PC sales. In fact, some industry analysts did not expect Legend to survive, much less become a leader in the third-largest and fastest-growing computer market in the world. The key to Legend's success is its multifaceted distribution system, along with competitive pricing and knowledge of the local market. With China's notoriously inefficient transportation system, companies must rely on a large number of local distributors to deliver products and provide additional services.

Legend sells through 1,800 distributors, 800 of whom were added in 1999. It also owns retail stores that sell its computers, makes repairs, and provides training for first-time buyers. The training is a crucial part of Legend's channel strategy; only 1 out every 175 Chinese consumers currently owns a computer. Legend understands the need to assist buyers more than foreign producers do and thus supplements in-store training with tutorials included with its PCs.

Legend is broadening its distribution by joining forces with Microsoft and IBM in the software and systems-integration markets. IBM's general manager for distribution notes that, "On one hand, we compete with Legend. But on the other hand, they are our second-largest partner in China."

Legend's success has other manufacturers rethinking their channel strategies. Compaq, IBM, Dell Computer Corporation, and Toshiba are among those modifying their channel strategies. Dell will pursue its strategy of selling direct to the Chinese consumer via both the Internet and toll-free telephone networks, while Toshiba, IBM, and Compaq are strengthening their ties with local distributors. The one thing these companies have in common is that they are trying to catch a local company who truly understands how and where the Chinese consumer wishes to purchase personal computers. **Source:** Dexter Roberts, Joyce Barnathan, and Bruce Einhorn, "How Legend Lives Up to Its Name," *Business Week,* February 15, 1999.

| **Exhibit 13–1** | *Consumer and business-to-business marketing channels* |

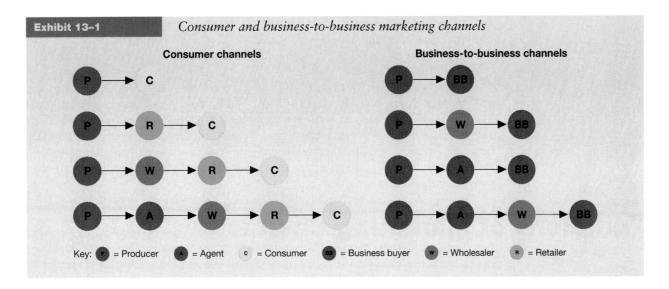

The Legend profile introduces several issues of interest in this chapter. First, the right product produced at the right time must be matched with the right means of distributing it to the marketplace. Second, the right means of distribution often changes over time. Third, understanding buyer needs is crucial for success.

In this chapter, we explore the **marketing channel,** or channel of distribution, defined as a combination of organizations and individuals (channel members) who perform the required activities to link producers of products to users of those products to accomplish marketing objectives.[1] In thinking about marketing channels, keep in mind that products can be goods, services, or ideas. Producers could be manufacturers, service organizations, or idea-generating groups or companies. Some alternative consumer and business-to-business channels are shown in Exhibit 13–1.

Different types of marketing channels require the services of **intermediaries,** often referred to as *middlemen,* who are directly involved in the purchase or sale of products as they flow from the originator to the user. Intermediaries include retailers, which sell to ultimate consumers, and wholesalers, which sell to retailers, other wholesalers, government buyers, manufacturers, and other business customers. Retailers and wholesalers are discussed in detail in subsequent chapters.

We introduce various types of marketing channels in this chapter. Some companies, such as Burger King, reach their customers through franchising. Computer producers, such as Tandy, may sell through their own retail stores (Radio Shack); others, such as Dell and Gateway, sell directly to the consumer via the Internet, telephone, and mail order. Decisions on marketing channels are prime elements in a Firm's overall marketing strategy and a factor in pricing, product, and marketing-communications considerations.

Importance of Marketing Channels

Since marketing channels determine how and where customers buy, the establishment of and any subsequent change in channels is indeed critical. Other marketing variables can be manipulated frequently, and changes are often easy to make. Marketers can raise and lower prices, vary advertising media and messages, and add and delete products from their market offerings without revolutionizing the way they do business.

Making major changes in marketing channels is not so easy. Marketing channels are harder to change because other parties, such as retailers and wholesalers, may play important roles in the channel. For example, several manufacturers receive a sizeable portion of their sales volume from Wal-Mart. Home appliance manufacturers National Presto Industries and Toastmaster get more than 30 percent of their sales volume from Wal-Mart, and National Picture & Frame, a supplier of mirrors and frames, gets 36 percent of its revenue from the discounter. Where would these companies make up the lost volume if they decided not to sell through Wal-Mart? It would require a marketing miracle for these companies to sell as much merchandise without Wal-Mart.[2]

Marketers are sometimes bound to their channels when significant sunk costs are involved. For example, the franchise system of McDonald's and company-owned outlets such as Exxon's convenience stores represent huge dollar investments. Such investments are made only after much forethought, and abandoning them is the last resort. For these reasons, marketing channels take on more of a sense of permanence—change is certainly an option, but one that is not so likely to be frequently exercised as with other marketing variables.

Functions of Marketing Channels

By performing five critical functions, marketing channels play an important role in accomplishing the key marketing activities discussed in Chapter 1 (Exhibit 1–7). These functions, shown in Exhibit 13–2, include the management of marketing communications, inventory, physical distribution, market feedback, and financial risk. It is important to note that none of these functions can be eliminated, but they can be shifted from one channel member to another.

Marketing Communications

Channel members are frequently involved in marketing communications activities, which include advertising and public relations, sales promotion, personal selling, and direct marketing communications. Home Depot, for example, a leading retailer of home improvement products, aggressively advertises and provides a trained sales staff to assist customers. Home Depot also uses in-store displays to demonstrate the mechanics of various home improvement projects such as building decks or installing ceiling fans.

Inventory Management

Marketing channel members sometimes provide inventory management functions. For example, auto parts wholesalers must stock thousands of products, many of which sell for under a dollar each, to be a competitive supplier to the independent repair shop market. In contrast, a Corvette-only parts wholesaler may stock fewer products but offer virtually every part available for repairing Corvettes of all vintages.

Exhibit 13–2   *Key functions performed in marketing channels*

Marketing communications
- Advertising the product
- Providing point-of-purchase displays
- Providing a salesforce that offers information & service to customers

Market feedback
- Serving on manufacturer advisory boards
- Informing other channel members of competitive activity
- Participating in test market evaluations

Inventory management
- Ordering an appropriate assortment of merchandise
- Maintaining adequate stock to meet customer demand
- Storing merchandise in an appropriate facility

Financial risk
- Offering credit
- Managing risks related to product loss or deterioration
- Managing risks related to product safety & liability

Physical distribution
- Delivering products
- Coordinating delivery schedules to meet customer expectations
- Arranging for the return of defective merchandise

Physical Distribution

The actual movement of products and other physical distribution activities are important elements in a marketing channel. For example, it is not unusual for suppliers of raw materials and components to a high-volume, fast-paced manufacturing plant to be given windows of only a few minutes to make deliveries. The coordination of delivery times is thus a major issue in meeting customer expectations, and suppliers who cannot meet such operating demands will lose business.

Market Feedback

The *relationship perspective* is illustrated when channel members provide valuable information to other channel members, leading to better performance in the channel. One company that provides useful information to intermediaries is Armstrong World Industries, an industry leader in commercial and residential flooring and home improvement products. To better serve the fast-growing home center market with key accounts such as Lowes, Menard's, and Home Depot, Armstrong created a Corporate Retail Account (CRA) division. One goal of the CRA was to improve retailer profit margins, which Armstrong did by sharing its expertise in store merchandising, employee training, and managing information to support a computerized inventory control system.

Catering to the home center market has produced significant sales increases for Armstrong and positioned the company for future sales increases as these large retailers become an even more important channel for its products.[3]

Financial Risk

The last function performed in marketing channels relates to ownership of the products passing through the channel. With ownership, or taking title, come various forms of risk. Perishable products may deteriorate; thefts may occur; or nature may deal out a flood, fire, or some other disaster.

Another risk involves accounts receivable: Who gets stuck if the customer doesn't pay the bill? For example, suppliers to Filene's Basement Corporation, a retail clothing discount chain with most of its 51 stores in New England, took a great risk by continuing to extend credit after Filene's declared bankruptcy. Ultimately, some of these suppliers could lose a considerable amount of money if Filene's is unable to recover from bankruptcy. Since the chief competitors of Filene's, outlet malls and larger chains such as TJ Maxx, are gaining momentum in this particular market, it is not clear whether Filene's suppliers' risk taking will eventually pay off.[4]

The assumption of risk is part of the quest to make a profit. It is an essential part of the job for members of any marketing channel.

Contributions of Intermediaries

It can be fashionable to rail about the perverse influence of channel intermediaries, or middlemen. Wholesalers and retailers in the grocery industry are sometimes portrayed as antiheroes, for example, whereas farmers may be seen as economic victims.

Those who take these views typically feel that intermediaries reap unfair profits. It is true that short-term imbalances in the economic system may allow opportunistic retailers and wholesalers to capture largely unearned windfall profits. For example, hotels may inflate prices for rooms, food, and beverages to maximize profits from a captive market, say, fans attending the Super Bowl.

In the long run, however, intermediaries must justify their existence on economic and societal terms to survive. An intermediary must be able to perform some marketing channel activity better than any other channel member. For example, Spiegel, Inc., a major intermediary for apparel and home furnishings manufacturers, has a catalog division and more than 275 stores in the US. Spiegel provides a

A retail intermediary, Target performs a wide range of functions, including advertising, selling, managing inventory, delivering merchandise, providing feedback to suppliers, and assuming financial risk.

wide range of marketing channel activities to boost sales in its stores, including sales and advertising support, store displays, inventory ordering and storage, delivery, and consumer credit. Manufacturers such as Sony, RCA, Calvin Klein, and Reebok benefit from the channel activities of Spiegel and other retailers. Without retail intermediaries, these manufacturers would have to build their own stores or sell directly to consumers through catalogs or some other means. If they could market more effectively and efficiently without Spiegel, good business sense says they would do so. Obviously, Spiegel is performing some of the marketing channel functions better than the manufacturers could.

Justifying their existence is painfully necessary for intermediaries in the highly competitive grocery products industry. Large supermarket chains following the *productivity perspective* continue to move away from independent wholesalers to their own distribution networks in an effort to control costs and improve product availability. Even Fleming, the world's largest grocery wholesaler, is struggling to maintain its financial well-being. Fleming's customer base, small independent grocers, is losing business to the large chains. At the same time, large manufacturers such as Procter & Gamble have cut back on discounts and promotional allowances. Since wholesalers such as Fleming traditionally kept a sizable portion of these moneys, profit margins are under even more pressure. Fleming and other wholesalers will have to be more efficient to survive, and many are also looking at expansion into international markets as means of generating more sales volume.[5]

In the vast majority of cases, intermediaries are not profiteering parasites; they are simply businesses trying to compete by adding value to the market offering. Given far-flung global markets, intense competition, and specialized support services, intermediaries are likely to remain integral in most marketing channels.

Types of Marketing Channels

The major alternatives available for structuring a marketing channel include direct and indirect channels, single and multiple marketing channels, and vertical marketing systems.

Hanoch Eiron, Channels Manager
Software Engineering Systems Division
Hewlett-Packard

As Channels Manager in a software division of Hewlett-Packard, Hanoch is responsible for improving selling efficiencies and developing new sales channels. Prior to joining HP, Mr. Eiron was General Manager with Franz, Inc., a California software manufacturer. He earned an MBA from U.C. Berkeley and an undergraduate degree from Tel-Aviv University, Israel.

"Manufacturers are constantly trying to improve the productivity of their channels. One way to do this is to use indirect channels rather than a direct sales orgaization. While direct channels are often necessary for specialized products, they are expensive—as much as 30 cents for each dollar of revenue generated. If manufacturers can decrease the level of specialization necessary to sell their products, indirect channels can boost productivity."

Channel management sometimes requires that existing channels be modified. Gateway County store has begun opening its own retail stores in the United States to supplement its traditional direct marketing channel.

Direct and Indirect Marketing Channels

A marketing channel may be direct or indirect. A **direct channel** describes movement of the product from the producer to the user without intermediaries. An **indirect channel** requires intermediaries between the originator and the user to perform some functions related to buying or selling the product to make it available to the final user. A given company might employ both direct and indirect channels.

DIRECT CHANNELS   Direct channels frequently occur in the marketing of medical and professional services, where the use of an intermediary is often impractical. Direct channels are also frequently used in business-to-business markets, where production equipment, components, and subassembly manufacturers sell directly to finished product manufacturers. Exhibit 13–3 gives some examples of direct marketing channels. Increasingly, consumer goods manufacturers are adding direct channels via the Internet for at least some of their products to reach ultimate consumers. For example, Mattel, Polaroid, and Levi Strauss have active Web sites where consumers can bypass traditional retailers and buy directly from the company.[6]

Some of the more spectacular marketing success stories come out of companies using direct channels of distribution. Dell Computer Corporation, a great example of the *entrepreneurial perspective,* sells over 75 percent of its products directly to customers. Dell has earned many industrywide awards for product quality and customer satisfaction, including a designation as one of *Fortune*'s "most admired" companies. Using a customer-focused approach, Dell sells more than $18 billion worth of computers, software, and accessories worldwide, the majority of which go to demanding, large business customers. The first company to offer customers direct, toll-free technical phone support and next-day on-site support, Dell management believes its close relationships with customers are the key to its success.[7]

Direct channels can also be used to market services. For example, X.com is selling its Standard & Poor 500 index mutual fund exclusively on a direct basis via the Internet. Investors pay no transaction or brokerage fees. X.com can offer the no-fee mutual fund because of cost savings compared to selling through brokers. The Internet-only fund also introduces investors to other X.com products and services.[8]

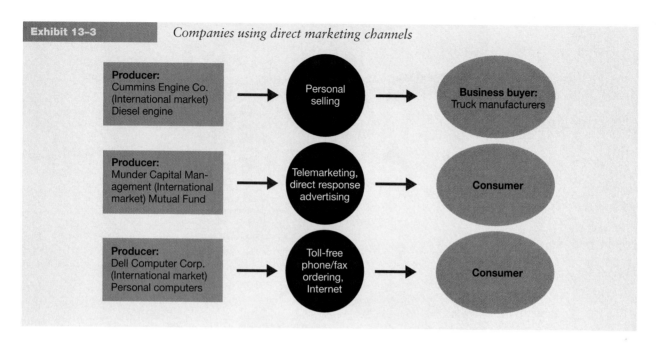

Exhibit 13–3   *Companies using direct marketing channels*

Cummins Engine Company successfully uses direct channels in business-to-business markets. Cummins's salespeople must be knowledgeable about maintenance costs, engine operating costs, and other technical data to effectively sell directly to truck manufacturers such as Chrysler, Navistar, Kenworth, and Volvo-GM.

INDIRECT CHANNELS   Despite the increasing popularity of direct channels, most consumer purchases (homes, automobiles, groceries, appliances, clothing) are still made in an indirect marketing channel, where there is some intermediary between the producer and the end user. Indirect channels are also important in some business-to-business settings.

Two examples of indirect marketing channels are shown in Exhibit 13–4. Orgill Brothers, one of the world's largest hardware wholesalers, is an important intermediary for thousands of manufacturers that want to reach small- and medium-

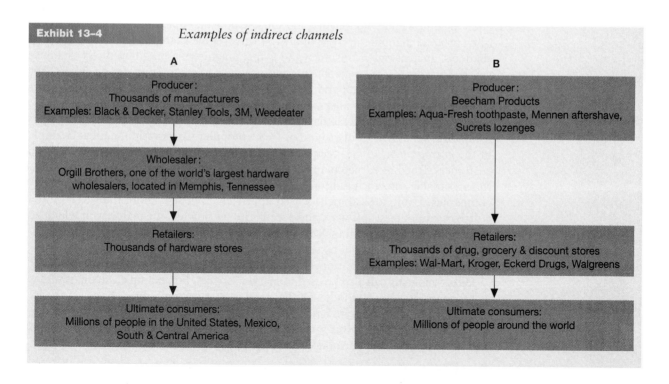

Exhibit 13–4   *Examples of indirect channels*

Most consumers buy houses in an indirect marketing channel with the assistance of a real estate agent. Others may buy in a direct channel from producers such as Rocky Mountain Log Homes.

sized retail hardware stores. It would not be economically feasible for most manufacturers to provide the sales support to individual hardware stores that Orgill Brothers provides. Example B is Beecham Products, which uses indirect channels to sell to ultimate consumers through retail intermediaries.

Single and Multiple Marketing Channels

Some companies use a **single-channel strategy** to reach their customers; others rely on a **multiple-channels strategy.** Some companies with multiple products or brands may use a single-channel strategy in one situation and a multiple-channels strategy in another. A single-channel strategy involves the use of only one means of reaching customers. For example, Nexxus shampoo is distributed exclusively through hair care professionals. Prell shampoo, widely available at discount, drug, and grocery stores, is a product distributed through multiple channels. Liz Claiborne uses a multiple-channels strategy to reach different market segments. Its Elisabeth stores serve large-size customers; First Issue stores sell a full product line under the First Issue label; and outlet stores market unsold inventory from past seasons. Liz Claiborne merchandise is also widely distributed in department and specialty stores.

As markets become increasingly fragmented, more firms use a multiple-channels strategy to appeal to as many potential buyers as possible. The basic idea is to allow customers to buy the way they want to and where they want to.

Hanoch Eiron discusses why the popularity of multiple channels in increasing:

"The move to multiple channels in many industries is driven by market fragmentation and buyer preferences. For example, in the computer industry, there are significant markets for home computers and business computers. Within these two broad categories, individual buyers have different preferences. Some like to buy in a retail store, some on the Internet or toll-free phone system, some from a local dealer, some directly from the manufacturer sales specialist. A manufacturer that uses only a single channel will most likely miss sale opportunities. Multiple channels let customers buy like they want to."

Vertical Marketing Systems

Emphasis on the *relationship perspective* has contributed to the growth of vertical marketing systems. These systems are centrally coordinated, highly integrated operations that work together to serve the ultimate consumer. The word *vertical* refers to the flow of the product from the producer to the customer. This flow is usually thought of as "down the channel" or "downstream," meaning that the product flows down from the producer to the customer.

Vertical marketing systems are now used in a sizable majority of the total sales of consumer goods. Exhibit 13–5 gives examples of the three basic types of vertical marketing systems: corporate, contractual, and administered channel systems.[9]

Exhibit 13–5

Types of vertical marketing systems

Channel systems

Corporate

Forward integration:
 Polo, Laura Ashley, Gulf States
 Paper Corp.

Backward integration:
 Winn-Dixie grocery chain

Description
One channel member owns
one or more other channel
members

Contractual

Wholesaler-sponsored voluntary groups:
 Ace Hardware, Western Auto

Retailer-sponsored cooperative groups:
 Affiliated Grocers, Cotter & Company
 (True Value Hardware)

Franchise systems:
 McDonald's, Holiday Inns, Personnel
 Pool of America

Description
Channel members operate according to
contractual agreement

Administered

Abbott Labs, General Electric, Rolex

Description
Channel members operate
according to agreed-upon plan

CORPORATE CHANNEL SYSTEMS Vertical coordination in a corporate channel system is achieved through ownership of two or more channel members on different levels of distribution. A corporate channel system in which one channel member owns one or more of its buyers downstream is called **forward integration.** Some of the companies that have used forward integration to open their own stores are Polo, Esprit, and Laura Ashley.

Business-to-business marketers also use forward integration. For example, Gulf States Paper Corporation, a manufacturer of assorted food-service products such as paper plates, bowls, and serving trays, owns a chain of wholesale paper distributors in the southeastern United States.

Other companies attempt to improve the efficiency and effectiveness of their marketing channels through ownership of one or more of their suppliers, not their buyers. This practice is called **backward integration.** The Winn-Dixie grocery store chain, for example, acquired its own cattle farms, coffee plantations, and ice cream manufacturing facilities for better control of the price and availability of key food products.

The global integration of marketing channels allows companies to take advantage of the strengths of various countries or regions of the world to maximize marketing efforts. For example, a company might manufacture its products in low-wage countries and use forward integration to establish retail distribution in more lucrative markets. This has been the channel strategy used by S. C. Fang Brothers, a Hong Kong textile manufacturing firm with a global sales base of more than $450 million. Fang Brothers was successful making T-shirts for The Gap and blouses for Calvin Klein, but it saw another retail opportunity. The company seized that opportunity in the late 1980s when it opened Episode stores in the United States. Fang Brothers opened 26 retail stores in the United States and then sold its successful retail operation to Mother Works, Inc., in 1966.[10]

CONTRACTUAL CHANNEL SYSTEMS Contractual systems may allow some channel members to gain clout in the marketplace and compete effectively with large corporate systems. Coordination between independent firms is achieved through contractual agreements rather than through ownership of channel members upstream or downstream. In this way, contractual channel members try to improve their buying power, gain economies of scale, and realize greater efficiencies through the standardization of operating procedures. The three primary types of contractual channels are wholesaler-sponsored voluntary groups, retailer-owned cooperative groups, and franchise systems.

Wholesaler-sponsored voluntary groups consist of independent retailers that operate under the name of a sponsoring wholesaler. Examples of wholesaler-sponsored voluntary groups are Ace Hardware and Western Auto. The wholesaler (Ace Hardware) buys in quantity, makes deliveries to the individual stores, and offers a variety of services that benefit its retailers. These services may include merchandising, advertising, and pricing support based on quantities purchased. Ace Hardware retailers buy most of their merchandise from the group wholesaler and pool their funds for advertising.

Retailer-owned cooperative groups operate like wholesaler-sponsored voluntary groups, but the retailers actually own the wholesaler. Affiliated Grocers and Cotter & Company's True Value are two well-known examples of this type of system.

The third type of contractual channel system is the **franchise system.** One party, the **franchisor,** grants another party, the **franchisee,** the right to distribute and sell

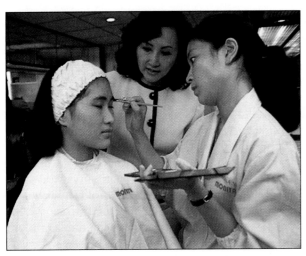

Cheng Ming Ming used forward integration to sell her own brands of beauty products through an international chain of beauty schools and salons that extends from Southeast Asia and China to the United States.

specified goods and services. The franchisee agrees to operate according to marketing guidelines set forth by the franchisor under a recognized trademark or trade name.

Franchise systems have been responsible for the growth of some of the most recognizable names in the business world, such as McDonald's and Holiday Inn. Nonretail franchise operations are also prominent, with companies such as Snelling & Snelling and Accoun-Temps in the personnel placement business and the Coca-Cola bottlers at the wholesale level. Exhibit 13–6 lists some other examples of nonretail franchise organizations. Retail franchising is discussed in more detail in Chapter 14.

ADMINISTERED CHANNEL SYSTEMS   A system designed to control a line or classification of merchandise is called an **administered channel system.** Here, channel members agree on a comprehensive noncontractual plan, and no channel member owns another. The parties in an administered system may work very closely to reduce joint operating costs for advertising, data processing, inventory control, order entry, or delivery schedules.

One example of an administered channel system is Agco Corporation's dealer network, which numbers 8,500 around the world. Agco has distribution rights to several leading brands of farm tractors, including Massey Ferguson, Agco Allis, and Landini, and supports its dealers with business planning, training, cash incentives, and constant communication. A key component of this administered system is Dealer Central, a telemarketing operation in Agco's Georgia headquarters. Dealers can call in for technical advice and product and parts availability when Agco's territory managers are not readily available. Agco's administered channel system has made the company a huge success even though the market for tractors has been fairly depressed in recent years.[11]

In the retail sector, successful administered marketing channels include General Electric and Rolex. Both companies have reputations for quality products backed

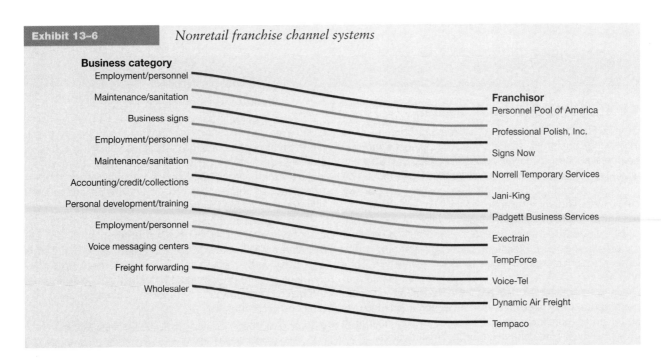

Exhibit 13–6   *Nonretail franchise channel systems*

Business category	Franchisor
Employment/personnel	Personnel Pool of America
Maintenance/sanitation	Professional Polish, Inc.
Business signs	Signs Now
Employment/personnel	Norrell Temporary Services
Maintenance/sanitation	Jani-King
Accounting/credit/collections	Padgett Business Services
Personal development/training	Exectrain
Employment/personnel	TempForce
Voice messaging centers	Voice-Tel
Freight forwarding	Dynamic Air Freight
Wholesaler	Tempaco

by highly effective marketing plans and activities. As a result, retailers are usually quite receptive to suggestions made by General Electric and Rolex for pricing and display practices. For more about how General Electric works, see "Earning Customer Loyalty: GE Supports the Small Dealer."

Managing Marketing Channels

The management of marketing channels requires decision making and action in the six areas shown in Exhibit 13–7. First, the firm formulates its marketing objectives and strategy. Only then can managers develop marketing-channel strategies and objectives. Various channel alternatives are then evaluated to determine capabilities, costs, compatibility with other marketing variables, and their availability to the firm. Next, the firm establishes its channel structure and implements the channel strategy. Finally, the firm must constantly evaluate channel performance, which may lead to adjustment in one or more of the other five management areas shown in the exhibit.

Formulate Marketing Objectives and Strategy

Marketing channels often represent a significant dollar investment, and established channels can be difficult to change without risking lost sales volume. As a result, it is imperative that a firm develop marketing-channel objectives and strategy only after formulating its overall marketing objectives and strategy.

Lexus by Toyota has become one of the biggest success stories in the luxury car market by positioning the exclusivity of the brand. The Lexus marketing strategy called for extending the marketing channel beyond existing Toyota dealers to a relatively small number of selected Lexus dealerships. With less competition between dealers, maintaining higher prices to support the exclusive image is not as problematic as when a geographic market is flooded with competing dealers. Higher prices mean higher profit margins, which makes it possible for dealers to provide exceptional service to its customers, an objective that is also compatible with the overall marketing strategy. By ensuring that other marketing-mix variables were compatible with the chosen marketing channel, and that the entire mix was compatible with the exclusive image of the product, Lexus has become a huge success.[12]

Earning Customer Loyalty

GE supports the small dealer

General Electric's appliance sales to large discounters were increasing, but profit margins were dropping as the discounters pushed for lower prices from GE. Brand loyalty was also slipping, as discount shoppers focus mostly on price. As a result, GE revamped its channel support for small independent appliance dealers in an attempt to strengthen profit margins and brand loyalty.

GE realized that small dealers needed advice on store merchandising and business planning, something the larger discount stores were able to do for themselves. They also needed quick access to product-knowledge information and flexible, quick delivery from GE since they could not afford to carry large inventories. GE began offering discount stores more low-priced appliances and concentrated on higher-quality merchandise for its small dealers. Small dealers were also given a much-improved ordering system

called Premier Plus, which featured next-day delivery. In addition, small dealers were given business-planning software, store-remodeling kits, and access to store-improvement loans. In many cases, GE obtained commitments from retailers such as share of business, sales volume, and breadth of product coverage granted to GE.

GE's channel strategies are paying off in the small-dealer category, which still accounts for approximately 40 percent of total appliance sales. One GE retailer says, "GE bends over backwards to help satisfy the customer." And independent dealers are noticeably holding their own against the discounters, with many reporting increased sales volume and profit margins.

Source: Steven Wheeler and Evan Hirsh, *Channel Champions* (San Francisco: Jossey-Bass Publishers, 1999), pp. 157–60.

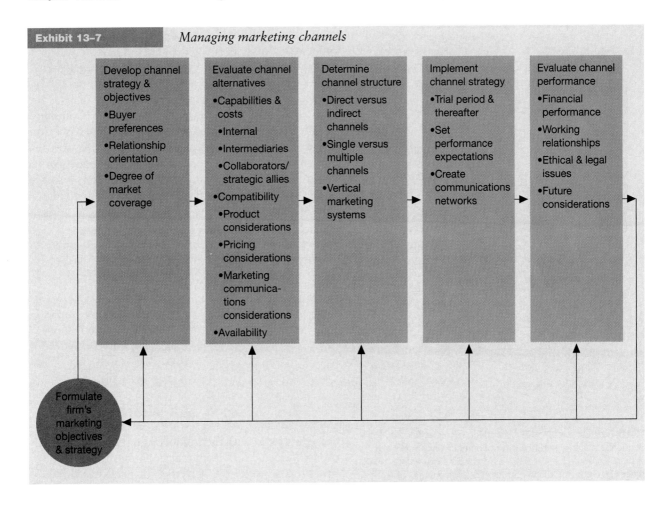

| Exhibit 13–7 | *Managing marketing channels* |

Develop channel strategy & objectives
- Buyer preferences
- Relationship orientation
- Degree of market coverage

Evaluate channel alternatives
- Capabilities & costs
  - Internal
  - Intermediaries
  - Collaborators/ strategic allies
- Compatibility
  - Product considerations
  - Pricing considerations
  - Marketing communications considerations
- Availability

Determine channel structure
- Direct versus indirect channels
- Single versus multiple channels
- Vertical marketing systems

Implement channel strategy
- Trial period & thereafter
- Set performance expectations
- Create communications networks

Evaluate channel performance
- Financial performance
- Working relationships
- Ethical & legal issues
- Future considerations

Formulate firm's marketing objectives & strategy

Develop Channel Objectives and Strategy

Channel objectives should be specifically stated, measurable, and consistent with the firm's marketing objectives. Objectives are often stated in terms of sales volume, profitability, market share, costs, number of wholesale or retail outlets, or geographic expansion. **Channel strategy** then is an expression of a general action plan and guidelines for allocating resources to achieve the channel objective.

The development of channel strategy involves decisions in three key areas: buyer preferences, relationship orientation, and the degree of market coverage.

BUYER PREFERENCES   Buyer preferences are important in determining channel strategy. Understanding the logic behind letting customers buy the way they want to is a hallmark of both established marketing leaders and entrepreneurs who beat the odds by breaking into long-established markets. Sellers of thousands of products, most notably books, recorded music, computers, and financial investments have found that millions of consumers worldwide prefer to buy on-line. Sellers of these products who did not fully appreciate buyer preferences are now playing catch-up. For example, sales growth at bookseller Amazon.com far outstrips growth through traditional bookstores, many of which are actually reporting declining sales. Sales through on-line brokerages such as E*trade and Charles Schwab are growing rapidly, while Merrill Lynch expects sales volume through its full-service brokers to decrease over time; in a move that reinforces the importance of paying attention to buyer preferences in the channels area, Merrill Lynch finally introduced an on-line option to its clients.[13]

RELATIONSHIP ORIENTATION   Most successful organizations try to establish strong relationships with others in their channel—not only because it is profitable

Every day. we rely on leaders like you.

At Johnson & Johnson, we know the value of partnering with businesses owned by the brightest leaders around.

That's why we're committed to creating new partnerships through our Minority and Women Business Supplier Outreach Program.

To learn more, log on to www.jnj.com.

Johnson & Johnson

The benefits of a relationship perspective can extend beyond economic advantage to the promotion of socially desirable results. For example, Johnson & Johnson has an active program to develop close partnerships with minority and female suppliers.

in the long run, but also because they believe that to do otherwise would be risky. Recall from Chapter 5 that a relationship orientation between buyers and sellers is a major trend, and that negotiations between parties often seek an outcome whereby both can win. This is the case with Frito-Lay and Oberto Sausage Company, who have signed a channels agreement that has Frito-Lay distributing Oberto products in 400,000 stores in the United States. Frito-Lay gets a meat product for its snack-food line, and Oberto gets an immediate boost in retail distribution. Both parties will reap increased sales from the agreement.[14]

Hanoch Eiron comments on the importance of manufacturers working with others in the channel: "Good working relationships with channel intermediaries is absolutely essential for success. Manufacturers should view their wholesalers and retailers as extensions of their companies, and use a team approach to maximizing channel performance. This is sometimes difficult, as these intermediaries sell competing manufacturers' brands. It is necessary that a manufacturer's objectives are compatible with those of the intermediary, and that there is a strong commitment to work together toward common objectives."

DEGREE OF MARKET COVERAGE Market coverage has to do with the number of outlets used to market a product. Market coverage commonly takes one of three forms: intensive, selective, or exclusive distribution. With **intensive distribution,** the product or service is distributed through every available outlet. For example, PepsiCo has long used intensive distribution with its soft drinks, selling through all sorts of retail stores, vending machines, restaurants, and concessionaires. Pepsi is now competing aggressively with Coke to intensify its sales to restaurants, theaters, sports arenas, and schools in the fountain-sales category.

Selective distribution involves selling a product in only some of the available outlets. This is commonly used when after-the-sale service is necessary, as with home appliances. Maytag, for example, sells appliances via selective distribution, and the company is even more selective in designating certain dealers as authorized service centers. In a metropolitan area of a million residents, Maytag products might be sold through a dozen retail stores, only two or three of which are designated as authorized service centers.

Exclusive distribution occurs when only one outlet is used in a geographic marketplace. Honda's Acura division, like Lexus, uses exclusive distribution to create distinctive dealerships for its upscale automobiles. Saturn is using the lure of exclusive market areas in Japan to expand in a tough market for its automobiles.

The Internet offers manufacturers another exclusive channel alternative for products that are typically distributed intensively or selectively. For example, IBM stopped selling its Aptiva computers through stores, deciding to sell them exclusively on the Internet.[15] Procter & Gamble, a distributor for fragrance manufacturer Hugo Boss, introduced a new men's cologne exclusively on-line for a three-month introductory period.[16] Rock bands Depeche Mode and the Cranberries have been successful with exclusive on-line distribution for designated portions of their concert tours.[17]

Evaluate Channel Alternatives

As shown in Exhibit 13–7, the evaluation of channel alternatives requires analysis in three related channel areas: capabilities and costs, channel compatibility with other marketing variables, and availability.

Thinking Critically

Rebecca Wetzel has just been appointed to a newly created position, manager of retail dealer development for HomeRight, a major home appliance company. She is responsible for providing training for retail salespeople and advice to dealers in the areas of merchandising, store promotions, and advertising. In the past, the HomeRight salesforce had provided these support activities to the retail dealers. In her first few weeks on the job, Rebecca visited several dealers in different markets and found that the retail support provided by the salesforce had been inconsistent—good in some cases, bad in others.

- What should Rebecca do within her own company to begin building a solid retail support program?

- To maximize dealer support and increase sales, what suggestions can you make to Rebecca for getting input from HomeRight dealers?

CHANNEL CAPABILITIES AND COSTS Marketers must determine exactly who will perform the various channel activities and at what cost. Establishing marketing channels can be expensive and difficult to reverse, so firms should carefully assess the costs and capabilities of each channel alternative.

The evaluation of channel alternatives often begins with an assessment of how the firm's internal resources might be used to accomplish channel activities. This naturally leads to subsequent examination of how intermediaries could fit in, if at all. Sometimes, firms join forces with others in the channel. For example, Starbucks is moving its products beyond its own coffeehouses to the grocery shelves by joining forces with companies already strong in distribution through grocery stores. In one venture, PepsiCo is distributing Starbuck's Frappuccino. In other arrangements, Dreyer's Grand Ice Cream is distributing several flavors of Starbuck's coffee ice cream and Kraft Foods is distributing packaged coffee.[18]

With the explosion of commercial applications on the Internet, channel partnerships between high-technology firms are popular. Internet companies have turned to large retailers to increase distribution of their products and services. Yahoo! and Kmart, Best Buy and Microsoft, Wal-Mart and America Online are examples.[19] In these arrangements, both parties recognize the capabilities of the other as a channel partner. Wal-Mart has one million visitors to its stores each week, approximately five times the number of America Online subscribers, so their partnership means AOL gets more exposure than it otherwise would. Wal-Mart, meanwhile, gets a well-known technology company that can help it build its own Internet marketing business.[20]

CHANNEL COMPATIBILITY Channel alternatives need to be compatible with other marketing variables affecting a firm's offering, including product, pricing, and marketing communications factors. For example, product perishability, consumer sensitivity to purchase price, and the nature of point-of-sale promotion could affect the compatibility of a particular marketing channel. Research suggests that channel variables such as amount and kind of shelf space and feature displays may interact with both price and perceived quality to affect purchase intentions or sales volume. In one study, store brands were rated much higher in attractive supermarkets than in less attractive stores. Two-thirds of shoppers who tasted store-brand jelly in a high-image store rated it very good or excellent. Only 38 percent rated it just as positively in an older, less appealing store.[21]

PRODUCT CONSIDERATIONS A product-related consideration is the product's desired image. Consider the case of OshKosh B'Gosh Inc. OshKosh, a maker of children's clothing, traditionally relied on expensive department stores and specialty stores for retail distribution, in keeping with its high-quality image. When OshKosh expanded into Sears and JC Penney stores, the company was concerned that such a move would affect its image and, subsequently, sales in upscale department stores where image is important.

OshKosh hoped to avoid problems with the upscale department stores by offering them exclusive, higher-profit items such as a novelty denim line. OshKosh was trying to minimize a possible product/channel incompatibility by differentiating its product offerings to two different types of retail customers.

PRICING CONSIDERATIONS Which marketing channels are appropriate can also depend on pricing strategies and tactics. One company that matches its marketing channel with its pricing strategy is Daewoo, who is selling its cars directly to consumers on the Internet. While there are several Web sites where consumers can buy cars, Daewoo is the first to offer direct-to-consumer sales on the Internet. This gives Daewoo a low-cost channel and allows them to reinforce its low-price offering to the consumer.[22]

MARKETING COMMUNICATIONS CONSIDERATIONS Compatibility with marketing communications plans and strategies also determines the suitability of various marketing channels. Sony, in an attempt to showcase its full product line better, supplements its independent dealer network with its own Sony Gallery of

Some companies join forces to move products through marketing channels. PepsiCo is distributing flavors of Starbuck's Frappuccino.

Consumer Electronics in Chicago, New York, and Los Angeles. Reebok now sells directly to colleges and high schools while continuing to sell through its traditional retail channel. Reebok took this action to address a lack of representation among American basketball players, a market dominated by Nike.

AVAILABILITY Another important issue in the evaluation of various channel alternatives is whether the channel is available under reasonable conditions. Quite often, new companies may have a hard time establishing an appropriate marketing channel. The right channel may simply be unavailable, or the desired channel is too expensive.

For large, powerful sellers, channel availability is less of a problem. Indeed, a firm with the financial wherewithal can simply purchase a channel of distribution. Such is the case with Kodak through its subsidiary Qualex Inc., a wholesale photofinisher. Qualex often buys competing photo labs outright; in other cases, it negotiates contracts to manage labs, thus opening the door for increased sales of Kodak film and paper. Kodak's Qualex now has the photofinishing business at Wal-Mart, Kmart, Walgreen's, and Eckerd Drug Stores. By becoming more aggressive with Qualex, Kodak has secured approximately 80 percent of the wholesale photofinishing market.[23]

Determine Channel Structure

The fourth phase of managing marketing channels shown in Exhibit 13–7 is to determine channel structure. The major decisions here concern whether to use direct or indirect channels, a single channel or multiple channels, or one of the many forms of vertical marketing systems. Firms often mix direct and indirect channels, and many firms use multiple channels, especially to reach new markets.

Implement Channel Strategy

The first four phases of managing marketing channels concentrate on planning the appropriate channel strategy and structure. The task now is to implement channel strategy. The full-scale implementation of a new channel strategy is often preceded by a trial period. Other important implementation tasks include setting performance expectations and creating communications networks.

Casey Jones Rides The OshKosh® Line Into Fashion History.

OshKosh B'Gosh's latest fashion trend is sweeping across America like the Cannonball Express. And babies everywhere are getting on board. For the store nearest you, call 1-800-782-4674.

Casey Reed Jones, age 14 months, Napa, California.

Baby B'gosh
BY OSHKOSH B'GOSH

The Biggest Name In Kids' Clothes.

To protect its high-quality image after expanding sales to Sears and JC Penney, Oshkosh offered upscale department stores exclusive, profitable merchandise.

RUN A TRIAL PERIOD The results of a trial period may indicate that a change is warranted, or just the opposite—that an existing strategy should stay in effect. In the Frito-Lay/Oberto Sausage example given earlier, a six-month trial period in Dallas tripled Oberto's sales, which led to the national distribution agreement between the two companies. Despite the explosion in marketing on the Internet, some businesses concluded after a trial period that this channel was not right for them. HarpCity, a retailer specializing in harmonicas, shut down its Web site after a trial convinced them that an incremental increase in sales was simply not worth the effort in this case.[24]

SET PERFORMANCE EXPECTATIONS As marketing-channel members have become more interdependent, the setting of performance expectations has evolved into more of a joint decision process, rather than one party's dictating standards to another. Procter & Gamble, one of the world's most powerful and effective marketing organizations, has learned the advantages of jointly setting performance standards with its wholesale and retail accounts. More than a hundred P&G key-customer marketing teams see reaching agreement on performance standards with their customers as an important part of their mission.[25]

Lack of agreement on performance standards could indicate that some other channel arrangement might be appropriate. If a channel is set up without advance agreement on performance standards, evaluation of channel performance becomes much more difficult.

CREATE COMMUNICATIONS NETWORKS   Another crucial aspect of channel strategy implementation is to establish communications networks among channel members. Sophisticated computer and communications technologies have greatly enhanced the capabilities of channel members to share important information on a timely basis, maintain goodwill, and solve problems in the mutual interest of channel members. For an example of how a computerized network facilitates communications among channel members, see "Using Technology: Saab Upgrades Dealer Communications."

The importance of ensuring adequate communications in the marketing channel is seen in the case of the National Franchise Council, an organization supported by the 15 largest franchise companies and overseen by the Federal Trade Commission. The council sponsors a traveling reform school, giving remedial training to franchise companies that have miscommunicated with franchise owners and potential owners. Among the companies learning how to better communicate with their channel partners are Atlanta-based Aaron Rents Inc., Noble Roman's Pizza of Minneapolis, and AlphaGraphics, headquartered in Tucson, Arizona.[26]

Evaluate Channel Performance

The evaluation of channel performance, the last area in Exhibit 13–7, can necessitate changes in any of the other decision areas. Evaluating marketing channels requires attention to four key areas: financial performance, working relationships with other channel members, ethical and legal issues, and future plans.

FINANCIAL EVALUATION   For the short run, channel members may be willing to operate at low levels of financial performance. Over time, however, financial results must be positive to sustain relationships in the channel.

An interesting example here involves Procter & Gamble. After years of offering significant discounts and costly promotions to retailers in the grocery trade, P&G concluded its marketing channel was too expensive. One step the company took

Using Technology

Saab upgrades dealer communications

Saab Cars USA is using IRIS (Intranet Retail Information Center), a state-of-the-art communications system to assist its dealers in achieving higher levels of customer satisfaction. The new system integrates three existing internal networks, thus allowing dealers quicker access to parts distribution, financing, and warranty information. In implementing the system, costs and simplicity were key concerns. Retailers own their own dealerships and typically do not have a sufficient level of computer expertise to design and operate sophisticated computer networks. Saab lowered implementation, training, and maintenance costs by making it easy for dealers to access and retrieve information. Simple navigation is one operating principle—information is never more than two clicks away. Another principle is that all applications need to be self-explanatory in order to reduce training costs. A third principle is quick response, with a three-second maximum for any transaction.

Retailers are delighted with the new system. Since they can get the information they need in a timely manner, they can answer customer questions more efficiently and improve customer service in several areas. IRIS has been so successful that Saab is considering expanding it into all 54 countries in which it operates.

Source: Jerry Rode, "Road Map to Competitive Advantage!" *Communication News*, April 1999, pp. 38, 41.

was to drastically reduce discounts and other trade promotions. This angered some of P&G's retailer customers, but some analysts think the company was deliberately shifting some of its distribution from grocery stores to discount stores, where the everyday-low-price policy is more welcome.

EVALUATE WORKING RELATIONSHIPS Three related concepts—power, conflict, and cooperation—are important in evaluation of working relationships among channel members. A firm may gain power in a variety of ways and use it to enhance its position in the marketing channel. Conflict among channel members is natural and sometimes constructive, but it can become destructive if it rages out of control. As power is wielded and conflicts ensue, channel members often find cooperation is essential if they are to flourish and survive.

CHANNEL POWER   Channel members may gain **channel power** in many ways.[27] For example, a giant retailer like Kmart offers vendors the opportunity to sell their products in more than 2,000 stores in the United States. In effect, Kmart is in a position to use **reward power** when it agrees to buy from a vendor—the reward being widespread distribution and the high probability of large sales volumes. Other examples of reward power might be a manufacturer's granting exclusive distribution rights to a wholesaler, offering special credit terms to deserving customers, or extending lenient returned-goods policies.

Some companies have achieved the status of channel leaders because of their expertise in marketing. K-Mart is a channel leader in many countries of the world, including Czech Republic.

Another form of power is **legitimate power,** which lies in ownership or contractual agreements. Holiday Inn has a certain amount of legitimate power over its franchisees through contractual agreements, for example, and Polo controls one of its channels by ownership of its own retail stores.

Power developed through the accumulation of expertise and knowledge is called **expert power.** Large retailers have gained a tremendous amount of expert power using point-of-sale scanners to gauge product movements, price sensitivities, and trade promotion effectiveness. In fact, retailers can know more about how manufacturers' products are doing in the marketplace than do the manufacturers. This expertise gives large retailers more power to negotiate favorably with their suppliers.

Power based on the desire of one channel member to be associated with another channel member is called **referent power.** For example, a jewelry store may wish to be selected as an exclusive dealer for Rolex watches. The store's desire would put Rolex in a powerful position with such a retailer.

Another form of power sometimes seen in channel relationships is **coercive power.** A manufacturer that threatens to cut off a distributor's credit unless the distributor pays its bills more promptly exemplifies coercive power. The use of coercive power can become abusive and even illegal. For instance, a distributor's coercing a manufacturer into dropping a competing distributor might be ruled a conspiracy in restraint of trade, a violation of federal antitrust legislation. Another example involves Microsoft, who is in the midst of an ongoing legal battle with the federal government. Prosecutors allege that the company abused its power, forcing unwilling customers to install its Windows operating system in computers or face retaliation from the software giant.

All channel members must develop some sort of power to survive. Some may build enough power to act as a **channel leader,** that is, a channel member with enough power to control others in the channel. Current channel leaders include Wal-Mart, Kroger, and General Electric. Large, successful organizations can gain buying power and selling power by controlling economic assets and resources, but smaller companies can also build power, especially by developing knowledge and expertise to gain expert power.

Thinking Critically

For the past three months, Ted Lucas had been trying to set up a business relationship with Williams Supply, an automobile repair parts wholesaler. The owner, Mr. Williams, had been promising Ted that he would begin stocking some of Ted's products, but would never make a commitment. After another failed attempt to set up Williams as a wholesaler, Ted made several sales calls on Williams's customers to see if he could convince them to buy from one of Ted's current wholesalers. Several of Williams's customers indicated they would be glad to switch their business, especially since Ted was offering a special price deal for new business through his current wholesaler. When Mr. Williams learned what had happened, he angrily told Ted that any chance of their doing business together was lost forever.

- Ted used coercive power in this situation. Was it justified?
- Assuming that Ted wants to resume his efforts to sell through Williams Supply, what should he do next?

CHANNEL CONFLICT   It is inevitable that channel members experience conflict with one another. **Channel conflict** may result from poor communications, a struggle over power in the channel, or incompatible objectives. For example, most buyers want to buy at as low a price as they can reasonably negotiate, whereas most sellers want to sell at as high a price as reasonably possible. Exhibit 13–8 provides several examples of routine channel conflict.

Channel conflict is commonplace in a competitive market where profitability is a requirement for survival, pointing up the importance of cooperation in resolving conflict to avoid senseless disagreements that can drain channel members' resources.

CHANNEL COOPERATION   **Channel cooperation** can help to reduce the amount of conflict and to resolve conflicts once they do occur.

The incentive to cooperate with other channel members is clearly strongest if all parties agree on their functional roles, and if agreement on performance standards has been reached prior to or early in the business relationship. When channel members do not agree on these matters, conflicts may be settled according to where the power lies. But conflicts settled only by the exercise of power often resurface, especially if the loser in the prior conflict gains an edge in the power dimension. As we suggest frequently in this book, more and more companies are embracing cooperation and building relationships as a superior way to ensure lasting market strength.

ETHICAL AND LEGAL ISSUES   The management of marketing channels calls attention to a number of ethical and legal issues, some of which are illustrated in Exhibit 13–9. Certainly, some channel conflicts have ethical and legal implications. And, strange as it might sound, cooperation taken to the extreme may also present problems, especially if agreements between channel members violate the key laws affecting marketing discussed in Chapter 2.

Because of the range of marketing activities that occur within any marketing channel, the potentially relevant legal issues for channels are numerous. Laws pertaining to pricing, product liability, and truth in advertising are a few examples of thousands of international, federal, state, and local regulations that might pertain to a given channel situation. Our discussion here focuses on the legal environment as it affects channel structure and selected buyer–seller interactions.

Producers may want to set up channel arrangements to ensure their products are given substantial market support by either wholesalers or retailers. One producer might wish to set up **exclusive territories,** so that no other reseller in a given geographic area sells a particular brand of a product. Another might enact **exclusive dealing agreements,** which would restrict a reseller from carrying a competing product line.

Another possibility is **tying contracts,** which require a reseller to buy products besides the one it really wants to buy. For example, a copier manufacturer may also require a customer to buy ink cartridges on the grounds that the printer can reach acceptable performance standards only if the specified cartridge is used.

Exclusive territories, exclusive dealing agreements, and tying contracts are legally acceptable unless they have anticompetitive effects or tend to create monopolies. A substantial reduction in competition through such arrangements is a violation of federal or state antitrust laws.

FUTURE CONSIDERATIONS   The final requirement in the evaluation of channel performance is to cast an eye to the future. Essentially, the firm should ask itself one key question: How well can this channel be expected to perform in the future? The answers can have far-reaching implications, as marketers make necessary changes in pursuit of their long-term goals.

Sometimes customers are the impetus for change in marketing channels. Consider the health care industry, in which major corporations have long been supporters of insurance-company-sponsored health maintenance organizations (HMOs) as a means of providing employee health benefits. The idea behind HMOs

Exhibit 13–8	*Examples of channel conflict*			
Who is upset?	**With whom?**	**Why?**		**Consequences**
Tommy Hilfiger	Wal-Mart	Wal-Mart's sale of imitation Hilfiger clothing		Wal-Mart is fined and ordered (by federal court) to cease
Bayer	Rite Aid drugstores	Unauthorized deductions from invoices		Reduce profits for Bayer
Auto dealers	General Motors	Use of dealer money for national advertising		Lawsuit against GM
Music distributors	Music retailers	Sale of used CDs cuts sales of new CDs, deprives artists of royalties		Sony, Warner Music, and others halted co-op advertising allowances to retailers that sell used CDs

Exhibit 13–9	*Examples of ethical and legal problems in marketing channels*
Situation	**Ethical/Legal Problem**
Large retailer threatens to stop buying unless supplier grants unreasonably low prices.	Unfair use of coercive power (unethical)
Powerful producer of consumer goods dictates how its products will be displayed without regard for space constraints in smaller stores.	Unfair use of coercive power (unethical).
Large wholesaler demands supplier replace its male sales rep with a female because the purchasing agent does not like to deal with men.	Unfair use of coercive power (unethical, potentially illegal).
Desperate to sign up new franchises, franchisor's sales rep downplays financial risk of owning franchise.	Deceptive communications (unethical, potentially illegal).
Wholesaler requests supplier stop selling to competing wholesaler; supplier grants request.	Excessive cooperation among channel members (illegal).
Two manufacturing companies agree not to sell to a particular wholesaler in an effort to damage the wholesaler's business.	Excessive cooperation among channel members (illegal).
Salesperson agrees to give retailer a lower price than competing retailers, based solely on friendship.	Excessive cooperation among channel members (illegal).

is to keep the costs of health care low; but now large companies such as General Mills, Honeywell, Pillsbury, American Express, and Dayton Hudson think the HMOs they helped create have gotten too big and bureaucratic and are stifling competition and medical innovation. As a result, these companies are now cutting out the HMO-intermediary as they contract directly with medical groups and hospitals. Hospitals and physician groups are also signing up consumers directly, which could lead to a substantial restructuring of the channels for basic health care, a structure in which HMOs have far less clout in the marketplace.[28]

Changing marketing channels is a major undertaking, and companies do not change if they are convinced the tried-and-true channel will get the job done. In the current environment characterized by changing consumer preferences, intense competition, and information-technology innovation, expect more companies to alter their channels.

Summary

1. **Explain the functions and key activities of marketing channels.** A marketing channel, sometimes referred to as a *channel of distribution,* is a combination of organizations that perform the activities required to link producers to users to accomplish particular marketing objectives.

   The primary goal of a marketing channel is to allow companies to reach their customers with the right product at the right time, to meet customer expectations, and to stimulate profitable sales volume. The key functions of marketing channels are marketing communications, inventory management, physical distribution, market feedback, and the assumption of financial risk.

2. **Discuss the role of intermediaries in marketing channels.** Intermediaries, often called *middlemen,* provide key marketing channel functions. To survive in the economic system, an intermediary must perform its particular functions more efficiently than any other channel member.

3. **Distinguish between direct and indirect marketing channels.** Direct marketing channels use no intermediaries to move products from producers to end users. Indirect marketing channels use at least one intermediary before the product reaches its final destination. Despite the dramatic growth of direct marketing channels, most products reach ultimate consumers through indirect marketing channels.

4. **Illustrate how some firms use multiple channels successfully.** As markets become increasingly specialized and companies seek to globalize their marketing efforts, the use of multiple channels is growing. Several examples of companies using multiple channels were presented in the chapter.

5. **See how marketing-channel decisions are related to other key marketing decision variables.** Marketing-channel strategies and objectives must be based on a firm's overall marketing strategies and objectives. After a channel strategy has been developed, different channel alternatives can be evaluated for capabilities, costs, and availability. Channel alternatives can also be evaluated for compatibility with product, pricing, and marketing communications variables.

6. **Understand how power, conflict, and cooperation affect the operation of a marketing channel.** Channel members develop power based on such factors as economic strength or market knowledge. In some instances, this power may be abused, leading to conflict between channel members.

   Conflict can also result from poor communications or incompatible goals among channel members. It is becoming increasingly necessary that channel members cooperate to resolve conflict and pursue mutually beneficial goals.

7. **Give examples of ethical and legal issues encountered in the operations of marketing channels.** The unfair use of power can raise ethical concerns. For example, a large buyer might try to force a small supplier to grant unreasonably low prices as a condition for continuing to be a supplier.

   If taken to the extreme, cooperation between channel members can be a violation of the law, as competition may be unfairly constrained. Certain arrangements between channel members may violate antitrust laws if they reduce competition. Exclusive territories, exclusive dealing agreements, and tying contracts are examples of potentially illegal channel arrangements.

Understanding Marketing Terms and Concepts

Thinking About Marketing

1. What are the key activities performed in a marketing channel?

2. How do indirect marketing channels differ from direct marketing channels? How do intermediaries contribute to marketing channels?

3. Explain the concepts of forward and backward integration.

4. How do franchisees and franchisors work together in a franchise system?

5. Review "Earning Customer Loyalty: GE Supports the Small Dealer." Citing specific points in the boxed insert to support your answer, what type or types of power did GE use to support its dealers?

6. Describe the varying degrees of market coverage—intensive distribution, exclusive distribution, and selective distribution—and give examples of each.

7. Channels must be compatible with the other elements of the marketing mix. Give examples that reflect compatibility between channels and product, pricing, and marketing communications considerations.

8. How might channel members build their power bases relative to other members of the channel?

9. Review "Using Technology: Saab Upgrades Dealer Communications." What are the advantages of IRIS to Saab dealers and consumers?

10. How can poor communication, abuse of power, and too much cooperation in marketing channels create ethical and legal problems?

Applying Marketing Skills

1. Discuss the advantages and disadvantages to the consumer of buying these products in alternative channels as opposed to grocery stores:

Product	Alternative channel
Citrus fruit	Farmers' market
Rib-eye steaks	Specialty meat market
Milk	Home delivery
Popcorn	Movie theater
Bottled soft drink	Vending machine

2. Assume you own the concession rights for the New York Yankees' home baseball games. What factors should you consider and what specific information would you need in deciding whether to buy soft-drink cups from a local distributor, who buys the cups from a Taiwanese manufacturer, or directly from the manufacturer?

3. Beth Norman is a sales rep for a leading manufacturer of commercial air-conditioning systems. She currently sells to three distributors in Dallas, who in turn sell exclusively to building contractors. One of Beth's distributors, Maverick Supply Company, has produced disappointing sales results for Beth during the past six months. Upon investigation, Beth discovered that Maverick bought heavily from one of her chief competitors. How might Beth use the five power bases discussed in this chapter to regain her lost position with Maverick?

Using the www in Marketing

Activity One As explained in the chapter opener, Legend Holdings uses multiple channels of distribution to sell personal computers in China. Access the Legend Web site at www.legends-holdings.com (note that some of the links are available only in Chinese) and respond to these questions.

1. Legend and IBM have signed a "Cooperation Memorandum." What are the benefits to both parties? Can you find other examples of channel cooperation on the Legend site?

2. Legend uses a direct marketing channel, including "1+1 Specialty Shops" to reach the home PC market. What are the advantages of Legend's direct channel for this market? Are there any disadvantages?

Activity Two Visit the Rite Aid Web site at www.riteaid.com. As a major drugstore chain, Rite Aid depends on hundreds of suppliers. After you have investigated the Supplier Central, News, Investor Relations, and Corporate Info links on the site, answer the following questions.

1. What evidence can you find that Rite Aid might be a channel leader? Which types of channel power (reward, legitimate, expert, referent, and coercive) does Rite Aid use in dealing with its suppliers?

2. What criteria does Rite Aid use in selecting suppliers? How do these criteria relate to improving value for Rite Aid's retail customers?

3. How important is it for Rite Aid's suppliers to be technologically competent in terms of managing the flow of products to Rite Aid?

Making Marketing Decisions
Case 13-1 Will CarMax Revolutionize Used-Car Channels?

Consumer dissatisfaction is the driving force behind a revolution in the automobile industry. Consumers enjoy having a new automobile, but they hate the buying experience. This is especially true in the used-car market, where sales practices are so bad that jokes and even movies ridicule dealers. Enter CarMax, a creation of electronics giant Circuit City.

In direct contrast to most used-car dealers, CarMax offers a huge inventory, a pleasant showroom, a food court, a children's play area, low-pressure salespeople, and no-haggle pricing. Customers can use computer kiosks to search for the right vehicle, and CarMax backs its vehicles with a five-day, 500-mile money-back guarantee.

CarMax has attracted a lot of attention, some of which translates into competitive activity. Local used-car dealers have responded by improving service and taking advantage of CarMax's no-haggle policy to undercut prices. Republic Industries, the parent company of AutoNation, a CarMax competitor, bought ADT, Ltd., the second-largest auto auction company in the United States. This gives AutoNation a direct link to the supply of late-model used cars, which are increasingly hard to find. Through one of its investors, AutoNation also has access to cars from Greater Auto Auctions, the fourth-largest auction company in the United States.

Increasingly, consumers are turning to the Internet for both new- and used-car purchases. While state franchise laws make it practically impossible for dealers to sell directly to consumers, the major manufacturers are setting up Web sites to facilitate sales through their dealers. Third-party on-line car companies, including Autobytel.com Inc. and Microsoft's CarPoint have become a much larger factor in the market. CarsDirect.com, backed by Dell Computer Corporation founder Michael Dell, is also a competitive force to be reckoned with. Forester Research predicts that by 2003 almost a half million cars per year will be sold via the Internet.

Used-car sellers are also feeling the competitive pressure from new-car dealers. Generous lease deals are attracting some customers who might typically buy used cars. These lease deals also keep a huge number of late-model autos in the market, which helps keep prices down.

CarMax was one of the first companies to see the opportunity for a new marketing channel in the used-car market. The company realized that consumers had gotten used to better shopping experiences—on the Internet and through other venues—for most products and services that exist in superstores, shopping malls, and catalogs. In recent years, mass-market distribution for everything from home electronics to vacation packages had brought prices down. Consumers are more demanding that prices be as low as possible, but they expect great selection and service. In short, they have discovered that they can get what they want at a reasonable price, with retailers such as department store Nordstrom's and on-line bookseller Amazon.com becoming the new standard. Auto industry analysts believe that these same consumers will shape the future of used-car marketing channels.

Heading into the year 2000, CarMax has yet to achieve its goal of revolutionizing the used-car market. The original plan called for 80 to 90 stores by 2001, and currently the company operates just 29 stores. AutoNation, its largest direct competitor, has more stores and has a more visible advertising and Web presence. CarMax, like AutoNation, is adding new-car dealerships to its retail mix. Undaunted, CarMax's president predicts the company will begin making a profit in the near future. He says, "We know the concept works, we just have to tweak it."

Questions

1. What marketplace conditions led to the emergence of CarMax?

2. What are the biggest threats facing CarMax as it attempts to become the preferred outlet for used automobiles? How can the company address these threats?

3. How can independent, local used-car dealers respond to CarMax and other used-car chains?

SOURCES: Fara Warner, "New Tactics Shake Up Online Auto Retailing," *The Wall Street Journal,* October 18, 1999, p. B1; Earle Eldridge, "Circuit City Fine-Tuning Its Used Car Chain Idea," *USA TODAY,* February 24, 1999, p. B8; Fara Warner, "Cars Direct.com Bets on One-Stop, Desktop Showroom," *The Wall Street Journal,* May 17, 1999, p. B4; Joann Muller, Keith Naughton, and Larry Armstrong, "Old Carmakers Learn New Tricks," *Business Week,* April 12, 1999, pp. 116–18; and Joann Muller, "Meet Your Local GM Dealer: GM," *Business Week,* October 11, 1999, p. 48.

Case 13-2 Caterpillar's Channels Span the Globe

Caterpillar is well positioned to further strengthen its reputation as a worldwide leader in the construction and mining equipment industry. The company has more than held its own against Japanese rivals Hitachi and Komatsu in recent years. Sales volume is strong, despite the fact that most of Cat's sales are in sectors where the economy is in recession—Asia, Latin America, and the

Middle East. In 1999, Cat's salesforce was recognized as one of the best in the world by *Sales & Marketing Management* magazine, primarily for its success in building close relationships with its 195 dealers in 200 countries. This is consistent with Caterpillar's Worldwide Code of Conduct, which identifies close, long-lasting relationships with dealers as a key priority.

Having parts and service readily available is important to Caterpillar customers, and the dealers play an important role in adding value after the sale. The typical Caterpillar dealer stocks 40,000 to 50,000 parts and has a huge investment in warehouses, fleets of trucks, service bays, highly trained technicians, and service equipment. Many provide around-the-clock service.

Caterpillar supports its dealers in several ways. Caterpillar rejects the notion of selling directly to end users with three exceptions: newly opened markets of formerly socialist countries, original equipment manufacturers, and the U.S. government. Even in these cases, dealers provide most of the after-sales service and support.

Caterpillar also supports its dealers by providing financing on equipment purchased, and offering programs on inventory control, equipment management, and maintenance programs. Additional support is available to dealers in quality management and continuous improvement, training on a wide variety of topics, and localized marketing programs.

Cat is also encouraging its dealers to open Cat-branded rental stores and reduce the amount of inventory held at the dealer level. Though both of these moves will hurt Cat's short-run profits, it will strengthen the dealers' competitiveness. In the long run, Cat should benefit from these tactics.

Another important element in the management of Caterpillar's marketing channel is a comprehensive communications program. According to Mr. Fites, "We communicate fully, frequently, and honestly. There are no secrets between our dealers and us." To communicate effectively, it is imperative that mutual trust exists

between Caterpillar and its dealers. Trust is essential because of the sensitive nature of some of the information that is exchanged, including financial data and strategic plans. Technology plays an important role in communications, as dealer employees have real-time access to continually updated databases of service information, sales forecasts, and customer satisfaction surveys.

Communications are further enhanced by personal visits and other routine contacts between people at dealerships and all levels of Caterpillar. Top Caterpillar executives meet annually with key dealers at regional conferences to discuss sales goals for each product line and the activities necessary to achieve the goals.

Caterpillar management is candid in pointing out that relationships with dealers are not perfect. For example, problems arise over pricing policies and dealer service-territory boundaries. When conflicts do arise, the chances of a mutually agreeable resolution are high, as Caterpillar and its dealers respect one another. By making its dealers its partners, Caterpillar has strengthened its position as a world leader in its industry and has positioned itself well for future success.

Questions

1. What are the advantages to Caterpillar of using its dealer network rather than selling directly to equipment users?

2. Caterpillar sells directly to end users in just three cases: newly opened markets in formerly socialist countries, original-equipment manufacturers, and the U.S. government. Why would Caterpillar sell direct in these situations? Since some dealers might resent Caterpillar's selling direct in these situations, how might Caterpillar minimize any conflict that might arise?

3. How does Caterpillar contribute to its partnership with dealers? How do the dealers contribute?

SOURCES: "Best Sales Forces 1999: Caterpillar," *Sales & Marketing Management,* July 1999, p. 64; Bruce Upbin, "Sharpening the Claws," *Forbes,* July 26, 1999, reprinted at www.forbes.com; Paul Gordon, "Caterpillar Banks on Turnaround in Dealers' Inventory Cuts," *The Pueblo Chieftan,* October 39, 1999, as reprinted in *Lexis-Nexis Academic Universe,* November 4, 1999; Donald V. Fites, "Make Your Dealers Your Partners," *Harvard Business Review,* March–April, 1996, pp. 84–95; and information from Caterpillar's home page at http://www.caterpillar.com.

Part Fourteen

Retailing

After studying this chapter, you should be able to:

1 Understand the economic importance of retailing and its role in the marketing channel.

2 Cite evidence of the globalization of retailing.

3 Discuss some of the advances in retailing technology.

4 Explain the reasons behind the growth of nonstore retailing.

5 Describe key factors in the retail marketing environment, and understand how they relate to retail strategy.

6 Cite important ethical and legal issues facing retailers.

www.walmart.com

Beginning with its legendary founder, Sam Walton, Wal-Mart has shown it knows how to build and run a formidable retail operation. The world's largest retailer by a wide margin, Wal-Mart is poised to further strengthen its leading position by following decades-old retailing principles while simultaneously pursuing ambitious growth initiatives in the global markets and in cyberspace.

To get off to a fast start in the twenty-first century, Wal-Mart will open 305 stores and superstores, another 25 Sam's Club stores, 10 Neighborhood Market grocery stores, and as many as 10 new distribution centers. This gives Wal-Mart 3,154 stores in the United States , with an additional 1,074 in international markets. New CEO Lee Scott expects company sales to reach $200 million in 2000; when he joined the company in 1980, its sales were at only $1.2 million.

As Wal-Mart looks to the future, it will continue to focus on cutting operating costs, providing high levels of customer service, and offering everyday-low-prices. In addition, its international expansion will continue to pick up steam, as signaled by its acquisition of Asda Group, the third-largest British supermarket chain. Wal-Mart is also expanding its on-line retailing effort, establishing a site from which customers can shop for 600,000 items and travel services. Customers will soon also be able to buy from Wal-Mart's on-line pharmacy.

In building a retail powerhouse, Wal-Mart sticks to old-fashioned customer service while expanding rapidly. Traditional stores, called brick-and-mortar stores, or stores with doors, are important to Wal-Mart's expansion both in the United States and around the world. On-line expansion (clicks and bytes) is also important to Wal-Mart. With Wal-Mart, it's not bricks versus clicks. It is both bricks and clicks—and a focus on the customer—that keeps Wal-Mart in front of its competitors.

Sources: Emily Nelson, "Wal-Mart Revamps Its Online Store, Prepares for Service in AOL Alliance," *The Wall Street Journal,* January 3, 2000, p. A12; Wendy Zellner, "Someday, Lee, This May Be All Yours," *Business Week,* November 15, 1999, pp. 84–92; Del Jones, "Small-Town Fellow Reaches Top of Retail as Wal-Mart CEO," *USA Today,* January 17, 2000, p. 3B; and Kerry Capell, Heidi Dawley, Wendy Zellner, and Karen Nickel Anhalt, "Wal-Mart's Not-So-Secret British Weapon," *Business Week,* January 24, 2000, p. 132.

Retailing, an important part of many marketing channels, includes all the activities involved in selling products and services to the ultimate, or final, consumer. This chapter explains the importance of retailing in the U.S. economy, discusses the functions retailers perform within the channel, and illustrates different types of retailers. Several trends in retailing are discussed: globalization, advances in technology, the focus on customer service, and nonstore retailing. We explore factors in the retail environment—both controllable and uncontrollable—that a firm must constantly monitor and coordinate to ensure a successful retail strategy. Finally, we examine some important ethical and legal issues in retailing.

The Role of Retailing

The role of retailing is to supply products and services directly to the final consumer. Retailers are differentiated from wholesalers according to the primary source of sales. **Retail sales** are sales to final consumers; **wholesale sales** are those to other businesses that in turn resell the product or service, or use it in running their own businesses. To be classified as a retailer, a firm's retail sales must equal or exceed 50 percent of its total revenues. Firms with less than 50 percent retail sales are classified as wholesalers. Wal-Mart was reminded of the distinction when its Sam's Wholesale Club was forced to change its name to Sam's Club in states in which its retail sales exceeded the 50 percent benchmark.

Economic Importance

Retailing is a major force in the economy. Approximately 2.2 million retailers in operation in the United States employ 21 million people, about one-eighth of the total U.S. labor force. Retailers generate an astonishing $2.6 trillion in annual revenues. This translates into a $9,600 retail expenditure for every man, woman, and child in the United States.[1] Leading retailers are shown in Exhibit 14–1.

Retailing also includes a diverse range of **service retailers.** Service retailers include dry cleaners, photo developers, shoe repair shops, banks, fitness clubs, movie

Exhibit 14–1	Leading retailers		
Company	**Sales ($ millions)**	**Profits ($ millions)**	**Employees (thousands)**
1. **Wal-Mart** Bentonville, Ark.	139,208	4,430	910
2. **Sears, Roebuck** Chicago, Ill.	41,322	1,048	324
3. **Kmart** Troy, Mich.	33,674	568	279
4. **Dayton Hudson** Minneapolis, Minn.	30,951	935	165
5. **JCPenney** Dallas, Tex.	30,678	594	250
6. **Kroger** Cincinnati, Ohio	28,203	411	140
7. **Safeway** Pleasanton, Calif.	24,484	807	170
8. **American Stores** Salt Lake City, Utah	19,867	234	121
9. **Albertson's** Boise, Idaho	16,005	567	100
10. **Federated Dept. Stores** Cincinnati, Ohio	15,833	662	662

Source: "Fortune One Thousand Ranked within Industries," *Fortune,* April 26, 1999, pp. F59–F60. Copyright 1999 Time Inc. Reprinted with permission.

theaters, game arcades, rental businesses (automobiles, furniture, appliances, videos), tourist attractions, hotels and restaurants, automotive repair shops, and some providers of health care services. Spending for services fuels increasing consumer-spending growth rates, as spending on products has underperformed the rest of the economy for quite some time.

Retailers' Uniqueness in the Channel

Retailers differ from other marketing channel members in that they handle smaller but more frequent customer transactions; they also provide assortments of products. A pleasant shopping environment is also more important in most forms of retailing than at other levels in the channel. Creation of a pleasant shopping atmosphere entails additional expense, which contributes to higher prices.

SELL SMALLER QUANTITIES MORE FREQUENTLY Retailers offer products in the sizes suitable and convenient for household consumption. Besides buying smaller sizes, most consumers buy products frequently because they lack sufficient storage space and funds to maintain large inventories of products. The average convenience store transaction is for only a few dollars, for example, but the average convenience store handles thousands of transactions per week.

PROVIDE ASSORTMENTS Retailers assemble assortments of products and services to sell. If retailers did not do so, shoppers would have to go to the bakery for bread, the butcher shop for meat, the dairy for milk, and the hardware store for lightbulbs; and a simple shopping trip could take hours to complete. By providing assortments, retailers offer the convenience of one-stop shopping for a variety of products and services. The typical supermarket carries over 15,000 different items made by more than 500 different manufacturers.

An assortment of items seen by the customer as reasonable substitutes for each other is defined as a **category**. Discount retailers that offer a complete assortment

Atmospherics are an important part of retailing. The Mall of America near Minneapolis uses a variety of dramatic atmospheric factors to attract and stimulate consumers.

and thus dominate a category from the customer's perspective are called **category killers**. These include Toys "Я" Us, Home Depot, and Circuit City. Since category killers dominate a category of merchandise, they can negotiate excellent prices from suppliers and be assured of dependable sources of supply.

EMPHASIZE ATMOSPHERICS Atmospherics refers to a retailer's combination of architecture, layout, color scheme, sound and temperature monitoring, special events, prices, displays, and other factors that attract and stimulate consumers. Retailers spend millions of dollars to create the retail atmospheres that enhance their respective images and the products and services they offer for sale. NikeTown, Planet Hollywood, F.A.O. Schwartz, and Express are pioneers in the use of atmospherics in retailing. As NikeTown and Planet Hollywood have learned, however, changing the atmosphere is important to keep customers coming back. Declining numbers of customers at Planet Hollywood suggest that no matter how interesting consumers find the environment on the first visit, they may treat it like a museum—"Great! I really enjoyed it and may come back someday. Now where are we going?"

In response to an increasingly hard-to-impress consumer, retailers are seeking active involvement of shoppers, that is, they are trying to give the shopper a memorable experience, or "shoppertainment." For example, Vans Inc., a California-based sporting-goods retailer, opened a 60,000-square-foot, $4 million skate park and off-road bicycle track at the Ontario Mills Mall near Los Angeles. In doing so, Van's becomes an exciting place for customer recreation, not just a place to buy gear.[2] The same is true with Bass Pro Shops store near Chicago where shoppers can check out the monster fish in the 27,000-gallon aquarium and practice their outdoor skills at the trout pond, archery range, or rifle range. For many retailers, there is doubt that the consumer has become an important role player in creating the right atmospherics and shopping experience.[3]

The best-known retail operation to gain headlines for its atmospherics is Mall of America, located in suburban Minneapolis. Opened in 1992, the Mall of America has a two-story miniature golf course, a 300-foot walk-through aquarium, Knott's Camp Snoopy (an amusement park with more than 20 attractions), and a Lego Imagination Center, complete with dinosaurs 20 feet tall. These features create an exciting atmosphere for shoppers who roam the 4.2-million-square-foot facility (2.5 million square feet of retail shopping space). Mall of America draws more than 42 million people per year, more than Walt Disney World and the Grand Canyon combined.[4]

Atmospherics, though expensive to create, can generate considerable benefits for retailers. Atmospherics can boost the number of consumers who visit a retail location. Indeed, some retailers are trying to make their stores a "destination" for shoppers, a place a shopper will make a special effort to reach. Atmospherics can also boost the average time a shopper spends at the location and the average amount spent on each shopping trip. Atmospherics often allow retailers to charge higher prices. Compare the atmosphere of a discount store to that of a full-line traditional department store or an exclusive specialty shop, for example.

Types of Retailers

Retailers can be classified according to the type of merchandise and services sold, location, various strategic differences, and method of ownership. Here we examine different ownership categories to provide an overview of several types of retailers.

Some significant retail enterprises, such as military exchange stores and public utility appliance stores, operate outside the realm of private enterprise. Within the private sector, there are several major retail ownership categories, including independent retailers, chains, franchising, leased departments, and cooperatives.

Independent Retailers

Independent retailers own and operate only one retail outlet. Independent retailers account for more than three-fourths of all retail establishments, a testament to Americans' desires to own and operate their own businesses and a relative lack of barriers to entry. There are no formal education requirements, no specific training requirements, and few legal requirements to owning a retail business. This ease of entry likely accounts for the unpreparedness and the high failure rate experienced by new retailers.

Independent retailer ABT Electronics and Appliances in Illinois competes effectively against chains such as Circuit City and Best Buy by offering higher-end merchandise and impeccable customer service.

Chains

A **retail chain** owns and operates multiple retail outlets. Examples are Nordstrom, Mervyn's, Musicland, Pappagallo, The Gap, and JCPenney. By far, chain stores sell more merchandise than any other category of retailers. Their major advantage is the ability to service large, widespread target markets by selling a large assortment of products and services. For an illustration of how a successful chain operates, see "Earning Customer Loyalty: bebe Builds Its Brand."

Franchising

Retail franchising is a form of chain ownership in which a franchisee pays the franchisor (parent company) fees or royalties and agrees to run the franchise by prescribed norms, in exchange for use of the franchisor's name. Well-known franchisors include

Many leading franchisors are expanding their international operations. 7-Eleven subsidiary operates this popular franchise in Japan.

McDonald's, Holiday Inn, Avis, Mrs. Fields', and Jiffy Lube. According to the International Franchise Association, about 3,000 franchise companies operate in the United States. Franchising operations employ 8.5 million workers at approximately 558,000 separate establishments. Franchises generate approximately a trillion dollars per year in sales.[5]

Franchising is also a major retailing force outside the United States. McDonald's decided to go international in 1967, and now has almost 12,000 units in 113 countries outside the United States.[6] The largest market for franchising outside the United States is Europe, with franchising popular in France, Germany, and the United Kingdom. Japan is the most active franchising market in the Asia-Pacific region; there is a significant amount of franchising in Australia, Hong Kong, Singapore, Indonesia, Malaysia, and India; and franchising is also well-established in Canada and Mexico.[7]

While many successful international franchised retailers are U.S.-based, there is an increasing number of expansion-minded franchisors outside the United States who view the world as their market. For example, Canada's Tim Horton's bakery/coffee restaurants, Taiwan's Kumon Math and Reading Centers, and Australian-based Cash Converters—a second-hand-store operator—are all highly rated by *Entrepreneur* magazine as leading international franchised retailers.[8]

Earning Customer Loyalty

bebe builds its brand

California-based bebe Stores Inc., a 100-store vertical retailer makes its own clothes, as does Gap, Inc. But unlike Gap, bebe has achieved success by attracting a more narrowly defined market of women in their twenties and thirties. While Gap successfully markets to men, women, and children through its various stores, including Gap, Old Navy, and Gap Kids, bebe sells sexy, trendy clothing to its market, which includes actress Calista Flockhart—television's Ally McBeal—and major film star Julia Roberts.

A key bebe strategy is to listen to the market and respond quickly. In one instance, bebe had planned to sell 1,000 pairs of Capri pants in its winter season. When 800 pairs were sold the first week, company buyers switched production away from suits to order another 50,000

pairs of Capri pants, all of which sold during the season. This kind of responsiveness has allowed bebe to build a loyal, growing customer base.

The company has opened a Web site to reinforce its store operations, and it plans to build its brand in other ways; bebe brand shoes, watches, and eyewear can now be purchased in upscale department stores, and bebe has taken its first steps toward global retailing with store openings in London and Vancouver. As a result of its loyal customer base, bebe generates approximately $800 per square foot in sales, more than double most of its competitors. Staying close to customers obviously has its rewards.

Source: Gabrielle Saveri, "This Is No Fashion Victim," *Business Week*, May 31, 1999, p. 89.

Exhibit 14–2	*Top 20 international retail franchise companies*	
	1. McDonald's	11. Radio Shack
	2. Yogen Fruz Worldwide (fast food)	12. Arby's
	3. Subway	13. Dairy Queen
	4. Kentucky Fried Chicken	14. Dunkin' Donuts
	5. Kumon Math & Reading Centers	15. Coldwell Banker
	6. Wendy's International	16. Baskin-Robbins
	7. TCBY Treats	17. Jazzercize, Inc.
	8. Taco Bell Corp.	18. GNC Franchising
	9. Blockbuster Video	19. Service Master
	10. Mail Boxes Etc.	20. Re/Max International

Source: Selected from "America's Top 200 International Franchises," *Entrepreneur* magazine Web site at www.entrepreneurmag.com/international/200intl_rank.hts, January 9, 2000.

The arrangements between franchisors and franchisees illustrate the benefits of a relationship perspective. In return for fees or royalties, the franchisee may receive management training, participation in cooperative buying and advertising, and assistance in selecting an appropriate location. The franchisor benefits in turn from a constant stream of income, fast payment for goods and services, and strict control over franchised operations that encourages consistency among outlets.

Franchising systems are popular because they offer the franchisee a proven business and the franchisors the ability to establish a national presence with the funds provided by the sale of franchises. Although risk is a factor in any business, franchising has a better track record than most start-ups. Approximately half of new U.S. businesses fail during the first five years, whereas almost 90 percent of franchises survive.[9]

Exhibit 14–2 presents some of the best-known franchise operations. These franchise companies were selected by *Entrepreneur* magazine based on financial strength and stability, size, growth rate, years in business and in franchising, and start-up costs.

Leased Departments

Leased departments are sections in a retail store that the owner rents to a second party. Typically, department stores rent their jewelry, shoe, hairstyling, and cosmetic departments. For example, Fox Photo leases space in Kroger grocery stores; travel agencies and hair salons often lease space in department stores; and cosmetics such as Estée Lauder and Clinique are sold through leased space in clothing stores.

As with franchising agreements, a leased-department arrangement benefits both lessor (the department store) and lessee. The lessor receives rental fees, can reduce inventory investment and subsequent risk, gains expertise in a specialized area, and enjoys the benefits derived from the store traffic generated by the leased department. Lessees benefit by operating in an established location with the assurance of store traffic and advertising.

Cooperatives

Responding to competitive pressures exerted by the buying power of chain stores, independent retailers sometimes band together to form **retail cooperatives**. Although each store remains independently owned, the retail cooperative generally adopts a common name and storefront. The stores participate in joint purchasing, shipping, and advertising, which allows cost savings normally enjoyed by chain outlets. Retail cooperatives include Sentry Hardware, Associated Grocers, and Ace Hardware.

Global retailing can be quite sophisticated, as is the case with this Kmart in Mexico, which offers fresh tortillas along with a large variety of food and nonfood items. In contrast, global retailing may be quite simple, as is the case with the Mars kiosk in Moscow.

Trends in Retailing

We have seen dramatic examples of change in retailing, such as the decline, then reemergence, of Sears as a retail power. JCPenney Company continues to struggle, caught between upscale department stores on one hand and discount stores on the other. Penney's private clothing label, Arizona Jean Co., has been losing out to national brands Tommy Hilfiger and Ralph Lauren in the department stores, while the discounters are selling clothes comparable to Penney's at much lower prices.[10] At the beginning of the decade, industry analysts predicted that retailing would be quite different 10 years later. Indeed, retailing has changed dramatically. Notable current trends in the retailing environment include global retailing, the increasing use of technology, a renewed emphasis on customer service, and the rapid expansion of nonstore retailing.

Global Retailing

With domestic markets becoming saturated and sales growth slowing, many retailers are exhibiting a global perspective. U.S.-based retailers have long been the leaders in global expansion, with, for example, McDonald's, Kentucky Fried Chicken, Radio Shack, and Wal-Mart being among the more progressive companies and L.L. Bean, Eddie Bauer, and The Gap expanding in Japan with great success.

Retailers from other countries are becoming more active in global retailing. In recent years, retailers based outside the United States have become more aggressive in global marketing. A fine example is Europe's largest retailer, France's Carrefour. Carrefour, after a major merger in 1999, now operates 8,800 stores in 26 countries. Poised to fight Wal-Mart around the world, Carrefour has been a pioneer in store design, softening the look of its gigantic stores with wood floors and softer lighting. Carrefour is known for selling groceries, clothing, and other merchandise under one roof. Many of their stores also offer a myriad of services, such as watch-repair services, cell-phone service, and travel services. Although Carrefour is not expected to challenge Wal-Mart in terms of sales volume, the company has already proven to be a formidable competitor against Wal-Mart in several markets, including those of Brazil and Argentina. In addition to the markets in these two countries, Carrefour is the leading retailer in France, Taiwan, Spain, Portugal, Greece, and Belgium.[11]

Technological Advances

Retailers have embraced the technological perspective, and advances in retail technology have developed at a phenomenal pace. A familiar example is the scanner linked to computerized inventory systems that greatly improve a retailer's efficiency level. Scanners speed the checkout process, reduce computational errors, and instantaneously input the transaction into the inventory system. This allows retailers to precisely track sales on a per-item basis, minimize out-of-stock problems, and judge the effectiveness of various pricing and marketing communications tactics. Other technological advances that directly influence customers include automated cash registers that can issue temporary charge cards and gift certificates, provide customer information, and process customer payments, as well as passenger computer terminals and the aircraft satellite systems that make in-flight shopping possible.

Self-checkout counters speed up the checkout process for customers while giving store managers greater flexibility with staffing.

Wireless computer technology is finding many applications in retailing: Electronics Boutique uses wireless registers to check customers out during peak times; Wal-Mart uses wireless technology to check product availability in the stockroom and in surrounding stores; ski resorts are using wireless scanners so that skiers can go directly to the lift rather than stand in a separate line to buy a lift ticket; and F.A.O. Schwartz is experimenting with a handheld scanner that allows adult shoppers with credit cards to scan the labels of toys they want to buy, drop off the scanner, and receive the goods by home delivery in a few days.[12] Retailers have long tried to find ways to reduce the amount of time customers must wait in line to pay, and wireless technology is helping to achieve this objective. Technology, most notably the Internet, has also affected nonstore retailing, to be discussed shortly. For an example of how technology can assist a department store's on-line customers, see "Using Technology: Le Printemps Rolls to Success."

Customer Service in Retailing

Customer service refers to the activities that increase the quality and value customers receive when they shop and purchase merchandise. Retailers rush to give lip service to the importance of customer service, but many still fall woefully short of

Using Technology

Le Printemps rolls to success

In Paris, the department store Le Printemps is combining low tech with high tech to better serve its on-line customers. Four Rollerblading salespeople, called "Webcamers," maneuver about the large store, equipped with wireless networking gear and video cameras. As they skate, they broadcast live to the store's Web site, *www.webcamer.com*. As customer requests come in, a Webcamer skates off to find the merchandise. Along the way, they type in size and color information. Once the merchandise is located, the Webcamer displays it for the customer via the Webcam.

The store receives between 30 and 100 requests per day, some of which are from pranksters who enjoy seeing the Webcamers taking long jaunts around the store. But Le Printemps, which uses the Webcamers as much for show as for selling, is not concerned about the pranksters. The company figures even the pranksters are helping debug the system.

For Le Printemps, Wecamers offer an inexpensive alternative to putting up an on-line catalog for its 1.5 million items. Though there have been some temporary glitches with the technology, Le Printemps will continue rolling up sales with its high-tech Webcamers.

Source: Kevin J. Delaney, "Where the E in E-Shopping Stands for 'Extreme,' " *The Wall Street Journal,* October 14, 1999, pp. B1, B17. Permission conveyed through the Copyright Clearance Center.

Speaking from Experience

Laurie Clyne
District Team Leader
Mervyn's Department Stores

Laurie Clyne, District Team Relations Leader with Mervyn's Department Stores, is responsible for managing the human resource function for 22 retail stores (2500 employees) in five states. Laurie earned a BA degree in Organizational Communication from Ohio State University.

"Technology plays a critical role in ensuring that our guests are presented with accurate pricing information. Since we stock thousands of items, this could be a complex process without the right technology. Hand held scanners (we call them scanning guns) allow our Team Members to check and change prices on our merchandise quickly and easily. The ultimate benefit is to the guest who knows the price marked on the item matches the signing on the rack and the advertised price which matches the price at the check-out register."

Thinking Critically

- If everyone agrees that customer service is important to retail success, why is good service still an exception to the rule?
- What can retailers do to ensure good service?

providing it. Today's consumers are tougher, more informed, and so sensitive to poor service they often walk away and never come back to a store rather than point out the service problem to the retailer. Worse yet, the average consumer with a service problem tells several other people about the problem.

Different types of retailers offer a variety of customer services to correspond with the image they need to project. Exhibit 14–3 compares some department store services with those offered by the typical discount store.

Store loyalty is the major reward of customer service, a benefit that builds on itself, as customers well served are customers retained. The Lark, a Chicago-area clothing retailer that sells brands such as Tommy Hilfiger and Ralph Lauren in low-income inner-city locations, has built a solid business based on loyal customers. The owner, 49-year-old Leonard Rothchild, learned the importance of customer service from his father, a butcher who owned a meat market. Rothchild believes that good customer service begins with treating employees well. He also believes in treating

| **Exhibit 14–3** | *Customer services offered by retailers* |

	Department, specialty stores	Discount stores		Department, specialty stores	Discount stores
Accept credit cards	●	●	Installment payments	●	◐
Alter merchandise	●	○	Lay-away plans	●	○
Assemble merchandise	●	○	Parking	●	●
Assist with merchandise to car	◐	○	Personal shopper	◐	○
Bridal registry	●	○	Play areas for children	◐	◐
Check cashing	●	◐	Provisions for special needs— wheelchairs, translators, etc.	◐	○
Child care facilities	◐	○	Repair services	◐	○
Convenient hours	●	●	Rest rooms	●	●
Credit	●	◐	Return privileges	●	●
Delayed billing	◐	○	Rooms to check coats, packages	◐	○
Delivery to home	◐	○			
Demo merchandise	●	◐	Sessions on using merchandise	◐	○
Display merchandise	●	●	Special orders	◐	○
Dressing rooms	●	○	Special showings	◐	○
Gift wrap	◐	○	Warranties	●	●
Information/assistance to select merchandise	●	◐			

● Frequently ◐ Occasionally ○ Rarely

Source: Adapted from Michael Levy and Barton A. Weitz, *Retailing Management,* 3rd ed. (Burr Ridge, IL: Richard D. Irwin, 1998), p. 571. © 1998 Irwin/McGraw-Hill. Reprinted with permission of the publisher.

customers equally, an important issue for The Lark's predominantly black customer base, as many report that they do not receive courteous service from suburban mall stores. By concentrating on personalized customer service, Rothchild has competed quite successfully with larger stores. He noted that "A national chain is like a battleship and turns in a wide arc. We can turn in a tight radius."[13]

Retailers can provide good service without necessarily providing personal service. Automated teller machines, credit card–processing gas pumps, and point-of-sale audiovisual materials in home improvement stores are examples of how technology can assist in providing customer service.

Nonstore Retailing

Traditional retailing is generally thought of as the selling of products and services in stores or some other physical structure. In contrast, **nonstore retailing** refers to sales outside a physical structure. Although stores account for almost 90 percent of all retail sales, the growth rate of nonstore retailing has far surpassed that of store-based retailing in the past few years.

Nonstore retailing offers consumers the convenience of selecting and purchasing merchandise according to their own schedules. Merchandise is delivered directly to consumers or shipped to convenient vending locations, methods that particularly appeal to consumers with few store choices, busy people who care little for shopping, those who are bored or dissatisfied with store shopping, and consumers with limitations on movement, such as some nondrivers or disabled people. There are disadvantages of nonstore retailing. Customers cannot try on merchandise, test it out, or have it altered before delivery. In addition, some nonstore retailers offer limited assortments.

The three most common forms of nonstore retailing are direct retailing, direct selling, and vending machine sales. Direct retailing is discussed in more detail in Chapter 19.

DIRECT RETAILING   **Direct retailing** is the portion of direct marketing in which ultimate consumers, not business customers, do the buying. **Direct marketing** can be defined as "the distribution of goods, services, information, or promotional benefits to targeted consumers through interactive communication while tracking response, sales, interests, or desires through a computer database."[14] The consumer is exposed to the merchandise through a nonpersonal medium (catalogs, TV shopping programs, interactive electronic networks), and then purchases the merchandise by mail or telephone. Familiar direct retailers include Amazon.com, Etoyz, Cdnow, L.L. Bean, Spiegel, Fingerhut, Lands' End, and Lillian Vernon. More recently, TV home shopping has become a legitimate form of retailing and major retailers Spiegel, Nordstrom, Bloomingdale's, and The Sharper Image are involved in TV home-shopping programs.

Direct retailing sales growth has been steadily outpacing growth for total retail sales for several years. It is estimated that direct retailing will top $1.2 trillion in sales in 2004, up a third from direct retail sales in 2000.[15] More than half of the U.S. adult population buys from at least one direct retailer each year, with clothing being the most popular item. Catalogs remain the most popular direct retailing method, followed by magazines, noncatalog direct mail, newspapers, and television. Interactive media, including on-line computer systems and interactive TV, make up a small, but growing, percentage of direct retailing.

Without question, the most attention-getting sector of direct retailing in recent years is that conducted over the Internet. While retail sales over the Internet, often referred to as **e-retailing**, presently

tuesday, 11:15 p.m.
buying a new dress.

bluefly

www.bluefly.com
the outlet store in your home

Consumers can buy almost anything via nonstore retailing. Bluefly.com offers designer fashions for women, men, and children.

account for less than 2 percent of total retail sales, it is forecasted that this figure will hit 7 percent in 2004.[16] For some product categories, e-retailing will indeed be a significant form of retailing. By 2004, Forrester Research predicts, e-retailing will account for half of all software sales, 40 percent of all computer hardware, and 25 percent of all recorded music.[17] Other popular categories will include books, consumer electronics, event tickets, leisure travel, and flowers.

E-retailing, like all retail sectors, is extremely competitive. Analysts predict that a shakeout in e-retailing is underway, and that some well-known e-retailers may disappear. Value America and Egghead, two well-known e-retailers are among those struggling to survive. Competitive intensity will increase as traditional brick-and-mortar stores expand their e-retailing activities. As noted in the chapter opener, Wal-Mart is rapidly expanding its on-line retailing capability. Home Depot, Toys "Я" Us, Nordstrom, Gap Inc., Macy's, and Barnes and Noble are also expanding their Internet marketing efforts. To maintain a competitive market position, Internet-only retailers such as Amazon.com and Cdnow are expanding their product offerings, linking with related e-retailers, and using price specials and promotions to drive traffic to their sites.

Retailers may use **portals,** or virtual shopping malls, to generate more traffic for their individual store Web sites. For example, Yahoo! Shopping links 7,500 merchants in its portal. Retailers such as Eddie Bauer, Brooks Brothers, and Office Max pay a monthly fee ranging from $100 to $300 to list up to 1,000 items at the portal, plus a commission of 2 to 15 percent on each sale.[18]

E-retailing offers several advantages compared with shopping in a store. Consumers can order from stores around the world 24 hours a day from home or from any location with Internet access. There is no waiting in line to check out, nor the hassle of transporting purchases home. On the other hand, there is not the instant gratification that comes with a store purchase, and some consumers are worried about credit card security when buying on-line. Others find navigation around e-retail Web sites to be cumbersome and slow. On balance, a growing number of consumers enjoy shopping on-line, and growth will likely be dramatic in the coming years.

DIRECT SELLING In **direct selling,** salespeople reach consumers directly or by telephone primarily at home or at work. A small amount of direct selling is done in other locations, including exhibitions, theme parks, and fairs. Industry statistics reveal that 70 percent of all U.S. direct sales occur in the home, 11 percent over the phone, and another 11 percent in the workplace. Direct selling generates $23 billion in annual sales. There are 9.7 million salespeople in direct selling, almost all of whom are independent contractors, not employees of the selling companies. Approximately 9 out of 10 direct salespeople work part-time.[19] Mary Kay, Avon, Cutco Cutlery, and Tupperware are familiar examples of companies that use direct selling.

VENDING MACHINE SALES Vending machines allow customers to purchase and receive merchandise from a machine. Estimates of industry size range from $19 billion to $28 billion annually, with offerings of predominantly beverages, food, and candy.[20] Vending machines are frequently located at work sites, hospitals, schools, tourist destinations, and travel facilities.

Several direct-selling companies are expanding their efforts in international markets. One of the leaders, Avon, is enjoying spectacular growth in Taiwan.

Understanding retail strategy: Important controllable and uncontrollable factors

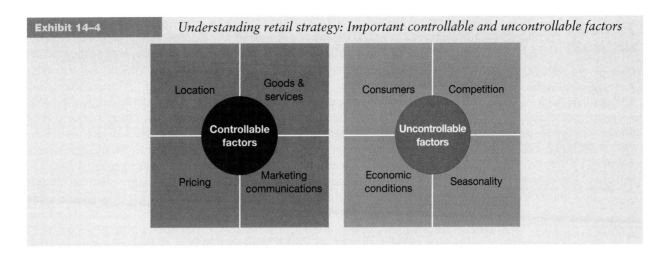

Developing Retailing Strategy
The scope of retail products and services and the demands of consumers combine to produce a constantly changing business environment. A successful retailer must effectively manipulate the factors it can control to survive in a largely uncontrollable environment. A few uncontrollable and controllable factors of interest to retailers are listed in Exhibit 14–4.

Uncontrollable Factors
A number of constantly changing factors in the retail environment are beyond the retailer's control. To survive, retailers must constantly monitor and adapt to changing, uncontrollable factors in the marketing environment such as legal restrictions, discussed later in the chapter, and advances in technology. The important uncontrollable factors we describe here are consumers, competition, economic conditions, and seasonality.

CONSUMERS Consumer demographics and lifestyles undergo constant changes, which retailers must recognize to satisfy the needs of their customers. For example, approximately half the U.S. adult working population is female. This means the traditional female role of housekeeper and shopper has all but disappeared. Retailers adapted to this change by offering longer store hours, time-saving appliances, and prepackaged, self-service items. Because many women have the buying power to make major independent purchases such as automobiles, retailers of big-ticket items now target this segment directly with marketing communications. Similarly, consumer product ads are directed to men and teenagers, who now do much of the routine grocery shopping.

Laurie Clyne reinforces the importance of building value for consumers: "At Mervyn's, we know our guests are busy. To ensure that they can shop quickly, we provide centralized checkouts at the entrances to our stores. This allows our guests to shop the entire store and make purchases, handle exchanges, and process returns only once—when they are ready to leave. This time-saving convenience builds value into each transaction."

COMPETITION Whether from new entries into the marketplace or from existing marketers, retail competition is fierce. One indicator of competition intensity is retail bankruptcies. Among those declaring bankruptcy in recent years were Service Merchandise, Montgomery Ward, Filene's Basement, Caldor, Bradlee's, Levitz Furniture, and catalog retailer J. Peterman. And small independent retailers, especially bookstores, have been hit especially hard by competition. Independent booksellers saw their market share drop by 50 percent in the past decade. Some independents tried to form regional chains to compete with the larger national chains; Taylor's in

Dallas, Oxford Books in Atlanta, and Cleveland's Booksellers tried this tactic, for example, but all have since gone out of business.[21] Competitive pressure from large chains such as Borders and Barnes and Noble, warehouse clubs, and on-line booksellers such as Amazon.com is intensifying even further, and the outlook for independent bookstores is grim.

Although the major chains have hurt smaller chains and independents, they, too, are feeling the effects of increased competition. For example, Claire's Stores, Inc., has 1,990 stores specializing in the market of 9- to 20-year-old females, with costume jewelry and accessories as primary products. Claire's has moved aggressively to take sales away from Gadzooks, a 300-store chain that appeals to the 13- to 19-year-old "grunge" female consumer with products such as baggy denims, thumb rings, and fake tatoos. The teenage consumer is hard to please, and Claire's has taken advantage of some merchandising mistakes by Gadzooks to expand its sales base.[22] Another example of intense competition between large chains is Kohl's department stores' assault on Sears and JCPenney. Kohl's keeps its overhead costs low and sells brand-name merchandise such as Bugle Boy apparel and Oneida flatware at lower prices than those found in higher-overhead department stores. The strategy Kohl's uses has produced sales-growth results far superior to that of other regional and national chains.[23]

To survive, retailers try to improve the productivity of their operations, attract new customers, and get existing customers to buy more. This sometimes requires redefining the business, as has occurred with Radio Shack. Radio Shack was having a hard time getting brand-name products into its stores. Management was also unhappy with the lower operating margins on the sale of electronics equipment caused by price competition from Best Buy and other discounters. Noting that manufacturers were not satisfied with their lack of dedicated selling space in larger retail stores, Radio Shack felt that manufacturers would respond to a well-trained sales staff, something not found in the discount stores. Radio Shack refurbished its stores and partnered with Compaq, Sony, and Sprint to better diversify its product sales mix. As a result, audio and video equipment have been displaced by telephones and electronic parts, accessories, and batteries as the top sellers. Radio Shack now sells more wireless telephones than Best Buy, Circuit City, Sears, and Montgomery Ward combined.[24] Another key element of Radio Shack's redefinition of its retailing strategy is to become a leading access point to the Internet via Microsoft's Internet service. The Radio Shack experience serves as a reminder that retailers must sometimes undergo substantial changes in order to remain competitive.

In a broad sense, there are two major types of competition: intratype and intertype. **Intratype competition** describes competition among retailers that use the same type of business format. McDonald's, Wendy's, and Burger King are intratype competitors, for example; they are all fast-food restaurants. **Intertype competition** prevails among retailers using different types of business to sell the same products and services. The intertype competitors of McDonald's would include all other food retailers, ranging from vending machines to fine restaurants. Retail businesses that appreciate both types of competition tend to be better prepared to face challenges and avoid the pitfalls of marketing myopia—that is, too narrowly defining the scope of their business.

ECONOMIC CONDITIONS   Economic conditions are another factor beyond the retailer's control. In recent years, the economy has been robust, and the retailing industry has enjoyed strong sales increases. Retail sales grew 8 percent in 1999, and are expected to grow another 6 percent in 2000.[25] Relatively low mortgage rates and high consumer confidence levels have spurred sales of home furnishings and building supply stores such as Home Depot and Restoration Hardware. Somewhat contrary to conventional logic, the growth in consumer incomes is associated with increasing sales by discount retailers. Sales growth at outlet malls is on a dramatic upswing, and discount stores have increased their lead over department stores in total market share.[26] One reason for discount-store growth in good economic times is the creation of upscale brands that attract wealthier consumers, who then purchase a wide variety of products. For example, Kmart uses the Martha Stewart line of housewares in this manner.

SEASONALITY   **Seasonality** refers to demand fluctuations related to the time of the year, which may be moderated or exacerbated by unpredictable changes in weather and in consumer preferences. Retailers specializing in clothing, sporting equipment, amusement parks, fresh food, hotels, and car rentals are particularly affected by seasonality. A retailer may minimize the effects of seasonality by adjusting some controllable variables within its retail strategy mix. For example, some retailers initiate special promotions to encourage consumers to buy during the off-season. Other retailers, like sporting goods stores, alter their product mix by focusing on different products for different seasons.

Controllable Factors

The four categories of controllable factors we discuss are location, the goods and services the retailer offers, the prices the retailer charges for products and services, and the marketing communications consumers receive.

LOCATION   The old saying—and experts confirm it—is that the three most important factors in retailing are location, location, and location. To most retailers, location *is* the most crucial factor and the least flexible element of retail strategy. A retailer can modify prices, products and services, and marketing communications relatively easily, but a poor location is difficult for even the best merchant to overcome. Moving is complicated by lease agreements, the transfer of inventory from one location to another, and perhaps even the sale of the building if the retailer owns it.

Evaluation of prospective locations requires analysis of strategic compatibility, accessibility, legal considerations, and economic factors. Key questions related to each of these criteria are presented in Exhibit 14–5.

In broad terms, retail sites are defined as isolated locations, unplanned business districts, or planned shopping centers. **Isolated locations** are freestanding locations,

Retailers, especially those operating in large urban areas, are concerned that shoppers may shop less frequently or only shop during certain hours of the day because they are fearful of crime. This shopping mall in Miami uses additional security measures to ensure shopper safety.

Exhibit 14–5	*Selected criteria to consider when evaluating retail locations*		
Strategic compatibility	**Accessibility**	**Legal considerations**	**Economic factors**
• Is the site located near target markets? • Is the type of shopping center or mall appropriate for the store? • What is the age and condition of the site? • Will adjacent stores complement/compete with the store?	• What are the road patterns and conditions surrounding the site? • Do any natural or artificial barriers impede access to the site? • Does the site have good visibility from the street? • Is there a good balance between too much and too little traffic flow? • Is it easy to enter/exit the parking lot? • Is the number/quality of parking spaces adequate? • Is the site accessible by mass transit? • Can vendor deliveries be easily made?	• Is the site zoning compatible with the store? • Does the store's design meet building codes? • Are the store's external signs compatible with zoning ordinances and building codes?	• What are the occupancy costs? • What will the cost of improvements and other one-time costs incurred during initial occupancy be? • Are the amenities available at the site worth the cost?

Source: Adapted from Michael Levy and Barton A. Weitz, *Retailing Management,* 2nd ed. (Burr Ridge, IL: Richard D. Irwin, 1995), p. 205. © 1995 Richard D. Irwin, Inc. Reprinted with permission of the publisher.

that is, there are no adjoining buildings. These are best suited for large retailers that can attract and hold a large customer base on their own and for convenience-related businesses such as gasoline stations and fast-food restaurants.

Unplanned business districts are made up of independently owned and managed retail operations. They generally evolve in a more spontaneous fashion than do planned business districts. Among the types of unplanned business districts are central business districts, secondary business districts, neighborhood business districts, and string locations. **Central business districts,** commonly known as downtown areas, represent the greatest concentration of office buildings and retail stores. **Secondary business districts** are defined by the intersection of two major thoroughfares. They make good locations because of this traffic flow.

Located in the midst of residential areas, **neighborhood business districts** consist of a small grouping of stores, with the largest generally being a supermarket or variety store. **String locations** are groupings of stores that sell similar goods and services. Automobiles and mobile homes are often sold in string locations.

Planned shopping centers are centrally owned and managed, have ample parking availability, and offer a variety of stores. There are approximately 44,000 planned shopping centers in the United States,[27] and their growth over the last 40 years has been dramatic. Smaller shopping centers have recently attracted an increasing number of shoppers, while the popularity of larger malls is declining.[28]

GOODS AND SERVICES   Another controllable factor in the retail strategy is the goods and services offered for sale. Retailers must decide on the number of product lines to carry, referred to as width or variety. They must also decide on the assortment of each product line, called length or depth. These decisions require several considerations. Major product considerations include compatibility (how well the product fits in with existing inventory), attributes (such as bulk, required service, selling levels), and profitability. Market considerations include stage in the product life cycle, market appropriateness (a product's appeal to the store's current target market), and competitive conditions. Finally, supply considerations such as product availability and supplier reliability need to be explored.

Retailers must be alert to the effects of changes in their product mix and open to a redefinition of competitors. For example, the practice of adding unrelated prod-

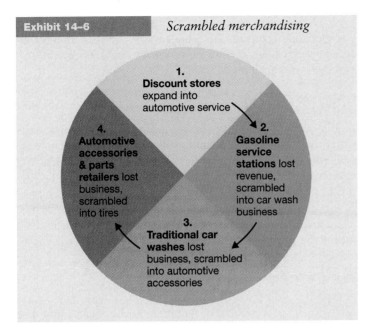

Exhibit 14–6   *Scrambled merchandising*

1.
Discount stores expand into automotive service

2.
Gasoline service stations lost revenue, scrambled into car wash business

3.
Traditional car washes lost business, scrambled into automotive accessories

4.
Automotive accessories & parts retailers lost business, scrambled into tires

uct categories to existing product lines is referred to as **scrambled merchandising.** In the not-too-distant past, grocery stores predominantly sold food items. Today, consumers can buy motor oil or rent movies at grocery stores. Scrambled merchandising allows grocery stores to obtain higher profit margins than the traditional 1 to 2 percent made on food items. Consumers, in turn, enjoy the extra convenience of one-stop shopping provided by a wide array of merchandise; in effect, they have received improved quality and value in their overall shopping experience.

Scrambled merchandising has had a chain-reaction effect something like that shown in Exhibit 14–6. When discount stores aggressively expanded into automotive service, traditional gasoline service stations lost revenue and scrambled into the car wash business. Traditional car-wash operations then expanded their sale of automotive accessories, causing lost volume for traditional automotive accessory and parts retailers. These retailers responded by scrambling into tires to supplement their lost sales on accessories.

Amazon.com provides an example of scrambled merchandising in e-retailing. Originally a bookseller, Amazon expanded into music and videos, then followed with a wide range of products, including electronics, computers, sports equipment, tools, software, and other offerings—a total of 500,000 products. Amazon is making these products available through its zShops concept, where independent vendors pay a small monthly fee to link with Amazon. As Amazon scrambles its merchandise to the extreme, it excludes only pornography, firearms, and human organs from its mix.[29]

PRICING   Retailers also control the final prices they charge consumers for their products and services. Retail prices are ultimately based on the store's target market, the desired store image, and the congruence between price and other elements of the retail mix (location, quality of products and services, marketing communications). Although price-conscious consumers may appear to dominate in many markets, successful retailers are found at all price ranges, from high to low.

Everyday-low-pricing (EDLP) strategies, pioneered by Wal-Mart in the 1980s, are now used by many retailers. With EDLP, retailers demand low prices from their suppliers, minimize costly advertising and promotions, and keep their retail prices consistently low to lure consumers. Now, many retailers are adopting "low-price leader" or "value pricing" programs. These programs feature low competitive prices across the board and a continual mix of special offers to keep consumers coming back.

Giant Food Incorporated uses extensive advertising as part of its marketing communications program. It also gains favorable publicity from outdoor advertising, as seen at Baltimore Oriole's Park at Camden Yards.

MARKETING COMMUNICATIONS   Decisions about the mix of marketing communications are also controllable. These decisions specify how the retailer allocates resources among personal selling, advertising, public relations, direct marketing, and sales promotion. Retailers such as The Limited emphasize personal in-store selling and do very little advertising; convenience stores promote sales by placing signs in their windows; others promote "a sale a week."

Marketing communications influence **store image,** the picture shoppers conjure up of a store's identity. This image is a composite of shoppers' perceptions of the store's

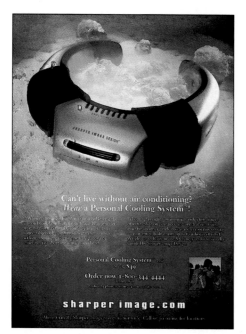

Sharper Image, a specialty retailer of innovative products, serves a global market through its Web site and stores in the United States and Switzerland.

location, goods, and services sold, and atmospherics. Essentially, store image is a reflection of consumers' feelings about a store. It affects consumer perceptions of the quality of products and services offered, prices, and the store's fashionability.

Types of Strategy Mix

Retailers differentiate themselves from one another according to the **strategy mix** they pursue. The elements of the retail strategy mix are the controllable variables we have discussed: location, products and services, pricing, and marketing communications. Exhibit 14–7 describes a range of retailers and their strategy mixes. Although a multitude of combinations exist, specialty stores, department stores, and convenience stores are the more obvious examples of retailers that combine the strategy mix variables in different ways to achieve their desired positions in the marketplace.

SPECIALTY STORES Specialty stores sell a narrow variety of products but offer a deep assortment of product choices. Typical examples of specialty stores are The Limited, Radio Shack, and The Sharper Image.

Because many specialty stores are not large enough to generate sufficient customer traffic on their own, most are commonly located in shopping clusters (malls, shopping centers) where their product selections complement goods provided by neighboring retailers. The marketing communications mix of a specialty store generally includes personal selling along with advertising that emphasizes the uniqueness of offerings and the depth of assortment. Specialty stores are also known for their medium to high prices.

DEPARTMENT STORES Department stores are characterized by a wide variety of merchandise and extensive depth of assortment, and they offer customers one-stop convenience for multiple shopping needs. Operations are typically organized around sales departments such as apparel, home furnishings, cosmetics, and housewares. Employees also work within centralized functional departments such as buying, merchandising, and advertising. Some of the more well-known department stores are Bloomingdale's, Dillard's, and Macy's.

Department stores generally occupy **anchor positions** in shopping centers, shopping malls, or downtown areas; that is, they are strategically placed at different ends of the shopping cluster. Because department stores generate a lot of customer traffic, this placement creates a traffic flow throughout the entire shopping facility.

Marketing communications for department stores focus on product selection and quality; services offered such as alterations, gift wrapping, and credit; shopping atmosphere; and store image. Department stores are heavy users of newspaper advertising, catalogs, direct mail, and personal selling. As do specialty stores, department stores commonly charge at or above competitive prices.

CONVENIENCE STORES Convenience stores have developed their own unique marketing mix. They carry a modest variety and shallow assortment of products. Prices are high, which consumers tolerate because of the ease of shopping offered by such retailers. Convenience stores often occupy **interceptor locations** between residential areas and the closest supermarket. Marketing communications are predominantly limited to the store's sign and banners displayed in the front windows.

Two convenience stores, Circle K and 7-Eleven, have been in bankruptcy, and the entire industry faces a predicted decline in new-store growth over the next decade. The industry's problems can be traced to three main sources. First, the industry is overbuilt, with the proliferation of convenience stores constructed by major oil companies such as Shell, Texaco, and BP. Second, as drugstores and supermarkets extend

Exhibit 14–7	*Examples of retail strategy mixes*				
Type of Retailer	**Location**	**Merchandise**	**Prices**	**Atmosphere and Services**	**Marketing Communications**
Convenience store	Neighborhood	Medium width and low depth of assortment; average quality	Average to above average	Average	Moderate
Superstore	Community shopping center or isolated site	Full assortment of supermarket items, plus health and beauty aids and general merchandise	Competitive	Average	Heavy use of newspapers and flyers; self-service
Warehouse store	Secondary site, often in industrial area	Moderate width and low depth; emphasis on national brands purchased at discounts	Very low	Low	Little or none
Specialty store	Business district or shopping center	Very narrow width of assortment; extensive depth of assortment; average to good quality	Competitive to above average	Average to excellent	Heavy use of displays; extensive salesforce
Department store	Business district, shopping center, or isolated store	Extensive width and depth of assortment; average to good quality	Average to above average	Good to excellent	Heavy use of ads; catalogs; direct mail; personal selling
Full-line discount store	Business district, shopping center, or isolated store	Extensive width and depth of assortment; average to good quality	Competitive	Slightly below average to average	Heavy use of newspapers; price-oriented; moderate salesforce
Factory outlet	Out-of-the-way site or discount mall	Moderate width, but very poor depth of assortment; some irregular merchandise; low continuity	Very low	Very low	Little; self-service

Source: Adapted from Barry Berman and Joel R. Evans, *Retail Management: A Strategic Approach,* 5th ed. (New York: Macmillan, 1992), pp. 98–99. Copyright © 1992 by Macmillan College Publishing Company, Inc. Reprinted with permission of the publisher.

their hours of operation, convenience stores have increasing difficulty differentiating themselves on convenience. Moreover, increases in the minimum wage, store rents, and other general expenses have dramatically increased operating costs. Even though sales through convenience stores are increasing, profit margins are declining.[30] Profit margins on merchandise are increasing, but this increase is more than offset by declining profit margins on motor fuel. Convenience stores have had difficulty passing on wholesale-price increases for motor fuel to the ultimate consumer.

To survive, many convenience stores have repositioned themselves as quick-service eateries specializing in "one-handed" food—items you can eat with one hand while driving with the other, such as hot dogs, corn dogs, pizza, burritos, and egg rolls.

MARGIN AND TURNOVER STRATEGY MIXES   Besides type of store, another distinction between retailers is gross margin and inventory turnover. **Gross margin** refers to sales revenue less the retailer's cost of goods sold. A retailer with higher margins makes more from each dollar of sales. **Inventory turnover** refers to how quickly merchandise is sold; it describes the number of times the retailer sells its average inventory during the year. Margin and turnover concepts are illustrated in Appendix A at the end of the text.

There are three strategic combinations of gross margin and inventory turnover among successful retailers. Jewelry stores exemplify a high-margin/low-turnover strategy. They realize high profits per sale but make fewer sales. Such retailers are also noted for their attention to personal service and attractive atmospheres that help support the merchandise.

Grocery stores use a low-margin/high-turnover strategy. They typically have a net profit margin of 1 to 2 percent but turn merchandise over very quickly. The third option is high-margin/high-turnover, demonstrated by convenience stores.

Laurie Clyne points out that teamwork can be an important part of a successful retail strategy: "Many companies claim to emphasize teamwork, but at Mervyn's it is our core strategy for getting the job done. The bottom line with teamwork at Mervyn's is in how we evaluate our team—performance reviews, pay raises, and bonuses are heavily weighted on team results at all levels in the company. And although we recognize that the effort and contribution of the individual is important, we know that our collective efforts count even more and is what leads us to success."

Ethical and Legal Issues in Retailing

Retailers engage in highly visible activities, and their marketing communications are similarly visible and thus subject to a fair amount of scrutiny. Ethical or legal violations that retailers have been accused of include deceptive advertising, dishonest sales practices, charging unreasonably high prices to disadvantaged consumers, selling potentially harmful products without adequate control, and selling prohibited products to underage consumers.

Additional factors pose special concerns for retailers: consumer fraud, supplier labor practices, shoplifting, slotting allowances, the use of personal customer information, and ecological considerations.

Consumer Fraud

Retailers that adopted the customer-is-always-right concept are having second thoughts when it comes to liberal return policies. Known in the industry as return churn or boomerang buying, return fraud is a growing problem for retailers. Fraudulent returns cost retailers more than a billion dollars annually. L.L. Bean notices more requests for returns in the spring, when yard sales pick up and old boots and camping equipment are bought cheap and then returned with a request for a full refund. Best Buy sells a lot of laptop computers during finals week in college towns, only to encounter a flood of returns after the term ends. And some customers take merchandise off the shelf, then proceed to customer service for a refund, claiming that the receipt has been lost. Others use retailers as free rental centers for big-screen TV sets, snow blowers, and formal apparel. Retailers are fighting back, cutting down on the time during which returns are accepted and being more insistent that the customer has a receipt. Fraudulent consumers drive up the cost of retailing, which ultimately translates into higher prices for honest consumers.

Supplier Labor Practices

Many retailers, including Wal-Mart, JCPenney, Talbots, and Macy's, have been part of a controversy involving the working conditions in their supplier manufacturing facilities. Referred to as sweatshops, these facilities are located primarily in low-wage countries in Asia and Eastern Europe. Sweatshop workers, many of whom are underage, are subjected to adverse working conditions and extremely low wages.

A storm of bad publicity began in the mid 1990s and continues today, with retailers, manufacturers, and celebrity spokespersons receiving unwanted exposure. Since then, many retailers have strengthened existing policies and adopted new procedures to address the sweatshop issue. The U.S. Department of Labor has commended several retailers for their active role in eliminating sweatshops, including Express, Nordstrom, The Limited, Patagonia, Nicole Miller, Lane Bryant, and Liz Claiborne. Nonetheless, the issue is far from resolved, and college students are among the most outspoken critics of retail-supplier labor practices. Campus protests at the University of Michigan, Georgetown University, and Duke University highlighted student dissatisfaction with sweatshop operations, and students on 100 campuses have joined a protest group called the United Students Against Sweatshops.[31] The issues surrounding sweatshop-produced merchandise are likely to remain key ethical issues for retailers well into the future.

Shoplifting

Retailers lose approximately $16 billion a year to shoplifting by customers and employees.[32] Nationwide, the incidence of shoplifting has increased sharply in recent years. Experts claim the primary contributors to increased shoplifting are fewer clerks per store and new floor layout arrangements that divide stores into separate boutiques. This type of layout creates barriers between departments, which makes it easier for shoplifters to conceal their activities. Specialty clothing stores, drugstores, convenience stores, and department stores are hit hardest by shoplifting. Items most frequently stolen are fashion accessories, costume jewelry, fine jewelry, recorded music, health and beauty aids, sporting goods, radios, and television sets.

Manufacturers are taking steps to reduce shoplifting in retail stores. Johnson & Johnson, Eastman Kodak, and Procter & Gamble are developing security-alarm tags for products ranging from film and cameras to Pampers and Tylenol. These three companies have formed the Consumer Products Manufacturers' Consortium to develop the tags and institute a global standard for the tags that can be used by all retailers and manufacturers.[33] The consortium hopes to have the participation of most retailers by 2003. If successful, the system could have a major impact on shoplifting in drug and grocery stores, where currently only 30 percent of all products are protected by security tags. Some methods for deterring shoplifting are detailed in Exhibit 14–8.

Slotting Allowances

Another retailing issue that has legal or ethical implications is the use of slotting allowances. **Slotting allowances** are fees manufacturers pay to retailers or wholesalers to obtain shelf or warehouse space for their products. In other words, retailers and wholesalers receive money from manufacturers in exchange for allocation of shelf space.

Slotting allowances, a common practice in grocery retailing, are controversial. They were first instituted to keep manufacturers from introducing not-so-new

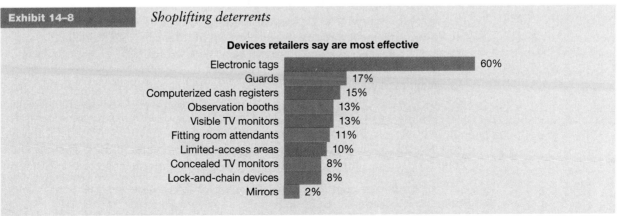

| Exhibit 14–8 | *Shoplifting deterrents* |

Devices retailers say are most effective

Device	Percentage
Electronic tags	60%
Guards	17%
Computerized cash registers	15%
Observation booths	13%
Visible TV monitors	13%
Fitting room attendants	11%
Limited-access areas	10%
Concealed TV monitors	8%
Lock-and-chain devices	8%
Mirrors	2%

Source: Arthur Young-IMRA 6th Annual Study of Security and Shrinkage. From Dale Lewison, *Retailing,* 4th ed. (New York: Macmillan, 1991), p. 310.

brands or bogus product-line extensions. Colorado State University professor Joseph P. Cannon notes that "the reason slotting fees came about was the number of new products, making it more difficult to evaluate them. Test marketing fell by the wayside because of the [importance of] speed to market and also because if you test your product, your competitors can see it before you go national."[34] Even though test marketing is less popular than in the past, slotting fees are more established than ever. Large manufacturers resist paying these questionable fees, but large wholesalers and retailers insist slotting fees be paid as a condition of doing business. In effect, slotting allowances place manufacturers in direct opposition to their customers: wholesalers and retailers.

Overall, slotting allowances are predominantly associated with negative consequences. They may increase conflict between channel members and reduce competitiveness at some levels. Large channel members can demand slotting allowances that increase their profit margins, while the smaller members must fend for themselves.

Slotting allowances may also reduce customer service by forcing fewer brand choices, higher retail prices, and less prepurchase information. This could ultimately threaten the quality of product provided to the consumer.

Use of Customer Information

Advances in database technology provide retailers greater access to and storage of consumer information and purchase histories. For example, when a customer calls Spiegel to check a catalog order, the service rep has instant access, via an order number, to the customer's previous sales and service transactions. This information can be used to sell other products and service warranties and to process orders more efficiently.

Are retailers free to use such information for any purpose, or is the customer's right to privacy being violated? Although this question is the subject of much debate, public sentiment favors the protection of consumer privacy. Some of the major videotape rental firms no longer maintain records of customers' past rentals. Other companies that fear adverse publicity will quite likely take a right-to-privacy stance.

Ecological Considerations

Retailers have begun to pay more attention to how their operations affect the environment. Wal-Mart, for example, has created Environmental Demonstration Stores in Kansas, Oklahoma, and California. These stores feature recycled construction materials, solar energy, and ozone-friendly air-conditioning systems. Local Wal-Mart stores have a "Green Coordinator," a specially trained associate who coordinates efforts to make the store environmentally responsible.[35] Home Depot also shows its awareness of ecological issues by announcing its refusal (beginning in 2002) to sell wood from environmentally endangered areas. Home Depot sells more lumber than any other company in the world, and its move has been hailed by environmentalists as a "great victory for the forests."[36]

Another indication that retailers are becoming more concerned with environmental issues is a move to ban smoking in shopping malls. Since the Environmental Protection Agency released a report on the dangers of secondhand smoke, shopping centers across the country have not waited for legal prompting; instead, they have taken the initiative to ban smoking.

Like all marketing institutions, retailers are finding that following an ethical perspective can be good for business. They are also acutely aware that questionable ethical practices can lead to consumer protest, tarnished images, and lost sales. Consumers must also take some responsibility for correcting some of the ethical problems in retailing. Shoplifting and consumer fraud hurt retailer profits. They also hurt honest consumers in the form of higher prices and inconvenient security measures.

Summary

1. Understand the economic importance of retailing and its role in the marketing channel. The role of retailing in the marketing channel is to provide products and services to the ultimate, or final consumer. Retailing is an important economic activity in that (1) there are approximately 2.2 million retailers in the United States; (2) nearly 21 million people, one-eighth of the U.S. labor force, are employed in retail or retail-related activities; and (3) retailers generate approximately $2.6 trillion in sales. Retailers differ from other channel members in that they sell smaller quantities more frequently, offer assortments of products, and emphasize atmospherics in their selling.

2. Cite evidence of the globalization of retailing. McDonald's, Wal-Mart, The Gap, Radio Shack, France's Carrefour, and L.L. Bean are but a few companies expanding retail operations around the globe. Markets in countries with highly developed economies such as the United States are somewhat saturated, thus retailers are increasingly eager to expand to less-competitive markets.

3. Discuss some of the advances in retailing technology. Retailing has benefited from various technologies in recent years. Automated cash registers, electronic kiosks, Universal Product Code scanners, and wireless computers are some examples of technology put to good use in retailing. The explosive growth in nonstore retailing is fueled in part by computer and communications technology.

4. Explain the reasons behind the growth of nonstore retailing. Busy people like to shop at their preferred times in the convenience of their own homes. Successful catalog retailing has encouraged consumers to try other forms of nonstore retailing such as TV shopping and on-line shopping. The growth of nonstore retailing is probably also the result of consumer boredom and dissatisfaction with some traditional retail stores.

5. Describe key factors in the retail marketing environment, and understand how they relate to retail strategy. Controllable factors include location, products and services, pricing, and marketing communications. Uncontrollable factors are consumers, competition, economic conditions, and seasonality. To be successful, retailers must effectively manipulate the controllable factors to manage the environment created by always-changing uncontrollable factors.

6. Cite important ethical and legal issues facing retailers. Routine legal restrictions govern practically every aspect of retailing. Contemporary ethical and legal issues of special concern are consumer fraud, supplier labor practices, shoplifting, the use of slotting allowances, the use of customer information, and ecological considerations. Consumer fraud in the form of unwarranted return of merchandise costs retailers more than a billion dollars a year, which ultimately is passed on to consumers. Some progressive retailers began monitoring the labor practices of their suppliers after sweatshop practices made the headlines, resulting in negative publicity for retailers, suppliers, and celebrity spokespersons. Employee, consumer, and supplier theft all figure into shoplifting. Slotting allowances are fees manufacturers pay to retailers or wholesalers to obtain shelf or warehouse space for their products. It's an ethically questionable practice and may be illegal. Other concerns are the retailer's use of customer information versus the individual's right to privacy, and the ecological impact of retail operations.

Understanding Marketing Terms and Concepts

Thinking About Marketing

1. What evidence can you cite supporting the economic importance of retailing?

2. How do retailers differ from other members in the channel of distribution?

3. How can retailers improve customer service by using technology?

4. Review "Earning Customer Loyalty: bebe Builds Its Brand." Realizing that consumer tastes can change quickly, how can fashion retailers get timely ideas for new fashions?

5. Review "Using Technology: Le Printemps Rolls to Success." How does this concept create value for consumers?

6. What uncontrollable factors affect the retail environment? What can retailers do to minimize the impact of these factors on sales?

7. What types of locations are possible alternatives for retailers? Briefly define each type of location.

8. List and describe the three types of nonstore retailing. What are the advantages and disadvantages of nonstore retail operations?

9. Discuss the benefits of retail franchising from both the franchisor's and franchisee's point of view.

10. Discuss some of the key ethical and legal issues in retailing.

Applying Marketing Skills

1. Retailers that sell secondhand merchandise, such as flea markets or Salvation Army stores, have been doing relatively well in recent years. Can you explain their success in terms of economic conditions and consumer preferences discussed in this chapter?

2. Tune in to a television shopping program once a week for a month, and analyze the products sold and the sales methods used. In particular, assess the following issues:
- What is the primary pricing strategy?
- What role do celebrities play in the programming?
- Can you generalize about the size and colors offered in apparel sales?
- Is it important to have merchandise with easy-to-demonstrate features?

3. For each of the following types of retail operations, suggest complementary products, either goods or services, that could logically be added to the merchandise mix:
- A small coffee shop that features light desserts, pastries, espresso, cappuccino, and gourmet coffees.
- A small independent bookstore located near a retirement community.
- A large parking garage adjacent to a downtown office building.
- A hairstyling salon.
- A pet supplies store.

Using the www in Marketing

Activity One　　L.L. Bean is a successful retailer in both store and non-store formats. One reason for L.L. Bean's success is excellent customer service. Visit the Web site at http://www.llbean.com and identify customer services not typically available from retail stores (refer to Exhibit 14–3 for services typically offered by retail stores). How do these services build stronger customer relationships?

Activity Two　　Compare on-line retailers at the Virtual Reality mall, http://www.vr-mall.com. Select any two of the retailers listed and answer these questions:

1. How would you describe the target market for each retailer? This will require some speculation on your part, but describe the likely demographic and lifestyle characteristics of the intended target markets for each retailer.

2. Which of the two retailers has done the best job in appealing to its target market with its on-line offerings? Please support your answer.

Making Marketing Decisions
Case 14–1 Zane's Cycles Takes On the Big Bikers

Chris Zane, owner of Zane's Cycles in New Haven, Connecticut, is not popular with his competitors. Maybe it is his combative attitude they don't like. He has told other dealers that he would put them out of business, and he has. It is an understatement to call him confident, given that he has said "Let Wal-Mart come—I'm ready." By paying attention to customers and delivering superior value, Zane has become the top bike retailer in New Haven at a time when small retailers in most markets are fighting for their lives.

Although small retailers like Chris Zane account for more than half of the $3.5 billion (in annual sales) bike market, they are feeling the heat from discount stores and mass retailers. There is another emerging threat to independents like Zane: the category killers. The largest chain, based in Chapel Hill, North Carolina, is Performance, Inc. Performance has 33 stores and a catalog operation. The founder and CEO of Performance said, "Because we are in a niche, we're a category killer in a 5,000-square-foot box, unlike Home Depot in their huge boxes."

To Zane, category killers and discounters pose a real threat, but he uses creativity and superior customer service to stay ahead of the pack. He said, "I'll give you lifetime service, guarantee you the lowest price, fix you a cappuccino." He began taking market share from other stores a decade ago by offering one-year service guarantees, whereas competitors offered only 30-day guarantees. Later he extended the guarantee to the life of the bike, and made the offer retroactive. "We wanted to make existing customers our apostles," said Zane. Although such an offer seems expensive for the retailer, Zane says the cost is minuscule compared with the lifetime value of his customers, who continue to buy accessories and perhaps more bikes over the years.

Zane has expanded his thinking on giveaways and does not charge customers for parts that cost less than a dollar. Costing him only $150 per year, this reinforces his goal of building customers for a lifetime. With so many freebies, some customers began to be skeptical about initial bike prices. According to Zane, customers would say, "Sure, you're giving me lifetime free service, but what are you charging me for this bike?" In response, Zane implemented a 90-day price guarantee. If the customer can find the bike cheaper in Connecticut within 90 days, Zane meets the price plus 10 percent. This guarantee rarely cost Zane money, and the results have been most positive. Sales have been increasing at 25 percent per year, and Zane's was named New Haven's best bicycle shop for 1993–1998 by the readers of the local newspaper.

Zane has used marketing communications to build his image while doing good for the community. Through the New Haven Regional Injury Prevention Program, he provides bike helmets to needy children in the area. Connecticut law requires that all children under the age of 12 wear helmets when biking, but many cannot afford them. By providing the kids with helmets, Zane helps the community and builds the image of his business at the same time.

Zane is aware that bike shoppers want expert advice, great service, a fair price, and a pleasant shopping experience. His store boasts a custom-made 14-foot mahogany coffee bar and a play area for children. He commissioned the coffee bar after realizing that customers found his store uninviting with its high ceilings and white walls. Customers thought the store looked more like a chain store than a homegrown business. By listening to customers, Zane is surviving, even prospering, despite the presence of the larger retailers.

Though Zane only employs 18 people in his shop, he has become a big voice to those interested in improving retail operations. On behalf of St. John's University and PRISMA Telephone & Communications in Germany, he was a guest speaker at an international conference on "Creating Customers for Life." Visitors to his store would definitely agree that when it comes to customer service, Chris Zane practices what he preaches.

Questions

1. What types of customers will most likely be attracted to the Zane's Cycles store?
2. Are there any disadvantages to Zane's offering a free lifetime service program?
3. Is superior customer service the best weapon in Zane's fight with discounters and category killers?

SOURCES: Donna Fenn "Leader of the Pack" *Inc.,* February 1996, pp. 31–38; Michael Barrier, "Wheels of Change in Bicycle Retailing," *Nation's Business,* February 1996, pp. 40–42; and information from the Zane's Cycles Web site at www.zanes.com, January 20, 2000.

Case 14–2 Can Dot Com Save Sears?

Sears, once the world's leading retailer, spent the 1990s on a roller-coaster comeback bid. Having lost its number-one status to Wal-Mart, Sears also suffered a blow to its bedrock, Middle America image when its automotive repair personnel were found guilty of performing unnecessary repairs and systematically overcharging customers. The company paid millions in fines and endured months of bad publicity. By 1996, however, Sears was riding high, having undergone a cost-cutting program on one hand while upgrading their stores on the other. Most analysts thought Sears would enter the twenty-first century as a premier retailer. Now, it appears that the turnaround has stalled, and the future of Sears is not clear—at least to investors. Sears stock fell almost 50 percent in 1999.

What happened to derail the Sears comeback? Sears had begun promoting its apparel and soft-goods products (for example, bed sheets and towels) with an advertising theme of "The Softer Side of Sears." The campaign worked well for a while but eventually lost its momentum. Apparel sales doubled over a three-year period, then remained flat for two consecutive years. During this time, discount stores, especially Target, made immense progress in these product categories. Wal-Mart also improved its apparel offerings, and the edge gained by Sears quickly disappeared. According to retail consultant Ken Harris, "Target is occupying the space Sears used to own. It's no badge of shame to shop at a Target store. They have demonstrated how to appeal to the upper-middle-class community of shoppers and make them feel good about going into their stores. Sears lost that. They're a bit tattered and trying to get that back."

During its turnaround, Sears aggressively expanded its private credit card business. The Sears card is the world's largest in terms of number of cardholders, thanks to a 56 percent increase in new cards issued in the mid-1990s. By the end of the 90s, however, Sears had cut back on new cards issued, because debt write-offs from unpaid credit cards had soared. To make matters worse, federal and state authorities charged that Sears had illegally coerced bankrupt credit card debtors into paying their past-due bills.

Heading into the twenty-first century, Sears dumped its "Softer Side" campaign. Replacing it with a more aggressive, value-oriented ad theme, "The Good Life at a Great Price. Guaranteed." Analysts, who had begun joking that the "Softer Side of Sears" referred to its earnings and stock price, were pleased with the new theme. The new theme positions Sears directly against Wal-Mart and Target in trying to assure consumers that they will receive good value from Sears.

Perhaps the biggest piece of Sears's twenty-first-century strategy is its e-retailing venture, Sears.com. For a company that many feel has become outdated, e-retailing seems like a huge challenge. Top management at Sears feels the "dot com" operation will contemporize the Sears image and invigorate its brands. It will also allow Sears to focus on the home market and introduce other well-known brands to supplement its own brands via the Internet. By focusing on the home, Sears plans to stay away from apparel, toys, and sporting goods at Sears.com. The company plans instead to be an on-line category killer for the home, focusing on home-oriented appliances, tools, and gadgets. Sears.com also offers outsourcing for repair and installation services.

As for the future of its e-retailing site, Sears spokespersons are vague. They acknowledge that consumers may well wish to shop across virtually all product lines, but they will not confirm future plans. The company has taken steps to ensure little conflict between store operations and its e-retailing site. All 850 Sears stores have kiosks that allow customers to visit sears.com and make purchases. When products are sold at sears.com, local Sears salespeople share in the commission.

Consulting firm Ernst & Young believes that Sears has a fighting chance for success in e-retailing. According to Ernst & Young, e-retailing requires two things: a wide assortment of products and a recognizable brand name that implies a wide assortment. Sears certainly has both of these things going for it. Then again, it also had these factors in its favor with its traditional stores and failed to fully capitalize on its strengths. Will past lessons help Sears succeed in the twenty-first century?

Questions

1. A customer orientation is a key to success in retailing. How would you rate Sears in this area in recent years? Are the needs for e-retail customers and store customers different? How can a giant retailer like Sears stay close to the customer?

2. What potential problems could Sears encounter in operating both an e-retail site and its traditional stores? What new opportunities might Sears realize by operating both?

3. Sears has always appealed to Middle America—that is, middle-class, family-oriented consumers. At present, is this a good target market for e-retailing? How about in the future?

SOURCES: Bernhard Warner, "Sears' Comeback Bid," *The Industry Standard,* November 22–29, 1999, pp. 212–20; Greg Farrell, "Ads Show Another Side of Sears," *USA Today,* August 18, 1999, p. 3B; Robert Berner, "Come See the Softer Side of Sears—Its Earnings," *The Wall Street Journal,* July 23, 1998, pp. B1, B12; and information from the Sears Web site at www.sears.com, January 20, 2000.

Wholesaling and Logistics Management

After studying this chapter, you should be able to:

1 Understand wholesaling and describe the three basic categories of wholesalers.

2 Identify and discuss the roles of different types of full-service and limited-function wholesalers.

3 Explain differences among the functions of agents, brokers, and commission merchants.

4 Understand the differences between manufacturers' sales branches and offices.

5 Appreciate how slow growth rates and globalization will affect wholesaling in the future.

6 Define logistics management and explain its key role in marketing.

7 Understand logistics activities, including warehousing, materials handling, inventory control, order processing, and transporting.

8 Discuss how some of the key ethical and legal issues affect logistics.

www.grainger.com

W.W. Grainger, Inc., was founded in 1927 to meet the needs of customers who required products faster than manufacturers could deliver. Today, Grainger is a leading business-to-business wholesaler, providing over 210,000 products to more than 1.5 million commercial, industrial, contractor, and institutional customers around the world. Grainger represents some of the top suppliers in the world, including companies such as Fuji, Champion, Nutone, Briggs & Stratton, General Electric, and John Deere. The company's vision statement provides direction for its business: "To be a primary source through the breadth of our offering and a focus on the lowest total cost solution for each of our customers."

Grainger serves its customers from 350 branches with 11,800 employees, 1,500 of whom are full-time field sales representatives. A satellite network links all of the branches and nine distribution centers. Grainger truly covers the market, with 70 percent of all U.S. businesses located within 20 minutes of a Grainger branch.

A key part of Grainger's marketing communications effort is its catalog, which lists 78,000 products. Now available on CD-ROM, Grainger's catalog reaches 2.6 million customers annually. E-commerce is also important to Grainger; on-line sales will reach $200 million in 2000. The company also has an on-line auction site and another site featuring six different companies offering thousands of products not stocked by Grainger. Only Cisco Systems, IBM, and Dell Computer Corporation sell more over the Internet.

Grainger clearly listens to its customers. The company uses surveys and focus groups to get feedback about product availability and service quality. Grainger's "No Excuses" policy empowers its employees to solve problems and ensure customer satisfaction. It has earned the trust of its customers, being named a preferred, distinguished, or select supplier for organizations such as Abbot Laboratories, Campbell Soup Company, 3M, Motorola, Tyson Foods, and Yale University.

Respect for the environment is another noteworthy aspect of Grainger's approach to business. Its catalog is printed with soy-based, nonpetroleum ink, and the color section and index are printed on recycled paper. Grainger also works with its paper suppliers to replenish natural resources; two trees are planted for every one that must be cut to print the catalog. The catalog also features many energy-saving products, identified with the "Energy Right" symbol.

The world of wholesaling, in contrast to retailing, does not often feature glamorous products. Nor are wholesaling companies part of our daily lives. Rather, it is from behind the scenes that Grainger and other leading wholesalers build value for their customers and keep the wheels of commerce rolling.

Source: Douglas A. Blackmon, "Selling Motors to Mops, Unglamorous Grainger Is a Web-sales Star," *The Wall Street Journal*, December 13, 1999, pp. B1, B8; and Grainger home page and related links available at http://www.grainger.com.

In this chapter we discuss two key areas related to the marketing channel and the other marketing mix elements: wholesaling and logistics management. Briefly, **wholesalers** are intermediaries in the marketing channel that sell to customers other than individual or household consumers. **Logistics management** is the planning, implementation, and movement of goods, services, and related information from point of origin to point of consumption. Increasingly, logistics management involves supply-chain management, discussed in Chapter 5.

Wholesalers are often involved in all five key functions of the marketing channel: marketing communications, inventory management, physical distribution, provision of market feedback, and assumption of financial risk. Logistics management also has some relevance to those functions, but it normally relates more specifically to inventory management and physical distribution activities. Logistics is an important function for wholesalers, especially if they handle the products they are reselling. For an illustration, see "Being Entrepreneurial: Ship Fast or Perish."

Wholesaling

WE *DELIVER* IT ALL
WITH ONE CALL

HARVEST

PROCESS

TRANSPORT

CUSTOMER
SERVICE

IPSWICH SHELLFISH GROUP

Ipswich Shellfish Group is a wholesaler that sells fresh seafood to restaurants and grocers worldwide.

Wholesaling is an important aspect of the marketing channel strategy for many firms. It refers to the marketing activities associated with selling products to purchasers that resell the products, use them to make another product, or use them to conduct business activities. Wholesaling does not include transactions with household and individual consumers, nor does it include the small purchases businesses occasionally make from retail stores. Essentially, wholesalers sell to manufacturers and industrial customers, retailers, government agencies, other wholesalers, and institutional customers such as schools and hospitals.

We mentioned in Chapter 13 that all intermediaries in a marketing channel, including wholesalers, must justify their existence by performing at least one function better than any other channel member. For wholesalers, this often means adding value to goods and services as they pass through the channel. For example, Computer Associates, a leading software company, uses **value-added resellers (VARs)** to sell to small- and medium-sized business customers. Many of these customers do not have their own computer departments to design, implement, and maintain management information systems, so they need VARs to do it for them. Computer Associates VARs add value in many ways, including showing customers how to integrate existing systems with new technology, training customer employees, and providing technical support.

Being Entrepreneurial

Ship fast or perish

Chesapeake Bay Gourmet, a small family-owned seafood distributor, has met with great success selling "homemade and handmade" crab cakes on QVC's television shopping network. To meet customer expectations, it is imperative that orders are processed and shipped within 48 hours. Since the frozen crab cakes are perishable, logistics management is more complicated than would be the case with nonperishable goods.

In its first QVC exposure, a seven-minute spot generated orders for 24,000 crab cakes, the largest order ever for Chesapeake Bay Gourmet. Its largest order to date through QVC totaled almost 20 tons of crab cakes to be shipped di-

rectly to customers. QVC accounts for about half of the company's sales revenue, and late shipping would jeopardize the business.

To manage the logistics, Chesapeake uses special frozen-food packaging and handling. Delivery trucks arrive one after another beginning at 3:00 A.M. By the end of the day, shipping is complete. Chesapeake must also take special care to manage its logistics both with retail customers such as Harry & David's and with its Internet sales. In the specialty perishable foods business, fast shipping is a must.

Source: Connie Gentry, "Logistics IT Moves Food Faster," *Inbound Logistics,* August 1999, pp. 23–30.

Don Becker
President
Becker Marketing Services

Before founding his packaging wholesaling company, Don Becker worked in sales, product management and sales management with Procter & Gamble and Mobil Corporation. He is a graduate of Drury College in Springfield, Missouri. Don is well aware of the need for wholesalers to constantly justify their position in the marketing channel.

"We have to add value to the products we buy from manufacturers in order to justify our position in the channel. How? By being the absolute product specialist in our custom polyethylene packaging niche—the go-to-guy for our customers, by providing the largest line of custom products available in the marketplace (perhaps 20–30 times what any one single manufacturer could provide), and by buying with such clout that we are competitive even when we have to compete with other manufacturers, and by servicing our customers better than our competition."

Types of Wholesalers

According to the U.S. Department of Commerce, the three basic categories of wholesalers are merchant wholesalers; agents, brokers, and commission merchants; and manufacturers' sales branches and offices. Exhibit 15–1 shows the three categories and the main types of wholesalers within each. Independent wholesalers that take title to the products they sell are called **merchant wholesalers.** Wholesalers in the second category, agents, brokers, and commission merchants, do not take title to the products bought or sold. They are sometimes referred to as *functional middlemen.* Those in the third category, manufacturers' sales branches and offices, are owned by producers or manufacturing firms.

MERCHANT WHOLESALERS According to the *Census of the Wholesale Trade,* published by the Department of Commerce, there are more than 375,000 merchant wholesalers based in the United States, accounting for 83 percent of the wholesale establishments in the country.[1] Merchant wholesalers, often called *distributors,* are categorized as either full-service wholesalers or limited-function wholesalers.

Exhibit 15–1   *Categories and types of wholesalers*

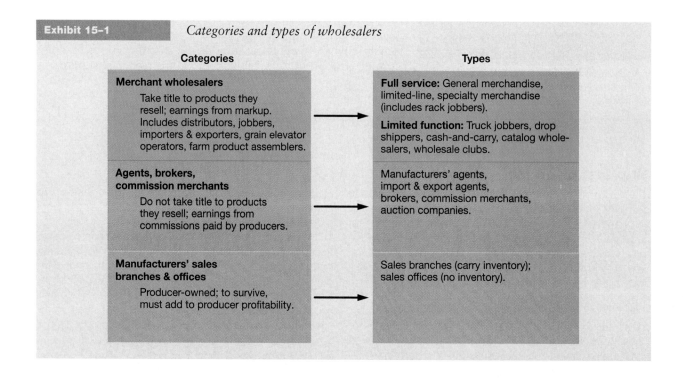

Categories	Types
Merchant wholesalers Take title to products they resell; earnings from markup. Includes distributors, jobbers, importers & exporters, grain elevator operators, farm product assemblers.	**Full service:** General merchandise, limited-line, specialty merchandise (includes rack jobbers). **Limited function:** Truck jobbers, drop shippers, cash-and-carry, catalog wholesalers, wholesale clubs.
Agents, brokers, commission merchants Do not take title to products they resell; earnings from commissions paid by producers.	Manufacturers' agents, import & export agents, brokers, commission merchants, auction companies.
Manufacturers' sales branches & offices Producer-owned; to survive, must add to producer profitability.	Sales branches (carry inventory); sales offices (no inventory).

Exhibit 15–2	*Functions performed by wholesalers*				
Type of Wholesaler	**Marketing Communications***	**Inventory Mgmt. and Storage**	**Physical Distribution**	**Market Feedback/ Advisory Board**	**Financial Risk/ Offer Credit†**
Full-service merchant wholesalers	Yes	Yes	Yes	Yes	Yes
Truck jobbers	Yes	Yes	Yes	Sometimes	Sometimes
Drop shippers	No	No	Yes	Yes	Yes
Cash and carry	No	Yes	No	Sometimes	No
Catalog wholesalers	Yes	Yes	Yes	Sometimes	Sometimes
Wholesale clubs	Sometimes	Yes	No	Sometimes	No
Mfrs.' agents	Sometimes	Sometimes	Sometimes	Yes	No
Auction companies	Yes	Sometimes	No	No	No
Import and export agents	Sometimes	Sometimes	Sometimes	Yes	No
Brokers	No	No	No	Yes	No
Commission merchants	Yes	Yes	Sometimes	Yes	Sometimes
Mfrs.' sales branches	Sometimes	Yes	Yes	Yes	Yes
Mfrs.' sales offices	Sometimes	No	No	Yes	Yes

Note: Refer to Exhibit 13–1 for multiple examples of each functional area.

*By definition, all wholesalers are involved in at least one form of marketing communications (selling).

†All wholesalers not classified as agents, brokers, or commission merchants incur financial risk when they assume ownership, or take title, to the products they subsequently resell. This exhibit refers to the financial risk taken by wholesalers that offer credit to their customers.

FULL-SERVICE WHOLESALERS   Full-service wholesalers by definition perform a wide range of services for their customers and the parties from which they purchase. These wholesalers might perform all key activities in an entire marketing channel (as in Exhibit 15–2), whereas limited-function wholesalers are likely to specialize in only a few activities.

Full-service wholesalers include general merchandise, limited-line, and specialty-line wholesalers. For a better idea of services available from full-service wholesalers, see Exhibit 15–3. **General merchandise wholesalers** carry a wide variety of products

W.W. Grainger, featured in the chapter opener, provides an example of the technological perspective with its use of an electronic catalog that reaches more than 2.5 million customers around the world.

Exhibit 15-3	*Services provided by full-service wholesalers/distributors*	
Distributor Services	**To Manufacturer**	**To Retailer**
Sensible buying	• Market feedback improves production planning, reducing costs of raw materials, components.	• Distributor buying clout passed on through low prices. • Dealing with only one or two wholesalers cuts purchasing costs, leads to one-stop shopping.
Distribution flow	• Reduces storage needs, moves products faster, cuts inventory costs. • Products stored closer to retailer for faster delivery; may cut need for costly distribution centers.	• Weekly deliveries reduce need for product storage, increase selling space. • Faster turnover increases profits.
Timely delivery	• Large orders, retail delivery fleets & coordinated back-haul programs reduce transportation costs, keeping product prices competitive.	• Regular deliveries permit better planning, cut receiving costs. • Fast restocking of high-demand products for immediate display.
Traffic-building promotion	• Centralized co-op programs maximize ad dollar at local level. • Increases consumer awareness, establishes products, builds market share.	• Direct-mail circulars, ads, etc., build retail traffic, increase store capabilities, save administrative effort. • Co-op programs save time, money.
Marketing	• Reduces selling costs, frees executive time as distribs serve many retail accounts; products receive wider representation.	• Retail sales training, merchandising, display, layout improve with distrib aid. • Computer systems provide price stickers, program margin requirements, optimize profits. • Hundreds of mfrs' products in one retail location.

and provide extensive services for their customers. A typical example is Alabama Paper Company, which serves retail, industrial, and business customers throughout Alabama from its Birmingham warehouse. Its diverse product line, in excess of 5,000 items, includes consumer electronics, fishing and hunting merchandise, industrial adhesives and packaging materials, office supplies, and home improvement items. As a full-service wholesaler, Alabama Paper performs many marketing channel functions and provides services for its customers and their suppliers.

Limited-line wholesalers do not stock as many products as general merchandise wholesalers, but they offer more depth in their product offering. Among merchant wholesalers, **specialty-line wholesalers** carry the most narrow product assortment—usually a single product line or part of one. To justify their existence, specialty-line wholesalers must be experts on the products they sell.

Rack jobbers, a category of specialty-line wholesalers, sell to retail stores. They set up and maintain attractive store displays and stock them with goods sold on consignment (the retailer pays for the goods only when sold). Rack jobbers are also called *service merchandisers,* a term that better captures the service-oriented aspects of their roles. Retailers depend on rack jobbers particularly in the provision of health and beauty aids, hosiery, and books and magazines. Some rack jobbers might be considered limited-function wholesalers if they carry very small inventories or fail to provide other services listed in Exhibit 15–2.

LIMITED-FUNCTION WHOLESALERS   Exhibit 15–1 shows five primary types of **limited-function wholesalers:** truck jobbers, drop shippers, cash-and-carry wholesalers, catalog wholesalers, and wholesale clubs. As Exhibit 15–2 shows, these wholesalers do not offer the comprehensive services of full-service wholesalers.

Producers of fast-moving or perishable goods that require frequent replenishment often use **truck jobbers.** These limited-service wholesalers deliver within a particular geographic area to ensure freshness of certain goods (bakery, meat, dairy). Marketers often choose truck jobbers, with their quick delivery and frequent store visits, to wholesale miscellaneous high-margin items such as candy, chewing gum, cigarettes, novelty items, and inexpensive toys sold in retail stores. Retailers hate to

Exhibit 15-3	Services provided by full-service wholesalers/distributors (concluded)	
Distributor Manages Assets	**Manufacturer Benefits**	**Retailer Benefits**
Product inventory	• Storage and delivery costs reduced to minimum. • Feedback on item movement improves production planning and use of assets.	• Turnover improved, promotional impact maximized, cash flow/return on investment increased. • In stock, good prices, superior service.
Physical plant	• Majority of plant used for production, not storage. • Need for regional redistribution facilities reduced or eliminated.	• More productive use of square footage ensured by lower inventory requirements, distributor printouts on product movement and margin management. • Market impact from merchandising assistance, in-store displays, signing, customer traffic flow.
Cash flow and credit	• Receivables minimized, credit risks reduced. • Administrative workload reduced.	• Cash flow accelerated through more-frequent small purchases, less cash tied up in inventory. • Best credit terms, extended dating, less paperwork.
People	• Can concentrate on manufacturing and marketing; distributors take product to market. • Concentrating on distributor customers enhances strong relationships with fewer customers.	• Selling techniques, product knowledge enhanced through distributor training, sales aids. • One-on-one contact with distributor management to seize market opportunities.

Source: Adapted with permission of the International Hardware Distributors Association.

be out of these items, for consumers will usually buy them at the next-most-convenient store instead.

Drop shippers arrange for shipments directly from the factory to the customer. Although they do not physically handle the product, drop shippers do take title and all associated risks while the product is in transit. They also provide the necessary sales support. Drop shippers operate in a wide variety of industries, including industrial packaging, lumber, chemicals, and petroleum and heating products.

As the term implies, **cash-and-carry wholesalers** do not deliver the products they sell, nor do they extend credit. Small retailers and other businesses whose limited sales make them unprofitable customers for larger wholesalers are the primary customers for cash-and-carry wholesalers. For example, cash-and-carry wholesalers are common in coastal towns, serving restaurant and grocery customers who make daily trips to the wholesaler to purchase fresh seafood.

Catalog wholesalers serve both major population centers and remote geographic locations and offer an alternative to cash-and-carry wholesalers. Most catalog wholesalers use delivery services such as UPS and require prepayment by check, money order, or credit card. Catalog wholesalers such as BrownCor International have established a large customer base by offering a wide range of competitively priced products, including office furniture, equipment and supplies, directional signs, packaging materials, and shelf and storage systems. These products can be conveniently ordered using toll-free telephone or fax systems.

Wholesale clubs are a growing phenomenon. These enterprises, which also serve retail customers under the same roof, are especially popular with small-business customers, civic and social organizations, and church groups. Wholesale club members pay an annual fee that entitles them to make tax-free purchases at lower-than-retail prices. As leaders such as Costco, Pace Warehouse, and Sam's Club enjoy rapid expansion, wholesale clubs are making major inroads into markets once dominated by older forms of wholesaling, such as office supply and institutional food wholesalers. They are also taking business away from certain types of retailers, such as supermarkets and tire dealers.

Sam's Club, a division of Wal-Mart, expanded rapidly by acquiring competitive wholesale clubs and opening new clubs in the United States and Mexico. Its clubs are large enough to incorporate departments selling fresh produce, meat, and bakery items.

AGENTS, BROKERS, AND COMMISSION MERCHANTS Almost 48,000 agent, broker, and commission merchant organizations operate at the wholesale level, making up approximately 11 percent of all wholesale establishments. As Exhibit 15–1 indicates, these wholesalers do not take title to the products they resell. They perform a limited number of marketing channel activities, emphasizing sales or purchases (see Exhibit 15–2). Since these wholesalers perform so few marketing channel functions, they must be very knowledgeable and build strong relationships with their customers and suppliers to generate income through commissions.

AGENTS Manufacturers' agents, also called manufacturers' representatives or reps, constitute the largest group in this wholesale merchant category. There are more than 29,000 manufacturers' agents in the country, all of which sell related but noncompeting product lines for manufacturers. For example, Ruddell and Associates, a San Francisco firm, sells Christmas ornaments, greeting cards, candles, books, calendars, and novelty items to gift stores, all furnished by different manufacturers. Manufacturers' agents frequently work by contract with the companies they represent; they usually have exclusive rights to represent each manufacturer within a specified geographic area.

Agent wholesalers, including auction houses, do not take title to the products they sell. Sothebys, auction house and appraisers since 1796, has offices and galleries worldwide, including New York, London, Brussels, and Stockholm.

Another type of agent is the auction company, of which there are approximately 1,300 in the United States. Auction companies, also called **auction houses,** sell merchandise at a given time and place to the highest bidder. They typically promote the sale of the merchandise through advertising that specifies the time, date, and location of the auction, along with a description of the merchandise to be sold and the auction rules.

Auction houses are a popular way to sell livestock, tobacco, used automobiles, and art and antiques. Famous art auctioneers are Sotheby's, Phillips, and Christie's, where works by noted artists sometimes fetch millions of dollars. Both the London-based Christie's and the New York–based Sotheby's are expanding into new international markets and searching for ways to further use the Internet for live auctions. Sotheby's has teamed up with Amazon.com to create an on-line auction service, which Sotheby's expects to be highly profitable despite lower commissions than can be earned from live auctions.[2] An **on-line auction company** uses a computer network, typically the Internet to bring buyers and sellers together. On-line auction companies typically charge a nominal listing fee and collect a 5 percent commission on goods sold.

The explosive growth of on-line auction sites will have a significant impact on wholesaling in the near future. Currently, on-line auction sites are dominated by person-to-person and business-to-person transactions. However, the business-to-business sector, including wholesaling, is showing signs of rapid growth. The leading on-line auction company, eBay, has invested in TradeOut.com, which runs an on-line auction house for excess business materials. TradeOut lists IBM, Caterpillar, and Abbott Labs among its customers, a sign that on-line auctions have proved to be a viable wholesale alternative to major companies. By 2002, on-line auctions will generate an estimated $53 billion in annual sales, with iMark, DoveBid, and OnSale, Inc., joining TradeOut as major on-line auction houses.[3]

On-line auctions can lower prices for business consumers as eager sellers compete for the business. Alabama-based Gulf Telephone bought $1 million worth of fiber-optic cable over a three-day period. A Gulf Telephone spokesperson estimated that the company saved 40 percent over its traditional method of buying through a broker and that normally it would have taken three weeks to buy the cable.[4]

Two other types of agents, import and export, specialize in international trade. **Import agents**—approximately 600 in the United States—find products in foreign countries to sell in their home countries. For example, cut flowers, available at lower cost outside the United States, are flown into the country daily. On a typical day, import agents arrange air cargo shipments from the Netherlands and South America to bring tulips, carnations, and roses to the United States. In many countries, it is extremely difficult (or even illegal) to try to sell products from another country without going through an import agent or similar intermediary.

On the other hand, **export agents** locate and develop markets abroad for products manufactured in their home countries. Basically, they function as manufacturers' agents in the home country and are paid commissions by the companies they represent. There are more than 1200 export agents in the United States. Export agents offer several advantages for companies seeking new markets, especially smaller companies. They offer exporters an opportunity to increase market exposure and sales volume with very little financial investment or risk.

BROKERS   Brokers are intermediaries that bring buyers and sellers together. They are paid a commission by either the buyer or the seller, depending on which party they represent in a given transaction. Unlike manufacturers' agents, brokers do not enter into contracts for extended periods with the parties they represent. Instead, they work on a transaction-by-transaction basis. There are approximately 8,600 wholesale broker firms in the United States, many of them in food and agricultural businesses.

COMMISSION MERCHANTS   Commission merchants provide a wider range of services than agents or brokers, often engaging in inventory management, physical distribution, and promotional activities, and offering credit and market feedback to the companies they represent. More than 6,700 commission merchants operate in the United States, primarily working to sell agricultural products for farmers.

MANUFACTURERS' SALES BRANCHES AND OFFICES   More than 29,000 manufacturer-owned wholesalers operate in the United States. Approximately 58 percent of these, or 17,000 are **manufacturers' sales branches,** which maintain inventory and perform a wide range of functions for the parent company. Manufacturers' sales branches handle delivery and act as an extension of the manufacturer to provide credit, market feedback, and promotional assistance.

Manufacturers' sales offices are the other significant type of producer-owned wholesaler, with more than 12,000 outlets in the United States. Sales offices do not maintain inventory, but they perform a limited range of functions, including assisting with sales and service, providing market feedback, and handling billing and collection of products sold.

Developments in Wholesaling

Three developments in wholesaling deserve special attention: the continuing struggle to grow, the globalization of wholesaling, and the increasing emphasis on developing relationships with others in the marketing channel.

WHOLESALERS FACE SLOW GROWTH   Wholesalers play an important role in the world economy, but growth is difficult to achieve. As power retailers such as Kroger, Office Depot, and Wal-Mart take over a larger share of the retail market, there has been an associated increase in retailers' buying directly from manufacturers, thus eliminating wholesalers.

Wholesalers' positions in markets served by retailers could grow even more precarious. Industry observers see power in the channel continuing to shift toward retailers. As shown in Exhibit 15–4, chains, wholesalers, and manufacturers generally agree that power is shifting in the grocery industry. Wholesalers are split on which way the power is shifting—35 percent say toward retailers, 65 percent say manufacturers. The point is that wholesalers are caught in a crossfire between retailers and manufacturers, with both sectors eager to improve their own profitability.

Other circumstances have threatened wholesalers, including a move to reduce overall health care costs. This puts pressure on a wide variety of wholesalers to reduce their costs; in addition, sales growth is decreasing as hospitals and other health

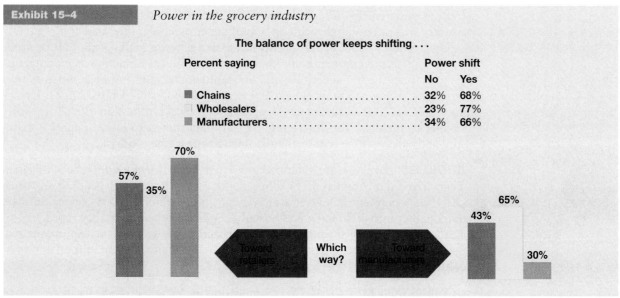

Exhibit 15–4   *Power in the grocery industry*

The balance of power keeps shifting . . .

Percent saying	Power shift	
	No	Yes
■ Chains	32%	68%
□ Wholesalers	23%	77%
■ Manufacturers.........................	34%	66%

57%
35%
70%
65%
43%
30%

Toward retailers   Which way?   Toward manufacturers

Source: "Trade Relations/ECR," *Progressive Grocer Annual Report,* April 1996, p. 21.

Thinking Critically

Brothers Office Supply is a traditional office-supply company, operating in a midwestern college town of 100,000. In addition to office supplies, Brothers sells high-quality office furniture. The company also sells calculators and electronic organizers, but it does not sell computers. Brothers' primary target market has been small- and medium-sized companies. Business was good until Sam's Club opened a store nearby last year. Rumor has it that Office Depot will open within the coming year.

- How can Brothers Office Supply compete with these lower-priced competitors?

care facilities are trying to reduce their usage of supplies and delaying major purchases more so than in the past. Travel agents have also felt the pressure, with airlines' cutting their commissions. Further, traditional wholesalers are facing more competition from transportation and distribution companies that are expanding the scope of their operations by offering services traditionally performed by wholesalers.

Wholesalers have taken several steps to combat tough market conditions. Some have grown through acquisition of other wholesalers; others, such as grocery wholesaler Supervalu, have expanded into retailing. Many others, including Fleming and Wetterau, are expanding into international markets and focusing on building customer value through stronger relationships with customers and suppliers.

GLOBALIZATION OF WHOLESALING   In response to tougher conditions in domestic markets, many American wholesalers have moved into international markets. Viking Office Products, a midsize catalog wholesaler, faced intense competition in the United States from Office Depot and Corporate Express. To continue growing, Viking expanded to nine European countries and Australia. Viking now does a majority of its business outside the United States and has been cited as a model for wholesaler expansion into international markets.[5]

As U.S. wholesalers become more prominent in international trade, they are following a pattern of development shown in Exhibit 15–5. This pattern suggests that international wholesalers play an important role in servicing the needs of a country with a simple economy. As the country's economy reaches the advanced stage, however, the role of conventional wholesalers becomes less important. Finally, when the country becomes part of a global economy, international wholesalers reemerge as an important element in the economic system. The United States, along with its primary trading partners, is part of a growing global economy, a factor that may help wholesalers maintain or expand their base of business.

RELATIONSHIPS IN WHOLESALING   Many wholesalers are turning to partnerships with suppliers and customers to strengthen their market positions. Exemplifying the partnership approach is the highly successful Ingram Micro Inc., a large wholesale distributor of computer products. Ingram has designed storefront Web sites for the value-added resellers in its national distribution network that buy through Ingram. These Web sites feature the VARs' own brand. Customers who access the VAR sites see Ingram's enormous inventory, wide range of services, and 24-hour delivery system. To the customer, the full scope of the local VAR's offering, as supplemented by Ingram, is readily apparent. The local VAR gets the credibility of a major corporation without the high overhead.[6]

Manufacturers are also finding that partnering with wholesalers can pay off. Square D, a major manufacturer of electrical products and industrial controls, generates 85 percent of its sales revenue through 2,000 North American wholesalers.

| **Exhibit 15–5** | *Cyclical wholesaling patterns by stages of economic development* |

Stages of Economic Development	Wholesaling Patterns
Simple economy	Dominance of international wholesalers (channels controlled by all-purpose wholesale merchants)
Expanding economy	Emergence of interregional wholesalers (regional specialization)
Maturing economy	Growth of specialized wholesalers (product-line and functional specialization)
Advanced economy	Decline of conventional wholesalers and regrouping by wholesalers (channels controlled by large-scale retailers and manufacturers)
Global economy	Reemergence of international wholesalers

Source: Mushtaq Luqmani, Donna Goehle, Zahir A. Quraeshi, and Ugur Yavas, "Tracing the Development of Wholesaling Thought and Practice," *Journal of Marketing Channels,* April 1991, p. 95. Reprinted with permission of The Hawworth Press, Inc.

Square D partners with its wholesalers, which are typically small and lacking big budgets, to provide training. The self-paced training program includes CD-ROMs, videos, and workbooks to teach sales skills and product knowledge to distributor personnel. The program is a huge success, with 96 percent of the participating wholesalers indicating that the training has had a positive impact on business. This pays off with increased sales for Square D, a company that sees its dealers as a competitive edge.[7]

Don Becker, owner of Becker Marketing Services, Inc., fully understands the importance of strong relationships with suppliers and customers: "It's only natural that there will be some friction and conflict in a marketing channel. As a wholesaler, my company is often caught in the middle, with the supplier pushing me in one direction and the customer pulling me in another. Our people have been able to establish strong relationships with most of our customers and suppliers. When it looks like we're heading for a major disagreement, I remind customers and suppliers that we are in this together, and that everybody has to benefit. Sometimes, I'll sacrifice, sometimes the customer compromises, and sometimes the supplier has to pitch in something extra—all for the good of the long-term relationship."

Logistics Management

Logistics management, as defined at the beginning of the chapter, deals with the movement of goods, services, and related information from point of origin to point of consumption. The importance of logistics management has increased in today's environment, marked by the use of speed as a competitive edge (to deliver customers' orders, for example), development of exciting new computer technologies, and increased realization that overall operating costs are extremely sensitive to the various costs of handling and holding inventory.

In progressive companies, logistics management has moved far beyond shipping and receiving to become a differentiating factor in marketing strategy. Logistics is instrumental in meeting such challenges as increasing responsiveness to customers, maintaining market position, stemming price erosion, and maintaining competitiveness in domestic and international markets. Consumers and business buyers are increasingly saying "I want it now!" More and more marketers are providing quality products at competitive prices. But that is not enough unless the product is available at the right time in the right place. As electronic commerce becomes more prevalent, marketers face the challenge of developing new logistics systems to deal directly with customers rather than always relying on wholesalers and traditional retail stores for distribution. Technology is a key element in meeting this challenge, as illustrated in "Using Technology: eToys Puts Work before Play."

Logistics management relies on a variety of methods for moving products and materials, including cargo planes and oceangoing supertankers. In some cases, simple means of transportation are used, such as with this Coca-Cola delivery van in China and this dogsled for newspaper delivery in North Dakota.

Exhibit 15-6	*Customer expectations of suppliers' logistics systems*

- Ease of inquiry and order entry
- Reliable, timely delivery information
- Accurate, undamaged, complete order fulfillment
- On-time delivery
- Error-free, especially with invoicing
- Responsive postsale support
- Claims handled with ease

Source: Compiled from Patrick M. Byrne, "Eight Forces for Global Change," *Travel and Distribution,* April 1992, pp. 53–54; and "Preston Trucking Company, Inc.: Customer Service Is a Process," *Customer Service Manager's Letter,* September 10, 1992, p. 6.

Importance of Logistics to Marketing

The drive to enhance customer satisfaction while simultaneously improving productivity and profitability has put logistics in the spotlight in the marketing efforts of many successful firms. Volvo GM Heavy Truck Corporation, for example, revamped its logistics system to solve a problem of excessive stockouts for repair parts. Dealers were losing business because they could not get parts on a timely basis. Volvo GM, working with FedEx logistics services, set up a distribution center in Memphis, Tennessee, to stock a full line of repair parts. Dealers now call toll-free, and repair customers are willing to pay premium prices for prompt service available via FedEx. Stockouts are down, dealer revenue is increasing, and Volvo GM has eliminated three warehouses, cutting its total inventory by 15 percent. Perhaps most important, both dealer and customer satisfaction has increased significantly.[8]

To keep customers satisfied, a logistics system should be easy to use and dependable and offer timely information. These attributes are detailed in Exhibit 15–6.

Key Activities in Logistics

Logistics includes five key functions: warehousing, materials handling, inventory control, order processing, and transporting raw materials and finished products from origin to destination. In the best logistics systems, these areas are carefully coordinated to gain customer satisfaction at an affordable cost.

Using Technology

eToys puts work before play

A Web pioneer in toy retailing, eToys has some formidable competitors. Toys "R" Us has a fast-growing Web site, and the always-competitive Amazon.com added toys to its site in early 1999. Logistics supported by technology will play a key role for eToys and other Web-based toy retailers in their fight for marketplace dominance. EToys has installed a sophisticated backup computer system to guard against network failure and increased its warehouse capacity 1,600 percent. In addition to its original 20,000-square-foot warehouse in California, eToys now has a 300,000-square-foot building in Utah, where inventory is stacked 60 feet high.

When a customer enters an order on the eToys Web site, a computer screen alerts employees as to which items should be put on a conveyor belt. A laser scanner matches the correct items to each customer's order. An automated process moves the customer's order to a packing station,

where the computer-generated packing slip is checked for accuracy before the order is sealed and shipped. The system is similar to the one used by L.L. Bean, a long-time catalog clothing retailer.

Despite its best efforts, eToys is not doing anything that competitors cannot duplicate. The company does have a head start on its competitors, however, as it was founded two years before most of them. Having been through the Christmas rush each year has given eToys a wealth of experience. With the hard work the company has always been noted for and the latest technology driving its systems, eToys should continue to be a major player in the toy market.

Source: Matt Krantz, "Stocking a Giant Toybox," *USA TODAY,* November 24, 1999, pp. B1–B2.

WAREHOUSING   Companies can choose private or public warehouses or distribution centers. *Private warehouses* are operated by the company using the warehouse. *Public warehouses* are for-hire facilities available to any business requiring storage or handling of goods. Public warehouses charge fees for storage and handling (receiving and moving goods out of storage).[9]

An interesting warehousing arrangement that captures the primary advantages of both private and public warehouses is used by Baldor Electric Company, an Arkansas-based manufacturer of motors, fans, and conveyor belts. Baldor stores the bulk of its inventory in 31 warehouses, each owned and operated by independent sales representatives. With this arrangement, Baldor avoids the expense of ownership but enjoys some measure of control, since the owners have an incentive to run the warehouses efficiently.[10]

Distribution centers are superwarehouses that serve a large geographic area. These automated warehouses do more than store products; they receive, process, and ship customer orders. Technological advances have allowed companies to save money and provide better service through distribution centers. Among the many companies using distribution centers are manufacturers such as Nike, Komatsu Dresser (heavy equipment), and Troll Associates (children's books), and retailers such as 50-Off Stores, Athlete's Foot, Williams-Sonoma, Wal-Mart, McCrory Stores, and General Motors.

With the increased volume of on-line buying, many companies are utilizing distribution centers that specialize in e-commerce. Fingerhut, originally a catalog retailer, now operates a distribution center in St. Cloud, Minnesota, to store products and fill orders for its own retail Web site and for other retailers, including Wal-Mart's on-line sales division. This distribution center receives up to 100 truckloads of merchandise daily, and processes as many as 30,000 items per hour for shipment. A dedicated fleet of trucks makes daily deliveries to local post offices across the nation, where items are mailed to the customer. This arrangement is far less expensive than paying postal rates for each package from St. Cloud to its final destination.[11]

MATERIALS HANDLING   Materials-handling activities include receiving, identifying, sorting, and storing products, and retrieving the goods for shipment. The use of technology is extremely important in this area of logistics. Bar coding is among the most noteworthy of the technological advances in materials handling, particularly in distribution centers. **Bar coding,** which allows a product to be identified by its computer-coded bar pattern, is used in a variety of logistics functions.

Lego Systems, Inc., sells its popular snap-together toys through major retailers such as Toys "R" Us, Target, and Kmart. To better serve these customers, Lego uses bar coding as the key element in its automated distribution center. Bar coding enables conveyors and automated warehouse trucks to move products into, around, and out of the building. It also generates advance shipping notices, inventory status reports, and customer invoices. Lego has improved shipping times, order accuracy, and fill rate (completeness orders) with its bar-code-driven distribution center while shipping 500,000 cases of product per month.[12]

A promising new technology called radio frequency identification (RFID) may eventually replace bar codes. Developed by Motorola, this technology allows the printing of radio antennas that can be affixed to products in place of a bar code. The advantage is that an entire container of diverse items could be scanned instantly at a distance, rather than up close, and one item at a time, as is the case with bar codes. The application of RFID to warehousing, order processing, and shipping seems inevitable now that costs for producing the radio tags are declining.[13]

Logistics includes warehousing, materials handling, inventory control, order processing, and transporting products to customers. This Unilever facility conducts all of the major logistical functions for retail customers in Nigeria.

INVENTORY CONTROL   Another key area of logistics is inventory control, which attempts to ensure adequate inventory to meet customer needs without incurring additional costs for carrying excess stock. Two such inventory control systems are in place in many industries: just-in-time and quick-response systems. Rarely used before 1990, these systems are now commonplace.

Just-in-time (JIT) inventory control systems apply primarily to the materials-handling side of logistics. These systems deliver raw materials, subassemblies, and component parts to manufacturers shortly before the scheduled manufacturing run that will consume the incoming shipment, thus the JIT label. Automobile manufacturers are among the most enthusiastic users of JIT systems, and suppliers often locate manufacturing or distribution facilities near automobile plants to provide prompt service at a reasonable cost.

Don Becker comments on the JIT process: "In the years I have had my own company, as a middleman (broker) selling to other middlemen (stocking wholesale distributors), it has been very important for us to select and sell our products to wholesale distributors that believe in buying in large quantities (of custom produced product), and providing JIT to their customers, the end users. By JIT, I mean the end user customer calling for an order and the wholesale distributor delivering the order in one hour, if necessary. By our linking ourselves to the right distributor, we have been able to build a large business satisfying hundreds of end user customers."

Quick-response (QR) inventory control systems are used by companies that provide retailers with finished goods. Quick-response systems are based on frequent but small orders, since inventory is restocked according to what has just been sold—yesterday, or even today in some systems. By melding strategy and technology, retailers such as Wal-Mart, Kmart, and Dillard's have matched up with vendors like Procter & Gamble, Gitano, and baby-clothes manufacturer Warren Featherstone to improve both responsiveness to the marketplace and productivity. Exhibit 15–7 describes the key steps required to implement a QR system.

Participants in quick-response systems must join together in a logistics partnership. A true partnership is necessary because buyers and sellers share sensitive information and must maintain constant communication. In fact, QR systems require so much information exchange that they take massive investments to implement. Bar coding and point-of-retail-sale scanning devices are needed. **Shipping container marking (SCM)** systems must be installed so tracking information can be fed into a computerized information system. This system is referred to as an **electronic data interchange (EDI)**.

EDIs are becoming increasingly popular for firms operating in global markets. For example, VF Corporation, makers of Lee and Wrangler jeans, developed an EDI system linking the company with retailers around the world. In Europe, VF is now printing bar codes on all garment hang tags and equipping customers there with handheld computers complete with built-in scanners and modems. This allows smaller retailers, as is typically the case in Europe, to participate in VF's EDI program even if they do not have a centralized computer system.[14] The basic goal remains the same: Have the product on the shelf when the customer is ready to buy.

Exhibit 15–7	*Key activities in quick-response systems*

- Retailers track sales and inventory for each item (stock-keeping unit).
- Automatic replenishment systems monitor stock to support smaller, more frequent shipments.
- Retailers assume responsibility for inventory carrying costs.
- Vendors commit to high level of service, stressing shipping accuracy and on-time delivery.
- Retailers share data with vendors to help plan production and commit to specific volume of purchases.
- Vendors mark shipping containers to speed delivery through distribution center to stores.

Source: Adapted from "Quick Response: What It Is; What It's Not," *Chain Store Age Executive,* March 1991, pp. B4, B5. Used by permission from *Chain Store Age Executive,* March 1991. Copyright Lebhar-Friedman, Inc., 425 Park Avenue, New York, NY 10022.

Exhibit 15–8	*Potential benefits of quick-response inventory control*

- Reduced negotiating costs for both buyer and seller.
- Increased responsiveness to marketplace needs.
- Stability of supply to the buyer and demand to the seller.
- Smoothing of production runs (fewer peaks and valleys).
- Decreased investment in inventory and storage space.
- Fewer out-of-stock occurrences.
- Higher levels of customer satisfaction.

Thinking Critically

Jean Robbins is a sales representative for Cribben Paper and Plastics Supply Company, a wholesaler to the garment manufacturing industry. One of Jean's customers is a large Arrow shirt manufacturing plant. The plant buys preprinted bags in which the shirts will be displayed and sold in retail stores. Cribben maintains a stock of the shirts in its warehouse and ships to Arrow on a JIT basis. Recently, the plant manager has threatened to buy directly from the bag manufacturer in truckload quantities, approximately 1,000 cases, or a month's supply. He claims he can get the bags at a 20 percent discount by buying direct.

- What should Jean do to keep her business with Arrow?

With a true partnership agreement, technology such as electronic data interchanges, and other resources such as personnel and training, QR systems offer the potential benefits shown in Exhibit 15–8.

Although JIT and QR systems offer impressive advantages, they can present drawbacks as well. Wal-Mart, for example, became frustrated with late and incomplete deliveries from Rubbermaid and removed Rubbermaid's Little Tikes toys from its shelves. Wal-Mart then stocked its shelves with toys from Fisher Price Inc. According to a Wal-Mart spokesperson, "The issue at Rubbermaid has never been about the products themselves. It has been about getting those products into the hands of consumers."[15] Wal-Mart's ordeal serves as a reminder that marketers are never completely insulated from inventory control problems, whatever the technological advances. Cautious marketers may shun quick-response systems in favor of carrying extra inventory, at a cost.

ORDER PROCESSING   Order-processing activities are critical to ensure that customers get what they order, when they want it, properly billed, and with appropriate service to support its use or installation. Accuracy and timeliness are key goals of order-entry processes. QR and JIT systems automatically handle order-processing activities. In other situations, order processing includes order entry, order handling, and scheduling for delivery. The term *order* here refers either to a customer's purchase order or to an order transmitted by a salesperson. Order handling entails procedures such as communicating the order to the shipping department or warehouse, clearing the order for shipping, or scheduling it for production. Eventually, the order is selected from stock, packaged, and scheduled for delivery. The order documentation becomes part of the customer's file of transactions with the seller. See Appendix A for mathematical calculations related to the determination of order quantities.

TRANSPORTING   The final logistics activity we consider in this chapter is transporting, which starts with selecting modes of transportation for delivery of products or materials. Shippers have five basic ways to move products and materials from one point to another—rail, truck, air, pipeline, and water transport—and each has its advantages and disadvantages. Logistics managers must assess each mode for costs, reliability, capacity, ability to deliver to customer receiving facilities, transit time, and special handling requirements such as refrigeration and temperature control, safety controls, and the capacity to deliver undamaged goods.

RAILROADS   Railroads carry approximately 40 percent of all U.S. freight, most of which is heavyweight, bulk cargoes. Railcars are the major shipping mode for coal, grain, and chemicals.[16]

Rail transport is fairly reliable but subject to interruption due to periodic labor disputes. These interruptions are usually short, and the federal government has often intervened to prevent massive shutdowns of rail service.

In recent years, the railroad industry has undergone a major consolidation, with several mergers between large rail companies. Burlington Northern merged with Santa Fe, Union Pacific purchased Southern Pacific, and Norfolk Southern and CSX jointly purchased Conrail. At present, Burlington Northern Santa Fe has proposed

McKesson Drug's distribution center in St. Louis, Missouri, features bar-code scanners for routing orders through an automated system that selects the items to be shipped, prints the customer invoice and sends the products to the shipping docks.

Creating and continuously enhancing customer value is a key focus of logistics companies. In this ad, Asiana Cargo promises customer satisfaction to its customers throughout the world.

a merger with Canadian National Railway, pending approval of government regulators.[17] Since this wave of mergers began in the late 1990s, shippers have complained about shipping delays and poor customer service from railroad companies. Some industry analysts predict that the mergers will not be good for shippers, as the rail companies may approach monopoly status and thus not feel a need to improve service. This remains to be seen, but purchasers of transportation services are monitoring the situation.[18]

TRUCKS   Trucks can deliver almost anywhere, particularly important for customers that lack a rail siding. Their fairly fast transit time makes trucks extremely effective and efficient for delivery to destinations within 500 miles. Although generally reliable, trucks can be negatively affected by inclement weather. Trucking has also been hampered at times by labor strikes, more so than have railroads.

Technology, especially in mobile communications and tracking equipment, plays an important role for successful trucking companies such as Roadway Express, J.B. Hunt, and M.S. Carriers. The human factor is important too. From a marketing point of view, the top priority for most trucking firms is recruiting, training, and retaining drivers. Considering the role that logistics can play in increasing customer satisfaction and profitability, trucking firms should emphasize hiring dependable drivers who can enhance customer relationships.

Given the increased demand for truck drivers due to more Internet shopping, it will not be easy for trucking firms to hire and retain good drivers. The boom in on-line shopping will increase traffic, which makes the truck driver's job that much more difficult, another reason it will be hard to attract drivers. Sharon Nichols of the Western Highway Institution says, "You're seeing a real change in how trucking companies set schedules and work drivers so that they are more frequently at home instead of being gone several weeks at a time."[19]

AIR FREIGHT   Air freight is tops in speed but highest in transportation cost. Sometimes air freight is an integral part of a company's operations, as with catalog businesses or firms marketing perishable items from faraway destinations, such as Maine lobster delivered to seafood restaurants in California. In other situations, a firm may justify the cost of air freight to take advantage of a marketing opportunity. For example, Sweden's Sandvik Coromant Company competes in the U.S. market for industrial metal-cutting tools and parts and always ships via air freight.

Both the relationship and global perspectives are illustrated with YFM Direct, a strategic alliance between Yellow Freight System and Royal Mass Group of The Netherlands. YFM provides truck delivery of trans-Atlantic shipments throughout North America and Western Europe.

Even though air freight is 10 times more expensive than shipping by boat, Coromant chooses that mode to compete more effectively. Further, the company points out that the higher cost of air freight is far less than the cost to both maintain inventories in the United States and pay inventory carrying costs during a two-week ocean transit.[20]

PIPELINES   Pipelines, such as the Alaska Pipeline, transport chemicals, gases, liquefied fossil fuels, and petroleum products. They offer fairly low-cost, reliable transportation to a limited number of destinations. Although the operation of a pipeline uses little energy, pipeline construction arouses environmental concerns about the land under which the line must travel.

WATER   Water transport is a good, low-cost alternative for large quantities of bulky products that must be shipped long distances. This includes bulk shipments of agricultural products, automobiles to and from foreign countries, and petroleum from distant oil-producing nations.

In the United States, water transport is available primarily in the eastern part of the country. The Mississippi River carries a large proportion of the country's water transport, and other rivers serve Cincinnati and Chicago. Rivers are also shipping routes for large amounts of cargo along the Gulf Coast between New Orleans and Houston, and between the Pacific Ocean and Portland, Oregon.

In the Great Lakes region, freighters carry huge shipments of raw materials—such as iron ore to Detroit—to service the automobile manufacturing industry. Other destinations served via the Great Lakes include Milwaukee, Buffalo, Chicago, and Toronto. The St. Lawrence Seaway, stretching from Lake Ontario to Montreal, can handle both barge traffic and oceangoing vessels. This project was jointly financed by the United States and Canada, with Canada providing approximately three-fourths of the necessary funds.

INTERMODAL   Although one mode of transportation may get the job done for a given shipper, **intermodal shipping** is often the choice. This involves the use of two or more modes of transportation. Loaded trailers, for example, may travel piggyback on railcars or in "stack trains."

North Carolina-based Spencer Gifts often uses intermodal shipping to service its 500 stores. It sometimes flies products in from Asia, holds them on the West Coast until needed, and then uses combinations of rail, air, and truck shipping to complete the job. Gold Kist uses intermodal shipping to get frozen chickens to Asia, and JC Penney has been converting to intermodal transportation. Some modes such as railcars can move products economically; others, such as trucks, can complete the delivery in a timely fashion. Industry analysts expect that intermodal shipping will increase in the future.[21]

Ethical and Legal Issues in Logistics

The legal environment for logistics is shaped by thousands of local, state, national, and international laws, tax codes, and tariff regulations that govern the movement of materials and products. The Interstate Commerce Commission, Federal Maritime Commission, and Department of Transportation are the major U.S. regulatory agencies.

One aspect of the legal environment that has affected logistics since the late 1970s is **deregulation**, which seeks to promote free competition among carriers. The pioneering laws affecting the transportation industry are the Airline Deregulation Act of 1978, the Staggers Rail Act of 1980, and the Motor Carrier Act of 1980.

A fierce debate raged prior to the passage of deregulation legislation. The proponents of deregulation predicted it would bring about a rather utopian marketplace, giving shipping customers more choices among competing shippers and, as a result, better service and lower shipping costs. Opponents predicted an economic disaster for both shippers and carriers, marked by mass exit of shippers from the marketplace and declining service levels to some communities.[22]

Two decades after deregulation, the effects are mixed. In the sluggish economic era of the 1980s and early 1990s, deregulation created a chaotic atmosphere and forced many companies into bankruptcy. For other companies, deregulation presented an opportunity to operate more efficiently. It allowed many to globalize their marketing efforts, improve customer service, and create business partnerships, all ingredients for success in the modern economy.

According to a survey of 453 shipping companies, deregulation has led to more ethical behavior in the trucking industry. Approximately 87 percent of the respondents believe that ethical standards of trucking company salespeople increased since the passage of the Motor Carrier Act.[23] A few comments from respondents indicate how ethical standards have evolved:

- The growth of coordinated shipping effort among previously decentralized corporate business units reduced local options to shift business for nonbusiness reasons, thus cutting incentives for unethical conduct.

- Most of the marginal operators that depended on questionable activities to gain business have been eliminated due to competition resulting from deregulation.

- Carriers are more image conscious and they realize there is more attention being paid to the carrier's service and performance than there was previously. "A slap on the back and a fifth under the table" no longer get the job done.

As suggested by the previous discussion, firms should view ethical considerations as an integral part of logistics management. Shippers and carriers face safety issues such as the handling of hazardous materials and the safety of oversized truck trains, trucking rigs pulling two 28-foot trailers. As the trucking industry grows faster than the highway infrastructure, traffic congestion is a growing concern for safety and air-quality reasons. Such issues raise ethical and legal questions.

Shippers have a responsibility to protect their employees and the general public from unsafe practices and materials. It is obvious that some materials such as explosives or corrosive chemicals would require special handling; but other less-obvious products might also pose dangers. Ignorance or negligence can be costly, as in the deadly 1996 Value Jet airlines crash, which was caused by improper shipping of oxygen tanks. The shipper of the oxygen tanks, Sabre Tech, has been found guilty of negligence and faces a multimillion-dollar fine. In addition, the FBI is conducting a criminal investigation. In another instance, the FAA has recommended that Bath & Body Works be fined $750,000 for shipping cosmetics that leaked inflammable ethyl alcohol aboard cargo flights.[24]

As logistics managers and wholesalers face the future, they must surely see the exciting prospect of playing an ever-increasing critical role in marketing. Change and adaptation will be necessary for survival of individual firms, and the management of information will play a key role for survivors. But wholesalers and logistics managers have tremendous technology at their disposal and can remain strong links in the chain that ultimately delivers customer satisfaction, profitability, and success.

Summary

1. **Understand wholesaling and describe the three basic categories of wholesalers.** An important part of marketing, wholesaling refers to the activities associated with selling products to purchasers that resell the products, use them to make another product, or use them to conduct business activities.

   The three basic categories of wholesalers are merchant wholesalers; agents, brokers, and commission merchants; and manufacturers' sales branches and offices. Some of these wholesalers provide a wide range of services, while others offer a narrow range of specialized services.

2. **Identify and discuss the roles of different types of full-service and limited-function wholesalers.** There are three main types of full-service wholesalers: general merchandise, limited-line, and specialty-line wholesalers. Of these, general merchandise wholesalers carry the broadest assortment of products and provide extensive services to their customers. These services may involve promotional assistance, inventory management and storage, physical distribution, market feedback, assumption of financial risk, and offering of credit.

   The two others carry progressively smaller and more-specialized assortments and provide different levels of service. Limited-function wholesalers include truck jobbers, drop shippers, cash-and-carry wholesalers, catalog wholesalers, and wholesale clubs. Of these, catalog wholesalers and wholesale clubs showed the most growth in recent years.

3. **Explain differences among the functions of agents, brokers, and commission merchants.** Agents, brokers, and commission merchants concentrate on making sales or purchases. They do not take title to the products they resell. These types of wholesalers must be quite knowledgeable in order to develop strong relationships with their customers and suppliers. They are paid a commission, a percentage of the value of each completed sale or purchase.

4. **Understand the differences between manufacturers' sales branches and offices.** Manufacturers' sales branches maintain inventory, handle delivery, and act as an extension of the manufacturer for a wide variety of services. Manufacturers' sales offices offer a narrower range of services, primarily because they do not maintain inventory.

5. **Appreciate how slow growth rates and globalization will affect wholesaling in the future.** Slow growth rates in most developed economies are putting a significant amount of pressure on wholesalers, which often face declining profit margins. As large retail chains gain more power and increase direct purchases from manufacturers, wholesalers can expect tough operating conditions to continue.

   To cope with slow growth, wholesalers often enter into relationships with manufacturers, customers, and in some cases, other wholesalers. Global markets offer more potential of growth for some wholesalers. As trade between nations becomes easier, wholesalers will have opportunities that have been difficult to realize in the past. Further, as developing economies grow, wholesalers that have the capability to conduct business outside the domestic marketplace can benefit by supplying them.

6. **Define logistics management and explain its key role in marketing.** Logistics management describes the planning, implementing, and controlling of the movement of goods, services, and related information from point of origin to point of consumption. In recent years, logistics management has grown more important in overall marketing strategies, because customer satisfaction is greatly affected by factors such as responsiveness to special shipping requirements and condition of delivered merchandise.

7. **Understand logistics activities, including warehousing, materials handling, inventory control, order processing, and transporting.** Some firms use independently owned public warehouses; others operate their own private warehouses or distribution centers. Materials-handling activities include receiving, identifying, sorting, storing, and retrieving goods for shipment. Inventory control is used to meet customer stock requirements without incurring excessive costs of carrying inventory. Just-in-time and quick-response systems are examples of inventory control programs used in a wide variety of industries.

   Order processing, triggered by the customer's purchase order, includes order entry, order handling, and delivery scheduling. The final part of logistics is transporting, which requires decisions about how to ship the product. Shippers may choose among rail, truck, air, pipeline, and water transport, or some combination of these modes.

8. **Discuss how some of the key ethical and legal issues affect logistics.** The continued push for deregulation in freight delivery is having both positive and negative effects. Ultimately, the aim of deregulation is to create more competition among carriers, which should lead to lower costs for shippers and perhaps lower prices for consumers.

These benefits are not possible, however, without some negative consequences. For example, smaller trucking firms are disappearing, creating job losses and the possibility of poorer service to smaller communities. There is also great concern over the environmental impact of transportation on the quality of air, water, and land.

Understanding Marketing Terms and Concepts

Thinking About Marketing

1. What is wholesaling? What are the three basic categories of wholesalers?

2. Review "Being Entrepreneurial: Ship Fast or Perish." Contrast the logistics activities of Chesapeake Bay Gourmet when it is filling QVC orders with what you think would take place when filling orders from local restaurants.

3. Which category of wholesalers does not take title to products they resell? What types of wholesalers fall into this category?

4. How do manufacturers' agents differ from manufacturers' branch offices?

5. In the grocery industry, are wholesalers becoming more or less powerful in the marketing channel?

6. Why has logistics management become more important in marketing during recent years?

7. Review "Using Technology: eToys Puts Work before Play." How can the technologies described in this insert improve customer satisfaction?

8. What are the key activities in logistics management?

9. What are the benefits of a quick-response inventory control system?

10. What are the five basic ways to move products and materials from one point to another? What are the key factors to be considered when choosing among these modes of transport?

Applying Marketing Skills

1. Assume you are the traffic manager for a large manufacturer of consumer goods. Your company is designing a quick-response delivery system for several large retail accounts. The system includes railcar delivery to distribution centers, direct-to-store truck delivery in a few isolated locations, and emergency service by air freight. What can you do to get feedback from your customers to aid in the design and implementation of the system?

2. During the Midwestern flood of 1993, grain shippers that normally use barges for transport had to resort to other modes of transportation. Which other modes would be logical for shipping grain? How would massive flooding affect these modes?

3. An established rock group is thinking about firing its agent of five years. The agent gets 10 percent of all concert revenues and 1 percent of all other band-related profits, including those from merchandising agreements,

commercial work, and paid TV appearances. The band members basically feel the agent is not really earning his seven-figure annual income. How would you advise the band? What factors should be considered before hiring

another agent or, alternatively, eliminating the agent in favor of a less-expensive salaried manager? [*Hint: this exercise pertains to the wholesaling portion of the chapter.*]

Using the www in Marketing

Activity One
Grainger, described in the chapter opener, is a leading business-to-business wholesaler. Review the Grainger Web site at http://www.grainger.com and answer these questions.

1. In which category of wholesalers does Grainger fit? Within the chosen category, which type is Grainger (refer to Exhibit 15–1).

2. What services does Grainger offer its international customers? Do these services add value to the tangible products sold by Grainger?

Activity Two
Many countries are signing on the Internet to facilitate trade with other countries. Check the Trade Commission of Mexico Web site at http://www.mexico-trade.com. This site lists more than

2,000 Mexican exporters classified by industry sector. There is also a comprehensive resource guide covering Mexico's economic, legal, and political systems.

1. Select three exporters that you think would be promising for national distribution in the United States, and give your reasoning. To complete this portion of the exercise, click on the "Directory of Exporters" link, then on the "Home Page Query" link.

2. Write a brief report on what exporters to Mexico should know about Mexico's economic, legal, and political systems. To complete this report, you can explore several links from the home page, including "Mexico Investment Guide," "Information on NAFTA," and "Legal Resources/Information on Mexico/Latin America."

Making Marketing Decisions
Case 15-1 Fleming Companies: A Giant in Trouble

The 1990s were a tough time for U.S. food wholesalers who serve a dying breed of customers: independent grocery stores. Most had to cut prices in an effort to keep their customers from buying direct from manufacturers, already a common practice among large chains. As prices eroded, so did profits. Fleming Companies, the second-largest food wholesaler with more than $15 billion in sales, experienced hard times along with the rest of the industry. In the past, Fleming had made a lot of its profits by pocketing manufacturers' promotional allowances and discounts rather than passing on the savings to grocers. As leading manufacturers such as Procter & Gamble shifted to everyday-low-pricing, they cut back on discounts and promotional allowances, which had a negative impact on wholesaler profits.

To chart the course for the future, Fleming management moved aggressively on two fronts: to increase the efficiency of its distribution system and to increase sales outside the United States. To increase the efficiency of the distribution system, Fleming announced in 1993 that it would reduce the number of its distribution centers from 33 to 25. Late in 1999, the company still had 32 distribution centers, and was backing off the commitment to reduce the total to 25. Critics acknowledge that it was a good idea to reduce the number of distribution centers, as it makes sense to drive as much volume as possible through each center. But they also argue that Fleming moved too far too fast, and

that the company did not get enough input from customers before moving to change the distribution system.

Another concern for Fleming is customer relationships, which have been strained in recent years. The attempt to revamp the distribution system has left some customers confused and unsure of what to expect from Fleming.

On a positive note, 80 percent of Fleming's customers are using its recently implemented business-to-business e-commerce application, VISIONET. VISIONET enables better communications regarding orders, promotions, and marketing bulletins among Fleming, its vendors, and its retailers. Fleming also announced a major supply contract with Kmart in 1999 and increased sales to key accounts Target Super Center and Raley's Supermarkets & Drug Centers.

Despite these gains, sales volume has declined since the mid-1990s, and Fleming must continue to focus on controlling its costs to once again become profitable. In the first three quarters of 1999, Fleming lost $40.9 million; on the other hand, Fleming reports that significant progress is being made toward achieving its Low Cost Pursuit program goals of reducing annual operating costs by $100 million. As part of this program, a reorganization announced late in 1999 will eliminate 700 jobs from the company's 39,000-person workforce. And, to offset a less-than-spectacular performance in the United States, Fleming has decided to increase its international operations. Mexico is a particularly attractive market, with an economy growing at a double-digit rate annually and with NAFTA helping to facilitate trade between the United States and Mexico. In addition to Mexico, Fleming is pushing growth initiatives in South and Central America, the Caribbean, Japan, and other Pacific Rim countries.

Questions

1. What are the primary factors leading to Fleming's problems?

2. Why did Fleming decide to move aggressively into markets outside the United States?

3. What obstacles might a U.S.-based wholesaler face in expanding into distant markets?

Sources: Wendy Zellner, "A Warehouse Full of Woes at Fleming," *Business Week,* September 23, 1996, pp. 100–102; information from Fleming's Web site at http://www.fleming.com; "Fleming Announces Strategic Organizational Plan to Maximize Efficiency and Enhance Customer Support," company news release, October 20, 1999; and Calmetta Y. Coleman, "Kmart Expands Pact with Supervalu, Fleming," *The Wall Street Journal,* July 22, 1999, p. B13.

Case 15-2 *Columbia Sportswear: A Logistics Leader*

Founded in 1938, Columbia Sportswear is one of the world's largest marketers of outdoor clothing and skiwear. The chairman of the board, 75-year-old Gert Boyle, is often featured in Columbia's off-beat, humorous TV ads. These ads typically show Ms. Boyle putting her son and company president through outdoor ordeals to test the durability of Columbia's products. Headquartered in Portland, Oregon, Columbia owns and operates sales offices in North America, Europe, and Asia. Columbia also owns and operates retail stores in the United States, Korea, Japan, and Australia.

As a global marketer heading into the twenty-first century, Columbia's distribution system was in need of an overhaul. The market for outdoor clothing was attracting new competitors, some of whom are among the leading marketers of brand-name clothing. Both Polo and Tommy Hilfiger had expanded their lines beyond dress and casual dress clothing to include parkas, windbreakers, and fleece products. Large retail chains were also gaining marketplace clout and demanding fast, accurate delivery from their suppliers. In response, Columbia enhanced and expanded its distribution center in Portland's Rivergate Industrial District; the purpose of the $34 million center is simple enough—to store incoming products from subcontractors in Asia until they are repackaged and shipped to customers in the United States.

At 643,000 square feet, the new facility, which opened in 1999, is more than double the size of the previous distribution center. It is so large that personnel use adult-sized tricycles to get around. Highly automated, the center needed no new employees beyond the 300 who operated the old center. According to Columbia president Tim Boyle, "More and more retailers are asking suppliers to fulfill customized orders, which takes more time, space, and resources. We are committed to offering these value-added services to our customers, and the Rivergate expansion will help us achieve that goal, while giving us the ability to lower our per-unit processing costs over time."

The new facility features five miles of conveyor belts that bring products to the order processing area, rather than employees' having to go to the product storage areas for retrieval. The facility utilizes the Rapid Unit Replenishment System, which allows storage of partial cases of products in a mechanized carousel. Partial cases can be retrieved quickly and forwarded to the packing area when less-than-a-case orders are filled. This can improve order efficiency and accuracy by up to 30 percent. The control system allows tracking of all processes and products throughout the distribution center, and computers and radio technologies allow the center to operate in a paperless environment.

With its new system in place, Columbia can now receive and process 1,500 cartons per hour, versus 5,000 per day with the old system. The company can now fulfill approximately 450 simultaneous orders, more than double the capacity with the previous system. Improvements in shipping now allow Columbia to ship 2,200 cartons per hour. These improvements have led to improved customer satisfaction and contributed to impressive sales growth. The director of distribution at Columbia comments: "Part of our growth can be tied to the fact that we provide excellent customer services. The combination of our highly trained, motivated, and dedicated people and our state-of-the-art facility will allow us to continue to provide our customers with the high level of service they have come to expect."

In the planning stages, Columbia considered outsourcing its distribution function to logistics specialists. By keeping the distribution center in-house, Columbia is able to provide specialized service for retail accounts. Some retailers want price tags added, and some want product shipped on hangers ready for display on retail racks. By owning its own facility, Columbia can control the process and provide customized services—a definite advantage in a highly competitive market.

Questions

1. What are the advantages of Columbia's automated system for retailers? For Columbia?

2. In this situation, Columbia spent $34 million for its new distribution center. What factors should be considered to determine whether or not the system is a good investment?

3. As technology evolves, what factors should Columbia consider before changing its current system?

Soruces: Jeff Manning, "Columbia Shifts into High Gear," *The Oregonian,* April 9, 1999, as printed at www.oregonianlive.com; and information from Columbia's Web site at www.columbia.com.

Chapter Sixteen

An Overview of Marketing Communications

After studying this chapter, you should be able to:

1 Discuss the objectives of marketing communications.

2 Understand the marketing communications mix and its role.

3 Explain the key elements of the marketing communications process.

4 Discuss the seven steps in the marketing communications planning process.

5 Demonstrate awareness of some of the key ethical and legal issues related to marketing communications.

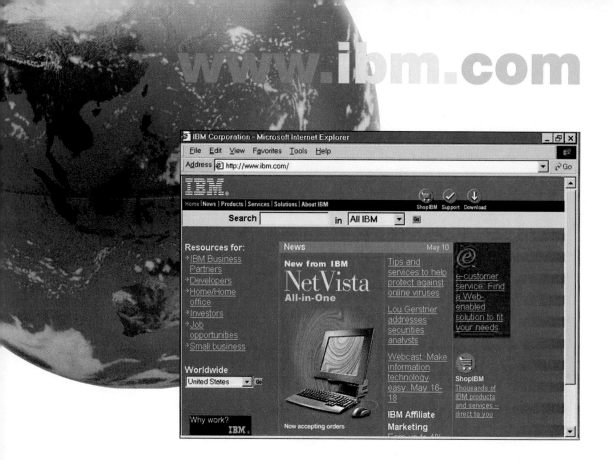

IBM has always been well-known for highly effective marketing communications. Its salespeople are among the best in the world, especially at handling large national and international clients. When the company rolled out its new business intelligence initiative, it used a classic integrated marketing communications campaign involving a wide variety of media and methods. Business intelligence (BI) involves gathering, managing, and analyzing a company's customers. IBM combines hardware, software, and consulting services to provide BI solutions for its clients.

The goal of IBM's integrated effort was to establish the company as a leader in the BI field. Implementing the communications program required several months' work by 170 IBM employees, along with creative support from ad agency Ogilvy & Mather Worldwide. IBM clients L.L. Bean, Kiwi Brands, and the National Basketball Association were also involved in developing the campaign.

To make a big impression in the market, IBM combined advertising, direct mail, public relations, Web advertising, and personal selling. Print ads were run in *The Wall Street Journal, USA Today,* and *Business Week.* Ads were also placed in trade publications for the banking, retail, and insurance industries. Radio ads were aired in the top 10 markets in North America, and TV commercials ran during prime time. Direct mail was sent to 250,000 executives in six industries. Sales representatives followed up a week later on 10,000 key executives. IBM's Web site introduced a page devoted to BI, and banner ads were run on 40 target-industry Web sites and several related information-technology sites. Public relations efforts involving IBM employees were targeted to industry analysts and industry publications.

The IBM business intelligence integrated marketing communications campaign began just a few months before this book went to press, and it will take some time to determine its ultimate effectiveness. Evidence of its initial effectiveness, however, can be seen on IBM's Web site, where more than 100 BI success stories are posted. Satisfied clients include Safeway, McDonald's Canada, Bell Atlantic, MCI, Domino's Pizza, and Cadbury Chocolates. Early signs thus indicate that IBM is getting the word out, then backing it up with excellent performance. **Sources:** Chad Kaydo, "Big Blue's Media Blitz," *Sales & Marketing Management,* December 1999, p. 80; and IBM's Web site at www.ibm.com, January 31, 2000.

Marketing communications, sometimes referred to as *promotion,* involve marketer-initiated techniques directed to target audiences in an attempt to influence attitudes and behaviors. The IBM example mentions several forms of marketing communications, reminding us that different techniques are appropriate in different situations. It also illustrates the importance of careful planning prior to implementing a major marketing communications effort. As is increasingly the case in contemporary marketing, IBM used the Web in conjunction with traditional media, public relations, and salespeople to get its message to target audiences. This example also reinforces the importance of the relationship perspective with IBM's collaboration with key customers and its advertising agency in the development of the comprehensive communications program. Further, it is important to note that a solid marketing communications program may be in place for a significant amount of time before the payoff of increased sales is realized. IBM's communications program for its business intelligence program is off to a good start, but only time will tell if it is successful.

Marketers may use one or all of several marketing communications methods. There are five major categories: advertising, public relations, sales promotion, personal selling, and direct marketing communications. Together they constitute the **marketing communications mix,** often referred to as the *promotional mix.*

This chapter explores these five major categories, as well as the major objectives of marketing communications and the way the communications process works and is implemented. We discuss how the marketing environment, including ethical and legal concerns, can influence the marketing communications effort.

The Role of Marketing Communications

The ultimate goal of marketing communications is to reach some audience to affect its behavior. There may be intermediate steps on the path to that goal, such as developing favorable consumer attitudes. Exhibit 16–1 lays out the three major objectives of marketing communications: to inform, to persuade, or to remind the marketer's audience.

Informing

Informing present or potential customers about a product is an important marketing communications function. Any time a new product is launched and promoted, marketing communications serve to inform audience members (the target market) about it. For example, RCA used marketing public relations to inform the market about Christina Aguilera's new album prior to its release. RCA hired a team to hit sites popular with teenagers, such as www.gurl.com and www.bolt.com, to chat about the album. As the release date neared, RCA supported the album with advertising targeted to retailers and ultimate consumers. The album debuted at number one on the charts.[1]

Marketing communications also serves an important role when new companies are founded and are seeking to build brand awareness. Advertising in the 2000 NFL Super Bowl, the major advertising event of the year, was dominated by recently founded electronic commerce or dot com companies. It is estimated that start-up dot com companies routinely spend as much as 90 percent of the money they raise in public offerings on advertising and marketing. The importance of informing the

Exhibit 16–1

The marketing communications mix

One major objective of marketing communications is to inform both customers and potential customers. The United States Mint used this print ad to announce the availability of the one-dollar coin.

Marketing communications are also used to remind consumers and reinforce positive perceptions. This ad reminds millions of consumers of America Online's status as the world's leading internet service provider.

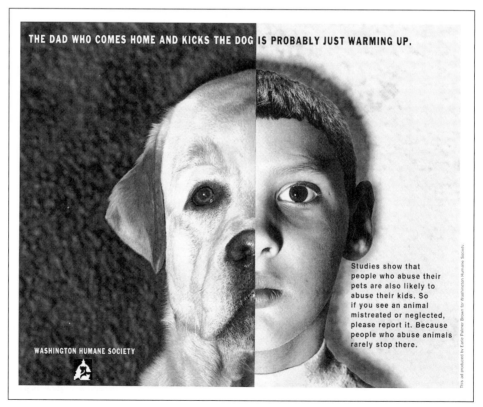

Marketing communications can be used to persuade others to take action. In this case, the Washington Humane Society attempts to persuade concerned citizens to report abused or neglected animals by pointing out a correlation between animal abuse and child abuse.

Dorothy Brazil Clark
Ralston Purina
Director, Market Research and
Strategic Planning

Dorothy Brazil Clark, Director, Market Research and Strategic Planning, at Ralston Purina in St. Louis is well aware of the need to maintain close relationships with customers at a reasonable cost. Her previous experience includes business development and sales with Norden Laboratories, a subsidiary of SmithKline Beecham. Dorothy earned her B.A. degree from the University of Iowa, and an MBA from the University of Missouri.

"Competitive leadership has never been more challenging than in today's marketplace. Those who succeed in leading their respective fields will win the battle by directly linking the message (the objective), medium (all marketing communications components) and the target (minds of the intended consumers who must be receptive to the message), all at a cost compatible with bottom line objectives."

public in a timely fashion is reinforced by a Priceline.com executive who states, "A lot of companies are saying 'We have to make it big, fast, or we're not going to make it at all.' "[2]

Persuading

Marketing communications may concentrate on persuading customers to purchase a firm's market offering. For instance, producers of the Broadway rock musical *Footloose* used marketing communications to overcome stinging critical reviews such as "flavorless marshmallow" and "theatrical nowheresville." To counter the negative publicity, an advertising campaign, developed specifically for MTV, was launched and consequently filled the theater, generating $500,000 in weekly sales.[3]

Persuasive advertising is also used by nonprofit and government organizations. For example, Canada's health ministry has run ads to persuade cigarette smokers to quit. The ad copy is blunt, with messages such as "Smoking can kill you" and "Cigarettes cause mouth cancer." Focus groups of smokers say that such are helpful in persuading them to quit.[4]

Reminding

When consumers are aware of a firm's brand and have positive attitudes toward it, a reminding objective may be appropriate. Although consumers may be sold on the product, they are still vulnerable to competitors' appeals. Marketing communications can remind consumers of a product's benefits and reassure them they are making the right choice. CDnow uses **permission marketing** to remind its on-line customers of new audio and video releases and special promotions. Permission marketing occurs when the customer grants the marketer permission to send regular updates of interest to the consumer. E-mail is typically used for permission marketing, but regular mail or a fax could also be employed for this purpose.

Personal selling is another way to remind buyers of the value of continuing the relationship and making repeat purchases. Among the best at using personal selling for all three objectives of marketing communications, including reminding, are Dell Computer, GE Capital, Pfizer, Xerox, America Online, and General Mills.[5]

The Marketing Communications Mix

To inform, persuade, and remind targeted consumers effectively, marketers rely on one or more of the five major elements of the marketing communications mix. We discuss these briefly here and in more detail in subsequent chapters.

Advertising

Advertising is nonpersonal, paid for by an identified sponsor, and disseminated through mass channels of communication to promote the adoption of goods, services, persons, or ideas. Marketers use media such as television, radio, outdoor signage, magazines, newspapers, and the Internet to advertise. Its ability to reach a mass audience often makes advertising an efficient method for communicating with a large target market.

Traditionally, advertising has been the most recognized form of marketing communications largely because of its high visibility. We cannot escape the advertising that surrounds us in our daily lives. This high visibility is achieved through enormous expenditures. Advertising expenditures are growing at less than 5 percent a year worldwide. The fastest-growing advertising markets include China, Taiwan, New Zealand, Australia, Italy, and Canada.[6] Advertising via the Internet is growing rapidly, with leading advertisers including Microsoft, IBM, Compaq Computer, General Motors, and Excite.[7] Some of the most creative advertising is being done by Internet marketers, as illustrated in "Being Entrepreneurial: Start-ups Show Creative Side."

This ad illustrates the combination of sales promotion and advertising. The sales promotion message (instant prizes) is part of a magazine ad for Gillette Mach3 razors.

Public Relations

The **public relations** function identifies, establishes, and maintains mutually beneficial relationships between an organization and the various publics on which its success or failure depends.[8] Employees, customers, stockholders, community members, and the government are examples of various publics for many firms.

A key aspect of public relations is publicity. **Publicity** refers to non-paid-for communications about the company or product that appear in some media form, often the news media. Since the firm cannot completely control the message being disseminated, publicity may generate more believable messages than paid-for communications such as advertising. Many firms hire outside agencies to handle their public relations and publicity requirements.

Sales Promotion

Sales promotion includes communications activities that provide extra value or incentives to ultimate consumers, wholesalers, retailers, or other organizational customers and that can stimulate im-

Being Entrepreneurial

Start-ups show creative side

Ad-industry veterans still fondly recall the creative revolution that occurred in the 1960s. Now they claim that advertising is undergoing its second revolution, led by start-up Internet marketers. In the 1960s, the ad revolution was accompanied by social unrest and sexual liberation. The current revolution is fueled by the booming information-technology economy, which is also having a noticeable cultural impact.

Several start-up companies grabbed their share of the limelight with unusual advertising. Monster.com, a job-finding service, used solemn-faced children declaring their intention to spend their careers sucking up to the boss in dead-end, boring jobs. Outpost.com features an executive who fires gerbils from a cannon in an attempt to get

viewers to remember his company's name. E-Trade shows a stockbroker making cold calls trying to drum up business, then asks, "If your broker is so good, why does he still have to work for a living?"

The new wave of advertising offers entertainment value to some television viewers, and ad agencies across the country are enjoying the opportunity to be creative with a whole new set of clients. One industry observer sums it up this way: "I think people are getting away from commercials that are obscure and so subtle that nobody gets it and going back to the crazy, exaggerated nonsense that makes advertising fun and sells products."

Source: Greg Farrell, "Wacky Internet Ads Ride Creative Wave," *USA Today,* June 9, 1999, pp. 1–2B.

mediate sales.[9] Sales promotion attempts to stimulate product interest, trial, or purchase. Coupons, samples, premiums, point-of-purchase displays, sweepstakes, contests, rebates, and trade show exhibits are all examples of sales promotion.

Consumer sales promotion is directed at ultimate users of the product or service; *trade sales promotion* is directed at retailers, wholesalers, or other business buyers. Marketers spend comparable amounts of money for consumer sales promotion and advertising. Expenditures for trade sales promotion are significantly higher than for either advertising or consumer trade promotion (see Exhibit 16–2). This may be surprising to most people, for the behind-the-scenes promotion activities to business buyers are not easily observable outside an industry.

Dorothy Brazil Clark points out the need to understand marketing communications as an integrated process focused on targeted consumers: "The requisite for good marketing communications in a world that demands end-to-end service is a total understanding of both communicator and the organizations involved as well as the place each occupies during all phases of the process. Successful management of the communication process then demands complete mastery of the process and its components, synchronization between existing components and a dismantling of the 'mass market' concept in favor of one emphasizing a family of segmented consumer groups."

Marketers typically use sales promotion in conjunction with other marketing communications elements. For example, sales promotion programs such as sweepstakes or contests may use advertising to spread the word to mass consumer markets. Marketers also frequently link sales promotion with many forms of direct marketing, especially direct mail, or include it as part of a trade show (product giveaways, merchandise imprinted with ad messages or logos).

Unlike some other forms of marketing communications, sales promotion is usually intended to produce immediate results. This probably explains why marketers have increasingly turned to sales promotion to improve sales volume and market share in a wide variety of highly competitive markets.

Professional salespeople play an important role in the marketing communications effort for complex products. Shown is a marketing representative for Health Images, Inc., who educates physicians on the use of MRI (magnetic resonance imaging) equipment.

Personal Selling

Personal selling involves interpersonal communications between a seller and a buyer to satisfy buyer needs to the mutual benefit of both parties. The personal nature of this method distinguishes it from nonpersonal forms of marketing communication. Personal selling

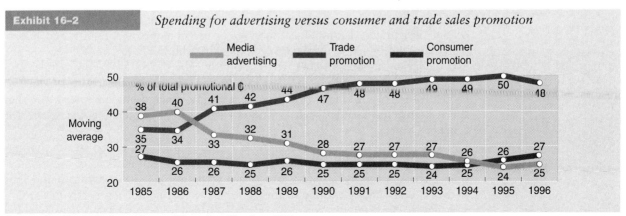

| Exhibit 16–2 | *Spending for advertising versus consumer and trade sales promotion* |

Source: Cox Direct 20th Annual Survey of Promotional Practices, 1998.

Thinking Critically

Advertising, personal selling, sales promotion, public relations, and direct marketing can be used singularly or in combinations to achieve marketing communications objectives. For each of the following situations, specify which marketing communications tools would be most appropriate.

- Attempting to sell a foreign government a dozen cargo planes.
- Raising money to support academic programs at your college or university.
- Informing an existing set of customers about a product modification.
- Trying to convince a local Chevrolet dealer to donate a vehicle to be used as grand prize in a drawing to benefit United Way.
- Informing the general public of a product recall.

allows immediate feedback, enabling a message to be tailored to fit the buyer's individual needs. Its dynamic nature and flexibility make personal selling an excellent communications medium for establishing and nurturing customer relationships.

Personal selling is an important element of marketing communications when the product is complex. The sale of medical equipment to hospitals and physicians would be practically impossible without well-informed salespeople who can provide the necessary details to prospective buyers.

Direct Marketing Communications

Direct marketing communications is a process of communicating directly with target customers to encourage response by telephone, mail, electronic means, or personal visit. Popular methods of direct marketing communications include direct mail, telemarketing, direct-response broadcast advertising, on-line computer shopping services, cable television shopping networks, infomercials, and in some instances, outdoor advertising.

Direct marketing communications are used by all types of marketers, including retailers, wholesalers, manufacturers, and service providers. A fast-growing segment of the marketing communications field, direct marketing often uses precise means of identifying members of a target audience and compiling customer/prospect databases with postal addresses, telephone numbers, account numbers, e-mail addresses or fax numbers to allow access to the buyers.

Integrated Marketing Communications

Today's highly competitive business environment puts considerable pressure on marketing communications to reach and spur busy, value-conscious consumers to buy. As a result, marketers are increasingly turning to **integrated marketing communications (IMC),** which is the strategic integration of multiple means of communicating with target markets to form a comprehensive, consistent message. According to an expert in the field, this involves using new media along with more established forms of marketing communications: " . . . My cry is to integrate, not isolate. Yes, we need to explore and develop the new media and new approaches, but we need to do that within the context of what exists and what is likely to evolve. We need to integrate the new media with the old, melding e-commerce and across-the-counter commerce."[10]

In one sense, marketing communications are integrated horizontally, or across various methods of communications. For example, the advertising message must be consistent with the personal selling message. But a campaign can also be integrated vertically, extending from the marketer down through the marketing channel. For example, salespeople are often dispatched to retailers to arrange for adequate inventory levels and to assist in setting up in-store displays.

Another aspect of integrated marketing communications is that it considers any contact with a brand, product, or company to be part of marketing communications. As a result of integrated marketing communications, consumers could see a product in a movie, a commercial message or brand name on a T-shirt, and a company name prominently displayed on a hot-air balloon. Television viewers see the cast of "Friends" sipping Diet Coke and moviegoers see BMW automobiles and motorcycles in James Bond movies. In addition, we notice that Dallas Cowboys football star Troy Aikman wears Logo brand hats when doing interviews and that sports arenas have names such as United Center, Pepsi Center, GM Place, and Air Canada Center.

These sorts of marketing communications are sometimes called **stealth marketing,** because their intent is not as blatant as some forms of marketing communications such as advertising. Such efforts are actually publicity generators and thus part of the marketing communications mix as we define it. These activities are increasing as marketers try to find new ways to reach audiences that may have be-

Sponsorship programs can be an important element of integrated marketing communications. In this ad, General Motors, an Olympics sponsor, suggests that its expertise was valuable for the Olympics and could benefit business customers.

Credibility is critical in marketing communications. Soccer phenom Mia Hamm is a highly credible presenter of marketing communications messages for Nike.

come jaded by too much advertising, sales promotion, and other traditional methods of communicating with a target audience.

Sponsorship programs, an investment in causes and events to support overall corporate objectives and marketing objectives,[11] may be an important part of an integrated marketing communications strategy. Sponsors may back a single event, such as the Olympics or the World Series, or multiple events, as Buick does with golf tournaments on the PGA tour. Sponsorships are also used quite effectively by small businesses.

Coca-Cola and Procter & Gamble are masters at integrating their marketing communications efforts. Both are well-known for consumer advertising. Their sales promotion efforts, in the form of coupons, sweepstakes, and contests are also familiar to millions of consumers. The average consumer, however, does not see their highly trained salespeople who call on wholesalers and retailers. Both P&G and Coke have used direct marketing effectively. Like many others, Coca-Cola and P&G also manage sophisticated public relations and publicity efforts to support their marketing communications campaigns.

The Marketing Communications Process

Communication is the process of establishing shared meaning, exchanging ideas, or passing information between a source and a receiver. Exhibit 16–3 shows how the marketing communications process works. Note that the intended target for any basic communication is the **receiver.** This could be a purchasing agent listening to a sales presentation, a consumer reading a magazine ad, or another of the various publics served by the marketer, such as stockholders or government officials.

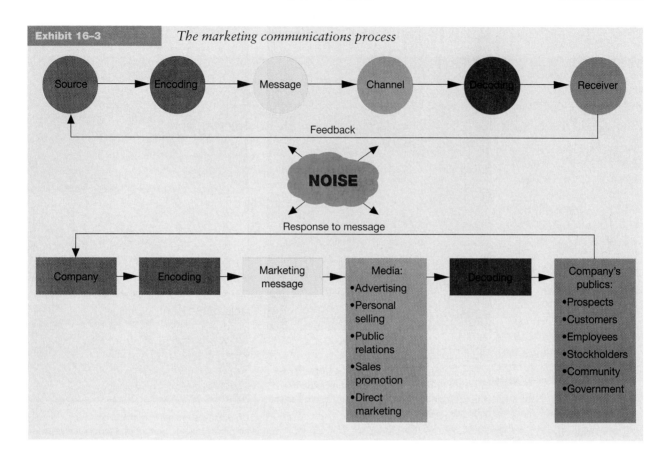

Exhibit 16–3 *The marketing communications process*

Sources of Marketing Communications

The marketer is the **source,** or message sender of marketing communications. Two types of sources normally play a role in marketing communications, the message sponsor and the message presenter. The **message sponsor** is typically the organization attempting to market its goods, services, or ideas. The **message presenter,** perhaps a salesperson, actor, or television personality, actually delivers the message. For instance, Nike is a message sponsor, whereas Tiger Woods is one of Nike's message presenters.

Communications Messages

The source sends a message through a channel to a receiver. The **marketing communications message** represents what the company is trying to convey about its products. A **message channel** is the means by which the message is conveyed. In advertising, message channels are often referred to as *media,* a reference to advertising vehicles such as newspapers, television, magazines, outdoor, and radio. Mail, telephones, audio- and videocassettes, salespeople, and computer networks and disks are also examples of message channels.

Encoding and Decoding

The source does the **encoding** by choosing the words, pictures, and other symbols used to transmit the intended message. **Decoding** is the process by which the receiver deciphers the meaning of the words, pictures, and other symbols used in the message. When the message is not decoded as the source intended, a lack of communication results. For example, a consumer may find the copy in a magazine ad too technical and thus not understand the message.

Feedback

Feedback is the part of the receiver's response that is communicated to the sender. Depending on the nature of the communication, the sender can assess feedback to judge the effectiveness of the communication. Personal selling and many forms of sales promotion offer relatively quick feedback. Feedback is not so immediate for mass advertising and public relations, and only subsequent sales figures or marketing research will indicate the effectiveness of the message.

Noise

Noise is any distraction or distortion during the communication process that prevents the message from being effectively communicated. Competing messages and interruptions, such as a telephone call during a salesperson's sales presentation, constitute noise. Noise can even come from within the message itself, sometimes at quite an expense. For example, consumer feedback indicated excessive noise in Calvin Klein ads, especially for Klein fragrances cKbe and cKone. Said one observer: "Can we please stop portraying our youth as bulimic heroin addicts?" The Calvin Klein ads were singled out by Ad Track, *USA Today*'s poll on the popularity and effectiveness of national advertising campaigns, as some of the worst advertising of the year.[12]

Marketing Communications Planning
There are seven key tasks in **marketing communications planning:** marketing plan review; situation analysis; communications process analysis; budget development; program development; integration and implementation of the plan; and monitoring, evaluating, and controlling the marketing communications program. These are diagrammed in Exhibit 16–4.

Marketing Plan Review

Marketing communications planning draws heavily on the firm's overall marketing strategy and marketing objectives. A review of the marketing plan is thus a logical place to start the process of marketing communications planning. The marketing plan often contains detailed information that is useful for marketing communications planning.

Situation Analysis

An analysis of the marketing communications situation considers how internal factors, such as the firm's capabilities and constraints, and other marketing mix variables will affect marketing communications. The situation analysis is also concerned with the marketing environment now and in the future. For example, competitive, economic, and social factors affect marketing communications. The political and legal environments, discussed later in this chapter, are also addressed in the situation analysis.

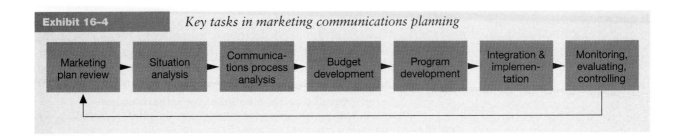

Exhibit 16–4   *Key tasks in marketing communications planning*

Marketing plan review → Situation analysis → Communications process analysis → Budget development → Program development → Integration & implementation → Monitoring, evaluating, controlling

THE COMPETITIVE ENVIRONMENT   Marketing communications are often used to foil the actions of competitors. For example, competitive strategy affected marketing communications for OAO Pikra, a soft-drink manufacturer in the Siberian region of Russia. Coke and Pepsi had been the top sellers until Pikra introduced Crazy Cola, a Coke parody. Coke and Pepsi had been winning the battle with Crazy Cola with advertising and in-store merchandising until Pikra introduced a new ad campaign targeting the youth market. One particularly popular ad featured teens in hip retro clothing dancing in a disco. Now, according to the company's president, "Coke may be the world leader, but we're number one here."[13]

THE ECONOMIC ENVIRONMENT   Budgets for marketing communications often decline in hard economic times, yet some well-known firms have benefited from increasing their marketing communications expenditures under adverse economic conditions. Such continuous marketing communications help to maintain market leadership. Campbell's, Coca-Cola, Ivory, Kellogg's, Kodak, Lipton, and Wrigley have all maintained an unwavering commitment to promoting their brands in good and bad times, and each is a leader in its market category.

The economic environment may cause firms to reconsider which components of the marketing communications mix to emphasize. One significant change in the economic environment is that electronic commerce has become a much more important part of the U.S. economy in recent years. As a result, major marketing organizations such as Procter & Gamble, Walt Disney, Philip Morris, AT&T, and Johnson & Johnson will increase their proportion of spending on Internet advertising. A survey of 1,800 corporate executives indicates that in the three-year period of 2000–2003, a higher percentage of marketing communications budgets will be dedicated to Internet advertising, direct mail advertising, and sales promotion.[14]

THE SOCIAL ENVIRONMENT   Communications messages often reflect social trends. For instance, many marketers communicate supposed environmental benefits of their products. Similarly, consumer interest in health and fitness has led marketers to promote the healthful aspects of many products. Social conditions can also affect a firm's marketing communications. For example, Timberland addressed racism in an ad campaign for its boots. The ad copy featured the statement "Give Racism the Boot" and was run in Europe and the United States to speak out against hatred and intolerance on a global basis. Proceeds from the sale of posters, T-shirts, and buttons were used to support community service programs.

Keeping current with behavioral changes in the target market is an important requirement of situation analysis. For example, the traditional target market for household products such as groceries, cleaning supplies, and health and beauty aids has changed dramatically. With 70 percent of women holding jobs outside the home, men have become extremely active in this market. Research by Yankelovich, a major consumer research firm, reveals that 74 percent of men shop for groceries on a regular basis. Over half of male grocery shoppers said they found grocery shopping a frustrating and time-consuming experience.[15] Marketing communications can help reduce the frustration for both male and female shoppers. For example, in-store displays and sampling programs can be made user-friendly and help buyers make good purchase decisions. In addition, reminder services can be implemented, not only for gifts, but for groceries and personal necessities. Ads can inform the buyer of new products, alternative uses for products, and special prices.

We have dozens of less painful ways to show your Mom you care.

She owns a special place in your heart. And perhaps there's no better way to show her than with roses from Bailey's Nursery. Why not get Mom a potted rose plant. It's the permanent way to show your mom how much you care. There, that didn't hurt a bit. Phone orders, call 348-6353, or stop by 3415 Boggy Creek Road. *Bailey's Nursery*

Marketers recognize that women are buying products traditionally bought by men and vice versa. This ad uses a humorous approach to encourage male patronage of a florist shop.

Dorothy Brazil Clark is mindful of the importance of approaching diverse markets with appropriately tailored marketing communications: "Those aspiring to be market leaders must successfully forge new communication pathways focused on and mirroring the diversity and pluralism reflected in the collective social, economic, political, and technological impact on both domestic and international environments. These customized pathways can serve as the integrating forces that connect the organization with its intended audiences."

MARKETING MIX CONSIDERATIONS Compatibility of product, price, and channel characteristics with marketing communications is essential. The physical characteristics of a product or product package (color, size, shape, texture, ingredients) and its brand name communicate a lot to consumers. For instance, the bright colors on the Cheer detergent package imply it is powerful enough to get clothes bright and clean without fading them. Brand names such as Arrid Extra Dry, Finesse, Ivory, Total, Huggies, Sheer Energy, and Angel Soft convey certain messages about the products.

The product's price also conveys a message. Consumers often use price as an indicator of product quality. The $15,900 price tag on a Rolex President watch indicates more than the cost of the watch; it also conveys a message of quality and prestige. Although both Rolex and Timex watches keep good time, each conveys a different message with its pricing strategy, and each has built an image consistent with its price.

The chosen marketing channel also communicates to the consumer. For instance, Wal-Mart and Neiman-Marcus each conveys a different message. Wal-Mart stands for everyday low prices—products that are very expensive and of the finest quality are typically not found there. Consumers generally assume items sold at Neiman-Marcus are of high quality because of the store's well-established image. The prices of products at Neiman-Marcus help convey that message.

Communications Process Analysis

In this step, marketers analyze the various elements of the basic communications model shown in Exhibit 16–4. Objectives for marketing communications are also set in this part of the planning process.

APPLYING THE BASIC COMMUNICATIONS MODEL Marketers try to understand the decoding processes of potential receivers of marketing communications in order to create effective messages and select appropriate message channels. For example, will the consumer need detailed information from a well-trained salesperson to make a favorable decision? Or can simple point-of-sale displays achieve the desired results?

SETTING MARKETING COMMUNICATIONS OBJECTIVES Exhibit 16–5 lists several general marketing communications objectives. Like all business objectives, a marketing communications objective should be stated as specifically as possible to help gauge the effectiveness of marketing communications efforts. It is also necessary to set objectives for each marketing communications effort, assuming separate programs are developed for individual products, product lines, geographic areas, customer groups, or different time periods. For example, greeting-card marketer Hallmark might run separate sales promotion programs to correspond with major occasions such as Christmas, Mother's Day, and Halloween.

Budget Development

Determining the optimal amount to spend on marketing communications involves considerable subjective judgment. Further, it is hard to measure precise results achieved by most forms of marketing communications. For example, some corporations spend more than $100,000 per year on rent, food, and drink for skyboxes at National Football League stadiums. Selected customers are invited to the games, at which they are hosted by company representatives. Although the companies use this form of entertainment to enhance customer relationships, it is virtually impossible to calculate the precise results of these expenditures. Likewise, it is difficult to tie concrete dollar results to most advertising and public relations expenditures.

| Exhibit 16–5 | *Examples of marketing communications objectives* |

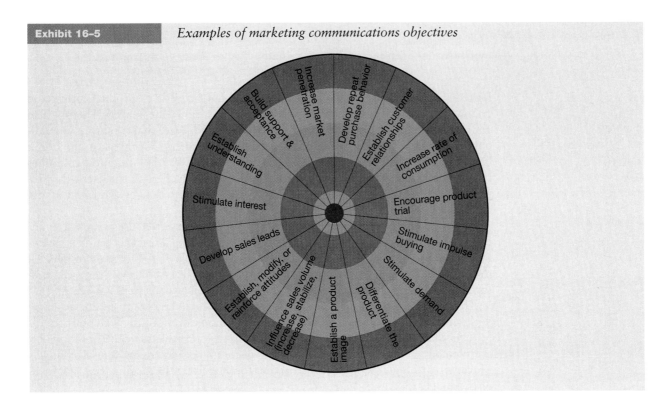

INFLUENCES ON BUDGETING The budget depends on the size of the company, its financial resources, the type of business, the market dispersion, the industry growth rate, and the firm's position in the marketplace. As shown in Exhibit 16–6, marketing communications expenditures also vary by industry.

The marketing communications budgets for business marketers are generally quite different than budgets for consumer products and service companies. For example, business marketers spend a majority of their marketing communications dollars on personal selling, whereas consumer marketers spend more on other forms of communications, with various forms of advertising leading the way.

BUDGETING METHODS Firms typically use any of four methods to determine the marketing communications budget: **percentage of sales, competitive parity, all-you-can-afford,** and **objective-task.**

PERCENTAGE OF SALES Using the preceding year (or even a longer period) as a basis, a company can set its marketing communications budget as a percentage of sales. A drawback is that the assumed causal sequence of effects is reversed; that is, expenditures for marketing communications should partially determine sales levels, rather than past sales levels determining marketing communications expenditures.

Firms can also budget according to percentage of forecasted sales. When doing so, they often use industry standards such as those shown in Exhibit 16–6 as guidelines for determining a percentage. Percentage-of-sales approaches ensure some stability in planning, but they fail to consider competitive and economic pressures.

COMPETITIVE PARITY Some firms set marketing communications budgets to equal the percentage allocated by other companies in the industry. This approach at least acknowledges competitive actions. The disadvantage is it assumes that the competition is correct, that marketing communications dollars are spent with equal effectiveness across companies, and that other firms have similar objectives and resources. These assumptions may be dangerous oversimplifications of actual conditions.

ALL-YOU-CAN-AFFORD Sometimes firms spend what they can afford, or some amount left over after covering other costs. Such a budgeting technique fails to consider a firm's objectives and to commit expenditures necessary to achieve them. This

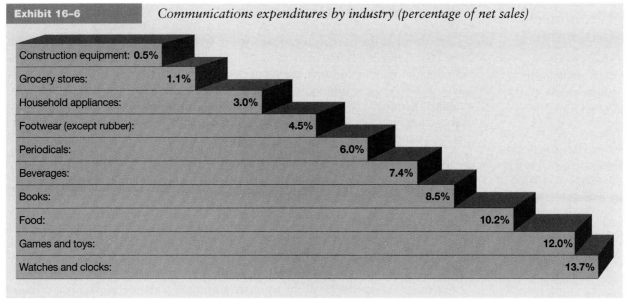

Exhibit 16–6	*Communications expenditures by industry (percentage of net sales)*

Construction equipment: 0.5%
Grocery stores: 1.1%
Household appliances: 3.0%
Footwear (except rubber): 4.5%
Periodicals: 6.0%
Beverages: 7.4%
Books: 8.5%
Food: 10.2%
Games and toys: 12.0%
Watches and clocks: 13.7%

Source: *Advertising Age* Web site at www.adage.com/dataplace, January 26, 2000.

is a questionable approach for the firm struggling to make a profit, because reduction of marketing communications expenditures may prevent any improvement and actually speed a downturn.

OBJECTIVE-TASK More detailed than the other budgeting methods, this approach sets the budget at the level necessary to achieve stipulated marketing communications objectives. The objective-task method forces identification of tasks that must be achieved to meet established objectives and provides a way to evaluate results. It has the advantage of requiring management to spell out its assumptions about the relationships among dollars spent, exposure levels, product trial, and continuing consumer purchases.[16]

Research indicates that marketing managers rely heavily on historical data—for example, last year's sales results—in allocating dollars to various marketing communications tools. This may be an acceptable practice in stable business environments; in many marketing environments, however, there is significant variation from year to year in consumer tastes, economic conditions, and competitive activity. When managers are operating in such unstable environments, they will likely be more successful if they rely more on objective-task, or zero-based, budgeting.[17]

Marketing Communications Program Development

Developing a marketing communications program involves developing general marketing communications strategies and allocating budgets to specific programs. A firm must decide the proper uses of explicit and implicit communications. And it must decide whether to adopt a push strategy, a pull strategy, or a combination strategy.

EXPLICIT AND IMPLICIT COMMUNICATIONS Marketing communications may be either explicit or implicit. **Explicit communications** convey a distinct, clearly stated message through personal selling, advertising, public relations, sales promotion, direct marketing, or some combination of these methods. **Implicit**

This ad illustrates how both explicit and implicit marketing communications can be part of the same message. Just like the watch, this rodeo cowboy can "take a licking and keep on ticking."

communications are what the message connotes about the product itself, its price, or the places it is sold. Fuji, for example, tried to alter its image after landing a contract to do all of the photofinishing work for Wal-Mart. Fuji was fearful that Wal-Mart buyers might not like the fact that Fuji is a Japanese company, so it developed a campaign to highlight Fuji's connections to the United States—5,000 employees, a billion dollars in manufacturing facilities, and sponsorship of U.S. athletes, including Olympic gold medalist Dan O'Brien. With Wal-Mart's encouragement, Fuji used advertising, in-store displays, and contests to promote the company as "part of the American landscape."[18] In this instance, the implicit communication is that Fuji is every bit as American as its most important customer, Wal-Mart, and its chief competitor, Kodak. As the Fuji example indicates, implicit and explicit communications can both be important in communicating a complete, consistent message.

PUSH, PULL, AND COMBINATION STRATEGIES   A **push strategy** involves convincing intermediary channel members to "push" the product through the channel to the ultimate consumer. The company directs its marketing communications efforts toward promoting and selling the product to a reseller, which then does the same to another reseller or to the ultimate consumer. Personal selling is a primary tool in this method. Sales promotion and advertising directed at channel members may also be used. For example, manufacturers may provide sales incentives to retailers or place ads in retailer-oriented trade magazines.

A **pull strategy** attempts to get consumers to "pull" the product from the manufacturing company through the marketing channel. The company concentrates its marketing communications efforts on the consumer; that is, it hopes to stimulate interest and demand for the product at the end-user level. If consumers want and ask for the product, resellers are more likely to carry and distribute it. A firm with a new and unproven product might find a pull strategy useful if distributors are reluctant to carry the product. The firm then uses advertising and sales promotion tools such as coupons to get many consumers to go to the retail store and request the product, thus pulling it through the channel.

Many firms practice a **combination strategy,** aiming marketing communications at both resellers and ultimate consumers. Nabisco, for example, uses personal selling and trade promotions to sell its products to grocery retailers. At the same time, it makes extensive use of advertising and sales promotion directed at ultimate consumers. Strict reliance on either a push or a pull strategy does not take full advantage of the power of marketing communications. A firm with limited resources, however, may not be able to follow both strategies and may emphasize one over the other.

Integration and Implementation

Implementation is setting the marketing communications plan into action. Depending on which tools the firm uses, it creates ads, purchases media time and space, and begins its sales promotion programs. If appropriate, the firm's personal selling, public relations, and direct marketing components also direct their efforts toward achieving the marketing communications objectives. The key aspect of implementation is coordination.

Monitoring, Evaluating, and Controlling

Firms can use a variety of methods to monitor, evaluate, and control marketing communications. For example, a firm might monitor sales promotion by the number of coupons redeemed or measure the effectiveness of a new personal selling strategy by looking at the number of new accounts opened by the salesforce. After an advertising campaign, a firm might run tests to see if consumers noticed the ad. Researchers could ask how many of those who noticed the ad linked the company name to it or actually read it. They might also ask consumers about their attitude toward the company and the product both before and after a marketing communi-

Money isn't everything.

It takes people, too. For example the people who initiated the Shell Youth Training Academy in South Central Los Angeles. This school helps inner-city high school students develop academic and social skills by providing them with both classroom training and paid, on-the-job experience. It's been so successful, Shell has started a second academy in Chicago.

Shell volunteers are frequently found helping repair, paint and fix up buildings that provide services to both young and old, like the Martin Luther King, Jr. Community Center in Houston. Shell employees

refurbished classrooms and the senior center, and established a state-of-the-art playground for the children of the neighborhood.

And whenever there's a need for disaster relief, Shell people go above and beyond to help their neighbors through earthquakes, hurricanes and floods with relief stations that provide essentials during tough times.

These are just a few of the hundreds of community projects across the nation where Shell employees are donating so much more than money.   **Shell**

Marketing communications can be used to communicate a corporation's role in socially responsible activities, which may also encourage other people to make contributions that will benefit society. This ad explains how Shell employees volunteer their time to worthwhile causes and projects.

cations program to see what effect, if any, the program had.

Marketers often rely on surveys and tests to evaluate marketing communications. Sometimes they look at sales results and attribute fluctuations in sales volume to the marketing communications, while largely ignoring the effects of other factors. Unfortunately, this narrow view prevails in many business settings.

Even though it may be difficult to measure the absolute effectiveness of most marketing communications, marketers have certainly not given up on the task. Quite the opposite is true, in fact, as marketers are increasingly under pressure to justify money spent on communications. Marketers are experimenting with interactive technology, which may offer some hope for better evaluation of marketing communications. This practice can raise ethical questions, as discussed in "Using Technology: Has DoubleClick Gone Too Far?"

Ethical and Legal Considerations
Exhibit 16–7 notes the ways the five areas of marketing communications may be subject to criticism from an ethical and legal viewpoint. Much to the dismay of upright professional marketers, ethical problems and legal violations in marketing communications continue. The good news is that an *ethical perspective* is also evident in marketing communications. In fact, marketing communications are frequently used to encourage responsible behavior such as contributing to charitable causes, practicing safe driving, and supporting community action programs. Marketing communications are also used to inform buyers about legal issues with reminders like "buckle up, it's the law," or "you must be 21 years old to purchase this product."

An example of marketing communications contributing to society is the Target stores' "Take Charge of Education" program, whereby a percentage of sales is returned to participating schools in local communities. Target generates a consider-

Using Technology

Has DoubleClick gone too far?

Web surfers often assume their identities are unknown unless they register when they visit sites. For Web advertisers, this anonymity represents lost opportunities to connect with potential buyers. From a strict business point of view, the more specifics marketers have about individuals who visit their sites, the better. They can follow up directly with high-potential consumers and develop more accurate consumer profiles, which can aid in more precise segmentation and improved market offerings.

DoubleClick can remove the surfer's anonymity by assigning electronic tracking devices called "cookies" to the consumer's Web browser. Unbeknownst to most consumers, the cookie follows consumers as they surf from site to site. Also without most consumers' knowledge, their identity is confirmed through Abacus, a huge database owned by DoubleClick that maintains names, phone numbers, addresses, and retail buying practices of 90 percent of American households.

Consumer groups are protesting DoubleClick's surreptitious discovery and sharing of private information with marketing organizations. A legal battle is underway as consumer privacy advocates have filed lawsuits and complaints with the Federal Trade Commission. Depending on the outcomes of regulatory and legal processes, consumers will lose some of their privacy rights or marketers will have to pull back from some tracking mechanisms. Either way, on-line marketing will be significantly affected.

Source: Diana Murphy, "Ad Company Is Watching Where You Go," *The Coloradoan,* January 28, 2000, pp. 8, 7.

Exhibit 16-7	*Ethical and legal concerns in marketing communications*
Marketing Communications Element	**Ethical/Legal Concerns**
Advertising	• Using deceptive advertising • Reinforcing unfavorable ethnic/racial/sex stereotypes • Encouraging materialism & excessive consumption
Public relations	• Lack of sincerity (paying lip service to worthwhile causes) • Using economic power unfairly to gain favorable publicity • Orchestrating news events to give false appearance of widespread support for corporate position
Sales promotion	• Offering misleading consumer promotions • Paying slotting allowances to gain retail shelf space • Using unauthorized mailing lists to reach consumers
Personal selling	• Using high-pressure selling • Failing to disclose product limitations/safety concerns • Misrepresenting product benefits
Direct marketing communications	• Invading privacy by telemarketing • Using consumer database information without authorization of consumers • Creating economic waste with unwanted direct mail

able amount of favorable publicity with this program, and promotes the program on its Web site, in-store signage, and some of its advertising. The program has returned more than $17 million to deserving schools, students, and teachers.[19] Such programs remind us that marketing communications are essential not only to profit-seeking marketers, but also to groups that support the improvement of our society. In some instance, the two constituencies overlap.

Legal—but Ethical?

Some marketing communications may be technically legal but raise significant ethical questions. For example, after four decades of self-imposed restrictions, the liquor industry has begun advertising on television. Critics, citing problems arising from excessive consumption of alcohol, are outraged. Citing lost market share to beer and wine manufacturers, liquor companies argue that they are legally entitled to use advertising to promote their businesses.[20]

Similarly, alcohol ads using lifestyle themes to appeal to youth are ethically questionable. Beer manufacturers such as Anheuser-Busch and Miller Brewing Company, however, are trying to promote responsible drinking and curb teenage consumption. Anheuser-Busch has pulled its beer ads from MTV, moving the spots to VH-1, which has a target market of 25- to 49-year-olds. Although there was not a legal issue involved, industry analysts said Anheuser-Busch made the move to avoid criticism of marketing to underage drinkers.[21] Anheuser-Busch and its chief competitor, Miller Brewing Company, also sponsor Web sites to promote responsible drinking.[22]

Critics of legalized gambling have tried to attack the industry by supporting restrictions on advertising of state lotteries and other gambling activities. The American Advertising Federation opposes restrictions on advertising for gambling, claiming that restrictions on truthful, nondeceptive advertising could lead to the curtailment of advertising other products, services, and activities.[23]

Deception in Marketing Communications

Exhibit 16-7 indicates that many problems relate to deception of consumers. Although this may happen in any area of the promotion mix, deceptive advertising is a prime concern. **Deceptive advertising,** communications intended to mislead consumers by making false claims or failing to disclose important information, is a major focus of the Federal Trade Commission (FTC), the government agency responsible for overseeing American business practices.

Deceptive advertising often involves false pricing offers, apparently to appeal to consumers' desire to get something for nothing. The Better Business Bureau, for example, found that several marketers misused the word "free" in ads for personal computers. Some ads required the purchase of three years of Internet service, and the PCs were refurbished, not new. Others required registering for a chance to win a free PC in exchange for receiving continuous on-screen ads. One on-line offer required a $20 enrollment fee to receive a free PC. The company address turned out to be a residence, and the Web site was shut down shortly thereafter.[24]

Another area of concern is substantiation of claims made in marketing communications. For example, the FTC found the Bayer Corporation guilty of making unsubstantiated claims in their ads that recommended taking an aspirin a day for the prevention of strokes and heart attacks. While a daily aspirin regimen might be good for some people, it may be of little or no benefit to others. Some people might even suffer adverse reactions from taking an aspirin every day. Bayer was ordered to conduct a $1 million consumer education campaign urging consumers to consult a physician before beginning a daily aspirin regimen.[25] All marketers, including salespeople, should be able to substantiate any claims made regarding a product's performance.

Additional Regulatory Concerns

Additional FTC guidelines can affect marketing communications. The FTC requires that any claims made about product performance be capable of verification. Although the FTC provides for **comparative advertising** (which compares one product with other products), it also requires that comparative claims be supported. If Pontiac wants to claim that its Bonneville costs thousands of dollars less than Lexus or BMW, it must make the basis for comparison clear to the consumer.

Product endorsers must be qualified to make judgments and must actually use the product being endorsed. Moreover, any demonstrations used in advertisements must be accurate representations and not images that are misleading.

Packaging and labeling practices of food and drug marketers are heavily scrutinized by consumers and regulatory agencies. At the national level, the Food and Drug Administration (FDA) keeps a watchful eye on health-related messages. In 1991, the FDA's regulatory power was extended by legislation that required manufacturers to disclose dietary and nutritional information on product labels about the amounts of fat, sugar, cholesterol, additives, and certain other elements in the product. The National Advertising Association Review Board (NARB) is also active in monitoring health and nutritional claims. In a recent case, the NARB found that Kellogg's had not substantiated implied claims that K-Sentials cereals provide a unique blend of vitamins and minerals or that all K-Sentials cereals contained additional calcium. Kellogg's agreed to modify their packaging and television, print, and Web advertising to correct the problems.[26]

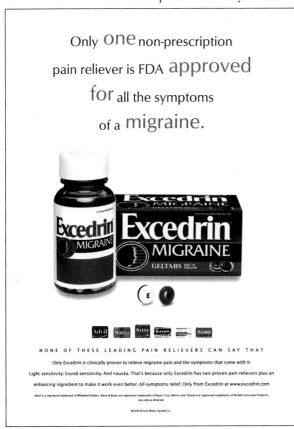

Only **one** non-prescription pain reliever is FDA **approved** **for** all the symptoms of a **migraine**.

NONE OF THESE LEADING PAIN RELIEVERS CAN SAY THAT

Only Excedrin is clinically proven to relieve migraine pain and the symptoms that come with it: Light sensitivity. Sound sensitivity. And nausea. That's because only Excedrin has two proven pain relievers plus an enhancing ingredient to make it work even better. All-symptoms relief. Only from Excedrin at www.excedrin.com

Advil is a registered trademark of Whitehall-Robins. Aleve & Bayer are registered trademarks of Bayer Corp. Motrin and Tylenol are registered trademarks of McNeil Consumer Products. Use only as directed.

©2000 Bristol-Myers Squibb Co.

Marketers who use comparative advertising must be able to substantiate their claims. In this instance, Whitehall Laboratories uses comparative advertising to claim that Advil is gentler on the stomach than aspirin and that it works better on headache pain than Extra Strength Tylenol.

Effects of Globalization

The increasing globalization of marketing often requires adjustment of the communications mix from country to country to avoid legal and ethical problems. From country to country, differences in language, culture, legal and ethical norms, and availability of various media are usually significant: Telemarketing laws, for example, in some European countries are far more stringent than are those in the United States. The use of humor and sex in marketing communications across countries and cultures can be a high-risk tactic due to the potential of misunderstandings' occurring. Sales promotion techniques that involve contests and giveaways are regulated quite differently in various countries. And of particular importance, effective advertising messages in one country may be offensive to residents of other countries, and what constitutes acceptable personal selling behavior also varies significantly across countries and cultures; for example, in many Latin and Far Eastern countries, establishing a personal relationship prior to developing a business relationship is crucial.

Recall that the global perspective also includes a recognition of multiculturalism within a given market or country. In a growing number of countries around the world, including the United States, marketing communications are addressing multicultural aspects of the market. Marketers must take special precautions not to perpetuate unfavorable stereotypes of ethnic and racial groups; often, these precautions include hiring ad agencies, research firms, and other specialists to guide their marketing communications efforts. Even so, consumers may be offended, which reinforces the importance of paying careful attention to cultural differences in marketing communications.

Summary

1. **Discuss the objectives of marketing communications.** The primary objective of marketing communications is to reach an audience to affect its behavior. In general, the three major objectives of marketing communications are to inform, to persuade, and to remind. The emphasis placed on one of the five primary communications methods to achieve these objectives depends on the company's marketing and communications strategy.

2. **Understand the marketing communications mix and its role.** Marketing communications allow marketers to reach current and potential customers. Advertising, public relations, sales promotion, personal selling, and direct marketing are the primary categories of marketing communications. Each of these tools has its unique advantages, providing a variety of techniques for reaching consumers. It is important that marketing communications be consistent with a firm's overall corporate and marketing strategy. Marketing communications must be coordinated with product, price, and channel factors to reach the desired target audience effectively.

3. **Explain the key elements of the marketing communications process.** Communication occurs when there is shared meaning between source and receiver. Communication is considered effective to the extent that the source gets a desired response from the receiver. From a marketing communications per-

spective, a firm as the source sends a marketing communications message through any of several message channels to its target audience, the receiver. The firm encodes the message by putting it into words, pictures, or symbols that best convey the message. Target audience members then decode the message by determining the meaning of the words, pictures, and symbols. Sometimes the intended message is not received if there is noise in the communications process.

4. **Discuss the seven steps in the marketing communications planning process.** The key tasks of marketing communications planning include marketing plan review, situation analysis, communications process analysis, budget development, program development, integration and implementation of the plan, and monitoring, evaluating, and controlling the marketing communications process.

5. **Demonstrate awareness of some of the key ethical and legal issues related to marketing communications.** All areas of marketing communications have come under criticism for unethical and illegal activities. Some of the more frequently publicized problems include deceptive advertising, inability to substantiate comparative claims, unfair reinforcement of ethnic, racial, and sex stereotypes, and encouragement of materialistic values.

Understanding Marketing Terms and Concepts

Thinking About Marketing

1. Briefly define marketing communications and describe the elements of the marketing communications mix.

2. What is sponsorship? What are some of its advantages and disadvantages? Give an example of sponsorship, and comment on its effectiveness.

3. What is the goal of marketing communications? Name three major objectives of marketing communications. For each objective, give an example of how an actual firm uses marketing communications to reach it.

4. Refer to "Being Entrepreneurial: Start-ups Show Creative Side." Attention-getting ads can help build brand identity. As start-up companies mature, how might their marketing communications change to more directly encourage short-term results?

5. What factors could cause a marketing communications message to be decoded differently from the way the source intended?

6. Briefly describe the steps in marketing communications planning.

7. How can other aspects of the marketing mix affect the marketing communications mix?

8. What influences the amount of money a company might spend on marketing communications?

9. Refer to "Using Technology: Has DoubleClick Gone Too Far?" Do you think it is acceptable for marketers to accumulate, share, and sell consumer information without the consumer's knowledge?

10. Give several examples of ethical or legal issues related to marketing communications.

Applying Marketing Skills

1. Select a major marketer of consumer goods that has advertised on national television within the past month. Try to identify approaches other than television advertising that have been part of this company's recent marketing communications mix.

2. Identify several specific examples of marketing communications that you feel are either ethically or legally questionable. What elements in each communication

cause the problem? How could each communication be improved to remove any doubt about its ethical or legal acceptability?

3. Choose a product you are familiar with, and illustrate how product, pricing, and marketing-channel factors influence the marketing communications activities for the product.

Using the www in Marketing

Activity One   The IBM Web site at http://www.ibm.com offers an opportunity to learn more about the company's marketing communications efforts. After reaching the IBM home page, click on "IBM press room" to see how IBM conducts public relations activities over the Internet. Investigate the philanthropy, public affairs, and environment links in the "About IBM" section to examine the company's role as a socially responsible corporation. As you investigate IBM's Web site, answer these questions.

1. How many of the following elements of marketing communications can you identify?

    a. Advertising

    b. Public relations

    c. Sales promotion

    d. Direct-marketing communications

2. Can you find information that would be useful in support of IBM's personal selling efforts?

3. How useful do you think the IBM site would be to existing customers, prospective customers, and potential stockholders?

Activity Two   Part of being a professional is keeping up with your field. In today's environment, this increasingly means staying abreast of international developments. Trade publications are useful for this purpose. For example, *Advertising Age* is one of the most widely read trade sources for all forms of marketing communications. Access the Web site http://www.adage.com and click on menu items of interest. Be sure to investigate the Ad Age International menu.

1. What developments are occurring outside the United States that you find noteworthy?

2. Check the Ad Age Dataplace to see if there is information related to international advertising and marketing.

Making Marketing Decisions
Case 16-1 Seagram Creeps, Other Distillers to Follow?

In 1996, Seagram Company ended the liquor industry's 50-year voluntary ban on television advertising. After much private debate, Seagram decided to "creep" into television advertising with limited advertising in one market: Corpus Christi, Texas. Given the amount of controversy generated by its "creep" strategy, Seagram executives are probably glad they did not initially go with an alternative "splash" campaign, which would have entailed a heavier advertising schedule in multiple markets.

The controversial aspects of liquor ads on TV revolve primarily around social questions. Opponents argue that drinking alcohol leads to increased social costs as a result of alcoholism, more automobile accidents, acts of violence, and employee absenteeism, and that alcohol, when consumed in excessive amounts, contributes to physical and mental disorders. Particularly troublesome to critics is that they feel that liquor companies target young, and in some cases, underage consumers.

Although Seagram and other liquor companies deny targeting young consumers, there is a fair amount of evidence to the contrary. The Seagram ads in Corpus Christi depicted two dogs participating in a graduation ceremony, which caused the president of Mothers Against Drunk Driving to comment, "For the industry to say they're not targeting young people is absurd."

Certainly print advertising by liquor companies includes blatant appeals to consumers under 21 years of age, a group that accounts for 30 percent of the United States population. *Spin* magazine, with 48 percent of its readership under 21 years of age, is a popular medium for liquor advertisers, as is *Allure* (with 44 percent underage readers) and Rolling Stone, with 35 percent underage.

Four years after Seagram's controversial TV ads, the liquor industry is on the verge of dramatically increasing its television advertising. The Distilled Spirits Council of the United States asked ad agency Bozell Worldwide to develop an advertising strategy to help reverse declining sales over the past two decades. On average, adult Americans drink 1.8 gallons of liquor per year, compared with 3 per year in 1980. Bozell, the creator of the famous milk-moustache ads asking "Got milk?", suggests that distillers increase their television advertising by 1,300 percent. Since the major networks have generally refused to run liquor ads, cable stations would be the key media vehicle.

There are some risks to liquor companies if they persist with television advertising. Their strategy was unveiled just as the federal government increased its scrutiny of liquor marketing. The FTC reviewed ad content and media placement of eight major advertisers of beer, liquor, and wine. The FTC recommended improvements in self-regulatory codes and will undoubtedly investigate further the age profiles of television programs and print media where alcoholic beverages are advertised. Since there is bipartisan political support against advertising liquor on television, an increase may bring counter measures such as increased taxes on alcohol, point-of-sale restraints, and restrictions on ad content. It appears that these are risks that the liquor companies are willing to take.

Questions

1. The U.S. government may enact regulations to prohibit liquor advertisements on television. How would liquor companies argue against such regulation?

2. Should liquor companies withhold advertising on television in an attempt to be more socially responsible?

3. How could liquor companies convince the public and government officials that their ads are not targeted toward consumers under the age of 21?

SOURCES: Vanessa O'Connell, "Distillers Weigh TV Ads Urging More Drinking," *The Wall Street Journal,* February 23, 1999, pp. B1, B4; Jeff Perlman, "AAF Welcomes FTC Decision on Alcohol Advertising Codes," from the American Advertising Association's Web site at www.aaf.org, January 24, 2000; Yumiko Ono, "Creep or Splash? Seagram Memo Plots Ad Move," *The Wall Street Journal,* June 18, 1996, pp. B1, B7; and Owen Ullmann, "The Spirited Brawl ahead over Liquor Ads on TV," *Business Week,* December 16, 1996, p. 47.

Case 16-2 SmithKline Beecham/Glaxo: Savvy Sponsors

 SmithKline Beecham Consumer Healthcare (SKB) has a vested interest in persuading consumers to stop smoking cigarettes. Its NicoDerm and Nicorette products are the leading over-the-counter smoking-cessation brands. For several years, SKB has effectively used sponsorship of stop-smoking events, music concerts, air shows, and automobile racing to promote these brands.

Perhaps the best-known event sponsored by SKB is the annual Great American Smokeout, held in partnership with the American Cancer Society. First held in 1976, the Great American Smokeout gives smokers an opportunity to give up smoking for the day, and, hopefully, for good. The Smokeout and New Year's Day are the most popular quitting times of the year. Recent spokespersons for the Great American Smokeout include *Will & Grace* television star Debra Messing, basketball star Alonzo Mourning, and U.S. Women's Soccer hero Brandi Chastain. These and other celebrities hosted "Countdown to the Great American Smokeout" pep rallies.

SKB has also enjoyed a long-running sponsorship tie with CART motor sports. To promote NicoDerm and Nicorette products, a support theme has been used. Just as CART driver Dennis Vitolo needs family and team support to win races, smokers need support to quit. SKB uses the same theme in the air shows it sponsors.

One of SKB's newest sponsorship programs links its quit-smoking products with country music. SKB likes the clean, wholesome image both of country music in general and of its featured performer, Martina McBride. SKB also likes the broad demographic profile of the country-music-fan adult—all age groups and a fairly even distribution of males and females. Further, sponsoring country music concerts allows SKB to gain a presence not reached by CART or through air shows. SKB actually offered consumers a free concert ticket with a purchase of Nicorette or NicoDerm.

To evaluate the effectiveness of its sponsorship programs, SKB focuses on sales volume; the company compares sales during sponsorship periods with sales during nonsponsorship periods. SKB also assesses incremental profits earned after the costs of the program are factored in. Further, the company is testing whether sales are better with an exclusive retail partner or with a large number of stores. It takes a lot less time and money to secure the cooperation of an exclusive retailer, so SKB wants to know if it is worth the extra effort and expense of gaining the cooperation of multiple retail partners.

SKB supports all of its sponsored events with the NicoVan to provide on-the-scene educational guidance and explanations to quit-smoking prospects. The company is also looking at how to link sponsorship areas together. For example, the CART Champ Car might feature promotional messages about the concerts, and vice versa.

In June 2000, the expected merger of SKB with Glaxo Wellcome Inc. will make Glaxo SmithKline the world's leading research-based pharmaceutical company. It will also add Wellcome's Zyban, another leading smoking-cessation brand to the product line. Zyban, unlike Nicorette and NicoDerm, is nicotine-free, and Glaxo has often used sponsorship to promote the product. Glaxo has partnered on occasion with the American Lung Association, and it sponsors select events on the Senior PGA men's golf tour. Most of its sponsorships coincide with the New Year, and Glaxo uses these sponsored events to entertain doctors, sales representatives, and hospital administrators. Additional marketing communications include some TV advertising and exposure in *Business Week,* the presenting sponsor for one of the golf tournaments.

SKB and Glaxo have enjoyed healthy sales growth for Nicorette, NicoDerm, and Zyban. Company spokespersons acknowledge that part of the companies' success is due to the number of people interested in quitting smoking, which is larger than ever before. But they also credit in part their integrated marketing communications programs, especially their sponsorship of high-visibility events.

Questions

1. In addition to the methods identified, how else could SKB and Glaxo measure the effectiveness of their sponsorship programs?

2. After the two companies merge, should Nicorette, NicoDerm, and Zyban be promoted together or separately? What are the pros and cons of joint promotion?

3. What ideas can you offer for integrating communications across sponsorship venues (i.e., country music concerts, air shows, CART auto racing, and golf tournaments)?

SOURCES: "SmithKline Creates Country Music Event to Promote Smoking Cessation Products," *IEG Sponsorship Report,* February 22, 1999, pp. 7–8; information from SmithKline Beecham's Web site at www.sb.com, January 31, 2000; and information from Glaxo Wellcome's Web site at www.glaxowellcome.com, January 31, 2000.

Chapter Seventeen

Advertising and Public Relations

After studying this chapter, you should be able to:

1 Understand the characteristics, functions, and types of advertising.

2 Realize how people process advertising information and how it affects buyer behavior.

3 Discuss approaches to developing advertising campaigns.

4 Describe different advertising objectives and the message strategies used to achieve them.

5 Understand the decisions involved in selecting media and scheduling advertising.

6 Explain how marketers assess advertising effectiveness.

7 Appreciate the roles of public relations and publicity in marketing.

www.british-airways.com

British Airways is by far the largest carrier of passengers between the United Kingdom and the United States, with over 40 percent market share of transatlantic flights. The airline's main base is Heathrow, and it is one of only two airlines that flies the Concorde, the world's only supersonic aircraft. It is also among the largest cargo-handling airlines in the world.

After several turbulent years, BA is shrinking its capacity by going to smaller planes and fewer routes. The efforts are designed to increase profitability by recasting British Airlines as the preferred choice for business and corporate travelers. As long as the airline dominates British airports, it will be able to charge premium prices for a large portion of transatlantic travel. In addition, the firm is determined to return to its tradition of innovation. These changes include seats that can turn into beds and face the rear of the plane and that are connected with multichannel entertainment centers. New television advertisements concentrate on customer service and benefits. The challenge for Saatchi's, BA's advertising agency, is to maintain the airline's premium positioning in the marketplace while still being concerned with the sale of unsold seats through Internet auctions and price-search avenues. This is a difficult task, as the airline's primary target audience is busy, watches little TV, and is overexposed to advertising.

The firm is also using advertising on the Internet as additional communication methods to generate sales. Specifically, British Airways is advertising on the Internet using unobtrusive "pop-up" advertising technology such that its ads occur on sites after the text has been processed. These Web ads promote the possibility of free airline tickets, using animation to grab viewer attention after the reader has been involved on-site for a period of time.

BA has also begun a series of direct-response advertisements, which include direct-response phone numbers, that promote holiday travel to 100 city destinations in Europe, the Middle East, and North America.

Information about all aspects of BA's marketing mix can be obtained from the firm's site (http://www.british-airways.com). For example, the site provides in-depth descriptions of the types of planes the airline uses, the services offered, special ticket prices to certain locations, and the locations that can be reached. Details about the company's use of media and press releases are available from the site's media and public relations archives.

Sources: Matt Carmichael, "British Airways Pops Up in Most Unobtrusive Way," *Advertising Age,* October 11, 1999, p. 64; Ian Darby, "Joshua Fights for the Battle of BA Long-Haul," *Marketing,* September 2, 1999, p. 11; Janet Guyon, "British Airways Takes," *Fortune,* September 27, 1999, pp. 214–17; Danny Rogers, "Will BA Take Off Again?" *Marketing,* August 26, 1999, pp. 18–19; Jane Hodges, "Agency.com Wins BA Work; Bring on the Fish and Chips," *Advertising Age,* September 2, 1996, p. 22; Claire Murphy, "Why Airlines Face Revolution," *Marketing,* June 20, 1996, p. 16; Jay Palmer, "Transatlantic Tie," *Barron's,* June 17, 1996, p. 14; and Steven J. Viuker, "High Stakes," *Barron's,* June 10, 1996, p. 20.

The British Airways marketing program is a good example of how marketers use different advertising media and communications approaches to reach their desired target segments. To handle its Internet presence, BA has selected an advertising agency that specializes in designing interactive Web sites. The airline promotes its services through both traditional advertising and other marketing communications, such as public relations and sales promotions, along with the interactive aspects of its Web site.

In this chapter, we explore issues associated with advertising, the most visible marketing activity. We discuss the related topic of public relations as well.

The Nature of Advertising

Advertising Defined

Advertising is the activity consumers most associate with the term *marketing*. **Advertising** is defined as a marketing communications element that is persuasive, nonpersonal, paid for by an identified sponsor, and disseminated through mass channels of communication to promote the adoption of goods, services, persons, or ideas.[1]

Effective advertising can present information about new or existing products, demonstrate meaningful uses of the product, and establish or refresh the brand's image.[2] It can reach a diverse or wide audience with repeated communications and gives a company the opportunity to dramatize its products and services in a colorful way.

Advertising stimulates demand, helps build brand success, develops and shapes buyer behavior, and gives the seller a measure of certainty about the level of sales. In addition, it informs buyers about product characteristics and availability and makes markets more competitive.[3]

In many markets, first-time purchasers are rare. Here advertising is critically important in affecting brand shares by inducing switching or retaining customers who otherwise might switch. Brand switching is generated from advertising through building brand awareness or altering consumer beliefs about brands.[4]

Advertising performs other functions as well. Some advertising supports personal selling efforts. For example, many companies advertise to increase consumer awareness of products, making later personal selling efforts easier. Such advertising, if executed effectively, generates sales leads and communicates product advantages to prospective buyers.

Advertising and the Marketing Concept

It is important to remember that advertising is expensive and must be targeted effectively to achieve a firm's objectives. Firms do not have unlimited budgets; thus, the allocation of these funds must be made with a clear view of target markets and, hence, the audience for the organization's advertising. Further, conceiving product offerings on the basis of consumer needs and benefits is not sufficient without some form of communication, frequently advertising. That is, communication (advertising) *and* desired product attributes are both integral aspects of the marketing concept.

The Advertising Industry

Advertising is a huge industry, with annual global expenditures close to $300 billion worldwide. General Motors, Procter & Gamble, and Daimler Chrysler each spend more than $1 billion on media advertising.[5] Exhibit 17–1 presents the amount advertisers spend in the United States on each medium.

Two of the fastest growing media are magazines and cable TV networks. In fact, their growth has caused average nightly audience shares of the major networks (ABC, NBC, CBS) to drop to under 50 percent, hence network advertising revenues have dropped by more than 10 percent.[6]

Exhibit 17–1	Total national advertising spending by type of medium	
Rank	**Medium**	**Expenditures ($ millions)**
1	Network TV	$16,272.0
2	Newspapers	16,130.9
3	Spot TV*	15,486.8
4	Magazines	13,780.2
5	Cable TV networks	6,672.0
6	Syndicated TV	2,691.6
7	National newspapers	2,658.2
8	National spot radio	2,039.8
9	Outdoor	1,727.0
10	Sunday magazine	1,029.4
11	Network radio	824.0
	Subtotal print media	43,162.2
	Subtotal broadcast media	33,598.7
	Total	79,312.0

*Spot TV refers to purchased time on selected television stations affiliated with one of the major networks.
Source: R. Craig Endicott, "Top 100 Mega Brands," *Advertising Age,* November 8, 1999, p. S4. Copyright Crain Communications, Inc. 1999.

Exhibit 17–2	World's top five advertising organizations

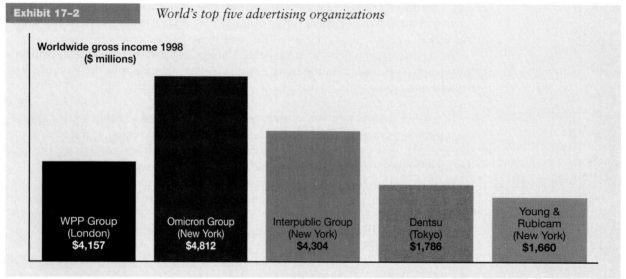

**Worldwide gross income 1998
($ millions)**

| WPP Group (London) $4,157 | Omicron Group (New York) $4,812 | Interpublic Group (New York) $4,304 | Dentsu (Tokyo) $1,786 | Young & Rubicam (New York) $1,660 |

Source: "Top 25 Global Ad Organizations," *Advertising Age,* April, 19, 1999, p. S18. Copyright Crain Communications, Inc. 1999.

Ad Agencies

Many advertisers hire **advertising agencies** to create ad campaigns and to purchase media time and space. Exhibit 17–2 lists the world's top five advertising organizations as measured by gross income. All of them employ many people in organizations worldwide, and three have their central offices in London or Tokyo.

Ad agencies employ creative people who develop unique advertising messages and media specialists who provide media planning and scheduling. Creative strategies and a proven track record clearly are good reasons to hire an ad agency. To limit costs and save on commissions, however, some large companies such as Benetton have in-house advertising functions to handle everything from creative design to media decisions. Other companies, such as Procter & Gamble, now buy their own media space and time instead of relying entirely on ad agencies. Other companies, such as IBM, Bayer, 3M, and Campbell Soup, have pared down the number of agencies used globally. This consolidation further enhances the "single voice" aspects of integrated marketing communications.

The choice of a competent ad agency is especially important for firms targeting new global markets. One U.S. soap manufacturer, for example, simply dubbed its commercials—showing people singing in the shower—into Polish TV ads. Poles laughed heartily at the advertiser's naiveté: There are very few showers in Polish homes, and because hot water is so limited, no Pole would take a leisurely shower. Marketers can avoid such gaffes by establishing close partnerships with a capable advertising agency.[7] Coca-Cola has shifted its $1.6 billion worldwide account to the Leo Burnett and the McCann-Erickson agencies.

Historically, agencies have been able to charge a 15 percent commission of their gross billings for time and space purchased for their clients. More recently, accountability and economic pressures have led to alternative compensation plans. First, many firms now charge rates below 15 percent. Second, some agencies use a labor-based system based on the number of hours worked. Third, in some instances, advertisers pay their agencies under an incentive program based on the extent to which the advertiser's objectives are met. Driver's Mart, which owns a network of used-car dealerships and spends $40 million on advertising, pays its agency a commission for every car sold.[8] The U.S. Army also has shifted to a pay-for-performance plan in which its advertising agency will be paid based upon recruitment success.

P&G has also decided to pay its agencies according to increases and decreases in sales, instead of paying labor-based fees or commissions based on media spending. The sheer size of the company's ad budget has resulted in significant attention to this shift toward pay for performance. In contrast, advertising executives worry about the other factors that affect sales and factors that are not under ad agency control. For instance, if an agency does great work, but the company fails to run the ads frequently enough, should the agency suffer? Conversely, if a company designs a great product that would sell without a lot of advertising, should the ad agency benefit?[9]

Industry in Transition

Today, marketers increasingly question each advertising expenditure. Targeting mass markets with advertising alone no longer makes sense for many companies.

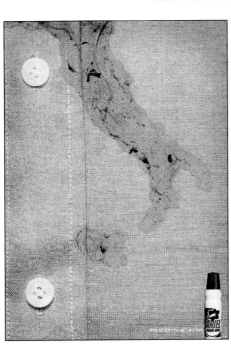

Ariel recognizes cultural influences in its advertising that promotes stain remover capability.

Simply buying air time during a specific TV program or buying a certain page in a specific magazine is not enough to reach targeted audiences. Advertisers often must use multimedia campaigns, combining television, print ads, videos, billboards, trade shows, direct mail, and activities such as event sponsorship into an *integrated marketing communications program.*[10]

Globalization of marketing efforts is another example of changing times. In many instances, both product and advertising must meet local market needs and fit in with cultural practices. Religious-dominant areas such as Saudi Arabia and Iran, areas with multiple cultural influences such as Japan and Korea, and more-homogeneous areas such as Sweden and Australia each require different advertising communications.[11] For example, Kraft advertised its processed cheese slices using a common theme (milk content) but different advertising styles and presentations to match the consumer preferences and uniqueness in Canada, the United Kingdom, Australia, and Spain.[12]

Japanese advertisers favor "soft selling" and often use indirect messages. The typical Western emphasis on product merit and use of spokespeople directly stating brand advantages are missing in much Japanese advertising.[13] And surprisingly, given the Japanese attraction to Western culture, the appearance of American images and settings has increased only modestly in Japanese advertising. Foreign advertisers in Japan should recognize these differences.

Speaking from Experience

Jim Ensign
Senior Vice President
Doe-Anderson, Inc.

Doe-Anderson, Inc., is an integrated marketing communications company, providing advertising, public relations, direct marketing, promotion, and interactive media counseling and services for national and international clients. Companies such as Valvoline, Sony Music and Entertainment, Allied Domecq Distilled Spirits, and National City Corporation use Doe-Anderson's integrated approach to develop marketing programs for their brands. Jim is the director of the advertising media planning and placement department and is also director of Doe-Anderson's Interactive Group, which develops Internet marketing programs and Web sites.

Jim earned a BS degree in business administration from Miami University in 1984 and held management positions at both Foote, Cone & Belding and Bayer, Bess, Vanderwarker in Chicago before joining Doe-Anderson, Inc., in Louisville, Kentucky, in 1992.

"We approach our clients' marketing communications challenges from a 'media neutral' basis. That is, we are never predisposed to believe that the best way to accomplish the goal is advertising. We go through a rigorous analysis of the challenge, the consumer, the competition, and the client's capabilities, and develop integrated programs that will best accomplish the goal—this may include no or little advertising, or may rely heavily on advertising."

Technological changes keep the advertising industry in transition as well. The extension of cable TV, the widespread penetration of VCRs, and remote-control capability all suggest some loss of effectiveness of TV commercials. Remote-control use, in particular, has given rise to **commercial zapping,** or changing the channels during commercials.[14] One study revealed that ads aired during competing sports events encountered audience losses up to 50 percent. Zapping is heaviest during news and late-night programming.[15] In addition, younger viewers and members of higher-income households are more likely to get up and do something else during TV commercial breaks.[16]

What then does this transition mean for advertising? The future looks brightest for media that reach target audiences more efficiently than broad-based ones like network TV. The winners are expected to be radio stations, specialized cable networks, new kinds of in-store advertising, and weekly newspapers, all of which appeal to specific rather than to broad audiences.[17]

Internet Advertising

Internet advertising is predicted by Forrester Research to reach $22 billion by 2004, surpassing magazines and trailing only television, newspapers, and direct mail. The evolution of the Internet as a meaningful channel of commercial communications is profoundly affecting the way firms do business. For example, advertising designed to establish consumer brand images will no longer focus primarily upon the 30-second commercial complemented by some print advertising. Advertisers and agencies alike are now required to consider all contacts with consumers in efforts to develop strong brands and brands that can be effective across borders. Advertisers on the Web have already begun to move beyond simple measurement of impressions. Now, through companies like AdKnowledge and Personify, purchasing behavior and the margins associated with purchases are being used to evaluate Internet advertising.[18]

The latest trend in network advertising is termed "rich media." Rich-media ads let Web users do everything from order merchandise to play video games without leaving the ad site. For example, the Tanqueray page enables Web surfers to play nine holes of golf when they visit the site. These rich-media advertisements provide direct-selling capabilities as well. As such, this sophisticated approach to Internet advertising has been found more effective than simple banner ads and animation. However, the use of banner advertising continues to grow, and research by Andersen Consulting reveals that banner ads, if placed in the right context, are effective at getting consumers to respond.[19]

The increasing number of specialized cable channels enables marketers to more effectively reach target markets with unique characteristics. ESPN2, for example, is an efficient means of reaching the sports enthusiast.

Advertising can be used to enhance corporate images. Here, LivePerson.com promotes their ability to enhance customer service for their clients.

Classifications of Advertising

Advertising can be classified by target audience, geographic area, medium, and purpose, as shown in Exhibit 17–3.[20] The special types discussed here are corporate image advertising, corporate advocacy advertising, public service advertising, classified advertising, direct-response advertising, business-to-business advertising, and cooperative advertising.

Corporate image advertising, directed toward the general public or investors and stockholders, promotes an organization's image and role in the community as a corporate citizen, independent of any product or service. **Corporate advocacy advertising** announces a stand on some issue related to the firm's operation, often one threatening the company's well-being. For example, Exxon addressed environmental issues in advocacy advertising following its Alaska oil spill.

Public service advertising is donated by the advertising industry to promote activities for some social good. For example, the World Wildlife Fund presents environmental public service advertisements. Frequently, marketers donate advertising time to drug and alcohol abuse prevention efforts, such as the "Just Say No" program and Mothers Against Drunk Driving (MADD).

Direct-response advertising (discussed in more detail in Chapter 20) is intended to elicit immediate action, often a purchase. Direct response ads on TV typically request immediate calls to telephone numbers shown on the TV screen. Direct-response ads also appear in magazines and direct mail. **Classified advertising,** mainly in newspapers, typically promotes transactions for a single item or service.

Firms use **business-to-business advertising** to promote their products or services directly to other firms. Most business advertising involves print ads in trade periodicals or direct mail sent to targeted buyers. In trade or business-to-business advertising, just as in consumer advertising, product benefits must be highlighted and a solution offered to prospects' problems. A significant portion of business-to-business advertising

Exhibit 17–3	*Classifications of advertising*		
By target audience	**By geographic area**	**By medium**	**By purpose**
Consumer advertising: Aimed at people who buy the product for their own or someone else's personal use.	**Local (retail) advertising:** Advertising by businesses whose customers come from only one city or local trading area.	**Print advertising:** Newspaper, magazine.	**Product advertising:** Intended to promote goods and services.
Business advertising: Aimed at people who buy or specify goods and services for use in business:	**Regional advertising:** Advertising for products sold in one area or region, but not the whole country.	**Broadcast (electronic) advertising:** Radio, TV.	**Nonproduct (corporate or institutional) advertising:** Intended to promote firm's mission or philosophy rather than a product.
• **Industrial:** Aimed at people who buy or influence the purchase of industrial products.	**National advertising:** Advertising aimed at customers in several regions of the country.	**Out-of-home advertising:** Outdoor, transit.	**Commercial advertising:** Intended to promote goods, services, or ideas with the expectancy of making a profit.
• **Trade:** Aimed at wholesalers and retailers who buy for resale to their customers.	**International advertising:** Advertising directed at foreign markets.	**Direct-mail advertising:** Advertising sent through the mail.	**Noncommercial advertising:** Sponsored by or for a charitable institution, civic group, or religious or political organization.
• **Professional:** Aimed at people licensed to practice under a code of ethics or set of professional standards.			**Action advertising:** Intended to bring about immediate action on the part of the reader.
• **Agricultural (farm):** Aimed at people in the farming or agricultural business.			**Awareness advertising:** Intended to build the image of a product or familiarity with the product's name and package.

should also be devoted to building and nurturing the brand images for the company as well as promoting/developing/enriching its key products and services."[21] Some business marketers, such as Ricoh Copiers, IBM, and Federal Express, advertise on TV in time slots likely to reach sophisticated adult audiences.

Cooperative advertising entails manufacturers contributing to a local dealer or retailer's advertising expense. The amount is based on the quantity of product the retailer purchases. The local marketer typically runs manufacturer-developed advertising that includes the outlet's name and logo.

Consumer Ad Processing
How then does advertising actually influence consumers? In this section, we explain how consumers process advertisements and how ads affect consumer attitudes and decisions.

Hierarchy of Effects

Advertising's influence on consumers is often explained by using the **hierarchy of effects,** or information-processing, model. This sequence of effects—exposure, attention, comprehension, acceptance, retention—is shown in Exhibit 17–4. Of course, every consumer does not consciously, or even subconsciously, go through a sequence of steps for all ads. Yet each stage of this hierarchy represents a specific goal for advertisers to pursue.

A marketer achieves *message exposure* by placing ads in appropriate media, such as magazines, TV programs, or newspapers, which gives the consumer the opportunity to process the message. According to the "mere exposure" hypothesis, positive evaluation of a brand can occur simply from repeated exposure to an advertisement.

Exhibit 17–4   *Advertising hierarchy of effects*

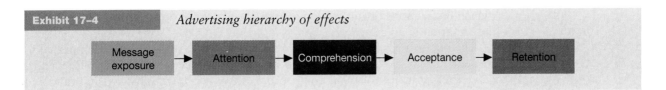

Consumer *attention* is the next step. The ad must stimulate the consumer to direct mental effort toward it. The primary attention-getting properties of an ad are its physical characteristics. For print ads, these include size, number of colors, and brightness. Motion, attention-getting models, and novelty also help grab attention.[22]

Attention does not necessarily mean the consumer will process a message further. *Message comprehension,* the next stage, means the consumer understands the ad's meaning. Comprehension includes categorization of the stimulus or advertised brand based upon prior information stored in memory. Elaboration of the information included in the ad furthers comprehension. Comprehension is enhanced to the extent the individual is motivated at the time of exposure and has some prior product category knowledge. Ad information that appears first (primacy effects) and last (recency effects) is often most comprehended.

Then, *message acceptance* must occur for the consumer to develop favorable attitudes about the advertised product or service and its subsequent purchase. Message acceptance includes both cognitive thoughts or responses related to the information in the ad as well as feelings, or affective responses, that occur because of the advertisement.

Message retention occurs when the consumer stores ad information in long-term memory, which is critical for affecting later purchase decisions and behavior.

Selective perception can occur at any stage. Exposure varies when consumers change channels during commercial breaks on television. *Selective attention* occurs when consumers notice certain ads but not others. Advertisers and advertising creative personnel expend considerable effort in developing ads that generate attention. Color, sexual images, attractive celebrity endorsers, and humor are frequently employed to garner attention.

Selective comprehension involves consumer interpretation of information provided in ads. Persuasion researchers have documented the tendency of individuals to perceive incoming information consistent with their own opinions and preferences. For example, an ad that disparages a consumer's favorite brand may be seen as biased or untruthful and its claims not accepted. *Selective retention* relates to what parts of the advertised information consumers actually remember. Given the low-involvement nature of ad encounters, messages are often kept simple and advertisers frequently use mnemonics, such as symbols, rhymes, and unique images, that assist the learning and remembering of brand information.

Influences on Ad Processing

Buyers' needs influence their processing of advertising messages. For example, a firm with a pressing need for waste removal would pay more attention to ads for this service than to aesthetic ads from a plant service to beautify the corporate office.

In addition, the buyer's motivation, ability, and opportunity to process brand information come into play. These concepts serve as important filters between advertising input (e.g., message content, media scheduling, and repetition) and the consumer. Consumer responses include thoughts or cognitions, affective feelings, and experiences.[23] First, *motivation* is related to the concept of consumer involvement, or the personal relevance or importance of the marketing communications message. Motivation is the desire to process the information. When motivation is low, potential customers pay little attention and remember minimal information, if any. *Ability* implies the buyer knows enough about the product category to understand the advertised message.[24] *Opportunity* is the extent to which distractions or limited exposure time affect the buyer's attention to brand information in an ad.

The opportunity for processing any single brand advertisement is diminished to the extent that the ad is surrounded by ads for competing brands. Consequently, advertisers attempt to avoid competitors' ads when buying advertising time and space. Competitive interference effects are particularly likely to occur for new brands. Since consumers' stored memory is limited, it is much more difficult for them to remember product information from ads for new brands in heavily advertised product categories. In contrast, well-known brands are less affected by competitive brand advertising; hence, they have important advantages in maintaining market share in the face of competing new brands.[25]

Product involvement may also affect the extent to which advertising is processed. Highly involved consumers are more likely to process the information in advertising and to notice differences in product attributes as advertised. In addition, extended problem solving is more likely; hence, complex advertisements may be more effective, since thoughtful processing of information is common in high-involvement situations.[26]

One well-known theory of persuasion, the **elaboration likelihood model,** includes individual motivation and ability to elaborate information in advertisements as determinants of two different "routes" to persuasion. Specifically, when consumer motivation and ability are high, persuasive message arguments are more thoroughly processed and the strength of the arguments influence persuasion in what is termed the "central route" to persuasion. However, when motivation and ability are low, peripheral cues become important in enhancing persuasion. In these cases, aspects of advertisements such as pictures and the use of celebrity and/or attractive models are important. In these latter cases, persuasion occurs through what is labeled the "peripheral route" to persuasion.[27]

Developing an Advertising Campaign

An ad campaign requires an analysis of the marketing situation, the target market involved, and the firm's overall communication objectives. As Exhibit 17–5 shows, once the firm has selected its target market, it must determine advertising objectives, determine the advertising budget, design the creative strategy, select and schedule media, and evaluate advertising effectiveness.

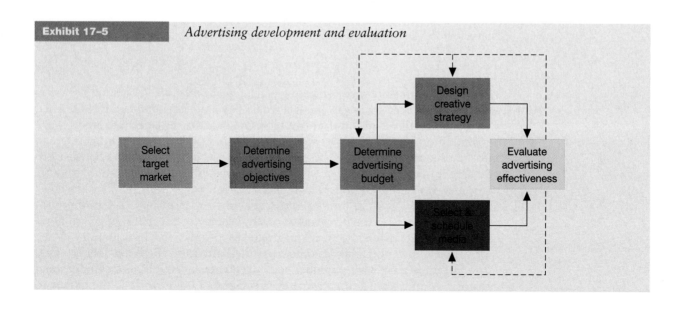

Exhibit 17-5   *Advertising development and evaluation*

Selecting Target Markets

The development of an effective advertising campaign is dependent upon the selection of target markets that the company can effectively serve. As explained in both Chapter 3 and Chapter 7, the selection of which target markets to serve is based upon a number of factors related to the marketplace and the advertiser. The most important of these determining factors include the firm's core competencies, its overall vision, and the potential of the intended targets in terms of long-term sales and profits. For the placement of advertising during TV programs, the shows are selected for their ability to deliver exposure to intended target markets. Segments that advertisers are trying to reach are traditionally identified by age, income, gender, education, and ethnicity. The youth are often the focus for their ability to establish what is trendy, while the older baby boomers offer attractive markets because of their substantial disposable incomes.

Determining Advertising Objectives

Advertising objectives should be realistic, precise, measurable, and consistent with the firm's overall marketing and communications objectives. One objective might be to increase brand awareness from 10 to 35 percent of all consumers within a particular market—say, cereal eaters between the ages of 18 and 55. Another might be to increase sales or market share, say, to achieve a sales growth of 2 percent in the next quarter. Setting objectives enhances the firm's ability to evaluate the effectiveness of its advertising expenditures.

The dot coms are spending extraordinary amounts of money on media advertising to build brand positioning and market share. For example, Hot.jobs spent $12 million of $16 million raised from venture capitalists to start operations on broadcast and outdoor media. In some cases, advertising objectives may be tied to other variables, such as market awareness, that are indirectly tied to sales objectives. In the face of low share for some of its products, Minolta used advertising to increase awareness of its entire line of products. Likewise, IBM recently spent $75 million on a global print campaign developed by Ogilvy & Mather just to improve the awareness of its technology services and consulting.[28]

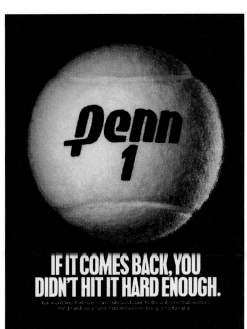

Advertisements often make use of novel pictorial displays to get attention and generate brand awareness. These ads are effective at encouraging information processing after initial exposure.

Determining Advertising Budget

The size of the advertising budget depends on the size of the company, its financial resources, the industry growth rate, market dispersion, and the firm's position in the marketplace. Smaller firms usually spend less; dominant firms may spend a disproportionately large amount to maintain market share and discourage competition. And a growing industry may warrant higher advertising budgets to build awareness, sales, and market share.

As explained in Chapter 16, budgets are often based on percentage of sales, competitive parity, all the firm can afford, or allocation by objectives, the recommended approach.

Designing Creative Strategy

Creative strategy combines the "what is said" with the "how it is said." Typically, the advertiser specifies the general content or theme of the message and the ad agency works with the company to develop the presentation.

Usually, the theme is the product's primary benefit or competitive advantage, presented in an attention-getting message the target audience can comprehend and remember. As competition for audience attention increases, highly creative and entertaining commercials become commonplace.[29]

Increasingly, advertisers are recognizing the influence of cultural diversity on advertising. As noted earlier, this is particularly true for international advertising, where standardization of advertising across national lines is on the decline. In addition, national advertisers often use specialized campaigns to target minority and other groups.

On occasion, failures in creative execution occur. Chrysler botched the introduction of its Intrepid by the use of very high-tech advertisements that only briefly showed the car at the end of the commercial. Sometimes questionable advertising is unintentionally humorous. For example, one sleep aid promoted the cautionary message "may cause drowsiness," while one snack brand advertised its contest as "You could be a winner! No purchase necessary. Details inside."[30]

MESSAGE STRATEGY ALTERNATIVES   Advertising messages can make objective or subjective claims. **Objective claims** describe product features or performance in measurable terms, such as "Chevy mid-sized vans are available with V-6 or V-8 engines." Objective claims often promote the benefits customers receive from the price paid. For example, Reebok advertises the custom fit from its pump technology. AT&T advertises service reliability for its monthly charges.

Subjective claims are not measurable, often stress image enhancement, and may include *puffery,* which is simply some level of acceptable exaggeration, such as Budweiser's "the King of beers" or Del Monte's "super natural" advertising phrases.[31]

Some advertising for brands with high awareness and high penetration is designed to increase usage by current customers. This type of advertising is termed **expansion advertising** and is intended to encourage "substitution in use." Advertising messages such as "use A-1 to grill burgers" or "consume Special K as an afternoon snack" have been found effective for encouraging expanded usage.[32]

Another strategy used by advertisers emphasizes the product's relative competitive value in the marketplace. Such value-based advertising is now prevalent in many consumer goods categories. The danger in heavy reliance on advertising messages that focus predominantly on value or price claims is that these strategies increase consumer sensitivity to price and make price differences more salient to buyers.[33]

Jim Ensign, Senior Vice President, Doe-Anderson, Inc., discusses the characteristics of effective advertising: "The advertising messages we create for our clients must accomplish at least two things to be successful. First, the messages must be *relevant* to the consumer. Advertising will never make a person interested in a product or a service if it does not appeal to or address a preexisting need or desire. Second, the message must be presented in an unexpected manner or environment. In the United States, adults are exposed to over 5,000 "promotional" messages every day. To break through the clutter, the message must stand out in an appealing way."

Message strategies frequently attempt to convey a distinct product image or quality appeal. Timex ads, for example, consistently focus on product quality; Lexus ads appeal to buyers' self-images. Some messages appeal to the hedonistic, or pleasure-seeking, side of consumers.

Comparative advertising relates a sponsored brand to a competitive brand on at least one product attribute. Objective attribute comparisons seem to be most effective at enhancing consumer attitudes about the sponsoring brand. Well-known comparisons include MCI against AT&T; Subaru against Volvo; Toshiba computers against Compaq; Maxwell House coffee against Folgers; American Express credit cards against Visa; Pizza Hut versus Domino's; and Weight Watchers diet meals against Lean Cuisine.[34] In some countries, like Greece and Argentina, comparative advertising is restricted to brand X comparisons. In Japan, comparative advertising is not used at all.

Typically, the advertiser claims superiority of its product on the most important features being compared. By not claiming superiority on a less important attribute, the advertiser implies admission of a slight shortcoming, which may actually enhance the credibility of the other claims. An advertiser may also enhance a lesser-

Thinking Critically

Comparative advertisements are frequently used in the United States. However, questions have been raised by advertising researchers regarding their effectiveness. The conventional wisdom is that comparative ad messages are most effective for secondary brands or at least not for the dominant brand in a market or product category.

- What aspects of consumer information processing might account for this view of when comparative claims are best used?

known product by comparing it with a well-known product. Comparative claims may represent either direct comparative advertising or indirect comparative advertising. In direct comparative advertisements, the advertised brand is compared overtly with a named competitor or competitors. Indirect claims involve no mention of competing brand names but assert generally that the advertised brand is superior or better.

Message strategies with *emotional appeals* attempt to evoke feelings, moods, and memories. Diet Pepsi and Dr Pepper commercials, for example, associate warm feelings with their brands. Marketers of insurance, tires, and automobiles may use *fear appeals* related to safety. The "baby in a tire" theme, produced by DDB Needham Advertising Agency of New York for Michelin Tires, recognizes the value of such advertising. The Club, an auto-theft device, stresses fear in its advertisements. And deodorant, shampoo, and toothpaste ads frequently play on the consumer's desire to be liked or to avoid disapproval.

A *celebrity endorsement* may be an element of the creative message strategy. Well-known spokespersons, such as Elizabeth Taylor, Tim Allen, and Tiger Woods, can enhance the persuasive impact of a message.

The milk-mustache appeals have been very effective at encouraging attitude change among consumers toward the use of milk and its nutritional benefits. These ads have included models, actors, and athletes as celebrity endorsers. This strategy is not without some risk, however, as evidenced by problems encountered by former frequent endorsers Michael Jackson, Madonna, Burt Reynolds, and O. J. Simpson.

Humor appeals can increase consumer attention and recall. The Energizer Bunny campaign created by TBWA Chiat Day agency has been rated as the most effective by consumers.[35] The most traditional of Super Bowl advertisers, Anheuser-Busch, relies heavily upon humor and has been particularly successful when animals are used in its ads to generate humorous situations. In fact, the company's ads, including the 2000 entry in which a dog gleefully chases a Budweiser truck until crashing into a parked service van, have won two recent Super Bowl Ad Meter competitions.[36]

Celebrities are often selected for advertisements because of their perceived expertise. The Nuprin–Steve Young pairing promoting solutions for aches and pains from athletic competition is one example. In other instances, celebrity endorsements are intended to help consumers identify with the product. For example, ads

Earning Customer Loyalty

Leo Burnett's repeat business

More than anything else, Leo Burnett, the global, Chicago-based advertising agency, is dedicated to keeping its clients from leaving the agency. Leo Burnett's customer retention rate is among the highest in the advertising industry. As part of this commitment, clients and employees are treated as the firm's most important assets. The agency's success is based on creating value that ties the clients to the agency—value generated from the development of creative ad campaigns that are effective at achieving client objectives.

Creativity is a sensitivity to human nature and an ability to communicate it, and the best creative advertising comes from an understanding of what people are thinking and feeling. It is this understanding of client customers—that is, a thorough commitment to the principles of the marketing concept—that enables Leo Burnett to earn client loyalty and, hence, maintain the agency's own customer base. However, even the best agencies lose business. So when

Leo Burnett lost portions of the United Airlines, McDonald's, and Miller Lite accounts, the company retooled itself and reorganized under one large umbrella. These changes enabled Burnett to successfully compete for and win the rights to handle the consolidated brand duties for Heinz convenience meal products. In addition, Delta Airlines, seeking a fresh start under new leadership, moved its business to Leo Burnett.

Source: Nikhil Deogun, "Media and Marketing: Coca-Cola Rethinks Its Ad Strategy," *The Wall Street Journal,* July 13, 1999, p. B2; Stuart Elliott, "Another Revamping at Leo Burnett," *The New York Times,* October 25, 1999, p. C22; Stuart Elliott, "2 Big Advertisers Consolidate Work," *The New York Times,* March 29, 1999, p. C11; Daniel McGinn, "Pour on the Pitch," *Newsweek,* May 31, 1999, p. 50; Dottie Enrico, "Advertisers Shift to Global Agencies," *USA Today,* February 28, 1996, p. 3B; Mark Gleason, "Bruised Burnett Says Loss Is Frustrating," *Advertising Age,* October 21, 1996, p. 58; Frederick F. Reichheld, *The Loyalty Effect: The Hidden Force behind Growth, Profits, and Lasting Value* (Cambridge, MA: Harvard Business School Press, 1996); and Terence A. Shimp, *Advertising, Promotion, and Supplemental Aspects of Integrated Marketing Communications,* 5th ed. (Fort Worth, TX: Dryden Press, 2000).

Emotional appeals that evoke feelings of warmth and caring are an effective means of instilling positive brand attitudes.

Fear appeals are often used to encourage support for programs related to violence, drug use, and other social issues.

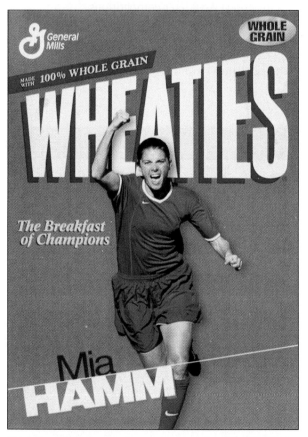

Celebrity endorsers are a frequent means of getting attention and generating positive attitudes toward sponsored brands.

Humor also generates interest and attitude change as an advertising message strategy. American Dairy Farmers incorporates humor in the promotion of cheese products.

that include professional athletes appeal to young people who dream of successful sports careers themselves.

Regardless of the punch celebrity endorsements or humor can have, however, the message still must reflect some competitive advantage, unique product benefit, and value.[37]

One strategy alternative that is controversial in terms of both the ethical issues involved and practical effectiveness is **subliminal advertising.** Although initially related to ad messages presented at a rate or level below thresholds of conscious awareness, this practice today most often involves the embedding of hidden symbols, such as sexual images or brand information, in advertisements. A number of books have been written on the dangers of subliminal advertising, but evidence supporting its practical effectiveness is virtually nonexistent. Most important, the very fact that such messages are embedded or concealed make the subliminal information extremely weak relative to more vivid stimuli.[38]

A growing phenomenon is the **advertorial,** a special advertising section with some nonadvertising content included in magazines. Advertorials are typically sold as special deals to advertisers that would not normally advertise in the magazine. An example is the "Guide to Entertainment" presented in *The New Yorker,* paid for by Chrysler. Advertorials offer advertisers a way to stand out in a cluttered media environment.[39] Television's counterpart is the **infomercial,** a 30-minute ad that resembles a talk show or news program. This form of direct marketing is now frequently seen on both network and cable TV.

A new form of advertising, **product placement advertising,** combines the efforts of marketers with moviemakers. Noteworthy examples include Apple in *Forest Gump* and Dr Pepper in *101 Dalmations.* Likewise, Dodge Ram has a starring role in *Twister.* Both obtained considerable product exposure within a unique medium. A related phenomenon is the use of joint advertising efforts to promote movies and products. Milk producers used *The Phantom* for a milk-mustache ad. PepsiCo and *Star Wars* have been featured in joint advertising, much like the long-term agreement between McDonald's and Disney.[40]

Selecting and Scheduling Media

Media planning involves decisions on *media class* (television, magazines) and *media vehicles* (specific television programs, specific magazines). Marketers must then decide on *media schedules* (frequency, timing of ads).

MEDIA CLASSES   There are seven classes of advertising media: television, magazines, newspapers, radio, outdoor, transit, and direct mail. There are advantages and disadvantages of these, and the effectiveness of each approach depends on its unique capabilities.

Television, magazines, and radio are useful in building brand awareness. TV, in particular, can reach mass markets. And with the advent of cable and specialized networks, TV can target specific markets at a relatively cheap cost per individual exposure. Television commercials, however, are expensive in total. The most expensive buys for the 1999–2000 season, for example, were for 30-second slots during *ER* ($545,000) and *Friends* ($510,000); keep in mind, too, that these figures include only air time, not production costs.[41] Moreover, since TV ads typically last 15 to 30 seconds and are surrounded by other messages, consumers can easily tune them out.

Magazines can present complex and factual information. Messages can be read leisurely, have a long life, have pass-along exposure, and can be targeted to specific audiences. But magazine ads are subject to interference from competing ads and take a substantial time to develop and introduce.

Newspaper advertising is excellent for local retail sales promotions. It can be developed quickly and can effectively target particular locations. But newspapers contain many ads and do not typically generate much audience involvement. The

Billboards are useful as a means of building brand-name awareness. Billboard advertising is common in many mass transit vehicles.

production quality of newspaper advertising is fairly low, though newspaper inserts do enable higher quality. For retailers, however, newspaper advertising is an effective communications medium.

Radio advertising can be quite cost-effective, the commercials can be targeted to specific audiences, and repetition of messages is possible. However, radio messages are subject to channel zapping and of course have no visual impact. Further, radio messages have a short life and typically generate only minimal involvement.

Outdoor advertising consists mainly of billboards constructed on leased property and rented to advertising companies. Billboards reach large numbers of consumers effectively and inexpensively. Billboard advertising is useful in supporting TV and radio campaigns and is particularly effective for building awareness of new brands. The average American now spends more time driving than eating meals, and two-thirds of that time is spent driving alone. U.S. outdoor advertising includes more than 400,000 billboards, plus billboard-sized ads placed on 37,000 buses. The costs for billboards are based upon traffic counts and the average number of daily impressions.[42] However, billboards present only limited message content, the span of exposure is brief, and messages must be viewed at a distance.

Jim Ensign, Senior Vice President, Doe-Anderson, Inc., comments on the use of the Internet and advertising: "The Internet, specifically the World Wide Web, is being integrated into all of our clients' marketing communications programs. In fact, a number of our clients are 'dot coms,' conducting their business primarily on the Web. We are rarely using the Web as only an 'advertising' medium. We are using it as an incredible tool to provide alternative sales channels, customer service, public relations, and direct marketing."

Transit advertisements—signs and messages on or in public buses and trains—are billboards on wheels. Transit ads inside vehicles are low in cost and provide frequent and lengthy exposure to riders. But message space is limited and typically reaches a restricted audience. The vehicle environment may detract from the prestige of the advertiser or message, and crowded conditions during rush hours may limit the opportunity to process the messages.

Direct mail, among the fastest-growing means of advertising today, has several significant advantages. It can reach narrow markets and enable the advertiser to elaborate on ad claims. Direct mail is also important in support of business-to-business marketing communications programs and is available to small and large companies. When coupled with toll-free numbers or return envelopes, direct mail can generate direct-response sales. But the frequency of direct-mail advertising can limit its effectiveness. Many consumers perceive such ads as junk mail and don't pay much attention to them. The success of direct-mail campaigns depends on the quality of the mailing lists used to target customers. In addition, printing, mailing, and development costs can make direct-mail marketing expensive.

MEDIA VEHICLES   Once the marketer has selected the media class, it must choose the specific advertising vehicles (specific magazines, radio, TV shows). The selection depends on the cost-effectiveness of a particular outlet for reaching desired market audiences. Factors include audience size and composition and the cost of running the ad. Advertisers seek to find audiences that contain high proportions of target customers. It is in making these decisions that demographics (i.e., characteristics of audiences) are often so important. Firms such as Simmons Research Bureau can help here. For example, an advertiser can request data exposure or magazine readership for women with incomes over $30,000 who regularly purchase tennis

"Drive":30
1.) Title card: "I Can Be Better" With Tiger Woods. Brought to you by the new Air Zoom TW.
Anncr. (VO): I can be better with Tiger Woods, Brought to you by the new Air Zoom TW.

2.) (Cut to Tiger)
Tiger: Today's topic . . . tee height.

3.) (Cut to close-up of golf ball on tee)
Tiger (VO): I like to tee off my ball just above the club head.

4.) (Cut to Tiger watching to see where his golf ball lands)
SFX: Sprinkler comes on.

5.) (He keeps watching . . .)
SFX: Lawn mower.
(. . . and watching)

6.) Tiger: Experiment and you'll find the tee height that's right for you.
Title card: Nike and Tiger Woods logo.

TV story boards are used to display the sequence and content of advertisements. Here, a humorous theme is employed using Tiger Woods as the spokesperson for Nike.

equipment. Similar sources for TV and newspaper audiences are provided by Arbitron, A. C. Nielsen, and MediaMark.

A common method to evaluate vehicles within a specific medium is by **cost per thousand (CPM)**. For magazines, the formula is:

$$CPM = [(\text{magazine page cost} \times 1{,}000)/\text{circulation}].$$

Using data for 2000 from www.mediastart.com, assume *Sports Illustrated* charges an insertion cost of $180,000 for a full-page, four-color advertisement and has a paid circulation of 3,281,395. The CPM for *SI* would be:

$$[(\$180{,}000 \times 1{,}000)/3{,}281{,}395] = \$54.85$$

Marketers can calculate this value for other magazines in that class and make comparisons for the decision. Rate and circulation statistics can be obtained from *Standard Rate & Data Services: Consumer Magazines.* Although this is a useful decision tool, CPM figures cannot be used to make comparisons across media and do not account for the quality of the audience, pass-along readership, the appropriateness of the media vehicle for the product category, or the nature of the editorial content.

An alternative to the CPM concept is CPM-TM, or the cost per thousand to reach a desired target market segment. Consider again the *SI* example and assume that Cadillac, a frequent sponsor of golf events, wishes to reach men with incomes over $50,000. This group makes up 40 percent of *Sports Illustrated* readership. The effective circulation then is only 1,312,558, and the CPM-TM increases to $137.14. This figure reflects more closely the cost-efficiency of reaching an important target segment for Cadillac.

MEDIA SCHEDULES   The most basic concepts in media scheduling are reach and frequency. **Reach** refers to the number of different people or households exposed to an ad or campaign over a specified time period (usually four weeks). **Frequency** refers to the number of times a person or household is exposed to a communications vehicle. Advertisers must address the basic question: Emphasize reach or frequency? When advertising is for a new brand, reach may be the paramount objective. Messages presenting detailed information or vying with heavily advertised competitors need greater frequency or repetition.

Increased repetition relative to competing brands has been shown effective at increasing top-of-mind awareness and brand preference. As such, advertising expenditures and brand equity are related in many mature product categories, such as cereal, soft drinks, and beer. Since advertising is often directed at consumers with existing knowledge and preferences, increased repetition helps maintain the ready accessibility of brand associations in the minds of consumers.[43]

One rule of thumb has been that three exposures are required for impact; that is, three exposures on average per individual are thought necessary to generate adequate message processing. More recently, practitioners have begun to realize that for large, well-known consumer brands, two repetitions within a purchase cycle may be sufficient. In truth, there are a large number of variables that affect advertising frequency, including how old the brand is and how well-known it is among its target audiences.[44]

For TV advertising, several conclusions regarding media schedules and the amount of advertising were recently offered in a summary of a large number of tests of the effectiveness of split-cable advertising. Specifically:

1. Brands in categories in a growth mode are more likely to benefit from increased TV advertising.

2. Increased advertising added to either the front end or back end of a media plan is more likely to result in higher sales than is increased advertising distributed throughout the plan.

3. Increased spending is generally only effective when coupled with changes in creative executions.

4. Increased spending for new brands or line extensions is more effective than similar increases for established brands.[45]

Thinking Critically

The objectives of many consumer ads for individual brands seen on national network and cable programs are to build brand recognition, attitudes, and sales. Hence, the effectiveness of these ads will eventually be considered in light of brand performance (i.e., sales, market share).

- What criteria or outcomes might be used to evaluate the effectiveness of corporate image campaigns? Of corporate advocacy advertising?

- How might a business-to-business company evaluate its own trade advertising when personal selling is the business's primary means of promotion?

Interestingly, the findings from a series of additional split-cable studies conducted by Frito-Lay confirmed these conclusions. Moreover, their results showed a significant increase in sales within the first three months for the effective campaigns (i.e., those campaigns resulting in significant increases in sales compared with comparison control areas in which the campaigns were not run).[46]

Advertisers are becoming increasingly concerned about reducing the waste of reaching consumers outside intended market segments. In response, media have taken steps to improve their efficiency. *Time, Reader's Digest, Newsweek,* and other magazines, for example, have invested heavily in "selective binding" technology, which permits targeting of advertising to subscribers in specific zip code areas.

Evaluating Advertising Effectiveness

The evaluation of advertising typically includes pretesting or copytesting, posttesting, and sales effectiveness research. Given today's bottom-line emphasis, firms are making the evaluation of advertising effectiveness a much more important task.

PRETESTING In general, **pretesting** proposed print and broadcast ads is done by evaluating consumer reactions through direct questioning and focus groups. Marketers evaluate the ads for overall likability, consumer recall of information, message communication, and their effects on purchase intentions and brand attitudes.

Research Systems Corporation (RSC) evaluates advertising for marketers and ad agencies.[47] From 500 to 600 randomly chosen consumers view TV pilot programs and a number of commercials, including the ones being evaluated. Before the screening, participants are shown various consumer products and are asked to indicate which they would like to receive. After the screening, a second questionnaire is administered. A persuasion score is computed for each commercial, which indicates the differences in percentages of consumers selecting the advertised product before and after the screening. Respondents are also called 48 hours later to explore estimates of recall. These viewer reactions are used to predict sales effectiveness of the ads.

POSTTESTING Marketers use **posttesting** through recall and attitude tests and inquiry evaluations to assess the effectiveness of an ad campaign. In **unaided recall tests** for print ads, respondents are questioned with no prompting about ads included in magazines. In **aided recall tests,** subjects are given lists of ads and asked which they remembered and read. An **inquiry evaluation** comes from the number of consumers responding to requests in an ad, such as using coupons or asking for samples or more product information.

Using Technology

Tailor-made advertising

TiVo of Silicon Valley has developed a smart digital video recorder and programming service that allows consumers instant access to their favorite shows or programs of interest on demand. With TiVo, you can watch what you want, when desired. The TiVo boxes, which sell for under $500, record broadcasts onto a high-capacity computer disk. TiVo has important implications for advertisers as well. Specifically, the product lets viewers pick alternative versions of ads being broadcast. Advertisements can be localized and tailored based on the interests of viewers. In addition, consumers can search and find information relevant to their preferences. As such, the technology personalizes the television-watching experience. General Motors has already partnered with TiVo to display car ads that match viewer likes and dislikes. For example, when a viewer who loves sports cars tunes to a program with a GM ad for minivans, the TiVo product substitutes a stored ad for Corvette.

Sources: "Companies Consider Ways to Target TV Advertising," *Marketing News,* March 15, 1999, p. 5; http://www.tivo.com; J. William Gurley, "How the Web Will Warp Advertising," *Fortune,* November 9, 1998, pp. 119–20; and Erin Strout, "The End of Advertising?" *Sales & Marketing Management,* January 2000, p. 15.

Starch Message Report Services provides awareness and readership data about ads carried in consumer and business magazines. Burke Market Research administers a day-after-recall program (DAR) for TV commercials. DAR is the percentage of individuals in an audience who recall something specific about the ad being posttested. High levels of recall do not necessarily result in increased sales, however.

SALES EFFECTIVENESS EVALUATIONS Sales effectiveness evaluations are the most stringent tests of advertising efficiency. They assess whether the advertising resulted in increased sales. Given the many factors that affect sales and the number of competing messages, sales effectiveness evaluations are difficult, and marketers and ad agencies can differ on measures of results. Increasingly, however, evaluations of advertising effectiveness based on brand awareness will no longer be sufficient. Advertising evaluations instead will be based on its contributions to sales growth.

Some newer programs combine awareness and sales data to evaluate advertising effectiveness. For example, ASI Monitor combines three data sets: (1) traditional ad awareness and attitude telephone surveys, (2) Nielsen household panel purchase data, and (3) Nielsen Monitor Plus data that include gross rating point (GRP) measures. The GRP measures incorporate both reach and frequency information. This tracking program allows advertisers to determine if advertising messages are getting through to consumers as schedules are run over time and the effects of that advertising on sales.[48]

Recognizing the need to provide quality advertising that improves company performance, DDB Needham rebates a substantial portion of its fee if sales for an advertised product do not improve. If ad campaigns are successful, DDB Needham receives a bonus in addition to its fee.[49] A. C. Nielsen has been a leader in studying the effects of advertising on sales. In one Nielsen study using matched samples of 4,000 households, results showed that for 9 of 10 packaged goods investigated, households exposed to magazine ads were more likely to purchase the advertised product than were those who had not seen the magazine ads. A. C. Nielsen is also developing measurement procedures for assessing the global effectiveness of Internet ads and audiences via a service called Nielsen/NetRatings.[50]

An understanding of the effectiveness of direct TV advertising on purchase behavior is emerging as advertisers study the results of their practices as part of direct-response television messages. For example, the effects of 1-800 direct-response advertising mostly disappear within eight hours. Response to daytime advertising is highest in the hour in which the ad is run. It is important to note that the sales effects differ substantially by station and creative design.[51]

Ethical and Legal Issues in Advertising

Advertising provides many useful functions for buyers, advertisers, and society. For buyers, benefits include comparative information about the availability and the characteristics of products and brands. For advertisers, advertising builds long-term brand recognition, introduces new products, and enhances corporate images. For society, advertising increases economic efficiency by enabling products to be sold in mass markets at lower unit costs and to be distributed over wide geographic areas.

Advertising does have its critics, however, and abuses do occur. In some instances, advertising malpractice has received considerable notoriety. Several years ago, Volvo Cars of North America altered cars in its "monster truck crushing" ads, for example. Other ethical issues related to advertising are more subtle. We discuss them below.

Is Advertising Manipulative?

Some critics charge that advertising stimulates needs and wants by creating unrealistic ideals about appearance and social identity. And indeed, students of marketing agree that advertising is intended to influence buyer behavior. Are ads that are designed to emphasize the idea that happiness and well-being are dependent upon physical attractiveness ethical? Hair-loss remedies and surgical "lift" procedures are frequently advertised with their messages and themes tied to enhanced self-esteem.[52] But if it's so easy to manipulate people into buying, why do so many products fail? It would seem more likely that instead of being manipulated by advertising, the reverse is true, and buyers exercise control over the marketplace by the choices they make with their discretionary income.

Is Advertising Deceptive or Misleading?

The Federal Trade Commission (FTC), which monitors marketplace abuses, prohibits advertising messages that deceive consumers by presenting false claims, by omitting relevant information, or by giving misleading impressions that result in faulty decisions.

In some instances the FTC requires **corrective advertising** to remedy misleading impressions or information in an ad. The offending advertiser or marketer must develop and pay for advertising that counters the misperceptions. Corrective advertising is required most often when there have been outright misrepresentations of fact, rather than presentation of half-truths.

In one of the earliest cases, Warner-Lambert was required in 1975 to spend $10 million in advertising to correct misleading claims about the ability of Listerine mouthwash to combat colds.[53] Volvo was instructed to run corrective ads in local newspapers, *USA Today,* and *The Wall Street Journal* to explain its withdrawal of ads misrepresenting the effect of the "monster truck crushing" demonstration discussed above.[54] The FTC required Volkswagen (and Audi) to run a series of full-page national magazine ads to inform consumers about product performance problems. The magazine advertising was required to reach a nonduplicated audience of at least 75 million adults. The FTC has also become very involved with the deception that can occur from "implied claims" included in the advertising of dietary-supplement products. As an example cited in *The Wall Street Journal,* scientific evidence is required to back up the implied heart-benefit claim from the assertion that "90 percent of cardiologists regularly take a certain product." Balance Bar, an energy food product, was forced to alter its claims of being proven clinically effective for the general population.[55]

How Does Advertising Affect Children?

The youth market offers tremendous potential to business, and much advertising is directed toward children. Advertisers know young consumers influence parental decisions and exert significant buying power themselves. Concerns about advertising to children center largely on three important issues:

- Children's ability to understand advertising's intent to persuade.
- The nutritional value of food and candy products marketed to children.
- The influence of advertising on children's demands to parents for advertised products.

On the other hand, some opponents of limits on advertising to children argue that:

- Parents are better able than the FTC to help children interpret information and make decisions.
- Children know that fruits and vegetables are more nutritious than sugared foods.
- Banning TV advertising to children limits free speech.[56]

In response to criticisms about questionable program content that carries advertising designed to appeal to children, Procter & Gamble and other major advertisers, such as IBM, GM, Sears, and Johnson & Johnson, are paying the Time-Warner WB network to develop and air shows with less sex and violence. Concerns about advertising and marketing to children relate to the Internet as well. In fact, on-line marketer deception has increased calls for legislation to protect both children's privacy as well as the future of e-commerce.[57]

Is Advertising Intrusive?

Many people are irritated by unwelcome advertising messages that threaten their right to privacy. Most observers agree the marketplace is cluttered with advertising messages and that any one ad has limited ability to influence consumers. Yet recognition of this limitation only reinforces pressures to increase ad repetition.

Related questions have to do with methods of ad communications delivery. Is it ethical for infomercials to package commercial messages as regular programming? What about the practice of allowing TV advertisers into school classrooms? Intrusiveness concerns about technology also extend to junk faxes and "spam advertising." Specifically, the same laws that require telemarketers to maintain "do-not-call" lists—the Telephone Consumer Protection Act—also prohibit marketers from sending unsolicited advertisements to facsimile machines. Several state legislatures have passed laws and federal legislation has been drafted governing unsolicited e-mail, or "spam advertising." [58]

Cause-Related Advertising

An extension of corporate advocacy advertising is the concept of **cause-related marketing (CRM)**, or social advertising. Cause-related marketing is the increasingly common phenomenon of companies' aligning themselves with causes, such as AIDS research, drug-abuse prevention, gay rights, racial harmony, and conservation. The real objectives of these campaigns vary from solely economic (i.e., the cause affiliation is entirely strategic) to solely social where there is extraordinary commitment to the cause. One well-known example is the campaign of Benetton shock ads that combine both economic and social objectives. The ads, which highlight issues such as AIDS, the Bosnia conflict, and the plight of refugees, are designed to both get attention and position Benetton as a cutting-edge social marketer. Sears stopped selling Benetton clothes for a period in 2000, in reaction to Benetton's campaign tied to capital punishment. For these programs to work, the objectives for the campaign should be long term, the cause should fit the company, and the employees should believe the issues are important.[59] While most cause-related marketing is designed to enhance corporate image perceptions, P&G is tying CRM to individual brands, such as Ariel and Daz, in efforts to build trust among consumers by linking individual brands to environmental causes. Also, this example tied to P&G in Europe, New Covent Garden Soup linked with a homeless charity to raise funds through sales of its soup to help refurbishment of their kitchens.[60]

Advertising Harmful Products

The use of advertising to market harmful products, such as cigarettes and alcohol, is frequently criticized. Regulations, both legislated and self-imposed, exist, but critics often argue for further restrictions on such advertising. In markets without restrictions, tobacco advertisers frequently connect smoking with glamour, excitement, and the great outdoors.

The Joe Camel campaign was quite successful in raising brand recognition, particularly among children and adolescents. In response to much criticism of the ads, however, Camel recently agreed to discontinue the use of the well-recognized cartoon character. Substantial opposition has arisen also to Seagram's announced plans to advertise its liquor products on TV.[61]

Public Relations

Public relations (PR) is often used as a complement to support advertising, personal selling, and sales promotions for disseminating marketing communications. PR communications are not overtly sponsored in the typical advertising sense and are a useful support to other forms of marketing communications. PR is an attempt to improve a company's relationship with its publics. Public relations may focus on customers, employees, stockholders, community members, news media, or the government. Most large corporations operate central PR departments to carry out coordinated public relations programs, and smaller companies with limited resources must also deal with PR issues. AT&T and other companies support scientific studies to reduce fears about links between the use of cellular phones and cancer.[62] The Pharmaceutical Manufacturers' Association recently instituted an $8 million print campaign to inform the public that life-saving drugs represent only 5 percent of national health care costs.

As advertising becomes less effective, companies of all sizes try to build public awareness and loyalty by supporting customer interests. The general public increasingly demands that companies behave responsibly toward society as a whole and that they have obligations to more than their customers and stockholders. Profit maximization and social responsibility need not be incompatible, however. Today, companies show greater concern for employee welfare, minority advancement, community improvement, environmental protection, and other causes. A PR department plays a critical role in planning, coordinating, and promoting these visionary activities for an organization.[63] Some companies have effectively embodied public relations principles into their overall marketing communications program. For example, Members Only fashion company funded over $100 million worth of social consciousness–raising advertising about drug abuse and voter registration. More recent advertising promotes care for the homeless.

Public Relations Functions

Most frequently, PR functions support a firm's products and services. Often, however, public relations activity addresses corporate image and social responsibility. Exxon Corporation's varied program to maintain and improve its corporate image is a good example. Its PR activity ranges from an ongoing campaign about environmental damage from the Alaskan oil spill targeted toward the scientific community to charitable support of the Special Olympics.[64] The remarkable turnaround of Sears during 1995 and 1996 is attributed in part to its effective use of PR communications in rebuilding relationships with the financial community and the media.

Public relations functions include press relations; product promotions; internal and external corporate communications; lobbying to promote, defeat, or circumvent legislation and regulations; advising management about public issues and company positions and image; and overall, responding to a variety of occurrences in the marketplace.[65] Driven by the Internet, the thrust of public relations firms is moving more from influencing the press to influencing companies. PR firms and PR departments within companies are acquiring new skills as they work with dot com companies to build business strategies and to establish marketplace presence and positioning. These dot com companies often start with PR work, even before advertising, in efforts to generate word-of-mouth communications. Gaining positive exposure among investors and analysts is crucial to young high-tech companies' survival.[66] Public relations can be **proactive** or **reactive,** as shown in Exhibit 17–6.

Publicity

Publicity, the generation of information by a company to the news media, has a narrower focus than public relations. The primary publicity techniques are news releases, press conferences, and feature articles, often presented in the business press.

One advantage of publicity is its relatively high credibility, because the messages are not paid for by a commercial sponsor. Information about a company presumably must be newsworthy to be published by an objective source. However, publicity messages may be revised by the media, then released at times most convenient to the broadcaster or publisher. Unfortunately, some publicity may be negative news

Exhibit 17–6	*Proactive and reactive marketing public relations*
Proactive marketing PR	**Reactive marketing PR**
• Product release announcements, statements by firm's spokespeople, even sponsorship, articles in business press. • Corporate image enhancement and development of goodwill; corporate advocacy advertising supports certain position on given social issue. • Cause-related marketing in which firm contributes specified amount to designated cause when customers buy firm's products.	• Firm's response to negative events and damaging publicity. • Negative information comes from news media, consumer advocacy groups, government agencies; usually related to product defects or problematic company practices. • Success depends on firm's ability to align its interests with the public's interests so both are served.

Public relations can support the communications efforts for all types of organizations. Large firms, such as Coca-Cola, should have the proactive plans in place to use if negative events occur.

stories beyond the firm's control, as when product tamperings occurred for Tylenol and Diet Pepsi. A firm's PR department must be prepared to react constructively and without delay when unfortunate events occur.

One very effective publicity stunt was the April Fools' joke by Taco Bell. The company announced in full-page ads in six major city newspapers and *USA Today* that it had purchased the Liberty Bell. At the end of the day, Taco Bell made a retraction and offered to give $50,000 to help restore the Liberty Bell. Even those most initially irate at the apparent inappropriate corporate sponsorship were amused. More important to Taco Bell, the company received at least 400 TV mentions, including network evening news coverage. This represented millions of dollars in exposure for $300,000 in media costs.[67]

As companies such as Intel and Polaris Software, which saw flaws in their products exposed to the world via the Internet, have learned, negative publicity can spread extremely fast via the new technology. Ameritech Corp., Quaker Oats Co., and Allstate Corp. have gone so far as to monitor Internet discussion groups or chat rooms in efforts to learn of negative comments about their products and services.[68]

Proactive PR requires that the firm formulates a crisis plan for communications in the event of an emergency. Such a plan should try to determine what unfortunate events might occur and specify who will speak for the company and who will be the audience. In times of emergency, one primary audience likely will be the news media. In instances of product recall, an important audience will be retailers.[69]

Summary

1. **Understand the characteristics, functions, and types of advertising.** Advertising, like other promotional elements, plays an important role in the total marketing communications program. Advertising is impersonal, paid for by an identified sponsor, and disseminated through mass channels of communication to promote the adoption of goods, services, persons, or ideas.

   Advertising can serve a number of functions, including heightening consumer awareness, disseminating information about a product's attributes or social value, shaping product images or emotional responses, persuading buyers to purchase, or reminding consumers about products, brands, or firms.

   Advertisements can be classified according to the target audience, geographic area, medium, and purpose. Corporate image advertising promotes an organization's image and role in the community as a corporate citizen. Other types are corporate advocacy, public service, classified, direct-response, business-to-business, and cooperative advertising.

2. **Realize how people process advertising information and how it affects buyer behavior.** Advertisements rely on successive stages of processing by a targeted individual: exposure (presenting the information to a receiver), attention (the conscious direction of a receiver's mental effort toward the advertising stimulus), comprehension (the degree to which the receiver correctly understands the intended message), acceptance (the degree to which the receiver accepts or yields to the message), and retention (the extent to which the receiver can recall or recognize the message at a later time).

   The relationships between these stages, and therefore the effectiveness of the advertising itself, may be affected by consumer needs as well as consumer motivations, opportunities, and abilities to process the information.

3. **Discuss approaches to developing advertising campaigns.** The steps in developing an ad campaign are (1) determining advertising objectives, (2) determining advertising budget, (3) designing appropriate creative strategies, (4) selecting and scheduling media, and (5) evaluating ad effectiveness.

4. **Describe different advertising objectives and the message strategies used to achieve them.** Advertising objectives should be consistent with the organization's overall marketing objectives and be realistic, precise, and measurable. Advertising objectives may be to inform, to persuade, or to remind.

   Many different message strategies can be used to achieve the advertising objective. One strategy is to compare the advertised brand to another. Celebrity endorsements, humor, and fear appeals are other tactics used to enhance the persuasive impact of advertisements.

5. **Understand the decisions involved in selecting media and scheduling advertising.** Decisions on media class involve choosing the most appropriate media channels, such as television, magazines, or radio. This choice depends on both the size and characteristics of the firm's target markets and the characteristics of the message itself.

   Decisions on media vehicles refer to the selection of the specific outlets within the chosen media class. These decisions usually depend on factors such as cost and the size and characteristics of the audience. Reach and frequency are important considerations in making these decisions.

6. **Explain how marketers assess advertising effectiveness.** Effectiveness evaluations involve some combination of pretesting, posttesting, and sales response research. Pretesting usually involves evaluating consumer reactions to proposed advertisements. Posttesting is used to measure the effectiveness of the chosen strategy during or after the ad campaign. Posttesting may include aided or unaided recall measurements, attitude evaluations, and sales impact effects.

7. **Appreciate the roles of public relations and publicity in marketing.** Public relations functions include the dissemination of press releases, product promotion efforts, and corporate communications, as well as lobbying and advising corporate executives about public issues affecting the firm. Publicity refers to the dissemination of nonpaid communication in news outlets and represents only a part of the larger activity of public relations.

   Marketing-oriented public relations can be proactive or reactive. Proactive marketing public relations refers to the initiation of positive public relations; it may take the form of corporate image advertising, advocacy advertising, or cause-related marketing. Reactive marketing public relations refers to defending an organization from negative and potentially damaging information, including negative events and adverse publicity.

Understanding Marketing Terms and Concepts

Thinking About Marketing

1. What different functions can advertising perform?

2. What are advertising agencies, and what services do they provide?

3. Explain why advertising expenditures have declined during recent years.

4. Define the following: business-to-business advertising; corporate image advertising; corporate advocacy advertising; direct-response advertising; and corrective advertising.

5. What steps are involved in a consumer's processing of advertisements? Why is understanding this sequence of these stages important to advertisers?

6. What can advertisers do to increase exposure, attention, and retention? How does audience involvement influence these processes?

7. Identify the steps involved in the development of an advertising campaign.

8. What are media class decisions, and how do they differ from media vehicle decisions?

9. Contrast pretesting with posttesting in the evaluation of advertising effectiveness. Explain the problem with using sales results as a measure of advertising effectiveness.

10. Explain the differences between advertising and public relations.

Applying Marketing Skills

1. Collect two examples each of: (a) corporate image advertising; (b) corporate advocacy advertising; (c) public service advertising; (d) comparative advertising; (e) classified advertising; (f) direct-response advertising; and (g) business-to-business advertising.

2. Consider the differences across magazine, radio, television, and outdoor advertising. Describe how each works to get consumers' attention and ensure retention.

3. The current average issue circulation for *People* magazine is 3,224,770. The cost for a one-page ad in a regular issue is $82,390. Estimate the CPM for that magazine. Compare it with similar data for *Time:* page cost, $113,700; circulation, 2,962,168. What might you advise a potential advertiser of personal computers? Of cosmetics?

Using the www in Marketing

Activity One   Consider the current Web site of British Airways, the company whose home page introduced the chapter.

1. How would you characterize the company's image based upon the Web site? Using examples, what elements of British Airways' communication mix are mentioned?

2. Examine the site of one of British Airways' competitors. How do the advertising strategies differ?

Activity Two   The Federal Trade Commission is the regulatory body that governs advertising at the federal level and rules on a case-by-case basis regarding deceptive advertising. Consider the information available on the Internet regarding the ongoing activities of the FTC:

1. What guidelines are available that define or describe what constitutes deceptive advertising?

2. Refer to a recent cease-and-desist order in which a company was prevented from further deceptive practices. In this case, what circumstances led the FTC to find the company's advertising deceptive?

3. Consider the Division of Advertising Practices of the Bureau of Consumer Protection. What are the primary areas of focus for its law-enforcement activities?

4. What guidelines are offered regarding advertising substantiation (i.e., test results or data that support ad claims)? Consider the May Department Stores (of Denver) case. What was deceptive about their price advertising?

Making Marketing Decisions
Case 17-1 Pizza Wars: Advertising Better Ingredients

Pizza Hut controls 22 percent of the pizza market with 7,132 stores and is part of the $8.5 billion-a-year company Tricon, which also includes Taco Bell and Kentucky Fried Chicken. Papa John's controls only 5 percent of the market with one-fourth the number of stores. However, as Pizza Hut lost share during the 1990s, Papa John's grew stronger, and Pizza Hut remains concerned. The confrontation between the two has been harsh and interesting to view. The complete fallout from their negative advertising regarding the freshness of ingredients and from the play on each other's advertising messages is as yet unknown. It is important to note that competition between the two pizza firms is about more than just ingredients. In the past five years, pizza sales have risen just 3.6 percent per year. With sales expected to remain flat in the industry, pressures to damage competitors are great.

In a recent settlement, Papa John's was required to pay Pizza Hut for damages for false and misleading advertising. The slogan in question was "Better ingredients. Better pizza." The judge also enjoined the Louisville-based company from further use of the advertising slogan. Such general claims typically are associated with the acceptable use of puffery. However, since Papa John's mentioned Pizza Hut in the ads, the judgment was made that the context of the claims no longer qualified as puffery. Papa John's is reconsidering

their advertising and making adjustments, but plans to appeal the case.

Marketers developing new campaigns must be aware of the potential for liability from comparative advertising claims. Advertisers must be able to document all claims made against competitors. Prior use of vague and general statements will not necessarily justify a slogan's future use. TV networks, which had cleared the Papa John's ads, will have to consider competitive claims more carefully.

Questions

1. Why is advertising "better ingredients and better pizza" deceptive? Comment on the role of puffery in comparative ads for firms with very similar offerings. What rules govern advertising practice under the federal Lanham Act?

2. What is the current status of the *Papa John's* v. *Pizza Hut* case?

3. How does advertising support the marketing of retail pizza sales?

4. Can aggressive advertising like that used by these pizza marketers have negative effects like the outcome of many negative political advertising campaigns?

SOURCES: Stuart Elliot, "Papa John's Ordered to Pay Pizza Hut," *The New York Times,* January 5, 2000, p. C5; James Heckman, " 'Puffery' Claims No Longer So Easy to Make," *Marketing News,* February 14, 2000, p. 6; J. Dee Hill, "Papa John's Seeking a New Tag after Court Fight," *Adweek,* November 29, 1999, p. 2; Daniel Roth, "This Ain't No Pizza Party," *Fortune,* November 9, 1998, p. 158.

Case 17-2 Toyota: Advertising Drives to Success in Europe

More and more international companies are moving away from global standardized advertising—that is, presenting the same advertising campaign in every country in which the company conducts business. A standardized strategy often fails to provide the most effective advertising for a given geographical area, because each area has its own distinctive political, legal, and cultural characteristics. The use of advertising suited to the particular characteristics of a country may be more effective.

Toyota has always taken an unstandardized approach, tailoring its advertising on a country-by-country basis. It lets the local marketers handle all the aspects of advertising for their particular area on the theory that they know the market best. Toyota simply supplies the local advertisers with the necessary raw materials (information pertinent for promoting Toyota vehicles) to develop effective advertisements for their area. This system has been effective for Toyota, which enjoys a significant market share in countries in North America, Asia, and Europe.

Eased trade conditions within Europe could allow Toyota to reevaluate just how integrated (if at all) it wants to make its advertising. Today, Toyota uses an integrative European approach to its advertising for only one brand, the Lexus luxury automobile, which has met with some success. The company might also find it profitable to reduce the number of advertising agencies it works with in Europe. Becoming more standardized in its advertising could offer Toyota certain economies of scale.

Of course, the issue of cultural differences would remain. Consumers in France still differ from those in Italy or the United Kingdom. But the European Union is bound to increase European consumers' familiarity with the culture of the other European countries, particularly when it comes to business and consumer considerations. Although every country will maintain its own identity and cultural values, their marketplace identities are at least converging somewhat.

Additional growth will occur in Europe as barriers limiting imports from Japan fall away. Under export restraint conditions so far, Japanese car dealers have been forced to promote largely their most expensive brands. Now dealers are learning how to sell higher volumes of lower-margin models. Two other phenomena are occurring in the advertising and marketing strategy for Toyota in Europe. First, Toyota Europe has contracted with Saatchi & Saatchi Advertising to handle strategic brand issues for all of Europe. This change suggests a move toward a consolidation of advertising support for Toyota in Europe. Second, the number of dealers receiving new cars has been reduced substantially, with the affected smaller dealers serving as partners providing only service and the taking of new orders. With these changes, the time could be right for Toyota to implement a more standardized advertising program across Europe.

Questions

1. Enumerate and explain the advantages and disadvantages to Toyota of using an integrative, standardized approach versus maintaining its current approach to advertising in Europe.

2. What would you recommend Toyota do regarding its advertising in Europe? Why?

3. Explain the impact that differing cultural values, legal considerations, and economic considerations have on international advertising.

4. Explain why Toyota should or should not promote the Lexus differently from its other automobile brands.

SOURCES: "Bates Saatchi to Open Kosovo Agency," *Advertising Age,* August 2, 1999, p. 41; David Kiley, "A New Set of Wheels," *American Demographics,* August 1999, pp. 38–39; Diana T. Kurylko, "Toyota to Consolidate Its Dealers in Europe," *Automotive News,* December 6, 1999, p. 55; "Choppy Waters: Japanese Cars in Europe," *The Economist,* December 10, 1994, p. 66; "Face-to-Face: With Hiroshi Okuda, Executive Vice President of Toyota," *Japanese Motor Business,* 3rd quarter 1994, pp. 6–16; and Jo-Anne Walker, "Toyota Poaches Director of Marketing from Ford," *Marketing Week,* March 29, 1996, p. 9.

Chapter Eighteen

Consumer and Trade Sales Promotion

After studying this chapter, you should be able to:

1 Explain the role and significance of sales promotion in the marketing communications mix.

2 Understand why sales promotion use and expenditures have increased in recent years.

3 Discuss the objectives and techniques of consumer sales promotion.

4 Discuss the objectives and techniques of trade sales promotion.

5 Explain the limitations of sales promotion.

6 Realize how deceptive and fraudulent sales promotion victimizes both consumers and marketers.

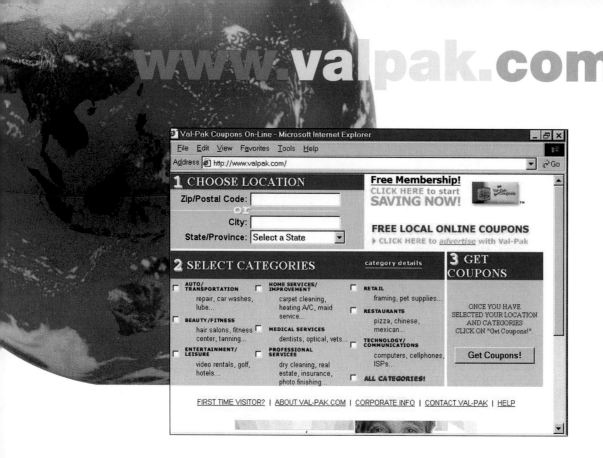

www.valpak.com

Val-Pak Direct Marketing Systems, Inc., is the oldest and largest local cooperative direct-mail company. Founded in 1969 in St. Petersburg, Florida, by an unemployed autoworker, Val-Pak now serves a customer base of 100,000 businesses through 250 field offices. Val-Pak mails 13 billion coupons annually in its familiar blue envelopes to 50 million consumers and small businesses. Its customer-advertisers share the cost of the mailing. Val-Pak is now part of Cox Enterprises, the ninth-largest U.S.-based media company in terms of revenues.

Val-Pak is also the leading distributor of on-line coupons. By accessing Val-Pak's Web site, consumers can download free coupons from a broad range of product and service categories, which are redeemable at local businesses across the United States and Canada. To further its on-line coupon-distribution business, Val-Pak has partnered with Yahoo!, a major Internet access company with 50 million users. Consumers can get Val-Pak coupons directly from Yahoo! or from the Val-Pak site. Popular brands promoted on-line include Goodyear, Fantastic Sam's, Subway, and Jiffy Lube.

While becoming a leader in sales promotion, Val-Pak has also been a good corporate citizen. The company supported the Jerry Lewis "Stars Across America!" telethon for the Muscular Dystrophy Association (MDA) by distributing, in custom-printed envelopes, 39 million fund-raising inserts prior to the event. Field offices contributed to the fund-raising efforts through special events such as bowl-a-thons and auctions.

Although primarily viewed as a direct-mail company, Val-Pak utilizes all forms of marketing combinations to grow its business. A franchise organization, Val-Pak depends on franchise salespeople to continue to sell the customers on direct-mail sales promotion and advertising. The company also benefits from public relations efforts, with support for events such as the MDA telethon generating favorable publicity. With growth expected in alternative media and direct marketing, and the continued important role of sales promotion, Val-Pak is well positioned for the future.

Source: Val-Pak Web site, http://www.valpak.com.

As the Val-Pak example illustrates, sales promotion is designed to boost sales. **Sales promotion** consists of media and nonmedia marketing communications employed for a predetermined, limited time to stimulate trial, increase consumer demand, or improve product availability.[1] Common sales promotion tools are coupons, samples, displays, contests, and sweepstakes. Sales promotion may be directed at ultimate consumers, retailers, or wholesalers. **Consumer sales promotion** is directed at consumers, and **trade sales promotion** is directed at resellers.

This chapter examines the growing role of sales promotion in marketing communications. The objectives, techniques, and limitations of consumer and trade sales promotion are explored. The chapter also looks at ethical and legal issues related to sales promotion.

The Role of Sales Promotion

A unique characteristic of sales promotion is that it offers an incentive for action. A consumer might receive a rebate for making a purchase, for instance, or a retailer may be offered an allowance for purchasing a specific quantity of a product within a specified time period. In contrast to many forms of advertising, sales promotion is oriented toward achieving short-term results. Sales promotion activities rarely stand alone, however; they are typically combined with other forms of marketing communications to create an integrated program.

Effective sales promotion, like all forms of marketing communications, should result from adequate planning as discussed in Chapter 16. Since sales promotion seeks results in the near future, it is possible to set specific, measurable objectives and to accurately monitor results. It should also be understood, however, that since sales promotion often works in conjunction with other communications, coordination of messages and timing is crucial for success. Exhibit 18–1 presents the primary considerations in sales-promotion planning.

SPEED LIMIT 444,312,000 MPH

"I have a Flashcom DSL connection and this is surely the future for internet connectivity. Anyone any place that can get this technology into their home or office is foolish not to order it today! It's fabulous!"

JOHN C. DVORAK
PC MAGAZINE

FREE SETUP
FREE EQUIPMENT
FREE INSTALLATION
FREE FIRST MONTH
SERVICE

FINALLY, INTERNET ACCESS THAT MOVES AT THE SPEED IT SHOULD.

Introducing internet access that is up to 100 times faster.

Experience the fastest internet yet. With DSL from Flashcom, once you're setup you're always on, so there's no wait to connect, no busy signals, and no dropped calls. Plus it works on the same line as your phone so you don't have to pay for a dedicated line, and you can talk while you surf.

CALL NOW 1.877.FLASHCOM (352.7426) www.flashcom.com

Flashcom
COVAD   THE DSL SPECIALISTS

Sales promotion is used to reach a variety of markets and buyers. This Flashcom promotion emphasizes free services and equipment to both business customers and ultimate consumers.

The Significance of Sales Promotion

The role of advertising declined during the latter half of the 1980s and the early 1990s. During this same era, the importance of sales promotion grew. Advertising expenditures have rebounded, yet sales promotion remains a strong part of the marketing communications mix. The marketing environment of recent years and the outlook in coming years suggest a healthy future for sales promotion.

Reasons for the Growth of Sales Promotion

The combined expenditures on consumer and trade sales promotion are almost triple the expenditures on advertising. Observers see no end to increased spending on sales promotion. What has motivated the growth of sales promotion in recent years? Changes in the marketing environment—consumer attitudes, demographic shifts, and lifestyle changes—are favorable for sales promotion, as are emerging technology and changes in retailing. Also, marketers are under pressure to perform well in the short term and are increasingly accountable for achieving measurable results.

CONSUMER FACTORS With the U.S. population growing at less than 1 percent annually, most mature products see only modest growth in per-capita consumption.

| Exhibit 18–1 | *The 10 commandments of creative sales promotion* |

1. **Set specific objectives.** Undisciplined, undirected creative work is a waste of time and resources.

2. **Know how basic promotion techniques work.** A sweepstakes shouldn't be used to encourage multiple purchases or a refund to get new customers. A price-off deal can't reverse a brand's downward sales trend.

3. **Use simple, attention-getting copy.** Most promotions are built around a simple idea: "save 75 cents." Emphasize the idea, and don't try to be cute.

4. **Use contemporary, easy-to-track graphics.** Don't expect to fit 500 words and 20 illustrations into a quarter-page, freestanding insert.

5. **Clearly communicate the concept.** Words and graphics must work together to get the message across.

6. **Reinforce the brand's advertising message.** Tie promotions to the brand's ad campaign.

7. **Support the brand's positioning and image.** This is especially important for image-sensitive brands and categories, like family-oriented Kraft.

8. **Coordinate promotional efforts with other marketing plans.** Be sure to coordinate schedules and plans. A consumer promotion should occur simultaneously with a trade promotion; a free-sample promotion should be timed in conjunction with the introduction of a new line.

9. **Know the media you work through.** Determine which media will work best. Should samples be distributed in stores, door-to-door, or through direct mail? Does the promotion need newspaper or magazine support?

10. **Know when to break the other nine commandments.** A confident, creative person knows when breaking these rules is the smartest way to go.

Source: Adapted with permission from William F. Arens and Courtland L. Bovee, *Contemporary Advertising,* 7th ed. (Burr Ridge, IL: Richard D. Irwin, 1999), p. 505. © 1999, McGraw-Hill/Irwin. Reproduced with permission from McGraw-Hill Companies.

The natural result is increased competition for market share. Sales promotion techniques, particularly price breaks, are therefore key.

Today's busy consumer cares less about shopping. If two spouses work outside the home, shopping time is limited. This makes consumers inevitably more responsive to sales promotion deals that encourage multiple purchases and to in-store displays.

Another factor in favor of sales promotion is simply that consumers like it. Shoppers get a lot of satisfaction from getting a good deal, and they are accustomed to special sales, rebates, and other forms of sales promotion. According to a study of the grocery industry, approximately 80 percent of consumers said it is very important that stores accept manufacturers' coupons and offer sale prices, and one in five shoppers said they would switch stores if their preferred store stopped having sales or specials.[2] Retailers find that sales promotion is often the necessary stimulus to increase, or even maintain, sales in today's competitive environment.

IMPACT OF TECHNOLOGY   There is ample evidence of technology as a stimulus for the growth of sales promotion. Computerized scanning devices let retailers know what is and what is not selling every day. They also provide quick input on which brands are most profitable. In the case of trade sales, portable computers in the hands of field salespeople let vendors track product movement practically instantaneously. As a result, both retailers and manufacturers can measure the effectiveness of various sales promotion programs very quickly. Manufacturers can thus adjust or eliminate unproductive programs, freeing up investment for more productive ones. Practically all major consumer-goods manufacturers, including PepsiCo, H.J. Heinz, and Procter & Gamble use scanner-tracked promotional programs.

INCREASED RETAIL POWER   Huge retailers such as Wal-Mart and Kmart wield tremendous clout by virtue of their immense purchasing power. Sales promotions directed at both retailers and consumers make the manufacturer's product more appealing.

As retailers gain more power, they have tried to increase sales of their own private-label products. Although retailers can tout their private labels while limiting in-store promotions for national brands, they cannot do much about sales-promotion efforts such as couponing. No doubt the struggle of national brand marketers against private labels has contributed to the growth of sales promotion.

The private-label trend is also occurring in European markets, where a lingering recession has compelled consumers to seek more value for their money. Private-label products are increasing in France, Switzerland, and Italy. To combat private-label sales, multinationals such as Unilever and Nestlé are promoting both their traditional brands and "Eurobrands," products designed for the entire European market.

Consumer Sales Promotion

Consumer sales promotion, with techniques such as coupons and rebates, helps pull a product through the channel of distribution. Both small and large companies can effectively use it with either new or existing products. Sometimes sales promotion may increase interest in mature or mundane products by imparting a sense of urgency to buy before the promotion ends.

Sales promotion can play an important role in stimulating consumers to try the product. In this ad, the free coupon will encourage consumers to try vitamins specifically formulated for runners.

Objectives of Consumer Promotions

Sales promotion may accomplish a variety of objectives, all related to affecting present or prospective consumers' behavior. As Exhibit 18–2 shows, objectives may be to stimulate trial; increase consumer inventory and consumption; encourage repurchase; neutralize competitive promotions; increase the sales of complementary products; stimulate impulse purchasing; and allow for flexible pricing.

STIMULATE TRIAL   Marketers commonly use sales promotion to stimulate product trial—to get consumers to try a product. This is particularly so for newly introduced or improved products. The decision to buy a new product entails risk, which may prompt buyer resistance. Sales promotion techniques that reduce consumer cost, such as coupons, rebates, or samples, help alleviate this risk. When Hershey wanted to encourage trial of its Hershey's Dark candy bar, for example, it offered buyers coupons redeemable for a free candy bar. In the minds of most people, no cost means no risk.

INCREASE CONSUMER INVENTORY AND CONSUMPTION
Sales promotion sometimes encourages consumers to increase their inventory or consumption of a product by enticing them to buy more than they would in the absence of a special incentive. The idea is that people tend to consume greater quantities of a product if it is on hand. For instance, a buy-one-get-one-free special on potato chips may stimulate consumers to buy more than normal. Because chips can get stale if not eaten within a certain time, and since they are around the house, people are likely to eat more than they normally would. Also, the more inventory of a given brand that consumers have, the less interest they have in stocking up on a competitor's brand.

Exhibit 18-2	*Objectives of consumer sales promotion*
	• Stimulate trial.
	• Increase consumer inventory and consumption.
	• Encourage repurchase.
	• Neutralize competitors.
	• Increase sales of complementary products.
	• Stimulate impulse purchasing.
	• Allow flexible pricing.

IMPULSE POWER.

GIANT SIZE **duraflame**

INTRODUCING
DURAFLAME FIRELOGS'
NEW, EYE-CATCHING
GIANT SIZE CASE PACKAGE.

duraflame

Sales promotion can help to neutralize competitive promotions. PETsMART used this promotion to minimize the impact of on-line competitors' promotions.

ENCOURAGE REPURCHASE   Sales promotion offers a variety of ways to help establish repeat-purchase patterns, on which the product's survival ultimately depends. Kodak uses it ProRewards program to encourage repeat purchases from professional photographers. With each film purchase, the photographers earn points that can be redeemed for personal and business-related merchandise. Bell Atlantic runs a similar program for business-telephone customers and reports that the percentage of customers who cease purchasing is 30 percent lower than that of customers who are not enrolled in the reward program.[3] Other examples of repeat-purchase promotions are the special price incentives magazines use to gain subscription renewals and the on-the-package coupons for future discounts that companies such as Domino's and Pizza Hut feature.

NEUTRALIZE COMPETITIVE PROMOTIONS   Sometimes marketers use sales promotions to combat competitive promotions. Consider the perennial battle between Coca-Cola and Pepsi-Cola, for example. Both firms constantly use promotions to attract consumers. As a result, the two firms often compete on price. Promotions to neutralize other retailers are also commonplace in the fast-food industry.

INCREASE SALES OF COMPLEMENTARY PRODUCTS   Using sales promotion to attract buyers to one product can increase sales of a complementary product. A rebate Gillette offered for its Sensor razor, for example, allowed consumers to get the product for practically nothing. Gillette hoped to cash in on sales of its Sensor razor blades, a complementary product the consumer must buy on a recurring basis. The promotion worked as planned, and Sensor is now a leading brand.

STIMULATE IMPULSE PURCHASING   Many people do not take the time to develop shopping lists. This tends to increase impulse purchasing. As the term implies, an impulse purchase is unplanned. It satisfies a strong desire to acquire a product quickly, without a lot of forethought. Retailers use special feature displays to generate impulse purchases.

ALLOW PRICE FLEXIBILITY   Sales promotion facilitates tailored price changes, which allow marketers to pursue opportunities as they arise. Suppose a manufacturer has set relatively high list prices, intending to appeal to the least price-sensitive segment of the market. Later the manufacturer can appeal to price-sensitive segments of the market through sales promotions. Automobile manufacturers follow this strategy despite the advent of no-haggle pricing.

Speaking from Experience

Kevin Marie Nuss
Churchill Downs
Vice President,
Sales and Marketing

Kevin Marie Nuss is Vice President of Sales and Marketing for Churchill Downs, the home of the Kentucky Derby. Her responsibilities include advertising, promotions, group sales, sponsorships, licensing, and merchandising for the Churchill Downs and Sports Spectrum facilities. She earned a B.A. in English from the University of Louisville. Kevin comments on the different objectives for consumer sales promotions:

"Consumer sales promotions can be used to achieve several objectives. We use some promotions to encourage casual race fans to come to Churchill Downs. These promotions are intended to generate new customers by providing other activities for customers in addition to horse racing. For example, the Kentucky Microbrew and Barbecue Festival is a promotion during which customers can sample different microbrewery and barbecue products from Kentucky in the Churchill Downs Infield during the race day. Other promotions are directed to increase frequency of attendance. This year we gave away Churchill Downs T-shirts on Mother's Day. Customers wearing these T-shirts receive free admission to Churchill Downs during the remainder of the meet."

Consumer Sales Promotion Techniques

Most people recognize the familiar consumer sales promotion techniques and have probably participated in some. Exhibit 18–3 lists some popular ones.

PRICE DEALS A **price deal** is a temporary reduction in the price of a product. Marketers may use price deals to introduce a new or improved brand, to convince current users to purchase more, or to encourage new users to try an established brand. There are two primary types of price deals: cents-off deals and price-pack deals. **Cents-off deals** offer a brand at less than the regular price. Sometimes the manufacturer's package itself specifies a price reduction in dollars or cents or by a certain percentage, say 25 percent off. Such deals are often promoted in the store in some manner and may also be advertised.

Price-pack deals offer consumers something extra through the packaging itself. Perhaps they can buy a package of Martha White brownie mix that is 20 percent bigger than usual or a box of Double-Chex with 40 percent more cereal for the price of the normal size.

Marketers would be smart not to overuse price deals, however. If a brand is frequently offered on a price deal, consumers come to expect it. They hold off purchasing the product until the company offers another deal. Frequent deals on the same product eventually erode its normal retail selling price and may diminish its brand value.

Price deals are also commonplace with nonpackaged goods such as consumer durables and services. They are also used extensively by on-line retailers in an attempt to attract customers and build market share. In an attention-getting promotion, Vitamins.com offered first-time buyers $25 off any order of $25.01 or more, with no charge for shipping.[4]

COUPONS A **coupon** is typically a printed certificate giving the bearer a stated price reduction or special value on a specific product, generally for a specific period of time. Coupons allow the manufacturer to reduce the product's price at any time. They are particularly useful in encouraging new-product trials.

Couponing is the most popular consumer sales promotion tool in the U.S. packaged-goods industry; it is also a significant factor in Canada, Italy, and the United Kingdom. Approximately 85 percent of Americans clip and save coupons, and coupons influence shopping and brand-choice decisions. In a recent survey, more than half (52 percent) of the respondents strongly agreed with the statement, "I usually look through my coupons when planning a shopping trip"; 43 percent strongly agreed with the statement, "I often purchase a brand name for which I have a coupon."[5]

Members of coupon-using households are more educated, have higher incomes, live in urban areas, and are less loyal to brands or particular stores. Furthermore, households tend to be consistent in their use of coupons across product classes. Consumers 18 to 44 years old tend to be the heaviest coupon users, redeeming an average of eight per week. There is also a correlation between coupon use and household expenditures for packaged goods, with heavy coupon users spending more than light users.[6]

Exhibit 18–3	*Consumer sales promotion techniques*
	• Price deals
	• Coupons
	• Rebates
	• Cross-promotions
	• Contests, sweepstakes, games
	• Premiums
	• Sampling
	• Advertising specialties

The outlook for couponing is favorable, as most marketers expect large numbers of consumers to continue to respond to price appeals. On the other hand, some manufacturers, including market leader Procter & Gamble, have reduced couponing expenditures, primarily because they feel it is a wasteful means of promoting their products.

The number of coupons distributed and redeemed have been on the decline since the early 1990s, yet more than 80 percent of consumers continue to use coupons. Only 2 percent of the several hundred billion coupons distributed annually are redeemed. Analysts point out that couponing has been negatively affected by manufacturers' use of shorter expiration periods on coupons and their attempts to get consumers to make multiple purchases to take advantage of coupons. Electronic promotions and a strong economy in the United States have also contributed to a decline in the use of coupons.[7] Nonetheless, coupons are expected to be a primary consumer-sales-promotion tool well into the future. One reason for this is that some major companies have introduced couponing into their sales promotions. Ford and General Motors, for example, have used coupons in the $500–$1,000 range to promote the sale of their cars and trucks.

Coupons may be distributed in several ways. The most popular method is through the **freestanding insert (FSI)**, a preprinted coupon (sometimes contained in an ad) placed into a separate publication, such as a newspaper. FSIs represent more than 80 percent of the coupons distributed in the United States annually. In-store handouts deliver about 5 percent of all coupons; coupons in or on the package also make up approximately 5 percent. The remainder of coupons are distributed by direct mail, magazine, newspaper, and miscellaneous methods such as distribution at special events and via the Internet.[8]

One technique to distribute in-store coupons, **on-shelf couponing,** uses a dispenser mounted near the manufacturer's particular product. Retailers also use in-store **checkout dispensers.** Catalina Marketing, the leading dispenser company, operates checkout dispensers in supermarkets around the world. Although coupons dispensed through Catalina are more expensive to manufacturers than those in newspapers, consumers redeem in-store coupons at a much higher rate. Using checkout scanner data about the consumer's purchases, the Catalina system dispenses coupons for similar products or beyond-the-store promotions. For example, a consumer who buys baby food might receive a coupon for Sears Portrait Studios.

On-line couponing, the distribution of coupons on the Internet, is a growing phenomenon. Catalina is also in this business, as are companies such as Val-Pak and other entrepreneurial ventures.

REBATES   A **rebate** is a cash reimbursement to a buyer for purchasing a product. The consumer typically must mail a rebate form, the purchase receipt, and some proof of purchase (often the universal product code) to the manufacturer within a certain time frame. Although consumers often purchase as a direct result of a rebate offer, many forget to send for the reimbursement or run out of time. Incentives such as coupons are easier to use, and rebates may not offer consumers the instant gratification that makes other incentives attractive.

Rebates serve several functions. They act as an economic appeal to attract customers, particularly price-conscious buyers. They have a deadline, thus consumers are encouraged to act by a certain time. They also offer a good way to reduce the perceived risk in trying a new brand, as a lower price represents less risk to most consumers.

Rebates also encourage increased consumption. The Quaker Oats Company, for instance, may offer a rebate

Issuing coupons to consumers during checkout at the grocery store is growing in popularity. Catalina Marketing's Checkout Direct dispenser compiles customer profiles using check-cashing-card data and issues coupons to match predicted future purchases.

Rebates are a popular consumer sales promotion tool. In this case, FISKARS uses a rebate as part of a seasonal sales promotion program.

on the purchase of two or more packages of instant oatmeal when the typical purchase is for only one package. Offering a rebate also allows the manufacturer to maintain a brand's original price while enjoying the benefits of a temporary price reduction. Manufacturers are also assured that the savings goes directly to the consumer, rather than to the retailer.[9] This is an advantage to the manufacturer that wishes to build brand loyalty with the ultimate consumer.

Some manufacturers are extending the use of rebates to Internet sites that specialize in promoting products with rebates. For example, freeafterrebate.com offers a variety of products free, excluding shipping and taxes, to buyers when the consumer returns a rebate form downloaded from the site.[10]

Kevin Marie Nuss, Vice President of Sales and Marketing, Churchill Downs, discusses the value of cross-promotions:

"Cross-promotions can be beneficial to all participating companies. We partner with different companies in a variety of cross-promotions. One example is a cross-promotion with a local dry cleaners and pizza restaurant. These partners sold reduced-price admission to our Festival in the Field promotion. This increased their business and gave our event exposure in their advertising efforts. Both partners sold all of their tickets, so we knew we would have a big crowd for the event. Another example is with Tricon Global Restaurants. Tricon sponsors the Junior Jockey Club for children. Participating families receive coupons for Taco Bell, KFC, and Pizza Hut products. This cross-promotion increases the attendance at Churchill Downs and also increases business at Tricon's different restaurants."

CROSS-PROMOTIONS   A cross-promotion, sometimes called a *tie-in*, is the collaboration of two or more firms in a sales promotion. Cross-promotions enhance the communications effort of all the participating firms. For example, Toys "R" Us has run cross-promotions with fast-food chain McDonald's, in which McDonald's customers get a coupon worth three to nine dollars off of a purchase from a Toys "R" Us retail store or Web site.[11] Cross-promotions have been particularly popular with on-line retailers who link with well-known brand marketers to get more exposure for their own name. CDNOW, for example, has run cross-promotions with GAP and Oldsmobile's Alero.

Cross-promotions offer several advantages. Relationships forged between strong brands reinforce the image of each. The image of a new product, or one with low

Earning Customer Loyalty

Tommy Hilfiger and Nintendo team up

Tommy Hilfiger's "Boys/Kids" teamed with Nintendo in one of the most successful back-to-school promotions in retailing history. Hilfiger is a major clothing brand in the 8- to 20-year-old age range department-store market, with a 20 percent market share. Nintendo is the leading marketer in the world-wide video-game market. Both were trying to overcome tough market conditions. Back-to-school sales forecasts were lower than usual, and Nintendo was facing intense competition from Sony Playstation. By teaming up in a cross-promotion, both Hilfiger and Nintendo came out winners.

For the promotion, Nintendo integrated the Hilfiger logo into its snowboarding game, and Hilfiger designed Tommy Nintendo sweatshirts, jackets, and T-shirts. Nintendo interactive displays were set up in Hilfiger display areas within 1,000 retail stores in 125 key U.S. markets. A national contest for Hilfiger and Nintendo merchandise and snowboarding trips drew 30,000 entries, and three million consumers sampled Nintendo video games at the in-store stations. Both companies exceeded their goals for the promotion. Hilfiger sales totaled $19 million during the two-week promotion, almost doubling the previous year's sales. Nintendo experienced the highest return of consumer rebates in its history. With successful promotions like this one, it is no surprise that today both brands are among the top five teenage brands.

Source: Promotion Marketing Association, "Reggie Super Award Winner, 1999: Get Ready to Fly," from the PMA Web site at www.pmalink.org, January 6, 2000.

Delivering product samples along with the newspaper is becoming more popular with marketers. America Online, a frequent user of sampling, provides free installation disks with a specified amount of free on-line services with this promotion.

market share, may be enhanced through association with a leading brand. Also, the resources pooled in a cross-promotion enable larger incentives to be offered and generate more fanfare in introducing the promotion to consumers. For more on cross-promotions, see "Earning Customer Loyalty: Tommy Hilfiger and Nintendo Team Up."

CONTESTS, SWEEPSTAKES, AND GAMES   A **contest** offers prizes based on the skill of contestants. Participants must use a skill or some ability to address a specified problem to qualify for a prize. Kodak has used photo contests successfully for decades, and contests are popular in association with major sporting events such as the Olympics and the Super Bowl. ABC Television ran a highly successful "What's Wrong with This Episode?" contest for its Drew Carey sitcom in conjunction with April Fools' Day to increase the number of viewers heading into a ratings period. The contest attracted 250,00 participants, more than half of whom entered on the show's Web site. Prizes included trips to Los Angeles, where the show is produced, and to Cleveland, the setting for the show. Other prizes were trips to the Rock and Roll Hall of Fame, tickets, to a Cleveland Indians baseball game, and various merchandise, such as Drew's pool table from the show. The contest episode increased total viewership by 8 percent and ratings by 30 percent over the previous week.[12]

A **sweepstakes** offers prizes based on a chance drawing of participants' names. Sweepstakes have strong appeal because they are easier to enter and take less time than contests and games. Wendy's "Summer of 99" sweepstakes, highlighting its 99-cent Super Value Menu, offered customers a chance to win their choice of 99 prizes. They entered the drawing of their choice, each for a specific prize, by filling out forms available in the stores. By law, purchase cannot be a requirement to enter a sweepstakes.

Games are similar to sweepstakes, but they cover a longer period. They encourage consumers to continue playing in order to win. M&M Mars "Chew the Clue" promotion for its Starburst candy brand is an example of the game format. The game asked customers, primarily teenagers, to identify a "mystery flavor" of a specially wrapped piece of candy included in each pack of Starburst candy over a 12-week period. All consumers who correctly guessed the flavor won a prize. All entrants were eligible to win major prizes at the end of the game, including a trip to Hawaii and vacation-gear backpacks. More than five million consumers played the game, and the number of teens identifying Starburst as one of "the coolest brands" nearly doubled.[13]

Contests, sweepstakes, and games can create interest and motivate consumption by encouraging consumer involvement. They are often used in integrated marketing communications programs along with in-store displays (part of trade promotion) and advertising. The future for these types of promotions is promising. Consumers seem to enjoy the friendly competition, and technology is lending a hand. Contests and games frequently appear on the Internet, where marketers are trying to get consumers to spend more time, thus increasing involvement and interest in the product or service. Automobile and truck manufacturers have been active in this area, including Jeep and Ford. Ford's scavenger hunt on the Internet, targeted to college students, led searchers on an extensive tour of the Ford Web site, following clues in several areas such as environmental issues, financing, careers with Ford, and new-vehicle information.[14]

PREMIUMS   An item given free or at a bargain price to encourage the consumer to buy is called a **premium**. Prepaid phone cards, for example, are often used as premiums. These cards, one of the most popular premiums in recent years, are imprinted with the company or brand logo, thus reminding the consumer of the sponsor every time the card is used. In addition, callers will often hear a short promotional message when they dial the free access number to use the card.

Premiums are intended to improve the product's image, gain goodwill, broaden the customer base, and produce quick sales. Premiums that require saving in-pack coupons or proofs of purchase to be redeemed can create consumer loyalty. For instance, Hormel Foods offered *Pinocchio* videos at discounted prices with the purchase of any five qualifying products.

In a variety of industries, the use of premiums is well established but not growing. For many Internet marketers, however, the popularity of premiums is increasing. Mary Wisner, a customer at BravoGifts.com, for example, bought a pair of North Face computer bags worth $75 by paying shipping costs of $4.95. In completing her Christmas shopping, Ms. Wisner found so many premiums on the Internet that she donated many of them to charities.[15] The heavy use of premiums by on-line retailers is an obvious attempt to wrest customers away from retail stores. It is also an expensive means of promotion and cannot continue indefinitely.

Research comparing the effectiveness of premiums with that of price discounts suggests that marketers might want to experiment with premiums, especially if their competitors are heavy users of price promotions. For example, a free spatula worth $3.99 at retail generated more consumer interest than a $2 price discount on pizza; and an offer of $2,500 worth of camping gear had a higher impact on consumer interest in buying a $28,500 utility vehicle than did a $2,000 discount on the vehicle. Since these premiums can be acquired by marketers at wholesale prices, the return on investment in these promotions can be highly attractive. Further, there is less danger of eroding brand image, which sometimes occurs with price-based promotions.[16]

SAMPLING   A **sample** is a small size of a product made available to prospective purchasers, usually free of charge. Marketers use samples to demonstrate a product's value or use and encourage future purchase. Sampling reduces the consumer's perception of risk by allowing product trial before purchase of a full-size version.

Marketers find sampling particularly useful for new brands with features that are difficult to describe adequately through advertising. Samples also draw heightened attention to a brand. For instance, Nabisco's A.1. Steak Sauce used extensive sampling in a 30-week "A.1. Rolling Steakhouse" tour. Using a mobile steak house and grilling vehicles designed to look like A.1. bottles, 500,000 samples were distributed in visits to 263 retail stores and cooking events. The promotion was well received by both retailers and consumers, with sales increasing by 5 percent, a significant amount in such a competitive market.[17]

Although usually mailed to prospective customers, samples may be distributed door-to-door; at trade shows, movies, and special events; or in store. They sometimes accompany the purchase of a related product, such as a free sample of laundry detergent with the purchase of a washing machine.

Sampling can be expensive, thus marketers must determine the most cost-effective manner of distribution. This depends on the target audience and the size of the sample. Although larger samples cost more, the sample should be big enough for consumers to make an adequate evaluation.

ADVERTISING SPECIALTIES   An **advertising specialty** is an item of useful or interesting merchandise given away free of charge and typically carrying an imprinted name or message. These items are typically low in cost, although some can be expensive. Examples of advertising specialties include pens or pencils, calendars, hats, jackets, coffee mugs, notebooks, key chains, golf and T-shirts, and totebags.[18]

Specialty advertising has several common uses. It can reinforce other advertising media to strengthen a message. It can also produce or foster high levels of brand recognition when the item has a relatively long life. A unique specialty advertising item can attract interest among target audience members and perhaps stimulate action. In addition, a useful specialty item can create a positive attitude toward the provider. Poor-quality merchandise, however, may detract from the marketer's image.

Thinking Critically

Assume you are a brand manager for a specialty manufacturer with only one product, a high-priced toothpaste with extraordinary whitening power. The product has been highly successful in Europe, and now you are planning national distribution in the United States. If you could only use one consumer-sales promotion technique of those shown in Exhibit 18.3, which one would you use? Support your reasoning.

For an illustration of how advertising specialties can be used to promote a political candidate, see "Being Entrepreneurial: New Candidate Beats the Odds."

Trade Sales Promotion

Trade sales promotion at the wholesale and retail level helps push products through the marketing channel. Unlike consumer sales promotion, trade promotion is not easily observed by ultimate consumers. Although consumer sales promotions are very visible, in fact they are dwarfed by the magnitude of trade sales promotion. Marketers spend approximately twice as much money on trade promotion.

Exhibit 18–4

Objectives of trade sales promotion

- Gain/maintain distribution.
- Influence resellers to promote product.
- Influence resellers to offer price discount.
- Increase reseller inventory.
- Defend against competitors.
- Avoid reduction of normal prices.

Objectives of Trade Promotions

Sales promotions aimed at the trade have many and varied objectives. As listed in Exhibit 18–4, common trade promotion objectives are to gain or maintain distribution; influence resellers to promote a product; influence resellers to offer a price discount; increase reseller inventory; defend a brand against competitors; and avoid reduction of normal prices.[19] Trade promotions may be conducted by manufacturers, service providers, or wholesalers, all directing their efforts toward other channel members, most notably retailers.

GAIN OR MAINTAIN DISTRIBUTION Sales promotion influences resellers to carry a product. Manufacturers selling directly to retailers may strike special introductory deals to get established with the retailer. Later, sales promotion may help maintain distribution in the face of competition or a flat sales period. Such is the case in the soft-drink market, in which Coke and Pepsi use sales promotion on a regular basis. Other incentives, such as providing free in-store displays, may encourage retailers to purchase by reducing their perceived risk. A trade show is another example of sales promotion that may provide a way to introduce the product to potential distributors and gain their business.

INFLUENCE RESELLERS TO PROMOTE THE PRODUCT Getting a product into a reseller's inventory is not always enough to realize sales objectives. In other words, it's not enough to get the product on the shelf; it may take sales promotion to move it off the shelf. Ways manufacturers can influence retailers to promote a product include offering incentives to the retail salesforce, splitting advertising costs

---

Being Entrepreneurial

New candidate beats the odds

Kathy Jorgensen, a political novice, used specialty advertising to help her win a seat on the Putnam County School Board in Florida. Her opponent was a 16-year incumbent who had run unopposed the previous 12 years. Further, Ms. Jorgensen's political party was outnumbered three to one among registered voters in the area. Using a slogan of "She'll Make a Difference," Ms. Jorgensen spent most of her campaign promotion funds on advertising specialties, tangible items that voters would save and see many times before the election.

Ms. Jorgensen and her supporters distributed 2,500 memo pads at community events and in local retail stores.

The fronts of the pads were printed with her name, campaign slogan, photo, and the election date; the backs of the pads featured her platform ideas; and the insides of the pads were printed with the school calendar. The memo pads, along with 1,000 standard placards and three automobile signs, brought Ms. Jorgensen significant local exposure and helped increase her name recognition among voters. After the election, Ms. Jorgensen attributed her victory to the use of relatively inexpensive advertising-specialty products.

Source: The Advertising Specialty Institute Web site at www.promomart.com, January 7, 2000.

Lamb Weston used a rebate and the chance to win a dream vacation—a Hawaii cruise for two—as extra incentives for restaurant operators to try Twister Fries. This promotion was designed to simultaneously maintain and build distribution through Lamb Weston distributors.

with the retailer, furnishing free display materials, or various other techniques. Quaker State, for example, could encourage service station attendants to promote the sale of motor oil by paying them 25 cents per can sold during a contest period. At the end of the contest, the attendant with the most sales would receive two free tickets to a NASCAR race. The basic idea is for additional sales volume to offset expenses involved in running the promotion or for sales to clear the dealers' inventory to make way for more profitable sales in the future.

INFLUENCE RESELLERS TO OFFER A PRICE DISCOUNT   Sometimes the manufacturer gives wholesalers and retailers allowances or discounts so that its product will be offered at a reduced price. The manufacturer hopes the lower price will lead to increased sales. This often occurs with end-of-season merchandise. For example, fishing equipment manufacturer Zebco might offer sporting goods stores a clearance price on factory-premarked rods and reels and a special display barrel with promotional signs indicating "Rod & Reel Riot! $12.99 While They Last!"

INCREASE RESELLER INVENTORY   Suppliers do not want channel members to run out of stock. A product being out of stock results in more than lost sales; it creates dissatisfaction among customers seeking to make a purchase. Sometimes a manufacturer may want to shift products to wholesalers or retailers because of the costs involved in holding inventory. The other channel members, of course, are well aware of the cost and risks of holding excess inventory, and the supplier may grant them special deals in exchange for doing so. Such an approach is commonplace in the greeting card industry, in which suppliers offer retailers special pricing and deferred payment in exchange for their booking orders well in advance.

DEFEND AGAINST COMPETITORS   Just as at the consumer level, sales promotion can stave off competitors at the trade level. An incentive may prompt channel members to choose one firm's brand over a competing one.

Trade sales promotion techniques

- Trade allowances
- Dealer loaders
- Trade contests
- Point-of-purchase displays
- Trade shows
- Training programs
- Push money

Kevin Marie Nuss, Vice President of Sales and Marketing, Churchill Downs, talks about the use of trade sales promotions: "Many companies use their sponsorship of the Kentucky Derby as basis for various trade sales promotions. Companies, such as Pepsi-Cola, establish contests for their retailers. The winning retailers are provided tickets to the Kentucky Derby and entertained at the Marquee Village at Churchill Downs. The equine division of Bayer takes a different approach. The company set up a tent at the Churchill Downs backstretch stable area for the two weeks before the Kentucky Derby. The tent contained displays and information about Bayer equine pharmaceutical products. This mini-trade show was visited by many veterinarians and horsemen during the two-week period."

AVOID PRICE REDUCTIONS Rather than reduce the price of a product permanently, marketers may use some form of trade promotion to offer channel members a temporary price reduction. If there is a momentary oversupply of product on the market, for example, a manufacturer might elect to maintain sales volume by offering a "1 free with 10" program of short duration. In effect, the customer gets a discount in the form of free goods, but the manufacturer avoids a permanent price reduction.

Trade Sales Promotion Techniques

Trade sales promotion techniques can be applied independently or in combinations. And firms often link trade sales promotion with consumer sales promotion and other elements of the communications mix. Some frequently used trade sales promotion techniques are shown in Exhibit 18–5.

TRADE ALLOWANCES Trade allowances are short-term special allowances, discounts, or deals granted to resellers as an incentive to stock, feature, or in some way participate in the cooperative promotion of a product. There are several kinds of allowances, including slotting allowances, which we discussed in Chapter 14. Another type, the *buying allowance,* is payment of a specified amount of money to a reseller for purchasing a certain amount of a product during a particular period. The payment may be by check or as a credit against an invoice. A manufacturer usually offers a buying allowance to increase the size of the reseller's order.

A *display allowance* is money or a product provided to a retailer for featuring the manufacturer's brand in an agreed-upon in-store display. An *advertising allowance* is money paid a reseller for including the manufacturer's product, along with other products, in the reseller's advertising efforts. Somewhat similar to this, *cooperative advertising* occurs when the manufacturer helps finance the reseller's advertising efforts featuring only the manufacturer's product. For example, Pioneer may help a local electronics store pay for a newspaper ad featuring Pioneer products.

DEALER LOADERS A dealer loader is a premium given to a reseller to encourage development of a special display or product offering. Loader techniques help ensure proper stock and display of the item, of particular interest to many manufacturers at certain seasons or holidays.

There are two common types of loaders. A *buying loader* is a gift, such as a free trip, for buying, displaying, and selling a certain amount of a product within a specified time. A *display loader* allows the reseller to keep some or all of the display when the promotion ends. A tennis racket manufacturer, for example, might allow qualifying retailers to keep an expensive, custom-produced lighted display featuring action photos of top players to help promote sales.

TRADE CONTESTS A trade contest typically associates prizes with sales of the sponsor's product. As do consumer contests, trade contests generate interest, which makes them useful for motivating resellers. Effective trade contests should be held periodically rather than all the time—otherwise, they lose some of their motivating potential. Effective contests can boost short-term sales and improve relations be-

Thinking Critically

Assume you are a sales representative for a consumer packaged-goods company that sells through grocery wholesalers. Your company is offering a limited-time buying allowance. One of your customers requests a higher allowance, which you deny. The customer then suggests that he will buy a huge additional order if you will allow him to claim $200 off the next invoice for "damaged goods" on his last order, even though the goods arrived unharmed. It is within your authority to allow customers to claim deductions for damaged goods up to $250 per claim. What would you do and what would be the implications of your decision?

Point-of-purchase displays call attention to featured products. JELLO uses this floor display to boost sales with a free offer of Super Bowl molds which give young consumers a fun way to enjoy the product.

tween manufacturer and reseller. Volkswagen has used trade contests to help establish the Passat as a popular choice in the luxury category. Its "Passat Mentor" program rates dealer salespeople according to sales results and customer satisfaction indicators. Top salespeople are awarded special status and trip prizes, including the opportunity to test-drive the latest-model Passat at high speeds on the Phoenix International Raceway track.[20]

POINT-OF-PURCHASE DISPLAYS   Point-of-purchase displays are generally used at the retail level to call customer attention to a featured product. Point-of-purchase displays are popular in grocery, drug, and discount stores and in the restaurant, food service, and tavern industry. Typically provided free or at low cost by the manufacturer to the reseller, point-of-purchase displays attract consumers while they shop, encouraging purchase of the particular product. With much of retailing self-service today, point-of-purchase displays support the retail sales effort by highlighting the product and offering information. Given that consumers make many purchase decisions in the store rather than before entering it, these displays can be important selling tools.

A disadvantage of displays is that manufacturers must assemble and place them. Retailers are busy, and they are deluged with point-of-purchase materials, many of which never make it to the sales floor. Displays often become unused throwaways, an unnecessary waste in marketing communications. Displays come in many varieties, including special racks, display cartons, banners, signs, price cards, video and computer monitors, mechanical dispensers, and robots. The names given to several popular point-of-purchase displays by retailers are shown in Exhibit 18–6, along with their descriptions.

TRADE SHOWS   A **trade show** is a periodic, semipublic event sponsored by trade, professional, and industrial associations at which suppliers rent booths to display products and provide information to potential buyers. Trade shows are big business, attracting more than 100 million visitors in the United States per year.[21] They are also extremely important in many overseas markets, including Europe, the Middle East, Africa, Asia, and Latin America. In many of these markets, trade shows are a more influential part of the marketing process than in the United States.

Marketers can use trade shows to accomplish any number of objectives, including demonstrating products, acquiring new-prospect leads, making sales, providing information, comparing competing brands, introducing new products, enhancing the corporate image, and strengthening relationships with existing customers.

Some shows are simply too large for customers to effectively visit each exhibit. Many companies use preshow mailings or phone calls to boost exhibit traffic. Companion promotional products are also effective for generating traffic and creating a

Exhibit 18–6	*Types of point-of-purchase displays*
	Sign Language
AISLE INTERRUPTER	Cardboard sign that juts into the middle of the aisle.
DANGLER	Sign hanging down from a shelf that sways when shoppers pass.
DUMP BIN	Box-shaped display holding products loosely dumped inside.
GLORIFIER	Small plastic "stage" that elevates one product above the rest.
WOBBLER	A jiggling sign.
LIPSTICK BOARD	Plastic surface on which messages are written with crayons.
NECKER	Coupon hanging on a bottle neck.
Y.E.S. UNIT	"Your Extra Salesperson," a fact sheet that pulls down like a shade.

Source: Yumiko Ono, "Wobblers and Sidekicks Clutter Stores, Irk Retailers," *The Wall Street Journal,* September 8, 1998, pp. B1, B3.

Trade shows allow marketers to accomplish several objectives as they gain exposure with interested prospects and strengthen relationships with existing customers. This photo is from the annual Comdex trade show, one of the world's largest, which brings computer-industry buyers and sellers together.

memorable exhibit. For example, Newell Group Purchasing, a hardware supplier, mailed a puzzle tray without the pieces to 5,500 Ace Hardware Dealers prior to a major trade show. The idea was to get the dealers to visit eight different Newell booths at the show to pick up the missing pieces to the puzzle. Dealers who collected the missing pieces were then eligible for a drawing for round-trip airfare to and from the next trade show. In spite of a decline in overall show attendance from the prior year, traffic at Newell's booths increased 10 percent.[22]

Passing out T-shirts or other specialty advertising items carrying the company's name and logo or constructing an unusual and eye-catching display can also generate booth traffic. It is important for companies to have well-trained salespeople available at a trade show. In addition, follow-up after the show is critical.

Major trade shows are held in large cities; thus lodging and associated expenses for company personnel can be expensive. To hold travel expenses to a minimum, many companies prefer regional trade shows. Even in Chicago, home to several major international trade shows, most conventioneers are attending smaller events, with 1,000 or fewer participants, and most are traveling less than 400 miles to attend.[23]

TRAINING PROGRAMS   Some manufacturers sponsor or pay for training programs for customer employees. Armstrong Tile, for example, a manufacturer of floor tile, provides sales training to teach some of its key dealer personnel how to sell or use its products.

Marketers may also provide training on a number of other topics, including retail and wholesale management procedures, safety issues, or current technical developments in an industrial field. Training programs are expensive, and results are often hard to measure. To be effective, training should be continual, or at least periodically reinforced, thus adding to the expense. Even though it is expensive, training can build productive relationships with customers.

Trade sales promotion sometimes includes reseller training. In this photo, Hewlett-Packard dealers receive training at the company's facility in Mexico City.

PUSH MONEY   **Push money,** also called **spiffs,** is what a manufacturer pays to retail salespeople to encourage them to promote its products over competitive brands. Push money may also be used to encourage the retail sale of specific products in the manufacturer's line. This extra incentive helps to get the manufacturer's brand special representation or favored treatment. The disadvantage is that the retail salesperson's extra enthusiasm for the manufacturer's product may wane once the spiff is eliminated, especially if another manufacturer offers a new spiff.

Limitations of Sales Promotion

Although sales promotion can accomplish a variety of objectives, there are certain things it cannot do. Sales promotion can help boost sales, but it typically cannot reverse a genuine declining sales trend. If sales are slipping, marketers should evaluate and perhaps change the product's marketing strategy. Attempting to use sales promotion as a quick fix may temporarily postpone worsening of the problem, but it cannot eliminate it.

In a similar vein, marketers cannot reasonably expect sales promotion to convert rejection of an inferior product into acceptance. Consumers judge a product on whether it satisfies their needs. Products that do not meet consumer needs naturally fade from the market over the course of time.

Beyond its inability to improve a brand's image, sales promotion may even weaken the brand image. As a sales promotion develops a life of its own, perceived product differentiation can be blurred; consumers may come to see the deal as more important than any other real or perceived brand difference. In essence, buyers reach a point at which they fail to see any differences among brands, and the marketer has unwittingly created short-run price-oriented behavior. In the soft-drink market, for instance, many consumers see Coca-Cola and Pepsi-Cola as interchangeable and decide which of the two they will purchase primarily on the basis of price (which is the better deal?).

Sales promotion, far more than other marketing activity, has also been blamed for encouraging competitive retaliation. Promotions can be developed quickly, and one company can respond to a competitor's sales promotion with its own. Quick response may stave off the potential of sales lost to the competitor's promotion. Although a promotion battle benefits consumers, two firms that compete head-to-head often both lose profits. Other forms of marketing communications are less likely to evoke such quick retaliatory efforts.

Sales promotion can result in manufacturers' gaining short-term volume but sacrificing profit. Special incentives and deals promote **forward buying,** both among distributors and consumers. That is, people buy more than they need at the deal price. They purchase enough to carry them to the next deal, when once again they can stock up at low prices. Thus, the manufacturer may sell more at the expense of less profit.

To overcome this problem, manufacturers are increasingly using **pay-for-performance trade promotions,** through which retailers are rewarded for making sales to consumers rather than making purchases from manufacturers. Scanner data can be used to measure results, and the incentive to overload warehouses to take advantage of lower prices during deal periods is reduced.

Ethical and Legal Issues in Sales Promotion

The American Marketing Association Code of Ethics stipulates the "avoidance of sales promotion that uses deception or manipulation." Sales promotion provides an environment ripe for exploitation, and many of the ethical and legal problems in marketing communications are related to questionable promotions. Deception and fraud are the primary issues. Global marketing poses added ethical concerns because of requirements specific to different cultures. Deceptive sales promotion costs consumers millions of dollars annually, not to mention the time spent pursuing worthless "free" offers of unethical businesses.

A popular consumer sales promotion tool, the sweepstakes, is often used deceptively. As a result, a variety of regulatory agencies, including the U.S. Postal Service and the Federal Trade Commission, actively police sweepstakes. In addition, all 50 states have various combinations of gambling, lottery, and consumer protection laws that regulate sweepstakes. At least nine states regulate the use of simulated checks, and separate restrictions exist for sweepstakes promoting tobacco, liquor, milk, and time-share lodging.

The impact of legal and regulatory forces on some sweepstakes operators is having a significant financial impact. Publisher's Clearing House, a major sweepstakes company, is revising its sweepstakes offerings and paying out millions of dollars to settle a class-action lawsuit.[24] American Family Publishers, which paid fines of $6.9 million in 40 states and the District of Columbia, has filed for Chapter 11 protection under the U.S. Bankruptcy Code.[25] With a flurry of lawsuits and newly proposed laws, it is clear that legal authorities have little tolerance for deceptive sweepstakes promotions.

Caution is the best policy when designing a sweepstakes program. In fact, the same could be said for any sales promotion—to ensure that manufacturers, wholesalers, and retailers steer clear of unethical or illegal activity. Basically, marketers must tell consumers the truth and clearly spell out the action necessary to enter the sweepstakes. In addition, marketers must take responsibility for the fair and equitable treatment of buyers and nonbuyers during a promotion, taking care not to make it significantly more difficult for nonbuyers to enter. Finally, a legitimate sweepstakes program entails honest distribution of prizes, which may require the services of a sweepstakes management company to avoid insider rigging.

Fraud

Another significant problem involves coupon and rebate fraud, with manufacturers the intended victims. Exhibit 18–7 points out some of the ways cheaters can profit from coupons and mail-in offers. Industry analysts say that unethical retailers are responsible for a majority of fraudulent coupon claims.

Manufacturers have resorted to high-tech methods to combat coupon fraud. To circumvent coupon counterfeiting, special inks produce the word *void* on coupons exposed to the light used in copier machines. New checkout scanner technology now polices misredemption at the store level. Even low-tech methods, such as shortening the redemption period, are used.

The most widespread effect of fraud and deceptive sales promotions is that, in the long run, consumers pay more for products than they would otherwise. Consumers also pay through taxes for the considerable government regulation needed to combat fraud and deception.

Diverting

Consumers are not the only victims of unethical and illegal sales promotion. Manufacturers can also be the targets of fraud. A controversial, yet commonplace, activity is **diverting** (also called *arbitraging*), or secretly purchasing a product where it is less expensive, usually as a result of a trade promotion, and reselling in areas where prices are higher.

Diverters use up-to-the-minute computerized information to find out where the deals are, purchase merchandise for shipment to a buyer authorized by the manufacturer to receive the deal, then divert all or part of the shipment to an unauthorized location while the goods are in transit. Diverters include both intermediaries and chain stores. Intermediaries are fairly tight-lipped about diverting, and some even maintain secret operations in the offices of legitimate wholesalers and supermarket chains.

Diverting can distort supply and demand and cause marketing strategies to backfire on manufacturers. Industry analysts believe diverting is inevitable so long as manufacturers offer the same products at different prices in different geographic markets. Some manufacturers, most notably Procter & Gamble, have instituted a one-price nationwide policy to reduce diverting.

Exhibit 18–7	*Examples of coupon and rebate fraud*

The Fake Storefront

A scam artist rents space cheap, sets up a store, then starts sending in coupons to manufacturers for payment. Pretty soon the store's shelves are bare, but the "owner" is still sending in coupons obtained illegally.

Stuffing the Ballot Box

A retailer legitimately obtains cash from clearinghouses and manufacturers for coupons handed in by shoppers, but boosts the take illegally by sending in extra coupons purchased at steep discounts from various sources, such as unscrupulous printers.

Playing the Middleman

An ambitious operator makes money supplying other operators—collecting coupons by the pound and selling them to retailers, buying and selling proofs of purchase, or counterfeiting coupons and proofs of purchase.

The Redemption Scam

Manufacturers offer big cash rebates on large items to shoppers who mail in forms, together with proofs of purchase-receipts, labels, or box tops. A con artist uses the rebate forms and proofs of purchase, real or counterfeit, to illicitly collect refunds without buying products.

Global Concerns

The *global perspective* requires marketers to make an extra effort to become familiar with local laws and customs. In Spain, for example, it is legal to require the purchase of the product for entry in sales promotion contests, whereas such a requirement is illegal in most other European countries. Further, according to an expert on sales promotion in Spain, the Spanish people are generally keen on gambling and participate heavily in promotional games of chance. Logically, sales promotion in Spain is extremely popular, more so than in other European countries with stricter regulations. As a result, it is impossible to design a sales-promotion campaign for the entire European market—marketers must adapt programs to the appropriate legal framework.

In Canada, a variety of laws affect sales promotion. For example, if entry into a contest requires that the consumer send in a UPC label, entrants are also allowed to submit a handwritten facsimile of the label. In Quebec, language laws require that most marketing communications be in French. Also, most contests must be structured to require that entrants answer a skill-testing question to be eligible for a prize.

These examples from Spain and Canada are reminders that marketing activities should be conducted to meet varying applicable local requirements, often a composite of national, state (or province), and local laws. As most sales promotion tools involve mass distribution of written documents, extreme caution should be used to ensure compliance with relevant laws.

Summary

1. Explain the role and significance of sales promotion in the marketing communications mix. Sales promotion is one way firms may communicate with intended target audiences. Sales promotion uses media and nonmedia marketing communications for a predetermined, limited time at either consumer, retailer, or wholesaler level to stimulate trial, increase consumer demand, or improve product availability. Sales promotion is unique in that it offers an extra incentive for action. Its importance is evidenced by the considerable amount of money firms invest in it.

2. Understand why sales promotion use and expenditures have increased in recent years. Expenditures in sales promotion have been fueled by changes in consumer demographics, lifestyles and attitudes, technological advances, a shift of power to retailers, a focus of firms on the short term, and an increasing emphasis on accountability for results.

Many shoppers today are busy and price-conscious, making sales promotion attractive. Scanning technology allows both retailers and manufacturers an opportunity to gauge the effectiveness of promotions quickly and accurately, thus reinforcing the use of sales promotion. Retailers have gained considerable power in the marketing channel in recent years, and manufacturers are virtually required to engage in sales promotion to increase or maintain distribution. Since sales promotion is generally short term, it fits with the time horizon most favored today in business. Finally, the results of sales promotion are easier to assess than the results of advertising, prompting its use in an era of accountability.

3. Discuss the objectives and techniques of consumer sales promotion. Consumer sales promotion attempts to stimulate trial, increase consumer inventory and consumption, encourage repurchase, neutralize competitive promotions, increase the sales of complementary products, stimulate impulse purchasing, and allow for flexible pricing policies. Consumer sales promotion techniques include price deals, coupons, rebates, cross-promotions, contests, sweepstakes, games, premiums, sampling, and advertising specialties.

4. Discuss the objectives and techniques of trade sales promotion. Trade sales promotion can help gain or maintain distribution, influence retailers to promote a product or to offer a price discount, increase reseller inventory, defend against competitors, and avoid price reductions. Popular trade sales promotion techniques involve trade allowances, dealer loaders, trade contests, point-of-purchase displays, trade shows, training programs, and push money.

5. Explain the limitations of sales promotion. Sales promotion cannot permanently reverse a genuine decline in sales, nor can it work to capture enduring acceptance of an inferior product. Overused sales promotion may actually weaken a brand image rather than strengthen it. Because it is short term and often highly visible, sales promotion can spur retaliation from competitors, which tends to diminish its effectiveness. In addition, consumers and resellers may engage in forward buying to take advantage of sales promotions, possibly causing the manufacturer to gain volume at the expense of declining profitability.

6. Realize how deceptive and fraudulent sales promotion victimizes both consumers and marketers. Deceptive sales promotion costs consumers millions of dollars annually. Moreover, manufacturers pay consumers and resellers hundreds of millions a year for fraudulently submitted rebates and coupons. The average consumer eventually pays a higher price for products to cover the cost of fraud in sales promotion. In addition, taxpayers have a heavier burden due to the increased costs of regulation at the federal, state, and local levels.

Understanding Marketing Terms and Concepts

Thinking About Marketing

1. What factors have contributed to the growth in sales promotion?

2. What are the objectives of consumer sales promotion?

3. Define and briefly discuss these consumer sales promotion techniques: price deals, coupons, rebates, cross-promotions, contests, sweepstakes, games, premiums, sampling, and advertising specialties.

4. How do the objectives of trade sales promotion differ from those of consumer sales promotion?

5. Define and briefly discuss these trade sales promotion techniques: trade allowances, dealer loaders, trade contests, point-of-purchase displays, trade shows, training programs, and push money.

6. How would these parties be affected if consumer and trade sales promotions on grocery products were banned by law? (*a*) consumers; (*b*) retailers; (*c*) manufacturers with their own brands.

7. Discuss the issue of deception in sales promotion, and give examples of deceptive sales promotion.

8. Discuss the problem of coupon and rebate fraud, and identify several ways unscrupulous operators could exploit manufacturers through fraud.

9. Refer to "Earning Customer Loyalty: Tommy Hilfiger and Nintendo Team Up." What factors should a company consider before joining with another company to promote its brand?

10. Refer to "Being Entrepreneurial: New Candidate Beats the Odds." How did Ms. Jorgensen build awareness for her brand (i.e., her own name)?

Applying Marketing Skills

1. Consult the Sunday edition of a local newspaper. Identify examples of as many consumer trade promotion techniques as possible. You may find examples of price deals, coupons, rebates, cross-promotions, contests, sweepstakes, games, premiums, and even sampling. Select one example from each category of consumer sales promotion techniques that you have identified, and try to determine the main objective of the promotion: stimulating trial, increasing consumer inventory and consumption, encouraging repurchase, neutralizing competitive promotions, or increasing the sale of complementary products.

2. Look again at the Sunday newspaper. Collect a minimum of 10 coupons or other sales-promotion materials intended to stimulate trial of a new product. You may need to review the paper for a couple of weeks to collect 10 examples. Now, visit local retailers to determine whether the new products are in stock. If the product is in stock, note any other point-of-purchase materials that encourage a purchase. If the product is not in stock, see if you can find out why.

3. Assume you are the owner of a small independent bookstore in a large metropolitan area. You face heavy competition from large national chains such as B. Dalton, Walden Books, and Bookstar. Your clientele is more upscale, educated, and intellectual than that of your competition. You are attempting to develop a sales-promotion program to encourage your clientele to become loyal customers. Explain how you would choose one or more consumer sales promotion techniques to accomplish this objective.

Using the www In Marketing

Activity One   As mentioned in the chapter opener, Val-Pak is best known for mailing coupons to consumers. Access the company's Web site at http://www.valpak.com, then answer these questions:

1. Coupons are available on the Val-Pak Web site. What are the advantages and disadvantages of distributing coupons on-line as compared with traditional methods such as distributing them in the newspaper, via direct mail, or in a store?

2. Do you see any evidence that Val-Pak uses sales promotion at its Web site? If not, how could Val-Pak use sales promotion to build awareness and usage of its services?

Activity Two   Specialty advertising products are often used in sales promotion. One Web site that can be useful in planning sales promotions is PromoMart, developed on behalf of the Advertising Specialty Institute.

1. Access the PromoMart site at http://www.promomart.com. Click on the "Promotional Ideas and Info," icon,

then the "Ideas Stores" icon, to learn about successful campaigns that use specialty advertising items.

2. Select three ideas that you think are good examples of sales promotion, and explain why you chose them.

Making Marketing Decisions
Case 18-1 *Women on Their Way by Wyndham*

Headquartered in Dallas, Texas, Wyndham International, Inc., is one of the world's largest hotel operators. Wyndham owns, leases, manages, and franchises more than 300 properties in the United States, Caribbean, Europe, and Canada. The company has 35,000 employees. Wyndham serves both business and leisure travelers and has become particularly well-known for catering to female business travelers, a fast-growing segment of the business travel market. In 1985, women made up 10 percent of the business travel market. By 2000, women accounted for 50 percent of business travel.

Wyndham began intensifying its efforts to develop the female business traveler market in 1995, when it held its first annual "Women on Their Way Contest." Contest entrants were asked to describe how they would improve business travel for women. Over the years, many suggestions from customers have been implemented at Wyndham properties. Women indicated they would like to have a comfortable, private place for conversation, not the hotel bar or lobby. Wyndham responded with its signature library in its Garden Hotel properties, a location convenient to the lobby and bar, but distinctly separate from these facilities. Guest suggestions led to an option of receiving prenotification by phone before room-service delivery, a safety and courtesy measure.

During the past five years, Wyndham generated a lot of publicity with its contest and learned valuable information about the female business traveler. This information serves as the basis for an ongoing relationship marketing program between Wyndham and its female customers. As part of the relationship marketing program, Women on Their Way members (membership also open to males) receive an e-mail newsletter featuring travel news and special promotional offers.

In addition to its annual contest to determine the best idea for improving travel for female businesspeople, Wyndham uses other sales-promotion tools to provide incentives and add value for its customers. Price deals such as two nights for one and special weekend rates help Wyndham boost sales volume, and cross-promotions with major airlines are also popular.

When Wyndham registers a guest for the Women on Their Way program, the company learns how often the person travels, how much travel is business or leisure, whether children accompany the guest, and with which airlines the guest flies. Prospective members also indicate if they are members of the National Association of Business Owners or the National Association of Female Executives.

There are signs that Wyndham's Women on Their Way program is helping position the company as a specialist in meeting the needs of traveling women. The program has been featured on international television via Cable News Network (CNN). Overall bookings are up for the Wyndham chain, though it is hard to tie booking results directly to the program. It is also difficult to tie specific results of the program to increased sales volume, because Wyndham has grown rapidly since it began the program in 1995, causing an overall increase in bookings. Inquiries to Wyndham's Web site are increasing, and feedback from guests and the female executive advisory board continues to be positive. Cary Broussard, director of the program, says: "Women are watching us—they want to see if we're putting our money where our mouth is. So far, I don't think they've been disappointed."

Questions

1. Explain how Wyndham uses a sales promotion tool, the annual contest, to better define and meet the needs of its female guests.

2. Wyndham often engages in cross-promotions with airlines and other travel-related companies. What other cross-promotion opportunities do you see for Wyndham?

3. What other sales-promotion objectives and tools could you recommend for Wyndham?

4. The results of sales promotion should be measurable. What can Wyndham do to better measure the sales-promotion aspects of its Women on Their Way program?

SOURCES: Tricia Campell, "How Wyndham Targets Women," *Sales & Marketing Management*, October 1, 1998, p. 42; and information from Wyndham's Women on Their Way Web site at www.womenbusinesstravelers.com.

Case 18-2 Pepsi, Virgin Atlantic, Hilton, and Microsoft: Even the Best Can Blow It!

 What do Pepsi, Virgin Atlantic, Hilton, and Microsoft have in common? For one thing, they market some of the best brands in the world. For another, they all engage extensively in successful sales promotions. For still another, all four companies have made big mistakes with sales promotions in recent years that cost them dearly—in terms of money, time, and image.

Pepsi made headlines with a botched promotion in the Philippines, which promised to pay one million pesos (about $40,000 U.S.) to anyone holding a bottle cap printed with the winning number. Due to a computer error, 800,000 caps were printed with the winning number, rather than the single winning cap. Angry consumers rioted in the streets, then filed hundreds of lawsuits and thousands of criminal complaints against Pepsi. The original budget for the promotion was $2 million; the actual costs including fines, topped out at over $13 million.

Pepsi also made news with its biggest-ever Pepsi Stuff campaign, in which the number of customers redeeming proofs-of-purchase for merchandise exceeded the forecast by 50 percent. This caused some customers not to get their Pepsi Stuff and an early cancellation of the promotion. During the promotion, Pepsi made unwanted headlines when it jokingly offered a $24 million Harrier jet as a piece of Pepsi Stuff. Pepsi had to withdraw the offer after five investors raised $3.5 million to buy enough Pepsi points to buy the jet.

Virgin Atlantic, a British airline company headed by the flamboyant Richard Branson, entered into a cross-promotion with the producers of the hit movie *Austin Powers: The Spy Who Shagged Me.* One thousand contest winners were to receive round-trip flights from the United States to London. The contest was held over a 10-hour period on a computer slot machine on the Web. There were several problems with the promotion. The starting time was changed unbeknownst to millions of potential players. Virgin made the change at the last minute so as not to penalize players on the West Coast in the United States, many of whom would have still been sleeping at the original 9:00 A.M. EST start time. Even with a revised (later) start time, a computer glitch prevented players from beginning to play until 12:45 P.M.

The contest rules stated that 100 trips would be given away each hour for 10 consecutive hours, yet some players received a message after one hour that all trips

had already been won. According to a Virgin Atlantic spokesperson, this occurred due to computer-programming error. During the 10-hour contest, the Web site received 18 million hits, but only half a million stayed to play the game. That is unfortunate for Virgin, as the company gained important consumer information from players that will be useful in future promotions. Nonetheless, a Virgin spokesperson indicated that the company was pleased with the results, adding that "in Austin Powers speak, that's grooooovy, baby."

Hilton made a costly sales promotion mistake on behalf of its riverboat Flamingo Hilton Casino when it mailed small-time gamblers coupons for redemption instead of properly sending them to a smaller group of high rollers. Estimated cost of the mistake is a million dollars. The high-roller coupons allow a player to get $75 worth of chips for $25, whereas regular coupons are good for $30 in chips for $25. When casino operators eventually began denying patrons the right to use the overly discounted coupons, angry players protested to management, giving the casino a public relations opportunity they would rather have avoided.

Microsoft is in the business of making money, not giving it away. But the software giant unintentionally gave some consumers $400 in free merchandise at Office Depot and Best Buy if they signed up for three years of Microsoft Network Internet service. Believing that state laws in California and Oregon might forbid the offer, Microsoft revoked a requirement that customers return the merchandise if they canceled the service in those two states. Some consumers then took the rebate and canceled their Internet service with Microsoft. Microsoft canceled the rebate offer in the two states, and says it has not calculated how many consumers exploited the loophole in the rebate offer.

Questions:

1. For each of these four companies, what steps could have been taken to prevent these sales-promotion mistakes?

2. In the Microsoft case, were the customers in California and Oregon who canceled the Internet service rightfully entitled to the free merchandise?

3. Following these sales-promotion mistakes, what public-relations efforts should each company have taken?

SOURCES: "Microsoft Suspends $400 Rebate Program in Two States," from the *New York Times* Web site at www.nytimes.com, January 8, 2000; Doug Tucker, "They Meant the Other Coupon," *Marketing News,* May 10, 1999, p. 29; Lark Borden, "Virgin Atlantic Sorts Out Free-Trip Giveaway Glitches," *The Coloradoan,* June 18, 1999; and Amie Smith, "Learning from the Mistakes of Others—A Sample of Disasters and How to Avoid Them," *Promo,* August 1998, pp. S8–S9.

Chapter Nineteen

Personal Selling and Sales Management

After studying this chapter, you should be able to:

1 Understand the role and importance of personal selling in the marketing communications mix.

2 See how the key steps in personal selling depend on a relationship perspective.

3 Identify the similarities and differences in the job responsibilities of salespeople and sales managers.

4 Describe the key activities in sales management.

5 Appreciate important ethical issues faced by salespeople and sales managers.

www.pfizer.com

Started in 1849, Pfizer has grown to be a worldwide pharmaceutical company with 1999 sales in excess of $16 billion. *Forbes* magazine named Pfizer its 1998 Company of the Year, and *Fortune* magazine ranked Pfizer as both the best company to work for in the pharmaceutical industry and the 20th best across all industries. These successes have come under the leadership of CEO William Steere.

Steere started as a Pfizer sales representative in San Francisco 40 years ago. He was then promoted to district sales manager and, after 12 other promotions, was named CEO in 1991. During his tenure as CEO, Pfizer has advanced from 13th in worldwide prescription drug sales to 2nd.

Pfizer's success is due to many factors. Steere divested unrelated businesses so the company could focus largely on pharmaceuticals. Now drug sales represent 90 percent of total company sales, with the other 10 percent coming from animal health products. Pfizer also spends heavily on research and development, the efforts of which have produced a number of new drugs that have been successful in the marketplace; for example, Viagra was the most successful prescription drug launch in history. The R&D labs have a number of new drugs in the pipeline: Six new products were introduced in the last six years, but the company expects to introduce eight new drugs in the next three years.

Developing new drugs is one thing; making them successful in the marketplace is another. This is largely the role of Pfizer's award-winning salesforce. The Pfizer salesforce is the largest in the industry, with 5,400 sales representatives in the United States and more than 17,000 worldwide. A survey of U.S. physicians ranked Pfizer's salesforce first overall in terms of their disease-and-product knowledge, credibility, and service. This was the fifth straight year Pfizer was ranked first, which is a record for the pharmaceutical industry.

The basic role of Pfizer salespeople is to provide physicians with reliable information about drugs so that they can confidently prescribe them to their patients. As described by CEO Steere: "The sales representatives are the ultimate technology transfer between our laboratories and the practicing physician. Doctors get a lot of information from our representatives, ranging from technical information on new products to new information on older drugs." The Pfizer salesforce is so good that other pharmaceutical companies have partnered with Pfizer to bring new products to market. For example, Pfizer salespeople helped launch Warner-Lambert's cholesterol-lowering drug, Lipitor, and G. D. Searle's arthritis drug, Celebrex.

With new products in the pipeline and growth in the size of its highly regarded salesforce, the future looks bright for Pfizer. However, as in many other industries, there is tremendous consolidation going on in the pharmaceutical industry. For example, if the merger between Glaxo Wellcome and SmithKline Beecham is finalized, as expected, it will produce the largest pharmaceutical company in the world, with combined sales in excess of $23 billion annually. Pfizer has made an aggressive bid for a strategic combination with Warner-Lambert. If this deal were consummated, the combination would have sales of more than $26 billion annually. **Sources:** www.pfizer.com, January 26, 2000; and Malcolm Campbell, "Fantastic Pfizer," *Selling Power,* May 1999, pp. 50–56.

The Pfizer example highlights the important role that personal selling can play in a firm's marketing strategy. Continuously introducing new drugs is critical to success in the pharmaceutical industry and requires both a concerted R&D effort and a strong marketing effort. Although Pfizer does advertise to physicians and consumers and inform them about diseases and new drug products, the Pfizer salesforce is critical to the success of new-product launches. Pfizer salespeople develop close relationships with physicians, and physicians rely on them as an important source of information about new drug products. It is also interesting to note that the company's CEO himself—William Steere—started his career as a Pfizer salesperson and that his first promotion was to district sales manager.

Personal selling is another element of the marketing communications mix, the face-to-face interaction between a seller and a buyer for the purpose of satisfying buyer needs to the benefit of both. This chapter describes the roles of professional salespeople and illustrates various types of sales jobs. We look at the key personal selling activities, especially the way salespeople work with customers to establish mutually beneficial relationships.

The remainder of the chapter deals with sales management. In simple terms, **sales management** provides leadership and supervision of an organization's personal selling function. Besides managing sales personnel, sales managers develop and implement sales strategy. As in other areas of marketing, personal selling and sales management roles are being redefined to meet the challenges of today's competitive, customer-driven marketplace.

We also discuss ethical issues in personal selling and sales management. Salespeople are among the most visible representatives of an organization's marketing effort, and they operate under considerable pressure to generate sales revenue. Because of these factors, it is extremely important for salespeople and sales managers to be aware of their ethical and legal responsibilities.

The Multiple Roles of Salespeople

Salespeople fulfill multiple roles that contribute to the overall success of a business. We look at these roles in two ways: as contributions to the marketing effort, and as functional roles (the different types of personal selling jobs).

Contributions of Personal Selling to Marketing

Personal selling is an important element of a firm's marketing strategy. Colgate–Palmolive salespeople work closely with Wal-Mart to market products to consumers.

Personal selling contributes to a firm's marketing efforts by producing sales revenue, meeting buyer expectations, and providing marketplace information. The key to successful marketing lies in understanding customer requirements and then matching a firm's offerings to those requirements. Because salespeople are often the most direct link between a firm and its customers, they can heavily influence whether or not the firm succeeds.

PRODUCING SALES REVENUE Salespeople make perhaps their most important contribution to the marketing function as revenue producers. Businesses scrambling for survival in a highly competitive world have become more profit-oriented in recent years. To produce an adequate bottom-line profit, it is imperative to achieve a suitable top-line, or sales revenue, figure. And salespeople are on the front line, supported of course by marketing research, product development, distribution, and other areas of the business. Sales personnel, along with management, are the prime bearers of the burden of contributing to profit by producing revenue.

Gerald J. Bauer
Sales Competency Leader and
Field Marketing Manager (ret.)
Du Pont Company

Gerald Bauer recently retired from Du Pont where he held a variety of positions, including sales, sales management, product management, industry management, customer service management, purchasing management, and sales training. He continues to work for Du Pont as a consultant and trainer. Jerry earned a BBA and MBA in marketing from the University of Toledo. Jerry highlights the increasing importance of the sales function throughout a company.

"We have come to realize at Du Pont that sales is not just an individual effort by salespeople. Anyone involved at the customer interface or in support of the customer plays a key role in overall sales success. The actions of a customer service representative, a technical representative, a truck driver, or a CEO can make or break the sale. Processes and systems need to be made customer-friendly to give our customer team efficient and effective support. Roles need to be clear, and redundancy eliminated. At Du Pont, we realize that our competitive advantage comes from our organizational capacity and capability. The combined capability of people is hard to duplicate, and the people of Du Pont are our strength."

MEETING BUYER EXPECTATIONS To succeed in a competitive marketplace, salespeople must—at a minimum—meet buyer expectations. Salespeople are at the heart of the *relationship perspective*. There is no question that the competitive environment has given buyers more clout in dealing with salespeople. According to the National Association of Purchasing Managers, buyers are less likely to tolerate salespeople who waste their time with poorly prepared sales presentations or who will not address their concerns.[1] Dennis Ferguson, a buyer for California-based Rayley's supermarkets, advises salespeople: "I'm busier than ever. Don't tell me what I already know. Tell me why and how your product . . . will disappear off the shelf."[2]

Exhibit 19–1 presents a number of dos and don'ts for salespeople. As suggested by the exhibit, many buyers today take a no-nonsense attitude when dealing with salespeople. They expect straightforward, honest communication. In short, they expect salespeople to live up to high professional standards.

PROVIDING MARKETPLACE INFORMATION Because personal selling involves face-to-face interaction with buyers, salespeople can get immediate feedback from customers. Just as marketplace feedback can help in a firm's development of future products and promotional programs, direct customer feedback adds value to the personal selling function. Feedback to the company can include information on competition and analysis of existing and potential customers and markets, which is useful in sales forecasting.

Job Roles of Salespeople

Although all personal selling involves face-to-face interactions with customers, there are distinct differences in the nature of these interactions. Salespeople's contributions to the overall company effort may be made in a variety of job roles. Exhibit 19–2 classifies personal selling jobs into two major categories: business-to-business and direct-to-consumer.

BUSINESS-TO-BUSINESS SALES Business-to-business selling involves the sale of products and services that are resold by the customer, used as part of the customer's manufacturing process, or used to facilitate the operation of the customer's business. Business selling involves three major types of salespeople: sales support, new business, and existing business.

New technologies can help salespeople perform their job roles more productively. The use of laptop computers turns a car into a virtual office for salespeople.

Exhibit 19–1	*What buyers expect from salespeople*

DOS

- Know your product and its competition better than the buyer does
- Be a tough, but open, negotiator.
- Have the backing of your company to make strategic partnerships.
- Understand the customer's future plans and offer ideas about how your company can help further them.
- Be willing to change your processes and products.
- Offer something unique—a technological change, a new way of delivering, or a large price concession.
- Get to know all the people interested in the product, from purchasing managers to engineers.
- Keep on top of potential product problems.
- Be able to explain how your company plans to improve the quality and reliability of its products.

DON'TS

- Use industry buzzwords without knowing what you're talking about.
- Portray your company as quality-conscious if it's not.
- Focus exclusively on short-term sales goals.
- Talk about strategic alliances without having the support of your company.
- Say, "We want your business, and we'll make it up later."
- Try to persuade purchasers to buy something that doesn't meet their needs.
- Simply talk pricing.
- Give a canned presentation.
- Come without ideas.
- Know the competition.
- Fly by the seat of your pants.
- Offer product today that you're not likely to have tomorrow.
- Roll over dead in negotiations.

Source: Linda Corman, "The World's Toughest Customers," *Selling,* September 1993, p. 53.

Exhibit 19–2	*Types of personal selling jobs*

Business-to-Business	
Sales support:	Promote the product or provide technical service. Includes missionaries and detailers.
New business:	Focus on sales growth by selling new products or new customers. Some salespeople are trade-show specialists, and some work in the field (out of the office).
Existing business:	Maintain and enhance relationships with an established customer base. Includes salespeople who follow an established route, writing up routine orders.
Direct-to-Consumer	
	Represent the seller in transactions with ultimate consumers. Includes retail salespeople and representatives of direct selling firms and most real estate and financial services.

Sales support salespeople are not directly involved in concluding customer purchases. Rather, they support the personal selling function by promoting a product or providing technical support. Sales support salespeople may work in coordination with other salespeople who actually solicit customer purchases, and their activities can be modified to meet the needs of individual customers.

One primary type of sales support job is that of the *missionary.* Missionary salespeople, like religious missionaries, work at the grassroots level to spread the "gospel," that is, help promote their company's products. In this instance, the grass roots level means with product users or with a channel intermediary such as a retail store. Broker organizations often use sales support personnel to visit individual grocery stores, assisting in merchandising and providing point-of-purchase sales information, thereby providing support to build sales volume for the broker's products. Textbook salespeople, such as those from Irwin/McGraw-Hill are a type of missionary salespeople.

In the pharmaceutical industry, highly specialized missionaries, or *detailers,* work for most major drug firms. Detailers call on medical professionals and provide them with technical information and product samples to encourage doctors to

Technical support salespeople must be experts in the use of highly technical products and possess effective sales skills. This salesperson from U.S. Surgical is demonstrating the use of suture products to medical personnel.

write prescriptions for the company's drugs. Pfizer salespeople represent a good example of detailers.

Technical support salespeople are an important element of the sales support function. They have expertise in areas such as design and installation of complex equipment and may provide specialized training to customer employees. Technical support salespeople are especially effective in sales teams formed to address customer needs. For example, the shipping and weighing division of Pitney Bowes sells sophisticated computerized systems that weigh, rate, and track packages for customers like Fed Ex and UPS. The Pitney Bowes sales team includes a sales rep and two sales support personnel—a shipping expert and a sales engineer.[3]

Members of the salesforce who concentrate on selling new products or selling to new customers are called **new-business salespeople.** These people are extremely important to companies focusing on sales growth. Suppose a newly established franchising firm depends on the sale of new franchises to achieve its growth objectives. Salespeople representing the franchising company may then travel the country in search of new franchisees.

Many salespeople are assigned to work with established customers to produce a steady stream of sales revenue. **Existing-business salespeople,** sometimes called *order takers,* include wholesaler reps who follow an established route, writing up fairly routine orders from their customers.

Business-to-business salespeople often represent some combination of the sales support, new-business, and existing-business roles. For example, salespeople from General Mills serve all three functions. They seek new business when new grocery retailers enter the market or when General Mills introduces a new product; they work with existing grocery chains and co-ops to maximize sales of existing and new products; and they provide sales support as they visit individual grocery stores to maximize the General Mills presence at the point of sale.

DIRECT-TO-CONSUMER SALES   **Direct-to-consumer salespeople** sell to individuals who personally use the products and services. This category includes over 4.5 million retail salespeople and over a million others who sell residential real estate and financial securities to ultimate consumers. Several additional million direct-to-consumer salespeople represent firms such as Avon, Mary Kay, Tupperware, Nu-Skin, Amway, and other direct-selling companies.

The Sales Process: A Relationship Approach

Whatever their role, salespeople try to maximize their effectiveness in the **sales process,** which involves initiating, developing, and enhancing long-term, mutually satisfying relationships with customers. This view of selling—called **relationship selling**—is a departure from the old approach that focused more on a salesperson's ability to make a compelling, and often manipulative, sales presentation than on customer needs. Exhibit 19–3 describes its components.

Exhibiting Trust-Building Attributes

To succeed in relationship selling, salespeople must have certain attributes. Although specific attributes vary depending on the sales context, the ability to build trust is basic. Research has shown that five attributes help to build relationships with customers. Salespeople must be customer-oriented, honest, dependable, competent, and likable.[4] Teresa McBride, head of a consulting firm that is the nation's fastest-growing Hispanic-owned business, said the smartest sales policy is one

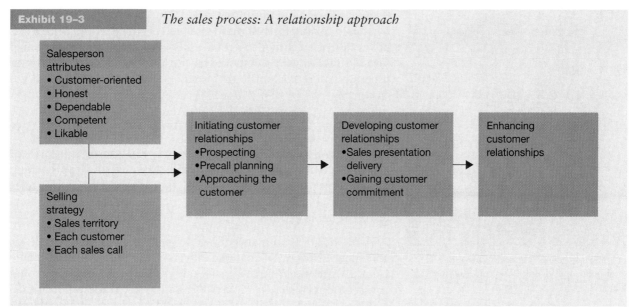

Source: Thomas N. Ingram, Raymond W. LaForge, and Charles H. Schwepker, Jr., *Sales Management: Analysis and Decision Making,* 3rd ed. (Fort Worth, TX: The Dryden Press/Harcourt Brace Jovanovich, 1997), p. 57. Copyright © 1997 by The Dryden Press, reproduced by permission of the publisher.

Salespeople should develop selling strategies for each customer and for each sales call. Successfully executing these strategies often requires salespeople to perform a variety of activities.

based on honesty. By following a trust-based sales strategy, the 31-year-old McBride doubled sales revenue to Fortune 500 clients in a single year.[5]

Developing a Selling Strategy

It is not enough for salespeople to exhibit the right attributes; they must also develop a selling strategy, an overall plan for a course of action. As part of integrated marketing communications programs, selling strategies should be developed at three levels: sales territory, customer, and individual sales call.

A sales territory, usually defined geographically, consists of specific customers and prospects assigned to a specific salesperson. Salespeople need an overall territory strategy regarding the amount of time to spend working with current customers versus trying to generate new customers. Lisa Paolozzi uses a specific territory strategy to sell successfully for FIND/SVP, a market research and consulting company. She spends Mondays and Tuesdays cold-calling prospects and making appointments with existing customers. The rest of the week she makes sales calls to customers and prospects. This approach allows her to plan effective coverage of the customers and prospects in her territory as well manage her time better.[6] Salespeople should also have a territory strategy focusing on specific customer needs they can satisfy. The territory strategy of an advertising sales rep for *Sports Illustrated,* for example, might be to provide high-quality, cost-effective print advertising to those who wish to reach an active, upscale audience.

Selling strategy should next be developed for each customer within a given sales territory. The *Sports Illustrated* salesperson might focus on the manufacturer of Prince tennis racquets and develop an advertising plan to coincide with tennis Grand Slam events: the Australian Open, the French Open, Wimbledon, and the U.S. Open. The salesperson might develop entirely different sales strategies for other sporting goods manufacturers, depending on the needs of the customer.

Finally, each sales call, or every meeting with the customer, should be guided by a strategy compatible with customer needs. By developing a specific plan of action for each sales call, the salesperson capitalizes on a major advantage of personal selling as

Salespeople play an important role in the pharmaceutical industry. Different strategies are used for different customers.

a marketing communications tool. The *Sports Illustrated* salesperson, for example, would probably have to meet with Prince executives individually and in groups, along with ad agency personnel several times to gain a commitment for the Grand Slam advertising program and to customize the program to the specific needs of the customer.

Initiating Customer Relationships

Exhibit 19–3 breaks initiating customer relationships into three primary activities: prospecting, precall planning, and approaching the customer. These activities, like the other parts of the sales process, are highly interrelated. They are not necessarily separately distinguishable actions.

PROSPECTING   **Prospecting** is defined as the seller's search for and identification of qualified buyers. Potential prospects come from a variety of sources, including existing customers, personal contacts, directories, computerized databases, trade publications, and trade shows. Prospects may respond to advertising by placing a telephone call or writing for more information. Such responses, called *inquiries,* are often assigned to salespeople for follow-up.

A qualified buyer must be reasonably accessible to the seller, able to afford the purchase, and at least willing to consider making it. To define qualified prospects, salespeople or companies may establish additional criteria involving elements such as geographical proximity, marketplace function (sales only to wholesalers, for example), or minimum sales-volume levels.

PRECALL PLANNING   In **precall planning,** the salesperson focuses on learning more about the customer's situation. Salespeople might visit the prospect's place of business to learn more about their needs. BellSouth, a major telecommunications company headquartered in Atlanta, instructs its salespeople to follow up a qualifying call with an information-gathering meeting with the prospect. After the proper information is gathered, the BellSouth account rep plans a sales presentation to be delivered at a later date.

A sales rep must consider a multitude of factors in planning a specific sales presentation. A good idea is to formulate a measurable *sales call objective* to guide the planning process. This should specify the desired customer action resulting from the call; for instance, "the customer will place an order of 400 units for immediate shipment."

Planning involves selecting a format for the sales presentation. In most cases, a two-way dialog between the buyer and the seller may be facilitated by an *organized sales presentation,* a mental or written outline developed by the salesperson. The outline should be flexible enough to allow **adaptive selling;** that is, the salesperson must be able to adjust her or his behavior to respond appropriately to the situation and to address the issues that are most important to the customer.[7]

A format at the other extreme from adaptive selling is a *canned sales presentation.* In effect, this is a fully scripted presentation that the sales rep memorizes; it could even be an automated presentation using audiovisual media. Although generally ineffective in business-to-business personal selling, canned presentations have worked well in consumer settings such as the sale of encyclopedias to families. Although they may be complete and logical, the relative inflexibility of canned presentations limits their usefulness.

Word processing supported by graphics facilitates another presentation format, the *written sales proposal.* Long used in major sales, written sales proposals can now easily be tailored to individual customers with diverse needs. Sales proposals are usually accompanied by face-to-face meetings between the buying and selling parties to define product specifications and negotiate details.

During precall planning, salespeople also decide how to use sales tools such as brochures, audiovisual support material, and computer technology. As an example, Dun's Marketing Services, a subsidiary of Dun & Bradstreet, greatly improved the effectiveness of its sales presentations by using a computer to demonstrate how its BusinessLine product works.

Precall planning requires a salesperson to think about communicating to customers how various product or service features translate into explicit benefits. A **feature** is merely a statement of fact about some aspect of a product or service. A **benefit** describes what the feature can do for the customer. For example, one feature of a Mitsubishi portable fax machine is a built-in speakerphone. The benefit of the speakerphone is that it allows hands-free conversation. Effective salespeople communicate more about benefits than features, focusing on those of particular interest to each customer.

APPROACHING THE CUSTOMER   The final phase of initiating the relationship is approaching the customer. This involves arranging the sales call, usually by making an appointment, and extends into the first sales call when introductions are made and the salesperson attempts to develop the basis for further sales activity. Common courtesy and business etiquette can help make a good initial impression. Improper behavior, on the other hand, can diminish the salesperson's opportunity to proceed in the sales process. Examples of behaviors to avoid are shown in Exhibit 19–4.

Developing Customer Relationships

After successfully approaching the customer, the salesperson can begin to develop the customer relationship. To do this, he or she must deliver an effective sales presentation or, more likely, multiple sales presentations. The relationship is established when the customer makes a commitment to take an action such as making a purchase.

SALES PRESENTATION DELIVERY   To make a successful sales presentation, the salesperson must achieve **source credibility**—that is, the customer must perceive its needs being satisfied by the combination of the salesperson, the product or service, and the salesperson's company. The salesperson's personal characteristics such as dress, appearance, and manner may be important in achieving source credibility.

Certain sales approaches can also help achieve source credibility. Prospect-oriented questioning and active listening, as illustrated in Exhibit 19–5, is very important.[8] The salesperson should be careful not to overstate any claims about the product or service and should be prepared to substantiate any that are made. Using third-party evidence such as letters from satisfied customers, called *testimonials,* can

---

Exhibit 19–4	*Approaching the customer: Violations of ethics and etiquette*

A survey of 250 secretaries, administrative assistants, and other "gatekeepers" responsible for scheduling appointments for visiting salespeople revealed these violations of sales etiquette and sales ethics:

- Arriving unannounced to make a sales call.
- Pretending to know the decision maker.
- Treating secretaries disrespectfully.
- Being reluctant to state the purpose of the proposed visit.
- Arriving late for appointments.
- Being overly persistent in attempts to get an appointment.
- Wasting time with unnecessary conversation.
- Failing to cancel appointments that cannot be met.

Source: Thomas N. Ingram, Michael D. Hartline, and Charles A. Schwepker, "Gatekeeper Perceptions: Implications for Improving Sales Ethics and Professionalism," *Proceedings of the Academy of Marketing Science,* 1992, pp. 328–32.

| **Exhibit 19–5** | *Questioning and listening in sales* |

- Remember that you cannot possibly suggest solutions for your clients if you have not listened to what they have said.
- When you are a good listener, you run less chance of dominating the conversation and losing the client's attention.
- You will always learn something valuable from listening. In building customer relationships, this learning process never stops.
- Listening provides feedback on how your sales presentation is going. React to what the prospect is telling you. Clarify the prospect's message when necessary.
- Plan and organize your presentation so you know which questions to ask. Make your questions clear and concise to avoid confusing the client.
- During the presentation, take notes to ensure appropriate follow-up activities or to plan for the next call.

Source: Phillip Schembra, "Often Overlooked Listening Habits," *The Selling Advantage,* January 1991, p. 3; and Phillip Schembra, "A Checklist on Asking Questions," *The Selling Advantage,* July 1991, p. 3.

enhance source credibility. Finally, pointing out guarantees and warranties that reduce the buyer's risk can assist in establishing source credibility.

Jerry Bauer, Sales Competency Leader and Field Marketing Manager, Du Pont Company, (ret.) talks about the importance of questioning and listening during a sales presentation: "Many people think that the key to a successful sales presentation is for a salesperson to be a good talker. At Du Pont, we think the key to sales success is to be a good listener. We emphasize this point in our sales training by saying that salespeople should talk about 20 percent of the time and listen 80 percent of the time. This might be a little stretch, but it encourages salespeople to focus on the listening aspect of the job. A parallel skill is the ability to ask good questions. Questioning and listening skills are a focal point of our sales training at Du Pont."

During the sales presentation, the sales rep should expect to resolve buyer concerns before the customer makes a commitment to buy. Buyer concerns, called *objections,* come in many forms ("Your price is too high"; "I don't like the color"; "I am happy with my current supplier") and must be dealt with successfully to make a sale. Objections are a form of *sales resistance,* which also includes unspoken customer concerns. To the extent possible, the salesperson should anticipate these concerns and formulate appropriate customer-oriented responses prior to the sales presentation. Salespeople must understand that questions and concerns are part of the buyer's attempt to make a sound purchase decision; addressing these concerns is an integral element in the sales process.

Many buyer concerns arise when a sales rep has not taken enough time to qualify a buyer and thus calls on a marginal prospect, perhaps one who cannot afford the product or will derive only limited benefits from a purchase. Under any set of circumstances, salespeople should treat buyer questions with patience and respect. Exhibit 19–6 details some ideas on how to deal with customers' unreasonable concerns and objections.

GAINING CUSTOMER COMMITMENT   In most cases, a buyer can choose from among a number of potential sellers; hence, sales reps are responsible for gaining customer commitment. This remains true even when the seller is the only available alternative, for a customer may elect to make no purchase at all.

A successful relationship between buyer and seller requires a firm commitment from both parties. Essentially, customer commitment involves an economic transaction between the buyer and the seller (customer buys when salesperson closes a sale), or an agreement between the two parties that moves them toward such a transaction. Some customer commitments take the form of a purchase order. Other examples are agreeing to continue sales negotiations, signing a long-term distribution contract, or accepting the seller's suggestion to maintain specified inventory levels to meet local demand.

Exhibit 19–6	*Dealing with unreasonable customer concerns and objections*

When a customer lodges a completely unjustified objection, one that is knowingly untrue or unreasonable, salespeople can follow these guidelines for responding.

- Allow customers to retain their dignity. State your position politely.

- Do not argue with a customer. Winning an argument can have detrimental effects on the relationship.

- Appeal to the customer's sense of fair play. Tell the customer you want to do what is right, and try to reach agreement on a course of action to be taken.

- Stand firm, so long as your position is based on facts.

- Do not use company policy as a reason for your position. This tends to invite criticism of the policy.

- If absolutely necessary, be prepared to say no to an unreasonable demand. Agreeing to an unreasonable demand can open the door for more of the same, which will ultimately endanger or ruin the relationship.

Source: Adapted from: *Making . . . Serving . . . Keeping Customers* (Chicago: The Dartnell Corporation, 1990).

To gain a commitment, a professional salesperson must be willing to spend the time necessary to give the customer all the pertinent information. Further, professional salespeople understand that when buyers do not want to make a commitment, it is because they see a commitment as simply not in their best interest at that time.

Relationship-oriented salespeople must walk a fine line between being persuasive and being overly persistent or pushy in an attempt to gain commitment. Buyers do not like being pressured into making decisions they feel are premature, and salespeople must realize that decisions made under pressure are likely to create postpurchase doubts. This can jeopardize the relationship and even lead to its termination.

Enhancing Customer Relationships

The final phase of the sales process shown in Exhibit 19–3 is enhancing customer relationships. The purpose of this step is to ensure that customer expectations are met or exceeded, so that an ongoing, mutually satisfying relationship between the buyer and seller may continue. This stage involves postsale follow-up activities such as entering and expediting customer orders, providing training for the customer's employees, assisting in merchandising and installation activities, and solving customer problems.

Salespeople can enhance the relationship by continuing to provide timely information, alerting the customer to forthcoming product improvements, monitoring customer satisfaction and making improvements as necessary, showing the customer additional ways to use the product, and acting as a consultant to the prospect's business. It is not unusual for salespeople to become confidants of customers, offering opinions when asked on a wide range of topics, some of which are unrelated to the sales offering.

Earning Customer Loyalty

Getting customer feedback

Texas Nameplate Company (TNC) is the smallest company to win the Malcolm Baldrige Quality Award. TNC generates about $4 million in annual sales. It focuses on retaining customers by being viewed as a trusted and valuable supplier. The company uses customer visits and response cards to get feedback from customers and to take corrective action when problems are identified. For example, twice a year, salespeople get a printout of customers who

have not made a purchase during the previous 12 months. The salespeople visit these customers to solve problems and reestablish the relationship. Last year this approach recovered 78 inactive accounts. TNC's approach is working, as more than 62 percent of customers have been doing business with TNC for more than 10 years.

Source: Michelle Marchetti, "Home-Style Selling," *Sales & Marketing Management,* August 1999, p. 16.

Salespeople should seek feedback from customers, rather than wait for problems to surface. Asking questions such as "How are we doing as your supplier?" is important, as well as follow-up action to continually build value for the customer. Salespeople must never take existing customers' business for granted. The added value to customers can be reinforced through periodic business reviews, where salespeople and perhaps their management meet with customers to analyze sales and profit performance and identify areas for future emphasis. The importance of enhancing customer relationships is illustrated in "Earning Customer Loyalty: Getting Customer Feedback."

Sales Management Activities

Sales managers must move their salesforces toward the ideal. Typically, successful sales managers were successful salespeople before being promoted. They usually continue some form of personal selling after becoming managers, perhaps selling to their own set of customers, accompanying salespeople on sales calls, or serving as a member of a selling team. Exhibit 19–7 presents management activities, including developing a sales strategy, designing the sales organization, developing and directing the salesforce, and evaluating effectiveness and performance.

These activities require more of sales managers than is expected of salespeople. Whereas salespeople concentrate mainly on relationships with customers, sales managers must work well with customers, salespeople, and many other people in the company to do a good job.

Developing a Sales Strategy

The starting point for sales management is developing a sales strategy to execute the firm's marketing strategy. A marketing strategy emphasizes the development of a marketing mix to appeal to defined target markets. A sales strategy focuses on how to sell to specific customers within those target markets.[9] Two key elements of a sales strategy are a relationship strategy and a sales channel strategy.

DEVELOPING A RELATIONSHIP STRATEGY   Although there is a clear trend toward a *relationship perspective*, especially in business-to-business selling, different types of relationships are possible. Buyers have different needs and desire to purchase in different ways for different products. Therefore, it is important that the selling firm develop specific **relationship strategies** for specific customer groups. Most firms will need to develop relationship strategies for three to five different customer groups. Exhibit 19–8 presents four basic relationship strategies.

The relationship strategies range from a transaction relationship to a collaborative relationship, with a solutions relationship and partnership relationship in between. As a company moves from transaction to collaborative relationships, the focus changes from just selling products to adding more value, the time frame of the relationship becomes longer, the products become more customized, and the number of customers becomes fewer. Also, the cost to serve customers becomes higher and there is a greater need for commitment between the buying and selling organization.

Thinking Critically

Select a familiar product that is sold through personal selling by a field salesforce:

- What other sales channels might be used in conjunction with personal selling by a field salesforce?
- What are the advantages and disadvantages of each sales channel?
- What are the key challenges facing sales managers when multiple sales channels are used?

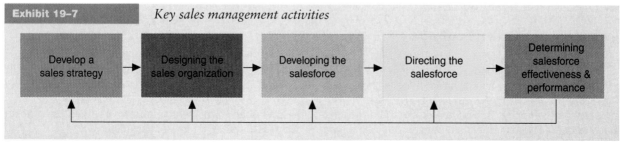

Exhibit 19–7   *Key sales management activities*

Develop a sales strategy → Designing the sales organization → Developing the salesforce → Directing the salesforce → Determining salesforce effectiveness & performance

Source: Adapted from Thomas N. Ingram, Raymond W. LaForge, and Charles H. Schwepker, Jr., *Sales Management and Decision Making,* 3rd ed. (Fort Worth, TX: The Dryden Press, 1997), p. 3. Copyright © 1997 by The Dryden Press, reproduced by permission of the publisher.

Exhibit 19–8	*Relationship selling strategies*			
	Transaction Relationship	**Solutions Relationship**	**Partnership Relationship**	**Collaborative Relationship**
Goal	Sell products		⟶	Add Value
Time frame	Short		⟶	Long
Offering	Standardized		⟶	Customized
Number of Customers	Many		⟶	Few
Cost to serve	Low		⟶	High
Commitment	Low		⟶	High

Source: Thomas N. Ingram, Raymond W. LaForge, and Charles H. Schwepker, Jr., *Sales Management: Analysis and Decision Making,* 3rd ed. (Fort Worth, TX: The Dryden Press, 1997), p. 140.

Team selling is being used by more firms to better meet the needs of large and important customers. Baxter employs multifunctional sales teams as part of its customer contact strategy.

The key strategic decision is to balance the customer's preference with the cost to serve the customer. In general, lower-cost methods are used in transaction relationships and the highest-cost methods in collaborative relationships. For example, allowing customers to purchase directly from the Internet can be a cost-effective way to serve customers in a transaction relationship. At the other extreme, many companies such as IBM use expensive multifunctional global account teams to serve collaborative relationship customers. Different approaches are typically used for the intermediate solutions and partnership relationship strategies. Thus, relationship and sales channel strategies are closely related.

DEVELOPING A SALES CHANNEL STRATEGY

A **sales channel strategy** addresses how the company initiates and maintains contact with customers. It may involve the use of a company field salesforce, telemarketing, independent sales reps, distributors, the Internet, and/or trade shows.[10] Such a strategy should ensure that customers receive the necessary attention from the salesforce. A sales channel strategy must be both effective (get the job done) and efficient (at a reasonable cost).

The traditional sales strategy is to have a field salesperson perform all selling activities to all customers. This can be an effective approach, but is typically very costly. Therefore, many sales organizations are looking for ways to replace expensive field selling with less-costly sales channels such as telemarketing or the Internet. The potential benefits from this approach are clear. Let's assume the cost of a personal sales call is $250 and the cost of a telephone sales call is $25; each time a personal sales call is replaced by a telephone sales call, the company saves $225. The savings are even greater if the personal sales call is replaced by an electronic interaction over the Internet.

For small customers and many transaction relationships, field selling can be totally replaced by using telemarketing, the Internet, or other sales channels. In other cases, field selling might be integrated with telephone selling or the Internet. For example, prospecting might be performed over the phone or the Internet. Once good prospects are identified, a salesperson makes personal sales calls to establish solutions, partnership, or collaborative relationships. Then, various service and re-ordering activities are performed over the telephone or the Internet. A couple of examples illustrate how companies are doing this:

- Applied Industrial Technologies distributes 1.5 million different industrial products through 380 branch offices with 900 field salespeople and 1,400 inside salespeople. Annual sales are over $1.5 billion. The field salespeople work with customers to determine their needs in order to negotiate pricing agreements. Each customer is then provided a private Extranet that can be used to purchase products, check on the status of orders, and get various types of information. Customers can also order or receive information over the phone from the inside salespeople. This approach allows customers to select the sales channel they want for each interaction. And, as customers interact more over the telephone and—especially—the Internet, Applied's costs to serve these customers goes down.[11]

- Xerox is integrating the Internet into a complicated sales channel strategy that includes retail stores, distributors, and field salespeople. Smaller transaction-type customers typically purchase supplies and smaller systems from retail stores. These customers can now purchase on-line from the Xerox Web site. If they have questions, the site provides toll-free numbers to reach Xerox service people. Field salespeople establish different types of relationships with larger customers; however, once the relationship is established, much of the customer service functions are being performed electronically through private Extranets developed for each customer.[12]

These examples are representative of the types of sales channel strategies being implemented by many companies. The trend is to use different sales channels for different types of customer relationships and to replace more-expensive with less-expensive sales channels whenever possible.

Although these trends apply to most customers, many companies use various types of **team selling** for their very best customers. These sales teams are typically multifunctional and can include people from different management levels. Normally used in partnership or collaborative relationships with key customers, these approaches are often called *national account, major account,* or *global account* programs. Team selling is an expensive sales channel, but can produce significant sales and profit growth in some situations. The approach used at Kele & Associates, a manufacturer of building automation peripherals, is illustrative. The company developed a national account program two years ago. Sales teams consisting of members from marketing, sales, accounting, and information technology plan and execute customized strategies to serve the company's best customers. The sales team analyzes each customer's business to identify ways Kele can add more value to the relationship. The strategy has been successful in growing business with these customers.[13]

Designing the Sales Organization

To implement a successful selling strategy, the company must design an appropriate sales organization and adjust it according to subsequent strategic changes. Some key questions to address in designing the sales organization include:

- Should the salesforce be generalists (salespeople who sell the entire product line) or specialists (only sell specific products or only sell to specific customers)?

- If specialists are used, should they be product specialists, market or customer specialists, or functional (new-business or existing-business) specialists?

- Should tight control be maintained with a centralized salesforce, or should sales activities and decision making be moved closer to the customer with a decentralized salesforce?

- How much total selling effort is needed to provide adequate sales coverage? How large should the salesforce be?

Sales managers can use new technologies to help make better sales organization design decisions. Mapping software, such as Terr Align, is useful in designing effective sales territories.

- How should specific customers and geographic areas be assigned to salespeople to form sales territories?
- How should *salesforce turnover* (the proportion of salespeople who leave their jobs) be factored into sales organization design decisions?

All these decisions are complex, and they may be addressed with any number of analytical tools. Computer algorithms and sophisticated decision models can give some quantitative input. Dictaphone, for example, used a computerized mapping program to realign sales territories when its poorly designed territories caused high salesforce turnover. The reconfiguration reduced salesforce turnover and improved morale and productivity.[14]

Developing the Salesforce

There are three main activities in developing the salesforce: recruiting, selecting, and training salespeople.

RECRUITING AND SELECTING *Recruiting* is the process of finding prospective job candidates; *selecting* involves choosing the candidates to be hired. Recruiting and selecting salespeople are challenging tasks. According to one survey, over 30 percent of 645 firms reported "some difficulty" or "great difficulty" in recruiting salespeople. There simply are not enough well-educated and skilled workers. For example, for its salesforce, pharmaceutical firm G. D. Searle recruits registered nurses and pharmacists, of which there are severe shortages in the United States.[15] Approximately 60 percent of all sales reps in the pharmaceutical industry are pharmacy school graduates, but the difficulty of recruiting pharmacists may cause some firms to seek candidates with nonpharmaceutical backgrounds.[16]

Another problem is lack of time to recruit qualified salespeople. In one survey, sales executives said that because of a lack of time, they sometimes rely on "warm body" recruiting—hiring under pressure to fill a vacancy.[17]

Observers predict that to meet the challenges in recruiting and selecting salespeople, companies will hire more part-time and older salespeople and increase efforts to diversify their salesforces ethnically and culturally. The number of women entering sales is also expected to continue to grow.

TRAINING There are two categories of sales training: initial and continual. Newly hired salespeople receive *initial training*, which typically focuses on product knowledge and sales techniques. *Continual training* for all salespeople is becoming more standard as firms attempt to stay current and competitive in an ever-changing environment. "Using Technology: More Training for Less" presents an example of how new technologies can improve sales training.

Sales training is a key for companies interested in continual improvement. At Union Pacific, for example, salespeople go through 21 courses over a five-year period to learn to deliver total quality management, including the improvement of customer relationships. The first year focuses on product knowledge and selling skills. The second year concentrates on working effectively in teams. In the third year, salespeople learn how to be team leaders. Then training moves to advanced stages of total quality management. According to Fred Henderson, vice president of sales and marketing, "We had to create a company strategy that was focused on the true requirements of the customer and the marketplace, and then build a training strategy to take it there."[18]

Sales training is conducted in a variety of ways. During a sales training session, Astra/Merck Group Pharmaceutical specialists discuss how they can most effectively respond to changing customer needs in the health care industry.

Directing the Salesforce

Directing salespeople to meet goals and objectives consumes much of the typical sales manager's time. These activities include motivation, supervision, and leadership of the salesforce.

Who's your sales rep of the year?

(Make your award on the basis of profit, not revenue.)

When you have Cognos Business Intelligence, you'll come up with the right answer in minutes, because you'll be able to see beyond the surface. You'll see in an instant who's contributing the most to the bottom line by selling high-margin products—so you can start rewarding the reps who are making the biggest contribution to your profit line. It's just one way you can use Business Intelligence from Cognos to make better decisions every day, everywhere within your enterprise.

Only Cognos has the applications, the know-how, the track record, and the support services to put Business Intelligence to work throughout your enterprise. To find out how innovative companies around the world have already profited from our Business Intelligence leadership, ask for our free book, *The Multidimensional Manager*, by visiting our Web site at www.cognos.com/fortune or by calling 1-800-426-4667, ext 2099.

COGNOS
Better Decisions Every Day™

www.cognos.com/fortune

Many sales organizations offer salespeople a variety of different rewards as incentives. Cognos helps sales organizations identify the most profitable salespeople to be recognized with different rewards.

MOTIVATION Salesforce motivation involves maximizing the effort salespeople direct toward specific objectives and helping them persist in the face of adversity. Most sales companies offer a variety of financial and nonfinancial rewards in their salesforce motivation programs.

Money remains the most sought-after reward among salespeople, with the opportunity for promotion into management also highly desired.[19] Most companies pay salespeople a combination of salary and incentives. Incentive pay could include commissions, bonuses, or both. About three-fourths of U.S. firms use a combination pay plan; less than 15 percent pay a straight salary; and some 10 percent pay by straight commission.[20] Salesperson compensation has been increasing in recent years. A study of 93,000 salespeople from 800 companies found the following median levels of compensation for salespeople: $36,000 for entry-level sales rep; $46,000 for intermediate sales rep; and $63,700 for senior sales rep.[21]

Incentive pay can have dramatic effects on salesforce motivation. Creative Works, a Northbrook, Illinois, school supply company, established an additional 2 percent bonus on top of the existing 5 percent commission for the addition of new customers. The company also introduced a one-dollar-per-case bonus on the opening order of any new products sold to new or existing accounts. In one year, sales jumped from $700,000 to $3 million and the customer base grew from 80 to 200.[22]

Most companies also use sales contests and formal recognition programs to motivate their salesforces. Such programs may offer exotic travel, merchandise, or high-visibility award ceremonies in addition to money as an incentive.

SUPERVISION AND LEADERSHIP Supervision of a salesforce deals with direction of day-to-day operations. Computerized **sales automation systems** are one way to assist sales managers in routine supervisory chores such as processing salespeople's call reports, itineraries, and expense reports.

Using Technology

More training for less

Many companies are using new technologies to provide cost-effective sales training. Consider two examples:

- Intel's Business Conferencing Group used a multipoint videoconference to train 40 sales reps in the United States and Europe in the use of its new Team-Station 4.0 videoconferencing system. The full-day program linked 20 sales offices and some reps in their homes. The videoconference was interactive, so all participants could ask questions at any time. Participants rated the sales training program as being very effective, and the cost savings compared with bringing everyone to the same location were substantial.

- Fisher Scientific Salespeople often show up for sales training in their pajamas. Because the training programs are on the Web, salespeople can receive them in their homes, cars, hotel rooms, or wherever they bring their laptop computers. Salespeople can receive product training, take an exam, or post messages to product experts wherever and whenever they want. The company saves money on travel costs, and the salespeople save valuable selling time.

Sources: Don Labriola, "Videoconferencing in Action," *Sales and Field Force Automation*, September 1999, p. 74; and Melinda Ligos, "Point, Click, and Sell," *Sales & Marketing Management*, May 1999, pp. 51–56.

Leadership activities, on the other hand, use more subtle communication to influence salespeople to achieve the company's overall objectives. One leadership function is *coaching*, or providing guidance and feedback on a regular basis to direct salespeople's activities. Another important leadership activity is conducting sales meetings that unite a salesforce in an effort to meet common goals.

The supervision and leadership of salespeople is very much a human endeavor, despite the help of technology. Sales managers routinely deal with human relations problems such as drug and alcohol abuse, sexual harassment, employee job stress, expense-account fraud, and any number of other people problems. Salespeople are no different from any other group of employees when it comes to problem areas.

Jerry Bauer, Sales Competency Leader and Field Marketing Manager, Du Pont Company, (ret.) discusses the importance of leadership within the sales function: **"With a constant eye on achieving profitable growth, we are having to change the way we manage our salesforces at Du Pont. Downsizing has led to larger spans of control and more self-managed teams. Mentoring and networking are becoming more and more important. We are looking for leaders who can provide a compelling vision. We want sales leaders who can build self-esteem, emotional involvement, and the knowledge, skills, and abilities of their team, and also instill a sense of excitement. You might say we are moving from 'sales management' to 'strategic leadership.' "**

Evaluating Performance and Effectiveness

Sales managers must establish standards by which performance and effectiveness are measured, evaluate performance and effectiveness against these standards, and then take appropriate follow-up action. *Salesperson performance* refers to how well individual salespeople meet job expectations. An evaluation of *salesforce effectiveness* is in fact an assessment of the entire sales organization. Factors within and outside the sales organization, such as product quality or competitors, can also influence salesforce effectiveness.

SETTING STANDARDS   Standards by which performance and effectiveness are assessed usually relate to quantitative outcomes, or *quotas,* such as total sales volume, gross margin, market share, number of new accounts added, and accounts retained. These quotas typically are based on a forecast developed at least in part by the sales manager.

Sales managers must also get the job done within a specified budget. Given the high costs of personal selling, achieving objectives within budget constraints is a constant challenge. For example, the median cost per sales call exceeds $200, despite increased efforts to trim sales costs. Travel-related costs, such as lodging and meals, continue to climb, along with salespeople's pay levels.[23]

It is becoming increasingly difficult to raise selling price only because of increasing sales costs. Thus, to maintain favorable sales-expense-to-sales-revenue ratios, most salespeople are asked to sell more each year, whether economic conditions are favorable or not.

EVALUATING PERFORMANCE   To evaluate individual salesperson performance, sales managers may take a behavior-based perspective, an outcome-based perspective, or a combination of the two. A *behavior-based perspective* defines the sales behaviors expected, such as how many sales calls to make or which sales presentation tactics to use. The salesperson is then evaluated on how well he or she executes the behaviors. An *outcome-based perspective* focuses on the results of sales behavior, such as total sales volume. As relationship selling spreads, the behavior-based perspective to evaluate salesperson performance is gaining more acceptance than the outcome-based approach.

ANALYZING EFFECTIVENESS   Managers may analyze sales, costs, profitability, and productivity to evaluate the effectiveness of the sales organization. They compare figures of one year with those of the previous year to gauge progress. Managers also compare their own salesforce effectiveness with that of competitors, if

Exhibit 19–9	*Example of a salesforce effectiveness evaluation*			
	District 1	**District 2**	**District 3**	**District 4**
Sales	$10,000,000	$12,000,000	$10,000,000	$12,000,000
Selling expenses	$ 1,000,000	$ 1,200,000	$ 1,500,000	$ 1,500,000
Sales calls	5,000	4,500	4,500	6,000
Proposals	100	105	120	120
Number of salespeople	10	15	10	15
Sales per salesperson	$ 1,000,000	$ 800,000	$ 1,000,000	$ 800,000
Expenses per salesperson	$ 100,000	$ 80,000	$ 150,000	$ 100,000
Calls per salesperson	500	300	450	400

Source: Adapted from Thomas N. Ingram and Raymond W. LaForge, *Sales Management: Analysis and Decision Making,* 2nd ed. (Fort Worth, TX: The Dryden Press/Harcourt Brace Jovanovich, 1992), p. 533. Copyright © 1992 by The Dryden Press, reproduced by permission of the publisher.

possible. For example, in the packaged-grocery business, market share data by brand are readily available, and comparisons with key competitors are commonplace.

A simple example of salesforce productivity analysis is shown in Exhibit 19–9. Note that District 2 is tied for the lead with District 4 in total sales volume. Also, the sales per salesperson and expenses per salesperson figures in District 2 compare favorably with the other districts. Yet the number of sales calls made per salesperson is low. This may explain why expenses are low, but it may also suggest that salespeople in District 2 may not be providing adequate contact with their customers.

Numbers, then, do not tell the whole story; analysis of the numbers can, however, suggest areas worth further investigation by the sales manager. By combining quantitative analysis with personal observation, information from customers, and review with salespeople, sales managers can evaluate the effectiveness of their salesforces.

Ethical and Legal Issues in Personal Selling

Because personal selling activities are highly visible, ethical and legal issues are extremely important for salespeople and sales managers. In building trust-based customer relationships, ethical behavior is even more critical. Major professional groups such as Sales and Marketing Executives International, the American Marketing Association, and the Direct Selling Association have adopted strict codes of ethics for salespeople, as have many companies. An example is shown in Exhibit 19–10.

Sales managers must take responsibility for the proper behavior of their salespeople, and they must also lead by example. They must know the laws related to buyer–seller interactions, the gathering of competitive information, and the management of personnel.

To be on the safe side, salespeople should be honest in their dealings with customers and be informed of relevant laws governing their business situation. All salespeople are subject to some form of contract law, which regulates transactions. Purchase orders are binding contracts, as are oral commitments made by a salesperson. An extensive review of 50 years of legal cases revealed that salespeople can, by inappropriate oral statements, create undesirable legal obligations for their firms. Problems include creation of unintended warranties, understatement of warning messages, disparagement of competitors' offerings without substantiation, misrepresentation of company offerings, and illegal interference with business relationships.[24]

Exhibit 19–10	*Code of ethics for professional salespeople*

As a Certified Professional Salesperson, I pledge to the following people and organizations:

The Customer. In all customer relationships, I pledge to:

Maintain honesty and integrity in my relationships with customers and prospective customers.

Accurately represent my product or service in order to place the customer or prospective customer in a position to make a decision consistent with the principle of mutuality of benefit and profit to the buyer and seller.

Keep abreast of all pertinent information that would assist my customers in achieving their goals as they relate to my product(s) or service(s).

The Company. In relationships with my employer, co-workers, and other parties whom I represent, I will:

Use their resources that are at my disposal for legitimate business purposes only.

Respect and protect proprietary and confidential information entrusted to me by my company.

The Competition. Regarding those with whom I compete in the marketplace, I promise:

To obtain competitive information only through legal and ethical methods.

To portray my competitors and their products and services only in a manner that is honest, that is truthful, and that reflects accurate information that can or has been substantiated.

Source: Excerpted from *Sales and Marketing Executives International Certified Professional Salesperson Code of Ethics* (Cleveland: Sales and Marketing Executives International, 1994).

Exhibit 19–11	*Unethical sales behaviors*

Research indicates sales behaviors that are unethical in the eyes of customers:

- Exaggerates the features and benefits of his/her products/services.
- Lies about availability to make a sale.
- Lies about the competition to make a sale.
- Sells products/services people don't need.
- Is interested only in own interests, not the clients'.
- Gives answers when doesn't really know the answers.
- Lies about competitors.
- Falsifies product testimonials.

- Passes the blame for something he/she did onto someone else.
- Poses as a market researcher when conducting telephone sales.
- Misrepresents guarantees/warranties.
- Makes oral promises that are not legally binding.
- Does not offer information about an upcoming sale that will include merchandise the customer is planning to buy.
- Accepts favors from customers so the seller will feel obliged to bend the rules/policies of the seller's company.
- Sells dangerous or hazardous products.

Source: Rosemary R. Lagace, Thomas N. Ingram, and Michael Borom, "An Exploratory Study of Salesperson Unethical Behavior: Scale Development and Validation," forthcoming in the *Proceedings,* American Marketing Association Summer Educators' Conference, 1994.

Exhibit 19–11 presents some specific sales behaviors deemed unethical by buyers. Salespeople interested in developing lasting relationships with their customers should refrain from those behaviors, for research suggests that buyers will go out of their way to avoid doing business with salespeople they see as unethical.[25]

There are also numerous ethical and legal issues relevant to relationships between sales managers and salespeople. For example, the Civil Rights Act of 1964 prohibits discrimination based on age, race, color, religion, sex, or national origin. The act has implications for recruiting and selecting salespeople and evaluating and rewarding their performance. The Americans with Disabilities Act of 1992 also affects recruiting and other sales management functions, as do guidelines for minimizing sexual harassment issued by the Equal Employment Opportunity Commission.

This is only a brief discussion of the ethical and legal consequences of marketers' actions. Given the pressure on the sales function to generate revenue, it is particularly important for sales managers to know and adhere to the laws of the marketplace and the workplace. They should be models, provide adequate training, and monitor, reinforce, and direct sales personnel. In developing trust-based relationships with customers, marketers should follow these guidelines not just because of laws or because it's the right thing to do—but because it is also a sound business practice.

Personal Selling and Sales Management in the Future

Future   The changes in the business environment are having an important effect on personal selling and sales management. Salespeople and sales managers will have to have different skills to be successful in the future. Two studies by MOHR Development suggest the competencies needed by salespeople and sales managers in the future.[26] Salesperson competencies involve the ability to:

1. Align customers' strategic objectives with your company's so both gain.
2. Go beyond product needs to assess business potential and add value to the relationship.
3. Understand the financial impact of the decisions made by your company and the client's organization.
4. Organize company resources to build customer-focused relationships.
5. Develop consultative problem solving and a willingness to change.
6. Establish a vision of a committed customer/supplier relationship.
7. Utilize self-appraisal and continuous learning by requesting feedback from customers, colleagues, and managers.

Sales manager competencies involve the ability to:

1. Provide strategic vision.
2. Organize company resources by leveraging relationships.
3. Influence company strategy.
4. Coach effectively.
5. Diagnose performance.
6. Select high-potential salespeople.
7. Leverage technology.
8. Demonstrate personal selling effectiveness.

These competencies indicate what it will take to be successful in the future. Notice the focus on developing relationships with customers by salespeople and developing relationships with salespeople by sales managers. Both salespeople and sales managers must possess communication and "people" skills as well as understand the strategic and financial aspects of business. And, the need to understand and be able to use technology effectively will be extremely important.

Summary

1. **Understand the role and importance of personal selling in the marketing communications mix.** Personal selling is a valuable part of the promotion mix and the overall marketing effort of many companies. Salespeople fulfill the extremely important role of generating revenue. In today's competitive environment, paying close attention to customer needs and expectations is necessary, and personal selling can help in this endeavor. Salespeople provide crucial marketplace information to their companies, which may further improve the marketing effort.

2. **See how the key steps in personal selling depend on a relationship perspective.** The sales process involves three steps: initiating, developing, and enhancing customer relationships. To initiate customer relationships, salespeople must first locate qualified potential customers through prospecting. They must then plan the initial sales call and the way to approach the customer.

   In developing customer relationships, salespeople must be able to deliver effective sales presentations. During a sales call, it is extremely important that the salesperson use questioning and listening skills to attend to all of the customer's requirements and to gain a commitment from the customer.

   To enhance relationships with customers, salespeople must be customer-oriented and continue to meet or exceed customer expectations. Relationship selling also requires that salespeople formulate and implement different strategies for different customers and that they minimize wasted time in each sales call.

   To be successful in relationship selling, salespeople gain the trust of their customers. To build trust, salespeople should be customer-oriented, honest, dependable, competent, and likable.

3. **Identify the similarities and differences in the job responsibilities of salespeople and sales managers.** Along with their other job duties, sales managers are usually involved in personal selling to some degree. Using an athletic team analogy, the salespeople are the players, and the sales manager is the coach. The sales manager must do everything necessary to field a competitive sales team year after year, including developing the team strategy. Salespeople concentrate on taking care of their customers; sales managers must work not only with customers, but also with others in the company to ensure success.

4. **Describe the key activities in sales management.** The key job activities of sales managers are developing a sales strategy, designing the sales organization, developing the salesforce, directing the salesforce, and evaluating performance and effectiveness. Sales managers must recruit and select salespeople and provide them with sufficient resources to be effective. Most sales managers play an active role in training their salespeople. They must also help motivate salespeople to reach their full potential and evaluate their performance. Sales managers must accomplish all these activities in a rapidly changing environment, which means they may need to adapt sales strategies to remain competitive.

5. **Appreciate important ethical issues faced by salespeople and sales managers.** Salespeople can develop trust with their customers by avoiding a range of unethical sales behaviors. Examples are lying, selling customers products they do not need, withholding information, and selling dangerous products.

   Sales managers lead by example. They must not abuse the power of their positions in dealing with their employees. Sales managers must also be prepared to deal with human relations issues such as drug abuse, sexual harassment, and employee job stress. Ignoring such issues would be less than ethical.

Understanding Marketing Terms and Concepts

Thinking About Marketing

1. Discuss the three major roles salespeople play in the overall marketing effort.

2. How are the roles of sales support salespeople different from those of new-business salespeople?

3. Give several examples of different types of direct-to-consumer salespeople.

4. To practice relationship selling, salespeople must be able to cultivate the trust of their customers. What attributes should salespeople have to cultivate the trust of their customers?

5. The first step in the sales process is to initiate customer relationships. Discuss the three primary activities during this initial step.

6. Review "Earning Customer Loyalty: Getting Customer Feedback." What happens to a company if customers are dissatisfied with its products or services?

7. How important is ethical behavior by salespeople in dealing with customers? Think about trust-building salesperson attributes, and consult Exhibits 19–3 and 19–10 before completing your answer.

8. Consult "Using Technology: More Training for Less." What other technologies could be used to improve sales training?

9. Describe the key responsibilities of sales managers in each of the five activity areas shown in Exhibit 19–7.

10. How are the recruitment and selection of salespeople related to designing the salesforce?

Applying Marketing Skills

1. Review the unethical sales behaviors in Exhibit 19–11. Can you recall from your own experiences as a consumer examples of any of those behaviors? In those instances, did you eventually come to trust the salesperson? Did you make purchases? What kind of sales behavior could you suggest for salespeople who wish to earn the trust of their customers?

2. When a commitment is not readily forthcoming from a prospect, some salespeople might use a "buy now" method to get the sale, which gives the buyer a good reason to make an immediate purchase. For example, the salesperson might suggest that the buyer can avoid a planned price increase by placing an immediate order. If no such price increase is actually planned, has the salesperson acted unethically? What if the buyer has been promising to place an order for months, but never has, and now seems to be stalling?

3. Visit a retail store with the aim of getting some details about a product you plan to buy at some future date. Evaluate the listening skills of the salesperson you encounter. Is the salesperson a good listener or not? How was the salesperson's credibility affected by his or her listening skills?

Using the www in Marketing

Activity One   Visit the Pfizer Web site (http://www.pfizer.com):

1. What are the requirements to become a sales representative for Pfizer?

2. Has the strategic merger between Pfizer and Warner-Lambert taken place? If so, what changes are being made? If not, why was the merger not completed?

3. How is Pfizer involved in e-commerce? Who can purchase what products from this site?

Activity Two   Review the Web site www.sales.com. You can register for free and get detailed information or browse the site to get basic information.

1. What sales tools are available to help salespeople develop relationships with customers?

2. How could sales managers use this site to help them in training salespeople?

3. How could this site be used to establish careers in sales?

Making Marketing Decisions
Case 19–1 Saturn: Taking a STEP to Equip Its Salesforce

In the late 1980s, the American automobile industry was struggling. Consumers were unhappy with product quality, pricing, advertising, and inane industry sales practices. Foreign automakers were continuing to build market share at the expense of domestic manufacturers. In this environment, General Motors departed from tradition and offered a "different kind of car from a different kind of company." The Saturn success story had begun.

By 1993, Saturn had become a force to be reckoned with. Sales were soaring, and GM was eager to transplant Saturn's winning ways to other divisions. Industry analysts cited several reasons for Saturn's rise to prominence: no-haggle pricing, customer-oriented selling, elimination of confusing rebates, and basically, a good car for a reasonable price.

Many competitors followed Saturn's lead with a one-price, no-haggle selling strategy. American automobile manufacturers also improved product quality, and many dealers adopted one-price policies similar to Saturn's. In the face of intensified competition, Saturn's salesforce has helped to sustain the company's edge in the marketplace. A key element in equipping the salesforce is the Saturn Training and Education Partnership, or STEP, a comprehensive program designed to develop job skills.

The STEP program reinforces five key values Saturn wants to instill in all facets of its operations: customer enthusiasm, excellence, teamwork, trust and respect, and constant improvement.

To reinforce these values in sales training, Saturn established the objectives for STEP long before its first dealership opened. Sales managers refined the program with salespeople from dealers who were interested in becoming Saturn dealers, and then with salespeople who had been hired to staff the still-unopened Saturn outlets.

The STEP program requires salespeople to abandon the conventional way of selling cars, which often involves high-pressure manipulative sales techniques. Instead, Saturn's sales philosophy casts the salesperson in a consultative role to build customer enthusiasm, with six key elements: listening to the customer; creating an environment of mutual trust; exceeding customer expectations; creating a "win-win" culture; following up to ensure that customer expectations are met; and constantly improving customer perceptions of quality.

The sales training consists of self-study modules and seminars. The self-study portion, which takes about 11 hours to complete, features learning activities based on short reading assignments and video vignettes. The short assignments can easily be completed one at a time, allowing training to be interspersed with other job activities.

Saturn measures the effectiveness of its training in three ways. For each module, trainees provide a written evaluation of materials, methods, and trainers. Each module is followed by a written test. Sixty days later, trainees are evaluated in a performance check that requires demonstration of the skills developed in training. All indicators point to a successful sales training program.

Questions

1. Did Saturn face any risks in implementing its STEP program?

2. Would previous sales experience be an asset to a Saturn job candidate? If so, what kind of experience?

3. How would Saturn's recruiting, selection, motivation, and evaluation of sales performance likely differ from that of a high-volume, conventional automobile dealer's sales operation?

4. How does the Saturn Web site (http:www.saturncars.com) supplement the efforts of Saturn salespeople?

SOURCES: "STEP . . . Training to Integrate the Saturn Difference," *Marketing Journal,* Winter 1993, pp. 1–2; Dorothy Cottrell, Larry Davis, Pat Detrick, and Marty Raymond, "Sales Training and the Saturn Difference," *Training and Development,* December 1992, pp. 38–43; Andrea Sawyers, "No-Haggle Pricing Hits Full Throttle," *Advertising Age,* March 22, 1992, p. S10, and Saturn Web site (http://www.saturncars.com) January 2000.

Case 19–2 IBM: Executing a Global Strategy

 IBM has developed a global strategy designed to meet the needs of its customers around the world. The strategy focuses on developing long-term relationships with customers and partnerships with distributors. Successfully executing this strategy requires teamwork among IBM's worldwide sales organization of about 140,000 salespeople and sales managers in 130 countries. Achieving this teamwork has been difficult due to the old way salespeople were compensated.

IBM's salesforce compensation program had three basic weaknesses. First, many large, multinational customers bought IBM products in one country and then shipped them to subsidiaries and divisions in other countries. Under the old compensation program, the salespeople making the sale were the only ones receiving incentive compensation. Salespeople in other countries received no compensation and, thus, were not willing to help with the sale or provide service to the customer's subsidiaries or divisions in different countries.

Second, the old compensation program relied heavily on the use of sales contests to motivate salespeople. The sales contests typically focused on generating sales in the short run. Therefore, salespeople were not rewarded for solving customer problems, providing service, or developing long-term relationships.

Third, salespeople received a lower commission for sales through distributors than for direct sales to a customer. This put IBM salespeople and distributors into direct competition with each other. Instead of being partners, they were competitors.

These problems led IBM to drastically change its salesforce compensation plan. The new plan awards 20 percent of incentive pay for team performance in a region or industry group, 60 percent for personal sales to end users and distributors, and 20 percent for sales contests.

Annual bonuses are based on profitability and customer satisfaction. Salespeople also receive a higher commission for sales to distributors.

The new salesforce compensation program is designed to promote teamwork, personal productivity, and customer satisfaction. All IBM salespeople around the world are compensated in the same way. The plan is intended to ensure that IBM's new strategy is executed successfully.

Questions

1. Why did IBM need to change its salesforce compensation plan?

2. How does the new compensation plan help to execute IBM's new strategy?

3. Do you think IBM should have the same compensation plan for salespeople worldwide or customize the compensation to different international markets? Why?

4. What problems do you see with the new plan? What improvements would you suggest?

SOURCE: Michele Marchetti, "Global Gamble," *Sales & Marketing Management,* July 1996, pp. 65–69.

Chapter Twenty

Direct Marketing Communications

After studying this chapter, you should be able to:

1 Understand the objectives of direct marketing communications, and describe its distinguishing characteristics.

2 Discuss the factors driving the growth in direct marketing communications.

3 Understand traditional direct marketing communications techniques such as direct mail, broadcast and print media, and telemarketing.

4 Recall examples of the use of technology such as electronic media in direct marketing communications.

5 Understand some of the ethical and legal issues facing marketers who use direct marketing communications.

In 1984, Dennis and Ann Pence left big-company management positions in New York City and moved to Sandpoint, Idaho, to launch a catalog retail business called Coldwater Creek. In the beginning, Coldwater Creek was a home business that consisted of taking orders on one telephone and shipping merchandise from a combination storage room/closet. Today it is a multichannel retailer with annual sales in excess of $300 million. In addition to its spacious headquarters campus in Sandpoint, Coldwater Creek now has a distribution center in West Virginia, a telemarketing center in Coeur d'Alene, Idaho, and retail stores in Sandpoint, Jackson (Wyoming), Seattle, and Kansas City.

Coldwater mails more than 150 million catalogs per year under three names: North Country, Spirit of the West, and Coldwater Creek Home. Its offerings include women's apparel, jewelry, gift items, home accessories, and furniture. The target audience is the same for all three catalogs and the Coldwater Web site: professional women 35–55 years of age, well-educated, with more discretionary income than time available for shopping.

The Coldwater Creek formula for success is to be driven by the customer. To ensure that customers receive outstanding service and enjoy a pleasant buying experience, the firm relies on technology, strong relationships with vendors, and direct marketing communications. Orders are received 365 days a year, 24 hours a day, by telephone, mail, fax, and the Internet. Telephone calls are answered in an average of three seconds, and orders are processed immediately. Approximately 90 percent are shipped the same day, and almost 100 percent within

24 hours. This fast, courteous service coupled with unusual, high-quality merchandise produces satisfied and loyal customers.

The Coldwater Creek Web site adds an important dimension to its marketing communications mix. Customers can learn about the company and its history and philosophy. Catalogs can be requested, stores browsed, and orders placed. And, customers can e-mail comments or questions directly to the company. Coldwater's customers are increasingly using the Web to place orders. As this shift continues, Coldwater is reducing catalog circulations to unproductive customers, thereby freeing up millions of dollars that can be devoted to better serving active customers.

Selecting the right customers, determining their needs, and working hard to satisfy those needs are critical to Coldwater Creek's success. At the heart of the Coldwater operation is a sophisticated computer system that keeps up with the details of the business. It tracks customers and interactions, and forecasts sales far enough in advance to help vendors schedule production more effectively and efficiently. This enhances the firm's relationships with suppliers. While the business details are handled by computer, customers only talk to people and are never put on hold. Coldwater Creek has used this blend of high-tech, high-touch to become a leading direct marketing company. **Sources:** Coldwater Creek Web site at http://www.Coldwater-Creek.com; Jeanette Hye, "Coldwater Call Center Gets 'Thin Client Server,'" *Women's Wear Daily,* December 15, 1999, p. 17; "Coldwater Creek Eyes Retail, Web," *Women's Wear Daily,* October 11, 1999, p. 20; and Grant Luckenbill, "Coldwater Expands, Retools Operations," *DM News,* July 19, 1999, p. 8.

Avon is best known for direct selling through several hundred thousand sales representatives. The company also uses a variety of direct marketing communications methods, including direct-response magazine ads and telemarketing as part of its worldwide integrated marketing communications effort.

In Chapter 16, we saw that most marketers use more than one way to communicate with their target markets. These multiple means of reaching target markets are sometimes developed into integrated marketing communications (IMC) programs. At the heart of many of these programs lies direct marketing communications. This chapter discusses the role and characteristics of direct marketing communications and examines the reasons for its growth. Direct marketing communications (DMC) methods are discussed, including a variety of interactive methods such as mail, video, telephone, salesperson, and computer. The chapter concludes with a discussion of ethical and legal issues in direct marketing communications.

Role of Direct Marketing Communications

Direct marketing communications have two primary objectives. The first is to establish relationships by soliciting a direct and immediate response from prospects or customers. Customer response could be a purchase, a request for additional information from the marketer, or a reply that furnishes data related to the customer's desires and interests. The second, and increasingly important, objective of DMC is to maintain and enhance customer relationships, whether those relationships have been established by direct marketing communications or by some other means.

Direct marketing communications techniques are used to reach both individual consumers and businesses. For example, in the United States, direct marketing generates almost 700 billion dollars in annual sales in business-to-business markets and 840 billion in sales to ultimate consumers.[1] In business-to-business markets, direct marketing is extensively used for business services, chemicals and allied products, real estate, and wholesaling. The most important tools in business-to-business direct marketing from a sales volume perspective are telephone marketing and direct mail, which account for more than 70 percent of all sales.[2] Newspaper, television, **on-line direct marketing** and radio also are used in business-to-business direct marketing. On-line direct marketing is that portion of electronic business, such as marketing on the Internet, that meets the definition of direct marketing communications given in Chapter 16: communicating directly with target customers to encourage response. It is important to note that not all electronic marketing involves on-line direct marketing.

Popular products bought by consumers via direct marketing include software, computers, recorded music, books, personal gift items, home decorating products, and clothing. In consumer markets, the largest sales generators are direct mail, telephone marketing, newspaper, and television.[3] On-line direct marketing is still relatively small from a sales-volume point of view but is growing at approximately 7 percent per year—roughly the growth rate for most other forms of direct marketing to ultimate consumers.

Direct marketing can be an important ingredient in integrated communications strategies. For example, Toyota is marketing its Lexus automobile brand using a combination of direct marketing, media advertising, and personal selling. Potential buyers are invited by direct mail to attend lavish "A Taste of Lexus" parties, where they enjoy the creations of celebrity chefs and test-drive the cars on a private race course. The direct marketing part of this communications program is carefully developed, with the mailing list for invitations to the parties drawn from the subscription list of *Vanity Fair* and *Conde Nast*.[4]

In the business-to-business area, Hewlett-Packard uses direct marketing in conjunction with other forms of marketing communications such as mass-media advertising, personal selling, sales promotion (trade shows), and public relations to sell computers. Sales by telephone make up an especially important part of Hewlett-Packard's direct marketing efforts.

Characteristics of Direct Marketing Communications

Several characteristics distinguish direct marketing from other marketing communications methods. First, direct marketing targets a carefully selected audience, as opposed to a mass audience. Second, it typically involves two-way communication; direct responses from customers make it interactive. Finally, direct-response results are quite measurable—marketers can determine what works and what does not.

Customer Databases

A key element of direct marketing communications is the use of a list or database of current or potential customers. **Lists** of names and addresses may also provide telephone numbers and data on demographics, lifestyles, brand and media preferences, and consumption patterns. Business-to-business lists may also indicate company characteristics such as annual sales, key decision makers, credit and purchasing history, and current suppliers. Lists can be developed from customer-transaction records, newspapers, trade show registration, or other sources that identify specific groups of customers or prospects. Rather than compiling its own lists, a company can purchase (in some cases), rent, reproduce, or use a list on a one-time basis.

Lists, often in the form of sophisticated computerized databases, allow direct marketers to focus on a precisely defined target market, as opposed to using mass-market appeals. **Database marketing,** or the use of computer database technologies to design, create, and manage customer lists, has become commonplace.[5] For an illustration of how databases aid in marketing communications, see Exhibit 20–1.

Customer databases can be quite large. For example, Database America's All Business File enables direct marketers to choose from more than 11 million companies in various segments, and consumer databases are often larger.

Companies use database information to deliver marketing communications tailored to the unique needs of a target audience. Dell Computer Corporation relies on its database-driven "Buyerwatch" program to keep customers up-to-date and to alert them to service and sales information. The key to the program is a Web page for each customer. The customer Web pages facilitate order tracking and access to technical support and parts information. The customer can monitor his or her own replacement needs, but Dell also uses the customer Web sites to communicate special deals and new upgrades keyed to each customer's system configuration. With Buyerwatch, small customers can get the same level of support as large corporate and government accounts.[6] For more on how databases are used in direct marketing communications, see "Using Technology: Frito-Lay Uses Database to Sell Chips."

Marketers are increasingly taking advantage of technological advances in their direct marketing programs. Metromail fits nicely with this movement by providing computerized databases and related services to facilitate direct marketing.

Immediate-Response Orientation

Direct marketing communications often have deadlines for action and offer special incentives for taking immediate action. An example would be a direct-mail piece from a bank saying, "Call now for superlow 7 percent mortgages. Free property survey. Offer expires June 1." Other marketing communications methods are not

Customer databases aid communications planning, integration, and execution

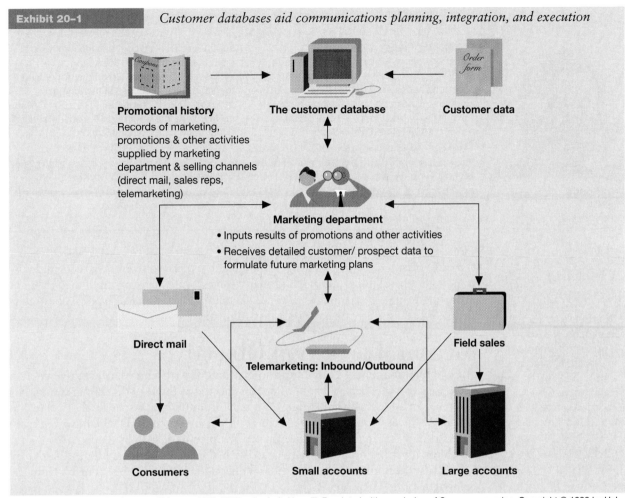

Promotional history

Records of marketing, promotions & other activities supplied by marketing department & selling channels (direct mail, sales reps, telemarketing)

The customer database

Customer data

Marketing department
- Inputs results of promotions and other activities
- Receives detailed customer/ prospect data to formulate future marketing plans

Direct mail

Telemarketing: Inbound/Outbound

Field sales

Consumers

Small accounts

Large accounts

Source: First appeared in *Success,* February 1993. Written by Jody Hewgill. Reprinted with permission of *Success* magazine. Copyright © 1993 by Hal Holdings Corporation.

Using Technology

Frito-Lay uses database to sell chips

When Frito-Lay introduced Baked Lays, their low-fat potato chip, the product was an immediate hot seller. On closer analysis, however, the good news was not so good after all. Sales for Baked Lays were coming from existing customers who were buying them instead of regular Lay's potato chips, not from new customers. The new product was cannibalizing the traditional product, not bringing in new business.

Frito-Lay worked with Catalina Marketing Group to identify households in its 48 million household database that had purchased six different low-fat products in the past six months. Four million households were selected. When these consumers used their credit cards at checkout counters, they automatically received a coupon for a free bag of

Balanced Lays. Forty percent of these consumers redeemed the coupons, and 25 percent of that 40 percent bought another bag at full price. These numbers represent a respectable 6 percent market share among the four million identified households.

Frito-Lay then followed up with a variety of offers for those who did not respond at all, those who only redeemed the free coupon, and those who both redeemed the coupon and made a purchase. In this case, the key to targeted promotion and sales success is using the database to identify and communicate with potential consumers.

Source: Lynn Dougherty, "Cutting the Fat," *1 to 1 Update,* a supplement to *Direct,* November 1999, p. 10.

Don Condit
President
Condit Communications

Don Condit, President of Condit Communications in Fort Collins, Colorado, specializes in business-to-business marketing communications. Before founding his own company, Don worked with Poppe Tyson Advertising in New York for 10 years as a senior copywriter and as an account supervisor. Don's work has won him honors, including the American Marketing Association's coveted Gold Effie, for having the year's most successful marketing program. Don, a graduate of Hamilton College in New York, comments on the advantages of direct marketing communications:

"The ability to measure results precisely is always a key advantage of direct marketing communications, particularly when compared to space advertising. For business-to-business clients in intensely competitive markets, another huge advantage is the ability to act covertly. To assess the scope and intent of our campaigns, competitors must rely on reports from field salespeople, a method that can be slow and inaccurate."

Thinking Critically

Courtney Knowlton, marketing manager for a popular women's magazine, is preparing a direct mail campaign to attract new subscribers. She is interested in getting the highest possible rate (the ratio of positive responders to the total number of pieces mailed). She has carefully prepared high-quality copy and removed the names of current subscribers from her mailing list. What additional suggestions can you give Courtney to maximize a positive response rate?

typically oriented toward gaining an immediate response from prospects and customers. Publicity, for example, and many forms of advertising are aimed more at achieving results over a period of time. Personal selling seeks a response, but salespeople typically cultivate customers for some time.

Measurable Action Objectives

Although all marketing communications should try to achieve measurable results, their objectives are generally not as action-specific as those of direct marketing. For instance, an advertising campaign for a new brand may have the goal of achieving brand awareness among 65 percent of its target audience. In DMC, however, marketers usually set much more specific action objectives, such as a purchase or a request for information. Achievement of such objectives can then be measured by calculating the number of purchases or requests for information that result from the campaign.

Action objectives allow the marketer to test several different forms of a direct marketing communication. The marketer can then adjust the message and the medium to achieve optimum results, consistent with the *productivity perspective*. For example, Astrology.net wanted to increase the number of people signing up to receive daily horoscopes by e-mail. The company developed seven different e-mail solicitation letters and began sending them at 9:00 A.M. By noon, two of the letters were doing well. At 2:00 P.M., these two were sent to a new test group, along with a newly created letter. The new letter produced the highest sign-up rate, and by the next morning it was sent to the entire target market.[7] Astrology's direct marketing communications effort was highly successful, thanks to the ability to measure results of different alternatives.

Growth of Direct Marketing Communications

Direct marketing communications have become a larger part of the total marketing communications picture in recent years. From 2000 to 2004, direct marketing is forecast to increase in efficiency with annual sales growing steadily at almost 9 percent.[8] By a large margin, direct marketers spend more money on telephone sales than any other direct medium, followed by direct mail. Other direct marketing activities such as infomercials, interactive shopping networks, and on-line direct marketing have become factors in this decade, and expenditures in these areas are growing.

Total direct marketing expenditures will reach an estimated $241 billion by 2004, split fairly evenly between business and consumer markets. Expenditures on direct marketing are growing at a healthy rate, with the 1999–2004 growth rate expected to be 6.4 percent.[9] In the remainder of this section, we will examine the global growth of DMC and some of the catalysts behind the growth.

Expansion into global markets is one reason for the growth of direct marketing communications. For more than three decades, Johnson & Hayward, Inc., has been involved in direct marketing communications on a global basis.

Global Direct Marketing Communications

Direct marketing communications are becoming more important in global marketing efforts. This has been true for U.S.-based marketers who have faced a fairly saturated domestic market for several years. It is becoming more commonplace for direct marketers outside the United States to expand their operations, including entry into the U.S. market. Even though the U.S. market may be crowded in some product categories, unique international offerings have a good chance of success in the United States. For example, Le Club des Createurs de Beaute, a global marketer of cosmetics and fragrances, entered the U.S. market with an initial mailing of 800,000 catalogs, which produced a higher-than-expected response. The annual catalog is also distributed in Japan, Belgium, Germany, and the United Kingdom.[10]

Asia has been a particularly attractive region for direct marketing efforts. Neiman Marcus, Patagonia, Eddie Bauer, J. Crew, and Victoria's Secret have been highly successful with their catalogs in Japan, Singapore, and Hong Kong. Japan Airlines uses direct marketing communications in its dealings with its 150,000-member JAL Family Club, and Citibank has a highly successful direct marketing program in its Hong Kong market.[11]

Other growth areas for direct marketing include Germany and the United Kingdom. In Germany, expenditures on direct marketing have been growing faster than in the United States. On-line direct marketing is growing rapidly in Germany, where on-line shoppers spend far more than do on-line shoppers in France and the United Kingdom. Although there are only eight million Internet users in Germany compared with 106 million in the United Kingdom, on-line sales in Germany total $290 million (U.S.), compared with $170 million (U.S.) for Britain.[12] On the other hand, business-to-business direct marketing is one of the hottest growth areas for direct marketing communications in the United Kingdom.[13]

Both Germany and the United Kingdom have been popular with expansion-minded U.S. direct marketers. For example, Quill, an office-supply marketer owned by Staples, Inc., has expanded in the United Kingdom and in Germany in the first wave of a country-by-country European expansion.[14] Quill will face strong competition from Viking Office Products, an Office Depot subsidiary, which also expanded its direct marketing efforts in several international markets, including the United Kingdom.[15]

Growth Catalysts

The increase in customized products, fragmented markets, and product price sensitivity; shrinking audiences for network television and newspapers; and emphasis on immediate sales all contribute to the expansion of direct marketing communications. Marketers are now forced to identify their target markets more specifically in order to reach them more effectively.

Other forces also contribute to the growth of direct marketing communications. Changes in lifestyles create a need for convenient, time-saving, and dependable ways to shop. Two-worker families have more discretionary income but less time. These conditions make shopping at home, at one's leisure, very appealing. The ease of communication between buyer and seller, combined with the increased use of credit cards and acceptable products, makes direct purchasing an attractive alternative for many consumers.

A major reason for the growth in direct marketing communications has been advancing technology, which allows more precise construction and manipulation of customer databases. **Predictive modeling** on a database allows the marketer to reach a desired target more effectively, thus avoiding waste and enhancing profits. Sophisticated computerized statistical techniques known as *neural networks* can calculate weights for customer characteristics such as age, income, education, or time on the job. Using artificial intelligence, neural networks "learn" which targets are more likely to respond by examining data examples and calculating the relationships between predictor characteristics and known results.

Direct Marketing Communications Techniques

Direct marketing communications include direct mail and some forms of broadcast advertising, such as infomercials and direct-response television and radio advertising. Direct-response advertising appears in newspapers and magazines as well. Other techniques include telemarketing and supplementary electronic media.

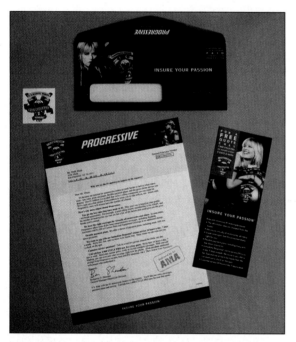

Direct mail can be a simple one-piece flyer or a more sophisticated multiple-piece mailer. Progressive Insurance Agency used direct mail to solicit business from Harley-Davidson owners.

Direct Mail

Direct Mail includes any form of advertising addressed to prospects through public or private delivery services. It can range in complexity from a simple flyer to a package including a letter, multipage brochure, video, and response card. The direct-mail response rate per thousand people reached is generally higher than for any other advertising medium, which may explain why both small companies and industry giants such as IBM, General Motors, Lockheed, and American Express use direct mail. Advantages and disadvantages of direct mail are summarized in Exhibit 20–2.

Direct mail has considerable flexibility in its self-contained message and the form used to convey it. A message could be written on a postcard or conveyed by videocassette. Moreover, direct mail can appeal to a narrow audience and be designed to suit a prospect's specific needs. Midwest Corvette Specialties, for example, can reach Corvette owners through its parts magazine. Working from a list of Corvette owners, the company avoids advertising to consumers who have no interest in its products.

Don Condit, President of Condit Communications, offers these thoughts on what makes for effective direct mail: "In direct mail we often search for gimmicks to make a piece of mail resemble a personal letter written for one reader. But the best device of all is copy that truly speaks to each reader personally—about relevant issues with a voice that is direct, honest, and disarming. By splitting copy, we can tailor each piece of mail for each audience segment and achieve the most important direct-mail success of all—readership."

Exhibit 20-2	*Advantages and disadvantages of direct mail*
Advantages	**Disadvantages**
• Self-contained message	• High cost per exposure
• Flexibility in message content and form of delivery	• Potential delivery delays
• Thorough coverage of target market	• Lack of support from other media
• Fewer distractions from other media	• "Junk mail" easy to ignore
• A large number of consumers like to make mail-order purchases	• Seen as wasteful, harmful to environment

The marketer can achieve nearly 100 percent coverage of the intended target market with direct mail, with fewer distractions than in some other media. For example, television or radio commercials are broadcast along with other ads and the regular programming. And magazine ads are juxtaposed with articles and other ads. A direct-mail piece, however, is typically viewed with less competition.

Perhaps the biggest advantage of direct mail is its potential effectiveness. In an average year, more than 40 percent of U.S. adults place orders by mail for goods or services, and approximately 11 percent order specifically as a result of offers made in direct-mail pieces.[16] Purchases resulting from direct mail are more frequent among higher-income consumers, prompting upscale businesses not known for using direct mail to do so. For example, upscale retailer Neiman Marcus has used a special Christmas catalog for years, and Nordstrom has increased its catalog mailings to the upscale female shopper. Other prominent upscale direct mail marketers include Robert Redford's Sundance, The Sharper Image, Herrington, and clothing retailer The Territory Ahead.

Direct mail does have its flaws, however. It has one of the highest costs per thousand of any form of advertising. And it suffers potential delivery delays; it may take up to six weeks for bulk mail to reach its destination. In addition, consumers can easily ignore it, tossing the junk mail without ever being exposed to its message. And finally, consumers increasingly view direct mail as wasteful and harmful to the environment.

Office Depot's house organ *Business News* is a full-color, 40-page magazine of how-to's and free advice mailed to more than a million businesspeople.

TYPES OF DIRECT MAIL Direct mail comes in many formats, as shown in Exhibit 20–3. The most common form of direct mail is the *sales letter,* which typically includes the recipient's name and may be mailed with brochures, price lists, and reply cards and envelopes. *Postcards* generally offer discounts, announce sales, or generate customer traffic. Postcards may be combined with a larger piece, such as a magazine cover or product information sheet. The idea is to cut through mailbox clutter with the larger piece, yet have an economical, easy way for the consumer to respond. This combination—called Double Postcard Plus, or DPC+—gives marketers a chance to deliver descriptive messages and compelling graphics not possible with an unaccompanied postcard. Even though costs are higher, more favorable response rates make it feasible in some situations.

Some companies produce publications referred to as *house organs* for mailing to particular audiences. These may be newsletters, consumer magazines, stockholder reports, or dealer publications. American Express distributes its *Your Business* quarterly, free of charge, to more than one million customers carrying the American Express Small Business Corporate Card. The publication gives card owners useful information not found elsewhere in hopes they

Exhibit 20–3	*Types of direct mail*

Sales letter: typically includes recipient's name; may be mailed with brochures, price lists, reply cards, and envelopes.

Postcards: generally used to offer discounts, announces sales, or generate customer traffic.

Catalogs: describe and often picture the product sold.

Video catalogs: serve same purpose as print catalog, but are on videocassettes.

Promotional videocassettes and audiocassettes: used to send product information to selected audiences.

Promotional interactive computer disks: allow the recipient to select information of interest.

Leaflets and flyers: typically single pages that can be folded and included with sales letters.

Statement stuffers: ads included in other mail such as bank or credit card statements or shipped with catalog orders.

Catalog sales are on the increase. Consumers like the convenience, simplicity, and reliability of catalog buying.

will keep and use the travel service's charge card. Increasingly popular are electronic house organs in the form of e-mail newsletters. For example, egghead.com, a computer supplies and software dealer, communicates weekly with 6.2 million active on-line buyers. Other marketers can buy space in the newsletter for advertising or direct marketing purposes.

By 2004, sales from printed *catalogs* will reach $125 billion.[17] Lands' End, Eddie Bauer, Patagonia, and JCPenney produce well-known catalogs. Catalogs offer a comfortable, convenient alternative to in-store shopping. Consumers enjoy browsing through the pages and using the simple, reliable means such as the mail, telephone, or fax to place orders. Most catalog retailers have well-trained staffs and efficient delivery systems, which further enhances the shopping experience. Catalogs also play a major role in business-to-business direct marketing, particularly in the office supply and furnishings category.

Catalogs, pioneered by general merchandise retailers such as Sears, are more likely to appeal to a niche market today. In the home furnishings market, successful niche catalogers include L.L. Bean Home, Linen Source, Restoration Hardware, Pottery Barn, and Hold Everything.

Promotional videocassettes and *audiocassettes* filled with product information are becoming popular direct-mail pieces. CD-ROMs offer several advantages, including more storage space and the capability of including audio and video. Island Hideways, Inc., a rental agent for villas and boats in the Caribbean, used CD-ROMs to give consumers an exciting way to find just the right vacation spot. A single disk contained 2,500 photographs, half an hour of music, 21 maps, the equivalent of 200 pages of text, and spreadsheet programs to help guests calculate the costs of different packages of condos, villas, boats, and resorts.[18]

Leaflets or *flyers* are typically single pages printed on one or both sides of standard-sized paper (8 1/2 by 11 inches) and folded. *Statement stuffers* are ads included in other mail such as bank or credit card statements.

BUSINESS-TO-BUSINESS DIRECT MAIL   All the forms of direct mail discussed above are frequently used in business-to-business marketing. With the increasing costs of sales calls, marketers use direct mail to generate sales leads, solicit sales, and provide after-sale support and service information. Novartis Seeds Inc., for example, uses direct mail to communicate with 7,000 farmers to stay in touch over an extended sales cycle, during which farmers often change their orders due to weather and marketplace changes.[19] For an indication of what makes a successful business-to-business direct mail piece, see Exhibit 20–4.

Exhibit 20–4   *Business-to-business mailings: Executive opinions*

When top marketing executives at companies with sales in excess of $500 million & more than 5,000 employees were asked what they liked in business-to-business mail-order catalogs, key findings were:

90 percent believe lots of pictures are the most helpful feature a catalog can offer

65 percent favor detailed tables of contents

65 percent say their firms order from 1 out of every 10 catalogs they receive

45 percent like order forms that are telephone-user friendly

65 percent appreciate fax order forms

Only 15 percent find case histories & testimonials worthwhile

60 percent say most catalogs are a waste of money

Source: "Survey: Marketers Like Faxes and Pictures," *Direct,* June 1992, p. 16. Reprinted with permission of *Direct* magazine, a Cowles Business Media publication.

Broadcast Media

Although used mostly for mass advertising, television and radio are also used for direct marketing communications. Infomercials and direct-response advertising on TV and radio are popular DMC formats.

INFOMERCIALS Infomercials are extended (usually 30-minute) commercials cast in a television-show format. Mixing information and entertainment, they strive to look more like a regular TV program than a commercial. Infomercials have become well established on cable television, generating well over a billion dollars a year in sales. Popular product categories for infomercials include health and fitness equipment, cosmetics, small kitchen appliances, and hair and personal care items. Familiar infomercial offerings include Ab Rocker, Total Gym, Torso Gym, Tan Perfect, Enforma System, Ronco appliances, and Tae Bo fitness techniques.

The infomercial format provides an opportunity to stand out in a cluttered environment. A 30-second commercial is more likely to get lost in the shuffle than a 30-minute one. In addition, an infomercial's length makes it possible to explain an advertised product more fully. For instance, Alien brand golf clubs featured a newly designed pitching wedge so unconventional-looking that buyers in retail stores would probably not want to try it. But with the infomercial format, there was enough time to show how well the club worked. With the assistance of celebrity presenter Jerry Pate, a well-known golfer and professional golf television commentator, the Alien became a huge success. Alien later followed the infomercial route when it introduced another unconventional club, the driving iron, to compete with much larger traditional clubs.

By featuring a direct-response telephone number, an infomercial guarantees a quick means for measuring results. Moreover, information obtained from those ordering can be used to develop a database.

Infomercials also have certain disadvantages. For one thing, airing is confined largely to cable TV and late-night programming on major networks, perhaps making it difficult to reach the target market with the desired message. Although potentially cost-effective, average production costs for infomercials are high, approximately $300,000.[20] Thus, production costs added to air-time costs make infomercials more expensive than most direct marketing communications methods.

Finally, infomercials have a poor image. Many suffer from exaggerated claims, low-quality production standards, and unprofessional presentation. Moreover, there is some concern that they are deceptive by appearing in the guise of programs. Infomercials for some products have drawn fire from the public, such as Eli Lilly's infomercial for its antidepressant, Prozac. While people recognize that depression is a serious problem and that public discussion might eventually lead to better treatments, they were upset at the overt sales pitch for the drug via an infomercial.[21] Problems such as these may be overcome as the format develops and attracts more credible sponsors.

DIRECT-RESPONSE TELEVISION ADVERTISING Direct-response television advertising includes an 800 or 900 telephone number and an address for placing orders in a typical 30-, 60-, or 90-second commercial. Unlike typical mass advertising, direct-response ads attempt to get an immediate answer from the consumer. Music is often featured in direct-response television ads with major advertisers such as Time Life Music (*AM Gold* and *Ultra Mix*) and Millennium Partners (*Swing is King*). Other major products advertised for direct response on television include Intuit's Quicken financial software, Mead Johnson's Boost Vanilla Shake, Glaxo Wellcome's Flonase, Sears's tools, and E*Trade's electronic stock-trading site. NBC uses direct response on its own network to sell program-related items. For example, NBC sold 260,000 copies of the CD for its miniseries, *The 60s*, 200,000 in retail stores and 60,000 copies through direct response.[22]

Although sometimes aired on network television, direct-response commercials are more widely broadcast on cable TV. Cable TV allows effective targeting of audiences through special-interest programming. Bass Pro Shops, a Springfield,

Missouri, catalog retailer, for example, uses direct-response advertising on popular cable-TV fishing programs. As with infomercials, this form of DMC enables database building and immediate assessment of results.

DIRECT-RESPONSE RADIO ADVERTISING   **Direct-response radio advertising** also offers the ability for immediate feedback through a telephone number or address provided with the commercial. In addition, it can be directed toward a very targeted audience and is relatively inexpensive compared with other forms of direct marketing communications. Radio, however, is not a particularly dynamic medium. Radio audiences tend to be too preoccupied with other things to focus on an address or a telephone number. Certainly a listener hearing a radio commercial while driving cannot easily record an address.

Print Media

Although not so tightly targeted as other direct marketing communications media, newspapers and magazines can also provide an opportunity for direct response. Consumers can respond to ads carrying an address, order form, coupon, or telephone number. The response can be either to purchase or to request additional information. One way to use direct-response print advertising is with a freestanding insert (FSI), discussed in Chapter 18.

Magazines may include other forms of direct marketing communications. Some marketers insert reply cards into magazines. **Reader-response cards** are sometimes used in conjunction with ads to allow consumers to request additional information. Readers wanting more information on a product would circle a number on the card corresponding to the product's ad in the magazine and send the card to the magazine's publisher. Another magazine insert is the floppy disk. *Forbes* magazine, for example, included a disk that contained information from such advertisers as American Express, Chevrolet, Embassy Suites, and Merrill Lynch, among others. America Online has used disk inserts extensively to attract new subscribers.

Telemarketing

Busy Body uses telemarketing as part of its communications mix. A toll-free number for inbound telemarketing is featured in print ads and on the company's Web site. Inbound telemarketing gives customers an alternative to purchasing in Busy Body stores or on the Web.

Telemarketing is an interactive direct marketing communications approach that uses telephone calls to initiate, develop, and enhance relationships with customers. On a cost-per-contact basis, telemarketing is less expensive than personal selling, but much more expensive than mass advertising and direct mail. However, its high return often justifies the added expense. According to the Direct Marketing Association, telemarketing sales will exceed $800 billion by the year 2004.[23]

Outbound telemarketing, sometimes called *teleselling,* occurs when the marketer actively solicits customers or prospects. Inbound telemarketing occurs when a customer calls the marketer to obtain information or place an order. Either case offers the advantage of two-way conversation, allowing the respondent to ask questions and give answers and the marketer to tailor a message to the individual needs of the prospect.

Very popular in business-to-business marketing, telemarketing can be effective in expanding international marketing operations. Gateway, the direct supplier of computers, established a telemarketing center in Dublin, Ireland, as a first step toward entry into European markets. Holiday Inn and Radisson have established telemarketing operations in Australia to handle the entire Asia Pacific region, and Apple serves Europe with telemarketing centers in France, the United Kingdom, and Germany.[24]

Technology has made telemarketing very productive. **Predictive dialing systems** save telemarketers as much as 20 minutes an hour by passing over answering machines, busy signals, and no answers. Predictive dialers automatically dial a designated amount of numbers per minute. Completed calls are immediately passed on to a live telemarketer, who simultaneously receives customer information on a computer terminal.

Unfortunately, telemarketing does not have a good image. Consumers view telemarketers as uninvited nuisances. In one survey by Louis Harris & Associates for the National Consumers League, 49 percent of adults said they were "completely fed up" with telemarketing.[25] In another Harris survey, 47 percent said that telemarketing is always an intrusion, never an opportunity.[26] Other common complaints are that telemarketing is an invasion of privacy, uses misleading tactics, and is a waste of time. Consumer organizations routinely warn consumers to be wary of telemarketing. Some go beyond warnings, urging consumers to take the offensive against telemarketing. For example, Junkbusters offers an antitelemarketing script at its Web site (www.junkbusters.com) under the question, "Telemarketers always use a script: why shouldn't you?" Junkbuster's script is recommended as "what to say when they call if you don't want junk calls."[27]

Unfortunately for legitimate companies, consumers do have to exercise caution when dealing with telemarketers. The National Consumers League identifies the top telemarketing fraud schemes in Exhibit 20–5. Telemarketers, then, should provide short, compelling messages, as most people will not spend more than a few minutes on the phone for an uninvited sales call.

Electronic Media

Several other electronic forms of direct marketing communications are available besides broadcast media. Although not used as often as other methods, interactive computer services, kiosks, and fax machines are growing in popularity.

INTERACTIVE COMPUTER SERVICES   As illustrated throughout this book, **interactive computer networks** are increasingly used for direct marketing communications. Traditional networks work via modem over telephone lines. Wireless Internet services, which utilize communications satellites, are also available, and simple Web-access appliances, not full-blown computers, are becoming a factor in this form of direct marketing communications.

As the rapid growth of electronic commerce continues, it is logical to expect more direct marketing communications via the Internet. This is because a key ingredient of DMC, the use of customer databases, is facilitated by electronic commerce. That is, once consumers buy electronically, they become part of that seller's customer database and may be receptive to direct communications. The obvious

Thinking Critically

Blake Stanley, Director of Promotions for a book retailer, is contemplating running a contest for consumers on his company's Web site. Winners would receive free books and merchandise. Currently, Blake's company enjoys sales from around the globe on its Web site. Since this is the first time that Blake has considered running a contest, he is wondering if any precautions are appropriate. What advice can you share with Blake?

Exhibit 20–5

National Consumers League's top ten telemarketing fraud list

1. *Work-at-home schemes*—Kits sold with false promises of profits.
2. *Prizes/sweepstakes*—Phony prize awards requiring payment of fees first.
3. *Telephone slamming*—Consumers' phone service is switched without their knowledge or consent.
4. *Advance fee loans*—Empty promises of loans requiring payment of fees in advance.
5. *Magazine sales*—Fake sales or renewals for magazine subscriptions that are never received.
6. *Telephone cramming*—Billing consumers for optional services they never ordered.
7. *Credit card offers*—Phony promises of credit cards requiring payment of fees in advance.
8. *Travel/vacation offers*—Offers of free trips or discount travel that never materialize.
9. *Credit card loss protection*—Unnecessary insurance sold using scare tactics or misrepresentations.
10. *Investments*—Stocks and other investments that don't pan out as promised.

Source: The National Consumers League's National Fraud Information Center at www.natlconsumersleague.org, February 6, 2000.

low cost of transmitting electronic messages when compared with other forms of direct marketing communications and the global reach of this medium provide strong incentives for marketers to use this communications tool.

Some cautionary notes are worth considering. First, although the total number of Internet users is large and growing, not all are relevant for direct marketers. Further, on-line users are very particular about unsolicited advertising that arrives by e-mail, called *spam*. Consumers receiving spam often react angrily, boycotting the spammer and "flaming" the offender. Flaming involves negative responses to the advertiser, such as deluging them with thousands of reply messages or sending e-mail "bombs" containing huge files that tie up computers for hours.

Another area of concern is that the Internet is suffering from congestion. Users complain that it takes too long to navigate the vast array of sites, and this could diminish the viability of computer networks as a communications vehicle. One additional concern is that computer vandals or "hackers" may interfere with a Web site's operation, even closing it down. In early 2000, hackers closed down some of the most popular Web sites for several hours, including Amazon.com, Yahoo!, and eBay. The FBI has warned marketers that their Web sites are only as secure as the other Web sites they link to, thus well protected sites can still be vandalized through less-protected linking sites.

Despite the uncertainties, direct marketing communications via interactive computer networks is growing rapidly. It is an ideal medium for computer-equipped consumers who want to stay in touch with retailers and service providers. Companies encourage this link by publicizing their Web addresses in ads and on product packaging. Another alternative is to use a company such as ReplyNet Inc. that specializes in distributing promotional information only to those consumers who request it.

Interactive computer services are also available for business-to-business marketers. Boise Cascade, for example, uses e-mail to encourage sales through its on-line office-supplies catalog. The response rate for Boise Cascade's e-mail promotions is 12 percent, compared with an average response rate of 1 percent on standard direct mail.[28]

Don Condit, President of Condit Communications, comments on the growth of the Internet in marketing communications: "The value of promotion over the Internet will grow more slowly for clients selling expensive capital equipment than it will for others. For each client, the rate of growth will also vary from one target audience to another. Pharmaceutical process engineers, for example, are already accustomed to using the Internet to find new equipment choices and alternate vendors, while engineers in the food-processing industry will not rely on the Internet for years to come."

INTERACTIVE COMPUTER KIOSKS   Another electronic marketing medium is the **interactive computer kiosk,** usually located in retail stores. These kiosks typically use touch-screen technology that allows the consumer to access specific information of interest. Some interactive computer kiosks include catalogs (video or paper) featuring items not stocked in the retail store, with a direct toll-free number for placing orders. Cities frequented by tourists sometimes use kiosks to help sightseers find their way around. These kiosks are often used as direct marketing communications vehicles for restaurants, hotels, and other services and attractions of interest to travelers. In Rome, visitors can access kiosks in 10 of the city's 15 McDonald's to learn about the Vatican and other destinations.[29]

Catalog retailers are also using computer kiosks to gain additional exposure and sales from mall shoppers. In Chicago and in metropolitan areas of Delaware, 30 kiosks sell merchandise from catalogers Hammacher Schlemmer, Lands' End, JCPenney, and the Wine Enthusiast. Each cataloger sells 50 to 100 items, with quarterly updates to allow changes in merchandise, presentation, or pricing.[30]

FAX MACHINES   Fax machines allow customers to transmit written documents via telephone. However, their use as a direct marketing communications tool has been restricted primarily to business-to-business customers. Direct marketers routinely use fax machines to receive customer orders. New technology called **fax-on-demand systems** allows instant response to 800-number requests for information using a fax. In these systems, a fax machine receives the request for information and immediately faxes the information back to the requester. For example, Compaq Computer Corporation's PaqFax system manages 80,000 incoming calls per month and faxes 1,250 pages of documents each day. It is the first option on the Compaq customer-support hot line and gives callers a chance to fulfill their own requests.[31]

One problem with using fax machines in business-to-business marketing communications is that most businesses do not want to tie up their incoming fax lines with unsolicited information. It is now a fairly common practice to send unsolicited marketing communications after normal business hours, a practice made easy by the delayed-dialing capabilities of most fax machines. Some states, including Texas, Oregon, and Florida, prohibit the transmission of unsolicited fax communications.

Many business-to-business marketers, including accounting firms and equipment manufacturers, depend on disseminating information as a means of attracting clients. Some of these marketers find an advantage in transmitting information in written, rather than audio or video form. Many prospective customers would rather read a customized report than listen to one, since it is easier to access important parts of the written report. Prices, product availability, shipping schedules, and other marketing mix variables can change frequently, and the fax is extremely accommodating when such changes occur. Many fax documents are never in hard copy form, but exist in computer files that can be changed with the flick of a key stroke just before dissemination. Now that the same function can be accomplished with e-mail, direct marketing communications via fax is declining in importance.

Interactive media such as fax-on-demand, electronic mail, and interactive voice-response systems are increasingly being put to use to build stronger relationships with customers. For an example, see "Earning Customer Loyalty: Norwegian Cruise Line Depends on the Fax."

Ethical and Legal Issues in Direct Marketing Communications

In this section, we discuss three key areas of ethical and legal concern in direct marketing communications: invasion of privacy, deceptive practices, and waste of natural resources.

Earning Customer Loyalty

Norwegian cruise line depends on the fax

Miami-based Norwegian Cruise Lines operates 10 cruise ships with a total of 14,500 berths. To generate last-minute reservations for unsold berths shortly before departure times, Norwegian sends out 60,000 to 70,000 fax pages each week to travel agents. The faxes feature special prices and other promotions, and are used in tandem with direct mail to cultivate relationships with travel agents as Norwegian's preferred suppliers.

Norwegian's fax program is targeted to travel agents who have been most productive in the past. Clark Reber, Norwegian's director of sales, notes that travel agents are deluged with faxes, so to avoid complaints, they do not send unsolicited faxes. Mr. Reber notes that faxes can be broadcast quickly, and he has found that travel agents are more likely to read them than direct mail or e-mail. Norwegian's faxes are broadcast via the Internet, which offers considerable cost savings over regular phone lines. Also, the faxes cost only 15 cents compared with about $1 for each direct mailing. The fax program is positive for all parties. Norwegian sells berths that otherwise would most likely be unsold, travel agents get incremental income, and consumers with flexible schedules get a bargain price for a luxury cruise.

Source: Jim Emerson, "Come Aboard," *Teledirect,* a supplement to *Direct,* November 1999, pp. T1, T4–T5.

Invasion of Privacy

As consumer databases become more sophisticated, there is growing concern among some buyers about invasion of privacy. Most people do not object to a company storing information on its own customers for information-management purposes. One survey indicates that on-line consumers will share personal information to get a customized product or service: 92 percent said they would reveal personal interests and hobbies, and 73 percent said they would willingly provide demographic information.[32] Consumers have also shown they will trade private information to take advantage of special offers. For example, when Free-PC announced it would give away free personal computers in exchange for private information, its Web site was swamped with more than a million inquiries.[33]

When they are unsure of how their information will be used, however, consumers are less than eager to share. Consumer surveys indicate that adults are concerned with a loss of control over how their personal information is used by companies and that they do not wish to receive more advertising messages as a result of divulging their personal information. Some are also concerned that detailed profiling of individual consumer behaviors could lead to discrimination by marketers. For example, if a company learns that a consumer shops a lot but does not buy much, the company can leave him or her on hold on help lines and not offer the consumer special deals.[34]

The privacy of children is a particularly sensitive issue. Consumer groups point out that on-line services may surpass television in influencing children's lives in the future and believe that some marketers manipulate children. For example, companies offer prizes for personal information—such as e-mail addresses and birthdays—that will be used in direct marketing communications. Critics believe that marketers should fully disclose how such information will be used and get parental consent if information will be identifiable by individuals rather than aggregated into group data.[35]

U.S. marketers are leery of legislative attempts to regulate potential threats to consumer privacy. Consumers in other countries, however, are accustomed to strict privacy statutes. European Union (EU) countries guarantee European citizens absolute control over their private information. If a company wants a consumer's personal information, they must get the individual's permission and explain how the information will be used. The European Union is pressuring marketers from other countries to follow the strict laws adopted by the European Union. According to EU law, no company can transmit personal data about EU citizens to countries whose privacy laws are not as strict as those in the European Union. EU law also prohibits data tags, or "cookies," that track customer preferences on the Web and does not allow marketers to use databases obtained from another marketer to solicit business.[36]

To ward off potential legislative action, some direct marketing companies are taking actions to avoid invading consumers' privacy. Fewer firms make their in-house lists available for rental to other companies. McDonald's, Fisher-Price, and Citicorp, for example, no longer rent their customer lists. Many firms allow consumers to choose whether or not they are included on lists made available to other firms. Others ask consumers how often they would like to receive mail solicitations.

Deceptive Practices

Attempts at telemarketing legislation have increased at least in part to address numerous telemarketing abuses (see Exhibit 20–6). Consumers exhibit high levels of trust in sellers when they order and pay for a product sight unseen. Direct-response marketers rely on this trust. Yet, certain direct-marketing activities have damaged that trust.

After 25 years, marketers have finally convinced consumers that 800-number telephone calls are toll-free. But some marketers ask 800-number callers to punch codes into their telephones that, unbeknownst to them, convert the call to a billable

Exhibit 20-6	*Telemarketing sales rule*

All businesses conducting outbound telemarketing must comply with the Telemarketing Sales Rule after passage of the Telemarketing and Consumer Fraud and Abuse Prevention Act of 1994. Major provisions of the rule include:

- Telemarketers must disclose costs associated with the purchase, limitations, restrictions, and refund/cancellation policies.
- Abusive acts are prohibited, including profane language and calling people who have indicated that they do not wish to be contacted.
- A "do not call" list must be maintained by the company using telemarketing. Telemarketers are restricted from making calls before 8:00 A.M. and after 9:00 P.M. local time.
- Companies must maintain records on transactions for a period of 24 months.
- The Telemarketing Sales rule is enforced by both the Federal Trade Commission and by a state's Attorney General, who can impose penalties of $10,000 per violation per day.

Source: Laura Hansen, "Dialing for Dollars," *Marketing Tools,* January–February 1997, pp. 47–51.

900 number. Another abuse comes from sweepstakes marketers that promote 900-number calls for prizes worth much less than the cost of the call.

Automatic number identification and **caller ID intrusion** systems pose additional ethical and legal problems. These systems let incoming telephone numbers of respondents to an ad or a promotion be identified at the onset of the call without the caller's consent or knowledge. Not only is this a possible invasion of privacy, but it also presents an opportunity to capture and sell unlisted numbers.

Waste of Natural Resources

People are concerned about the environmental consequences of marketing decisions, thus increasing attention on use of natural resources. In the direct-mail industry, consumer complaints and regulatory interest concerning junk mail have motivated discussion about excessive contributions to landfills, impact on timber production and harvesting, and the economic waste associated with rising paper costs.

It is commonly known that consumers do not want to receive all their unsolicited mail. One survey indicated that receiving "junk mail," or unsolicited direct-mail advertising, was the most annoying common consumer experience. On a 10-point scale, with 10 representing "completely fed up," 59 percent of those surveyed gave junk mail a 10.[37] Two alternatives are easily available to marketers that want to cut down on waste by minimizing undeliverable and unwanted direct-mail pieces. First, a marketer can increase the accuracy of a mailing list by running it through the U.S. Postal Service's national file on changes of address. By using this service, which has change-of-address information on 100 million people, mailers could cut down on undeliverable pieces and perhaps qualify for lower postage rates in the process.

In addition, direct marketers could better inform consumers of their right to remove their names from mailing lists. The Direct Marketing Association coordinates a "preference" program that allows consumers to stop mail and telephone solicitation if they so choose. There may be some way marketers can make consumers more aware of this program, which would eventually lead to less unwanted mail and more efficient direct marketing communications.

Cutting out waste in DMC requires that consumers join with concerned companies to bring about the desired changes. This is true of most ethical and legal problems facing marketing. For example, when asked about invasion of privacy, the president of the National Consumers League said, "Are consumers being exploited? Most certainly. Is it an invasion of privacy? Probably not. Most consumers are willing to disclose the information." Whether we are talking about invasion of privacy, deceptive practices, waste of natural resources, or any other significant ethical or legal issue in marketing, the consumer must take an active role in effecting favorable change.

Summary

1. **Understand the objectives of direct marketing communications, and describe its distinguishing characteristics.** Direct marketing communications are directed at target audiences using one or more media. One objective of direct marketing communications is to elicit a response by telephone, mail, or personal visit from a prospect or customer. Another objective, to maintain and enhance customer relationships, is growing in importance.

   Direct marketing is distinguished from other marketing communications methods in several ways. First, it uses customer databases, or lists, to target an audience precisely. Next, it is oriented more toward an immediate response than are most other forms of marketing communications. Finally, its objectives are specific consumer actions, so results are highly measurable.

2. **Discuss the factors driving the growth in direct marketing communications.** Increasingly fragmented markets make the narrowly focused methods of direct marketing quite attractive. Changes in lifestyles have created a need for convenient, time-saving, and dependable ways to shop. Perhaps one of the biggest motivators of growth in direct marketing communications has been the emergence of database marketing, which gives marketers a more in-depth understanding of productive target customers.

3. **Understand traditional direct marketing communications techniques such as direct mail, broadcast and print media, and telemarketing.** Direct mail is the most popular method, and it comes in a variety of forms, from postcards to video catalogs. Print and broadcast media are used for direct-response advertising, and the infomercial has become a significant

means of communicating directly with the target market. Inbound and outbound telemarketing have become extremely popular, even though outbound telemarketing is a nuisance to many consumers. Each of these methods has unique capabilities and limitations, one reason marketers typically use multiple methods to reach a given audience.

4. **Recall examples of the use of technology such as electronic media in direct marketing communications.** Interactive computer services, interactive computer kiosks, and fax machines are three examples of relatively new technology now widely used in direct marketing communications. These tools offer immediate information to consumers and business-to-business buyers, and sometimes allow the customer to do business with the seller after normal business hours.

5. **Understand some of the ethical and legal issues facing marketers who use direct marketing communications.** As database lists become more sophisticated, there is increased concern about invasion of privacy. Abuse of consumers' privacy is likely to lead to legislation to curb it. Telemarketing has come under the heaviest attacks, as unethical marketers use deceptive methods in dealing with consumers. Actions can and should be taken to avoid unwarranted or abusive intrusion. Junk mail has been accused of wasting natural resources. Concerned marketers, consumers, and associations such as the Direct Marketing Association must work together to curb these problems. Otherwise, it is certain that some consumers will be victimized and that legislation will be enacted to address the issues.

Understanding Marketing Terms and Concepts

Thinking About Marketing

1. Define direct marketing communications and describe their distinguishing characteristics.

2. What is database marketing? How has it contributed to the growth of direct marketing communications?

3. Describe advantages and disadvantages of direct mail.

4. What is an infomercial? What types of products do you think would benefit most from using this type of advertising and why?

5. What is an interactive computer service? How does it differ from an interactive computer kiosk?

6. Refer to "Using Technology: Frito-Lay Uses Database to Sell Chips." Develop at least one appropriate measurable action objective for each of the three groups of consumers: those who did not respond at all; those who only redeemed the free coupon; and those who both redeemed the coupon and made the purchase.

7. Refer to "Earning Customer Loyalty: Norwegian Cruise Line Depends on the FAX." How does this fax program illustrate these key marketing perspectives: productivity; customer value; and the relationship perspectives?

8. Database marketing has come under attack from those who believe it is an invasion of privacy. Should marketers be concerned about this? What can be done to deal with consumers' concerns? Explain.

9. Review the Telephone Sales Rule in Exhibit 20–6. Is it necessary to have federal government intervention to regulate telemarketing?

10. What can direct marketers do to cut down on the waste generated by their communications methods?

Applying Marketing Skills

1. Working in groups of three to five students, analyze two current infomercials to see if they meet the standards of conduct as set forth by the National Infomercial Marketing Association:

   a. A "paid advertisement" disclosure must appear at the beginning and end of each infomercial and at each ordering opportunity.

   b. The name of the sponsor must be disclosed.

   c. There can be no misrepresentations as to format, no false claims or deception through omission, and no indecent or offensive material.

   To what extent do the members of the group agree on the last point? Summarize your opinions for class discussion.

2. Assume you are the chair of an alumni fund-raising committee for your college or university. The committee is charged with the task of contacting approximately 30,000 alumni to solicit donations for a new library. The goal is to raise $1 million from the alumni within the next 18 months. The first order of business is to determine what form of communication is to be used in the campaign. The alumni are scattered across the United States, and approximately 10 percent live in a variety of foreign countries. Which means of reaching these alumni would you recommend the committee consider? Briefly explain your reasoning.

   a. Direct mail

   b. Telemarketing

   c. Personal selling

   d. Direct-response television advertising

   e. E-mail

   f. Fax solicitation

3. Which types of direct marketing communications would you choose for each task?

   a. Informing your customers of an upcoming sale in your retail store.

   b. Introducing yourself and your company to new prospects in your sales territory.

   c. Inviting current customers to visit your booth at a trade show next month.

   d. Demonstrating a new software program offered by your company.

   e. Familiarizing European construction managers with your latest piece of earth-moving equipment.

   f. Bringing your 1,200 dealers up-to-date on a variety of happenings in your company.

Using the www in Marketing

Activity One   Visit the Coldwater-Creek Web site (http://www.Coldwater-Creek.com).

1. How does this Web site fit with Coldwater Creek's other direct marketing communications efforts?

2. Identify examples of how Coldwater Creek implements an ethics perspective.

3. What Web site improvements can you recommend to Coldwater Creek?

Activity Two   Trade associations often use the Internet to provide valuable information to consumers and managers. The Direct Marketing Association maintains a comprehensive Web site at http://www.the-dma.org. What evidence can you find that the Direct Marketing Association promotes an ethical perspective in the practice of direct marketing?

Making Marketing Decisions

Case 20-1 Cisco Revolutionizes Marketing with the Internet

Cisco Systems is best known for providing computer networking products that help other companies use the Internet and corporate intranets. The California-based company is becoming famous for another reason—its Web site, Cisco Connection Online (http://www.cisco.com), is having the biggest impact in business today. Cisco uses the Internet to deliver most of its customer support, and to fill more than 80 percent of its purchase orders.

Cisco Connection is bringing the company more revenue, and it is also producing significant cost savings. Savings in phone charges, printing, mailing, express shipping, and time spent by technical support personnel add up to approximately $500 million per year. These resources can be redirected into important company priorities, including key-account management for large customers. Since existing customers can order on-line, account managers can work more on defining their customers' long-term strategic needs and spend less time on administrative and logistical tasks. Among Cisco's other corporate priorities are the acquisition of other companies to achieve growth targets and the building of strategic partnerships with other industry leaders such as Microsoft, IBM, EDS, Motorola, and Hewlett-Packard.

There are several customer-oriented features of Cisco Connection Online. The system's Troubleshooting Engine helps customers diagnose and fix problems. The Software Center lets customers upgrade their systems electronically, while Bug Alert transmits information about potential software problems within 24 hours of discovery. The Status Agent allows customers to track shipments with FedEx tracking numbers via a hotlink to FedEx's Web site. The Marketplace feature facilitates placing an order, with the proper prices and discounts automatically entered by the computer.

Cisco's Web site is maintained and constantly updated by every department that communicates with customers, including marketing, public relations, engineering, customer service, and technical support. This allows the company to move fast. For example, the day a new product is introduced, all press releases, product manuals, and marketing information goes automatically to the Web where it is easily retrieved by anyone who needs the information.

Cisco is using company intranets to further boost work efficiency by facilitating team interactions. Rather than saving documents to their own computers, people save documents to the group's Web site. The entire work process is based on group interaction supported by a Web site. Valuable information flows quickly between the Internet and various work-group intranets. Cisco is rapidly growing, and its use of interactive computer technologies is fueling the growth.

Cisco CEO John Chambers learned the importance of sales and customer service early in his career with IBM, and he firmly believes that technology—in this instance, the Internet—is the way to deliver customer value. Under his leadership, Cisco has joined a group of major suppliers and service providers to hasten the use of wireless Internet usage. Even more so than the computer-bound Internet, wireless technology promises a whole new world for direct marketing communications to global customers.

Questions

1. How does Cisco Connection Online supplement the person selling effort at Cisco?

2. Cisco is trying to improve customer relationships with its use of the Internet and company intranets. While these technologies are saving the company a lot of money, are customer relationships being improved?

3. How are Cisco's direct marketing communications through computer networks affecting other areas in the company's marketing effort such as marketing channels, pricing, and product management?

SOURCES: Information from Cisco's Web site at www.cisco.com, February 8, 2000; and Andy Reinhardt, "Meet Cisco's Mr. Internet," *Business Week Online,* September 13, 1999.

Case 20–2 Sam Goody Replays Its Way to Success

Sam Goody, a music and video retail chain, has long used a customer loyalty program to encourage repurchases and to give regular customers extra value. At one point, however, this program, called Replay, began experiencing serious problems, causing large numbers of customer defections. Inbound telemarketing representatives were overwhelmed with customer complaints. Record-keeping was poor, preventing qualified customers from receiving rebate checks when they made major purchases in a timely manner. As membership in Replay dropped, store managers became reluctant to promote the program. Sam Goody's loyalty program was quite simply having the opposite-than-hoped-for effect.

Sam Goody improved its loyalty program with the help of database marketing specialists from Minnesota-based

Group 3 Marketing. The basic idea of Replay remained the same: that it is a consumer club offering its members discounts and other promotions, reviews, information about new releases, and related information. In return, members pay $7.99 a year to belong. To improve the program, the frequency of direct mail contact with members increased and the content of the mailings became far more customized.

Now bimonthly newsletters and four to five postcards are sent out monthly. The newsletters generate in-store or on-line responses of 16 to 18 percent, while the postcards typically generate a 5 to 7 percent response. The newsletters are more customized than the postcards, with message content dependent upon customer information from the database. In most cases, content is tailored to music and film preferences, birthdays, proximity to retail stores, and recent purchases. Postcards usually focus on new-product releases.

Basic demographic data is captured when members join Replay, and purchase information is gathered when the membership card is swiped in the store. This data is transferred electronically every day to Group 3 Marketing; on-line purchases are automatically recorded into the database.

One page of each newsletter is predominantly tailored to the individual Replay member. Personalized information includes accumulated point balances, gift-certificate rewards status, and product information that matches the member's interests. Other customized material is included in free-standing inserts.

Each Sam Goody's store receives a report on the purchasing activity of its 50 top-spending customers. When these customers make purchases, their names appear on the electronic cash register screens. This allows store personnel to greet the key customers by name and to eventually recognize them as they enter the store. In some cases, this leads to personalized in-store service deserving of a top customer.

Sam Goody's uses the Replay database to send e-mail promotions and special offers to members, but only after the member has signed up for these notices. When they sign up on-line, members have an option to receive their newsletters on-line. This option will save Sam Goody a significant amount of money in the years to come, as more and more consumers will opt for on-line direct marketing communications.

The tuned-up Replay program has been so successful that Musicland, Sam Goody's parent company, has rolled it out to their other retail chains. These include On Cue, Sun Coast, and Media Play stores. Store managers now give their enthusiastic support to Replay, and promotional signage for Replay is prominent in the stores. Musicland is looking to expand the on-line aspect of the program. With a meaningful database, user-friendly interface, and highly customized direct marketing communications, the future looks good for Replay.

Questions

1. How could Sam Goody use the information from its database to enhance in-store promotions and personal selling?

2. How could Sam Goody use its database to improve market segmentation and target marketing?

3. What methods could you recommend to assess the effectiveness of the various direct marketing communications vehicles used in Sam Goody's Replay program?

SOURCES: Jim Emerson, "Turnaround: Sam Goody Revives and Expands Sagging Loyalty Program," *Direct,* November 1999, pp. 1, 11; and information from Sam Goody's Web site at www.samgoody.com, February 8, 2000.

Chapter Twenty-One

Electronic Commerce

After studying this chapter, you should be able to:

1 Explain the differences between e-business, e-commerce, and e-marketing.

2 Discuss the benefits of e-commerce to buyers and sellers.

3 Describe the current activity and trends in B2C and B2B e-commerce.

4 Discuss key e-commerce marketing issues in each area of the marketing mix.

5 Explain how the Internet and related technologies can help marketers improve the productivity of their activities.

6 Describe how e-commerce marketers can build long-term trust-based relationships with their customers.

7 Understand the important legal and ethical issues associated with marketing practice and e-commerce.

CyberAtlas provides Internet statistics and market research for those interested in electronic commerce. One of the most useful aspects of this Web site is the Latest Market Research section. This section lists the titles and short summaries of recent articles on various e-commerce topics. The articles are listed in chronological order with the most recent first. A click on the article title will produce the complete article. At the end of each article, it is possible to format the article for printing or to e-mail it to a friend. Typical e-commerce topics covered in this section are e-commerce advertising, demographics, traffic patterns, geographics, and retailing. Some of the articles provide useful statistics that are updated on a regular basis. For example, a report ranking e-commerce retailers in the United States and presenting a variety of statistics about each company is a monthly feature. There is also an Archives section, so it is possible to access articles presented in the past.

Specific types of e-commerce information can be accessed in various ways. The Search CyberAtlas function allows a user to type in one or more keywords and receive a listing of available materials related to these words. E-commerce information is also categorized in several ways to facilitate access. The Big Picture offers information according to general e-commerce statistics, demographics, geographics, hardware, and traffic patterns. The Markets section is organized according to broad industry categories, such as advertising, education, finance, professional, retail, and travel. A click on a category in either the Big Picture or Markets sections produces a listing of information related to the desired category.

CyberAtlas also offers a free weekly newsletter. The electronic newsletter highlights new developments on the CyberAtlas Web site and brief information about developments in e-commerce. The only thing needed to subscribe to the newsletter is an e-mail address. It is also possible to interact electronically with CyberAtlas by sending an e-mail from the Send Us feedback section.

The features of CyberAtlas discussed to this point are free. Most of the free materials represent summaries from large e-commerce market research studies. The All NetResearch section offers the opportunity to purchase complete reports of e-commerce studies conducted by different companies. Several of the most recent ones are normally listed on the CyberAtlas home page. However, a complete listing of all reports available from All NetResearch can be obtained by clicking on the hotlink to its Web site. Most of these reports are quite long and provide much more detailed statistics than the summary reports offered for free by CyberAtlas. **Source:** http://cyberatlas.internet.com, April 17, 2000.

The Internet can be used to perform various business and marketing activities. Garden.com represents an example of e-business, e-commerce, and e-marketing.

CyberAtlas provides a great deal of valuable information about the use of the Internet in various business activities. Business use of the Internet is relatively new, although it continues to grow at a rapid pace. Therefore, some of the terminology describing these activities is loosely defined and many terms are used interchangeably. The most common and popular terms are e-business, e-commerce, and e-marketing.

We present specific definitions for each of these terms. **Electronic business (e-business)** is defined as the use of the Internet to conduct business activities. This is the broadest term, since it encompasses all business activities performed on the Internet. **Electronic commerce (e-commerce)** is defined as the use of the Internet for buying and selling products that are transported either physically or digitally from location to location. Thus, e-commerce is the subset of e-business concerned specifically with buying and selling activities on the Internet. **Electronic marketing (e-marketing)** is defined as the use of the Internet to perform marketing activities. All e-marketing activities are considered e-business, but only those e-marketing activities focusing on buying and selling transactions are part of e-commerce. *E-commerce* is currently the most popular term, but many think *e-business* will gradually replace it since e-business includes all Internet business activities.[1]

Previous chapters have examined the use of the Internet in all aspects of marketing. All of this coverage falls within the domain of e-business and e-marketing, and some of it is also e-commerce, since it focuses directly on buying and selling activities. The purpose of this chapter is to emphasize e-commerce. We discuss the benefits of e-commerce to buyers and sellers, present statistics concerning e-commerce activity and trends, and examine key e-commerce issues with particular attention to legal and ethical issues.

Benefits of E-commerce

E-commerce offers many benefits to buyers and sellers. Consider the following purchasing situation:[2]

Mary wants to buy a *Harry Potter* book for her daughter. She could go to the local bookstore, compare the *Harry Potter* books in the store, and purchase one of these books at a stated price. Or, she might get on the Internet and start at a portal, such as Netscape.com. She could then select a search engine, such as GoTo.com, and receive a listing of Web sites with information about *Harry Potter* books. She could then look at various sites. She might go to a site like "Nancy's Magical Harry Potter Page" where she would find book reviews, discussion groups, and other information about *Harry Potter* books. She would find a link to eToys.com, and if she clicked on it, she would find that eToys has a special price on *Harry Potter* books. She could order one or more books from eToys, or she might decide to go to another bookstore site, such as Amazon.com, and compare book prices and availability. Based on all of this information, she could purchase the books she wants from the site offering the most attractive option.

E-commerce provides many benefits to buyers and sellers. The Barnes & Noble Web site illustrates some of those benefits related to *Harry Potter* books.

This situation illustrates the major differences between traditional commerce and e-commerce. Let's examine this situation to identify the benefits of e-commerce to buyers and sellers.

Benefits to Buyers

In the traditional commerce situation, Mary would have to travel to a retail book-store when it was open for business. She could look at the *Harry Potter* books the store had on its shelves and compare the books based on the information on the book covers. A salesperson at the store may or may not be able to provide her with additional, useful information. She could then decide to purchase one or more of the available *Harry Potter* books at the prices charged by this particular bookstore. If she wanted to comparison shop, she would have to travel to other stores and re-peat the above process.

In the e-commerce situation, Mary could shop whenever she wanted from wher-ever she could access the Internet. She could easily get a tremendous amount of in-formation about all *Harry Potter* titles, and much of this information would be from *Harry Potter* readers and not just from book sellers. She could then readily compare prices and delivery options from different sites and decide which was most attractive to her. She could then make a purchase and receive the books in a few days.

The key benefits of e-commerce to buyers are evident from comparing the above purchasing situations and are summarized in Exhibit 21–1. One of the most im-portant buyer benefits is convenience. Buyers can engage in e-commerce 24 hours a day and seven days a week from any location with Internet access. There are no time and place limitations for buyers. Buyers can shop whenever it is most conve-nient for them and not just when sellers are open for business.

Another important benefit is that buyers have more choices in e-commerce. Buy-ers are not limited to only what is available from a few sellers; they have access to a tremendous variety of products offered by a large number of sellers. Related to increased choice, is the substantial amount of information available to buyers in e-commerce. Some of this additional information is about alternative products, but buyers can also get detailed information about each specific alternative product. And, much of this information is from other buyers or organizations that are try-ing to help buyers make the best purchasing decisions and not just sell them prod-ucts. Buyers are also not just passive recipients of information, but people who can interact electronically to get answers to specific questions by participating in dis-cussion groups, chat rooms, and/or bulletin boards, or by sending e-mails.

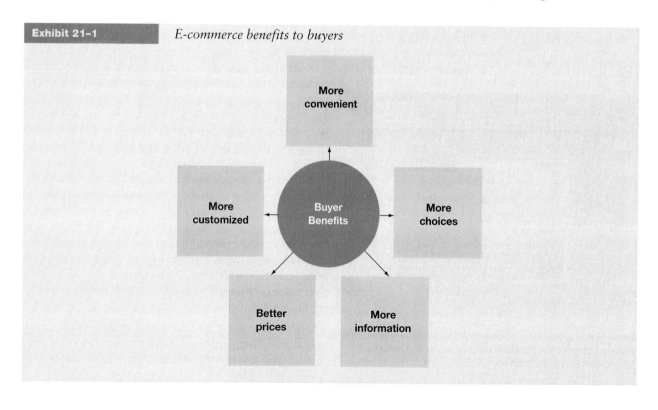

Exhibit 21–1   *E-commerce benefits to buyers*

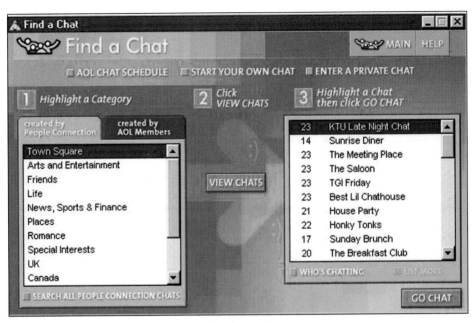

Buyers can get useful information about products from various sources on the Internet. Chat rooms provide an opportunity to interact with others about different products.

Another important benefit is that e-commerce encourages price competition. Since buyers have easy access to the products and prices offered by different sellers, comparison shopping is facilitated. Therefore, if sellers are not price competitive, buyers readily find this out and shop elsewhere. In addition, various services to interject price competition have been introduced on the Internet. These include auctions, such as eBay, name-your-price sites, such as Priceline, and sites that present direct price comparisons of different sellers of a particular product, such as Quotesmith for insurance. All of these developments make it easier for buyers to get the best prices for the products purchased in e-commerce.

A final benefit is that buyers can customize the shopping experience as well as many products in order to meet their individual needs. Buyers have control over what is viewed at an Internet site; this allows them to access only the information desired and customize the shopping experience to meet their particular needs. Buyers can also customize many products. As presented in Chapter 2, buyers of Dell computers can build the exact computer they desire, determine how and when it will be shipped, and keep track of its progress from production through delivery. Computer service information is also available electronically, so buyers can access this service information whenever needed.

When all of the benefits of e-commerce are considered, the net effect is that e-commerce increases the power of the buyer in most transactions. In traditional commerce, sellers often have more power because buyers have only limited information and there are typically only a few alternative sellers. In e-commerce, buyers can assemble a great deal of information and purchase from a large number of suppliers. This increases the power of buyers and makes them more "product and price makers" and less "product and price takers."[3]

Benefits to Sellers

In the traditional commerce situation, the bookstore where Mary shopped drew most of its customers from

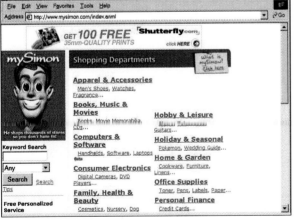

E-commerce makes it easier for buyers to evaluate different purchasing alternatives. mySimon.com facilitates comparison shopping.

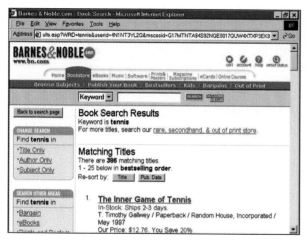

E-commerce allows sellers to serve customers from anywhere at any time. Barnes & Noble's Web site illustrates this for a customer interested in tennis books.

a geographic trading area around the store location. The bookstore served these customers during defined hours on specific days. Most sales came from books in the store's inventory, although special orders could be placed for customers. Since inventory is costly, the bookstore faced the difficult task of trying to carry the books desired by its customers while simultaneously minimizing inventory costs. The bookstore's expenses for advertising and for rent for its building were quite high. Prices for books had to cover these costs—but also remain competitive—to generate the level of sales required to earn a profit.

The e-commerce situation is much different for the seller. E-commerce book sellers can serve customers around the clock from any geographic location. These sellers can offer almost any book in print and do not usually keep these books in their own inventory. In addition, it is relatively easy for e-commerce book sellers to provide customers with a great deal of information about specific books, to interact with customers electronically, to collect and assemble information about customers, and to suggest books consistent with a customer's reading habits and interests. Although there are costs for Web design and operation, and some physical facilities are required, these costs are normally lower than those faced by traditional bookstores. The net result is that e-commerce book sellers can typically offer customers a better book selection, a more convenient shopping experience, and lower prices than can traditional bookstores.

The major benefits of e-commerce to sellers are illustrated both in the situations just described and in Exhibit 21–2. Some of the benefits to sellers are similar to those for buyers. For example, the ability to serve customers with no geographic or

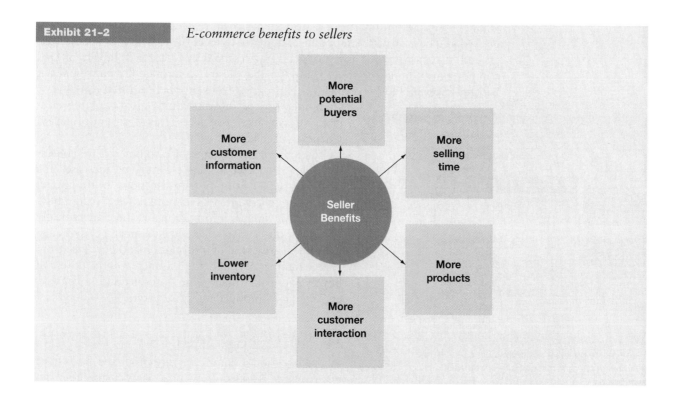

Exhibit 21-2   *E-commerce benefits to sellers*

temporal limitations expands the business opportunities available to sellers and provides convenience to buyers. Similarly, being able to offer a large product selection with limited inventory is an attractive business model that simultaneously provides buyers with tremendous product choice. Electronic communication also makes it possible for sellers to cost-effectively interact with buyers, collect customer information, and provide additional product information and convenient service.

The e-commerce model has many benefits for sellers. Costs for inventory, physical facilities, and marketing are often lower than those in traditional businesses selling similar products. Although e-commerce sellers face costs in other areas and it takes time to build an electronic infrastructure and customer base, the e-commerce seller has the potential to be very profitable.

E-commerce Activity and Trends

Thinking Critically

The text presents the key benefits of e-commerce to buyers and sellers. However, no business or marketing approach is without limitations. Therefore, think about e-commerce and address the following questions:

- What are the major problems faced by buyers in purchasing from e-commerce sellers?

- What are the major challenges faced by e-commerce sellers?

- Why are some e-commerce sellers not performing as well as expected?

There are two major types of e-commerce. One type is businesses selling to consumers over the Internet. This is normally referred to as **business-to-consumer (B2C) e-commerce.** Mary purchasing *Harry Potter* books over the Internet is an example of B2C e-commerce. The other type is businesses selling to other businesses or organizations over the Internet. **Business-to-business (B2B) e-commerce** is the term for this type of e-commerce. Dell selling computers to your university over the Internet is an example. We will now examine the current activity and expected trends for each type of e-commerce.

B2C E-commerce

We previously discussed consumer buying behavior (Chapter 4) and retailing (Chapter 14). B2C e-commerce builds on the key concepts covered in these chapters but only includes consumer buying from businesses over the Internet. Another term used to describe these activities is **e-retailing,** since B2C e-commerce is retailing over the Internet.

The level of B2C e-commerce is largely dependent upon the number of active Internet users. There were approximately 130.6 million active Internet users worldwide at the end of 1999. This figure is expected to increase to 361.9 million by the year 2003. About 42 percent of these Internet users currently come from the United States, but the U.S. percentage of worldwide Internet usage is expected to decline. Worldwide Internet usage percentages for 2003 are projected at 36.9 percent United States, 30 percent Western Europe, 27 percent Asia-Pacific, and 5.3 percent Latin America. Most of the growth in Internet usage will come from Asia-Pacific, Western Europe, and Latin America.[4] Although all Internet users are not purchasers, the total number and growth of Internet users provides a general assessment of the current level and future growth potential for e-commerce.

E-commerce statistics reflect this relationship. A recent study found the United States to be the leader in e-commerce accounting for 54 percent of on-line buyers. The United States also leads in the percentage of adults who have bought on-line (31 percent), followed by Sweden (21 percent), Switzerland (19 percent), Canada (18 percent), and Australia (14 percent). E-commerce also varies by countries within regions. For example, the percentage of adults buying on-line in Germany (14 percent) and the Netherlands (11 percent) is relatively high; the percentages are much lower in other European countries, such as France (5 percent), Italy (3 percent), and Spain (2 percent). The items most frequently purchased on-line include books (37 percent), computer equipment and software (21 percent), CDs (20 percent), and clothing (17 percent).[5] Interestingly, a recent study found that the longer consumers have been on-line, the more they spend per transaction. Those who have been on-line five years spend twice as much as those who recently became Internet users. And, 61 percent of Internet shoppers plan to increase their on-line spending by about 43 percent. Only 7 percent indicated their e-commerce activity would decrease.[6]

This snapshot of B2C e-commerce suggests continued growth in the future. This growth will vary geographically and be focused in specific product lines. But, even

B2C e-commerce is growing rapidly around the world. Printemps appeals to international customers for fashion products.

with this growth, B2C e-commerce will still represent a relatively small portion of the total retail market. Estimates differ, but in the United States, B2C e-commerce may reach just 15 to 20 percent of total retail sales.

B2B E-commerce

Although B2C e-commerce is the most visible, e-commerce is larger and growing more rapidly in the B2B area. B2B e-commerce is fundamentally changing the way businesses do business with each other. The basic concepts covered in Chapter 5 about business purchasing behavior apply, but the Internet is changing how some activities are being performed. For example, purchasing managers still evaluate potential suppliers based on various criteria. However, much of the evaluation process for some products now takes place electronically, instead of in person. Companies such as GE, Cisco, Oracle, Ford, and GM are moving as much of their purchasing as possible to the Internet.

The worldwide B2B market was estimated to be $145 billion in 1999. It is expected to grow to $403 billion in 2000 and reach $3.95 trillion by the end of 2003. Even though growth in B2B e-commerce is rapid, it will only account for about 7 percent of the total $105 trillion in worldwide business-to-business commerce expected in 2004. And, B2B e-commerce growth is faster in some areas than others. For example, more than 65 percent of U.S. B2B e-commerce purchases in 2003 are expected to come from six sectors: retail, motor vehicles, shipping, industrial equipment, high tech, and government.[7]

One major trend driving growth in the B2B area is the establishment of on-line procurement exchanges to bring buyers and sellers from a particular industry, geographic area, or affinity group together. An example is the on-line exchange being developed by more than a dozen oil and chemical companies. Participating companies include Royal Dutch/Shell Group, BP Amoco PLC, Dow Chemical, and Mitsubishi. The total procurement of these 14 companies is more than $125 billion annually, with 40 percent in North and South America, 40 percent in Europe, and 20 percent in Asia. When the exchange is operational, it is expected to cut purchasing costs for the participating companies by as much as 30 percent.[8]

Speaking from Experience

John Parker
Director of Business Operations
Quixtar, Inc.

Quixtar.com is based on a new business model designed to allow registered members to shop from a unique array of products or to develop a Web-based business as an Independent Business Owner. John Parker is Director of Business Operations for Quixtar. His responsibilities include Business Operations, Business Relations, and Public Relations for the privately-held company founded in 1999. He earned his Business Administration degree in Finance from the University of Notre Dame. Although John is involved in all of the e-commerce trends, he thinks companies need to integrate aspects of traditional commerce with e-commerce to be successful.

"Many Web companies are discovering that much of the 'old economy' infrastructure really is necessary to satisfy 'new economy' customers. Companies have to be able to provide responsive customer service and to deliver products to customers in a reliable and timely manner. Quixtar's arrangements with sister-company Amway Corp. provide easy access to warehousing and distribution services that are needed to get products into the hands of customers quickly. Also, we're able to provide a level of customer service that many e-commerce companies never realized would be required. Even in the kind of technological age we are entering, there's a need to be connected with real people who can provide assistance and support."

E-commerce is changing many aspects of business. Inventa recognizes the different changes in B2C and B2B business.

Although B2C and B2B e-commerce activities will grow significantly in the future, not all companies will succeed. Many e-commerce companies are having trouble earning a profit, and investors are finally showing some skepticism about the stock evaluations for these companies. As in traditional commerce, many issues need to be addressed by e-commerce companies in order for those companies to be successful. We now examine the key issues facing companies involved in e-commerce.

Key E-business Marketing Issues

As indicated in earlier discussions, e-commerce and the broader area of e-business are having a significant impact on consumer and business marketing. Business analysts believe that e-business as we know it now will become an integral part of most business operations in the near future. Some companies already see e-business as an integrating mechanism for all of its business activities. For an example of how Ford Motor Company uses e-business across several functional areas, see Exhibit 21–3. Despite progressive efforts from companies such as Ford, most aspects of e-business are fairly new to marketers and the key issues for managing e-business processes deserve special consideration. In this section, we will review key marketing issues in each area of the marketing mix: marketing communications; product; channels; and pricing. We will then discuss two key marketing priorities in e-business, improving productivity and building long-term trust-based customer relationships. The final section of the chapter delves into ethical and legal issues particularly relevant for e-business.

Marketing Communications

In this section, we will discuss several important marketing communications issues in e-business. First, emerging technologies that will enhance marketing communications in the near future are discussed. We then turn our attention to the basic issues of attracting customers to e-business sites, improving customer involvement once they are attracted to sites, encouraging return visits and purchases, implementing ongoing dialogues with customers, and ensuring that e-business communications are integrated with other marketing communications.

EMERGING TECHNOLOGY   Emerging technologies are bringing marketers new alternatives for communicating with customers. For example, Sprint, AT&T,

Exhibit 21–3	*Ford Motor Company's e-business approach*

Ford has launched an e-business strategy to rewire the automaker. The ultimate vision: To use the Net to do everything from ordering a car to linking 30,000 suppliers. Here is the game plan:

What	How	Goal
RETAILING	Set up BuyerConnection Web site and joined MSN CarPoint site, where consumers can order custom-assembled cars, track their progress, and apply for financing.	Reduce working capital by shrinking excess inventories and wipe out costly rebates needed to move unwanted cars off dealer lots, thus saving up to $650 per car.
CUSTOMER SERVICE	OwnerConnection Web site lets owners get on-line help, manage their warranty service, and check on financing.	Improve service with 24-hour access. Gather better data on customer problems. And cut costs with automated help.
SUPPLIERS	Launched auto-exchange Web site for on-line purchasing and swapping of information between 30,000 suppliers and 6,900 dealers.	Save up to $8.9 billion a year in discounts and reduced transaction costs on parts, raw materials, and supplies. Speed data exchange with partners while collecting up to $3 billion a year in exchange fees.
MARKETING	Teaming up with Yahoo!, TeleTech, CarPoint, iVillage, and bolt.com to monitor the interests and buying patterns of Web-surfing customers.	Improve factory efficiency by anticipating customer demand. Funnel data on customer preferences to car designers.
DIGITAL DASHBOARD	Equip new cars with Web access, satellite phone services, and e-mail capabilities.	Make Ford the carmaker for an Internet generation. Collect millions of dollars in fee-based services.
FINANCING	Shift more of the activities of Ford Credit to the Net for on-line financing and collections.	Cut service costs by 15 to 20 percent, while boosting revenues by reaching new customers.
WIRED WORKERS	Offering all 350,000 employees a computer, printer, and Net access for $5 a month.	Makes the workforce Web-savvy so it will quickly adopt the Internet initiatives, while enabling the CEO to send weekly e-mail to employees.

Source: Kathleen Kerwin, Marcia Stepanek, and David Welch, "At Ford, E-Commerce Is Job 1," *Business Week,* February 28, 2000, p. 76.

and Nextel are among the companies that offer wireless Web services via cell phones, and Motorola is installing Web technology into all of its new cell phones. With wireless technology, cell phone users can access Yahoo!, Fox Sports, MapQuest, and a fast-growing list of Web companies. Slow download speeds are a constraint, but tremendous improvements are expected sometime in 2001. Currently, it takes 20 minutes to download a three-minute song coded in MP3; with the pending improvements, it would take one minute. As connection speeds improve, the commercial application for wireless technology will explode.[9]

Technology improvements for desk-bound Web users are also imminent. For example, **broadband Internet technology,** a super-fast connection to the Web via cable modem, digital subscriber lines, or satellites, will allow marketers to greatly enhance e-business activities. Broadband is 50 times faster than a 56K modem, thus allowing users to download huge files quickly. This will allow marketers to increase multimedia and interactive aspects of their messages. By 2003, industry experts predict that a quarter of U.S. households will have broadband technology. This is good news for e-business, since broadband subscribers spend significantly more time online than do modem users.[10]

Using new technologies to communicate with customers is a challenge for marketers, if for no other reason than that the pace of new technology development is staggering. Nonetheless, marketers generally have no choice but to try to keep abreast of new methods of communicating with customers. To those marketers who can lead the charge, marketplace performance can be impressive, though short-term profitability can be problematic. Amazon.com and CDNOW have certainly found this to be the case.

ATTRACTING CUSTOMERS   The continuation of the adoption of computer and communications technology guarantees a growing potential market for e-business. However, this by no means guarantees that the number of on-line shoppers will grow for any particular marketer. In fact, a lot of on-line shoppers drop out of the market after trying it for a while. Since 1997, researchers at the University of Pennsylvania's Wharton School have tracked the on-line purchases of 1,000 shoppers who bought in that year. The research shows that 15 percent did not make an on-line purchase in 1998 but did increase their catalog spending. Those that did continue on-line shopping spent 117 percent more in 1998 than in 1997, but only 25 percent more in 1999 than in 1998.[11] For marketers, this means they must work hard to attract shoppers to their sites—and quite likely even harder to keep them coming back.

To attract shoppers, many on-line merchants are using extensive promotions. Others have partnered with popular search engines or **portals.** Portals, also discussed in Chapter 14, offer general Internet functions and direct visitors to additional sites. Having a strong identity at a portal, such as Yahoo! with 120 million monthly users, can obviously help steer traffic to an individual company site. Marketers should be aware, however, that consumers are increasingly going directly to a company Web site of their choice rather than using a search engine or portal to find what they want. One study indicates that more than half of those users monitored went directly to favorite company sites, bypassing portals and search engines.[12] This implies that Internet marketers must quickly establish an identity to drive traffic to their sites.

To reach consumers who do use portals, a widespread method is **banner advertising.** These ads are "clickable" should the viewer want more information about the product or service being advertised. Banner ads are the most popular ads on the Internet, but consumers seem to be tiring of them. In the early days of e-commerce in 1997, approximately 2 percent of Web visitors clicked on one or more banner ads at portal sites. That number dropped to .5 percent in 1999 and is expected to drop further.[13] Thus, other forms of marketing communications are becoming more important to drive shoppers to Web sites.

One alternative favored by many dot com companies is conventional advertising—for example, Super Bowl ads—to increase awareness for their sites. Even well-established Internet marketers such as Amazon.com have increased their use of traditional advertising, and Autobytel uses a 35-person national salesforce to drive traffic to its Web site. Other companies that introduce their e-business capabilities to their customers via the salesforce include Airborne Express, Bank One, and Liberty Mutual Insurance.[14]

John Parker, Director of Business Operations, Quixtar, discusses the approach his company uses to build traffic for Quixtar.com: "Many e-commerce companies rely on large advertising expenditures to build site traffic. The Quixtar business model does not include any advertising. Quixtar's marketing budget rewards Independent Business Owners (IBOs) who generate sales volume at Quixtar.com. We've built a tremendous site, but unless people know about it, that investment is wasted. Our IBOs not only spread the word about the site, but they also go on-line with their clients and prospects, helping them understand how to shop on the site and how the site can help them develop their own business. This is what we call our "High-Tech, High-Touch" approach. High tech is necessary, but high touch is what makes our model work."

IMPROVING CUSTOMER INVOLVEMENT AND RETURN VISITS   Once customers are attracted to e-commerce and e-business sites, marketers try to keep them involved long enough to accomplish communications and sales objectives. One strategy to boost customer interactions—or to increase **site stickiness**—is to incorporate search capabilities into the site so that customers can easily find the information they are seeking. Using alternative spellings of products and brands can facilitate customer navigation of the site. In an increasing number of cases, multilingual sites are also needed. Another strategy is to provide a site map that illustrates where key blocks of information are stored.

Some on-line marketers try to build site stickiness by increasing **personalization** of communications. Portals have long offered this feature whereby visitors can customize the look and content of the portal's home page. American Express, Lands' End, Fidelity Investments, and Sun Microsystems are examples of nonportal marketers who do a good job in facilitating personalization for their site visitors.[15] A step beyond personalization is **building on-line communities** where customers who share interests can interact with other like-minded customers. For example, Virgin Megastores sponsors an on-line community for customers who wish to share music reviews and discuss their favorite performing artists.

Whether or not visitors return to e-commerce sites is largely a function of the perceived value they receive when they do visit. There is little time to return to poorly designed sites, sites lacking sufficient information, or those that ultimately do not deliver a good value for the time and money spent by the consumer. As noted in Chapter 4, consumers who shop on the Web are impatient, wish to be in control, and are quick to shift to another Web site if they cannot quickly find what they want. CD-NOW is aware of how on-line shoppers behave and has designed its site accordingly. The site, which can be customized according to a customer's preferences, is long on information and short on advertising. Searches are easy to conduct, and buying recorded music is a simple process. Shipping confirmation is an automatic process, and if necessary, returns are easily accomplished. All of these site attributes enhance marketing communications and provide increased value for the customer. An approach for creating value for consumers in different countries is presented in "Earning Customer Loyalty: Bol.com Recognizes Country Differences."

IMPLEMENTING ONGOING DIALOGUE Permission marketing, first discussed in Chapter 16, directly connects the marketer with the customer—with the customer's permission. This frequently results in an ongoing dialogue between buyer and seller. Permission marketing is commonly conducted via e-mail, which can also be used in a number of other ways to establish dialogue with customers. Palm Computing Inc., manufacturer of the Palm Pilot, uses e-mail to regularly send messages to 400,000 customers. Palm sends about 30 messages per month, but no more than two per customer. Messages typically introduce new product accessories, tips for using the Pilot, or events of potential interest to the customer.[16]

Amazon.com uses e-mail permission marketing to alert current customers of new book releases that may be of interest to the customer. Recently, one of the authors received an e-mail from Amazon stating, "As someone who's purchased a book by sportscaster Bob Costas, you might like to know that his newest book is available with a 30% discount at the following Web link. . . ." Personally speaking, this sort

Earning Customer Loyalty

Bol.com recognizes country differences

Www.bol.com is trying to duplicate in Europe the success of Amazon.com, but by recognizing important differences between the countries it serves (e.g., Britain, France, Germany, Spain, Switzerland, and the Netherlands). The firm's strategy is based upon the need to incorporate localized differences into the options offered to consumers from different countries. Sites are also available in Malaysia, Singapore, and Hong Kong, with Japan and Italy forthcoming. For the current European sites, countries are so different in many respects that separate sites for each country greatly facilitate customer loyalty. These differences among cultures include, for example, the willingness to provide credit card information; in some areas of Europe, sole reliance on

the credit card for purchases would eliminate 60 percent of potential customers. Bol.com customers can purchase books, music, and gifts, like the products sold by Amazon.com, but the country of choice is selected as the shopper enters the "bol.com store." As such, this Internet marketer is able to capitalize upon unique cultural and language differences in establishing each site. Such segmentation principles are basic to the implementation of marketing strategies designed to enhance customer loyalty.

Sources: Michael Kavanagh, "Guardian Strikes Bertelsmann Deal," *Marketing Week*, February 4, 1999, p. 35; Adrienne Mand, "Euro E-comm: Giant Bertelsmann Tests Site," *Adweek*, November 30, 1998, p. 33; http://www.bol.com/index.html; Andrew Ross Sorkin, "Bol.com Serves Local Flavors All Over Europe," *The New York Times*, March 29, 2000, p. 6.

On-line marketers try to establish ongoing dialogues with their best customers. Cyber Dialogue assists some on-line marketers in identifying valuable customers and the establishment of dialogue with these customers.

of communication is appreciated and encourages return visits to Amazon's site. E-mail can also be used for company newsletters, for reminders of special events and promotions, and for numerous customer service applications.

Getting customers' permission to converse with them via e-mail is becoming more important since unsolicited e-mail, or **spam,** is increasingly unpopular. Many targets of spam feel that it is an intrusion and a waste of time. Others are concerned at the incidence of fraudulent information in some spam. Further, spam, or junk e-mail, adds to the overall cost of electronic communications. Internet service providers such as America Online and Lycos have to charge higher user fees to cover the costs of more equipment to prevent system overloads that can occur with spam bulk e-mails.[17] To date, 14 states have enacted laws regulating the use of spam, and several pieces of legislation are pending in Congress. More so from a consumer preference perspective than from growing legal restraints, most marketers would be well advised to avoid junk e-mail.

Ongoing dialogue can also be established via Internet sales presentations. MCI uses Internet-delivered presentations to simultaneously reach customers in multiple markets. Participants in the Internet sales conferences are attracted by banner ads on other Web sites. They register for the conference, and can get answers to their real-time questions during the conference.[18]

For companies with seasonal or annual business cycles, maintaining an ongoing dialogue with customers can help keep them active until the next selling season comes around. This is particularly crucial for companies that have encountered service problems, such as some electronic retailers following higher-than-expected sales levels during holiday rush seasons. Toys " Я " Us opened two new distribution centers in 2000 and communicated with previous on-line customers to let them know that the new distribution centers should alleviate service problems during future rush periods.[19]

ENSURING INTEGRATED MARKETING COMMUNICATIONS Marketers must take care to ensure that messages disseminated over the Internet are consistent with other messages disseminated via other media, the salesforce, and channel partners. As an example, Val-Pak (see opener for Chapter 18), a direct-mail specialty company, sends consumers coupons redeemable at local retail stores. Val-Pak also has a Web site that offers consumers coupons good at local retail stores. For marketers using Val-Pak, the fact that the company offers consistent communications messages in both direct-mail and electronic media is an advantage over single media alternatives. According to the director of Internet business development for Val-Pak's parent company, Cox Target Media, "Val-Pak coupons on-line puts a one-two punch in our advertisers' messages in front of the consumers."[20]

It is equally important that messages put forth on the Internet are consistent with the firm's overall image and marketing strategy. There have been some noteworthy exceptions to this obvious principle of integrated marketing communications. Priceline.com, an on-line consumer bidding site, has used actor William Shatner as a leather-jacketed lounge singer in its television ads. Many industry observers rate the ads highly, and Priceline has also put the ads on its Web site due to popular demand. Priceline executives feel that the ads are effective and point out that Priceline is tied with Amazon.com as the third most-recognizable Internet brand name.[21] Consumers, however, give the ads mixed reviews: 14 percent say they like the ads a lot; 26 percent dislike the ads; 25 percent think the ads are effective.[22] While the ads have generated a fair amount of publicity for Priceline, they do not seem to complement Priceline's print ads or overall marketing strategy. Whether the ads are effective or not is a matter of opinion. The key issue here is that the ads could well be more effective if they reinforced other elements of Priceline's marketing communications.

The 2000 Super Bowl served as a powerful reminder that marketing communications should reinforce the other communications of a firm, as well as a firm's marketing strategy. Dot com companies dominated television advertising during the game's broadcast, and analysts generally gave them failing grades. Pets.com was the only dot com advertiser to run a top-five ad, and most finished far down in the rankings. Among the comments from advertising industry experts: "Eager for instant attention, the dot-coms spent millions of dollars but walked off with little more than bruised egos and red faces"; "The dot-com commercials had more incomplete passes than the game"; and "They're spending all the money and they aren't even memorable. I can't tell you what they are."[23]

Done right, the Web offers marketers exciting opportunities to integrate marketing communications with **hybrid campaigns** that blend traditional media with the Web to make the consumer an active participant. Tommy Hilfiger, for example, ran print ads in its "Unreleased Cuts" campaign featuring models from an on-line talent contest for musicians without recording contracts. The print ads invited consumers to go to tommy.com to play "record executive for the day" and help select a winner of a $10,000 recording session. Ford Motor Company used TV ads to steer consumers to its Web site where they could "direct" commercials for the Focus automobile. Nike developed "whatever.com" ads that sent consumers to its Web site to select the endings for three incomplete TV ads.[24]

With the advent of Web communication, the area of public relations offers new opportunities and new challenges for marketers. Web sites can become 24-hour-a-day public relations agents with press releases and other content favorable to the company. Publicity generated on third-party Web sites can be a big plus as well. For example, a business's becoming the Yahoo! "Daily Pick" can mean thousands of incremental visitors are driven to that company's site.[25]

The Web also offers unique challenges to marketers in the publicity area. Competitors can enter the sites of complaint groups—which are fairly common—pretending to be dissatisfied customers with legitimate complaints. The very fact that complaint sites are commonplace may encourage a higher volume of complaints than in the past. It is far cheaper and generally less time-consuming to complain online than to write a letter or reach a responsive party on the phone.

Of course, companies should make it easy for unhappy customers to resolve their complaints. On the other hand, some marketers fear that electronic communications makes it far too easy to portray a routine problem as some sort of customer service travesty. One opportunistic entrepreneur is counting on consumers' propensity to complain, developing an on-line complaint business named sucks.com.[26] Founder Dan Parisi spent about $100,000 to register the names of 500 of the largest companies in the world combined with the sucks.com suffix. Such developments have marketers and public relations professionals worried. To defend against possible damage to brand image and brand equity, companies should register variations of their brand names. For example, in a defensive move, U-Haul registered the name Uhaulsucks.com among other names related to their company name.

The Web has also been the source of some potentially damaging unfounded rumors. One hoax detailed how Tommy Hilfiger, while appearing on *The Oprah Winfrey Show,* reportedly said that he did not want African Americans wearing his clothing brand. Hilfiger had never appeared on the program. Another totally false rumor circulating on the Web was that Mrs. Field's Cookies sponsored a party for the jurors who acquitted O.J. Simpson of murder charges.[27] Many such rumors or unfounded complaints are ignored by the target companies. In other cases, companies must fight back to protect their reputations. In these cases, the Web can be a powerful tool.

Product-Related Issues

The Internet and related technologies affect numerous product decision areas. For example, marketing research can be conducted over the Internet, and the Internet is the fastest-growing source of secondary data. As such, the Internet can be a useful vehicle for determining customer preferences and developing new products. The Internet can be the delivery mechanism for digital products. Software and recorded music are increasingly transmitted to customers in digital downloadable files. In many cases, the Web has allowed companies to offer new products or services as a result of their expertise in Web site design, site security, and the procedural aspects of running a Web site.

Of the countless number of product-related issues in e-commerce, we will discuss two issues of particular importance to marketers in this section. First, we will consider the importance of customer service in e-commerce. Second, we will look at the threat posed by marketers of imitation products.

CUSTOMER SERVICE IN E-COMMERCE   Customer service is a major component of any market offering. This is especially true for on-line marketers and their customers. Ultimate consumers who buy in traditional stores can examine products and interact with store personnel face-to-face in the event of a service problem. Business-to-business buyers and sellers often interact extensively through off-line methods. For companies who rely primarily on the Web to communicate with customers, customer service becomes extremely important for success.

While much was made of some companies' inability to ship complete orders during the Christmas 1999 season, approximately 85 percent of surveyed customers said they were satisfied with their on-line shopping experiences during the Christmas season.[28] Most progressive companies, however, would not settle for an 85 percent satisfaction rate when it comes to customer service. There is an increasing amount of evidence that Internet marketers have realized that customer service must improve and that they are taking appropriate steps to achieve improvements. There is also growing evidence that in many cases the Web can help deliver better customer service while possibly reducing service costs.

Customer service properly defined for e-commerce moves well beyond reactive activities such as resolving complaints and processing customer returns. Good customer service takes the offensive, designing processes that anticipate and prevent problems before they occur. Customer service professionals insist that customer satisfaction be monitored and that they be empowered to ensure satisfaction. Cisco, the world's most valuable company in terms of market value, quadrupled its sales in the 1997–2000 time period while only doubling its customer support staff. Cisco has been successful in the customer service area by shifting a lot of routine inquiries, such as order-tracking, to its Web site.[29]

Most marketing organizations have not yet integrated the Web into their customer service operations. According to McKinsey and Company and Forrester Research, only 8 percent of the almost 70,000 customer service call centers in the United States are Web-enabled. That is changing, however. By 2002, 60 percent of brokerage houses and 50 percent of banks will use the Internet for some aspects of customer service.[30] For those companies who are striving for better e-commerce customer service, it is important to recognize that customer expectations continue to rise. This means that Internet marketers must become faster at providing the information shoppers need. Surveys show that a sizable percentage of firms do not respond to e-mail inquiries, do not furnish e-mail addresses for customer service personnel, or take more than five days to respond to inquiries. Further, only a small percentage of e-commerce sites offer a functional "help" button.[31] Clearly, we expect that those who succeed in e-commerce will show substantial improvements in customer service in the immediate future.

IMITATION PRODUCTS Imitation products threaten brand image and brand equity built by legitimate marketers. This has been a chronic problem over the years, and now the Internet offers yet another avenue for unscrupulous imitators. The lack of strict regulatory guidelines for the Internet makes this threat particularly ominous. The FBI has established a consortium to fight Internet fraud, but their parent agency, the U.S. Justice Department, is taking a wait-and-see approach. According to a spokesperson, the Justice Department will take no action unless complaints are lodged more frequently.[32] Local police monitor the sale of counterfeit products in flea markets and retail stores, but they are not sure they have jurisdiction over Internet sales.

Makers of luxury goods are the favorite target of counterfeit manufacturers. As a rule, genuine luxury-goods makers do not sell their products on the Internet, nor do they authorize others to do so. Cartier, Gucci, Chanel, Coach, Luis Vuitton, and Tommy Hilfiger are among those companies victimized by counterfeit marketers. For advice on how to spot fake versions of these brands, see Exhibit 21–4.

Marketers have several options for fighting the sale of fake brands. Rolex takes the legal route, tracking down imitators and filing lawsuits. In one search of popular auction site eBay, Rolex discovered 747 of its watches on sale, many of which were fake. Some companies, including Louis Vuitton, Gucci, and Cartier, provide toll-free numbers for consumers to call if they suspect a product is an imitation.[33] Others use their own Web sites to stress that their products are not for sale on the Web. When counterfeiters are discovered, a cease and desist letter is typically issued, which may cause the Web site operator to quit selling the product but probably not

Exhibit 21–4	*How to spot fake products sold on the Web*

Company	Warning signs
Cartier	Cartier does sell on the Web; fake watches often lack engraved Cartier signature on the back of the watch.
Chanel	No authorized dealers on-line.
Coach	Some authentic Coach handbags are sold on the Web, but not by authorized dealers; fake products often use low-grade, smelly leather.
Luis Vuitton	Fake products often use an "LX" logo, which can be easily confused with the genuine "LV" logo.
Gucci	No authorized Internet dealers; bags marked "Made in Russia" or "Made in India" are fake, as all genuine Gucci bags are made in Italy.
Tommy Hilfiger	No authorized Internet dealers; Hilfiger watches are fake—Hilfiger doesn't make watches.

Source: Rebecca Quick, "Sleaze E-commerce," *The Wall Street Journal*, May 14, 1999, pp. W1, W10.

shut down the site. Indeed, this is a tough fight for luxury-goods makers, as many consumers seek out and support these dubious sites.

Key E-commerce Channels Issues

As the use of the Web as a channel grows dramatically, two major issues emerge. One is the potential for electronic channels to completely transform entire industries and individual companies. The second major issue is how to integrate electronic channels with existing channels. This section takes a closer look at both of these issues.

TRANSFORMATION WITH ELECTRONIC CHANNELS   The channels for entire industries can be transformed with electronic channels. Take for example the automobile industry. The Big Three manufacturers, Ford, DaimlerChrysler, and General Motors, have combined forces to set up a single portal for automotive suppliers. This will allow suppliers to work through a single on-line exchange. The Big Three also use the site for auctioning surplus equipment and supplies and are encouraging their suppliers to use the site to negotiate better deals on their on-line purchases.[34] If successful, this move could restructure industry channels by encouraging more direct sales and thus fewer sales through the wholesale sector.

Another, perhaps even bigger, channels transformation could occur if the key players in entertainment, communications, and Internet sectors join forces. With the merger of AOL and Time Warner, for example, a media giant (Time Warner) brings its products to the delivery system or marketing channel (AOL). Thus, movies, music, periodicals, books, and television shows can gain an entirely new channel. What are the long-term implications for traditional resellers such as movie houses and bookstores? As the computer and other Net appliances gain penetration in the households of the world, such combinations could indeed transform the channels in several industries.

In the broadly defined entertainment and educational markets, companies such as Sony, Disney, Viacom (MTV, CBS, and Simon and Schuster) and Seagram (Universal Studios) are called **content providers.** AOL, Yahoo!, MSN, and Earthlink are among the portals through which hundreds of millions of consumers receive the content. Completing the channel structures are **pipes,** or the means used to get the content to the portals. Pipes include AT&T, MCI, Cablevision, and Comcast.[35] Some of these content providers, pipes, and portals are trying to become vertically integrated—that is, linked through ownership. Others are seeking channel partners to integrate operations from point of origin to point of consumption. As mergers and partnerships occur, the channels in the entertainment and educational sectors could be dramatically transformed.

INTEGRATING ELECTRONIC CHANNELS   When electronic channels are added to existing channels, marketers must strive to minimize conflict with other channel members. In many cases, this extends to encouraging cooperation between members of alternative channels so that channels are complementary. Multiple channels are often devised to meet the needs of different market segments or customer classification. This is one factor fueling the growth of electronic channels, as some consumers and business customers prefer to buy electronically. Electronic channels can also be an attractive alternative to the seller, as on-line transactions are often less expensive than other types of transactions, especially face-to-face transactions.

The addition of electronic channels can be threatening to people who work in alternative channels. For example, employees of a retail store who receive incentive pay for in-store sales may not embrace a company selling the same products on the Web. Lids Corporation, a

Integrating electronic channels with existing channels is an important task for most firms. Net Vendor helps companies do this successfully.

mall retailer best known for its extensive offering of hats and caps, added the Web as a sales channel with the full support of its in-store staff. Lids put together an educational program for employees in its 400 stores. Once the store employees were informed about the Web's ability to offer customers an additional 7,000 products and were taught how to assist on-line customers, Lids unveiled an incentive plan that let in-store employees earn money from on-line sales. Within a few months, 10 percent of store visitors became Web buyers—a sure sign that Lids had successfully integrated electronic channels into its existing channel.[36]

Pricing Issues in E-commerce

In this section, we will discuss two pricing issues particularly relevant to the e-commerce marketplace. First is the increase in price sensitivity brought about through the Web and related technology. The second issue concerns the use of price promotions, including some related accounting reporting issues.

PRICE SENSITIVITY IN E-COMMERCE   The most pervasive impact of the Web in the pricing area is that of more disclosure. For sellers on the Web, the whole world, including their competitors and suppliers, can easily see and compare prices. Both economic theory and consumer studies strongly suggest that the more buyers know about a seller's price relative to other sellers' prices, the more price sensitive they become. Marketers of hard-to-differentiate products and resellers of products available in multiple stores will encounter a higher proportion of price-sensitive consumers than will marketers of specialty goods.

Since Web shoppers can rely on software robots ("bots" as discussed in Chapter 4) to surf the Web for the best price rather than having to conduct their own searches, it is reasonable to expect that price sensitivity in many product categories will increase in the future. Marketers have mixed feelings about bots. Some resent them and try to block bots from their Web sites. These marketers may contact the bot's parent company and request an end to the bot's visits. Or they may employ their own software robots to encounter visiting bots and limit their access to the site. Some company Web sites block surfers whose browsers hide the surfer's address.[37] In the end, however, it is hard to completely block bots. Further, blocking bots can give consumers the impression that a company is not price competitive. As a result, many successful on-line marketers, including Amazon.com, welcome bots to their sites. As the number of e-commerce sites multiplies, consumers will have a harder time searching sites on their own, so the use of bots is expected to

Being Entrepreneurial

BizBuyer.com automates RFQs

Some business buyers issue requests for quotes (RFQs) the old-fashioned way. They develop the specifications for the product or service desired, contact current suppliers for quotes, search directories for other bidders, and try to get the word out through direct mail and phone calls. Others turn to BizBuyer.com, a California-based Web company that brings small businesses with services to sell together with potential buyers. The entire process is conducted on-line.

Vendors like BizBuyer because they gain new customers at a low cost of sales. Potential customers are already engaged in an active search for services, something that can be said only for a small percentage of prospects listed in other sources such as the Yellow Pages. BizBuyer helps inform potential buyers about the service they are seek-

ing by providing them with on-line buyer guides that explain industry terminology and give tips on how to assess alternative vendors. Further, BizBuyer requires potential buyers to define their needs in detail. The sales cycle moves fast because buyers can post 24 hours a day and bids are taken on a first-come, first-served basis.

Ultimately, the success of BizBuyer will depend on the quality of vendors it attracts. BizBuyer checks the credit and reputation of every vendor before allowing them to respond to RFQs. They also have a system so that buyers can rate vendors' quality, and this information is available to all potential buyers.

Source: Dana James, "Request for Cash," *Marketing News,* March 27, 2000, p. 11.

increase. For marketers of many products, the message is clear—if e-commerce is part of the plan, then be resolved to be price competitive.

Internet technology is also having an impact on business-to-business pricing. The "name-your-own-price" model, popularized by priceline.com in consumer markets, is gaining ground in business-to-business markets. Government buyers and other business purchasers who buy on bid can take advantage of Web sites that specialize in the facilitation of price quotes from a large number of vendors. For an example of such a site, see "Being Entrepreneurial: BizBuyer.com Automates RFQs."

MANAGING THE PRICE-PROMOTION MIX   Extensive use of price promotions by Internet marketers poses some interesting challenges for management. Sales promotions, including price promotions, are designed for short-term use to boost site traffic and sales. As many traditional retailers can attest, once consumers get used to price promotions, they may not shop unless a promotion is in effect. Internet merchants used a multitude of expensive promotions to build business in late 1999 and may consequently have a hard time returning to more profitable pricing levels. Free shipping, a particularly popular price promotion, offers one example. According to e-commerce experts from Forrester Research, "Free shipping is a costly promotion for snagging customers. But since retailers have started down this path, they will have a tough time turning back because consumers take shipping costs seriously."[38] This will be a more serious problem in the future, as bulkier products such as computers and other home electronics are forecasted to become a larger part of the mix of products sold on-line.

In the early years of e-commerce, price promotions were favored to build market share. However after the steep decline in stock prices for many Internet sellers in early 2000, the emphasis began to shift from volume to profitability. When price promotions are employed as a standard business practice rather than as a sales promotion, the profitability goal becomes even harder to attain. The lesson here is the same for dot coms as it has been for traditional merchants over the years—it is hard to make a profit when you give away too much in the way of promotions. Ultimately successful Internet marketers will be those who provide superior value. Some will be able to do that by operating at lower costs than their competitors do, but many will succeed by offering superior products, information, and service.

Another aspect of managing price promotions comes at the marketing/accounting/top management interface. In standard accounting practice, discounts (including price promotions) are deducted from total sales to yield net sales. Net sales less cost of goods equals gross margin. CDNOW, in a break from accepted accounting practice, charges its on-line coupons off as a marketing expense, not as a price discount. If a customer buys a $25 video and uses a $10 coupon, CDNOW books $25 in revenue, and books the $10 coupon as a marketing expense. As this book went to press, the Securities and Exchange Commission was contemplating a requirement that coupon values be subtracted; otherwise, sales revenue is overstated.[39]

E-commerce marketers face all of the traditional challenges of traditional marketers and more. Strategy that links the target market with the appropriate marketing mix is still the key to success. As e-commerce matures, two areas are becoming especially important for those firms that will succeed. These areas relate to two key marketing perspectives: improving productivity and establishing long-term trust-based relationships with customers.

Improving Productivity   E-commerce firms have faced the reality that they

must focus on profitability, not just sales volume. In the period from March 10, 2000, through April 11, 2000, the Hambrecht & Quist Internet Index fell 33 percent, indicating that investors were losing faith in Internet-based companies.[40] Investors had become concerned about how much money it was taking to generate sales volume and the resulting lack of profit in the sector. According to Merrill Lynch, up to three-fourths of all Internet companies face elimination through

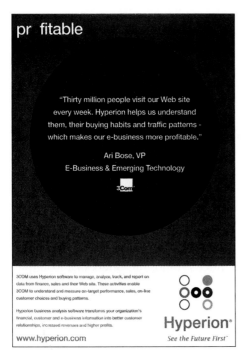
This ad relates how Hyperion helps 3Com improve the profitability of its e-business operations.

bankruptcy or consolidation. *Business Week* magazine offered this opinion: "Companies with unique models that are specific to the Web, like priceline.com and eBay, are considered likely winners, while those with great customer service and new revenue streams like Amazon.com are also well-positioned. But across the board, companies will have to show a clear path to profitability and the ability to manage costs. Now that's a blast from the past."[41]

For most Internet-based companies, the pressure to improve profitability falls largely on marketing, where most expenses originate. The good news is that the Web and related technology can help improve productivity and profitability. This is true both for Internet-based companies as well as for those who use the Web as a major business tool. As shown in Exhibit 21–5, the Lucent Technologies Power Systems unit used the Web to improve operations, cut costs, and improve sales.

Countless companies have found the Internet to be a cost-effective way to process orders and service requests. Citibank provides its customers e-commerce services that generate significant savings. According to Citibank's vice president for e-commerce, Vibhav Panadiker, "By processing orders over the Internet, many of our customers have been able to reduce costs by as much as 75 percent. When both front-end and back-end processes are automated, reducing costs per order from $150 to $40 is quite possible."[42]

The Web can also be more productive in some cases as an alternative to an existing marketing practice. MarketHome Inc., a direct-mail company based in California, began using Web-based e-mail campaigns instead of the traditional postal mode. MarketHome is now a believer in the Web, as its return-on-investment was five to six times greater than the previous method. According to a spokesperson, MarketHome has clients that have generated up to $1 million in revenue from a $6,000 investment in direct marketing on the Web.[43]

The Web can also take over routine activities, thus freeing current personnel to concentrate on higher-stakes activities. This is the case at Carlson Wagonlit Travel, where lower-fare airline flights, such as short shuttle trips, are booked entirely on the Web. This allows Carlson's outbound telemarketing personnel to concentrate on high-potential customers.[44]

Improving marketing productivity will be a key to survival and success for most e-commerce companies. They will also need to establish long-term trust-based customer relationships to remain competitive.

Exhibit 21–5	*Lucent improves productivity with the Web*	
Lucent Web Advantage		
How Lucent uses the Net to help it cut costs and turn information into business opportunities.		
Challenge	**Solution**	**Payoff**
Needed to slash costs without slashing jobs.	**Use the Web** to automate clerical functions and paperwork.	**Helped to reduce costs** from 24.2% of revenue in 1996 to 21.3% this year.
Customers who wanted Lucent to prepare cost-benefit analyses on equipment had to wait days or weeks.	**Internal Web sites** let customers prepare their own cost-benefit reports, using special Q&A templates.	**Customers bypass** the waiting list that delayed work by days, giving Lucent an edge over rivals on customer service.
It used to take days for the salesforce to get key information about competitors' contract wins and losses.	**Internal Web site** and business intelligence software keep sales teams up-to-date on competitors' movements.	**Salesforce** can tap data instantly via their laptops, helping them to customize and close deals in hours rather than days.
Administrative costs at Lucent's Texas-based Power Systems unit were rising.	**Internal Web sites** were created to speed transactions and eliminate paperwork on product orders.	**Unit's sales** rose 20% and headcount fell 16% during FY$_{99}$, thanks to convenience and faster service.

Source: Steve Rosenbush, "Lucent in a Rush," *Business Week*, E.BIZ, December 13, 1999, pp. EB46.

Building Relationships in E-commerce

Mutually beneficial, long-term buyer–seller relationships are based on economics and trust. Economics essentially defines the value proposition—that is, does the customer receive sufficient value from the seller to maintain the business relationship? Our discussion of the marketing mix issues in e-commerce, including customer service, pricing, and product considerations, serves as a reminder that a relationship will not exist unless the seller is providing adequate value.

Trust is also a key element in the establishment of ongoing relationships. This is an especially crucial area for e-commerce marketers, as many potential consumers have some reservations about the trustworthiness of on-line marketers. Current on-line customers generally find e-commerce marketers to be highly reliable and worthy of customer trust. Yet on-line sales are made to only a small percentage of consumers. To expand this number, trust building is essential. As shown in Exhibit 21–6, trust-based collaboration between buyers and sellers is based on five building blocks: site security; merchant legitimacy; fulfillment; tone; and customer control.[45]

Site Security

A significant number of potential e-commerce customers are reluctant to share credit card and other personal information necessary to buy on-line. There are also concerns about viruses that could be contracted when visiting Web sites. These fears are multiplied when hackers break into e-commerce sites. Early in 2000, hackers showed just how vulnerable sites can be by breaking into Yahoo!, eBay, Amazon.com., and E*Trade. These sites were shut down for hours at a time, and consumers worried that their credit card information may have been captured by the hackers.

To maximize site security, site operators use **encryption** to convert readable messages into an unreadable format unless the reader is authorized by the system. **Authentication,** which verifies the identity of users and hardware, is also essential for secure sites. **Data integrity** is required, meaning that data cannot be corrupted by viruses, destroyed, or changed without authorization. The process of **nonrepudiation** is another key element in building site security; this precludes the later denial of a valid transaction by either the buyer or seller. **Customer privacy** (discussed in the last section of this chapter), protects the data from unauthorized viewing.[46] With these processes and safeguards in place, e-commerce marketers can offer their customers a reasonably safe site, perhaps even a guaranteed-safe site.

Merchant Legitimacy

Marketers of well-established, high-quality branded merchandise have an advantage in achieving merchant legitimacy. So do leading retailers who have added e-commerce to their store base. Examples include Barnes and Noble, Kmart, and Toys " Я " Us. Many business-to-business companies already had achieved legitimacy, or credibility, with customers before moving into e-commerce. For most start-ups and marketers of lesser-known brands or unbranded merchandise, offering risk-free trial periods and strong customer satisfaction guarantees could be effective.

Marketing communications can also affect the perceived legitimacy of lesser-known e-commerce merchants. Referring again to

Exhibit 21–6

Building trust on-line

Trust

Differentiators — Consumer collaboration

Tone | Customer control

Fulfillment

Basic building blocks — State-of-the-art security | Merchant legitimacy

Source: Sandeep Dayal, Helene Landesberg, and Michael Zeisser, "How to Build Trust On-line," *Marketing Management,* Fall 1999, p. 65.

Online marketers must pay close attention to site security in order to build trust-based customer relationships. RSA Security offers its expertise in Web security in this ad.

Super Bowl advertising, the most expensive ad time on television, many start-ups were trying to establish legitimacy in the minds of their target customers. While most start-ups failed to establish legitimacy with their Super Bowl ads, some did move a step closer. Examples include OurBeginning.com and Computer.com, with both reporting millions of new visitors to their sites in the days following the Super Bowl.

Fulfillment

Fulfillment refers to meeting customer expectations in an efficient manner. Customer service again comes to the forefront, and it is important to note that customer service is not restricted to after-the-sale status. The Boston Consulting Group reports that 80 percent of on-line purchasers have experienced at least one failed purchase during their past 12 months of shopping and that 25 percent of all attempted on-line purchases fail. Typical reasons for failure include technical problems with the Web site, difficulties in finding products, and delivery problems after the sale.

Lands' End and Gap offer good examples of how to ensure fulfillment. Lands' End overhauled its site in 1999—and doubled its sales. The site features multiple opportunities for the customer to interact with the company, including electronic chats with customer service agents 24 hours a day.[47] The Gap site is also customer-friendly and allows shoppers to compare the fit of items, say a loose fit versus a classic fit. By encouraging interaction and dialogue, Lands' End and Gap do a good job fulfilling customer expectations.

Tone

Web site content and dialogue with customers should always be friendly and straightforward. This is absolutely as important in electronic exchanges as it is in other communications exchanges such as between a salesperson and the customer. Web site design, content, and navigation should be coordinated and customer-focused. Disclosures and policies related to purchases and delivery should be clearly identifiable and easy to interpret.

At L.L. Bean's Web site, all of these points are covered in an inviting, simple format. The site features a "Start Here Go Anywhere" button, a "Need Help?" icon, a simplified purchase process, and interesting content to explain how their hiking boots and other apparel and equipment meets the needs of their shoppers. Further, the tone is straightforward. For example, the site speaks directly to site security and consumer privacy issues: "llbean.com is a *secure* site that respects your *privacy.*"

Control

Customer trust is more easily achieved if the customer has a significant amount of control over the interaction. For example, at CDNOW, customers have an option of "one-click" buying or of checking and even rechecking order details before making the purchase. Allowing customers the option of sharing their personal information with other marketers is another way to grant the customer control. Alternative ways of doing this are discussed later in the ethical and legal discussion.

Personalization is another way to give customers more control. When consumers can receive relevant information in their preferred format—and even products tailored to individual tastes—the customer gains control. Actually, this a mutually beneficial occurrence, as it works to the benefit of the marketer as well as the customer.

The model shown in Exhibit 21–5 includes the basic elements for trust building between buyers and sellers in e-commerce. For any given situation, additional considerations could also be important. For example, in business-to-business arrangements, companies might be sharing sensitive data and might have additional security concerns such as the extent of employee access to the data. In the final section of the chapter, we discuss some of the key ethical and legal issues in e-commerce. Along with the factors discussed in this section, proper response to these issues is critical to the trust-building process.

John Parker, Director of Business Operations, Quixtar, talks about the importance of trust in building customer relationships: "Earning customer trust is critical for e-commerce businesses. One reason on-line shoppers trust Quixtar.com is that it's not an anonymous Web site to them, as many e-commerce sites are. People shopping at Quixtar.com are affiliated with Quixtar as an Independent Business Owner, or they know someone who is. This personal connection to the site helps shoppers feel more secure and adds a layer of personal trust that many faceless sites don't have. Security of personal information is also crucial to maintaining customer trust. We do not sell or share customer information with anyone under any circumstances. Strict adherence to this policy helps us establish long-term relationships with customers."

Ethical and Legal Issues

The newness of the Internet coupled with rapid growth, as well as the absence of regulations and guidelines to govern individual and marketer practices, have led to a number of ethical and legal questions. These questions include concerns about privacy, weblining, and fraudulent practices. Other important, and as yet to be determined, controversies center upon the role of state and national governments in the determination of Internet legislation and taxes.

Privacy

Because of the vast amount of data that can be collected on the Internet and because of the global nature of the Internet, private citizens, privacy groups, and governments worldwide have expressed concerns regarding the privacy of individuals and other users of the Internet. Currently, the most discussed issues include the profiling of web surfer activity in efforts to track advertising effectiveness and to target customers; the sharing of private information about individuals; and, concerns related to the rights and privacy of children and teens.[48] The privacy issue attracted significant attention recently in the wake of DoubleClick's disclosure that it planned to cross-reference previously anonymous data about on-line shopping habits with real names of people and addresses. This capability was made possible from information obtained through a direct-marketing company.[49]

The U.S. government is still willing to allow private industries the opportunity to devise sufficient privacy rights policies. However, these efforts have fallen short of expectations thus far.[50] Failure to address these privacy issues will undoubtedly lead to government intervention. This possibility has already occurred in the European Union through its Data Protection Directive. The directive bars transmission of personal information to other countries that do not have parallel safety guards.[51] These concerns are not unfounded. For example, a 1999 FTC study of Web merchants found that 90 percent of the companies polled collected personal information but that only 10 percent actually followed established Fair Information Practices—a philosophical framework for privacy protection that has been generally adopted worldwide over the past 25 years.[52]

The Federal Trade Commission has identified five core principles of privacy protection that are widely accepted in the United States, Canada, and Europe:[53]

- *Notice*—Making consumers aware before any personal information is gathered.

- *Choice*—The opportunity to consent to or forbid any secondary uses of information.

- *Access*—The ability to review any information gathered without significant delay.

Thinking Critically

Consider the Web site for a business-to-business firm, such as www.cisco.com, and the ability of the firm to interact with its suppliers and customers.

- What effects will e-commerce relationships between manufacturers and their existing suppliers have on other suppliers trying to obtain new business from those same manufacturers?

- Should business-to-business firms that engage in weblining be obligated to inform customers the status of their account (e.g., A, B, C), and, if so, why?

- *Integrity and security*—Personal information is processed accurately.
- *Enforcement*—Consumer should have recourse if any of the above core principles is violated.

In response to pressures regarding the use of information obtained on the Web, many companies have posted privacy polices that disclose how they collect, use, and share data with partners or advertisers. In addition, opt-in and opt-out choices are made available to consumers. The more stringent opt-in choice forbids the gathering and sale of data unless permission is given.[54]

The worst fears about privacy on the Internet lie in the use of **cookies**—tiny computer files, stored on users' PCs, that Web sites use to track visitors to their sites. By assigning each site visitor a unique cookie, accurate tallies of behavior can be determined. This information can also be used to evaluate advertising effectiveness and to then develop strategies for targeting individual shoppers with advertising.[55] Web sites desire to obtain demographic information because advertisers are willing to pay 7 to 10 times as much for the ability to direct messages to prescreened audiences.[56]

Another domain that has attracted consistent concern since the inception of the Internet is the effects of the Web on the rights and privacy of children and teens. In response to these concerns, the Children's Online Privacy Protection Act was passed. Sites that target visitors under the age of 13 will now have to obtain parental permission before collecting personal information.[57]

Weblining

The Internet lets companies identify high- and low-value customers, such that deals and special services can be targeted only to the most profitable customers. The positive aspects of this practice, now termed **weblining**, include increased profitability for the firm and enhanced services and prices for the most-valued customers. The downside aspects of the practice are troublesome. Specifically, people may be judged by their predicted behavior rather than by their actual behavior. Moreover, low-profit customers may have to pay more for products, and the needs of these less-profitable customers get less attention. To the extent that weblining affects the disadvantaged, the practice may unfairly discriminate.[58]

Sanwa Bank in California is only one of a number of banks where customer service representatives use Net-based programs to categorize customers as being A, B, or C customers. The least-valued Cs are the ones most likely to end up on hold when they call in for service. Weblining is growing in B2B marketing as well. Once an e-business identifies a customer, it knows how profitable it is to do business with that customer. E-businesses then focus their promotions and special services on their best customers, while giving ordinary customers higher costs and less service. This is consistent with efforts to maximize profits but raises questions of equal treatment. Other critics question the accuracy of the analysis programs underlying weblining practices.[59]

Fraud

Fraud and questionable practices on the Internet, both by individuals and by companies, have grown rapidly. For example, one-fourth of all consumer complaints identified by the Federal Trade Commission are now about the Internet, up from just 3 percent in 1997. Internet Fraud Watch, operated by the National Consumers' League, reported an increase of more than 600 percent in reports of fraud between 1997 and 1998. The Net has become a breeding ground for credit card fraud, auction rip-offs, get-rich schemes, and e-commerce sites that fail to deliver as promised.[60] The top ten scams on the Internet, as identified by *Business Week*, are listed in Exhibit 21–7.

Fraud on the Internet is attributable to both individuals and e-businesses. Regarding the former, individuals have used eBay's auction site to sell questionable-

Exhibit 21–7	*The top ten scams on the Internet*
1. Auction Fraud	You've topped the last bidder for the 1950 Gibson guitar. You send the check, but the guitar never arrives. When the goods do come, they're counterfeit or faulty.
2. Internet Access	Fly-by-night internet service providers offer too little bandwidth—or not Net connection at all—to far too many consumers.
3. Sales Fraud of Computers	This rip-off is so common it has its own category. Scammers feed on the urge by consumers to pay nearly nothing for such high-tech gear as PCs, laptop computers, or scanners. Often you get nothing.
4. All Other Sales Fraud	Shady e-commerce sites with enticing come-ons that promise huge savings on everything from televisions to old records—but never deliver.
5. Web Site Design	You just have to get your business on the Net. Be careful: Some folks promise to build a snazzy Web site, but don't.
6. Porn Sites	You can get railroaded into one of these sites. And before you know it, your phone bill is in the four-digit range because the site operator hijacked your Web connection to run up the tab.
7. Get-Rich-Quick	Just when authorities had begun to believe they had seen the end of these scams, the Net has revived pyramid schemes and other old frauds.
8. Sham Franchises	You pay serious dough for the exclusive rights to deliver widgets in your area. Guess what? No one wants them.
9. Work-at-Home	You answered the ad, and you've done the work. But the check's always in the mail.
10. Travel	That free trip you won sounds fantastic—and it turns out to be a fantasy, all right. You end up paying.

Source: Dan Carney, "Fraud on the Internet," *Business Week E.Biz,* April 3, 2000, p. EB62.

quality items, and a few purchases have been paid for but goods never delivered. Credit card scam artists use bogus credit cards to buy e-tickets picked up at the airport to avoid detection of differing addresses. In other instances, businesses prey on other small businesses. For example, Web page design companies have bilked small companies by charging exorbitant fees for Internet design work. Fraudulent "pump and dump" stock offerings begin with naïve consumers' buying a stock touted on the Internet via "spam" e-mail.[61]

In reaction to these abuses, both government and industry cybersleuths have begun to fight back. It should be noted that those individuals charged with identifying and prosecuting Internet abuses are becoming more and more effective. The FTC has become quite vigilant in investigating instances of fraud, deceptive advertising practices, and privacy abuses. The Securities and Exchange Commission has proposed an automated surveillance system that will search the Internet for "get-rich-quick schemes" and even monitor chat rooms for evidence of fraudulent appeals.[62]

Legislation

Given the newness of the Internet and the complex issues involved with e-commerce, regulations and legislation are still evolving. Most U.S. legislation so far has been supportive of the Internet industry. A listing of the most current legislation is presented in Exhibit 21–8. Briefly, this legislation, much of which is still pending, limits the poaching of Internet addresses, restricts Web gambling sites, gives digital signatures the legal weight of paper-and-pencil signatures, and continues tax credits that benefit technology and Internet companies.[63]

The situation in Europe is much more complex and restrictive. As examples, Denmark bans advertising to children, France bans advertising in English, and Germany bans comparative advertising. The European Union has also imposed limits

Exhibit 21–8	*Legislation affecting Internet commerce*		
	What It Does	**Pro**	**Con**
American Inventors Protection Act	Reduces patent fees, guarantees a 17-year patent term, and reduces litigation costs for patent owners.	Internet companies that hold many patents benefit.	Small businesses and inventors say it tips the balance in favor of big business.
Anticybersquatting Consumer Protection Act	Curbs poaching of trade-marked names for Internet addresses and imposes $100,000 fine on "dot-con artists" who profiteer.	E-commerce community believes business will grow only if trademark holders feel protected on-line.	Cyber-rights groups say individual domain-name holders and small businesses are in peril.
Internet Gambling Prohibition Act of 1999	Senate measure bans Web gambling sites, violators face fines of $20,000 and jail terms to four years; House has not yet approved companion measure.	Organized gambling was the primary supporter.	Internet gambling houses, many of which are located offshore, would lose out. Sports sites won exemption of fantasy sports games.
Millennium Digital Commerce Act/Electronic Signatures in Global and National Commerce Act	Would give digital signatures the legal weight of pen-and-paper counterparts; House and Senate measures still need to be reconciled before going to the president.	E-commerce companies see on-line signatures clearing the way for instant Internet transactions and contracts.	Consumer groups fear House version allows businesses to notify consumers by e-mail rather than letters.
Satellite Home Viewer Improvement Acts	Allows satellite-TV carriers to compete with cable companies by running local stations; does not ban Internet companies from doing the same.	Local broadcasters benefit; they won the right to charge potentially higher rates to satellite carriers than cable companies.	Excluding Net companies is a blow to the National Association of Broadcasters and the Motion Picture Association.
Ticket to Work and Work Incentive Act	Provides companies with a five-year extension of the research and development tax credit.	Benefits every technology and Internet lobbying group.	Technology lobbies were seeking a permanent extension but failed due to congressional restrictions.

Source: Elizabeth Wasserman, "Score Another Round for the Internet Industry," *The Industry Standard,* December 6, 1999, p. 66 (www.thestandard.com).

on the transference of data to third countries where assurances of privacy are inadequate. In one court case, Lands' End's traditional 100 percent guarantee for any clothing worn out was found to be unlawful.[64] In other areas of the world, such as China, governments are suspicious of Internet commerce because of perceived threats to government control.[65]

Taxes

The imposition of sales taxes on e-commerce continues to be debated. As long as the Web site operator has no physical presence in a state, the on-line marketer can currently avoid charging any sales tax applied in that state. Proponents of a tax-free Internet argue that e-commerce offers extensive opportunities for new growth and innovation and that governments should not threaten this growth through the addition of sales taxes. In addition, traditional retailers are going on-line more and more and the convenience of consumers should be paramount. Other detractors of Internet taxes argue that most e-commerce results from business-to-business sales, most of which are exempt from sales taxes because the goods involve purchases for resale or manufacturing or for nontaxable business services.[66]

Opposition to tax-free Internet sales comes from (1) state and local governments that receive 36 percent of their tax revenues from sales taxes and that consequently worry about future loss of government revenues and (2) some traditional brick-and-mortar retail establishments that feel they are being placed at a severe competitive disadvantage because they are required to charge and collect sales taxes. Others argue that the failure to tax Internet sales is bad social policy. This position is based upon the fact that Internet sales come disproportionately from wealthier individuals—those least in need of a tax break. According to one study, on-line shoppers have average household incomes of $56,320 compared with an average of $22,940 for families without Net access.[67]

The actual impact of imposing sales taxes on Internet revenues remains unclear. One study found that imposing taxes on the Internet would cut sales by 25 percent; most economists feel the impact of taxes would in reality be much less than that. So far, the amount of state revenues being lost is small, as e-retailing accounts for a still small percentage of total retail sales. However, state governments are concerned about the challenge and potential losses in the face of predictions that depict continuing rapid rates of growth of e-commerce retail sales.[68]

Summary

1. **Explain the differences between e-business, e-commerce, and e-marketing.** E-business includes all business activities conducted over the Internet, and e-marketing includes all marketing activities conducted over the Internet. E-commerce is restricted to using the Internet directly for buying and selling products. E-commerce is part of e-business and e-marketing.

2. **Discuss the benefits of e-commerce to buyers and sellers.** Buyers benefit from e-commerce through more-convenient shopping, more choices, better information, better prices, and the ability to customize both the shopping experience and some purchases. Sellers benefit from an expanded market of potential customers and the ability to offer buyers many product alternatives, to collect information about customers, to meet the specific needs of customers, to communicate with customers, and to have lower costs in some areas.

3. **Describe the current activity and trends in B2C and B2B e-commerce.** Both B2C and B2B e-commerce are growing rapidly; growth differs for different areas and types of products. B2C will expand as more consumers in more countries use the Internet; the longer the Internet usage, the more products purchased electronically. B2B is growing faster than B2C. This will likely continue as more firms move their purchasing activities to the Internet and purchase products electronically from specific firms or from the procurement exchanges being established.

4. **Discuss key e-commerce marketing issues in each area of the marketing mix.** In the marketing communications area, we discussed emerging technologies such as wireless Web services and broadband Internet technology, both of which will allow marketers to reach more customers with more exciting messages. Other important issues include how to attract customers, how to improve customer involvement to generate return visits, and how to implement ongoing dialogue with customers. The integration of e-commerce communications with other marketing communications was also discussed. In the product area, the discussion was devoted to the importance of customer service and the threat posed by marketers of imitation products. Key issues in the channels area include the Web's ability to completely transform the channels for entire industries and the integration of electronic channels with other channels. Our pricing coverage focuses on how the Internet is increasing price sensitivity in consumer and business markets and on issues related to managing the price-promotion mix.

5. **Explain how the Internet and related technologies can help marketers improve the productivity of their activities.** Internet marketers must concentrate on improving profitability, which as a rule has not been acceptable to date. Most expenses for e-commerce firms originate in marketing. Some e-commerce marketers are reporting productivity improvements in order processing, and some forms of marketing on the Web are showing superior return-on-investment figures compared with previously used alternatives. Using the Web for routine activities can also free up personnel to work on higher-stakes activities.

6. **Describe how e-commerce marketers can build long-term trust-based relationships with their customers.** E-commerce marketers can build trust by building site security and earning the reputation of a legitimate merchant. They must complete the fulfillment process, which ensures that customer expectations are met. It is also important to communicate with customers in a friendly, helpful tone and to allow the customer to control a significant portion of the buyer–seller interaction.

7. **Understand the important legal and ethical issues associated with marketing practice and e-commerce.** The important legal and ethical issues include concerns about privacy, weblining, and fraud. Other important, and as yet to be determined, controversies center upon the role of state and national governments in the determination of legislation and taxes. Privacy concerns revolve around information obtained by companies and other organizations regarding customer addresses, clickstream patterns, financial data, and credit information. The Internet also allows companies to identify high- and low-value customers, such that deals and specials services can be targeted only to the most profitable customers. The positive aspects of this practice of weblining include increased profitability for the firm and enhanced services and prices for most-valued customers. Concerns have arisen, however, regarding the effects of weblining on less-fortunate customers. Fraudulent practices include credit card fraud, auction rip-offs, get-rich schemes, and e-commerce sites that fail to

deliver as promised. Proponents of a tax-free Internet argue that e-commerce offers extensive opportunities for new growth and innovation. Proponents of Internet taxes argue that traditional retailers are placed a competitive disadvantage and that state and local governments will suffer from lost revenues.

Understanding Marketing Terms and Concepts

Thinking About Marketing

1. How are the benefits of e-commerce different and similar for consumers versus organizational buyers?

2. How would you convince a local retailer to become involved in e-commerce?

3. What are the three most important trends you see for e-commerce in the next three years?

4. What can marketers do to attract customers to their e-commerce sites and to keep them coming back? How does trust building figure into these efforts?

5. How can the Internet transform the marketing channels for an entire industry?

6. Refer to "Being Entrepreneurial: BizBuyer.com Automates RFQs." What are the advantages of listing with a service such as BizBuyer for vendors? For buyers?

7. Why is it crucial for e-commerce marketers to improve productivity, and how might this be accomplished?

8. Refer to "Earning Customer Loyalty: Bol.com Recognizes Country Differences." Compare the differences in the sites for Britain and Germany. What segmentation principles are incorporated into the European-based dot com marketer?

9. What are the benefits associated with weblining that accrue to companies engaging in the practice? What ethical questions arise from the practice of weblining?

10. Contrast some of the problems associated with consumer fraud with the problems associated with marketer fraud.

11. What are the likely outcomes from the ongoing debate surrounding privacy concerns and marketer activity on the Internet?

Applying Marketing Skills

1. The growth of on-line retail sales is expected to soon reach $3 trillion. Yet, despite established brand names and marketplace presence, many traditional retailers have had difficulty in competing on-line. What aspects of marketing on-line from businesses to consumers cause problems for traditional intermediaries? Specifically, what has Kmart done to enhance its ability to compete effectively for on-line sales?

2. How do the Web sites of Ford and GM facilitate purchases from their suppliers? What cost reductions are possible from such e-commerce exchanges? What effects will e-commerce in B2B situations have on the maintenance of long-term exchange relationships? That is, will e-commerce for B2B companies strengthen or weaken efforts to develop lasting relationships among supply-chain partners?

3. Go to the www.shop.org site and consider the information presented regarding the state of on-line shopping. What are the key trends driving on-line industry sales growth? What lessons have been learned from the e-commerce experience of successful companies? What can be learned from the comparison between "Strictly Internet" and multichannel retailers? Describe the performance results from the most recent "State of On-line Retailing" annual report.

Using the www in Marketing

Activity One   Go to the CyberAtlas home page (http://cyberatlas.internet.com).

1. Select an e-commerce topic that interests you and use the search engine to identify information about this topic available from CyberAtlas.

2. Use information available from CyberAtlas to update the e-commerce statistics presented in the chapter.

3. What is your assessment of the CyberAtlas Web site? How could it be made more useful?

Activity Two   There are several other sites that provide e-commerce information similar to that of CyberAtlas. Go to eMarketer (http://estats.com) and The Standard (http://thestandard.net).

1. Compare and contrast the CyberAtlas, eMarketer, and The Standard Web sites. Which site do you think is the most useful? Why?

2. Search the CyberAtlas, eMarketer, and The Standard Web sites for the same e-commerce topic. Which site provides the most material on the topic? Does any site have information not available from the other sites?

3. How could marketers involved in e-commerce make use of these three Web sites?

Making Marketing Decisions

Case 21-1 Toys "Я" Us: Competing against Both Bricks and Clicks

In the extreme version of predictions regarding Internet efficiency, the characteristics of the Internet will lead to markets where retailer location is irrelevant and consumers are fully informed of prices and products. Such arguments support the success of early on-line retailers like Amazon.com. A frequently asked question is, Why have so many off-line businesses with well-recognized brand names been so slow to respond? The primary reasons appear to be fear that new channels (i.e., the Internet) merely cannibalize revenues from existing sources; existing salesforces and intermediaries are threatened; capital markets favor the "pure plays" of new on-line retailers; and existing distribution systems are not designed to focus on single packages delivered to individual households.

These issues and problems faced Toys "Я" Us as the firm sought to develop a presence on the Internet. Started in 1948, with the first toy supermarket opened in 1957, Toys "Я" Us has evolved into an $11 billion-plus-dollar business, with 1,450 stores worldwide. Traditionally, Toys "Я" Us has battled Kmart, Target, and Wal-Mart. During the late 1990s, even more formidable competition arose from eToys, the on-line retailer of toys and related children's products. According to Media Metrix on-line tracking data, eToys was the second-most-visited on-line site for the holiday shopping season in 1999. In 1998, in anticipation of the emergence of eToys, Toysrus.com was formed to enable shoppers to purchase on-line. It is important to note that returns to Toys "Я" Us were

facilitated by allowing consumers to return problem purchases to any of their conveniently located retail stores. In addition, the Web site for Toys "Я" Us now includes search engines to assist in the identification of desired gifts and procedures for enhanced delivery.

CEO Robert Nakasone addressed the threat from eToys aggressively. First, the firm established a separate on-line unit rather than attempting to refine its previous in-house capabilities. In addition, the firm combined with venture capitalist Benchmark Capital and moved the new on-line endeavor from its New Jersey headquarters to Northern California. These rather drastic actions were intended to quickly expand their competitive abilities in the face of the emergence of eToys and other on-line competition.

Questions

1. What accounts for the initial success of on-line competitor eToys?

2. What competitive advantages does Toys "Я" Us have over eToys because of its long-term marketplace presence?

3. How can Toys "Я" Us sell effectively on the Internet and still maintain satisfactory relationships with its brick-and-mortar retail outlets?

4. What trends in e-commerce are likely to cause additional problems for Toys "Я" Us?

SOURCES: Erik Brynjolfsson and Michael D. Smith, "Frictionless Commerce? A Comparison of Internet and Conventional Retailers," *Management Science,* 2000 (forthcoming); Nanette Byrnes and Paul C. Judge, "Internet Anxiety," *Business Week,* June 28, 1999, pp. 79–88; and John Peet, "E-Commerce: Shopping around the Web," *The Economist,* February 26, 2000, pp. 15–16.

Case 21-2 DoubleClick: Tracking Advertising or Individual Behavior

DoubleClick describes its core purpose as "being in the business of making advertising work on the Web." The firm sells and manages on-line advertisements for thousands of Web sites. To relieve marketers from the aggravation of inserting ads on thousands of sites, DoubleClick stores ads from its advertisers on central computers and coordinates the placement of the ads. DoubleClick relies heavily upon cookies placed on computers, generally when a site is visited for the first time. As such, DoubleClick is an industry leader in using technology and media expertise to create solutions that help advertisers employ the Web for selling products and building relationships with customers. Recent events, however, have placed considerable pressures upon the New York–based firm. The first involves the furor and concern over individual privacy. Second, many large, well-known marketers want to maintain control of Web-based customer information related to their own advertising.

Considering the first of these two issues, privacy concerns and the monitoring of consumer behavior on the Web remain contested issues. In early 2000, DoubleClick generated a heated reaction from critics when the firm purchased an off-line database for $1.7 billion and announced plans to match previously anonymous on-line behavior with names, addresses, and other personal information. In the face of considerable pressures, the firm canceled its initial plans but has not ruled out linking on-line profiles with off-line identities. Specifically, a series of lawsuits and FTC investigations caused the change in plans of DoubleClick. By joining the two databases, DoubleClick had hoped to create a perfect marketing tool to sell to advertisers. Such a merger of data sources would be effective at guiding one-to-one marketing campaigns with advertising tailored at the individual level.

Privacy standards are expected to emerge from industry groups such as the Internet Advertising Bureau and the American Association of Advertising Agencies. The FTC will undoubtedly influence the standards as well. Major Internet privacy bills are already being considered by Congress, while most state legislatures are considering regulations. DoubleClick has hired a consumer expert to oversee its privacy activities. In addition, DoubleClick has begun to promote its "opt-out" option as a reasonable solution for consumers and marketers. It is important to note that data collectors intent upon offering data-based target marketing must convince the public of the benefits of participating.

Pressures on DoubleClick are also being applied from the marketer side. General Motors, Ford Motor Company, IBM, and Procter & Gamble are leading a list of companies that are trying to block Internet ad companies like DoubleClick from controlling data regarding movement on the Internet related to their sites and their customers. Even well-known ad agencies like WPP Group's J. Walter Thompson have arranged to obtain exclusive use of the data from DoubleClick associated with their ad campaigns.

Questions

1. What are the ethical issues associated with the primary focus of DoubleClick?

2. What environmental influences are likely to affect the future of the firm's business in both Europe and the United States?

3. How might the advertising industry assist DoubleClick in its efforts to ensure consumer privacy?

SOURCES: "Crisis Rx for DoubleClick," *Advertising Age,* February 28, 2000, p. 58; "DoubleClick Blinks," *Newsweek,* March 13, 2000, p. 72; Anita Hamilton, "Data Mining: DoubleClick's Double Take," *Time,* March 13, 2000, p. 95; http://www.doubleclick.com...any_info/about_doubleclick/overview.htm, March 27, 2000; Kathryn Kranhold and Michael Moss, "Keep Away from My Cookies, More Marketers Say," *The Wall Street Journal,* March 20, 2000, pp. B1, B6; Patrick Thibodeau, "Dotcoms Wary of Privacy Bills: DoubleClick Furor May Push Regulation Drive," *Computerworld,* March 13, 2000, p. 1; Fred Vogelstein, "Minding One's Business," *U.S. News & World Report,* March 13, 2000, p. 45; and Rick Whiting, "DoubleClick Gets Double Trouble with Database Plan," *Information Week,* March 6, 2000, p. 24.

Appendix A

Applications of Mathematical and Financial Tools to Marketing Decisions

Marketing decisions are often enhanced by the use of mathematical and financial analyses. These computations are helpful in setting prices, evaluating financial aspects of the firm, evaluating suppliers, determining inventory order quantities, and estimating segment potentials. Analysis of the firm's income statement is crucial for control and performance evaluation. This appendix describes and presents example calculations for some of the most frequently used mathematical and financial tools.

Supplier Selection

Business buyers frequently use weighted indexes to evaluate suppliers. As explained in Chapter 5, buyers base decisions regarding selection of suppliers or vendors on the criteria they consider most important. Exhibit A–1 shows a simplified weighted index approach for evaluating two suppliers, A and B. This example is from the experiences of General Electric and its purchases of electrical wiring devices.

In this example, five criteria are used to evaluate two suppliers: quality performance, delivery performance, technical capability, quoted price, and service factors. Price and delivery performance are weighted most heavily. These weights reflect a consensus of managerial judgment and past experiences with purchases of this type of product. Each supplier is evaluated on a 1-to-10 scale for each attribute, with 10 being the best possible rating. The scores are multiplied by an importance weight for

Exhibit A–1	*Simplified weighted decision matrix*				
		Supplier A		**Supplier B**	
Evaluation Criteria	**Importance Weight**	**Score**	**Total**	**Score**	**Total**
Quality performance	16%	9.6	154	9.3	149
Delivery performance	22	8.1	178	7.6	167
Technical capability	8	10.0	80	8.0	64
Quoted price	44	7.5	330	9.3	409
Service factors	10	6.4	64	8.8	88
Overall total	**100%**	—	**806**	—	**877**

each criterion. The "total" columns are summed to produce a score for each supplier. In this case, supplier B, with an overall total score of 877, is selected as the preferred vendor.

Estimating Segment Potentials

The "Survey of Buying Power" published annually by *Sales & Marketing Management* magazine, enables the computation of the *buying power index (BPI)* for individual geographic market segments. Frequently used to evaluate market segment potentials, the BPI is a measure of a particular market's ability to buy. The index converts three basic elements—population, effective buying income (EBI), and retail sales—into a measure of a market's ability to purchase, expressed as a percentage of the total U.S. potential. The three elements are weighted as follows: 0.2, population; 0.3, U.S. retail sales potential; and 0.5, EBI, or effective buying income. The latter weight reflects the importance of income to buying potential. The BPI for a market can be computed as:

$$BPI = (0.5)(EBI) + (0.3) \text{ (Retail sales \%)} + (0.2) \text{ (Population \%)}$$

The computations in Exhibit A–2 provide an example. Specifically, a skiing equipment company in West Virginia is considering expanding its sales operations into one of two neighboring states, Pennsylvania or Kentucky. The company offers premier equipment that it sells at premium prices. Their equipment is targeted toward young adults, aged 25 to 45 years old, with an EBI of at least $35,000.

The figures in Exhibit A–2 suggest that Pennsylvania offers the greatest potential as a market. However, other factors, such as the cost of living, competition, and the legal environment, may differ between these two states as well. Consequently, BPI comparisons should be used in conjunction with other information.

Exhibit A–2	*Evaluating geographic target segments*		
	Pennsylvania	**Kentucky**	**United States**
Households aged 25–45	1,805,780	590,118	41,231,931
Households EBI > $35,000	2,046,065	483,254	42,555,244
General merchandise stores' sales ($000)	$9,230,884	$3,448,368	$182,310,557

To construct a customized BPI for evaluating each state, the company made the following calculations:

Step 1. The ratio of each state's markets to those of the entire United States are:

Pennsylvania	Kentucky
% of households aged 25–45:	% of households aged 25–45:
1,805,780/41,231,931 = .043	590,118/41,231,931 = .014
% of households EBI > $35,000:	% of households EBI > $35,000:
2,046,065/42,555,244 = .048	483,254/42,555,244 = .011
% of general merchandise stores' sales:	% of general merchandise stores' sales:
$9,230,884/$182,310,557 = .051	$3,448,368/$182,310,557 = .019

Step 2. The company assigns importance weights as follows:

Households aged 25–45	(20%) or .20
Households EBI > $35,000	(50%) or .50
General merchandise stores' sales	(30%) or .30

Note: These weights sum to 1.0.

Step 3. The BPI is the weighted sum of the three components:

Pennsylvania

$(.20 \times .043) + (.50 \times .048) + (.30 \times .051) = .0479$

Kentucky

$(.20 \times .014) + (.50 \times .011) + (.30 \times .019) = .0140$

Price Determination

In this section of the appendix, we discuss the break-even formula, elasticities of demand, and methods for computing retail markups. First, we present break-even formulas for quantity (units) and revenue (dollars). Second, we look at examples of other forms of elasticity and discuss profit maximization. Third, we explain markups and markdowns.

Break-Even Analysis

The traditional break-even formula is based on the premise that the break-even point in units occurs when total revenues equal total costs. The break-even quantity in units is defined as:

$$Q(BE) = \frac{\text{Fixed costs}}{\text{Price} - \text{Variable cost per unit}}$$

The break-even point in dollars is computed as:

$$Q(BE\$) = \frac{\text{Fixed costs}}{1 - (\text{Variable cost} / \text{Price})}$$

The *BEP* in units is derived as follows. Remember that the *BEP* occurs where total costs equal total revenues:

$$TR = TC$$
$$P \times Q = FC + (VC \times Q)$$
$$\text{and } TC = FC + (VC \times Q)$$
$$P \times Q - VC \times Q = FC$$
$$Q(P - VC) = FC$$

Therefore, the *BEP* in units is $Q(BEP) = FC/(P - VC)$.

This analysis can be extended by considering the effects of different prices and quantity demanded. For example, the data presented in Exhibit A–3 show how the break-even quantity can vary as prices rise and demand declines. Notice the inverse relationship between price and demand. In this example, total fixed cost is $15,000 and variable cost per unit is $7.

This "sensitivity analysis" allows managers to consider alternative assumptions and conditions. It greatly enhances the managerial usefulness and realism of the break-even approach.

Elasticity

Price elasticity represents the change in quantity demanded from a change in price. Elasticities greater than 1 indicate elastic demand; that is, a 1 percent change in price causes a greater percentage change in demand. Inelastic demand occurs when a 1 percent price change results in less than a 1 percent change in demand. A commonly used computational approach for estimating elasticity is to compute the arc

Exhibit A–3						Break-even points from different prices and quantity demanded	
Price	Quantity Demanded (000s)	Total Revenue ($000)	Total Fixed Costs ($000)	Total Variable Costs ($000)	Total Costs ($000)	Break-Even Quantity (000s)	Profit ($000)
$10	5.0	$50.0	$15.0	$35.0	$50.0	5.00	$ 0.0
11	4.8	52.8	15.0	33.6	48.6	3.75	4.2
12	4.7	56.4	15.0	32.9	47.9	3.00	8.5
13	4.6	59.8	15.0	32.2	47.2	2.50	12.6
14	4.0	56.0	15.0	28.0	43.0	2.14	13.0
15	3.4	51.0	15.0	23.8	38.8	1.87	12.2

elasticity, where the price elasticity of demand is measured over a range using the average price and quantity as the base.

Arc elasticity of demand is computed as follows:

$$E_d = \frac{(Q_2 - Q_1)/[(Q_1 + Q_2)/2]}{(P_2 - P_1)/[(P_1 + P_2)/2]}$$

For example, at the price of $6 per ticket, the average moviegoer demands two tickets per month. At a price of $4 per ticket, the average moviegoer purchases six tickets per month. The price elasticity for this example is:

$$E_d = \frac{(6 - 2)/[(6 + 2)/2]}{(4 - 6)/[(4 + 6)/2]} = -2.5$$

Therefore, the price elasticity of demand over this price range is elastic. Remember that price elasticities are normally negative and that typically the negative sign, while shown here, is omitted.

Cross-price elasticity reflects quantity changes in one good or service caused by changing prices of other goods or services. This concept is useful for examining relationships among complementary goods (printers, personal computers) and substitutes (competitive brands, items in a product line, and pure substitutes such as videotape rental charges and movie prices). Conceptually, cross elasticity can be expressed as:

$$E_c = \frac{\text{Change in quantity demanded for product A}}{\text{Change in price for product B}}$$

If E_c is positive, products A and B are substitutes. If E_c is negative, the two products are complementary.

Assume the price of a Kodak 35-millimeter camera is $145 and a comparable Minolta is $149. Further, assume the quantities demanded for the Kodak and Minolta cameras at these prices are 50,000 and 100,000 units, respectively. When Kodak lowers its price to $142, the demand increases to 60,000. The Minolta demand, however, declines to 95,000 units. The cross-price elasticity for the Minolta camera is:

$$E_c = \frac{-5,000/100,000}{-\$3/\$145} = 2.42$$

In this example, the two cameras are substitutes; hence, decreasing the price of one brand decreases the demand for the other.

Profit Maximization

The traditional economic perspective on price setting is based on the premise that profits are maximized when marginal revenue equals marginal cost. Marginal revenue is the amount obtained from selling one additional unit of a product—this is usually the price paid for the unit. Marginal cost is the cost of producing and selling one additional unit of a product.

The cost and revenue data presented in Exhibit A–4 can be used to analyze these relationships for a hypothetical manufacturer of personalized T-shirts. The corresponding cost and revenue curves are depicted in Exhibit A–5. Note that in columns 4, Marginal Revenue, and 7, Marginal Cost, the manufacturer continues to expand output as long as marginal revenue exceeds marginal cost. Any expansion in output beyond this point would increase costs more than it would revenue. Therefore, the optimal output is four units priced at $6. Profits are maximized at that level:

$$\text{Profits} = TR - TC = \$24 - \$18 = \$6$$

Exhibit A–5 plots these findings. It shows that profits are maximized when price equals $6 and quantity equals 4. Notice that marginal costs initially decline as output increases. The shaded profit area is computed by multiplying unit profit times quantity of output:

$$\begin{aligned} \text{Profits} &= (AR - ATC) \times Q \\ &= (\$6 - \$4.50) \times 4 \\ &= \$6 \end{aligned}$$

Exhibit A-4   *Sales and cost information for personalized T-shirts*

(1) Quantity Q	(2) Price P	(3) Total revenue $TR = Q \times P$	(4) Marginal revenue MR	(5) Total cost TC	(6) Average total cost $ATC = \dfrac{TC}{Q}$	(7) Marginal cost MC	(8) Profit $\pi =$ $TR - TC$
0	$10	$ 0		$ 2.00	—		$ -2.00
1	9	9	$ 9	9.00	$9.00	$ 7.00	0.00
2	8	16	7	14.00	7.00	5.00	2.00
3	7	21	5	15.00	5.00	1.00	6.00
4	6	24	3	18.00	4.50	3.00	6.00
5	5	25	1	22.50	4.50	4.50	2.50
6	4	24	-1	30.00	5.00	7.50	-6.00
7	3	21	-3	49.00	7.00	19.00	-28.00

Exhibit A-5   *Intersection of marginal cost and marginal revenue curves*

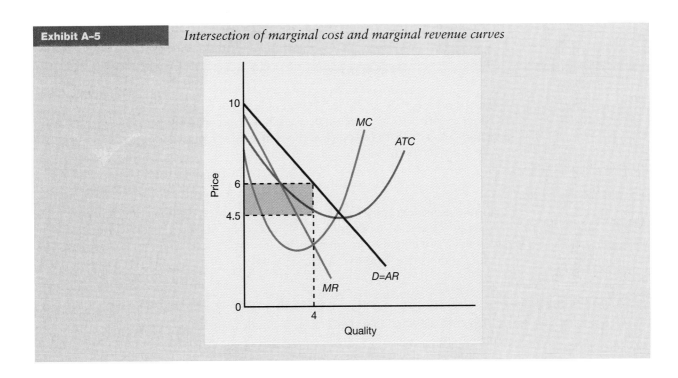

In this case, unit profit is the difference between average revenue and average total cost.

Markups and Markdowns

Retail markups can be computed on either cost or the selling price. Markup as a percentage of cost is calculated as:

$$\text{Markup} = \frac{\text{Selling price} - \text{Cost}}{\text{Cost}}$$

Assume, for example, that a new Wilson tennis racket costs a retailer $90 and the markup is $50. Therefore, the selling price is $140. The markups on cost and price are:

Markup on cost = $50/$90 = 56%
Markup on price = $50/$140 = 36%

Frequently, retailers desire to convert markup percentages on cost to markup percentages on price and vice versa. The computational procedures for making these conversions are:

$$\text{Markup on cost} = \frac{\text{Markup on selling price}}{100\% - \text{Markup on selling price}}$$

$$\text{Markup on price} = \frac{\text{Markup on cost}}{100\% + \text{Markup on cost}}$$

Price reductions are common practice in retailing. In these instances, the retailer may wish to know what the percentage markdown is:

$$\text{Markdown on initial selling price} = \frac{\text{Initial selling price} - \text{Reduced sale price}}{\text{Initial selling price}}$$

$$\text{Markdown on reduced sale price} = \frac{\text{Initial selling price} - \text{Reduced sale price}}{\text{Reduced sale price}}$$

Return on Inventory Investment

Retailers evaluate merchandising performance of departments using the *gross margin return on inventory investments (GMROI)*. The GMROI combines the effects of both profits and turnover. Since both are considered, the GMROI enables comparison between retail store areas that differ in turnover and gross margin. It is computed as:

$$GMROI = \frac{\text{Gross margin}}{\text{Net sales}} \times \frac{\text{Net sales}}{\text{Average inventory}} = \frac{\text{Gross margin}}{\text{Average inventory}}$$

Average inventory is usually expressed in terms of costs.

Inventory turnover, which is also used to evaluate how well investments in inventory are used, is the number of times inventory turns over or is sold, typically in a year. Inventory turnover is computed as:

$$\text{Inventory turnover} = \frac{\text{Costs of goods sold}}{\text{Average inventory cost}}$$

where average inventory equals (Beginning inventory + Ending inventory)/2. If for example, the cost of goods sold during a year was $600,000 and the average inventory was $200,000, then inventory turnover was 3. This value can be compared with that of competitive firms to evaluate inventory investment and firm performance.

Balancing Physical Distribution Costs

One of the objectives of a distribution system is to provide adequate levels of customer service at reasonable costs. Companies would like to carry high inventories so they can fill orders promptly and maintain high service levels. As inventories increase, however, costs to the firm rise as well. These relationships are depicted graphically in Exhibit A–6.

As Exhibit A–6 shows, total costs represent the sum of two offsetting costs. Order-processing costs, which decline as average inventory increases, include setup costs, manufacturing costs, and administrative costs. Inventory-carrying costs increase as average inventory increases. Carrying costs include storage, insurance, investment, and obsolescence costs. The *economic order quantity (EOQ)* model offers one approach for determining inventory order quantities that balance these costs. Specifically, the EOQ model can be derived from the total cost relationships presented in Exhibit A–6 as follows:

$$\text{Total costs} = \text{Carrying costs} + \text{Ordering costs} = \frac{QCI}{2} + \frac{RS}{Q}$$

where

Q = order quantity,
C = unit cost,
I = opportunity cost (%),
R = annual demand, and
S = ordering, setup cost.

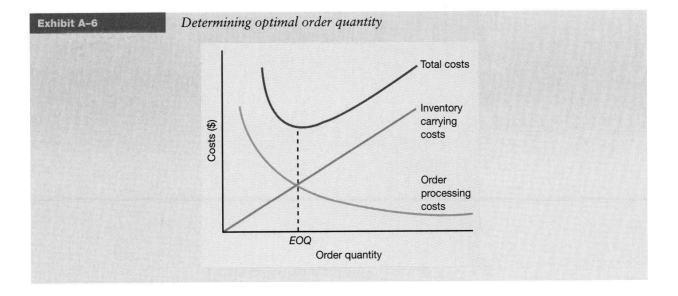

Note that ($Q/2$) is the average inventory and (R/S) is the number of orders required per year. The objective is to select the quantity that minimizes the total cost curve (see Exhibit A–6). Therefore, using basic calculus, the above equation can be differentiated with respect to Q:

$$TC'(Q) = \frac{CI}{2} + (-1)\frac{RS}{Q^2} = 0$$

By setting the above to zero and solving for Q, the EOQ model is derived:

$$EOQ = \sqrt{\frac{2RS}{CI}}$$

The model assumes that the pattern of demand is constant, that the lead time from order to delivery is constant, that all the order is received in a batch, and that stockouts do not occur. This approach can easily be modified to include the maintenance of safety stocks to further enhance service levels.

As an example, assume a manager wishes to determine the economic order quantity for a product that costs $3 and has annual sales of 600 units. The ordering cost is $80, and the opportunity cost of capital is 20 percent.

$$EOQ = \sqrt{\frac{2(600)(\$80)}{(\$3)(.2)}} = 400 \text{ units}$$

Total inventory costs for this product then would be:

$$TC = \frac{400}{2}(3)(.2) + \frac{600}{400}(80) = 120 + 120 = \$240$$

Income Statement and Performance Ratios   The

income statement summarizes the firm's revenues and expenses over an accounting period, usually 12 months beginning either July 1 or January 1. The income statement shown in Exhibit A–7 is for a manufacturer and marketer of aluminum components for compact disc manufacturers. (Income statements can also be developed for specific brands or projects.) Total and net sales are shown at the top of the statement. Net sales ($780,212) are determined by subtracting returns, allowances, and discounts from total sales. Gross profit is the amount remaining after costs of goods sold are subtracted from net sales. Operating income ($106,558) is the amount of funds available after operating expenses have been subtracted from gross profits. Net income is the final amount left after nonoperating items (interest expenses) and corporate income taxes have been paid.

Exhibit A-7	*Income statement for year ended December 31, 2000*		
Sales revenue			$839,490
Less: Returns & allowances		$ 43,345	
Discounts		15,933	
Total			59,278
Net sales			780,212
Less: Cost of goods sold			416,296
Gross profits on sales (gross margin)			363,916
Operating expenses			
Salaries		$136,000	
Rent		19,000	
Miscellaneous office		2,046	
Marketing		52,812	
Depreciation		30,000	
Insurance		2,320	
Utilities		4,750	
Payroll taxes		9,230	
Bad debts		1,200	
Total operating expenses			257,358
Operating income			106,558
Nonoperating items			
Interest expense		$9,600	
Purchase discounts lost		534	
Total nonoperating items			10,134
Net income before corporate income taxes			96,424
Less: Corporate income taxes			48,212
NET INCOME			$48,212
Net income per weighted share of common stock outstanding			5.3487

This statement is useful in evaluating the performance of the firm. From the income statement, a number of frequently used ratios can be determined. Performance ratios based on the income statement include gross margin ratio, net income ratio, cost-of-goods-sold ratio, operating expense ratio, sales efficiency ratio, and return on investment (ROI).

$$\text{Gross margin ratio} = \frac{\text{Gross margin}}{\text{Net sales}} = \frac{\$363,916}{\$780,212} = 47\%$$

This ratio represents the percentage of sales revenue available to cover operating expenses and profit objectives.

$$\text{Net income ratio} = \frac{\text{Net income}}{\text{Net sales}} = \frac{\$48,212}{\$780,212} = 6\%$$

The net income ratio reflects the percentage of each sales dollar that is profit before corporate income taxes.

$$\text{Cost-of-goods-sold ratio} = \frac{\text{COGS}}{\text{Net sales}} = \frac{\$416,296}{\$780,212} = 53\%$$

This ratio reflects the percentage of sales used to manufacture goods sold. If it is high, costs are either excessive or prices may be too low.

$$\text{Operating expense ratio} = \frac{\text{Total expenses}}{\text{Net sales}} = \frac{\$257,358}{\$780,212} = 33\%$$

This ratio reflects the company's operating efficiency and represents the percentage of each dollar needed to cover expenses.

$$\text{Sales efficiency ratio} = \frac{\text{Net sales}}{\text{Gross sales}} = \frac{\$780,212}{\$839,490} = 93\%$$

This ratio reflects adjustments to gross sales from returns, allowances, and discounts.

$$\text{Return on investment (ROI)} = \frac{\text{Net profit before taxes}}{\text{Total investment}}$$

Information regarding total investment from the firm's balance sheet is required to compute ROI. ROI figures can be compared with industry averages and opportunity costs of investing elsewhere to evaluate the firm's performance.

Appendix B

Developing a Marketing Plan

A general strategic planning process is presented in Chapter 3. The basic stages include: examine the current situation, identify potential threats and opportunities, set objectives, and develop strategies. This appendix illustrates the types of information typically appearing in each section of a product marketing plan.

Business units within the firm have their own product marketing plans that focus on specific target markets and marketing mixes for each product. As explained in Chapter 3, product marketing plans typically include both strategic decisions (or what to do) and execution decisions (or how to do it). Marketing plans may be developed for a single brand, a product line, or a business unit that markets multiple product lines. For a product, a product line, or a business unit, the general strategic planning process includes the following stages: (1) examine the current situation; (2) identify potential threats and opportunities; (3) set objectives; and (4) develop strategies. These stages may overlap in that work is simultaneously underway regarding each stage. The plans themselves will also include projected financial outcomes and procedures for plan performance monitoring and control.

Overall, planning is a process directed toward making decisions with tomorrow in mind. As such, planning is a means of preparing for future decisions so that they can be made rapidly, economically, and with as little disruption to the business as possible.[1] Marketing plans may be for new products and services being introduced or for existing products or services. Regardless of the type of plan, all plans will be reviewed at least annually for needed revisions. Properly developed marketing plans can provide considerable benefits to firm performance. Plans:[2]

- Act as a road map to guide future decisions.
- Assist in management control and implementation of strategy.
- Assist in helping obtain resources for implementation.
- Stimulate thinking and encourage better use of resources.
- Help in the organization and assignment of responsibilities, tasks, and timing.
- Inform new employees of their roles in implementing existing plans and reaching objectives.
- Help generate awareness of strengths, weaknesses, opportunities, and threats.

The Marketing Plan[3]

The following outline is consistent with the general planning procedure summarized above and depicted earlier in Exhibit 3–2. Frequently cited content issues and topics are enumerated for each stage in this section. Later in the appendix, an example plan for a particular situation is presented.

Parts of the Marketing Plan

1. Executive summary
2. Situation analysis
3. Marketing objectives
4. Market selection: Target markets
5. Marketing strategy
6. Marketing mix: Action programs (specifics of marketing mix implementation)
7. Budgets, control, and accountability

Part 1: Executive Summary

A. The summary should present a description of the product/service, its target market and its *need* within that market. The summary should also present an overview of the main points of the plan (i.e., the marketing mix and the sales and profits for the first two years).

B. The relationship between the organization's mission, objectives, and strategy and the marketing plan should be clearly expressed.

C. The summary should emphasize an action orientation.

Part 2: Situation Analysis

INTERNAL ANALYSIS

A. Describe the company's *current* product(s) or service(s).

   1. What are their sales in dollars?

   2. What is their share of the market?

   3. How do they compare to the competition?

B. Analyze and describe the company's internal strengths.

C. Analyze and describe the company's internal weaknesses.

D. Analyze and describe the company's potential opportunities.

E. Analyze and describe the company's potential threats.

F. Describe why the company is suited to develop the product/service being considered (e.g., company resources, existing customers, etc).

EXTERNAL ANALYSIS (EXTERNAL ENVIRONMENT)

A. Describe important external conditions and/or trends affecting the industry:

Social	Legal/Regulatory
Technological	Competitive
Economic	Institutional

   1. Is the size of the market of the product category increasing or decreasing and how quickly?

   2. Why has the market remained stable or changed?

B. Do these conditions create opportunities for the product/service? Do these conditions pose threats to the product/service?

Part 3: Marketing Objectives

A. What are the corporate marketing objectives of the company?

B. What are the specific marketing objectives of the product/service under evaluation?

C. Are the objectives of the marketing plan compatible with the overall marketing objectives of the company and/or business unit?

Part 4: Market Selection and Target Markets

A. Describe the firm's possible market segments.

    1. What are the characteristics (age, geography, income, lifestyles, etc.) of each of the market segments?

    2. Assess the potential of each market segment.

B. Describe the chosen target market(s).

    1. Why was this target market selected?

    2. How does the product or service meet the needs of the target market?

C. Describe the purchase decision behavior of the target market(s). (Who, why, when, how should be answered.)

D. What is the general sales forecast for the target market of the product/service?

Part 5: Marketing Strategy

A. Who are the competitors and/or what are the product substitutes for the product?

B. Does the organization have an obvious competitive advantage? If yes, what is it? (Consider brand names, service, price, distribution, technology, personnel.)

C. Provide a complete competitive analysis for the product/service. This should include the following:

    1. Major competitors' strengths and weaknesses.

    2. Brand positioning and competitive advantage.

    3. Market share.

D. Does the product/service have a competitive advantage? If yes, explain your competitive strategy.

E. How will the product or service be positioned?

Part 6: The Marketing Mix Product/Service

A. What is the total product concept for this good or service? Describe the product/service in terms of features and benefits.

B. Will it satisfy consumers' needs? How will the consumer use the product? Will consumers purchase the product?

C. How does the product differ from that of the competition?

D. Describe the package (size, color, label, etc.) and its benefits.

E. Are any product modifications expected as the product moves through the product life cycle?

F. Are any warranties or guarantees offered?

G. What is the test marketing process for the product/service?

Part 6B: Action Program—Pricing

A. What is the overall pricing policy for the organization?

B. What are the organization's pricing objectives?

C. What is the pricing structure (pricing method, approach, and strategy) for this product or service?

D. How does the pricing structure for the product or service compare with that of the competition?

E. What is the target market's evaluation of price and its ability to purchase? Will there be significant demand at this price? What is the estimated effect of lowering or raising the price of the product or service?

F. What is the competition's likely reaction to the pricing strategy for the product or service at this price level?

G. What (if any) price promotions (sales, discounts, allowances, etc.) will be used during the year?

Part 6C: Action Program—Distribution

A. What is the current distribution strategy?

B. How effective are the current distribution channels? Will these same channels be used for the new product/service? Why?

C. What (if any) new distribution channels should be added to accommodate the new product/service?

D. Does the competition use any distribution channels not currently being used by the planning organization?

E. What (if any) expected future developments could affect how, what, when, or where consumers will purchase this product/service?

Part 6D: Action Program— Marketing Communications

A. What are the communications objectives for the organization's product or service?

B. What is the overall promotional strategy for the organization? Describe in terms of structure, tasks, and strategy (push/pull).

C. How much money is allocated for the promotional budget? How will it be divided?

D. What are the copy and media strategies for this product or service? How does the advertising differ from any competitors?

E. What is the role of personal selling in the promotional mix? What is the ratio of advertising spending to personal selling spending? Does this ratio reflect the importance given to personal selling in the overall promotional strategy?

F. What is the role of sales promotion? What is the ratio of advertising expenditures to sales promotion expenditures? Does this ratio reflect the importance given to sales promotion in the overall promotional strategy?

G. What types of sales promotion will be used?

H. What are the objectives of the public relations program?

Part 7: Budgets, Control, and Accountability

A. For the product or service being planned for, develop a time line that will explain the following:

1. What will be accomplished and how much will it cost?

2. Who will do it?

3. When will it be done?

B. How will results be measured? (Consider sales analysis, market share analysis, and cost analysis, etc.) What information is needed for comparison of actual and planned results?

C. Who will be responsible for monitoring and controlling the marketing plan? Who is accountable for significant deviations from the plan?

D. Develop a pro forma statement for the first two years of sales and detail the income and expenses in both quantitative and qualitative format.

Notes

1. Subhash C. Jain, *Marketing Planning Strategy,* 4th ed. (Cincinnati, OH: South-Western Publishing Company, 1993), p. 5.

2. William A. Cohen, *The Marketing Plan* (New York, NY: John Wiley and Sons, 1995), p. 2.

3. The marketing plan outline included in this appendix is an adaptation of the marketing plan exercise used by Professor Anne M. Devine, Alverno College, Business and Management Division, 3401 S. 39th Street, Milwaukee, WI 53234-3922. We are indebted to Professor Devine for her permission to include this plan in the appendix.

Glossary

ABILITY the consumer's knowledge about the product category sufficient to understand the advertised message, *399*

ACCEPTABLE PRICE RANGE the range of prices buyers are willing to pay for a product; prices above the range may be judged unfair, while prices below the range may generate concerns about quality, *282*

ACCESSIBILITY the degree to which a firm can reach intended target segments efficiently with its products and communications, *154*

ADAPTIVE SELLING a salesperson's adjustment of his or her behavior between and during sales calls to respond appropriately to the situation and address issues important to the customer, *450*

ADMINISTERED CHANNEL SYSTEM system designed to control a line or classification of merchandise; channel members agree on a comprehensive plan but no channel member owns another member, *303*

ADOPTION PROCESS the steps consumers follow in deciding whether to use a new product, *212*

ADVERTISING the element of the marketing communications mix that is nonpersonal, paid for by an identified sponsor, and disseminated through mass channels of communication to promote the adoption of goods, services, persons, or ideas, *372*

ADVERTISING AGENCY a company that develops advertising messages and provides media planning and scheduling for marketers, *394*

ADVERTISING ALLOWANCE money paid a reseller for including the manufacturer's product, along with other products, in the reseller's advertising efforts, *432*

ADVERTISING SPECIALTY an item of useful or interesting merchandise given away free and typically carrying an imprinted name or message; for example, a pen, calendar, or coffee mug, *429*

ADVERTORIAL a special advertising section with some editorial (nonadvertising) content included in magazines, *405*

AFFECT REFERRAL a choice heuristic in which consumers elicit from memory their overall evaluation of products and choose the alternative for which they have the most positive feelings, *84*

AIDED RECALL TESTS posttesting in which consumers are given lists of ads and asked which they remembered and read, *409*

AIO STATEMENTS survey responses concerning activities, interests, and opinions (AIO), used in psychographic research, *160*

ALL-YOU-CAN-AFFORD BUDGETING a method for determining the marketing communications budget that involves spending whatever's left over after other costs without considering the firm's objectives, *380*

AMERICANS WITH DISABILITIES ACT (ADA) a U.S. law passed in 1990 to prohibit discrimination against consumers with disabilities, *38*

ANCHOR POSITION retail stores, often department stores, that are strategically placed in malls, shopping centers, or downtown shopping areas to attract customers and stimulate traffic flow throughout the shopping area, *334*

ARBITRAGING see diverting, *436*

ATMOSPHERICS a retailer's combination of architecture, layout, color scheme, sound and temperature monitoring, special events, prices, displays, and other factors that attract and stimulate customers, *320*

ATTENTION the consumer's mental notice directed at a marketing communication (such as an ad), often stimulated by its physical characteristics; the second step in the information-processing model, *399*

ATTITUDES learned predispositions to respond favorably or unfavorably to a product or brand; based on beliefs about its attributes (price, service level, quality), *83–84*

AUCTION HOUSE a company that sells merchandise at a given time and place to the highest bidder, *351*

AUTHENTICATION a way to verify the identity of users and hardware in order to secure Web sites, *509*

AUTOMATIC NUMBER IDENTIFICATION a system that identifies incoming phone numbers of respondents to an ad or promotion at the beginning of the call without the caller's knowledge, *483*

BACKWARD INTEGRATION a corporate marketing channel system in which the channel member owns one or more of its suppliers upstream (as opposed to forward integration, where it owns buyers downstream), *302*

BAIT AND SWITCH advertising a product at an attractively low price to get customers into the store but not making it available, so customers must trade up to a more expensive version, *287*

BALANCED MATRIX ORGANIZATION an approach to new-product development in which a project manager oversees the project and shares responsibility and authority with functional managers, *214*

BANNER ADVERTISING ads on a Web site that are "clickable" should a viewer want more information about the product or service being advertised, *499*

BAR CODING a computer-coded bar pattern that identifies a product; see also **Universal Product Code**, *356*

BASES OF SEGMENTATION the distinguishing characteristics of market segments (such as demographics, benefits sought) within a firm's overall product or service market, *156*

BASIC PRICE MIX   the basic components that define the size and means of payment exchanged for goods and services; less comprehensive than the price promotion mix, *244*

BATTLE OF THE BRANDS   intense competition between manufacturer and distributor brands, *191*

BEHAVIOR-BASED PERSPECTIVE   a way of evaluating salesperson performance that defines the sales behaviors expected, such as how many calls to make or which presentation tactics to use; see also **outcome-based perspective**, *459*

BENEFIT   what a product feature can do for a particular customer; for example, a speakerphone built into a fax machine is a feature, but the fact that it allows hands-free conversation is a benefit, *451*

BENEFIT SEGMENTATION   segmenting the market by the attributes or benefits consumers need or desire, such as quality, service, or unique features, *161*

BEST-VALUE STRATEGY   purchasing the lowest-cost brand available with the desired level of quality, *259*

BIDS   in government markets, written proposals from qualified suppliers in response to published governmental requirements or specifications, *114*

BRAND   a name, term, sign, symbol, design, or combination that a firm uses to identify its products and differentiate them from those of competitors, *188*

BRAND AWARENESS   when target consumers know about a brand and it comes to mind when thinking about the product category; for example, Kleenex comes to mind when thinking about tissues, *189*

BRAND COMPETITORS   direct competitors that offer the same types of products (for example, Domino's Pizza and Pizza Hut), *41*

BRAND EQUITY   the value a brand has in the marketplace due to reputation and goodwill, *189*

BRAND IDENTITY   the brand concept from the brand owner's viewpoint; the specific aspects of the brand that the marketer wants to communicate to consumers, *189*

BRAND IMAGE   consumers' impression about a brand, *189*

BRAND LOYALTY   when consumers purchase a specific brand all or most of the time, *189*

BRAND MARK   the element of a brand that cannot be vocalized (for example, the MGM lion or the Texaco star), *188*

BRAND NAME   the element of a brand that can be vocalized (for example, IBM, Tide, Coke), *188*

BRANDING   identifying a firm's products to distinguish them from competitors' similar products, *188*

BREAK-EVEN ANALYSIS   calculation of the number of units that must be sold at a certain price for the firm to cover costs (break even); revenues earned past the break-even point contribute to profits, *274*

BROADBAND INTERNET TECHNOLOGY   a superfast connection to the Web via cable modem, digital subscriber lines, or satellites, *498*

BROKER   an intermediary that brings buyers and sellers together and is paid a commission by whichever party it represents in a given transaction, *351*

BUILDING ON-LINE COMMUNITIES   a step beyond personalization where customers who share interests can interact with other like-minded customers on a Web site, *500*

BUNDLING   marketing two or more products in a single package at one price (for example, computer systems or ski weekends), *280*

BUSINESS ANALYSIS   the stage of new-product development where initial marketing plans are prepared, including a tentative marketing strategy and estimates of sales, costs, and profitability, *209*

BUSINESS FIRMS   manufacturers of tangible goods and firms that provide services such as health care, entertainment, and transportation, *103*

BUSINESS LEVEL   the smaller units within a complex organization that are managed as self-contained businesses, *51*

BUSINESS NETWORKS   strategic alliances among suppliers, distributors, and the marketing firm, *55*

BUSINESS PRODUCTS   goods and services purchased by a firm for its own use (as opposed to consumer products), *182*

BUSINESS STRATEGIC PLAN   a plan for how each business unit in the corporate family intends to compete in the marketplace, given the vision, objectives, and growth strategies of the corporate strategic plan, *52*

BUSINESS-TO-BUSINESS ADVERTISING   promoting products or services directly to other firms, often through print ads in trade periodicals or direct-mail promotions to targeted potential buyers, *397*

BUSINESS-TO-BUSINESS BUYING BEHAVIOR   the decision making and other activities of organizations as buyers, *103*

BUSINESS-TO-BUSINESS (B2B) E-COMMERCE   businesses selling to other businesses or organizations over the Internet, *495*

BUSINESS-TO-CONSUMER (B2C) E-COMMERCE   businesses selling to consumers over the Internet, *495*

BUYING ALLOWANCE   payment of a specified amount of money to a reseller for purchasing a certain amount of a product during a particular period, *432*

BUYING CENTER   business purchasing decision makers made up of people throughout all levels of the organization, not just the purchasing department; the buying center makeup may vary as purchasing decisions change, *113*

BUYING LOADER   a dealer premium in the form of a gift, such as a free trip, for buying, displaying, and selling a certain amount of a product within a specified time, *432*

BUYING POWER INDEX (BPI)   a measure of a particular market's relative ability to buy, based on population, effective buying income, and retail sales and expressed as a percentage of the total U.S. potential, *36*

CALLER ID INTRUSION   see **automatic number identification**, *483*

CANNED SALES PRESENTATION   a fully scripted presentation that the sales rep memorizes, or even an audiovisual presentation, that is not adaptable to individual customers, *450*

CANNIBALIZATION   when a new product takes sales away from existing products, which leads merely to a shift in the company's sales instead of a gain, *231*

CAPITAL PRODUCTS   expensive items that are used in business operations but do not become part of any finished product; examples include physical facilities (office buildings) and accessory equipment (copiers and forklifts), *184*

CASH-AND-CARRY WHOLESALER a limited-function wholesaler that does not extend credit for or deliver the products it sells; its primary customers are small retailers, *349*

CATALOG WHOLESALER a limited-function wholesaler that offers a wide range of competitively priced products that customers order by phone or fax, *349*

CATEGORY an assortment of items seen by the customer as reasonable substitutes for each other, *320*

CATEGORY KILLERS discount retailers that offer a complete assortment and can thus dominate a product category, giving them the clout to negotiate excellent prices from suppliers and be assured of dependable sources of supply, *320*

CAUSAL RESEARCH experiments in which researchers manipulate independent variables and observe the dependent variable(s) of interest to identify cause-and-effect relationships, *127*

CAUSE-RELATED MARKETING companies aligning themselves with causes, such as drug-abuse prevention and environmental conservation, *412*

CELEBRITY ENDORSEMENT the use of a famous spokesperson, say a sports or movie star, to promote a product, *403*

CENTRAL BUSINESS DISTRICT a downtown area representing a city's greatest concentration of office buildings and retail stores, *332*

CENTS-OFF DEAL an offering of a brand at less than the regular price, *425*

CHANNEL CONFLICT conflict between members of a marketing channel, which may stem from poor communication, a power struggle, or incompatible objectives, *311*

CHANNEL COOPERATION a cooperative spirit among members of a marketing channel that helps reduce and resolve conflicts, *311*

CHANNEL LEADER a marketing channel member with enough power to control others in the channel, *310*

CHANNEL OBJECTIVES specific, measurable goals of a marketing channel that are consistent with the firm's

marketing objectives and are often stated in terms of sales volume, profitability, market share, cost, number of wholesale or retail outlets, or geographic expansion, *305*

CHANNEL OF DISTRIBUTION see **marketing channel**, *295*

CHANNEL POWER ways marketing channel members can gain control to enhance their position, including reward power, legitimate power, expert power, and referent power, *310*

CHANNEL STRATEGY an expression of a general action plan and guidelines for allocating resources to achieve the objective of a marketing channel, *305*

CHECKOUT DISPENSERS make coupons available to customers in supermarkets. Although they are more expensive than newspaper coupons, they tend to be redeemed at a higher rate, *426*

CHILD PROTECTION ACT a U.S. law passed in 1990 to regulate advertising on children's TV programs, *38*

CHILD SAFETY ACT a U.S. law passed in 1966 that prohibits the marketing of dangerous products to children, *38*

CHILDHOOD CONSUMER SOCIALIZATION the process by which young people acquire skills, knowledge, and attitudes to help them function as consumers in the marketplace, *87*

CLASSIFIED ADVERTISING advertising that typically promotes transactions for a single item or service and usually appears in newspapers, *397*

CLAYTON ACT a U.S. law passed in 1914 that prohibits anti-competitive activities, *38*

CLUSTER SAMPLING a probability sampling technique in which units are organized into similar clusters, such as neighborhoods; clusters are then selected randomly and each house in the selected clusters is included in the sample, *135*

COACHING the leadership function of providing guidance and feedback on a regular basis to direct salespeople's activities, *459*

CO-BRANDING when two brand names appear on the same product; for example, a VISA card with your university's name, *192*

COERCIVE POWER power a member of a marketing channel uses to pressure another member to do something; for example, a manufacturer threatens to cut off a distributor's credit unless the distributor pays its bills more promptly, *310*

COGNITIVE DISSONANCE a consumer's postpurchase doubt about the appropriateness of a purchase decision; caused by an imbalance of information because each alternative has attractive features; most likely to occur when the purchase is important and visible, the perceived risk is high, and the decision involves a long-term commitment, *96*

COLLABORATIVE VENTURE an arrangement in which two or more firms share in the rights to market specified products; may take the form of a strategic partnership, strategic alliance, joint venture, or licensing agreement, *204*

CO-MARKETING ALLIANCES contractual arrangements between different companies offering complementary products in the marketplace or possessing complementary technology, *70*

COMBINATION STRATEGY aiming marketing communications at both resellers and ultimate consumers in a push–pull approach, *382*

COMMERCIAL ZAPPING changing the channels during TV commercials, *396*

COMMERCIALIZATION the stage of new-product development after the product tests successfully and the firm introduces it on a full-scale basis, *211*

COMMISSION MERCHANT a wholesaler that provides a wider range of services than do agents or brokers, often engaging in inventory management, physical distribution, and promotional activities and offering credit and market feedback to the companies it represents, *351*

COMMUNICATION the process of establishing shared meaning, exchanging ideas, or passing information between a source and a receiver, *375*

COMPARATIVE ADVERTISING advertising that compares a sponsored brand with a competitive brand on at least one product attribute (such as MCI versus AT&T services), *385, 402*

COMPETITIVE ADVANTAGE trying to get consumers to purchase one's products instead of competitors' products, through either lower prices or differentiation, *63*

COMPETITIVE ENVIRONMENT
all the organizations that attempt to serve the same customers, including both brand competitors and product competitors, *41*

COMPETITIVE PARITY BUDGETING   a budgeting method for marketing communications based on the percentage allocated by other companies in the industry, *380*

COMPETITIVE PRICING STRATEGIES   pricing strategies based on a firm's position in relation to its competition; includes penetration pricing, limit pricing, and price signaling, *278*

COMPETITIVE STRATEGY-POSITIONING CONTINUUM
competitive strategies are described as existing on a continuum anchored by "low cost leadership" on one end and "differentiation" on the other, *251*

COMPOSITE OF SALESFORCE ESTIMATES   a means of forecasting sales in which sales reps give forecasts for their territories, which can then be combined, *167*

CONCENTRATED STRATEGY   a strategy in which a firm seeks a large share of one or a few profitable segments of the total market, often concentrating on serving the selected segments innovatively and creatively, *165*

CONCEPT DEVELOPMENT   the process of shaping and refining the idea for a new product into a complete description, *207*

CONCEPT TESTS   having the concept for a new product evaluated by potential customers, *208*

CONSOLIDATED METROPOLITAN STATISTICAL AREA (CMSA)   the largest designation of geographic areas based on census data; the 20 largest market areas in the United States that contain at least two PMSAs, *159*

CONSUMER ATTITUDES   learned predispositions to respond favorably or unfavorably to a product or brand, *83*

CONSUMER BEHAVIOR   the mental and emotional processes and the physical activities people engage in when they select, purchase, use, and dispose of products or services to satisfy particular needs and desires, *77*

CONSUMER CREDIT PROTECTION ACT   a U.S. law

passed in 1968 that requires full disclosure of financial charges for loans, *38*

CONSUMER DECISION PROCESS   a four-step process: (1) recognizing a need or problem, (2) searching for information, (3) evaluating alternative products or brands, and (4) purchasing a product, *81*

CONSUMER INFORMATION PROCESSING   represents the cognitive processes by which consumers interpret and integrate information from the environment, *82*

CONSUMER LEARNING   a process that changes consumers' knowledge or behavior patterns through marketing communications or experience, *94*

CONSUMER PRODUCT SAFETY COMMISSION (CPSC)   an agency of the U.S. government that protects consumers from unsafe products, *39*

CONSUMER PRODUCTS   goods and services purchased by consumers for their own personal use (as opposed to business products), *182*

CONSUMER PROTECTION LAWS   laws that state what firms must do to give consumers the information they need to make sound purchasing decisions or to make sure the products they buy are safe, *38*

CONSUMER RIGHTS   four inherent rights of consumers: (1) to safety, (2) to be informed, (3) to choose, and (4) to be heard, *38*

CONSUMER SALES PROMOTION   sales promotion directed at ultimate users of the product or service (as opposed to trade sales promotion), *421*

CONSUMERISM   a social movement in which consumers demand better consumer information, quality, service, dependability, and fair prices, *34*

CONTENT PROVIDERS
companies who send information through the Web, *505*

CONTEST   a sales promotion that offers prizes based on the skill of contestants, *427*

CONTINUAL TRAINING   ongoing sales training that helps firms stay current and competitive in an ever-changing environment, *457*

CONTRIBUTION MARGIN   is the quantity P-VC where P+ unit price and Q (BEP) = break-even quantity, *274*

CONVENIENCE PRODUCTS
consumer may prefer a specific brand but does not want to spend much time shopping for it; will buy another brand if preferred one is not available; normally low-priced, often-purchased goods, *183*

CONVENIENCE STORE   retail store that carries a modest variety and shallow assortment of products and has high prices but offers a convenient location and hours, *334*

CONVERSION RATES   statistical measurement that is used to describe the percent of shoppers who are converted into buyers, *82*

COOKIES   tiny computer files, stored on users' PCs, that Web sites use to track visitors to their sites, *512*

COOPERATIVE ADVERTISING
advertising for a local dealer or retailer whose expense is contributed to by the manufacturer, *398*

CORE COMPETENCY   the unique bundle of skills that are possessed by individuals across the organization and that provide the basis for competitive advantage, *58*

CORE PURPOSE   the company's reason for being or its idealistic motivation for doing work, *56*

CORE VALUES   the small set of guiding principles that represent the enduring tenets of the organization, *56*

CORPORATE ADVOCACY ADVERTISING   advertising that announces a stand on some issue related to the firm's operation, often one threatening the company's well-being, *397*

CORPORATE IMAGE ADVERTISING   advertising directed toward the general public or investors and stockholders promoting an organization's image and role in the community as a corporate citizen, independent of any product or service, *397*

CORPORATE LEVEL   the highest level in any organization, at which managers address issues concerning the overall organization and their decisions and actions affect all other organizational levels, *51*

CORPORATE STRATEGIC PLAN
a plan that determines what a company is and wants to become and that guides strategic planning at all organizational levels; it involves developing a corporate vision, formulating corporate objectives, allocating resources, determining how to

achieve desired growth, and establishing business units, *52*

CORPORATE VISION the basic values of an organization, specifying what it stands for, where it wants to go, and how it plans to get there, and addressing the organization's markets, principal products or services, geographic domain, core technologies, objectives, basic philosophy, self-concept, and desired public image, *56*

CORRECTIVE ADVERTISING advertising the FTC mandates to remedy misleading impressions and information in an ad, *411*

COST PER THOUSAND (CPM) a factor in evaluating the cost effectiveness of a particular outlet for reaching desired market audiences, *408*

COUNTERSEGMENTATION combining market segments to appeal to a broad range of consumers and assuming an increasing consumer willingness to accept fewer product and service variations for lower prices, *165*

COUNTERTRADE trade between developed and less-developed countries that involves barter and exchanges instead of just currency, *243*

COUPON a printed certificate giving the bearer a stated price reduction or special value on a specific product, generally for a specific time period; especially useful in encouraging new-product trials; may be distributed in an ad, in a freestanding insert, or on the store shelf, *425*

CREATIVE STRATEGY combining what is said in an ad with how it is said; typically the marketer specifies the general theme of the message and the ad agency develops the presentation, *401*

CROSS ELASTICITY OF DEMAND the relation of the percentage change in quantity demanded for one product to percentage price changes for other products; a price increase for one brand of cola will increase demand for a substitute brand, but a price increase for computers will decrease demand for printers, a complementary product, *271*

CROSS-FUNCTIONAL TEAMWORK having employees from different functional areas of a firm work together to satisfy customer needs, *69*

CROSS-PROMOTION the collaboration of two or more firms in a sales promotion; also called a **tie-in,** *427*

CROSS-SECTIONAL STUDY a survey of customers administered at a

given time to assess, for example, perceived satisfaction with service, *127*

CULTURAL ENVIRONMENT factors and trends related to how people live and behave, including the values, ideas, attitudes, beliefs, and activities of specific population subgroups; a component of the social environment, *31*

CULTURE the values, ideas, attitudes, and symbols people adopt to communicate, interpret, and interact as members of a society; a society's way of life, learned and transmitted from one generation to the next, that includes both abstract and material elements. Culture determines the most basic values that influence consumer behavior patterns and can be used to distinguish subcultures that represent substantial market segments and opportunities, *84*

CUSTOMARY PRICE pricing strategies that modify the quality, features, or service of a product without adjusting the price; customary price beliefs reflect consumers' strongly held expectations about what the price of a product should be, *281*

CUSTOMER LOYALTY CONCEPT a focus beyond customer satisfaction toward customer retention as a way to generate sales and profit growth, *5*

CUSTOMER PRIVACY any way in which data is protected from unauthorized viewing on a Web site, *509*

CUSTOMER SERVICE the assistance a firm provides to help a customer with the purchase or use of a product or service; providing exceptional customer service can give a firm a marketing advantage, *193*

CUSTOMER VALUE what a customer gets (benefits from product use, related services) for what a customer gives (price paid, time to shop), *6*

CUSTOMER VALUE PERSPECTIVE an emphasis on giving customers more of what they want for less than they have to give, *17*

CUSTOMIZED MARKETING STRATEGY implementing a different marketing mix for each target market country in international marketing, *68*

CYCLE TIME the total elapsed time to complete a business process, *106*

DATA INTEGRITY a condition required to ensure security, meaning that

data cannot be corrupted by viruses, destroyed, or changed without authorization, *509*

DATA MINING the process by which market cells are derived from company databases by the use of sophisticated analytical and statistical procedures that discover interesting patterns within company data sets, *153*

DATABASE MARKETING the collection and use of individual customer-specific information stored on a computer to make marketing more efficient, *141, 470*

DEALER LOADER a premium given to a reseller to encourage development of a special display or product offering, *432*

DECEPTIVE ADVERTISING communications intended to mislead consumers by making false claims or failing to disclose important information, *384*

DECLINE STAGE the fourth and final stage of the product life cycle, when falling sales and profits persist, *226*

DECODING the process in communications by which the receiver deciphers the meaning of the words, pictures, and other symbols used in the message, *376*

DEMAND CURVE relationship that shows how many units a market will purchase at a given price in a given time period; generally, customers buy more units as prices drop and fewer units as prices rise, *270*

DEMOGRAPHIC ENVIRONMENT the size, distribution, and growth rate of groups of people with different traits that relate to buying behavior; a component of the social environment, *28*

DEPARTMENT STORE a retail store characterized by a wide variety of merchandise and extensive depth of assortment; typically organized around sales departments like apparel, cosmetics, and housewares, *334*

DEREGULATION promotes free competition, in some cases by means of legislation. It is one aspect of the legal environment, *360*

DERIVED DEMAND demand for business-to-business products that is dependent upon demand for other products in consumer markets, as when increased consumer demand for new automobiles causes the demand for products used to make them to also go up, *104*

DESCRIPTIVE RESEARCH
research directed by one or more formal research questions or hypotheses, usually involving a survey or questionnaire, *126*

DIFFERENTIAL PRICING   selling the same product to different buyers at a variety of prices; such price discrimination works because there are differences in reactions to price among consumers or consumer segments, *277*

DIFFERENTIAL RESPONSIVENESS   the degree to which market segments exhibit varying responses to different marketing mix combinations, *155*

DIFFERENTIATED STRATEGY
using different marketing strategies for different segments; either marketing a unique product and communications campaign to each segment, or marketing a common product to different segments with various communication strategies, *164*

DIFFERENTIATION   offering consumers products or services that are better than the competition; one way to gain a competitive advantage, *164*

DIFFUSION PROCESS   the adoption of an innovative product form over time, *224*

DIRECT CHANNEL   the movement of the product from the producer to the user without intermediaries, *299*

DIRECT INVESTMENT   investing in production, sales, distribution, and/or other operations in a foreign country; requires a large investment of resources but gives the marketer much control over operations, *67*

DIRECT MAIL   any form of advertising addressed to prospects through public or private delivery services, including everything from a simple flyer to a package that contains a letter, multipage brochure, video, and response card, *474*

DIRECT MARKETING   distributing goods, services, information, or promotional benefits to carefully targeted consumers through interactive (two-way) communication while tracking response, sales, interests, or desires through a computer database, *327*

DIRECT MARKETING CHANNEL
a way to move the product from producer to user without intermediaries, *p. 299*

DIRECT MARKETING COMMUNICATIONS   a process of communications directly with target customers to encourage response by telephone, mail, electronic means, or personal visit; examples of DMC methods include direct mail, telemarketing, computer shopping services, TV shopping networks, and infomercials, *376, 469*

DIRECT-RESPONSE ADVERTISING   advertising intended to elicit immediate purchase; for example, TV commercials that show a toll-free phone number, *397*

DIRECT-RESPONSE RADIO ADVERTISING   radio ads that provide a phone number or address to elicit immediate feedback from the consumer, *478*

DIRECT-RESPONSE TELEVISION ADVERTISING   TV ads that include an 800 or 900 phone number and an address for placing orders in an attempt to get an immediate answer from the consumer, *477*

DIRECT RETAILING   the portion of direct marketing in which ultimate consumers, not business consumers, do the buying (see also **direct marketing**), *327*

DIRECT SELLING   a method in which salespeople reach consumers directly or by telephone primarily at home or at work and sell through personal demonstration and explanation, *328*

DIRECT-TO-CONSUMER SALESPEOPLE   sales reps who sell to individuals who personally use the products and services; they include retail salespeople, real estate agents, and financial securities agents, *448*

DISCOUNTS   reductions from the market price; for example, cash discounts for prompt payment or quantity discounts for large orders. See also **trade sales promotion allowances**, *284*

DISPLAY ALLOWANCE   money or a product provided to a retailer for featuring the manufacturer's brand in an agreed-on in-store display, *432*

DISPLAY LOADER   a dealer premium that lets the reseller keep some or all of the display when the promotion ends, *432*

DISTRIBUTION CENTER   an automated "superwarehouse" that serves a large geographic area and receives, processes, and ships customer orders in addition to storing products, *356*

DISTRIBUTOR BRAND   a brand sponsored by a distributor such as a wholesaler or retailer; the distributor is responsible for the product's quality and marketing. Also called a **store brand**, **private brand**, or **private label**, *191*

DIVERSIFICATION STRATEGY
expanding into new products and new markets; the riskiest growth strategy, since the company cannot build directly on its strengths in its current markets or products, *60*

DIVERTING   secretly purchasing a product where it is less expensive, usually due to a trade promotion, and reselling it where prices are higher, *436*

DOWNWARD STRETCH STRATEGY   adding products to the lower end of a product line; for example, IBM entered the market with high-priced microcomputers and later added lower-priced ones, *230*

DROP SHIPPER   a limited-function wholesaler that arranges for shipments directly from the factory to the customer; it does not physically handle the product but does take title and all associated risks while the product is in transit, as well as provide sales support, *349*

DUMPING   selling a product in a foreign country at a price lower than in the home country and lower than its marginal cost of production, *256*

DURABILITY   the stability of market segments and whether distinctions between them will diminish or disappear as the product category or the markets mature, *155*

EARLY ADOPTERS   the second group to adopt a new product (after innovators); they represent about 13.5 percent of a market, *224*

EARLY MAJORITY   the third group to adopt a new product (after innovators and early adopters); they represent about 34 percent of a market, *224*

ECONOMIC ENVIRONMENT
factors and trends that are related to the production of goods and services and population incomes and that affect the purchasing power of markets, *35*

EFFICIENT ASSORTMENT   the practice of reducing the number of brands or sizes without affecting sales or consumers' perceptions of variety, *172*

ELABORATION LIKELIHOOD MODEL   a theory of persuasion that includes individual motivation and the ability to elaborate information in advertisements as determinants of two different "routes" of persuasion, *400*

ELASTIC DEMAND   demand for a product that changes substantially in response to small changes in price; when demand is elastic, a small decrease in price may substantially increase total revenues, 270

ELECTRONIC BUSINESS (E-BUSINESS) use of the Internet to conduct business activities, 491

ELECTRONIC COMMERCE (E-COMMERCE) use of the Internet for buying and selling products that are transported either physically or digitally from location to location, 491

ELECTRONIC DATA INTERCHANGE (EDI) a computerized system that allows exchange of information between parties; part of a quick-response inventory control system, 357

ELECTRONIC MARKETING (E-MARKETING) use of the Internet to perform marketing activities, 491

EMBARGO prohibition against trade with a particular country, imposed by the UN or individual governments, 37

EMOTIONAL APPEALS ad message strategies that attempt to evoke feelings, moods, and memories to sell a product, 403

ENCODING the process in communications by which the source chooses the words, pictures, and other symbols used to transmit the intended message, 376

ENCRYPTION in order to maximize site security, Web site operators use this to convert readable messages into an unreadable format unless the reader is authorized by the system, 509

ENTREPRENEURIAL PERSPECTIVE an emphasis on innovation, risk taking, and proactiveness in all marketing activities, 17

ENTRY STRATEGY the approach used to begin marketing products internationally; options run the gamut from exporting to joint ventures to direct investment, 66

ENVIRONMENTAL PROTECTION AGENCY (EPA) agency of the U.S. government whose goal is to protect the environment, 39

ENVIRONMENTAL SCANNING identifying relevant factors and trends and assessing their potential impact on the organization's markets and marketing activities, 27

E-RETAILING retail sales over the Internet, 327, 495

ETHICS PERSPECTIVE addressing the morality of marketing decisions and practicing social responsibility, 34

ETHNIC PATTERNS the norms and values of specific groups or subcultures, which may be formed around nationality, religion, race, or geographic factors, 86

ETHNOGRAPHIC RESEARCH technique in which market researchers record how consumers actually use products, brands, and services from day to day by entering their homes, observing consumption behavior, and recording pantry and garbage content, 134

EUROPEAN UNION (EU) the world's largest consumer market, consisting of 16 European nations: France, Germany, Italy, the Netherlands, Belgium, Luxembourg, Britain, Ireland, Denmark, Greece, Spain, Portugal, Sweden, Finland, Norway, and Austria, 257

EVERYDAY-LOW-PRICING (EDLP) suppliers reduce discounts and promotions to retailers; and retailers demand low prices from suppliers and minimize advertising and sales promotions to keep prices consistently low, 333

EXCHANGE the transfer of something tangible or intangible, actual or symbolic, between two or more social actors, 9

EXCHANGE RATE the price of one country's currency in terms of another country's currency, 247

EXCLUSIVE DEALING AGREEMENT a marketing channel arrangement between producer and reseller that restricts the reseller from carrying a competing product line, 311

EXCLUSIVE DISTRIBUTION using only one outlet in a geographic marketplace, 306

EXCLUSIVE TERRITORIES a marketing channel arrangement between a producer and a reseller that prohibits other resellers from selling a particular brand in a given geographic area, 311

EXISTING-BUSINESS SALESPEOPLE sales reps who work with established customers, writing up fairly routine orders, to provide a steady stream of sales revenue, 448

EXPANSION ADVERTISING advertising designed to increase usage by current customers with high awareness and high penetration, 402

EXPERT OPINION a qualitative approach to forecasting sales in which

analysts ask executives within the company or other experts to provide forecasts based on their own judgments, 167

EXPERT POWER power a member of a marketing channel gains by accumulating expertise and knowledge; for example, large retailers have gained much expert power using point-of-sale scanners to gauge product movements, price sensitivities, and trade promotion effectiveness, 310

EXPLICIT COMMUNICATIONS a distinct, clearly stated message conveyed through personal selling, advertising, public relations, sales promotion, direct marketing, or some combination of these methods, 381

EXPLORATORY RESEARCH research carried out to gain greater understanding or develop preliminary background and suggest hypotheses for a detailed follow-up study; may involve literature reviews, case analyses, interviews, and focus groups, 126

EXPORT AGENT a wholesaler that locates and develops markets abroad for products manufactured in its home country, operating on commission, 351

EXPORTING selling products to buyers in international markets, either directly or through intermediaries, 67

EXTENSIVE PROBLEM SOLVING using considerable mental effort and a substantial search for information, usually in response to a high-involvement decision, 83

EXTERNAL REFERENCE PRICES prices charged by other retailers or comparison prices a retailer provides to enhance perceptions of the advertised price, 260

EXTERNAL SECONDARY DATA secondary data that are collected from outside the firm and may be proprietary (provided by commercial marketing research firms) or nonproprietary (available from public sources), 128

EXTERNAL SOURCING acquiring specific brands from another firm or purchasing the entire firm to obtain ownership of its products, 203

FAD a subcategory of fashion that has a very short product life, 226

FAIR CREDIT REPORT ACT a U.S. law passed in 1970 to regulate the reporting and use of credit information, *38*

FAIR DEBT COLLECTIONS PRACTICE ACT a U.S. law passed in 1970 to regulate methods for collecting on debts, *38*

FAIR PACKAGING & LABELING ACT a U.S. law passed in 1965 to regulate the packaging and labeling of products, *38*

FAMILY BRAND NAME STRATEGY branding all items in a product line or even the entire product mix with a family name or the company name, *234*

FAMILY LIFE CYCLE the sequence of steps a family goes through, from young single adults to the married couple whose children have left home; household consumption patterns vary greatly across the family life cycle, *88*

FASHION a component of style whose products reflect what is currently popular, *226*

FAX-ON-DEMAND SYSTEMS allow instant response to 800-number requests for information. In these systems, a fax machine receives the request for information and immediately faxes the information back to the requester, *481*

FEAR APPEAL a type of emotional appeal used in an ad message strategy; for example, Michelin's "baby in a tire" theme, *403*

FEATURE a statement of fact about some aspect of a product or service (as opposed to a benefit, which is what the feature can do for the customer), *451*

FEDERAL COMMUNICATIONS COMMISSION (FCC) agency of the U.S. government that regulates the interstate communications industry, *39*

FEDERAL TRADE COMMISSION (FTC) agency of the U.S. government that regulates business practices; established by the Federal Trade Commission Act of 1914, *39*

FEEDBACK the part of the receiver's response that is communicated to the sender, *377*

FIELDWORK the process of contacting respondents, conducting interviews, and completing surveys in market research, *136*

FIVE Cs of pricing five critical influences on pricing decisions—costs, customers, channels of distribution, competition, and compatibility, *252*

FIXED COSTS costs that cannot be changed in the short run and do not vary with the quantity produced; they include plant investments, interest, and the costs of production facilities. See also **variable costs**, *272*

FLYER a single-page piece of direct mail printed on one or both sides of 8 1/2 × 11-inch paper and folded, *476*

FOB ORIGIN PRICING a form of geographic pricing in which buyers are charged the unit cost of goods plus shipping costs, which vary with location; in FOB (free on board), the goods are placed on a carrier and shipped to the customer, who pays the transportation charges, *284*

FOCUS GROUP an exploratory research method in which a moderator leads 8 to 12 people in a focused, in-depth discussion on a specific topic; used most for examining new-product concepts and advertising themes, investigating the criteria underlying purchase decisions, and generating information for developing consumer questionnaires, *130*

FOOD AND DRUG ADMINISTRATION (FDA) an agency of the U.S. government that regulates the food, drug, and cosmetics industries; established by the Food, Drug & Cosmetic Act of 1938, *39*

FORWARD BUYING when distributors or consumers stock up on enough of a product at a deal price to carry them over to the next sale, *435*

FORWARD INTEGRATION a corporate marketing channel system in which a channel member owns one or more of its buyers downstream (as opposed to backward integration, where it owns suppliers upstream), *302*

FRANCHISE SYSTEM a contractual marketing channel system where the franchisor grants a franchisee the right to distribute and sell specified goods and services and the franchisee agrees to operate according to marketing guidelines set forth by the franchisor under a recognized trademark or trade name, *302*

FRANCHISEE party that is granted rights (by the franchisor) to distribute and sell specified goods and services, *302*

FRANCHISOR parent company that grants rights to a franchisee to distribute and sell its goods and services, *302*

FREESTANDING INSERT (FSI) a preprinted ad, usually containing a

coupon, placed in a separate publication, such as a newspaper, *421*

FREIGHT ABSORPTION PRICING a form of geographical pricing in which the seller absorbs freight costs, *284*

FREQUENCY the number of times a person or household is exposed to a communication vehicle such as an ad, *408*

FULL-SERVICE WHOLESALER a wholesaler that performs a wide range of services for its customers and the parties from which it purchases, *347*

FUNCTIONAL LEVEL the various functional areas within a business unit, where most of the unit's work is performed (for example, marketing and accounting are functional areas), *52*

FUNCTIONAL MIDDLEMAN a wholesaler that does not take title to the products it sells, *346*

GAME a sales promotion that offers prizes like sweepstakes but covers a longer time period, *428*

GATEKEEPERS decision makers who control the flow of information and communication among buying-center participants, *113*

GENERAL AGREEMENT ON TARIFFS AND TRADE (GATT) an agreement under which countries meet periodically to negotiate matters related to trade and tariffs; in 1993, GATT was signed by 108 countries representing 80 percent of all global trade, *37*

GENERAL MERCHANDISE WHOLESALER a wholesaler that carries a wide variety of products and provides extensive services for its customers, *347*

GENERICS products that are not branded; they are labeled only by their generic name (tomato soup) and usually cost less and may be of lower quality than their branded competitors, *190*

GEODEMOGRAPHICS the combination of geographic information and demographic characteristics; used in segmenting and targeting specific segments, *159*

GLOBAL PERSPECTIVE a view of the marketplace that includes searching for marketing opportunities around the world, competing internationally, and working with multicultural suppliers, employees, channel participants, and customers, *28*

GLOBAL STRATEGY a corporate level strategy that views the whole world as a global market, *68*

GOING-RATE PRICING pricing at or near industry averages; strategy often when companies compete on the basis of attributes or benefits other than price, *279*

GOODS physical products such as cars, golf clubs, soft drinks, or other concrete entities (in contrast to services, which are nonphysical products), *180*

GOVERNMENT MARKET federal, state, and local government organizations that purchase goods and services for use in many activities, *114*

GROSS DOMESTIC PRODUCT (GDP) the total size of a country's economy measured in the amount of goods and services produced, *35*

GROSS MARGIN sales revenue minus the retailer's cost of goods sold, *335*

GROWTH STAGE the second stage in the product life cycle, when sales and profits increase rapidly, *226*

HIERARCHY OF EFFECTS see information-processing model, *398*

HIGH-INVOLVEMENT DECISIONS purchasing decisions that involve high levels of importance or personal relevance, thorough information processing, and substantial differences between alternatives, *82*

HYBRID CAMPAIGNS ad campaigns that blend traditional media with the Web to make the consumer an active participant, *502*

IDEA GENERATION the initial stage of the new-product development process, requiring creativity and innovation to generate ideas for potential new products, *206*

IDEA SCREENING evaluating the pool of new-product ideas to reduce it to a smaller, more attractive set, based on consistency with the company vision and strategic objectives, potential market acceptance, fit with the firm's capabilities, and possible long-term contribution to profit, *207*

IMPLICIT COMMUNICATIONS what the marketing message connotes about the product, its price, or the places it is sold, *381*

IMPORT AGENT a wholesaler that finds products in foreign countries to sell in its home country; in many countries, it is illegal to sell imported products without going through an import agent or similar intermediary, *351*

IMPULSE PURCHASES impulse purchases are decisions made with little or no cognitive effort; choices made on the spur of the moment without prior problem recognition, but possibly with strong positive feelings, *84*

INCENTIVE PAY commissions, bonuses, or both; about 75 percent of U.S. firms use a combination pay plan, less than 15 percent pay a straight salary, and 10 percent pay straight commission, *458*

INCOME-BASED PRICING the determination of price based upon the income to be generated by the product under consideration, *275*

INDEPENDENT RETAILERS retailers that own and operate only one retail outlet; they account for more than three-fourths of all U.S. retail establishments, *321*

INDIRECT CHANNEL a way to move the product from producer to user with the help of intermediaries that perform functions related to buying or selling the product, *299*

INDIVIDUAL BRAND NAME STRATEGY establishing specific and different brand names for each individual product in a product line, *234*

INDIVIDUAL PRODUCT any brand or variant of a brand in a company's product line, *221*

INELASTIC DEMAND the demand that exists when price changes do not result in significant changes in the quantity of a product demanded, *270*

INFOMERCIAL a program-length TV ad that resembles a talk show or news program, *405, 477*

INFORMATION-PROCESSING MODEL the sequence of advertising's effects: (1) exposure, (2) attention, (3) comprehension, (4) acceptance, and (5) retention; also called the **hierarchy-of-effects model**, *398*

INFORMATIONAL INFLUENCE an interpersonal process, based on

consumers' desire to make informed choices and reduce uncertainty, in which they seek information and advice from people they trust, *89*

INITIAL TRAINING sales training that focuses on product knowledge and sales techniques, *457*

INNOVATORS consumers who are most willing to try new products (about the first 2.5 percent of product adopters), *212, 224*

INQUIRY EVALUATION posttesting of an ad based on the number of consumers responding to requests in it, such as using coupons or asking for samples or more product information, *409*

INSTITUTIONAL ENVIRONMENT all the organizations involved in marketing products and services, including marketing research firms, ad agencies, wholesalers, retailers, suppliers, and customers, *41*

INSTITUTIONAL MARKET includes organizations such as profit or nonprofit hospitals, educational and religious institutions, and trade associations, *103*

INTEGRATED MARKETING COMMUNICATIONS the strategic integration of multiple means of communicating with target markets to form a comprehensive, consistent message; communications are integrated horizontally (across various methods of communications) and vertically (from the marketer down through the marketing channel), *374*

INTENSIVE DISTRIBUTION distributing a product or service through every available outlet, *306*

INTERACTIVE COMPUTER KIOSK an electronic marketing medium, usually located in retail stores, that uses touch-screen technology to let the consumer access information of interest, *480*

INTERACTIVE COMPUTER SERVICES systems that allow consumers and marketers to communicate with each other through phone lines and a personal computer, *479*

INTERCEPTOR LOCATION a location between a residential area and the closest supermarket, where a convenience store does business, *334*

INTERMARKET SEGMENTS well-defined, similar clusters of customers across national boundaries that let firms standardize marketing programs and offerings for each segment globally, *150*

INTERMEDIARIES middlemen directly involved in the purchase or sale of products as they flow from originator to user; they include retailers and wholesalers, *295*

INTERMODAL SHIPPING using two or more modes of transportation to ship products; for example, loaded trailers may travel piggyback on railcars, *360*

INTERNAL DEVELOPMENT a way to generate new products in which a firm creates the products itself, possibly subcontracting product design, engineering, or test marketing or working in partnership with another firm, *204*

INTERNAL REFERENCE PRICES comparison price standards that consumers remember and use to judge the fairness of prices; they include the expected price, the price last paid, the average retail price, and the price the consumer would like to pay now, *260*

INTERNAL SECONDARY DATA secondary data collected within a firm, including accounting records, salesforce reports and customer feedback, *128*

INTERSTATE COMMERCE COMMISSION (ICC) agency of the U.S. government that regulates interstate transportation, *39*

INTERTYPE COMPETITION competition among retailers that use different business formats to sell the same products; for example, McDonald's intertype competitors include all food retailers, from vending machines to fine restaurants, *330*

INTRATYPE COMPETITION competition among retailers that use the same business format, *330*

INTRODUCTION STAGE the first stage in the product life cycle, when a new product is launched into the marketplace; it continues the commercialization stage of the new-product development process, *225*

INVENTORY TURNOVER the number of times a retailer sells its average inventory during the year, or how quickly merchandise is sold, *335*

INVOLVEMENT the level of importance, interest, or personal relevance generated by a product or a decision, which varies by the decision at hand and by the person's needs or motives, *82*

ISO 9000 the International Standards Organization's 25-page set of quality standards; certification shows that a company meets world standards, *40*

ISOLATED LOCATIONS freestanding retail sites where there are no adjoining buildings; best suited for large retailers that can attract a customer base on their own or for convenience businesses, *331*

JOINT VENTURE an arrangement between two or more organizations to market products internationally, through licensing agreements, contract manufacturing deals, or equity investments in strategic partnerships, *67*

JUST-IN-TIME (JIT) INVENTORY CONTROL SYSTEM a system that delivers raw materials, subassemblies, and component parts to manufacturers shortly before the scheduled manufacturing run that will consume the incoming shipment, *357*

LABEL a printed description of a product on a package, *192*

LAGGARDS the final group to adopt a new product; they represent about 16 percent of a market, *224*

LANHAM TRADEMARK ACT a U.S. law passed in 1946 that protects trademarks and brand names, *38*

LATE MAJORITY the fourth group to adopt a new product; they represent about 34 percent of a market, *224*

LEASED DEPARTMENTS sections in a retail store that the owner rents to another party; typically department stores rent their jewelry, shoe, hairstyling, and cosmetic departments, *323*

LEGITIMATE POWER power a member of a marketing channel gains through ownership or contractual agreements, *310*

LICENSING the right to use a trademark in exchange for paying royalties on the sale of the licensed product, *192*

LIFESTYLE RESEARCH a person's pattern of living, as expressed in activities, interests, and opinions; lifestyle traits are more concrete than personality traits and more directly linked to the acquisition, use, and disposition of goods

and services. See also **psychographic research**, *160*

LIFETIME VALUE OF A LOYAL CUSTOMER the sales or profits generated from a customer who purchases a firm's product throughout their lifetime or some other extended time period, *5*

LIMIT PRICING a competitive pricing strategy that involves setting prices low to discourage new competition, *278*

LIMITED-FUNCTION WHOLESALER a truck jobber, drop shipper, cash-and-carry wholesaler, catalog wholesaler, or wholesale club that does not offer the comprehensive service of a full-service wholesaler, *348*

LIMITED-LINE WHOLESALER a full-service wholesaler that does not stock as many products as a general merchandise wholesaler but has more depth in its product offering, *348*

LIMITED PROBLEM SOLVING a situation between routinized response behavior and extensive problem solving; the consumer understands the relevant product attributes but may need some new information to, say, evaluate a new brand in a familiar product class, *83*

LINE-FILLING STRATEGY adding products in various places within a product line to fill gaps that may not be at either the high or the low end, *231*

LISTS databases of current or potential customers that include their names, addresses, telephone numbers, and perhaps data on demographics, lifestyles, brand and media preferences, and consumption patterns, *470*

LOGISTICS MANAGEMENT planning, implementing, and moving raw materials and products from point of origin to point of consumption, *345*

LONGITUDINAL RESEARCH research conducted over time, typically on a panel of consumers or stores, *127*

LOW-INVOLVEMENT DECISIONS purchase decisions that involve fairly little personal interest, relevance, or importance and simple decision processes, *82*

MAGNUSSON-MOSS ACT a U.S. law passed in 1975 to regulate warranties, *38*

MAIL SURVEYS marketing research method that involves sending questionnaires via mail, often to large, geographically diverse groups of people, *132*

MAJOR ACCOUNTS key, high-potential customers, *456*

MAJORITY FALLACY pursuing large "majority" market segments because they offer potential gains while overlooking the fact that they also may attract overwhelming competition, *165*

MALL INTERCEPT INTERVIEWS market research method in which consumers are interviewed one-on-one while shopping, *133*

MANUFACTURER BRAND a brand sponsored by the product's manufacturer, who is responsible for its quality and marketing. Also called a national brand or regional brand, *191*

MANUFACTURERS' AGENT a merchant wholesaler that sells related but noncompeting product lines for various manufacturers; also called **manufacturers' rep**, *350*

MANUFACTURER'S SALES BRANCH a manufacturer-owned wholesaler that maintains inventory and performs a wide range of functions for the parent company, *352*

MANUFACTURER'S SALES OFFICE a producer-owned wholesaler that differs from the manufacturer's sales branch in that it does not maintain inventory or perform as many functions for the parent company, *352*

MARGINAL COSTS costs that are incurred in producing one additional unit of output; they typically decline early due to economies of scale but increase as the firm approaches capacity, *272*

MARGINAL REVENUE the additional revenue a firm will receive if one more unit of product is sold (MR is usually the price of the product), *272*

MARKET a group of people or organizations with needs to satisfy or problems to solve, the money to satisfy needs or solve problems, and the authority to make expenditure decisions, *26*

MARKET COVERAGE the number of outlets used to market a product; may involve intensive, selective, or exclusive distribution, *306*

MARKET EXPANSION STRATEGY a corporate growth strategy of marketing existing products to new markets (different market segments in the same geographic area or the same

target market in different geographic areas), *59*

MARKET FORECAST the amount of sales predicted based on the marketing effort (expenditures) put forth by all the companies competing to sell a particular product or service in a specific period, *166*

MARKET MAVENS people who share with other consumers their knowledge about kinds of products, places to shop, and other facets of the market, *91*

MARKET PENETRATION STRATEGY achieving corporate growth objectives with existing products within existing markets, by persuading current customers to purchase more of the product or by capturing new customers, *59*

MARKET POTENTIAL the maximum amount of industry sales possible for a product or service for a specific period, *166*

MARKET SCOPE how broadly a business views its target market, *62*

MARKET SEGMENTATION dividing the market for a product into subsets of customers who behave in the same way, have similar needs, or have similar characteristics that relate to purchase behavior, *149*

MARKET SHARE a firm's percentage of the total market or total industry sales of a product, *249*

MARKET TESTS marketing a new product in test locations using the planned promotion, pricing, and distribution strategies, *167*

MARKETING the process of planning and executing the conception, pricing, promotion, and distribution of ideas, goods, and services to create exchanges that satisfy individual and organizational goals, *3*

MARKETING AS A SOCIETAL PROCESS a process that facilitates the flow of goods from producers to consumers in a society, *7*

MARKETING CHANNEL a combination of organizations and individuals (channel members) who perform the activities required to link producers to users to products to accomplish marketing objectives; also called **channel of distribution**, *295*

MARKETING COMMUNICATIONS marketer-

initiated techniques directed to target audiences in an attempt to influence attitudes and behaviors; its three main objectives are to inform, persuade, and remind consumers; also called promotion, *369*

MARKETING COMMUNICATIONS ACTIVITIES activities that include advertising and public relations, sales promotion, personal selling, and direct marketing, *371–375*

MARKETING COMMUNICATIONS MESSAGE what the company is trying to convey about its products, *376*

MARKETING COMMUNICATIONS MIX the combination of advertising, public relations, sales promotion, personal selling, and direct marketing; also called the promotional mix, *369*

MARKETING COMMUNICATIONS PLANNING a seven-step process: (1) marketing plan review, (2) situation analysis, (3) communications process analysis, (4) budget development, (5) program development, (6) integration and implementation of the plan, and (7) monitoring, evaluating, and controlling the marketing communications program, *377*

MARKETING CONCEPT the interrelated principles that (1) an organization's basic purpose is to satisfy customer needs, (2) satisfying customer needs requires integrated, coordinated efforts throughout the organization, and (3) organizations should focus on long-term success, *4*

MARKETING DECISION SUPPORT SYSTEM (MDSS) a comprehensive entity that encompasses all data, activities, and computerized elements used to process information relevant to marketing decisions; designed to enhance managerial decision making and firm performance by providing timely, relevant internal and external information, *140*

MARKETING ENVIRONMENT the uncontrollable environment within which marketers must operate, encompassing social, economic, competitive, technological, legal/political, and institutional environments; all factors outside an organization that can affect its marketing activities, *25*

MARKETING MANAGEMENT specific strategic decisions for individual products and the day-to-day activities needed to execute these strategies successfully, *55*

MARKETING MIX   the overall marketing effort to appeal to the target market, consisting of decisions in four basic areas: product, pricing, communications, and distribution, *10*

MARKETING PHILOSOPHY   an organization's emphasis on satisfying customers' needs; a focus on the marketing concept, *4*

MARKETING RESEARCH activities linking marketer, customer, and public through information used to identify marketing opportunities; generate, refine, and evaluate marketing actions; monitor marketing performance; and improve understanding of marketing as a process. Marketing research specifies the information required to address these issues, designs the methods for collecting information, manages and implements the data collection process, analyzes the results, and communicates the findings and implications, *123*

MARKETING RESEARCH DESIGNS   general strategies or plans of action for addressing research problems, data collection, and analysis, *126*

MARKETING RESEARCH PROCESS   a six-step sequence: (1) problem definition, (2) determination of research design, (3) determination of data collection methods, (4) development of data collection forms, (5) sample design, and (6) analysis and interpretation, *125*

MARKETING STRATEGIC PLAN a functional plan for how marketing managers will execute the business strategic plan, addressing the general target market and marketing mix, *53*

MARKETING STRATEGIES selecting a target market and developing a marketing mix to satisfy that market's needs, *10*

MARKUP PRICING   pricing where markup is the difference between the cost of an item and the retail price, expressed as a percentage, *273*

MASS CUSTOMIZATION   the ability of complex manufactured products to be made to order; possible because of advances in manufacturing and information technology, *152, 186*

MATURITY STAGE   the third stage of the product life cycle, when competition intensifies and sales growth slows, *226*

MEASURABILITY   the degree to which the size and purchasing power of market segments can be assessed, *154*

MEDIA CLASS   one of seven classes of advertising media: TV, magazines, newspapers, radio, outdoor, transit, and direct mail, *405*

MEDIA SCHEDULE   the frequency and timing of ads and commercials. See also **reach** and **frequency**, *408*

MEDIA VEHICLE   a specific TV program, magazine, or the like in any of the seven media classes, *407*

MERCHANT WHOLESALER   an independent distributor that takes title to the products it sells; may be either a full-service or a limited-function wholesaler, *346*

MESSAGE ACCEPTANCE   the point where the consumer develops favorable attitudes about the advertised product and subsequent purchase; step 4 in the information-processing model, *399*

MESSAGE CHANNEL   the means by which a company conveys its message about its products; for example, advertising vehicles like newspapers, TV, and billboards, *376*

MESSAGE COMPREHENSION the point where the consumer understands an ad's meaning; step 3 in the information-processing model, *399*

MESSAGE EXPOSURE   what a marketer achieves by placing ads in appropriate media, giving consumers the opportunity to process the message; step 1 in the information-processing or hierarchy of effects model, *398*

MESSAGE PRESENTER   a person, perhaps a salesperson, actor, or TV personality who actually delivers the message, *376*

MESSAGE RETENTION   the point where a consumer stores ad information in long-term memory, which is critical for affecting later purchase decisions and behavior; step 5 in the information-processing model, *399*

MESSAGE SPONSOR   the organization that is attempting to market its goods, services, or ideas, *376*

METROPOLITAN STATISTICAL AREA (MSA)   a geographic area identified by census data to contain a city with a population of at least 50,000 or be an urbanized area with 50,000 people that is part of a county of at least 100,000 residents, *159*

MICROMARKETING   using computer analysis of census and demographic data to identify clusters of households that share similar consumption patterns (for example, the PRIZM market segmentation system), *170*

MIDDLEMEN   see **intermediaries**, *295*

MISSION STATEMENT   an element in the strategic planning process that expresses the company's basic values and specifies the boundaries within which business units, marketing, and other functions must operate, *56*

MISSIONARY SALESPEOPLE sales support personnel who work at the grassroots level to promote their company's products; especially important in the grocery and pharmaceutical markets, *447*

MODIFIED REBUY DECISIONS business purchasing decisions that call for the evaluation of new alternatives; could involve considering new suppliers for current purchase needs or new products offered by current suppliers; an example is the purchase of complex component parts from a new supplier, *112*

MOTIVATION   the desire to process ad information; a state or condition within a person that prompts goal-directed behavior; it generally occurs when some need or problem is recognized and it can affect information search, information processing, and purchase behavior, *92, 399*

MULTINATIONAL STRATEGY recognizes national differences and views the collection of other countries as a portfolio of markets, *68*

MULTIPLE-CHANNELS STRATEGY   distributing a product through more than one channel to reach customers (for example, Prell shampoo is widely available at discount, drug, and grocery stores), *301*

NATIONAL BRAND   see **manufacturer brand**, *191*

NEGATIVE DISCONFIRMATION an experience where a purchase does not turn out as well as the consumer expected, *94*

NEGOTIATED PRICING   pricing in which negotiation between vendor and supplier replaces multiple bids; common for large investments. See also **sealed-bid pricing**, *284–285*

NEIGHBORHOOD BUSINESS DISTRICT a small grouping of stores, the largest usually a supermarket or variety store, located in the midst of a residential area, *332*

NETWORK ORGANIZATIONS firms involved in many different types of organizational partnerships, including strategic alliances, joint ventures, and vendor partnering, *4*

NEURAL NETWORKS sophisticated statistical techniques that can use a database to calculate weights for such traits as age, income, education, or time on the job, *474*

NEW-BUSINESS SALESPEOPLE members of the salesforce who concentrate on selling new products or selling to new customers, *448*

NEW-TASK DECISIONS business purchasing decisions that occur when the buying problem is new and a great deal of information must be gathered; relatively infrequent decisions for a company, and the cost of making a wrong decision is high, *111*

NOISE any distraction or distortion during the communications process that prevents the message from being communicated effectively, *377*

NONPRICE COMPETITION competition between brands for sales based on factors other than price, such as quality, service, or specific product features, *250*

NONPROBABILITY SAMPLING market research in which selection of the sample is based on the researcher's or field worker's judgment, *135*

NONPROPRIETARY SECONDARY DATA secondary data that are available from libraries, computer databases, and other public sources, *128*

NONREPUDIATION a process that precludes the later denial of a valid transaction by either buyer or seller and is a key element in building Web site security, *509*

NONSTORE RETAILING the selling of products and services outside a physical structure through, for example, direct marketing, direct selling, or vending machine sales, *327*

NORMATIVE INFLUENCE a strategy in which marketers show consumers the favorable conditions that can occur when their brands are used or the unfavorable consequences that can occur when not used, *90*

NORMS the expectations, real or imagined, of other individuals or groups of people, *89*

NORTH AMERICAN FREE TRADE AGREEMENT (NAFTA) a treaty that eliminates many trade barriers among the United States, Mexico, and Canada, *37*

NORTH AMERICAN INDUSTRIAL CLASSIFICATION SYSTEM (NAICS) a numerical scheme developed by the federal government for categorizing businesses, *104*

OBJECTIONS buyer concerns about a product, *452*

OBJECTIVE CLAIMS advertising messages that describe product features or performance in measurable terms, often reflecting a quality/value perspective, *402*

OBJECTIVE PRICE see price, *243*

OBJECTIVE-TASK BUDGETING a budgeting method for marketing communications based on achieving stipulated objectives, identifying tasks to meet those objectives, and evaluating results, *380*

OBSERVATION RESEARCH market research technique where a researcher or a video camera monitors customer behavior, or anonymous shoppers evaluate the quality of services offered, *133*

ODD–EVEN PRICING setting prices at just below an even amount (for example, contact lenses for $199.95 instead of $200), *280*

ON-LINE AUCTION COMPANY a firm that uses a computer network, typically the Internet, to bring buyers and sellers together, *351*

ON-LINE COUPONING refers to the distribution of coupons on the Internet, *426*

ONLINE DIRECT MARKETING that portion of electronic business that is communicating directly with target customers to encourage response, *469*

ON-SHELF COUPONING distributing coupons via a dispenser mounted near the manufacturer's product on a store shelf, *426*

OPERATIONAL PRODUCTS products that are used in a firm's activities but do not become part of any finished product; examples include lightbulbs, cleaning materials, and services (such as accounting or advertising), *185*

OPINION LEADERS people who influence consumer behavior through word-of-mouth communications based on their interest or expertise in particular products, *91*

OPPORTUNITIES areas where a company's performance might be improved; typically ranked by managers so the most important can be addressed first in the next strategic planning stage, *26*

OPPORTUNITY the extent to which distractions or limited exposure time affect the buyer's attention to brand information in an ad, *399–400*

ORDER in order processing, either a customer's purchase order or an order transmitted by a sales rep, *358*

ORDER TAKERS see existing-business salespeople, *448*

ORGANIZATION OF PETROLEUM EXPORTING COUNTRIES (OPEC) a loose federation of many of the oil-producing countries, designed to influence market prices and short-term profits for crude oil, *257*

ORGANIZED SALES PRESENTATION a mental or written outline developed by the salesperson that is flexible enough to allow adaptive selling, *451*

OUTCOME-BASED PERSPECTIVE a way of evaluating salesperson performance that focuses on the results of sales behavior, such as total sales volume; see also **behavior-based perspective**, *459*

OUTSOURCING a firm's decision to purchase products and services from other companies rather than to make the products or perform the services internally; examples include components for computers, shipping, telecommunications, payroll administration, *106*

PACKAGE the container or wrapper for a product, including the label, *192*

PARTITIONED PRICING a pricing strategy in which a firm divides the price of a product or service into parts in lieu of charging a single price; the parts are often termed *base price* and *surcharge*, 280

PAY-FOR-PERFORMANCE TRADE PROMOTION a sales promotion in which retailers are rewarded for making sales to consumers rather than purchases from manufacturers, 435

PENETRATION PRICING setting a low initial price to encourage initial product trial, stimulate sales growth and lower unit production costs, increase total revenues, and enhance profits, 248, 278

PERCEIVED MONETARY PRICE the consumer's subjective perception of whether the price of a product is high or low, fair or unfair (in contrast to objective price), 258

PERCEIVED VALUE the buyer's overall assessment of a product's utility based on what is received and what is given; the quality per dollar, 258

PERCENTAGE OF SALES BUDGETING a budgeting method for marketing communications based on the preceding year's or forecasted coming year's sales, 380

PERCEPTUAL MAPS spatial representations of consumer perceptions of products or brands, used to evaluate brand positions in a market, 170

PERIODIC DISCOUNTING offering occasional discounts to take advantage of consumer segments' differing price sensitivity; includes price skimming, 278

PERMISSION MARKETING marketing that occurs when the customer grants the marketer permission to send regular updates of interest to the consumer via e-mail, 371, 500

PERSONAL INTERVIEWS one-on-one interactions—between a consumer, customer, or respondent and a market researcher—to gather data, 132

PERSONAL SELLING the element of the marketing communications mix that involves face-to-face interactions between seller and buyer to satisfy buyer needs for their mutual benefit, 373, 445

PERSONALITY a person's consistent response to his or her environment, linked to susceptibility to persuasion and social influence and thereby to purchase behavior, 91

PERSONALIZATION a way for marketers to build site stickiness by customizing the look and content of a portal's home page, 500

PIPES the means used to get content from Web content providers into portals, 505

PLANNED SHOPPING CENTER a retail center that is centrally owned and managed, has ample parking, and offers a variety of stores, 332

PLUS-ONE DIALING method of telephone interview where a phone number is randomly selected from the local directory and a digit or digits added to it; allows inclusion of unlisted numbers in the sample, 132

POINT-OF-PURCHASE DISPLAY a sales promotion, often provided free by the manufacturer to the retailer, to call customer attention to a featured product, 432

POLITICAL/LEGAL ENVIRONMENT factors and trends related to governmental activities and specific laws and regulations that affect marketing practice, 36

PORTALS search engines that offer general Internet functions and that direct visitors to additional sites, 328, 499

POSITIONING developing an overall image for a product or brand by designing a marketing program, including the product mix, that a market segment will perceive as desirable, 169

POSITIVE DISCONFIRMATION an experience where a purchase turns out better than a consumer expected, 94

POSTTESTING recall and attitude tests and inquiry evaluations marketers use to assess the effectiveness of an ad campaign, 409

PRECALL PLANNING focusing on learning more about the customer's situation before making a sales call, 450

PREDATORY DUMPING dumping intended to drive rivals out of business, 256

PREDATORY PRICING charging very low prices to drive competition from the market and then raising prices once a monopoly has been established, 287

PREDICTIVE DIALING SYSTEMS automated dialing machines that make telemarketing more productive by passing over answering machines, busy signals, and no answers and passing live calls on to a live telemarketer, 479

PREDICTIVE MODELING manipulating a customer database to reach a desired target more effectively, using neural networks and other technologies, 474

PRELAUNCH ACTIVITIES marketing research studies conducted before commercialization of a new product, 215

PREMIUM an item given free or at a bargain price to encourage the consumer to buy, 428

PREMIUM PRICING setting higher prices on one or more product versions; a popular strategy for beer, clothing, appliances, and cars, 280

PRESTIGE PRICING keeping prices high to maintain an image of product quality and appeal to buyers who associate premium prices with high quality, 251

PRETESTING evaluating consumer reactions to proposed ads through focus groups and direct questioning, based on overall likability, consumer recall of information, message communication, and effects on purchase intentions and brand attitudes, 409

PRICE the amount of money a buyer pays a seller in exchange for products and services, 243

PRICE-AVERSION STRATEGY buying the lowest-priced brand (in contrast to the best-value strategy, which takes quality into account), 259

PRICE COMPETITION competition between brands for sales based on price alone; most common for similar brands and for customers with limited budgets and weak brand loyalties; see also **nonprice competition**, 250

PRICE DEAL a temporary reduction in the price of a product, in the form of a cents-off or price-pack deal, used to introduce a new brand, convince current users to purchase more, or encourage new users to try an established brand, 425

PRICE DISCRIMINATION selling the same product to different customers at different prices; restricted in the United States by the Robinson-Patman Act; see also **differential pricing**, 256

PRICE ELASTICITY OF DEMAND the responsiveness of customer demand to changes in a product's price, 245

PRICE-PACK DEAL a product that offers consumers something extra through the packaging itself; for example, a box of cereal with 20 percent more cereal for the regular price, 425

PRICE PROMOTION MIX the basic price plus such supplemental components as sale prices, temporary discounts, coupons, and favorable payment and credit terms; encourages purchase behavior by strengthening the basic price during relatively short periods of time, *244*

PRICE/QUALITY RELATIONSHIP the extent to which a consumer associates a higher product price with higher quality, *259*

PRICE-SEEKING STRATEGY purchasing the highest-priced brand to maximize expected quality, *259*

PRICE-SENSITIVITY MEASUREMENT (PSM) a pricing approach that incorporates input from potential buyers, who read a product description and then plot on a scale the prices they would pay, yielding price estimates high enough to reflect the product's perceived value but low enough to avoid sticker shock, *275*

PRICE SIGNALING a competitive pricing strategy that puts high prices on low-quality products, *278*

PRICE SKIMMING setting prices high initially to appeal to consumers who are not price sensitive, then lowering prices sequentially to appeal to the next market segments, *249, 278*

PRICE THRESHOLD the point at which buyers notice a price increase or decrease; the threshold level depends on a product's average price (for example, a 10¢ reduction on a 50¢ product is more meaningful than on a $10 product), *282*

PRIMARY DATA data collected for a particular research problem—for example, survey information; typically more current and relevant than secondary data but more expensive to gather, *127*

PRIMARY DEMAND general demand for a new product form, which marketing tries to generate at the introduction stage of the product life cycle, *227*

PRIMARY METROPOLITAN STATISTICAL AREA (PMSA) a major urban area, often located within a CMSA, that has at least one million inhabitants, *159*

PRIVATE BRAND see distributor brand, *191*

PRIVATE LABEL see distributor brand, *191*

PRIVATE RESPONSE a complaint in which a dissatisfied consumer bad-mouths a product to friends or family, *95*

PRIVATE WAREHOUSE a warehouse operated by the company that uses it, *356*

PRIZM potential rating index by ZIP markets, which divides every neighborhood in the United States into one of 40 distinct cluster types that reveal consumer data; PRIZM+4 uses ZIP+4 codes for even greater detail covering individual demographics, individual credit records, model-specific auto registration, and purchase behavior data from private sources, *170*

PROACTIVE PR a form of public relations that is positive and opportunity seeking, such as product release announcements, event sponsorship, and placement of articles in the business press, *413*

PROBABILITY SAMPLING market research in which each person in the population has a known, nonzero chance of being selected by some objective procedure; such unbiased selection increases the sample's representativeness, *135*

PROBLEM DEFINITION the first step in the marketing research process; identifying the difference between the way things should be and the way they are or identifying the issues that need to be investigated, *126*

PRODUCT an idea, a physical entity (a good), a service, or any combination that is an element of exchange to satisfy individual or business objectives, *179*

PRODUCT COMPETITORS companies that offer different kinds of products to satisfy the same basic need (for example, Domino's Pizza and Kentucky Fried Chicken both attempt to satisfy a consumer need for fast food but offer somewhat different products and services from each other), *41*

PRODUCT DESIGN the styling, aesthetics, and function of a product, which affect how it works, how it feels, and how easy it is to assemble, fix, and recycle, *187*

PRODUCT DIFFERENTIATION circumstance in which a firm's offerings differ or are perceived to differ from those of competing firms on any attribute, including price, *152*

PRODUCT EXPANSION STRATEGY marketing new products to the same customer base, *60*

PRODUCT LIFE CYCLE (PLC) the advancement of a product through the stages of introduction, growth, maturity, and decline, *223*

PRODUCT LINE a group of individual products that are closely related in some way, *221*

PRODUCT-LINE CONTRACTION deleting individual products from a product line, *232*

PRODUCT-LINE LENGTH the number of products in any one product line, *222*

PRODUCT-LINE PRICING offering multiple versions of the same product, with those priced at the low end used to build traffic and those at the high end creating a quality image for the entire product line, *243*

PRODUCT MARKETING PLANS plans within each business unit that focus on specific target markets and marketing mixes for each product and include both strategic decisions (what to do) and execution decisions (how to do it), *53*

PRODUCT MIX the total assortment of products and services marketed by a firm, *221*

PRODUCT-MIX CONSISTENCY the relatedness of the different product lines in a product mix; for example, all of Schwab's product lines are investment-related, but J&J sells everything from contact lenses to baby powder, *223*

PRODUCT-MIX WIDTH the number of product lines in a company's product mix, *222*

PRODUCT PLACEMENT ADVERTISING the combined efforts of marketers with moviemakers, such that product exposure is obtained among moviegoers, *405*

PRODUCTION PHILOSOPHY an organization's emphasis on the production function, valuing activities related to improving production efficiency or producing sophisticated products and services, *4*

PRODUCTION PRODUCTS raw materials and components that become part of some finished product (for example, steel and paper), *185*

PRODUCTIVITY PERSPECTIVE getting the most output for each marketing dollar spent, by doing the same things better and/or doing different things, *298*

PROJECT MATRIX ORGANIZATION an approach to new-product development in which a project manager has primary responsibility and authority, and functional managers assign personnel as needed, *214*

PROJECT TEAM ORGANIZATION an approach to new-product development in which a project manager heads a core group of people selected from various functional areas; managers from the different functional areas are not formally involved, *214*

PROJECTIVE TECHNIQUES market research methods, such as word association or sentence completion, that let researchers elicit feelings that normally go unexpressed, *133*

PROMOTIONAL INTERACTIVE COMPUTER DISKS a relatively new format for direct-mail campaigns in which the information is presented on disk and the consumer can respond, *479*

PROPRIETARY SECONDARY DATA data provided by commercial marketing research firms that sell their services to other firms; examples are diary panels and scanner data, *129*

PROSPECTING the seller's search for and identification of qualified buyers, defined as buyers who are reasonably accessible to the seller, able to afford the purchase, and willing to consider making it, *450*

PROTOTYPE DEVELOPMENT converting the concept for a new product into an actual product, using the information obtained from concept tests to design a tangible product that can be tested further, *209*

PSYCHOGRAPHIC RESEARCH a concept for dividing a market into lifestyle segments on the basis of consumer interests, values, opinions, personality traits, attitudes, and demographics to develop marketing communications and product strategies, *92, 160*

PSYCHOLOGICAL PRICING the recognition that buyers' perceptions and beliefs affect their evaluations of prices, *280*

PUBLIC RELATIONS (PR) the element of the marketing communications mix that identifies, establishes, and maintains mutually beneficial relations between an organization and the various publics on which its success or failure depends—for example, customers, employees, stockholders, community members, and the government, *372, 412*

PUBLIC RELATIONS FUNCTIONS press relations; product promotions; internal and external corporate communications; lobbying to promote, defeat, or circumvent legislation and regulations; advising management about public issues and company positions and image; and overall responding to various occurrences in the marketplace, either reactively or proactively, *413*

PUBLIC SERVICE ADVERTISING (PSAs) advertising donated by the ad industry to promote activities for some social good, *397*

PUBLIC WAREHOUSE a for-hire facility available to any business that requires storage or handling of goods, *356*

PUBLICITY information about the company or product that appears, unpaid for, in the news media; primary publicity techniques are news releases, press conferences, and feature articles, often presented in the business press, *372, 413*

PUFFERY advertising that contains claims including acceptable exaggeration, *402*

PULL STRATEGY concentrating marketing communications on consumers to stimulate demand in an attempt to get consumers to "pull" a product from the manufacturing company through the marketing channel, *382*

PUSH MONEY what a manufacturer pays retail salespeople to encourage them to promote its products over competitive brands or to sell specific products in the manufacturer's line, *434*

PUSH STRATEGY directing marketing communications toward intermediary channel members to "push" a product through the channel to the ultimate consumer, *382*

QUALITATIVE DATA open-ended responses obtained from in-depth interviews, focus groups, and some observation studies; characterized by depth of response and richness of description, *131*

QUALITY the totality of features and characteristics of a product or service that bear on its ability to satisfy stated or implied needs, *186*

QUALITY FUNCTION DEPLOYMENT (QFD) a procedure in the new-product development process that links specific consumer requirements with specific product characteristics, *209*

QUANTITATIVE DATA information collected using more structured response formats that can be more easily analyzed and projected to larger populations, *132*

QUICK-RESPONSE (QR) INVENTORY CONTROL SYSTEM a system for providing retailers with finished goods in which inventory is restocked according to what has just been sold, based on small but frequent orders, *357*

QUOTAS the quantitative outcomes (such as total sales volume, gross margin, market share, number of new accounts added, and accounts retained) used to assess sales reps' performance and effectiveness, *459*

RACK JOBBER a specialty-line wholesaler that sells to retail stores, setting up and maintaining attractive store displays and stocking them with goods sold on consignment, *348*

RANDOM-DIGIT DIALING a method of telephone interviewing where, for example, four random digits are added to three-digit telephone exchanges to reach consumers, *132*

REACH the number of different people or households exposed to an ad or campaign over a specified time period (usually four weeks), *408*

REACTIVE PR a form of public relations that addresses negative events or changes in the marketplace that adversely affect the firm, such as negative publicity from product defects or employee behavior, *413*

READER-RESPONSE CARDS card inserts in magazines, used in conjunction with ads, that make it easy for readers to send for more information on a product, *478*

REBATE cash reimbursement for purchasing a product, in which the buyer must mail a rebate form, the receipt, and proof of purchase to the manufacturer within a certain time, *426*

RECEIVER the intended target for any basic communication; for example, a purchasing agent listening to a sales presentation or a consumer reading a magazine ad, *375*

RECIPROCITY when firm A purchases from supplier B who in turn buys A's own products and services, *115*

REFERENCE GROUPS interpersonal influences beyond the

family, including friends and co-workers, *89*

REFERENT POWER power a member of a marketing channel gains through another member's desire to be associated with it, *310*

REGIONAL BRAND see manufacturer brand, *191*

RELATED DIVERSIFICATION branching out into new products and markets that have something in common with existing operations (for example, a video rental store diversifying into music retailing), *60*

RELATIONSHIP MARKETING developing, maintaining, and enhancing long-term profitable relationships with customers, *17*

RELATIONSHIP PERSPECTIVE building partnerships with firms outside the organization and encouraging teamwork among different functions within the organization to develop long-term customer relationships, *140, 297*

RELATIONSHIP SELLING see relationship marketing, *448*

RELATIONSHIP STRATEGY a framework for working with customers based on relationship selling; it includes the counselor strategy, the supplier strategy, and the systems-designer strategy, *454*

RELIABILITY reflects the consistency of responses or the extent to which results are reproducible, *139*

REPOSITIONING developing new marketing programs to shift consumer beliefs and opinions about an existing brand; see also **positioning**, *170*

RESELLER MARKET firms that purchase goods and in turn sell them to others at a gain; includes wholesalers and retailers, *115*

RESERVATION PRICE the highest price a person is willing to pay for a product; one form of a consumer's internal reference price, *260*

RETAIL CHAIN a retailer that owns and operates multiple retail outlets; chains represent 20 percent of all retailers and account for 50 percent of all retail sales, *322*

RETAIL COOPERATIVE a group of stores that remain independently owned but adopt a common name and storefront and band together to increase their buying power, *323*

RETAIL FRANCHISING a form of chain ownership in which a franchisee pays the franchisor (parent company) fees or royalties and agrees to run the franchise by prescribed norms in exchange for use of the franchisor's name, *322*

RETAIL SALES sales to final consumers, as opposed to wholesale sales; a firm's retail sales must be at least half of its total revenues for it to be classified a retailer, *319*

RETAIL STRATEGY MIX the controllable variables of location, products and services, pricing, and marketing communications, *334*

RETAILER-OWNED COOPERATIVE GROUP a contractual marketing channel system in which the retailers own the wholesaler, *302*

RETAILING all of the activities involved in selling products and services to the final consumer; retailers include independents, chains, franchises, leased departments, cooperatives, and various forms of nonstore retailers, *319*

RETURN ON INVESTMENT (ROI) ratio of income before taxes to total operating assets associated with a product, such as plant and equipment and inventory, *250*

REWARD POWER power a member of a marketing channel gains when it can offer another member widespread distribution, special credit terms, or some other reward, *310*

ROBINSON-PATMAN ACT a U.S. law passed in 1936 to prohibit price discrimination, *38*

ROLLOUT STUDIES marketing research studies performed on a new product after it has been introduced, *215*

ROUTINIZED RESPONSE BEHAVIOR a quick, habitual decision with limited search for information in response to some need, *82*

SALES AUTOMATION SYSTEMS computerized systems sales managers use for routine supervisory chores such as processing sales reps' call reports, itineraries, and expense reports, *458*

SALES CHANNEL STRATEGY addresses how a company initiates and maintains contact with customer through the use of a company field salesforce, telemarketing, independent sales reps, distributors, or trade shows, *455*

SALES EFFECTIVENESS EVALUATIONS the most stringent tests of advertising efficiency, they assess whether the advertising resulted in increased sales, *410*

SALES MANAGEMENT managers who oversee the personal selling function, managing sales personnel and developing and implementing sales strategy, *445*

SALESFORCE EFFECTIVENESS how well the entire sales organization is performing, including an evaluation of individual salespeople's performance, *459*

SALESFORCE TURNOVER the proportion of salespeople who leave their jobs, *457*

SALES POTENTIAL the maximum amount of sales a specific firm can obtain for a specified time period, *166*

SALES PROCESS the process of initiating, developing, and enhancing long-term, mutually satisfying relationships with customers, *448*

SALES PROMOTION the element of the marketing communications mix that provides extra value or incentives to consumers, wholesalers, retailers, or other organizational customers to stimulate product interest, trial, or purchase; media and nonmedia marketing communications employed for a predetermined, limited time to stimulate trial, increase consumer demand, or improve product availability, *372, 421*

SALES RESISTANCE customer concerns about a product, both spoken (objections) and unspoken, *452*

SALES SUPPORT SALESPEOPLE employees who support the personal selling function by promoting a product or providing technical support, working in coordination with the salespeople who actually solicit customer purchases, *447*

SALES TERRITORY usually defined geographically, a territory consists of specific customers assigned to a specific salesperson, *449*

SALESPERSON PERFORMANCE how well individual salespeople meet job expectations, evaluated from a behavior-based perspective, an outcome-based perspective, or a combination of the two, *459*

SAMPLE a small size of a product made available to prospective purchasers, usually free, to demonstrate a product's value or use and encourage future purchase, *429*

SAMPLE SIZE   the size of a sample in market research, based on the anticipated response rate, variability in the data, cost, and time considerations and desired level of precision, *136*

SAMPLING FRAME   the outline or working description of the population used in sample selection for market research, *135*

SANCTIONS   restrictions imposed by the UN or individual governments to limit trade with specific countries, *37*

SCANNER DATA   a type of proprietary data derived from UPC bar codes, *129*

SCRAMBLED MERCHANDISING   adding unrelated product categories to existing product lines, *333*

SEALED-BID PRICING   pricing in which sellers submit sealed bids for providing their products or services and the buyer chooses among them. See also **negotiated pricing**, *285*

SEASONALITY   product demand fluctuations related to the time of year, which may be affected by unpredictable changes in weather and in consumer preferences, *331*

SECOND-MARKET DISCOUNTING   a form of differential pricing in which different prices are charged in different market segments (for example, foreign markets), *277*

SECONDARY BUSINESS DISTRICT   a concentration of retail stores defined by the intersection of two major thoroughfares, *332*

SECONDARY DATA   proprietary and nonproprietary data already collected for some other purpose and available from various sources (such as library research); typically cheaper than collecting primary data but may be less current or relevant, *128*

SECONDARY DEMAND   demand for a specific brand of new product form, which marketing tries to generate after competing brands are introduced, *227*

SELECTING   choosing the candidates to be hired for a sales job, *457*

SELECTIVE DISTRIBUTION   involves selling a product in only some of the available outlets and is commonly used when after-the-sale service is necessary, such as in the home appliance industry, *306*

SELECTIVE PERCEPTION   information is only partially processed or is misinterpreted due to limited exposure, attention, or comprehension; caused most often by the consumer's limited ability and motivation to see and process everything, *399*

SELF-CONCEPT   a person's overall perception and feelings about himself or herself; consumers buy products that are consistent with or that enhance their self-concept, *91*

SELLING PHILOSOPHY   an organization's emphasis on the selling function to the exclusion of other marketing activities, *4*

SELLING STRATEGY   an overall plan for a salesperson's course of action, developed at three levels: sales territory, customer, and individual sales call, *449*

SERVICE MERCHANDISER   see **rack jobber**, *348*

SERVICE RETAILERS   all retailers that sell services, from rental businesses to movie theaters, hotels, and car repair shops, *319*

SERVICES   nonphysical products such as a haircut, a football game, or a doctor's diagnosis (in contrast to goods, which are physical products), *180*

SHERMAN ACT   a U.S. law passed in 1890 to prohibit monopolistic practices, *38*

SHIPPING CONTAINER MARKING (SCM)   feeds information into a computerized tracking system to facilitate shipping of products, *357*

SHOPPING PRODUCTS   categories of items within which consumers do not know exactly what they want and are willing to spend time shopping; usually expensive items such as cars, TVs, *183*

SIMPLE RANDOM SAMPLING   a probability sampling approach in which each unit has an equal chance of being selected, *135*

SIMULATED TEST MARKETING   evaluating a new-product prototype in situations set up to be similar to those where consumers would actually purchase or use the product (for example, intercepting shoppers at a high-traffic location in a mall), *211*

SINGLE-CHANNEL STRATEGY   using only one means to reach customers (for example, Nexxus shampoo is distributed exclusively through hair care professionals), *301*

SINGLE-SOURCE DATA   data produced by proprietary systems that combine information on product purchase behavior with TV viewing behavior, *129*

SITE STICKINESS   a term used to describe a marketer's goal of boosting customer interactions and time spent on a site, *499*

SLOTTING ALLOWANCES   fees manufacturers pay to retailers or wholesalers to obtain shelf or warehouse space for their products, *337*

SOCIAL CLASSES   relatively homogenous divisions within a society that contain people with similar values, needs, lifestyles, and behavior. Usually divided into four classes: upper, middle, working, and lower, *87*

SOCIAL ENVIRONMENT   all factors and trends related to groups of people, including their number, characteristics, behavior, and growth projections, *27*

SOCIAL RESPONSIBILITY   minimizing social costs, such as environmental damage, and maximizing the positive impact of marketing decisions on society, *84*

SOCIALIZATION   absorbing a culture, a process that continues throughout life and produces many specific preferences of products and services, shopping patterns, and interactions with others, *85*

SOURCE   the message sender; in marketing communications, the marketer, *103, 376*

SOURCE CREDIBILITY   the state in which a customer perceives that its needs are satisfied by the combination of the sales rep, the product or service, and the rep's company, *451*

SOURCES   companies or individuals who sell products and services directly to buying organizations; also called **suppliers** or **vendors**, *p. 103*

SPAM   unsolicited e-mail, *501*

SPECIALTY-LINE WHOLESALER   a wholesaler that sells only a single product line or part of a line but is an expert regarding those products, *348*

SPECIALTY PRODUCTS   items for which consumers want a specific brand and are willing to hunt for it; they won't switch brands (as with convenience products) or shop to evaluate alternatives (as for shopping products), *184*

SPIFF see push money, *434*

SPONSORSHIP investments in causes and events to support overall corporate and marketing objectives, *375*

STANDARD INDUSTRIAL CLASSIFICATION (SIC) SYSTEM a federal government numerical scheme for categorizing businesses from general industry groupings to specific product categories, *105*

STANDARD TEST MARKETING testing a new-product prototype and its marketing strategy in actual market situations, *211*

STANDARDIZED MARKETING STRATEGY implementing the same product, price, distribution, and communications programs in all international markets, *67*

STATEMENT STUFFERS promotional pieces that are included in other mail, such as bank or credit card statements, *476*

STATISTICAL DEMAND ANALYSIS forecasting sales from equations in which price, promotion, distribution, competitive, and economic factors are independent variables, *168*

STEALTH MARKETING involves a wide range of publicity generators, from product placement in movies and television to the naming of sports facilities, such as the United Center in Chicago, *374*

STORE BRAND see distributor brand, *191*

STORE IMAGE the picture shoppers have of a store's identity, composed of their perceptions of its location, goods and services sold, and atmospherics, *333*

STRAIGHT REBUY DECISIONS most common type of business purchasing decision in which products and services are simply repurchased; delivery, performance, and price are critical considerations, *112*

STRATEGIC BUSINESS UNIT (SBU) a unit of a company that focuses on a single product or brand, a line of products, or a mix of related products that meet a common market need and whose management oversees the basic business functions, *60*

STRATEGIC MARKETING marketing activities that encompass three

functions: (1) helping to orient everyone in the organization toward markets and customers, (2) helping to gather and analyze information needed to examine the current situation, identify trends in the marketing environment, and assess their potential impact, and (3) helping to develop corporate, business, and marketing strategic plans, *54*

STRATEGY MIX one way by which retailers differentiate themselves from one another. This consists of the following (all controllable) elements: location, product and services, pricing, and marketing mixes, *334*

STRATIFIED SAMPLING a probability sampling technique in which the population is divided into mutually exclusive groups, such as consumers with different income levels, and random samples are taken from each group, *135*

STRING LOCATION a grouping of stores that sell similar goods and services (for example, cars or mobile homes), *332*

STYLE a unique form of expression that is defined by a product's characteristics and has a fluctuating life cycle, *226*

SUBJECTIVE CLAIMS advertising claims that are not measurable and often stress image enhancement, *402*

SUBLIMINAL ADVERTISING initially related to ad messages presented at a rate or level below thresholds of conscious awareness, this practice today most often involves the embedding of hidden symbols in advertisements, *405*

SUBSTANTIALNESS the degree to which identified target segments are large enough and have sufficient sales and profit potential to warrant separate marketing programs, *154*

SUPPLIERS see sources, *103*

SUPPLY-CHAIN MANAGEMENT the "effort involved in producing and delivering a final product from the supplier's supplier to the customer's customer," usually by cutting across organizational and company boundaries, In order to better serve the customer and gain a competitive advantage, *103*

SURROGATE SHOPPERS those who are a commercial enterprise, consciously engaged and paid, by a consumer or other interested partner on behalf of the consumer, to perform any or all of the activities involved in consumer decision making, *82*

SURVEY OF BUYERS' INTENTIONS sales forecast based on surveys of what either consumers or organizational buyers say they will do; such surveys are most reliable when the buyers have well-formed intentions and are willing to disclose them accurately, *167*

SWEEPSTAKES a sales promotion that offers prizes based on a chance drawing of participants' names, *428*

TARGET COSTING a pricing process that combines both cost and customer input into pricing decisions; determines what the manufacturing costs must be to achieve desired profits and customer features, as well as acceptable market prices, *253*

TARGET MARKET a defined group of consumers or organizations with whom a firm wants to create marketing exchanges, *10*

TARGET-RETURN PRICING a cost-oriented approach that sets prices to achieve a desired rate of return, with cost and profit estimates based on some expected volume or sales level, *274*

TARGETING selecting which segments in a market are appropriate to focus on and designing the means to reach them, *152*

TEAM SELLING a sales approach in which a company assigns accounts to sales teams of specialists according to the customers' purchase-information needs, *456*

TECHNICAL SUPPORT SALESPEOPLE the people in sales support who have expertise in areas such as design and installation of complex equipment and may provide specialized training to customer employees, *448*

TECHNOLOGICAL ENVIRONMENT factors and trends related to innovations that affect the development of new products or the marketing process, *40*

TECHNOLOGY PERSPECTIVE using new and emerging technologies as sources for new products and services and to improve marketing practice, *17*

TELEMARKETING an interactive direct marketing communications approach that uses the phone to initiate, develop, and enhance relationships with customers, *478*

TEST MARKETING testing the prototype of a new product and its marketing strategy in simulated or actual market situations, *211*

TESTIMONIALS third-party evidence, such as letters from satisfied customers, that enhance source credibility, *451*

THIRD-PARTY RESPONSE a complaint about a product in which the consumer takes legal action or files a complaint with a consumer-affairs agency instead of dealing just with the company, *95*

THREATS trends in the marketing environment that might adversely affect a company's situation; typically ranked by managers so the most important threats can be addressed first in the next strategic planning stage, *26*

TIE-IN see cross-promotion, *427*

TOTAL COSTS the sum of variable costs and fixed costs, *272*

TOTAL REVENUE total sales, or unit price multiplied by the quantity of the product sold; (before-tax) profits equal total revenue minus total costs, *272*

TRADE ALLOWANCE the amount a manufacturer contributes to a local dealer or retailer's advertising expense, *432*

TRADE CONTEST a sales promotion at the reseller level that associates prizes with sales of the sponsor's product, *432*

TRADE SALES PROMOTION sales promotion directed at retailers, wholesalers, or other business buyers to help push products through the marketing channel, *421*

TRADE SALES PROMOTION ALLOWANCES concessions a manufacturer allocates to wholesalers or retailers to promote its products (for example, supermarkets' cooperative advertising), *284*

TRADE SHOW a periodic, semipublic event sponsored by a trade, professional, or industrial association at which suppliers rent booths to display products and provide information to potential buyers, *433*

TRADEMARK a brand or part of a brand that is registered with the U.S. Patent and Trademark Office, giving the owner exclusive rights to use the brand, *188*

TRANSACTION MARKETING producing sales in the short run at any cost, *455*

TRANSACTION VALUE the perceived merits of the deal itself; retailers provide comparison pricing in an effort to boost products' transaction value by raising shoppers' internal price standard, *261*

TREND ANALYSIS a quantitative forecasting approach that examines historical sales data for predictable patterns (also known as time-series analysis), *167*

TRUCK JOBBER a limited-function wholesaler that delivers within a small geographic area to ensure freshness of goods (for example, bakery, meat, dairy), *348*

TWO-WAY STRETCH STRATEGY adding products at both the low and the high end of a product line, *231*

TYING CONTRACT a marketing channel arrangement in which a manufacturer requires a reseller to buy products in addition to the one it really wants, *311*

UNAIDED RECALL TESTS posttesting in which consumers are questioned with no prompting about ads, *409*

UNDIFFERENTIATED STRATEGY marketing a single product using a single promotional mix for the entire market; most often used early in the life of a product category, *164*

UNIFORM DELIVERED PRICE a form of geographical pricing in which each customer, no matter where located, is charged the same average freight amount, *284*

UNIT PRICING price information presented on a per-unit weight or volume basis so shoppers can compare prices across brands and across package sizes within brands, *287*

UNIVERSAL PRODUCT CODE (UPC) bar code that is scanned at grocery checkouts and can provide secondary data for marketing research, *129*

UNPLANNED BUSINESS DISTRICT shopping area that evolved spontaneously and is made up of independently owned and managed retail operations; types include central business districts, secondary business districts, neighborhood business districts, and string locations, *332*

UNRELATED DIVERSIFICATION branching out into products or services that have nothing in common with existing operations, *60*

UPWARD STRETCH STRATEGY adding products at the higher end of a product line; for example, Japanese carmakers entered the U.S. market at the low end and gradually added higher-priced cars, *231*

U.S.–CANADA TRADE ACT a law passed in 1988 to allow free trade between the United States and Canada, *38*

UTILITARIAN INFLUENCE compliance with the expectations of others to achieve rewards or avoid punishments (for example, peer disapproval), *89*

VALIDITY refers to the extent to which the measures or questions used in a study truly reflect the concepts being studied, *139*

VALUE-ADDED RESELLERS (VARs) intermediaries that add value to goods and services as they pass through the marketing channel, *345*

VALUE-EXPRESSIVE INFLUENCE a desire to enhance self-concept through identification with others (for example, by purchasing a product endorsed by a celebrity), *89*

VALUE IN USE (VIU) an approach for determining the economic value that a product has relative to an existing competitive offering, *276*

VALUE-IN-USE PRICING basing pricing on customer estimates of the costs if the service could not be obtained (for example, downtime costs if a computer could not be repaired), *253*

VALUES shared beliefs or cultural norms about what is important or right, which directly influence how consumers view and use products, brands, and services, *85*

VALUES AND LIFESTYLES PROGRAM (VALS) a lifestyle program from SRI International that segments consumers into eight groups: actualizers, fulfillers, believers, achievers, strivers, experiencers, makers, and strugglers, *161*

VARIABLE COSTS costs that change with the level of output, such as wages and raw materials; see also **fixed costs**, *272*

VENDORS see **sources**, *103*

VERTICAL MARKETING SYSTEMS centrally coordinated, highly integrated operations in which the product flows down the channel from producer to ultimate consumer; the basic vertical types are corporate, contractual, and administered channel systems, *301*

VIDEO CATALOG a direct-mail catalog in videocassette form, *476*

VOICE RESPONSE a complaint about a product in which the customer seeks satisfaction directly from the seller, *95*

WEBLINING the positive aspects of the Internet's ability to allow companies to identify high- and low-value customers so that deals and special services can be targeted only to the most profitable customers, *512*

WHOLESALE CLUB a club whose members pay an annual fee that entitles them to make tax-free purchases at lower-than-retail prices, *349*

WHOLESALE SALES sales to other businesses that resell the product or service or use it in running their own businesses (as opposed to retail sales), *319*

WHOLESALER-SPONSORED VOLUNTARY GROUP a contractual marketing channel system consisting of independent retailers that operate under the name of a sponsoring wholesaler, *302*

WHOLESALERS firms that sell to manufacturers and industrial customers, retailers, government agencies, other wholesalers, and institutional customers such as schools and hospitals, *345*

WHOLESALING refers to the marketing activities associated with selling products to purchasers who resell the products, use them to make another product, or use them to conduct business activities, *345*

WRITTEN SALES PROPOSAL a detailed written presentation of a product's capabilities, benefits, and costs, often tailored to the individual customer, *450*

ZONE PRICING a form of geographical pricing in which customers within one area (say, the Northeast) are charged one freight price and more-distant zones are charged higher freight amounts, *284*

Notes

Chapter One

[1]Peter D. Bennett, ed., *Dictionary of Marketing Terms* (Chicago: American Marketing Association, 1988), p. 54.

[2]Nevin J. "Dusty" Rhodes, "Marketing a Community Symphony Orchestra," *Marketing News,* January 29, 1996, p. 2.

[3]Cyndee Miller, "How a Bank Marketed Itself and Its Town," *Marketing News,* July 12, 1996, pp. 8, 12.

[4]Chad Rubel, "Marketing Briefs," *Marketing News,* November 20, 1995.

[5]H. Lee Murphy, "How Campaign 2000 Will Be Different," *Marketing News,* November 8, 1999, pp. 8–9.

[6]Chad Rubel, "Managers Buy Into Quality When They See That It Works," *Marketing News,* March 25, 1996, p. 14.

[7]For different perspectives concerning the marketing concept, see Franklin S. Houston, "The Marketing Concept: What It Is and What It Is Not," *Journal of Marketing,* April 1986, pp. 81–87; Frederick E. Webster, Jr., "The Rediscovery of the Marketing Concept," *Business Horizons,* May–June 1988, pp. 29–39; Lynn W. McGee and Rosann L. Spiro, "The Marketing Concept in Perspective," *Business Horizons,* May–June 1988, pp. 40–45; and Ajay K. Kohli and Bernard J. Jaworski, "Market Orientation: The Construct, Research Propositions, and Managerial Implications," *Journal of Marketing,* April 1990, pp. 1–18.

[8]James L. Heskett, Thomas O. Jones, Gary W. Loveman, W. Earl Sasser, Jr., and Leonard A. Schlesinger, "Putting the Service-Profit Chain to Work," *Harvard Business Review,* March–April 1994, pp. 165–66.

[9]Ibid., p. 164.

[10]Laura Struebling, "Customer Loyalty: Playing for Keeps," *Quality Progress,* February 1996, pp. 25–26.

[11]Thomas O. Jones and Earl Sasser, Jr., "Why Satisfied Customers Defect," *Harvard Business Review,* November–December 1995, pp. 91–93.

[12]Heskett et al., "Putting the Service-Profit Chain to Work," pp. 166–67.

[13]Dexter Roberts, "A Tale of Two Families," *Business Week,* June 28, 1999, pp. 52–56.

[14]William L. Wilkie and Elizabeth S. Moore, "Marketing's Contribution to Society," *Journal of Marketing,* Special Issue 1999, pp. 198–218.

[15]Avraham Shama, "Management under Fire: The Transformation of Managers in the Soviet Union and Eastern Europe," *The Executive,* February 1993, pp. 22–35.

[16]See Franklin S. Houston and Jule B. Gassenheimer, "Marketing and Exchange," *Journal of Marketing,* October 1987, pp. 3–18, for a more complete discussion of exchange and marketing.

[17]Richard P. Bagozzi, "Toward a Formal Theory of Marketing Exchange," in *Conceptual and Theoretical Developments in Marketing,* eds. O. C. Ferrell, Stephen W. Brown, and Charles W. Lamb, Jr. (Chicago: American Marketing Association, 1979), p. 434.

[18]This section draws heavily from the historical analysis and marketing evolution conceptualization presented in Ronald A. Fullerton, "How Modern Is Modern Marketing? Marketing's Evolution and the Myth of the 'Production Era,' " *Journal of Marketing,* January 1988, pp. 108–25.

[19]Arch W. Shaw, *An Approach to Business Problems* (Cambridge: Harvard University Press, 1916), p. 104.

Chapter Two

[1]Polly LaBarre, "How Skandia Generates Its Future Faster," *Fast Company,* December–January 1997, p. 58.

[2]Nafis Sadik, "World Population Continues to Rise," *The 1992 Information Please Almanac* (Boston: Houghton Mifflin, 1991), p. 131.

[3]John W. Wright, *The Universal Almanac 1993* (Kansas City, MO: Andrews and McMeel, 1992), p. 326.

[4]Ibid., p. 279.

[5]Dan Morse, "Follow the Demographics, Franchising Experts Agree," *The Wall Street Journal Interactive Edition,* December 21, 1999, pp. 1–4.

[6]Dom Del Prete, "Wall Street Bullish on Mature Adults," *Marketing News,* December 6, 1993, pp. 1–2.

[7]Michele Marchetti, "Talkin' 'bout My Generation," *Sales & Marketing Management,* December 1995, p. 66.

[8]"They Understand Your Kids," *Fortune,* Autumn–Winter 1993, pp. 29–30.

[9]Tom W. Smith, *The Emerging 21st Century American Family,* National Opinion Research Center, University of Chicago, GSS Social Change Report No. 42, November 24, 1999, p. 28.

[10]Laura Zinn, Heather Keets, and James B. Treece, "Home Alone—with $660 Billion," *Business Week,* July 29, 1990, pp. 76–77.

[11]Joseph Weber, "What's Not Cookin' at Campbell's," *Business Week,* September 23, 1996, p. 40.

[12]Amy Hilliard-Jones, "Consumers of Color Are Changing the American Marketplace," *Marketing News,* November 18, 1996, p. 8.

[13]Ibrahim Sajid Malick, "New Americans: The Overlooked $400 Billion Market," *Marketing News,* July 15, 1996, p. 9.

[14]Hilliard-Jones, "Consumers of Color," p. 8.

[15]Malick, "New Americans," p. 9.

[16]Maria Puente and Martin Kasindorf, "Blended Races Make a True Melting Pot," *USA Today,* September 7, 1999, pp. 1A and 13A.

[17]Erika Rasmusson, "Marketing en Espanol," *Sales & Marketing Management,* September 1999, p. 16.

[18]Cyndee Miller, "She Succeeds Royally Even in a Bear Market," *Marketing News,* July 29, 1996, p. 2.

[19]Tim Triplett, "Increase in Women Golfers Sparks Marketing Interest," *Marketing News,* June 3, 1996, pp. 2, 14.

[20]"To Your Health," *Modern Maturity,* January–February 1999, p. 23.

[21]Susan Hansen, "Herbal-Tonic Bottler Has Healthy Start," *INC.,* June 1999, pp. 21–22.

[22]Marvin Cetron and Owen Davies, *Crystal Globe* (New York: St. Martin's Press, 1991), pp. 353–54.

[23]"Edison Environmental Awards," *Marketing News*, May 6, 1996, p. E14.

[24]Ronald Grover, Joyce Barnathan, Dexter Roberts, and Stan Crock, "Go East, Media Moguls," *Business Week*, March 22, 1999, p. 40.

[25]John Ward Anderson, "Thundering Herd," *The Courier-Journal* (Louisville, KY), January 2, 1994, p. A8.

[26]Jay M. Tannon, "NAFTA Is Good News for U.S. Trade," *Business First*, November 29, 1993, p. 7.

[27]Amy Borrus, Bill Javetski, John Parry, and Brian Bremner, "Change of Heart," *Business Week*, May 20, 1996, pp. 48–49.

[28]Cyndee Miller, "Opening the Vietnam Market," *Marketing News*, April 12, 1993, pp. 1–2; David Rogers, "In the New Vietnam, Baby Boomers Strive for Fun and Money," *The Wall Street Journal*, January 7, 1994, pp. A1–A5; Urban C. Lehner, "U.S. Firms Head for Vietnam, but Find Asian, European Firms Already There," *The Wall Street Journal*, February 10, 1994, p. A14; and James Walsh, "Peace Finally at Hand," *Time*, February 14, 1994, pp. 34–36.

[29]Sheri Prasso and Paul Magnusson, "Welcome Back?" *Business Week*, August 16, 1999, p. 54.

[30]Joyce Barnathan and David Lindorff, "Hong Kong's New Boss," *Business Week*, December 23, 1996, pp. 50–54.

[31]Mike France, Peter Burrows, Linda Himelstein, and Michael Moeller, "Does a Breakup Make Sense?" *Business Week*, November 22, 1999, pp. 38–41.

[32]Tony Czuczka, "Bonn, Germany," *Associated Press*, July 5, 1996, pp. 1–2.

[33]Robert S. Greenberger, "Syria Enjoys Economic Boom, Boosted by Freedom Allowed under Law No. 10," *The Wall Street Journal*, January 4, 1994, p. A5.

[34]Maxine S. Lans, "New Laws on Green Marketing Are Popping Up All the Time," *Marketing News*, February 15, 1993, pp. 22, 24.

[35]Elyse Tanouye, "Warner-Lambert Drug Is Approved for Epilepsy Cases," *The Wall Street Journal*, January 4, 1994, p. B12.

[36]Stephen Baker, "Did Smithkline Find the Smoking Gun?" *Business Week*, April 29, 1996, p. 44.

[37]Jonathan B. Levine, "What EC Business? You Have Two Choices," *Business Week*, October 19, 1992, pp. 58–59.

[38]"The List: Adapt or Die," *Business Week*, July 26, 1999, p. 6.

[39]John Carey, "U.S. Innovation Ain't What It Used to Be," *Business Week*, March 22, 1999, p. 6.

[40]Marvin Cetron and Owen Davies, *Crystal Globe* (New York: St. Martin's Press, 1991), pp. 329–34.

[41]"Know Thy Enemy," *Success*, June 1996, p. 10.

[42]Cetron and Davies, *Crystal Globe*, p. 358.

[43]G. Pascal Zachary, "Global Growth Attains a New, Higher Level That Could Be Lasting," *The Wall Street Journal*, March 13, 1997, pp. A1 and A8.

Chapter Three

[1]Tom Peters, *Liberation Management* (New York: Alfred A. Knopf, 1992), p. 45.

[2]Michael H. Morris and Leyland F. Pitts, "The Contemporary Use of Strategy, Strategic Planning, and Planning Tools by Marketers: A Cross-National Comparison," *European Journal of Marketing*, 1993, pp. 36–57.

[3]Ronald Grover and Eric Schine, "Can Hilton Draw a Full House?" *Business Week*, June 8, 1992, pp. 88–89.

[4]Francy Blackwood, "Dissecting the Service," *Selling*, March 1996, pp. 26–28; *Hoover's Company Profile Database* (Austin, TX: The Reference Press, 1996); and Malcolm Fleschner, "Copy This, Copy This, Copy This," *Selling Power*, March 1996, pp. 22–26.

[5]Adapted from William Keenan, Jr., "America's Best Sales Forces: Six at the Summit," *Sales & Marketing Management*, June 1990, pp. 66–72; Brian Dumaine, "PG Rewrites the Marketing Rules," *Fortune*, November 6, 1989, pp. 34–48; and Alecia Swasy, "In a Fast-Paced World, Procter & Gamble Sets Its Store in Old Values," *The Wall Street Journal*, September 21, 1989, pp. A1–A2.

[6]Philip Kotler, *Marketing Management*, The Millennium Edition (Upper Saddle River, NJ: Prentice Hall); Anil Menon, Sundar G. Bharadwaj, Phani Tej Adidam, and Steve W. Edison, "Antecedents and Consequences of Marketing Strategy Making: A Model and a Test," *Journal of Marketing*, April 1999, pp. 18–40; and Charles H. Noble and Michael P. Mokwa, "Implementing Marketing Strategies: Developing and Testing a Managerial Theory," *Journal of Marketing*, October 1999, pp. 57–73.

[7]Frederick E. Webster, Jr., "The Changing Role of Marketing in the Corporation," *Journal of Marketing*, October 1992, pp. 1–17.

[8]Ibid., p. 10.

[9]Ravi S. Achrol and Philip Kotler, "Marketing in the Network Economy," *Journal of Marketing*, Special Issue 1999, pp. 146–47.

[10]George S. Day and David B. Montgomery, "Charting New Directions for Marketing," *Journal of Marketing*, Special Issue 1999, pp. 3–13.

[11]Christine Moorman and Roland T. Rust, "The Role of Marketing," *Journal of Marketing*, Special Issue 1999, p. 180.

[12]Adapted from John A. Pearce II and Fred David, "Corporate Mission Statements: The Bottom Line," *Academy of Management Executive*, May 1987, p. 109.

[13]James C. Collins and Jerry I. Porras, "Building Your Company's Vision," *Harvard Business Review*, September–October 1996, pp. 65–77.

[14]http://www.benjerry.co.uk/aboutbj/mission.htm.

[15]http://www.whirlpool.com/whr/ics/story/vision.html.

[16]Gilbert Fuchsberg, " 'Visioning' Missions Becomes Its Own Mission," *The Wall Street Journal*, January 7, 1994, pp. B1, B4.

[17]http://www.boeing.com/companyoffices/aboutus/mission/index.html.

[18]Linda Himelstein, "The Soul of a New Nike," *Business Week*, June 17, 1996, pp. 70–71.

[19]Ian P. Murphy, "Survey Finds Safe Growth Is Priority for New Products," *Marketing News*, July 15, 1996, p. 15.

[20]Terry Lefton, "Nike's New Golf Balls Aim Straight up Fairway," *Brandweek*, January 18, 1999, p. 5; and Chuck Stogel, "Nike Restages Golf Push for '00," *Brandweek*, June 28, 1999, p. 34.

[21]"Tootsie Roll Industries," *Fortune*, January 10, 1994, p. 109.

[22]David W. Cravens, *Strategic Marketing* (Homewood, IL: Richard D. Irwin, 1994), pp. 46–47.

[23]Gary McWilliams, "DEC's Comeback Is Still a Work in Progress," *Business Week*, January 18, 1993, p. 75.

[24]Julia Flynn, David Greising, Kevin Kelly, and Leah Nathans Spiro, "Smaller but Wiser," *Business Week*, October 12, 1992, pp. 28–29.

[25]Webster, "The Changing Role of Marketing in the Corporation," p. 10.

[26]George S. Day, *Analysis for Strategic Marketing Decisions* (St. Paul, MN: West Publishing Company, 1995), pp. 202–5.

[27]Philip Kotler, *Marketing Management: Analysis, Planning, Implementation, and Control*, 8th ed. (Englewood Cliffs, NJ: Prentice Hall, 1994), p. 76.

[28]John A. Byrne, "Strategic Planning," *Business Week*, August 26, 1996, pp. 46–52; Peter Elstrom, "Did Motorola Make the Wrong Call?" *Business Week*, July 29, 1996, pp. 66–68; Gary Hamel and C. K. Prahalad, *Competing for the Future* (Boston: Harvard Busi-

ness School Press, 1994); Webster, "The Changing Role of Marketing," pp. 1–17; and John O. Whitney, "Strategic Renewal for Business Units," *Harvard Business Review,* July–August 1996, pp. 84–98.

[29]Andrea Rothman, Gail DeGeorge, and Eric Sheine, "The Season of Upstart Startups," *Business Week,* August 31, 1992, pp. 68–69.

[30]"General Excellence: Southwest Airlines," *Sales & Marketing Management,* August 1993, p. 38.

[31]Kevin Kelly, Wendy Zellner, and Aaron Bernstein, "Suddenly Big Airlines Are Saying: 'Small Is Beautiful,' " *Business Week,* January 17, 1994, p. 37.

[32]Pierre Sparaco, "Swissair Expands Partnership Network," *Aviation Week and Space Technology,* August 23, 1999, p. 56.

[33]Joseph B. White, "GM Saturn Unit Trumpets Profit Turned in 1993," *The Wall Street Journal,* January 6, 1994, p. A4.

[34]David Sedgwick, "Saturn Cadillac Evolves, as GM Keeps Trucking," *Automotive News,* August 16, 1999, p. 20.

[35]Edmund Faltermayer, "Competitiveness: How U.S. Companies Stack Up Now," *Fortune,* April 18, 1994, pp. 52–64.

[36]Gary McWilliams, "Wang's Great Leap out of Limbo," *Business Week,* March 7, 1994, pp. 68–69.

[37]"Cadbury Buys Spanish Concern," *The Wall Street Journal,* April 22, 1994, p. A6.

[38]Kathy Rebello and Neil Gross, "A Juicy New Apple?" *Business Week,* March 7, 1994, pp. 88–90; "Ciba-Geigy Plans China Venture," *The Wall Street Journal,* April 22, 1994, p. A6; and Brian Coleman and Bridget O'Brian, "Delta Airlines, Virgin Atlantic Forge Alliance," *The Wall Street Journal,* April 13, 1994, p. A4.

[39]David M. Szymanski, Sundar G. Bharadwaj, and P. Rajan Varadarajan, "Standardization versus Adaptation of International Marketing Strategy: An Empirical Investigation," *Journal of Marketing,* October 1993, pp. 1–17; Subhash C. Jain, "Standardization of International Marketing Strategy: Some Research Hypotheses," *Journal of Marketing,* January 1989, pp. 70–79; and John A. Quelch and Edward J. Hoff, "Customizing Global Marketing," *Harvard Business Review,* May–June 1986, pp. 59–68.

[40]Quelch and Hoff, "Customizing," p. 59.

[41]James E. Ellis, "Why Overseas? 'Cause That's Where the Sales Are," *Business Week,* January 10, 1994, p. 63.

[42]Richard A. Melcher and Stewart Toy, "On Guard, Europe," *Business Week,* December 14, 1992, pp. 54–55.

[43]Ellis, "Why Overseas?" p. 63.

[44]Sally Solo, "How to Listen to Consumers," *Fortune,* January 11, 1993, pp. 77–78.

[45]Michael R. Czinkota and Ilka A. Ronkainen, *International Marketing,* 4th ed. (Fort Worth, TX: Dryden Press, 1995), pp. 263–65; and Jean-Pierre Jeannet and H. David Hennessey, *Global Marketing Strategies,* 3rd ed. (Boston: Houghton Mifflin Company, 1995), p. 336.

[46]David A. Aaker and Erich Joachimsthaler, "The Lure of Global Branding," *Harvard Business Review,* November–December 1999, p. 138.

[47]Edward F. McQuarrie and Shelby McIntyre, "The Customer Visit: An Emerging Practice in Business-to-Business Marketing," *Marketing Science Institute,* May 1992, p. 10.

[48]Ginger Trumfio, "Kodak Adjusts Its Focus," *Sales & Marketing Management,* January 1994, p. 20.

[49]Maricris G. Briones, "Strange Bedfellows," *Marketing News,* August 17, 1998, p. 2.

[50]Louis Bucklin and Sanjit Sengupta, "Organizing Successful Co-Marketing Alliances," *Journal of Marketing,* April 1993, pp. 32–46; Manohar U. Kalwani and Narakesari Narayandas, "Long-Term Manufacturer–Supplier Relationships: Do They Pay Off for Supplier Firms?" *Journal of Marketing,* January 1995,

pp. 1–16; and Robert M. Morgan and Shelby D. Hunt, "The Commitment–Trust Theory of Relationship Marketing," *Journal of Marketing,* July 1994, pp. 20–38.

[51]Maricris G. Briones, "Strange Bedfellows," *Marketing News,* August 17, 1998, p. 2.

[52]Bernard Simonin and Julie Ruth, "Is a Company Known by the Company It Keeps? Assessing the Spillover Effects of Brand Alliances on Consumer Brand Attitudes," *Journal of Marketing Research,* February 1998, pp. 30–42; "Credit Card Co-Branding on the Rise: Survey," *Supermarket News,* June 5, 1998, p. 21; Harriet Marsh, "P&G Enters the Age of Alliances," *Marketing,* February 11, 1999, p. 18; R. Venkatesh and Vijay Mahajan, "Products with Branded Components: An Approach for Premium Pricing and Partner Selection," *Marketing Science* 16, no. 2 (1997), pp. 146–65.

Chapter Four

[1]http://www.EconoMagic.com/beana.htm

[2]Annetta Miller, "The Millennial Mind-Set: It's Here, It's Clear, Get Used to It," *American Demographics,* January 1999, pp. 60–65; and Cheryl Russell, "The New Consumer Paradigm," *American Demographics,* April 1999, pp. 51–58.

[3]http://www.infores.com/public/marketing/press/new/n18schro.htm December 3, 1999; Craig Karman, "Companies to Watch," *The Wall Street Journal,* November 29, 1999, p. R6.

[4]Tom W. Smith, "The Emerging 21st Century American Family," *GSS Social Exchange Report No. 42* (Chicago, IL: National Opinion Research Center, University of Chicago, November 24, 1999), p. 28.

[5]Frank Rose, "If It Feels Good, It Must Be Bad," *Fortune,* October 21, 1991, p. 100.

[6]"The Procter & Gamble Company: Global Opportunities and Growth," *1995 Annual Report,* Cincinnati, OH.

[7]*What the Customer Wants: The Wall Street Journal's Guide to Marketing in the 1990s* (New York: Dow Jones, 1990), p. vi.

[8]Bernard J. Jaworski and Ajay K. Kohli, "Market Orientation: Antecedents and Consequences," *Journal of Marketing,* July 1993, p. 53.

[9]Peter R. Dickson, "Toward a General Theory of Competitive Rationality," *Journal of Marketing,* January 1992, p. 70.

[10]Robert Hof, Heather Green, and Paul Judge, "Going, Going, Gone," *Business Week,* April 12, 1999, pp. 30–32; Sloane Lucas, Lycos, mySimon Tout New User Guides," *Brandweek,* August 9, 1999, p. 31; Michael Schrage, "The Tangled Web of E-Deception," *Fortune,* September 27, 1999, p. 296; Erica Goode, "The On-Line Consumer? Tough, Impatient, and Gone in a Blink," *The New York Times,* September 22, 1999, p. 22; and Edward C. Baig, "The Biggest Used-Car Lot of All," *Business Week,* August 9, 1999, pp. 96–98.

[11]J. Jeffrey Inman and Russell S. Winer, "Where the Rubber Meets the Road: A Model of In-Store Decision Making," *Report No. 98-122* (Cambridge, MA: Marketing Science Institute, October 1998), p. v.

[12]Stanley C. Hollander and Kathleen M. Rassuli, "Shopping with Other People's Money: The Marketing Management Implications of Surrogate-Mediated Consumer Decision-Making," *Journal of Marketing* 63 (April 1999), pp. 102–18; and Paco Underhill, "What Shoppers Want," *Inc.,* July 1999, pp. 72–82.

[13]J. Paul Peter and Jerry C. Olson, *Consumer Behavior and Marketing Strategy,* 3rd ed. (Homewood, IL: Richard D. Irwin, Inc., 1993), p. 57.

[14]James F. Engel, Roger D. Blackwell, and Paul W. Miniard, *Consumer Behavior,* 7th ed. (Ft. Worth, TX: Dryden Press, 1993), pp. 276–77.

[15]Thomas S. Robertson, "Low-Commitment Consumer Behavior," *Journal of Advertising Research,* April 1976, pp. 19–24.

[16]Jeffrey J. Stoltman, James W. Gentry, Kenneth A. Anglin, and Alvin C. Burns, "Situational Influences on the Consumer Decision Sequence," *Journal of Business Research,* November 1990, p. 196.

[17]Marcia Mogelonsky, "America's Hottest Markets," *American Demographics,* January 1996, p. 22.

[18]John C. Mowen, *Consumer Behavior,* 2nd ed. (New York: Macmillan Publishing Company, 1990), pp. 332–33; and Dennis W. Rook, "The Buying Impulse," *Journal of Consumer Research,* September 1987, pp. 189–99.

[19]Stephen J. Hoch and George F. Lowenstein, "Time-Inconsistent Preferences and Consumer Self-Control," *Journal of Consumer Research,* March 1991, pp. 492–502.

[20]Geert Hofstede, "Culture and Organizations," *International Studies of Management and Organizations* 10, no. 4 (1981), pp. 15–41; Martin S. Roth, "The Effects of Culture and Socioeconomics on the Performance of Global Brand Image Strategies," *Journal of Marketing Research,* May 1995, p. 172; and Mikael Sandergaard, "Hofstede's Consequences: A Study of Reviews, Citations, and Replications," *Organizational Studies* 15, no. 3 (1994), pp. 447–56.

[21]Lynn R. Kahle, Sharon E. Beatty, and Pamela Homer, "Alternative Measurement Approaches to Consumer Values: The List of Values (LOV) and Values and Life Style (VALS)," *Journal of Consumer Research,* December 1986, p. 406.

[22]Engel et al., *Consumer Behavior,* p. 87.

[23]Joel Garreau, *The Nine Nations of North America* (Boston: Houghton Mifflin, 1981).

[24]Mowen, *Consumer Behavior,* pp. 618–19.

[25]Michael M. Phillips, "Selling by Evoking What Defines a Generation," *The Wall Street Journal,* August 13, 1996, p. B1.

[26]Richard P. Coleman, "The Continuing Significance of Social Class to Marketing," *Journal of Consumer Research,* December 1983, pp. 265–80.

[27]Jerry C. Olson, *Consumer Behavior and Marketing Strategy,* 3rd ed. (Homewood, IL: Richard D. Irwin, 1993), p. 490.

[28]Greg J. Duncan, Timothy M. Smeeding, and Willard Rogers, "The Incredible Shrinking Middle Class," *American Demographics,* May 1992, p. 38.

[29]Rebecca Piirto Heath, "The New Working Class," *American Demographics,* January 1998, p. 52.

[30]Mowen, *Consumer Behavior,* p. 527; and Scott Ward, "Consumer Socialization," *Journal of Consumer Research,* September 1974, pp. 1–14.

[31]James U. McNeal, "Tapping the Three Kid's Markets," *American Demographics,* April 1998, pp. 37–41.

[32]Robert Bontilier, "Pulling the Family's Strings," *American Demographics,* August 1993, p. 46.

[33]Chip Walker, "Can TV Save the Planet?" *American Demographics,* May 1996, pp. 42–48.

[34]William D. Danko and Charles M. Schaninger, "An Empirical Evaluation of the Gilly-Enis Updated Household Life Cycle Model," *Journal of Business Research,* August 1990, p. 39; Mary C. Gilly and Ben M. Enis, "Recycling the Family Life Cycle: A Proposal for Redefinition," in *Advances in Consumer Research,* vol. 9, ed. Andrew Mitchell (Ann Arbor, MI: Association for Consumer Research, 1982), pp. 271–76; Patrick Murphy and William Staples, "A Modernized Family Life Cycle," *Journal of Consumer Research,* June 1979, pp. 12–22; and Charles M. Schaninger and William D. Danko, "A Conceptual and Empirical Comparison of Alternative Household Life Cycle Models," *Journal of Consumer Research,* March 1993, pp. 580–94.

[35]Tom W. Smith, "The Emerging 21st Century American Family," *GSS Social Exchange Report No. 42,* (Chicago, IL: National Opinion Research Center, University of Chicago, November 24, 1999), p. 28.

[36]Diane Crispell, "Dual-Earner Diversity," *American Demographics,* July 1995, pp. 32–37, 55; and Marcia Mogelonsky, "The Rocky Road to Adulthood," *American Demographics,* May 1996, pp. 26–35, 56.

[37]Hal Espen, "Levi's Blues," *New York Times Magazine,* March 21, 1999, p. 54.

[38]Terry L. Childers and Akshay Rao, "The Influence of Familial and Peer-Based Reference Groups on Consumer Decisions," *Journal of Consumer Research,* September 1992, p. 204; and William O. Bearden and Michael J. Etzel, "Reference Group Influence on Product and Brand Purchase Decisions," *Journal of Consumer Research,* September 1982, p. 184.

[39]Edward B. Keller, "Customers Provide Due Influence for Product," *Marketing News,* June 7, 1999, p. H37.

[40]Lawrence F. Feick and Linda L. Price, "The Market Maven: A Diffuser of Marketplace Information," *Journal of Marketing,* January 1987, pp. 83–97.

[41]Chip Walker, "Word of Mouth," *American Demographics,* July 1995, p. 38.

[42]"Poor College Students Ain't What They Used to Be," *Marketing News,* August 16, 1999, p. 3.

[43]M. Joseph Sirgy, "Self-Concept in Consumer Behavior: A Critical Review," *Journal of Consumer Research,* December 1982, pp. 287–88.

[44]Beth A. Walker and Jerry L. Olson, "Means-End Chains: Connecting Products with Self," *Journal of Business Research,* March 1991, p. 111.

[45]Stephen J. Hoch and George F. Lowenstein, "Time-Inconsistent Preferences and Consumer Self-Control," *Journal of Consumer Research,* March 1991, pp. 492–502; and Sirgy, "Self-Concept in Consumer Behavior," pp. 288–89.

[46]Harold H. Kassarjian and Mary Jane Sheffet, "Personality and Consumer Behavior: An Update," in *Perspectives in Consumer Behavior,* 4th ed., eds. H. H. Kassarjian and T. S. Robertson (Englewood Cliffs, NJ: Prentice Hall, 1990), pp. 281–363.

[47]John L. Lastovicka, "On the Validation of Lifestyle Traits: A Review and Illustration," *Journal of Marketing Research,* February 1982, p. 126.

[48]William L. Wilkie, *Consumer Behavior* (New York: John Wiley & Sons, 1986), p. 307.

[49]Abraham H. Maslow, *Motivation and Personality,* 2nd ed. (New York: Harper and Row, 1970).

[50]Russell W. Belk, "An Exploratory Assessment of Situational Effects in Buyer Behavior," *Journal of Marketing Research,* May 1974, p. 156.

[51]Gordon C. Brunner, "Music, Mood, and Marketing," *Journal of Marketing,* October 1990, pp. 94–104; and Ronald E. Milliman, "Using Background Music to Affect the Behavior of Supermarket Shoppers," *Journal of Marketing,* Summer 1982, pp. 86–91.

[52]Brian Wansink and Michael L. Ray, *How Expansion Advertising Affects Brand Usage Frequency: A Programmatic Evaluation,* MSI Report Summary, Report No. 93–126 (Cambridge, MA: Marketing Science Institute, 1993), p. 1.

[53]Stephen J. Hoch and John Deighton, "Managing What Consumers Learn from Experience," *Journal of Marketing,* April 1989, pp. 1–20.

[54]Walter R. Nord and J. Paul Peter, "A Behavior Modification Perspective on Marketing," *Journal of Marketing,* Spring 1980, p. 41; and Michael L. Rothschild and William C. Gaidis, "Behavioral Learning Theory: Its Relevance to Marketing and Promotions," *Journal of Marketing,* Spring 1981, pp. 70–78.

[55]Susan Fournier and David Glen Mick, "Rediscovering Satisfaction," *Journal of Marketing* 63 (October 1999), pp. 5–23.

[56]Richard L. Oliver, "A Cognitive Model of the Antecedents and Consequences of Satisfaction Decisions," *Journal of Marketing Research,* November 1980, pp. 460–61.

[57]Richard L. Oliver, "Cognitive, Affective, and Attribute Bases of the Satisfaction Response," *Journal of Consumer Research,* December 1993, p. 419.

[58]Marsha L. Richins and Peter H. Bloch, "Post-Purchase Product Satisfaction: Incorporating the Effects of Involvement and Time," *Journal of Business Research,* September 1991, pp. 145–58.

[59]Kelly Shermach, "Don't Grow Complacent when Your Customers Are 'Satisfied,' " *Marketing News,* May 20, 1996, p. 7.

[60]Timothy L. Keiningham, Melinda K. M. Goddard, Terry G. Vavra, and Andrew J. Iaci, "Customer Delight and the Bottom Line," *Marketing Management,* Fall 1999, pp. 57–63; Steve Lewis, "All or Nothing: Customers Must Be 'Totally Satisfied,' " *Marketing News,* March 2, 1998, p. 11; and Don Peppers and Martha Rogers, "When Extreme Isn't Enough," *Sales & Marketing Management,* February 1999, p. 26.

[61]Jagdip Singh, "Consumer Complaint Intentions and Behavior: Definitional and Taxonomical Issues," *Journal of Marketing,* January 1988, pp. 93–107.

[62]For a detailed discussion of managerial reactions to complaint behavior, see Alan J. Resnik and Robert R. Harmon, "Consumer Complaints and Managerial Response: A Holistic Approach," *Journal of Marketing,* Winter 1983, pp. 86–97; see also Howard Schlossberg, "Customer Satisfaction: Not a Fad, but a Way of Life," *Marketing News,* June 10, 1991, p. 18; and Judith Waldrop, "Educating the Customer," *American Demographics,* September 1991, p. 45.

[63]Waldrop, "Educating the Customer," p. 45.

[64]Stephanie Anderson Forest, "Customers 'Must Be Pleased, Not Just Satisfied,' " *Business Week,* August 3, 1992, p. 52.

[65]Waldrop, "Educating the Customer," p. 44.

[66]For additional explanation regarding the role of cognitive dissonance in marketing and consumer behavior, see William H. Cummings and M. Venkatesan, "Cognitive Dissonance and Consumer Behavior: A Review of the Evidence," *Journal of Marketing Research,* August 1976, pp. 303–8; and Pradeep K. Korgaonkar and George P. Moschis, "An Experimental Study of Cognitive Dissonance, Product Involvement, Expectations, Performance, and Consumer Judgments of Product Performance," *Journal of Advertising* 11, no. 3 (1982), pp. 32–44.

[67]Mowen, *Consumer Behavior,* p. 764.

[68]Carolyn Gatten, "Social Issues Guide Consumer Buying," *Marketing News,* December 9, 1991, p. 80.

[69]Kirk Davidson, "Like Marketers, Consumers Have Responsibilities," *Marketing News,* March 3, 1998, p. 24.

Chapter Five

[1]Martha C. Cooper, Douglas M. Lambert, and Janus D. Pugh, "Supply Chain Management: More than a New Name for Logistics," *The International Journal of Logistics Management* 8, no. 1 (1997), p. 2.

[2]James Weir, "Governments Find Outwork Can Work Out," *The Dominion* (Wellington, New Zealand), November 3, 1999, p. 26.

[3]"Outsourcing, the Union, and Business," *Purchasing Today,* May 1999, p. 4.

[4]"Toyota Promises Custom Order in Five Days," *USA Today,* August 6, 1999, p. B1.

[5]Judy Strauss and Raymond Frost, *Marketing on the Internet* (Upper Saddle River, New Jersey: Prentice Hall, 1999), p. 176.

[6]"Gerber Drops Suppliers Who Use Genetically Altered Crops," *The Coloradoan* (Fort Collins, Colorado), July 31, 1999, p. B7.

[7]Don Peppers and Martha Rogers, "In Vendors They Trust," *Sales & Marketing Management,* November 1999, pp. 30–32.

[8]Mike Green, "Technology in Manufacturer/Retailer Integration: Wal-Mart and Procter & Gamble," *Velocity,* Spring 1999, pp. 12–17.

[9]Information from Herman Miller Web site at www.herman-miller.com/company/environment/conservation.html.

[10]For a revised and expanded version of this typology, see Michele D. Bunn, "Taxonomy of Buying Decision Approaches," *Journal of Marketing,* January 1993, pp. 38–56; see also Patrick J. Robinson, Charles W. Faris, and Yoram Wind, *Industrial Buying and Creative Marketing* (Boston: Allyn and Bacon, 1967).

[11]Barry Rehfeld, "How Large Companies Buy," *Personal Selling Power,* September 1993, p. 31.

[12]Elizabeth Wilson, Gary L. Lillien, and David T. Wilson, "Developing and Testing a Contingency Paradigm of Group Choice in Organizational Buying," *Journal of Marketing Research,* November 1991, pp. 452–53.

[13]Kevin R. Fitzgerald, "What Makes a Superior Supplier?" *Velocity,* Spring 1999, pp. 22–24, 49.

[14]Jonathan Moore and Bruce Einhorn, "A Business-to-Business E-Boom," *Business Week,* October 25, 1999, p. 62.

[15]*Statistical Abstract of the United States* (Washington, D.C.: U.S. Department of Commerce, 1998), p. 341.

[16]Information from on-line version of *Commerce Business Daily,* (Washington, D.C.: U.S. Department of Commerce), December 5, 1999, at www.cbd.net.

[17]Gregory T. Gundlach and Patrick E. Murphy, "Ethical and Legal Foundations of Relational Marketing Exchanges," *Journal of Marketing,* October 1993, pp. 35–46; and Craig Smith and John A. Quelch, *Ethics in Marketing* (Homewood, IL: Richard D. Irwin, 1983), pp. 40–43.

Chapter Six

[1]Vincent P. Barabba, "The Market Research Encyclopedia," *Harvard Business Review,* January-February 1990, p. 105.

[2]"AMA Board Approves New Marketing Definition," *Marketing News,* March 1, 1985, pp. 1, 14.

[3]John Tarsa, "Ocean Spray Marketing Research: Delivering Insights in a Customer-Supplier Relationship," *Marketing Research: A Magazine of Management and Application,* September 1991, p. 8.

[4]Hilton Barrett, "Ultimate Goal Is to Anticipate the Needs of Market," *Marketing News,* October 7, 1996, p. 10; and Paul Gerhold, "Defining Marketing (or Is It Market?) Research," *Marketing Research: A Magazine of Management and Application* 5, no. 4, p. 67.

[5]Ty Albert, "Mindset Clearly Has Changed," *Marketing News,* December 6, 1999, p. 17.

[6]Sara Eckel, "Intelligence Agents," *American Demographics,* March 1999, p. 53; Ann M. Raider, "Programs Make Results out of Research," *Marketing News,* June 21, 1999, p. 14; Jagdish Sheth and Rajendra S. Sisodia, "Feeling the Heat—Part 2," *Marketing Management* 3, no. 4 (Winter 1995), p. 22.

[7]Simon Chadwick, "The Research Industry Grows Up and Out," *Marketing News,* June 8, 1998, p. 9.

[8]Adapted from Gilbert A. Churchill, Jr., *Marketing Research: Methodological Foundations,* 5th ed. (Chicago: Dryden Press, 1991), p. 9.

[9]Earl Babbie, *The Practice of Social Research,* 5th ed. (Belmont, CA: Wadsworth, 1989), p. 80.

[10]See William R. Dillon, Thomas J. Madden, and Neil A. Firtle, *Marketing Research in a Marketing Environment,* 2nd ed. (Homewood, IL: Richard D. Irwin, 1990), p. 29; and Churchill, *Marketing Research,* pp. 130–43.

[11]See, for example, Johan K. Johansson and Ikujiro Nonaka, "Market Research the Japanese Way," *Harvard Business Review,* May–June 1987, pp. 16–18, 22; and Tim Powell, "Despite Myths, Secondary Research Is Valuable Tool," *Marketing News,* September 2, 1991, p. 28.

[12]Alvin C. Burns and Ronald F. Bush, *Marketing Research,* 2nd ed. (Upper Saddle River, NJ: Prentice Hall), p. 143.

[13]Ed Campbell, "CD-ROMs Bring Census Data In-House," *Marketing News,* January 1992, p. 15.

[14]Lawrence N. Gold, "The Coming of Age of Scanner Data," *Marketing Research: A Magazine of Management and Application,* Winter 1993, p. 23.

[15]For several recent descriptions, Joseph M. Winski, "Gentle Rain Turns to Torrent," *Advertising Age,* June 3, 1991, p. 34; Blair Peters, "The 'Brave New World' of Single Source Information," *Marketing Research: A Magazine of Management and Applications,* December 1990, pp. 13–21; and "Nielsen, NPD Start Single Source Service," *Marketing News,* August 28, 1987, p. 1.

[16]Thomas G. Exter, "The Next Step Is Called GIS," *American Demographics,* May 1992, p. 2.

[17]Jack Szergold, "Getting the GIS of Things," *Management Review,* July 1993, p. 6.

[18]David Churbuck, "Geographics," *Forbes,* January 6, 1992, pp. 262–67; and Eric Schine, "Computer Maps Pop Up All over the Map," *Business Week,* July 26, 1993, p. 75.

[19]See Bobby J. Calder, "Focus Groups and the Nature of Qualitative Marketing Research," *Journal of Marketing Research,* August 1977, pp. 353–64; and Edward F. Fern, "The Use of Focus Groups for Idea Generation: The Effects of Group Size, Acquaintanceship, and Moderator on Response Quantity and Quality," *Journal of Marketing Research,* February 1982, pp. 1–13.

[20]Judith Langer, "15 Myths of Qualitative Research: It's Conventional, But Is It Wisdom," *Marketing News,* March 1, 1999, pp. 13–14.

[21]Jonathan Jameson, "Marketing: Back to the Basics," *Restaurant Business,* September 1, 1991, p. 82; and Cyndee Miller, "Right Package Sets Mood for Image-Driven Brands," *Marketing News,* August 5, 1991, p. 2.

[22]Jack Honomichl, "Legislation Threatens Research by Phone," *Marketing News,* June 24, 1991, p. 4.

[23]Stephen W. McDaniel, Perry Verille, and Charles S. Madden, "The Threats to Marketing Research: An Empirical Reappraisal," *Journal of Marketing Research,* February 1985, pp. 74–80; and Howard Gershowitz, "Entering the 1990s—The State of Data Collection—Telephone Data Collection," *Applied Marketing Research,* Spring 1990, pp. 16–19.

[24]Michael P. Cronin, "On-the-Cheap Market Research," *Inc.,* June 1992, p. 108.

[25]Pamela Rogers, "One-on-Ones Don't Get the Credit They Deserve," *Marketing News,* January 2, 1991, p. 9.

[26]Susan Kraft, "Who Slams the Door on Research?" *American Demographics,* September 1991, p. 9.

[27]Alan J. Bush and Joseph F. Hair, Jr., "Mall Intercept versus Telephone Interviewing Environment," *Journal of Marketing Research,* May 1985, pp. 158–68.

[28]Howard Schlossberg, "Shoppers Virtually Stroll through Store Aisles to Examine Packages," *Marketing News,* June 6, 1993, p. 2.

[29]Robert Hayes, "Internet-based Surveys Provide Fast Results," *Marketing News,* April 13, 1998, p. 13; Dana James, "Precision Decision," *Marketing News,* September 27, 1999, pp. 23–25; Phil Levine, Bill Ahlauser, Dale Kulp, and Rick Hunter, "Internet Interviewing," *Marketing Research: A Magazine of Management and Application,* Summer 1999, pp. 33–36; Seymour Sudman and Edward Blair, "Sampling in the Twenty-First Century," *Journal of the Academy of Marketing Science* 27, no. 2, p. 275.

[30]Sharon Hollander, "Projective Techniques Uncover Real Consumer Attitudes," *Marketing News,* January 4, 1988, p. 34.

[31]Stephen Groves and Raymond P. Fisk, "Observational Data Collection Methods for Services Marketing: An Overview," *Journal of the Academy of Marketing Science,* Summer 1992, pp. 217–24.

[32]William B. Helmreich, "Louder than Words: On-Site Observational Research," *Marketing News,* March 1, 1999, p. 16.

[33]Rebecca Piirto, "Socks, Ties, and Videotape," *American Demographics,* September 1991, p. 6.

[34]Shelby D. Hunt, Richard D. Sparkman, Jr., and James B. Wilcox, "The Pretest in Survey Research: Issues and Preliminary Findings," *Journal of Marketing Research,* May 1982, pp. 269–73.

[35]Sudman and Blair, "Sampling in the Twenty-First Century," *Journal of the Academy of Marketing Science,* Vol. 27(2), p. 275.

[36]Gershowitz, "Entering the 1990s."

[37]Peter S. Tuckel and Harry W. O'Neil, "Call Waiting," *Marketing Research: A Magazine of Management and Application,* Spring 1995, p. 7.

[38]Thomas L. Greenbaum, "Focus Group by Video Next Trend of the 90s," *Marketing News,* July 29, 1996, p. 4; Leslie M. Harris, "Technology, Techniques Drive Focus Group Trends," *Marketing News,* February 27, 1995, p. 8; Beth Schneider, "Using Interactive Kiosks for Retail Research," *Marketing News,* January 2, 1995, p. 13; Barbara A. Schuldt and Jeff W. Totten, "Electronic Mail vs. Mail Response Rates," *Marketing Research: A Magazine of Management and Application* 6, no. 1, p. 36; and Gary S. Vazzana and Duane Bachmann, "Fax Attracts," *Marketing Research: A Magazine of Management and Application* 6, no. 2, p. 19.

[39]Daphre Chandler, "Eight Common Pitfalls of International Research," in *The Resurgence of Research in Decision Making: 1992 CASRO Annual Journal* (Port Jefferson, NY: The Council of American Survey Research Organizations, 1992), pp. 81–85.

[40]Elizabeth Loken, "Probing Japanese Buyers' Minds," *Business Marketing,* 1987, pp. 85–86.

[41]Neil Helgeson, "Research Isn't Linear When Done Globally," *Marketing News,* July 19, 1999, p. 13.

[42]William R. Dillon, Thomas J. Madden, and Neil Firtle, *Essentials of Marketing Research* (Homewood, IL: Richard D. Irwin, Inc. 1993), pp. 293–95.

[43]Howard N. Gundee, "Council Joins Industrial Effort to Support Research," *Marketing News,* January 4, 1993, p. 22.

[44]McDaniel, Verille, and Madden, "Threats to Marketing Research."

[45]Wade Lettwich, "How Researchers Can Win Friends and Influence Politicians," *American Demographics,* August 1993, p. 9.

[46]"The Persistence of Surveying," *Marketing News,* September 28, 1992, p. 4.

[47]Ishmael P. Akaah and Edward A. Riordan, "Judgments of Marketing Professionals about Ethical Issues in Marketing Research: A Replication and Extension," *Journal of Marketing Research,* February 1989, p. 113.

[48]Patrick E. Murphy and Gene R. Laczniak, "Emerging Ethical Issues Facing Marketing Researchers," *Marketing Research,* June 1992, pp. 6–7.

[49]Mary B. W. Taylor, "Schools Profit from Offering Pupils for Market Research," *The New York Times,* April 5, 1999, pp. A1, A16.

[50]Tom Eisenhart, "After 10 Years of Marketing Decision Support Systems, Where's the Payoff?" *Business Marketing,* June 1990, pp. 46–48, 50.

[51]Alan J. Greco and Jack T. Hogue, "Developing Marketing Decision Support Systems," *Journal of Business and Industrial Marketing,* Summer–Fall 1990, p. 28; and Alan J. Greco and Jack T. Hogue, "Developing Marketing Decision Support Systems in Consumer Goods Firms," *Journal of Consumer Marketing,* Winter 1990, pp. 56–64.

[52]Rajerdra S. Sisodia, "Marketing Information and Decision Support Systems for Services," *Journal of Services Marketing*, Winter 1992, p. 53.

[53]Randolph E. Bucklin, Donald R. Lehmann, and John D. C. Little, *From Decision Support to Decision Automation: A 2020 Vision*, Marketing Science Institute, Report no. 98-119 (Cambridge, MA: June 1998).

[54]Lisa Beneson, "Bull's Eye Marketing," *Success*, February 1993, pp. 43–44.

[55]Rochelle Kass, "Know Your Customers," *Bank Systems and Technology*, November 1992, p. 35.

[56]James Heckman, "You Have Tools to Boost Your Budget," *Marketing News*, September 13, 1999, p. 4.

[57]Jagdish Sheth and Rajendra S. Sisodia, "Feeling the Heat—Part 2," p. 22.

[58]George R. Milne and Maria-Eugenia Boza, *A Business Perspective on Database Marketing and Consumer Privacy Practices*, Marketing Science Institute, Report no. 98-110 (Cambridge, MA: June 1998); Joseph Phelps, Glen Nowak, and Elizabeth Ferrell, *Marketers' Information Practices and Privacy Concerns: How Willing Are Consumers to Provide Personal Information for Shopping Benefits?* Marketing Science Institute, Report no. 99-112, (Cambridge, MA: June 1999).

Chapter Seven

[1]For an in-depth review, see Gary L. Lilien and Philip Kotler, *Marketing Decision Making: A Model Building Approach* (New York: Harper and Row, 1983); and Peter R. Dickson and James L. Ginter, "Market Segmentation, Product Differentiation, and Marketing," *Journal of Marketing*, April 1987, pp. 1–10.

[2]Faye Brookman, "Companies Invest in Customer Loyalty," *Marketing News*, March 2, 1998, p. 12.

[3]Karen Blumenthal, "Compaq Is Segmenting Home-Computer Market," *The Wall Street Journal*, July 16, 1996, p. A3; Bradley Johnson, "Compaq's Ads Go Global," *Advertising Age*, June 24, 1996, pp. 1, 48; and John F. Yarbrough, "Salvaging a Lousy Year," *Sales & Marketing Management*, July 1996, pp. 70–73.

[4]Harper W. Boyd, Jr., and Orville C. Walker, Jr., *Marketing Management: A Strategic Approach* (Homewood, IL: Richard D. Irwin, 1990), p. 186.

[5]Cyndee Miller, "Researcher Says U.S. Is More of a Bowl than a Pot," *Marketing News*, May 10, 1993, p. 6; and Cynthia Webster, "The Effects of Hispanic Subcultural Identification on Information Search Behavior," *Journal of Advertising Research*, September–October 1992, pp. 54–62.

[6]Daniel F. Hansler and Donald R. Riggin, "Geodemographics: Targeting the Market," *Fund Raising Management*, December 1989, pp. 35–43.

[7]Saeed Samiee, "A Conceptual Framework for International Marketing," in *International Business: Inquiry: An Emerging Vision*, eds. B. Toyne and Douglas Nigh (Columbia, SC: USC Press, 1994); see also Theodore Leavitt, "The Globalization of Markets," *Harvard Business Review*, May–June 1983, pp. 99–102; and Saeed Samiee and Kendall Roth, "The Influence of Global Marketing Standardization on Performance," *Journal of Marketing*, April 1992, pp. 1–17.

[8]Ugar Yavas, Bronislaw J. Verhage, and Robert T. Green, "Global Consumer Segmentation versus Local Market Orientation: Empirical Findings," *Marketing International Review*, 1992, pp. 266–68.

[9]Alpa Agarwal, "Profiting from India's Strong Middle Class," *Marketing News*, October 7, 1996, p. 6; and Cyndee Miller, "Teens Seen as the First Truly Global Consumers," *Marketing News*, March 27, 1995, p. 9.

[10]Peter D. Bennett, ed., *Dictionary of Marketing Terms* (Chicago: American Marketing Association, 1988), p. 199.

[11]Marian B. Wood and Evelyn Ehrlich, "Segmentation: Five Steps to More Effective Business-to-Business Marketing," *Sales & Marketing Management*, April 1991, p. 60.

[12]James H. Gilmore and B. Joseph Pine, II, "The Four Faces of Mass Customization," *Harvard Business Review*, January–February 1997, pp. 91–101; and Suresh Kotha, "From Mass Production to Mass Customization: The Case of the National Industrial Bicycle Company of Japan," *European Management Journal*, October 1996, pp. 442–50.

[13]Philip Kotler, *Kotler on Marketing: How to Create, Win, and Dominate Markets* (New York, NY: The Free Press, 1999); Philip Kotler, *Marketing Management*, Millennium ed. (Englewood Cliffs, NJ: Prentice Hall, Inc., 2000); Marc Logman, "Marketing Mix Customization and Customizability," *Business Horizons*, November–December 1997, pp. 39–44; "The Right Stuff: America's Move to Mass Customization," *1998 Annual Report*, Federal Reserve Bank of Dallas; and Mike McNamee, "Isn't There More to Life than Plastic," *Business Week*, November 22, 1999, pp. 173–76.

[14]Gary L. Berman, "The Hispanic Market: Getting Down to Cases," *Sales & Marketing Management*, October 1991, p. 66.

[15]Shirley Young, Leland Ott, and Barbara Feign, "Some Practical Considerations in Market Segmentation," *Journal of Marketing Research*, August 1978, pp. 405–12.

[16]Marcia Mogelonsky, "Watching in Tongues," *American Demographics*, April 1998, pp. 4–52.

[17]Ronald Grover, "Old Rockers Never Die—They Just Switch to CDs," *Business Week*, August 17, 1992, p. 54.

[18]Maria Mallory, "Working Up to a Major Market," *Business Week*, March 23, 1992, p. 70.

[19]Roger J. Calantone and Alan G. Sawyer, "The Stability of Benefit Segments," *Journal of Marketing Research*, August 1978, pp. 395–404.

[20]Howard Schlossberg, "Success with Seniors Depends on Dialogue and Long-Range Plans," *Marketing News*, January 4, 1993, p. 2.

[21]Henry Assael, "Segmenting Markets by Response Elasticity," *Journal of Advertising Research*, April 1976, pp. 27–35.

[22]Hartmarx, *Annual Report* (Chicago: Hartmarx Corporation, 1992).

[23]"The American Dream Is Alive and Well—In Mexico," *Business Week*, September 30, 1991, p. 102.

[24]Ibrahim Sajid Malick, "New Americans: The Overlooked $400 Billion Market," *Marketing News*, July 15, 1996, p. 9.

[25]Philip Kotler, *Marketing Management: Analysis, Planning, Implementation, and Control*, 8th ed. (Englewood Cliffs, NJ: Prentice Hall, 1994), p. 265.

[26]See Yoram Wind and Richard Cardoza, "Industrial Market Segmentation," *Industrial Marketing Management*, March 1974, pp. 153–66, for a similar outline of business-to-business segmentation bases.

[27]Jon Berry, "An Empire of Niches," *Superbrands*, 1991, p. 22.

[28]"Diversity in America," *A Supplement to American Demographics*, 1999, pp. 1–10.

[29]Peter Francese, "America at Mid-Decade," *American Demographics*, February, 1995, pp. 23–31; and Peter Zollo, "Talking to Teens," *American Demographics*, November 1995, pp. 22–28.

[30]Susan Mitchell, *American Generations: Who They Are and How They Live*, 2nd ed. (Ithaca, NY: New Strategist Publications, 1998).

[31]Laura Koss-Feder, "Want to Catch Gen X? Try Looking on the Web," *Marketing News*, June 8, 1998, p. 20.

[32]Francese, "America at Mid-Decade"; Cyndee Miller, "Boomers Come of Age," *Marketing News*, January 15, 1996, pp. 1, 6; Karen Ritchie, "Marketing to Generation X," *American Demographics*, April 1995, pp. 34–39; and Zollo, "Talking to Teens."

33James Heckman, "Today's Game Is Keep-Away," *Marketing News,* July 5, 1999, pp. 1, 7; and James U. McNeal, "Tapping the Three Kids Markets," *American Demographics,* April 1998, pp. 37–41.

34Lisa Modisette and Steve Huson, "Customer Knowledge Is Power," *Cellular Business,* September 1996, p. 98.

35Daniel F. Hansler and Don L. Riggen, "Geodemographics: Targeting the Market," *Fund Raising Management,* December 1989, p. 35.

36Eric A. Cohen, "Demos Alone Don't Sell Products," *Marketing News,* June 21, 1999, p. 16.

37Nick Fuller, "Finding Cable's Target," *Marketing,* February 18, 1992, p. 27.

38Susan Mitchell, "Birds of a Feather," *American Demographics,* February 1995, pp. 40–41.

39William D. Wells and Douglas J. Tigert, "Activities, Interests, and Opinions," *Journal of Advertising Research,* August 1971, pp. 27–35; and William D. Wells, "Psychographics: A Critical Review," *Journal of Marketing Research,* May 1975, pp. 196–213. See also Allen M. Clark, " 'Trends' That Will Impact New Products," *Journal of Consumer Marketing,* Winter 1991, pp. 29–34; P. Valette-Florence and A. Jolibert, "Social Values, AIO, and Consumption Patterns: Exploratory Findings," *Journal of Business Research,* March 1990, pp. 109–22; and Steven Hoch, "Who Do We Know: Predicting the Interests and Opinions of the American Consumer," *Journal of Consumer Research,* December 1988, pp. 315–24.

40Wells and Tigert, "Activities, Interests, and Opinions," p. 30.

41Brian Davis and Warren A. French, "Exploring Advertising Usage Segments among the Aged," *Journal of Advertising Research,* February–March 1989, pp. 22–29.

42Paul C. Judge, "Are Tech Buyers Different," *Business Week,* January 26, 1998, pp. 64, 68; Carol Morgan and Doren Levy, "To Their Health: Rx Companies Are Trying to Figure Out the Best Method for Reaching Aging Boomers," *Brandweek,* January 19, 1999, pp. 30–33; and Linda P. Morton, "Segmenting Publics: An Introduction," *Public Relations Quarterly,* Fall 1998, p. 33.

43Michael Gates, "VALS Changes with the Times," *Incentive,* June 1989, p. 27.

44Martha Farnsworth Riche, "Psychographics for the 1990s," *American Demographics,* July 1989, p. 30.

45Russell I. Haley, "Benefit Segmentation: A Decision-Oriented Tool," *Journal of Marketing,* July 1968, pp. 30–35.

46Ibid.; and Paul E. Green, Abba M. Krieger, and Catherine M. Schagger, "Quick and Simple Benefit Segmentation," *Journal of Advertising Research,* June–July 1985, pp. 9–17.

47William J. McDonald, "Internet Customer Segments: An International Perspective," *American Marketing Association Summer Educators' Proceedings,* Summer 1996, pp. 311–42.

48Michael Anthony, "More Customers or Right Customers: Your Choice," *Marketing News,* August 31, 1998, p. 13.

49Kristaan Helson, Kamel Jedidi, and Wayne S. DeSarbo, "A New Approach to Country Segmentation Utilizing Multinational Diffusion Patterns," *Journal of Marketing,* October 1993, p. 61.

50David A. Chambers, "Data Technology Boosts Popularity of Lifestage Marketing," *Marketing News,* October 28, 1991, p. 16.

51Robert H. Waterman, Jr., "Successful Small- and Medium-Sized Firms Stress Creativity, Employ Niche Strategy," *Marketing News,* March 15, 1984, p. 24.

52Boyd and Walker, Jr., *Marketing Management,* p. 294.

53John B. Mahaffie, "Why Forecasts Fail," *American Demographics,* March 1995, pp. 34–40.

54Raymond Serafin and Cleveland Horton, "Buick Ads Target Zip Codes," *Advertising Age,* April 1, 1991, pp. 1, 36.

55Lisa Napoli, "Staying with the Pitch," *New York Times,* February 23, 1998, p. 5; Joseph Pereira, "Sneaker Company Targets Out-of-Breath Baby Boomers," *The Wall Street Journal,* January 16, 1998, p. B1; and B. G. Yovovich, "Scanners Reshape Grocery Business," *Marketing News,* March 16, 1998, pp. 1, 11.

56Martin R. Lautman, "The ABCs of Positioning," *Marketing Research: A Magazine of Management and Applications,* Winter 1993, p. 12.

57Judann Pollack, "Snackwell's Rallies with New Focus," *Advertising Age,* January 25, 1999, p. 16.

58Mita Sujan and James R. Bettman, "The Effects of Brand Positioning Strategies on Consumers' Brand and Category Perceptions: Some Insights from Schema Research," *Journal of Marketing Research,* November 1989, p. 454.

59Jason M. Sherman, "Reducing the Risks of Target Marketing," *Marketing News,* November 11, 18, 1996, p. 12.

60Paula Munier Lee, "The Micromarketing Revolution," *Small Business Reports,* February 1990, pp. 73–82.

61Howard Schlossberg, "Packaged Goods Experts: Micromarketing the Only Way to Go," *Marketing News,* July 6, 1992, p. 8.

62James Heckman, "Today's Game Is Keep-Away," pp. 1, 7; and Allyson L. Stewart-Allen, "Rules for Reaching Euro Kids Are Changing," *Marketing News,* June 7, 1999, p. 10.

63N. Craig Smith and John A. Quelch, *Ethics in Marketing* (Homewood, IL: Richard D. Irwin, 1993), pp. 188–95.

64Marcia Mogelonsky, "Product Overload?" *American Demographics,* August 1998, pp. 65–69; and "What's New," *Marketing News,* March 2, 1998, p. 2.

65Barbara Kahn and Leigh McAlister, *Grocery Revolution: The New Focus on the Consumer* (Reading, MA: Addison Wesley, 1997) pp. 66–67.

Chapter Eight

1Adapted from Peter D. Bennett, ed., *Dictionary of Marketing Terms* (Chicago: American Marketing Association, 1988), p. 153.

2"Business-to-Business Product: Hewlett-Packard," *Sales & Marketing Management,* August 1993, p. 42.

3Tricia Campbell, "A Card for the Future," *Sales & Marketing Management,* December 1999, p. 15.

4Tom Peters, *Liberation Management* (New York: Alfred A. Knopf, 1992), p. 295.

5Wendy Zellner, "Penney's Rediscovers Its Calling," *Business Week,* April 5, 1993, pp. 51–52.

6"Pen Wars," *Forbes,* January 6, 1992, pp. 88–89.

7Laura Johannes, "Smart Marketing Helps Biogen Match Schering," *The Wall Street Journal,* December 19, 1996, p. B8.

8Brian Dumaine, "Design That Sells and Sells and . . . ," *Fortune,* March 11, 1991, pp. 86–94.

9Seanna Browder, "In This Dogfight, Boeing's Gutsy Maneuver Paid Off," *Business Week,* December 2, 1996, p. 46.

10Oscar Suris, "How Ford Cut Costs on Its 1997 Taurus, Little by Little," *The Wall Street Journal,* July 18, 1996, p. B1.

11Bruce Nussbaum, "Winners: The Best Product Designs of the Year," *Business Week,* June 3, 1996, p. 73.

12Diane Brady, "Hilton? Conrad? Hey! Is the Name 'Trump' in Use by Anyone?" *The Wall Street Journal,* September 10, 1996, p. B10.

13Deborah Michelle Sanders, "Master of Your Domain," *Success,* June 1996, p. 54.

14James Heckman, "Trademarks Protected through New Cyber Act," *Marketing News,* January 3, 2000, pp. 6–7.

15Cyndee Miller, "And Baby Gets Brands," *Marketing News,* March 11, 1996, p. 18.

[16]Erich Joachimsthaler and David A. Aaker, "Building Brands without Mass Media," *Harvard Business Review,* January–February 1997, pp. 39–50.

[17]Don E. Schultz, "Brand-Building Different from Gaining Trial," *Marketing News,* January 3, 2000, p. 12.

[18]Meghan Henterly, "Retailers Hope Private Brands Will Boost Profits," *The Courier-Journal* (Louisville, KY), June 2, 1996, p. E2.

[19]Stephen E. Frank, "To More Bankers, 'Bank' Is a Bad Word," *The Wall Street Journal,* November 15, 1996, p. B9.

[20]Diana T. Kurylko, "Product Namer Attempts to Capture a Car's Feeling," *Business First,* April 5, 1993, pp. 30–31.

[21]Valerie Reitman, "P&G Uses Skills It Has Learned at Home to Introduce Its Brands to the Russians," *The Wall Street Journal,* April 14, 1993, pp. B1, B3.

[22]Steve Rivkin, "The Name Game Heats Up," *Marketing News,* April 22, 1996, p. 8.

[23]Nancy Armour, "Notre Dame Unique in Sports Marketing," *Marketing News,* May 20, 1996, p. 13.

[24]Kelly Shermach, "Proper Design Aids Sales of Do-It-Yourself Products," *Marketing News,* September 11, 1995, p. 12.

[25]Kathleen Deveny, "Toothpaste Makers Tout New Packaging," *The Wall Street Journal,* October 10, 1992, pp. B1, B10.

[26]Michael Connor, "Services Research Should Focus on Service Management," *Marketing News,* September 13, 1993, pp. 36, 41.

[27]"The List: Going the Distance," *Business Week,* August 12, 1996, p. 4.

[28]James B. Miller, "Bailing Out Customers," *Sales & Marketing Management,* January 1994, p. 29.

[29]John R. Graham, "Customer Service Redefined: It's What You Know, Not What You Sell," *Marketing News,* January 3, 1994, p. 25.

[30]Martin Everett, "Relate Is Good, Elate Is Better," *Sales & Marketing Management,* January 1994, pp. 31–32.

Chapter Nine

[1]Christopher Power, Kathleen Kerwin, Ronald Glover, Keith Alexander, and Robert D. Hof, "Flops," *Business Week,* August 16, 1993, p. 82.

[2]"Try It, They May Buy It," *The Wall Street Journal,* November 14, 1996, p. A1.

[3]Alan Farnham, "America's Most Admired Company," *Fortune,* February 7, 1994, pp. 50–54.

[4]Sharon Walsh, "Fast-Food Competition Brings New Products and Strategies," *The Courier-Journal,* January 12, 1997, p. E4.

[5]Power et al., "Flops," p. 77.

[6]Rahul Jacob, "Beyond Quality and Value," *Fortune,* Autumn–Winter 1993, pp. 8–11.

[7]"Shortening the Product Pipeline," *Sales and Marketing Management,* January 1999, p. 71.

[8]Cyndee Miller, "Little Relief Seen for New Product Failure," *Marketing News,* June 21, 1993, pp. 1, 10.

[9]Brenton R. Schlender, "How Sony Keeps the Magic Going," *Fortune,* February 24, 1993, pp. 76–84.

[10]www.newellco.com and www.rubbermaid.com, January 12, 2000.

[11]Suein Hwang, "Colgate-Palmolive Profit Rose 11% in Third Quarter," *The Wall Street Journal,* October 22, 1993, p. B5.

[12]Stephen D. Moore, "French Drug Maker Reaps Profits with Offbeat Strategy," *The Wall Street Journal,* November 14, 1996, p. B3.

[13]Thomas D. Kuczmarski, *Managing New Products: Competing through Excellence* (Englewood Cliffs, NJ: Prentice Hall, 1988), pp. 37–39.

[14]Power et al., p. 77.

[15]www.3M.com, January 14, 2000.

[16]Dori Jones Young, "When the Going Gets Tough, Boeing Gets Touchy-Feely," *Business Week,* January 17, 1994, pp. 65–67.

[17]Power et al., "Flops," p. 77.

[18]"Mercury's Mystique Tries No-Tuneup Tack," *The Courier-Journal,* February 3, 1994, p. D1.

[19]Kevin Kelly, "The New Soul of John Deere," *Business Week,* January 31, 1994, pp. 64–66.

[20]Quentin Hardy, "How a Wife's Question Led Motorola to Chase Global Cell-Phone Plan," *The Wall Street Journal,* December 16, 1996, pp. A1, A10.

[21]Amy Borrus, "Click Here to Pay Your Parking Ticket," *Business Week,* January 17, 2000, pp. 76, 78.

[22]Linda Rochford and Thomas R. Wotruba, "New Product Development under Changing Economic Conditions," *Journal of Business and Industrial Marketing* 8, no. 3 (1993), pp. 4–12.

[23]David Leonhardt, "It Was a Hit in Buenos Aires—So Why Not Boise?" *Business Week,* September 7, 1998, pp. 56–58.

[24]Kathleen Devery, "Failure of Its Oven Lovin' Cookie Dough Shows Pillsbury Pitfalls of New Products," *The Wall Street Journal,* July 17, 1993, pp. B1, B8.

[25]Jerry Flint, "The Car Chrysler Didn't Build," *Forbes,* August 12, 1996, pp. 89–91.

[26]Power et al., "Flops," p. 80.

[27]Christopher Power, "Will It Sell in Podunk? Hard to Say," *Business Week,* August 10, 1992, p. 46.

[28]William R. Dillon, Thomas J. Madden, and Neil H. Firtle, *Essentials of Marketing Research* (Homewood, IL: Richard D. Irwin, 1993), p. 732.

[29]Ian P. Murphy, "Ameritech Test Towns Market Innovation," *Marketing News,* November 18, 1996, pp. 2, 12.

[30]"Up Front," *Business Week,* April 19, 1999, p. 8.

[31]Warren B. Brown and Necmi Karagozoglu, "Leading the Way to Faster New Product Development," *The Executive,* February 1993, pp. 36–47.

[32]Kyle Pope, "Compaq Is Set to Introduce 'Subnotebook,' " *The Wall Street Journal,* February 2, 1994, p. 85.

[33]"Winning the New Product Launch," *On Target Research,* 1999, pp. 14–15.

[34]Wendy Bounds, "Camera System Is Developed but Not Delivered," *The Wall Street Journal,* August 7, 1996, p. B1.

[35]"Survey Reveals Better Planning Is Needed in New Product Development," *Quality Progress,* February 1996, pp. 16–17.

[36]This section draws heavily from Robert G. Cooper and Elko J. Kleinschmidt, "Stage Gate Systems for New Product Success," *Marketing Management* 1, no. 4, pp. 20–26.

[37]Richard Gibson, "A Cereal Maker's Quest for the Next Grape-Nuts," *The Wall Street Journal,* January 23, 1997, B1–2.

[38]Roy Furchgott, "The Best Products of 1999," *Business Week,* December 20, 1999, pp. 104–18.

Chapter Ten

[1]Peter Bennett, *Dictionary of Marketing Terms* (Chicago: American Marketing Association, 1988), p. 156.

[2]Ibid.

[3]www.palm.com, January 17, 2000.

[4]Ibid.

[5]Cyndee Miller, "Another Win for Retro: Designer Jeans Are Back," *Marketing News,* June 3, 1996, pp. 18–19.

[6]Dana James, "Rejuvenating Mature Brands Can Be Stimulating Exercise," *Marketing News,* August 16, 1999, pp. 16–17.

[7]Laura Johannes, "Hasbro Unveils Toys It Says Will Remain 99.9% Germ-Free," *The Wall Street Journal*, January 28, 1997, p. B8.

[8]Christy Fisher, "Line Extension No Recipe for Success in Candy," *Advertising Age*, January 31, 1994, pp. 3, 38.

[9]Robert McNatt, "Honda Could Use a Little Pickup," *Business Week*, January 18, 1999, p. 6.

[10]Ian P. Murphy, "Yoo-Hoo Adds Flavors to Its Marketing Mix," *Marketing News*, February 3, 1997, p. 2.

[11]Gabriella Stern, "Makers of Frozen Diet Entrees Start Some Diets of Their Own," *The Wall Street Journal*, January 4, 1994, pp. B1, B7.

[12]Elizabeth A. Lesly, "Borden Faces Facts: It's Time to Shed the Flab," *Business Week*, November 9, 1992, p. 44.

[13]Geoffrey Smith and Nathans Spiro, "Fidelity Jumps Feet First into the Fray," *Business Week*, May 25, 1992, pp. 104–6.

[14]"Circuit City Stores Plans to Try Its Hand at Peddling a New Product—Used Cars," *The Wall Street Journal*, April 7, 1993, p. B6.

[15]Greg Bowens, "Wiping the Mess from Gerber's Chin," *Business Week*, February 1, 1993, p. 32.

[16]Ronald Grover, "Coors Is Thinking Suds 'R' Us," *Business Week*, June 8, 1992, p. 34.

[17]William C. Symonds, "The Big Trim at Gillette," *Business Week*, November 8, 1999, p. 42.

[18]Kyle Pope, "Texas Instruments Sees Path on Information Highway," *The Wall Street Journal*, March 9, 1994, p. B4.

[19]Allen D. Shocker, Rajendra K. Srivastava, and Robert W. Ruekert, "Challenges and Opportunities Facing Brand Management: An Introduction to the Special Issue," *Journal of Marketing Research*, May 1994, pp. 149–58.

[20]Srinivas K. Reddy, Susan L. Holak, and Subodh Bhat, "To Extend or Not to Extend: Success Determinants of Line Extensions," *Journal of Marketing Research*, May 1994, pp. 243–62.

[21]Gene R. Laczniak and Patrick E. Murphy, *Ethical Marketing Decisions: The Higher Road* (Boston, MA: Allyn and Bacon, 1993), p. 81.

[22]Fred W. Morgan, "Incorporating a Consumer Product Safety Perspective into the Product Development Process," in N. Craig Smith and John A. Quelch, eds., *Ethics in Marketing* (Homewood, IL: Richard D. Irwin, 1993), pp. 351–59.

[23]Douglas Lavin, "Chrysler Corp. Discloses a Third Recall of Its Neon Model for Brake Problem," *The Wall Street Journal*, April 8, 1994, p. A3; and "Some Crayon Brands Are Recalled by U.S., Citing Lead Levels," *The Wall Street Journal*, April 7, 1994, p. A8.

[24]Mary Agnes Carey, "Popcorn at Movies Gets Thumbs Down for Being Full of Fat," *The Wall Street Journal*, April 26, 1994, p. A5.

[25]Laczniak and Murphy, *Ethical Marketing Decisions*, p. 89.

[26]Marcus W. Brauchli, "Chinese Flagrantly Copy Trademarks of Foreigners," *The Wall Street Journal*, June 20, 1994, pp. B1, B5.

[27]Laczniak and Murphy, *Ethical Marketing Decisions*, p. 103.

Chapter Eleven

[1]Stuart Sinclair, "A Guide to Global Pricing," *Journal of Business Strategy*, May–June 1993, p. 16.

[2]Walter van Waterschoot and Christophe Van den Butle, "The 4P Classification of the Marketing Mix Revisited," *Journal of Marketing*, October 1992, p. 90.

[3]Michael V. Marn and Robert Rosiello, "Managing Price, Gaining Profit," *Harvard Business Review*, September–October 1992, p. 86.

[4]David R. Bell and James M. Lattin, "Shopping Behavior and Consumer Preference for Store Price Format: Why 'Large Basket' Shoppers Prefer EDLP," Marketing Science Institute, Report no. 98-114 (Cambridge, MA: 1998); and Susan Keane, "Beyond EDLP/HiLo: A New Look at Retailer Pricing," *Insights from MSI*, Marketing Science Institute (Cambridge, MA: 1999), pp. 7–8.

[5]Marn and Rosiello, "Managing Price, Gaining Profit," p. 84.

[6]Hermann Simon, "Pricing Opportunities and How to Exploit Them," *Sloan Management Review*, Winter 1992, p. 56; and Gerard J. Tellis, "The Price Elasticity of Selective Demand: A Meta-Analysis of Econometric Models of Sales," *Journal of Marketing Research*, November 1988, p. 331–41.

[7]Kent B. Monroe, *Pricing: Making Profitable Decisions* (New York: McGraw-Hill, 1990), pp. 8–10; and Paul W. Farris and John A. Quelch, "In Defense of Price Promotion," *Sloan Management Review*, Fall 1987, p. 63.

[8]Philip Kotler, *Marketing Management: Analysis, Planning, Implementation, and Control*, 8th ed. (Englewood Cliffs, NJ: Prentice Hall, 10th edition, 2000, p. 458.

[9]John G. Lynch and Dan Ariely, "Electronic Shopping for Wine: How Search Costs Affect Consumer Price Sensitivity, Satisfaction with Merchandise, and Retention," Marketing Science Institute, Report no. 99-104 (Cambridge, MA: 1999).

[10]Pam Black, "All the World's an Auction," *Business Week*, February 8, 1999, pp. 120–21; and Gene Koretz, "Inflation's New Adversary," *Business Week*, October 4, 1999, p. 30.

[11]Tommy Hanrahan, "Price Isn't Everything," *The Wall Street Journal*, July 12, 1999, p. R20; Gene Koretz, "Inflation's New Adversary," *Business Week*, October 4, 1999, p. 30; and Gary McWilliams, "Dealer Loses?" *The Wall Street Journal*, July 12, 1999, p. R20.

[12]Sinclair, "A Guide to Global Pricing," p. 16.

[13]Maricris G. Briones, "The Euro Starts Here," *Marketing News*, July 20, 1998, pp. 1, 39.

[14]Michael D. Mondello, "Naming Your Price," *Inc.*, July 1992, p. 80.

[15]Thomas T. Nagle, *The Strategy and Tactics of Pricing: A Guide to Profitable Decision Making* (Englewood Cliffs, NJ: Prentice Hall, 1989), p. 8.

[16]"Cruise Lines Deep in Discounts," *Advertising Age*, February 3, 1992, p. 16.

[17]Zachary Schiller, "Procter & Gamble Hits Back," *Business Week*, July 19, 1993, p. 20.

[18]Alison Rea, "Why Rising Bank Fees Are Backfiring," *Business Week*, August 19, 1996, p. 66.

[19]Peter R. Dickson, *Marketing Management* (Fort Worth, TX: Dryden Press, 1994), p. 476.

[20]Robert Jacobson and David A. Aaker, "Is Market Share All That It's Cracked Up to Be?" *Journal of Marketing*, Fall 1985, pp. 11–22.

[21]Greg Bowers, "Wiping the Mess from Gerber's Chin," *Business Week*, February 1, 1993, p. 32.

[22]Richard Gibson, "Kellogg's Cutting Prices on Some Cereals in Bid to Check Loss of Market Share," *The Wall Street Journal*, June 10, 1996, p. A3.

[23]Monroe, *Pricing*, p. 8.

[24]Marn and Rosiello, "Managing Price, Gaining Profit," pp. 84–85.

[25]Nagle, *Strategy and Tactics of Pricing*, pp. 114–15.

[26]Simon, "Pricing Opportunities," p. 64.

[27]"Sheraton's New Pricing Makes Rivals Cry Foul," *Advertising Age*, May 11, 1992, p. 6.

[28]Michael Porter, *Competitive Strategy* (New York, NY: Free Press, 1980); Joel E. Urbany, "Pricing Strategies and Determination," *Marketing: Best Practices* (Fort Worth, TX: The Dryden Press, 2000), p. 510.

[29]Mondello, "Naming Your Price," p. 80.

[30]Doug Carroll, "Price Wars Make Airlines Shrink," *USA Today*, November 24, 1993, p. 18B.

[31]Allan J. McGrath, "Ten Timeless Truths about Pricing," *Journal of Business and Industrial Marketing,* Summer–Fall 1991, p. 17.

[32]Ralph G. Kauffman, "The Future of Purchasing and Supply: Strategic Cost Management," *Purchasing,* September 1999, pp. 33–35; Leslie Kaufman, "Downscale Moves Up," *Newsweek,* July 27, 1998, pp. 32–33; and Zachary Schiller, Greg Burns, and Karen Lowry Miller, "Make It Simple," *Business Week,* September 9, 1996, pp. 96–104.

[33]Raymond Serafin, "U.S. Cars Build Share with Value Pricing," *Advertising Age,* July 12, 1993, p. 4; and Wendy Zeller, "Penney's Rediscovers Its Calling," *Business Week,* April 5, 1993, p. 51.

[34]Donald F. Blumberg, "What Is Your Service Really Worth?" *Success,* July–August 1992, p. 13.

[35]Robert Hales and David Staley, "Mix Target Costing, QFD for Successful New Products," *Marketing News,* January 2, 1995, p. 18.

[36]Stephen J. Hoch, Byung-Do Kim, Alan L. Montgomery, and Peter E. Rossi, "Determinants of Store-Level Price Elasticity," *Journal of Marketing Research* 32 (February 1995), pp. 17–29; and Barbara E. Kahn and Leigh McAlister, *Grocery Revolution: The Focus on the Consumer* (Reading, MA: Addison-Wesley, 1997), pp. 185–92.

[37]Monroe, *Pricing,* p. 204.

[38]Peggy Simpson, "Poles Shop Till Prices Drop," *Business Week,* August 19, 1996, p. 4.

[39]Gene Koretz, "Inflation's New Adversary," *Business Week,* October 4, 1999, p. 30.

[40]Makoto Abe, "Behavioral Explanations for Asymmetric Price Competition," Marketing Science Institute, Report no. 98-123 (Cambridge, MA: 1998); George Cressman, Jr., "Utility Pricing: It's All in the Packaging," *Marketing News,* May 24, 1999, p. 12; and Nikhilm Deogun, "Coke and Pepsi Call Off Pricing Battle," *The Wall Street Journal,* June 12, 1997, p. A3.

[41]Susan M. Broniarczyk and Joseph W. Alba, "The Importance of the Brand in Brand Extension," *Journal of Marketing Research,* May 1994, pp. 214–25. For recent reviews, see David A. Aaker and Kevin Lane Keller, "Consumer Evaluations of Brand Extensions," *Journal of Marketing,* January 1990, pp. 27–41; and C. Whan Park, Sandra Milberg, and Robert Lawson, "Evaluation of Brand Extensions: The Role of Product Feature Similarity and Brand Concept Consistency," *Journal of Consumer Research,* September 1991, pp. 185–93.

[42]Joseph Weber, "Drug Prices: So Much for Restraint," *Business Week,* March 4, 1996, p. 40.

[43]Kent B. Monroe and Susan M. Petroshius, "Buyers' Perceptions of Price: An Update of the Evidence," in *Perspectives in Consumer Behavior,* 3rd ed., ed. H. H. Kassarjian and T. S. Robertson (Glenview, IL: Scott, Foresman, 1991), p. 44.

[44]Valarie Zeithaml, "Consumer Perceptions of Price, Quality, and Value: A Means-End Model and Synthesis of Evidence," *Journal of Marketing,* July 1988, p. 10; and Peter R. Dickson and Alan G. Sawyer, "The Price Knowledge and Search of Supermarket Shoppers," *Journal of Marketing,* July 1990, pp. 42–53.

[45]Zeithaml, "Consumer Perceptions," p. 14.

[46]Kent B. Monroe and R. Krishnan, "The Effect of Price on Subjective Product Evaluations," *Perceived Quality: How Consumers View Stores and Merchandise,* ed. Jacob Jacoby and Jerry Olson (Lexington, MA: Lexington Books, 1985), pp. 209–32.

[47]Gary Levin, "Price Rises as Factor for Consumers," *Advertising Age,* November 8, 1993, p. 37.

[48]Leonard Berry, "Strengthening the Service Brand," *Marketing Science Institute Review* (Cambridge, MA: Marketing Science Institute, Spring 1998), p. 4.

[49]Robert A. Peterson and William R. Wilson, "Perceived Risk and Price-Reliance Schema and Price–Perceived-Quality Mediators," in *Perceived Quality: How Consumers View Stores and Merchandise,* ed. Jacob Jacoby and Jerry Olson (Lexington, MA: Lexington Books, 1985), pp. 247–68. Studies of firm behavior reveal that pursuit of product-quality strategies can improve profitability and that price and quality are related at the firm level. See Robert Jacobson and David A. Aaker, "The Strategic Role of Product Quality," *Journal of Marketing,* October 1987, pp. 31–44.

[50]Donald R. Lichtenstein and Scot Burton, "The Relationship between Perceived and Objective Price Quality," *Journal of Marketing Research,* November 1989, pp. 429–43.

[51]Gerard J. Tellis and Gary J. Gaeth, "Best Value, Price Seeking, and Price Aversion: The Impact of Information and Learning on Consumer Choices," *Journal of Marketing,* April 1990, pp. 34–45.

[52]Niraj Dawar, "The Signaling Impact of Low Introductory Price on Perceived Quality and Trial," *Marketing Letters* 8, no. 3, p. 252.

[53]Robert Jacobson and Carl Obermiller, "The Formation of Expected Future Price: A Reference Price for Forward-Looking Consumers," *Journal of Consumer Research,* March 1990, p. 421.

[54]Noreen M. Klein and Janet E. Oglethorpe, "Cognitive Reference Points in Consumer Decision Making," in *Advances in Consumer Research,* vol. 14, ed. M. Wallendorf and J. Anderson (Provo, UT: Association for Consumer Research, 1987), pp. 183–97.

[55]Margaret C. Campbell, "Perceptions of Price Unfairness: Antecedents and Consequences," *Journal of Marketing Research* 36 (May 1999), pp. 187–99.

[56]Joel E. Urbany and Peter R. Dickson, *Consumer Knowledge of Consumer Prices: An Exploratory Study and Framework,* Marketing Science Institute, Report no. 90-112 (Cambridge, MA: 1990), p. 18.

[57]Dickson and Sawyer, "Price Knowledge and Search," p. 42–53.

[58]Aradha Krishna, "Effect of Dealing Patterns on Consumer Perceptions of Deal Frequency and Willingness to Pay," *Journal of Marketing Research,* November 1991, pp. 441–51.

[59]Abhijit Biswas and Edward A. Blair, "Contextual Effects of Reference Prices in Retail Advertisements," *Journal of Marketing,* July 1991, p. 4.

[60]Richard Thaler, "Mental Accounting and Consumer Choice," *Marketing Science,* Summer 1985, pp. 199–214.

[61]Dhruv Grewal, Kent B. Monroe, and R. Krishnan, "The Effects of Price-Comparison Advertising on Buyers' Perceptions of Acquisition Value, Transaction Value, and Behavioral Intentions," *Journal of Marketing* 62 (April 1998), pp. 46–59.

Chapter Twelve

[1]Diane Brady, "Insurers Step Gingerly into Cyberspace," *Business Week,* November 22, 1999, pp. 160–62; Adrian J. Slywotzky, "The Age of the Choiceboard," *Harvard Business Review,* January–February 2000, pp. 40–41; and Jennifer Tanaka, "The Never-Ending Search for the Lowest Price," *Newsweek,* June 7, 1999, p. 86.

[2]Harper W. Boyd, Jr., and Orville C. Walker, Jr., *Marketing Management: A Strategic Approach* (Homewood, IL: Richard D. Irwin, 1990), p. 461.

[3]Michael Parkin, *Microeconomics,* 2nd ed. (Reading, MA: Addison-Wesley, 1992), p. 109.

[4]Philip Kotler, *Marketing Management: Analysis, Planning, Implementation, and Control,* 8th ed. (Englewood Cliffs, NJ: Prentice Hall, 1994), p. 495.

[5]Rockney G. Walters, "Assessing the Impact of Retail Price Promotions on Product Substitution, Complementary Purchase, and Interstore Sales Displacement," *Journal of Marketing,* April 1991, p. 17.

[6]Paul A. Samuelson and William D. Nordhaus, *Economics,* 14th ed. (New York: McGraw-Hill, 1992), p. 210.

[7]Ford S. Worthy, "Japan's Smart Secret Weapon," *Fortune,* August 12, 1991, pp. 72–73.

[8]Allen L. Appell, "Income-Based Pricing: An Additional Approach to Teaching the Subject of Pricing in Marketing Courses," *Marketing Education Review* 7 (Summer), pp. 61–64.

[9]George E. Cressman, Jr., "Show Customers the New Offering's Value," *Marketing News,* March 29, 1999, p. 18.

[10]John B. Elmer, " '3-D' Pricing Helps to Overcome Marketing Myopia," *Marketing News,* August 5, 1991, p. 6; and Peter H. van Westenoorp, "Price Sensitivity Meter (PSM)—A New Approach to Study Consumer Perception of Prices," *NSS, N. V. Nederlanouse Stichting voor Statistiek (NSS),* 1975, pp. 140–67.

[11]Timothy Matanovich, Gary L. Lilien, and Arvind Rangaswamy, "Engineering the Price-Value Relationship," *Marketing Management,* Spring 1999, pp. 48–53.

[12]The organization and content of this section are based on the typology and discussion of Gerard J. Tellis, "Beyond the Many Faces of Price: An Integration of Pricing Strategies," *Journal of Marketing,* October 1986, pp. 146–60.

[13]Kent B. Monroe, *Pricing: Making Profitable Decisions,* 2nd ed. (New York: McGraw-Hill, 1990), p. 490.

[14]Evan I. Schwartz, *Digital Darwinism: 7 Breakthrough Business Strategies for Surviving in the Cutthroat Web Economy* (New York, NY: Broadway Books, 1999).

[15]Kotler, *Marketing Management,* p. 512.

[16]Gerard J. Tellis and Gary J. Gaeth, "Best Value, Price-Seeking, and Price Aversion: The Impact of Information and Learning on Consumer Choices," *Journal of Marketing,* April 1990, p. 36.

[17]Tellis, "Beyond the Many Faces of Price," p. 153.

[18]Teresa Andreoli, "Value Retailers Take the Low-Income Road to New Heights," *Discount Store News,* February 19, 1996, pp. 1, 19.

[19]Monroe, *Pricing,* p. 304.

[20]Joseph P. Guiltinan, "The Price Bundling of Services: A Normative Framework," *Journal of Marketing,* April 1987, p. 74.

[21]Gary J. Gaeth, Irwin P. Levin, Goutam Ghakraborty, and Aron Levin, "Consumer Evaluation of Multi-Product Bundles: An Information Integration Analysis," *Marketing Letters,* December 1990, p. 47; and Francis J. Mulhern and Robert P. Leone, "Implicit Price Bundling of Retail Products: A Multiproduct Approach to Maximizing Store Profitability," *Journal of Marketing,* October 1991, pp. 63–76.

[22]Thomas J. DiLorenzo, "The Economic Joy of Bundling," *The Wall Street Journal,* July 29, 1998, p. A15; Dilip Soman and John T. Gourville, *Transaction Decoupling: The Effects of Price Bundling on the Decision to Consume,* Marketing Science Institute, Report no. 98–131 (Cambridge, MA: 1998).

[23]Tim Clark, "Four H-P Success Story Strategies," *Business Marketing,* July 1993, pp. 18, 20.

[24]Vicki Morwitz, Eric A. Greenleaf, and Eric J. Johnson, "Divide and Prosper: Consumers' Reactions to Partitioned Prices," *Journal of Marketing Research* 35 (November 1998), pp. 453–63.

[25]Robert Schindler, "How to Advertise Price," in *Attention, Attitude, and Affect in Response to Advertising,* ed. E. M. Clark, T. C. Brock, and D. W. Stewart (Hillsdale, NJ: Lawrence Erlbaum Associates, 1994), pp. 251–69.

[26]Cornelia Pechmann, "Do Consumers Overgeneralize One-Sided Comparative Price Claims, and Are More Stringent Regulations Needed?" *Journal of Marketing Research* 33 (May 1996), pp. 150–62.

[27]Kotler, *Marketing Management,* p. 514.

[28]Barbara E. Kahn and Leigh McAlister, *Grocery Revolution: New Focus on the Consumer* (Reading, MA: Addison-Wesley, 1997), pp. 69–72.

[29]For research regarding acceptable price limits, see Peter R. Dickson and Alan G. Sawyer, "The Price Knowledge and Search of Supermarket Shoppers," *Journal of Marketing,* July 1990, pp. 42–53; Rustan Kosenko and Don Rahtz, "Buyer Market Price Knowledge on Acceptable Price Range and Price Limits," in *Advances in Consumer Research,* vol. 15, ed. Michael J. Houston (Provo, UT: Association for Consumer Research, 1987), pp. 328–33; and Patricia Sorce and Stanley M. Widrick, "Individual Differences in Latitude of Acceptable Prices," in *Advances in Consumer Research,* vol. 18, ed. Rebecca H. Holman and Michael R. Soloman (Provo, UT: Association for Consumer Research, 1991), pp. 802–5.

[30]Margaret C. Campbell, "Perceptions of Price Unfairness: Antecedents and Consequences," *Journal of Marketing Research* 36 (May 1999), pp. 187–99; Daniel Kahneman, Jack L. Knetrch, and Richard Thaler, "Fairness and the Assumptions of Economics," *Journal of Business* 59, no. 4 (1986), pp. S285–S300; and Wendy Zeller, "Straightened Up and Flying Right," *Business Week,* April 5, 1999, p. 42.

[31]Roberta Maynard, "Taking Guesswork Out of Pricing," *Nation's Business,* December 1997, pp. 27–29.

[32]Kate Fitzgerald, "Target Accuses Wal-Mart in Ads," *Advertising Age,* March 29, 1993, pp. 1, 50.

[33]Alan Radding, "Big Blue Takes Aim at Toshiba, Compaq," *Advertising Age,* March 25, 1991, pp. 1, 48; Kathy Rebello and Stephanie Anderson, "They're Slashing as Fast as They Can," *Business Week,* February 17, 1992, p. 40; and Hal Lancaster and Michael Allen, "Compaq Computer Finds Itself Where It Once Put IBM," *The Wall Street Journal,* January 13, 1992, p. B4.

[34]Kathleen Madigan, Joseph Weber, and Geoffrey Smith, "The Latest Mad Plunge of the Price Slashers," *Business Week,* May 11, 1992, p. 36.

[35]Kenneth M. Culpepper, "Utility Deregulation: Margin of Error Is Small, Margin of Profit Is Thin," *Direct Marketing,* May 1998, p. 60; and Stephanie Gallagher, "Flipping the Switch on Competition," *Kiplinger's Personal Finance Magazine,* March 1999, p. 45.

[36]Robert C. Blattberg, Richard Briesch, and Edward J. Fox, "How Promotions Work," *Marketing Science* 14, no. 3, pp. G123–4.

[37]Michael J. Zenor, Bart J. Bronnenberg, and Leigh McAlister, *The Impact of Marketing Policy on Promotional Price Elasticities and Baseline Sales,* Marketing Science Institute, Report no. 98–101 (Cambridge, MA: 1998).

[38]Hugh M. Cannon and Fred W. Morgan, "A Strategic Pricing Framework," *Journal of Business and Industrial Marketing,* Summer–Fall 1991, p. 62.

[39]Monroe, *Pricing,* p. 427.

[40]Michael L. Mellot, "Systematic Approach to Pricing Increases Profits," *Marketing News,* May 24, 1993, p. 3.

[41]Jim Hansen, "Fees for Loans: Just Part of the Marketing Equation," *Credit Union Executive,* November–December 1992, pp. 42–45; Clifford L. Ratza, "A Client-Driven Model for Service Pricing," *Journal of Professional Services Marketing* 8, no. 2 (1993), pp. 55–64; and Madhav N. Segal, "An Empirical Investigation of the Pricing of Professional Services," *Journal of Professional Services Marketing,* 1991, pp. 169–81.

[42]Kristen Young, "When Morris Took Flight, Fares Fell," *USA Today,* August 30, 1993, pp. 1B–2B.

[43]Guiltinan, "The Price Bundling of Services," p. 74.

[44]Zachary Schiller, Susan Garland, and Julia Flynn Siler, "The Humana Flap Could Make All Hospitals Feel Sick," *Business Week,* November 4, 1991, p. 34.

[45]Gwendolyn K. Ortmeyer, "Ethical Issues in Pricing," in *Ethics in Marketing,* ed. N. Craig Smith and John A. Quelch (Homewood, IL: Richard D. Irwin, 1993), p. 401; and Andrea Rothman, "The Airlines Get Out the Good China," *Business Week,* February 3, 1992, p. 66.

[46]Marc Rice, "Profiteering Claimed as Wood Prices Rise," *The Commercial Appeal,* August 28, 1992, pp. B4–B5; and "Home Depot Offers Storm Victims Break," *The Commercial Appeal,* August 29, 1992, p. B4.

[47]*Code of Federal Regulations*, 16, 233.0 FTC, Office of the Federal Register, National Archives and Records Administration, Washington, DC, pp. 26–30.

[48]"News Release," Colorado Department of Law, Attorney General, June 21, 1989, pp. 2–3.

[49]Dan Morse, "Breakthrough Product Visits Funeral Homes," *The Wall Street Journal*, January 7, 2000, p. A1.

[50]Nagle, *Strategy and Tactics of Pricing*, p. 324.

[51]Adam Bryant, "Aisle Seat Bully," *Newsweek*, May 24, 1999, p. 56; Anna Wilde Mathews and Scott McCartney, "U.S. Sues American Air in Antitrust Case," *The Wall Street Journal*, May 15, 1999, pp. A3, A6; and Wendy Zeller, "Straightened Up and Flying Right," *Business Week*, April 5, 1999, p. 42.

[52]Ortmeyer, "Ethical Issues in Pricing," pp. 396–97.

Chapter Thirteen

[1]Adapted from Peter D. Bennet, ed., *Dictionary of Marketing Terms*, 2nd ed. (Chicago: American Marketing Association, 1995), p. 167.

[2]Matthew Schifrin, "The Big Squeeze," *Forbes*, March 11, 1996, pp. 45–46.

[3]Steven Wheeler and Evan Hirsh, *Channel Champions* (San Francisco: Jossey-Bass Publishers, 1999), pp. 61–63.

[4]"Filene's Basement Seeks Protection," *Business Week*, September 6, 1999, p. 42.

[5]"Fleming Reports Higher Adjusted Earnings for Fourth-Quarter and Full-Year 1999," from Fleming's Web site at *www.fleming.com*, February 28, 2000.

[6]Paul Davidson, "Manufacturers Squeeze the Hand That Sell Them," *USA TODAY*, June 4, 1999, p. B1.

[7]Information from Dell Computer Corporation's Web site at *www.dell.com*, February 28, 2000.

[8]Ann Tergesen, "Here Come the E-Funds," *Business Week*, January 31, 2000, p. 125.

[9]Bennett, *Dictionary of Marketing Terms*, p. 300.

[10]Information furnished by Episode Stores, March 28, 1997.

[11]Geoffey Brewer, "Wheeler Dealers," *Sales & Marketing Management*, June 1995, pp. 39–42, 44. Information from Agco Corporation home page at *www.agcocorp.com*, February 28, 2000.

[12]Wheeler and Hirsh, *Channel Champions*, pp. 30–33.

[13]Charles Gasparino and Rebecca Buckman, "Facing Internet Threat, Merrill to Offer Trading Online for Low Fees," *The Wall Street Journal*, June 1, 1999, pp. A1, A10.

[14]"Frito-Lay Signs National Distribution Agreement with Oberto Sausage Company, Leader in Billion-Dollar Meat Snack Business," *PR Newswire*, November 4, 1999, as printed at *www.hoovers.com*.

[15]"No Aptivas Sold Here," *Business Week*, November 1, 1999, p. 53.

[16]Dennis Berman, "Scratch, Sniff, then Click," *Business Week*, September 27, 1999, p. 8.

[17]Bruce Haring, "More Musicians Relish Selling Tour Tickets Exclusively On Line," *USA TODAY*, March 31, 1999, p. D1.

[18]Vanessa O'Connell, "Starbucks, Kraft Align for Pact to Sell Coffee," *The Wall Street Journal*, September 28, 1998, p. B6.

[19]Paul Davidson, "Net Giants, Superstores Teaming Up," *USA TODAY*, December 17–19, 1999, p. D1.

[20]Rachel Beck, "Retailers, Internet Firms Set Alliances," *The Coloradoan*, December 17, 1999, p. B2.

[21]Pamela Sebastian, "Business Bulletin," *The Wall Street Journal*, October 31, 1996, p. A1.

[22]James R. Healey, "Daewoo Plans Internet Auto Sales Route," *USA TODAY*, February 3, 1999, p. D3.

[23]Wendy Bounds, "Kodak Rebuilds Photofinishing Empire, Quietly Buying Labs, Wooing Retailers," *The Wall Street Journal*, June 4, 1996, pp. B1, B5.

[24]Edward Harris, "Some Companies Hop Off Internet Bandwagon," *The Wall Street Journal*, June 10, 1999, p. B12.

[25]Mike Graen, "Technology in Manufacturer/Retailer Integration: Wal-Mart and Procter & Gamble," *Velocity*, Spring, 1999, pp. 12–17.

[26]Dan Morse, "First Firms Undergo Franchise Council's Reform School," *The Wall Street Journal*, August 10, 1999, p. B2.

[27]The types of power discussed in this section can be traced back to John French, Jr., and Bertram Raven, "The Bases of Social Power," in *Studies in Social Power*, D. Cartwright, ed. (Ann Arbor, MI: University of Michigan Press, 1959), pp. 150–67.

[28]Keith H. Hammonds, "The Healer's Revenge," *Business Week*, June 15, 1998, pp. 68–72.

Chapter Fourteen

[1]*Statistical Abstract of the United States* (Washington, D.C.: U.S. Department of Commerce, 1998), pp. 765–68.

[2]Janet Ginsburg and Kathleen Morris, "Xtreme Retailing," *Business Week*, December 20, 1999, pp. 120–28.

[3]Ibid.

[4]Information from Mall of America's Web site at www.mallofamerica.com, January 9, 2000; and Miguel Helft, "Meanwhile, Back at the Mall," *The Industry Standard*, December 6, 1999, pp.76, 80.

[5]Information from www.franchiseinfomall.com, January 9, 2000.

[6]Laura Tiffany, "The Wild Frontier," *Entrepreneur International*, March 1999, as it appeared in *Entrepreneur International* magazine on-line at www.entrepreneurmag.com, January 9, 2000.

[7]Information from www.franchiseinfomall.com, January 9, 2000.

[8]Tiffany, "The Wild Frontier."

[9]Information from www.franchiseinfomall.com, January 9, 2000.

[10]Stephanie Anderson, "A Penney Saved?" *Business Week*, March 29, 1999, pp. 64–66; and Lorrie Grant, "Penney's Chain Fights for Survival," *USA Today*, February 25, 1999, p.3B.

[11]Carol Matlack, Inka Resch, and Wendy Zellner, "En Garde, Wal-Mart," *Business Week*, September 13, 1999, pp. 54–55.

[12]Salina Khan, "Gadgets Help You Get Out of Line," *USA Today*, December 20, 1999, p. 3B.

[13]Robert Berner, "Urban Rarity: Stores Offering Spiffy Service," *The Wall Street Journal*, July 25, 1996, pp. B1, B9.

[14]Stan Rapp, "Getting the Words Right," *Direct*, July 1993, p. 98.

[15]Information from the Direct Marketing Association Web site at www.the-dma.org, January 10, 2000.

[16]Maryann Jones Thompson, "E-Retailers Vie for $185 Billion," *The Industry Standard*, November 22–29, 1999, p. 167.

[17]Ibid.

[18]Elinor Abreu, "Shop and Surf," *The Industry Standard*, November 22–29, 1999, p. 205–7.

[19]Information from the Direct Selling Association Web site at www.dsa.org, January 12, 2000.

[20]Information from the National Automatic Merchandising Association Web site at www.vending.org, January 12, 2000.

[21]Keith L. Alexander, "Local Booksellers Battle Big Chains," *USA Today*, April 30, 1999, p. 10B; and Bob Minzeshelmer, "Even Small Chains Are Swallowed in Battle of Bookstore Giants," *USA Today*, August 12, 1999, p. 7D.

[22]Emily Nelson and Alejandro Bodipo-Memba, "Gadzooks! Claire's stores Moves In on a Rival," *The Wall Street Journal*, September 17, 1998, p. B1.

[23]Lorrie Grant, "Thriving Kohl's Turns Up Pressure on Rivals," *USA Today,* October 14, 1999, p. 12B.

[24]Evan Ramstad, "Inside Radio Shack's Surprising Turnaround," *The Wall Street Journal,* June 8, 1999, pp. B1, B16.

[25]Elaine Walker, "Analysts Say Retail Sales Expected to Slow This Year," *Amarillo Globe News,* as presented at www.amarillonet.com, January 18, 2000.

[26]Rene Wisely, "Outlet Malls Surge," *The Coloradoan,* July 19, 1999, p. B2.

[27]Information from the International Council of Shopping Centers Web site at www.icsc.org, January 22, 2000.

[28]Ibid.

[29]James Lardner, "A Flea Market for Webheads," *U.S. News & World Report,* October 11, 1999, pp. 50–52.

[30]Information from the National Association of Convenience Stores Web site at www.csstorecentral.com, January 22, 2000.

[31]Aaron Bernstein, "Sweatshop Reform: How to Solve the Standoff," *Business Week,* May 3, 1999, pp. 186–90.

[32]Tara Parker-Pope, "Consortium to Develop Security Tags for Items Sold in Groceries, Drug Stores," *The Wall Street Journal,* March 10, 1999, p. B3.

[33]Ibid.

[34]Stephen Bitsoli, "The Practice and Money behind Displaying Goods," *The Macomb Daily,* December 12, 1999, p. 1C; and Paul N. Bloom, Gregory T. Gundlach, and Joseph P. Cannon, *Slotting Allowances and Fees: Schools of Thought and the Views of Practicing Managers,* Marketing Science Institute working paper no. 99–106, (1999).

[35]Information from Wal-Mart's Web site at www.walmart.com, January 22, 2000.

[36]James Pilcher, "Home Depot to Stop Selling Old-Growth Wood," *The Coloradoan,* August 27, 1999, p. B2.

Chapter Fifteen

[1]1997 *Economic Census* (Washington, D.C.: U.S. Census Bureau, January 21, 2000), pp. 7–24.

[2]Alexandra Peers and George Anders, "Web Auctions Get Haute," *The Wall Street Journal,* June 17, 1999, pp. B1, B4.

[3]George Anders, "Ebay Purchases Stake in TradeOut.com," *The Wall Street Journal,* November 1, 1999, p. B6.

[4]Keith L. Alexander, "Online Business Auctions Bypass Liquidators," *USA Today,* November 15, 1999, p. 19E.

[5]"Viking Office Products," from *West of Wall Street,* February 1996, p. 5; and information from the Viking Office Products Web site at www.viking.com.

[6]Rochelle Garner, "Eliminating Turf Wars," *Sales & Marketing Management,* June 1999, p. 56.

[7]Michele Marchetti, "Peace Offering," *Sales & Marketing Management,* September 1999, pp. 59–67.

[8]James A. Narus and James C. Anderson, "Rethinking Distribution," *Harvard Business Review,* July–August 1996, pp. 112–20.

[9]Peter D. Bennett, ed., *Dictionary of Marketing Terms* (Chicago: American Marketing Association, 1998), p. 213.

[10]Norton Paley, "Romancing Your Customers," *Sales & Marketing Management,* March 1996, pp. 30–32.

[11]Rebecca Quick, "Behind Doors of a Warehouse: Heavy Lifting of E-Commerce," *The Wall Street Journal,* September 3, 1999, p. B1.

[12]Dennis Bathory-Kitsz, "Lego Plays with Really Big Toys, Builds Blockbuster DC," *Consumer Goods Manufacturer,* January–February 1995, p. 19.

[13]Kevin Maney, "High-Tech Tags Mean Days of Bar Codes May Be Numbered," *USA Today,* March 31, 1999, p. 3B.

[14]Liz Seymour, "Custom Tailored for Service: VF Corporation," *Hemispheres,* March 1996, pp. 25–28.

[15]Andrew Osterland, "Fixing Rubbermaid Is No Snap," *Business Week,* September 20, 1999, p. 110.

[16]David Field, "Railroad Goliaths Propose $6B Merger," *USA Today,* December 21, 1999, p. 3B.

[17]Ibid.; and Jim Brennan, "Prepare Now for Next Wave of Rail Mergers," *Inbound Logistics,* December 1999, p. 18.

[18]Brennan, "Prepare Now"; and Earle Eldridge, "Rail Glitches Delay Delivery of Sport Utilities," *USA Today,* December 14, 1999, p. 1B.

[19]"Internet Shopping Could Spur Truck-Driver Shortage," *The Coloradoan,* December 28, 1999, p. B4.

[20]Robert J. Bowman, "Weighty Matters," *World Trade,* May 1995, pp. 84–87.

[21]Robert J. Bowman, "Long Distance Run," *World Trade,* May 1995, pp. 54–64.

[22]The text discussion of the effects of deregulation draws on James P. Rakowski, R. Neil Southern, and Judith L. Jarrell, "The Changing Structure of the U.S. Trucking Industry: Implications for Logistics Managers," *Journal of Business Logistics,* January 1993, pp. 111–29.

[23]Kenneth C. Schneider and James C. Johnson, "Professionalism and Ethical Standards in a Deregulated Environment: A Case Study of the Trucking Industry," *Journal of Personal Selling and Sales Management,* Winter 1992, pp. 33–43.

[24]Gary Stoller, "FAA Seeks $2.25M Fine from Shipper," *USA Today,* May 1, 1998, p. 1B.

Chapter Sixteen

[1]Erin White, " 'Chatting' a Singer up the Pop Charts," *The Wall Street Journal,* October 5, 1999, pp. B1, B4.

[2]Kathleen Morris, "The Name's the Thing," *Business Week,* November 15, 1999, p. 36.

[3]Larry Light, "The Great Hyped Way," *Business Week,* May 3, 1999, p. 131–35.

[4]Julian Beltrame, "Warning: These Cigarette Labels Could Really Gross You Out," *The Wall Street Journal,* June 7, 1999, p. B2.

[5]"Here's to the Winners," *Sales & Marketing Management,* July 1999, pp. 46–70.

[6]Information from *Advertising Age*'s Web site at www.adage.com, January 24, 2000.

[7]Ibid.

[8]Scott M. Cultrip, Allen H. Center, and Glen M. Broom, *Effective Public Relations,* 6th ed. (Englewood Cliffs, NJ: Prentice Hall, 1985), p. 4.

[9]George E. Belch and Michael A. Belch, *Introduction to Advertising and Promotion: An Integrated Marketing Communications Perspective,* 3rd ed. (Homewood, IL: Richard D. Irwin, 1995), p. 12.

[10]Don E. Schultz, "New Media, Old Problem: Keeping Marcom Integrated," *Marketing News,* March 25, 1999, p. 12.

[11]T. Bettina Cornwell, "Sponsorship-Linked Marketing Development," *Sport Marketing Quarterly* 4, no. 4 (1995), pp. 13–24.

[12]Melanie Wells, "Humor Pays Off When Toying with Emotions," *USA Today,* December 9, 1996, pp. B1, B2.

[13]Betsy McKay, "Siberian Soft-Drink Queen Outmarkets Coke and Pepsi," *The Wall Street Journal,* August 23, 1999, pp. B1, B4.

[14]Marjorie Valin, "Nationwide Survey of Top Executives Reveals Mixed Attitudes Toward Advertising in Shifting Business Environment," from the American Advertising Federation's Web site at www.aaf.org, January 24, 2000.

[15]"Real Men Don't Browse," *Marketing Tools,* July 1998, p. 10.

[16]Adapted from Philip Kotler, *Marketing Management: Analysis, Planning, and Control,* 8th ed. (Englewood Cliffs, NJ: Prentice Hall, 1994), pp. 612–13.

[17]George S. Low and Jakki J. Mohr, *Brand Managers' Perceptions of the Marketing Communications Budget Allocation Process,* Marketing Science Institute, (Cambridge, MA: 1998), pp. 35–38.

[18]Wendy Bounds, "Fuji Tries to Develop All-American Image," *The Wall Street Journal,* October 1, 1996, p. B4.

[19]Information from Target's Web site at www.target.com, January 26, 2000.

[20]Vanessa O'Connell, "Distillers Weigh TV Ads Urging More Drinking," *The Wall Street Journal,* February 23, 1999, pp. B1, B4.

[21]Chuck Ross, "Anheuser-Busch Pulls Beer Ads off MTV Network," *Advertising Age,* December 23, 1996, pp. 1, 27.

[22]Information from Miller Brewing Company-sponsored Web site at www.thinkwhenyoudrink.com, January 26, 2000, and Anheuser-Busch's Web site at www.anheuser-busch.com, January 26, 2000.

[23]Marjorie Valin, "AAF, Media and Advertising Groups Tell Gambling Commission: Don't Tread on 1st Amendment," from the American Advertising Federation's Web site at www.aaf.org, January 27, 2000.

[24]"Be Cautious of Free PC Offers," from the Better Business Bureau's Web site at www.bb.org, January 27, 2000.

[25]"Bayer Settles FTC Charges," from the Federal Trade Commission's Web site at www.ftc.gov, January 27, 2000.

[26]"Kellogg's Agrees to Modify Ad Claims," from the Web site of the Council of Better Business Bureau's National Advertising Division at www.caru.org/nad99, January 27, 2000.

Chapter Seventeen

[1]Charles H. Patti and Charles F. Frazer, *Advertising: A Decision-Making Approach* (Chicago: Dryden Press, 1988), p. 4.

[2]Laurie Petersen, "A Short-Sighted View of Advertising," *Adweek's Marketing Week,* November 11, 1991, p. 9.

[3]John Kenneth Galbraith, "Economics and Advertising: Exercise in Denial," *Advertising Age,* November 9, 1988, p. 81.

[4]John Deighton, Caroline M. Henderson, and Scott A. Nelson, "The Effects of Advertising on Brand Switching and Repeat Purchasing," *Journal of Marketing Research,* February 1994, p. 28.

[5]"Top 200 Brands," *Advertising Age,* May 6, 1996, p. 34.

[6]Dean M. Krugman and Roland T. Rust, "The Impact of Cable and VCR Penetration on Network Viewing: Assessing the Decade," *Journal of Advertising Research,* January–February 1993, pp. 67–73; and Joe Mandese, "Nets Get Less for More," *Advertising Age,* March 2, 1992, p. 1.

[7]Mel Mandell, "Getting the Word Out," *World Trade,* November 1993, p. 30.

[8]Iris Cohen Selinger, "Big Profits, Risks with Incentive Fees," *Advertising Age,* May 15, 1995, p. 3; and Mark Gleason, "Driver's Mart Pacing Agency Pay to Sales, *Advertising Age,* May 6, 1996, p. 3.

[9]Paul Allen, "New Ad Agency Model Needed to Cope with Info Overload," *Marketing News,* August 31, 1998, p. 4; Sarah Lorge, "Paying Ad Agencies their Due," *Sales & Marketing Management,* November 1999, p. 13; and Daniel McGinn, "Pour on the Pitch," *Newsweek,* May 31, 1999, pp. 5–51.

[10]Allan J. Magrath, "The Death of Advertising Has Been Greatly Exaggerated," *Sales & Marketing Management,* February 1992, p. 23.

[11]Sergey Frank, "Avoiding the Pitfalls of Business Abroad," *Sales & Marketing Management,* March 1992, p. 57.

[12]James M. Kolts, "Adaptive Marketing," *Journal of Consumer Marketing,* Summer 1990, pp. 39–40.

[13]C. Anthony Di Benedetto, Marik Tamate, and Rajan Chandran, "Developing Creative Advertising Strategy for the Japanese Marketplace," *Journal of Advertising Research,* January–February 1992, pp. 39–48.

[14]Fred S. Zufryden, James H. Pendrick, and Avu Sankaralingam, "Zapping and Its Impact on Brand Purchase Behavior," *Journal of Advertising Research,* January–February 1993, p. 58.

[15]Joanne Lipman, "TV Ad Deals to Set Big Price Increases," *The Wall Street Journal,* June 25, 1992, p. B8.

[16]Judith Waldrap, "And Now a Break from Our Sponsor," *American Demographics,* August 1993, pp. 16–18.

[17]Dana Wechsler Linden and Vicki Contavespi, "Media Wars," *Forbes,* August 19, 1991, p. 38.

[18]Kathryn Kranhold, "Banner Ads Deliver More Punch and Purchases than Thought," *The Wall Street Journal Interactive Edition,* November 24, 1999; and Randall Rothenberg, "An Advertising Power, but Just What Does Doubleclick Do?" *The New York Times,* September 22, 1999, p. 14.

[19]Maricris G. Briones, "Rich Media May Be Too Rich for Your Blood," *Marketing News,* March 29, 1999, p. 4; Laurie Freeman, "Advertising Fundamentally Changes Definition," *Marketing News,* December 6, 1999, p. 15; Janet Ginsburg and Kathleen Morris, "Extreme Retailing," *Business Week,* December 20, 1999, p. 123; and J. William Gurley, "How the Web Will Warp Advertising," *Fortune,* November 9, 1998, pp. 119–20.

[20]William F. Arens and Courtland L. Bovée, *Contemporary Advertising,* 5th ed. (Burr Ridge, IL: Richard D. Irwin, 1994), p. 8.

[21]Jim Garner, "Sneakers, Soap, and Semiconductors," *Marketing News,* March 1, 1999, p. 55; and Bob Lamons, "Resolve to Promote Your Firm's Brand Image in the New Millennium," *Marketing News,* January 17, 2000, p. 4.

[22]Scott B. MacKenzie, "The Role of Attention in Mediating the Effect of Advertising on Attribute Importance," *Journal of Consumer Research,* September 1986, pp. 174–95.

[23]Demetrious Vakratsas and Tim Ambler, "How Advertising Works: What Do We Really Know?" *Journal of Marketing,* January 1999, pp. 26–43.

[24]Deborah J. MacInnis, Christine Moorman, and Bernard J. Jaworski, "Enhancing and Measuring Consumers' Motivation, Opportunity, and Ability to Process Brand Information from Ads," *Journal of Marketing,* October 1991, pp. 32–53.

[25]Robert J. Kent, "Competitive Interference Effects in Consumer Memory for Advertising: The Role of Brand Familiarity," *Journal of Marketing,* July 1994, pp. 97–105.

[26]James F. Engel, Roger D. Blackwell, and Paul W. Miniard, *Consumer Behavior,* 7th ed. (Fort Worth, TX: Dryden Press, 1993), p. 277.

[27]Richard E. Petty, John T. Cacioppo, and David Schumann, "Central and Peripheral Routes to Advertising Effectiveness: The Moderating Role of Involvement," *Journal of Consumer Research* 10 (September 1983), pp. 135–46.

[28]Seema Nayyar and Jennifer Lach, "We're Being Watched," *American Demographics,* October 1998, pp. 53–58; and Bill Stoneman, "Beyond Rocking the Ages," *American Demographics,* May 1998, pp. 45–49.

[29]Joann Lublin, "As VCRs Advance, Agencies Fear TV Viewers Will Zap More Ads," *The Wall Street Journal,* January 4, 1991, p. B3.

[30]Tom Dougherty, "Create Great Advertising for the Millennuim," *Marketing News,* March 15, 1999, p. 2; Jean Halliday, "Chrysler Officials Admit to Flubbing the Intrepid Relaunch," *Advertising Age,* June 18, 1998, p. 10; and George F. Will, "The Perils of Brushing," *Newsweek,* May 10, 1999, p. 92.

[31]Gary T. Ford, Darlene B. Smith, and John L. Swasy, "Consumer Skepticism of Advertising Claims: Testing Hypotheses from Eco-

nomics of Information," *Journal of Consumer Research,* March 1990, pp. 433–41.

[32]Brian Wansik and Michael L. Ray, "Advertising Strategies to Increase Usage Frequencies," *Journal of Marketing,* January 1996, pp. 31–46.

[33]Ajay Karla and Ronald C. Goodstein, "The Impact of Advertising Positioning Strategies on Consumer Price Sensitivity, *Journal of Marketing Research,* May 1998, pp. 210–24.

[34]Thomas E. Barry, "Comparative Advertising: What Have We Learned in Two Decades?" *Journal of Advertising Research,* March–April 1993, p. 20.

[35]"Humor Remains Top Tool for Ad Campaign," *USA Today,* September 30, 1996, p. 3B.

[36]Bruce Horowitz, "Most Dot-Coms Don't Have Super Night," *USA Today,* January 31, 2000, p. 1.

[37]Scott Hume, "Best Ads Don't Rely on Celebrities," *Advertising Age,* May 25, 1992, p. 20; and Kevin Goldman, "Candice Bergen Leads the List of Top Celebrity Endorsers," *The Wall Street Journal,* September 17, 1993, pp. B1, B6.

[38]Timothy E. Moore, "Subliminal Advertising: What You See Is What You Get," *Journal of Marketing,* Spring 1982, pp. 27–47; and Terence A. Shimp, *Advertising, Promotion, and Supplemental Aspects of Integrated Marketing Communications,* 4th ed. (Fort Worth, TX: Dryden Press, 1997), pp. 310–12.

[39]Scott Donaten, "Advertorials Are Like a Drug," *Advertising Age,* March 9, 1992, p. S16.

[40]David Leonhardt, Peter Burrows, and Bill Vlasic, "Cue the Soda Can," *Business Week,* June 24, 1996, pp. 64–65.

[41]Joe Mandese, "Prime-Time Price Woes," *Advertising Age,* September 20, 1999, p. 1.

[42]Brad Edmondson, "In the Driver's Seat," *American Demographics,* March 1998, pp. 46–52.

[43]Giles D'Souza and Ram C. Rao, "Can Repeating an Advertisement More Frequently than the Competition Affect Brand Preference in a Mature Market?" *Journal of Marketing,* April 1995, p. 39.

[44]Joe Mandese, "Revisiting Ad Reach, Frequency," *Advertising Age,* November 27, 1995, p. 46.

[45]Leonard M. Lodish et al., "How TV Advertising Works: A Meta-Analysis of 389 Real World Split Cable TV Advertising Experiments," *Journal of Marketing Research,* May 1995, p. 138.

[46]Dwight R. Riskey, "How TV Advertising Works: An Industry Response," *Journal of Marketing Research,* May 1997, pp. 202–3.

[47]Cyndee Miller, "Study Says 'Likability' Surfaces as Measure of TV Ad Success," *Marketing News,* January 7, 1991, p. 14.

[48]Laurence N. Gold, "Advertising Tracking: New Tricks of the Trade," *Marketing Research: A Magazine of Practice and Application* 5, p. 42.

[49]Faye Rice, "A Cure for What Ails Advertising?" *Fortune,* December 16, 1991, p. 121.

[50]Lorraine Calvacca, "Making a Case for the Glossies," *American Demographics,* July 1999, p. 36; Juliana Koranteng, "A. C. Nielsen to Offer Data on Net Ad Effectiveness," *Advertising Age International,* October 1999, p. 4; "Net Ads on Pace for $4 Billion Year," *Content Factory,* November 4, 1999, http://www.comtexnews.com; and "Net Newbie @ Plan Still Undiscovered," *Business Week,* January 17, 2000, p. 115.

[51]Gerard J. Tellis, Rajesh K. Chandy, and Pattana Thaivanich, *Decomposing the Effects of Direct TV Advertising: Which Ad Works, When, Where, and How Often?* Marketing Science Institute, MSI Working Paper No. 99-118 (Cambridge, MA: 1999).

[52]D. Kirk Davidson, "Marketing This 'Hope' Sells Our Profession Short," *Marketing News,* July 20, 1998, p. 6.

[53]William L. Wilkie, Dennis L. McNeill, and Michael B. Mazis, "Marketing's 'Scarlet Letter': The Theory and Practice of Corrective Advertising," *Journal of Marketing,* Spring 1984, pp. 11–31.

[54]Raymond Serafin and Gary Levin, "Ad Industry Suffers Crushing Blow," *Advertising Age,* November 12, 1990, pp. 1, 76, 77.

[55]Judann Pollack, "Energy Bar Ad Claims Challenged in Court," *Advertising Age,* April 21, 1998, p. 3; Michael Schrage, "The Tangled Web of E-Deception," *Fortune,* September 27, 1999, p. 296; and Rochelle Sharp, "On Implied Claims for Supplements," *The Wall Street Journal,* November 19, 1998, p. B7.

[56]David A. Aaker, Rajeev Batra, and John G. Myers, *Advertising Management,* 4th ed. (Englewood Cliffs, NJ: Prentice Hall, 1992), p. 557.

[57]"Anything for a Ratings Boost," *Marketing News,* September 13, 1999, p. 2; and Kathryn C. Montgomery, "Gov't Must Take the Lead in Protecting Children," *Advertising Age,* June 22, 1998, p. 40.

[58]Maxine Lans Retsky, "Junk Faxes Subject to Telemarketing Laws," *Marketing News,* April 26, 1999, p. 7.

[59]Minette E. Drumwright, "Company Advertising with a Social Dimension," Report #96-110, Marketing Science Institute, (Cambridge, MA: 1996), p. i; and Bob Garfield, "This Heavy-Handed Ad Exploits Someone New," *Advertising Age,* May 10, 1993, p. 50.

[60]Allyson L. Stewart-Allen, "Europe Ready for Cause-Related Campaigns," *Marketing News,* July 6, 1998, p. 9; and "Why P&G Is Linking Brands to Good Causes," *Marketing,* August 26, 1999, p. 11.

[61]Kirk Davidson, "Look for Abundance of Opposition to TV Liquor Ads," *Marketing News,* January 6, 1997, pp. 4, 30; Ian P. Murphy, "Competitive Spirits: Liquor Industry Turns to TV Ads," *Marketing News,* December 12, 1996, pp. 1, 17; and Tar Parker-Pope, "Tough Tobacco-Ad Rule Light Creative Fires," *The Wall Street Journal,* October 9, 1996, p. B1.

[62]Donald P. Robin and R. Eric Reidenbach, "Social Responsibility, Ethics, and Marketing Strategy: Closing the Gap between Concept and Application," *Journal of Marketing,* January 1987, pp. 44–58.

[63]Patricia Winters, "Drugmakers Portrayed as Villains, Worry about Image," *Advertising Age,* February 22, 1993, p. 1; Kate Fitzgerald, "Health Concerns Don't Slow Down Cellular Phones," *Advertising Age,* February 8, 1993, p. 4; Annetta Miller, "Do Boycotts Work?" *Newsweek,* July 6, 1992, p. 56; and Howard Schlossberg, "Members Only to Introduce Homeless in Cause Marketing," *Marketing News,* July 20, 1992, p. 6.

[64]Caleb Solomon, "Exxon Attacks Scientific Views of *Valdez* Oil Spill," *The Wall Street Journal,* April 15, 1993, p. B1.

[65]Philip Kotler, *Marketing Management: Analysis, Planning, Implementation, and Control,* 8th ed. (Englewood Cliffs, NJ: Prentice Hall, 1994), pp. 676–77.

[66]Adriana Cento, "7 Habits for Highly Effective Public Relations," *Marketing News,* March 16, 1999, p. 8; Dana James, "Dot-Coms Demand New Kind of Publicity," *Marketing News,* November 22, 1999, p. 6; and Kathleen V. Schmidt, "Public Relations," *Marketing News,* January 17, 2000, p. 13.

[67]Bob Lamons, "Taco Bell Rings in the New Age of Publicity Stunts," *Marketing News,* May 20, 1996, p. 15.

[68]Joseph B. Cahill, "Net Chats: Big Business Is Listening," *Crain's Chicago Business,* April 8, 1996, pp. 1, 53; and Helen Roper, "Letters from Cyberhell," *Inc. Technology,* September 1995, pp. 67–70.

[69]Joan McGrath and Myrna Pedersen, "Don't Wait for Disaster; Have a Crisis Plan Ready," *Marketing News,* December 2, 1996, p. 6.

Chapter Eighteen

[1]Adapted from Peter D. Bennett, ed., *Dictionary of Marketing Terms* (Chicago: American Marketing Association, 1988), p. 179.

[2]"Clean and Cheap Carries Weight with Shoppers," *Progressive Grocer Annual Report,* April 1996, p. 28.

[3]Chad Kaydo, "How to Build a B-to-B Frequency Program," *Sales & Marketing Management*, April 1999, p. 80.

[4]Larry Armstrong, "E-tailers Keep Giving Away the Store," *Business Week*, January 10, 2000, p. 44.

[5]*20th Annual Survey of Promotional Practices* (Largo, Florida: Cox Direct, 1998), p. 11.

[6]Ibid., p. 19; and "Adults Love Coupons," *Marketing News*, August 26, 1996, p. 1.

[7]Matthew Klein, "The Silence of the Scissors," *Marketing Tools*, May 1998, p. 64.

[8]"Targeted Couponing Slows Redemption Slide," *Marketing News*, February 12, 1996, p. 11; and *1996 Statistical Fact Book* (New York: Direct Marketing Association, 1996), p. 156.

[9]Bill Wolfe, "Buyers, Manufacturers Benefit from Rebates," *The Coloradoan*, May 1, 1999, p. B2.

[10]Information from www.freeafterrebate.com, January 6, 2000.

[11]Lorrie Grant, "Toy E-tailers Lure Consumers with Deals," *USA TODAY*, November 23, 1999, p. 3B.

[12]Promotion Marketing Association, Inc., "Reggie Gold Award Winner, 1999: What's Wrong with this Episode Contest, the Drew Carey Show," from www.pmalink.com, January 6, 1999.

[13]Promotion Marketing Association, Inc., "Reggie Silver Award Winner, 1999: Starburst Chew the Clue," from www.pmalink.com, January 6, 1999.

[14]"Thousands Follow Clues, Find the Answers in Ford's Internet Scavenger Hunt," *PR Newswire*, The PointCast Network http://www.pointcast.com, June 19, 1996.

[15]Armstrong, "E-tailers Keep Giving the Store Away."

[16]David Vaczek, "Hard, Cold Merchandise," *PROMO Magazine*, May 1999, pp. S3–S5.

[17]Promotion Marketing Association, Inc., "Reggie Gold Award Winner, 1999: A.1. Rolling Steakhouse Tour," from www.pmalink.com, January 6, 1999.

[18]David Hardesty, "Top Ten Selling Promotional Products: An Analysis of What Promotional Products Distributors Sell," *Promotional Products Business*, January 2000, pp. 204–210, 268.

[19]Adapted from Robert C. Blattberg and Scott A. Neslin, *Sales Promotion, Concepts, Methods, and Strategies* (Englewood Cliffs, NJ: Prentice Hall, 1990), p. 314.

[20]Vincent Alonzo, "Showering Dealers with Incentives," *Sales & Marketing Management*, October 1999, pp. 24–26.

[21]Information from the Specialty Advertising Institute, www.promomart.com., January 7, 2000.

[22]Jeff Tanner, *Curriculum Guide to Trade Show Marketing* (Bethesda, MD: Center for Exhibition Industry Research, 1995), p. T12.

[23]"Publisher's Clearing House Settles Suit over Practices," *The Coloradoan*, August 27, 1999, p. B2.

[24]Erin White, "Sweepstakes Concern Seeks Creditor Shield," *The Wall Street Journal*, November 1, 1999, p. B8; and Kathleen V. Schmidt, "American Family Bankruptcy," *Marketing News*, November 22, 1999, p. 3.

[25]Gene Korprowski, "Think Small," *Marketing Tools*, January–February 1997, p. 26.

Chapter Nineteen

[1]Derrick C. Schnebelt, "Turning the Tables," *Sales & Marketing Management*, January 1993, pp. 22–23.

[2]David Topus, "Keep It Short . . . and Smart," *Selling*, August 1993, p. 30.

[3]Tom Murray, "Team Selling: What's the Incentive?" *Sales & Marketing Management*, June 1991, pp. 89–92.

[4]Jon M. Hawes, Kenneth E. Mast, and John E. Swan, "Trust Earning Perceptions of Sellers and Buyers," *Journal of Personal Selling and Sales Management*, Spring 1989, pp. 1–8.

[5]Ingrid Abramowitz, "The Trust Factor," *Success*, March 1993, p. 18.

[6]Stuart Miller, "Beating the Clock—and Records," *Sales & Marketing Management*, February 1997, pp. 20–21.

[7]Rosann L. Spiro and Barton A. Weitz, "Adaptive Selling: Conceptualization, Measurement, and Nomological Validity," *Journal of Marketing Research*, February 1990, pp. 61–69.

[8]"Pipe Down," *Sales & Marketing Management*, January 1994, p. 22.

[9]David W. Cravens, Thomas N. Ingram, and Raymond W. LaForge, "Evaluating Multiple Sales Channel Strategies," *Journal of Business and Industrial Marketing*, Summer–Fall 1991, pp. 37–48.

[10]Ibid.

[11]Chad Kaydo, "You've Got Sales," *Sales & Marketing Management*, October 1999, pp. 30–34.

[12]Ibid., pp. 36–38.

[13]Erin Stout, "Planning to Profit from National Accounts," *Sales & Marketing Management*, October 1999, p. 107.

[14]Bob Attanasio, "How PC-Based Sales Quotas Boost Productivity and Morale," *Sales & Marketing Management*, September 1991, pp. 148–50.

[15]"Taking Aim at Tomorrow's Challenges," *Sales & Marketing Management*, September 1991, pp. 66–67.

[16]Francy Blackwood, "A Prescription for Change," *Selling*, August 1993, pp. 22–25.

[17]William Keenan, Jr., "Time Is Everything," *Sales & Marketing Management*, August 1993, pp. 60–62.

[18]"Sales Training Points the Way toward Successful Total Quality Management," *Sales and Marketing* (newsletter of the American Society of Training and Development), Winter 1993, pp. 1, 6.

[19]Lawrence B. Chonko, John F. Tanner, Jr., William A. Weeks, and Melissa R. Schmitt, *Reward Preferences of Salespeople*, Center for Professional Selling, Baylor University, Research Report no. 91–3 (Waco, TX: 1991).

[20]"Compensation and Expenses," *Sales & Marketing Management*, June 28, 1993, p. 65.

[21]Christen P. Heide, "New Dartnell Survey," *Marketing Times*, Summer 1996, p. 1.

[22]"Bonuses for Breaking New Ground," *Inc.*, March 1993, p. 27.

[23]"Compensation and Expenses," p. 65.

[24]Karl A. Boedecker, Fred W. Morgan, and Jeffrey J. Stoltman, "Legal Dimensions of Salespersons' Statements: A Review and Managerial Suggestions," *Journal of Marketing*, January 1991, pp. 70–80.

[25]I. Frederick Trawick, John E. Swan, Gail McGee, and David R. Rink, "Influence of Buyer Ethics and Salesperson Behavior on Intention to Choose a Supplier," *Journal of the Academy of Marketing Science*, Winter 1991, pp. 17–23.

[26]Reported in Bernard L. Rosenbaum, "What You Need for Success in the 21st Century," *Selling*, November 1999, pp. 8–9.

Chapter Twenty

[1]"DM Ad Expenditures, Revenue, Employment Will Outpace U.S. Economy According to Forecasts in WEFA's 1999 Economic Impact Study," *Direct Connection*, Winter 1999–2000, p. 5.

[2]"Economic Impact: U.S. Direct Marketing Today," from the Direct Marketing Association's Web site at www.the-dma.org, January 10, 2000.

[3]Ibid.

[4]Frederic M. Biddle, "Luxury-Car Makers Try the Party Scene," *The Wall Street Journal*, August 4, 1999, p. B8.

[5]Peter D. Bennett, ed., *Dictionary of Marketing Terms*, 2nd ed. (Chicago: American Marketing Association, 1995), p. 75.

[6]"The Visible Marketer," *Direct*, December 1999, p. 48.

[7]Thom Weidlich, "This Is a Test," *Direct*, July 1999, pp. 1, 49–51.

[8]"Economic Impact: U.S. Direct Marketing Today."

[9]Ibid.

[10]"Transplants: Two catalogs Expand Their Markets," *Direct*, June 1999, pp. 98–99.

[11]Richard H. Levey, "Home Market," *Direct*, June 1999, pp. 1, 39–40.

[12]Ray Schultz, "Live from Germany: The New DM Boom," *Direct*, December 1999, p. 13.

[13]Claire Coyne, "UK Turns Up B-to-B Mail Volume," from the Direct Marketing Association's Web site www.the-dma.org, February 3, 2000.

[14]Ray Schultz, "Quill Enters the British Market," *Direct*, May 15, 1999, p. 20.

[15]Jim Emerson, "Viking Goes One-Up," *1 to 1 Update*, a supplement to *Direct*, November 1, 1999, p. 17.

[16]*1996 Statistical Fact Book* (New York: Direct Marketing Association, 1996), p. 41.

[17]"Economic Impact: U.S. Direct Marketing Today."

[18]Tony Seideman, "Multimedia Is the Message," *Inc. Technology*, no. 3 (1996) pp. 82–83.

[19]Chad Kaydo, "Planting the Seeds of Marketing Success," *Sales & Marketing Management*, August 1998, p. 73.

[20]Erika Rasmusson, "Speeding Growth with Infomercials," *Sales & Marketing Management*, August 1998, p. 77.

[21]"Experts Saddened by Medication Infomercial," *Marketing News*, June 7, 1999, p. H33.

[22]Jonathan Boorstein, "Must-Sell TV," *Direct*, June 1999, pp. 1, 47–48.

[23]"Economic Impact: U.S. Direct Marketing Today."

[24]From an advertisement for the Third Annual International Call Center Summit, held April 15–17, 1996, Reston, VA.

[25]"USA Snapshots," *USA Today*, July 14, 1999, p. 1A.

[26]"USA Snapshots," *USA Today*, May 3, 1999, p. 1A.

[27]"JunkBusters Anti-Telemarketing Script," from the JunkBusters Web site at www.junkbusters.com, February 6, 2000.

[28]Jim Emerson, "From the Web to the Desk," in *Email Dispatch*, a supplement to *Direct*, September 1999, pp. E10–E12.

[29]Monica Larner, "When in Rome, Download," *Business Week*, November 25, 1996, p. 8.

[30]Risa Bauman, "CD Catalog Kiosks Tested in Two Areas," *Direct*, June 1993, p. 55.

[31]"Case Study—Technical Support at Compaq Computer," from FaxBack's Web site at www.faxback.com, February 6, 2000.

[32]"USA Snapshots," *USA Today*, December 16, 1998, p. 1B.

[33]Leslie Miller, "On-Line Quid Pro Quo: A Freebie for Your Info," *USA Today*, March 31, 1999, p. 4D.

[34]Heather Green, Norm Alster, Amy Borus, and Catherine Yang, "Privacy: Outrage on the Web," *Business Week*, February 14, 2000, pp. 38–40; and Edward C. Baig, Marcia Stepanek, and Neil Gross, "Special Report: Privacy," *Business Week*, April 5, 1999, pp. 84–90.

[35]For more on the privacy of children and advertising, see the National Consumers League Web site at www.natlconsumersleague.org.

[36]Thom Weidlich, "Up in the Air in Europe," *Direct*, May 15, 1999, p. 13; and Stephen Baker, Marsha Johnston, and William Echikson, "Europe's Privacy Cops," *Business Week*, November 2, 1998, pp. 49–51.

[37]"No. 1 Nuisance: Junk Mail," *Direct*, December 1999, p. 6.

Chapter Twenty-One

[1]These definitions are adapted from material presented in Marilyn Greenstein and Todd M. Feinman, *Electronic Commerce: Security, Risk Management, and Control* (Boston, MA: Irwin/McGraw-Hill, 2000), pp. 1–2.

[2]This situation is adapted from Nicholas G. Carr, "Hypermediation: Commerce as Clickstream," *Harvard Business Review*, January–February 2000, pp. 46–47.

[3]Adrian J. Slywotzky, "The Age of the Choiceboard," *Harvard Business Review*, January–February 2000, pp. 40–41.

[4]These statistics are presented in "U.S. Internet Dominance Slipping," cyberatlas.internet.com, March 29, 2000.

[5]Reported in "eCommerce Goes Global," http://www.emarketer.com/estats, April 13, 2000.

[6]Reported in "The Longer Online, the More They Spend," http://www.emarketer.com/estats, April 14, 2000.

[7]Reported in "B2B E-Commerce: $403 Billion in 2000," http://cyberatlas.internet.com, January 26, 2000.

[8]Bhushan Bahree, "Fourteen Oil, Chemical Firms Join to Form On-line Exchange," *The Wall Street Journal Interactive Edition*, April 12, 2000, pp. 1–3.

[9]Kevin Maney, "Wireless Option Opens Door to a New E-World," *USA Today*, February 18–20, 2000, pp. 1–2A.

[10]Dana James, "Broadband Horizons," *Marketing News*, March 13, 2000, pp. 1, 9.

[11]Gene Koretz, "E-Shoppers Take a Breather," *Business Week*, March 20, 2000, p. 32.

[12]"Online and On Target," *Business Week*, April 3, 2000, p. 10.

[13]John Buskin, "Online Persuaders," *The Wall Street Journal*, July 12, 1999, pp. R12, R26.

[14]Ginger Conlon, "How to Move Customers Online," *Sales & Marketing Management*, March 2000, pp. 27–28.

[15]Jane E. Zarem, "Watch and Learn," *1 to 1 Online*, February 2000, p. 59.

[16]Chad Kaydo, "As Good as It Gets," *Sales & Marketing Management*, March 2000, pp. 55–60.

[17]Maxine Lans Retsky, "Spam Getting Trickier for Marketers to Use," *Marketing News*, March 13, 2000, p. 13.

[18]Sarah Lorge, "The Value of Virtual Presentations," *Sales & Marketing Management*, November 1999, p. 113.

[19]"Toys Я Us Online to Open Additional Centers," *USA Today*, April 11, 2000, p. 1B.

[20]Jonathan Boorstein, "Co-ops.com," *Direct*, March 1, 2000, pp. 66–67.

[21]Donna Rosato and Matt Krantz, "Priceline.com's Stock Gets Pumped Up," *USA Today*, March 15, 2000, p. 3B.

[22]Michael McCarthy, "Priceline's Campy Ads Polarize Audience," *USA Today*, March 13, 2000, p. 5B.

[23]"Few Ads Scored Touchdowns during Super Bowl," *The Wall Street Journal*, February 1, 2000, p. B8; and Bruce Horovitz, "Most Dot-Coms Don't Have a Super Night," *USA Today*, January 31, 2000, p. 1B.

[24]Michael McCarthy, "Companies Are Sold on Interactive Ad Strategy," *USA Today*, March 3, 2000, p. 1B.

[25]Michael Krauss, "Good PR Critical to Growth on the Web," *Marketing News*, January 18, 1999, p. 8.

[26]Greg Farrell, "From Sour Grapes to Online Whine," *USA Today*, April 7, 2000, p. 1B.

[27]Ibid.

[28]McKinsey and Company, "@ Your Service," *Business 2.0,* March 2000, pp. 427–28.

[29]Ibid.

[30]Ibid.

[31]Bill Meyers, "Service with an E-Smile," *USA Today,* October 12, 1999, p. 1B.

[32]Rebecca Quick, "Sleaze E-commerce," *The Wall Street Journal,* May 14, 1999, pp. W1, W10.

[33]Ibid.

[34]"Big 3 to Pool Online Buying Efforts," from MSNBC News Services Web site at www.msnbc.com, February 25, 2000.

[35]William Holstein and Fred Vogelstein, "You've Got a Deal!" *U.S. News & World Report,* January 24, 2000, pp. 34–40.

[36]Dan Hanover, "Channel Conflict? Put a Lid on It," *Sales & Marketing Management,* March 2000, p. 86.

[37]Karen Solomon, "Revenge of the Bots," *The Industry Standard,* November 22–29, pp. 263–71.

[38]Michael White, "Free Shipping May Come Back to Haunt E-retailers," *The Coloradoan,* December 31, 1999, p. B2.

[39]Matt Krantz, "CDNOW Gains in Question," *USA Today,* December 16, 1999, p. 1B; and Catherine Yang, "Earth to Dot-Com Accountants," *Business Week,* April 3, 2000, p. 40.

[40]Heather Green, Norm Alster, and Arlene Weintraub, "The Dot.Coms Are Falling to Earth," *Business Week,* April 17, 2000, pp. 48–49.

[41]Ibid.

[42]Ginger Conlon, "Just Another Channel?" *Sales & Marketing Management,* January 2000, pp. 23–24.

[43]Ibid.

[44]Ibid.

[45]Sandeep Dayal, Helene Landesberg, and Michael Zeisser, "How to Build Trust Online," *Marketing Management,* Fall 1999, pp. 64–69.

[46]International Data Corporation, "An IDC White Paper: eSecurity," from IDC's Web site at www.idc.com, April 6, 2000.

[47]Lorrie Grant, "E-Retailers Need to Debug Shopping," *USA Today,* March 8, 2000, p. 2B.

[48]Nanette Byrnes and Paul C. Judge, "Internet Anxiety," *Business Week,* June 28, 1999, pp. 88–98.

[49]Richard B. Schmitt, "Online Privacy: Alleged Abuses Shape New Law," *The Wall Street Journal,* February 29, 2000, p. B1.

[50]Marilyn Greenstein and Todd M. Feinman, *Electronic Commerce: Security, Risk Management and Control* (Boston, MA: Irwin/McGraw-Hill, 2000), p. 73.

[51]"Time to Move on Internet Privacy," *Business Week,* February 28, 2000, p. 174.

[52]Heather Green, Mike France, Marcia Stepanek, and Amy Borrus, "It's Time for Rules in Wonderland," *Business Week,* March 20, 2000, pp. 84–85.

[53]Greenstein and Feinman, *Electronic Commerce:* p. 73.

[54]Green, France, Stepanek, and Borrus, "It's Time for Rules in Wonderland," p. 85.

[55]Thomas E. Weber, "The Man Who Baked the First Web Cookies Chews Over Their Fate," *The Wall Street Journal,* February 28, 2000, p. B1.

[56]http://www.nytimes.com/library/tech/00/03/biztech/articles/31yahoo.html.

[57]Dru Sefton, "Teen Girls Feel the Net Effect," *USA Today,* February 28, 2000, p. A3.

[58]Marcia Stepanek, "Weblining," *Business Week,* April 3, 2000, pp. EB26–EB34.

[59]Edward C. Baig, Marcia Stepanek, and Neil Gross, "Privacy: The Internet Wants Your Private Info. What's in It for You?" *Businessweek Online,* April 5, 1999; and http://www.eco.utexas.edu/faculty/Norman/long/auto-info.html.

[60]Dan Carney, "Fraud on the Internet," *Business Week E.Biz,* April 3, 2000, pp. EB58–68; Kathleen Murphy, "Government, Industry Target Web Fraud," *Internet World,* May 17, 1999, p. 3.

[61]Carney, "Fraud on the Internet," pp. EB58–EB60.

[62]Mathew Moss, "SEC's Plan to Snoop for Crime on Web Sparks a Debate over Privacy," *The Wall Street Journal,* March 28, 2000, p. B1.

[63]Maxine Lans Retsky, "FTC Order Rule Applies to E-Commerce," *Marketing News,* January 18, 1999, p. 7; Glenn Simpson, "As FTC Rides Herd on the Web, Marketers Begin to Circle the Wagons," *The Wall Street Journal,* February 29, 2000, p. B1; and Elizabeth Wasserman, "Score Another Round for the Internet Industry," *The Industry Standard,* December 6, 1999, p. 66 (www.thestandard.com).

[64]John Peet, "E-Commerce: Shopping around the Web," *The Economist,* February 26, 2000, p. 53.

[65]Ibid.

[66]Sheila R. Cherry, "e-Taxes for e-Tail," *Insight on the News,* January 31, 2000, p. 10; Howard Gleckman, "The Great Internet Tax Debate," *Business Week,* March 27, 2000, pp. 228–36; "Internet Taxes an End Run," *Business Week,* June 28, 1999, p. 47; and Peet, "E-Commerce: Shopping around the Web," pp. 50–53.

[67]Andy Reinhardt, "No Net Taxes: A Break for the Well-Off," *Business Week,* January 17, 2000, p. 39.

[68]Howard Gleckman, "The Great Internet Tax Debate," *Business Week,* March 27, 2000, pp. 228–36.

Photo Credits

Prologue
Photo/Steve Case: Wide World Photos
All other artwork in prologue: Courtesy America Online

Chapter 1
Courtesy of Amazon.com, p. 2
Courtesy DDB Needham/Dallas, p. 3
Courtesy Friday's Hospitality WorldWide, p. 6
Greg Girard/Contact Press Images, p. 8
Courtesy Colgate-Palmolive Company, p. 9
Courtesy Colgate-Palmolive Company, p. 9
These materials have been reproduced by McGraw-Hill with the permission of e-Bay Inc. COPYRIGHT © EBAY, INC. ALL RIGHTS RESERVED, p. 10
Courtesy AC Nielsen, p. 12
Stock Montage, Inc., p. 15
Stock Montage, Inc., p. 15
Stock Montage, Inc., p. 15

Chapter 2
Courtesy Dell Computer, p. 24
Courtesy IBM, p. 28
Copyright © Eastman Kodak Company, p. 32
Courtesy Hong Kong & Shanghai Banking Corporation Limited, p. 32
Michael Kevin Daly/The Stock Market, p. 33
Courtesy Land's End, Inc., p. 33
Courtesy Young & Rubicam, Frankfurt, p. 34
Courtesy The Gillette Company, p. 35
Courtesy Telxon; Agency: Hitchcock, Fleming & Assoc., p. 40

Chapter 3
Courtesy Honeywell International, Inc., p. 50
Courtesy ABB, p. 51
© Brian Smale, p. 57
Courtesy Wieden & Kennedy/Amsterdam, p. 61
Courtesy The Clorax Company, p. 61
Greg Girard/Contact Press Images, p. 63
Courtesy United Airlines, p. 64
Courtesy Peapod, p. 66
Courtesy Toyota Motor Corporate Services of North America, Inc., p. 67
© Joe Stewardson, p. 68
Courtesy Hewlett-Packard Company, p. 69

Chapter 4
Copyright © Eastman-Kodak Company, p. 76
Courtesy McDonald's Corporation, p. 78

Courtesy Hallmark Cards, Inc., p. 78
Courtesy Unilever United States, Inc., p. 83
Courtesy Latina Magazine, p. 86
Used with the permission of Oscar Mayer Foods, a division of Kraft Foods, Inc., p. 87
Courtesy Swatch Watch Group, Inc., p. 89
Wada Mitsurio/The Gamma Liaison Network, p. 90
Courtesy Buick, p. 95
Advertisement courtesy of Anheuser-Busch, Inc., p. 96

Chapter 5
Courtesy Tum Yeto, p. 102
Courtesy GE Capital Services, p. 106
Courtesy Lucent Technologies, p. 109
Courtesy ITT Industries, p. 111
Courtesy Colgate-Palmolive Company, p. 112
Courtesy Tyson Foods, Inc., p. 115
Courtesy Siemens AG, p. 115

Chapter 6
Courtesy Information Resources, Inc., p. 122
Courtesy Nestle USA, Inc., p. 123
Courtesy South Seas Plantation, p. 127
Courtesy AC Nielsen, p. 128
Courtesy Colgate-Palmolive Company, p. 129
Courtesy AC Nielsen, p. 129
Courtesy Demographics On Call, p. 130
Stock Boston, p. 132
© Bill Whitehead, p. 135
Courtesy Saatchi & Saatchi/Singapore, p. 138
L.L. Bean, Inc., p. 142

Chapter 7
Courtesy SRI International, p. 148
Courtesy Ford Motor Company, p. 149
Courtesy Evian; agency: Paradiset DDB/Sweden, p. 151
Courtesy Que Pasa.com, p. 154
Courtesy Hartmarx Corporation, p. 154
Courtesy Hartmarx Corporation, p. 154
Courtesy Fallon McElligott, p. 159
Courtesy Andersen Consulting, p. 161
Courtesy J.C. Penney Co., p. 161
Courtesy Hasbro, Inc., p. 168
Kinko's Inc. 2000. Kinko's is a registered trademark of Kinko's Corporation and is used by permission. All copyrights and trademarks are the property of the respective owners and are used by permission. All rights reserved, p. 170

575

Chapter 17

Courtesy British Airways, p. 392
Courtesy Saatchi & Saatchi, p. 395
Courtesy ESPN, Inc., p. 397
Courtesy LivePerson, p. 397
Courtesy Penn Racquet Sports, p. 401
Courtesy Canon U.S.A., Inc., p. 404
Courtesy Gun Coalition Against Violence, p. 404
M. Hruby, p. 404
Courtesy Dairy Management, Inc.; agency: DDB Needham/Chicago, p. 404
Financial Times "Tram" by Delaney Lund Knox Warren & Partners-London, p. 406
Courtesy Nike, Inc., p. 407
Wide World Photos, p. 414

Chapter 18

Courtesy Val-Pak, p. 420
Courtesy Flash.com; agency: The Woo Agency; creative director: Richard Perlmutter; senior art director: Valerie Moizel, p. 421
Courtesy Road Runner Sports, p. 423
pet.smart, p. 424
Catalina Marketing photo, p. 426
Courtesy Fiskars, p. 427
© John Abbott, p. 428
Courtesy Lamb Weston, Inc.: agency: Strahan Advertising, Inc., p. 431
Courtesy Kraft Foods, Inc., p. 433
Einzig Photographers, Inc., p. 434
Keith Dannemiller/SABA, p. 434

Chapter 19

Courtesy Pfizer, Inc., p. 444
Courtesy Colgate-Palmolive Company, p. 445

Courtesy Hunt-Wesson, Inc., p. 446
Courtesy United States Surgical Corporation, p. 448
Mark Tuschman/The Stock Market, p. 449
Courtesy Bristol-Myers Squibb Pharmaceutical, p. 450
© Will Panich, p. 455
Courtesy of Metron, Inc. Terr Align is a registered trademark of Metron, Inc., p. 456
Courtesy Merck & Co., Inc., p. 457
Courtesy Cognos Incorporated, p. 458

Chapter 20

Courtesy Coldwater Creek, p. 468
Courtesy Avon, p. 469
Courtesy Info, USA, p. 470
Courtesy Johnson & Hayward, Inc., p. 473
Courtesy Liggett-Stashower Direct, p. 474
Courtesy Office Depot, Inc., p. 475
M. Hruby, p. 476
Courtesy Busy Body, Inc., p. 477

Chapter 21

Courtesy Cyber Atlas, p. 490
Courtesy Garden.com, p. 491
Courtesy barnes & noble.com, p. 491
Courtesy America Online, p. 493
Courtesy mySimon, Inc., p. 493
Courtesy barnes & noble.com, p. 494
Courtesy Inventa Corporation, p. 497
Courtesy Cyber Dialogue, p. 501
Courtesy Netvendor, p. 505
Courtesy Hyperion, p. 508
Courtesy RSA Security, Inc., p. 510

Name Index

Company Index

Subject Index